Net inc. with purchase: FIFO, $252,000; LIFO, $150,000
DP 2 No check figure
FSP 1 Gross margin, FIFO, $2,472.2 million
FSP 2 No check figure

9-1A Dept.–Land improv., $1,883; Office bldg., $12,953; Storage bldg., $1,037; Furniture, $9,017
9-2A No check figure
9-3A Depr. 19X5: SL, $18,000; UOP, $13,500; DDB, $2,960; SYD, $6,000
9-4A Depr. Exp. 19X3, before closing, $3,867
9-5A No check figure
9-6A Cost of new truck, $17,867
9-7A Part 1. Depletion, $441,000
9-1B Depr.–Land improv., $2,865; Home office bldg., $24,878; Garage, $1,425; Furniture, $11,644
9-2B No check figure
9-3B Dept. 19X6: SL, $9,000; UOP, $9,720; DDB, $1,901; SYD, $2,571
9-4B Depr. Exp. 19X5, before closing, $9,688
9-5B No check figure
9-6B Cost of new truck, $22,690
9-7B Depletion, $738,000

10-1A No check figure
10-2A No check figure
10-3A Wage exp., $19,207
10-4A Total annual cost of employee, $69,474
10-5A 3. Cash payment, $54,292; 4. Cash payment, $36,311
10-6A Total liab., $363,532
10-7A Net pay, $1,617
10-8A No check figure
10-1B No check figure
10-2B No check figure
10-3B Salary exp., $9,695
10-4B Total annual cost of employee, $59,710
10-5B 3. Cash payment, $12,543; 4. Cash payment, $11,455
10-6B Total liab., $285,738
10-7B Net pay, $1,926
10-8B No check figure
DP No check figures
FSP No check figures
CP, Pt 3 Lakeway total assets, revised, $1,914,000; Lakeway net inc., revised, $241,600

11-1A 19X7 Interest exp., $106,667
11-2A 4. Interest exp., $26,850
11-3A 9/30/X4 Bond Carrying Amount, $164,464
11-4A 12/31/X3 Bond carrying amount, $451,280
11-5A 12/31 Interest exp. (bonds), $93,000
11-6A No check figure
11-7A No check figure
11-1B 19X5 Interest exp., $135,000
11-2B 4. Interest exp., $53,500
11-3B 9/30/X4 Bond carrying amount, $106,801
11-4B 12/31/X3 Bond carrying amount, $315,785
11-5B 12/31 Interest exp. (bonds), $21,750
11-6B No check figure
11-7B No check figure
DP 1 EPS Plan A, $1.86

DP 2 No check figure
FSP No check figures

12-1A No check figure
12-2A Total stock. equity, $240,000
12-3A Total stock. equity, $446,800
12-4A Total stock. equity: Advantage, $578,000; Vanguard, $567,000
12-5A 6. Pfd. div., $212,080
12-6A Total assets, $513,000; return on common, .087
12-7A 2. 19X3 Div. Pay.: Pfd., $35,000; Com. $230,000
12-8A BV per share: Pfd., $52.55; Com. $8.43
12-9A Taxable income: 19X7 $215,000; 19X8 $265,000
12-1B No check figure
12-2B Total stock. equity, $115,000
12-3B Total stock. equity, $327,500
12-4B Total stock. equity: Navarro, $331,000; Action, $445,000
12-5B 6. Pfd. div., $22,500,000
12-6B Total assets, $797,000; return on common, .064
12-7B 2. 19X3 Div. Pay.: Pfd., $2,500; Com. $24,500
12-8B BV per share: Pfd., $28.20; Com. $7.16
12-9B Taxable income: 19X3 $200,000; 19X4 $230,000
DP 1 Total stock. equity: Plan 1, $515,200; Plan 2, $500,200
DP 2 No check figure
FSP 1 2. Avg. issue price of common, $2.11
FSP 2 No check figure

13-1A No check figure
13-2A Total stock. equity: Dec. 31, 19X8, $438,000; Dec. 31, 19X9, $525,000
13-3A 2. Debit to Re, 1.3 mil.; 4. End bal., T/Stock, $213.5 mil.; 7. EPS = $4.46
13-4A No check figure
13-5A Total stock. equity, $546,080
13-6A Total stock. equity, $531,000
13-7A RE, June 30, 19X4, $112,000; EPS = $3.40
13-8A EPS = $3.07; stock. equity, $1,778,945
13-1B No check figure
13-2B Total stock. equity: Dec. 31, 19X6, $374,250; Dec. 31, 19X7, $391,850
13-3B 2. Debit to RE, $28.3 mil.; 4. End bal., T/Stock, $222.2 mil.; 7. EPS = $1.95
13-4B No check figure
13-5B Total stock. equity, $762,700
13-6B Total stock. equity, $629,000
13-7B RE, Dec. 31, 19X3, $146,000; EPS = $.56
13-8B EPS = $1.63; stock. equity, $528,130
DP No check figures
FSP No check figures

14-1A Loss of Sale on Inv., Jan. 14, $13,400
14-2A Inv. in Affiliates, 12/31, $11,549,000
14-3A Consol. Total assets, $830,000
14-4A Consol. Total assets, $899,000
14-5A 2. Long-term investments, $605,550
14-6A Cost of bond, $487,444
14-7A A. Loss, $100; B. Adj., $98,000
14-1B Gain on Sale of Inv., Feb. 6, $5,513
14-2B Inv. in Affiliates, 12/31, $84,595,000

14-7B ...
DP No check figures
FSP No check figures
CP, Pt. 4 Total liab.: Current, $71,250; Long-term, $289,536; Total S/E: $675, 874

15-1A No check figure
15-2A Increase in cash, $21,300
15-3A Net cash inflow from operations, $77,800
15-4A Net cash inflow from operations, $77,800
15-5A Net cash inflow from operations, $110,200
15-6A Net cash inflow from operations, $86,100
15-7A Net cash inflow from operations, $100,800
15-8A Net cash inflow from operations, $65,900
15-1B No check figure
15-2B Decrease in cash, $10,500
15-3B Net cash inflow from operations, $99,400
15-4B Net cash inflow from operations, $99,400
15-5B Net cash inflow from operations, $126,000
15-6B Net cash inflow from operations, $40,500
15-7B Net cash inflow from operations, $37,200
15-8B Net cash inflow from operations, $88,400
DP 1 No check figure
DP 2 Net cash inflow from operations, $170,000
FSP 1 2a. Collections, $11,021.9 mil.; 2b. Payments to employees, $802.9 mil.
FSP 2 No check figure
Appendix:
15A-1 Transaction analysis total debits, Panel A, $1,555,900
15A-2 Transaction analysis total debits, Panel A, $115,100
15A-3 Transaction analysis total debits, Panel A, $255,300
15A-4 Transaction analysis total debits, Panel A, $1,398,800

16-1A Per 2–Actual NI exceeds budget, $2,000
16-2A June net inc., $4,300
16-3A Net inc., 6 months, $5,192
16-4A Ending cash, July, $12,350
16-5A Total assets, $119,100; Owner's equity, $88,600
16-6A Dec. 31, 19X3, Net inc. $37,000
16-7A Net inc. $42,470; Total assets, $222,670
16-1B Per. 2–Actual NI exceeds budget, $2,000
16-2B Sept. net inc., $1,600
16-3B Net inc. 6 months, $32,210
16-4B Ending cash, Oct., $10,070
16-5B Total assets, $109,100; Owner's equity, $85,700
16-6B Dec. 31, 19X6, Net inc., $11,000
16-7B Net inc. $40,150; Total assets, $180,550
DP 1 Cash bal. before financing, $1,578
DP 2 Ending cash: Cotton, $285; Linen, $0

17-1A No check figure
17-2A 3. B/E sales = $750,000; 5. Income = $90,000
17-3A A. Unit contrib. margin, $1.50; B. Contrib. margin ratio, .471

(continued on back cover)

PRINCIPLES OF
FINANCIAL
&
MANAGEMENT
ACCOUNTING

A CORPORATE APPROACH

Charles T. Horngren
Stanford University

Walter T. Harrison, Jr.
Baylor University

Michael A. Robinson
Baylor University

 PRENTICE HALL Englewood Cliffs, New Jersey 07632

Library of Congress Cataloging-in-Publication Data

Horngren, Charles T.,
    Principles of financial and management accounting: a corporate
approach / Charles T. Horngren, Walter T. Harrison, Jr., Michael A.
Robinson.
        p.   cm.
    Includes indexes.
    ISBN 0-13-037748-1
    1. Corporations—Accounting.   2. Managerial accounting.
I. Harrison, Walter T.   II. Robinson, Michael A.   III. Title.
HF5686.C7H66   1994
658.15'11—dc20   93-31194
                                                         CIP

Managing Editor: Rob Dewey
Editor in Chief: Joseph Heider
Production Editor: Carol Burgett
Managing Editors, Production: Kris Ann Cappelluti, Joyce Turner
Cover Design: Rosemarie Paccione
Cover Art: *Magna I,* 1990, Bronze, height: 20″, © Joseph A. McDonnell, 1992
Copy Editor: Marie Lines, Margo Quinto
Buyers: Trudy Pisciotti, Herb Klein
Editorial Assistants: Linda Albelli, Renee Pelletier

For our wives: Joan, Nancy, and Roberta

Printed in the United States of America

10 9 8 7 6 5 4 3 2 1

ISBN: 0-13-037748-1

Prentice-Hall International (UK) Limited, *London*
Prentice-Hall of Australia Pty. Limited, *Sydney*
Prentice-Hall Canada Inc., *Toronto*
Prentice-Hall Hispanoamericana, S.A., *Mexico City*
Prentice-Hall of India Private Limited, *New Delhi*
Prentice-Hall of Japan, Inc., *Tokyo*
Simon & Schuster Asia Pte. Ltd., *Singapore*
Editora Prentice-Hall do Brasil, Ltda., *Rio de Janeiro*

PHOTO CREDITS

1	Stacy Pick/Stock, Boston
50	David Lawrence/The Stock Market
103	Tom Tracy/The Stock Market
149	Butch Martin/The Image Bank
214	Courtesy of Nordstrom
274	Courtesy of Citibank Diners Club, Inc.
331	Shostal/Superstock
395	Charles Gupton/Stock, Boston
439	Superstock
484	Courtesy of American Airlines
529	Jon Feingersh/The Stock Market
571	Teri Stratford
615	Courtesy of Texas Instruments
659	Reggie C. Parker/FPG International
706	Alan Carey/The Image Works
768	Courtesy of Lexus
809	Courtesy of Chrysler Corporation
846	Peter Yates/SABA
888	Jon Feingersh/The Stock Market
934	Arnulf Husmo/Tony Stone Images
974	Gabe Palmer/The Stock Market
1016	Joe Bator/The Stock Market
1056	Courtesy of Chrysler Corporation
1093	Ken Levine/Allsport
1136	Gianalberto Cigolini/The Image Bank
1171	Courtesy of Hewlett Packard
1210	Courtesy of Superstock

Brief Contents

Contents

Part Three
Accounting for Noncash Assets and Current Liabilities

Preface

Principles of Financial and Management Accounting provides full introductory coverage of both financial and management accounting. We have written the book for use throughout a two-semester or three-quarter sequence of accounting courses.

In content and emphasis, instructors will find that **Principles of Financial and Management Accounting** is in the mainstream for courses in introductory accounting. This book focuses on the most widely used accounting theory and practice. This text and its supplements supply the most effective tools available for learning fundamental accounting concepts and procedures.

Clarity and Accuracy

Two themes have directed our writing of this text—*clarity* and *accuracy*. We believe that we have produced the clearest prose, learning objectives, exhibits, definitions, and assignment material for courses in principles of accounting. Students will find this book easy to study. We have assumed that students have no previous education in accounting or business.

The contributions of many reviewers who teach introductory accounting courses have guided us in writing an accurate text. We and the publishers have sought input on our work from an unprecedented number of accounting educators and students in order to publish a book that meets your strict demands for accuracy.

This demand for accuracy did not stop with the text. The authors and publisher have taken extraordinary care and incurred extraordinary cost to ensure that the supplements are accurate. The *Solutions Manual*, in particular, went through a rigorous review process. The authors' solutions were checked by two independent reviewers, reconciled by the supplements coordinator, and then checked again through a Lotus program. The final typeset solutions were reworked one last time by a third independent reviewer.

The Business Context of Accounting

To enhance our presentation of accounting, we set out to create a business context for the student. As often as possible, we have integrated actual companies and their business data into our text narrative and assignment material. Students reading about companies familiar to them find the material interesting and also develop a deeper appreciation for accounting's importance in today's business world. When information drawn from real companies would be too advanced for introductory students, we illustrated the accounting point at hand by using realistic examples, building a framework of relevance that makes learning the topic more inviting to the students.

Each chapter opens with a description of an actual business situation. We call these *vignettes*, and most are drawn from the business press. We also bring students inside the world of business through three of our supplements: ABC News videos, *New York Times* articles, and Disclosure software (which presents financial data from publicly traded companies).

Distinctive Features

Assignment Material

Principles of Financial and Management Accounting has voluminous assignment material. Exercises and problems are referenced to chapter learning objectives. In addition, chapters conclude with a special feature called Extending Your Knowledge. This section includes Decision Problems and an Ethical Issue case.

Chapter-Opening Vignettes

Each chapter opens with an actual business situation. We believe that emphasis on the real-world environment of business promotes student interest and learning. These vignettes are referred to as appropriate throughout the text.

Recommendations of the Accounting Education Change Commission

The recommendations of this important group have inspired us in several ways.

* Chapter 1 includes a discussion of ethics in business, and, as we mentioned, all chapters include an Ethical Issue case for student analysis.
* To sharpen students' decision-making skills, financial ratios are interspersed throughout the text. For example, Chapter 4 introduces the current ratio and the debt ratio, Chapter 5 covers the gross margin percentage and inventory turnover, and Chapter 8 discusses the acid-test ratio and days' sales in receivables. Other ratios appear throughout the book as appropriate (Chapter 27, Using Accounting Information to Make Business Decisions, presents all important financial ratios, including those discussed elsewhere in the text.)
* To meet the challenge of improving students' communications skills, we include in all chapters new assignment material that requires essay answers.

Four-Color Design

The four-color design enlivens and eases learning. A strong program of visual features—exhibits and tables—helps reinforce the text. Note that the two-tone beige tint in exhibits denotes financial statements. The green tint in exhibits identifies ledgers, journals, work sheets, and the like. The learning objectives appear in a textured tint panel at the chapter's opening and in the text margin. Key headings appear in blue. And full-color photos tied to the chapter-opening vignettes begin every chapter.

Two-tone beige denotes financial statements	Green identifies ledgers, journals, work sheets, and so on	Pale texture highlights learning objectives

Management Accounting

Management accounting chapters follow a logical order. Chapter 16 begins our study of management accounting by demonstrating how budgets are prepared. Chapter 17 introduces a model of cost-volume-profit relationships, an important planning tool of managers. Our first two chapters on management accounting are confined to nonmanufacturing organizations. In this way, we can explore two major tools (budgets and the cost-volume-profit model) without contending with the many new terms associated with manufacturing organizations.

Chapter 18 extends our discussion of cost behavior introduced in Chapter 17. We discuss three methods used by accountants to determine cost behavior patterns and show how knowledge of these patterns is important for decision making, planning, and control.

Chapters 19 and 20 describe the two major types of manufacturing accounting systems: job order and process. We focus on the methods used by accountants to cost products for inventory valuation and income determination. Chapters 21 and 22 pursue management accounting tools in more depth. We show how accounting information is used to evaluate the performance of both business segments and their managers.

Chapter 23 introduces students to several accounting and management techniques that have gained widespread acceptance in recent years. We discuss activity-based costing, just-in-time (JIT) production systems, life-cycle budgeting, target costing, and total quality management (TQM). The overall themes of this chapter are the need for accurate information for management decisions and the need for continuous improvement of business processes to remain competitive.

In Chapters 24 and 25, we illustrate the use of accounting information in specific business decisions. The focus is short-term in the first chapter and long-term in the second. In Chapter 26, we discuss transfer pricing in both domestic and international contexts. We then extend our previous discussions of performance evaluation by demonstrating two methods used to assess the profitability of entire businesses and their major divisions.

Chapter Organization

1. Each chapter begins with a vignette, as we have described. Learning objectives also appear at the start of every chapter. These objectives are keyed to the relevant chapter material and are also referenced to the exercises and problems.

2. Most chapters offer two *Summary Problems for Your Review*. Each *Summary Problem* includes its fully worked-out solution. These features, which generally appear at the halfway point and at the end of each chapter, provide students with immediate feedback and serve as key review aids.

3. Each chapter presents three important tools for student review. A text *Summary* recaps the chapter discussion. *Self-Study Questions* allow students to test their understanding of the chapter. The text that supports the answer is referenced by page number, and the answers appear before the Assignment Material. *Accounting Vocabulary* presents the key terms introduced in the chapter, complete with their definitions.

4. *Assignment Material* is more varied and plentiful than in competing texts. *Questions* (covering the major definitions, concepts, and procedures) may be assigned as homework or used to promote discussion in class. *Exercises,* identified by topic area and learning objectives, cover the full spectrum of the chapter text. *Problems,* also identified by topic area and learning objectives, come in A and B sets. The two sets allow instructors to vary assignments from term to term and to solve the A or B problem in class and assign the related problem for homework. Those exercises and problems that can be solved using the Lotus 1-2-3® templates are designated by a black computer disk.

5. Each chapter ends with an *Extending Your Knowledge* section. Under this heading are presented:

> *two *Decision Problems,* which help students to develop critical thinking skills. Analysis, interpretation, and determining a course of action are ordinarily required.
>
> *an *Ethical Issue* case, which presents a business scenario that challenges the ethical conduct of the accountant and asks the student to resolve the dilemma. Many of these cases also challenge students' accounting skills.
>
> *two *Financial Statement Problems* (for most chapters). The first problem links the chapter's subject matter directly to the actual financial statements in the annual report of The Goodyear Tire & Rubber Company, which appears in Appendix C. Students answer the second financial statement problem using data taken from the annual report of another company. Instructors may refer students to annual reports kept in the library or contained in Disclosure's Compact D™/ SEC Academic Edition.

The Supplements Package

We have a far-reaching package of teaching and learning tools to supplement the text. A team of contributors devoted hundreds of hours to perfecting the supplements. Our supplements coordinator, who is a professional accounting teacher, together with a full-time development editor worked with the contributors to ensure maximum instructional value, accuracy, and consistency with the text and within the supplements package.

Resources from the Business World _____

The three supplements we describe here—unique to **Principles of Financial and Management Accounting** and Prentice Hall—show students how the accounting they are learning in the classroom works in the context of actual business.

ABC News/PH Video Library for *Principles of Financial and Management Accounting*

Video is the most dynamic of all the supplements you can use to enhance your class. The quality of the video material and how well it relates to your course can make all the difference. For these reasons, Prentice Hall and ABC News have decided to work together to bring you the best and most comprehensive video ancillaries available in the college market.

Through its wide variety of award-winning programs—*Nightline, Business World, On Business, This Week with David Brinkley, World News Tonight,* and *The Health Show*—ABC offers a resource for feature and documentary-style videos related to text concepts and applications. The programs have extremely high production quality, present substantial content, and are hosted by well-versed, well-known anchors. Prentice Hall, its authors, and its editors provide the benefit of having selected videos on topics that will work well with this course and text and give the instructor teaching notes on how to use them in the classroom. "The ABC News/PH Video Library for **Principles of Financial and Management Accounting**" offers video material for selected topics in the text. A video guide is provided to integrate the videos into your lecture.

The New York Times

The New York Times and Prentice Hall are sponsoring "Themes of the Times," a program designed to enhance student access to current information of relevance in the classroom. Through this program, the core subject matter provided in the text is supplemented by a collection of time-sensitive articles from one of the world's most distinguished newspapers, *The New York Times*. These articles demonstrate the connection between what is learned in the classroom and what is happening in the world around us. To enjoy the wealth of information of *The New York Times* daily, a reduced subscription rate is available. For information, call toll-free: 1-800-631-1222.

Prentice Hall and *The New York Times* are proud to co-sponsor "Themes of the Times." We hope it will make the reading of both textbooks and newspapers a dynamic learning process.

Compact D™/SEC Academic Edition

Through an exclusive arrangement with Disclosure, Prentice Hall is providing adopters of this text with a software disk containing detailed profiles and financial data for 100 publicly traded companies. By combining this wealth of data with computer-search capabilities, students can analyze companies of their choosing. Financial statement problems written specifically for use with the Compact D™/SEC Academic Edition are included in most chapters.

Acknowledgments

The authors and publisher wish to thank our many reviewers, whose contributions have meant so much to this project.

Reviewers

John Blahnik, Lorain County Community C.
Walter DeAguero, Saddleback C.
Graig Griffiths, Blinn C.
Donald Minyard, Samford U.
Marilyn Okleshen, Mankato State U.
Sandra Penn, Wayne State U.
Robert Ripley, San Diego City C.
Audrey Taylor, Wayne State U.
Vicki Vorell, Cuyahoga Community C.
Steven Wong, San Jose City C.

Questionnaire Respondents

Fouad Ainajjar, Wayne State U.
Frank Beigbeder, Rancho Santiago C.

John Blahnik, Lorain County Community C.
Walter DeAguero, Saddleback C.
Sue Garr, Wayne State U.
John Keros, Eastern Michigan U.
Donald Minyard, Samford U.
Marilyn Okleshen, Mankato State U.
Sandra Penn, Wayne State U.
Sue Ravenscroft, Eastern Michigan U.
Robert Ripley, San Diego City C.
Leo Ruggle, Mankato State U.
Raymond Shaffer, Youngstown State U.
Audrey Taylor, Wayne State U.
John Varga, Orange Coast C.
Alan Vogel, Cuyahoga Community C.
Vicki Vorell, Cuyahoga Community C.
Steven Wong, San Jose City C.

The authors also wish to thank Eric Carlsen for his assistance with the computer sections of this text and W. Morley Lemon for his contributions to the Decision Problems.

Among the many people at Prentice Hall who helped to publish this book are: Linda Albelli, Lisamarie Brassini, Carol Burgett, Kris Ann Cappelluti, Terri Daly, Patti Dant, Diane deCastro, Stephen Deitmer, Rob Dewey, Anne DiBisceglie, Patrice Fraccio, David Gillespie, Joseph Heider, Herb Klein, Lori Morris-Nantz, Judy Perkinson, Trudy Pisciotti, Joyce Turner, and Patricia Wosczyk.

Charles T. Horngren
Walter T. Harrison, Jr.
Michael A. Robinson

Accounting and Its Environment

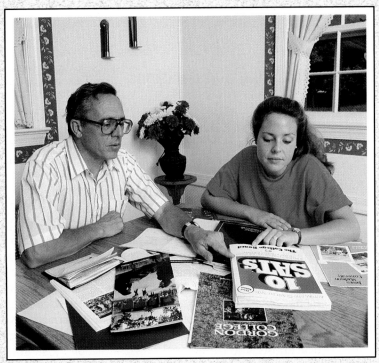

Melissa Roberts is making college plans for next year. She must choose from two alternatives. She can stay at home and attend the Community College of Denver or enroll in the University of Colorado and live on campus. By staying at home she can save on room and board expense. Also, she can keep her job at Kinko's, the photocopying store, where she earns money for her car payments. If she instead chooses to attend the University of Colorado, she cannot live at home. Her family can help her with tuition and fees, but Melissa will be on her own to cover room, board, and personal expenses. Would she be able to find a job at the university to pay these personal expenses? Would she have to sell her car? Of course, Melissa must determine which school offers the better education. The university is more expensive, but will she be able to land a job paying her a higher salary if she chooses the university over the community college?

Each year millions of students face similar decisions. They weigh the costs and the benefits of the various educational choices. They must estimate how much their education will be worth and how much it will cost. Financing the education includes determining what the family can afford, what the student may earn while in school, and what amount, if any, must be borrowed. These financial considerations are accounting matters. As you read Chapter 1, consider how Melissa might use accounting information in deciding which school to attend. Also think over how people in nearly every walk of life can apply accounting information in making decisions in their daily lives.

Accounting and Decisions

Accounting has been called "the language of business." Perhaps a better term is "the language of financial decisions." The better you understand the language, the better you can manage the financial aspects of living. Personal financial planning, investments, loans, car payments, income taxes, and many other aspects of daily life are based on accounting. A recent survey indicates that business managers believe it is more important for college students to learn accounting than any other business subject. Other surveys show that persons trained in accounting and finance make it to the top of their organizations in greater numbers than persons trained in any other field. Indeed, accounting is an important subject.

Regardless of your roles in life—student, head of household, investor, manager, politician—you will find a knowledge of accounting helpful. The major purpose of this book is to help you learn to use accounting information to make informed decisions. Individuals who can do so have a great advantage over those who cannot.

OBJECTIVE 1

Develop a working vocabulary for decision making

What Is Accounting?

Accounting is the system that measures business activities, processes that information into reports, and communicates these findings to decision makers. **Financial statements** are the documents that report on an individual's or an organization's business in monetary amounts.

Is our business making a profit? Should we start up a new line of women's clothing? Are sales strong enough to warrant opening a new branch outlet? The most intelligent answers to business questions like these use accounting information. Decision makers use the information to develop sound business plans. As new programs affect the business's activities, accounting takes the company's financial pulse rate. The cycle continues as the accounting system measures the results of activities and reports the results to decision makers.

Bookkeeping is a procedural element of accounting just as arithmetic is a procedural element of mathematics. Increasingly, people are using computers to do much of the detailed bookkeeping work at all levels—in households, businesses, and organizations of all types. Exhibit 1-1 illustrates the role of accounting in business.

Users of Accounting Information: The Decision Makers

Decisions beg for information. The more important the decision, the greater the need for relevant information. Virtually all businesses and most individuals keep accounting records to aid decision making. Most of the material in this book describes business situations, but the principles of accounting apply to the financial considerations of individuals as well. The following sections discuss the range of people and groups who use accounting information and the decisions they make.

Individuals.   People use accounting information in day-to-day affairs to manage their bank accounts, to evaluate job prospects, to make investments, and to decide whether to rent or to buy a house.

Businesses.   Managers of businesses use accounting information to set goals for their organizations, to evaluate their progress toward those goals, and to take corrective action if necessary. Decisions based on accounting information may include which building and equipment to purchase, how much merchandise inventory to keep on hand for sale to customers, and how much cash to borrow.

Investors and Creditors.   Investors provide the money that businesses need to begin operations. To decide whether to help start a new venture, potential investors evaluate what income they can reasonably expect on their investment. This means analyzing the financial statements of the new business. Those people who do invest monitor the progress of the business by analyzing the company's financial statements and by keeping up with its developments in the business press—for example, *The Wall Street Journal, Business Week, Forbes,* and *Fortune,* and the business section of the *New York Times.* Accounting reports are a major source of information for the business press.

EXHIBIT 1-1   *The Accounting System: The Flow of Information*

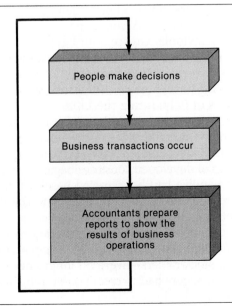

Before making a loan, potential lenders determine the borrower's ability to meet scheduled payments. This evaluation includes a projection of future operations, which is based on accounting information.

Government Regulatory Agencies. Most organizations face government regulation. For example, the Securities and Exchange Commission (SEC), a federal agency, requires businesses to disclose certain financial information to the investing public. The SEC, like many government agencies, bases its regulatory activity in part on the accounting information it receives from firms.

Taxing Authorities. Local, state, and federal governments levy taxes on individuals and businesses. The amount of the tax is figured using accounting information. Businesses determine their sales tax based on their accounting records that show how much they have sold. Individuals and businesses compute their income tax based on how much money their records show they have earned.

Nonprofit Organizations. Nonprofit organizations—such as churches, most hospitals, government agencies, and colleges that operate for purposes other than to earn a profit—use accounting information in much the same way that profit-oriented businesses do. Both profit organizations and nonprofit organizations deal with budgets, payrolls, rent payments, and the like—all from the accounting system.

Other Users. Employees and labor unions may make wage demands based on the accounting information that shows their employer's reported income. Consumer groups and the general public are also interested in the amount of income that businesses earn. For example, during times of fuel shortages consumer groups have charged that oil companies have earned "obscene profits." On a more positive note, newspapers report "improved profit pictures" of companies as the nation emerges from an economic recession. Such news, based on accounting information, is related to our standard of living.

The Development of Accounting Thought

Accounting has a long history. Some scholars claim that writing arose in order to record accounting information. Account records date back to the ancient civilizations of China, Babylonia, Greece, and Egypt. The rulers of these civilizations used accounting to keep track of the cost of labor and materials used in building structures like the great pyramids.

Accounting developed further as a result of the information needs of merchants in the city-states of Italy during the 1400s. In that commercial climate the monk Luca Pacioli, a mathematician and friend of Leonardo da Vinci, published the first known description of double-entry bookkeeping in 1494.

The pace of accounting development increased during the Industrial Revolution as the economies of developed countries began to mass-produce goods. Until that time, merchandise had been priced based on managers' hunches about cost, but increased competition required merchants to adopt more sophisticated accounting systems.

In the nineteenth century, the growth of corporations, especially those in the railroad and steel industries, spurred the development of accounting. Corporation owners—the stockholders—were no longer necessarily the managers of their business. Managers had to create accounting systems to report to the owners how well their businesses were doing.

The role of government has led to still more accounting developments. When the federal government started the income tax, accounting supplied the concept of "income." Also, government at all levels has assumed expanded roles in health, education, labor, and economic planning. To ensure that the information that it uses to make decisions is reliable, the government has required strict accountability in the business community.

The Accounting Profession

OBJECTIVE 2
Identify different aspects of the accounting profession

Positions in the field of accounting may be divided into several areas. Two general classifications are *public accounting* and *private accounting*.

Public accountants are those who serve the general public and collect professional fees for their work, much as doctors and lawyers do. Their work includes auditing, income tax planning and preparation, and management consulting. These specialized accounting services are discussed in the next section. Public accountants are a small fraction (about 10 percent) of all accountants. Those public accountants who have met certain professional requirements are designated as **Certified Public Accountants (CPAs).**

Private accountants work for a single business, such as a local department store, the McDonald's restaurant chain, or the Eastman Kodak Company. Charitable organizations, educational institutions, and government agencies also employ private accountants. The chief accounting officer usually has the title of controller, treasurer, or chief financial officer. Whatever the title, this person usually carries the status of vice-president.

Some public accountants pool their talents and work together within a single firm. Most public accounting firms are called *CPA firms* because most of their professional employees are CPAs. CPA firms vary greatly in size. Some are small businesses, and others are medium-sized partnerships. The largest CPA firms are worldwide partnerships with over 2,000 partners. Such huge firms are necessary because of the size and complexity of operations of some of their clients. For instance, Price Waterhouse, one of the six largest American CPA firms, has reported that its annual audit of one particular client would take one accountant 630,720 hours of effort—that equals 72 years of nonstop work! Another Price Waterhouse client owns 300 separate corporate entities. All their records are combined into a single set of financial statements. Such time-consuming tasks make a large staff of accountants a necessity.

The six largest American accounting firms, often called the Big Six, are, in alphabetical order,

Arthur Andersen & Co.   Ernst & Young
Coopers & Lybrand   KPMG Peat Marwick
Deloitte & Touche   Price Waterhouse & Co.

Although these firms employ only about 12 percent of the 350,000 CPAs in the United States, they audit the financial statements of approximately 85 percent of the 2,600 largest corporations. The top partners in large accounting firms earn about the same amount as the top managers of other large businesses.

Exhibit 1-2 shows the accounting positions within public accounting firms and other organizations. Of special interest in the exhibit is the upward movement of accounting personnel, as the arrows show. In particular, note how accountants may move from positions in public accounting firms to similar or higher positions in industry and government. This is a frequently traveled

EXHIBIT 1-2 *Accounting Positions within Organizations*

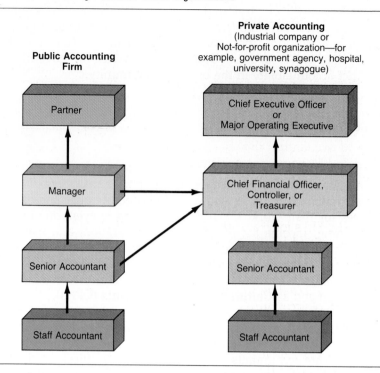

career path. Because accounting deals with all facets of an organization—such as purchasing, manufacturing, marketing, and distribution—it provides an excellent basis for gaining broad business experience.

Accounting Organizations and Designations

The position of accounting in today's business world has created the need for control over the professional, educational, and ethical standards for accountants.

The *American Institute of Certified Public Accountants (AICPA)* is the national professional organization of CPAs. A CPA is a professional accountant who earns this title through a combination of education, qualifying experience, and an acceptable score on a written national examination that takes approximately 2½ days. The AICPA prepares and grades the examination and gives the results to the individual states, which then issue licenses that enable qualifying people to practice accounting as CPAs. CPAs must also be of high moral character and must conduct their professional practices according to a code of professional conduct. Other nations have similar arrangements, but some use the designation *Chartered Accountant* in place of *Certified Public Accountant*.

The AICPA also develops accounting and auditing principles. The Auditing Standards Board of the AICPA formulates generally accepted auditing standards, which govern the way CPAs perform audits. The AICPA publishes a monthly professional journal, the *Journal of Accountancy*.

State societies of CPAs are professional organizations, much like the AICPA, but their jurisdictions are limited to their respective states. Each state has a state board of accountancy, which administers the state laws that regulate the practice of accounting within its borders. State boards of accountancy, not the AICPA, issue CPA certificates to qualifying individuals.

The *Financial Accounting Standards Board (FASB)* is the body that formulates **generally accepted accounting principles (GAAP)**. These principles, which we discuss later in this chapter, are the most important accounting guidelines. The FASB issues documents called *financial accounting standards,* which are to financial accounting what government laws are to our general conduct. The FASB, composed of seven members, is governed by the Financial Accounting Foundation and is not a part of the AICPA or any other organization.

The *Institute of Management Accountants (IMA),* formerly the *National Association of Accountants (NAA),* focuses on the practice of management accounting, the branch of accounting that is designed to help manage a business. A *CMA*—Certified Management Accountant—earns this designation much as a CPA does but under the direction of the IMA. The IMA publishes the journal *Management Accounting.*

Like the IMA, the *Financial Executives Institute (FEI)* is active in management accounting. The FEI's journal is the *Financial Executive.*

The *CIA*—Certified Internal Auditor—receives this designation from the *Institute of Internal Auditors (IIA).* This organization publishes the journal *The Internal Auditor.*

The *American Accounting Association (AAA)* focuses on the academic and research aspects of accounting. A high percentage of its members are professors. The AAA publishes the quarterly journals *The Accounting Review, Accounting Horizons,* and *Issues in Accounting Education.*

The *Securities and Exchange Commission (SEC)* is an agency of the United States government with the legal power to set and enforce accounting and auditing standards. The SEC has delegated much of this authority to the private sector (through the FASB and the AICPA).

The *Internal Revenue Service (IRS),* another federal agency, has the responsibility of enforcing the tax laws and of collecting the revenue needed to finance the operations of the government. Since it focuses primarily on taxes, the main impact of the IRS is on taxation.

Ethical Considerations in Accounting and Business _____

Ethical considerations pervade all areas of accounting and business. Think over the following situation, which challenged the ethical conduct of the accountant.

Texaco Corporation was recently the defendant in a lawsuit that threatened to put the company out of business. The managers and accountants of Texaco had reason to downplay this lawsuit for fear that customers would stop buying the company's products, that Texaco's stock price would fall, and that banks would stop loaning money to the company. Should Texaco have disclosed this sensitive information? Generally accepted accounting principles required Texaco to describe this situation in its financial statements, and the company's auditor was required to state whether the Texaco disclosure was adequate.

A common thread running through all accounting situations is the need to provide *information.* Our entire economic system is based on an orderly flow of honest information for decision making. Accountants are a vital link in this information chain. Whether or not an accountant provides honest information will make or break a career. The most important asset of an accountant (or any professional) is the quality of the person's reputation. Opinion polls rank accountants among the most honest professionals.

By what criteria do accountants address questions that challenge their ethical conduct? The American Institute of Certified Public Accountants (AICPA), the Institute of Management Accountants (IMA), and most large companies have codes of ethics that bind their members and employees to high levels of ethical conduct.

AICPA Code of Professional Conduct

The Code of Professional Conduct was adopted by the members of the AICPA to provide guidance in performing their professional duties. The Preamble to the Code of Conduct states, "[A] certified public accountant assumes an obligation of self-discipline above and beyond the requirements of laws and regulations . . . an unswerving commitment to honorable behavior, even at the sacrifice of personal advantage." Key terms in the Code include *self-discipline, honorable behavior, moral judgments, the public interest, professionalism, integrity,* and *technical and ethical standards.*

IMA Standards of Ethical Behavior

The opening paragraph of the IMA Standards of Ethical Conduct states, "Management accountants have an obligation to the organizations they serve, their profession, the public, and themselves to maintain the highest standards of ethical conduct." The Ethical Standards include sections on competence, confidentiality, integrity, objectivity, and resolution of ethical conflict. The requirements for a high level of professional conduct are similar to those in the AICPA code. The IMA standards, however, are written from the perspective of a management accountant rather than from the perspective of an independent auditor.

The Boeing Company's Business Conduct Guidelines

Most corporations impose standards of ethical conduct on their employees. One example is the guidelines formulated by the Boeing Company, a leading manufacturer of aircraft. In the introduction to Boeing's set of business conduct standards, the chairperson of the board and chief executive officer state, "We owe our success as much to our reputation for integrity as we do to the quality and dependability of our products and services. This reputation is fragile and can easily be lost." For example, Boeing could be ruined if shoddy work led to plane crashes.

Specialized Accounting Services

Because accounting affects people in many different fields, public accounting and private accounting include specialized services.

Public Accounting

Auditing is the accounting profession's most significant service to the public. An audit is the independent examination that ensures the reliability of the accounting reports that management prepares and submits to investors, creditors, and others outside the business. In carrying out an audit, CPAs from outside a business examine the business's financial statements. If the CPAs believe that these documents are a fair presentation of the business's operations, the CPAs give a professional opinion stating that the firm's financial statements are in accordance with GAAP. Why is the audit so important? Creditors considering loans want assurance that the facts and figures the borrower submits are reliable. Stockholders, who have invested in the company, need to know that the financial picture management shows them is complete. Government agencies need accurate information from businesses.

Tax accounting has two aims: complying with the tax laws and minimizing the taxes to be paid. Because federal income tax rates range as high as 31 percent for individuals and 34 percent for corporations, reducing income tax is an important management consideration. Tax work by accountants consists of preparing tax returns and planning business transactions in order to minimize taxes. CPAs advise individuals on what types of investments to make and on how to structure their transactions.

Management consulting is the catchall term that describes the wide scope of advice CPAs provide to help managers run a business. As CPAs conduct audits, they look deep into a business's operations. With the insight they gain, they often make suggestions for improvements in the business's management structure and accounting systems. (We discuss these areas of accounting in the next section.) Management consulting is the fastest-growing service provided by accountants.

Private Accounting

Cost accounting analyzes a business's costs to help managers control expenses. Traditionally, cost accounting has emphasized manufacturing costs, but it is increasingly concerned with the cost of selling the goods. Good cost accounting records guide managers in pricing their products to achieve greater profits. Also, cost accounting information shows management when a product is not profitable and should be dropped.

Budgeting sets sales and profit goals and develops detailed plans—called budgets—for achieving those goals. Many companies regard their budgeting activities as one of the most important aspects of their accounting systems. Some of the most successful companies in the United States have been pioneers in the field of budgeting—Procter & Gamble and General Electric, for example.

Information systems design identifies the organization's information needs, both internal and external. Using flow charts and manuals, designers develop and implement the system to meet those needs. Accounting information systems help control the organization's operations.

Internal auditing is performed by a business's own accountants. Large organizations—Motorola, Bank of America, and 3M among them—maintain a staff of internal auditors. These accountants evaluate the firm's own accounting and management systems. Their aim is to improve operating efficiency and to ensure that employees and departments follow management's policies, plans, and procedures.

Exhibit 1-3 summarizes these accounting specializations. They may also be grouped under the headings financial accounting and management accounting.

Financial accounting provides information to people outside the firm. Creditors and stockholders, for example, are not part of the day-to-day management of the company. Likewise, government agencies, such as the SEC, and the general public are external users of a firm's accounting information. This book deals primarily with financial accounting.

Management accounting generates confidential information for internal decision makers, such as top executives, department heads, college deans, and hospital administrators. Other books cover management accounting.

EXHIBIT 1-3 *Public and Private Accounting*

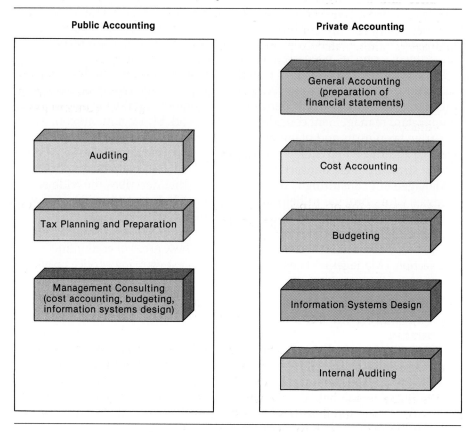

Types of Business Organizations

Businesses take one of three forms of organization, and in some cases the accounting procedures depend on the organization form. Therefore, you should understand differences between a proprietorship, a partnership, and a corporation.

A **proprietorship** has a single owner, called the proprietor, who is usually also the manager. Proprietorships tend to be small retail establishments and individual professional businesses, such as those of physicians, attorneys, and accountants. A proprietor is personally liable for the debts and obligations of the business. However, from the accounting viewpoint each proprietorship is distinct from its proprietor. Thus the accounting records of the proprietorship do not include records of the proprietor's personal affairs.

A **partnership** joins two or more individuals together as co-owners. Each owner is a partner. Many retail establishments, as well as some professional organizations of physicians, attorneys, and accountants, are partnerships. Like proprietors, partners are personally liable for the debts of their business. Most partnerships are small and medium-sized, but some are gigantic, exceeding 2,000 partners. Accountants treat the partnership as a separate organization, distinct from the personal affairs of each partner. Accounting for partnerships is covered in Appendix D.

A **corporation** is a business owned by **stockholders.** The corporation is the dominant form of business organization in the United States. Although proprietorships and partnerships are more numerous, corporations transact more business and are larger in terms of total assets, income, and number of employees. Most well-known companies, such as CBS, General Motors, and American Airlines, are corporations. Their full names include *Corporation* or *Incorporated* (abbreviated *Corp.* and *Inc.*) to indicate that they are corporations, for example, CBS, Inc. and General Motors Corporation. Some corporations bear the name "Company," such as Ford Motor Company. This title does not clearly identify the organization as a corporation because a proprietorship and a partnership can also bear the name "Company." This book concentrates on corporations.

Characteristics of a Corporation _____

We now look at the principal features of a corporation to distinguish this form of business organization from proprietorships and partnerships.

Separate Legal Entity

A **corporation** is a business entity formed under state law. The state grants a **charter,** which is the document that gives the state's permission to form a corporation.

A corporation is a distinct entity from a legal perspective. We may consider the corporation as an artificial person that exists apart from its owners, who are called **stockholders** or **shareholders.** The corporation has many of the rights that a person has. For example, a corporation may buy, own, and sell property. Assets and liabilities in the business belong to the corporation. The corporation may enter into contracts, sue, and be sued.

The ownership interest of a corporation is divided into shares of **stock.** A person becomes a stockholder by purchasing the stock of the corporation. The corporate charter specifies how much stock the corporation can issue (sell) and lists the other details of its relationship with the state.

Continuous Life and Transferability of Ownership

Most corporations have continuous lives regardless of changes in the ownership of their stock. Stockholders may transfer stock as they wish. They may sell or trade the stock to another person, give it away, bequeath it in a will, or dispose of it in any other way they desire. The transfer of the stock does not affect the continuity of the corporation. Proprietorships and partnerships, on the other hand, terminate when their ownership changes.

No Mutual Agency

Mutual agency of the owners is not present in a corporation as it is in a partnership. This means that the stockholder of a corporation cannot commit the corporation to a contract (unless he or she is also an officer in the business). For this reason, a stockholder need not exercise the care that partners must in selecting co-owners of the business.

Limited Liability of Stockholders

A stockholder has **limited liability** for corporation debts. Unlike proprietors and partners, a stockholder has no personal obligation for corporation liabilities. The most that a stockholder can lose on an investment in a corporation's stock is the cost of the investment. On the other hand, proprietors and partners are personally liable for the debts of their businesses.

The combination of limited liability and no mutual agency means that persons can invest limited amounts in a corporation without fear of losing all their personal wealth because of a business failure. This feature enables a corporation to raise more capital from a wider group of investors than proprietorships and partnerships.

Separation of Ownership and Management

Stockholders own the business, but a board of directors—elected by the stockholders—appoints corporate officers to manage the business. Thus stockholders may invest $1,000 or $1 million in the corporation without having to manage the business or disrupt their personal affairs.

However, this separation between owners—stockholders—and management may create problems. Corporate officers may decide to run the business for their own benefit and not to the stockholders' advantage. Stockholders may find it difficult to lodge an effective protest against management policy because of the distance between them and management.

Corporate Taxation

Corporations are separate taxable entities. They pay a variety of taxes not borne by proprietorships or partnerships. These taxes include an annual franchise tax levied by the state. The franchise tax is paid to keep the corporation charter in force and enables the corporation to continue in business. Corporations also pay federal and state income taxes. Corporate earnings are subject to **double taxation.** First, corporations pay their own income taxes on corporate income. Then, the stockholders pay personal income tax on the cash dividends that they receive from corporations. This is different from proprietorships and partnerships, which pay no business income tax. Instead, the tax falls solely on the owners.

Government Regulation

Strong government regulation is an important disadvantage to the corporation. Because stockholders have only limited liability for corporation debts, outsiders doing business with the corporation can look no further than the corporation itself for any claims that may arise against the business. To protect persons who loan money to a corporation or who invest in its stock, states monitor the affairs of corporations. For many corporations, this government regulation is expensive.

Organization of a Corporation

Creation of a corporation begins when its organizers, called the **incorporators,** obtain a charter from the state. The charter includes the authorization for the corporation to issue a certain number of shares of stock, which are shares of ownership in the corporation. The incorporators pay fees, sign the charter, and file the required documents with the state. Then the corporation comes into existence. The incorporators agree to a set of **bylaws,** which act as the constitution for governing the corporation.

The ultimate control of the corporation rests with the stockholders, who receive one vote for each share of stock they own. The stockholders elect the members of the **board of directors,** which sets policy for the corporation and appoints the officers. The board elects a chairperson, who usually is the most powerful person in the corporation. The board also designates the president, who is the chief operating officer in charge of managing day-to-day operations. Most corporations also have vice-presidents in charge of sales, manufacturing, accounting and finance, and other key areas. Often the president and one or more vice-presidents are also elected to the board of directors. Exhibit 1-4 shows the authority structure in a corporation.

A corporation keeps a subsidiary record of its stockholders. The business must notify the stockholders of the annual stockholder meeting and mail them dividend payments (which we discuss later in this chapter). Large companies use a registrar to maintain the stockholder list and a transfer agent to issue stock certificates. Banks provide these registration and transfer services. The transfer agent handles the change in stock ownership from one shareholder to another.

OBJECTIVE 3

Apply accounting concepts and principles to business situations

Accounting Concepts and Principles _____

As stated previously, the rules that govern how accountants measure, process, and communicate financial information are called generally accepted accounting principles, or GAAP.

EXHIBIT 1-4 *Authority Structure in a Corporation*

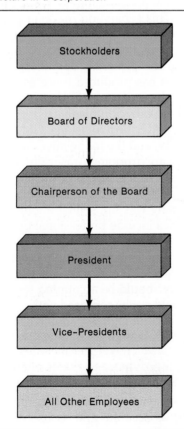

The term *accounting principles* is broader than you might at first think. Generally accepted accounting principles include not only principles but also concepts and methods that identify the proper way to produce accounting information. Generally accepted accounting principles are very much like the law—a set of rules for conducting behavior in a way acceptable to the majority of people. GAAP rests on a conceptual framework written by the Financial Accounting Standards Board. The primary objective of financial reporting is to provide information useful for making investment and lending decisions. To be useful, information must be relevant, reliable, and comparable. Accountants strive to meet these goals in the information they produce. Your study of this course will expose you to the generally accepted methods of accounting. First, however, you need to understand the *entity concept*, the *reliability principle*, the *cost principle*, the *going-concern concept*, and the *stable-monetary-unit concept*. These are basic to your first exposure to accounting.

The Entity Concept

The most basic concept in accounting is that of the **entity**. An accounting entity is an organization or a section of an organization that stands apart from other organizations and individuals as a separate economic unit. From an accounting perspective, sharp boundaries are drawn around each entity so as not to confuse its affairs with those of other entities.

Consider Mazzio, a pizzeria owner whose bank account shows a $20,000 balance at the end of the year. Only half of that amount—$10,000—grew from the business's operations. The other $10,000 arose from the sale of the family motorboat. If Mazzio follows the entity concept, he will account for the money generated by the business—one economic unit—separately from the money generated by the sale of an item belonging not to the business but to himself—a second economic unit. This separation makes it possible to view the business's financial position clearly.

Suppose Mazzio disregards the entity concept and treats the full $20,000 amount as attributable to the pizzeria's operations. He will be misled into believing that the business has produced twice as much cash as it has. The steps needed to improve the business will likely not be taken.

Consider GM, a huge organization made up of its Chevrolet, Buick, Oldsmobile, Cadillac, Pontiac, and Saturn divisions. GM considers each division as a separate accounting entity, and the following example shows why. Suppose sales in the Buick division are dropping drastically. GM will want to come up with an immediate solution to the problem. But if sales figures from all five divisions were treated as a single lump-sum amount, then management would not even know the company was not selling enough Buicks.

Other accounting entities include professional organizations such as a law firm, a doctor's practice, a hospital, a church or synagogue, a college or university, and a family household. Each entity may have a number of subentities. For example, universities have various colleges like law and business as subentities. Each subentity should be accounted for separately. In summary, business transactions should not be confused with personal transactions. Similarly, the transactions of different entities should not be accounted for together. Each entity should be evaluated separately.

The Reliability (or Objectivity) Principle

Accounting records and statements are based on the most reliable data available so that they will be as accurate and as useful as possible. This is the **reliability principle.** Reliable data are verifiable. They may be confirmed by any independent observer. Ideally, then, accounting records are based on information that flows from activities that are documented by objective evidence. Without the reliability principle, also called the *objectivity principle,* accounting records would be based on whims and opinions and would be subject to dispute.

Suppose that you start a stereo shop, and to have a place for operations, you transfer a small building to the business. You believe the building is worth $155,000. To confirm its value, you hire two real estate professionals, who appraise the building at $147,000. Is $155,000 or $147,000 the more reliable estimate of the building's value? The real estate appraisal of $147,000 is, because it is supported by independent, objective observation.

The Cost Principle

The **cost principle** states that assets and services that are acquired should be recorded at their actual cost (also called historical cost). Even though the purchaser may believe the price paid is a bargain, the item is recorded at the price paid in the transaction.

Suppose your stereo shop purchases some stereo equipment from a supplier who is going out of business. Assume you get a good deal on this purchase and pay only $2,000 for merchandise that would have cost you $3,000 elsewhere. The cost principle requires you to record this merchandise at its actual cost of $2,000, not the $3,000 that you believe the equipment to be worth.

The cost principle also holds that the accounting records should maintain the historical cost of an asset for as long as the business holds the asset. Why? Because cost is a reliable measure. Suppose your store holds the stereo equipment for six months. During that time, stereo prices increase, and the equipment can be sold for $3,500. Should its accounting value—the figure "on the books"—be the actual cost of $2,000 or the current market value of $3,500? According to the cost principle, the accounting value of the equipment remains at actual cost, $2,000.

As we continue to explore accounting, we will discuss other principles that guide accountants.

The Going-Concern Concept

Another reason for measuring assets at historical cost is the **going-concern concept,** which holds that the entity will remain in operation for the foreseeable future. Most assets, such as supplies, land, buildings, and equipment, are acquired to use rather than to sell. Under the going-concern concept, accountants assume that the business will remain in operation long enough to use existing assets for their intended purpose. The market value of an asset—the price for which the asset can be sold—may change many times during the asset's life. Therefore, an asset's current market value may not be relevant for decision making. Moreover, historical cost is a more reliable accounting measure for assets.

To better understand the going-concern concept, consider the alternative, which is to *go out of business.* You have probably seen stores advertise a "Going Out of Business" sale. The entity is trying to sell all its assets. In that case, the relevant measure of the assets is their current market value. However, going out of business is the exception rather than the rule, and for this reason accounting records list assets at their historical cost.

We often think of a loaf of bread, a suit of clothes, and a month's apartment rent in terms of dollar value. In the United States, accountants record transactions in dollars because the dollar is the medium of exchange. British accountants record transactions in terms of the pound sterling, and in Japan transactions are recorded in yen.

Unlike a liter, a mile, or an acre, the value of a dollar changes over time. A rise in prices is called inflation, and during inflation a dollar will purchase less milk, less toothpaste, and less of anything else. When prices are relatively stable—when there is little inflation—a dollar's purchasing power is also stable. Most periods of United States history have been characterized by a low rate of inflation.

Accountants assume that the dollar's purchasing power is relatively stable. The **stable-monetary-unit concept** is the basis for ignoring the effect of inflation in the accounting records. It allows accountants to add and subtract dollar amounts as though each dollar had the same purchasing power. For example, Nike, Inc., manufacturer of athletic shoes, reported land of $10.8 million in 1989. During 1990, Nike purchased land of $0.4 million and at the end of 1990 reported land of $11.2 million. Accountants for Nike added the costs of the new and the old land, effectively ignoring changes in the purchasing power of the dollar.

Accountants have devised ways to take inflation into account. When inflation accelerates, the FASB can require companies to show inflation-adjusted amounts in reports.

OBJECTIVE 4

Use the accounting equation to describe an organization's financial position

The Accounting Equation

Financial statements tell us how a business is performing and where it stands. We will see several financial statements in this course of study. But how do accountants arrive at the items and amounts that make up the financial statements?

The most basic tool of the accountant is the accounting equation. This equation presents the assets of the business and the claims to those assets. **Assets** are the economic resources of a business that are expected to be of benefit in the future. Cash, office supplies, merchandise, furniture, land, and buildings are examples. Claims to those assets come from two sources.

Liabilities are "outsider claims," which are economic obligations—debts—payable to outsiders. These outside parties are called *creditors*. For example, a creditor who has loaned money to a business has a claim—a legal right—to a part of the assets until the business pays the debt. "Insider claims" are called **owners' equity** or **capital.** These are the claims held by the owners of the business. An owner has a claim to the entity's assets because he or she has invested in the business. Owners' equity is measured by subtracting liabilities from assets.

The accounting equation shows the relationship among assets, liabilities, and owners' equity. Assets appear on the left-hand side of the equation. The legal and economic claims against the assets—the liabilities and owners' equity—appear on the right-hand side of the equation:

$$\text{ASSETS} = \text{LIABILITIES} + \text{OWNERS' EQUITY}$$

Let's take a closer look at the elements that make up the accounting equation. Suppose you run a business that supplies meat to fast-food restaurants.

Some customers may pay you in cash when you deliver the meat. Cash is an asset. Other customers may buy on credit and promise to pay you within a certain time after delivery. This promise is also an asset because it is an economic resource that will benefit you in the future when you receive cash from the customer. The meat supplier calls this promise an **account receivable**. If the promise that entitles you to receive cash in the future is formally written out, it is called a **note receivable**. All receivables are assets.

The fast-food restaurant's promise to pay you for the meat it purchases on credit creates a debt for the restaurant. This liability is an **account payable** of the restaurant, which means that the debt is not written out. Instead it is backed up by the reputation and the credit standing of the restaurant and its owner. A written promise of future payment is called a **note payable**. All payables are liabilities.

Owners' equity is the amount of the assets that remains after subtracting liabilities. We often write the accounting equation to show that the owners' claim to business assets is a residual:

$$\text{ASSETS} - \text{LIABILITIES} = \text{OWNERS' EQUITY}$$

Owners' Equity

The owners' equity of a corporation—called **stockholders' equity**—is divided into two main categories, paid-in capital and retained earnings. For a corporation the accounting equation can be written as

$$\text{ASSETS} = \text{LIABILITIES} + \text{STOCKHOLDERS' EQUITY}$$

$$\text{ASSETS} = \text{LIABILITIES} + \text{PAID-IN CAPITAL} + \text{RETAINED EARNINGS}$$

Paid-in, or **contributed, capital** is the amount invested in the corporation by its owners. The basic component of paid-in captial is common stock, which the corporation issues to its stockholders as evidence of their ownership.

Retained earnings is the amount earned by income-producing activities and kept for use in the business. Two types of transactions that affect retained earnings are revenues and expenses. **Revenues** are increases in retained earnings from delivering goods or services to customers. For example, a laundry's receipt of cash from a customer for cleaning a coat brings in revenue and increases the laundry's retained earnings. **Expenses** are the decreases in retained earnings that result from operations. For example, the wages that the laundry pays its employees is an expense and decreases retained earnings.

Businesses strive for profitability. When revenues exceed expenses, the result of operations is a profit or net income. When expenses exceed revenues, the result is a net loss. If the business is successful in earning a net income, it may pay dividends, the third type of transaction that affects retained earnings. **Dividends** are distributions to stockholders of assets (usually cash) generated by net income. Dividends are not expenses because they are decided after expenses and revenues are recorded. First the business measures its net income or net loss. Then a corporation may (or may not) pay dividends. Exhibit 1-5 shows the relationships among retained earnings, revenues, expenses, net income or net loss, and dividends.

The owners' equity of proprietorships and of partnerships is different. These types of business make no distinction between paid-in capital and retained earnings. Instead, the equity of each owner is accounted for under the single heading of Capital—for example, Gary Lyon, Capital for a proprietorship. The partnership of Pratt and Muesli has a separate record for the capital of each partner: Pratt, Capital and Muesli, Capital.

EXHIBIT 1-5 *Components of Retained Earnings*

Accounting for Business Transactions

In accounting terms, a **transaction** is any event that *both* affects the financial position of the business entity *and* may be reliably recorded. Many events may affect a company, including (1) elections, (2) economic booms and recessions, (3) purchases and sales of merchandise inventory, (4) payment of rent, (5) collection of cash from customers, and so on. However, the accountant records only events with effects that can be measured reliably as transactions.

Which of the above five events would the accountant record? The answer is events (3), (4), and (5) because their dollar amounts can be measured reliably. Dollar effects of elections and economic trends cannot be measured reliably, so they would not be recorded even though they may affect the business more than events (3), (4), and (5).

To illustrate accounting for business transactions, let's assume that Gary and Monica Lyon open a travel agency that they incorporate as Air and Sea Travel, Inc. We now consider 11 events and analyze each in terms of its effect on the accounting equation of Air and Sea Travel. Transaction analysis is the essence of accounting.

Transaction 1.   The Lyons invest $50,000 of their money to begin the business. Specifically, they deposit $50,000 in a bank account entitled Air and Sea Travel, Inc. As evidence of the corporation, Air and Sea Travel issues common stock to Gary and Monica Lyon. The stock is printed on certificates and issued by the corporation. It provides tangible evidence that the Lyons have an ownership interest in the corporation. The effect of this transaction on the accounting equation of the business entity is

OBJECTIVE 5

Use the accounting equation to analyze business transactions

	Assets	=	Liabilities + Stockholders' Equity	Type of SE Transaction
	Cash		Common Stock	
(1)	+50,000		+50,000	Owner investment

The first transaction increases both the assets, in this case Cash, and the stockholders' equity of the business, Common Stock. The transaction involves no liabilities of the business because it creates no obligation for Air and Sea Travel to pay an outside party. To the right of the transaction we write "Owner investment" to keep track of the reason for the effect on stockholders' equity.

Note that the amount on the left side of the equation equals the amount on the right side. This equality must hold for every transaction.

Transaction 2.   Air and Sea Travel purchases land for a future office location, paying cash of $40,000. Regardless of the Lyons' belief about the true value of the land, it is recorded at $40,000 because of the *cost principle* and the *reliability principle.* Actual cost is a reliable measure of an asset. The effect of this transaction on the accounting equation is

	Assets			Liabilities + Stockholders' Equity	Type of SE Transaction
	Cash	+	Land	Common Stock	
(1)	50,000			50,000	Owner investment
(2)	−40,000	+	40,000		
Bal.	10,000		40,000	50,000	
		50,000		50,000	

The cash purchase of land increases one asset, Land, and decreases another asset, Cash, by the same amount. After the transaction is completed, Air and Sea Travel has cash of $10,000, land of $40,000, no liabilities, and stockholders' equity of $50,000. Note that the sums of the balances (which we abbreviate Bal.) on each side of the equation are equal. This equality must always exist— $50,000 after the first two transactions.

Transaction 3.   The business buys stationery and other office supplies, agreeing to pay $500 within thirty days. This transaction increases the assets and the liabilities of the business. Its effect on the accounting equation is

	Assets				Liabilities + Stockholders' Equity	
	Cash	+	Office Supplies +	Land	Accounts Payable +	Common Stock
Bal.	10,000			40,000		50,000
(3)			+500		+500	
Bal.	10,000		500	40,000	500	50,000
		50,500			50,500	

The asset affected is office supplies, and the liability is called an account payable. The term *payable* signifies a liability. Because Air and Sea Travel is obligated to pay $500 in the future, but signs no formal promissory note, we record the liability as an Account Payable, not as a Note Payable. We say that purchases supported by the general credit standing of the buyer are made on *open account.*

Transaction 4. The purpose of business is to increase assets and stockholders' equity through revenues. Revenues increase retained earnings, a component of stockholders' equity, because they increase the business's assets but not its liabilities. As a result, the owners' interest in the assets of the business increases. Exhibit 1-5 shows that revenues increase the retained earnings of the business. Air and Sea Travel earns service revenue by providing travel arrangement services for customers. Assume the business earns $5,500 and collects this amount in cash. The effect on the accounting equation is an increase in the asset Cash and an increase in Retained Earnings, as follows:

	Assets				Liabilities + Stockholders' Equity			Type of SE Transaction
	Cash	Office + Supplies +	Land	=	Accounts Payable +	Common Stock +	Retained Earnings +	
Bal.	10,000	500	40,000		500	50,000		
(4)	+ 5,500						+5,500	Service revenue
Bal.	15,500	500	40,000		500	50,000	5,500	
		56,000				56,000		

This revenue transaction caused the business to grow, as shown by the increase in total assets and total liabilities and stockholders' equity.

Transaction 5. Air and Sea Travel performs services for customers who do not pay immediately. In return for the services, Air and Sea receives the customers' promise to pay the $3,000 amount within one month. This promise is an asset to Air and Sea Travel, an account receivable because the business expects to collect the cash in the future. In accounting, we say that Air and Sea performed this service *on account*. When the business performs service for a client or a customer, the business earns revenue regardless of whether it receives cash immediately or expects to collect cash later. This $3,000 of service revenue is as real to the business as the $5,500 of revenue that was collected immediately in the preceding transaction. Air and Sea Travel records an increase in the asset Accounts Receivable and an increase in Retained Earnings as follows:

	Assets					Liabilities + Stockholders' Equity			Type of SE Transaction
	Cash	+ Accounts Receivable +	Office Supplies +	Land	=	Accounts Payable +	Common Stock +	Retained Earnings	
Bal.	15,500	0	500	40,000		500	50,000	5,500	
(5)		+3,000						+3,000	Service revenue
Bal.	15,500	3,000	500	40,000		500	50,000	8,500	
		59,000					59,000		

Again, this revenue transaction caused the business to grow.

Transaction 6. In earning revenue a business incurs expenses. Expenses include office rent, salaries paid to employees, newspaper advertisements, and utility payments for light, electricity, gas, and so forth. During the month, Air and Sea Travel pays $2,700 in cash expenses: office rent, $1,100; employee salary, $1,200 (for a part-time assistant); and total utilities, $400. The effect on the accounting equation is

	Assets					Liabilities + Stockholders' Equity				Type of SE Transaction
	Cash	+ Accounts Receivable	+ Office Supplies	+ Land	=	Accounts Payable	+ Common Stock	+ Retained Earnings		
Bal.	15,500	3,000	500	40,000		500	50,000	8,500		
(6)	− 2,700							−1,100		Rent expense
								−1,200		Salary expense
								− 400		Utilities expense
Bal.	12,800	3,000	500	40,000		500	50,000	5,800		
		56,300					56,300			

Because expenses have the opposite effect of revenues, they cause the business to shrink, as shown by the smaller amounts of total assets and total liabilities and stockholders' equity.

Each expense should be recorded in a separate transaction. Here, for simplicity, they are recorded together. Note that even though the figure $2,700 does not appear on the right-hand side of the equation, the three individual expenses add up to a $2,700 total. As a result, the "balance" of the equation holds, as we know it must.

Transaction 7. Air and Sea pays $400 to the store from which it purchased $500 worth of office supplies in Transaction 3. In accounting, we say that the business pays $400 *on account.* The effect on the accounting equation is a decrease in the asset Cash and a decrease in the liability Accounts Payable as follows:

	Assets					Liabilities + Stockholders' Equity		
	Cash	+ Accounts Receivable	+ Office Supplies	+ Land	=	Accounts Payable	+ Common Stock	+ Retained Earnings
Bal.	12,800	3,000	500	40,000		500	50,000	5,800
(7)	− 400					−400		
Bal.	12,400	3,000	500	40,000		100	50,000	5,800
		55,900					55,900	

The payment of cash on account has no effect on the asset Office Supplies because the payment does not increase or decrease the supplies available to the business.

Transaction 8. The Lyons remodel their home at a cost of $30,000, paying cash from personal funds. This event is a *nonbusiness* transaction. It has no effect on Air and Sea Travel's business affairs and therefore is not recorded by the business. It is a transaction of the *personal* entity, the Lyon family, not the business entity, Air and Sea Travel. We are focusing solely on the business entity, and this event does not affect it. This transaction illustrates an application of the *entity concept.*

Transaction 9. In Transaction 5, Air and Sea Travel performed service for customers on account. The business now collects $1,000 from a customer. We say that Air and Sea collects the cash *on account.* It will record an increase in the asset Cash. Should Air and Sea Travel also record an increase in service revenue? No, because Air and Sea Travel already recorded the revenue when it performed the service in Transaction 5. The phrase "collect cash on account" means to record an increase in Cash and a decrease in the asset Accounts Receivable. The effect on the accounting equation is

		Assets				Liabilities +	Stockholders' Equity	
	Cash	Accounts + Receivable	Office + Supplies +	Land	=	Accounts Payable +	Common Stock +	Retained Earnings
Bal.	12,400	3,000	500	40,000		100	50,000	5,800
(9)	1,000	−1,000						
Bal.	13,400	2,000	500	40,000		100	50,000	5,800
		55,900					55,900	

Total assets are unchanged from the preceding transaction's total. Why? Because Air and Sea Travel merely exchanged one asset for another. Also, stockholders' equity is unchanged.

Transaction 10.   An individual approaches Mrs. Lyon about selling a parcel of the land owned by the Air and Sea Travel entity. She and the other person agree to a sale price of $22,000, which is equal to the business's cost of the land. Air and Sea Travel sells the land and receives $22,000 cash. The effect on the accounting equation is

		Assets				Liabilities +	Stockholders' Equity	
	Cash	Accounts + Receivable	Office + Supplies +	Land	=	Accounts Payable +	Common Stock +	Retained Earnings
Bal.	13,400	2,000	500	40,000		100	50,000	5,800
(10)	+22,000			−22,000				
Bal.	35,400	2,000	500	18,000		100	50,000	5,800
		55,900					55,900	

Transaction 11.   The corporation declares a dividend and pays Gary and Monica Lyon $2,100 cash for their personal use. The effect on the accounting equation is

		Assets				Liabilities +	Stockholders' Equity		Type of SE Transaction
	Cash	Accounts + Receivable	Office + Supplies +	Land	=	Accounts Payable +	Common Stock +	Retained Earnings	
Bal.	35,400	2,000	500	18,000		100	50,000	5,800	
(11)	− 2,100							−2,100	Dividends
Bal.	33,300	2,000	500	18,000		100	50,000	3,700	
		53,800					53,800		

The dividend decreases the asset Cash and also the stockholders' equity of the business.

Does the dividend decrease the business entity's holdings? The answer is yes because the cash paid to the stockholders is no longer available for Air and Sea Travel business use. The dividend does *not* represent a business expense, however, because the cash is paid to the owners for their personal use. We record this decrease in stockholders' equity as Dividends.

Evaluating Business Transactions

Exhibit 1-6 summarizes the 11 preceding transactions. Panel A of the exhibit lists the details of the transactions, and Panel B presents the analysis. As you study the exhibit, note that every transaction maintains the equality:

ASSETS = LIABILITIES + STOCKHOLDERS' EQUITY

EXHIBIT 1-6   *Analysis of Transactions of Air and Sea Travel, Inc.*

Panel A—Details of transactions

1. The owners invested $50,000 cash in the business.
2. Paid $40,000 cash for land.
3. Purchased $500 of office supplies on account payable.
4. Received $5,500 cash from customers for service revenue earned.
5. Performed services for customers on account, $3,000.
6. Paid cash expenses: rent, $1,100; employee salary, $1,200; utilities, $400.
7. Paid $400 on the account payable created in Transaction 3.
8. Owners paid personal funds to remodel home. Not a transaction of the business.
9. Received $1,000 on the account receivable created in Transaction 5.
10. Sold land for cash equal to its cost of $22,000.
11. Declared and paid a dividend of $2,100 to the stockholders.

Panel B—Analysis of transactions

		Assets				Liabilities +	Stockholders' Equity		Type of SE Transaction
	Cash	+ Accounts Receivable	+ Office Supplies +	Land		Accounts Payable +	Common Stock +	Retained Earnings	
(1)	+50,000						+50,000		Owner investment
Bal.	50,000						50,000		
(2)	−40,000			+40,000					
Bal.	10,000			40,000			50,000		
(3)			+500			+500			
Bal.	10,000		500	40,000		500	50,000		
(4)	+ 5,500							+ 5,500	Service revenue
Bal.	15,500		500	40,000		500	50,000	5,500	
(5)		+3,000						+ 3,000	Service revenue
Bal.	15,500	3,000	500	40,000		500	50,000	8,500	
(6)	− 2,700				=			− 1,100	Rent expense
								− 1,200	Salary expense
								− 400	Utilities expense
Bal.	12,800	3,000	500	40,000		500	50,000	5,800	
(7)	− 400					−400			
Bal.	12,400	3,000	500	40,000		100	50,000	5,800	
(8)	Not a transaction of the business								
(9)	+ 1,000	−1,000							
Bal.	13,400	2,000	500	40,000		100	50,000	5,800	
(10)	+22,000			−22,000					
Bal.	35,400	2,000	500	18,000		100	50,000	5,800	
(11)	− 2,100							− 2,100	Dividends
Bal.	33,300	2,000	500	18,000		100	50,000	3,700	
			53,800				53,800		

Financial Statements

The analysis of the transactions complete, what is the next step in the accounting process? How does an accountant present the results of the analysis? We now look at the **financial statements,** which are formal reports of financial information about the entity. The primary financial statements are the (1) balance sheet, (2) income statement, (3) statement of retained earnings, and (4) statement of cash flows. In this chapter, we discuss and illustrate the first three statements. We show the statement of cash flows in the appendix to the chapter and cover the statement in detail in Chapter 15.

The **balance sheet** lists all the *assets, liabilities,* and *stockholders' equity* of an entity as of a specific date, usually the end of a month or a year. The balance sheet is like a snapshot of the entity. For this reason, it is also called the **statement of financial position**.

The **income statement** presents a summary of the *revenues* and *expenses* of an entity for a specific period of time, such as a month or a year. The income statement, also called the **statement of earnings** or **statement of operations**, is like a moving picture of the entity's operations during the period. The income statement holds perhaps the most important single piece of information about a business—its net income, which is revenues minus expenses. If expenses exceed revenues, the result is a net loss for the period.

The **statement of retained earnings** presents a summary of the changes that occurred in the retained earnings of the entity during a specific time period, such as a month or a year. An increase in retained earnings arises from net income earned during the period. A decrease results from dividends to the owner and from a net loss for the period. Net income or net loss comes directly from the income statement. Dividends are capital transactions between the business and its owner, so they do not affect the income statement.

Each financial statement has a heading, which gives the name of the business (in our discussion, Air and Sea Travel, Inc.), the name of the particular statement, and the date or time period covered by the statement. A balance sheet taken at the end of year 19X4 would be dated December 31, 19X4. A balance sheet prepared at the end of March 19X7 is dated March 31, 19X7.

An income statement or a statement of retained earnings covering an annual period ending in December 19X5 is dated For the Year Ended December 31, 19X5. A monthly income statement or statement of retained earnings for September 19X9 has in its heading For the Month Ended September 30, 19X9, Month Ended September 30, 19X9, or For the Month of September 19X9.

Exhibit 1-7 illustrates all three statements. Their data come from the transaction analysis in Exhibit 1-6. We are assuming the transactions occurred during the month of April 19X1. Study the exhibit carefully, because it shows the relationships among the three financial statements. The chapter appendix gives the statement of cash flows for April 19X1.

Observe the following in Exhibit 1-7:

1. The *income statement* for the month ended April 30, 19X1
   a. Reports all *revenues* and all *expenses* during the period. Revenues and expenses are reported only on the income statement.
   b. Reports *net income* of the period if total revenues exceed total expenses, as in the case of Air and Sea Travel's operations for April. If total expenses exceed total revenues, the result is a *net loss.*
2. The *statement of retained earnings* for the month ended April 30, 19X1
   a. Opens with the retained earnings balance at the beginning of the period.

EXHIBIT 1-7 *Financial Statements of Air and Sea Travel, Inc.*

Air and Sea Travel, Inc.
Income Statement
Month Ended April 30, 19X1

Revenues:		
Service revenue		$8,500
Expenses:		
Salary expense	$1,200	
Rent expense	1,100	
Utilities expense	400	
Total expenses		2,700
Net income		$5,800

Air and Sea Travel, Inc.
Statement of Retained Earnings
Month Ended April 30, 19X1

Retained earnings, April 1, 19X1	$ 0
Add: Net income for the month	5,800
	5,800
Less: Dividends	2,100
Retained earnings, April 30, 19X1	$3,700

①

②

Air and Sea Travel, Inc.
Balance Sheet
April 30, 19X1

Assets		Liabilities	
Cash	$33,300	Accounts payable	$ 100
Accounts receivable	2,000	**Stockholders' Equity**	
Office supplies	500		
Land	18,000	Common stock	50,000
		Retained earnings	3,700
		Total stockholders' equity	53,700
		Total liabilities and stockholders'	
Total assets	$53,800	equity	$53,800

b. Adds *net income* (or subtracts *net loss,* as the case may be). Net income (or net loss) comes directly from the income statement, which includes the effect of all the revenues and all the expenses for the period (see the first arrow in the exhibit).

c. Subtracts *dividends.*

d. Ends with the retained earnings balance at the end of the period.

3. The *balance sheet* at April 30, 19X1, the end of the period
   a. Reports all *assets, liabilities,* and *stockholders' equity* of the business at the end of the period. No other statement reports assets and liabilities.

b. Balances. That is, total assets equal the sum of total liabilities plus total stockholders' equity. This balancing feature gives the balance sheet its name. It is based on the accounting equation.

c. Reports the ending retained earnings balance, taken directly from the statement of retained earnings (see the second arrow).

4. The statement of cash flows for the month ended April 30, 19X1, reports the cash effects of the operating, investing, and financing transactions for the period. This statement is illustrated in the chapter appendix.

Summary Problem for Your Review

Jill Smith opens an apartment-locator business near a college campus. She names the corporation Campus Apartment Locators, Inc. During the first month of operations, May 19X1, the business engages in the following transactions:

a. Smith invested $35,000 of personal funds to acquire the common stock of the corporation.

b. Purchased on account office supplies costing $350.

c. Paid cash of $30,000 to acquire a lot next to the campus. She intends to use the land as a future building site for her business office.

d. Located apartments for clients and received cash of $1,900.

e. Paid $100 on the account payable she created in transaction b.

f. Paid $2,000 of personal funds for a vacation for her family.

g. Paid cash expenses for office rent, $400, and utilities, $100.

h. Sold office supplies to another business for its cost of $150.

i. Declared and paid a cash dividend of $1,200.

Required

1. Analyze the preceding transactions in terms of their effects on the accounting equation of Campus Apartment Locators, Inc. Use Exhibit 1-6 as a guide, but show balances only after the last transaction.

2. Prepare the income statement, statement of retained earnings, and balance sheet of the business after recording the transactions. Use Exhibit 1-7 as a guide.

SOLUTION TO REVIEW PROBLEM

Panel A. Details of transactions

a. Smith invested $35,000 cash to acquire the common stock of the corporation.

b. Purchased $350 of office supplies on account.

c. Paid $30,000 to acquire land as a future building site.

d. Earned service revenue and received cash of $1,900.

e. Paid $100 on account.

f. Paid for a vacation with personal funds—not a transaction of the business.

g. Paid cash expenses for rent, $400, and utilities, $100.

h. Sold office supplies for cost of $150.

i. Paid dividends of $1,200.

Panel B.   Analysis of transactions

	Assets				Liabilities +	Stockholders' Equity		Type of SE Transaction
	Cash	+ Office Supplies +	Land		Accounts Payable +	Common Stock +	Retained Earnings	
(a)	+35,000					+35,000		Owner investment
(b)		+350			+350			
(c)	−30,000		+30,000					
(d)	+ 1,900			=			+ 1,900	Service revenue
(e)	− 100				−100			
(f)	Not a business transaction							
(g)	− 500						− 400	Rent expense
							− 100	Utilities expense
(h)	+ 150	−150						
(i)	− 1,200						− 1,200	Dividends
Bal.	5,250	200	30,000		250	35,000	200	
		35,450				35,450		

Financial Statements of Campus Apartment Locators, Inc.

Campus Apartment Locators, Inc.
Income Statement
Month Ended May 31, 19X1

Revenues:		
Service revenue.....................................		$1,900
Expenses:		
Rent expense	$400	
Utilities expense	100	
Total expenses....................................		500
Net income..		$1,400

Campus Apartment Locators, Inc.
Statement of Retained Earnings
Month Ended May 31, 19X1

Retained earnings, May 1, 19X1	$ 0
Add: Net income for the month	1,400
	1,400
Less: Dividends.....................................	1,200
Retained earnings, May 31, 19X1	$ 200

Campus Apartment Locators, Inc.
Balance Sheet
May 31, 19X1

Assets		Liabilities	
Cash....................	$ 5,250	Accounts payable	$ 250
Office supplies	200	**Stockholders' equity**	
Land	30,000	Common stock	35,000
		Retained earnings........	200
		Total stockholders' equity.	35,200
		Total liabilities	
Total assets..............	$35,450	and stockholders' equity	$35,450

Summary

Accounting is a system for measuring, processing, and communicating financial information. As the "language of business," accounting helps a wide range of decision makers. Accounting dates back to ancient civilizations, but its importance to society has been greatest since the Industrial Revolution. Today, accountants serve as CPAs, CMAs, or CIAs in all types of organizations. They offer many specialized services for industrial companies, including general accounting, cost accounting, budgeting, system design, and internal auditing. CPAs in public practice deal with auditing, tax planning and preparation, and management consulting.

The three basic forms of business organization are the proprietorship, the partnership, and the corporation. Corporations dominate business in the United States, although proprietorships and partnerships are more numerous. A corporation is owned by the stockholders. Ethical considerations pervade all areas of accounting and business.

Generally accepted accounting principles—GAAP—guide accountants in their work. Among these guidelines are the entity concept, the reliability principle, the cost principle, the going-concern concept, and the stable-monetary-unit concept.

In its most common form, the accounting equation is

$$\text{ASSETS} = \text{LIABILITIES} + \text{OWNERS' EQUITY}$$

Transactions affect a business's assets, liabilities, and owner's equity. Therefore, transactions are analyzed in terms of their effect on the accounting equation.

The owners' equity of a corporation is called stockholders' equity and is composed of paid-in captial represented by common stock and retained earnings.

The *financial statements* communicate information for decision making by the entity's managers, owners, and creditors and by government agencies. The *income statement* presents a moving picture of the entity's operations in terms of revenues earned and expenses incurred during a specific period. Total revenues minus total expenses equal net income. Net income or net loss answers the question, How much income did the entity earn or how much loss did it incur during the period? The *statement of retained earnings* reports the increases and decreases in retained earnings from net income (or net loss) and dividends during the period. The *balance sheet* provides a snapshot of the entity's financial standing in terms of its assets, liabilities, and stockholders' equity at a specific time. It answers the question, What is the entity's financial position? The *statement of cash flows* reports the cash effects of the operating, investing, and financing transactions.

Self-Study Questions

Test your understanding of the chapter by marking the best answer for each of the following questions:

1. To become a CPA, a person must *(p. 6)*
   a. Graduate from college with a master's degree
   b. Obtain four years of accounting experience
   c. Pass a national examination
   d. Pass an accounting examination that differs from state to state

2. The organization that formulates generally accepted accounting principles is *(p. 7)*
   a. American Institute of Certified Public Accountants (CPAs)
   b. Internal Revenue Service
   c. Financial Accounting Standards Board
   d. Institute of Management Accountants
3. Which of the following forms of business organization is an "artificial person" and must obtain legal approval from a state to conduct business? *(p. 11)*
   a. Law firm   c. Partnership
   b. Proprietorship   d. Corporation
4. The economic resources of a business are called *(p. 16)*
   a. Assets   c. Liabilities
   b. Owners' equity   d. Receivables
5. A corporation has assets of $140,000 and liabilities of $60,000. How much is its stockholders' equity? *(p. 17)*
   a. $0   c. $140,000
   b. $80,000   d. $200,000
6. The purchase of office supplies (or any other asset) on account will *(p. 19)*
   a. Increase an asset and increase a liability
   b. Increase an asset and increase stockholders' equity
   c. Increase one asset and decrease another asset
   d. Increase an asset and decrease a liability
7. The performance of service for a customer or client and immediate receipt of cash will *(p. 20)*
   a. Increase one asset and decrease another asset
   b. Increase an asset and increase stockholders' equity
   c. Decrease an asset and decrease a liability
   d. Increase an asset and increase a liability
8. The payment of an account payable (or any other liability) will *(p. 21)*
   a. Increase one asset and decrease another asset
   b. Decrease an asset and decrease stockholders' equity
   c. Decrease an asset and decrease a liability
   d. Increase an asset and increase a liability
9. The report of assets, liabilities, and stockholders' equity is called the *(p. 24)*
   a. Financial statement
   b. Balance sheet
   c. Income statement
   d. Statement of retained earnings
10. The financial statements that are dated for a time period (rather than a specific time) are the *(pp. 24–25)*
    a. Balance sheet and income statement
    b. Balance sheet and statement of retained earnings
    c. Income statement and statement of retained earnings
    d. All financial statements are dated for a time period

Answers to the Self-Study Questions follow the Accounting Vocabulary.

Accounting Vocabulary

Accounting, like many other subjects, has a special vocabulary. It is important that you understand the following terms. They are explained in the chapter and also in the glossary at the end of the book.

Accounting. The system that measures business activities, processes that information into reports and financial statements, and communicates the findings to decision makers (*p. 2*).

Account payable. A liability backed by the general reputation and credit standing of the debtor (*p. 17*).

Account receivable. An asset, a promise to receive cash from customers to whom the business has sold goods or for whom the business has performed services (*p. 17*).

Asset. An economic resource that is expected to be of benefit in the future (*p. 16*).

Auditing. The examination of financial statements by outside accountants, the most significant service that CPAs perform. The conclusion of an audit is the accountant's professional opinion about the financial statements (*pp. 8–9*).

Balance sheet. List of an entity's assets, liabilities, and owners' equity as of a specific date. Also called the Statement of financial position (*p. 24*).

Board of directors. Group elected by the stockholders to set policy for a corporation and to appoint its officers (*p. 13*).

Budgeting. Setting of goals for a business, such as its sales and profits, for a future period (*p. 9*).

Bylaws. Constitution for governing a corporation (*p. 12*).

Capital. Another name for the Owners' equity of a business (*p. 16*).

Certified Public Accountant (CPA). A professional accountant who earns this title through a combination of education, experience, and an acceptable score on a written national examination (*p. 5*).

Charter. Document that gives the state's permission to form a corporation (*p. 11*).

Corporation. A business owned by stockholders that begins when the state approves its articles of incorporation. A corporation is a legal entity, an "artificial person," in the eyes of the law (*p. 11*).

Cost accounting. The branch of accounting that analyzes and helps control a business's costs (*p. 9*).

Cost principle. States that assets and services are recorded at their purchase cost and that the accounting record of the asset continues to be based on cost rather than current market value (*p. 15*).

Dividend. Distribution by a corporation to its stockholders (*p. 17*).

Double taxation. Corporations pay their own income taxes on corporate income. Then the stockholders pay personal income tax on the cash dividends that they receive from corporations (*p. 12*).

Entity. An organization or a section of an organization that, for accounting purposes, stands apart from other organizations and individuals as a separate economic unit. This is the most basic concept in accounting (*p. 14*).

Expense. Decrease in retained earnings that occurs in the course of delivering goods or services to customers or clients (*p. 17*).

Financial accounting. The branch of accounting that provides information to people outside the business (*p. 9*).

Financial statements. Business documents that report financial information about an entity to persons and organizations outside the business (*pp. 24–26*).

Generally accepted accounting principles (GAAP). Accounting guidelines, formulated by the Financial Accounting Standards Board, that govern how businesses report their financial statements to the public (*p. 7*).

Going-concern concept. Accountants' assumption that the business will continue operating in the foreseeable future (*p. 15*).

Income statement. List of an entity's revenues, expenses, and net income or net loss for a specific period. Also called the Statement of operations and the Statement of earnings (*p. 24*).

Incorporators. Persons who organize a corporation (*p. 12*).

Information systems design. Identification of an organization's information needs, and development and implementation of the system to meet those needs (*p. 9*).

Internal auditing. Auditing that is performed by a business's own accountants to evaluate the firm's accounting and management systems. The aim is to improve operating efficiency and to ensure that employees follow management's procedures and plans *(p. 9)*.

Liability. An economic obligation (a debt) payable to an individual or an organization outside the business *(p. 16)*.

Limited liability. No personal obligation of a stockholder for corporation debts. The most that a stockholder can lose on an investment in a corporation's stock is the cost of the investment *(pp. 11–12)*.

Management accounting. The branch of accounting that generates information for internal decision makers of a business, such as top executives *(p. 9)*.

Net earnings. Another name for Net income or Net profit *(p. 17)*.

Net income. Excess of total revenues over total expenses. Also called Net earnings or Net profit *(p. 17)*.

Net loss. Excess of total expenses over total revenues *(p. 17)*.

Net profit. Another name for Net income or Net earnings *(p. 17)*.

Note payable. A liability evidenced by a written promise to make a future payment *(p. 17)*.

Note receivable. An asset evidenced by another party's written promise that entitles you to receive cash in the future *(p. 17)*.

Owners' equity. The claim of owners of a business to the assets of the business. Also called Capital *(p. 16)*.

Paid-in capital. A corporation's capital from investments by the stockholders. Also called Contributed capital *(p. 17)*.

Partnership. A business with two or more owners *(p. 10)*.

Private accountant. Accountant who works for a single business, such as a department store or General Motors *(p. 5)*.

Proprietorship. A business with a single owner *(p. 10)*.

Public accountant. Accountant who serves the general public and collects fees for work, which includes auditing, income tax planning and preparation, and management consulting *(p. 5)*.

Reliability principle. Requires that accounting information be dependable (free from error and bias). Also called the Objectivity principle *(pp. 14–15)*.

Retained earnings. A corporation's capital that is earned through profitable operation of the business *(p. 17)*.

Revenue. Increase in retained earnings that is earned by delivering goods or services to customers or clients *(p. 17)*.

Shareholder. Another name for Stockholder *(p. 11)*.

Stable-monetary-unit concept. Accountants' basis for ignoring the effect of inflation and making no adjustments for the changing value of the dollar *(p. 16)*.

Statement of financial position. Another name for the Balance sheet *(p. 24)*

Statement of operations. Another name for the Income statement *(p. 24)*.

Statement of retained earnings. Summary of the changes in the retained earnings of an entity during a specific period *(p. 24)*.

Stockholder. A person who owns the stock of a corporation *(p. 11)*.

Stockholders' equity Owners' equity of a corporation. *(p. 17)*.

Transaction. An event that affects the financial position of a particular entity and may be reliably recorded *(p. 18)*.

Answers to Self-Study Questions

1.	c	6.	a.
2.	c	7.	b
3.	d	8.	c
4.	a	9.	b
5.	b	10.	c

ASSIGNMENT MATERIAL _____

Questions

1. Distinguish between accounting and bookkeeping.
2. Identify five users of accounting information and explain how they use it.
3. Where did accounting have its beginning? Who wrote the first known description of bookkeeping? In what year?
4. Name two important reasons for the development of accounting thought.
5. Name three professional titles of accountants. Also give their abbreviations.
6. What organization formulates generally accepted accounting principles? Is this organization a government agency?
7. Name the three principal types of services provided by public accounting firms.
8. How do financial accounting and management accounting differ?
9. Give the name(s) of the owner(s) of a proprietorship, a partnership, and a corporation.
10. Why do ethical standards exist in accounting? Which organization directs its standards toward independent auditors? Which organization directs its standards more toward management accountants?
11. Why is the entity concept so important to accounting?
12. Give four examples of accounting entities.
13. Briefly describe the reliability principle.
14. What role does the cost principle play in accounting?
15. If *assets = liabilities + owners' equity*, then how can *liabilities* be expressed?
16. Explain the difference between an account receivable and an account payable.
17. Identify the items that make up the balance of retained earnings.
18. What role do transactions play in accounting?
19. What is a more descriptive title for the balance sheet?
20. What feature of the balance sheet gives this financial statement its name?
21. What is another title of the income statement?
22. Which financial statement is like a snapshot of the entity at a specific time? Which financial statement is like a moving picture of the entity's operations during a period of time?
23. What information does the statement of retained earnings report?
24. What piece of information flows from the income statement to the statement of retained earnings? What information flows from the statement of retained earnings to the balance sheet?

Exercises

Exercise 1-1   *Explaining the income statement and the balance sheet*   **(L.O. 1,2)**

Felix and Charlotte Jiminez want to open a Mexican restaurant in Oklahoma City. In need of cash, they ask City Bank & Trust for a loan. The bank's procedures require borrowers to submit financial statements to show the likely results of operations for the first year and the likely financial position at the end of the first year. With little knowledge of accounting, Felix and Charlotte don't know how to proceed. Explain to them what information the statement of operations (the income statement) and the statement of financial position (the balance sheet) provides. Indicate why a lender would require this information.

Exercise 1-2   *Business transactions*   *(L.O. 3)*

For each of the following items, give an example of a business transaction that has the described effect on the accounting equation:

a.   Increase one asset and decrease another asset.
b.   Decrease an asset and decrease owners' equity.
c.   Decrease an asset and decrease a liability.
d.   Increase an asset and increase owners' equity.
e.   Increase an asset and increase a liability.

Exercise 1-3   *Transaction analysis*   *(L.O. 3)*

Kreitze Contractors, Inc., a corporation, or Darren Kreitze, the major stockholder, experienced the following events. State whether each event (1) increased, (2) decreased, or (3) had no effect on the total assets of the business. Identify any specific asset affected.

a.   Borrowed money from the bank.
b.   Cash purchase of land for a future building site.
c.   Kreitze purchased additional stock in the business.
d.   Paid cash on accounts payable.
e.   Purchased machinery and equipment for a manufacturing plant; signed a promissory note in payment.
f.   Performed service for a customer on account.
g.   Declared and paid a cash dividend.
h.   Received cash from a customer on account receivable.
i.   Kreitze used personal funds to purchase a swimming pool for his home.
j.   Sold land for a price equal to the cost of the land; received cash.

Exercise 1-4   *Accounting equation*   *(L.O. 4)*

Compute the missing amount in the accounting equation of each of the following three entities:

	Assets	Liabilities	Stockholders' Equity
Entity A	$?	$41,800	$34,400
Entity B	65,900	?	34,000
Entity C	61,700	29,800	?

Exercise 1-5 *Accounting equation* **(L.O. 4)**

Oriole Travel Agency balance sheet data, at May 31, 19X2, and June 30, 19X2, were as follows:

	May 31, 19X2	June 30, 19X2
Total assets	$150,000	$195,000
Total liabilities	109,000	131,000

Required

Below are three assumptions about investments and dividends during June. For each assumption, compute the amount of net income or net loss of the business during June 19X2.

a. The owners invested $30,000 in the business and received no dividends.
b. The owners made no additional investments in the business but received cash dividends of $6,000.
c. The owners invested $8,000 in the business and received dividends of $6,000.

Exercise 1-6 *Transaction analysis* **(L.O. 5)**

Indicate the effects of the following business transactions on the accounting equation. Transaction *a* is answered as a guide.

a. Invested cash of $1,800 to purchase the common stock of the business.
   Answer: Increase asset (Cash)
   Increase owners' equity (Common Stock)
b. Performed legal service for a client on account, $650.
c. Purchased on account office furniture at a cost of $500.
d. Received cash on account, $400.
e. Paid cash on account, $250.
f. Sold land for $12,000, which was our cost of the land.
g. Paid $90 cash to purchase office supplies.
h. Performed legal service for a client and received cash of $2,000.
i. Paid monthly office rent of $700.

Exercise 1-7 *Transaction analysis; accounting equation* **(L.O. 3,5)**

Allison LaChappelle opens a medical practice to specialize in child care. During her first month of operation, January, her practice, entitled Allison LaChappelle, Professional Corporation (P.C.), experienced the following events:

Jan. 6	LaChappelle invested $120,000 in the business by opening a bank account in the name of Allison LaChappelle, P.C.
9	Paid cash for land costing $90,000. She plans to build an office building on the land.
12	Purchased medical supplies for $2,000 on account.
15	Officially opened for business.
15–31	Treated patients and earned service revenue of $6,000, receiving cash.
15–31	Paid cash expenses: employee salaries, $1,400; office rent, $1,000; utilities, $300.
28	Sold supplies to another physician for cost of $500.
31	Paid $1,500 on account.

Required

Analyze the effects of these events on the accounting equation of the medical practice of Allison LaChappelle, P.C. Use a format similar to that of Exhibit 1-6 in the chapter, with headings for Cash; Supplies; Land; Accounts Payable; Common Stock; and Retained Earnings.

Exercise 1-8 *Business organization, transactions, and net income* (L.O. 3,5)

The analysis follows for the transactions that Allied Leasing Corporation engaged in during its first month of operations. The company buys equipment that it leases out to earn revenue. The owners of the business made only one investment to start the business and received no dividends from Allied.

	Cash +	Accounts Receivable +	Lease Equipment =	Accounts Payable +	Common Stock +	Retained Earnings
a.	+ 46,000				+ 46,000	
b.			+ 80,000	+ 80,000		
c.	+ 1,600					+ 1,600
d.		+ 500				+ 500
e.	− 10,000			− 10,000		
f.	− 850		+ 850			
g.	+ 150	− 150				
h.	− 2,000					− 2,000

Required

1. Describe each transaction.
2. If these transactions fully describe the operations of Allied Leasing during the month, what was the amount of net income or net loss?

Exercise 1-9 *Business organization, balance sheet* (L.O. 3,6)

Presented below are the balances of the assets and liabilities of Long-Gone Delivery Service as of September 30, 19X2. Also included are the revenue and expense figures of the business for September.

Delivery service revenue ....$ 4,100	Delivery equipment $15,500
Accounts receivable 900	Supplies................... 600
Accounts payable 750	Note payable 8,000
Common stock............. 5,100	Rent expense 500
Salary expense 2,000	Cash 650
	Retained earnings .... ?

Required

1. What type of business organization is Long-Gone Delivery Service? How can you tell?
2. Prepare the balance sheet of Long-Gone Delivery Service as of September 30, 19X2. Not all amounts are used.

Exercise 1-10 *Income statement and dividends* (L.O. 3,6)

Presented below are the balances of the assets, liabilities, stockholders' equity, revenues, and expenses of Technical Consultants Inc., at December 31, 19X3, the end of its first year of business. During the year the owners invested $15,000 in the business.

Note payable	$ 30,000	Rent expense	$21,000
Utilities expense	5,800	Cash	3,600
Accounts payable	3,300	Office supplies	4,800
Retained earnings.........	17,100	Salary expense	39,000
Service revenue...........	131,000	Salaries payable	2,000
Accounts receivable	9,000	Property tax expense	1,200
Supplies expense	4,000	Common stock	10,000
Office furniture	45,000	Dividends	?

Required

1. Prepare the income statement of Technical Consultants Inc., for the year ended December 31, 19X3. Not all amounts are used.
2. What was the amount of the dividends during the year?

Problems   *Group A*

Problem 1-1A   *Analyzing a loan request* *(L.O. 1,2,3)*

As an analyst for Midlantic Bank, it is your job to write recommendations to the bank's loan committee. Sigma Enterprises has submitted the following summary data to support the company's request for a $300,000 loan.

Income Statement Data (Summarized):	19X5	19X4	19X3
Total revenues	$790,000	$730,000	$720,000
Total expenses	640,000	570,000	540,000
Net income	$150,000	$160,000	$180,000

Selected Statement of Retained Earnings Data:	19X5	19X4	19X3
Dividends	$190,000	$180,000	$170,000

Balance Sheet Data (Summarized):	19X5	19X4	19X3
Total assets	$630,000	$600,000	$560,000
Total liabilities	$390,000	$320,000	$260,000
Total stockholders' equity	240,000	280,000	300,000
Total liabilities and stockholders' equity	$630,000	$600,000	$560,000

Required

Should the bank loan $300,000 to Sigma Enterprises? Write a one-paragraph recommendation to the loan committee.

Problem 1-2A   *Entity concept, transaction analysis, accounting equation* *(L.O. 3,5)*

Kathy Wood practiced law with a large firm, a partnership, for ten years after graduating from law school. Recently she resigned her position to open her own law office, which she operates as a professional corporation. The name of the new entity is Kathy Wood, Attorney and Counselor, Professional Corporation (P.C.).

Wood recorded the following events during the organizing phase of her new business and its first month of operations. Some of the events were personal and did not affect the law practice. Others were business transactions and should be accounted for by the business.

July 1   Wood sold 1,000 shares of Eastman Kodak stock, which she had owned for several years, receiving $88,000 cash from her stockbroker.

July 2   Wood deposited the $88,000 cash from sale of the Eastman Kodak stock in her personal bank account.

3   Wood received $135,000 cash from her former partners in the law firm from which she resigned.

5   Wood deposited $130,000 cash in a new business bank account entitled Kathy Wood, Attorney and Counselor, Professional Corporation. The business issued common stock to Ms. Wood.

6   A representative of a large company telephoned Wood and told her of the company's intention to transfer its legal business to the new entity of Kathy Wood, Attorney and Counselor.

7   Wood paid $550 cash for letterhead stationery for her new law office.

9   Wood purchased office furniture for the law office, agreeing to pay the account payable, $11,500, within three months.

23   Wood finished court hearings on behalf of a client and submitted her bill for legal services, $6,100. She expected to collect from this client within one month.

30   Wood paid office rent expense, $1,900.

31   The business declared and paid a dividend of $3,500.

Required

1.   Classify each of the preceding events as one of the following:
    a. Business transaction to be accounted for by the business of Kathy Wood, Attorney and Counselor, Professional Corporation.
    b. Business-related event but not a transaction to be accounted for by the business of Kathy Wood, Attorney and Counselor, Professional Corporation.
    c. Personal transaction not to be accounted for by the business of Kathy Wood, Attorney and Counselor, Professional Corporation.
2.   Analyze the effects of the above events on the accounting equation of the business of Kathy Wood, Attorney and Counselor, Professional Corporation. Use a format similar to Exhibit 1–6.

Problem 1-3A   *Balance sheet* (L.O. 3,6)

The bookkeeper of Glass Travel Agency, Inc., prepared the balance sheet of the company while the accountant was ill. The balance sheet contains numerous errors. In particular, the bookkeeper knew that the balance sheet should balance, so he plugged in the stockholders' equity amount needed to achieve this balance. However, the stockholders' equity amount is not correct. All other *amounts* are accurate.

Glass Travel Agency, Inc.
Balance Sheet
Month Ended October 31, 19X7

Assets		Liabilities	
Cash....................	$ 1,400	Notes receivable	$11,000
Advertising expense	300	Interest expense	2,000
Land	30,500	Office supplies	800
Salary expense...........	3,300	Accounts receivable	1,600
Office furniture	4,700	Note payable	20,000
Accounts payable	3,000	**Stockholders' Equity**	
Utilities expense	1,100		
		Stockholders' equity......	8,900
Total assets..............	$44,300	Total liabilities	$44,300

Required

1. Prepare the correct balance sheet as of October 31, 19X7. Compute total assets and total liabilities. Then take the difference to determine correct stockholders' equity.

2. Identify the accounts listed above that should not be presented on the balance sheet and state why you excluded them from the correct balance sheet you prepared for Requirement 1.

Problem 1-4A *Balance sheet, entity concept (L.O. 3,6)*

Matt Thomas is a realtor. He buys and sells properties on his own, and he also earns commission as a real estate agent for buyers and sellers. He organized his business as a corporation on March 10, 19X2, by investing $70,000 to acquire the business's common stock. Consider the following facts as of March 31, 19X2:

a. Thomas has $5,000 in his personal bank account, and the business has $9,000 in its bank account.

b. Office supplies on hand at the real estate office total $1,000.

c. The business spent $15,000 for an Electronic Realty Associates (ERA) franchise, which entitled the business to represent itself as an ERA agent. ERA is a national affiliation of independent real estate agents. This franchise is a business asset.

d. The business owes $48,000 on a note payable for some undeveloped land that was acquired for a total price of $90,000.

e. Thomas owes $65,000 on a personal mortgage on his own home, which he acquired in 19X1 for a total price of $90,000.

f. Thomas owes $950 on a personal charge account with Macy's.

g. The business acquired furniture for $12,000 on March 26. Of this amount, the business owes $6,000 on open account at March 31.

Required

1. Prepare the balance sheet of the real estate business of Matt Thomas, Realtor, Inc., at March 31, 19X2.

2. Identify the personal items given in the preceding facts that would not be reported on the balance sheet of the business.

Problem 1-5A *Transaction analysis for an actual company (L.O. 4,5)*

A recent balance sheet of Xerox Corporation, the manufacturer of copiers and other office equipment, is summarized as follows, with amounts in thousands. For example, Cash of $266,600,000 is presented as $266,600.

Xerox Corporation
Balance Sheet
December 31, 19XX
(thousands)

Assets		Liabilities	
Cash	$ 266,600	Notes payable	$1,985,500
Accounts receivable ...	1,466,900	Accounts payable	390,300
Merchandise		Other liabilities	2,107,600
inventories	1,469,800	Total liabilities	4,483,400
Land, buildings, and			
equipment..........	2,659,700	**Stockholders' equity**	5,333,300
Other assets	3,953,700	Total liabilities	
		and stockholders'	
Total assets	$9,816,700	equity	$9,816,700

Suppose the company had the following transactions and events (amounts in thousands) during January of the following year:

a. Received cash investment from owners, $160.
b. Purchased inventories on account, $400.
c. Paid cash on account, $136.
d. Sold equipment to another company on account, $670. The equipment had cost $670.
e. Learned that a national television news program would show members of Congress using Xerox copy machines as part of a senate investigation. The value of this advertisement to the company is estimated to be $1,000.
f. Borrowed cash, signing a note payable, $550.
g. Purchased equipment for cash, $380.
h. Collected cash on account from customers, $289.
i. Received special equipment from an owner as an investment in the company. The value of the equipment was $119.

Required

1. Showing all amounts in thousands, analyze the January transactions of Xerox. Use a format similar to Exhibit 1-6.
2. Prove that assets = liabilities + stockholders' equity after analyzing the transactions.

Problem 1-6A   *Business transactions and analysis*   **(L.O. 5)**

Amalfi Company was recently formed. The balance of each item in the company's accounting equation is shown below for February 8 and for each of nine following business days.

		Cash	Accounts Receivable	Supplies	Land	Accounts Payable	Stockholders' Equity
Feb.	8	$3,000	$7,000	$ 800	$11,000	$3,800	$18,000
	12	2,000	7,000	800	11,000	2,800	18,000
	14	6,000	3,000	800	11,000	2,800	18,000
	17	6,000	3,000	1,100	11,000	3,100	18,000
	19	3,000	3,000	1,100	11,000	3,100	15,000
	20	1,900	3,000	1,100	11,000	2,000	15,000
	22	7,900	3,000	1,100	5,000	2,000	15,000
	25	7,900	3,200	900	5,000	2,000	15,000
	26	7,700	3,200	1,100	5,000	2,000	15,000
	28	2,600	3,200	1,100	10,100	2,000	15,000

Required

Assuming a single transaction took place on each day, describe briefly the transaction that was most likely to have occurred, beginning with February 12. Indicate which accounts were affected and by what amount. No revenue or expense transactions occurred on these dates.

Problem 1-7A   *Income statement, statement of retained earnings, balance sheet* **(L.O. 6)**

Presented below are the amounts of (a) the assets, liabilities, and common stock of Millwood Delivery Service, Inc., as of December 31 and (b) the revenues and expenses of the company for the year ended on that date. The items are listed in alphabetical order.

Accounts payable $14,000	Land ....$ 8,000
Accounts receivable 6,000	Note payable 31,000
Building 13,000	Property tax expense 2,000
Cash 4,000	Rent expense 14,000
Common stock 10,000	Salary expense 38,000
Equipment 21,000	Service revenue............ 100,000
Interest expense 4,000	Supplies 13,000
Interest payable 1,000	Utilities expense 3,000

The beginning amount of retained earnings was $2,000, and during the year dividends were $32,000.

Required

1. Prepare the income statement of Millwood Delivery Service, Inc., for the year ended December 31 of the current year.
2. Prepare the statement of retained earnings of the company for the year ended December 31.
3. Prepare the balance sheet of the company at December 31.

Problem 1-8A *Transaction analysis, accounting equation, financial statements* **(L.O. 5,6)**

Kathy Starr owns and operates an interior design studio called Starr Designers, Inc. The following amounts summarize the financial position of her business on April 30, 19X5:

	Assets =				Liabilities +	Stockholder's Equity		Type of SE Transaction
	Cash +	Accounts Receivable +	Supplies +	Land	= Accounts Payable +	Common Stock +	Retained Earnings	
Bal.	720	2,240		23,100	4,400	10,000	11,660	

During May 19X5 the business completed the following transactions:

a. Starr received $12,000 as a gift and deposited the cash in the business bank account. The business issued common stock to Starr.
b. Paid off the beginning balance of accounts payable.
c. Performed services for a client and received cash of $1,100.
d. Collected cash from a customer on account, $750.
e. Purchased supplies on account, $120.
f. Consulted on the interior design of a major office building and billed the client for services rendered, $5,000.
g. Received cash of $1,700 and issued common stock to Starr.
h. Recorded the following business expenses for the month:
   1. Paid office rent—$1,200
   2. Paid advertising—$860.
i. Sold supplies to another interior designer for $80, which was the cost of the supplies.
j. Declared and paid dividends of $2,400.

Required

1. Record the effects of the above transactions on the accounting equation of Starr Designers, Inc. Adapt the format of Exhibit 1-6.
2. Prepare the income statement of Starr Designers, Inc., for the month ended May 31, 19X5. List expenses in decreasing order by amount.

3. Prepare the statement of retained earnings of Starr Designers, Inc., for the month ended May 31, 19X5.
4. Prepare the balance sheet of Starr Designers, Inc., at May 31.

(Group B)

Problem 1-1B *Analyzing a loan request (L.O. 1,2,3)*

As an analyst for Salt Lake Bank, it is your job to write recommendations to the bank's loan committee. Lomoni Company has submitted the following summary data to support its request for a $100,000 loan.

Income Statement Data (Summarized):	19X5	19X4	19X3
Total revenues	$850,000	$760,000	$720,000
Total expenses	640,000	570,000	540,000
Net income	$210,000	$190,000	$180,000

Selected Statement of Retained Earnings Data:	19X5	19X4	19X3
Dividends	$160,000	$140,000	$120,000

Balance Sheet Data (Summarized):	19X5	19X4	19X3
Total assets	$730,000	$660,000	$590,000
Total liabilities	$240,000	$220,000	$200,000
Total stockholders' equity	490,000	440,000	390,000
Total liabilities and stockholders' equity ..	$730,000	$660,000	$590,000

Required

Should the bank loan $100,000 to Lomoni Company? Write a one-paragraph recommendation to the loan committee.

Problem 1-2B *Entity concept, transaction analysis, accounting equation (L.O. 3,5)*

Melvin Dexter practiced law with a large firm, a partnership, for five years after graduating from law school. Recently he resigned his position to open his own law office, which he operates as a professional corporation. The name of the new entity is Melvin Dexter, Attorney, Professional Corporation (P.C.).

Dexter recorded the following events during the organizing phase of his new business and its first month of operations. Some of the events were personal and did not affect his law practice. Others were business transactions and should be accounted for by the business.

May 4 Dexter received $50,000 cash from his former partners in the law firm from which he resigned.

   5 Dexter deposited $50,000 cash in a new business bank account, entitled Melvin Dexter, Attorney, P.C. The business issued common stock to Dexter.

   6 Dexter paid $300 cash for letterhead stationery for his new law office.

   7 Dexter purchased office furniture for his law office. Dexter agreed to pay the account payable, $5,000, within six months.

   10 Dexter sold 500 shares of IBM stock, which he and his wife had owned for several years, receiving $75,000 cash from his stockbroker.

May 11 Dexter deposited the $75,000 cash from sale of the IBM stock in his personal bank account.

12 A representative of a large company telephoned Dexter and told him of the company's intention to transfer its legal business to the new entity of Melvin Dexter, Attorney, P.C.

29 Dexter finished court hearings on behalf of a client and submitted his bill for legal services, $4,000. Dexter expected to collect from this client within two weeks.

30 Dexter paid office rent expense, $1,000.

31 The business declared and paid a dividend of $2,000.

Required

1. Classify each of the preceding events as one of the following:
   a. Business transaction to be accounted for by the business of Melvin Dexter, Attorney, P.C.
   b. Business-related event but not a transaction to be accounted for by the business of Melvin Dexter, Attorney, P.C.
   c. Personal transaction not to be accounted for by the business of Melvin Dexter, Attorney, P.C.
2. Analyze the effects of the above events on the accounting equation of the business of Melvin Dexter, Attorney, P.C. Use a format similar to Exhibit 1-6.

Problem 1-3B *Balance sheet* (L.O. 3,6)

The bookkeeper of Getz Auction Co. prepared the balance sheet of the company while the accountant was ill. The balance sheet contains numerous errors. In particular, the bookkeeper knew that the balance sheet should balance, so he plugged in the stockholders' equity amount needed to achieve this balance. However, the stockholders' equity amount is not correct. All other *amounts* are accurate.

Getz Auction Co.
Balance Sheet
Month Ended July 31, 19X3

Assets		Liabilities	
Cash....................	$ 2,000	Accounts receivable	$ 3,000
Office supplies	1,000	Service revenue..........	35,000
Land	20,000	Property tax expense	800
Advertising expense	2,500	Accounts payable	8,000
Office furniture	10,000	**Stockholders' Equity**	
Note payable	16,000		
Rent expense	4,000	Stockholders' equity......	8,700
Total assets..............	$55,500	Total liabilities	$55,500

Required

1. Prepare the correct balance sheet as of July 31, 19X3. Compute total assets and total liabilities. Then take the difference to determine correct stockholders' equity.
2. Identify the accounts listed above which should *not* be presented on the balance sheet and state why you excluded them from the correct balance sheet you prepared for Requirement 1.

Problem 1-4B *Balance sheet, entity concept* (L.O. 3,6)

Sue Kerault is a realtor. She buys and sells properties on her own, and she also earns commission as a real estate agent for buyers and sellers. She organized her business as a corporation on September 24, 19X4, by investing $90,000 to acquire the business's common stock. Consider the following facts as of November 30, 19X4:

a. Kerault owes $80,000 on a note payable for some undeveloped land that was acquired by the business for a total price of $140,000.

b. The business spent $15,000 for a Century 21 real estate franchise, which entitles it to represent itself as a Century 21 agent. Century 21 is a national affiliation of independent real estate agents. This franchise is a business asset.

c. Kerault owes $120,000 on a personal mortgage on her personal residence, which she acquired in 19X1 for a total price of $170,000.

d. Kerault has $10,000 in her personal bank account, and the business has $12,000 in its bank account.

e. Kerault owes $1,800 on a personal charge account with Neiman-Marcus Specialty Department Store.

f. The business acquired furniture for $17,000 on November 25. Of this amount, the business owes $6,000 on open account at November 30.

g. Office supplies on hand at the real estate office totaled $1,000.

Required

1. Prepare the balance sheet of the real estate business of Sue Kerault, Realtor, Inc., at November 30, 19X4.
2. Identify the personal items given in the preceding facts that would not be reported on the balance sheet of the business.

Problem 1-5B *Transaction analysis for an actual company* (L.O. 4,5)

A recent balance sheet of Levi Strauss & Company, the world's largest seller of jeans and casual pants, is summarized as follows, with amounts in thousands. For example, Cash of $263,389,000 is presented as $263,389.

Levi Strauss & Company
Balance Sheet
November 25, 19XX
(thousands)

Assets		Liabilities	
Cash	$ 263,389	Notes payable	$ 83,361
Accounts receivable	339,798	Accounts payable	229,453
Merchandise inventories	387,660	Other liabilities	300,847
Property, plant, and equip. ..	330,455	Total liabilities	613,661
Other assets	99,800		
		Stockholders' equity	
		Stockholders' equity	807,441
		Total liabilities	
Total assets	$1,421,102	and stockholders' equity ...	$1,421,102

Suppose that the company had the following transactions and events (amounts in thousands) during December:

a. Received cash investments from owners, $18.
b. Received special equipment from an owner as an investment in the company. The value of the equipment was $90.
c. Borrowed cash, signing a note payable, $100.
d. Purchased equipment for cash, $125.
e. Purchased inventories on account, $90.
f. Paid cash on account, $54.
g. Sold equipment to another company on account, $14. The equipment had cost $14.
h. Discovered that the president of the United States was going to wear Levi blue jeans while giving his State of the Union address next January.
i. Collected cash on account from customers, $84.

Required:

1. Showing all amounts in thousands, analyze the December transactions of Levi Strauss. Use a format similar to Exhibit 1-6.
2. Prove that assets = liabilities + stockholders' equity after analyzing the transactions.

Problem 1-6B   *Business transactions and analysis* **(L.O. 5)**

Cardinale Company was recently formed. The balance of each item in the company's accounting equation is shown below for May 10 and for each of nine following business days.

	Cash	Accounts Receivable	Supplies	Land	Accounts Payable	Stockholders' Equity
May 10	$ 8,000	$4,000	$1,000	$ 8,000	$4,000	$17,000
11	11,000	4,000	1,000	8,000	4,000	20,000
12	6,000	4,000	1,000	13,000	4,000	20,000
15	6,000	4,000	3,000	13,000	6,000	20,000
16	5,000	4,000	3,000	13,000	5,000	20,000
17	7,000	2,000	3,000	13,000	5,000	20,000
18	16,000	2,000	3,000	13,000	5,000	29,000
19	13,000	2,000	3,000	13,000	2,000	29,000
22	12,000	2,000	4,000	13,000	2,000	29,000
23	8,000	2,000	4,000	13,000	2,000	25,000

Required

Assuming a single transaction took place on each day, describe briefly the transaction that was most likely to have occurred, beginning with May 11. Indicate which accounts were affected and by what amount. No revenue or expense transactions occurred on these dates.

Problem 1-7B   *Income statement, statement of retained earnings, balance sheet* **(L.O. 6)**

Presented below are the amounts of (a) the assets and liabilities, and common stock of Petoski Theater Corporation as of December 31 and (b) the revenues and expenses of the company for the year ended on that date. The items are listed below and on the facing page.

Accounts payable	$ 19,000	Land	$ 65,000
Accounts receivable	12,000	Note payable	85,000
Advertising expense	11,000	Property tax expense	4,000
Building	170,000	Rent expense	23,000

Cash	10,000	Salary expense	63,000
Common stock	100,000	Salaries payable	1,000
Furniture	20,000	Service revenue	200,000
Interest expense	9,000	Supplies	3,000

The beginning amount of retained earnings was $50,000, and during the year dividends were $65,000.

Required

1. Prepare the income statement of Petoski Theater Corporation for the year ended December 31 of the current year.
2. Prepare the statement of retained earnings of the company for the year ended December 31.
3. Prepare the balance sheet of the company at December 31.

Problem 1-8B *Transaction analysis, accounting equation, financial statements*
(L.O. 5,6)

Lisa Reed owns and operates an interior design studio called Reed Interiors, Inc. The following amounts summarize the financial position of her business on August 31, 19X2:

	Assets				= Liabilities +	Stockholders' Equity		Type of SE Transaction
	Cash	+ Receivable	+ Supplies +	Land	= Payable +	Stock	+ Earnings	
		Accounts			Accounts	Common	Retained	
Bal.	1,250	1,500		12,000	8,000	4,000	2,750	

During September 19X2 the following events occurred:

a. Reed inherited $15,000 and deposited the cash in the business bank account. The business issued common stock to Reed.
b. Performed services for a client and received cash of $700.
c. Paid off the beginning balance of accounts payable.
d. Purchased supplies on account, $500.
e. Collected cash from a customer on account, $1,000.
f. Received cash of $1,000 and issued common stock to Reed.
g. Consulted on the interior design of a major office building and billed the client for services rendered, $2,400.
h. Recorded the following business expenses for the month:
   1. Paid office rent—$900.
   2. Paid advertising—$100.
i. Sold supplies to another business for $150, which was the cost of the supplies.
j. Declared and paid dividends of $1,800.

Required

1. Record the effects of the above transactions on the accounting equation of Reed Interiors, Inc. Adapt the format of Exhibit 1-6.
2. Prepare the income statement of Reed Interiors, Inc., for the month ended September 30, 19X2. List expenses in decreasing order by amount.
3. Prepare the statement of retained earnings of Reed Interiors, Inc., for the month ended September 30, 19X2.
4. Prepare the balance sheet of Reed Interiors, Inc., at September 30, 19X2.

Extending Your Knowledge

Decision Problems

1. Using Financial Statements to Evaluate a Loan Request (L.O. 1,3)

The proprietors of two businesses, Dillard's Hardware Company and Leslie Falco Home Decorators, Inc., have sought business loans from you. To decide whether to make the loans, you have requested their balance sheets.

Dillard's Hardware Company
Balance Sheet
August 31, 19X4

Assets		Liabilities	
Cash....................	$ 1,000	Accounts payable	$ 12,000
Accounts receivable	14,000	Note payable	18,000
Merchandise inventory ..	85,000	Total liabilities	30,000
Store supplies	500		
Furniture and fixtures ...	9,000	**Stockholders' Equity**	
Building	90,000	Stockholders' equity.....	183,500
Land	14,000	Total liabilities	
		and stockholders'	
Total assets............	$213,500	equity	$213,500

Leslie Falco Home Decorators, Inc.
Balance Sheet
August 31, 19X4

Assets		Liabilities	
Cash....................	$11,000	Accounts payable	$ 3,000
Accounts receivable	4,000	Note payable	18,000
Office supplies	1,000	Total liabilities	21,000
Office furniture	6,000		
Land	19,000	**Owners' Equity**	
		Owners' equity	20,000
		Total liabilities	
Total assets.............	$41,000	and owners' equity	$41,000

Required

1. Based solely on these balance sheets, which entity would you be more comfortable loaning money to? Explain fully, citing specific items and amounts from the balance sheets.
2. In addition to the balance sheet data, what other financial statement information would you require? Be specific.

2. Using Accounting Information   (L.O. 1,2)

A friend learns that you are taking an accounting course. Knowing that you do not plan a career in accounting, the friend asks why you are "wasting your time." Explain to the friend:

1. Why you are taking the course.
2. How accounting information is used or will be used:
   a. In your personal life.
   b. In the business life of your friend, who plans to be a farmer.
   c. In the business life of another friend, who plans a career in sales.

Ethical Issue

An ethical issue of current importance centers on the nature of work that accounting firms perform. CPA firms audit the financial statements of companies in order to express a professional opinion on the reliability of those statements. For this audit opinion to be objective and unbiased, it is critical that the auditors be entirely independent of their clients. CPA firms also perform management advisory (consulting) services for clients. This work often includes designing accounting systems. In many cases the same CPA firm audits the financial statements of a company for which it has designed the accounting system.

Required

Discuss the ethical issue in this situation. Propose a solution.

Financial Statement Problems

1. Identifying Items from a Company's Financial Statements (L.O. 4)

This and similar problems in succeeding chapters focus on the financial statements of an actual company: The Goodyear Tire & Rubber Company. As you study each problem, you will gradually build the confidence that you can understand and use actual financial statements.

Refer to the Goodyear financial statements in Appendix C, and answer the following questions:

1. How much in cash (including cash equivalents) did Goodyear have on December 31, 1991?
2. What were total assets at December 31, 1991? At December 31, 1990?
3. Write the company's accounting equation at December 31, 1991, by filling in the dollar amounts:

ASSETS = LIABILITIES + STOCKHOLDERS' EQUITY

4. Identify net sales (revenue) for the year ended December 31, 1991. (Net sales means sales revenue after certain subtractions.)
5. How much net income or net loss did Goodyear experience for the year ended December 31, 1991? Was 1991 a good year or a bad year compared to 1990?

2. Identifying Items from an Actual Company's Financial Statements
(L. O. 4)

Obtain the annual report of an actual company of your choosing. Annual reports are available in various forms including the original document in hard copy, microfiche, and computerized databases such as that provided by Disclosure, Inc.

Answer these questions about the company. Concentrate on the current year in the annual report you select, except as directed for particular questions.

1. How much in cash (which may include cash equivalents) did the company have at the end of the current year? At the end of the preceding year? Did cash increase or decrease during the current year? By how much?
2. What were total assets at the end of the current year? At the end of the preceding year?
3. Write the company's accounting equation at the end of the current year by filling in the dollar amounts:

ASSETS = LIABILITIES + STOCKHOLDERS' EQUITY

4. Identify net sales revenue for the current year. The company may label this as *Net sales, Sales, Net revenue,* or other title. How much was the corresponding revenue amount for the preceding year?
5. How much net income or net loss did the company experience for the current year? For the preceding year?

Appendix:

Statement of Cash Flows for Air and Sea Travel, Inc.

Air and Sea Travel would also prepare a statement of cash flows to report the cash effects of its operating, investing, and financing transactions. Operating activities relate to all transactions affecting net income or net loss. Investing activities include buying and selling long-lived assets. Financing activities show the amounts of cash the entity received from its owners and creditors and the cash amounts paid to these two groups.

Each type of activity includes cash receipts and cash payments and results in a net cash inflow (receipts greater than payments) or a net cash outflow (payments greater than receipts). The statement of cash flows shows the net increase or decrease in cash of the entity during the period.

Air and Sea Travel, Inc., was incorporated as a business during April. During the month its cash went from zero to an ending amount of $33,300, an increase of the same amount. This is the bottom line of the statement that follows. Trace the increase to the bottom line of Exhibit 1-6. Study the statement mainly for *format*. We will cover the statement of cash flows in detail in Chapter 15.

Air and Sea Travel, Inc.
Statement of Cash Flows
Month Ended April 30, 19X1

Cash flows from **operating** activities:		
Receipts:		
Collections for customers ($5,500 + $1,000)		$ 6,500
Payments:		
To suppliers ($1,100 + $400 + $400)	$ (1,900)	
To employees	(1,200)	(3,100)
Net cash inflow from operating		
activities.		3,400
Cash flows from **investing** activities:		
Acquisition of land	$(40,000)	
Sale of land	22,000	
Net cash outflow from investing		
activities		(18,000)
Cash flows from **financing** activities:		
Issuance of common stock	$50,000	
Payment of dividends	(2,100)	
Net cash inflow from financing activities		47,900
Net increase in cash		$33,300

Chapter 2

Recording Business Transactions

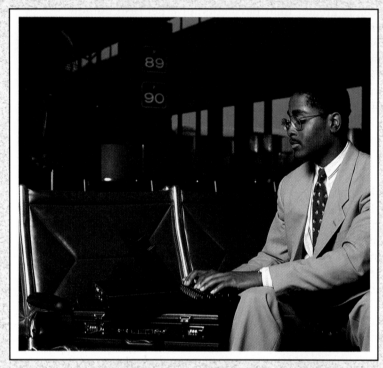

Grant Reynolds was the typical college graduate—bursting with energy and ideas. After finishing his studies at the University of Northern Iowa with a degree in marketing, he took a job with Marshall Field, a department store in Chicago. There he made the contacts in the marketing world needed to launch his own business for exporting lap-top computers to Eastern Europe. In its infancy, the business made only a few sales, but each sale was for a large amount. Grant's payroll consisted only of his own salary and the salary of an assistant. With only a few sales and a one-person staff, Grant simply kept informal accounting records in a notebook.

At the end of the first year of operations Grant noted that sales totaled $4.3 million. Grant was anxious to expand his business and needed a bank loan. However, he could not produce the financial statements the bank required. Grant's informal records did not give the bank the information it needed to evaluate his business and so make a decision on the loan. Grant had to hire a CPA to reconstruct the accounting records and create the financial statements to show how the business had performed and where it stood financially. As you read Chapter 2, consider the importance of keeping accurate business records and how accounting meets that need.

Chapter 1 illustrates how to account for business transactions by analyzing their effects on the accounting equation. That approach emphasizes accounting analysis, but it becomes unwieldy in day-to-day business if many transactions occur. In practice, accountants use a different approach to record accounting information. This chapter focuses on processing accounting information as it is actually done in practice.

The Account

The basic summary device of accounting is the **account.** This is the detailed record of the changes that have occurred in a particular asset, liability, or stockholders' equity during a period of time. Each account appears on its own page. For convenient access to the information in the accounts the pages are grouped together in a single book called the **ledger.** When you hear reference to "keeping the books" or "auditing the books," the word *books* refers to the ledger. The ledger may be a bound book, a loose-leaf set of pages, or a computer record.

In the ledger, the accounts are grouped in three broad categories, based on the accounting equation:

$$\text{ASSETS} = \text{LIABILITIES} + \text{STOCKHOLDERS' EQUITY}$$

Assets

Those economic resources that will benefit the business in the future are assets. The following asset accounts are common to many firms.

Cash. The Cash account shows the cash effects of a business's transactions. Cash means money and any medium of exchange that a bank accepts at face value. Cash includes currency, coins, money orders, certificates of deposit, and checks. The Cash account includes all cash items whether they are kept on hand, in a safe, in a cash register, or in a bank.

Notes Receivable. A business may sell its goods or services in exchange for a promissory note, which is a written pledge that the customer will pay the business a fixed amount of money by a certain date. The Notes Receivable account is a record of the promissory notes that the business expects to collect in cash.

Accounts Receivable. A business may sell its goods or services in exchange for an oral or implied promise for future cash receipt. Such sales are made on credit (on account). The Accounts Receivable account contains these amounts.

Prepaid Expenses. A business often pays certain expenses in advance. A prepaid expense is an asset because the business avoids having to pay cash in the future for the specified expense. The ledger holds a separate asset account for each prepaid expense. Prepaid Rent and Prepaid Insurance are prepaid expenses that occur often in business. Office Supplies are also accounted for as prepaid expenses.

Land. The Land account is a record of the land that a business owns and uses in its operations.

Building. The cost of a business's buildings—office, warehouse, garage, and the like—appear in the Building account.

Equipment, Furniture, and Fixtures. A business has a separate asset account for each type of equipment—Office Equipment and Store Equipment, for example. The Furniture and Fixtures account shows the cost of this asset.

Other asset categories and accounts will be discussed as needed. For example, many businesses have an Investments account for their investments in other companies.

Liabilities

Recall that a *liability* is a debt. A business generally has fewer liability accounts than asset accounts because a business's liabilities can be summarized under relatively few categories.

Notes Payable. This account is the opposite of the Notes Receivable account. Notes Payable represents the amounts that the business must pay because it signed a promissory note to purchase goods or services.

Accounts Payable. This account is the opposite of the Accounts Receivable account. The oral or implied promise to pay off debts arising from credit purchases of goods appears in the Accounts Payable account. Such a purchase is said to be made on account. Other liability categories and accounts are added as needed. Taxes Payable, Wages Payable, and Salary Payable are accounts that appear in many ledgers.

Stockholders' Equity

The owners' claims to the assets of the corporation are called *stockholders' equity*. In a proprietorship or a partnership, owner's equity is often split into separate accounts for the owner's capital balance and the owner's withdrawals. A corporation has a similar setup, but uses the Common Stock, Retained Earnings, and Dividends accounts.

Common Stock. This account represents the owners' investment in the corporation. A person invests in a corporation by purchasing common stock. The corporation issues a stock certificate imprinted with the name of the stockholder as proof of ownership.

Retained Earnings.   A business must earn a profit to remain in operation. The Retained Earnings account shows the cumulative net income earned by the corporation over its lifetime, minus cumulative net losses and dividends. The title Retained Earnings is thus well chosen. We will be using this account more in the chapters to follow and include it here merely for completeness.

Dividends.   The owners of a corporation demand cash from their business. After profitable operations, the board of directors may (or may not) declare a dividend to be paid in cash at a later date. Dividends are not required. They are optional and depend upon the action of the board of directors. The corporation keeps a separate account titled Dividends, which indicates a decrease in Retained Earnings.

Revenues.   The increase in stockholders' equity from delivering goods or services to customers or clients is called *revenue*. The ledger contains as many revenue accounts as needed. Air and Sea Travel, Inc., would have a Service Revenue account for amounts earned by providing travel arrangement service for clients. If the business loans money to an outsider, it will also need an Interest Revenue account for the interest earned on the loan. If the business rents a building to a tenant, it will need a Rent Revenue account. Increases in revenue accounts are *increases* in stockholders' equity.

Expenses.   The cost of operating a business is called *expense*. Expenses have the opposite effect of revenues, so they decrease stockholders' equity. A business needs a separate account for each category of its expenses, such as Salary Expense, Rent Expense, Advertising Expense, and Utilities Expense. Expense accounts are decreases in stockholders' equity.

Exhibit 2-1 shows how asset, liability, and stockholders' equity accounts can be grouped into the ledger. Typically, each account occupies a separate sheet or record.

Double-Entry Bookkeeping

Accounting is based on double-entry bookkeeping, which means that accountants record the *dual effects* of a business transaction. We know that each transaction affects two accounts. For example, Gary and Monica Lyon's $50,000 cash investment in the travel agency increased both the Cash account and the Common Stock account of the business. It would be incomplete to record only the increase in the entity's cash without recording the increase in its stockholders' equity.

Consider a *cash purchase of supplies*. What are the dual effects of this transaction? The purchase (1) decreases cash and (2) increases supplies. A *purchase of supplies on credit* (1) increases supplies and (2) increases accounts payable. A *cash payment on account* (1) decreases cash and (2) decreases accounts payable. All transactions have at least two effects on the entity.

The T-Account

How do accountants record transactions in the accounts? The account format used for most illustrations in this book is called the T-account. It takes the form of the capital letter "T." The vertical line in the letter divides the account into

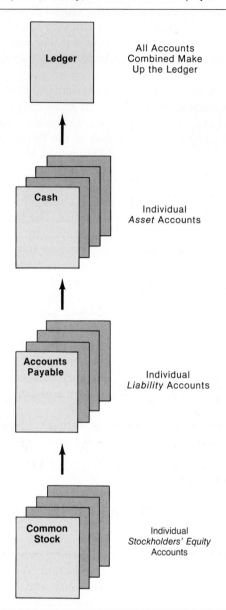

its left and right sides. The account title rests on the horizontal line. For example, the Cash account of a business appears in the following T-account format:

Cash

Left side	Right side
Debit	*Credit*

The left side of the account is called the **debit** side, and the right side is called the **credit** side. Often beginners in the study of accounting are confused by the words *debit* and *credit*. To become comfortable using them, simply remember this:

Debit = Left Side   Credit = Right Side

Even though *left side* and *right side* are more descriptive, *debit* and *credit* are too deeply entrenched in accounting to avoid using.[1]

Increases and Decreases in the Accounts

The type of an account determines how increases and decreases in it are recorded. For any given account, all increases are recorded on one side, and all decreases are recorded on the other side. Increases in *assets* are recorded in the left (the debit) side of the account. Decreases in assets are recorded in the right (the credit) side of the account. Conversely, increases in *liabilities* and *stockholders' equity* are recorded by *credits*. Decreases are recorded by *debits*.

This pattern of recording debits and credits is based on the accounting equation:

ASSETS = LIABILITIES + STOCKHOLDERS' EQUITY

Notice that assets are on the opposite side of the equation from liabilities and stockholders' equity. This explains why increases and decreases in assets are recorded in the opposite manner from liabilities and stockholders' equity. It also explains why liabilities and stockholders' equity are treated the same way: they are on the same side of the equal sign. Exhibit 2-2 shows the relationship between the accounting equation and the rules of debit and credit.

To illustrate the ideas diagrammed in Exhibit 2-2, reconsider the first transaction from the preceding chapter. Gary and Monica Lyon invested $50,000 in cash to begin the travel agency, and the business issued common stock to them as evidence of their ownership in the business. Which accounts of the business are affected? By what amounts? On what side (debit or credit)? The answer is that Assets and Common Stock would increase by $50,000, as the following T-accounts show.

Assets   =   Liabilities + Stockholders' Equity

Cash		Common Stock	
Debit for Increase, 50,000			**Credit for Increase, 50,000**

Notice that Assets = Liabilities + Stockholders' Equity, *and* that total debits = total credits.

EXHIBIT 2-2 *Accounting Equation and the Rules of Debit and Credit*

Accounting Equation:	Assets		=	Liabilities		+	Stockholders' Equity	
Rules of Debit and Credit:	Debit for Increase	Credit for Decrease		Debit for Decrease	Credit for Increase		Debit for Decrease	Credit for Increase

[1] The words *debit* and *credit* have a Latin origin (*debitum* and *creditum*). Pacioli, the Italian monk who wrote about accounting in the fifteenth century, used these terms.

The amount remaining in an account is called its *balance*. This initial transaction gives Cash a $50,000 debit balance and Common Stock a $50,000 credit balance.

The second transaction is a $40,000 cash purchase of land. This transaction affects two assets: Cash and Land. It decreases (credits) Cash and increases (debits) Land, as shown in the T-accounts:

Assets   =   Liabilities   +   Stockholders' Equity

Cash				Common Stock	
Balance 50,000	Credit for Decrease, 40,000				Balance 50,000

Land	
Debit for Increase, 40,000	

After this transaction, Cash has a $10,000 debit balance ($50,000 debit balance −$40,000 credit amount), Land's debit balance is $40,000, and the Common Stock account has a $50,000 credit balance.

Transaction 3 is a $500 purchase of office supplies on account. This transaction increases the asset Office Supplies and the liability Accounts Payable, as shown in the following accounts:

Assets   =   Liabilities   +   Stockholders' Equity

Cash		Accounts Payable		Common Stock	
Balance 10,000			Credit for Increase, 500		Balance 50,000

Office Supplies	
Debit for Increase, 500	

Land	
Balance 40,000	

Accountants create accounts as needed. The process of writing a new T-account in preparation for recording a transaction is called *opening the account*. For Transaction 1, we opened the Cash account and the Common Stock account. For Transaction 2, we opened the Land account, and for Transaction 3, Office Supplies and Accounts Payable.

Accountants could record all transactions directly in the accounts, as we have shown for the first three transactions. However, that way of accounting is not practical because it does not leave a clear record of each transaction. Suppose you need to know what account was debited and what account was credited in a particular transaction. Looking at each account in the ledger does not answer this question. Why? Because double-entry accounting always affects at least two accounts. Therefore, you may have to search through all the accounts in the ledger to find both sides of a particular transaction. To avoid this waste of time, accountants keep a record of each transaction in a journal and then transfer this information into the accounts.

The Debit-Credit Language of Accounting

As we have seen, *debit* means "left side" and *credit* means "right side." We say "Debit Cash for $1,000," which means to place $1,000 on the left side of the cash account. We record "a $500 debit to Accounts Payable" by entering the $500 in the left side of this account, which signals a decrease in a liability. When we speak of "crediting a liability account for $750," we mean to increase the account's balance by recording $750 on the right side of the account.

In everyday conversation, we sometimes use the word *credit* in a sense that is different from its technical accounting meaning. For example, we may praise someone by saying, "She deserves credit for her good work." In your study of accounting forget this general use. Remember that *debit means left side* and *credit means right side*. Whether an account is increased or decreased by a debit or credit depends on the type of account (see Exhibit 2-2).

Recording Transactions in Journals

In actual practice, accountants record transactions first in a book called the **journal.** A journal is a chronological record of the entity's transactions. In this section, we describe the recording process and illustrate how to use the journal and the ledger.

The recording process follows these five steps:

1. Identify the transaction from source documents, such as bank deposit slips, sales receipts, and check stubs.
2. Specify each account affected by the transaction and classify it by type (asset, liability, or stockholders' equity).
3. Determine whether each account is increased or decreased by the transaction.
4. Using the rules of debit and credit, determine whether to debit or credit the account.
5. Enter the transaction in the journal, including a brief explanation for the journal entry. Accountants write the debit side of the entry first and the credit side next.

We have discussed steps 1, 2, 3, and 4. Step 5, "Enter the transaction in the journal," means to write the transaction in the journal. This step is also called "making the journal entry," "preparing the journal entry," or "journalizing the transaction." A major part of learning accounting is understanding how to prepare journal entries.

Let's apply the five steps to journalize the first transaction of the accounting practice of Air and Sea Travel, Inc.—the $50,000 cash investment in the business.

Step 1. The source documents are the bank deposit slip. The Lyons' $50,000 check is drawn on their personal bank account, and the stock certificate is issued to the Lyons.

OBJECTIVE 3
Record transactions in the journal

Step 2. *Cash* and *Common Stock* are the accounts affected by the transaction. Cash is an asset account, and Common Stock is a stockholders' equity account.

Step 3. Both accounts increase by $50,000. Therefore, debit Cash: it is the asset account that is increased. Also, credit Common Stock: it is the stockholders' equity account that is increased.

Step 4. Debit Cash to record an increase in this asset account. Credit Common Stock to record an increase in this stockholders' equity account.

Step 5. The journal entry is

Date	Accounts and Explanation	Debit	Credit
Apr. 2	Cash	50,000	
	Common Stock		50,000
	Issued common stock to owners.		

Note that the journal entry includes (a) the date of the transaction, (b) the title of the account debited (placed flush left) and the title of the account credited (indented slightly), (c) the dollar amounts of the debit (left) and credit (right)—dollar signs are omitted in the money columns—and (d) a short explanation of the transaction.

A helpful hint: To get off to the best start when analyzing a transaction, you should first pinpoint its effects (if any) on cash. Did cash increase or decrease? Then find its effect on other accounts. Typically, it is easier to identify the effect of a transaction on cash than to identify the effect on other accounts.

The journal offers information that the ledger accounts do not provide. Each journal entry shows the complete effect of a business transaction. Let's examine the initial investment. The Cash account shows a single figure, the $50,000 debit. We know that every transaction has a credit, so in what account will we find the corresponding $50,000 credit? In this simple illustration, we know that the Common Stock account holds this figure. But imagine the difficulties an accountant would face trying to link debits and credits for hundreds of daily transactions—without a separate record of each transaction. The journal answers this problem and presents the full story for each transaction.

The journal can be a loose-leaf notebook, a bound book, or a computer listing. Exhibit 2-3 shows how a journal page might look with the first transaction entered.

EXHIBIT 2-3 *The Journal*

Journal			Page 6
Date	Accounts and Explanation	Debit	Credit
Apr. 2	Cash	50,000	
	Common Stock		50,000
	Issued common stock to owners.		

In these introductory discussions we temporarily ignore the date of each transaction in order to focus on the accounts and their dollar amounts.

Posting from the Journal to the Ledger

Posting means transferring the amounts from the journal to the appropriate accounts in the ledger. Debits in the journal are posted as debits in the ledger, and credits in the journal as credits in the ledger. The initial investment transaction of Air and Sea Travel is posted to the ledger as shown in Exhibit 2-4.

Flow of Accounting Data

Exhibit 2-5—at the top of the next page—summarizes the flow of accounting data from the business transaction to the ledger.

Illustrative Problem

In this section, we illustrate transaction analysis, journalizing, and posting. We continue the example of Air and Sea Travel, Inc., and account for six of the early transactions. Transactions that affect cash are the easiest to analyze. Therefore, when a transaction affects cash, we account for the cash effect first.

EXHIBIT 2-4 *Journal Entry and Posting to the Ledger*

Panel A—Journal Entry:

Accounts and Explanation	Debit	Credit
Cash	50,000	
Common Stock		50,000
Issued common stock to owners.		

Panel B—Posting to the Ledger:

Cash
50,000

Common Stock
50,000

OBJECTIVE 4
Post from the journal to the ledger

EXHIBIT 2-5 *Flow of Accounting Data*

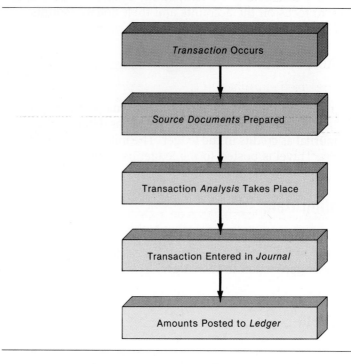

Transaction Analysis, Journalizing, and Posting

1. *Transaction:* The Lyons invested $50,000 to begin the travel agency, which in turn issued common stock to them.

    Analysis: The investment in the business increased its asset cash; to record this increase, debit Cash.
    The investment also increased the stockholders' equity of the corporation; to record this increase, credit Common Stock.

    Journal   Cash 50,000
    Entry: Common Stock   50,000
                  Issued common stock to owners.

    Ledger | Cash | | Common Stock |
    Accounts:
    | (1) 50,000 | | | (1) 50,000 |

2. *Transaction:* Paid $40,000 cash for land as a future office location.

    Analysis: The purchase decreased cash; therefore, credit Cash.
    The purchase increased the entity's asset land; to record this increase, debit Land.

    Journal   Land 40,000
    Entry: Cash   40,000
                  Paid cash for land.

Ledger
Accounts:

Cash			Land	
(1) 50,000	(2) 40,000		(2) 40,000	

3. *Transaction:* Purchased $500 office supplies on account payable.

   Analysis: The credit purchase of office supplies increased this asset; to record this increase, debit Office Supplies. The purchase also increased the liability, accounts payable; to record this increase, credit Accounts Payable.

   Journal Entry:
   Office Supplies 500
       Accounts Payable 500
   Purchased office supplies on account.

Ledger
Accounts:

Office Supplies			Accounts Payable	
(3) 500				(3) 500

4. *Transaction:* Paid $400 on the account payable created in the preceding transaction.

   Analysis: The payment decreased the asset cash; therefore, credit Cash. The payment also decreased the liability, accounts payable; to record this decrease, debit Accounts Payable.

   Journal Entry:
   Accounts Payable 400
       Cash 400
   Paid cash on account.

Ledger
Accounts:

Cash			Accounts Payable	
(1) 50,000	(2) 40,000		(4) 400	(3) 500
	(4) 400			

5. *Transaction:* The Lyons remodeled their personal residence. This is not a transaction of the travel agency, so no journal entry is made in the corporation's books.

6. *Transaction:* Paid dividends of $2,100.

   Analysis: The dividends decreased the entity's cash; therefore, credit Cash.
   The transaction also decreased the stockholders' equity of the entity and must be recorded by a debit to a stockholders' equity account. Decreases in the stockholders' equity of a corporation that result from distributions to owners are debited to a separate account entitled Dividends. Therefore, debit Dividends.

   Journal Entry:
   Dividends 2,100
       Cash 2,100
   Paid dividends.

Ledger Accounts:	Cash				Dividends	
	(1) 50,000	(2)	40,000		(6)	2,100
		(4)	400			
		(6)	2,100			

As each journal entry is posted to the ledger, it is keyed by date or by transaction number. In this way, a trail is provided through the accounting records so that any transaction can be traced from the journal to the ledger and, if need be, back to the journal. This linking allows the accountant to locate efficiently any information needed.

Ledger Accounts after Posting

We next illustrate how the accounts look when the amounts of the preceding transactions have been posted. The accounts are grouped under the accounting equation's headings.

Note that each account has a balance figure. This amount is the difference between the account's total debits and its total credits. For example, the balance in the Cash account is the difference between the debits, $50,000, and the credits, $42,500 ($40,000 + $400 + $2,100). Thus the Cash balance is $7,500. The balance amounts are not journal entries posted to the accounts, so we set an account balance apart by horizontal lines.

If the sum of an account's debits is greater than the sum of its credits, that account has a debit balance, as the Cash account does here. If the sum of its credits is greater, that account has a credit balance, as Accounts Payable does.

Assets		=	Liabilties		+	Stockholders' Equity	
Cash			**Accounts Payable**			**Common Stock**	
(1) 50,000	(2) 40,000	(4) 400	(3) 500			(1) 50,000	
	(4) 400		Bal. 100			Bal. 50,000	
	(6) 2,100						
Bal. 7,500							

Office Supplies		**Dividends**	
(3) 500		(6) 2,100	
Bal. 500		Bal. 2,100	

Land	
(2) 40,000	
Bal. 40,000	

Trial Balance

A **trial balance** is a list of all accounts with their balances. It provides a check on accuracy by showing whether the total debits equal the total credits. A trial balance may be taken at any time the postings are up to date. Exhibit 2-6 is the trial balance of the general ledger of Air and Sea Travel, Inc., after the first six transactions have been journalized and posted.

EXHIBIT 2-6 *Trial Balance*

Air and Sea Travel, Inc.
Trial Balance
April 30, 19X1

Account Titles	Balance	
	Debit	Credit
Cash..........................	$ 7,500	
Office supplies	500	
Land	40,000	
Accounts payable		$ 100
Common stock		50,000
Dividends.....................	2,100	
Total........................	$50,100	$50,100

The word *trial* is well chosen. The list is prepared as a *test* of the accounts' balances. The trial balance shows the accountant whether the total debits and total credits are equal. In this way it may signal accounting errors. For example, if only the debit (or only the credit) side of a transaction is posted, the total debits will not equal the total credits. If a debit is posted as a credit or vice versa, debits and credits will be out of balance. For example, if the $500 debit in Office Supplies is incorrectly posted as a credit, total debits will be $49,600 and total credits will be $50,600. The trial balance alerts the accountant to such errors in posting.

Some errors may not be revealed by the trial balance. For example, a $1,000 cash payment for supplies may be credited to Accounts Payable instead of to Cash. This error would cause both Cash and Accounts Payable to be overstated, each by $1,000. However, because an asset and a liability are overstated by the same amount, the trial balance would still show total debits equal to total credits. Also, if an accountant erroneously recorded a $5,000 transaction at only $500, the trial balance would show no error. However, total debits and total credits would both be understated by $4,500 (that is, $5,000 − $500).

Do not confuse the trial balance with the balance sheet. Accountants prepare a trial balance for their internal records. The company reports its financial position—both inside and outside the business—on the balance sheet, a formal financial statement.

Summary Problem for Your Review

On August 1, 19X5, Liz Shea opens a business that she names Shea's Research Service, Inc. During the entity's first ten days of operations, the following transactions take place:

a. To begin operations, Shea deposits $60,000 of personal funds in a bank account entitled Shea's Research Service, Inc., and the business issues common stock to her.

b. Pays $40,000 cash for a small house to be used as an office.

c. Purchases $250 in office supplies on credit (that is, on account).

d. Pays cash of $6,000 for office furniture.

e. Pays $150 on the account payable created in transaction *c*.
f. Pays a dividend of $1,000.

Required

1. Prepare the journal entries to record these transactions. Key the journal entries by letter.
2. Post the entries to the ledger.
3. Prepare the trial balance of Shea's Research Service, Inc., at August 10, 19X5.

SOLUTION TO REVIEW PROBLEM

Requirement 1

Accounts and Explanation	Debit	Credit
a. Cash	60,000	
Common Stock		60,000
Issued common stock to owner.		
b. Building	40,000	
Cash...		40,000
Purchased building for an office.		
c. Office Supplies	250	
Accounts Payable		250
Purchased office supplies on account.		
d. Office Furniture	6,000	
Cash...		6,000
Purchased office furniture.		
e. Accounts Payable......................................	150	
Cash...		150
Paid cash on account.		
f. Dividends..	1,000	
Cash...		1,000
Paid dividends.		

Requirement 2

Assets

Cash				Office Supplies	
(a)	60,000	(b)	40,000	(c)	250
		(d)	6,000		
		(e)	150	Bal.	250
		(f)	1,000		
Bal.	12,850				

Office Furniture		Building	
(d)	6,000	(b)	40,000
Bal.	6,000	Bal.	40,000

Liabilities

Accounts Payable

(e)	150	(c)	250
		Bal.	100

Stockholders' Equity

Common Stock

(a)	60,000
Bal.	60,000

Dividends

(f)	1,000		
Bal.	1,000		

Requirement 3

Shea's Research Service, Inc.
Trial Balance
August 10, 19X5

Account Title	Balance	
	Debit	Credit
Cash.....................................	$12,850	
Office supplies	250	
Office furniture	6,000	
Building	40,000	
Accounts payable		$ 100
Common Stock		60,000
Dividends..............................	1,000	
Total	$60,100	$60,100

Details of Journals and Ledgers

To focus on the main points of journalizing and posting, we purposely omitted certain essential data. In actual practice, the journal and the ledger provide additional details that create a "trail" through the accounting records for future reference. For example, an accountant may need to verify the date of a transaction or to determine whether a journal entry has been posted to the ledger. Let's take a closer look at the journal and the ledger.

Journal. Exhibit 2-7, Panel B, presents the journal format most often used by accountants. Note that the journal page number appears in the upper-right corner.

As the column headings indicate, the *journal* displays the following information:

1. The *date,* which is very important because it indicates when the transaction occurred. The year appears first. It is not necessary to repeat it for each journal entry. The year appears only when the journal is started or when the year has changed. Note that the year appears with an X in the third column. We present the year in this way because the dates we choose are for illustration only. Thus 19X1 is followed by 19X2, and so on. We will use this format throughout the book. Like the year, the month is entered only once. The second date column shows the day of the transaction. This column is filled in for every transaction.

EXHIBIT 2-7 *Details of Journalizing and Posting*

Panel A—Illustrative Transactions

Date	Transaction
April 2, 19X1	Gary and Monica Lyon invested $50,000 in the travel
	agency, which issued common stock to the owners.
3	Paid $500 cash for office supplies.

Panel B—Journal

Page 1

Date	Accounts and Explanation	Post Ref.	Debit	Credit
19X1				
Apr. 2	Cash	11	50,000	
	Common Stock	31		50,000
	Initial investment			
3	Office Supplies	13	500	
	Cash	11		500
	Purchased office supplies.			

① ② ③ ④

Panel C—Ledger

Cash   Account No. 11

Date	Item	Jrnl. Ref.	Debit	Date	Item	Jrnl. Ref.	Credit
19X1				19X1			
Apr. 2		J.1	50,000	Apr. 3		J.1	500

Office Supplies   Account No. 13

Date	Item	Jrnl. Ref.	Debit	Date	Item	Jrnl. Ref.	Credit
19X1							
Apr. 3		J.1	500				

Common Stock   Account No. 31

Date	Item	Jrnl. Ref.	Debit	Date	Item	Jrnl. Ref.	Credit
				19X1			
				Apr. 2		J.1	50,000

2. The *account title* and explanation of the transaction. You are already familiar with this presentation from Exhibit 2-3.
3. The *posting reference*, abbreviated Post. Ref. How this column helps the accountant becomes clear when we discuss the details of posting.
4. The *debit* column, which shows the amount debited.
5. The *credit* column, which shows the amount credited.

Ledger.   Exhibit 2-7, Panel C, presents the *ledger* in T-account format. Each account has its own page in the illustrative ledger. Our example shows Air and Sea Travel's Cash account. This account maintains the basic format of the T-account but offers more information.

The account title appears at the top of the ledger page. Note also the account number at the upper-right column. Each account has its own identification number. We will look later at how accountants assign account numbers.

The column headings identify the ledger account's features.

1. The *date*.
2. The *item* column. This space is used for any special notation.
3. The *journal reference* column, abbreviated *Jrnl. Ref.* The importance of this column becomes clear when we discuss the mechanics of posting.
4. The *debit* column, with the amount debited.
5. The *credit* column, with the amount credited.

Posting

We know that posting means moving information from the journal to the ledger accounts. But how do we handle the additional details that appear in the journal and the ledger formats that we have just seen? Exhibit 2-7 illustrates the steps in full detail. Panel A lists the first two transactions of Air and Sea Travel; Panel B presents the journal; and Panel C shows the ledger.

Since the flow of accounting data moves from the journal to the ledger, the accountant first records the journal entry, as shown in Panel B. The transaction data are given in Panel A, except for the Post. Ref. number. Let's trace the arrows to follow the details of posting.

Arrow 1 traces the date, Apr. 2, 19X1, from the journal to the ledger account Cash.

Arrow 2 begins at the journal's page number, Page 1, and ends in the journal reference column, Jrnl. Ref., of the ledger. The J. 1 entry in that column stands for "Journal (page) 1." Why bother with this detail? If an accountant is using the Cash account and needs to locate the original journal entry, the journal page number tells where to look.

Arrow 3 indicates that the accountant posts the debit figure—$50,000 in this journal entry—as a debit figure in the account.

Arrow 4 points to a posting detail. Once the accountant has posted a dollar figure to the appropriate account, that account's number is entered in the journal's Post. Ref. column. This step indicates that the information for that account has been posted from the journal to the ledger. A blank Post Ref. column for a journal entry means that the entry has not yet been posted to the ledger account.

Having performed these steps for the debit entry, the accountant then posts the credit entry to the ledger. After posting, the accountant draws up the trial balance, as we discussed earlier.

Four-Column Account Format

The ledger accounts illustrated in Exhibit 2-7 are in two-column T-account format, with the debit column placed left and the credit column placed right. The T-account clearly distinguishes debits from credits and is often used for illustrative purposes that do not require much detail.

Another standard format has four amount columns, as illustrated for the Cash account in Exhibit 2-8. The first pair of amount columns are for the debit and credit amounts, and the second pair of amount columns are for the account's balance. This four-column format keeps a running balance in the account and for this reason is used more often in actual practice.

In the exhibit, Cash has a debit balance of $50,000 after the first transaction is posted and a debit balance of $49,500 after the second transaction.

Chart of Accounts

As you know, the general ledger contains the business's accounts grouped under the headings Assets, Liabilities, Stockholders' Equity, Revenues, and Expenses. To keep track of their accounts, organizations have a **chart of accounts,** which lists all the accounts and their account numbers. These account numbers are used as posting references, as illustrated by arrow 4 in Exhibit 2-7. It is easier to write the account number, 11, in the posting reference column of the journal than to write the account title, Cash. Also, this numbering system makes it easy to locate individual accounts in the ledger.

Assets are often numbered beginning with 1, liabilities with 2, stockholders' equity with 3, revenues with 4, and expenses with 5. The second digit in an account number indicates the position of the individual account within the category. For example, Cash may be account number 11, which is the first asset account. Accounts Receivable may be account number 12, the second asset account. Accounts Payable may be account number 21, the first liability account. All accounts are numbered using this system.

Many organizations have so many accounts that they use three- or four-digit account numbers. For example, account number 101 may be Cash on Hand, account number 102 may be Cash on Deposit in First National Bank, and account number 103 may be Cash on Deposit in Lakewood Bank. In the assignment material we use various numbering schemes to correspond to the variety found in practice.

EXHIBIT 2-8 *Account in Four-Column Format*

Account Cash		Jrnl. Ref.	Debit	Credit	Balance	Account No. 11
Date	Item	Jrnl. Ref.	Debit	Credit	Debit	Credit
19X1						
Apr.2		J.1	50,000		50,000	
3		J.1		500	49,500	

EXHIBIT 2-9 *Chart of Accounts—Air and Sea Travel, Inc.*

Balance Sheet Accounts		
Assets	**Liabilities**	**Stockholders' Equity**
11 Cash	21 Accounts Payable	31 Common Stock
12 Accounts Receivable	22 Notes Payable	32 Retained Earnings
13 Office Supplies		33 Dividends
17 Office Furniture		
19 Land		

Income Statement Accounts	
Revenues	**Expenses**
41 Service Revenue	51 Rent Expense
	52 Salary Expense
	53 Utilities Expense

The chart of accounts for Air and Sea Travel, Inc., appears in Exhibit 2-9. Notice that the account numbers jump from 13 to 17. Gary Lyon realizes that later the business may need to add other supplies accounts—for example, Tax Forms Supplies. Any additional supplies account would logically appear after Office Supplies, and Tax Forms Supplies might be account number 14.

Normal Balances of Accounts

Accountants speak of an account's *normal balance,* which refers to the side of the account—debit or credit—where *increases* are recorded. This term also refers to the usual balance—debit or credit—in the account. For example, Cash and all other assets usually have a debit balance, so assets are *debit-balance* accounts. On the other hand, liabilities and owner's equity usually have a credit balance, so they are *credit-balance* accounts. Exhibit 2-10 illustrates the normal balances of assets, liabilities, and stockholders' equity.

An account that normally has a debit balance may occasionally have a credit balance. This indicates a negative amount of the item. For example, Cash will have a temporary credit balance if the entity overdraws its bank account. Similarly, the liability Accounts Payable—normally a credit balance account—will have a debit balance if the entity overpays its account. In other instances, the shift of a balance amount away from its normal column indicates an account-

EXHIBIT 2-10 *Normal Balances of Balance Sheet Accounts*

Assets	=	Liabilities	+	Stockholders' Equity
Normal Bal. Debit		Normal Bal. Credit		Normal Bal. Credit

ing error. For example, a credit balance in Office Supplies, Office Furniture, or Buildings indicates an error because negative amounts of these assets cannot exist.

As we have explained, stockholders' equity usually contains several accounts. In total, these accounts show a normal credit balance for the stockholders' equity of the business. Each individual stockholders' equity account has a normal credit balance if it represents an *increase* (for example, the Common Stock account and the Retained Earnings in Exhibit 2-11). However, if the individual stockholders' equity account represents a *decrease* in stockholders' equity, the account will have a normal debit balance (for example, the Dividends account in Exhibit 2-11).

EXHIBIT 2-11 *Rules of Debit and Credit and Normal Balances of Accounts*

Panel A—Rules of Debit and Credit:

Assets		=	Liabilities		+	Common Stock	
Debit for Increase	Credit for Decrease		Debit for Decrease	Credit for Increase		Debit for Decrease	Credit for Increase

						Retained Earnings	
						Debit for Decrease	Credit for Increase

						Dividends	
						Debit for Increase	Credit for Decrease

						Revenues	
						Debit for Decrease	Credit for Increase

						Expenses	
						Debit for Increase	Credit for Decrease

Panel B—Normal Balances:

	Debit	Credit
Assets	Debit	
Liabilities		Credit
Stockholders' equity-overall		Credit
Common stock		Credit
Retained earnings		Credit
Dividends	Debit	
Revenue		Credit
Expenses	Debit	

Additional Stockholders' Equity Accounts: Revenues and Expenses

The stockholders' equity category includes two additional types of accounts: revenues and expenses. As we have discussed, *revenues* are increases in stockholders' equity that result from delivering goods or services to customers. *Expenses* are decreases in stockholders' equity due to the cost of operating the business. Therefore, the accounting equation may be expanded as follows:

ASSETS = LIABILITIES + STOCKHOLDERS' EQUITY

(COMMON STOCK + RETAINED EARNINGS − DIVIDENDS) + (REVENUES − EXPENSES)

Revenues and expenses appear in parentheses because their impact on the accounting equation arises from their effect on stockholders' equity. If revenues exceed expenses, the net effect—revenues minus expenses—is *net income*, which increases stockholders' equity. If expenses are greater, the net effect is a net loss, which decreases stockholders' equity.

We can now express the rules of debit and credit in final form as shown in Exhibit 2-11, Panel A. Panel B shows the *normal* balances of the five types of accounts: *Assets, Liabilities, Stockholders' equity*, and its subparts, *Revenues* and *Expenses*.

All of accounting is based on these five types of accounts. You should become very familiar with the related rules of debit and credit and the normal balances of accounts.

Typical Account Titles

Thus far we have dealt with a limited number of transactions and accounts to introduce key concepts. Actual businesses engage in more transactions, requiring more accounts. Additional transactions are recorded in the same manner, with accounts added to the ledger as needed. The following summary describes some of the more common accounts grouped by financial statement and account category. As you work exercises and problems in this and future chapters, you will find these descriptions useful.

Balance Sheet—Assets, Liabilities, and Stockholders' Equity

Assets

Cash: Money on hand and in the bank.

Accounts receivable: Claim on open account against the cash of a client or a customer. (Open account means that no promissory note exists to support the receivable.)

Note receivable: Claim against the cash of another party, supported by a promissory note signed by the other party. (All receivables are assets, and any account with *receivable* in its title is an asset.)

Merchandise inventory: Merchandise that an entity sells in its business (such as clothing by a department store or stereos by a stereo shop).

Office supplies: Stationery, stamps, paper clips, staples, and so forth.

Office furniture: Desks, chairs, file cabinets, and so forth.

Office equipment: Typewriters, calculators, and other equipment used in a business office. A business may have other types of equipment, such as delivery equipment or store equipment.

Building: Building used in a business.

Land: Land on which a business building stands.

Liabilities

Accounts payable: Liability to pay cash to another party on open account.

Note payable: Liability to pay cash to another party, supported by a signed promissory note.

Salary or wage payable: Liability to pay an employee for work. (Most liabilities have the word *payable* in the account title, and any account with *payable* in its title is a liability.)

Stockholders' Equity

Common stock: Represents the owners' investments in the business as evidenced by stock certificates issued by the corporation.

Retained earnings: The cumulative net income of the business over its lifetime, minus cumulative net losses and dividends.

Dividends: Payments of assets to the owners of the business for their personal use.

Income Statement—Revenues and Expenses

Revenues

Service revenue: Revenue earned by performing a service (accounting service by a CPA firm, legal service by a law firm, laundry service by a laundry, and so forth).

Sales revenue: Revenue earned by selling a product (sales of hardware by a hardware store, food by a grocery store, and so forth).

Expenses

Rent expense: Expense for office rent and the rental of office equipment or the rental of any other business asset.

Salary or wage expense: Expense of having employees work for the business.

Utilities expense: Expense of using electricity, water, gas, and other items provided by utility companies.

Supplies expense: Expense of using supplies such as stationery, stamps, paper clips, and staples.

Advertising expense: Expense of advertising the business.

Interest expense: Expense of using borrowed money.

Property tax expense: Expense for property tax on business land, buildings, and equipment.

Illustrative Problem

Let's account for the revenues and expenses of the accounting practice of Sara Nichols, Attorney, Professional Corporation (P.C.), for the month of July 19X1. We follow the same steps illustrated earlier: analyze the transaction, journalize, post to the ledger, and prepare the trial balance. Revenue accounts and expense accounts work just like asset, liability, and stockholders' equity accounts. Each revenue and each expense account has its own page in the ledger and its own identifying account number.

Transaction Analysis, Journalizing, and Posting

1. **Transaction:** Sara Nichols invested $10,000 cash in a business bank account to open her law practice. The business issued common stock to Sara.

   Analysis: The asset cash is increased; therefore, debit Cash. The stockholders' equity of the business increased because of an owner investment; therefore, credit Common Stock.

   Journal Entry:
   ```
   Cash.................................  10,000
        Common Stock ..................          10,000
   Issued common stock to the owner.
   ```

   Ledger Accounts:

Cash	Common Stock
(1) 10,000	(1) 10,000

2. **Transaction:** Performed service for a client and collected $3,000 cash.

   Analysis: The asset cash is increased; therefore, debit Cash.

   The revenue account Service Revenue is increased; credit Service Revenue.

   Journal Entry:
   ```
   Cash.................................  3,000
        Service Revenue ................          3,000
   Performed service and received cash.
   ```

   Ledger Accounts:

Cash	Service Revenue
(1) 10,000	(2) 3,000
(2) 3,000	

3. **Transaction:** Performed service for a client and billed the client for $500 on account receivable. This means the client owes the business $500 even though the client signed no formal promissory note.

   Analysis: The asset accounts receivable is increased; therefore, debit Accounts Receivable.

   The revenue service revenue is increased; credit Service Revenue.

   Journal Entry:
   ```
   Accounts Receivable ..................  500
        Service Revenue ................          500
   Performed service on account.
   ```

   Ledger Accounts:

Accounts Receivable	Service Revenue
(3) 500	(2) 3,000
	(3) 500

4. *Transaction:* Performed accounting service of $700 for a client, who paid $300 cash immediately. Nichols billed the remaining $400 to the client on account receivable.

Analysis: The assets cash and accounts receivable are increased; therefore, debit both of these asset accounts.

The revenue service revenue is increased; credit Service Revenue for the sum of the two debit amounts.

Journal Entry:

Cash.................................	300	
Accounts Receivable	400	
Service Revenue		700

Performed service for cash and on account.

Note: Because this transaction affects more than two accounts at the same time, the entry is called a *compound entry*. No matter how many accounts a compound entry affects—there may be any number—total debits must equal total credits.

Ledger Accounts:

Cash	
(1) 10,000	
(2) 3,000	
(4) **300**	

Accounts Receivable	
(3) 500	
(4) **400**	

Service Revenue	
	(2) 3,000
	(3) 500
	(4) **700**

5. *Transaction:* Paid the following cash expenses: office rent, $900; employee salary, $1,500; and utilities, $500.

Analysis: The asset cash is decreased; therefore, credit Cash for the sum of the three expense amounts.

The following expenses are increased: Rent Expense, Salary Expense, and Utilities Expense. They should each be debited.

Journal Entry:

Rent Expense	900	
Salary Expense	1,500	
Utilities Expense	500	
Cash		2,900

Paid cash expenses.

Ledger Accounts:

Cash	
(1) 10,000	(5) 2,900
(2) 3,000	
(4) 300	

Rent Expense	
(5) 900	

Salary Expense	
(5) 1,500	

Utilities Expense	
(5) 500	

6. *Transaction:* Received a telephone bill for $120 and will pay this expense next week.

   Analysis: Utilities expense is increased; therefore, debit this expense.

   The liability accounts payable is increased; credit this account.

   Journal Entry:
   Utilities Expense   120
       Accounts Payable   120
   Received utility bill.

   Ledger Accounts:

Accounts Payable		Utilities Expense	
	(6) 120	(5) 500	
		(6) 120	

7. *Transaction:* Collected $200 cash from the client established in Transaction 3.

   Analysis: The asset cash is increased; therefore, debit Cash.

   The asset accounts receivable is decreased; therefore, credit Accounts Receivable.

   Journal Entry:
   Cash   200
       Accounts Receivable   200
   Received cash on account.

   Note: This transaction has no effect on revenue; the related revenue is accounted for in Transaction 3.

   Ledger Accounts:

Cash		Accounts Receivable	
(1) 10,000	(5) 2,900	(3) 500	(7) 200
(2) 3,000		(4) 400	
(4) 300			
(7) 200			

8. *Transaction:* Paid the telephone bill that was received and recorded in Transaction 6.

   Analysis: The asset cash is decreased; credit Cash.

   The liability accounts payable is decreased; therefore, debit Accounts Payable.

   Journal Entry:
   Accounts Payable   120
       Cash   120
   Paid cash on account.

   Note: This transaction has no effect on expense because the related expense was recorded in Transaction 6.

   Ledger Accounts:

Cash		Accounts Payable	
(1) 10,000	(5) 2,900	(8) 120	(6) 120
(2) 3,000	(8) 120		
(4) 300			
(7) 200			

9. *Transaction:* Paid dividend of $1,100.

Analysis: The asset cash decreased; credit Cash. The dividend decreased stockholders' equity; therefore, debit Dividends.

Journal Entry:

Dividends 1,100
    Cash 1,100
Paid dividends.

Ledger Accounts:

Cash			
(1)	10,000	(5)	2,900
(2)	3,000	(8)	120
(4)	300	**(9)**	**1,100**
(7)	200		

Dividends	
(9)	**1,100**

Ledger Accounts After Posting

Assets

Cash			
(1)	10,000	(5)	2,900
(2)	3,000	(8)	120
(4)	300	(9)	1,100
(7)	200		
Bal.	9,380		

Accounts Receivable			
(3)	500	(7)	200
(4)	400		
Bal.	700		

Liabilities

Accounts Payable			
(8)	120	(6)	120
		Bal.	0

Stockholders' Equity

Common Stock	
(1)	10,000
Bal.	10,000

Dividends	
(9)	1,100
Bal.	1,100

Stockholder's Equity

Revenue

Service Revenue	
(2)	3,000
(3)	500
(4)	700
Bal.	4,200

Expenses

Rent Expense	
(5)	900
Bal.	900

Salary Expense	
(5)	1,500
Bal.	1,500

Utilities Expense	
(5)	500
(6)	120
Bal.	620

Sara Nichols, Attorney, P.C.
Trial Balance
July 31, 19X1

Account Title	Balance	
	Debit	Credit
Cash	$ 9,380	
Accounts receivable....................	700	
Accounts payable......................		$ 0
Common stock		10,000
Dividends	1,100	
Service revenue		4,200
Rent expense	900	
Salary expense	1,500	
Utilities expense.....................	620	
Total	$14,200	$14,200

Analytical Use of Accounting Information

What dominates the accountant's analysis of transactions: the accounting equation, the journal, or the ledger? The accounting equation is most fundamental. In turn, the ledger is more useful than the journal in providing an overall model of the organization. Accountants and managers must often make quick decisions without the benefit of a complete accounting system: journal, ledger, accounts, and trial balance. For example, the owner of a company may be negotiating the purchase price of another business. For a quick analysis of the effects of transactions, accountants often skip the journal and go directly to the ledger. They compress transaction analysis, journalizing, and posting into one step. This type of analysis saves time that may be the difference between a good business decision and a lost opportunity.

OBJECTIVE 6
Analyze transactions without a journal

Let's take an example to see how it works. For instance, the first revenue transaction—Sara Nichols performed accounting service for a client and collected cash of $3,000—may be analyzed by debiting the Cash account and crediting the Service Revenue account directly in the ledger as follows:

Cash	Service Revenue
3,000	3,000

With this shortcut, the accountant can immediately see the effect of the transaction on both the entity's cash and its service revenue. Or you can take the quick analysis a step further—go straight to the financial statements. This transaction increased Cash on the balance sheet by $3,000. It also increased Service Revenue on the income statement—and owner's capital on the balance sheet—by $3,000. Modern computer-assisted accounting systems often have this "journal-less" feature.

Computers and Accounting

Computers have revolutionized accounting. Decades ago, big and expensive computers were available only to the large companies that could afford them. Today, prices for increasingly powerful microcomputers continue to drop, enabling smaller businesses to take advantage of accounting with computers. Microcomputers—also known as personal computers, like Apple, IBM PC, TRS, and Compaq—electronically handle much of the work done by hand in the past.

Just what benefits does a computer offer? An accountant must analyze every business transaction, whether the accounting system is manual—as we are presenting in these opening chapters—or computerized. Once the transaction has been analyzed, a computerized accounting package performs much the same actions as accountants do in a manual system. The computer automatically makes a journal entry, capturing the necessary information in a consistent format. A computer's ability to perform routine tasks and mathematical operations fast and without error frees accountants for decision making. On the market today is a wide variety of specialized computer programs—known as *software*—that require almost no computer programming expertise.

You may be wondering about the role of debits and credits in a computerized accounting system. The computer interprets debits and credits as increases or decreases by account type. For example, a computer reads a debit to Cash as an increase to that account. Debits and credits actually need not be used in a computerized system. They were originally designed to ensure accuracy in manual accounting systems. Still, debit and credit are so deeply ingrained in the vocabulary of accounting that we use them even when dealing with computerized accounting systems.

In addition to helping with accounting itself, microcomputers assist with many financial applications of accounting information and in business correspondence. Also, thanks to telecommunications, micros can tap into the information stored in larger computers across the globe. As we progress through the study of accounting, we will consider computer applications that fit the topics under discussion.

Summary Problem for Your Review

The trial balance of Tomassini Computer Service Center, Inc., on March 1, 19X2, lists the entity's assets, liabilities, and stockholders' equity on that date.

Account Title	Balance Debit	Balance Credit
Cash	$26,000	
Accounts receivable	4,500	
Accounts payable		$ 2,000
Common stock		10,000
Retained earnings		18,500
Total	$30,500	$30,500

During March the business engaged in the following transactions:

1. Borrowed $45,000 from the bank. Tomassini signed a note payable in the name of the business.
2. Paid cash of $40,000 to a real estate company to acquire land.
3. Performed service for a customer and received cash of $5,000.
4. Purchased supplies on credit, $300.
5. Performed customer service and earned revenue on account, $2,600.
6. Paid $1,200 on account.
7. Paid these cash expenses: salaries, $3,000; rent, $1,500; interest, $400.
8. Received $3,100 on account.
9. Received a $200 utility bill that will be paid next week.
10. Paid dividend of $1,800.

Required

1. Open the following accounts, with the balances indicated, in the ledger of Tomassini Computer Service Center, Inc. Use the T-account format.

   Assets—Cash, $26,000; Accounts Receivable, $4,500; Supplies, no balance; Land, no balance

   Liabilities—Accounts Payable, $2,000; Note Payable, no balance

   Stockholders' Equity—Common Stock, $10,000; Retained Earnings, $18,500; Dividends, no balance

   Revenues—Service Revenue, no balance

   Expenses—(none have balances) Salary Expense, Rent Expense, Utilities Expense, Interest Expense

2. Journalize the preceding transactions. Key journal entries by transaction number.

3. Post to the ledger.

4. Prepare the trial balance of Tomassini Computer Service Center, Inc., at March 31, 19X2.

5. Compute the net income or net loss of the entity during the month of March. List expenses in order from the largest to the smallest.

SOLUTION TO REVIEW PROBLEM

Requirement 1

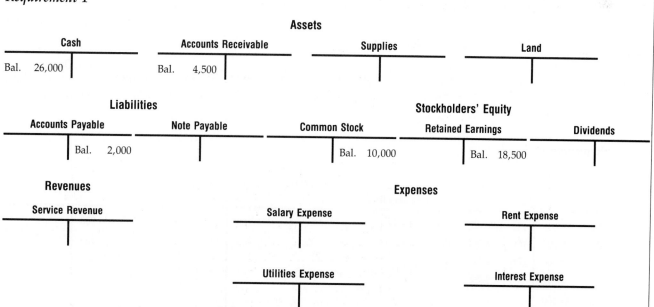

Requirement 2

Accounts and Explanation	Debit	Credit
1. Cash	45,000	
Note Payable...............................		45,000
Borrowed cash on note payable.		
2. Land	40,000	
Cash		40,000
Purchased land for cash.		
3. Cash	5,000	
Service Revenue............................		5,000
Performed service and received cash.		
4. Supplies	300	
Accounts Payable...........................		300
Purchased supplies on account.		
5. Accounts Receivable	2,600	
Service Revenue............................		2,600
Performed service on account.		
6. Accounts Payable	1,200	
Cash		1,200
Paid on account.		
7. Salary Expense	3,000	
Rent Expense	1,500	
Interest Expense	400	
Cash		4,900
Paid cash expenses.		
8. Cash	3,100	
Accounts Receivable		3,100
Received on account.		
9. Utilities Expense	200	
Accounts Payable...........................		200
Received utility bill.		
10. Dividends	1,800	
Cash		1,800
Paid dividend.		

Requirement 3

Assets

	Cash					Accounts Receivable				Supplies			Land	
Bal.	26,000	(2)	40,000		Bal.	4,500	(8)	3,100	(4)	300		(2)	40,000	
(1)	45,000	(6)	1,200		(5)	2,600			Bal.	300		Bal.	40,000	
(3)	5,000	(7)	4,900		Bal.	4,000								
(8)	3,100	(10)	1,800											
Bal.	31,200													

Liabilities

	Accounts Payable				Note Payable				Common Stock	
(6)	1,200	Bal.	2,000			(1)	45,000			Bal. 10,000
		(4)	300							
		(9)	200			Bal.	45,000			
		Bal.	1,300							

Stockholders' Equity

	Retained Earnings			Dividends	
		Bal. 18,500		1,800	
				Bal. 1,800	

Revenues

	Service Revenue		
		(3)	5,000
		(5)	2,600
		Bal.	7,600

	Salary Expense	
(7)	3,000	
Bal.	3,000	

	Utilities Expense	
(9)	200	
Bal.	200	

Expenses

	Rent Expense	
(7)	1,500	
Bal.	1,500	

	Interest Expense	
(7)	400	
Bal.	400	

Requirement 4

Tomassini Computer Service Center, Inc.
Trial Balance
March 31, 19X2

Account Title	Balance	
	Debit	Credit
Cash	$31,200	
Accounts receivable	4,000	
Supplies	300	
Land..............................	40,000	
Accounts payable		$ 1,300
Note payable		45,000
Common stock		10,000
Retained earnings		18,500
Dividends	1,800	
Service revenue		7,600
Salary expense....................	3,000	
Rent expense	1,500	
Utilities expense	200	
Interest expense	400	
Total.............................	$82,400	$82,400

Requirement 5

Net income for the month of March

Revenues:		
Service revenue		$7,600
Expenses:		
Salary expense	$3,000	
Rent expense	1,500	
Interest expense	400	
Utilities expense	200	
Total expenses		5,100
Net income		$2,500

Summary

The *account* can be viewed in the form of the letter "T." The left side of each account is its *debit* side. The right side is its *credit* side. The *ledger,* which contains a record for each account, groups and numbers accounts by category in the following order: assets, liabilities, stockholders' equity, and its subparts: revenues and expenses.

Assets and *expenses* are increased by debits and decreased by credits. *Liabilities, stockholders' equity,* and *revenues* are increased by credits and decreased by debits. The side—debit or credit—of the account in which increases are recorded is that account's normal balance. Thus the normal balance of assets and expenses is a debit, and the normal balance of liabilities, stockholders' equity, and revenues is a credit. Dividends, which decreases stockholders' equity, normally has a debit balance. *Revenues,* which are increases in stockholders' equity, have a normal credit balance. *Expenses,* which are decreases in stockholders' equity, have a normal debit balance.

The accountant begins the recording process by entering the transaction's information in the *journal,* a chronological list of all the business's transactions. The information is then posted—transferred—to the *ledger* accounts. Posting references are used to trace amounts back and forth between the journal and the ledger. Businesses list their account titles and numbers in a chart of accounts.

The *trial balance* is a summary of all the account balances in the ledger. When *double-entry accounting* has been done correctly, the total debits and the total credits in the trial balance are equal.

We can now trace the flow of accounting information through these steps:

Business Transaction → Source Documents → Journal Entry → Posting to Ledger → Trial Balance

Self-Study Questions

Test your understanding of the chapter by marking the best answer for each of the following questions.

1. An account has two sides called the *(p. 54)*
   - a. Debit and credit
   - b. Asset and liability
   - c. Revenue and expense
   - d. Journal and ledger

2. Increases in liabilities are recorded by *(p. 55)*
   a. Debits ·   ⌣ b. Credits
3. Why do accountants record transactions in the journal? *(p. 58)*
   a. To ensure that all transactions are posted to the ledger
   b. To ensure that total debits equal total credits
   ⊢ c. To have a chronological record of all transactions
   ⌣ d. To help prepare the financial statements
4. Posting is the process of transferring information from the *(p. 59)*
   a. Journal to the trial balance   c. Ledger to the financial
   b. Ledger to the trial balance   statements
                                      ⌵ d. Journal to the ledger
5. The purchase of land for cash is recorded by a *(p. 60)*
   ⌵ a. Debit to Cash and a credit to Land
   b. Debit to Cash and a debit to Land
   ⊥ c. Debit to Land and a credit to Cash
   d. Credit to Cash and a credit to Land
6. The purpose of the trial balance is to *(p. 62)*
   ⌵ a. Indicate whether total debits equal total credits
   b. Ensure that all transactions have been recorded
   c. Speed the collection of cash receipts from customers
   d. Increase assets and stockholders' equity
7. What is the normal balance of the Accounts Receivable, Office Supplies, and Rent Expense accounts? *(p. 69)*
   ⌵ a. Debit   b. Credit
8. A business has Cash of $3,000, Notes Payable of $2,500, Accounts Payable of $4,300, Service Revenue of $7,000, and Rent Expense of $1,800. Based on these data, how much are its total liabilities? *(p. 72)*
   a. $5,500   c. $9,800
   ⌵ b. $6,800   d. $13,800
9. Farber Company earned revenue on account. The journal entry to record this transaction is a *(p. 73)*
   a. Debit to Cash and a credit to Revenue
   ⌵ b. Debit to Accounts Receivable and a credit to Revenue
   c. Debit to Accounts Payable and a credit to Revenue
   d. Debit to Revenue and a credit to Accounts Receivable
10. The account credited for a receipt of cash on account is *(p. 75)*
    a. Cash   c. Service Revenue
    b. Accounts Payable   ⌵ d. Accounts Receivable

Answers to the Self-Study Questions follow the Accounting Vocabulary.

Accounting Vocabulary

Account. The detailed record of the changes that have occurred in a particular asset, liability, or owner equity during a period *(p. 51)*.

Chart of accounts. List of all the accounts and their account numbers in the ledger *(p. 68)*.

Credit. The right side of an account *(p. 54)*.

Debit. The left side of an account *(p. 54)*.

Journal. The chronological accounting record of an entity's transactions *(p. 57)*.

Ledger. The book of accounts *(p. 51)*.

Posting. Transferring of amounts from the journal to the ledger *(p. 59)*.

Trial balance. A list of all the ledger accounts with their balances *(p. 62)*.

ASSIGNMENT MATERIAL _____

Questions

1. Name the basic summary device of accounting. What letter of the alphabet does it resemble, and what are its two sides called?
2. Is the following statement true or false? Debit means decrease and credit means increase. Explain your answer.
3. Write two sentences that use the term *debit* in different ways.
4. What are the three *basic* types of accounts? Name two additional types of accounts. To which one of the three *basic* types are these two additional types of accounts most closely related?
5. Suppose you are the accountant for Smith Courier Service. Keeping in mind double-entry bookkeeping, identify the *dual effects* of Mary Smith's investment of $10,000 cash in her business.
6. Briefly describe the flow of accounting information.
7. To what does the *normal balance* of an account refer?
8. Complete the table by indicating the normal balance of the five types of accounts.

Account Type	Normal Balance
Assets	_____
Liabilities	_____
Stockholders' equity	_____
Revenues	_____
Expenses	_____

9. What does posting accomplish? Why is it important? Does it come before or after journalizing?
10. Label each of the following transactions as increasing stockholders' equity (+), decreasing stockholders' equity (−), or as having no effect on stockholders' equity (0). Write the appropriate symbol in the space provided.

___ a. Investment by owner ___ e. Cash payment on account
___ b. Revenue transaction ___ f. Dividends
___ c. Purchase of supplies on credit ___ g. Borrowing money on a note payable
___ d. Expense transaction ___ h. Sale of services on account

11. What four steps does posting include? Which step is the fundamental purpose of posting?
12. Rearrange the following accounts in their logical sequence in the ledger:

Notes Payable Cash
Accounts Receivable Common Stock
Sales Revenue Salary Expense

13. What is the meaning of the statement, Accounts Payable has a credit balance of $1,700?

14. Jack Brown Campus Cleaners launders the shirts of customer Bobby Baylor, who has a charge account at the cleaners. When Bobby picks up his clothes and is short of cash, he charges it. Later, when he receives his monthly statement from the cleaners, Bobby writes a check on Dear Old Dad's bank account and mails the check to Jack Brown. Identify the two business transactions described here. Which transaction increases the business's stockholders' equity? Which transaction increases the business's cash?

15. Explain the difference between the ledger and the chart of accounts.

16. Why do accountants prepare a trial balance?

17. What is a compound journal entry?

18. The accountant for Bower Construction Company mistakenly recorded a $500 purchase of supplies on account as a $5,000 purchase. He debited Supplies and credited Accounts Payable for $5,000. Does this error cause the trial balance to be out of balance? Explain your answer.

19. What is the effect on total assets of collecting cash on account from customers?

20. What is the advantage of analyzing and recording transactions without the use of a journal? Describe how this "journal-less" analysis works.

Exercises

Exercise 2-1   Using accounting vocabulary   (L.O. 1)

The trial balance of Auditron, Inc., lists Cash of $62,100. Write a short memo to explain the accounting process that produced this listing on the trial balance. Mention *debits, credits, journals, ledgers, posting,* and so on.

Exercise 2-2   Analyzing and journalizing transactions   (L.O. 2,3)

Analyze the following transactions in the manner shown for the December 1 transaction. Also record each transaction in the journal.

Dec. 1   Paid monthly rent expense of $1,000. (Analysis: The expense rent expense is increased; therefore, debit Rent Expense. The asset cash is decreased; therefore, credit Cash.)

1	Rent Expense......................................	1,000	
	Cash......................................		1,000

 4   Received $600 cash on account from a customer.
 8   Performed service on account for a customer, $1,100.
12   Purchased office furniture on account, $810.
19   Sold for $69,000 land that had cost this same amount.
24   Purchased building for $140,000; signed a note payable.
27   Paid the liability created on December 12.

Exercise 2-3   Journalizing transactions   (L.O. 3)

Vines Consulting Company, Inc., engaged in the following transactions during March 19X3, its first month of operations:

Mar. 1 John Vines invested $65,000 of cash to start the business. The corporation issued common stock to Vines.

2 Purchased office supplies of $200 on account.

4 Paid $25,000 cash for land to use as a future building site.

6 Performed service for customers and received cash, $2,000.

9 Paid $100 on accounts payable.

17 Performed service for customers on account, $1,600.

23 Received $1,200 cash from a customer on account.

31 Paid the following expenses: salary, $1,200; rent, $500.

Required

Record the preceding transactions in the journal of Vines Consulting Company, Inc. Key transactions by date and include an explanation for each entry, as illustrated in the chapter. Use the following accounts: Cash; Accounts Receivable; Office Supplies; Land; Accounts Payable; Common Stock; Service Revenue; Salary Expense; Rent Expense.

Exercise 2-4   *Posting to the ledger and preparing a trial balance* **(L.O. 4,5)**

1. After journalizing the transactions of Exercise 2-3, post the entries to the ledger, using T-account format. Key transactions by date as in the following example. Date the ending balance of each account Mar. 31.

Common Stock	
	Mar. 1 65,000

2. Prepare the trial balance of Vines Consulting Company, Inc., at March 31, 19X3.

Exercise 2-5   *Describing transactions and posting* **(L.O. 3,4)**

The journal of Scholes Company appears below.

Journal   **Page 5**

Date	Accounts and Explanation	Post Ref.	Debit	Credit
Aug. 5	Cash		530	
	Sales Revenue			530
9	Supplies		270	
	Accounts Payable			270
11	Accounts Receivable		2,100	
	Sales Revenue			2,100
14	Rent Expense		1,200	
	Cash			1,200
22	Cash		1,400	
	Accounts Receivable			1,400
25	Advertising Expense		350	
	Cash			350
27	Accounts Payable		270	
	Cash			270
31	Utilities Expense		220	
	Accounts Payable			220

Required

1. Describe each transaction. Example: Aug. 5—Cash sale.
2. Post the transactions to the ledger using the following account numbers: Cash, 11; Accounts Receivable, 12; Supplies, 13; Accounts Payable, 21; Sales Revenue, 41; Rent Expense, 51; Advertising Expense, 52; Utilities Expense, 53. Use dates, journal references, and posting references as illustrated in Exhibit 2-7. You may write the account numbers as posting references directly in your book unless directed otherwise by your instructor.
3. Compute the balance in each account after posting. The first debit amount of $530 is posted to Cash as an example:

Cash		
Aug. 5 J.5 530		

Exercise 2-6 *Journalizing transactions* **(L.O. 3)**

The first five transactions of Rosenthal Security Company have been posted to the company's accounts as follows:

Cash			Supplies		Equipment	
(1) 45,000	(3) 42,000		(2) 400		(5) 6,000	
(4) 7,000	(5) 6,000					

Land		Accounts Payable		Note Payable	
(3) 42,000			(2) 400		(4) 7,000

Common Stock	
	(1) 45,000

Required

Prepare the journal entries that served as the sources for the five transactions. Include an explanation for each entry as illustrated in the chapter.

Exercise 2-7 *Preparing a trial balance* **(L.O. 5)**

Prepare the trial balance of Rosenthal Security Company at September 30, 19X4, using the account data from the preceding exercise.

Exercise 2-8 *Preparing a trial balance* **(L.O. 5)**

The accounts of Japaridze Realty Company are listed below with their normal balances at September 30, 19X4. The accounts are listed in no particular order.

Account	Balance
Common Stock....................	$48,800
Advertising expense	650
Accounts payable....................	4,300
Sales commission revenue............	16,000
Land	23,000
Note payable.......................	25,000
Cash	7,000
Salary expense	6,000
Building	45,000
Rent expense	2,000
Dividends	4,000
Utilities expense....................	400
Accounts receivable.................	5,500
Supplies expense	300
Supplies	250

Required

Prepare the company's trial balance at September 30, 19X4, listing accounts in proper sequence, as illustrated in the chapter. Supplies comes before Building and Land. List the expense with the largest balance first, the expense with the next largest balance second, and so on.

Exercise 2-9 *Correcting errors in a trial balance* **(L.O. 5)**

The trial balance of Thai Enterprises at November 30, 19X9, does not balance:

Cash	$ 4,200	
Accounts receivable	2,000	
Supplies	600	
Land	46,000	
Accounts payable		$ 3,000
Common Stock		42,000
Service revenue		4,700
Salary expense	1,700	
Rent expense...................	800	
Utilities expense	300	
Total	$55,600	$49,700

Investigation of the accounting records reveals that the bookkeeper:

1. Recorded a cash revenue transaction by debiting Cash for the correct amount of $5,000 but failed to record the credit to Service Revenue.
2. Posted a $1,000 credit to Accounts Payable as $100.
3. Did not record utilities expense or the related account payable in the amount of $200.
4. Understated Cash and Common Stock, by $400 each.

Required

Prepare the correct trial balance at November 30, complete with a heading. Journal entries are not required.

Exercise 2-10 *Recording transactions without a journal* (L.O. 6)

Open the following T-accounts: Cash; Accounts Receivable; Office Supplies; Office Furniture; Accounts Payable; Common Stock; Dividends; Service Revenue; Salary Expense; Rent Expense.

Record the following transactions directly in the T-accounts without using a journal. Use the letters to identify the transactions.

a. Albert Peña opened an accounting firm by investing $8,800 cash and office furniture valued at $7,400. Organized as a professional corporation, the business issued common stock to Peña.
b. Paid monthly rent of $1,500.
c. Purchased office supplies on account, $800.
d. Paid employee salary, $1,800.
e. Paid $400 of the account payable created in *c*.
f. Performed accounting service on account, $1,700.
g. Declared and paid dividends of $2,000.

Exercise 2-11 *Preparing a trial balance* (L.O. 5)

After recording the transactions in Exercise 2-10, prepare the trial balance of Albert Peña, CPA, P.C., at May 31, 19X7.

Problems

(Group A)

Problem 2-1A *Analyzing a trial balance* (L.O.1)

The owners of McBee Service Company are selling the business. They offer the following trial balance to prospective buyers:

McBee Service Company Trial Balance December 31, 19XX		
Cash	$ 4,000	
Accounts receivable	11,000	
Prepaid expenses	4,000	
Land	31,000	
Accounts payable		$ 31,000
Note payable		20,000
Common Stock		30,000
Dividends...............................	21,000	
Sales revenue		47,000
Rent expense............................	14,000	
Advertising expense	3,000	
Wage expense	33,000	
Supplies expense	7,000	
	$128,000	$128,000

Your best friend is considering buying McBee Service Company. He seeks your advice in interpreting this information. Specifically, he asks whether this trial balance is the same as a balance sheet and an income statement. He also wonders whether McBee must be a sound company. After all, the accounts are in balance.

Required

Write a short note to answer your friend's questions. To aid his decision, state how he can use the information on the trial balance to determine whether McBee has earned a net income or experienced a net loss for the current period.

Problem 2-2A *Analyzing and journalizing transactions (L.O. 2,3)*

Lee Quinius practices medicine under the business title Lee Quinius, M.D., Professional Corporation. During April his medical practice engaged in the following transactions:

Apr. 1 Quinius deposited $75,000 cash in the business bank account. The business issued common stock to Quinius.

     5 Paid monthly rent on medical equipment, $700.

     9 Paid $42,000 cash to purchase land for an office site.

   10 Purchased supplies on account, $1,200.

   19 Paid $1,000 on account.

   30 Revenues earned during the month included $6,000 cash and $5,000 on account.

   30 Paid employee salaries ($2,400), office rent ($1,500), and utilities ($400).

   30 Borrowed $20,000 from the bank for business use. Quinius signed a note payable to the bank in the name of the business.

   30 Declared and paid dividends of $4,000.

Quinius's business uses the following accounts: Cash; Accounts Receivable; Supplies; Land; Accounts Payable; Notes Payable; Common Stock; Dividends; Service Revenue; Salary Expense; Rent Expense; Utilities Expense.

Required

1. Prepare an analysis of each business transaction of Lee Quinius, M.D., P.C., as shown for the April 1 transaction:

    Apr. 1 The asset Cash is increased. Increases in assets are recorded by debits; therefore, debit Cash.

          The stockholders' equity is increased. Increases in stockholders' equity are recorded by credits; therefore, credit Common Stock.

2. Prepare the journal entry for each transaction. Explanations are not required.

Problem 2-3A *Journalizing transactions, posting to T-accounts, and preparing a trial balance (L.O. 2,3,4,5)*

Marie Haley organized as a professional corporation and opened a law office on January 2 of the current year. During the first month of operations the business completed the following transactions:

Jan. 2 Haley deposited $40,000 cash in a business bank account entitled Marie Haley, Attorney, P.C. The business issued common stock to Haley.

     3 Purchased supplies, $500, and furniture, $2,600, on account.

     4 Performed legal services for a client and received cash, $1,500.

     7 Paid cash to acquire land for a future office site, $22,000.

11 Defended a client in court, billed the client, and received his promise to pay the $800 within one week.

15 Paid secretary salary, $650.

16 Paid for the furniture purchased January 3 on account.

17 Paid the telephone bill, $110.

18 Received partial payment from client on account, $400.

19 Prepared legal documents for a client on account, $600.

22 Paid the water and electricity bills, $130.

29 Received $1,800 cash for helping a client sell real estate.

31 Paid secretary salary, $650.

31 Paid rent expense, $700.

31 Declared and paid dividends of $2,200.

Required

Open the following T-accounts: Cash; Accounts Receivable; Supplies; Furniture; Land; Accounts Payable; Common Stock; Dividends; Service Revenue; Salary Expense; Rent Expense; Utilities Expense.

1. Record each transaction in the journal, using the account titles given. Key each transaction by date. Explanations are not required.

2. Post the transactions to the ledger, using transaction dates as posting references in the ledger. Label the balance of each account *Bal.*, as shown in the chapter.

3. Prepare the trial balance of Marie Haley, Attorney, P.C., at January 31 of the current year.

Problem 2-4A *Journalizing transactions, posting to accounts in four-column format, and preparing a trial balance* **(L.O. 2,3,4,5)**

The trial balance of the accounting practice of William Pittenger, C.P.A., at November 15, 19X3, was

William Pittenger, C.P.A., P.C.
Trial Balance
November 15, 19X3

Account Number	Account	Debit	Credit
11	Cash......................	$ 5,000	
12	Accounts receivable.........	8,000	
13	Supplies	600	
14	Land.......................	35,000	
21	Accounts payable		$ 4,400
31	Common Stock		20,000
32	Retained earnings...........		22,000
33	Dividends	2,100	
41	Service revenue.............		7,100
51	Salary expense..............	1,800	
52	Rent expense	700	
53	Utilities expense	300	
	Total......................	$53,500	$53,500

During the remainder of November, William Pittenger (private individual) or William Pittenger, C.P.A., P.C. completed the following transactions:

Nov. 16 Collected $4,000 cash from a client on account.
17 Performed tax services for a client on account, $1,700.
19 Paid utilities, $200.
21 Paid on account, $2,600.
22 Purchased supplies on account, $200.
23 Declared and paid dividends of $2,100.
23 Pittenger paid for the renovation of his residence with personal funds, $55,000.
24 Received $1,900 cash for audit work just completed.
30 Paid office rent, $700.
30 Paid employees' salaries, $1,800.

Required

1. Record the transactions that occurred during November 16 through 30 in *page 6* of the journal. Include an explanation for each entry.
2. Post the transactions to the ledger, using dates, account numbers, journal references, and posting references. Open the ledger accounts listed in the trial balance together with their balances at November 15. Use the four-column account format illustrated below. Enter *Bal.* (for previous balance) in the Item column, and place a check mark (✓) in the journal reference column for the November 15 balance, as illustrated for Cash:

Account	Cash				Account No. 11	
					Balance	
Date	Item	Jrnl. Ref.	Debit	Credit	Debit	Credit
Nov. 15	Bal.	✓			5,000	

3. Prepare the trial balance of William Pittenger, CPA, P.C. at November 30, 19X3.

Problem 2-5A *Journalizing, posting to T-accounts, preparing a trial balance (L.O. 2,3,4,5)*

Steakley Delivery Service, Inc., began operations during May of the current year. In a short period thereafter, the entity engaged in these transactions:

a. Lou Steakley, the incorporator, deposited $3,500 cash in a bank account entitled Steakley Delivery Service, Inc., and also invested in the business a delivery truck valued at $8,000. The corporation issued common stock to Steakley.
b. Purchased $40 fuel for the delivery truck, using a business credit card.
c. Paid $100 cash for supplies.
d. Completed a delivery job and received cash, $700.
e. Performed delivery services on account, $3,200.
f. Purchased advertising leaflets for cash, $200.
g. Paid the office manager salary, $950.
h. Received $1,000 cash for performing delivery services.
i. Received cash from customer on account, $1,800.
j. Purchased used office furniture on account, $600.
k. Paid office utility bills, $120.

l. Purchased $70 fuel on account for the truck.

m. Completed a delivery job and received the customer's promise to pay the amount due, $100, within ten days.

n. Paid cash to creditor on account, $200.

o. Paid $250 for repairs to the delivery truck.

p. Paid office manager the salary of $950 and office rent of $250.

q. Declared and paid dividends of $1,900.

Required

1. Record each transaction in the journal, using the account titles given. Key each transaction by letter. Explanations are not required.

2. Open the following T-accounts: Cash; Accounts Receivable; Supplies; Delivery Truck; Office Furniture; Accounts Payable; Common Stock; Dividends; Delivery Service Revenue; Salary Expense; Rent Expense; Repair Expense; Advertising Expense; Utilities Expense; Fuel Expense. Post the transactions to the ledger, keying transactions by letter. Label the balance of each account *Bal.*, as shown in the chapter.

3. Prepare the trial balance of Steakley Delivery Service, Inc., using the current date.

Problem 2-6A   *Correcting errors in a trial balance.* **(L.O. 2,5)**

The trial balance below does not balance. The following errors were detected:

a. The cash balance is understated by $400.

b. Office maintenance expense of $200 is omitted from the trial balance.

c. Rent expense of $200 was posted as a credit rather than a debit.

d. The balance of Advertising Expense is $300, but it is listed as $400 on the trial balance.

e. A $600 debit to Accounts Receivable was posted as $60.

f. The balance of Utilities Expense is understated by $60.

g. A $500 debit to the Dividends account was posted as a credit to Common Stock.

h. A $100 purchase of supplies on account was not journalized or posted.

i. A $5,600 credit to Service Revenue was not posted.

j. Office furniture should be listed in the amount of $1,300.

Hewitt Speed & Marine		
Trial Balance		
October 31, 19X1		
Cash	$ 3,800	
Accounts receivable	2,000	
Supplies	500	
Office furniture	2,300	
Land	46,800	
Accounts payable		$ 2,000
Note payable		18,300
Common Stock		32,100
Dividends	3,700	
Service revenue		4,900
Salary expense	1,000	
Rent expense	600	
Advertising expense	400	
Utilities expense	200	
Property tax	100	
Total	$61,400	$57,300

Required

Prepare the correct trial balance at October 31. Journal entries are not required.

Problem 2-7A *Recording transactions directly in the ledger, preparing a trial balance (L.O. 2,5,6)*

Ken Mazanec obtained a corporate charter from the state of Pennsylvania and started a cable television service. During the first month of operations Mazanec completed the following selected transactions:

a. Mazanec began the business with an investment of $30,000 cash and a building valued at $50,000. The corporation issued common stock to Mazanec.
b. Borrowed $25,000 from the bank; signed a note payable.
c. Paid $32,000 for transmitting equipment.
d. Purchased office supplies on account, $400.
e. Paid employee salary, $1,300.
f. Received $500 for cable TV service performed for customers.
g. Sold cable service to customers on account, $2,300.
h. Paid $100 of the account payable created in *d*.
i. Received a $600 bill for utility expense that will be paid in the near future.
j. Received cash on account, $1,100.
k. Paid the following cash expenses:
   (1) Rent on land, $1,000
   (2) Advertising, $800.
l. Declared and paid dividends of $2,600.

Required

1. Open the following T-accounts: Cash; Accounts Receivable; Office Supplies; Transmitting Equipment; Building; Accounts Payable; Note Payable; Common Stock; Dividends; Service Revenue; Salary Expense; Rent Expense; Advertising Expense; Utilities Expense.
2. Record the above transactions directly in the T-accounts without using a journal. Use the letters to identify the transactions.
3. Prepare the trial balance of Mazanec Cable TV Service, Inc., at January 31, 19X7.

(Group B)

Problem 2-1B *Analyzing a trial balance (L.O. 1)*

The owners of Wang Service Company are selling the business. They offer the trial balance shown at the top of the next page to prospective buyers. Your best friend is considering buying Wang Service Company. He seeks your advice in interpreting this information. Specifically, he asks whether this trial balance is the same as a balance sheet and an income statement. He also wonders whether Wang must be a sound company. After all, the accounts are in balance.

Required

Write a short note to answer your friend's questions. To aid his decision, state how he can use the information on the trial balance to determine whether Wang has earned a net income or experienced a net loss for the current period.

Wang Service Company
Trial Balance
December 31, 19XX

Cash	$ 18,000	
Accounts receivable	27,000	
Prepaid expenses	4,000	
Land	81,000	
Accounts payable		$41,000
Note payable		32,000
Common Stock		30,000
Dividends	18,000	
Sales revenue		104,000
Rent expense	26,000	
Advertising expense	3,000	
Wage expense	23,000	
Supplies expense	7,000	
	$207,000	$207,000

Problem 2-2B   *Analyzing and journalizing transactions*   *(L.O. 2,3)*

Good Times Theater Company owns movie theaters in the shopping centers of a major metropolitan area. Its principal stockholder and general manger, Jill Mead, engaged in the following business transactions:

Dec. 1 Mead invested $75,000 personal cash in the business by depositing this amount in a bank account entitled Good Times Theater Company. The corporation issued common stock to Mead.

2 Paid $55,000 cash to purchase land for a theater site.

5 Borrowed $250,000 from the bank to finance the construction of the new theater. Mead signed a note payable to the bank in the name of Good Times Theater Company.

7 Received $20,000 cash from ticket sales and deposited this amount in the bank. (Label the revenue as Sales Revenue.)

10 Purchased supplies for the older theaters on account, $1,700.

15 Paid theater employee salaries, $2,800, and rent on a theater building, $1,800.

15 Paid property tax expense on theater building, $1,200.

16 Paid $800 on account.

17 Declared and paid a cash dividend of $3,000.

Good Times uses the following accounts: Cash; Supplies; Land; Accounts Payable; Notes Payable; Common Stock; Dividends; Sales Revenue; Salary Expense; Rent Expense; Property Tax Expense.

Required

1. Prepare an analysis of each business transaction of Good Times Theater Company, as shown for the December 1 transaction:

Dec. 1 The asset Cash is increased. Increases in assets are recorded by debits; therefore, debit Cash.

The stockholders' equity of the entity is increased. Increases in stockholders' equity are recorded by credits; therefore, credit Common Stock.

2. Prepare the journal entry for each transaction. Explanations are not required.

Problem 2-3B   *Journalizing transactions, posting to T-accounts, and preparing a trial balance*   **(L.O. 2,3,4,5)**

Oliver Goldsmith opened a law office on September 3 of the current year. During the first month of operations, the business completed the following transactions:

Sep.   3   Goldsmith transferred $20,000 cash from his personal bank account to a business account entitled Oliver Goldsmith, Attorney, Professional Corporation. The corporation issued common stock to Goldsmith.

  4   Purchased supplies, $200, and furniture, $1,800, on account.

  6   Performed legal services for a client and received $1,000 cash.

  7   Paid $15,000 cash to acquire land for a future office site.

  10   Defended a client in court, billed the client, and received his promise to pay the $900 within one week.

  14   Paid for the furniture purchased September 4 on account.

  15   Paid secretary salary, $600.

  16   Paid the telephone bill, $120.

  17   Received partial payment from client on account, $700.

  20   Prepared legal documents for a client on account, $800.

  24   Paid the water and electricity bills, $110.

  28   Received $1,500 cash for helping a client sell real estate.

  30   Paid secretary salary, $600.

  30   Paid rent expense, $500.

  30   Declared and paid dividends of $2,000.

Required

Open the following T-accounts: Cash; Accounts Receivable; Supplies; Furniture; Land; Accounts Payable; Common Stock; Dividends; Service Revenue; Salary Expense; Rent Expense; Utilities Expense.

1. Record each transaction in the journal, using the account titles given. Key each transaction by date. Explanations are not required.
2. Post the transactions to the ledger, using transaction dates as posting references in the ledger. Label the balance of each account *Bal.*, as shown in the chapter.
3. Prepare the trial balance of Oliver Goldsmith, Attorney, P.C., at September 30 of the current year.

Problem 2-4B   *Journalizing transactions, posting to accounts in four-column format, and preparing a trial balance*   **(L.O. 2,3,4,5)**

The trial balance of the accounting practice of Elizabeth Staar, CPA, Professional Corporation, is dated February 14, 19X3.

  During the remainder of February, Staar or the business completed the following transactions:

Feb.   15   Collected $2,000 cash from a client on account.

  16   Performed tax services for a client on account, $900.

  18   Paid office utilities, $300.

  20   Paid on account, $1,000.

  21   Purchased supplies on account, $100.

  21   Declared and paid dividends of $1,200.

21 Staar paid for a swimming pool for her private residence, using personal funds, $13,000.

22 Received cash of $2,100 for audit work just completed.

28 Paid office rent, $800.

28 Paid employees' salaries, $1,600.

Elizabeth Staar, CPA, P.C.
Trial Balance
February 14, 19X3

Account Number	Account	Debit	Credit
11	Cash.................................	$ 4,000	
12	Accounts receivable	11,000	
13	Supplies	800	
14	Land	18,600	
21	Accounts payable		$ 3,000
31	Common Stock		10,000
32	Retained earnings.....................		20,000
33	Dividends............................	1,200	
41	Service revenue.......................		7,200
51	Salary expense........................	3,600	
52	Rent expense	800	
53	Utilities expense	200	
	Total................................	$40,200	$40,200

Required

1. Record the transactions that occurred during February 15 through 28 in *page 3* of the journal. Include an explanation for each entry.

2. Open the ledger accounts listed in the trial balance, together with their balances at February 14. Use the four-column account format illustrated below. Enter *Bal.* (for previous balance) in the Item column, and place a check mark (✓) in the journal reference column for the February 14 balance, as illustrated for Cash:

Account Cash   **Account No. 11**

					Balance	
Date	Item	Jrnl. Ref.	Debit	Credit	Debit	Credit
Feb. 14	Bal.	✓			4,000	

Post the transactions to the ledger, using dates, account numbers, journal references, and posting references.

3. Prepare the trial balance of Elizabeth Staar, CPA, P.C., at February 28, 19X3.

Problem 2-5B   *Journalizing, posting to T-accounts, and preparing a trial balance*
(L.O. 2,3,4,5)

Dwyer Delivery Service, Inc., completed the following transactions during its first month of operations:

a. Paul Dwyer, the incorporator of the business, began operations by investing in the business $5,000 cash and a truck valued at $10,000. The corporation issued common stock to Dwyer.

b. Paid $200 cash for supplies.

c. Used a company credit card to purchase $50 fuel for the delivery truck. (Credit Accounts Payable.)

d. Performed delivery services for a customer and received $600 cash.

e. Completed a large delivery job, billed the customer $2,000, and received a promise to be paid the $2,000 within one week.

f. Paid employee salary, $800.

g. Received $900 cash for performing delivery services.

h. Purchased fuel for the truck on account, $40.

i. Received $2,000 cash from a customer on account.

j. Paid for advertising in the local newspaper, $170.

k. Paid utility bills, $100.

l. Purchased fuel for the truck, paying $30 with a company credit card.

m. Performed delivery services on account, $800.

n. Paid for repairs to the delivery truck, $110.

o. Paid employee salary, $800, and office rent, $200.

p. Paid $120 on account.

q. Declared and paid a dividend of $1,900.

Required

1. Record each transaction in the journal, using the account titles given. Key each transaction by letter. Explanations are not required.

2. Open the following T-accounts: Cash; Accounts Receivable; Supplies; Delivery Truck; Accounts Payable; Common Stock; Dividends; Delivery Service Revenue; Salary Expense; Rent Expense; Advertising Expense; Fuel Expense; Repair Expense; Utilities Expense. Post the transactions to the ledger, keying transactions by letter. Label the balance of each account *Bal.*, as shown in the chapter.

3. Prepare the trial balance of Dwyer Delivery Service, Inc., using the current date.

Problem 2-6B *Correcting errors in a trial balance* *(L.O. 2,5)*

The trial balance in this problem does not balance. The following errors were detected:

a. The cash balance is understated by $300.

b. Property tax expense of $500 was omitted from the trial balance.

c. Land should be listed in the amount of $24,000.

d. A $200 purchase of supplies on account was not journalized or posted.

e. A $2,800 credit to Counseling Service Revenue was not posted.

f. Rent expense of $200 was posted as a credit rather than a debit.

g. The balance of Advertising Expense is $600, but it was listed as $500 on the trial balance.

h. A $300 debit to Accounts Receivable was posted as $30.

i. The balance of Utilities Expense is overstated by $70.

j. A $900 debit to the Dividends account was posted as a credit to Common Stock.

```
                Samaritan Counseling Center
                       Trial Balance
                       June 30, 19X2

Cash ...................................    $ 2,000
Accounts receivable......................    10,000
Supplies ................................       900
Office furniture.........................     3,600
Land ....................................    26,000
Accounts payable ........................               $ 4,000
Note payable ............................                14,000
Common Stock ............................                22,000
Dividends................................     2,000
Counseling service revenue ..............                 6,500
Salary expense ..........................     1,600
Rent expense.............................     1,000
Advertising expense .....................       500
Utilities expense .......................       300
Property tax expense.....................       100
Total ...................................   $48,000    $46,500
```

Required

Prepare the correct trial balance at June 30. Journal entries are not required.

Problem 2-7B   *Recording transactions directly in the ledger, preparing a trial balance*
(L.O. 2,5,6)

Diana Flori obtained a corporate charter from the state of Connecticut and started a consulting service. During the first month of operations the business completed the following selected transactions:

a. Flori began the business with an investment of $15,000 cash and a building valued at $60,000. The corporation issued common stock to Flori.
b. Borrowed $30,000 from the bank; signed a note payable.
c. Purchased office supplies on account, $1,300.
d. Paid $18,000 for office furniture.
e. Paid employee salary, $2,200.
f. Performed consulting service on account for client, $2,100.
g. Paid $800 of the account payable created in *c*.
h. Received a $900 bill for advertising expense to be paid in the near future.
i. Performed consulting service for customers and received cash, $1,600.
j. Received cash on account, $1,200.
k. Paid the following cash expenses:
    (1) Rent on land, $700.
    (2) Utilities, $400.
l. Declared and paid a dividend of $3,500.

Required

1. Open the following T-accounts: Cash; Accounts Receivable; Office Supplies; Office Furniture; Building; Accounts Payable; Note Payable; Common Stock; Dividends; Service Revenue; Salary Expense; Advertising Expense; Rent Expense; Utilities Expense.
2. Record each transaction directly in the T-accounts without using a journal. Use the letters to identify the transactions.
3. Prepare the trial balance of Flori Consulting Service, Inc., at June 30, 19X3.

Extending Your Knowledge

Decision Problems

1. Recording Transactions Directly in the Ledger, Preparing a Trial Balance, and Measuring Net Income or Loss   (L.O. 2,5,6)

You have been requested by a friend named Charles Sligh to give advice on the effects that certain business transactions will have on the entity he plans to start. Time is short, so you will not be able to do all the detailed procedures of journalizing and posting. Instead, you must analyze the transactions without the use of a journal. Sligh will continue the business only if he can expect to earn monthly net income of $3,500. Assume the following transactions have occurred:

a. Sligh deposited $6,000 cash in a business bank account, and the corporation issued common stock to Sligh.
b. Borrowed $4,000 cash from the bank and signed a note payable due within one year.
c. Paid $300 cash for supplies.
d. Purchased advertising in the local newspaper for cash, $800.
e. Purchased office furniture on account, $1,500.
f. Paid the following cash expenses for one month: secretary salary, $1,400; office rent, $400; utilities, $300; interest, $50.
g. Earned revenue on account $4,300.
h. Earned revenue and received $2,500 cash.
i. Collected cash from customers on account, $1,200.
j. Paid on account, $1,000.
k. Declared and paid cash dividends, $900.

Required

1. Open the following T-accounts: Cash; Accounts Receivable; Supplies; Furniture; Accounts Payable; Notes Payable; Common Stock; Dividends; Service Revenue; Salary Expense; Advertising Expense; Rent Expense; Utilities Expense; Interest Expense.
2. Record the transactions directly in the accounts without using a journal. Key each transaction by letter.
3. Prepare a trial balance at the current date. List expenses with the largest amount first, the next largest amount second, and so on. The business name will be Sligh Apartment Locators.
4. Compute the amount of net income or net loss for this first month of operations. Would you recommend that Sligh continue in business?

2. Using the Accounting Equation   (L.O. 2)

Although all the following questions deal with the accounting equation, they are not related:

1. Explain the advantages of double-entry bookkeeping over single-entry bookkeeping to a friend who is opening a used book store.
2. When you deposit money in your bank account, the bank credits your account. Is the bank misusing the word *credit* in this context? Why does the bank use the term *credit* to refer to your deposit, and not *debit*?

3. Your friend asks, "When revenues increase assets and expenses decrease assets, why are revenues credits and expenses debits and not the other way around?" Explain to your friend why revenues are credits and expenses are debits.

Ethical Issue

Community Chest, a charitable organization in Mojave, New Mexico, has a standing agreement with Encino State Bank. The agreement allows Community Chest to overdraw its cash balance at the bank when donations are running low. In the past, Community Chest managed funds wisely and rarely used this privilege. Greg Osborn has recently become the president of Community Chest. To expand operations, Osborn is acquiring office equipment and spending large amounts for fund-raising. During his presidency, Community Chest has maintained a negative bank balance of approximately $1,000.

Required

What is the ethical issue in this situation? State why you approve or disapprove of Osborn's management of Community Chest funds.

Financial Statement Problems

1. Journalizing Transactions for an Actual Company (L.O. 2,3)

This problem helps to develop skill in recording transactions by using an actual company's account titles. Refer to The Goodyear Tire & Rubber Company financial statements in Appendix C. Assume Goodyear completed the following selected transactions during November 1991:

Nov. 5 Earned sales revenue on account, $55,000.
9 Borrowed $500,000 by signing a note payable (long-term debt).
12 Purchased equipment on account, $70,000.
17 Paid $110,000, which represents payment of $100,000 long-term debt due within one year plus interest expense of $10,000.
19 Earned sales revenue and immediately received cash of $16,000.
22 Collected the cash on account that was earned on November 5.
24 Paid rent of $14,000 for three months in advance.
28 Received a home-office electricity bill for $1,000, which will be paid in December (this is an administrative and general expense).
30 Paid off half the account payable created on November 12.

Required

Journalize these transactions using the following account titles taken from the financial statements of Goodyear: Cash; Accounts Receivable; Prepaid Expenses; Equipment; Long-term Debt Due Within One Year; Trade Accounts Payable; Long-Term Debt; Sales Revenue; Selling, Administrative, and General Expense; Interest Expense. Explanations are not required.

2. Journalizing Transactions for an Actual Company (L.O. 2,3)

Obtain the annual report of an actual company of your choosing. Assume the company completed the following selected transactions during May of the current year:

May 3 Borrowed $350,000 by signing a short-term note payable (may be called *short-term debt* or other account title).

5 Paid rent for six months in advance, $4,600.

9 Earned revenue on account, $74,000.

12 Purchased equipment on account, $33,000.

17 Paid a telephone bill, $300 (this is Selling Expense).

19 Paid $90,000 of the money borrowed on May 3.

26 Collected one half of the cash on account from May 9.

30 Paid the account payable from May 12.

Required

1. Journalize these transactions, using the company's actual account titles taken from its annual report. Explanations are not required.
2. Open a ledger account for each account that you used in journalizing the transactions. (For clarity, insert no actual balances in the accounts.) Post the transaction amounts to the accounts, using the dates as posting references. Take the balance of each account.
3. Prepare a trial balance.

Chapter 3

Measuring Business Income: The Adjusting Process

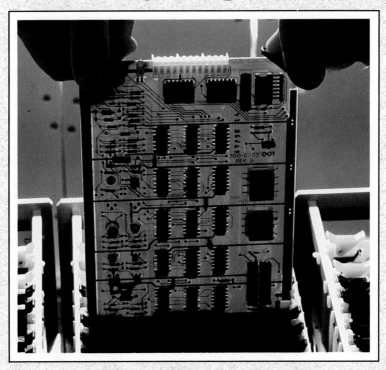

Hewlett-Packard Co., continuing to see strong sales of computers and printers despite the troubles facing many other big computer makers, said net income grew 40% in its fiscal second quarter on a 12% increase in revenue.

H-P said net income in the quarter ended April 30 was $326 million, compared with $233 million in the year-ago quarter. Second-quarter revenue was $4.18 billion, compared with $3.73 billion last year.

H-P's strong results, which met many analysts' expectations, illustrate a continued comeback for the Palo Alto, Calif., computer company, which two years ago had a profit decline because of uncompetitive products and growing expenses. Since then, H-P has introduced a string of successful computers, while many of its printers have proven more popular than expected.

SOURCE: Adapted from Stephen Kreider Yoder, "Hewlett-Packard Posts 40% Rise in Net for Quarter on 12% Gain in Revenue," *The Wall Street Journal*, May 19, 1992, p. B6.

The primary goal of business is to earn a profit. Many companies such as Hewlett-Packard expect to earn increasing amounts of profit each year. When they do, they expand the business, hire more employees, and make their owners happy. When profits fail to meet goals, the result can be layoffs, idle facilities, and unhappy owners.

Air and Sea Travel, Inc., the travel agency we discussed in the earlier chapters, earns business income by providing travel arrangement services for customers. Regardless of the type of activity, the profit motive increases an owner's level of interest in the business. As you read Chapter 3, consider how important income is to a business and how important accounting procedures are in measuring income.

At the end of each accounting period, the accountant prepares the entity's financial statements. The period may be a month, three months, six months, or a full year. Whatever the length of the period, the end accounting product is the same, the financial statements. And the most important single amount in these statements is the net income or net loss—the profit or loss—for the period. A double-entry accounting system produces not only the income statement but the other financial statements as well.

An important step in financial statement preparation is the trial balance that we discussed in Chapter 2. The trial balance includes the effects of the transactions that occurred during the period—the cash collections, purchases of assets, payments of bills, sales of assets, and so on. To measure its income properly, however, a business must do some additional accounting at the end of the period to bring the records up to date before preparing the financial statements. This process is called *adjusting the books,* and it consists of making special entries called *adjusting entries.* This chapter focuses primarily on these adjusting entries to help you better understand the nature of business income.

Accountants have devised concepts and principles to guide the measurement of business income. Chief among these are the concepts of accrual accounting, the accounting period, the revenue principle, and the matching principle. In this chapter, we apply these concepts and principles to measure the income and prepare the financial statements of Air and Sea Travel for the month of April.

Accrual-Basis Accounting versus Cash-Basis Accounting

OBJECTIVE 1

Distinguish accrual-basis accounting from cash-basis accounting

There are two widely used bases of accounting: the accrual basis and the cash basis. In **accrual-basis accounting**, an accountant recognizes the impact of a business event as it occurs. When the business performs a service, makes a sale, or incurs an expense, the accountant enters the transaction into the books, whether or not cash has been received or paid. In **cash-basis account-ing,** however, the accountant does not record a transaction until cash is received or paid. Cash receipts are treated as revenues, and cash payments are handled as expenses.

GAAP requires that a business use the accrual basis. This means that the accountant records revenues as they are earned and expenses as they are *incurred*—not necessarily when cash changes hands.

Using accrual-basis accounting, Air and Sea Travel <u>records revenue when the business performs services for a customer on account</u>. Air and Sea Travel has earned the revenue at that time because its work has generated an account receivable, a legal claim against the customer for whom the work was performed. By contrast, if Air and Sea Travel used <u>cash-basis accounting, it would not record revenue at the time it performed the service.</u> Air and Sea Travel would wait until it received cash from the customers.

Why does GAAP require that businesses use the accrual basis? What advantage does accrual-basis accounting offer? Suppose Air and Sea Travel's accounting period ends after it has earned the revenue but before it has collected the money due from the customer. If the business used the cash-basis method, its financial statements would not include this revenue or the related account receivable. As a result, the financial statements would be misleading. Revenue and the asset Accounts Receivable would be understated, and thus the business would look less successful than it actually is. If Air and Sea Travel wants to get a bank loan to open a new office, the understated revenue and asset figures might hurt its chances.

Air and Sea Travel, using accrual-basis accounting, treats expenses in a like manner. For instance, salary expense includes amounts paid to employees plus any amount owed to employees but not yet paid. Air and Sea Travel's use of the employee's service, not the payment of cash to the employee, brings about the expense. Under cash-basis accounting, it would record the expense only when it actually paid the employee.

Suppose the business Air and Sea Travel owes a secretary a salary and the financial statements are drawn up before the business pays. Expenses and liabilities would be understated, so the business would look more successful than it really is. This incomplete information would not provide an accurate accounting to potential creditors.

As these examples show, accrual accounting provides more complete information than does cash-basis accounting. This is important because the more complete the data, the better equipped decision makers are to reach intelligent conclusions about the firm's financial health and future prospects. Three concepts used in accrual accounting are the accounting period, the revenue principle, and the matching principle.

The Accounting Period

The only way to know for certain how successfully a business has operated is to close its doors, sell all its assets, pay the liabilities, and return any leftover cash to the owners. This process, called liquidation, is the same as going out of business. Obviously, it is not practical for accountants to measure business income in this manner. Instead, businesses need periodic reports on their progress. Accountants slice time into small segments and prepare financial statements for specific periods. Until a business liquidates, the amounts reported in its financial statements must be regarded as estimates.

The most basic accounting period is one year, and virtually all businesses prepare annual financial statements. For about 60 percent of large companies in a recent survey, the annual accounting period runs the calendar year from January 1 through December 31. Other companies use what is called a *fiscal year*, which ends on some date other than December 31. The year-end date is usually the low point in business activity for the year. Depending on the type of business, the fiscal year may end on April 30, July 31, or some other date. Retailers are a notable example. For example, J. C. Penney Company uses a fiscal year ending on January 31 because the low point in Penney's business activity has followed the after-Christmas sales during January.

Companies cannot wait until the end of the year to gauge their progress. The manager of a business wants to know how well the business is doing each month, each quarter, and each half year. Outsiders such as lenders also demand current information about the business. So companies also prepare financial statements for *interim* periods, which are less than a year. Monthly financial statements are common, and a series of monthly statements can be combined for quarterly and semiannual periods. Most of the discussions in this book are based on an annual accounting period. However, the procedures and statements can also be applied to interim periods as well.

OBJECTIVE 2

Apply the revenue and matching principles

Revenue Principle

The **revenue principle** tells accountants (1) *when* to record revenue by making a journal entry and (2) the *amount* of revenue to record. When we speak of "recording" something in accounting, the act of recording the item naturally leads to posting to the ledger accounts and preparing the trial balance and the financial statements. Although the financial statements are the end product of accounting and what accountants are most concerned about, our discussions often focus on recording the entry in the journal because that is where the accounting process starts.

The general principle guiding *when* to record revenue says to record revenue as it has been earned—but not before. In most cases, revenue is earned when the business has delivered a completed good or service to the customer. The business has done everything required by the agreement, including transferring the item to the customer. Two situations that provide guidance on when to record revenue follow. The first situation illustrates when *not* to record revenue. Situation 2 illustrates when revenue should be recorded.

Situation 1—Do not record revenue.   A customer of another travel agency expresses her intention to transfer her business to Air and Sea. Should Air and Sea Travel record any revenue based on this intention? The answer is no because no transaction has occurred.

Situation 2—Record revenue.   Next month Monica consults with this customer and tailors a vacation plan to her goals. After transferring the business plan to the client, Air and Sea Travel should record revenue. If the client pays for this service immediately, Air and Sea will debit Cash. If the service is performed on account, the business will debit Accounts Receivable. In either case, it should record revenue by crediting the Service Revenue account.

The general principle guiding the *amount* of revenue says to record revenue equal to the cash value of the goods or the service transferred to the customer. Suppose that in order to obtain a new customer, Air and Sea performs travel service for the price of $500. Ordinarily, the business would have charged $600 for this service. How much revenue should Air and Sea record? The answer is $500 because that was the cash value of the transaction. Air and Sea Travel will not receive the full value of $600, so that is not the amount of revenue to record. It will receive only $500 cash, and that pinpoints the amount of revenue earned.

Matching Principle

The **matching principle** is the basis for recording expenses. Recall that expenses, such as rent, utilities, and advertising, are the costs of operating a business. Expenses are the costs of assets that are used up in the earning of revenue. The matching principle directs accountants (1) to identify all expenses incurred during the accounting period, (2) to measure the expenses, and (3) to "match" the expenses against the revenues earned during that same span of time. To "match" expenses against revenues means to subtract the expenses from the revenues in order to compute net income or net loss.

There is a natural link between revenues and some types of expenses. Accountants follow the matching principle by first identifying the revenues of a period and the expenses that can be linked to particular revenues. For example, a business that pays sales commissions to its sales personnel will have commission expense if the employees make sales. If they make no sales, the business has no commission expense. Cost of goods sold is another example. When merchandise is sold, there must also be a cost—the cost incurred by the seller— assigned to the goods sold. If there are no sales, there can be no cost of goods sold.

Other expenses are not so easy to link with particular sales. Monthly rent expense occurs, for example, regardless of the revenues earned during the period. The matching principle directs accountants to identify these types of expenses with a particular time period, such as a month or a year. If Air and Sea Travel employs a secretary at a monthly salary of $ 1,900, the business will record salary expense of $1,900 each month. Because financial statements appear at definite intervals, there must be some cutoff date for the necessary information. Most entities engage in so many transactions that some are bound to spill over into more than a single accounting period. Air and Sea Travel prepares monthly statements for its business at April 30. How does the business account for a transaction that begins in April but ends in May? How does Air and Sea bring the accounts up to date for preparing the financial statements? To answer these questions, accountants use the time-period concept.

Time-Period Concept

Managers, investors, and creditors are making decisions daily and need periodic readings on the business's progress. To meet this need for information, accountants prepare financial statements at regular intervals. Virtually all companies report net income for an annual period and their assets, liabilities, and stockholders' equity at the end of the year. Most companies also prepare monthly and quarterly financial statements.

The **time-period concept** ensures that accounting information is reported at regular intervals. It interacts with the revenue principle and the matching principle to underlie the use of accruals. To measure income accurately, companies update the revenue and expense accounts immediately prior to the end of the period. Tootsie Roll Industries, Inc., the candy maker, provides an actual example of an expense accrual. At December 31, 1989, Tootsie Roll recorded employee compensation of $3.4 million that the company owed its workers for unpaid services performed before year end. Tootsie Roll's accrual entry was

1989		
Dec. 31	Salary (or Wage) Expense............. 3,400,000	
	Salary (or Wage) Payable	3,400,000

This entry serves two purposes. It assigns the expense to the proper period. Without the accrual entry at December 31, total expenses of 1989 would be understated and as a result net income would be overstated. Incorrectly, the expense would fall in 1990 when Tootsie Roll makes the next payroll disbursement. The accrual entry also records the liability for reporting on the balance sheet at December 31, 1989. Without the accrual entry, total liabilities would be understated.

At the end of the accounting period, companies also accrue revenues that have been earned but not collected. The remainder of the chapter discusses how to make the necessary adjustments to the accounts.

Adjustments to the Accounts

At the end of the period, the accountant prepares the financial statements. This end-of-the-period process begins with the trial balance that lists the accounts and their balances after the period's transactions have been recorded in the journal and posted to the accounts in the ledger. Exhibit 3-1 is the trial balance of Air and Sea Travel, Inc., at April 30, 19X1.

EXHIBIT 3-1 *Unadjusted Trial Balance*

Air and Sea Travel, Inc. Unadjusted Trial Balance April 30, 19X1		
Cash...	$24,800	
Accounts receivable	2,250	
Supplies......................................	700	
Prepaid rent	3,000	
Furniture.....................................	16,500	
Accounts payable		$13,100
Unearned service revenue......................		450
Common Stock		20,000
Retained earnings		11,250
Dividends....................................	3,200	
Service revenue		7,000
Salary expense................................	950	
Utilities expense	400	
Total..	$51,800	$51,800

This *unadjusted* trial balance includes some new accounts that will be explained in this section. It lists most, but not all, of the revenue and the expenses of the travel agency for the month of April. These trial balance amounts are incomplete because they omit certain revenue and expense transactions that affect more than one accounting period. That is why it is called an *unadjusted* trial balance. In most cases, however, we refer to it simply as the trial balance, without the "unadjusted" label.

Under the cash basis of accounting, there would be no need for adjustments to the accounts because all April cash transactions would have been recorded. The accrual basis requires adjusting entries at the end of the period in order to produce correct balances for the financial statements. To see why, consider the Supplies account in Exhibit 3-1.

Air and Sea Travel uses supplies in providing travel services for customers during the month. This reduces the quantity of supplies on hand and thus constitutes an expense, just like salary expense or rent expense. Gary and Monica Lyon do not bother to record this expense daily, and it is not worth their while to record supplies expense more than once a month. It is time-consuming to make hourly, daily, or even weekly journal entries to record the expense for the use of supplies. So how does the business account for supplies expense?

By the end of the month, the Supplies balance is not correct. The balance represents the amount of supplies on hand at the start of the month plus any supplies purchased during the month. This balance fails to take into account the supplies used (supplies expense) during the accounting period. It is necessary, then, to subtract the month's expenses from the amount of supplies listed on the trial balance. The resulting new adjusted balance measures the cost of supplies that are still on hand at April 30. This is the correct amount of supplies to report on the balance sheet. Adjusting entries in this way will bring the accounts up to date.

Adjusting entries assign revenues to the period in which they are earned and expenses to the period in which they are incurred. They are needed (a) to measure properly the period's income and (b) to bring related asset and liability accounts to correct balances for the financial statements. For example, an adjusting entry is needed to transfer the amount of supplies used during the period from the asset account Supplies to the expense account Supplies Expense. The adjusting entry updates both the Supplies asset account and the Supplies Expense account. This achieves accurate measures of assets and expenses. Adjusting entries, which are the key to the accrual basis of accounting, are made before preparing the financial statements.

The end-of-period process of updating the accounts is called *adjusting the accounts, making the adjusting entries,* or *adjusting the books.* Adjusting entries can be divided into five categories:

1. Prepaid expenses
2. Depreciation
3. Accrued expenses
4. Accrued revenues
5. Unearned revenues

Prepaid Expenses

Prepaid expenses is a category of miscellaneous assets that typically expire or are used up in the near future. Prepaid rent and prepaid insurance are examples of prepaid expenses. They are called prepaid expenses because they are expenses that are paid in advance. Salary expense and utilities expense, among others, are typically *not* prepaid expenses because they are not paid in advance.

Prepaid Rent.   Landlords usually require tenants to pay rent in advance. This prepayment creates an asset for the renter because that person has purchased the future benefit of using the rented item. Suppose Air and Sea Travel prepays three months' rent on April 1, 19X1, after negotiating a lease for the business office. If the lease specifies monthly rental amounts of $1,000 each, the entry to record the payment for three months is a debit to the asset account, Prepaid Rent, as follows:

Apr. 1   Prepaid Rent ($1,000 × 3)   3,000
                 Cash   3,000
             Paid three months' rent in advance.

After posting, Prepaid Rent appears as follows:

Prepaid Rent
Apr. 1   3,000

The trial balance at April 30, 19X1, lists Prepaid Rent as an asset with a debit balance of $3,000. Throughout April, the Prepaid Rent account maintains this beginning balance as shown in Exhibit 3-1.

At April 30 Prepaid Rent should be adjusted to remove from its balance the amount of the asset that has expired, which is one month's worth of the prepayment. By definition, the amount of an asset that has expired is *expense*. The adjusting entry transfers one-third, or $1,000 ($3,000 X 1/3), of the debit balance from Prepaid Rent to Rent Expense. The debit side of the entry records an increase in Rent Expense, and the credit records a decrease in the asset Prepaid Rent.

OBJECTIVE 3

Make the typical adjusting entries at the end of the accounting period

Apr. 30   Rent Expense ($3,000 × 1/3)   1,000
                  Prepaid Rent...........................   1,000
              To record rent expense.

After posting, Prepaid Rent and Rent Expense appear as follows:

Prepaid Rent		Rent Expense	
Apr. 1 3,000	Apr. 30 1,000	Apr. 30 1,000	
Bal. 2,000		Bal. 1,000	

Correct asset amount, $2,000 → **Total accounted for, $3,000** ← Correct expense amount, $1,000

The full $3,000 has been accounted for: two-thirds measures the asset, and one-third measures the expense. This is correct because two-thirds of the asset remains for future use, and one-third of the prepayment has expired. Recording this expense illustrates the matching principle. The same analysis applies to a prepayment of three months' insurance premiums. The only difference is in the account titles, which would be Prepaid Insurance and Insurance

Expense instead of Prepaid Rent and Rent Expense. This adjusting entry illustrates the matching principle.

Supplies. Supplies are accounted for in the same way as prepaid expenses. On April 2 Air and Sea Travel paid cash of $700 for office supplies:

Apr. 2 Supplies 700
             Cash   700
        Paid cash for supplies.

Assume that the business purchased no additional supplies during April. The April 30 trial balance, therefore, lists Supplies with a $700 debit balance, as shown in Exhibit 3-1.

During April, Air and Sea Travel used supplies in performing services for customers. The cost of the supplies used is the measure of *supplies expense* for the month.

Air and Sea Travel does not keep a continuous record of supplies used each day or each week during April. To keep these detailed records would be impractical. Instead, to measure the business's supplies expense during April, the Lyons count the supplies on hand at the end of the month. This is the amount of the asset still available to the business. Assume the count indicates that supplies costing $400 remain. Subtracting the entity's $400 supplies on hand at the end of April from the cost of supplies available during April ($700) measures supplies expense during the month ($300).

Cost of asset available during the period	−	Cost of asset on hand at the end of the period	=	Cost of asset used (expense) during the period
$700	−	$400	=	$300

The April 30 adjusting entry to update the Supplies account and to record the supplies expense for the month debits the expense and credits the asset as follows:

Apr. 30 Supplies Expense ($700 − $400) 300
            Supplies   300
        To record supplies expense.

After posting, the Supplies and Supplies Expense accounts appear as follows:

Supplies					Supplies Expense		
Apr. 2	700	Apr. 30	300		Apr. 30	300	
Bal.	400				Bal.	300	

Correct asset amount, $400 → **Total accounted for, $700** ← Correct expense amount, $300

The Supplies account then enters the month of May with a $400 balance, and the adjustment process is repeated each month.

The logic of the accrual basis is probably best illustrated by how businesses account for plant assets. **Plant assets** are long-lived assets, such as land, buildings, furniture, machinery, and equipment used in the operations of the business. As one accountant said, "All assets but land are on a march to the junkyard." That is, all plant assets but land decline in usefulness as they age. This decline is an *expense* to the business. Accountants systematically spread the cost of each plant asset, except land, over the years of its useful life. This process is called the recording of **depreciation.** The concept underlying accounting for plant assets and depreciation expense is the same as for prepaid expenses. In both cases the business purchases an asset that wears out or is used up. As the asset is used, more and more of its cost is transferred from the asset account to the expense account. The major difference between prepaid expenses and plant assets is the length of time it takes for the asset to lose its usefulness. Prepaid expenses usually expire within a year. Most plant assets remain useful for a number of years.

Consider Air and Sea Travel's operations. Suppose that on April 3 the business purchased furniture on account for $16,500:

Apr. 3	Furniture	16,500	
	Accounts Payable		16,500
	Purchased office furniture on account.		

After posting, the Furniture account appears as follows:

Furniture

Apr. 3	16,500

Using cash-basis accounting, the accountant for Air and Sea Travel would enter in the ledger the entire $16,500 as an expense for April. As a result, the financial statements for that month would be extremely misleading. Income would be significantly understated. Also, the cash-basis approach fails to take into consideration that the asset will be of benefit to Air and Sea Travel in future accounting periods.

In accrual-basis accounting, an asset is recorded when the furniture is acquired. Then, a portion of the asset's cost is transferred from the asset account to Depreciation Expense each period that the asset is used. This method matches the asset's expense to the revenue of the period, which is an application of the matching principle.

Gary and Monica Lyon believe the furniture will remain useful for five years and be virtually worthless at the end of its life. One way to compute the amount of depreciation for each year is to divide the cost of the asset ($16,500 in our example) by its expected useful life (5 years). This procedure gives annual depreciation of $3,300 ($16,500/5 years = $3,300 per year). Depreciation for the month of April is $275 ($3,300/12 months = $275 per month). Chapter 9 covers depreciation in more detail.

Depreciation expense for April is recorded by the following entry:

Apr. 30	Depreciation Expense—Furniture	275	
	Accumulated Depreciation—Furniture		275
	To record depreciation on furniture.		

You may be wondering why Accumulated Depreciation is credited instead of Furniture. The reason is that the original cost of the plant asset is an objective measurement, and that figure remains in the original asset account as long as the business uses the asset. Accountants may refer to that account if they need to know how much the asset cost. This information may be useful in a decision about whether to replace the furniture and the amount to pay. The amount of depreciation, however, is an *estimate*. Accountants use the **Accumulated Depreciation** account to show the cumulative sum of all depreciation expense from the date of acquiring the asset. Therefore, the balance in this account increases over the life of the asset.

Accumulated Depreciation is a **contra asset** account, which means an asset account with a normal credit balance. A **contra account** has two distinguishing characteristics: (1) it always has a companion account, and (2) its normal balance is opposite that of the companion account. In this case, Accumulated Depreciation accompanies Furniture. It appears in the ledger directly after Furniture. Furniture has a debit balance, and therefore Accumulated Depreciation, a contra asset, has a credit balance. All contra asset accounts have credit balances.

A business carries an accumulated depreciation account for each depreciable asset. If a business has a building and a machine, for example, it will carry the accounts Accumulated Depreciation—Building, and Accumulated Depreciation—Machine.

After posting the depreciation entry, the Furniture, Accumulated Depreciation, and Depreciation Expense accounts are

Furniture		Accumulated Depreciation—Furniture		Depreciation Expense	
Apr. 3 16,500			Apr. 30 275	Apr. 30 275	
Bal. 16,500			Bal. 275	Bal. 275	

The balance sheet shows the relationship between Furniture and Accumulated Depreciation. The balance of Accumulated Depreciation is subtracted from the balance of Furniture. The net amount of a plant asset (cost minus accumulated depreciation) is called its **book value,** as shown below for Furniture.

Plant Assets:

Furniture	$16,500
Less Accumulated depreciation	275
Book value.........................	$16,225

Because Accumulated Depreciation is subtracted from its companion account to determine the asset's book value, Accumulated Depreciation is also called a *valuation* account.

Suppose Air and Sea Travel owns a building that cost $48,000 and on which annual depreciation is $2,400. The amount of depreciation for one month would be $200 ($2,400/12), and the entry to record depreciation for April is

Apr. 30	Depreciation Expense—Building	200	
	Accumulated Depreciation—Building		200
	To record depreciation on building.		

The balance sheet at April 30 would report Air and Sea Travel's plant assets as shown in Exhibit 3-2. Now, however, let's return to the business's actual situation.

EXHIBIT 3-2 *Plant Assets on the Balance Sheet (April 30)*

Plant assets:			
Furniture		$16,500	
Less Accumulated depreciation ..		275	$16,225
Building		48,000	
Less Accumulated depreciation ..		200	47,800
Book value of plant assets			$64,025

Accrued Expenses

Businesses often incur expenses before they pay cash. Payment is not due until later. Consider an employee's salary. The employer's salary expense and salary payable grow as the employee works, so the liability is said to *accrue*. Another example is interest expense on a note payable. Interest accrues as the clock ticks. The term **accrued expense** refers to an expense that the business has incurred but not yet paid.

It is time-consuming to make hourly, daily, or even weekly journal entries to accrue expenses. Consequently, the accountant waits until the end of the period. Then an adjusting entry brings each expense (and related liability) up to date just before the financial statements are prepared.

Salary Expense. Most companies pay their employees at set times. Suppose Air and Sea Travel pays its employee a monthly salary of $1,900, half on the 15th and half on the last day of the month. Here is a calendar for April that has paydays circled:

APRIL

Sun.	Mon.	Tue.	Wed.	Thur.	Fri.	Sat.
					1	2
3	4	5	6	7	8	9
10	11	12	13	14	⑮	16
17	18	19	20	21	22	23
24	25	26	27	28	29	㉚

Assume that if either payday falls on a weekend, the business pays the employee on the following Monday. During April Air and Sea paid its employee's first half-month salary of $950 on Friday, April 15, and recorded the following entry:

Apr. 15   Salary Expense   950
                     Cash   950
              To pay salary.

After posting, the Salary Expense account is

Salary Expense	
Apr. 15 950	

The trial balance at April 30 (Exhibit 3-1) includes Salary Expense, with its debit balance of $950. Because April 30, the second payday of the month, falls on a Saturday, the second half-month amount of $950 will be paid on Monday, May 2. Without an adjusting entry, this second $950 amount is not included in the April 30 trial balance amount for Salary Expense. Therefore, at April 30 the accountant adjusts for additional *salary expense* and *salary payable* of $950 by recording an increase in each of these accounts as follows:

Apr. 30	Salary Expense	950
	Salary Payable.............................	950
	To accrue salary expense.	

After posting, the Salary Expense and Salary Payable accounts appear as follows:

Salary Expense			Salary Payable	
Apr. 15	950		Apr. 30	950
Apr. 30	950		Bal.	950
Bal.	1,900			

The accounts at April 30 now contain the complete salary information for the month. The expense account has a full month's salary, and the liability account shows the portion that the business still owes.

Air and Sea Travel will record the payment of this liability on May 2 by debiting Salary Payable and crediting Cash for $950. This payment entry does not affect April or May expenses because the April expense was recorded on April 15 and April 30. May expense will be recorded in a like manner. All accrued expenses are recorded with similar entries—a debit to the appropriate expense account and a credit to the related liability account.

Accrued Revenues

Businesses often earn revenue before they receive the cash because payment is not due until later. A revenue that has been earned but not yet received in cash is called an **accrued revenue.** Assume Air and Sea Travel is hired on April 15 by Guerrero Tour Company to perform services on a monthly basis. Under this agreement, Guerrero will pay Air and Sea $500 monthly, with the first payment on May 15. During April, Air and Sea will earn half a month's fee, $250. On April 30 the Air and Sea accountant makes the following adjusting entry to record an increase in Accounts Receivable and Service Revenue:

Apr. 30	Accounts Receivable ($500 × 1/2)	250
	Service Revenue	250
	To accrue service revenue.	

Recall that Accounts Receivable has an unadjusted balance of $2,250, and the Service Revenue unadjusted balance is $7,000 (Exhibit 3-1). Posting this adjusting entry has the following effects on these two accounts:

Accounts Receivable			Service Revenue	
	2,250			7,000
Apr. 30	250		Apr. 30	250
Bal.	2,500		Bal.	7,250

This adjusting entry illustrates accrual accounting and the revenue principle in action. Without the adjustment, Air and Sea Travel's financial statements would be misleading. All accrued revenues are accounted for similarly—by debiting a receivable and crediting a revenue.

Unearned Revenues

Some businesses collect cash from customers in advance of doing work for the customer. This creates a liability called **unearned revenue,** which is an obligation arising from receiving cash in advance of providing a product or a service. Only when the job is completed will the business have earned the revenue. Suppose Baldwin Investment Bankers engages Air and Sea Travel's services, agreeing to pay Air and Sea $450 monthly, beginning immediately. If Baldwin makes the first payment on April 20, Air and Sea Travel records this increase in the business's liabilities by recording:

Apr. 20   Cash   450
                     Unearned Service Revenue   450
             Received revenue in advance.

After posting, the liability account appears as follows:

Unearned Service Revenue	
	Apr. 20 450

Unearned Service Revenue is a liability because it represents Air and Sea Travel's obligation to perform service for the customer. The April 30 unadjusted trial balance (Exhibit 3-1) lists this account with a $450 credit balance prior to the adjusting entries. During the last 10 days of the month, Air and Sea will have earned one-third (10 days divided by April's total 30 days) of the $450, or $150. Therefore, the Air and Sea accountant makes the following adjustment to decrease the liability, Unearned Service Revenue, and to record an increase in Service Revenue:

Apr. 30   Unearned Service Revenue ($450 × 1/3)   150
                     Service Revenue   150
             To record unearned service revenue that has been
             earned.

This adjusting entry shifts $150 of the total amount from the liability account to the revenue account. After posting, the balance of Service Revenue is increased by $150 and the balance of Unearned Service Revenue has been reduced to $300:

Unearned Service Revenue			Service Revenue		
Apr. 30 150	Apr. 20 450				7,000
	Bal. 300			Apr. 30	250
				Apr. 30	150
				Bal.	7,400

Correct liability amount, $300 → | Total accounted for, $450 | ← Correct revenue amount, $150

Accounting for all types of revenues that are collected in advance follows the same pattern.

Summary of the Adjusting Process

Because one purpose of the adjusting process is to measure business income properly, each adjusting entry affects at least one income statement account—a revenue or an expense. The other side of the entry—a debit or a credit, as the case may be—is to a balance sheet account—an asset or a liability. This step updates the accounts for preparation of the balance sheet, which is the second purpose of the adjustments. No adjusting entry debits or credits Cash because the cash transactions are recorded earlier in the period. The end-of-period adjustment process is reserved for the noncash transactions that are required by accrual accounting. Exhibit 3-3 summarizes the adjusting entries.

Posting the Adjusting Entries _____

Exhibit 3-4 summarizes the adjusting entries of Air and Sea Travel at April 30. Panel A of the exhibit briefly describes the data for each adjustment, Panel B gives the adjusting entries, and Panel C shows the accounts. The adjustments are keyed by letter.

EXHIBIT 3-3 *Summary of Adjusting Entries*

Adjusting Entry	Type of Account Debited	Type of Account Credited
Prepaid expense, supplies	Expense	Prepaid expense, supplies (Asset)
Depreciation	Expense	Accumulated depreciation (Contra asset)
Accrued expenses	Expense	Payable (Liability)
Accrued revenues	Receivable (Asset)	Revenue
Unearned revenues	Unearned revenue (Liability)	Revenue

Adapted from Beverly Terry.

EXHIBIT 3-4   *Journalizing and Posting the Adjusting Entries*

Panel A—Information for Adjustments at April 30, 19X1

a. Accrued service revenue, $250.
b. Supplies on hand, $400.
c. Prepaid rent expired, $1,000.
d. Depreciation on furniture, $275.
e. Accrued salary expense, $950.
f. Amount of unearned service revenue that has been earned, $150.

Panel B—Adjusting Entries

a. Accounts Receivable 250
        Service Revenue   250
      To accrue service revenue.

b. Supplies Expense 300
        Supplies   300
      To record supplies used.

c. Rent Expense 1,000
        Prepaid Rent   1,000
      To record rent expense.

d. Depreciation Expense.......................... 275
        Accumulated Depreciation—Furniture........   275
      To record depreciation on furniture.

e. Salary Expense................................ 950
        Salary Payable   950
      To accrue salary expense.

f. Unearned Service Revenue..................... 150
        Service Revenue   150
      To record unearned revenue that has been earned.

Panel C—Ledger Accounts

Assets

Cash	
Bal. 24,800	

Accounts Receivable	
2,250	
(a) 250	
Bal. 2,500	

Supplies	
700	(b) 300
Bal. 400	

Prepaid Rent	
3,000	(c) 1,000
Bal. 2,000	

Furniture	
Bal. 16,500	

Accumulated Depreciation	
	(d) 275
	Bal. 275

Liabilities

Accounts Payable		Salary Payable		Unearned Service Revenue	
	Bal. 13,100	(e) 950		(f) 150	450
			Bal. 950		Bal. 300

Stockholders' Equity

Common Stock	Retained Earnings	Dividends
Bal. 20,000	Bal. 11,250	Bal. 3,200

Revenues

Service Revenue

	7,000
(a)	250
(f)	150
Bal.	7,400

Expenses

Rent Expense		Salary Expense		Supplies Expense	
(c) 1,000		950		(b) 300	
Bal. 1,000		(e) 950		Bal. 300	
		Bal. 1,900			

Depreciation Expense		Utilities Expense	
(d) 275		Bal. 400	
Bal. 275			

Adjusted Trial Balance

This chapter began with the trial balance before any adjusting entries—the unadjusted trial balance (Exhibit 3-1). After the adjustments are journalized and posted, the accounts appear as shown in Exhibit 3-4, Panel C. A useful step in preparing the financial statements is to list the accounts, along with their adjusted balances, on an **adjusted trial balance.** This document has the advantage of listing all the accounts and their adjusted balances in a single place. Exhibit 3-5 shows the preparation of the adjusted trial balance.

The format of Exhibit 3-5 is called a work sheet. We will take a long look at the accounting work sheet in the next chapter. For now simply note how clearly this format presents the data. The information in the Account Title column and in the Trial Balance columns is drawn directly from the trial balance. The two Adjustments columns list the debit and credit adjustments directly across from the appropriate account title. Each adjusting debit is identified by a letter in parentheses that refers back to the adjusting entry. For example, the debit labeled *a* on the worksheet refers back to the debit adjusting entry of $250 to Accounts Receivable in Panel B of Exhibit 3-4. Likewise for adjusting credits, the corresponding credit—labeled *a*—refers back to the $250 credit to Service Revenue.

OBJECTIVE 4

Prepare an adjusted trial balance

The Adjusted Trial Balance columns give the adjusted account balances. Each amount on the adjusted trial balance of Exhibit 3-5 is computed by combining the amounts from the unadjusted trial balance plus or minus the adjustments. For example, Accounts Receivable starts with a debit balance of $2,250. Adding the $250 debit amount from adjusting entry *a* gives Accounts Receivable an adjusted balance of $2,500. Supplies begins with a debit balance of $700. After the $300 credit adjustment, its adjusted balance is $400. More than one entry may affect a single account, as is the case for Service Revenue. If accounts are unaffected by the adjustments, they show the same amount on both trial balances. This is true for Cash, Furniture, Accounts Payable, and the Stockholders' Equity accounts.

EXHIBIT 3-5 *Preparation of Adjusted Trial Balance*

Air and Sea Travel, Inc.
Preparation of Adjusted Trial Balance
April 30, 19X1

Account Title	Trial Balance Debit	Trial Balance Credit	Adjustments Debit		Adjustments Credit		Adjusted Trial Balance Debit	Adjusted Trial Balance Credit
Cash	24,800						24,800	
Accounts receivable	2,250		(a)	250			2,500	
Supplies	700				(b)	300	400	
Prepaid rent	3,000				(c)	1,000	2,000	
Furniture	16,500						16,500	
Accumulated depreciation					(d)	275		275
Accounts payable		13,100						13,100
Salary payable					(e)	950		950
Unearned service revenue		450	(f)	150				300
Common stock		20,000						20,000
Retained earnings		11,250						11,250
Dividends	3,200						3,200	
Service revenue		7,000			(a)	250		7,400
					(f)	150		
Rent expense			(c)	1,000			1,000	
Salary expense	950		(e)	950			1,900	
Supplies expense			(b)	300			300	
Depreciation expense			(d)	275			275	
Utilities expense	400						400	
	51,800	51,800	2,925		2,925		53,275	53,275

Preparing the Financial Statements from the Adjusted Trial Balance

The April financial statements of Air and Sea Travel can be prepared from the information on the adjusted trial balance. Exhibit 3-6 shows how the accounts are distributed from the adjusted trial balance to the financial statements. The income statement (Exhibit 3-7) comes from the revenue and expense accounts. The statement of retained earnings (Exhibit 3-8) shows the reasons for the change in retained earnings during the period. The balance sheet (Exhibit 3-9) reports the assets, liabilities, and stockholders' equity.

Financial Statements

The accounts and the amounts for the income statement and the balance sheet are taken from the adjusted trial balance. The adjusted trial balance also provides the data for the statement of retained earnings. Exhibits 3-7, 3-8, and 3-9 illustrate these three financial statements, best prepared in the order shown: the income statement first, followed by the statement of retained earnings, and last, the balance sheet. The essential features of all financial statements are (1) the name of the entity, (2) the title of the statement, (3) the date or the period covered by the statement, and (4) the body of the statement.

EXHIBIT 3-6 Preparing the Financial Statements from the Adjusted Trial Balance

Account Title	Adjusted Trial Balance Debit	Adjusted Trial Balance Credit	
Cash	24,800		
Accounts receivable	2,500		
Supplies	400		
Prepaid rent	2,000		
Furniture	16,500		
Accumulated depreciation		275	Balance Sheet
Accounts payable		13,100	
Salary payable		950	
Unearned service revenue		300	
Common stock		20,000	
Retained earnings		11,250	Statement of
Dividends	3,200		Retained Earnings
Service revenue		7,400	
Rent expense	1,000		
Salary expense	1,900		
Supplies expense	300		Income Statement
Depreciation expense	275		
Utilities expense	400		
	53,275	53,275	

EXHIBIT 3-7 Income Statement

OBJECTIVE 5

Prepare the financial statements from the adjusted trial balance

Air and Sea Travel, Inc.
Income Statement
For the Month Ended April 30, 19X1

Revenue		
Service revenue..		$7,400
Expenses:		
Salary expense...	$1,900	
Rent expense...	1,000	
Utilities expense	400	
Supplies expense	300	
Depreciation expense.................................	275	
Total expenses...		3,875
Net income...		$3,525

EXHIBIT 3-8 Statement of Retained Earnings

Air and Sea Travel, Inc.
Statement of Retained Earnings
For the Month Ended April 30, 19X1

Retained earnings, April 1, 19X1	$11,250
Add: Net income	3,525
	14,775
Less: Dividends	3,200
Retained earnings, April 30, 19X1	$11,575

EXHIBIT 3-9 Balance Sheet

Air and Sea Travel, Inc.
Balance Sheet
April 30, 19X1

Assets			**Liabilities**		
Cash		$24,800	Accounts payable.......		$13,100
Accounts receivable.....		2,500	Salary payable..........		950
Supplies		400	Unearned service		
Prepaid rent		2,000	revenue		300
Furniture	$16,500		Total liabilities..........		14,350
Less Accumulated					
depreciation........	275	16,225	**Stockholders' Equity**		
			Common stock	$20,000	
			Retained earnings	11,575	
			Total stockholders'		
			equity		31,575
			Total liabilities and		
Total assets		$45,925	stockholders' equity ..		$45,925

On the income statement it is customary to list expenses in descending order by amount, as shown in Exhibit 3-7. However, Miscellaneous Expense, a catchall account for expenses that do not fit another category, is usually reported last regardless of its amount.

Relationships Among the Three Financial Statements _____

The arrows in Exhibits 3-7, 3-8, and 3-9 show the relationships among the income statement, the statement of retained earnings, and the balance sheet.

1. The income statement reports net income or net loss, figured by subtracting expenses from revenues. Because revenues and expenses are stockholders' equity accounts—subparts of Retained Earnings—their net figure is then transferred to the statement of retained earnings. Note that net income in Exhibit 3-7, $3,525, increases retained earnings in Exhibit 3-8. A net loss would decrease retained earnings.

2. Retained earnings is a balance sheet account, so the ending balance in the statement of retained earnings is transferred to the balance sheet. This amount is the final balancing element of the balance sheet. To solidify your understanding of this relationship, trace the $11,575 figure from Exhibit 3-8 to Exhibit 3-9.[1]

Microcomputers and the Accounting Process _____

Microcomputers have caused a revolution in the accounting departments of many companies. Like mainframe computers, these machines handle electronically much of the work done by hand in the past. Their prices continue to fall, enabling more small businesses to own one. Names like Apple, IBM PC, TRS, and Compaq have become almost household words.

Whether a system is manual or computerized, the steps in the accounting process are essentially the same: journalize transactions, post to the ledger, prepare the trial balance, make the adjustments, and present the financial statements. The ability of computers to perform mathematical operations rapidly and without errors comes in handy for such routine tasks as recording cash receipts and cash payments and keeping track of accounts receivable and accounts payable. Posting is also well suited for a computer because no analysis is involved. Debits in the journal are transferred as debits to the appropriate ledger accounts, and likewise for credits. The computer can be programmed to print the trial balance and the financial statements, relieving much of the tedium of preparing the statements. Accountants are freed up for decision making.

At any time during the period managers may request a forecast of the year's net income. The accountant can make several sets of estimates for the ending quantities of supplies, accrued salaries, unearned revenues, and all the other items that will be adjusted. Instantly the computer can produce several different sets of financial statements—one for each set of estimated data. Using these data managers can identify a lagging division in the business immediately, rather than at the end of the period, when the financial statements are issued. The manager can take steps needed to help the lagging division before its operations grow worse. Alternately, the company's bank may require forecasted financial statements before making a loan. Without a computer these forecasts may be expensive to obtain or even unavailable.

_____

[1]You may be wondering why the total assets on the balance sheet ($45,925 in Exhibit 3-9) do not equal the total debits on the adjusted trial balance ($53,275 in Exhibit 3-6). Likewise, the total liabilities and stockholders' equity on the balance sheet do not equal the total credits on the adjusted trial balance. The reason for these differences is that Accumulated Depreciation and Dividends are *subtracted* from their related accounts on the balance sheet but *added* in their respective columns on the adjusted trial balance.

Certain aspects of the accounting process almost demand the precision and speed of a computer. Weekly payrolls for example, require detailed computations on a regular basis—tailored to each employee's specific situation. Depreciation computations for a building with a 30-year useful life are complex and time-consuming. Computers greatly ease this work. As we progress through the study of accounting, we will point out computer applications that fit the topics under discussion.

Summary Problem for Your Review

The trial balance of Crane Service Co. pertains to December 31, 19X1, the end of its yearlong accounting period. Data needed for the adjusting entries are:

a. Supplies on hand at year end, $2,000.

b. Depreciation on furniture and fixtures, $20,000.

c. Depreciation on building, $10,000.

d. Salaries owed but not yet paid, $5,000.

e. Accrued service revenue, $12,000.

f. Of the $45,000 balance of unearned service revenue, $32,000 was earned during the year.

Crane Service Company
Trial Balance
December 31, 19X1

Cash	$ 198,000	
Accounts receivable	370,000	
Supplies	6,000	
Furniture and fixtures	100,000	
Accumulated depreciation—furniture and fixtures		$ 40,000
Building	250,000	
Accumulated depreciation—building		130,000
Accounts payable		380,000
Salary payable		
Unearned service revenue		45,000
Common stock		100,000
Retained earnings		193,000
Dividends	65,000	
Service revenue		286,000
Salary expense	172,000	
Supplies expense		
Depreciation expense—furniture and fixtures		
Depreciation expense—building		
Miscellaneous expense	13,000	
Total	$1,174,000	$1,174,000

Required

1. Open the ledger accounts with their unadjusted balances. Show dollar amounts in thousands (for example, the Accounts Receivable amount of $370,000 becomes a debit of 370).

2. Journalize Crane Service Company's adjusting entries at December 31, 19X1. Key entries by letter as in Exhibit 3-4.

3. Post the adjusting entries.

4. Write the trial balance on a sheet of paper, enter the adjusting entries, and prepare an adjusted trial balance, as shown in Exhibit 3-5.

5. Prepare the income statement, the statement of retained earnings, and the balance sheet. Draw the arrows linking the three statements.

SOLUTION TO REVIEW PROBLEM

Requirements 1 and 3

Assets

Cash	
Bal. 198	

Accounts Receivable	
370	
(e) 12	
Bal. 382	

Supplies	
6	(a) 4
Bal. 2	

Furniture and Fixtures	
Bal. 100	

Accumulated Depreciation— Furniture and Fixtures	
	40
	(b) 20
	Bal. 60

Building	
Bal. 250	

Accumulated Depreciation— Building	
	130
	(c) 10
	Bal. 140

Liabilities

Accounts Payable	
	Bal. 380

Salary Payable	
	(d) 5
	Bal. 5

Unearned Service Revenue	
(f) 32	45
	Bal. 13

Stockholders' Equity

Common Stock	
	Bal. 100

Retained Earnings	
	Bal. 193

Dividends	
Bal. 65	

Revenues

Service Revenue	
	286
	(e) 12
	(f) 32
	Bal. 330

Expenses

Salary Expense	
172	
(d) 5	
Bal. 177	

Supplies Expense	
(a) 4	
Bal. 4	

Depreciation Expense— Furniture and Fixtures	
(b) 20	
Bal. 20	

Depreciation Expense— Building	
(c) 10	
Bal. 10	

Miscellaneous Expense	
Bal. 13	

Requirement 2

	19X1			
a.	Dec. 31	Supplies Expense ($6,000 − $2,000)	4,000	
		Supplies		4,000
		To record supplies used.		

b.	31	Depreciation Expense—

b. 31 Depreciation Expense—
Furniture and Fixtures.................... 20,000
    Accumulated Depreciation—
    Furniture and Fixtures 20,000
To record depreciation expense on furniture
and fixtures.

c. 31 Depreciation Expense—Building............ 10,000
    Accumulated Depreciation—
    Building 10,000
To record depreciation expense on building.

d. 31 Salary Expense 5,000
    Salary Payable 5,000
To accrue salary expense.

e. 31 Accounts Receivable...................... 12,000
    Service Revenue 12,000
To accrue service revenue.

f. 31 Unearned Service Revenue................. 32,000
    Service Revenue 32,000
To record unearned service revenue that has
been earned.

Requirement 4

Crane Service Company
Preparation of Adjusted Trial Balance
December 31, 19X1
(amounts in thousands)

	Trial Balance		Adjustments		Adjusted Trial Balance	
	Debit	Credit	Debit	Credit	Debit	Credit
Cash	198				198	
Accounts receivable	370		(e) 12		382	
Supplies	6			(a) 4	2	
Furniture and fixtures	100				100	
Accumulated depreciation— furniture and fixtures		40		(b) 20		60
Building	250				250	
Accumulated depreciation—building		130		(c) 10		140
Accounts payable		380				380
Salary payable				(d) 5		5
Unearned service revenue		45	(f) 32			13
Common stock		100				100
Retained earnings		193				193
Dividends	65				65	
Service revenue		286		(e) 12 (f) 32		330
Salary expense	172		(d) 5		177	
Supplies expense			(a) 4		4	
Depreciation expense— furniture and fixtures			(b) 20		20	
Depreciation expense— building			(c) 10		10	
Miscellaneous expense	13				13	
	1,174	1,174	83	83	1,221	1,221

Requirement 5

Crane Service Company
Income Statement
For the Year Ended December 31, 19X1
(amounts in thousands)

Revenues:
   Service revenue $330
Expenses:
   Salary expense $177
   Depreciation expense—furniture &
      fixtures   20
   Depreciation expense—building   10
   Supplies expense   4
   Miscellaneous expense   13
   Total expenses   224
Net income $106

Crane Service Company
Statement of Retained Earnings
For the Year Ended December 31, 19X1
(amounts in thousands)

Retained earnings, January 1, 19X1 .... $193
Add: Net income   106
                                        299
Less: Dividends   65
Retained earnings, December 31, 19X1 ..... $234

Crane Service Company
Balance Sheet
December 31, 19X1
(amounts in thousands)

Assets			Liabilities		
Cash		$198	Accounts payable		$380
Accounts receivable		382	Salary payable		5
Supplies		2	Unearned service		
Furniture and fixtures	$100		revenue		13
Less Accumulated			Total liabilities		398
depreciation	60	40			
Building	250		**Stockholders' Equity**		
Less Accumulated			Common stock	$100	
depreciation	140	110	Retained earnings	234	
			Total stockholders'		
			equity		334
			Total liabilities and		
Total assets		$732	stockholders' equity		$732

Summary

In *accrual-basis accounting,* business events are recorded as they affect the entity. In *cash-basis accounting,* only those events that affect cash are recorded. The cash basis omits important events such as purchases and sales of assets on account. It also distorts the financial statements by labeling as expenses those cash payments that have long-term effects, like the purchases of buildings and equipment. Some small organizations use cash-basis accounting, but the generally accepted method is the accrual basis.

Accountants divide time into definite periods—such as a month, a quarter, and a year—to report the entity's financial statements. The year is the basic *accounting period,* but companies prepare financial statements as often as they need the information. Accountants have developed the *revenue principle* to determine when to record revenue and the amount of revenue to record. The *matching principle* guides the accounting for expenses. *Adjusting entries* are a result of the accrual basis of accounting. These entries, made at the end of the accounting period, update the accounts for preparation of the financial statements. One of the most important pieces of accounting information is net income or net loss, and the adjusting entries help to measure the *net income* of the period.

Adjusting entries can be divided into five categories: *prepaid expenses, depreciation, accrued expenses, accrued revenues,* and *unearned revenues.* To prepare the *adjusted trial balance,* enter the adjusting entries next to the *unadjusted trial balance.* This document can be used to prepare the income statement, the statement of retained earnings, and the balance sheet.

These three financial statements are related as follows: Income, shown on the *income statement,* increases retained earnings, which also appears on the *statement of retained earnings.* The ending balance of retained earnings is the last amount reported on the *balance sheet.*

Computers can aid the accounting process in a number of ways, chiefly by performing routine operations. Many adjusting entries, however, require analysis that is best done manually, without the computer.

Self-Study Questions

Test your understanding of the chapter by marking the best answer for each of the following questions.

1. Accrual-basis accounting *(p. 105)*
   a. Results in higher income than cash-basis accounting
   b. Leads to the reporting of more complete information than does cash-basis accounting
   c. Is not acceptable under GAAP
   d. Omits adjusting entries at the end of the period
2. Under the revenue principle, revenue is recorded *(p. 106)*
   a. At the earliest acceptable time
   b. At the latest acceptable time
   c. After it has been earned, but not before
   d. At the end of the accounting period
3. The matching principle provides guidance in accounting for *(p. 107)*
   a. Expenses   c. Assets
   b. Stockholders' equity   d. Liabilities
4. Adjusting entries *(p. 109)*
   a. Assign revenues to the period in which they are earned
   b. Help to properly measure the period's net income or net loss
   c. Bring asset and liability accounts to correct balances
   d. All of the above

5. A law firm began November with office supplies of $160. During the month, the firm purchased supplies of $290. At November 30 supplies on hand total $210. Supplies expense for the period is *(p. 111)*
   a. $210   c. $290
   √ b. $240   d. $450

6. A building that cost $120,000 has accumulated depreciation of $50,000. The book value of the building is *(pp. 113–114)*
   a. $50,000   c. $120,000
   √ b. $70,000   d. $170,000

7. The adjusting entry to accrue salary expense *(p. 115)*
   a. Debits Salary Expense and credits Cash
   b. Debits Salary Payable and credits Salary Expense
   c. Debits Salary Payable and credits Cash
   √ d. Debits Salary Expense and credits Salary Payable

8. A business received cash of $3,000 in advance for service that will be provided later. The cash receipt entry debited Cash and credited Unearned Revenue for $3,000. At the end of the period, $1,100 is still unearned. The adjusting entry for this situation will *(pp. 116–117)*
   √ a. Debit Unearned Revenue and credit Revenue for $1,900
   b. Debit Unearned Revenue and credit Revenue for $1,100
   c. Debit Revenue and credit Unearned Revenue for $1,900
   d. Debit Revenue and credit Unearned Revenue for $1,100

9. The links between the financial statements are *(pp. 121–122)*
   a. Net income from the income statement to the statement of retained earnings
   √ b. Ending retained earnings from the statement of retained earnings to the balance sheet
   c. Both of the above
   d. None of the above

10. Accumulated Depreciation is reported on the *(p. 122)*
    √ a. Balance sheet   c. Statement of retained earnings
    b. Income statement   d. Both a and b

Answers to the Self-Study Questions follow the Accounting Vocabulary.

Accounting Vocabulary

Accrual-basis accounting. Accounting that recognizes (records) the impact of a business event as it occurs, regardless of whether the transaction affected cash *(pp. 104–105)*.

Accrued expense. An expense that has been incurred but not yet paid in cash *(p. 114)*.

Accrued revenue. A revenue that has been earned but not yet received in cash *(p. 115)*.

Accumulated depreciation. The cumulative sum of all depreciation expense from the date of acquiring a plant asset *(p. 113)*.

Adjusted trial balance. A list of all the ledger accounts with their adjusted balances *(p. 119)*.

Adjusting entry. Entry made at the end of the period to assign revenues to the period in which they are earned and expenses to the period in which they are incurred. Adjusting entries help measure the period's income and bring the related asset and liability accounts to correct balances for the financial statements *(p. 109)*.

Book value of a plant asset. The asset's cost less accumulated depreciation *(p. 113)*.

Cash-basis accounting. Accounting that records only transactions in which cash is received or paid *(p. 105)*.

Contra account. An account with two distinguishing characteristics: (1) it always has a companion account, and (2) its normal balance is opposite that of the companion account *(p. 113)*.

Contra asset. An asset account with a normal credit balance. A contra account always has a companion account and its balance is opposite that of the companion account *(p. 113)*.

Depreciation. Expense associated with spreading (allocating) the cost of a plant asset over its useful life *(p. 112)*.

Matching principle. The basis for recording expenses. Directs accountants to identify all expenses incurred during the period, to measure the expenses, and to match them against the revenues earned during that same span of time *(p. 107)*.

Plant asset. Long-lived assets, like land, buildings, and equipment, used in the operation of the business *(p. 112)*.

Prepaid expense. A category of miscellaneous assets that typically expire or get used up in the near future. Examples include prepaid rent, prepaid insurance, and supplies *(p. 109)*.

Revenue principle. The basis for recording revenues, tells accountants when to record revenue and the amount of revenue to record *(p. 106)*.

Unearned revenue. A liability created when a business collects cash from customers in advance of doing work for the customer. The obligation is to provide a product or a service in the future. Also called Deferred revenue *(p. 116)*.

Answers to Self-Study Questions

1. b
2. c
3. a

4. d
5. b ($160 + $290 − $210 = $240)

6. b ($120,000 − $50,000 = $70,000)
7. d
8. a ($3,000 received − $1,100 unearned = $1,900 earned)
9. c
10. a

ASSIGNMENT MATERIAL _____

Questions

1. Distinguish the accrual basis of accounting from the cash basis.
2. How long is the basic accounting period? What is a fiscal year? What is an interim period?
3. What two questions does the revenue principle help answer?
4. Briefly explain the matching principle.
5. What is the purpose of making adjusting entries?
6. Why are adjusting entries made at the end of the accounting period, not during the period?
7. Name five categories of adjusting entries and give an example of each.
8. Do all adjusting entries affect the net income or net loss of the period? Include in your answer the definition of an adjusting entry.
9. Why does the balance of Supplies need to be adjusted at the end of the period?
10. Manning Supply Company pays $1,800 for an insurance policy that covers three years. At the end of the first year, the balance of its Prepaid Insurance account contains two elements. What are the two elements, and what is the correct amount of each?
11. The title Prepaid Expense suggests that this type of account is an expense. If so, explain why. If not, what type of account is it?

12. What is a contra account? Identify the contra account introduced in this chapter, along with the account's normal balance.

13. The manager of a Quickie-Pickie convenience store presents his entity's balance sheet to a banker to obtain a loan. The balance sheet reports that the entity's plant assets have a book value of $135,000 and accumulated depreciation of $65,000. What does *book value* of a plant asset mean? What was the cost of the plant assets?

14. Give the entry to record accrued interest revenue of $800.

15. Why is an unearned revenue a liability? Use an example in your answer.

16. Identify the types of accounts (assets, liabilities, and so on) debited and credited for the five types of adjusting entries.

17. What purposes does the adjusted trial balance serve?

18. Explain the relationship among the income statement, the statement of retained earnings, and the balance sheet.

19. Bellevue Company failed to record the following adjusting entries at December 31, the end of its fiscal year: (a) accrued expenses, $500; (b) accrued revenues, $850; and (c) depreciation, $1,000. Did these omissions cause net income for the year to be understated or overstated and by what overall amount?

20. Identify several accounting tasks for which it is efficient to use a micro-computer. What is the basic limitation on the use of a computer?

Exercises

Exercise 3-1 *Cash basis versus accrual basis* **(L.O. 1)**

The Oak Lodge had the following selected transactions during August:

Aug. 1 Prepaid damage and liability insurance for the year, $6,000.
    5 Paid electricity expenses, $700.
    9 Received cash for the day's room rentals, $1,400.
   31 Purchased six television sets, $3,000.
   31 Served a banquet, receiving a note receivable, $1,200.
   31 Made an adjusting entry for insurance expense (from Aug. 1).

Show how each transaction would be handled using the cash basis and the accrual basis. Under each column give the amount of revenue or expense for August. Journal entries are not required. Use the following format for your answer, and show your computations:

	Amount of Revenue or Expense for August	
Date	**Cash Basis**	**Accrual Basis**

Exercise 3-2 *Applying accounting concepts and principles* **(L.O. 2)**

Identify the accounting concept or principle that gives the most direction on how to account for each of the following situations:

a. Expenses of $2,600 must be accrued at the end of the period to properly measure income.

b. A customer states her intention to shift her business to a travel agency. Should the travel agency record revenue based on this intention?

c. The owners of a business desire monthly financial statements to measure the progress of the entity on an ongoing basis.

d. Expenses of the period total $6,100. This amount should be subtracted from revenue to compute the period's income.

Exercise 3-3 *Applying accounting concepts* **(L.O. 2)**

Write a short paragraph to explain in your own words the concept of depreciation as it is used in accounting.

Exercise 3-4 *Allocating prepaid expense to the asset and the expense* **(L.O. 2)**

Compute the amounts indicated by question marks for each of the following Prepaid Rent situations. Consider each situation separately.

	Situation			
	1	**2**	**3**	**4**
Beginning Prepaid Rent	$ 300	$ 500	$ 600	$ 900
Payments for Prepaid Rent during the year	900	?	?	1,100
Total amount to account for	?	?	1,500	2,000
Ending Prepaid Rent.................	200	600	500	?
Rent Expense	$?	$ 300	$1,000	$1,600

Exercise 3-5 *Journalizing adjusting entries* **(L.O. 3)**

Journalize the entries for the following adjustments at December 31, the end of the accounting period.

a. Interest revenue accrued, $4,100.
b. Unearned service revenue earned, $800.
c. Depreciation, $6,200.
d. Employee salaries owed for two days of a five-day workweek; weekly payroll, $9,000.
e. Prepaid insurance expired, $450.

Exercise 3-6 *Analyzing the effects of adjustments on net income.* **(L.O. 3)**

Suppose the adjustments required in Exercise 3-5 were not made. Compute the overall overstatement or understatement of net income as a result of the omission of these adjustments.

Exercise 3-7 *Recording adjustments in T-accounts* **(L.O. 3)**

The accounting records of Galvez Art Supply include the following unadjusted balances at May 31: Accounts Receivable, $1,200; Supplies, $600; Salary Payable, $0; Unearned Service Revenue, $400; Service Revenue, $5,100; Salary Expense, $1,200; Supplies Expense, $0.

Galvez's accountant develops the following data for the May 31 adjusting entries:

a. Supplies on hand, $100.
b. Salary owed to employee, $400.
c. Service revenue accrued, $350.
d. Unearned service revenue that has been earned, $250.

Open the foregoing T-accounts and record the adjustments directly in the accounts, keying each adjustment amount by letter. Show each account's adjusted balance. Journal entries are not required.

Exercise 3-8 *Adjusting the accounts* **(L.O. 3,4)**

Preparation of the Pack-n-Mail Service adjusted trial balance is incomplete. Enter the adjustment amounts directly in the adjustment columns of the text. Service Revenue is the only account affected by more than one adjustment.

Pack-n-Mail Service, Inc.
Preparation of Adjusted Trial Balance
October 31, 19X2

Account Title	Trial Balance Debit	Trial Balance Credit	Adjustments Debit	Adjustments Credit	Adjusted Trial Balance Debit	Adjusted Trial Balance Credit
Cash	3,000				3,000	
Accounts receivable	6,500				7,100	
Supplies	1,040				800	
Office furniture	19,300				19,300	
Accumulated depreciation		11,060				11,320
Salary payable						600
Unearned revenue		900				690
Common stock		10,000				10,000
Retained earnings		6,340				6,340
Dividends	6,200				6,200	
Service revenue		11,830				12,640
Salary expense	2,690				3,290	
Rent expense	1,400				1,400	
Depreciation expense					260	
Supplies expense					240	
	40,130	40,130			41,590	41,590

Exercise 3-9 *Journalizing adjustments* **(L.O. 3, 4)**

Make journal entries for the adjustments that would complete the preparation of the adjusted trial balance in Exercise 3-8. Include explanations.

Exercise 3-10 *Preparing the financial statements* **(L.O. 5)**

Refer to the adjusted trial balance in Exercise 3-8. Prepare Pack-n-Mail Service, Inc.'s, income statement and statement of retained earnings for the three months ended October 31, 19X2, and its balance sheet on that date. Draw the arrows linking the three statements.

Exercise 3-11 *Preparing the financial statements* **(L.O. 5)**

The accountant for MediCenter, Inc., has posted adjusting entries *a* through *e* to the accounts at September 30, 19X2. Selected balance sheet accounts and all the revenues and expenses of the entity are listed here in T-account form.

Accounts Receivable		Supplies		Accumulated Depreciation–Furniture	
23,000		4,000	(a) 2,000		5,000
(e) 4,500					(b) 3,000

Accumulated Depreciation–Building		Salary Payable		Service Revenue	
	33,000		(d) 1,500		135,000
	(c) 4,000				(e) 4,500

Salary Expense		Supplies Expense		Depreciation Expense–Furniture		Depreciation Expense–Building	
28,000		(a) 2,000		(b) 3,000		(c) 4,000	
(d) 1,500							

Required

Prepare the income statement of MediCenter, Inc., for the year ended September 30, 19X2. List expenses in order from the largest to the smallest.

Exercise 3-12 *Computing financial statement amounts* **(L.O. 5)**

The adjusted trial balances of Oakmont Corporation at December 31, 19X8, and December 31, 19X7, include these amounts:

	19X8	19X7
Supplies.....................	$ 1,500	$ 1,100
Salary payable	3,400	3,700
Unearned service revenue.....	17,200	16,300

Analysis of the Cash account at December 31, 19X8, reveals these cash disbursements and cash receipts for 19X8.

Cash disbursements for supplies	$ 9,100
Cash disbursements for salaries	84,800
Cash receipts for service revenue	731,200

Compute the amount of supplies expense, salary expense, and service revenue to report on the 19X8 income statement.

Problems

(Group A)

Problem 3-1A *Cash basis versus accrual basis* **(L.O. 1,2)**

Temporary Manpower Services experienced the following selected transactions during January:

Jan. 1 Prepaid insurance for January through March, $600.
   4 Purchased office equipment for cash, $1,400.
   5 Received cash for services performed, $900.
   8 Paid gas bill, $300.
   12 Performed services on account, $1,000.
   14 Purchased office equipment on account, $300.
   28 Collected $500 on account from January 12.
   31 Paid salary expense, $1,100.
   31 Paid account payable from January 14.
   31 Recorded adjusting entry for January insurance expense (see Jan. 1).

Required

1. Show how each transaction would be handled using the cash basis and the accrual basis. Under each column give the amount of revenue or expense for January. Journal entries are not required. Use the following format for your answer, and show your computations:

	Amount of Revenue or Expense for January	
Date	Cash Basis	Accrual Basis

2. Compute January net income or net loss under each method.
3. Indicate which measure of net income or net loss is preferable. Give your reason.

Problem 3-2A *Applying accounting principles* (L.O. 2)

Write a short memo to contrast the cash basis of accounting with the accrual basis. Mention the roles of the revenue principle and the matching principle in accrual accounting.

Problem 3-3A *Journalizing adjusting entries* (L.O. 3)

Journalize the adjusting entry needed on December 31, end of the current accounting period, for each of the following independent cases affecting Windsor Construction Contractors.

a. Windsor pays its employees each Friday. The amount of the weekly payroll is $2,100 for a five-day workweek, and the daily salary amounts are equal. The current accounting period ends on Monday.
b. Windsor has loaned money, receiving notes receivable. During the current year the entity has earned accrued interest revenue of $737 that it will receive next year.
c. The beginning balance of Supplies was $2,680. During the year the entity purchased supplies costing $6,180, and at December 31 the inventory of supplies on hand is $2,150.
d. Windsor is servicing the air-conditioning system in a large building, and the owner of the building paid Windsor $12,900 as the annual service fee. Windsor recorded this amount as Unearned Service Revenue. Ralph Windsor, the owner, estimates that the company has earned one-fourth of the total fee during the current year.
e. Depreciation for the current year includes: Office Furniture, $650; Equipment, $3,850; Trucks, $10,320. Make a compound entry.
f. Details of Prepaid Rent are shown in the account:

Prepaid Rent		
Jan. 1 Bal.	600	
Mar. 31	1,200	
Sep. 30	1,200	

Windsor pays office rent semiannually on March 31 and September 30. At December 31, $600 of the last payment is still an asset.

Problem 3-4A *Analyzing and journalizing adjustments* *(L.O. 3)*

Patricia Wood Court Reporting Company's unadjusted and adjusted trial balances at April 30, 19X1, are as follows:

Patricia Wood Court Reporting Company
Adjusted Trial Balance
April 30, 19X1

Account Title	Trial Balance		Adjusted Trial Balance	
	Debit	Credit	Debit	Credit
Cash	8,180		8,180	
Accounts receivable	6,360		6,540	
Interest receivable			300	
Note receivable	4,100		4,100	
Supplies	980		290	
Prepaid rent	1,440		720	
Building	66,450		66,450	
Accumulated depreciation		14,970		16,070
Accounts payable		6,920		6,920
Wages payable				320
Unearned service revenue		670		110
Common stock		25,000		25,000
Retained earnings		35,770		35,770
Dividends	3,600		3,600	
Service revenue		9,940		10,680
Interest revenue				300
Wage expense	1,600		1,920	
Rent expense			720	
Depreciation expense			1,100	
Insurance expense	370		370	
Supplies expense			690	
Utilities expense	190		190	
	93,270	93,270	95,170	95,170

Required

Journalize the adjusting entries that account for the differences between the two trial balances.

Problem 3-5A *Journalizing and posting adjustments to T-accounts; preparing the adjusted trial balance* *(L.O. 3,4)*

The trial balance of Insurors of Texas at October 31, 19X2, and the data needed for the month-end adjustments follow.

Adjustment data:

a. Prepaid rent still in force at October 31, $400.
b. Supplies used during the month, $440.

c. Depreciation for the month, $700.

d. Accrued advertising expense at October 31, $320. (Credit Accounts Payable.)

e. Accrued salary expense at October 31, $180.

f. Unearned commission revenue still unearned at October 31, $2,000.

Required

1. Open T-accounts for the accounts listed in the trial balance, inserting their October 31 unadjusted balances.

Insurors of Texas, Inc. **Trial Balance** **October 31, 19X2**		
Cash	$1,460	
Accounts receivable	14,750	
Prepaid rent....................	3,100	
Supplies	780	
Furniture	22,370	
Accumulated depreciation		$11,640
Accounts payable		1,940
Salary payable..................		
Unearned commission revenue ..		2,290
Common Stock		10,000
Retained earnings		14,140
Dividends......................	2,900	
Commission revenue............		8,580
Salary expense	2,160	
Rent expense...................		
Utilities expense	340	
Depreciation expense		
Advertising expense	730	
Supplies expense		
Total	$48,590	$48,590

---

2. Journalize the adjusting entries and post them to the T-accounts. Key the journal entries and the posted amounts by letter.

3. Prepare the adjusted trial balance.

Problem 3-6A *Preparing the financial statements from an adjusted trial balance*
(L.O. 5)

The adjusted trial balance of Tradewinds Travel Designers at December 31, 19X6, is shown on page 138.

Required

Prepare Tradewinds' 19X6 income statement, statement of retained earnings, and balance sheet. List expenses in decreasing order on the income statement and show total liabilities on the balance sheet. Draw the arrows linking the three financial statements.

Tradewinds Travel Designers, Inc.
Adjusted Trial Balance
December 31, 19X6

Cash	$ 3,320	
Accounts receivable	11,920	
Supplies	2,300	
Prepaid rent....................	600	
Office equipment	33,180	
Accumulated depreciation—office equipment		$16,350
Office furniture................	27,680	
Accumulated depreciation—office furniture		4,870
Accounts payable		3,640
Property tax payable		1,100
Interest payable		830
Unearned service revenue		620
Note payable...................		27,500
Common stock		10,000
Retained earnings		6,090
Dividends.....................	44,000	
Service revenue		127,880
Depreciation expense—office equipment	6,680	
Depreciation expense—office furniture	2,370	
Salary expense	39,900	
Rent expense..................	14,400	
Interest expense	3,100	
Utilities expense	2,670	
Insurance expense	3,810	
Supplies expense	2,950	
Total	$198,880	$198,880

Problem 3-7A *Preparing an adjusted trial balance and the financial statements (L.O. 3,4,5)*

The unadjusted trial balance of Joe Heider, Attorney, Professional Corporation, at July 31, 19X2, and the related month-end adjustment data are as follows:

Adjustment data:

a. Prepaid rent expired during the month. The unadjusted prepaid balance of $3,600 relates to the period July through October.
b. Supplies on hand at July 31, $500.
c. Depreciation on furniture for the month. The estimated useful life of the furniture is four years.
d. Accrued salary expense at July 31 for one day only. The five-day weekly payroll is $1,000.
e. Accrued legal service revenue at July 31, $700.

Required

1. Write the trial balance on a sheet of paper similar to Exhibit 3-5 and prepare the adjusted trial balance of Joe Heider, Attorney, P.C., at July 31, 19X2. Key each adjusting entry by letter.

2. Prepare the income statement, the statement of retained earnings, and the balance sheet. Draw the arrows linking the three financial statements.

Joe Heider, Attorney, P.C.
Trial Balance
July 31, 19X2

Cash	$14,600	
Accounts receivable	11,600	
Prepaid rent....................	3,600	
Supplies	800	
Furniture	16,800	
Accumulated depreciation		$ 3,500
Accounts payable		3,450
Salary payable.................		
Common Stock		25,000
Retained earnings		13,650
Dividends.....................	4,000	
Legal service revenue		8,750
Salary expense	2,400	
Rent expense...................		
Utilities expense	550	
Depreciation expense		
Supplies expense		
Total	$54,350	$54,350

Problem 3-8A *Journalizing and posting adjustments to four-column accounts; preparing the adjusted trial balance and the financial statements* **(L.O. 3,4,5)**

The trial balance of Foster Cleaning Service at July 31, 19X3, is shown on page 140, and the data needed to make the year-end adjustments are as follows:

Adjustment data:

a. At July 31 the business has earned $1,420 of service revenue that has not yet been recorded.

b. Supplies used during the year totaled $3,060.

c. Prepaid rent still in force at July 31 is $1,040.

d. Depreciation for the year is based on cleaning equipment costing $37,300 and an estimated useful life of 10 years.

e. The entity cleans the carpets of a large apartment complex that pays in advance. At July 31 the entity has earned $2,210 of the unadjusted balance of Unearned Service Revenue.

f. At July 31 the business owes its employees accrued salaries for two-thirds of a four-week payroll. Total payroll for the four weeks is $2,670.

Required

1. Open the accounts listed in the trial balance, inserting their July 31 unadjusted balances. Use four-column accounts. The following accounts have experienced no activity during the month, so their balances should be dated July 1: Supplies, Prepaid Rent, Accumulated Depreciation, and Unearned Service Revenue.

2. Journalize the adjusting entries, using page 4 of the journal.

3. Post the adjusting entries to the ledger accounts, using all posting references.

Foster Cleaning Service, Inc.
Trial Balance
July 31, 19X3

Account No.			
101	Cash	$ 1,010	
121	Accounts receivable	6,200	
131	Supplies	3,400	
133	Prepaid rent	1,890	
141	Cleaning equipment	37,300	
151	Accumulated depreciation		$ 14,360
201	Accounts payable		6,410
211	Salary payable		
221	Unearned service revenue		3,110
301	Common Stock		8,000
302	Retained earnings		6,310
303	Dividends	40,100	
401	Service revenue		91,060
501	Salary expense	32,150	
504	Depreciation expense		
506	Supplies expense		
509	Rent expense	6,000	
511	Utilities expense	1,200	
	Total	$129,250	$129,250

4. Prepare the adjusted trial balance at July 31.
5. Prepare the income statement, the statement of retained earnings, and the balance sheet. Draw the arrows linking the three financial statements.

(Group B)

Problem 3-1B *Cash basis versus accrual basis* **(L.O. 1,2)**

Samaritan Counseling Service had the following selected transactions during October:

Oct. 1 Prepaid insurance for October through December, $450.
   4 Purchased office equipment for cash, $800.
   5 Performed counseling services and received cash, $700.
   8 Paid advertising expense, $100.
   11 Performed counseling service on account, $1,200.
   19 Purchased office furniture on account, $150.
   24 Collected $400 on account for the October 11 service.
   31 Paid account payable from October 19.
   31 Paid salary expense, $600.
   31 Recorded adjusting entry for October insurance expense (see Oct. 1).

Required

1. Show how each transaction would be handled using the cash basis and the accrual basis. Under each column give the amount of revenue or expense for October. Journal entries are not required. Use the following format for your answer, and show your computations:

Amount of Revenue or Expense for October		
Date	Cash Basis	Accrual Basis

2. Compute October net income or net loss under each method.
3. Indicate which measure of net income or net loss is preferable. Give your reason.

Problem 3-2B Applying accounting principles (L.O. 2)

As the controller of Hillsborough Auto Glass Company, you have hired a new bookkeeper, whom you must train. Write a memo to explain why adjusting entries are needed to measure net income properly. Mention the accounting principles underlying the use of adjusting entries.

Problem 3-3B Journalizing adjusting entries (L.O. 3)

Journalize the adjusting entry needed on December 31, end of the current accounting period, for each of the following independent cases affecting Randolph Engineering Consulting Company.

a. Each Friday Randolph pays its employees for the current week's work. The amount of the payroll is $2,500 for a five-day work week. The current accounting period ends on Thursday.

b. Randolph has received notes receivable from some clients for professional services. During the current year, Randolph has earned accrued interest revenue of $8,575, which will be received next year.

c. The beginning balance of Engineering Supplies was $3,800. During the year the entity purchased supplies costing $12,530, and at December 31 the inventory of supplies on hand is $2,970.

d. Randolph is conducting tests of the strength of the steel to be used in a large building, and the client paid Randolph $27,000 at the start of the project. Randolph recorded this amount as Unearned Engineering Revenue. The tests will take several months to complete. Randolph executives estimate that the company has earned two-thirds of the total fee during the current year.

e. Depreciation for the current year includes: Office Furniture, $4,500; Engineering Equipment, $6,360; Building, $3,790. Make a compound entry.

f. Details of Prepaid Insurance are shown in the account:

Prepaid Insurance	
Jan. 1 Bal. 2,400	
Apr. 30 3,600	
Oct. 31 3,600	

Randolph pays semiannual insurance premiums (the payment for insurance coverage is called a *premium*) on April 30 and October 31. At December 31, $2,400 of the last payment is still in force.

Problem 3-4B Analyzing and journalizing adjustments (L.O. 3)

Ahmed Rashad Commission Sales Company's unadjusted and adjusted trial balances at December 31, 19X0, are shown on the following page.

Required

Journalize the adjusting entries that account for the differences between the two trial balances.

Ahmed Rashad Commission Sales Company
Adjusted Trial Balance
December 31, 19X0

Account Title	Trial Balance		Adjusted Trial Balance	
	Debit	Credit	Debit	Credit
Cash	3,620		3,620	
Accounts receivable	11,260		14,090	
Supplies	1,090		780	
Prepaid insurance	2,200		1,330	
Office furniture	21,630		21,630	
Accumulated depreciation		8,220		10,500
Accounts payable		6,310		6,310
Salary payable				960
Interest payable				280
Note payable		12,000		12,000
Unearned commission revenue		1,440		960
Common stock		5,000		5,000
Retained earnings		8,010		8,010
Dividends	29,370		29,370	
Commission revenue		72,890		76,200
Depreciation expense			2,280	
Supplies expense			310	
Utilities expense	4,960		4,960	
Salary expense	26,660		27,620	
Rent expense	12,200		12,200	
Interest expense	880		1,160	
Insurance expense			870	
	113,870	113,870	120,220	120,220

Problem 3-5B *Journalizing and posting adjustments to T-accounts; preparing the adjusted trial balance* **(L.O. 3,4)**

The trial balance of Griffin Realty, Inc., at August 31 of the current year is shown on the following page. The data needed for the month-end adjustments are:

a. Prepaid rent still in force at August 31, $620.
b. Supplies used during the month, $300.
c. Depreciation for the month, $400.
d. Accrued advertising expense at August 31, $110. (Credit Accounts Payable.)
e. Accrued salary expense at August 31, $550.
f. Unearned commission revenue still unearned at August 31, $1,670.

Required

1. Open T-accounts for the accounts listed in the trial balance, inserting their August 31 unadjusted balances.
2. Journalize the adjusting entries and post them to the T-accounts. Key the journal entries and the posted amounts by letter.
3. Prepare the adjusted trial balance.

Griffin Realty, Inc.
Trial Balance
August 31, 19X6

Cash	$ 2,200	
Accounts receivable	23,780	
Prepaid rent	2,420	
Supplies	1,180	
Furniture	19,740	
Accumulated depreciation		$ 3,630
Accounts payable		2,410
Salary payable		
Unearned commission revenue		2,790
Common stock		15,000
Retained earnings		24,510
Dividends	4,800	
Commission revenue		11,700
Salary expense	3,800	
Rent expense		
Utilities expense	550	
Depreciation expense		
Advertising expense	1,570	
Supplies expense		
Total	$60,040	$60,040

Problem 3-6B *Preparing the financial statements from an adjusted trial balance*
(L.O. 5)

The adjusted trial balance of Blaine Delivery Services at December 31, 19X8
follows:

Blaine Delivery Service, Inc.
Adjusted Trial Balance
December 31, 19X8

Cash	$ 8,340	
Accounts receivable	41,490	
Prepaid rent	1,350	
Supplies	970	
Equipment	70,690	
Accumulated depreciation—equipment		$ 22,240
Office furniture	24,100	
Accumulated depreciation—office furniture		18,670
Accounts payable		13,600
Unearned service revenue		4,520
Interest payable		2,130
Salary payable		930
Note payable		40,000
Common stock		12,000
Retained earnings		20,380
Dividends	48,000	
Service revenue		201,790
Depreciation expense—equipment	11,300	
Depreciation expense—office furniture	2,410	
Salary expense	102,800	
Rent expense	12,000	
Interest expense	4,200	
Utilities expense	3,770	
Insurance expense	3,150	
Supplies expense	1,690	
Total	$336,260	$336,260

Required

Prepare Blaine's 19X8 income statement, statement of retained earnings, and balance sheet. List expenses in decreasing order on the income statement and show total liabilities on the balance sheet. Draw the arrows linking the three financial statements.

Problem 3-7B *Preparing an adjusted trial balance and the financial statements*
(L.O. 3,4,5)

The unadjusted trial balance of Terri Peterson, Audio Therapist, Professional Corporation, at October 31, 19X2, and the related month-end adjustment data follow:

Terri Peterson, Audio Therapist, P.C.
Trial Balance
October 31, 19X2

Cash..	$16,300	
Accounts receivable	8,000	
Prepaid rent..	4,000	
Supplies	600	
Furniture..	15,000	
Accumulated depreciation		$ 3,000
Accounts payable		2,800
Salary payable		
Common stock		25,000
Retained earnings...................................		11,000
Dividends..	3,600	
Consulting service revenue		7,400
Salary expense......................................	1,400	
Rent expense		
Utilities expense	300	
Depreciation expense................................		
Supplies expense		
Total..	$49,200	$49,200

Adjustment data:

a. Prepaid rent expired during the month. The unadjusted prepaid balance of $4,000 relates to the period October through January.
b. Supplies on hand at October 31, $400.
c. Depreciation on furniture for the month. The furniture's expected useful life is five years.
d. Accrued salary expense at October 31 for one day only. The five-day weekly payroll is $1,500.
e. Accrued consulting service revenue at October 31, $1,000.

Required

1. Write the trial balance on a sheet of paper, using as an example Exhibit 3-5, and prepare the adjusted trial balance of Terri Peterson, Audio Therapist, P.C., at October 31, 19X2. Key each adjusting entry by letter.
2. Prepare the income statement, the statement of retained earnings, and the balance sheet. Draw the arrows linking the three financial statements.

Problem 3-8B

Journalizing and posting adjustments to four-column accounts; preparing the adjusted trial balance and the financial statements **(L.O. 3,4,5)**

The trial balance of Air-Tite Security Service, Inc., at May 31, 19X3, and the data needed to make the year-end adjustments follow.

Adjustment data:

a. At May 31 the business has earned $1,000 service revenue that has not yet been recorded.

b. Supplies used during the year totaled $5,650.

c. Prepaid rent still in force at May 31 is $330.

d. Depreciation for the year is based on tools and installation equipment costing $27,900 and having an estimated useful life of 9 years.

e. Air-Tite installs locks in a large apartment complex that pays in advance. At May 31 the entity has earned $3,600 of the unadjusted balance of Unearned Service Revenue.

f. At May 31 the business owes its employees accrued salaries for half a four-week payroll. Total payroll for the four weeks is $2,600.

Air-Tite Security Service, Inc.
Trial Balance
May 31, 19X3

Account No.			
101	Cash	$ 3,260	
112	Accounts receivable	14,700	
127	Supplies	7,700	
129	Prepaid rent	1,430	
143	Equipment	27,900	
154	Accumulated depreciation		$ 12,150
211	Accounts payable		4,240
221	Salary payable		
243	Unearned service revenue		5,810
301	Common stock		10,000
305	Retained earnings		7,080
311	Dividends	34,800	
401	Service revenue		80,610
511	Salary expense...........................	28,800	
513	Depreciation expense.....................		
515	Supplies expense		
519	Rent expense		
521	Utilities expense	1,300	
	Total....................................	$119,890	$119,890

Required

1. Open the accounts listed in the trial balance, inserting their May 31 unadjusted balances. Use four-column accounts. The following accounts have experienced no activity during the month, so their balances should be dated May 1: Supplies, Prepaid Rent, Accumulated Depreciation, and Unearned Service Revenue.

2. Journalize the adjusting entries, using page 7 of the journal.

3. Post the adjusting entries to the ledger accounts, using all posting references.

4. Prepare the adjusted trial balance at May 31.
5. Prepare the income statement, the statement of retained earnings, and the balance sheet. Draw the arrows linking the three financial statements.

Extending Your Knowledge

Decision Problems

1. Valuing a Business Based on its Net Income (L.O. 4,5)

Ace Black has owned and operated Black Biomedical Systems, Inc., a management consulting firm for physicians, since its beginning ten years ago. From all appearances the business has prospered. Black lives in the fast lane—flashy car, home located in an expensive suburb, frequent trips abroad, and other signs of wealth. In the past few years, you have become friends with him and his wife through weekly rounds of golf at the country club. Recently, he mentioned that he has lost his zest for the business and would consider selling it for the right price. He claims that his clientele is firmly established and that the business "runs on its own." According to Black, the consulting procedures are fairly simple and anyone could perform the work.

Assume you are interested in buying this business. You obtain its most recent monthly trial balance, which follows. Assume that revenues and expenses vary little from month to month and April is a typical month.

Your investigation reveals that the trial balance does not include the effects of monthly revenues of $1,100 and expenses totaling $2,100. If you were to buy Black Biomedical Systems, you would hire a manager so you could devote your time to other duties. Assume that this person would require a monthly salary of $2,000.

Black Biomedical Systems, Inc.		
Trial Balance		
April 30, 19XX		
Cash	$ 7,700	
Accounts receivable	4,900	
Prepaid expenses	2,600	
Plant assets	241,300	
Accumulated depreciation		$189,600
Land	138,000	
Accounts payable		11,800
Salary payable		
Unearned consulting revenue		56,700
Common stock		100,000
Retained earnings		37,400
Dividends	9,000	
Consulting revenue		12,300
Salary expense	3,400	
Rent expense		
Utilities expense	900	
Depreciation expense		
Supplies expense		
Total	$407,800	$407,800

Required

1. Is this an unadjusted or an adjusted trial balance? How can you tell?
2. Assume that the most you would pay for the business is thirty times the monthly net income you could expect to earn from it. Compute this possible price.
3. Black states that the least he will take for the business is the amount of ending total stockholders' equity. Compute this amount.
4. Under these conditions, how much should you offer for the business? Give your reason.

2. Explaining the concepts underlying the accrual basis of accounting (L.O. 1,2)

The following independent questions relate to the accrual basis of accounting:

1. It has been said that the only time a company's financial position is known for certain is when the company is ended and its only asset is cash. Why is this statement true?
2. A friend suggests that the purpose of adjusting entries is to correct errors in the accounts. Is your friend's statement true? What is the purpose of adjusting entries if the statement is wrong?
3. The text suggested that furniture (and each other plant asset that is depreciated) is a form of prepaid expense. Do you agree? Why do you think some accountants view plant assets this way?

Ethical Issue

The net income of Christopher's, a department store, decreased sharply during 1991. Matthew Christopher, owner of the store, anticipates the need for a bank loan in 1992. Late in 1991 he instructed the accountant to record a $4,500 sale of furniture to the Christopher family, even though the goods will not be shipped from the manufacturer until January 1992. Christopher also told the accountant not to make the following December 31, 1991, adjusting entries:

Salaries owed to employees.................	$1,800
Prepaid insurance that has expired	670

Required

1. Compute the overall effect of these transactions on the store's reported income for 1991.
2. Why did Christopher take this action? Is this action ethical? Give your reason, identifying the parties helped and the parties harmed by Christopher's action.
3. As a personal friend, what advice would you give the accountant?

Financial Statement Problems

1. Journalizing and Posting Transactions, and Tracing Account Balances to the Financial Statements (L.O. 3,4,5)

Goodyear Tire & Rubber Company—like all other businesses—makes adjusting entries prior to year end in order to measure assets, liabilities, revenues, and expenses properly. Examine Goodyear's balance sheet, paying particular attention to Prepaid expenses, Accrued payrolls and other compensation (similar to Salary payable), and Other current liabilities. The amount reported for

Other current liabilities is the sum of several accounts combined under this heading. Assume the Other current liabilities of $282.5 million at December 31, 1990, include two accounts with the following balances: Interest Payable, $110.0 million, and Unearned Sales Revenue, $172.5 million.

Required

1. Open T-accounts for these four accounts. Insert Goodyear's balances (in millions) at December 31, 1990. (Examples: Prepaid Expenses, $206.3; Interest Payable, $110.0.)
2. Journalize the following for 1991. Key entries by letter. Explanations are not required.

   Cash transactions (amounts in millions):
   a. Paid prepaid expenses, $184.6.
   b. Paid the December 31, 1990, accrued payrolls and other compensation.
   c. Paid the December 31, 1990, interest payable.
   d. Received $154.3 cash for unearned sales revenue.

   Adjustments at December 31, 1991 (amounts in millions):
   e. Prepaid expenses expired, $135.0. (Debit Administrative and General Expense.)
   f. Accrued payrolls and other compensation, $352.8. (Debit Selling Expense.)
   g. Accrued interest payable, $123.1.
   h. Earned sales revenue for which cash had been collected in advance, $97.7.
3. After these entries are posted, show that the balances in the four accounts opened in Requirement 1 agree with the corresponding amounts reported in the December 31, 1991, balance sheet.

2. Adjusting the Accounts of an Actual Company   *(L.O. 2)*

Obtain the annual report of an actual company of your choosing. Assume the company accountants *failed* to make four adjustments at the end of the current year. For illustrative purposes, we shall assume that the amounts reported in the company's balance sheet for the related assets and liabilities are *incorrect*.

   Adjustments omitted:
   a. Depreciation of equipment, $800,000
   b. Salaries owed to employees but not yet paid, $230,000
   c. Prepaid rent used up during the year, $100,000
   d. Accrued sales (or service) revenue, $140,000

Required

1. Compute the correct amounts for the following balance sheet items:
   a. Book value of plant assets
   b. Total liabilities
   c. Prepaid expenses
   d. Accounts receivable
2. Compute the amount of net income or net loss that the company would have reported if the accountants had recorded these transactions properly. Ignore income tax.

Chapter 4

Completing the Accounting Cycle

"Homer, if you don't get those invoices and check stubs to the office in Baton Rouge this week, you can just hang it up."

Ed Simpson, the owner of a Baton Rouge, Louisiana, construction company, was talking to his construction superintendent, Homer Huntley. . . . By the time Simpson left the small construction shack, Homer was furious. Muttering under his breath, "Bookkeepers! Don't they have anything better to do than ruin my day?" he started yanking invoices, check stubs, handwritten notes, and other papers off the nails he had driven into the shack's walls as a haphazard filing system for job records.

Homer stuffed the papers into a brown grocery bag he'd been using as a trash container, folded the bag's top, and fastened it with a nail pulled from the wall. . . . On his way home later that night, Homer stuffed the bag into a mail box outside the local post office.

Homer was understandably surprised when the company's bookkeeper called a few days later to say that he had received the bag. For years after that, the bag hung on the wall in the accounting office at Simpson Construction Company.

Source: Arthur Sharplin, "Brown Bag Bookkeeping," *Journal of Accountancy* (July 1986), p. 122. Used with the permission of the American Institute of Certified Accountants

Our humorous actual example illustrates how some small businesses keep their accounting records. As you study Chapter 4, consider the advantages of a more formal way of keeping records and completing the accounting cycle.

You have studied how accountants journalize transactions, post to the ledger accounts, prepare the trial balance and the adjusting entries, and draw up the financial statements. One major step remains to complete the accounting cycle—closing the books. This chapter illustrates the closing process for Air and Sea Travel, Inc., at April 30, 19X1. It also shows how to use three additional accounting tools that are optional. One of these optional tools is the accountant's work sheet. Building upon the adjusted trial balance, the work sheet leads directly to the financial statements, which are the focal point of financial accounting. The chapter also presents an example of an actual balance sheet to show how companies classify assets and liabilities to provide meaningful information for decision making.

Overview of the Accounting Cycle

The **accounting cycle** is the process by which accountants produce an entity's financial statements for a specific period of time. For a new business, the cycle begins with setting up (opening) the ledger accounts. Gary and Monica Lyon started Air and Sea Travel, Inc., from scratch on April 1, 19X1, so the first step in the cycle was to open the accounts. After a business has operated for one period, however, the account balances carry over from period to period. Therefore, the accounting cycle usually starts with the account balances at the beginning of the period, as shown in Exhibit 4-1. The exhibit highlights the new steps that we will be discussing in this chapter.

The accounting cycle is divided into work performed during the period—journalizing transactions and posting to the ledger—and work performed at the end of the period to prepare the financial statements. A secondary purpose of the end-of-period work is to get the accounts ready for recording the transactions of the next period. The greater number of individual steps at the end of the period may imply that most of the work is done at the end. Nevertheless, the recording and posting during the period takes far more time than the end-of-period work. Some of the terms in Exhibit 4-1 may be unfamiliar, but they will become clear by the end of the chapter.

EXHIBIT 4-1 *The Accounting Cycle*

During the period	1.	Start with the account balances in the ledger at the beginning of the period.
	2.	Analyze and journalize transactions as they occur.
	3.	Post journal entries to the ledger accounts.
End of the period	4.	Compute the unadjusted balance in each account at the end of the period.
	5.	**Enter the trial balance on the work sheet, and complete the work sheet.***
	6.	Using the work sheet as a guide, a. Prepare the financial statements. b. Journalize and post the adjusting entries. **c. Journalize and post the closing entries.**
	7.	**Prepare the postclosing, or afterclosing, trial balance. This trial balance becomes step 1 for the next period.**

*Optional

The Accountant's Work Sheet

Accountants often use a **work sheet,** a columnar document that is designed to help move data from the trial balance to the finished financial statements. The work sheet provides an orderly way to compute net income and arrange the data for the financial statements. By listing all the accounts and their unadjusted balances, it helps the accountant identify the accounts needing adjustment. Although it is not essential, the work sheet is helpful because it brings together in one place the effects of all the transactions of a particular period. The work sheet aids the closing process by listing the adjusted balances of all the accounts. It also helps the accountant discover potential errors.

The work sheet is not part of the ledger or the journal, nor is it a financial statement. Therefore, it is not part of the formal accounting system. Instead, it is a summary device that exists for the accountant's convenience.

Exhibits 4-2 through 4-6 illustrate the development of a typical work sheet for Air and Sea Travel, Inc. The heading at the top names the business, identifies the document, and states the accounting period. A step-by-step description of its preparation follows. Observe that steps 1 through 3 use the adjusted trial balance that was introduced in Chapter 3. Only steps 4 and 5 are entirely new.

Steps introduced in Chapter 3 to prepare the adjusted trial balance:

1. Write the account titles and their unadjusted ending balances in the Trial Balance columns of the work sheet and total the amounts.
2. Enter the adjustments in the Adjustments columns and total the amounts.
3. Compute each account's adjusted balance by combining the trial balance and adjustment figures. Enter the adjusted amounts in the Adjusted Trial Balance columns.

OBJECTIVE 1
Prepare a work sheet

New steps introduced in this chapter:

4. Extend the asset, liability, and stockholders' equity amounts from the Adjusted Trial Balance to the Balance Sheet columns. Extend the revenue and expense amounts to the Income Statement columns. Total the statement columns.

5. Compute net income or net loss as the difference between total revenues and total expenses on the income statement. Enter net income or net loss as a balancing amount on the income statement and on the balance sheet and compute the adjusted column totals. After completion, total debits equal total credits in the income statement columns and in the balance sheet columns.

1. Write the account titles and their unadjusted ending balances in the Trial Balance columns of the work sheet and total the amounts. Of course, total debits should equal total credits as shown in Exhibit 4-2. The account titles and balances come directly from the ledger accounts before preparing the adjusting entries. If the business uses a work sheet, there is no need for a separate trial balance. It is written directly onto the work sheet, as shown in the exhibit. Accounts are grouped on the work sheet by category and are usually listed in the order they appear in the ledger. By contrast, their order on the financial statements follows a different pattern. For example, the expenses on the work sheet in Exhibit 4-2 indicate no particular order. But on the income statement, expenses are ordered by amount with the largest first (see Exhibit 4-7).

Accounts may have zero balances (for example, Depreciation Expense). All accounts are listed on the trial balance because they appear in the ledger. Electronically prepared work sheets list all the accounts, not just those with a balance.

2. Enter the adjusting entries in the Adjustments columns and total the amounts. Exhibit 4-3 includes the April adjusting entries. These are the same adjustments that were illustrated in Chapter 3 to prepare the adjusted trial balance.

How does the accountant identify the accounts that need to be adjusted? By scanning the trial balance. Cash needs no adjustment because all cash transactions are recorded as they occur during the period. Consequently, Cash's balance is up to date.

Accounts Receivable is listed next. Has Air and Sea Travel earned revenue that it has not yet recorded? The answer is yes. The business arranges travel for a customer who pays a $500 fee on the 15th of each month. At April 30 Air and Sea Travel has earned half of this amount, $250, which must be accrued because Air and Sea has not yet billed it to the customer. To accrue this service revenue, Air and Sea Travel debits Accounts Receivable and credits Service Revenue on the work sheet in Exhibit 4-3. A letter is used to link the debit and the credit of each adjusting entry. By moving down the trial balance, the accountant identifies the remaining accounts needing adjustment. Supplies is next. The business has used supplies during April, so Air and Sea Travel debits Supplies Expense and credits Supplies. The other adjustments are analyzed and entered on the work sheet as shown in the exhibit.

The process of identifying accounts that need to be adjusted is aided by listing the accounts in their proper sequence. However, suppose one or more accounts is omitted from the trial balance. It can always be written below the first column totals—$51,800. Assume that Supplies Expense was accidentally omitted and thus did not appear on the trial balance. When the accountant identifies the need to update the Supplies account, he or she knows that the

EXHIBIT 4-2

Air and Sea Travel, Inc.
Work Sheet
For the Month Ended April 30, 19X1

Account Title	Trial Balance		Adjustments		Adjusted Trial Balance		Income Statement		Balance Sheet	
	Debit	Credit	Debit	Credit	Debit	Credit	Debit	Credit	Debit	Credit
Cash	24,800									
Accounts receivable	2,250									
Supplies	700									
Prepaid rent	3,000									
Furniture	16,500									
Accumulated depreciation		13,100								
Accounts payable										
Salary payable		450								
Unearned service revenue		20,000								
Common stock		11,250								
Retained earnings										
Dividends	3,200									
Service revenue		7,000								
Rent expense										
Salary expense	950									
Supplies expense										
Depreciation expense	400									
Utilities expense										
	51,800	51,800								

Write the account titles and their unadjusted ending balances in the Trial Balance columns of the work sheet, and total the amounts.

EXHIBIT 4-3

Air and Sea Travel, Inc.
Work Sheet
For the Month Ended April 30, 19X1

Account Title	Trial Balance Debit	Trial Balance Credit	Adjustments Debit	Adjustments Credit	Adjusted Trial Balance Debit	Adjusted Trial Balance Credit	Income Statement Debit	Income Statement Credit	Balance Sheet Debit	Balance Sheet Credit
Cash	24,800									
Accounts receivable	2,250		(a) 250							
Supplies	700			(b) 300						
Prepaid rent	3,000			(c) 1,000						
Furniture	16,500									
Accumulated depreciation				(d) 275						
Accounts payable		13,100								
Salary payable				(e) 950						
Unearned service revenue		450	(f) 150							
Common stock		20,000								
Retained earnings		11,250								
Dividends	3,200									
Service revenue		7,000		(a) 250						
				(f) 150						
Rent expense			(c) 1,000							
Salary expense	950		(e) 950							
Supplies expense			(b) 300							
Depreciation expense			(d) 275							
Utilities expense	400									
	51,800	51,800	2,925	2,925						

Enter the adjusting entries in the Adjustments columns, and total the amounts.

debit in the adjusting entry is to Supplies Expense. In this case, the accountant can write Supplies Expense on the line beneath the amount totals and enter the debit adjustment—$300—on the Supplies Expense line. Keep in mind that the work sheet is not the finished version of the financial statements, so the order of the accounts on the work sheet is not critical. When the accountant prepares the income statement, Supplies Expense can be listed in its proper sequence.

After the adjustments are entered on the work sheet, the amount columns should be totaled to see that total debits equal total credits. This provides some assurance that each debit adjustment is accompanied by an equal credit.

3. *Compute each account's adjusted balance by combining the trial balance and adjustment figures. Enter the adjusted amounts in the Adjusted Trial Balance columns.* Exhibit 4-4 shows the work sheet with the adjusted trial balance added.

This step is performed as it was in Chapter 3. For example, the Cash balance is up to date, so it receives no adjustment. Accounts Receivable's adjusted balance of $2,500 is computed by adding the trial balance amount of $2,250 to the $250 debit adjustment. Supplies' adjusted balance of $400 is determined by subtracting the $300 credit adjustment from the unadjusted debit balance of $700. An account may receive more than one adjustment, as does Service Revenue. The column totals should maintain the equality of debits and credits.

4. *Extend the asset, liability, and stockholders' equity amounts from the Adjusted Trial Balance to the Balance Sheet columns. Extend the revenue and expense amounts to the Income Statement columns. Total the statement columns.* Every account is either a balance sheet account or an income statement account. The asset, liability, and stockholders' equity accounts go to the balance sheet, and the revenues and expenses go to the income statement. Debits on the adjusted trial balance remain debits in the statement columns, and likewise for credits. Each account's adjusted balance should appear in only one statement column, as shown in Exhibit 4-5.

The income statement indicates total expenses in the debit column ($3,875) and total revenues ($7,400) in the credit column. The balance sheet shows total debits of $49,400 and total credits of $45,875. At this stage, the column totals should not necessarily be equal.

5. *Compute net income or net loss as the difference between total revenues and total expenses on the income statement. Enter net income or net loss as a balancing amount on the income statement and on the balance sheet and compute the adjusted column totals.* Exhibit 4-6 presents the completed work sheet, which shows net income of $3,525, computed as follows:

Revenue (total credits on the income statement .	$7,400
Expenses (total debits on the income statement).	3,875
Net income	$3,525

Net income of $3,525 is entered in the debit column of the income statement, and the income statement columns are totaled at $7,400. The net income amount is then extended to the credit column of the balance sheet. This is because an excess of revenues over expenses increases retained earnings, and increases in retained earnings are recorded by a credit. In the closing process, which we discuss later, net income will find its way into the Retained earnings account.

If expenses exceed revenue, the result is a net loss. In that event, the accountant writes the words Net loss on the work sheet. The loss amount should be entered in the credit column of the income statement and in the debit column of the balance sheet. This is because an excess of expenses over

EXHIBIT 4-4

Air and Sea Travel, Inc.
Work Sheet
For the Month Ended April 30, 19X1

Account Title	Trial Balance Debit	Trial Balance Credit	Adjustments Debit	Adjustments Credit	Adjusted Trial Balance Debit	Adjusted Trial Balance Credit	Income Statement Debit	Income Statement Credit	Balance Sheet Debit	Balance Sheet Credit
Cash	24,800				24,800					
Accounts receivable	2,250		(a) 250		2,500					
Supplies	700			(b) 300	400					
Prepaid rent	3,000			(c) 1,000	2,000					
Furniture	16,500				16,500					
Accumulated depreciation				(d) 275		275				
Accounts payable		13,100				13,100				
Salary payable				(e) 950		950				
Unearned service revenue		450	(f) 150			300				
Common stock		20,000				20,000				
Retained earnings		11,250				11,250				
Dividends	3,200				3,200					
Service revenue		7,000		(a) 250 (f) 150		7,400				
Rent expense			(c) 1,000		1,000					
Salary expense	950		(e) 950		1,900					
Supplies expense			(b) 300		300					
Depreciation expense			(d) 275		275					
Utilities expense	400				400					
	51,800	51,800	2,925	2,925	53,275	53,275				

Compute each account's adjusted balance by combining the trial balance and adjustment figures. Enter the adjusted amounts in the Adjusted Trial balance columns.

EXHIBIT 4-5

Air and Sea Travel, Inc.
Work Sheet
For the Month Ended April 30, 19X1

Account Title	Trial Balance		Adjustments		Adjusted Trial Balance		Income Statement		Balance Sheet	
	Debit	Credit	Debit	Credit	Debit	Credit	Debit	Credit	Debit	Credit
Cash	24,800				24,800				24,800	
Accounts receivable	2,250		(a) 250		2,500				2,500	
Supplies	700			(b) 300	400				400	
Prepaid rent	3,000			(c) 1,000	2,000				2,000	
Furniture	16,500				16,500				16,500	
Accumulated depreciation				(d) 275		275				275
Accounts payable		13,100				13,100				13,100
Salary payable				(e) 950		950				950
Unearned service revenue		450	(f) 150			300				300
Common stock		20,000				20,000				20,000
Retained earnings		11,250				11,250				11,250
Dividends	3,200				3,200				3,200	
Service revenue		7,000		(a) 250		7,400		7,400		
				(f) 150						
Rent expense			(c) 1,000		1,000		1,000			
Salary expense	950		(e) 950		1,900		1,900			
Supplies expense			(b) 300		300		300			
Depreciation expense			(d) 275		275		275			
Utilities expense	400				400		400			
	51,800	51,800	2,925	2,925	53,275	53,275	3,875	7,400	49,400	45,875

Extend the asset, liability, and stockholders' equity amounts from the Adjusted Trial Balance to the Balance Sheet columns. Extend the revenue and expense amounts to the Income Statement columns. Total the statement columns.

EXHIBIT 4-6

Air and Sea Travel, Inc.
Work Sheet
For the Month Ended April 30, 19X1

Account Title	Trial Balance Debit	Trial Balance Credit	Adjustments Debit	Adjustments Credit	Adjusted Trial Balance Debit	Adjusted Trial Balance Credit	Income Statement Debit	Income Statement Credit	Balance Sheet Debit	Balance Sheet Credit
Cash	24,800				24,800				24,800	
Accounts receivable	2,250		(a) 250		2,500				2,500	
Supplies	700			(b) 300	400				400	
Prepaid rent	3,000			(c) 1,000	2,000				2,000	
Furniture	16,500				16,500				16,500	
Accumulated depreciation				(d) 275		275				275
Accounts payable		13,100				13,100				13,100
Salary payable				(e) 950		950				950
Unearned service revenue		450	(f) 150			300				300
Common stock		20,000				20,000				20,000
Retained earnings		11,250				11,250				11,250
Dividends	3,200				3,200				3,200	
Service revenue		7,000		(a) 250		7,400		7,400		
				(f) 150						
Rent expense			(c) 1,000		1,000		1,000			
Salary expense	950		(e) 950		1,900		1,900			
Supplies expense			(b) 300		300		300			
Depreciation expense			(d) 275		275		275			
Utilities expense	400				400		400			
	51,800	51,800	2,925	2,925	53,275	53,275	3,875	7,400	49,400	45,875
Net income							3,525			3,525
							7,400	7,400	49,400	49,400

Compute net income or net loss as the difference between total revenues and total expenses on the income statement. Enter net income or net loss as a balancing amount on the income statement and on the balance sheet, and compute the adjusted column totals.

revenue decreases stockholders' equity, and decreases in stockholders' equity are recorded by a debit.

The balance sheet columns are totaled at $49,400. An out-of-balance condition indicates an error in preparing the work sheet. Common mistakes include arithmetic errors and carrying an amount to the wrong column, to the incorrect statement column, or extending a debit as a credit, or vice versa. Columns that balance offer some, but not complete, assurance that the work sheet is correct. For example, it is possible to have offsetting errors. Fortunately, that is unlikely.

The watchwords are: Work deliberately, and do not rush. By avoiding errors, you can save time and reduce frustration.

Microcomputer Spreadsheets

Computerized general ledger packages, which we discussed in the last chapter, have a disadvantage. With most general ledger packages, the trial balance, adjustments, and adjusted trial balance cannot appear on the computer screen at the same time. To counter this disadvantage, some software programs create an electronically prepared work sheet, also called a **spreadsheet** or an **electronic spreadsheet.** Lotus 1-2-3® is a popular electronic spreadsheet.

OBJECTIVE 2

Explain how a microcomputer spreadsheet can be used in accounting

An electronic spreadsheet is a grid of information *cells* named by row and column. Columns are designated alphabetically from left to right, rows numerically from top to bottom. For example, the cell in the third row from the top and the fourth column from the left is labeled D3. Spreadsheets typically can have thousands of rows and hundreds of columns. Accountants skilled in using electronic spreadsheets can use them for work sheet analysis.

An electronic spreadsheet has three types of information: numbers, labels, and formulas. For example, the title of an account on an electronic spreadsheet formatted as a worksheet would be entered in, say cells A3 and A4 as a label: Accounts receivable, as shown in the accompanying diagram. The unadjusted debit balance of $2,250 (also see the work sheet in Exhibits 4-4 through 4-6) would be entered as a number in the next column, B4. A credit balance for an account would appear in Column C. Column D would hold an adjustment if a debit ($250 in our example), and Column E would hold an adjustment if a credit. Column F would hold the adjusted trial balance for this account if a debit, and Column G would hold the adjusted trial balance if a credit.

How does the accountant get the correct amount displayed in Column F or Column G? Let's use a simplified example to illustrate. A formula is entered in cell F4 as follows: @ SUM(B4+D4)−E4. The formula itself would not appear in the cell. It would appear in the upper-left corner of the spreadsheet when the cursor (the electronic marker) is in that cell. What would appear is the numerical result of that formula, which is 2,500 (2,250 + 250 − 0). This is illustrated at the top of page 160.

The spreadsheet can be programmed to complete the entire work sheet after the accountant has entered the trial balance and the adjustment amounts. This is a big time saver because once the spreadsheet program is set up, it can be saved as a spreadsheet template. This can be used over and over again without the user having to rewrite the account titles or the cell formulas and do the arithmetic by hand. The spreadsheet can also be programmed to journalize and post the adjusting and closing entries and prepare the financial statements directly from the data on the work sheet.

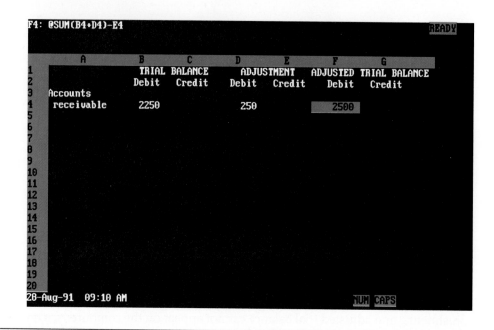

Summary Problem for Your Review

The trial balance of State Service Company at December 31, 19X1, the end of its year, is presented below:

State Service Company
Trial Balance
December 31, 19XI

Cash	$ 198,000	
Accounts receivable	370,000	
Supplies	6,000	
Furniture and fixtures	100,000	
Accumulated depreciation—furniture and fixtures		$ 40,000
Building	250,000	
Accumulated depreciation—building		130,000
Accounts payable		380,000
Salary payable		
Unearned service revenue		45,000
Common stock		100,000
Retained earnings		193,000
Dividends	65,000	
Service revenues		286,000
Salary expense	172,000	
Supplies expense		
Depreciation expense—furniture and fixtures		
Depreciation expense—building		
Miscellaneous expense	13,000	
Total	$1,174,000	$1,174,000

Data needed for the adjusting entries include:

a. Supplies on hand at year end, $2,000.
b. Depreciation on furniture and fixtures, $20,000.
c. Depreciation on building, $10,000.
d. Salaries owed but not yet paid, $5,000.
e. Accrued service revenue, $12,000.
f. Of the $45,000 balance of Unearned Service Revenue, $32,000 was earned during 19Xl.

Required

Prepare the work sheet of State Service Company for the year ended December 31, 19X1. Key each adjusting entry by the letter corresponding to the data given.

SOLUTION TO REVIEW PROBLEM

State Service Company
Work Sheet
For the Year Ended December 31, 19X1

Account Title	Trial Balance Debit	Trial Balance Credit	Adjustments Debit	Adjustments Credit	Adjusted Trial Balance Debit	Adjusted Trial Balance Credit	Income Statement Debit	Income Statement Credit	Balance Sheet Debit	Balance Sheet Credit
Cash	198,000				198,000				198,000	
Accounts receivable	370,000		(e) 12,000		382,000				382,000	
Supplies	6,000			(a) 4,000	2,000				2,000	
Furniture and fixtures	100,000				100,000				100,000	
Accumulated depreciation— furniture and fixtures		40,000		(b) 20,000		60,000				60,000
Building	250,000				250,000				250,000	
Accumulated depreciation— building		130,000		(c) 10,000		140,000				140,000
Accounts payable		380,000				380,000				380,000
Salary payable				(d) 5,000		5,000				5,000
Unearned service revenue		45,000	(f) 32,000			13,000				13,000
Common stock		100,000				100,000				100,000
Retained earnings		193,000				193,000				193,000
Dividends	65,000				65,000				65,000	
Service revenue		286,000		(e) 12,000 (f) 32,000		330,000		330,000		
Salary expense	172,000		(d) 5,000		177,000		177,000			
Supplies expense			(a) 4,000		4,000		4,000			
Depreciation expense— furniture and fixtures			(b) 20,000		20,000		20,000			
Depreciation expense— building			(c) 10,000		10,000		10,000			
Miscellaneous expense	13,000				13,000		13,000			
	1,174,000	1,174,000	83,000	83,000	1,221,000	1,221,000	224,000	330,000	997,000	891,000
Net Income							106,000			106,000
							330,000	330,000	997,000	997,000

Using the Work Sheet

As illustrated thus far, the work sheet helps to organize accounting data and to compute the net income or net loss for the period. It also aids in preparing the financial statements, recording the adjusting entries, and closing the accounts.

Preparing the Financial Statements

Even though the work sheet shows the amount of net income or net loss for the period, it is still necessary to prepare the financial statements. The sorting of accounts to the balance sheet and the income statement eases the preparation of the statements. The work sheet also provides the data for the statement of retained earnings. Exhibit 4-7 presents the April financial statements for Air and Sea Travel, Inc. (based on data from the work sheet in Exhibit 4-6).

The financial statements can be prepared directly from the adjusted trial balance as shown in Chapter 3. That is why completion of the work sheet is optional.

Recording the Adjusting Entries

The adjusting entries are a key element of accrual-basis accounting. The work sheet helps identify the accounts that need adjustments, which may be conveniently entered directly on the work sheet as shown in Exhibits 4-2 through 4-6. However, these work sheet procedures do not adjust the accounts in the ledger itself. Recall that the work sheet is neither a journal nor a ledger. Actual adjustment of the accounts requires journal entries that are posted to the ledger accounts. Therefore, the adjusting entries must be recorded in the journal as shown in Panel A of Exhibit 4-8. Panel B of the exhibit shows the postings to the accounts, with "Adj." denoting an amount posted from an adjusting entry. Only the revenue and expense accounts are presented here in order to focus on the closing process, which is discussed in the next section.

The adjusting entries could have been recorded in the journal when they were entered on the work sheet. However, it is not necessary to journalize them at that time. Most accountants prepare the financial statements immediately after completing the work sheet. They can wait to journalize and post the adjusting entries just before they make the closing entries.

Delaying the journalizing and posting of the adjusting entries illustrates another use of the work sheet. Many companies journalize and post the adjusting entries—as in Exhibit 4-8—only once annually, at the end of the year. The need for monthly and quarterly financial statements, however, requires a tool like the work sheet. The entity can use the work sheet to aid in preparing interim statements without entering the adjusting entries in the journal and posting them to the ledger.

Closing the Accounts

Accountants use the term **closing the accounts** to refer to the step at the end of the period that prepares the accounts for recording the transactions of the next period. Closing the accounts consists of journalizing and posting the closing entries. Closing sets the balances of the revenue and expense accounts back to zero in order to measure the net income of the next period. Closing is a clerical

EXHIBIT 4-7 *April Financial Statements of Air and Sea Travel, Inc.*

Air and Sea Travel, Inc.
Income Statement
For the Month Ended April 30, 19X1

Revenues:		
Service revenue		$7,400
Expenses:		
Salary expense	$1,900	
Rent expense	1,000	
Utilities expense	400	
Supplies expense	300	
Depreciation expense	275	
Total expenses		3,875
Net income		$3,525

Air and Sea Travel, Inc.
Statement of Retained Earnings
For the Month Ended April 30, 19X1

Retained earnings, April 1, 19X1	$11,250
Add: Net income	3,525
	14,775
Less: Dividends	3,200
Retained earnings, April 30, 19X1	$11,575

Air and Sea Travel, Inc.
Balance Sheet
April 30, 19X1

Assets			Liabilities		
Cash		$24,800	Accounts payable		$13,100
Accounts receivable		2,500	Salary payable		950
Supplies		400	Unearned service		
Prepaid rent		2,000	revenue		300
Furniture	$16,500		Total liabilities		14,350
Less Accumulated			**Stockholders' Equity**		
depreciation	275	16,225			
			Common stock	$20,000	
			Retained earnings	11,575	
			Total stockholders'		
			equity		31,575
			Total liabilities		
			and stockholders'		
Total assets		$45,925	equity		$45,925

procedure devoid of any new accounting theory. Recall that the income statement reports only one period's income. For example, net income for McDonald's, Inc., for 1993 relates exclusively to 1993. At December 31, 1993, McDonald's accountants close the company's revenue and expense accounts for that year. Because these accounts' balances relate to a particular accounting period

EXHIBIT 4-8 *Journalizing and Posting the Adjusting Entries*

Panel A—Journalizing: **Page 4**

Adjusting Entries

Apr. 30	Accounts Receivable	250	
	Service Revenue		250
30	Supplies Expense	300	
	Supplies		300
30	Rent Expense	1,000	
	Prepaid Rent		1,000
30	Depreciation Expense	275	
	Accumulated Depreciation		275
30	Salary Expense	950	
	Salary Payable		950
30	Unearned Service Revenue	150	
	Service Revenue		150

Panel B—Posting the Adjustments to the Revenue and Expense Accounts:

Revenue   Expenses

Service Revenue			Rent Expense			Salary Expense	
	7,000		Adj. 1,000			950	
Adj.	250				Adj.	950	
Adj.	150		Bal. 1,000				
					Bal. 1,900		
Bal. 7,400							

Supplies Expense		Depreciation Expense	
Adj. 300		Adj. 275	
Bal. 300		Bal. 275	

Utilities Expense	
400	
Bal. 400	

Adj. = Amount posted from an adjusting entry
Bal. = Balance

and are therefore closed at the end of the period, the revenue and expense accounts are called **temporary (nominal) accounts.** The Dividends account—although not a revenue or an expense—is also a temporary account because it is important to measure withdrawals for a specific period. The closing process applies only to temporary accounts.

To understand better the closing process, contrast the nature of the temporary accounts with the nature of the **permanent (real) accounts**—the assets, liabilities, and stockholders' equity. The permanent accounts are *not* closed at the end of the period because their balances are not used to measure income.

Consider Cash, Accounts Receivable, Supplies, Buildings, Accounts Payable, Notes Payable, Common Stock, and Retained Earnings. These accounts do not represent increases and decreases for a single period as do the revenues and expenses, which relate exclusively to only one accounting period. Instead, the permanent accounts represent assets, liabilities, and stockholders' equity that are on hand at a specific time. This is why their balances at the end of one accounting period carry over to become the beginning balances of the next period. For example, the Cash balance at December 31, 19X1, is also the beginning balance for 19X2.

Briefly, **closing entries** transfer the revenue, expense, and dividends balances from their respective accounts to the retained earnings account. As you know, revenues increase stockholders' equity (retained earnings), and expenses and dividends decrease it. It is when we post the closing entries that the Retained Earnings account absorbs the impact of the balances in the temporary accounts. As an intermediate step, however, the revenues and the expenses are transferred first to an account entitled **Income Summary,** which collects in one place the total debit for the sum of all expenses and the total credit for the sum of all revenues of the period. The Income Summary account is like a temporary "holding tank" that is used only in the closing process. Then the balance of Income Summary is transferred to Retained Earnings. The steps in closing the accounts of a corporation like Air and Sea Travel, Inc., are as follows:

1. Debit each revenue account for the amount of its credit balance. Credit Income Summary for the sum of the revenues. This entry transfers the sum of the revenues to the credit side of Income Summary.

2. Credit each expense account for the amount of its debit balance. Debit Income Summary for the sum of the expenses. This entry transfers the sum of the expenses to the debit side of Income Summary.

3. Debit Income Summary for the amount of its credit balance (revenues minus expenses) and credit the Retained Earnings account. If Income Summary has a debit balance, then credit Income Summary for this amount, and debit Retained Earnings. This entry transfers the net income or loss from Income Summary to the Retained Earnings account.

4. Credit the Dividends account for the amount of its debit balance. Debit the Retained Earnings account. Dividends are not expenses and do not affect net income or net loss. Therefore, this account is *not* closed to the Income Summary. This entry transfers the dividends amount to the debit side of the Retained Earnings account.

To illustrate, suppose Air and Sea Travel closes the books at the end of April. Exhibit 4-9 presents the complete closing process for the business. Panel A gives the closing journal entries, and Panel B shows the accounts after the closing entries have been posted.

The amount in the debit side of each expense account is its adjusted balance. For example, Rent Expense has a $1,000 debit balance. Also note that Service Revenue has a credit balance of $7,400 before closing. These amounts come directly from the adjusted balances in Exhibit 4-8, Panel B.

Closing entry 1, denoted in the Service Revenue account by *Clo.,* transfers Service Revenue's balance to the Income Summary account. This entry zeroes out Service Revenue for April and places the revenue on the credit side of Income Summary. Closing entry 2 zeroes out the expenses and moves their total ($3,875) to the debit side of Income Summary. At this point, Income Summary contains the impact of April's revenues and expenses; hence Income Summary's balance is the month's net income ($3,525). Closing entry 3 closes

EXHIBIT 4-9 *Journalizing and Posting the Closing Entries*

OBJECTIVE 4

Close the revenue, expense, and dividends accounts

Panel A-Journalizing:

		Closing Entries		Page 5
1.	Apr. 30	Service Revenue	7,400	
		Income Summary		7,400
2.	30	Income Summary	3,875	
		Rent Expense......................		1,000
		Salary Expense		1,900
		Supplies Expense		300
		Depreciation Expense		275
		Utilities Expense		400
3.	30	Income Summary ($7,400–$3,875)	3,525	
		Retained Earnings		3,525
4.	30	Retained Earnings	3,200	
		Dividends........................		3,200

Panel B-Posting:

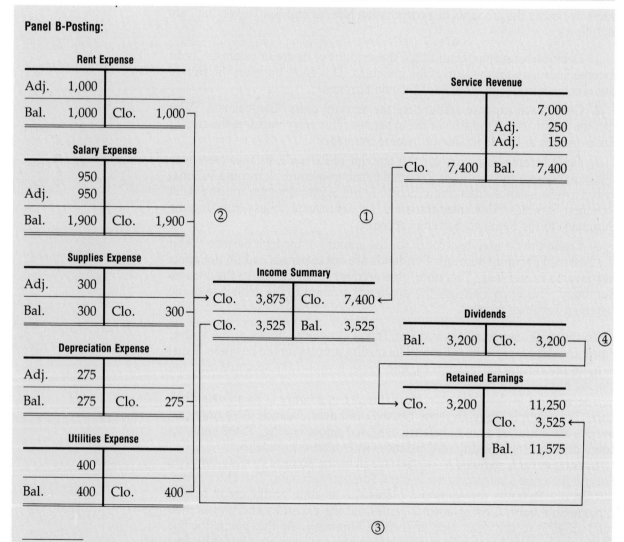

Adj = Amount posted from an adjusting entry
Clo. = Amount posted from a closing entry
Bal. = Balance

the Income Summary account by transferring net income to the credit side of Retained Earnings.[1] The last closing entry (entry 4) moves the dividends to the debit side of Retained Earnings, leaving a zero balance in the Dividends account.

After all the closing entries, the revenues, the expenses, and the Dividends account are set back to zero to make ready for the next period. The Retained Earnings account includes the full effects of the April revenues, expenses, and dividends. These amounts, combined with the beginning Retained Earnings balance, give Retained Earnings an ending balance of $11,575. Note that this Retained Earnings balance agrees with the amount reported on the statement of retained earnings and on the balance sheet in Exhibit 4-7. Also note that the ending balance of Retained Earnings remains. We do not close it out—because it is a balance sheet account.

Closing a Net Loss. What would the closing entries be if Air and Sea Travel business had suffered a net *loss* during April? Suppose April expenses totaled $7,700 and all other factors were unchanged. Only closing entries 2 and 3 would be altered. Closing entry 2 would transfer expenses of $7,700 to the debit side of Income Summary, as follows:

Income Summary			
Clo.	7,700	Clo.	7,400
Bal.	300		

Closing entry 3 would then credit Income Summary to close its debit balance and to transfer the net loss to Retained Earnings:

3.	Apr. 30	Retained Earnings	300	
		Income Summary		300

After posting, these two accounts would appear as follows:

Income Summary					Retained Earnings		
Clo.	7,700	Clo.	7,400	→ Clo.	300		11,250
Bal.	300	Clo.	300				

Finally, the Dividends balance would be closed to Retained Earnings as before.

Postclosing Trial Balance

The accounting cycle ends with the **postclosing trial balance** (see Exhibit 4-10). The postclosing trial balance is the final check on the accuracy of journalizing and posting the adjusting and closing entries. Like the trial balance that begins the work sheet, the postclosing trial balance is a list of the ledger's accounts and balances. This step ensures that the ledger is in balance for the start of the

---

[1] The Income Summary account is a convenience for combining the effects of the revenues and expenses prior to transferring their income effect to Retained Earnings. It is not necessary to use the Income Summary account in the closing process. Another way of closing the revenues and expenses makes no use of this account. In this alternative procedure, the revenues and expenses are closed directly to Retained Earnings.

EXHIBIT 4-10 *Postclosing Trial Balance*

Air and Sea Travel, Inc.
Postclosing Trial Balance
April 30, 19X1

Cash	$24,800	
Accounts receivable	2,500	
Supplies	400	
Prepaid rent	2,000	
Furniture	16,500	
Accumulated depreciation		$ 275
Accounts payable		13,100
Salary payable		950
Unearned service revenue		300
Common stock		20,000
Retained earnings		11,575
Total	$46,200	$46,200

next accounting period. The postclosing trial balance is dated as of the end of the accounting period for which the statements have been prepared.

Note that the postclosing trial balance resembles the balance sheet. It contains the ending balances of the permanent accounts—the balance sheet accounts: the assets, liabilities, and stockholders' equity. No temporary accounts—revenues, expenses, or dividends accounts—are included because their balances have been closed. The ledger is up-to-date and ready for the next period's transactions.

Reversing Entries

OBJECTIVE 5
Use reversing entries to save time

Reversing entries are special types of entries that ease the burden of accounting after adjusting and closing entries have been made at the end of a period. Reversing entries are used most often in conjunction with accrual-type adjustments such as accrued salary expense and accrued service revenue. GAAP does not require reversing entries. They are used only for convenience and to save time.

Reversing Entries for Accrued Expense.   Accrued expenses accumulate with the passage of time and are paid at a later date. At the end of the period the business makes an adjusting entry to record the expense that has accumulated up to that time.

To see how reversing entries work, return to the adjusting entries (Exhibit 4-8) that Air and Sea Travel used to update its accounting records for the April financial statements. At April 30—prior to the adjusting entries—Salary Expense has a debit balance of $950 from salaries paid during April. At April 30 the business owes its employee an additional $950 for service during the last part of the month. Assume for the purpose of this illustration that on May 5, the next payroll date, Air and Sea Travel will pay the $950 of accrued salary plus $100 in salary that its employee has earned in the first few days of May. The next payroll payment will be $1,050 ($950 + $100). However, to present the correct financial picture, the $950 in salary expense incurred in April must be included in the April statements, not in the May statements. Accordingly, the accountant makes the following adjusting entry on April 30:

Adjusting Entries

Apr. 30   Salary Expense   950
                    Salary Payable..........................   950

After posting, the Salary Payable and Salary Expense accounts appear as follows:

Salary Payable

	Apr. 30 Adj.* 950
	Apr. 30 Bal. 950

Salary Expense

Paid during April	950	
Apr. 30	950	
Apr. 30 Bal. 1,900		

---

*Entry explanations used throughout this discussion are
Adj. = Adjusting entry
Bal. = Balance
Clo. = Closing entry
CP   = Cash payment entry
CR   = Cash receipt entry
Rev. = Reversing entry

After the adjusting entry, the April income statement reports salary expense of $1,900, and the balance sheet at April 30 reports Salary Payable, a liability, of $950. The $1,900 debit balance of Salary Expense is eliminated by a closing entry at April 30, 19X1, as follows:

Closing Entries

April 30   Income Summary   1,900
                    Salary Expense   1,900

After posting, Salary Expense appears as follows:

Salary Expense

Paid during April CP 950	
Apr. 30 Adj. 950	
Apr. 30 Bal. 1,900	Apr. 30 Clo. 1,900

In the normal course of recording salary payments during the year, Air and Sea Travel makes the standard entry, as follows:

Salary Expense   XXX
        Cash   XXX

In our example, however, payday does not land on the day the accounting period ends, and Air and Sea Travel's accountant has made an adjusting entry to accrue salary payable of $950, as we have just seen. On May 5, the next payday, assume the total payroll is $1,050. Air and Sea credits Cash for $1,050, but what account—or accounts—should he debit? The cash payment entry is

May 5	Salary Payable	950	
	Salary Expense	100	
	Cash		1,050

This method of recording the cash payment is correct but inefficient because Air and Sea must refer back to the adjusting entries of April 30. Otherwise, the accountant does not know the amount of the required debit to Salary Payable (in this example, $950). Searching the preceding period's adjusting entries takes time, and in business, time is money. To avoid having to separate the debit of a later cash payment entry into two accounts, accountants have devised a technique called *reversing entries*.

Making a Reversing Entry.   A **reversing entry** switches the debit and the credit of a previous adjusting entry. A reversing entry, then, is the exact opposite of an adjusting entry. The reversing entry is dated the first day of the period following the adjusting entry.

Let's continue with our example of the May 5 cash payment of $1,050 for salaries. On April 30, Air and Sea Travel made the following adjusting entry to accrue Salary Payable:

Adjusting Entries

Apr. 30	Salary Expense	950	
	Salary Payable.............................		950

The reversing entry simply reverses the position of the debit and the credit:

Reversing Entries

May 1	Salary Payable	950	
	Salary Expense...........................		950

Notice that the reversing entry is dated the first day of the new period. It is the exact opposite of the April 30 adjusting entry. Ordinarily, the accountant who makes the adjusting entry also prepares the reversing entry at the same time. Air and Sea Travel postdates the reversing entry to the first day of the next period, however, so that it affects only the new period. Note how the accounts appear after the accountant posts the reversing entry:

Salary Payable

May 1 Rev. 950	Apr. 30 Bal. 950

Zero balance

Salary Expense

Apr. 30 Bal. 1,900	Apr. 30 Clo. 1,900

Zero balance

	May 1 Rev. 950

The arrow shows the transfer of the $950 credit balance from Salary Payable to Salary Expense. This credit balance in Salary Expense does not mean that the entity has negative salary expense, as might be suggested by a credit balance in an expense account. Instead, the odd credit balance is merely a temporary result of the reversing entry. The credit balance is eliminated on May 5, when the $1,050 cash payment for salaries is debited to Salary Expense in the customary manner:

May 5	Salary Expense 1,050	
	Cash	1,050

Then this cash payment entry is posted:

Salary Expense

May 5	CP	1,050	May 1	Rev.	950
May 5	Bal.	100			

Now Salary Expense has its correct debit balance of $100, which is the amount of salary expense incurred thus far in May. The $1,050 cash disbursement also pays the liability for Salary Payable. Thus the Salary Payable account has a zero balance, which is correct, as shown at the bottom of the preceding page.

The adjusting and reversing process is repeated period after period. Cash payments for salaries are debited to Salary Expense, and these amounts accumulate in that account. At the end of the period, the accountant makes an adjusting entry to accrue salary expense incurred but not yet paid. At the same time, the accountant also makes a reversing entry, which allows her to record all payroll entries in the customary manner—by routinely debiting Salary Expense. Even in computerized systems, making reversing entries is more efficient than writing a program to locate the amount accrued from the preceding period and making the more complicated journal entry. Reversing entries may be made for all types of accrued expenses.

Reversing Entries for Accrued Revenues   Certain revenues, such as services performed on a continuous basis and interest earned on notes receivable, accrue with the passage of time, just as expenses do. However, a business usually does not record accrued revenues daily, weekly, or even monthly. Thus at the end of the accounting period, the business may have to accrue revenue that will be collected later. Then, when cash is received, a second entry is needed.

To illustrate reversing entries for accrued revenue, recall that Air and Sea Travel performs services for customers on a monthly basis. At April 30, Air and Sea has earned $250 of service revenue that it will collect on May 15, along with an additional $250 for services performed in the first half of May. On April 30, Air and Sea made this adjusting entry:

Adjusting Entries

Apr. 30	Accounts Receivable 250	
	Service Revenue	250

At the same time, the accountant can make the following reversing entry, postdated to May 1:

Reversing Entries

May 1	Service Revenue 250	
	Accounts Receivable	250

The net effect of the reversing entry is that the accountant need not refer back to the April 30 adjusting entry when recording the May cash transaction. On May 15, when Air and Sea Travel receives $500 from the customer, the business can record the cash receipt as follows:

May 15   Cash   500
             Service Revenue   500

After this entry is posted, the accounts have their correct balances.

The appendix at the end of this chapter discusses the use of reversing entries for prepaid expenses and unearned revenues.

Classification of Assets and Liabilities

OBJECTIVE 6

Classify assets and liabilities as current or long-term

On the balance sheet, assets and liabilities are classified as either *current* or *long-term* to indicate their relative *liquidity*. **Liquidity** is a measure of how quickly an item may be converted to cash. Therefore, cash is the most liquid asset. Accounts receivable is a relatively liquid asset because the business expects to collect the amount in cash in the near future. Supplies are less liquid than accounts receivable, and furniture and buildings are even less so.

Users of financial statements are interested in liquidity because business difficulties often arise owing to a shortage of cash. How quickly can the business convert an asset to cash and pay a debt? How soon must a liability be paid? These are questions of liquidity. Balance sheets list assets and liabilities in the order of their relative liquidity.

Current Assets.   **Current assets** are assets that are expected to be converted to cash, sold, or consumed during the next 12 months or within the business's normal operating cycle if longer than a year. The **operating cycle** is the time span during which (1) cash is used to acquire goods and services, and (2) these goods and services are sold to customers, who in turn pay for their purchases with cash. For most businesses, the operating cycle is a few months. A few types of business have operating cycles longer than a year. Cash, Accounts Receivable, Notes Receivable due within a year or less, and Prepaid Expenses are current assets. Merchandising entities such as Sears, Penney's and K Mart have an additional current asset, Inventory. This account shows the cost of goods that are held for sale to customers.

Long-Term Assets.   **Long-term assets** are all assets other than current assets. They are not held for sale, but rather they are used to operate the business. One category of long-term assets is plant assets, or fixed assets. Land, Buildings, Furniture and Fixtures, and Equipment are examples of plant assets.

Financial statement users such as creditors are interested in the due dates of an entity's liabilities. The sooner a liability must be paid, the more current it is. Liabilities that must be paid on the earliest future date create the greatest strain on cash. Therefore, the balance sheet lists liabilities in the order in which they are due. Knowing how many of a business's liabilities are current and how many are long-term helps creditors assess the likelihood of collecting from the entity. Balance sheets usually have at least two liability classifications, *current liabilities* and *long-term liabilities*.

Current Liabilities.   **Current liabilities** are debts that are due to be paid within one year or within the entity's operating cycle if the cycle is longer than a year. Accounts Payable, Notes Payable due within one year, Salary Payable,

Unearned Revenue, and Interest Payable owed on notes payable are current liabilities.

Long-Term Liabilities. All liabilities that are not current are classified as **long-term liabilities.** Many notes payable are long-term. Other notes payable are paid in installments, with the first installment due within one year, the second installment due the second year, and so on. In this case, the first installment would be a current liability and the remainder a long-term liability.

An Actual Classified Balance Sheet

Exhibit 4-11 is a classified balance sheet of Grumman Corporation, a major maker of military aircraft. As you study the balance sheet, you will be delighted at how much of it you already understand. So far, you have been exposed

EXHIBIT 4-11 *Classified Balance Sheet*

Grumman Corporation Balance Sheet (adapted) December 31, 19XX	
	(dollar amounts in thousands)
Assets	
Current Assets	
Cash	$ 19,264
Marketable securities	95,115
Accounts receivable	801,953
Inventories	862,634
Prepaid expenses	35,077
Total current assets	1,814,043
Property, plant, and equipment, less accumulated depreciation [of $636,109]	587,408
Noncurrent assets	
Long-term receivables	60,335
Investments	28,398
Other	75,801
	164,534
Total	$2,565,985
Liabilities and Shareholders' Equity	
Current liabilities	
Short-term debt	$ 96,188
Accounts payable	276,538
Wages and employee benefits payable	74,887
Income taxes [payable]	99,553
Advances [unearned revenue current] and deposits	31,889
Other current liabilities	160,776
Total current liabilities	739,831
Long-term debt	802,078
Deferred income taxes	106,646
Other liabilities [such as unearned revenue, long-term]	95,175
Preferred stock	40,086
Common stock	290,530
Retained earnings	491,639
Total	$2,565,985

to almost all the assets and liabilities reported by this actual company. Marketable securities, among the current assets, are investments expected to be sold for cash within the next year. Noncurrent investments are expected to be held for a longer period. Grumman has two categories of receivables, current and noncurrent. The company reports the *book value*, or *net* amount, of property, plant, and equipment ($587,408,000), along with the amount of accumulated depreciation ($636,109,000). The original cost of the property, plant, and equipment is the sum of the two amounts, $1,223,517,000 ($587,408,000 + $636,109,000). Other assets and other liabilities are catchall categories for items that are difficult to classify.

Grumman Corporation, like many other companies, does not report a figure for total liabilities. This amount is the sum of total current liabilities, long-term debt, deferred income taxes (a topic covered in later accounting courses), and other liabilities: ($739,831,000 + $802,078,000 + $106,646,000 + $95,175,000 = $1,743,730,000). Grumman *labels its stockholders' equity as shareholders' equity* and has two classes of stock, preferred and common. Total shareholders' equity, not listed separately, is the sum of preferred stock, common stock, and retained earnings.

For your understanding, we have added bracketed explanation for several accounts. The bracketed items do not appear on the actual balance sheet.

Formats of Balance Sheets

The balance sheet of Grumman Corporation shown in Exhibit 4-11 lists the assets at the top, with the liabilities and the shareholders' equity below. This is the **report format.** The balance sheet of Air and Sea Travel, Inc., presented in Exhibit 4-7 lists the assets at the left, with the liabilities and the stockholders' equity at the right. That is the **account format.**

Either format is acceptable. A recent survey of 600 companies indicated that 56 percent use the account format and 44 percent use the report format.

Use of Accounting Information in Decision Making

The purpose of accounting is to provide information for decision making. Chief users of accounting information include managers, investors, and creditors. A creditor considering lending money must predict whether the borrower can repay the loan. If the borrower already has lots of debt, the probability of repayment is lower than if the borrower has a small amount of liabilities. To assess financial position, decision makers use ratios on various items drawn from a company's financial statements.

One of the most common financial ratios is the **current ratio**, which is the ratio of an entity's current assets to its current liabilities. The current ratio measures the ability to pay current liabilities with current assets. It is computed as follows:

$$\text{Current ratio} = \frac{\text{Total current assets}}{\text{Total current liabilities}}$$

A company prefers a high current ratio, which means that the business has plenty of current assets to pay current liabilities. An increasing current ratio from period to period indicates improvement in financial position.

A rule of thumb: A strong current ratio is 2.00, which indicates that the company has $2.00 in current assets for every $1.00 in current liabilities. A company with a current ratio of 2.00 would probably have little trouble paying its current liabilities. Most successful businesses operate with current ratios in the range between 1.50 and 2.00.

Grumman Corporation, the company in Exhibit 4-11, has a current ratio of 2.45 ($1,814,043/$739,831). What does this ratio value indicate about Grumman Corporation? The company appears to have sufficient current assets to pay all its current liabilities—a strong position.

How would a decision maker use the current ratio? A low current ratio would worry top managers of a company because it indicates difficulty in paying debts. Suppose the company needs to borrow money. If the bank agreed to loan money to a company with a current ratio of, say, .750—which it might not—the bank would place some restrictions on the borrower because of the company's risky financial position. For example, the lender might charge a high rate of interest and restrict dividends as part of the loan agreement. A decision maker considering investing in this business could recognize the company's risky position and might prefer to invest in another company instead. Lenders and investors would view a company such as Grumman Corporation as substantially less risky. Such a company could probably borrow money on better terms and also attract more investors.

A second aid to decision making is the **debt ratio**, which is the ratio of total liabilities to total assets. The debt ratio indicates the proportion of a company's assets that are financed with debt. This ratio measures a business's ability to pay both current and long-term debts—total liabilities. It is computed as follows:

$$\text{Debt ratio} = \frac{\text{Total liabilities}}{\text{Total assets}}$$

A low debt ratio is safer than a high debt ratio. Why? Because a company with a small amount of liabilities has low required payments. Such a company is unlikely to get into financial difficulty. By contrast, a business with a high debt ratio may have trouble paying its liabilities, especially when sales are low and cash is scarce. When a company fails to pay its debts, the creditors can take the business's assets away from the stockholders.

Grumman Corporation (Exhibit 4-11) has a debt ratio of .680 [.680 = ($739,831 + $802,078 + $106,646 + $95,175)/$2,565,985]. A debt ratio of .680 is fairly high in comparison to the norm of around .50. Lenders may place some restrictions on a borrower with liabilities of this magnitude. Very cautious people may be reluctant to invest in the company, and the managers of Grumman Corporation may feel pressure to reduce the company's debt.

In summary, a high current ratio is preferred over a low current ratio. Increases in the current ratio indicate improving financial position. By contrast, a low debt ratio is preferred over a high debt ratio. Improvement is indicated by a decrease in the debt ratio.

Financial ratios are an important aid to decisions. However, it is unwise to place too much confidence in a single ratio or any group of ratios. For example, a company may have a high current ratio, which indicates financial strength. It may also have a high debt ratio, which suggests weakness. Which ratio gives the more reliable signal about the company? Experienced managers, lenders, and investors evaluate a company by examining a large number of ratios over several years to spot trends and turning points. These people also consider other facts, such the company's cash position and its trend of net income. No single ratio gives the whole picture about a company.

As you progress through the study of accounting, we will introduce key ratios used for decision making. Chapter 27, Using Accounting Information to Make Business Decisions, summarizes all the ratios discussed throughout this textbook. Chapter 27 provides an overview of the use of ratios in decision making.

Detecting and Correcting Accounting Errors _____

You have now learned all the steps that an accountant takes from opening the books and recording a transaction in the journal through closing the books and the postclosing trial balance. Along the way, errors may occur. Accounting errors include incorrect journal entries, mistakes in posting, and transpositions and slides. This section discusses their detection and correction.

OBJECTIVE 7
Correct typical accounting errors

Incorrect Journal Entries. When a journal entry contains an error, the entry can be erased and corrected—if the error is caught immediately. Other accountants prefer to draw a line through the incorrect entry to maintain a record of all entries to the journal. After the incorrect entry is crossed out, the accountant can make the correct entry.

If the error is detected after posting, the accountant makes a *correcting entry*. Suppose Air and Sea Travel paid $5,000 cash for furniture and erroneously debited Supplies as follows:

Incorrect Entry

May 13	Supplies...................................	5,000	
	Cash		5,000
	Bought supplies.		

The debit to Supplies is incorrect, so it is necessary to make a correcting entry as follows:

Correcting Entry

May 15	Furniture	5,000	
	Supplies		5,000
	To correct May 13 entry.		

The credit to Supplies in the second entry offsets the incorrect debit of the first entry. The debit to Furniture in the correcting entry places the purchase amount in the correct account.

Incorrect posting. Sometimes an accountant posts a debit as a credit or a credit as a debit. Such an error shows up in the trial balance—total debits do not equal total credits.

Suppose a $100 debit to Cash is posted as a $100 credit. The trial balance's total debits are $200 too low. Total credits are correct. The difference is $200. Whenever a debit or credit has been misplaced, the resulting difference is evenly divisible by 2, as is the $200 figure in our example. Dividing that difference by 2 yields the amount of the incorrect posting, which in this case we know is $100. The accountant may then search the journal for the $100 entry and make the corrections.

Transpositions and Slides.   A **transposition** occurs when digits are reversed—for example, $85 is a transposition of $58. Transpositions cause errors that are evenly divisible by 9. In this particular case, the transposition causes a $27 error ($85 − $58), which is evenly divisible by 9 ($27/9 = $3).

A **slide** results from adding one or more zeroes to a number or from dropping off a zero, for example, writing $500 as $5,000 or vice versa. The difference of $4,500 ($5,000 − $500) is evenly divisible by 9 ($4,500/9 = $500). Transpositions and slides occur in the transfer of numbers, for example, from the journal to the ledger or from the ledger to the trial balance.

Incorrect postings, transpositions, and slides can be corrected by crossing out the incorrect amount and then inserting the correct amount in its appropriate place.

Summary Problem for Your Review

Refer to the data in the earlier Summary Problem for Your Review, presented on pages 160–161.

Required

1. Journalize and post the adjusting entries. (Before posting to the accounts, enter their balances as shown in the trial balance. For example, enter the $370,000 balance in the Accóunts Receivable account before posting its adjusting entry.) Key adjusting entries by *letter,* as shown in the work sheet solution to the first review problem. You can take the adjusting entries straight from the work sheet on page 161.
2. Journalize and post the closing entries. (Each account should carry its balance as shown in the adjusted trial balance.) To distinguish closing entries from adjusting entries, key the closing entries by *number.* Draw the arrows to illustrate the flow of data, as shown in Exhibit 4-9, page 166. Indicate the balance of the Retained Earnings account after the closing entries are posted.
3. Prepare the income statement for the year ended December 31, 19X1. List Miscellaneous Expense last among the expenses, a common practice.
4. Prepare the statement of retained earnings for the year ended December 31, 19Xl. Draw the arrow that links the income statement to the statement of retained earnings.
5. Prepare the classified balance sheet at December 31, 19X1. Use the report form. All liabilities are current. Draw the arrow that links the statement of retained earnings to the balance sheet.

SOLUTION TO REVIEW PROBLEM

Requirement 1

a. Dec. 31 Supplies Expense 4,000
                 Supplies   4,000

b.   31 Depreciation Expense—Furniture
                 and Fixtures 20,000
                       Accumulated Depreciation—
                       Furniture and Fixtures   20,000

c.   31 Depreciation Expense—Building............... 10,000
                       Accumulated Depreciation—Building   10,000

d.   31 Salary Expense................................ 5,000
                 Salary Payable   5,000

e.   31 Accounts Receivable.......................... 12,000
                 Service Revenue   12,000

f.   31 Unearned Service Revenue.................... 32,000
                 Service Revenue   32,000

Accounts Receivable		Supplies		Accumulated Depreciation—Furniture and Fixtures	
370,000		6,000	(a) 4,000		40,000
(e) 12,000					(b) 20,000

Accumulated Depreciation—Building		Salary Payable		Unearned Service Revenue	
	130,000		(d) 5,000	(f) 32,000	45,000
	(c) 10,000				

Service Revenue		Salary Expense		Supplies Expense	
	286,000	172,000		(a) 4,000	
	(e) 12,000	(d) 5,000			
	(f) 32,000	Bal. 177,000		Bal. 4,000	
	Bal. 330,000				

Depreciation Expense—Furniture and Fixtures		Depreciation Expense—Building	
(b) 20,000		(c) 10,000	
Bal. 20,000		Bal. 10,000	

Requirement 2

1.	Dec. 31	Service Revenue	330,000	
		Income Summary		330,000
2.	31	Income Summary	224,000	
		Salary Expense		177,000
		Supplies Expense		4,000
		Depreciation Expense— Furniture and Fixtures		20,000
		Depreciation Expense—Building .		10,000
		Miscellaneous Expense		13,000
3.	31	Income Summary ($330,000 − $224,000)	106,000	
		Retained Earnings		106,000
4.	31	Retained Earnings	65,000	
		Dividends		65,000

Salary Expense

	172,000			
(d)	5,000			
Bal.	177,000	(2)	177,000	

Supplies Expense

(a)	4,000			
Bal.	4,000	(2)	4,000	

Depreciation Expense– Furniture & Fixtures

(b)	20,000			
Bal.	20,000	(2)	20,000	

Depreciation Expense– Building

(c)	10,000			
Bal.	10,000	(2)	10,000	

Miscellaneous Expense

	13,000			
Bal.	13,000	(2)	13,000	

Income Summary

(2)	224,000	(1)	330,000	
(3)	106,000	Bal.	106,000	

Service Revenue

			286,000	
		(e)	12,000	
		(f)	32,000	
(1)	330,000	Bal.	330,000	

Dividends

Bal.	65,000	(4)	65,000	

Retained Earnings

(4)	65,000		193,000	
		(3)	106,000	
		Bal.	234,000	

Requirement 3

State Service Company
Income Statement
For the Year Ended December 31, 19X1

Revenues:		
Service revenue		$330,000
Expenses:		
Salary expense	$177,000	
Depreciation expense–furniture and fixtures	20,000	
Depreciation expense–building	10,000	
Supplies expense...................................	4,000	
Miscellaneous expense.............................	13,000	
Total expenses		224,000
Net income		$106,000

Requirement 4

State Service Company
Statement of Retained Earnings
For the Year Ended December 31, 19X1

Retained earnings January 1, 19X1..............................	$193,000
Add: Net income	106,000
	299,000
Less: Dividends	65,000
Retained earnings, December 31, 19X1	$234,000

Requirement 5

State Service Company
Balance Sheet
December 31, 19X1

Assets

Current assets:		
Cash		$198,000
Accounts receivable		382,000
Supplies..		2,000
Total current assets		582,000
Plant assets:		
Furniture and fixtures	$100,000	
Less Accumulated depreciation	60,000	40,000
Building..	250,000	
Less Accumulated depreciation	140,000	110,000
Total assets		$732,000

Liabilities

Current liabilities:		
Accounts payable		$380,000
Salary payable		5,000
Unearned service revenue		13,000
Total current liabilities		398,000

Stockholders' Equity

Common stock.....................................	$100,000	
Retained earnings	234,000	
Total stockholders' equity		334,000
Total liabilities and stockholders' equity		$732,000

Summary

The accounting cycle is the process by which accountants produce the financial statements for a specific period of time. The cycle starts with the beginning account balances. During the period, the business journalizes transactions and posts them to the ledger accounts. At the end of the period, the trial balance is prepared, and the accounts are adjusted in order to measure the period's net income or net loss.

Completion of the accounting cycle is aided by use of a *work sheet*. This columnar document summarizes the effects of all the activity of the period. It is neither a journal nor a ledger but merely a convenient device for completing the accounting cycle.

The work sheet has columns for the trial balance, the adjustments, the adjusted trial balance, the income statement, and the balance sheet. It aids the adjusting process, and it is the place where the period's net income or net loss is first computed. The work sheet also provides the data for the financial statements and the closing entries. However, it is not necessary. The accounting cycle can be completed from the less elaborate adjusted trial balance.

Microcomputer *spreadsheets* are extremely useful for tasks such as completing the accounting cycle. Their main advantage is that they can be programmed to print documents such as the work sheet and perform repetitious calculations without errors.

Revenues, expenses, and dividends represent increases and decreases in stockholders' equity for a specific period. At the end of the period, their balances are closed out to zero, and, for this reason, they are called *temporary accounts*. Assets, liabilities, and stockholders' equity are not closed because they are the *permanent accounts*. Their balances at the end of one period become the beginning balances of the next period. The final accuracy check of the period is the *postclosing trial balance*. *Reversing entries*, the opposite of prior-period adjusting entries, ease the accountant's work.

Four common accounting errors are *incorrect journal entries, incorrect postings, transpositions*, and *slides*. Techniques exist for detecting and correcting these errors.

The balance sheet reports current and long-term assets, current and long-term liabilities, and can be presented in report or account format. Two decision aids are the *current ratio*—total current assets divided by total current liabilities—and the *debt ratio*—total liabilities divided by total assets.

Self-Study Questions

Test your understanding of the chapter by marking the best answer to each of the following questions.

1. The focal point of the accounting cycle is the *(p. 150)*
   a. Financial statements
   b. Trial balance
   c. Adjusted trial balance
   d. Work sheet

2. Arrange the following accounting cycle steps in their proper order *(p. 151):*
   a. Complete the work sheet
   b. Journalize and post adjusting entries
   c. Prepare the postclosing trial balance
   d. Journalize and post transactions
   e. Prepare the financial statements
   f. Journalize and post closing entries

3. The work sheet is a *(p. 151)*
   a. Journal
   b. Ledger
   c. Financial statement
   d. Convenient device for completing the accounting cycle

4. The usefulness of the work sheet is *(p. 151)*
   a. Identifying the accounts that need to be adjusted
   b. Summarizing the effects of all the transactions of the period
   c. Aiding the preparation of the financial statements
   d. All of the above
5. Which of the following accounts is not closed? *(p. 164)*
   a. Supplies Expense   c. Interest Revenue
   b. Prepaid Insurance   d. Dividends
6. The closing entry for Salary Expense, with a balance of $322,000, is *(p. 166)*

   a. Salary Expense........................... 322,000
         Income Summary   322,000
   b. Salary Expense........................... 322,000
         Salary Payable   322,000
   c. Income Summary 322,000
         Salary Expense   322,000
   d. Salary Payable 322,000
         Salary Expense   322,000

7. The purpose of the postclosing trial balance is to *(p. 167)*
   a. Provide the account balances for preparation of the balance sheet
   b. Ensure that the ledger is in balance for the start of the next period
   c. Aid the journalizing and posting of the closing entries
   d. Ensure that the ledger is in balance for completion of the work sheet
8. Reversing entries are used to *(p. 170)*
   a. Avoid having to refer back to a preceding period's adjusting entry when recording a cash transaction of a later period
   b. Prepare the financial statements
   c. Close the accounts
   d. Bring accounts to their correct balances at the beginning of a new period
9. The classification of assets and liabilities as current or long-term depends on *(p. 172)*
   a. Their order of listing in the general ledger
   b. Whether they appear on the balance sheet or the income statement
   c. The relative liquidity of the item
   d. The format of the balance sheet—account format or report format
10. Ordinarily, a company prefers *(p. 175)*
   a. A high current ratio and a high debt ratio
   b. A high current ratio and a low debt ratio
   c. A low current ratio and a high debt ratio
   d. A low current ratio and a low debt ratio

Answers to the self-study questions follow the Accounting Vocabulary.

Accounting Vocabulary

Account format of the balance sheet. Format that lists the assets at the left, with liabilities and stockholders' equity at the right *(p. 174)*.

Accounting cycle. Process by which accountants produce an entity's financial statements for a specific period *(p. 150)*.

Closing entries. Entries that transfer the revenue, expense, and Dividends balances from these respective accounts to the Retained Earnings account (p. 165).

Closing the accounts. Step in the accounting cycle at the end of the period that prepares the accounts for recording the transactions of the next period. Closing the accounts consists of journalizing and posting the closing entries to set the balances of the revenue, expense, and Dividends accounts to zero (p. 162).

Current asset. An asset that is expected to be converted to cash, sold, or consumed during the next twelve months, or within the business's normal operating cycle if longer than a year (p. 172).

Current liability. A debt due to be paid within one year or one of the entity's operating cycles if the cycle is longer than a year (p. 172).

Current ratio. Current assets divided by current liabilities. Measures the ability to pay current liabilities from current assets (p. 174).

Debt ratio. Ratio of total liabilities to total assets. Tells the proportion of a company's assets that it has financed with debt (p. 175).

Income summary. A temporary "holding tank" account into which the revenues and expenses are transferred prior to their final transfer to the Retained Earnings account (p. 165).

Liquidity. Measure of how quickly an item may be converted to cash (p. 172).

Long-term asset. An asset other than a current asset (p. 172).

Long-term liability. A liability other than a current liability (p. 173).

Nominal account. Another name for a Temporary account—revenues, expenses, and Dividends—that are closed at the end of the period. (p. 164).

Operating cycle. Time span during which cash is paid for goods and services that are sold to customers who then pay the business in cash (p. 172).

Permanent accounts. Another name for a Real account—the assets, liabilities, and stockholders' equity accounts. These accounts are not closed at the end of the period because their balances are not used to measure income (pp. 164–165).

Postclosing trial balance. List of the ledger accounts and their balances at the end of the period after the journalizing and posting of the closing entries. The last step of the accounting cycle, the postclosing trial balance, ensures that the ledger is in balance for the start of the next accounting period (pp. 167–168).

Real account. Another name for a Permanent account—asset, liability, and stockholders' equity—that is *not* closed at the end of the period (pp. 164–165).

Report format of the balance sheet. Format that lists the assets at the top, with the liabilities and stockholders' equity below (p 174).

Reversing entry. An entry that switches the debit and the credit of a previous adjusting entry. The reversing entry is dated the first day of the period following the adjusting entry (p. 170).

Slide. An accounting error that results from adding one or more zeros to a number, or from dropping a zero. For example, writing $500 as $5,000 or as $50 is a slide. A slide is evenly divisible by 9. (p. 177).

Spreadsheet. Integrated software program that can be used to solve many different kinds of problems. An electronically prepared work sheet (p. 159).

Temporary account. Another name for a Nominal account. The revenue, expense, and Dividends accounts that relate to a particular accounting period and are closed at the end of the period are temporary accounts. (p. 164).

Transposition. An accounting error that occurs when digits are flip-flopped. For example, $85 is a transposition of $58. A transposition is evenly divisible by 9 (p. 177).

Work sheet. A columnar document designed to help move data from the trial balance to the financial statements (p. 151).

ASSIGNMENT MATERIAL _____

Questions

1. Identify the steps in the accounting cycle, distinguishing those that occur during the period from those that are performed at the end.
2. Why is the work sheet a valuable accounting tool?
3. Name two advantages the work sheet has over the adjusted trial balance.
4. Briefly explain how a microcomputer spreadsheet can be programmed to complete the work sheet.
5. Why must the adjusting entries be journalized and posted if they have already been entered on the work sheet?
6. Why should the adjusting entries be journalized and posted before making the closing entries?
7. Which types of accounts are closed?
8. What purpose is served by closing the accounts?
9. State how the work sheet helps with recording the closing entries.
10. Distinguish between permanent accounts and temporary accounts, indicating which type is closed at the end of the period. Give five examples of each type of account.
11. Is Income Summary a permanent account or a temporary account? When and how is it used?
12. Give the closing entries for the following accounts (balances in parentheses): Service Revenue ($4,700), Salary Expense ($1,100), Income Summary (credit balance of $2,000), Dividends ($2,300).
13. Briefly describe a reversing entry by stating what it is, when it is dated, and what it accomplishes.
14. Why are assets classified as current or long-term? On what basis are they classified? Where do the classified amounts appear?
15. Indicate which of the following accounts are current assets and which are long-term assets: Prepaid Rent, Building, Furniture, Accounts Receivable, Merchandise Inventory, Cash, Note Receivable (due within one year), Note Receivable (due after one year).
16. In what order are assets and liabilities listed on the balance sheet?
17. Name an outside party that is interested in whether a liability is current or long-term. Why is this party interested in this information?
18. A friend tells you that the difference between a current liability and a long-term liability is that they are payable to different types of creditors. Is your friend correct? Include in your answer the definitions of these two categories of liabilities.

19. Show how to compute the current ratio and the debt ratio. Indicate what ability each ratio measures, and state whether a high value or a low value is safer.

20. Give the name of the following accounting errors:
    a. Posted a $300 debit from the journal as a $300 credit in the ledger.
    b. Posted a $300 debit from the journal as a $3,000 debit in the ledger.
    c. Recorded a transaction by debiting one account for $3,100 and crediting the other account for $1,300.

21. How would you detect each of the errors in the preceding question?

22. Capp Company purchased supplies of $120 on account. The accountant debited Supplies and credited Cash for $120. A week later, after this entry has been posted to the ledger, the accountant discovers the error. How should he correct the error?

Exercises

Exercise 4-1   *Preparing a work sheet* **(L.O. 1)**

The trial balance of Makovic Pest Control, Inc., follows.

Additional information at September 30, 19X6:

a. Accrued salary expense, $200.
b. Prepaid rent expired, $900.
c. Supplies used, $2,250.
d. Accrued service revenue, $210.
e. Depreciation, $40.

Required

Complete Makovic's work sheet for September 19X6.

Makovic Pest Control, Inc.
Trial Balance
September 30, 19X6

Cash	$ 1,560	
Accounts receivable	2,840	
Prepaid rent	1,200	
Supplies	3,390	
Equipment	12,600	
Accumulated depreciation		$ 2,240
Accounts payable		1,600
Salary payable		
Common stock		10,000
Retained earnings		6,030
Dividends	3,000	
Service revenue		7,300
Depreciation expense		
Salary expense	1,800	
Rent expense		
Utilities expense	780	
Supplies expense		
Total	$27,170	$27,170

Exercise 4-2 *Journalizing adjusting and closing entries* (L.O. 3)

Journalize the adjusting and closing entries in Exercise 4-1.

Exercise 4-3 *Posting adjusting and closing entries* (L.O. 3)

Set up T-accounts for those accounts affected by the adjusting and closing entries in Exercise 4-1. Post the adjusting and closing entries to the accounts, denoting adjustment amounts by Adj., closing amounts by Clo., and balances by Bal. Double rule the accounts with zero balances after closing and show the ending balance in each account.

Exercise 4-4 *Preparing a postclosing trial balance* (L.O. 3)

Prepare the postclosing trial balance in Exercise 4-1.

Exercise 4-5 *Identifying and journalizing closing entries* (L.O. 4)

From the following selected accounts that Langefeld Catering Service reported in its June 30, 19X4, annual financial statements, prepare the entity's closing entries.

Retained earnings	$45,600	Interest expense	$ 2,200
Service revenue	92,100	Accounts receivable	26,000
Unearned revenues	1,350	Salary payable	850
Salary expense	12,500	Depreciation expense	10,200
Accumulated depreciation	35,000	Rent expense	5,900
Supplies expense	1,400	Dividends	40,000
Interest revenue	700	Supplies	1,100

Exercise 4-6 *Identifying and journalizing closing entries* (L.O. 4)

The accountant for Damon Reed, Attorneys, Professional Corporation, has posted adjusting entries *a* through *e* to the accounts at December 31, 19X2. All the revenue, expense, and stockholders' equity accounts of the entity are listed here in T-account form.

Accounts Receivable		Supplies		Accumulated Depreciation—Furniture	
23,000		4,000	(a) 2,000		5,000
(e) 3,500					(b) 1,100

Accumulated Depreciation—Building				Salary Payable	
	33,000				(d) 700
	(c) 6,000				

Common Stock		Retained Earnings		Dividends		Service Revenue	
	25,000		24,400	52,400			103,000
							(e) 3,500

Salary Expense		Supplies Expense		Depreciation Expense—Furniture		Depreciation Expense—Building	
28,000		(a) 2,000		(b) 1,100		(c) 6,000	
(d) 700							

Required

Journalize Reed's closing entries at December 31, 19X2.

Exercise 4-7 *Preparing a statement of retained earnings* **(L.O. 4)**

From the following accounts of Overhead Door Company, prepare the entity's statement of retained earnings for the year ended December 31, 19X5:

Retained Earnings				Dividends			
Dec. 31	41,000	Jan. 1	52,000	Mar. 31	8,000	Dec. 31	41,000
		Dec. 31	43,000	Jun. 30	8,000		
				Sep. 30	8,000		
				Dec. 31	17,000		

Income Summary			
Dec. 31	85,000	Dec. 31	128,000
Dec. 31	43,000		

Exercise 4-8 *Identifying and recording adjusting and closing entries* **(L.O. 3, 4)**

The trial balance and income statement amounts from the March work sheet of Bigelow Bonding Company are presented below.

Required

Journalize the adjusting and closing entries of Bigelow Bonding Company at March 31.

Account Title	Trial Balance		Income Statement	
Cash	$ 3,100			
Supplies	2,400			
Prepaid rent	1,100			
Office equipment	30,800			
Accumulated depreciation		$ 6,900		
Accounts payable		4,600		
Salary payable..................				
Unearned service revenue		4,400		
Common stock		7,500		
Retained earnings		7,300		
Dividends	1,000			
Service revenue		12,700		$16,000
Salary expense	3,000		$ 3,800	
Rent expense....................	1,200		1,400	
Depreciation expense			400	
Supplies expense			500	
Utilities expense	800		800	
	$43,400	$43,400	6,900	16,000
Net income			9,100	
			$16,000	$16,000

Exercise 4-9 *Journalizing reversing entries* **(L.O. 5)**

Return to Exercise 4-6. Identify the two adjustments for which reversing entries would be most useful. Journalize those reversing entries.

Exercise 4-10 *Journalizing and posting an accrued expense and the related reversing entry* **(L.O. 5)**

During 19X2 London Sales Company pays wages of $44,200 to its employees. At December 31, 19X2, the company owes accrued wages of $900 that will be included in the $1,200 weekly payroll payment on January 4, 19X3.

Required

1. Open T-accounts for Wage Expense and Wage Payable.
2. Journalize all wage transactions for 19X2 and 19X3, including adjusting, closing, and reversing entries. Record the $44,200 amount by a single debit to Wage Expense.
3. Post amounts to the two T-accounts, showing their balances at January 4, 19X3. Denote cash payment entries by *CP*, adjusting entries by *Adj.*, closing entries by *Clo.*, reversing entries by *Rev.*, and balances by *Bal.*

Exercise 4-11 *Preparing a classified balance sheet* **(L.O. 6)**

1. After solving Exercise 4-8, use the data in that exercise to prepare Bigelow Bonding Company's classified balance sheet at March 31 of the current year. Use the report format.
2. Compute Bigelow's current ratio and debt ratio at March 31. One year ago the current ratio was 1.20 and the debt ratio was .30. Indicate whether Bigelow's ability to pay its debts has improved or deteriorated during the current year.

Exercise 4-12 *Correcting accounting errors* **(L.O. 7)**

Prepare a correcting entry for each of the following accounting errors:

a. Adjusted prepaid rent by debiting Prepaid Rent and crediting Rent Expense for $700. This adjusting entry should have debited Rent Expense and credited Prepaid Rent for $700.
b. Debited Salary Expense and credited Cash to accrue salary expense of $500.
c. Recorded the earning of $3,200 service revenue collected in advance by debiting Accounts Receivable and crediting Service Revenue.
d. Accrued interest revenue of $800 by a debit to Accounts Receivable and a credit to Interest Revenue.
e. Recorded a $600 cash purchase of supplies by debiting Supplies and crediting Accounts Payable.
f. Debited Supplies and credited Accounts Payable for a $2,300 purchase of office equipment on account.

Problems   *(Group A)*

Problem 4-1A *Preparing a work sheet* **(L.O. 1)**

The trial balance of Agape Counseling Center, Inc., at May 31, 19X2, is shown on the following page.

Additional data at May 31, 19X2:

a. Accrued salary expense, $600.
b. Supplies on hand, $410.
c. Prepaid insurance expired during May, $390.
d. Accrued interest expense, $220.

e. Unearned service revenue earned during May, $4,400.
f. Accrued advertising expense, $60 (credit Accounts Payable).
g. Accrued interest revenue, $170.
h. Depreciation: furniture, $380; building, $160.

o.

Agape Counseling Center, Inc.
Trial Balance
May 31, 19X2

Cash	$ 1,670	
Notes receivable	10,340	
Interest receivable		
Supplies	560	
Prepaid insurance	1,790	
Furniture	27,410	
Accumulated depreciation—furniture		$ 1,480
Building	55,900	
Accumulated depreciation—building		33,560
Land	13,700	
Accounts payable		14,730
Interest payable		
Salary payable		
Unearned service revenue		6,800
Note payable, long-term		18,700
Common stock		20,000
Retained earnings		14,290
Dividends	3,800	
Service revenue		9,970
Interest revenue		
Depreciation expense—furniture		
Depreciation expense—building		
Salary expense	2,170	
Insurance expense		
Interest expense		
Utilities expense	490	
Property tax expense	640	
Advertising expense	1,060	
Supplies expense		
Total	$119,530	$119,530

Required

Complete Agape's work sheet for May.

Problem 4-2A *Preparing financial statements from an adjusted trial balance; journalizing the adjusting and closing entries* **(L.O. 3, 6)**

The adjusted trial balance of Lopez Consulting Service, Inc., at April 30, 19X2, the end of the company's fiscal year, is shown on the following page.

Adjusting data at April 30, 19X2, which have all been incorporated into the trial balance figures that follow:

a. Supplies used during the year, $6,880.
b. Prepaid insurance expired during the year, $5,370.
c. Accrued interest expense, $2,280.

d.   Accrued service revenue, $2,200.
e.   Depreciation for the year: equipment, $6,700; building, $3,210.
f.   Accrued wage expense, $830.
g.   Unearned service revenue earned during the year, $5,180.

Lopez Consulting Service, Inc.
Adjusted Trial Balance
April 30, 19X2

Cash	$ 2,370	
Accounts receivable	25,740	
Supplies	3,690	
Prepaid insurance....................	2,290	
Equipment	63,930	
Accumulated depreciation—equipment .		$ 28,430
Building	74,330	
Accumulated depreciation—building ...		18,260
Accounts payable		19,550
Interest payable		2,280
Wage payable		830
Unearned service revenue		3,660
Note payable, long-term...............		69,900
Common stock		20,000
Retained earnings....................		26,200
Dividends...........................	47,500	
Service revenue......................		99,550
Depreciation expense—equipment	6,700	
Depreciation expense—building........	3,210	
Wage expense	29,800	
Insurance expense	5,370	
Interest expense	8,170	
Utilities expense	5,670	
Property tax expense	3,010	
Supplies expense	6,880	
Total	$288,660	$288,660

Required

1.   Journalize the adjusting and closing entries.
2.   Prepare Lopez's income statement and statement of retained earnings for
     the year ended April 30, 19X2, and the classified balance sheet on that
     date. Use the account format for the balance sheet.
3.   Compute Lopez's current ratio and debt ratio at April 30, 19X2. One year
     ago the current ratio stood at 1.21, and the debt ratio was .82. Did Lopez's
     ability to pay debts improve or deteriorate during 19X2?

Problem 4-3A   *Taking the accounting cycle through the closing entries*   *(L.O. 3, 4)*

The unadjusted T-accounts of Dave Laufenberg, M.D., Professional Corpor-
tion, at December 31, 19X2, and the related year-end adjustment data follow:

Adjustment data at December 31, 19X2, include:

a.   Supplies on hand, $2,000.
b.   Depreciation for the year, $6,000.
c.   Accrued salary expense, $3,000.
d.   Accrued service revenue, $4,000.
e.   Unearned service revenue earned during the year, $2,000.

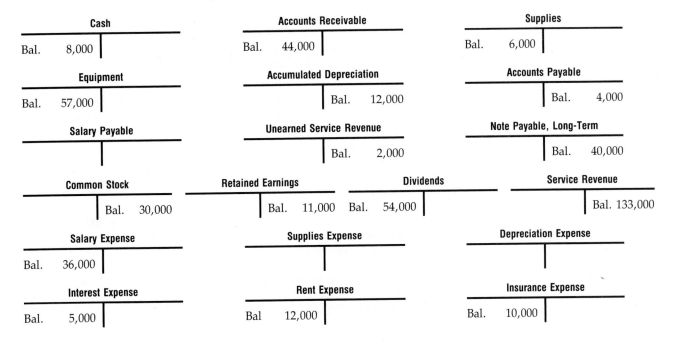

Cash		Accounts Receivable		Supplies	
Bal. 8,000		Bal. 44,000		Bal. 6,000	

Equipment		Accumulated Depreciation		Accounts Payable	
Bal. 57,000			Bal. 12,000		Bal. 4,000

Salary Payable		Unearned Service Revenue		Note Payable, Long-Term	
			Bal. 2,000		Bal. 40,000

Common Stock		Retained Earnings		Dividends		Service Revenue	
	Bal. 30,000		Bal. 11,000	Bal. 54,000			Bal. 133,000

Salary Expense		Supplies Expense		Depreciation Expense	
Bal. 36,000					

Interest Expense		Rent Expense		Insurance Expense	
Bal. 5,000		Bal 12,000		Bal. 10,000	

Required

1. Write the trial balance on a work sheet and complete the work sheet. Key each adjusting entry by the letter corresponding to the data given.
2. Prepare the income statement, the statement of retained earnings, and the classified balance sheet in account format.
3. Journalize the adjusting and closing entries.

Problem 4-4A *Completing the accounting cycle (L.O. 3, 4)*

This problem should be used only in conjunction with Problem 4-3A. It completes the accounting cycle by posting to T-accounts and preparing the post-closing trial balance.

Required

1. Using the Problem 4-3A data, post the adjusting and closing entries to the T-accounts, denoting adjusting amounts by *Adj.*, closing amounts by *Clo.*, and account balances by *Bal.*, as shown in Exhibit 4-9. Double underline all accounts with a zero ending balance.
2. Prepare the postclosing trial balance.

Problem 4-5A *Completing the accounting cycle (L.O. 3, 4, 6)*

The trial balance of Hubby Insurance Agency, Inc., at October 31, 19X0, and the data needed for the month-end adjustments are as follows:

Adjustment data:

a. Prepaid rent still in force at October 31, $2,000.
b. Supplies used during the month, $570.
c. Depreciation on furniture for the month, $250.
d. Depreciation on building for the month, $280.
e. Accrued salary expense at October 31, $310.
f. Unearned commission revenue still unearned at October 31, $4,700.

Hubby Insurance Agency, Inc.
Trial Balance
October 31, 19X0

Account Number	Account Title	Debit	Credit
11	Cash	$ 2,900	
12	Accounts receivable	12,310	
13	Prepaid rent	2,200	
14	Supplies	840	
15	Furniture	26,830	
16	Accumulated depreciation—furniture........		$ 3,400
17	Building	68,300	
18	Accumulated depreciation—building		9,100
21	Accounts payable........................		7,290
22	Salary payable..........................		
23	Unearned commission revenue		5,300
31	Common stock		50,000
32	Retained Earnings		35,490
33	Dividends	3,900	
41	Commission revenue		9,560
51	Salary expense	1,840	
52	Rent expense...........................		
53	Utilities expense	530	
54	Depreciation expense—furniture		
55	Depreciation expense—building		
56	Advertising expense	490	
57	Supplies expense		
	Total	$120,140	$120,140

Required

1. Open the accounts listed in the trial balance, inserting their October 31 unadjusted balances. Also open the Income Summary account, number 34. Use four-column accounts. Date the balances of the following accounts October 1: Prepaid Rent, Supplies, Building, Accumulated Depreciation—Building, Furniture, Accumulated Depreciation—Furniture, Unearned Commission Revenue, Common Stock, and Retained Earnings.

2. Write the trial balance on a work sheet and complete the work sheet of Hubby Insurance Agency, Inc., for the month ended October 31, 19X0.

3. Prepare the income statement, the statement of retained earnings, and the classified balance sheet in report format.

4. Using the work sheet data, journalize and post the adjusting and closing entries. Use dates and posting references. Use 12 as the number of the journal page.

5. Prepare a postclosing trial balance.

Problem 4-6A *Using reversing entries (L.O. 5)*

Refer to the data in Problem 4-5A.

Required

1. Open accounts for Salary Payable and Salary Expense. Insert their unadjusted balances at October 31, 19X0.

2. Journalize adjusting entry *e* and the closing entry for Salary Expense at October 31. Post to the ledger accounts.
3. On November 3, Hubby Insurance Agency, Inc., paid the next payroll amount of $470. Journalize this cash payment, and post to the accounts. Show the balance in each account.
4. Repeat requirements 1-3 using a reversing entry. Compare the balances of Salary Payable and Salary Expense computed using a reversing entry, with those balances computed without using a reversing entry (as appear in your answer to requirement 3).

Problem 4-7A *Journalizing adjusting and reversing entries* **(L.O. 5)**

The accounting records of Conner Company reveal the following information before adjustments at December 31, 19X6, the end of the accounting period.

a. On July 31 Conner deposited $25,000 in a savings account. The bank will pay Conner interest of $1,200 on January 31, 19X7. Of this amount, five sixths is earned in 19X6.
b. On November 29 Conner Company received a property tax bill from the city. The total amount, due on January 15, 19X7, is $3,900. Three fourths of this amount is property tax expense of 19X6.
c. Commissions owed to sales employees at December 31 are $2,565, and salaries owed to home office employees are $1,870.

Required

1. Journalize the adjusting entry needed for each situation at December 31, 19X6, identifying each entry by its corresponding letter.
2. Journalize reversing entries as needed. Use the corresponding letters for references. Date the entries.
3. Use the first situation that calls for a reversing entry to explain the practical value of the reversal.

Problem 4-8A *Preparing a classified balance sheet in report format* **(L.O. 6)**

The accounts of Gose & Pinkoff, CPAs, Professional Corporation, at March 31, 19X3, are listed in alphabetical order.

Accounts payable	$12,700	Interest payable	$ 200
Accounts receivable	11,500	Interest receivable	800
Accumulated depreciation—building	47,300	Note payable, long-term	3,200
		Note receivable, long-term	6,900
Accumulated depreciation—furniture	7,700	Other assets	1,300
		Other current assets	900
Advertising expense	2,300	Other current liabilities	1,100
Building	55,900	Prepaid insurance	600
Cash	1,400	Prepaid rent	4,700
Common stock	25,000	Retained earnings, March 31, 19X2	17,800
Current portion of note payable	800	Salary expense	16,400
Current portion of note receivable	3,100	Salary payable	1,400
		Service revenue	71,100
Depreciation expense	1,900	Supplies	3,800
Dividends	31,200	Supplies expense	4,600
Furniture	43,200	Unearned service revenue	2,800
Insurance expense	600		

Required

1. All adjustments have been journalized and posted, but the closing entries have not yet been made. Prepare the company's classified balance sheet in report format at March 31, 19X3. Use captions for total assets, total liabilities, total stockholders' equity, and total liabilities and stockholders' equity.
2. Compute Pinkoff's current ratio and debt ratio at March 31, 19X3. At March 31, 19X2, the current ratio was 1.28, and debt ratio was .32. Did the firm's ability to pay debts improve or deteriorate during 19X3?

Problem 4-9A *Analyzing and journalizing corrections, adjustments, and closing entries (L.O. 4, 7)*

The accountants of Polanski Catering Service encountered the following situations while adjusting and closing the books at February 28. Consider each situation independently.

a. The company bookkeeper made the following entry to record a $950 credit purchase of supplies:

Feb. 26   Equipment   950
                    Accounts Payable   950

Prepare the correcting entry, dated February 28.

b. A $390 credit to Accounts Receivable was posted as $930.
   (1) At what stage of the accounting cycle will this error be detected?
   (2) Describe the technique for identifying the amount of the error.

c. The $1,620 balance of Utilities Expense was entered as $16,200 on the trial balance.
   (1) What is the name of this type of error?
   (2) Assume this is the only error in the trial balance. Which will be greater, the total debits or the total credits, and by how much?
   (3) How can this type of error be identified?

d. The accountant failed to make the following adjusting entries at February 28:
   (1) Accrued service revenue, $700
   (2) Insurance expense, $460
   (3) Accrued interest expense on a note payable, $520
   (4) Depreciation of equipment, $3,300
   (5) Earned service revenue that had been collected in advance, $2,700
   Compute the overall net income effect of these omissions.

e. Record each of the adjusting entries identified in item *d*.

f. The revenue and expense accounts after the adjusting entries had been posted were Service Revenue, $95,330; Wage Expense, $29,340; Depreciation Expense, $6,180; Interest Expense, $4,590; Utilities Expense, $1,620; and Insurance Expense, $740. Two balances prior to closing were Retained Earnings, $75,150; and Dividends, $48,000. Journalize the closing entries.

(Group B)

Problem 4-1B *Preparing a work sheet (L.O. 1)*

The trial balance of Ross Painting Contractors, Inc., at July 31, 19X3, is shown on the next page. Additional data at July 31, 19X3, are as follows:

a. Accrued wage expense, $440.
b. Supplies on hand, $14,740.

c. Prepaid insurance expired during July, $500.
d. Accrued interest expense, $180.
e. Unearned service revenue earned during July, $4,770.
f. Accrued advertising expense, $100 (credit Accounts Payable).
g. Accrued service revenue, $1,100.
h. Depreciation: equipment, $430; building, $270.

Ross Painting Contractors, Inc. Trial Balance July 31, 19X3		
Cash	$ 4,200	
Accounts receivable	37,820	
Supplies	17,660	
Prepaid insurance	2,300	
Equipment	32,690	
Accumulated depreciation—equipment		$ 26,240
Building	36,890	
Accumulated depreciation—building		10,500
Land	28,300	
Accounts payable		22,690
Interest payable		
Wage payable		
Unearned service revenue		10,560
Note payable, long-term		22,400
Common stock		50,000
Retained earnings		12,130
Dividends	4,200	
Service revenue		17,190
Depreciation expense—equipment		
Depreciation expense—building		
Wage expense	6,200	
Insurance expense		
Interest expense		
Utilities expense	270	
Property tax expense	840	
Advertising expense	340	
Supplies expense		
Total	$171,710	$171,710

Required

Complete Ross's work sheet for July.

Problem 4-2B *Preparing financial statements from an adjusted trial balance; journalizing the adjusting and closing entries* **(L.O. 3, 6)**

The adjusted trial balance of Federal Security Couriers at June 30, 19X1, the end of the company's fiscal year, is on the next page.

Adjusting data at June 30, 19X1, which have all been incorporated into the trial balance that follows:
a. Supplies used during the year, $3,580.
b. Prepaid insurance expired during the year, $3,100.
c. Accrued interest expense, $680.
d. Accrued service revenue, $940.

e. Depreciation for the year: equipment, $6,300; building, $3,470.
f. Accrued wage expense, $770.
g. Unearned service revenue earned during the year, $6,790.

Federal Security Couriers
Adjusted Trial Balance
June 30, 19X1

Cash	$ 18,350	
Accounts receivable	26,470	
Supplies	1,290	
Prepaid insurance	1,700	
Equipment	55,800	
Accumulated depreciation—equipment		$ 16,480
Building	144,900	
Accumulated depreciation—building		16,850
Accounts payable		36,900
Interest payable		1,490
Wage payable		770
Unearned service revenue		2,300
Note payable, long-term		97,000
Common stock		25,000
Retained Earnings		42,390
Dividends	45,300	
Service revenue		108,360
Depreciation expense—equipment	6,300	
Depreciation expense—building	3,470	
Wage expense	18,800	
Insurance expense	3,100	
Interest expense	11,510	
Utilities expense	4,300	
Property tax expense	2,670	
Supplies expense	3,580	
Total	$347,540	$347,540

Required

1. Journalize the adjusting and closing entries.
2. Prepare Federal's income statement and statement of retained earnings for the year ended June 30, 19X1, and the classified balance sheet on that date. Use the account format for the balance sheet.
3. Compute Federal's current ratio and debt ratio at June 30, 19X1. One year ago the current ratio stood at 1.01, and the debt ratio was .71. Did Federal's ability to pay debts improve or deteriorate during 19X1?

Problem 4-3B *Taking the accounting cycle through the closing entries* **(L.O. 3, 4)**

The unadjusted T-accounts of Christine Ciancia, Psychologist, Professional Corporation, at December 31, 19X2, are given at the top of the next page. The related year-end adjustment data at December 31, 19X2, include:

a. Supplies on hand, $1,000.
b. Depreciation for the year, $9,000.
c. Accrued salary expense, $2,000.
d. Accrued service revenue, $1,000.
e. Unearned service revenue earned during the year, $5,000.

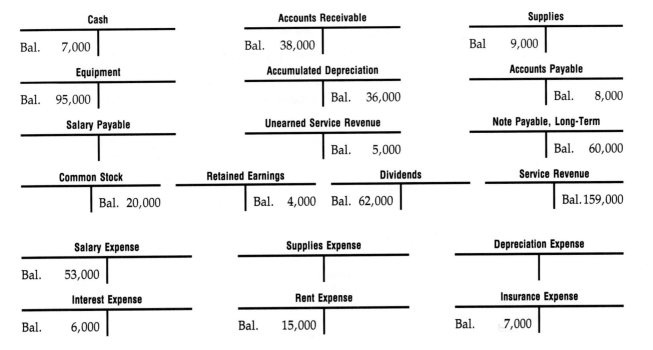

Cash		Accounts Receivable		Supplies	
Bal. 7,000		Bal. 38,000		Bal 9,000	

Equipment		Accumulated Depreciation		Accounts Payable	
Bal. 95,000			Bal. 36,000		Bal. 8,000

Salary Payable		Unearned Service Revenue		Note Payable, Long-Term	
			Bal. 5,000		Bal. 60,000

Common Stock		Retained Earnings		Dividends		Service Revenue	
	Bal. 20,000		Bal. 4,000	Bal. 62,000			Bal. 159,000

Salary Expense		Supplies Expense		Depreciation Expense	
Bal. 53,000					

Interest Expense		Rent Expense		Insurance Expense	
Bal. 6,000		Bal. 15,000		Bal. 7,000	

Required

1. Write the trial balance on a work sheet, and complete the work sheet. Key each adjusting entry by the letter corresponding to the data given.
2. Prepare the income statement, the statement of retained earnings, and the classified balance sheet in account format.
3. Journalize the adjusting and closing entries.

Problem 4-4B *Completing the accounting cycle* **(L.O. 3, 4)**

This problem should be used only in conjunction with Problem 4-3B. It completes the accounting cycle by posting to T-accounts and preparing the post-closing trial balance.

Required

1. Using the Problem 4-3B data, post the adjusting and closing entries to the T-accounts, denoting adjusting amounts by *Adj.*, closing amounts by *Clo.*, and account balances by *Bal.*, as shown in Exhibit 4-9. Double underline all accounts with a zero ending balance.
2. Prepare the postclosing trial balance.

Problem 4-5B *Completing the accounting cycle* **(L.O. 3, 4, 6)**

The trial balance of Nix Insurance Agency, Inc., at August 31, 19X9, and the data needed for the month-end adjustments follow.

a. Prepaid rent still in force at August 31, $1,050.
b. Supplies used during the month, $140.
c. Depreciation on furniture for the month, $370.
d. Depreciation on building for the month, $130.
e. Accrued salary expense at August 31, $460.
f. Unearned commission revenue still unearned at August 31, $7,750.

hasn't seen paid

Nix Insurance Agency, Inc.
Trial Balance
August 31, 19X9

Account Number	Account Title	Debit	Credit
11	Cash	$ 6,800	
12	Accounts receivable	17,560	
13	Prepaid rent	1,290	
14	Supplies	900	
15	Furniture	15,350	
16	Accumulated depreciation—furniture		$ 12,800
17	Building	89,900	
18	Accumulated depreciation—building		28,600
21	Accounts payable		6,240
22	Salary payable........................		
23	Unearned commission revenue		8,900
31	Common stock		20,000
32	Retained earnings		54,920
33	Dividends	4,800	
41	Commission revenue		7,800
51	Salary expense	1,600	
52	Rent expense..........................		
53	Utilities expense	410	
54	Depreciation expense—furniture		
55	Depreciation expense—building		
56	Advertising expense	650	
57	Supplies expense		
	Total	$139,260	$139,260

Required

1. Open the accounts listed in the trial balance, inserting their August 31 unadjusted balances. Also open the Income Summary account, number 34. Use four column accounts. Date the balances of the following accounts as of August 1: Prepaid Rent, Supplies, Furniture, Accumulated Depreciation—Furniture, Building, Accumulated Depreciation—Building, Unearned Commission Revenue, and Common Stock, and Retained Earnings.

2. Write the trial balance on a work sheet and complete the work sheet of Nix Insurance Agency, Inc., for the month ended August 31, 19X9.

3. Prepare the income statement, the statement of retained earnings, and the classified balance sheet in report format.

4. Using the work sheet data, journalize and post the adjusting and closing entries. Use dates and posting references. Use page 7 as the number of the journal page.

5. Prepare a postclosing trial balance.

Problem 4-6B   *Using reversing entries*   **(L.O. 5)**

Refer to the data in Problem 4-5B.

Required

1. Open accounts for Salary Payable and Salary Expense. Insert their unadjusted balances at August 31, 19X9.

2. Journalize adjusting entry *e* and the closing entry for Salary Expense at August 31. Post to the accounts.

3. On September 5, Nix Insurance Agency, Inc., paid the next payroll amount of $580. Journalize this cash payment, and post to the accounts. Show the balance in each account.

4. Repeat requirements 1–3 using a reversing entry. Compare the balances of Salary Payable and Salary Expense computed using a reversing entry, with those balances computed without using a reversing entry (as appear in your answer to requirement 3).

Problem 4-7B   *Journalizing adjusting and reversing entries* **(L.O. 5)**

Vidmar Company's accounting records reveal the following information before adjustments at December 31, 19X3, the end of the accounting period:

a. Wages owed to hourly employees total $3,400. Total salaries owed to salaried employees are $2,790. These amounts will be paid on the next scheduled payday in January 19X4.

b. On October 31 Vidmar loaned $40,000 to another business. The loan agreement requires the borrower to pay Vidmar interest of $2,400 on April 30, 19X4. One third of this interest is earned in 19X3.

c. On December 23 Vidmar Company received a property tax bill from the city. The total amount, due on February 1, 19X4, is $4,600. Half of this amount is property tax expense for 19X3.

Required

1. Journalize the adjusting entry needed for each situation at December 31, 19X3, identifying each entry by its corresponding letter.

2. Journalize reversing entries as needed. Use the corresponding letters for references. Date the entries appropriately.

3. Use the first situation that calls for a reversing entry to explain the practical value of the reversal.

Problem 4-8B   *Preparing a classified balance sheet in report format* **(L.O. 6)**

The accounts of Hankins Travel Agency, Inc., at December 31, 19X6, are listed in alphabetical order.

Accounts payable	$ 3,100	Interest payable	$ 600
Accounts receivable	4,600	Interest receivable	200
Accumulated deprecia-tion—building	37,800	Note payable, long-term .	27,800
Accumulated deprecia-tion—furniture	11,600	Note receivable, long-term	4,000
		Other assets	3,600
Advertising expense	2,200	Other current assets	1,700
Building	104,400	Other current liabilities . .	4,700
Cash	4,500	Prepaid insurance	1,100
Commission revenue	93,500	Prepaid rent	6,600
Common stock	20,000	Retained earnings, December 31, 19X5	30,300
Current portion of note payable	2,200	Salary expense	22,600
Current portion of note receivable	1,000	Salary payable	1,900
		Supplies	2,500
Depreciation expense . . .	1,300	Supplies expense	5,700
Dividends	47,400	Unearned commission revenue	3,400
Furniture	22,700		
Insurance expense	800		

Required

1. All adjustments have been journalized and posted, but the closing entries have not yet been made. Prepare the company's classified balance sheet in report format at December 31, 19X6. Use captions for total assets, total liabilities, total stockholders' equity, and total liabilities and stockholders' equity.

2. Compute Hankins's current ratio and debt ratio at December 31, 19X6. At December 31, 19X5, the current ratio was 1.52, and the debt ratio was .37. Did Hankins's ability to pay debts improve or deteriorate during 19X6?

Problem 4-9B *Analyzing and journalizing corrections, adjustments, and closing entries (L.O. 4, 7)*

Accountants for Osaka Catering Service encountered the following situations while adjusting and closing the books at December 31. Consider each situation independently.

a. The company bookkeeper made the following entry to record a $400 credit purchase of office equipment:

Nov. 12	Office Supplies	400	
	Accounts Payable		400

Prepare the correcting entry, dated December 31.

b. A $750 debit to Cash was posted as a credit.
   (1) At what stage of the accounting cycle will this error be detected?
   (2) Describe the technique for identifying the amount of the error.

c. The $35,000 balance of Equipment was entered as $3,500 on the trial balance.
   (1) What is the name of this type of error?
   (2) Assume this is the only error in the trial balance. Which will be greater, the total debits or the total credits, and by how much?
   (3) How can this type of error be identified?

d. The accountant failed to make the following adjusting entries at December 31:
   (1) Accrued property tax expense, $200
   (2) Supplies expense, $1,390
   (3) Accrued interest revenue on a note receivable, $950
   (4) Depreciation of equipment, $4,000
   (5) Earned service revenue that had been collected in advance, $5,300
       Compute the overall net income effect of these omissions.

e. Record each of the adjusting entries identified in item *d*.

f. The revenue and expense accounts, after the adjusting entries had been posted, were Service Revenue, $55,800; Interest Revenue, $2,000; Salary Expense, $13,200; Rent Expense, $5,100; Depreciation Expense, $5,550; Supplies Expense, $1,530; and Property Tax Expense, $1,190. Two balances prior to closing were Retained Earnings, $58,600; and Dividends, $30,000. Journalize the closing entries.

Extending Your Knowledge

Decision Problems

1. Completing the Accounting Cycle to Develop the Information for a Bank Loan   (L.O. 4, 6)

Two years ago, your friends Grant Thornton and Brent Snow founded Thornton & Snow Computing Service, Inc. The business has prospered. Thornton, who remembers that you took an accounting course while in college, comes to you for advice. He wishes to know how much net income his business earned during the past year. He also wants to know what the entity's total assets, liabilities, and stockholders' equity are. His accounting records consist of the T-accounts of his ledger, which were prepared by an accountant who moved to another city. The ledger at December 31 of the current year is

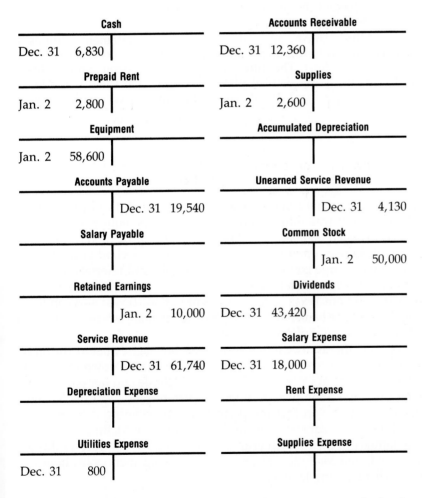

Thornton indicates that at the year's end customers owe the business $1,600 accrued service revenue, which it expects to collect early next year. These revenues have not been recorded. During the year Thornton & Snow collected $4,130 service revenue in advance from customers, but earned only $1,190 of that amount. Rent expense for the year was $2,400, and the business used up

$2,100 in supplies. Thornton estimates that depreciation on equipment was $5,900 for the year. At December 31 the business owes employees $1,200 accrued salary.

At the conclusion of your meeting, Thornton expresses concern that dividends during the year might have exceeded net income. To get a loan to expand the business, Thornton & Snow must show the bank that the business's retained earnings account has grown during the year. Has it? You and Thornton agree that you will meet again in one week. You perform the analysis and prepare the financial statements to answer his questions.

2. Finding an Error in the Work Sheets (L.O. 1, 7)

You are preparing the financial statements for the year ended October 31, 19X5 for Woodside Publishing Company, a weekly newspaper. You began with the trial balance of the ledger, which balanced, and then made the required adjusting entries. To save time, you omitted preparing an adjusted trial balance. After making the adjustments on the work sheet, you extended the balances from the trial balance, adjusted for the adjusting entries, and computed amounts for the income statement and balance sheet columns.

a. You added the debits and credits on the income statement and found that the credits exceeded the debits by $X. Did Woodside Publishing have a profit or a loss based on your finding?

b. You entered the balancing amount from the income statement columns in the balance sheet columns and found the total debits exceeded total credits in the balance sheet. The difference between the debits and credits is twice the amount ($2X) you calculated in question *a*. What is the likely cause of the difference? What assumption have you made in your answer?

Ethical Issue

McBride Associates, a management consulting firm, is in its third year of operations. The company was initially financed by owners' equity as the three partners each invested $30,000. The first year's slim profits were expected because new businesses often start slowly. During the second year McBride Associates landed a large contract with a paper mill, and referrals from that project brought in several other large jobs. To expand the business, McBride borrowed $100,000 from Texas National Bank of Lufkin, Texas. As a condition for making this loan the bank required McBride to maintain a current ratio of at least 1.50 and a debt ratio of no more than .50.

Business during the third year has been good, but slightly below the target for the year. Expansion costs have brought the current ratio down to 1.47 and the debt ratio up to .51 at December 15. Glenda McBride and her partners are considering the implication of reporting this current ratio to Texas National Bank. One course of action that the partners are considering is to record in December of the third year some revenue on account that McBride Associates will earn in January of their fourth year of operations. The contract for this job has been signed, and McBride will perform the management consulting services for the client during January.

Required

1. Journalize the revenue transaction, and indicate how recording this revenue in December would affect the current ratio and the debt ratio.

2. State whether it is ethical to record the revenue transaction in December. Identify the accounting principle relevant to this situation.

3. Propose for McBride Associates a course of action that is ethical.

Financial Statement Problems

1. Using An Actual Balance Sheet   (L.O. 6)

This problem, based on The Goodyear Tire & Rubber Company's balance sheet in Appendix C, will familiarize you with some of the assets and liabilities of this actual company. Answer these questions, using Goodyear's balance sheet.

1. Which balance sheet format does Goodyear use?
2. Name the company's largest current asset and largest current liability at December 31, 1991.
3. Compute Goodyear's current ratios at December 31, 1991, and December 31, 1990. Also compute the debt ratios at these dates. Did the ratio values improve or deteriorate during 1991? Refer to the income statement to explain why the ratio values improved or deteriorated.
4. Under what category does Goodyear report land, buildings, machinery, and equipment?
5. What was the cost of the company's plant assets at December 31, 1991? What was the book value of the plant assets? To answer this question, refer to the Properties and Plants note.

2. Using An Actual Balance Sheet   (L.O. 6)

Obtain the annual report of an actual company of your choosing. Answer these questions about the company:

1. Which balance sheet format does the company use?
2. Name the company's largest asset and largest liability at the end of the current year and at the end of the preceding year. Name the largest *current* asset and the largest *current* liability at the end of the current year and at the end of the preceding year.
3. Compute the company's current ratio at the end of the current year and the current ratio at the end of the preceding year. Also compute the debt ratio at the end of the current year and at the end of the preceding year. Did these ratio values improve or deteriorate during the current year? Does the income statement help to explain why the ratios improved or deteriorated? Give your reason.

Appendix

Prepaid Expenses, Unearned Revenues, and Reversing Entries

Chapters 1 through 4 illustrate the most popular way to account for prepaid expenses and unearned revenues. This appendix expands that coverage by illustrating an alternate approach to handling prepaid expenses and unearned revenues—equally appropriate—that calls for reversing entries.

Prepaid Expenses

Prepaid expenses are advance payments of expenses. Prepaid Insurance, Prepaid Rent, Prepaid Advertising, and Prepaid Legal Cost are prepaid expenses. Supplies that will be used up in the current period or within one year are also accounted for as prepaid expenses.

When a business prepays an expense—rent, for example—it can debit an *asset* account (Prepaid Rent) as follows:

Prepaid Rent.......................	XXX	
Cash		XXX

Alternatively, the accountant can debit an *expense* account in the entry to record this cash payment, as follows:

Rent Expense	XXX	
Cash		XXX

Regardless of the account debited, the business must adjust the accounts at the end of the period. Making the adjustment allows the business to report the correct amount of expense for the period and the correct amount of asset at the period's end.

Prepaid Expense Recorded Initially as an Asset

Prepayments of expenses provide a future benefit to the business, so it is logical to record the prepayment by debiting an *asset* account. Suppose on August 1, 19X6, the business prepays one year's rent of $6,000 ($500 per month). The cash payment is recorded:

19X6			
Aug. 1	Prepaid Rent..................	6,000	
	Cash		6,000

On December 31, the end of the accounting period, five months' prepayment has expired and must be accounted for as *expense*. The adjusting entry is

Adjusting Entries

19X6			
Dec. 31	Rent Expense ($6,000 × 5/12)	2,500	
	Prepaid Rent		2,500

The adjusting entry transfers $2,500 of the original $6,000 prepayment from Prepaid Rent to Rent Expense. This leaves a $3,500 debit balance in Prepaid Rent, which is seven months' rent still prepaid. After posting, the accounts appear as follows:

Prepaid Rent

19X6			19X6		
Aug. 1	CP	6,000	Dec. 31	Adj.	2,500
Dec. 31	Bal.	3,500			

Rent Expense

19X6		
Dec. 31	Adj.	2,500
Dec. 31	Bal.	2,500

The $2,500 balance of Rent Expense is closed to Income Summary, along with all other expenses and revenues, at the end of the accounting period.

No reversing entry is used under this approach. The asset account Prepaid Rent has a debit balance to start the new period. This is consistent with recording prepaid expenses initially as assets.

The balance sheet at December 31, 19X6, reports Prepaid Rent of $3,500 as an asset. The 19X6 income statement reports Rent Expense of $2,500 as an expense, which is the expired portion of the initial $6,000 rent prepayment. Keep this reporting result in mind as you study the next section.

Prepaid Expense Recorded Initially as an Expense

Prepaying an expense creates an asset. However, the asset may be so short-lived that it will expire in the current accounting period—within one year or less. Thus the accountant may decide to debit the prepayment to an expense account at the time of payment. Continuing with the rent example, the $6,000 cash payment on August 1 may be debited to Rent Expense:

```
19X6
Aug. 1   Rent Expense .................   6,000
             Cash ...................            6,000
```

At December 31 only five months' prepayment has expired, leaving seven months' rent still prepaid. In this case, the accountant must transfer $7/12$ of the original prepayment of $6,000, or $3,500, to Prepaid Rent. The adjusting entry decreases the balance of Rent Expense to $5/12$ of the original $6,000, or $2,500. The December 31 adjusting entry is

Adjusting Entries

```
19X6
Dec. 31   Prepaid Rent ($6,000 × 7/12) .....   3,500
              Rent Expense ............            3,500
```

After posting, the two accounts appear as follows:

Prepaid Rent

19X6		
Dec. 31 Adj.	3,500	
Dec. 31 Bal.	3,500	

Rent Expense

19X6			19X6	
Aug. 1 CP	6,000		Dec. 31 Adj.	3,500
Dec. 31 Bal.	2,500			

The balance sheet for 19X6 reports Prepaid Rent of $3,500, and the income statement for 19X6 reports Rent Expense of $2,500. Whether the business initially debits the prepayment to an asset account or to an expense account, the financial statements report the same amounts for prepaid rent and rent expense. The Rent Expense's balance is closed at the end of the period.

During the next accounting period, the $3,500 balance in Prepaid Rent will expire and become expense. It is efficient on the beginning date of the new year to make a *reversing entry* that transfers the ending balance of Prepaid Rent back to Rent Expense:

Reversing Entries

19X7			
Jan. 1	Rent Expense	3,500	
	Prepaid Rent		3,500

This reversing entry avoids later worry about which prepayments become expenses. The arrow shows the transfer of the debit balance from Prepaid Rent to Rent Expense after posting:

Prepaid Rent

19X6			19X7	
Dec. 31 Bal.	3,500		Jan. 1 **Rev.**	**3,500**

Zero balance

Rent Expense

19X6			19X6	
Aug. 1 CP	6,000		Dec. 31 Adj.	3,500
Dec. 31 Bal.	2,500		Dec. 31 Clo.	2,500
19X7				
Jan. 1 **Rev.**	**3,500**			

After the reversing entry, the $3,500 amount is lodged in the expense account. This is consistent with recording prepaid expenses initially as expenses. Because this $3,500 amount will become expense during 19X7, no additional adjustment is needed. Subsequent expense prepayments are debited to Rent Expense and then adjusted at the end of the period as outlined here. Reversing entries ease the work of the accounting process for all types of prepaid expenses that are recorded initially as expenses. Reversing entries are not used for prepaid expenses that are recorded initially as assets.

Comparing the Two Approaches to Recording Prepaid Expenses

In summary, the two approaches to recording prepaid expenses are similar in that the asset amount reported on the balance sheet and the expense amount reported on the income statement are the same. They differ, however, in the prepayment entries and the adjusting entries. When a prepaid expense is recorded initially as an asset, (1) the adjusting entry transfers the *used* portion of the asset to the expense account and (2) no reversing entry is used. When a prepaid expense is recorded initially as an expense, (1) the adjusting entry transfers the *unused* portion of the expense to the asset account and (2) a *reversing entry* transfers the amount of the asset account back to the expense account to start the new accounting period.

Unearned (Deferred) Revenues _____

Unearned (deferred) revenues arise when a business collects cash in advance of earning the revenue. The recognition of revenue is *deferred* until later when it is earned. Unearned revenues are liabilities because the business that receives cash owes the other party goods or services to be delivered later.

Recall the prepaid expense examples listed on p. 204—insurance, rent, advertising, and so on. Prepaid expenses create assets for the business that pays the cash. The business that receives the cash in advance, however, faces a liability. For example, the landlord who receives a tenant's rent in advance must provide future service to the tenant. This is a liability, and the cash the landlord receives is unearned rent revenue. Similarly, unearned revenue arises as magazine publishers sell subscriptions, colleges collect tuition, airlines sell tickets, and attorneys accept advance fees.

When a business receives cash before earning the related revenue, the business debits Cash. It can credit either a *liability* account or a *revenue* account. In either case, the business must make adjusting entries at the end of the period to report the correct amounts of liability and revenue on the financial statements.

Unearned (Deferred) Revenue Recorded Initially as a Liability

Receipt of cash in advance of earning revenue creates a liability, so it is logical to debit Cash and credit a liability account. Assume an attorney receives a $7,200 fee in advance from a client on October 1, 19X2. The attorney will earn this amount at the rate of $800 per month during the nine-month period ending June 30, 19X3. The attorney's cash receipt entry is

19X2			
Oct. 1	Cash	7,200	
	Unearned Legal Revenue ..		7,200

On December 31, 19X2, the end of the law firm's accounting period, three months of the fee agreement have elapsed. The attorney has earned ⅜ of the $7,200, or $2,400. The adjusting entry to transfer $2,400 to the revenue account is

Adjusting Entries

19X2
Dec. 31   Unearned Legal Revenue ($7,200 × ⅜)   2,400
            Legal Revenue.   2,400

After posting, the liability and revenue accounts are

Unearned Legal Revenue

19X2			19X2		
Dec. 31	Adj.	2,400	Oct. 1	CR	7,200
			Dec. 31	Bal.	4,800

Legal Revenue

			19X2		
			Dec. 31	Adj.	2,400
			Dec. 31	Bal.	2,400

The law firm's 19X2 income statement reports legal revenue of $2,400, while its balance sheet reports unearned legal revenue of $4,800 as a liability. During 19X3 the attorney will earn the remaining $4,800 and will then make an adjusting entry to transfer $4,800 to the Legal Revenue account. No reversing entry is used. The balance in the liability account is consistent with recording the unearned revenue initially as a liability.

Unearned (Deferred) Revenue Recorded Initially as a Revenue

Receipt of cash in advance of earning the revenue can be credited initially to a *revenue* account. If the business has earned all the revenue within the period during which it received the cash, no adjusting entry is necessary. However, if the business earns only a part of the revenue at the end of the period, it must make adjusting entries.

Suppose on October 1, 19X2, the law firm records the nine-month advance fee of $7,200 as revenue. The cash receipt entry is

19X2
Oct. 1   Cash   7,200
        Legal Revenue   7,200

At December 31 the attorney has earned only ⅜ of the $7,200, or $2,400. Accordingly, the firm makes an adjusting entry to transfer the unearned portion (⅝ of $7,200, or $4,800) from the revenue account to a liability account.

Adjusting Entries

19X2
Dec. 31   Legal Revenue ($7,200 × ⅝)   4,800
            Unearned Legal Revenue . .   4,800

The adjusting entry leaves the earned portion (3/9, or $2,400) of the original amount in the revenue account. After posting, the total amount ($7,200) is properly divided between the liability account ($4,800) and the revenue account ($2,400), as follows:

Unearned Legal Revenue

		19X2		
		Dec. 31	Adj.	4,800
		Dec. 31	Bal.	4,800

Legal Revenue

19X2			19X2		
Dec. 31	Adj.	4,800	Oct. 1	CR	7,200
			Dec. 31	Bal.	2,400

The attorney's 19X2 income statement reports legal revenue of $2,400, and the balance sheet at December 31, 19X2, reports as a liability the unearned legal revenue of $4,800. Whether the business initially credits a liability account or a revenue account, the financial statements report the same amounts for unearned legal revenue and legal revenue.

The law firm will earn the $4,800 during 19X3. On January 1, 19X3, it is efficient to make a reversing entry in order to transfer the liability balance back to the revenue account. By making the reversing entry, the accountant avoids having to reconsider the situation one year later, when the 19X3 adjusting entries will be made. The reversing entry is

Reversing Entries

19X3
Jan. 1   Unearned Legal Revenue.......   4,800
               Legal Revenue   4,800

After posting, the liability account has a zero balance. The $4,800 credit is now lodged in the revenue account because it will be earned during 19X3. The arrow in the following example shows the transfer from the liability account to the revenue account.

Unearned Legal Revenue

			19X2		
			Dec. 31	Adj.	4,800
19X3			19X2		
Jan. 1	**Rev.**	**4,800**	Dec. 31	Bal.	4,800

Zero balance

Legal Revenue

19X2			19X2		
Dec. 31	Adj.	4,800	Oct. 1	CR	7,200
Dec. 31	Clo.	2,400	Dec. 31	Bal.	2,400
			19X3		
			Jan. 1	**Rev.**	**4,800**

Subsequent advance receipts of revenue are credited to the Legal Revenue account. The year-end adjusting process is the same for every period.

Comparing the Two Approaches to Recording Unearned (Deferred) Revenues

The two approaches to recording unearned revenue are similar in that the liability amount reported on the balance sheet and the revenue amount reported on the income statement are the same. The approaches differ, though, in how adjustments are handled. When unearned revenues are recorded initially as liabilities, (1) the adjusting entry transfers to the revenue account the amount of the advance collection that has been *earned* during the period, and (2) *no* reversing entry is used. When unearned revenues are recorded initially as revenue, (1) the adjustment transfers to the liability account the amount of the advance collection that is still *unearned,* and (2) a *reversing entry* transfers the balance of the liability account to the revenue account to begin the next accounting period.

Summary

Prepaid expenses may be recorded initially in an *asset* account or an *expense* account. When prepaid expenses are recorded initially as an asset, no need exists for a reversing entry because the asset account balance will be adjusted at the end of the next period. However, when prepaid expenses are recorded initially as an expense, a reversing entry eases accounting for the expense of the new period. Regardless of the approach taken, the financial statements should report the same amount of asset and expense.

Unearned (deferred) revenues may be recorded initially as a *liability* or a *revenue.* Recording unearned revenues initially as liabilities causes no need for a reversing entry. However, when recording them initially as revenues, a reversing entry eases accounting. Either recording approach is acceptable as long as the *financial statements* report the *correct* amounts.

Appendix Assignment Material

Exercises

Exercise 4A-1   *Recording supplies transactions two ways*

At the beginning of the year supplies of $1,490 were on hand. During the year the business paid $3,300 cash for supplies. At the end of the year the count of supplies indicates the ending balance is $1,260.

Required

1. Assume the business records supplies by initially debiting an *asset* account. Therefore, place the beginning balance in the Supplies T-account and record the above entries directly in the accounts without using a journal.
2. Assume the business records supplies by initially debiting an *expense* account. Therefore, place the beginning balance in the Supplies Expense T-account and record the above entries directly in the accounts without using a journal.

3. Compare the ending account balances under the two approaches. Are they the same or different? Why?

Exercise 4A-2   *Recording unearned revenues two ways*

At the beginning of the year the company owed customers $6,450 for unearned sales collected in advance. During the year the business received advance cash receipts of $10,000. At year end the unearned revenue liability is $3,900.

Required

1. Assume the company records unearned revenues by initially crediting a liability account. Open T-accounts for Unearned Sales Revenue and Sales Revenue and place the beginning balance in Unearned Sales Revenue. Journalize the cash collection and adjusting entries and post their dollar amounts. As references in the T-accounts, denote a balance by *Bal.*, a cash receipt by *CR*, and an adjustment by *Adj.*
2. Assume the company records unearned revenues by initially crediting a revenue account. Open T-accounts for Unearned Sales Revenue and Sales Revenue and place the beginning balance in Sales Revenue. Journalize the cash collection and adjusting entries and post their dollar amounts. As references in the T-accounts, denote a balance by *Bal.*, a cash receipt by *CR*, and an adjustment by *Adj.*
3. Compare the ending balances in the two accounts. Explain why they are the same or different.

Exercise 4A-3   *Using reversing entries to account for unearned revenues*

One approach to recording unearned revenue in Exercise 4A-2 calls for a reversing entry. Identify that approach. Journalize and post the entries required in Exercise 4A-2 and also the closing and reversing entries. The end of the current period is December 31, 19X1. Use dates for all entries and postings except the cash collection, which is a summary of the year's transactions. As references in the ledger accounts, denote a balance by *Bal.*, cash receipts by *CR*, adjusting entries by *Adj.*, closing entries by *Clo.*, and reversing entries by *Rev.*

Exercise 4A-4   *Identifying transactions from a ledger account*

McGraw Company makes its annual insurance payment on June 30. Identify each of the entries (a) through (e) to the Insurance Expense account as a cash payment, an adjusting entry, a closing entry, or a reversing entry. Also give the other account debited or credited in each entry.

Insurance Expense

Date	Item	Debit	Credit	Balance Debit	Balance Credit
19X4					
Jan. 1	(a)	800		800	
June 30	(b)	1,240		2,040	
Dec. 31	(c)		410	1,630	
Dec. 31	(d)		1,630	—	
19X5					
Jan. 1	(e)	410		410	

Problems

Problem 4A-1 *Recording prepaid rent and rent revenue collected in advance two ways*

DeGroot Sales and Service completed the following transactions during 19X4:

Aug. 31 Paid $9,000 store rent covering the six-month period ending February 28, 19X5.

Dec. 1 Collected $2,200 cash in advance from customers. The service revenue will be earned $550 monthly over the period ending March 30, 19X5.

Required

1. Journalize these entries by debiting an asset account for Prepaid Rent and by crediting a liability account for Unearned Service Revenue. Explanations are unnecessary.
2. Journalize the related adjustments at December 31, 19X4.
3. Post the entries to the ledger accounts and show their balances at December 31, 19X4. Posting references are unnecessary.
4. Repeat Requirements 1 through 3. This time debit Rent Expense for the rent payment and credit Service Revenue for the collection of revenue in advance.
5. Compare the account balances in Requirements 3 and 4. They should be equal.

Problem 4A-2 *Journalizing adjusting and reversing entries*

The accounting records of Friedman, Inc., reveal the following information before adjustments at December 31, 19X7, end of the accounting period:

a. Friedman routinely debits Sales Supplies when it purchases supplies. At the beginning of 19X7 supplies of $800 were on hand, and during the year the company purchased supplies of $6,700. At year end the count of sales supplies on hand indicates the ending amount is $950.
b. Friedman collects revenue in advance from customers and credits such amounts to Sales Revenue because the revenue is usually earned within a short time. At December 31, 19X7, however, the company has a liability of $6,840 to customers for goods they paid for in advance.
c. Rentals cost the company $1,000 per month. The company prepays rent of $6,000 each May 1 and November 1 and debits Rent Expense for such payments.
d. The company prepaid $3,500 for television advertising that will run daily for two weeks—December 27, 19X7 through January 9, 19X8. Friedman debited Prepaid Advertising for the full amount on December 15.

Required

1. Journalize the adjusting entry needed for each situation at December 31, 19X7, identifying each entry by its corresponding letter.
2. Journalize reversing entries as needed. Use the corresponding letters for references. Date the entries appropriately.

Problem 4A-3 *Recording supplies and unearned revenue transactions two ways*

The accounting records of Stone Company reveal the following information about sales supplies and unearned sales revenue for 19X5:

Sales Supplies

19X5			
Jan. 1	Beginning amount on hand..................	$	420
Mar. 16	Cash purchase of supplies		3,740
Dec. 31	Ending amount on hand		290

Unearned Sales Revenue

19X5		
Jan. 1	Beginning amount on advance collections	6,590
July 22	Advance cash collection from customer	16,480
Nov. 4	Advance cash collection from customer	38,400
Dec. 31	Advance collections earned during the year ...	52,160

Required

1. Assume Stone Company records (a) supplies by initially debiting an asset account and (b) advance collections from customers by initially crediting a liability account.
   a. Open T-accounts for Sales Supplies, Sales Supplies Expense, Unearned Sales Revenue, and Sales Revenue. Insert the beginning balances in the appropriate accounts.
   b. Record the cash transactions during 19X5 directly in the accounts.
   c. Record the adjusting and closing entries at December 31, 19X5, directly in the accounts.
   d. If appropriate, record the reversing entries at January 1, 19X6, directly in the accounts.
2. Assume Stone Company records (a) supplies by initially debiting an expense account and (b) advance collections by initially crediting a revenue account. Perform steps *a* through *d* as in Requirement 1.
3. Using the following format, compare the amounts that would be reported for the above accounts in the 19X5 balance sheet and income statement under the two recording approaches of Requirements 1 and 2. Explain any

	Requirement 1	Requirement 2
Balance sheet at December 31, 19X5 reports:	$	$
Sales supplies............................		
Unearned sales revenue		
Income statement for year ended December 31, 19X5, reports:		
Sales revenue............................		
Sales supplies expense....................		

Chapter 5

Merchandising
and the Accounting Cycle

With department stores falling into Chapter 11 [bankruptcy] like dominoes, the rag trade [garment industry] should be the last place to find a superb growth company. But look at Donna Karan Co., the women's clothing concern, which projects net sales of $132 million this year, thanks mainly to the year-old DKNY line. That's up from $107 million last year and $7.4 million in 1985, Karan's first year in business. . . .

Karan clothing sells well, and wholesale buyers know it. . . . How does Karan do it? Says Neiman Marcus President and Chief Executive Terry Lundgren: "She cares about what is selling to the customer, not just what the store buyers are buying." Famous customers help, too. Candice Bergen and Diane Sawyer regularly wear Karan's wool jersey and crepe designs on television.

What's next? International expansion. Karan already sells 20 percent of her merchandise abroad, half of that to Japan. A Donna Karan shop opened in August in Hong Kong. . . . Next spring Karan debuts in France.

Karan says she will remain private for now. But with stellar growth and no long-term debt, Donna Karan, the company, would be even more welcome on Wall Street than it is in America's department and specialty stores.

Source: Katherine Weisman, "Designing Woman," *Forbes,* October 1, 1990, p. 261. Used with permission of Forbes, Inc.

How do the operations of Donna Karan Co. differ from the businesses we have studied so far? In the first four chapters Air and Sea Travel, Inc., provided an illustration of a business that earns revenue by selling its services. Service enterprises include Holiday Inns, American Airlines, physicians, lawyers, CPAs, the Atlanta Braves baseball team, and the twelve-year-old who cuts lawns in your neighborhood. A *merchandising entity* earns its revenue by selling products, called *merchandise inventory* or simply *inventory*. Donna Karan Co., a Goodyear tire store, a Safeway grocery, a Macy's department store, and an ice-cream shop are merchandising entities. Exhibit 5-1 shows the income statement for a merchandising business. You will notice that this income statement differs from those shown earlier.

The amount that a merchandiser earns from selling its inventory is called **net sales revenue,** often abbreviated as **sales revenue.** The income statement in Exhibit 5-1 reports net sales revenue of $680,000. The major revenue of a merchandising entity, sales revenue, represents the increase in stockholders' equity from delivering inventory to customers. The major expense of a merchandiser is *Cost of Goods Sold.* This expense's title is well chosen, because its amount represents the entity's cost of the goods (inventory) it has sold to customers. As long as inventory is held, it is an asset. When the inventory is sold to the customer, the inventory's cost becomes an expense. The excess of Sales Revenue over Cost of Goods Sold is called **gross margin** or **gross profit.** This important business statistic is often mentioned in the business press because it helps measure a business's success. A sufficiently high gross margin is often vital to success.

EXHIBIT 5-1 *A Merchandiser's Income Statement*

Midwest Supply Company Income Statement For the Year Ended December 31, 19X6		
Net sales revenue		$680,000
Cost of goods sold		370,000
Gross margin		310,000
Operating expenses:		
Salary expense............................	$130,000	
Rent expense	60,000	
Insurance expense	18,000	
Depreciation expense......................	14,000	
Supplies expense..........................	8,000	230,000
Net income		$ 80,000

The following illustration will clarify the nature of gross margin. Consider a concession stand at a football game. Assume the business sells a soft drink for $1.00 and the vendor's cost is $.20. Gross margin per unit is $.80 ($1.00 − $.20), and the overall gross margin is $.80 multiplied by the number of drinks sold. If the concession stand sells 400 drinks on a Saturday afternoon, its gross margin on drink sales is $320 (400 × $.80). The gross margin on all sales, including hot dogs, popcorn, and candy, is the sum of the gross margins on all the items sold. Sears's gross margin—and that of a Safeway store, a neighborhood drug store, and every other merchandiser—is computed in exactly the same way: Sales Revenue − Cost of Goods Sold = Gross Margin.

Margin in gross margin refers to the excess of revenue over expense. *Gross* indicates that the operating expenses (rent, depreciation, advertising, and so on) have not yet been subtracted. After subtracting all the expenses we have *net income*. Gross margin and net income are *not* accounts in the ledger, so we cannot make journal entries to them. Instead, they are remainders left over after subtracting expenses from revenues. Study Exhibit 5-1, focusing on the sales revenue, cost of goods sold, and gross margin. Note the separate category for operating expenses.

The Operating Cycle for a Merchandising Business _____

OBJECTIVE 1

Explain the operating cycle of a merchandising business

A merchandising entity buys inventory, sells the inventory to its customers, and uses the cash to purchase more inventory to repeat the cycle. Exhibit 5-2 diagrams the operating cycle for *cash sales* and for *sales on account*. For a cash sale—item *a* in the exhibit—the cycle is from cash to inventory, which is purchased for resale, and back to cash. For a sale on account—item *b*—the cycle is from cash to inventory to accounts receivable and back to cash.

Purchase of Merchandise Inventory _____

The cycle of a merchandising entity begins with cash, which is used to purchase inventory, as Exhibit 5-2 shows. **Purchases,** in the accounting sense, are only those items of merchandise inventory that a firm buys to resell to customers in the normal course of business. For example, a stereo center records in the Purchases account the price it pays for tape decks, turntables, and other items of inventory acquired for resale. A bicycle shop debits Purchases when it buys ten-speeds for its inventory. A grocery store debits Purchases when it buys canned goods, meat, frozen food, and other inventory. A $500 purchase on account is recorded as follows:

June 14	Purchases	500	
	Accounts Payable		500
	Purchased inventory on account.	

The Purchase Invoice: A Basic Business Document

Business documents are the tangible evidence of transactions. As we trace the steps that Austin Sound Stereo Center, an actual business, takes in ordering, receiving, and paying for inventory, we point out the roles that documents play in carrying on business.

EXHIBIT 5-2   *Operating Cycle of a Merchandiser*

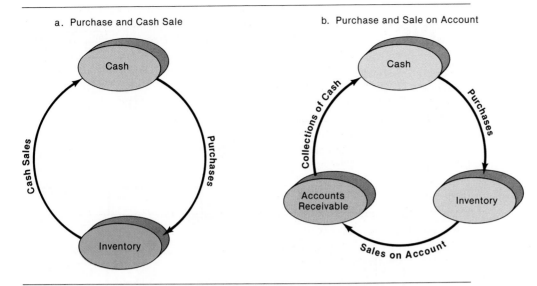

a. Purchase and Cash Sale

b. Purchase and Sale on Account

1. Suppose Austin Sound wants to stock JVC brand turntables, cassette decks, and speakers. Austin Sound prepares a *purchase order* and faxes it to JVC.
2. On receipt of the purchase order, JVC scans its warehouse for the inventory that Austin Sound ordered. JVC ships the equipment and mails the invoice to Austin on the same day. The **invoice** is the seller's request for payment from the purchaser. It is also called the *bill*.
3. Often the purchaser receives the invoice before the inventory arrives. Austin Sound does not pay immediately. Instead, Austin waits until the inventory arrives in order to ensure that it is (1) the correct type, (2) the quantity ordered, and (3) in good condition. After the inventory is inspected and approved, Austin Sound pays JVC the invoice amount.

Exhibit 5-3 is a copy of an actual invoice from JVC Corp. to Austin Sound Stereo Center. From Austin Sound's perspective, this document is a *purchase invoice*, whereas to JVC it is a *sales invoice*. The circled numbers that appear on the exhibit correspond to the following numbered explanations:

1. The seller is JVC Southwest Branch.
2. The invoice date is 05/27/92. The date is needed for determining whether the purchaser gets a discount for prompt payment (see item 5 below).
3. The purchaser is Austin Sound Stereo Center. The inventory is invoiced (billed) and shipped to the same address, 305 West Martin Luther King Blvd., Austin, Texas.
4. Austin Sound's purchase order (P.O.) date was 05/25/92.
5. Credit terms of the transaction are 3% 15, NET 30 DAYS. This means that Austin Sound may deduct 3 percent of the total amount due if Austin pays within 15 days of the invoice date. Otherwise, the full amount— net—is due in 30 days. (A full discussion of discounts appears in the next section.)
6. Austin Sound ordered six turntables, three cassette decks, and two speakers.
7. JVC shipped five turntables, no cassette decks, and no speakers.

EXHIBIT 5-3 *Business Invoice*

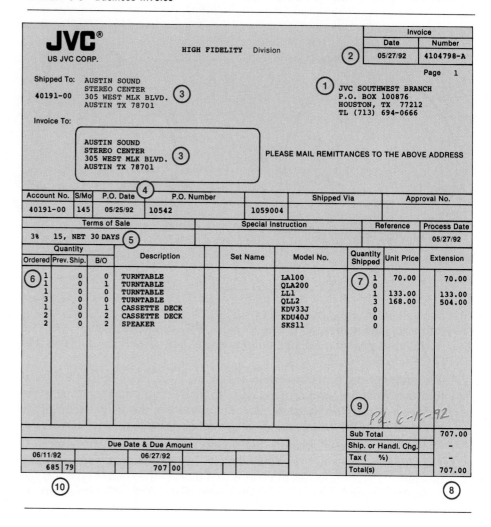

8. Total invoice amount is $707.

9. Austin Sound paid on 6-10-92. How much did Austin pay? (See item 10.)

10. Payment occurred 14 days after the invoice date—within the discount period. Therefore, Austin Sound paid $685.79 ($707 minus the 3 percent discount).

Discounts from Purchase Prices

There are two major types of discounts from purchase prices: quantity discounts and cash discounts (called purchase discounts).

Quantity Discounts.   A **quantity discount** works this way: the larger the quantity purchased, the lower the price per item. For example, JVC may offer no discount for the purchase of only one or two cassette decks and charge the list price—the full price—of $200 per unit. However, JVC may offer the following quantity discount terms in order to persuade customers to buy a larger number of cassette decks:

Quantity	Quantity Discount	Net Price Per Unit
Buy minimum quantity, 3 cassette decks	5%	$190 [$200 − .05($200)]
Buy 4–9 decks	10%	$180 [$200 − .10($200)]
Buy more than 9 decks..............	20%	$160 [$200 − .20($200)]

Suppose Austin Sound purchases five cassette decks from this manufacturer. The cost of each cassette deck is, therefore, $180. Purchase of five units on account would be recorded by debiting Purchases and crediting Accounts Payable for the total price of $900 ($180 X 5).

There is no quantity discount account, and there is no special accounting entry for a quantity discount. Instead, all accounting entries are based on the net price of a purchase after subtracting the quantity discount. If a quantity discount is also offered, the purchase discount is computed on the net purchase amount after subtracting the quantity discount.

Purchase Discounts. Many businesses also offer purchase discounts to their customers. A **purchase discount** is a reward for prompt payment. If a quantity discount is also offered, the purchase discount is computed on the net purchase amount after subtracting the quantity discount.

JVC's credit terms of 3% 15 NET 30 DAYS can also be expressed as 3/15 n/30. Terms of simply n/30 indicate that no discount is offered and that payment is due 30 days after the invoice date. Terms of *eom* usually mean that payment is due at the end of the current month. However, a purchase after the twenty-fifth of the current month on terms of *eom* can be paid at the end of the next month.

Let's use the Exhibit 5-3 transaction to illustrate accounting for a purchase discount. Austin Sound records this purchase on account as follows:

OBJECTIVE 2
Account for the purchase
and sale of inventory

May 27	Purchases	707.00	
	Accounts Payable		707.00
	Purchased inventory on account.		

Austin Sound paid within the discount period, so its cash payment entry is

June 10	Accounts Payable.........................	707.00	
	Cash ($707.00 × .97)		685.79
	Purchase Discounts ($707.00 × .03)		21.21
	Paid on account within discount period.		

Purchase Discounts, which has a credit balance, is a contra account to Purchases. We show how to report Purchase Discounts on the income statement later in the chapter.

Alternatively, if Austin Sound pays this invoice after the discount period, it must pay the full invoice amount. In this case, the payment entry is

June 29	Accounts Payable.........................	707.00	
	Cash		707.00
	Paid on account after discount period.		

Purchase Returns and Allowances

Most businesses allow their customers to *return* merchandise that is defective, damaged in shipment, or otherwise unsuitable. Or if the buyer chooses to keep damaged goods, the seller may deduct an *allowance* from the amount the buyer owes. Because returns and allowances are closely related, they are usually recorded in a single account, **Purchase Returns and Allowances.** This account, a contra account to Purchases, gives a record of the amount of returns and allowances for the period. Later in the chapter, we show how to report this account on the income statement.

Suppose the $70 turntable purchased by Austin Sound (in Exhibit 5-3) was not the turntable ordered. Austin returns the merchandise to the seller and records the purchase return as follows:

June 3	Accounts Payable	70.00	
	Purchase Returns and Allowances		70.00
	Returned inventory to seller.		

Now assume that one of the JVC turntables is damaged in shipment to Austin Sound. The damage is minor, and Austin decides to keep the turntable in exchange for a $10 allowance from JVC. To record this purchase allowance, Austin Sound makes this entry:

June 4	Accounts Payable	10.00	
	Purchase Returns and Allowances		10.00
	Received a purchase allowance.		

Observe that the return and the allowance had two effects. (1) They decreased Austin Sound's liability, which is why we debit Accounts Payable. (2) They decreased the net cost of the purchase, which is why we credit Purchase Returns and Allowances. It would be incorrect to credit Purchases because Austin Sound did in fact make the purchase. Changes because of returns and allowances are recorded in the contra account.

During the period, the business records the cost of all inventory bought in the Purchases account. The balance of Purchases is a *gross* amount because it does not include subtractions for purchase discounts, returns, or allowances. **Net purchases** is the remainder that is computed by subtracting the contra accounts as follows:

> **Purchases (*debit* balance account)**
> **− Purchase Discounts (*credit* balance account)**
> **− Purchase Returns and Allowances (*credit* balance account)**
> _____
> **= Net purchases (a *debit* subtotal, not a separate account)**

Transportation Costs

The transportation cost of moving inventory from seller to buyer can be significant. The purchase agreement specifies FOB terms to indicate who pays the shipping charges. The term *FOB* stands for *free on board* and governs when the legal title to the goods passes from seller to buyer. Under FOB *shipping point* terms, title passes when the inventory leaves the seller's place of business—the shipping point. The buyer owns the goods while they are in transit and therefore pays the transportation cost. Under FOB *destination* terms, title passes when the goods reach the destination, so the seller pays transportation cost.

	FOB Shipping Point	FOB Destination
When does title pass to buyer?	Shipping point	Destination
Who pays transportation cost?	Buyer	Seller

FOB shipping point terms are most common, so generally, the buyer bears the shipping cost. The buyer debits Freight In (sometimes called Transportation In) and credits Cash or Accounts Payable for the amount. Suppose the buyer receives a shipping bill directly from the freight company. The buyer's entry to record payment of the freight charge is:

March 3	Freight In	190	
	Cash		190
	Paid a freight bill.		

Under FOB shipping point terms, the seller sometimes prepays the transportation cost as a convenience and lists this cost on the invoice. The buyer would *not* debit Purchases for the combined cost of the inventory and the shipping cost. Rather, the buyer would debit Purchases for the cost of the goods and Freight In separately. A $5,000 purchase of goods, coupled with a related freight charge of $400, would be recorded as follows:

March 12	Purchases	5,000	
	Freight In	400	
	Accounts Payable		5,400
	Purchased inventory on account plus freight.		

Purchase discounts and quantity discounts are computed only on the cost of the inventory, *not* on the freight charges. Suppose the $5,000 credit purchase allows a $100 discount for early payment. The cash payment within the discount period would be $5,300 [net payment of $4,900 on the inventory ($5,000, less the $100 purchase discount), plus the freight charge of $400].

Sale of Inventory

The sale of inventory may be for cash or on account, as Exhibit 5-2 shows.

Cash Sale.   Sales of retailers like department stores, drug stores, gift shops, and restaurants are often for cash. A $3,000 cash sale is recorded by debiting Cash and crediting the revenue account, Sales Revenue, as follows:

Jan. 9	Cash	3,000	
	Sales Revenue		3,000
	Cash sale.		

Sale on Account.   Most sales by wholesalers, manufacturers, and retailers are made on account (on credit). A $5,000 sale on account is recorded by a debit to Accounts Receivable and a credit to Sales Revenue, as follows:

Jan. 11	Accounts Receivable	5,000	
	Sales Revenue		5,000
	Sale on account.		

The related cash receipt on account is journalized as follows:

Jan. 19 Cash 5,000
            Accounts Receivable....................   5,000
         Collection on account.

Sales Discounts, Sales Returns and Allowances

Sales Discounts and **Sales Returns and Allowances** are contra accounts to Sales Revenue, just as Purchase Discounts and Purchase Returns and Allowances are contra accounts to Purchases. Let's examine a sequence of the sale transactions of JVC.

On July 7, JVC sells stereo components for $7,200 on credit terms of 2/10 n/30. JVC's entry to record this credit sale follows:

July 7 Accounts Receivable 7,200
            Sales Revenue   7,200
         Sale on account.

Assume the buyer returns goods that cost $600. JVC records the sales return and the related decrease in Accounts Receivable as follows:

July 12 Sales Returns and Allowances 600
            Accounts Receivable.....................   600
         Received returned goods.

JVC grants a $100 sales allowance for damaged goods. JVC journalizes this transaction by debiting Sales Returns and Allowances and crediting Accounts Receivable as follows:

July 15 Sales Returns and Allowances 100
            Accounts Receivable.....................   100
         Granted a sales allowance for damaged goods.

After the preceding entries are posted, Accounts Receivable has a $6,500 debit balance, as follows:

Accounts Receivable			
July 7	7,200	July 12	600
		15	100
Bal.	6,500		

On July 17, the last day of the discount period, JVC collects half ($3,250) of this receivable ($6,500 X 1/2 = $3,250). The cash receipt is $3,185 [$3,250 − ($3,250 X .02)], and the collection entry is

July 17 Cash 3,185
         Sales Discounts ($3,250 X .02) 65
            Accounts Receivable   3,250
         Cash collection within the discount period.

Suppose JVC collects the remainder on July 28—after the discount period—so there is no sales discount. To record this collection on account, JVC debits Cash and credits Accounts Receivable for the same amount, as follows:

July 28	Cash	3,250	
	Accounts Receivable		3,250
	Cash collection after the discount period.		

Net sales is computed in a manner similar to net purchases. We subtract the contra accounts as follows:

> **Sales Revenue** (*credit* balance account)
> **− Sales Discounts** (*debit* balance account)
> **− Sales Returns and Allowances** (*debit* balance account)
> **= Net sales** (a *credit* subtotal, not a separate account)

Cost of Goods Sold

Cost of goods sold (COGS) is the largest single expense of most merchandising businesses. It is the cost of the inventory that the business has sold to customers. Another name for cost of goods sold is **cost of sales**. How is it computed?

Recall from Chapter 3 that supplies expense is computed as follows:

> **Beginning supplies**
> **+ Supplies purchased during the period**
> **= Supplies available for use during the period**
> **− Supplies on hand at the end of the period**
> **= Supplies expense**

Cost of goods sold is computed this same way, as shown in Exhibit 5-4.

By studying the exhibit, you will see that the computation and the diagram tell the same story. That is, a company's goods available for sale during a period come from beginning inventory plus the period's net purchases and freight costs. Either the merchandise is sold during the period, or it remains on hand at the end. The merchandise that remains is an asset, Inventory. The cost of the inventory that has been sold is an expense, Cost of Goods Sold.

Two main types of inventory accounting systems exist: the periodic system and the perpetual system. The periodic method is used by businesses that sell relatively inexpensive goods. A grocery store without an optical-scanning cash register does not keep a daily running record of every loaf of bread and every can of pineapple that it buys and sells. The cost of the record keeping would be overwhelming. Instead, grocers count their inventory periodically—at least once a year—to determine the quantities on hand. The inventory amounts are used to prepare the annual financial statements. Other businesses such as office supply outlets, restaurants, and department stores also use the periodic inventory system. The key idea is that detailed inventory records in the ledger are not necessary for controlling merchandise and managing day-to-day operations. In small businesses, the owner can visually inspect the goods on hand for control purposes.

Under the perpetual inventory system, the business maintains a running record of inventory on hand. This system achieves control over expensive

EXHIBIT 5-4 *Measurement of Cost of Goods Sold*

Computation:

$$
\begin{array}{l}
\textbf{Beginning inventory} \\
+\textbf{Net purchases} \\
+\textbf{Freight in} \\
\hline
=\textbf{Cost of goods available for sale} \\
-\textbf{Ending inventory} \\
\hline
=\textbf{Cost of goods sold}
\end{array}
$$

Diagram:

goods such as automobiles, jewelry, and furniture. The loss of one item would be significant, and this justifies the cost of a perpetual system. More and more businesses are using the perpetual system as computers become more flexible and less expensive. Even under a perpetual system the business counts the inventory on hand annually. The physical count establishes the correct amount of ending inventory and serves as a check on the perpetual records.

In this chapter, we illustrate the periodic inventory system because it highlights the relationship between inventory and cost of goods sold, as shown in Exhibit 5-4. This model for computing expense is used throughout accounting and is extremely useful for analytical purposes. Furthermore, the periodic system is used by many small businesses, such as those we illustrate in the early chapters of this book. Chapter 8 discusses the perpetual system.

Under the periodic system, as we have noted, the business does not keep a running record of the cost of its inventory on hand. Instead, it counts the goods on hand at the end of each year to determine the inventory to be reported on the balance sheet. This ending inventory amount becomes the beginning inventory of the next period and is used to compute cost of goods sold for the income statement. *In the periodic inventory system, entries to the Inventory account are made only at the end of the period.*

In this inventory system, cost of goods sold is *not* a ledger account like Salary Expense, Rent Expense, and the other operating expenses. Instead, it is the cost left over when we subtract the cost of ending inventory from the cost of goods available for sale. Cost of goods sold is computationally more complex than the other expenses.

Exhibit 5-5 summarizes the first half of the chapter by showing Austin Sound's net sales revenue, cost of goods sold—including net purchases—and gross margin on the income statement.

Note that arithmetic operations—addition and subtraction —move across the columns from left to right. For example, the figures for Sales Discounts and for Sales Returns and Allowances appear in a separate column. Their sum—$3,400—appears to the right, where it is subtracted from Sales Revenue. The net sales amount of $135,900 appears in the right-most column.

Contra accounts—discounts, returns and allowances, and the like—are frequently netted against their related accounts parenthetically. Thus many accountants would report sales in our example as follows:

Net sales revenue (net of sales discounts, $1,400,
    and returns and allowances, $2,000) $135,900

Purchases can also be reported at its net amount in the following manner:

Cost of goods sold:
Beginning inventory .... $ 40,500
Net purchases (net of purchase discounts, $3,000,
    and returns and allowances, $1,200) 85,100
Freight in 5,200
Cost of goods available for sale 130,800
Less: Ending inventory 42,000
Cost of goods sold .... $ 88,800

These presentations of *net* sales and *net* purchases underscore an important fact: published financial statements usually report only *net* amounts for these items because discounts and returns and allowances are relatively small in

EXHIBIT 5-5 *Partial Income Statement*

Austin Sound Stereo Center, Inc. Income Statement For the Year Ended December 31, 19X6			
Sales revenue.................			$139,300
Less: Sales discounts		$ 1,400	
Sales returns and allowances		2,000	3,400
Net sales			$135,900
Cost of goods sold:			
Beginning inventory			$ 40,500
Purchases		$89,300	
Less: Purchase discounts .	$3,000		
Purchase returns and allowances ...	1,200	4,200	
Net purchases			85,100
Freight in			5,200
Cost of goods available for sale.....................			130,800
Less: Ending inventory ...			42,000
Cost of goods sold			88,800
Gross margin			$ 47,100

OBJECTIVE 3

Compute cost of goods sold and gross margin

amount. For most businesses, these contra items are details of primary interest only to managers and therefore are not highlighted in the financial statements. For example, Colgate-Palmolive Company recently reported:

	19X9	19X8
Net sales	$5,038,813	$4,734,325
Cost of sales	2,843,050	2,725,218
Gross profit	$2,195,763	$2,009,107

Summary Problem for your Review

Brun Sales Company engaged in the following transactions during June of the current year:

June 3 Purchased inventory on credit terms of 1/10 net eom (end of month), $1,610.

9 Returned 40 percent of the inventory purchased on June 3. It was defective.

9 Sold goods for cash, $920.

15 Purchased merchandise of $5,100, less a $100 quantity discount. Credit terms were 3/15 net 30.

16 Paid a $260 freight bill on goods purchased.

18 Sold inventory on credit terms of 2/10 n/30, $2,000.

22 Received damaged merchandise from the customer to whom the June 18 sale was made, $800.

24 Borrowed money from the bank to take advantage of the discount offered on the June 15 purchase. Signed a note payable to the bank for the net amount.

24 Paid supplier for goods purchased on June 15, less all discounts.

28 Received cash in full settlement of the account from the customer who purchased inventory on June 18.

29 Paid the amount owed on account from the purchase of June 3.

30 Purchased inventory for cash, $900, less a quantity discount of $35.

Required

1. Journalize the above transactions. Explanations are not required.
2. Assume the note payable signed on June 24 requires the payment of $95 interest expense. Was the decision wise or unwise to borrow funds to take advantage of the cash discount?

SOLUTION TO REVIEW PROBLEM

Requirement 1

June 3 Purchases.   1,610
                 Accounts Payable   1,610

June 9	Accounts Payable ($1,610 X .40)...............	644		
	Purchase Returns and Allowances........		644	
9	Cash	920		
	Sales Revenue..........................		920	
15	Purchases ($5,100 − $100)	5,000		
	Accounts Payable......................		5,000	
16	Freight In..................................	260		
	Cash		260	
18	Accounts Receivable	2,000		
	Sales Revenue..........................		2,000	
22	Sales Returns and Allowances	800		
	Accounts Receivable		800	
24	Cash [$5,000 − .03($5,000)]..................	4,850		
	Note Payable..........................		4,850	
24	Accounts Payable...........................	5,000		
	Purchase Discounts ($5,000 X. 03)		150	
	Cash ($5,000 X .97)		4,850	
28	Cash [($2,000 − $800) X .98]..................	1,176		
	Sales Discounts [($2,000 − $800) X .02]	24		
	Accounts Receivable ($2,000 − $800)		1,200	
29	Accounts Payable ($1,610 − $644)	966		
	Cash		966	
30	Purchases ($900–$35)	865		
	Cash		865	

Requirement 2. The decision to borrow funds was wise because the discount ($150) exceeded the interest paid on the amount borrowed ($95). Thus the entity was $55 better off as a result of its decision.

The Adjusting and Closing Process for a Merchandising Business

A merchandising business adjusts and closes the accounts much as a service entity does. The steps of this end-of-period process are the same: If a work sheet is used, enter the trial balance, and complete the work sheet to determine net income or net loss. The work sheet provides the data for preparing the financial statements and for journalizing the adjusting and closing entries. After these entries are posted to the ledger, a postclosing trial balance can be prepared.

The Inventory account affects the adjusting and closing entries of a merchandiser. At the end of the period, before any adjusting or closing entries, the Inventory account balance is still the cost of the inventory that was on hand at the beginning date. It is necessary to remove this beginning balance and replace it with the cost of the ending inventory. Various acceptable bookkeeping techniques might be used to bring the inventory records up to date. In this chapter we illustrate the closing-entry method. In the chapter appendix we present an alternative approach, the adjusting-entry method.

To illustrate a merchandiser's adjusting and closing process, let's use Austin Sound's December 31, 19X6, trial balance in Exhibit 5-6. All the new accounts—Inventory, Freight In, and the contra accounts—are highlighted for emphasis. However, Inventory is the only account that is affected by the new closing procedures. Note that additional-data item *g* gives the ending inventory of $42,000.

EXHIBIT 5-6 *Trial Balance*

Austin Sound Stereo Center, Inc.
Trial Balance
December 31, 19X6

Cash	$ 2,850	
Accounts receivable	4,600	
Note receivable, current	8,000	
Interest receivable		
Inventory	**40,500**	
Supplies	650	
Prepaid insurance	1,200	
Furniture and fixtures	33,200	
Accumulated depreciation		$ 2,400
Accounts payable		47,000
Unearned sales revenue		2,000
Interest payable		
Note payable, long-term		12,600
Common stock		10,000
Retained earnings		15,900
Dividends	34,100	
Sales revenue		**138,000**
Sales discounts	**1,400**	
Sales returns and allowances	**2,000**	
Interest revenue		600
Purchases	**89,300**	
Purchase discounts		**3,000**
Purchase returns and allowances		**1,200**
Freight in	**5,200**	
Rent expense	8,400	
Depreciation expense		
Insurance expense		
Supplies expense		
Interest expense	1,300	
Total	$232,700	$232,700

Additional data at December 31, 19X6:

a. Interest revenue earned but not yet collected, $400.
b. Supplies on hand, $100.
c. Prepaid insurance expired during the year, $1,000.
d. Depreciation, $600.
e. Unearned sales revenue earned during the year, $1,300.
f. Interest expense incurred but not yet paid, $200.
g. Inventory on hand, $42,000.

Work Sheet of a Merchandising Business

The Exhibit 5-7 work sheet is similar to the work sheets we have seen so far, but a few differences appear. Note that this work sheet does not include adjusted trial balance columns. In most accounting systems, a single operation combines trial balance amounts with the adjustments and extends the adjusted balances directly to the income statement and balance sheet columns. Therefore, to reduce clutter, the adjusted trial balance columns are omitted. A second difference is that the merchandiser's work sheet includes inventory and purchase amounts (which are highlighted here). Let's examine the entire work sheet.

Account Title Columns. The trial balance lists a number of accounts without balances. Ordinarily, these accounts are affected by the adjusting process.

EXHIBIT 5-7 *Work Sheet*

Austin Sound Stereo Center, Inc.
Work Sheet
For the Year Ended December 31, 19X6

Account Title	Trial Balance Debit	Trial Balance Credit	Adjustments Debit	Adjustments Credit	Income Statement Debit	Income Statement Credit	Balance Sheet Debit	Balance Sheet Credit
Cash	2,850						2,850	
Accounts receivable	4,600						4,600	
Note receivable, current	8,000						8,000	
Interest receivable			(a) 400				400	
Inventory	40,500				40,500	42,000	42,000	
Supplies	650			(b) 550			100	
Prepaid insurance	1,200			(c) 1,000			200	
Furniture and fixtures	33,200						33,200	
Accumulated depreciation		2,400		(d) 600				3,000
Accounts payable		47,000						47,000
Unearned sales revenue		2,000	(e) 1,300					700
Interest payable				(f) 200				200
Note payable, long-term		12,600						12,600
Common stock		10,000						10,000
Retained earnings		15,900						15,900
Dividends	34,100						34,100	
Sales revenue		138,000		(e) 1,300		139,300		
Sales discounts	1,400				1,400			
Sales returns and allowances	2,000				2,000			
Interest revenue		600		(a) 400		1,000		
Purchases	89,300				89,300			
Purchase discounts		3,000				3,000		
Purchase returns and allowances		1,200				1,200		
Freight in	5,200				5,200			
Rent expense	8,400				8,400			
Depreciation expense			(d) 600		600			
Insurance expense			(c) 1,000		1,000			
Supplies expense			(b) 550		550			
Interest expense	1,300		(f) 200		1,500			
	232,700	232,700	4,050	4,050	150,450	186,500	125,450	89,400
Net income					36,050			36,050
					186,500	186,500	125,450	125,450

Examples include Interest Receivable, Interest Payable, and Depreciation Expense. The accounts are listed in the order they appear in the ledger. This eases the preparation of the work sheet. If additional accounts are needed, they can be written in at the bottom of the work sheet before net income is determined. Simply move net income down to make room for the additional accounts.

Trial Balance Columns. Examine the Inventory account, $40,500 in the trial balance. This $40,500 is the cost of the beginning inventory. The work sheet is designed to replace this outdated amount with the new ending balance, which in our example is $42,000 (additional-data item *g* in Exhibit 5-6). As we shall see, this task is accomplished later in the columns for the income statement and the balance sheet.

Adjustments Columns. The adjustments are similar to those discussed in Chapters 3 and 4. They may be entered in any order desired. The debit amount of each entry should equal the credit amount, and total debits should equal total credits.

Income Statement Columns. The income statement columns contain adjusted amounts for the revenues and the expenses. Sales Revenue, for example, is $139,300, which includes the $1,300 adjustment.

You may be wondering why the two inventory amounts appear in the income statement columns. The reason is that both beginning inventory and ending inventory enter the computation of cost of goods sold. Recall that beginning inventory is added to purchases and ending inventory is subtracted. Even though the resulting cost-of-goods-sold amount does not appear on the work sheet, all the components of cost of goods sold are evident there. *Placement of beginning inventory ($40,500) in the work sheet's income statement debit column has the effect of adding beginning inventory in computing cost of goods sold. Placing ending inventory ($42,000) in the credit column has the opposite effect.*

Purchases and Freight In appear in the debit column because they are added in computing cost of goods sold. Purchase Discounts and Purchase Returns and Allowances appear as credits because they are subtracted. Together, all these items are used to compute cost of goods sold—$88,800 on the income statement in Exhibit 5-5.

The income statement column subtotals on the work sheet indicate whether the business earned net income or incurred a net loss. If total credits are greater, the result is net income, as shown in the exhibit. Inserting the net income amount in the debit column brings total debits into agreement with total credits. If total debits are greater, a net loss has occurred. Inserting a net loss amount in the credit column would equalize total debits and total credits. Net income or net loss is then extended to the opposite column of the balance sheet.

Balance Sheet Columns. The only new item on the balance sheet is inventory. The balance listed is the ending amount of $42,000, which is determined by a physical count of inventory on hand at the end of the period.

Financial Statements of a Merchandising Business _____

OBJECTIVE 4

Prepare a merchandiser's financial statements

Exhibit 5-8 presents Austin Sound's financial statements. The *income statement* through gross margin repeats Exhibit 5-5. This information is followed by the **operating expenses,** which are those expenses other than cost of goods sold

EXHIBIT 5-8 *Financial Statements of Austin Sound*

Austin Sound Stereo Center, Inc.
Income Statement
For the Year Ended December 31, 19X6

Sales revenue			$139,300
Less: Sales discounts		$ 1,400	
Sales returns and allowances		2,000	3,400
Net sales revenue			$135,900
Cost of goods sold:			
Beginning inventory		$ 40,500	
Purchases	$89,300		
Less: Purchase discounts	$3,000		
Purchase returns and allowances	1,200	4,200	
Net purchases		85,100	
Freight in		5,200	
Cost of goods available for sale		130,800	
Less: Ending inventory		42,000	
Cost of goods sold			88,800
Gross margin			47,100
Operating expenses:			
Rent expense		8,400	
Insurance expense		1,000	
Depreciation expense		600	
Supplies expense		550	10,550
Income from operations			36,550
Other revenue and (expense):			
Interest revenue		1,000	
Interest expense		(1,500)	(500)
Net income			$ 36,050

Austin Sound Stereo Center, Inc.
Statement of Retained Earnings
For the Year Ended December 31, 19X6

Retained earnings, December 31, 19X5	$15,900
Add: Net income	36,050
	51,950
Less: Dividends	34,100
Retained earnings, December 31, 19X6	$17,850

Austin Sound Stereo Center, Inc.
Balance Sheet
December 31, 19X6

Assets

Current:		
Cash		$ 2,850
Accounts receivable		4,600
Note receivable		8,000
Interest receivable		400
Inventory		42,000
Prepaid insurance		200
Supplies		100
Total current assets		58,150
Plant:		
Furniture and fixtures	$33,200	
Less: Accumulated depreciation	3,000	30,200
Total assets		$88,350

Liabilities

Current:		
Accounts payable		$47,000
Unearned sales revenue		700
Interest payable		200
Total current liabilities		47,900
Long-term:		
Note payable		12,600
Total liabilities		60,500
Stockholders' Equity		
Common stock	$10,000	
Retained earnings	17,850	
Total stockholders' equity		27,850
Total liabilities and stockholders' equity		$88,350

that are incurred in the entity's major line of business—merchandising. Rent is the cost of obtaining store space for Austin Sound's operations. Insurance is necessary to protect the inventory. The business's store furniture and fixtures wear out, and that expense is depreciation. Supplies expense is the cost of stationery, mailing, packages, and the like, used in operations.

Many companies report their operating expenses in two categories. *Selling expenses* are those expenses related to marketing the company's products—sales salaries; sales commissions; advertising; depreciation, rent, utilities, and property taxes on store buildings; depreciation on store furniture; delivery expense, and the like. *General expenses* include office expenses, such as the salaries of the company president and office employees, depreciation, rent, utilities, property taxes on the home office building, and office supplies.

Gross margin minus operating expenses equals **income from operations,** or **operating income,** as it is also called. Many businesspeople view operating income as the most reliable indicator of a business's success because it measures the entity's major ongoing activities.

The last section of Austin Sound's income statement is **other revenue and expense.** This category reports revenues and expenses that are outside the main operations of the business. Examples include gains and losses on the sale of plant assets (not inventory) and gains and losses on lawsuits. Accountants have traditionally viewed Interest Revenue and Interest Expense as "other" items because they arise from loaning money and borrowing money—financing activities that are outside the operating scope of selling merchandise or, for a service entity, rendering services.

The bottom line of the income statement is net income, which includes the effects of all the revenues and gains less all the expenses and losses. We often hear the term *bottom line* used to refer to a final result. The term originated in the position of net income on the income statement.

A merchandiser's *statement of retained earnings* looks exactly like that of a service business. In fact, you cannot determine whether the entity is merchandising or service oriented from looking at the statement of retained earnings.

If the business is a merchandiser, the *balance sheet* shows inventory as a major current asset. In contrast, service businesses usually have minor amounts of inventory.

Adjusting and Closing Entries for a Merchandising Business

OBJECTIVE 5

Adjust and close the accounts of a merchandising business

Exhibit 5-9 presents Austin Sound's adjusting entries, which are similar to those you have seen previously.

The closing entries in the exhibit include two new effects. The first closing entry debits Inventory for the ending balance of $42,000 and also debits the revenue and expense accounts that have credit balances. For Austin Sound these accounts are Sales Revenue, Interest Revenue, Purchase Discounts, and Purchase Returns and Allowances. The offsetting credit of $186,500 transfers their sum to Income Summary. This amount comes directly from the credit column of the income statement on the work sheet (Exhibit 5-7).

The second closing entry includes a credit to Inventory for its beginning balance, and credits to the revenue and expense accounts with debit balances. These are Sales Discounts, Sales Returns and Allowances, Purchases, Freight In, and the expense accounts. The offsetting $150,450 debit to Income Summary comes from the debit column of the income statement on the work sheet.

The last two closing entries close net income from Income Summary and also close Dividends into the Retained Earnings account.

The entries to the Inventory account deserve additional explanation. Recall

		Journal		
		Adjusting Entries		
a.	Dec. 31	Interest Receivable	400	
		Interest Revenue.....................		400
b.	31	Supplies Expense ($650 − $100)	550	
		Supplies		550
c.	31	Insurance Expense	1,000	
		Prepaid Insurance		1,000
d.	31	Depreciation Expense	600	
		Accumulated Depreciation		600
e.	31	Unearned Sales Revenue	1,300	
		Sales Revenue		1,300
f.	31	Interest Expense	200	
		Interest Payable		200
		Closing Entries		
	Dec. 31	Inventory (ending balance)	42,000	
		Sales Revenue	139,300	
		Interest Revenue.......................	1,000	
		Purchase Discounts	3,000	
		Purchase Returns and Allowances	1,200	
		Income Summary		186,500
	31	Income Summary	150,450	
		Inventory (beginning balance)		40,500
		Sales Discounts		1,400
		Sales Returns and Allowances........		2,000
		Purchases		89,300
		Freight In		5,200
		Rent Expense		8,400
		Depreciation Expense		600
		Insurance Expense		1,000
		Supplies Expense		550
		Interest Expense		1,500
	31	Income Summary ($186,500 − $150,450)....	36,050	
		Retained earnings		36,050
	31	Retained Earnings	34,100	
		Dividends		34,100

that before the closing process Inventory still has the period's beginning balance. At the end of the period, this balance is one year old and must be replaced with the ending balance in order to prepare the financial statements at December 31, 19X6. The closing entries give Inventory its correct ending balance of $42,000, as shown here:

Inventory			
Jan. 1 Bal.	40,500	Dec. 31 Clo.	40,500
Dec. 31 Clo.	42,000		
Dec. 31 Bal.	42,000		

EXHIBIT 5-9B Ledger Accounts of Austin Sound Stereo Center, Inc.

Assets

Cash		Accounts Receivable		Note Receivable		Interest Receivable	
2,850		4,600		8,000		(A) 400	

Inventory		Supplies		Prepaid Insurance		Furniture and Fixtures	
40,500	(C) 40,500	650	(A) 550	1,200	(A) 1,000	33,200	
(C) 42,000		100		200			

Accumulated Depreciation	
	2,400
	(A) 600
	3,000

Liabilities

Accounts Payable		Unearned Sales Revenue		Interest Payable		Note Payable	
	47,000	(A) 1,300	2,000		(A) 200		12,600
			700				

Stockholders' Equity

Common Stock		Retained Earnings		Dividends		Income Summary	
	10,000	(C) 34,100	15,900	34,100	(C) 34,100	(C)150,450	(C)186,500
			(C) 36,050			(C) 36,050	
			17,850				

Revenues

Sales Revenue		Sales Discounts		Sales Returns and Allowances		Interest Revenue	
	138,000	1,400	(C) 1,400	2,000	(C) 2,000		600
	(A) 1,300					(A) 400	
(C)139,300	139,300					(C) 1,000	1,000

Expenses

Purchases		Purchase Discounts		Purchase Returns and Allowances		Freight In	
89,300	(C) 89,300	(C) 3,000	3,000	(C) 1,200	1,200	5,200	(C) 5,200

Rent Expense		Depreciation Expense		Insurance Expense		Supplies Expense	
8,400	(C) 8,400	(A) 600	(C) 600	(A) 1,000	(C) 1,000	(A) 550	(C) 550

Interest Expense	
1,300	
(A) 200	
1,500	(C) 1,500

A = Adjusting entry;   C = Closing entry

The inventory amounts for these closing entries are taken directly from the income statement columns of the work sheet. The offsetting debits and credits to Income Summary in these closing entries also serve to record the dollar amount of cost of goods sold in the accounts. Income Summary contains the cost of goods sold amount after Purchases and its related contra accounts and Freight In are closed.

Study Exhibits 5-7, 5-8, and 5-9 carefully because they illustrate the entire end-of-period process that leads to the financial statements. As you progress through this book, you may want to refer to these exhibits to refresh your understanding of the adjusting and closing process for a merchandising business.

Income Statement Format

We have seen that the balance sheet appears in two formats: the account format and the report format. There are also two basic formats for the income statement: *multiple-step* and *single-step*.

Multiple-Step Income Statement

The income statements presented thus far in this chapter have been multiple-step income statements. Austin Sound's multiple-step income statement for the year ended December 31, 19X6, appears in Exhibit 5-8. The **multiple-step format** contains subtotals to highlight significant relationships. In addition to net income, it also presents gross margin and income from operations. This format communicates a merchandiser's results of operations especially well because gross margin and income from operations are two key measures of operating performance.

OBJECTIVE 6

Recognize different formats of the income statement

EXHIBIT 5-10   *Single-Step Income Statement*

Austin Sound Stereo Center, Inc. Income Statement For the Year Ended December 31, 19X6	
Revenues:	
Net sales (net of sales discounts, $1,400, and returns and allowances, $2,000)	$135,900
Interest revenue	1,000
Total revenues	136,900
Expenses:	
Cost of goods sold	$ 88,800
Rent expense	8,400
Interest expense	1,500
Insurance expense	1,000
Depreciation expense	600
Supplies expense	550
Total expenses	100,850
Net income	$ 36,050

Single-Step Income Statement

The **single-step format** groups all revenues together and then lists and deducts all expenses together without drawing any subtotals. The single-step format has the advantage of listing all revenues together and all expenses together, as shown in Exhibit 5-10. Thus it clearly distinguishes revenues from expenses. The income statements in Chapters 1 through 4 were single-step. This format works well for service entities because they have no gross margin to report. A recent survey of 600 companies indicated that 56 percent use the single-step format and 44 percent use the multiple-step format.

Most published financial statements are highly condensed. Appendix C at the end of the book gives the income statement of The Goodyear Tire & Rubber Company. Notice that only seven categories of expenses are reported. Of course, condensed statements can be supplemented with desired details. For example, in Exhibit 5-10, the single-step income statement could be accompanied by a supporting schedule that gives the detailed computation of cost of goods sold.

Use of Accounting Information in Decision Making _____

Merchandise inventory is the most important asset to a merchandising business because it captures the essence of the entity. To manage the firm, owners and managers focus their energies on the best way to sell the inventory. They use several ratios to evaluate operations.

A key decision tool for a merchandiser relates to gross margin, which is net sales minus cost of goods sold. Merchandisers strive to increase the *gross margin percentage,* which is computed as follows:

For Austin Sound
(Exhibit 5-8)

$$\textbf{Gross margin percentage} = \frac{\textbf{Gross margin}}{\textbf{Net sales revenue}} = \frac{\$47,100}{\$135,900} = .347$$

The gross margin (or gross profit) percentage is one of the most carefully watched measures of profitability because it is fundamental to a merchandiser. For most firms, the gross margin percentage changes little from year to year, and a small downturn may signal an important drop in income. A small increase in the gross margin percentage usually indicates an increase in profitability.

Austin Sound's gross margin percentage of 34.7 percent compares favorably with the industry average for electronic retailers, which is 34.9 percent. By contrast, the average gross margin percentage is 14.1 percent for automobile dealers, 22.8 percent for grocery stores, and 55.7 percent for restaurants.

Owners and managers strive to sell inventory as quickly as possible because unsold merchandise drains profits. The faster the sales occur, the higher the income. The slower the sales, the lower the income. Ideally a business could operate with zero inventory. Most businesses, however, including retailers such as Austin Sound, must keep goods on hand for customers. Successful merchandisers purchase carefully to keep the goods moving through the business at a rapid pace. **Inventory turnover,** the ratio of cost of goods sold to average inventory, indicates how rapidly inventory is sold. Its computation follows:

$$\frac{\text{Inventory}}{\text{turnover}} = \frac{\text{Cost of goods sold}}{\text{Average inventory}} = \frac{\text{Cost of goods sold}}{(\text{Beginning inventory} + \text{ending inventory})/2} = \frac{\$88,800}{(\$40,500 + \$42,000)/2}$$

$$= 2.2 \text{ times per year}$$

Inventory turnover is usually computed for an annual period, and the relevant cost-of-goods-sold figure is the amount for the entire year. Average inventory is computed from the beginning and ending amounts. The resulting inventory turnover statistic shows how many times inventory was sold during the year. A high rate of turnover is preferred over a low turnover. An increase in the rate of turnover usually means higher profits.

Inventory turnover varies from industry to industry. Grocery stores, for example, turn their goods over faster than automobile dealers do. Drug stores have higher turnover than furniture stores do. Retailers of electronic products, such as Austin Sound, have an average turnover of 3.6 times per year. What does Austin Sound's turnover rate of 2.2 times per year indicate about its ability to sell inventory? It suggests that Austin Sound is not very successful. The lower one-fourth of electronics retailers average a turnover rate of 2.7, so Austin Sound's turnover of 2.2 looks rather bad.

Financial analysis is complex. For Austin Sound we see an acceptable gross margin percentage but a poor rate of inventory turnover. These two ratios do not provide enough information to yield an overall conclusion about the firm, but the illustration shows how owners and managers may apply ratios to evaluate a company.

Computers and Inventory

Inventory record keeping is a demanding manual accounting task, from the paperwork required in purchasing and selling inventory to the job of periodically counting it. Computers have dramatically reduced the time required to manage inventory and have greatly increased a company's ability to control its inventory.

A computerized system enhances accounting control over inventory because the computer can keep accurate and up-to-the-minute records of the number of units purchased, the number of units sold, and the quantities on hand. The computer can also issue purchase-order forms automatically when the quantity of inventory on hand falls below the minimum amount that management sets.

Computerized inventory systems are often integrated with accounts receivable and sales. When a prospective customer's order is entered into the computer, the computer checks warehouse records to see if the requested units are in stock. If so, details of the shipment are entered into the computer, which then multiplies the number of units shipped by the unit price. The computer checks the customer's credit standing. With approved credit, the computer then prints an invoice for the customer and calculates the debit to Accounts Receivable (for that specific customer), the credit to Sales Revenue, and the reduction in inventory quantity.

The computer can keep up-to-the-minute records, so managers can call up current inventory information at any time. This inventory system can substitute for a physical count when interim financial statements are needed. These are features of a perpetual inventory system, which is covered in more detail in Chapter 8.

Summary Problem for Your Review

The accompanying trial balance relates to King Distributing Company.

Required:

1. Make a single summary journal entry to record King's
   a. Unadjusted sales for the year, assuming all sales were made on credit.
   b. Sales returns and allowances for the year.
   c. Sales discounts for the year, assuming the cash collected on account was $329,000.
   d. Purchases of inventory for the year, assuming all purchases were made on credit.
   e. Purchase returns and allowances for the year.
   f. Purchase discounts for the year, $6,000. Cash paid on account was $188,400.
   g. Transportation costs for the year, assuming a cash payment in a separate entry.
2. Enter the trial balance on a work sheet and complete the work sheet.
3. Journalize the adjusting and closing entries at December 31. Post to the Income Summary account as an accuracy check on the entries affecting that account. The credit balance closed out of Income Summary should equal net income computed on the work sheet.
4. Prepare the company's multiple-step income statement, statement of retained earnings, and balance sheet in account format.
5. Compute the inventory turnover for 19X3. Turnover for 19X2 was 2.1. Would you expect King Distributing Company to be more profitable or less profitable in 19X3 than in 19X2? Give your reason.

Additional data at December 31, 19X3:

a. Supplies used during the year, $2,580.
b. Prepaid rent in force, $1,000.
c. Unearned sales revenue still not earned, $2,400. The company expects to earn this amount during the next few months.
d. Depreciation. The furniture and fixtures' estimated useful life is 10 years, and they are expected to be worthless when they are retired from service.
e. Accrued salaries, $1,300.
f. Accrued interest expense, $600.
g. Inventory on hand, $65,800.

Note: If your instructor assigned the appendix to this chapter, which illustrates the adjusting-entry method, turn to page 269 for the Alternate Solution to Review Problem. If you were not assigned the appendix, then study the Solution to Review Problem that follows.

King Distributing Company
Trial Balance
December 31, 19X3

Cash	$ 5,670	
Accounts receivable	37,100	
Inventory	60,500	
Supplies	3,930	
Prepaid rent	6,000	
Furniture and fixtures	26,500	
Accumulated depreciation		$ 21,200
Accounts payable		46,340
Salary payable		
Interest payable		
Unearned sales revenue		3,500
Note payable, long-term		35,000
Common stock		20,000
Retained earnings		3,680
Dividends	48,000	
Sales revenue		346,700
Sales discounts	10,300	
Sales returns and allowances	8,200	
Purchases	175,900	
Purchases discounts		6,000
Purchase returns and allowances		7,430
Freight in	9,300	
Salary expense	82,750	
Rent expense	7,000	
Depreciation expense		
Utilities expense	5,800	
Supplies expense		
Interest expense	2,900	
Total	$489,850	$489,850

SOLUTION TO REVIEW PROBLEM

Requirement 1

Sales, purchases, and related discount and return and allowance entries:

19X3

a.	Accounts Receivable	346,700	
	Sales Revenue		346,700
b.	Sales Returns and Allowances	8,200	
	Accounts Receivable		8,200
c.	Cash	329,000	
	Sales Discounts	10,300	
	Accounts Receivable		339,300
d.	Purchases	175,900	
	Accounts Payable		175,900
e.	Accounts Payable	7,430	
	Purchase Returns and Allowances		7,430
f.	Accounts Payable	194,400	
	Purchase Discounts		6,000
	Cash		188,400
g.	Freight In	9,300	
	Cash		9,300

Requirement 2

King Distributing Company
Work Sheet
For the Year Ended December 31, 19X3

Account Title	Trial Balance Debit	Trial Balance Credit	Adjustments Debit	Adjustments Credit	Income Statement Debit	Income Statement Credit	Balance Sheet Debit	Balance Sheet Credit
Cash	5,670						5,670	
Accounts receivable	37,100						37,100	
Inventory	60,500				60,500	65,800	65,800	
Supplies	3,930			(a) 2,580			1,350	
Prepaid rent	6,000			(b) 5,000			1,000	
Furniture and fixtures	26,500						26,500	
Accumulated depreciation		21,200		(d) 2,650				23,850
Accounts payable		46,340						46,340
Salary payable				(e) 1,300				1,300
Interest payable				(f) 600				600
Unearned sales revenue		3,500	(c) 1,100					2,400
Note payable, long-term		35,000						35,000
Common stock		20,000						20,000
Retained earnings		3,680						3,680
Dividends	48,000						48,000	
Sales revenue		346,700		(c) 1,100		347,800		
Sales discounts	10,300				10,300			
Sales returns and allowances	8,200				8,200			
Purchases	175,900				175,900			
Purchase discounts		6,000				6,000		
Purchase returns and allowances		7,430				7,430		
Freight in	9,300				9,300			
Salary expense	82,750		(e) 1,300		84,050			
Rent expense	7,000		(b) 5,000		12,000			
Depreciation expense			(d) 2,650		2,650			
Utilities expense	5,800				5,800			
Supplies expense			(a) 2,580		2,580			
Interest expense	2,900		(f) 600		3,500			
	489,850	489,850	13,230	13,230	374,780	427,030	185,420	133,170
Net income					52,250			52,250
					427,030	427,030	185,420	185,420

Requirement 3

Adjusting Entries

19X3

Dec. 31	Supplies Expense	2,580	
	Supplies		2,580
31	Rent Expense	5,000	
	Prepaid Rent		5,000
31	Unearned Sales Revenue................	1,100	
	Sales Revenue		1,100
31	Depreciation Expense ($26,500/10)	2,650	
	Accumulated Depreciation		2,650
31	Salary Expense........................	1,300	
	Salary Payable		1,300
31	Interest Expense	600	
	Interest Payable		600

Closing Entries

19X3

Dec. 31	Inventory (ending balance)	65,800	
	Sales Revenue	347,800	
	Purchase Discounts....................	6,000	
	Purchase Returns and Allowances	7,430	
	Income Summary		427,030
31	Income Summary	374,780	
	Inventory (beginning balance)		60,500
	Sales Discounts		10,300
	Sales Returns and Allowances		8,200
	Purchases		175,900
	Freight In........................		9,300
	Salary Expense		84,050
	Rent Expense		12,000
	Depreciation Expense		2,650
	Utilities Expense		5,800
	Supplies Expense..................		2,580
	Interest Expense		3,500
31	Income Summary ($427,030 − $374,780) ...	52,250	
	Retained Earnings		52,250
31	Retained Earnings	48,000	
	Dividends		48,000

Income Summary

Clo.	374,780	Clo.	427,030
Clo.	52,250	Bal.	52,250

Requirement 4

King Distributing Company
Income Statement
For the Year Ended December 31, 19X3

Sales revenue			$347,800
Less: Sales discounts		$ 10,300	
Sales returns and allowances		8,200	18,500
Net sales revenue			$329,300
Cost of goods sold:			
Beginning inventory			$60,500
Purchases		$175,900	
Less: Purchase discounts	$6,000		
Purchase returns and allowances	7,430	13,430	
Net purchases			162,470
Freight in			9,300
Cost of goods available for sale			232,270
Less: Ending inventory			65,800
Cost of goods sold			166,470
Gross margin			162,830
Operating expenses:			
Salary expense			84,050
Rent expense			12,000
Utilities expense			5,800
Depreciation expense			2,650
Supplies expense			2,580	107,080
Income from operations			55,750
Other expense:			
Interest expense			3,500
Net income			$ 52,250

King Distributing Company
Statement of Retained Earnings
For the Year Ended December 31, 19X3

Retained earnings, December 31, 19X2	$ 3,680
Add: Net income	52,250
	55,930
Less: Dividends	48,000
Retained earnings, December 31, 19X3	$ 7,930

King Distributing Company
Balance Sheet
December 31, 19X3

Assets

Current:		
Cash		$ 5,670
Accounts receivable		37,100
Inventory		65,800
Supplies		1,350
Prepaid rent		1,000
Total current assets		110,920
Plant:		
Furniture and fixtures	$26,500	
Less: Accumulated depreciation	23,850	2,650
Total assets		$113,570

Liabilities

Current:		
Accounts payable		$ 46,340
Salary payable		1,300
Interest payable		600
Unearned sales revenue		2,400
Total current liabilities		50,640
Long-term:		
Note payable		35,000
Total liabilities		85,640
Stockholders' Equity		
Common stock	$20,000	
Retained earnings	7,930	
Total stockholders' equity		27,930
Total liabilities and stockholders' equity		$113,570

Requirement 5

$$\text{Inventory turnover} = \frac{\text{Cost of goods sold}}{\text{Average inventory}} = \frac{\$166,470}{(\$60,500 + \$65,800)/2} = 2.6$$

The increase in the rate of inventory turnover from 2.1 to 2.6 suggests higher profits in 19X3 than in 19X2.

Summary

The major revenue of a merchandising business is *sales revenue,* or *sales.* The major expense is *cost of goods sold.* Net sales minus cost of goods sold is called *gross margin,* or *gross profit.* This amount measures the business's success or failure in selling its products at a higher price than it paid for them.

The merchandiser's major asset is *inventory.* In a merchandising entity the accounting cycle is from cash to inventory as the inventory is purchased for resale, and back to cash as the inventory is sold.

Cost of goods sold is unlike the other expenses in that it is not an account in the ledger. Instead, cost of goods sold is the remainder when beginning inventory and net purchases and freight in are added and ending inventory is subtracted from that sum.

The *invoice* is the business document generated by a purchase/sale transaction. Most merchandising entities offer *discounts* to their customers and allow them to *return* unsuitable merchandise. They also grant *allowances* for damaged goods that the buyer chooses to keep. Discounts and Returns and Allowances are *contra* accounts to both Purchases and Sales.

The end-of-period adjusting and closing process of a merchandising business is similar to that of a service business. In addition, a merchandiser makes inventory entries at the end of the period. These closing entries replace the period's beginning balance with the cost of inventory on hand at the end. A by-product of these closing entries is the computation of cost of goods sold for the income statement.

The income statement may appear in the *single-step format* or the *multiple-step format.* A single-step income statement has only two sections—one for revenues and the other for expenses—and a single income amount for net income. A multiple-step income statement has subtotals for gross margin and income from operations. Both formats are widely used in practice.

Two key decision aids for a merchandiser are the *gross margin percentage* and the *rate of inventory turnover.* Increases in these measures usually signal an increase in profits.

Self-Study Questions

Test your understanding of the chapter by marking the best answer for each of the following questions.

1. The major expense of a merchandising business is *(pp. 215, 223)*
   a. Cost of goods sold
   b. Depreciation
   c. Rent
   d. Interest
2. Sales total $440,000, cost of goods sold is $210,000, and operating expenses are $160,000. How much is gross margin? *(p. 215)*
   a. $440,000
   b. $230,000
   c. $210,000
   d. $70,000

3. A purchase discount results from *(p. 219)*
   a. Returning goods to the seller
   b. Receiving a purchase allowance from the seller
   c. Buying a large enough quantity of merchandise to get the discount
   d. Paying within the discount period
4. Which one of the following pairs includes items that are the most similar? *(p. 222)*
   a. Purchase discounts and purchase returns
   b. Cost of goods sold and inventory
   c. Net sales and sales discounts
   d. Sales returns and sales allowances
5. Which of the following is *not* an account? *(p. 223)*
   a. Sales revenue   c. Inventory
   b. Net sales   d. Supplies expense
6. Cost of goods sold is computed by adding beginning inventory and net purchases and subtracting X. What is X? *(p. 224)*
   a. Net sales   c. Ending inventory
   b. Sales discounts   d. Net purchases
7. Which account causes the main difference between a merchandiser's adjusting and closing process and that of a service business? *(p. 227)*
   a. Advertising Expense   c. Inventory
   b. Interest Revenue   d. Accounts Receivable
8. The major item on a merchandiser's income statement that a service business does not have is *(pp. 230–231)*
   a. Cost of goods sold   c. Salary expense
   b. Inventory   d. Total revenue
9. The closing entry for Sales Discounts is *(p. 233)*
   a. Sales Discounts
        Income Summary
   b. Sales Discounts
        Sales Revenue
   c. Income Summary
        Sales Discounts
   d. Not used because Sales Discounts is a permanent account, which is not closed.
10. Which income statement format reports income from operations? *(p. 235)*
   a. Account format   c. Single-step format
   b. Report format   d. Multiple-step format

Answers to the Self-Study Questions follow the Accounting Vocabulary.

Accounting Vocabulary

Cost of goods sold. The cost of the inventory that the business has sold to customers, the largest single expense of most merchandising businesses. Also called Cost of sales *(p. 223)*.

Cost of sales. Another name for Cost of goods sold *(p. 223)*.

Gross margin. Excess of sales revenue over cost of goods sold. Also called Gross profit *(p. 215)*.

Gross margin percentage. Gross margin divided by net sales revenue. A measure of profitability *(p. 236)*.

Gross profit. Excess of sales revenue over cost of goods sold. Also called

Gross margin *(p. 215)*.

Income from operations. Gross margin (sales revenue minus cost of goods sold) minus operating expenses. Also called Operating income *(p. 232)*.

Inventory turnover. Ratio of cost of goods sold to average inventory. Measures the number of times a company sells its average level of inventory during a year *(pp. 236–237)*.

Invoice. Seller's request for payment from a purchaser. Also called a bill *(p. 217)*.

Multiple-step income statement. Format that contains subtotals to highlight significant relationships. In addition to net income, it also presents gross margin and income from operations (p. 235).

Net purchases. Purchases less purchase discounts and purchase returns and allowances (p. 220).

Net sales revenue. Sales revenue less sales discounts and sales returns and allowances (p. 223).

Operating expenses. Expenses, other than cost of goods sold, that are incurred in the entity's major line of business. Examples include rent, depreciation, salaries, wages, utilities, property tax, and supplies expense (pp. 230–231).

Operating income. Another name for Income from operations (p. 232).

Other expense. Expense that is outside the main operations of a business, such as a loss on the sale of plant assets (p. 232).

Other revenue. Revenue that is outside the main operations of a business, such as a gain on the sale of plant assets (p. 232).

Purchases. The cost of inventory that a firm buys to resell to customers in the normal course of business (p. 216).

Purchase discount. Reduction in the cost of inventory that is offered by a seller as an incentive for the customer to pay promptly. A contra account to Purchases (p. 219).

Purchase returns and allowances. Decrease in a buyer's debt from returning merchandise to the seller or from receiving from the seller a reduction in the amount owed. A contra account to Purchases (p. 220).

Quantity discount. A purchase discount that provides a lower price per item the larger the quantity purchased (p. 218).

Sales discount. Reduction in the amount receivable from a customer, offered by the seller as an incentive for the customer to pay promptly. A contra account to Sales Revenue (p. 222).

Sales returns and allowances. Decrease in the seller's receivable from a customer's return of merchandise or from granting the customer an allowance from the amount the customer owes the seller. A contra account to Sales Revenue (p. 222).

Sales revenue. Amount that a merchandiser earns from selling inventory before subtracting expenses (p. 215).

Single-step income statement. Format that groups all revenues together and then lists and deducts all expenses together without drawing any subtotals (p. 236).

Answers to Self-Study Questions

1. a
2. b ($440,000 − $210,000 = $230,000)
3. d
4. d
5. b

6. c
7. c
8. a
9. c
10. d

ASSIGNMENT MATERIAL _____

Questions

1. Gross margin is often mentioned in the business press as an important measure of success. What does gross margin measure, and why is this important?
2. Describe the operating cycle for (a) the purchase and cash sale of inventory and (b) the purchase and sale of inventory on account.
3. Identify 10 items of information on an invoice.
4. What is the similarity and what is the difference between purchase discounts and quantity discounts?

5. Indicate which accounts are debited and credited for (a) a credit purchase of inventory and the subsequent cash payment and (b) a credit sale of inventory and the subsequent cash collection. Assume no discounts, returns, allowances, or freight.

6. Inventory costing $1,000 is purchased and invoiced on July 28 under terms of 3/10 n/30. Compute the payment amount on August 6. How much would the payment be on August 8? What explains the difference? What is the latest acceptable payment date under the terms of sale?

7. Inventory listed at $35,000 is sold subject to a quantity discount of $3,000 and under payment terms of 2/15 n/45. What is the net sales revenue on this sale if the customer pays within 15 days?

8. Name four contra accounts introduced in this chapter.

9. Briefly discuss the similarity in computing supplies expense and computing cost of goods sold.

10. Why is the title of cost of goods sold especially descriptive? What type of item is cost of goods sold?

11. Beginning inventory is $5,000, net purchases total $30,000, and freight in is $1,000. If ending inventory is $8,000, what is cost of goods sold?

12. Identify two ways that cost of goods sold differs from operating expenses such as Salary Expense and Depreciation Expense.

13. Suppose you are evaluating two companies as possible investments. One entity sells its services, and the other entity is a merchandiser. How can you identify the merchandiser by examining the two entities' balance sheets and their income statements?

14. You are beginning the adjusting and closing process at the end of your company's fiscal year. Does the trial balance carry the beginning or the ending amount of inventory? Will the balance sheet that you prepare report the beginning or the ending inventory?

15. Give the two closing entries for inventory (using no specific amount).

16. During the closing process, what accounts contain the amount of cost of goods sold for the period? Where is the final resting place of cost of goods sold?

17. What is the identifying characteristic of the "other" category of revenues and expenses? Give an example of each.

18. Name and describe the two income statement formats and identify the type of business to which each format best applies.

19. List eight different operating expenses.

20. Which financial statement reports sales discounts, sales returns and allowances, purchase discounts, and purchase returns and allowances? Show how they are reported, using any reasonable amounts in your illustration.

21. Does a merchandiser prefer a high or a low rate of inventory turnover? Give your reason.

Exercises

Exercise 5-1 *Journalizing purchase and sale transactions* **(L.O. 2)**

Journalize, without explanations, the following transactions of Gonzaga, Inc., during July:

July 3 Purchased $2,000 of inventory under terms of 2/10 n/eom (end of month) and FOB shipping point.

7 Returned $300 of defective merchandise purchased on July 3.

9 Paid freight bill of $110 on July 3 purchase.

July 10   Sold inventory for $2,200, collecting cash of $400. Payment terms on the remainder were 2/15 n/30.

12   Paid amount owed on credit purchase of July 3, less the discount and the return.

16   Granted a sales allowance of $800 on the July 10 sale.

23   Received cash from July 10 customer in full settlement of her debt, less the allowance and the discount.

Exercise 5-2   *Journalizing transactions from a purchase invoice* **(L.O. 2)**

ABC TIRE WHOLESALE DISTRIBUTORS, INC.
2600 Commonwealth Avenue
Boston, Massachusetts 02215

Invoice date: May 14, 19X3   **Payment terms:** 2/10 n/30

Sold to: Kendrick Tire Co,
4219 Crestwood Parkway
Lexington, Mass. 02173

Quantity Ordered	Description	Quantity Shipped	Price	Amount
6	P135-X4 Radials.........	6	$37.14	$ 222.84
8	L912 Belted-bias........	8	41.32	330.56
14	R39 Truck tires	10	50.02	500.20
	Total.......................................			$1,053.60

Due date: **Amount:**
May 24, 19X3 $1,032.53
May 25 through June 13, 19X3 $1,053.60

Paid:

As the manager of Kendrick Tire Company, you receive the accompanying invoice from a supplier.

Required

1. Record the May 15 purchase on account.
2. The R39 truck tires were ordered by mistake and therefore were returned to ABC. Journalize the return on May 19.
3. Record the May 22 payment of the amount owed.

Exercise 5-3   *Journalizing purchase transactions* **(L.O. 2)**

On April 30 Feldman Jewelers purchased inventory of $4,300 on account from a wholesale jewelry supplier. Terms were 3/15 net 45. On receiving the goods, Feldman checked the order and found $800 of items that were not ordered. Therefore, Feldman returned this amount of merchandise to the supplier on May 4.

To pay the remaining amount owed, Feldman had to borrow from the bank because of a temporary cash shortage. On May 14 Feldman signed a short-term note payable to the bank and immediately paid the borrowed funds to the wholesale jewelry supplier. On May 31 Feldman paid the bank the net amount of the invoice, which was borrowed, plus $30 interest.

Required

Record the indicated transactions in the journal of Feldman Jewelers. Explanations are not required.

Exercise 5-4 *Journalizing sale transactions* (L.O. 2)

Refer to the business situation in Exercise 5-3. Journalize the transactions of the wholesale jewelry supplier. Explanations are not required.

Exercise 5-5 *Computing the elements of a merchandiser's income statement* (L.O. 3)

Supply the missing income statement amounts in each of the following situations:

Sales	Sales Discounts	Net Sales	Beginning Inventory	Net Purchases	Ending Inventory	Cost of Goods Sold	Gross Margin
$98,300	(a)	$92,800	$32,500	$66,700	$39,400	(b)	$33,000
82,400	$2,100	(c)	27,450	43,000	(d)	$44,100	36,200
91,500	1,800	89,700	(e)	54,900	22,600	59,400	(f)
(g)	3,000	(h)	40,700	(i)	48,230	62,500	36,600

Exercise 5-6 *Computing cost of goods sold for an actual company* (L.O. 3)

For the year ended December 31, 19X9, House of Fabrics, a retailer of home-related products, reported net sales of $338 million and cost of goods sold of $154 million. The company's balance sheet at December 31, 19X8 and 19X9, reported inventories of $133 million and $129 million, respectively. What were House of Fabrics's net purchases during 19X9?

Exercise 5-7 *Preparing a merchandiser's multiple-step income statement* (L.O. 3,4,6)

Selected accounts of Payless Cashways Company are listed in alphabetical order.

Accounts receivable	$ 48,300	Purchases	$ 71,300
Accumulated deprecia-		Purchase discounts	3,000
tion	18,700	Purchase returns.	2,000
Freight in	2,200	Sales discounts	9,000
General expenses	23,800	Sales returns	4,600
Interest revenue	1,500	Sales revenue	201,000
Inventory, June 30	21,870	Selling expenses	37,840
Inventory, May 31	19,450	Unearned sales revenue .	6,500
Retained earnings, May 31	126,070		

Required

Prepare the business's multiple-step income statement for June of the current year. Compute the rate of inventory turnover. Last year the turnover was 2.8 times. Does this two-year trend suggest improvement or deterioration in profitability?

Exercise 5-8 *Preparing a single-step income statement for a merchandising business* (L.O. 3,4,6)

Prepare Payless Cashways' single-step income statement for June, using the data from the preceding exercise. In a separate schedule, show the computation of cost of goods sold.

Exercise 5-9 *Using work sheet data to prepare a merchandiser's income statement* **(L.O. 5,6)**

The trial balance and adjustments columns of the work sheet of Midway Auto Supply include the following accounts and balances at March 31, 19X2.

Account Title	Trial Balance Debit	Trial Balance Credit	Adjustments Debit	Adjustments Credit
Cash	2,000			
Accounts receivable	8,500		(a) 2,100	
Inventory	36,070			
Supplies	13,000			(b) 8,600
Store fixtures	22,500			
Accumulated depreciation		11,250		(c) 2,250
Accounts payable		9,300		
Salary payable				(d) 1,200
Note payable, long-term		7,500		
Common stock		20,000		
Retained earnings		13,920		
Dividends.....................	45,000			
Sales revenue		213,000		(a) 2,100
Sales discounts	2,000			
Purchases.....................	114,200			
Purchase returns		2,600		
Selling expense................	21,050		(b) 5,200	
			(d) 1,200	
General expense...............	10,500		(b) 3,400	
			(c) 2,250	
Interest expense	2,750			
Total	277,570	277,570	14,150	14,150

Ending inventory at March 31, 19X2, is $34,500.

Prepare the company's multiple-step income statement for the year ended March 31, 19X2. Compute the gross margin percentage and the inventory turnover for the year. Compare these figures with the gross margin percentage of .43 and the inventory turnover of 3.16 for 19X1. Does the two-year trend suggest improvement or deterioration in profitability?

Exercise 5-10 *Use work sheet data to prepare the closing entries of a merchandising business* **(L.O. 5)**

Use the data from Exercise 5-9 to journalize Midway Auto Supply's closing entries at March 31, 19X2.

Problems (Group A)

Problem 5-1A *Explaining the operating cycle of a retailer* **(L.O. 1)**

Macy's Department Store is one of the most famous retailers in the world. The women's sportswear department of Macy's purchases clothing from manufacturers such as Ruff Hewn, Jones New York, and Prophecy. Macy's advertising department is promoting end-of-year sales.

Required

You are the manager of the Macy's store in Dallas. Write a memo to a new employee in the women's sportswear department explaining how the company's operating cycle works.

Problem 5-2A *Accounting for the purchase and sale of inventory* (L.O. 2)

The following transactions occurred between American Hospital Supply and Prucare Medical Clinic during June of the current year.

June 8 American Hospital Supply sold $3,900 worth of merchandise to Prucare Medical Clinic on terms of 2/10 n/30, FOB shipping point. American prepaid freight charges of $200 and included this amount in the invoice total. (American's entry to record the freight payment debits Accounts Receivable and credits Cash.)

11 Prucare returned $600 of the merchandise purchased on June 8. American issued a credit memo for this amount.

17 Prucare paid $2,000 of the invoice amount owed to American for the June 8 purchase. This payment included none of the freight charge.

26 Prucare paid the remaining amount owed to American for the June 8 purchase.

Required

Journalize these transactions, first on the books of Prucare Medical Clinic and second on the books of American Hospital Supply.

Problem 5-3A *Journalizing purchase and sale transactions* (L.O. 2)

Davis Book Store engaged in the following transactions during July of the current year:

July 2 Purchased inventory for cash, $800, less a quantity discount of $150.

3 Purchased store supplies on credit terms of net eom (end of month), $2,300.

8 Purchased inventory of $3,000 less a quantity discount of 10 percent, plus freight charges of $230. Credit terms are 3/15 n/30.

9 Sold goods for cash, $1,200.

11 Returned $200 (net amount after the quantity discount) of the inventory purchased on July 8. It was damaged in shipment.

12 Purchased inventory on credit terms of 3/10 n/30, $3,330.

14 Sold inventory on credit terms of 2/10 n/30, $9,600, less a $600 quantity discount.

16 Paid the electricity and water bills, $275.

20 Received returned inventory from July 14 sale, $400 (net amount after the quantity discount). Davis shipped the wrong goods by mistake.

21 Borrowed the amount owed on the July 8 purchase. Signed a note payable to the bank for $2,655, which takes into account the return of inventory on July 11.

21 Paid supplier for goods purchased on July 8 less the discount and the return.

23 Received $6,860 cash in partial settlement of his account from the customer who purchased inventory on July 14. Granted the customer a 2 percent discount and credited his account receivable for $7,000.

30 Paid for the store supplies purchased on July 3.

Required

1. Journalize the above transactions.
2. Compute the amount of the receivable at July 31 from the customer to whom Davis sold inventory on July 14. What amount of cash discount applies to this receivable at July 31?

Problem 5-4A *Computing cost of goods sold and gross margin* **(L.O. 3)**

Selected accounts of Montpelier Supply Company had these balances at June 30, 19X9.

Purchases	$ 98,100
Selling expenses	29,800
Equipment	44,700
Purchase discounts	1,300
Accumulated depreciation—equipment.....	6,900
Note payable	30,000
Sales discounts........................	3,400
General expenses	16,300
Accounts receivable	22,600
Accounts payable	23,800
Cash	13,600
Freight in.............................	4,300
Sales revenue	173,100
Purchases returns and allowances	1,400
Salary payable	1,800
Retained earnings	36,000
Sales returns and allowances	12,100
Inventory: June 30, 19X8	33,800
June 30, 19X9	32,500

Required

1. Show the computation of Montpelier Supply's net sales, cost of goods sold, and gross margin for the year ended June 30, 19X9.
2. John Wilfong, manager of Montpelier Supply, strives to earn a gross margin percentage of 40 percent. Did he achieve this goal?
3. Did the rate of inventory turnover reach the industry average of 2.8?

Problem 5-5A *Preparing a merchandiser's financial statements* **(L.O. 3,4,6)**

The accounts of Curtis Mathes Home Entertainment Center are listed in alphabetical order.

Accounts payable	$27,380	Purchases	$273,100
Accounts receivable	31,200	Purchase discounts	4,670
Accumulated depreciation		Purchase returns and	
—office equipment	9,500	allowances.............	10,190
Accumulated depreciation		Salary payable	6,120
—store equipment	6,880	Sales discounts..........	8,350
Cash	12,320	Sales returns and	
Dividends	11,000	allowances.............	17,900
General expenses.........	75,830	Sales revenue	531,580
Interest expense.........	7,200	Selling expenses..........	84,600
Interest payable	3,000	Stockholders' equity, June	
Inventory: June 30........	190,060	30....................	73,720
July 31	187,390	Store equipment	47,500
Note payable, long-term ..	160,000	Supplies	4,350
Office equipment.........	79,000	Unearned sales revenue...	9,370

Required

1. Prepare the entity's multiple-step income statement for July of the current year.

2. Prepare the income statement in single-step format.
3. Prepare the balance sheet in report format at July 31 of the current year. Show your computation of the July 31 balance of stockholders' equity.

Problem 5-6A *Using work sheet data to prepare financial statements* **(L.O. 3,4,6)**

The trial balance and adjustments columns of the work sheet of Lawson Coffee Company include the following accounts and balances at September 30, 19X5:

Account Title	Trial Balance Debit	Trial Balance Credit	Adjustments Debit	Adjustments Credit
Cash....................	7,300			
Accounts receivable	4,360		(a) 1,800	
Inventory	31,530			
Supplies	10,700			(b) 7,640
Equipment	79,450			
Accumulated depreciation ..		29,800		(c) 9,900
Accounts payable		13,800		
Salary payable				(e) 200
Unearned sales revenue		3,780	(d) 2,600	
Note payable, long-term		10,000		
Common stock		50,000		
Retained earnings.........		8,360		
Dividends	35,000			
Sales revenue.............		242,000		(a) 1,800
				(d) 2,600
Sales returns	3,100			
Purchases	127,400			
Purchase discounts........		3,700		
Selling expense	40,600		(b) 7,640	
			(e) 200	
General expense	21,000		(c) 9,900	
Interest expense	1,000			
Total....................	361,440	361,440	22,140	22,140

Required

1. Inventory on hand at September 30, 19X5, is $32,580. Without entering the preceding data on a formal work sheet, prepare the company's multiple-step income statement for the year ended September 30, 19X5, and its September 30, 19X5, balance sheet. Show your computation of the ending balance of Retained Earnings.

2. Compute the gross margin percentage and the inventory turnover for 19X5. For 19X4, Lawson's gross margin percentage was .57 and the rate of inventory turnover was 4.2. Does the two-year trend in these ratios suggest improvement or deterioration in profitability?

Problem 5-7A *Preparing a merchandiser's work sheet* **(L.O. 5)**

Paschall Paint Company's trial balance relates to December 31 of the current year.

Additional data at December 31, 19XX:

a. Insurance expense for the year, $6,090.
b. Store fixtures have an estimated useful life of 10 years and are expected to be worthless when they are retired from service.

c. Accrued salaries at December 31, $1,260.
d. Accrued interest expense at December 31, $870.
e. Store supplies on hand at December 31, $760.
f. Inventory on hand at December 31, $99,350.

Paschall Paint Company
Trial Balance
December 31, 19XX

Cash	$ 2,910	
Accounts receivable.................	6,560	
Inventory	101,760	
Store supplies	1,990	
Prepaid insurance	3,200	
Store fixtures......................	63,900	
Accumulated depreciation		$ 37,640
Accounts payable...................		29,770
Salary payable		
Interest payable		
Note payable, long-term		37,200
Common stock		30,000
Retained earnings		33,120
Dividends	36,300	
Sales revenue		286,370
Purchases.........................	161,090	
Salary expense	46,580	
Rent expense	14,630	
Utilities expense...................	6,780	
Depreciation expense		
Insurance expense..................	5,300	
Store supplies expense..............		
Interest expense...................	3,100	
Total	$454,100	$454,100

Required

Complete Paschall's work sheet for the year ended December 31 of the current year.

Problem 5-8A *Journalizing the adjusting and closing entries of a merchandising business (L.O. 5)*

Required

1. Journalize the adjusting and closing entries for the data in Problem 5-7A.
2. Determine the December 31 balance of Retained Earnings.

Problem 5-9A *Preparing a merchandiser's work sheet, financial statements, and adjusting and closing entries (L.O. 3,4,5)*

The year-end trial balance of Wang Sales Company relates to July 31 of the current year.

Wang Sales Company
Trial Balance
July 31, 19XX

Cash	$ 3,120	
Notes receivable, current	6,900	
Interest receivable		
Inventory	104,000	
Prepaid insurance	2,810	
Notes receivable, long-term	19,300	
Furniture	16,000	
Accumulated depreciation		$ 12,000
Accounts payable.....................		14,360
Salary payable		
Sales commission payable		
Unearned sales revenue..............		4,090
Common stock		50,000
Retained earnings		52,270
Dividends	59,000	
Sales revenue		337,940
Sales discounts......................	3,440	
Sales returns and allowances	8,900	
Interest revenue		1,910
Purchases...........................	163,200	
Purchase discounts		2,100
Purchase returns and allowances......		5,760
Freight in	11,100	
Salary expense	39,030	
Sales commission expense.............	31,500	
Rent expense	10,000	
Utilities expense.....................	2,130	
Insurance expense....................		
Depreciation expense		
Total	$480,430	$480,430

Additional data at July 31, 19XX:

a. Accrued interest revenue, $350.
b. Prepaid insurance still in force, $310.
c. Furniture has an estimated useful life of eight years. Its value is expected to be zero when it is retired from service.
d. Unearned sales revenue still unearned, $1,900.
e. Accrued salaries, $1,640.
f. Accrued sales commissions, $1,430.
g. Inventory on hand, $102,600.

Required

1. Enter the trial balance on a work sheet, and complete the work sheet for the year ended July 31 of the current year.
2. Prepare the company's multiple-step income statement and statement of retained earnings for the year ended July 31 of the current year. Also prepare its balance sheet at that date. Long-term notes receivable should be reported on the balance sheet between current assets and plant assets in a separate section labeled Investments.
3. Journalize the adjusting and closing entries at July 31.

4. Post to the Retained Earnings account and to the Income Summary account as an accuracy check on the adjusting and closing process.

(Group B)

Problem 5-1B *Explaining the operating cycle of a retailer* *(L.O. 1)*

EyeMasters is a regional chain of optical shops in the southwestern United States. They specialize in offering a large selection of eyeglass frames, and they provide while-you-wait service. EyeMasters carries frames made by Logo Paris, Liz Claiborne, Ralph Lauren, and others. EyeMasters has launched a vigorous advertising campaign promoting its two-for-the-price-of-one frame sales.

Required

You are the president of this company. Write a memo to your store manager explaining how the company's operating cycle works.

Problem 5-2B *Accounting for the purchase and sale of inventory* *(L.O. 2)*

The following transactions occurred between Allcare Medical Supply and Greenview Clinic during February of the current year.

Feb. 6 Allcare Medical Supply sold $5,300 worth of merchandise to Greenview Clinic on terms of 2/10 n/30, FOB shipping point. Allcare prepaid freight charges of $300 and included this amount in the invoice total. (Allcare's entry to record the freight payment debits Accounts Receivable and credits Cash.)

10 Greenview returned $900 of the merchandise purchased on February 6. Allcare issued a credit memo for this amount.

15 Greenview paid $3,000 of the invoice amount owed to Allcare for the February 6 purchase. This payment included none of the freight charge.

27 Greenview paid the remaining amount owed to Allcare for the February 6 purchase.

Required

Journalize these transactions, first on the books of Greenview Clinic and second on the books of Allcare Medical Supply.

Problem 5-3B *Journalizing purchase and sale transactions* *(L.O. 2)*

Monarch Paper Company engaged in the following transactions during May of the current year:

May 3 Purchased office supplies for cash, $300.

7 Purchased inventory on credit terms of 2/10 net eom (end of month), $1,100.

8 Returned half the inventory purchased on May 7. It was not the inventory ordered.

10 Sold goods for cash, $450.

13 Sold inventory on credit terms of 2/15 n/45, $3,900, less $600 quantity discount offered to customers who purchased in large quantities.

16 Paid the amount owed on account from the purchase of May 7, less the discount and the return.

May 17 Received defective inventory returned from May 13 sale, $900, which is the net amount after the quantity discount.

18 Purchased inventory of $4,000 on account. Payment terms were 2/10 net 30.

26 Borrowed $3,920 from the bank to take advantage of the discount offered on May 18 purchase. Signed a note payable to the bank for this amount.

26 Paid supplier for goods purchased on May 18, less the discount.

28 Received cash in full settlement of his account from the customer who purchased inventory on May 13, less the discount and the return.

29 Purchased inventory for cash, $2,000, less a quantity discount of $400, plus freight charges of $160.

Required

1. Journalize the above transactions.
2. Assume the note payable signed on May 26 requires the payment of $30 interest expense. Was the decision wise or unwise to borrow funds to take advantage of the cash discount?

Problem 5-4B *Computing cost of goods sold and gross margin* **(L.O. 3)**

Selected accounts of Cargill Coin Collectors had these balances at November 30 of the current year.

Accumulated depreciation—furniture and fixtures	$ 13,600
Note payable	14,000
Purchase discounts	600
Sales discounts	2,100
General expenses	19,300
Accounts receivable	7,200
Purchases	132,000
Selling expenses	8,800
Furniture and fixtures	37,200
Purchase returns and allowances	900
Salary payable	300
Common stock	25,000
Retained earnings	27,800
Sales revenue	184,600
Sales returns and allowances	3,200
Inventory: November 30, 19X0	41,700
November 30, 19X1	39,500
Accounts payable	9,500
Cash	3,700
Freight in	1,600

Required

1. Show the computation of Cargill's net sales, cost of goods sold, and gross margin for the year ended November 30 of the current year.
2. Gretchen Sharp, manager of Cargill Coin Collectors, strives to earn a gross margin percentage of 25 percent. Did she achieve this goal?
3. Did the rate of inventory turnover reach the industry average of 3.4?

Problem 5-5B *Preparing a merchandiser's financial statements* **(L.O. 3,4,6)**

The accounts of Pure Milk Company are listed in alphabetical order.

Accounts payable	$ 16,950	Purchases $364,000
Accounts receivable	43,700	Purchase discounts 1,990
Accumulated depreciation		Purchase returns
—office equipment	22,450	and allowances......... 3,400
Accumulated depreciation		Salary payable 2,840
—store equipment	16,000	Sales discounts........... 10,400
Cash	7,890	Sales returns and
Dividends	9,000	allowances............. 18,030
General expenses.........	116,700	Sales revenue 731,000
Interest expense.........	5,400	Selling expenses.......... 132,900
Interest payable	1,100	Stockholders' equity,
Inventory: April 30	69,350	April 30 74,620
May 31........	71,520	Store equipment 88,000
Note payable, long-term ..	45,000	Supplies................ 5,100
Office equipment.........	58,680	Unearned sales revenue... 13,800

Required

1. Prepare the business's multiple-step income statement for May of the current year.
2. Prepare the income statement in single-step format.
3. Prepare the balance sheet in report format at May 31 of the current year. Show your computation of the May 31 balance of stockholders' equity.

Problem 5-6B *Using work sheet data to prepare financial statements* **(L.O. 3,4,6)**

The trial balance and adjustments columns of the work sheet of Scarlatti Development Company include the following accounts and balances at November 30, 19X4:

	Trial Balance		Adjustments	
Account Title	**Debit**	**Credit**	**Debit**	**Credit**
Cash	4,000			
Accounts receivable	14,500		(a) 6,000	
Inventory	47,340			
Supplies....................	2,800			(b) 2,400
Furniture	39,600			
Accumulated depreciation		4,900		(c) 2,450
Accounts payable		12,600		
Salary payable				(e) 1,000
Unearned sales revenue		13,570	(d) 6,700	
Note payable, long-term		15,000		
Common stock..............		40,000		
Retained earnings		20,310		
Dividends	42,000			
Sales revenue		164,000		(a) 6,000
				(d) 6,700
Sales returns................	6,300			
Purchases	73,200			
Purchase discounts		2,040		
Selling expense	28,080		(e) 1,000	
General expense	13,100		(b) 2,400	
			(c) 2,450	
Interest expense	1,500			
Total	272,420	272,420	18,550	18,550

1. Inventory on hand at November 30, 19X4, is $52,650. Without entering the preceding data on a formal work sheet, prepare the company's multiple-step income statement for the year ended November 30, 19X4, and its November 30, 19X4, balance sheet. Show your computation of the ending balance of Retained Earnings.
2. Compute the gross margin percentage and the rate of inventory turnover for 19X4. For 19X3, Scarlatti's gross margin percentage was .58, and inventory turnover was 1.1. Does the two-year trend in these ratios suggest improvement or deterioration in profitability?

Problem 5-7B *Preparing a merchandiser's work sheet* **(L.O. 5)**

Randall Apparel, Inc.'s trial balance relates to December 31 of the current year.

Additional data at December 31, 19XX:

a. Rent expense for the year, $10,200.
b. Store fixtures have an estimated useful life of 10 years and are expected to be worthless when they are retired from service.
c. Accrued salaries at December 31, $900.
d. Accrued interest expense at December 31, $360.
e. Inventory on hand at December 31, $80,200.

Required

Complete Randall Apparel, Inc.'s work sheet for the year ended December 31 of the current year.

Randall Apparel, Inc.
Trial Balance
December 31, 19XX

Cash	$ 1,270	
Accounts receivable	4,430	
Inventory	73,900	
Prepaid rent	4,400	
Store fixtures	22,100	
Accumulated depreciation		$ 8,380
Accounts payable		6,290
Salary payable		
Interest payable		
Note payable, long-term		18,000
Common stock		25,000
Retained earnings		30,920
Dividends	39,550	
Sales revenue		170,150
Purchases	67,870	
Salary expense	24,700	
Rent expense	7,700	
Advertising expense	4,510	
Utilities expense	3,880	
Depreciation expense		
Insurance expense	2,770	
Interest expense	1,660	
Total	$258,740	$258,740

Problem 5-8B Journalizing the adjusting and closing entries of a merchandising business
(L.O. 5)

Required

1. Journalize the adjusting and closing entries for the data in Problem 5-7B.
2. Determine the December 31 balance of Retained Earnings.

Problem 5-9B Preparing a merchandiser's work sheet, financial statements, and
adjusting and closing entries (L.O. 3,4,5)

The year-end trial balance of Weisner Sales Company pertains to March 31 of the current year.

Additional data at March 31, 19XX:

a. Accrued interest revenue, $1,030.
b. Insurance expense for the year, $3,000.
c. Furniture has an estimated useful life of 6 years. Its value is expected to be zero when it is retired from service.
d. Unearned sales revenue still unearned, $8,200.
e. Accrued salaries, $1,200.
f. Accrued sales commissions, $1,700.
g. Inventory on hand, $133,200.

Weisner Sales Company
Trial Balance
March 31, 19XX

Cash	$ 7,880	
Notes receivable, current	12,400	
Interest receivable		
Inventory	130,050	
Prepaid insurance	3,600	
Notes receivable, long-term	62,000	
Furniture	6,000	
Accumulated depreciation		$ 4,000
Accounts payable		12,220
Sales commission payable		
Salary payable		
Unearned sales revenue		9,610
Common stock		50,000
Retained earnings		122,780
Dividends	66,040	
Sales revenue		440,000
Sales discounts	4,800	
Sales returns and allowances	11,300	
Interest revenue		8,600
Purchases	233,000	
Purchase discounts		3,100
Purchase returns and allowances		7,600
Freight in	10,000	
Sales commission expense	78,300	
Salary expense	24,700	
Rent expense	6,000	
Utilities expense	1,840	
Depreciation expense		
Insurance expense		
Total	$657,910	$657,910

Required

1. Enter the trial balance on a work sheet, and complete the work sheet for the year ended March 31 of the current year.
2. Prepare the company's multiple-step income statement and statement of retained earnings for the year ended March 31 of the current year. Also prepare its balance sheet at that date. Long-term notes receivable should be reported on the balance sheet between current assets and plant assets in a separate section labeled Investments.
3. Journalize the adjusting and closing entries at March 31.
4. Post to the Retained Earnings account and to the Income Summary account as an accuracy check on the adjusting and closing process.

Extending Your Knowledge

Decision Problems

1. Using the Financial Statements to Decide on a Business Expansion (L.O. 4,6)

David Wheelis manages Heights Pharmacy, Inc., which has prospered during its second year of operation. In deciding whether to open another pharmacy in the area, David has prepared the current financial statements of the business.

Heights Pharmacy, Inc.
Income Statement
For the Year Ended December 31, 19X1

Sales revenue		$175,000
Interest revenue		24,600
Total revenue		199,600
Cost of goods sold:		
Beginning inventory	$ 27,800	
Net purchases	87,500	
Cost of goods available for sale	115,300	
Less: Ending inventory	30,100	
Cost of goods sold		85,200
Gross margin		114,400
Operating expenses:		
Salary expense	18,690	
Rent expense	12,000	
Interest expense	6,000	
Depreciation expense	4,900	
Utilities expense	2,330	
Supplies expense	1,400	
Total operating expense		45,320
Income from operations		69,080
Other expense:		
Sales discounts ($3,600) and returns ($7,100)		10,700
Net income		$ 58,380

Heights Pharmacy, Inc.
Statement of Retained Earnings
For the Year Ended December 31, 19X1

Retained earnings, January 1, 19X1	$15,000
Add: Net income	58,380
Retained earnings, December 31, 19X1 .	$73,380

Heights Pharmacy, Inc.
Balance Sheet
December 31, 19X1

Assets

Current:	
Cash	$ 5,320
Accounts receivable	9,710
Inventory	30,100
Supplies	2,760
Store fixtures	63,000
Total current assets	110,890
Other:	
Dividends	45,000
Total assets	$155,890

Liabilities

Current:	
Accumulated depreciation—store fixtures	$ 6,300
Accounts payable	10,310
Salary payable....................	900
Total current liabilities	17,510
Other:	
Note payable due in 90 days........	40,000
Total liabilities.....................	57,510

Stockholders' Equity

Common stock	$25,000	
Retained earnings	73,380	
Total stockholders' equity		98,380
Total liabilities and stockholders' equity		$155,890

David recently read in an industry trade journal that a successful pharmacy meets all of these criteria:

(a) The gross margin percentage is at least .50.

(b) The current ratio is at least 2.00.

(c) The debt ratio is no greater than .50.

Basing his opinion on the entity's financial statement data, David believes the business meets all three criteria. He plans to go ahead with his expansion plan and asks your advice on preparing the pharmacy's financial statements in accordance with generally accepted accounting principles. He assures you that all amounts are correct.

Required

1. Prepare a correct multiple-step income statement, a statement of retained earnings, and a balance sheet in report format.
2. Based on the corrected financial statements, compute correct measures of the three criteria listed in the trade journal.
3. Assuming the criteria are valid, make a recommendation about whether to undertake the expansion at this time.

2. Understanding the Operating Cycle of a Merchandiser   (L.O. 1,3)

A. Gayle Yip-Chuk has come to you for advice. Earlier this year she opened a record store in a plaza near the university she had attended. The store sells records, cassettes, and compact discs for cash and on credit cards and, as a special feature, on credit to certain students. Many of the students at the university are co-op students who alternate school and work terms. Gayle allows co-op students to buy on credit while they are on a school term, with the understanding that they will pay their account shortly after starting a work term.

Business has been very good. Gayle is sure it is because of her competitive prices and the unique credit terms she offers. Her problem is that she is short of cash, and her loan with the bank has grown significantly. The bank manager has indicated that he wishes to reduce Gayle's line of credit because he is worried that Gayle will get into financial difficulties.

Required

1. Explain to Gayle why you think she is in this predicament.
2. Gayle has asked you to explain her problem to the bank manager and to assist in asking for more credit. What might you say to the bank manager to assist Gayle?

B. The employees of Schneider Ltd. made an error when they performed the periodic inventory count at year end, October 31, 19X2. Part of one warehouse was not counted and therefore was not included in inventory.

Required

1. Indicate the effect of the inventory error on cost of goods sold, gross margin, and net income for the year ended October 31, 19X2.
2. Will the error affect cost of goods sold, gross margin, and net income in 19X3? If so, what will the effects be?

Ethical Issue

Kingston & Barnes, a partnership, makes all sales of industrial conveyor belts under terms of FOB shipping point. The company usually receives orders for sales approximately one week before shipping inventory to customers. For orders received late in December, Lisa Kingston and Meg Barnes, the managers, decide when to ship the goods. If profits are already at an acceptable level, they delay shipment until January. If profits are lagging behind expectations, they ship the goods during December.

Required

1. Under Kingston & Barnes's FOB policy, when should the company record a sale?

2. Do you approve or disapprove of Kingston & Barnes's means of deciding when to ship goods to customers? If you approve, give your reason. If you disapprove, identify a better way to decide when to ship goods. (There is no accounting rule against the Kingston & Barnes practice.)

Financial Statement Problems

1. Closing Entries for a Merchandising Corporation; Evaluating Ratio Data (L.O. 5)

This problem uses both the income statement (statement of income) and the balance sheet of The Goodyear Tire & Rubber Company in Appendix C. It will aid your understanding of the closing process of a business with inventories.

Assume that the inventory and closing procedures outlined in this chapter are appropriate for Goodyear. Further, use the amounts of inventories reported on the balance sheet. Ignore freight in, and assume net purchases for the year ended December 31, 1991, totaled $8,372.0 million.

Required

1. Using Net Purchases and amounts from the income statement, journalize Goodyear's closing entries for the year ended December 31, 1991. You will be unfamiliar with certain costs and expenses, but you should treat them all similarly.
2. What amount was closed to Retained Earnings? How is this amount labeled on Goodyear's income statement?
3. Compute Goodyear's gross margin percentages and inventory turnover rates during 1991 and 1990. (In addition to the information in the Goodyear report in Appendix C, you will also need the December 31, 1989, Inventories balance, which was $1,642.0 million.) Did these ratio values of Goodyear improve or deteriorate during 1991? Summarize these results in a sentence.

2. Identifying Items from an Actual Company's Financial Statements (L.O. 5)

Obtain the annual report of an actual company of your choosing. *Make sure that the company's balance sheet reports Inventories, Merchandise Inventories, or a similar asset category.* Answer these questions about the company:

1. What was the balance of total inventories reported on the balance sheet at the end of the current year? At the end of the preceding year? (If you selected a manufacturing company, you may observe more than one category of inventories. If so, name these categories and briefly explain what you think they mean.)
2. Give the company's journal entries to close Income Summary and Dividends.
3. Compute the company's gross margin percentage for the current year and for the preceding year. Did the gross margin percentage increase or decrease during the current year? Is this a favorable signal or an unfavorable signal about the company?
4. Compute the rate of inventory turnover for the current year. Would you expect your company's rate of inventory turnover to be higher or lower than that of a grocery chain such as Safeway or Kroger? Higher or lower than that of an aircraft manufacturer such as Boeing or McDonnell Douglas? State your reasoning.

Appendix

The Adjusting and Closing Process for a Merchandising Business: Adjusting-Entry Method

This appendix illustrates the adjusting-entry method for completing the accounting cycle of a merchandising business. In this approach we record the end-of-period inventory entries as adjustments rather than as closing entries. Except for this difference in handling inventory entries, the adjusting-entry method and the closing-entry method are identical. *No other adjusting or closing entries are affected by the approach taken, and the financial statements that result from both methods are the same.* Because of the way computers operate, computerized systems use the adjusting-entry method.

The Adjusting and Closing Process

To illustrate a merchandiser's adjusting and closing process, let's use Austin Sound's December 31, 19X6, trial balance in Exhibit 5-6, page 228. All the new accounts—Inventory, Freight In, and the contra accounts—are highlighted for emphasis. Inventory is the only new account that is affected by the adjusting procedures. Note that additional-data item *g* gives the ending inventory of $42,000.

Work Sheet of a Merchandising Business

The Exhibit 5A-1 work sheet is similar to the work sheets we have seen so far, but a few differences appear. Note that this work sheet does not include adjusted trial balance columns. In most accounting systems, a single operation combines trial balance amounts with the adjustments and extends the adjusted balances directly to the income statement and balance sheet columns. Therefore, to reduce clutter, the adjusted trial balance columns are omitted. A second difference is that the merchandiser's work sheet includes inventory and purchase amounts (which are highlighted). Let's examine the entire work sheet.

Account Title Columns.   The trial balance lists a number of accounts without balances. Ordinarily, these accounts are affected by the adjusting process. Examples include Interest Receivable, Interest Payable, and Depreciation Expense. The accounts are listed in the order they appear in the ledger. This eases the preparation of the work sheet. Note that Income Summary—used for the inventory adjustments—is listed between Dividends and Sales Revenue. If additional accounts are needed, they can be written in at the bottom of the work sheet before net income is determined. Simply move net income down to make room for the additional accounts.

Trial Balance Columns.   Examine the Inventory account, $40,500 in the trial balance. This $40,500 is the cost of the beginning inventory. The work sheet is designed to replace this outdated amount with the new ending balance, which in our example is $42,000 (additional-data item *g* in Exhibit 5-6). As we shall see, this task is accomplished through the adjusting process.

Adjustments Columns.   The adjustments are similar to those discussed in Chapters 3 and 4. They may be entered in any order desired. The debit amount

Austin Sound
Work Sheet
For the Year Ended December 31, 19X6

Account Title	Trial Balance Debit	Trial Balance Credit	Adjustments Debit	Adjustments Credit	Income Statement Debit	Income Statement Credit	Balance Sheet Debit	Balance Sheet Credit
Cash	2,850						2,850	
Accounts receivable	4,600						4,600	
Note receivable, current	8,000						8,000	
Interest receivable			(a) 400				400	
Inventory	40,500		(g2) 42,000	(g1) 40,500			42,000	
Supplies	650			(b) 550			100	
Prepaid insurance	1,200			(c) 1,000			200	
Furniture and fixtures	33,200						33,200	
Accumulated depreciation		2,400		(d) 600				3,000
Accounts payable		47,000						47,000
Unearned sales revenue		2,000	(e) 1,300					700
Interest payable				(f) 200				200
Note payable, long-term		12,600						12,600
Common stock		10,000						10,000
Retained earnings		15,900						15,900
Dividends	34,100						34,100	
Income summary			(g1) 40,500	(g2) 42,000	40,500	42,000		
Sales revenue		138,000		(e) 1,300		139,300		
Sales discounts	1,400				1,400			
Sales returns and allowances	2,000				2,000			
Interest revenue		600		(a) 400		1,000		
Purchases	89,300				89,300			
Purchase discounts		3,000				3,000		
Purchase returns and allowances		1,200				1,200		
Freight in	5,200				5,200			
Rent expense	8,400				8,400			
Depreciation expense			(d) 600		600			
Insurance expense			(c) 1,000		1,000			
Supplies expense			(b) 550		550			
Interest expense	1,300		(f) 200		1,500			
	232,700	232,700	86,550	86,550	150,450	186,500	125,450	89,400
Net income					36,050			36,050
					186,500	186,500	125,450	125,450

of each entry should equal the credit amount, and total debits should equal total credits.

The inventory adjustments are new. At the end of the period, accountants replace the beginning Inventory balance with the ending Inventory balance. Entry *g1* removes the beginning balance ($40,500) by crediting the Inventory account. The debit portion of entry *g1* transfers the beginning inventory amount to the Income Summary. This is done because beginning inventory becomes part of cost of goods sold during the year. Entry *g2* places the ending balance ($42,000) in the Inventory account with a debit. The credit to Income Summary signifies that the ending inventory amount is subtracted in computing cost of goods sold. Therefore, the two inventory adjustments prepare Inventory for the balance sheet and aid in computing cost of goods sold for the income statement.

Income Statement Columns. The income statement columns contain adjusted amounts for the revenues and the expenses. Sales Revenue, for example, is $139,300, which includes the $1,300 adjustment.

The two inventory amounts appear in the income statement columns alongside Income Summary because beginning inventory and ending inventory enter the computation of cost of goods sold. Recall that beginning inventory is added to purchases and ending inventory is subtracted. Even though the resulting cost-of-goods-sold amount does not appear on the work sheet, all the components of cost of goods sold are evident there. Placement of beginning inventory ($40,500) in the work sheet's income statement debit column has the effect of adding beginning inventory in computing cost of goods sold. Placing ending inventory ($42,000) in the credit column has the opposite effect.

Purchases and Freight In appear in the debit column because they are added in computing cost of goods sold. Purchase Discounts and Purchase Returns and Allowances appear as credits because they are subtracted. Together, all these items are used to compute cost of goods sold—$88,800 on the income statement in Exhibit 5-5, on page 225.

The income statement column subtotals on the work sheet indicate whether the business earned net income or incurred a net loss. If total credits are greater, the result is net income, as shown in the exhibit. Inserting the net income amount in the debit column brings total debits into agreement with total credits. If total debits are greater, a net loss has occurred. Inserting a net loss amount in the credit column would equalize total debits and total credits. Net income or net loss is then extended to the opposite column of the balance sheet.

Balance Sheet Columns. The only new item on the balance sheet is inventory. The balance listed is the ending amount of $42,000, which is determined by a physical count of inventory on hand at the end of the period. On the work sheet this amount comes from the $42,000 amount in the Adjustments Debit column.

Recall that the financial statements for a company are the same whether the adjusting-entry method or the closing-entry method is used. Exhibit 5-8, on page 231, presents Austin Sound's financial statements, which are based on the information in the work sheet. The text on pages 230–232 discusses these financial statements in detail.

Adjusting and Closing Entries for a Merchandising Business

OBJECTIVE 5

Adjust and close the accounts of a merchandising business

Exhibit 5A-2 presents Austin Sound's adjusting entries, which are similar to those you have seen previously. Adjustment *g1* transfers the beginning Inventory balance to Income Summary. Entry *g2* sets up the ending Inventory balance.

The first closing entry debits the revenue and expense accounts that have credit balances. For Austin Sound these accounts are Sales Revenue, Interest Revenue, Purchase Discounts, and Purchase Returns and Allowances. The offsetting credit of $144,500 transfers their sum to Income Summary.

The second closing entry credits the revenue and expense accounts with debit balances. These are Sales Discounts, Sales Returns and Allowances, Purchases, Freight In, and the expense accounts.

Journal

Adjusting Entries

a.	Dec. 31	Interest Receivable	400	
		Interest Revenue		400
b.	31	Supplies Expense ($650–$100)	550	
		Supplies............................		550
c.	31	Insurance Expense	1,000	
		Prepaid Insurance		1,000
d.	31	Depreciation Expense	600	
		Accumulated Depreciation		600
e.	31	Unearned Sales Revenue	1,300	
		Sales Revenue		1,300
f.	31	Interest Expense	200	
		Interest Payable		200
g1	31	Income Summary	40,500	
		Inventory		40,500
g2	31	Inventory	42,000	
		Income Summary		42,000

Closing Entries

	Dec. 31	Sales Revenue	139,300	
		Interest Revenue.........................	1,000	
		Purchase Discounts	3,000	
		Purchase Returns and Allowances	1,200	
		Income Summary		144,500
	31	Income Summary	109,950	
		Sales Discounts		1,400
		Sales Returns and Allowances		2,000
		Purchases		89,300
		Freight In		5,200
		Rent Expense		8,400
		Depreciation Expense.................		600
		Insurance Expense		1,000
		Supplies Expense		550
		Interest Expense		1,500
	31	Income Summary ($186,500–$150,450)*	36,050	
		Retained earnings		36,050
	31	Retained earnings.........................	34,100	
		Dividends		34,100

* The $186,500 amount is the sum of the $144,500 credit in the closing entry and the $42,000 credit in the g2 adjusting entry. The $150,450 amount is the sum of the $109,950 debit in the closing entry and the $40,500 debit in the g1 adjusting entry.

The last two closing entries close net income from Income Summary and also close Dividends into the Retained Earnings account.

The entries to the Inventory account deserve additional explanation. Recall that before the adjusting process Inventory still has the period's beginning balance. At the end of the period, this balance is one year old and must be replaced with the ending balance in order to prepare the financial statements at December 31, 19X6. The adjusting entries give Inventory its correct ending

EXHIBIT 5A-2B   *Ledger Accounts of Austin Sound Stereo Center, Inc.*

Assets

Cash	
2,850	

Accounts Receivable	
4,600	

Note Receivable	
8,000	

Interest Receivable	
(A) 400	

Inventory	
40,500	(A) 40,500
(A) 42,000	

Supplies	
650	(A) 550
100	

Prepaid Insurance	
1,200	(A) 1,000
200	

Furniture and Fixtures	
33,200	

Accumulated Depreciation	
	2,400
	(A) 600
	3,000

Liabilities

Accounts Payable	
	47,000

Unearned Sales Revenue	
(A) 1,300	2,000
	700

Interest Payable	
	(A) 200

Note Payable	
	12,600

Stockholders' Equity

Common Stock	
	10,000

Retained Earnings	
34,100	15,900
	(C) 36,050
	17,850

Dividends	
34,100	(C) 34,100

Income Summary	
(A) 40,500	(A) 42,000
(C)109,950	(C)144,500
(C) 36,050	

Revenues

Sales Revenue	
	138,000
	(A) 1,300
(C)139,300	139,300

Sales Discounts	
1,400	(C) 1,400

Sales Returns and Allowances	
2,000	(C) 2,000

Interest Revenue	
	600
	(A) 400
(C) 1,000	1,000

Expenses

Purchases	
89,300	(C) 89,300

Purchase Discounts	
(C) 3,000	3,000

Purchase Returns and Allowances	
(C) 1,200	1,200

Freight In	
5,200	(C) 5,200

Rent Expense	
8,400	(C) 8,400

Depreciation Expense	
(A) 600	(C) 600

Insurance Expense	
(A) 1,000	(C) 1,000

Supplies Expense	
(A) 550	(C) 550

Interest Expense	
1,300	
(A) 200	
1,500	(C) 1,500

(A) = Adjusting entry; (C) = Closing entry

balance of $42,000, as shown here:

Inventory

Jan. 1 Bal.	40,500	Dec. 31 Adj.	40,500
Dec. 31 Adj.	42,000		
Dec. 31 Bal.	42,000		

The inventory amounts for these adjusting entries are taken directly from the Adjustments columns of the work sheet. The offsetting debits and credits to Income Summary in these adjusting entries also serve to record the dollar amount of cost of goods sold in the accounts. Income Summary contains the cost-of-goods-sold amount after Purchases and its related contra accounts and Freight In are closed.

Study Exhibits 5A-1, 5A-2, and 5-8 carefully because they illustrate the entire end-of-period process that leads to the financial statements. As you progress through this book, you may want to refer to these exhibits to refresh your understanding of the adjusting and closing process for a merchandising business.

Return to the heading Income Statement Format on page 235.

Alternate Solution to Review Problem

Requirement 1

Sales, purchases, and related discount and return and allowance entries:

	19X3			
a.	Accounts Receivable	346,700	
	Sales Revenue		346,700
b.	Sales Returns and Allowances	8,200	
	Accounts Receivable		8,200
c.	Cash	329,000	
	Sales Discounts	10,300	
	Accounts Receivable		339,300
d.	Purchases	175,900	
	Accounts Payable		175,900
e.	Accounts Payable	7,430	
	Purchase Returns and Allowances		7,430
f.	Accounts Payable	194,400	
	Purchase Discounts		6,000
	Cash		188,400
g.	Freight In	9,300	
	Cash		9,300

King Distributing Company
Work Sheet
For the Year Ended December 31, 19X3

Account Title	Trial Balance Debit	Trial Balance Credit	Adjustments Debit	Adjustments Credit	Income Statement Debit	Income Statement Credit	Balance Sheet Debit	Balance Sheet Credit
Cash	5,670						5,670	
Accounts receivable	37,100						37,100	
Inventory	60,500		(g2) 65,800	(g1) 60,500			65,800	
Supplies	3,930			(a) 2,580			1,350	
Prepaid rent	6,000			(b) 5,000			1,000	
Furniture and fixtures	26,500						26,500	
Accumulated depreciation		21,200		(d) 2,650				23,850
Accounts payable		46,340						46,340
Salary payable				(e) 1,300				1,300
Interest payable				(f) 600				600
Unearned sales revenue		3,500	(c) 1,100					2,400
Note payable, long-term		35,000						35,000
Common stock		20,000						20,000
Retained earnings		3,680						3,680
Dividends	48,000						48,000	
Income summary			(g1) 60,500	(g2) 65,800	60,500	65,800		
Sales revenue		346,700		(c) 1,100		347,800		
Sales discounts	10,300				10,300			
Sales returns and allowances	8,200				8,200			
Purchases	175,900				175,900			
Purchase discounts		6,000				6,000		
Purchase returns and allowances		7,430				7,430		
Freight in	9,300				9,300			
Salary expense	82,750		(e) 1,300		84,050			
Rent expense	7,000		(b) 5,000		12,000			
Depreciation expense			(d) 2,650		2,650			
Utilities expense	5,800				5,800			
Supplies expense			(a) 2,580		2,580			
Interest expense	2,900		(f) 600		3,500			
	489,850	489,850	139,530	139,530	374,780	427,030	185,420	133,170
Net income					52,250			52,250
					427,030	427,030	185,420	185,420

Requirement 3

Adjusting Entries

19X3			
Dec. 31	Supplies Expense	2,580	
	Supplies		2,580
31	Rent Expense	5,000	
	Prepaid Rent.......................		5,000
31	Unearned Sales Revenue...............	1,100	
	Sales Revenue		1,100
31	Depreciation Expense ($26,500/10)	2,650	
	Accumulated Depreciation		2,650

	31	Salary Expense............................	1,300	
		Salary Payable		1,300
	31	Interest Expense	600	
		Interest Payable		600
	31	Income Summary	60,500	
		Inventory.........................		60,500
	31	Inventory	65,800	
		Income Summary		65,800

Closing Entries

19X3				
Dec.	31	Sales Revenue	347,800	
		Purchase Discounts.......................	6,000	
		Purchase Returns and Allowances	7,430	
		Income Summary....................		361,230
	31	Income Summary	314,280	
		Sales Discounts		10,300
		Sales Returns and Allowances		8,200
		Purchases...........................		175,900
		Freight In...........................		9,300
		Salary Expense		84,050
		Rent Expense		12,000
		Depreciation Expense		2,650
		Utilities Expense		5,800
		Supplies Expense.....................		2,580
		Interest Expense.....................		3,500
	31	Income Summary ($65,800 + $361,230 − $60,500 − $314,280)....................	52,250	
		Retained Earnings		52,250
	31	Retained Earnings	48,000	
		Dividends		48,000

Income Summary

Adj.	60,500	Adj.	65,800
Clo.	314,280	Clo.	361,230
Clo.	52,250	Bal.	52,250

Turn back to page 242 for the solution to requirement 4, which shows the financial statements for King Distributing Company.

Comprehensive Problem for Part One

Completing a Merchandiser's Accounting Cycle

The end-of-month trial balance of Lansing Building Materials, Inc., at January 31 of the current year follows:

<table>
<tr><td colspan="4" align="center">Lansing Building Materials, Inc.
Trial Balance
January 31, 19XX</td></tr>
<tr><th>Account Number</th><th>Account</th><th colspan="2" align="center">Balance</th></tr>
<tr><th></th><th></th><th>Debit</th><th>Credit</th></tr>
<tr><td>11</td><td>Cash ....</td><td>$ 6,430</td><td></td></tr>
<tr><td>12</td><td>Accounts receivable ....</td><td>19,090</td><td></td></tr>
<tr><td>13</td><td>Inventory ....</td><td>65,400</td><td></td></tr>
<tr><td>14</td><td>Supplies ....</td><td>2,700</td><td></td></tr>
<tr><td>15</td><td>Building ....</td><td>195,000</td><td></td></tr>
<tr><td>16</td><td>Accumulated depreciation—building ...</td><td></td><td>$ 36,000</td></tr>
<tr><td>17</td><td>Fixtures.............................</td><td>45,600</td><td></td></tr>
<tr><td>18</td><td>Accumulated depreciation—fixtures ....</td><td></td><td>5,800</td></tr>
<tr><td>21</td><td>Accounts payable ....</td><td></td><td>28,300</td></tr>
<tr><td>22</td><td>Salary payable ....</td><td></td><td></td></tr>
<tr><td>23</td><td>Interest payable ....</td><td></td><td></td></tr>
<tr><td>24</td><td>Unearned sales revenue ....</td><td></td><td>6,560</td></tr>
<tr><td>25</td><td>Note payable, long-term..............</td><td></td><td>87,000</td></tr>
<tr><td>31</td><td>Common stock ....</td><td></td><td>100,000</td></tr>
<tr><td>32</td><td>Retained earnings....................</td><td></td><td>44,980</td></tr>
<tr><td>33</td><td>Dividends...........................</td><td>9,200</td><td></td></tr>
<tr><td>41</td><td>Sales revenue ....</td><td></td><td>177,970</td></tr>
<tr><td>42</td><td>Sales discounts ....</td><td>7,300</td><td></td></tr>
<tr><td>43</td><td>Sales returns and allowances...........</td><td>8,140</td><td></td></tr>
<tr><td>51</td><td>Purchases ....</td><td>103,000</td><td></td></tr>
<tr><td>52</td><td>Purchase discounts ....</td><td></td><td>4,230</td></tr>
<tr><td>53</td><td>Purchase returns and allowances ....</td><td></td><td>2,600</td></tr>
<tr><td>54</td><td>Selling expense ....</td><td>21,520</td><td></td></tr>
<tr><td>55</td><td>General expense ....</td><td>10,060</td><td></td></tr>
<tr><td>56</td><td>Interest expense ....</td><td></td><td></td></tr>
<tr><td></td><td>Total ....</td><td>$493,440</td><td>$493,440</td></tr>
</table>

Additional data at January 31, 19XX:

a. Supplies consumed during the month, $1,500. One-half is selling expense, and the other half is general expense.

b. Depreciation for the month: building, $4,000; fixtures, $4,800. One-fourth of depreciation is selling expense, and three-fourths is general expense.

c. Unearned sales revenue still unearned, $1,200.

d. Accrued salaries, a general expense, $1,150.

e. Accrued interest expense, $780.

f. Inventory on hand, $60,720.

Required

1. Using four-column accounts, open the accounts listed on the trial balance, inserting their unadjusted balances. Date the balances of the following accounts January 1: Inventory; Supplies; Building; Accumulated Depreciation—Building; Fixtures; Accumulated Depreciation—Fixtures; Unearned Sales Revenue; Common Stock; and Retained Earnings. Date the balance of Dividends January 31.

2. Enter the trial balance on a work sheet, and complete the work sheet for the month ended January 31 of the current year. Lansing groups all operating expenses under two accounts, Selling Expense and General Expense. Leave two blank lines under Selling Expense and three blank lines under General Expense.

3. Prepare the company's multiple-step income statement and statement of retained earnings for the month ended January 31 of the current year. Also prepare the balance sheet at that date in report form.

4. Journalize the adjusting and closing entries at January 31, using page 3 of the journal.

5. Post the adjusting and closing entries, using dates and posting references.

6. Compute Lansing's current ratio and debt ratio at January 31, and compare these values with the industry averages of 1.9 for the current ratio and .57 for the debt ratio. Compute the gross margin percentage and the rate of inventory turnover for the month, and compare these ratio values with the industry averages of .26 for the gross margin percentage and .5 for inventory turnover. Does Lansing Building Materials appear to be stronger or weaker than the average company in the building materials industry?

Chapter 6

Accounting Information Systems
and Internal Control

iners Club was the first credit card company. It was started in 1952 as a club for frequent diners by a man who ran out of money at a restaurant.

Before 1984, [Diners Club service] representatives had to start a file for each card holder inquiry, keep track of the accumulating paperwork until it had all been received, make a decision, and then contact the card holder. All the files were kept on paper. The personal card group handles about 10,000 pieces of correspondence a month, so there was a lot of clerical effort maintaining the paper files.

With the image processing system [which can convert pictures, drawings, and written characters to machine-readable form], all correspondence to the personal card group is scanned at the mail room to digitize it. Each digitized image is stored on an optical storage system and given four indices for retrieval purposes—date received, date of credit card charge, account number, and amount. From there, only the electronic images are used; the paper is discarded.

Source: *I/S Analyzer* (formerly *EDP Analyzer*), May 1989, vol. 27, no. 5, p. 1. Used with permission of United Communications Group.

Diners Club needs a system to keep track of all its correspondence. By automating, the company was able to streamline its work. In the same way, accounting systems are designed to provide the information that managers need, at a cost the company can afford.

An **accounting information system**—often called simply an *information system*—is the combination of personnel, records, and procedures that a business uses to meet its routine needs for financial data. Because each business has different information demands, each uses a different accounting information system. For example, a jewelry store earns revenue by selling inventory, so the store's management usually wants an up-to-the-minute, accurate level of goods on hand for sale. A physician, however, earns revenue by providing service, and there is little or no inventory to control. The physician needs to keep track of the time spent on each patient. The jewelry store and the physician, then, need different information systems to answer the special sorts of questions that arise as they conduct their business. For maximum effectiveness, the information system is tailored to the business's specific needs.

A basic understanding of accounting systems—the glue that holds the various parts of an organization together—is important for managing and evaluating a business. Also, you do not want your employees to take advantage of you by manipulating your accounting system to cover theft. Business owners who are unfamiliar with accounting systems are victims of this practice to an alarming degree.

This chapter describes accounting information system designs and how they are implemented. It discusses and illustrates special journals and ledgers that accountants use to streamline information systems. The chapter also shows how managers structure duties to maintain control over operations.

Accounting System Design and Installation

System Design. An accounting information system begins with a design. The manager and the designer study the business's goals and organizational structure. They also identify management's information needs, breaking down the required information-processing tasks. The designer must consider the personnel who will operate the system, the documents and reports to be produced, and the equipment to be used. Almost every information system uses a computer for at least some tasks. Some CPA firms specialize in system design and install accounting systems for their clients.

System Installation. Installation includes selecting and training employees to operate the system, testing the system, and modifying it as needed. For a large system, installation may take months or even years. Often installation is more difficult than planned. Even after careful consideration in the design phase, unforeseen difficulties may emerge. If the system is not debugged, it will not perform its intended tasks.

Basic Model of Information Processing

Processing information means collecting, organizing, and processing data, and communicating the information to statement users. In addition, accounting data are used by managers. For example, accounts receivable might be analyzed to identify the biggest customers, who will receive special privileges. Exhibit 6-1 shows how the *basic model of information processing* relates to an accounting system.

1. The *source data* for the accounting system are the documents, such as invoices and canceled checks, that business transactions generate.
2. *Organizing and processing* data require transaction analysis, journalizing, posting, and preparation of the work sheet.
3. The output is *information—*the *financial statements.*

Notice that the system converts data to reports, fulfilling accounting's role of providing information.

An Effective Information System

OBJECTIVE 1

Describe the features of an effective information system

Each business's accounting information system follows the basic model shown in Exhibit 6-1. A well-designed information system offers control, compatibility, flexibility, and an acceptable cost/benefit relationship.

EXHIBIT 6-1 *Information-Processing Model and the Accounting System*

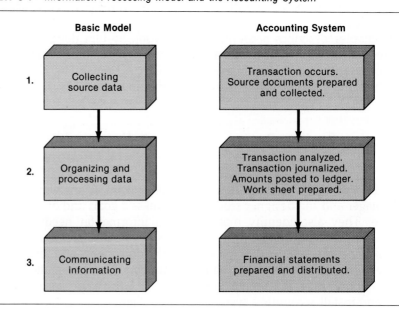

Control

A good accounting system gives management control over operations. *Internal controls* are the methods and procedures used to authorize transactions, safeguard assets, and ensure the accuracy of accounting records. For example, most companies exert tight controls over cash disbursements to avoid theft through unauthorized payments. Also, keeping accurate records of accounts receivable is the only way to ensure that customers are billed and collections are received on time. The accounting system controls assets to different degrees. Usually control over cash is tighter than control over supplies and prepaid expenses because cash is more open to theft. The final section of this chapter details internal control procedures.

Compatibility

An information system meets the compatibility guideline when it works smoothly with the business's particular structure, personnel, and special features. For example, one company may be organized by geographical region, another company by product line. The compatibility guideline means designing the information system with the company's needs and the human factor in mind.

Flexibility

Organizations evolve. They develop new products, sell off unprofitable operations, and adjust employee pay scales. Changes in the business often call for changes in the accounting system. A well-designed system meets the flexibility guideline if it can accommodate such changes without needing a complete overhaul. In most organizations, systems are rarely replaced in their entirety.

Acceptable Cost/Benefit Relationship

Control, compatibility, and flexibility can be achieved in an accounting system, but they cost money. At some point, the cost of the system outweighs its benefits. Identifying that point is the job of the accountant as systems analyst and of the manager as user of the information. For example, a company should buy a new computer only if the benefits exceed the computer's cost.

Computer Data Processing _____

Much data processing in business is done by computer. Computers offer significant advantages in accuracy and in the volume of accounting work that can be performed.

Components of a Computer System

The components of a computer data processing system are *hardware, software,* and *personnel.*

Hardware.   Computer **hardware** is the equipment that makes up the system. A **mainframe system** is characterized by a single computer that can handle a large volume of transactions very quickly. It can be used locally or by employees at various locations. Employees enter data into the mainframe through remote terminals. In large systems, the employees may be scattered all over the world yet have access to the same computer. Smaller computers, called **minicomputers,** operate like large systems but on a smaller scale.

A microcomputer system is based on a different concept. In a **microcomputer** system, each work station has its own computer, often called a personal computer (PC). These small computers can be connected so that employees can work on the same project together. A group of microcomputers connected for common use is called a *network.* Networked microcomputer systems achieve many of the benefits of a mainframe system. Micro systems are popular because they are more flexible and less expensive than large mainframes.

Software.   Computer **software** is the set of programs, or instructions, that causes the computer to perform the work desired. In a computer system, transactions are not entered into the accounting records by writing entries in a journal. They are entered by typing data on a keyboard similar to that of a typewriter. The keyboard is wired to the computer, which converts the typed data into instructions the computer uses to process the data. In some systems, the data are entered into the computer on punched cards.

Mainframe software includes programs written in computer languages such as FORTRAN, COBOL, and PL/1. Microcomputers use software based on computer languages such as BASIC and PASCAL. Other micro software is designed to do specialized tasks. For example, LOTUS 1-2-3 performs financial analysis, and dBASE III organizes, stores, and retrieves large quantities of data. Peachtree's Insight program processes data and prints the balance sheet, income statement, and subsidiary records of accounts receivable, accounts payable, and payroll, among many other accounting tasks. Microcomputer software is popular because much of it is menu-driven. This means that by following instructions—the "menu"—you can do complex tasks with little or no computer training.

Personnel.   Computer personnel in a mainframe system include a systems analyst, a programmer, and a machine operator. The *systems analyst* designs the system, based on managers' information needs and the available accounting data. It is the analyst's job to design systems that convert data into useful information—at the lowest cost. The *programmer* writes the programs (instructions) that direct the computer's actions. The computer *operator* runs the machine.

In microcomputer systems, the distinction between the programmer and the operator is blurred because an employee may handle both responsibilities. For example, a marketing manager may use a microcomputer to identify the territory needing an advertising campaign. The company treasurer may use a micro to analyze the effects of borrowing money at various interest rates. The controller may prepare the budget on a micro. These people may program the computer to meet their specific needs, and also operate the machine.

Batch versus On-Line Processing

Computers process data in two main ways, in batches and on-line. **Batch processing** handles similar transactions in a group, or batch. Payroll accounting systems use batch processing. Suppose each employee fills out a weekly time sheet showing the number of hours worked. Stored in the computer are the employee's hourly pay and payroll deductions. The machine operator enters the hours worked, and the computer multiplies hours by hourly pay to determine each employee's gross pay. The computer subtracts deductions to compute net pay and prints payroll checks for the net amount. It also prints the weekly payroll report and updates the ledger accounts—all in one batch operation.

On-line processing handles transaction data continuously, often from various locations, rather than in batches at a single location. In retail stores like Sears and Penney's, the cash register does more than make change. It also doubles as a computer terminal. When you charge merchandise at a Penney's store in the United States, the transaction is recorded at Penney's data-processing center in Dallas, Texas, directly from the store cash register. For any one transaction the computer in Dallas may perform the following steps:

1. Accounts receivable—
    a. Compares your account number with the list of approved accounts.
        Assume your account is approved.
    b. Adds the amount of this transaction to your previous balance and determines whether the new balance, including this transaction amount, exceeds your credit limit.
        Assume it does not exceed your credit limit.
    c. Debits the Accounts Receivable account and updates your personal account balance to include the effect of this transaction.
2. Sales Revenue—Credits the Sales Revenue account.
3. Inventory—
    a. Updates inventory records for the decrease due to this transaction.
    b. Prepares an order for replacement merchandise if the updated quantity on hand is below the reorder point.

The interactive nature of on-line processing—accounting for accounts receivable, sales, and inventory simultaneously—requires a large share of the computer's capacity. On-line processing, therefore, is used more in mainframe systems than in micro systems.

Overview of an Accounting Information System

The purpose of an accounting information system is to produce the financial statements and other reports used by managers, creditors, and interested people who evaluate the business. Each entity designs its system to achieve the goals of control, compatibility, flexibility, and an acceptable cost/benefit relationship. Exhibit 6-2 diagrams a typical accounting system for a merchandising business.

Special Accounting Journals

The journal entries illustrated so far in this book have been made in the *general journal*. In practice, however, it is inefficient to record all transactions there.

Think of using the general journal to debit Accounts Receivable and credit Sales Revenue for each credit sale made in a department store on a busy Saturday! Assuming you survived that, consider posting each journal entry to the

EXHIBIT 6-2 *Overview of an Accounting System*

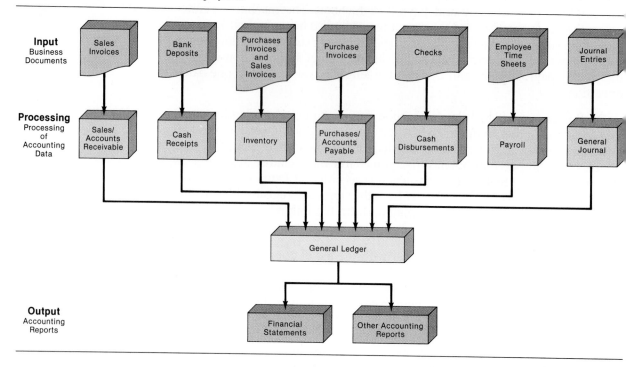

ledger. Not only would the work be tedious, but it would be time-consuming and expensive.

In fact, most of a business's transactions fall into one of four categories, so accountants use special journals to record these transactions. This system reduces the time and cost otherwise spent journalizing, as we will see. The four categories of transactions, the related special journal, and the posting abbreviations follow.

Transaction	Special Journal	Posting Abbreviation
1. Sale on account	Sales journal	S
2. Cash receipt	Cash receipts journal	CR
3. Purchase on account	Purchases journal	P
4. Cash disbursement	Cash disbursements journal	CD

Businesses use the **general journal** for transactions that do not fit one of the special journals. For example, adjusting and closing entries are entered in the general journal. Its posting abbreviation is J.

OBJECTIVE 2

Use the sales journal

Sales Journal

Most merchandisers sell at least some of their inventory on account. These *credit sales* are recorded in the **sales journal,** also called the *credit sales journal.* Credit sales of assets other than inventory—for example, buildings—occur infrequently and are recorded in the general journal.

Exhibit 6-3 illustrates a sales journal (Panel A) and the related posting to the ledgers (Panel B) of Austin Sound, the stereo shop introduced in Chapter 5.

EXHIBIT 6-3 *Sales Journal and Posting to Ledgers*

Panel A–Sales Journal:

		Sales Journal		Page 3
Date	**Invoice No.**	**Account Debited**	**Post Ref.**	**Accounts Receivable Dr. Sales Revenue Cr.**
19X6				
Nov. 2	422	Maria Galvez	✓	935
13	423	Brent Harmon	✓	694
18	424	Susan Levy	✓	907
27	425	Clay Schmidt	✓	783
30		Total		3,319
				(12/41)

Individual accounts receivable are posted daily.

Totals are posted at the end of the month.

Panel B–Posting to Ledgers:

Accounts Receivable Ledger

Maria Galvez

Date	Jrnl. Ref.	Debit	Credit	Balance
Nov. 2	S.3	935		935

Brent Harmon

Date	Jrnl. Ref.	Debit	Credit	Balance
Nov. 13	S.3	694		694

Susan Levy

Date	Jrnl. Ref.	Debit	Credit	Balance
Nov. 18	S.3	907		907

Clay Schmidt

Date	Jrnl. Ref.	Debit	Credit	Balance
Nov. 27	S.3	783		783

General Ledger

Accounts Receivable   No. 12

Date	Jrnl. Ref.	Debit	Credit	Balance
Nov. 30	S.3	3,319		3,319

Sales Revenue   No. 41

Date	Jrnl. Ref.	Debit	Credit	Balance
Nov. 30	S.3		3,319	3,319

The sales journal in Exhibit 6-3 (Panel A) has only one amount column, on the far right. Each entry in this column is a debit (Dr.) to Accounts Receivable and a credit (Cr.) to Sales Revenue, as the heading above this column indicates. For each transaction, the accountant enters the date, invoice number, and customer name along with the transaction amount. In practice the business must know the amount receivable from each customer.

Consider the first transaction. On November 2 Austin Sound sold stereo equipment on account to Maria Galvez for $935. The invoice number is 422. All this information appears on a single line in the sales journal. Note that no explanation is necessary. The transaction's presence in the sales journal means that it is a credit sale: debited to Accounts Receivable—Maria Galvez and credited to Sales Revenue. To gain any additional information about the transaction, a person looks up the actual invoice.

Posting to the General Ledger.   Note the term *general ledger*. The ledger we have used so far is the **general ledger,** which holds the accounts reported in the financial statements. However, we will soon introduce other ledgers.

Posting from the sales journal to the general ledger is done monthly. First, the amounts in the journal are summed. In Exhibit 6-3, the total credit sales for November are $3,319. Recall that this column has two headings, Accounts Receivable and Sales Revenue. When the $3,319 is posted to these accounts in the general ledger, the accountant enters their account numbers beneath the total in the sales journal. Note in Panel B of Exhibit 6-3 that the account number for Accounts Receivable is 12 and the account number for Sales Revenue is 41. These account numbers are written beneath the credit sales total in the sales journal to signify that the $3,319 has been posted to the two accounts. The $3,319 is a debit to Accounts Receivable and a credit to Sales Revenue, as the heading in the sales journal states.

Posting to the Subsidiary Ledger.   The $3,319 sum of the November debits does not identify the amount receivable from any specific customer. Most businesses would find it cumbersome to keep a separate accounts receivable account in the general ledger for each customer. A business may have thousands of customers. Imagine how many pages thick the general ledger for Sears would be. To streamline operations, businesses instead place the accounts of their individual credit customers in a subsidiary ledger, called the accounts receivable ledger. A **subsidiary ledger** is a book of accounts that provides supporting details on individual balances, the total of which appears in a general ledger account. The customer accounts are filed alphabetically.

Amounts in the sales journal are posted to the subsidiary ledger daily to keep a current record of the amount receivable from each customer. Suppose Maria Galvez telephones Austin Sound on November 11 to ask how much money she owes. The subsidiary ledger readily provides that information.

When each transaction amount is posted to the subsidiary ledger, a check mark is written in the posting reference column of the sales journal.

Journal References in the Ledgers.   When amounts are posted to the ledgers, the journal page number is written in the account to identify the source of the data. All transaction data in Exhibit 6-3 originated on page 3 of the sales journal, so all journal references in the ledger accounts are S.3. The S. indicates sales journal.

Trace all the postings in Exhibit 6-3. The most effective way to learn about accounting systems and special journals is to study the flow of data. The arrows indicate the direction of the information.

The arrows show the links between the individual customer accounts in the subsidiary ledger and the Accounts Receivable account. These links are summarized as follows:

Accounts Receivable debit balance $3,319

Customer	Balance
Maria Galvez	$ 935
Brent Harmon	694
Susan Levy	907
Clay Schmidt	783
Total accounts receivable	$3,319

Accounts Receivable in the general ledger is a **control account,** which is an account whose balance equals the sum of the balances of a group of related accounts in a subsidiary ledger. In this simple illustration, the Accounts Receivable balance is the total amount of credit sales. The individual customer accounts are subsidiary accounts. They are "controlled" by the Accounts Receivable account in the general ledger.

Let's look at the advantages the sales journal offers. Each transaction is entered on a single line, and the account titles do not have to be written. Also, the sales journal streamlines posting. Suppose Austin Sound had 400 credit sales for the month. How many postings to the general ledger would be made from the sales journal? There are only two, one to Accounts Receivable and one to Sales Revenue. How many postings would there be from the general journal? The total would be 800 (400 debits to Accounts Receivable and 400 credits to Sales Revenue).

Cash Receipts Journal

OBJECTIVE 4
Use the cash receipts journal

Cash transactions are common in most businesses because cash receipts from customers are the lifeblood of business. To streamline the recording of repetitive cash receipt transactions, accountants use the **cash receipts journal.**

Exhibit 6-4, Panel A, illustrates the cash receipts journal. The related posting to ledgers is shown in Panel B. The exhibit illustrates November transactions for Austin Sound.

Every transaction recorded in this journal is a cash receipt, so the first column is for debits to the Cash account. The next column is for debits to Sales Discounts on collections from customers. In a typical merchandising business, the main sources of cash are collections on account and cash sales. Thus the cash receipts journal has credit columns for Accounts Receivable and Sales Revenue. The journal also has a credit column for Other Accounts, which lists sources of cash other than cash sales and collections on account. This Other Accounts column is also used to record the names of customers from whom cash is received on account.

In Exhibit 6-4, cash sales occurred on November 6, 19, and 28. Observe the debits to Cash and the credits to Sales Revenue ($517, $853, and $1,802). On November 11 Austin Sound borrowed $1,000 from First Bank. Cash is debited, and Note Payable to First Bank is credited in the Other Accounts column because no specific credit column is set up to account for borrowings. For this transaction, it is necessary to write the account title, Note Payable to First Bank, in the Other Accounts/Account Title column to record the source of cash.

On November 14 Austin Sound collected $900 from Maria Galvez. Referring back to Exhibit 6-3, we see that on November 2 Austin Sound sold merchandise for $935 to Ms. Galvez. Assume that the terms of sale allowed a $35 discount for prompt payment and that she paid within the discount period. Austin's cash receipt is recorded by debiting Cash for $900 and Sales Discounts for $35 and by crediting Accounts Receivable for $935. Note that the customer's name appears in the Other Accounts/Account Title column. This enables the business to keep track of each customer's account in the subsidiary ledger.

Total debits should equal total credits in the cash receipts journal. This equality holds for each transaction and for the monthly totals. For example, the first transaction has a $517 debit and an equal credit. For the month, total debits ($6,134 + $35 = $6,169) equal total credits ($1,235 + $3,172 + $1,762 = $6,169).

EXHIBIT 6-4 *Cash Receipts Journal and Posting to Ledgers*

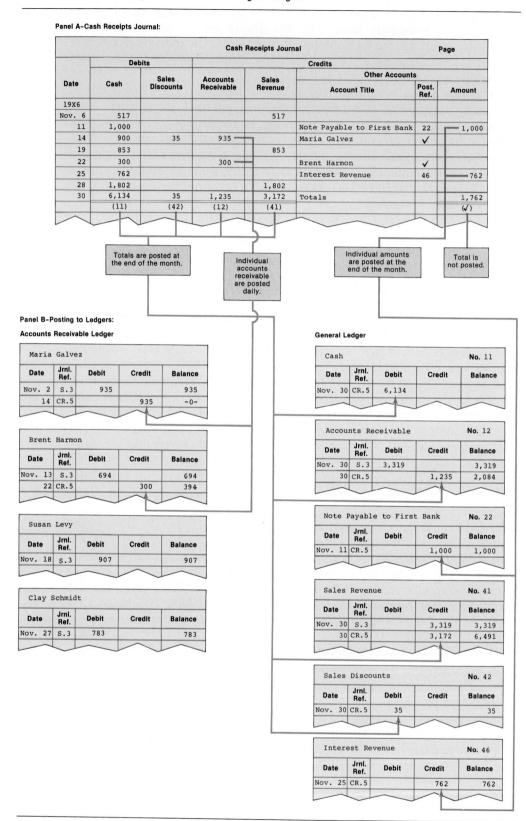

Posting to the General Ledger. The column totals are posted monthly. To indicate their posting, the account number is written below the column total in the cash receipts journal. Note the account number for Cash (11) below the column total $6,134, and trace the posting to Cash in the general ledger. Likewise, the Sales Discounts, Accounts Receivable, and Sales Revenue column totals are also posted to the general ledger.

The column total for *Other Accounts* is not posted. Instead, these credits are posted individually. In Exhibit 6-4, the November 11 transaction reads "Note Payable to First Bank." This account's number (22) in the Post. Ref. column indicates that the transaction amount was posted individually. The check mark, instead of an account number, below the column total indicates that the column total was not posted. The November 25 collection of interest revenue is also posted individually.

Posting to the Subsidiary Ledger. Amounts from the cash receipts journal are posted to the subsidiary accounts receivable ledger daily to keep the individual balances up to date. The postings to the accounts receivable ledger are credits. Trace the $935 posting to Maria Galvez's account. It reduces her balance to zero. The $300 receipt from Brent Harmon reduces his accounts receivable balance to $394.

After posting, the sum of the individual balances that remain in the accounts receivable ledger equals the general ledger balance in Accounts Receivable ($2,084). Austin Sound may prepare a November 30 list of account balances from the subsidiary ledger as a check of the accuracy of journalizing and posting:

Customer Accounts Receivable

Customer	Balance
Brent Harmon	$ 394
Susan Levy	907
Clay Schmidt	783
Total accounts receivable	$2,084

Keeping good accounts receivable records reduces errors and helps customer relations.

The cash receipts journal offers the same advantages as the sales journal: streamlined journalizing of transactions and fewer postings to the ledgers.

Summary Problem for Your Review

A company completed the following selected transactions during March:

Mar. 4 Received $500 from a cash sale to a customer.

6 Received $60 on account from Brady Lee. The full invoice amount was $65, but Lee paid within the discount period to gain the $5 discount.

9 Received $1,080 on a note receivable from Beverly Mann. This amount includes the $1,000 note receivable plus interest revenue.

Mar. 15 Received $800 from a cash sale to a customer.
24 Borrowed $2,200 by signing a note payable to Interstate Bank.
27 Received $1,200 on account from Lance Albert. Payment was received after the discount period lapsed.

The general ledger showed the following balances at February 28: Cash, debit balance of $1,117; Accounts Receivable, debit balance of $2,790; Note Receivable—Beverly Mann, debit balance of $1,000. The accounts receivable subsidiary ledger at February 28 contained debit balances as follows: Lance Albert, $1,840; Brady Lee, $65; Melinda Fultz, $885.

Required

1. Record the transactions in the cash receipts journal, page 7.
2. Compute column totals at March 31. Show that total debits equal total credits in the cash receipts journal.
3. Post to the general ledger and the accounts receivable subsidiary ledger. Use complete posting references, including the account numbers illustrated: Cash, 11; Accounts Receivable, 12; Note Receivable—Beverly Mann, 13; Note Payable—Interstate Bank, 22; Sales Revenue, 41; Sales Discounts, 42; Interest Revenue, 46. Insert a check mark (✓) in the posting reference column for each February 28 account balance.
4. Prove the accuracy of posting by showing that the total of the balances in the subsidiary ledger equals the general ledger balance in Accounts Receivable.

SOLUTION TO REVIEW PROBLEM

Requirements 1 and 2

Cash Receipts Journal   Page 7

| | Debits | | Credits | | | | |
| | | | | | Other Accounts | | |
Date	Cash	Sales Discounts	Accounts Receivable	Sales Revenue	Account Title	Post. Ref.	Amount
Mar. 4	500			500			
6	60	5	65		Brady Lee	✓	
9	1,080				Note Receivable—		
					Beverly Mann	13	1,000
					Interest Revenue	46	80
15	800			800			
24	2,200				Note Payable—		
					Interstate Bank	22	2,200
27	1,200		1,200		Lance Albert	✓	
31	5,840	5	1,265	1,300	Total		3,280
	(11)	(42)	(12)	(41)			(✓)

5,845   5,845

286   Part Two   Introduction to Accounting Systems

Requirement 3

Accounts Receivable Ledger

Lance Albert

Date	Jrnl. Ref.	Debit	Credit	Balance
Feb. 28	✓0			1,840
Mar. 27	CR.7		1,200	640

Melinda Fultz

Date	Jrnl. Ref.	Debit	Credit	Balance
Feb. 28	✓0			885

Brady Lee

Date	Jrnl. Ref.	Debit	Credit	Balance
Feb. 28	✓0			65
Mar. 6	CR.7		65	——

General Ledger

Cash   No. 11

Date	Jrnl. Ref.	Debit	Credit	Balance
Feb. 28	✓0			1,117
Mar. 31	CR.7	5,840		6,957

Accounts Receivable   No. 12

Date	Jrnl. Ref.	Debit	Credit	Balance
Feb. 28	✓0			2,790
Mar. 31	CR.7		1,265	1,525

Note Receivable-Beverly Mann   No. 13

Date	Jrnl. Ref.	Debit	Credit	Balance
Feb. 28	✓0			1,000
Mar. 9	CR.7		1,000	——

Note Payable-Interstate Bank   No. 22

Date	Jrnl. Ref.	Debit	Credit	Balance
Mar. 24	CR.7		2,200	2,200

Sales Revenue   No. 41

Date	Jrnl. Ref.	Debit	Credit	Balance
Mar. 31	CR.7		1,300	1,300

Sales Discounts   No. 42

Date	Jrnl. Ref.	Debit	Credit	Balance
Mar. 31	CR.7	5		5

Interest Revenue   No. 46

Date	Jrnl. Ref.	Debit	Credit	Balance
Mar. 9	CR.7		80	80

Requirement 4

Lance Albert	$ 640
Melinda Fultz	885
Total accounts receivable	$1,525

This total agrees with the balance in Accounts Receivable.

OBJECTIVE 5

Use the purchases journal

A merchandising business purchases inventory and supplies frequently. Such purchases are usually made on account. The **purchases journal** is designed to account for all purchases of inventory, supplies, and other assets *on account*. It can also be used to record expenses incurred on account.

Exhibit 6-5 illustrates Austin Sound's purchases journal (Panel A) and posting to ledgers (Panel B).[1]

The purchases journal in Exhibit 6-5 has amount columns for credits to Accounts Payable and debits to Purchases, Supplies, and Other Accounts. The Other Accounts columns accommodate purchases of items other than inventory and supplies. These columns make the journal flexible enough to accommodate a wide variety of transactions. Each business designs its purchases journal to meet its own needs for information and efficiency. Accounts Payable is credited for all transactions recorded in the purchases journal.

On November 2 Austin Sound purchased from JVC Corp. stereo inventory costing $700. The creditor's name (JVC Corp.) is entered in the Account Credited column. The purchase terms of 3/15 n/30 are also entered to help identify the due date and the discount available. Accounts Payable is credited and Purchases is debited for the transaction amount. On November 19 a credit purchase of supplies is entered as a debit to Supplies and a credit to Accounts Payable.

Note the November 9 purchase of fixtures from City Office Supply. Since the purchases journal contains no column for fixtures, the Other Accounts debit column is used. Because this was a credit purchase, the accountant enters the creditor name (City Office Supply) in the Account Credited column and writes "Fixtures" in the Other Accounts/Account Title column.

The total credits in the journal ($2,876) are compared to the total debits ($1,706 + $103 + $1,067 = $2,876) to prove the accuracy of the entries in the purchases journal.

To pay debts efficiently, a company must know how much it owes particular creditors. The Accounts Payable account in the general ledger shows only a single total, however, and therefore does not indicate the amount owed to each creditor. Companies keep an accounts payable subsidiary ledger that lists the creditors in alphabetical order, along with the amounts owed to them. Exhibit 6-5, Panel B, shows Austin Sound's accounts payable subsidiary ledger, which includes accounts for Audio Electronics, City Office Supply, and others. After posting at the end of the period, the total of the individual balances in the subsidiary ledger equals the balance in the Accounts Payable control account in the general ledger. This system is like the accounts receivable system discussed earlier in the chapter.

Posting from the Purchases Journal. Posting from the purchases journal is similar to posting from the sales journal and the cash receipts journal. Exhibit 6-5, Panel B, illustrates the posting process. Individual accounts payable in the *accounts payable subsidiary ledger* are posted daily, and column totals and other amounts are posted to the *general ledger* at the end of the month. In the ledger accounts, P.8 indicates the source of the posted amounts—that is, page 8 of the purchases journal. Use of the special purchases journal offers advantages over the general journal similar to those advantages discussed for the sales journal.

---

[1]This is the only special journal that we illustrate with the credit column placed to the left and the debit columns to the right. This arrangement of columns clearly links each entry to Accounts Payable with the individual supplier to be paid.

EXHIBIT 6-5 *Purchases Journal and Posting to Ledgers*

Panel A–Purchases Journal:

				Credit	Debits				
Date	Account Credited	Terms	Post. Ref.	Accounts Payable	Purchases	Supplies	Other Accounts		
							Account Title	Post. Ref.	Amount
19X6									
Nov. 2	JVC Corp.	3/15 n/30	✓	700	700				
5	Pioneer Sound	n/30	✓	319	319				
9	City Office Supply	2/10 n/30	✓	440			Fixtures	19	440
12	Audio Electronics, Inc.	n/30	✓	236	236				
13	JVC Corp.	3/15 n/30	✓	451	451				
19	City Office Supply Co.	2/10 n/30	✓	103		103			
23	O'Leary Furniture Co.	n/60	✓	627			Furniture	18	627
30	Totals			2,876	1,706	103			1,067
				(21)	(51)	(16)			(✓)

Purchases Journal — Page 8

Individual accounts payable are posted daily.

Totals are posted at the end of the month.

Total is not posted.

Individual amounts are posted at the end of the month.

Panel B–Posting to Ledgers:

Accounts Payable Ledger

Audio Electronics

Date	Jrnl. Ref.	Debit	Credits	Balance
Nov. 12	P.8		236	236

City Office Supply Co.

Date	Jrnl. Ref.	Debit	Credit	Balance
Nov. 9	P.8		440	440
19	P.8		103	543

JVC Corp.

Date	Jrnl. Ref.	Debit	Credit	Balance
Nov. 2	P.8		700	700
13	P.8		451	1,151

O'Leary Furniture Co.

Date	Jrnl. Ref.	Debit	Credit	Balance
Nov. 23	P.8		627	627

Pioneer Sound

Date	Jrnl. Ref.	Debit	Credit	Balance
Nov. 5	P.8		319	319

General Ledger

Supplies — No. 16

Date	Jrnl. Ref.	Debit	Credit	Balance
Nov. 30	P.8	103		103

Furniture — No. 18

Date	Jrnl. Ref.	Debit	Credit	Balance
Nov. 23	P.8	627		627

Fixtures — No. 19

Date	Jrnl. Ref.	Debit	Credit	Balance
Nov. 9	P.8	440		440

Accounts Payable — No. 21

Date	Jrnl. Ref.	Debit	Credit	Balance
Nov. 30	P.8		2,876	2,876

Purchases — No. 51

Date	Jrnl. Ref.	Debit	Credit	Balance
Nov. 30	P.8	1,706		1,706

OBJECTIVE 6

Use the cash
disbursements journal

Businesses make most cash disbursements by check. All payments by check are recorded in the **cash disbursements journal.** Other titles of this special journal are the *check register* and the *cash payments journal.* Like the other special journals, it has multiple columns for recording cash payments that occur frequently.

Exhibit 6-6, Panel A, illustrates the cash disbursements journal, and Panel B shows the postings to the ledgers of Austin Sound.

The cash disbursements journal in the exhibit has two debit columns—for Accounts Payable and Other Accounts—and two credit columns—for Cash and Purchase Discounts. It also has columns for the date and the check number of each cash payment. A debit column can be added for other frequently used accounts, such as Purchases.

All entries in the cash disbursements journal include a credit to Cash. Payments on account are debits to Accounts Payable. On November 15 Austin Sound paid JVC on account, with credit terms of 3/15 n/30 (for details, see the first transaction in Exhibit 6-5). Therefore, Austin took the 3 percent discount and paid $679 ($700 less the $21 discount).

The Other Accounts column is used to record debits to accounts for which no special column exists. For example, on November 3 Austin Sound paid rent expense of $1,200, and on November 8 the business purchased supplies for $61.

As with all other journals, the total debits ($3,161 + $819 = $3,980) should equal the total credits ($21 + $3,959 = $3,980).

Posting from the Cash Disbursements Journal.   Posting from the cash disbursements journal is similar to posting from the cash receipts journal. Individual creditor amounts are posted daily, and column totals and Other Accounts are posted at the end of the month. Exhibit 6-6, Panel B, illustrates the posting process.

Amounts in the Other Accounts column are posted individually (for example, Rent Expense—debit $1,200). When each Other Accounts amount is posted to the general ledger, the account number is written in the Post. Ref. column of the journal.

As a proof of accuracy, companies total the individual creditor balances in the accounts payable subsidiary ledger for comparison with the Accounts Payable balance in the general ledger:

Creditor Accounts Payable

Creditor	Balance
Audio Electronics	$ 236
City Office Supply	543
JVC Corp.	451
O'Leary Furniture	627
Pioneer Sound	200
Total accounts payable	$2,057

This total, computed at the end of the period, agrees with the Accounts Payable balance in Exhibit 6-6. Agreement of the two amounts indicates that journalizing and posting have been performed correctly and that the resulting account balances are correct.

Use of the cash disbursements journal streamlines journalizing and posting in the same way as for the other special journals.

EXHIBIT 6-6 *Cash Disbursements Journal and Posting to Ledgers*

Panel A—Cash Disbursements Journal:

				Debits		Credits	
Date	**Ck. No.**	**Account Debited**	**Post. Ref.**	**Other Accounts**	**Accounts Payable**	**Purchase Discounts**	**Cash**
19X6							
Nov. 3	101	Rent Expense	54	1,200			1,200
8	102	Supplies	16	61			61
15	103	JVC Corp.	✓		700	21	679
20	104	Pioneer Sound	✓		119		119
26	105	Purchases	51	1,900			1,900
30		Totals		3,161	819	21	3,959
				(✓)	(21)	(52)	(11)

Total is not posted.

Totals are posted at the end of the month.

Individual accounts payable are posted daily

Individual amounts are posted at the end of the month.

Panel B—Posting to Ledgers:

Accounts Payable Ledger

Audio Electronics

Date	Jrnl. Ref.	Debit	Credit	Balance
Nov. 12	P.8		236	236

City Office Supply

Date	Jrnl. Ref.	Debit	Credit	Balance
Nov. 9	P.8		440	440
19	P.8		103	543

JVC Corp.

Date	Jrnl. Ref.	Debit	Credit	Balance
Nov. 2	P.8		700	700
13	P.8		451	1151
15	CD.6	700		451

O'Leary Furniture Co.

Date	Jrnl. Ref.	Debit	Credit	Balance
Nov. 23	P.8		627	627

Pioneer Sound

Date	Jrnl. Ref.	Debit	Credit	Balance
Nov. 5	P.8		319	319
20	CD.6	119		200

General Ledger

Cash No. 11

Date	Jrnl. Ref.	Debit	Credit	Balance
Nov. 30	CR.5	6,134		6,134
30	CD.6		3,959	2,175

Supplies No. 16

Date	Jrnl. Ref.	Debit	Credit	Balance
Nov. 30	P.8	103		103
8	CD.6	61		164

Accounts Payable No. 21

Date	Jrnl. Ref.	Debit	Credit	Balance
Nov. 30	P.8		2,876	2,876
30	CD.6	819		2,057

Purchases No. 51

Date	Jrnl. Ref.	Debit	Credit	Balance
Nov. 30	P.8	1,706		1,706
26	CD.6	1,900		3,606

Purchase Discounts No. 52

Date	Jrnl. Ref.	Debit	Credit	Balance
Nov. 30	CD.6		21	21

Rent Expense No. 54

Date	Jrnl. Ref.	Debit	Credit	Balance
Nov. 3	CD.6	1,200		1,200

The Credit Memorandum—
A Basic Business Document

OBJECTIVE 7

Journalize return and allowance transactions

Customers sometimes bring merchandise back to the seller, and sellers grant sales allowances to customers because of product defects and for other reasons. The effect of sales returns and sales allowances is the same—both decrease net sales in the same way a sales discount does. The document issued by the seller to indicate having credited the customer's Account Receivable is called a **credit memorandum,** or **credit memo,** because the company gives the customer credit for the returned merchandise. When a company issues a credit memo, it records the transaction by debiting Sales Returns and Allowances and crediting Accounts Receivable.

Suppose Austin Sound sold two stereo speakers for $198 on account to Stephanie Baker. Later she discovered a defect and returned the speakers. Austin Sound would issue to Ms. Baker a credit memo like the one in Exhibit 6-7.

To record the *sales return,* Austin Sound would make the following entry in the general journal:

	General Journal			Page 9

Date	Accounts	Post Ref.	Debit	Credit
Nov. 6	Sales Returns and Allowances	43	198	
	Accounts Receivable—Stephanie Baker	12/✔		198
	Credit memo no. 27			

The debit side of the entry is posted to Sales Returns and Allowances. Its account number (43) is written in the posting reference column when $198 is posted. The credit side of the entry requires two $198 postings, one to

EXHIBIT 6-7 *Credit Memorandum*

Credit Memorandum	No. 27

Austin Sound
305 West Martin Luther King Blvd.
Austin, Texas 78701

Date November 6, 19X6

Customer Name Stephanie Baker

538 Rio Grande, Apt. 236

Austin, Texas 78703

Reason for Credit Defective merchandise returned

Description	Amount
2 Trailblazer JU170456 Speakers	$198

Accounts Receivable, the control account in the general ledger (account number 12), and the other to Stephanie Baker's account in the accounts receivable subsidiary ledger. These credit postings explain why the document is called a *credit memo*.

Observe that the posting references of the credit include two notations. The account number (12) denotes the posting to Accounts Receivable in the general ledger. The check mark (✓) denotes the posting to Ms. Baker's account in the subsidiary ledger. Why are two postings needed? Because this is the general journal. Without specially designed columns, it is necessary to write both posting references on the same line. Posting to the general ledger usually occurs monthly; and posting to the subsidiary ledger, daily.

Suppose Ms. Baker had paid cash. Austin Sound would either give her a credit memo or refund her cash. Austin Sound would record the cash refund in the *cash disbursements journal* as follows:

Cash Disbursements Journal Page 8

| | | | | Debits | | Credits | | |
Date	Ck. No.	Account Debited	Post Ref.	Other Accounts	Accounts Payable	Purchase Discounts	Cash
Nov. 6	106	Sales Returns and Allowances	43	198			198

A business with a high volume of sales returns, such as a department store chain, may find it efficient to use a special journal for sales returns and allowances.

The Debit Memorandum— A Basic Business Document

Purchase Returns occur when a business returns goods to the seller. The procedures for handling purchase returns are similar to those dealing with sales returns. The purchaser gives the merchandise back to the seller and receives either a cash refund or replacement goods.

When a business returns merchandise to the seller, it may also send a business document known as a **debit memorandum,** or **debit memo.** This document states that the buyer no longer owes the seller for the amount of the returned purchase. The buyer debits the Account Payable to the seller and credits Purchase Returns and Allowances. If the volume of purchase returns is high enough, the business may use a special journal for purchase returns.

Many businesses record their purchase returns in the general journal. Austin Sound would record its return of defective speakers to JVC as follows:

General Journal Page 9

Date	Accounts	Post Ref.	Debit	Credit
Nov. 6	Accounts Payable—JVC Corp..........	21/✓	144	
	Purchase Returns and Allowances....	53		144
	Debit memo no. 16			

Sales Tax

Most states and many cities levy tax on sales (sales tax). Sellers must add the tax to the sale amount, then pay the tax to the government. In most jurisdictions, sales tax is levied only on final consumers, so retail businesses usually do not pay sales tax on the goods they purchase for resale. For example, Austin Sound would not pay tax on a purchase of equipment from JVC, a wholesaler. However, when retailers like Austin Sound make sales, they must collect sales tax from the consumer. In effect, retailers serve as collecting agents for the taxing authorities. The amount of tax depends on the total sales.

Retailers set up procedures to collect the tax, account for it, and pay it on time. Invoices may be preprinted with a place for entering the sales tax amount, and the general ledger has an account entitled Sales Tax Payable. The sales journal may include a special column for sales tax, such as the one illustrated in Exhibit 6-8.

Note that the amount debited to Accounts Receivable ($3,484.95) is the sum of the credits to Sales Tax Payable ($165.95) and Sales Revenue ($3,319.00). This is so because the customers' payments—the Accounts Receivable figures—are partly for the purchase of merchandise (Sales Revenue) and partly for tax created by the sale. Individual customer accounts are posted daily to the accounts receivable subsidiary ledger, and each column total is posted at the end of the month. The check marks in the Posting Reference column show that individual amounts have been posted to the customer accounts. The absence of account numbers under the column totals shows that the total amounts have not yet been posted.

Another way to account for sales tax is to enter a single amount—which is the sum of sales revenue and sales tax—in the Sales Revenue account. This amount is what the customer pays the retailer. At the end of the period, the business computes the tax collected and transfers that amount from Sales Revenue to Sales Tax Payable through a general journal entry. This procedure eliminates the need for a special multicolumn journal.

Suppose a retailer's Sales Revenue account shows a $10,500 balance at the end of the period. This retailer chooses to enter the full amount of each sale—the actual sales revenue and the sales tax—as Sales Revenue. How does the retailer divide the total amount into its two parts?

To compute the actual sales revenue, the Sales Revenue balance is divided by 1 plus the tax rate. Assume that sales tax is 5 percent. Thus the retailer divides $10,500 by 1.05 (1 + .05), which yields $10,000. Subtracting the actual

EXHIBIT 6-8 *Sales Journal Designed to Account for Sales Tax*

Sales Journal Page 4

Date	Invoice No.	Account Debited	Post. Ref.	Accounts Receivable Dr.	Sales Tax Payable Cr.	Sales Revenue Cr.
19X6						
Nov. 2	422	Maria Galvez	✓	981.75	46.75	935.00
13	423	Brent Harmon	✓	728.70	34.70	694.00
18	424	Susan Levy	✓	952.35	45.35	907.00
27	425	Clay Schmidt	✓	822.15	39.15	783.00
30		Totals		3,484.95	165.95	3,319.00

sales revenue—the $10,000—from the $10,500 total yields $500, the sales tax. The retailer records sales tax with the following entry in the general journal:

		Post.		
Date	**Accounts**	**Ref.**	**Debit**	**Credit**
July 31	Sales Revenue	41	500	
	Sales Tax Payable	28		500
	To transfer sales tax to the liability account			

General Journal — **Page 9**

Balancing the Ledgers

At the end of the period, after all postings, equality should exist between:

1. Total debits and total credits of the account balances in the general ledger. These amounts are used to prepare the trial balance that has been used throughout Chapters 3 through 5.
2. The balance of the Accounts Receivable control account in the general ledger and the sum of individual customer accounts in the accounts receivable subsidiary ledger.
3. The balance of the Accounts Payable control account in the general ledger and the sum of individual creditor accounts in the accounts payable subsidiary ledger.

   This process is called **balancing the ledgers,** or proving the ledgers. It is an important control procedure because it helps ensure the accuracy of the accounting records. Equality between Accounts Receivable control and the accounts receivable subsidiary ledger was proved as shown on page 287. A simpler and less costly procedure is to total the individual customer balances on a calculator tape for comparison with Accounts Receivable control. Balancing the accounts payable ledger follows the same pattern as illustrated on page 289.

Documents as Journals

Many small businesses streamline their accounting systems to save money by using the actual business documents as the journals. For example, Austin Sound could let its sales invoices serve as its sales journal and keep all invoices for credit sales in a loose-leaf binder. At the end of the period, the accountant simply totals the sales on account and posts that amount to Accounts Receivable and Sales Revenue. Also, the accountant can post directly from invoices to customer accounts in the accounts receivable ledger. This "journal-less" system reduces accounting cost because the accountant does not have to write in journals and ledgers the information already in the business documents.

Summary Problem for Your Review

Identify the journal in which each of the following transactions would be recorded. Use journal abbreviations: sales journal = S; cash receipts journal = CR; purchases journal = P; cash disbursements journal = CD; general journal = J.

Cash sale_____

Sale on account_____

Loaned cash on note receivable_____

Received cash on account_____

Purchase of building on long-term note payable__

Paid cash on account_____

Cash purchase of inventory_____

Owner investment of cash in the business_____

Closing entries_____

Purchase of supplies on account_____

Receipt of cash on account_____

Adjusting entry for accrued salaries_____

Cash purchase of land_____

Credit purchase of inventory_____

Collection of interest revenue_____

Paid interest expense_____

Cash sale of equipment_____

Cash dividends_____

Owner investment of land in the business_____

SOLUTION TO REVIEW PROBLEM

Cash sale_____ **CR**

Sale on account_____ **S**

Loaned cash on note receivable_____ **CD**

Received cash on account_____ **CR**

Purchase of building on long-term note payable **J**

Paid cash on account_____ **CD**

Cash purchase of inventory_____ **CD**

Owner investment of cash in the business____ **CR**

Closing entries_____ **J**

Purchase of supplies on account_____ **P**

Receipt of cash on account_____ **CR**

Adjusting entry for accrued salaries_____ **J**

Cash purchase of land_____ **CD**

Credit purchase of inventory_____ **P**

Collection of interest revenue_____ **CR**

Paid interest expense_____ **CD**

Cash sale of equipment_____ **CR**

Cash dividends_____ **CD**

Owner investment of land in the business____ **J**

OBJECTIVE 8

Define internal control, and identify control strengths and weaknesses in a company's system

Internal Control

You learned earlier in the chapter that a well-designed accounting system helps managers control the business. We now look in more detail at internal control. **Internal control** is the organizational plan and all the related measures adopted by an entity to

1. Safeguard assets
2. Ensure accurate and reliable accounting records
3. Promote operational efficiency
4. Encourage adherence to company policies

Internal controls include administrative controls and accounting controls.

Administrative controls include the plan of organization, the methods, and the procedures that help managers achieve operational efficiency and adherence to company policies. Moreover, administrative controls help eliminate waste.

Accounting controls include the methods and procedures that safeguard assets, authorize transactions, and ensure the accuracy of the financial records. Of these elements, safeguarding assets is the most important. This section focuses on internal accounting controls, with emphasis on cash transactions.

The need for laws requiring internal control has received increased attention over the past twenty years. During that time many illegal payments, embezzlements, and other criminal business practices came to light. Concerned citizens wanted to know why the companies' internal controls had failed to alert management that these illegalities had occurred. To answer these growing worries, the U.S. Congress passed the Foreign Corrupt Practices Act. This act requires companies under SEC jurisdiction to maintain an appropriate system of internal control whether or not they have foreign operations.[2] Thus its title is a bit misleading.

Wise management has always kept a system of strong internal control, so before the law was enacted many businesses had already met the requirements for internal control policies. However, the Foreign Corrupt Practices Act has affected companies' approaches to internal control. Formerly, internal control was viewed as the accountant's responsibility. The act shifted responsibility for internal control to company managers. Furthermore, boards of directors, to comply with the act and with other SEC requirements, compile written evidence of management's evaluations and ongoing reviews of the internal control system.

Exhibit 6-9 presents excerpts from the General Mills Report of Management Responsibilities, included in its annual report. Note the frequent references to internal controls, audits, and ethical conduct. Observe that the chairman of the board of directors, who heads the entire organization, and the chief financial officer, who is one of the top three officers of the company, sign the statement. Likewise, management teams in other organizations state their responsibility for internal control in their annual reports.

Effective Systems of Internal Control

Whether the business is General Mills or a local department store, its system of internal controls, if effective, has the following noteworthy characteristics.

Competent and Reliable Personnel

Employees should be *competent* and *reliable*. Paying top salaries to attract top-quality employees, training them to do their job well, and supervising their work all help to build a competent staff. A business adds flexibility to its staffing by rotating employees through various jobs. If one employee is sick or on vacation, a second employee is already trained to step in and do the job.

---

[2] The Foreign Corrupt Practices Act contains specific prohibitions against bribery and other corrupt practices in addition to requiring the maintenance of accounting records in reasonable detail and accuracy.

Report of Management Responsibilities

The management of General Mills, Inc. includes corporate executives, operating managers, *controllers* and other personnel working full time on company business. These managers are responsible for the fairness and accuracy of our financial statements. . . . The statements have been prepared in accordance with generally accepted accounting principles. . . .

Management has established a system of *internal controls* that provides reasonable assurance that, in all material respects, assets are maintained and accounted for in accordance with management's authorization, and transactions are recorded accurately on our books. Our *internal controls* provide for appropriate separation of duties and responsibilities, and there are documented policies regarding utilization of company assets and proper financial reporting. These . . . policies demand high *ethical conduct* from all employees.

We maintain a strong *audit* program that independently evaluates the adequacy and effectiveness of *internal controls*. The independent *auditors,* internal *auditors,* and *controllers* have full and free access to the *Audit Committee* at any time.

KPMG Peat Marwick, independent certified public accountants, are retained to *audit* the consolidated financial statements. [Emphasis added]

H. B. Atwater, Jr.
Chairman of the Board and Chief Executive Officer

F. C. Blodgett
Vice Chairman of the Board,
Chief Financial and Administrative Officer

Source: General Mills, Inc., *1990 Annual Report,* p. 19.

Rotating employees through various jobs also promotes reliability. An employee is less likely to handle her job improperly if she knows that her misconduct may come to light when a second employee takes over the job. This same reasoning leads businesses to require that employees take an annual vacation. A second employee, stepping in to handle the position, may uncover any wrongdoing.

Assignment of Responsibilities

In a business with an effective internal control system, no important duty is overlooked. A model of such assignment of responsibilities appears in the corporate organizational chart in Exhibit 6-10.

Notice that the corporation has a vice-president of finance and accounting. Two other officers, the treasurer and the controller, report to the vice-president. The treasurer is responsible for cash management. The controller performs accounting duties.

Within this organization, the controller may be responsible for approving invoices for payment, and the treasurer may actually sign the checks. Working under the controller, one accountant may be responsible for property taxes, another accountant for income taxes. In sum, all duties are clearly defined and assigned to individuals who bear responsibility for carrying them out.

EXHIBIT 6-10 *Organization Chart of a Corporation*

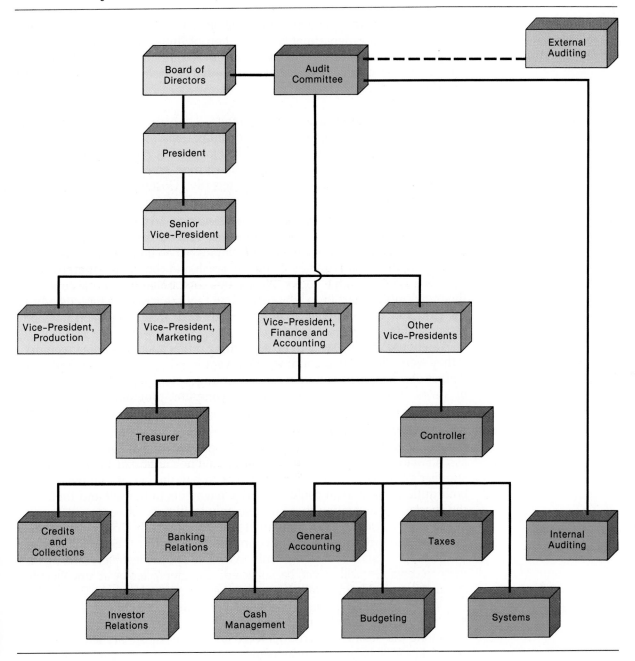

Proper Authorization

An organization generally has a written set of rules that outlines approved procedures. Any deviation from standard policy requires *proper authorization*. For example, managers or assistant managers of retail stores must approve customer checks for amounts above the store's usual limit. Likewise, deans or department chairpersons of colleges and universities must give the authorization for a freshman, sophomore, or junior to enroll in courses otherwise restricted to seniors.

Separation of Duties

Smart management divides the responsibilities for transactions between two or more people or departments. Separation of duties limits the chances for fraud and also promotes the accuracy of the accounting records. This crucial and often neglected component of the internal control system may be subdivided into four parts.

1. Separation of operations from accounting. The entire accounting function should be completely separate from operating departments so that objective records may be kept. For example, product inspectors, not machine operators, should count units produced by a manufacturing process. Accountants, not salespersons, should keep inventory records. Observe the separation of accounting from production and marketing in Exhibit 6-10.

2. Separation of the custody of assets from accounting. To reduce temptation and fraud, the accountant should not handle cash, and the cashier should not have access to the accounting records. If one employee had both cash-handling and accounting duties, this person could steal cash and conceal the theft by making a bogus entry on the books. We see this component of internal control in the organization chart in Exhibit 6-10. Note that the treasurer has custody of the cash and the controller accounts for the cash. Neither person has both responsibilities.

Warehouse employees with no accounting duties should handle inventory. If they were allowed to account for the inventory, they could steal it and write it off as obsolete. In a computerized accounting system, a person with custody of assets should not have access to the computer programs. Similarly, the programmer should not have access to tempting assets like cash.

3. Separation of the authorization of transactions from the custody of related assets. If possible, persons who authorize transactions should not handle the related asset. For example, the same individual should not authorize the payment of a supplier's invoice and also sign the check to pay the bill. If one person had both duties, that person could authorize payments to himself and then sign the checks. By separating these duties, only legitimate bills are paid.

For another example, an individual who handles cash receipts should not have the authority to write off accounts receivable. (Businesses that sell on credit declare certain of their accounts receivable as uncollectible, realizing that these receivables will never be collected. Chapter 7 looks at uncollectible accounts receivable in detail.) Suppose the company shown in Exhibit 6-10 employs V. Saucier. He works in Credits and Collections (under the treasurer) and handles cash receipts from customers.

Among the business's accounts receivable in the subsidiary ledger is Gina Kowalski's $500 balance. Saucier could label Kowalski's account as uncollectible, and the business might cease trying to collect from her. When Kowalski mails a $500 check to pay off her balance, Saucier forges the endorsement and pockets the money. Kowalski, of course, has no reason to notify anyone else at the business that she has mailed a check, so Saucier's crime goes undetected. This theft would have been avoided by denying Saucier either the access to cash receipts or the authority to declare accounts uncollectible.

4. Separation of duties within the accounting function. Independent performance of various phases of accounting helps to minimize errors and the opportunities for fraud. For example, in a manual system, different accountants keep the cash receipts journal and the cash disbursements journal. In a computer system, the employees who enter data into the computer do not also operate the machines.

Internal and External Audits

It is not economically feasible for auditors to examine all the transactions during a period, so they must rely to some degree on the accounting system to produce accurate accounting records. To gauge the reliability of the company's accounting system, auditors evaluate its system of internal controls. Auditors also spot the weaknesses in the system and recommend corrections. Auditors offer *objectivity* in their reports, while managers immersed in operations may overlook weaknesses.

Audits are internal or external. Exhibit 6-10 shows *internal auditors* as employees of the business reporting directly to the audit committee. Some organizations have the internal auditors report directly to the vice president. Throughout the year, they audit various segments of the organization. *External auditors* are entirely independent of the business. These people, employed by an accounting firm, are hired by an entity as outsiders to audit the entity as a whole. Both groups of auditors are independent of the operations they examine, and their reviews of internal controls are often similar.

An auditor may find that an employee has both cash-handling and cash-accounting duties or may learn that a cash shortage has resulted from lax efforts to collect accounts receivable. In such cases, the auditor suggests improvements. Auditors' recommendations assist the business in running smoothly and economically.

Documents and Records

Business *documents and records* vary considerably, from source documents like sales invoices and purchase orders to special journals and subsidiary ledgers. Specially designed records—for example, the special journals discussed in the last chapter—speed the flow of paperwork and enhance efficiency.

Documents should be prenumbered. A gap in the numbered sequence calls attention to a missing document.

Prenumbering cash sale receipts discourages theft by the cashier because the copy retained by the cashier, which lists the amount of the sale, can be checked against the actual amount of cash received. If the receipts are not prenumbered, the cashier can destroy the copy and pocket the cash sale amount. However, if the receipts are prenumbered, the missing copy can easily be identified.

Limitations of Internal Control

Most internal control measures can be overcome. Systems designed to thwart an *individual* employee's fraud can be beaten by two or more employees working as a team—colluding—to defraud the firm. Consider a movie theater. The ticket seller takes in the cash, and the ticket taker tears the tickets in half so they cannot be reused, retaining the torn ticket stub. But suppose they put a scheme together in which the ticket seller pockets the cash from ten customers and the ticket taker admits the customers without tickets. Who would catch them? The manager could take the additional control measure of counting the people in the theater and matching that figure against the number of ticket stubs retained. But that takes time away from other duties. As you see, the stricter the internal control system, the more expensive it becomes.

A system of internal control that is too complex may strangle people in red tape. Efficiency and control are hurt rather than helped. The more complicated the system, the more time and money it takes to maintain. Just how tight should an internal control system be? Managers must make sensible judgments. Investments in internal control must be judged in the light of the costs and benefits.

Computers and Internal Control

Computers have had both positive and negative effects on internal control. On the positive side, their speed of operation and high reliability increase efficiency. On the negative side, computer systems are less flexible than manual systems. Computers can take data in only one programmed format, whereas humans can process data if it is merely legible.

Effective internal control is as important to computer systems as it is to manual systems. For example, consider the separation of duties. Programmers should not be allowed to physically operate the computers. A computer consultant commented that he had opportunities to steal when he ran computer operations for a large bank. "I alone designed the dividend-payment operation, wrote the program for it, and ran the job on the machine. The operation was so big that it had a mistake tolerance of nearly $100,000. I could have paid at least half that much to myself, in small checks, and the money wouldn't even have been missed." To avoid theft, no one person should have complete control over system design, programming, and machine operation.

The computer has brought about an important development in cash payments. **Electronic funds transfer (EFT)** is a system that relies on electronic impulses—not paper documents—to account for cash transactions. To manage payroll, an employer enters the employee's name, pay rate, and any other needed data on a magnetic tape, which is transferred to a bank. The bank runs the tape, which automatically decreases the business's cash account and increases the employee's cash account. Some retailers use EFT to handle sales. Customers pay with a card that activates a computer. The computer automatically decreases the customer's bank account balance and increases the store's account balance.

EFT systems reduce the cost of processing cash transactions. However, this savings is achieved by reducing the documentary evidence of transactions. Traditional approaches to internal control have relied on documents, so EFT and other computer systems pose a significant challenge to managers and accountants who design and enforce internal control systems. Computer systems also create problems in protecting private information. For example, a group of students in Milwaukee gained access to highly confidential national defense data by computer! Such situations point to the need for computer security measures.

Summary

An efficient accounting system combines *personnel, records,* and *procedures* to meet a business's information needs. Processing accounting information means collecting data from source documents, organizing and recording the data, and communicating the information through the financial statements. Each business designs its accounting system to satisfy its particular information needs.

To be effective, the system must provide management with the information needed to *control* the organization. Also, the system must be *compatible* with the business's operations. As a business changes, the system must be *flexible* enough to handle new needs. Finally, the system must be *cost-beneficial*.

Computer data processing systems include *hardware, software,* and *personnel.* Hardware may consist of a mainframe computer or microcomputers. Computer operators use software to process data *on-line* or in *batches.*

Many businesses use special journals to account for repetitive transactions such as credit sales, cash receipts, credit purchases, and cash disbursements. Special journals reduce the amount of writing and posting required. Some businesses find it efficient to use source documents as journals.

Computer systems can be programmed to possess all the special journal features described in this chapter. The major goal of system design is efficient, routine handling of high volumes of transactions. Special journals were originally created to meet that objective. Similarly, computer systems can store records of sales, cash receipts, purchases, and cash disbursements and print special journals as desired.

Businesses use a subsidiary ledger to account for individual customer accounts receivable. The subsidiary ledger gives information on each customer's account. The total of the subsidiary ledger's individual account balances must match the balance in the Accounts Receivable control account in the general ledger. Companies may also keep a subsidiary ledger for accounts payable.

Internal controls should safeguard assets, ensure accurate accounting records, promote operational efficiency, and encourage adherence to company policies. An effective internal control system includes these features: *reliable personnel, clear-cut assignment of responsibility, proper authorization,* and *separation of duties,* which is the primary element of internal control. Many businesses use security devices, audits, and specially designed documents and records in their internal control systems.

Self-Study Questions

Test your understanding of the chapter by marking the best answer for each of the following questions.

1. Why does a jewelry store need a different kind of accounting system than a physician uses? *(p. 275)*
   a. They have different kinds of employees.
   b. They have different kinds of journals and ledgers.
   c. They have different kinds of business transactions.
   d. They work different hours.

2. Special journals help most by *(pp. 279, 280)*
   a. Limiting the number of transactions that have to be recorded
   b. Reducing the cost of operating the accounting system
   c. Improving accuracy in posting to subsidiary ledgers
   d. Easing the preparation of the financial statements

3. Galvan Company recorded 523 credit sale transactions in the sales journal. How many postings would be required if these transactions were recorded in the general journal? *(p. 283)*
   a. 523   c. 1,569
   b. 1,046   d. 2,092

4. Which two dollar-amount columns in the cash receipts journal will be used the most by a department store that makes half of its sales for cash and half on credit? *(p. 284)*
   a. Cash Debit and Sales Discounts Debit
   b. Cash Debit and Accounts Receivable Credit
   c. Cash Debit and Other Accounts Credit
   d. Accounts Receivable Debit and Sales Revenue Credit

5. Entries in the purchases journal are posted to the *(p. 288)*
   a. General ledger only
   b. General ledger and the Accounts payable ledger
   c. General ledger and the Accounts receivable ledger
   d. Accounts receivable ledger and the Accounts payable ledger

6. Every entry in the cash disbursements journal includes a *(p. 291)*
   a. Debit to Accounts Payable   c. Credit to Purchase Discounts
   b. Debit to an Other Account   d. Credit to Cash

7. Mazarotti Company has issued a debit memo. The related journal entry is *(p. 293)*
   a. Accounts Payable XXX
      Purchase Returns and Allowances XXX
   b. Purchase Returns and Allowances XXX
      Accounts Payable XXX
   c. Accounts Receivable XXX
      Sales Returns and Allowances XXX
   d. Sales Returns and Allowances XXX
      Accounts Receivable XXX

8. Balancing the ledgers at the end of the period is most closely related to *(p. 295)*
   a. Control   c. Flexibility
   b. Compatibility   d. Acceptable cost/benefit relationship

9. Which of the following is an element of internal control? *(p. 296)*
   a. Safeguarding assets
   b. Ensuring accurate and reliable accounting records
   c. Promoting operational efficiency
   d. Encouraging adherence to company policies
   e. All the above are elements of internal control

10. Which of the characteristics of an effective system of internal control is violated by allowing the employee who handles inventory to also account for inventory? *(p. 300)*
    a. Competent and reliable personnel   c. Proper authorization
    b. Assignment of responsibilities   d. Separation of duties

Answers to the Self-Study Questions follow the Accounting Vocabulary.

Accounting Vocabulary

Accounting information system. The combination of personnel, records, and procedures that a business uses to meet its need for financial data *(p. 275)*.

Balancing the ledgers. Establishing the equality of (a) total debits and total credits in the general ledger or (b) the balance of a control account in the general ledger and the sum of individual accounts in the related subsidiary ledger *(p. 295)*.

Batch processing. Computerized accounting for similar transactions in a group or batch *(p. 278)*.

Cash disbursements journal. Special journal used to record cash disbursements by check *(p. 290)*.

Cash receipts journal. Special journal used to record cash receipts *(p. 283)*.

Control account. An account whose balance equals the sum of the balances in a group of related accounts in a subsidiary ledger *(p. 283)*.

Credit memo. Document issued by a seller to indicate having credited a customer's account receivable account *(p. 292)*.

Debit memo. Business document issued by a buyer to state that the buyer no longer owes the seller for the amount of returned purchases (p. 293).

Electronic fund transfer (EFT). System that accounts for cash transactions by electronic impulses rather than paper documents (p. 302).

General journal. Journal used to record all transactions that do not fit one of the special journals (p. 280).

General ledger. Ledger of accounts that are reported in the financial statements (p. 282).

Hardware. Equipment that makes up a computer system (p. 278).

Internal control. Organizational plan and all the related measures adopted by an entity to safeguard assets, ensure accurate and reliable accounting records, promote operational efficiency, and encourage adherence to company policies (p. 296).

Mainframe system. Computer system characterized by a single computer (p. 278).

Microcomputer. A computer small enough for each employee (work station) to have its own (p. 278).

Minicomputer. Small computer that operates like a large system but on a smaller scale (p. 278).

On-line processing. Computerized accounting for transaction data on a continuous basis, often from various locations, rather than in batches at a single location (p. 279).

Purchases journal. Special journal used to record all purchases of inventory, supplies, and other assets on account (p. 288).

Sales journal. Special journal used to record credit sales (p. 280).

Software. Set of programs or instructions that cause the computer to perform the work desired (p. 278).

Subsidiary ledger. Book of accounts that provides supporting details on individual balances, the total of which appears in a general ledger account (p. 282).

Answers to Self-Study Questions

1. c
2. b
3. c [523 × 3 (one debit, one credit, and one to the accounts receivable ledger) = 1,569]
4. b
5. b
6. d
7. a
8. a
9. e
10. d

ASSIGNMENT MATERIAL

Questions

1. Briefly describe the two phases of implementing an accounting system.
2. Describe the basic information processing model of an accounting system.
3. What are the attributes of an effective information system? Briefly describe each attribute.
4. How does a mainframe computer system differ from a microcomputer system?
5. Describe an on-line computer processing operation for accounts receivable, sales, and inventory by a large retailer, such as Sears or Penney's.

6. Name four special journals used in accounting systems. For what type of transaction is each designed?

7. Describe the two advantages that special journals have over recording all transactions in the general journal.

8. What is a control account, and how is it related to a subsidiary ledger? Name two common control accounts.

9. Graff Company's sales journal has one amount column headed Accounts Receivable Dr. and Sales Revenue Cr. In this journal, 86 transactions are recorded. How many posting references appear in the journal? State what each posting reference represents.

10. Use S = Sales; CR = Cash Receipts; P = Purchases; CD = Cash Disbursements; and SRA = Sales Returns and Allowances to identify the special journal in which the following column headings appear. Some headings may appear in more than one journal.

Sales Revenue Cr._____   Invoice No._____

Accounts Payable Dr._____   Sales Discounts Dr._____

Cash Dr._____   Other Accounts Cr._____

Purchase Discounts Cr._____   Purchases Dr._____

Accounts Receivable Cr._____   Cash Cr._____

Check No._____   Credit Memo No._____

Other Accounts Dr._____   Accounts Payable Cr._____

Post. Ref._____   Accounts Receivable Dr._____

11. The accountant for Bannister Company posted all amounts correctly from the cash receipts journal to the general ledger. However, she failed to post three credits to customer accounts in the accounts receivable subsidiary ledger. How would this error be detected?

12. In posting from the cash receipts journal of Enfield Homebuilders, the accountant failed to post the amount of the sales revenue credit column. Identify two ways this error can be detected.

13. At what two times is posting done from a special journal? What items are posted at each time?

14. For what purposes are a credit memo and a debit memo issued? Who issues each document, the seller or the purchaser?

15. The following entry appears in the general journal:

Nov. 25   Sales Returns and Allowances ....?   539
                Accounts Receivable—B.Goodwin....?   539

Prepare likely posting references.

16. What is the purpose of balancing the ledgers?

17. Posting from the journals of McKedrick Realty is complete. However, the total of the individual balances in the accounts payable subsidiary ledger does not equal the balance in the Accounts Payable control account in the general ledger. Does this necessarily indicate that the trial balance is out of balance? Give your reason.

18. Assume that posting is completed. The trial balance shows no errors, but the sum of the individual accounts payable does not equal the Accounts Payable control balance in the general ledger. What two errors could cause this problem?

19. Which of the features of effective internal control is the most fundamental? Why?

20. Which company employees bear primary responsibility for a company's financial statements and for maintaining the company's system of internal control? How do these persons carry out this responsibility?

21. Identify features of an effective system of internal control.
22. Separation of duties may be divided into four parts. What are they?
23. How can internal control systems be circumvented?
24. Are internal control systems designed to be foolproof and perfect? What is a fundamental constraint in planning and maintaining systems?
25. Why should the same employee not write the computer programs for cash disbursements, sign checks, and mail the checks to payees?

Exercises

Exercise 6-1   Using the sales and cash receipts journals   (L.O. 2,4)

The sales and cash receipts journals of CompuGraphics Company include the following entries:

Sales Journal

Date	Account Debited	Post Ref.	Amount
Oct. 7	C. Carlson	✓	730
10	T. Muecke	✓	3,100
10	E. Lovell	✓	190
12	B. Goebel................................	✓	5,470
31	Total		9,490

Cash Receipts Journal

	Debits		Credits				
					Other Accounts		
Date	Cash	Sales Discounts	Accounts Receivable	Sales Revenue	Account Title	Post Ref.	Amount
Oct. 16					C. Carlson	✓	
19					E. Lovell	✓	
24	100			100			
30					T. Muecke	✓	

CompuGraphics makes all sales on credit terms of 2/10 n/30. Complete the cash receipts journal for those transactions indicated. Also, total the journal and show that total debits equal total credits. Assume that each cash receipt was for the full amount of the receivable.

Exercise 6-2   Classifying postings from the cash receipts journal   (L.O. 3,4)

The cash receipts journal of Schwarzkopf, Inc., is shown on the following page.

Required

Identify each posting reference (a) through (l) as (1) a posting to the general ledger as a column total, (2) a posting to the general ledger as an individual amount, (3) a posting to a subsidiary ledger account, or (4) an amount not posted.

	Debits				Credits		
					Other Accounts		
Date	**Cash**	**Sales Discounts**	**Accounts Receivable**	**Sales Revenue**	**Account Title**	**Post. Ref.**	**Amount**
Dec. 2	794	16	810		Swingline Co.	(a)	
9	1,291		1,291		Kamm, Inc.	(b)	
14	3,904			3,904		(c)	
19	4,480				Note Receivable	(d)	4,000
					Interest Revenue	(e)	480
30	314	7	321		L. M. Roose	(f)	
31	4,235			4,235		(g)	
31	15,018	23	2,422	8,139	Totals		4,480
	(h)	(i)	(j)	(k)			(l)

Exercise 6-3   *Identifying transactions from postings to the accounts receivable ledger* *(L.O. 3)*

An account in the accounts receivable ledger of Tyler Company follows.

John Babcock

					Balance	
Date		**Jrnl. Ref.**	**Dr.**	**Cr.**	**Dr.**	**Cr.**
May 1	....				703	
10	....	S.5	1,180		1,883	
15	....	J.8		191	1,692	
21	....	CR.9		703	989	

Required

Describe the three posted transactions.

Exercise 6-4   *Posting directly from sales invoices; balancing the ledgers* *(L.O. 3)*

Emery Printing Company uses its sales invoices as the sales journal and posts directly from them to the accounts receivable subsidiary ledger. During June the company made the following sales on account:

Date	Invoice No.	Customer Name	Amount
June 6	256	Emily Jacques	$ 716
9	257	Forrest Ashworth ...	798
13	258	Paul Scott	550
16	259	Jan Childres........	3,678
22	260	Emily Jacques	1,915
30	261	Jan Childres........	800
		Total	$8,457

Required

1. Open general ledger accounts for Accounts Receivable and Sales Revenue and post to those accounts. Use dates and use June Sales as the journal reference in the ledger accounts.
2. Open customer accounts in the accounts receivable subsidiary ledger and post to those accounts. Use dates and use invoice numbers as journal references.
3. Balance the ledgers.

Exercise 6-5 *Recording purchase transactions in the general journal and in the purchases journal* **(L.O. 5)**

During April, Ippolito, Inc., completed the following credit purchase transactions:

April 4 Purchased inventory, $1,604, from Textan Co.
       7 Purchased supplies, $107, from JJ Maine Corp.
    19 Purchased equipment, $1,903, from Liston-Fry Co.
    27 Purchased inventory, $2,210, from Milan, Inc.

Record these transactions first in the general journal—with explanations—and then in the purchases journal. Omit credit terms and posting references. Which procedure for recording transactions is quicker?

Exercise 6-6 *Posting from the purchases journal, balancing the ledgers* **(L.O. 3,5)**

The purchases journal of Odegaard Company follows.

Purchases Journal   Page 7

Date	Account Credited	Terms	Post. Ref.	Account Payable Cr.	Purchases Dr.	Supplies Dr.	Acct. Title	Post. Ref.	Amt. Dr.
							Other Accounts Dr.		
Sep. 2	Schaeffer Company	n/30		1,100	1,100				
5	Rolf Office Supply	n/30		175		175			
13	Schaeffer Company	2/10 n/30		347	347				
26	Marks Equipment Company	n/30		916			Equipment		916
30	Totals			2,538	1,447	175			916

Required

1. Open ledger accounts for Supplies, Equipment, Accounts Payable, and Purchases. Post to these accounts from the purchases journal. Use dates and posting references in the ledger accounts.
2. Open accounts in the accounts payable subsidiary ledger for Schaeffer Company, Rolf Office Supply, and Marks Equipment Company. Post from the purchases journal. Use dates and journal references in the ledger accounts.
3. Balance the Accounts Payable control account in the general ledger with the total of the balances in the accounts payable subsidiary ledger.

Exercise 6-7 *Using the cash disbursements journal* *(L.O. 6)*

During July Scott Products had the following transactions:

July 3 Paid $792 on account to Hellenic Corp., net of an $8 discount.
    6 Purchased inventory for cash, $817.
  11 Paid $375 for supplies.
  15 Purchased inventory on credit from Monroe Corporation, $774.
  16 Paid $8,062 on account to LaGrange Associates; there was no discount.
  21 Purchased furniture for cash, $960.
  26 Paid $3,910 on account to Graff Software. The discount was $90.
  31 Made a semiannual interest payment of $800 on a long-term note payable. The entire payment was for interest.

Required

1. Draw a cash disbursements journal similar to the one illustrated in this chapter. Omit the check number (Ck. No.) and posting reference (Post. Ref.) columns.
2. Record the transactions in the journal. Which transaction should not be recorded in the cash disbursements journal? In what journal does it belong?
3. Total the amount columns of the journal. Determine that the total debits equal the total credits.

Exercise 6-8 *Using business documents to record transactions* *(L.O. 6)*

The following documents describe two business transactions:

Invoice		
Date: August 14, 19X0		
Sold to: Zephyr Bicycle Shop		
Sold by: Schwinn Company		
Terms: 2/10 n/30		
Items Purchased Bicycles		
Quantity	Price	Total
4	$90	$360
2	70	140
5	60	300
Total		$800

Debit Memo		
Date: August 20, 19X0		
Issued to: Schwinn Company		
Issued by: Zephyr Bicycle Shop		
Items Returned Bicycles		
Quantity	Price	Total
1	$90	$ 90
1	$ 70	70
Total		$160
Reason: Wrong sizes		

Use the general journal to record these transactions and Zephyr's cash payment on August 21. Record the transactions first on the books of Zephyr Bicycle Shop and, second, on the books of Schwinn Company, which makes and sells bicycles. Round to the nearest dollar. Explanations are not required. Set up your answer in the following format:

Date   **Zephyr Journal Entries**   **Schwinn Journal Entries**

Exercise 6-9 *Detecting errors in the special journals* **(L.O. 2,3,4,6)**

Financial MicroSystems uses special journals for credit sales, cash receipts, credit purchases, and cash disbursements, and the subsidiary ledgers illustrated in this chapter. During March the accountant made four errors. State the procedure that will detect each error described in the following:

(a) Posted a $40 debit to Raoul Gortari's account in the accounts receivable subsidiary ledger as a $400 credit.

(b) Added the Cash Credit column of the cash disbursements journal as $4,176 and posted this incorrect amount to the Cash account. The correct total was $4,026.

(c) Recorded receipt of $500 on account from Eichler, Inc., as a credit to Accounts Receivable in the cash receipts journal. Failed to record "Eichler, Inc."

(d) Failed to post the total of the Accounts Receivable Dr./Sales Revenue Cr. column of the sales journal.

Exercise 6-10 *Journalizing return and allowance transactions* **(L.O. 7)**

Medoff Company records returns and allowances in its general journal. During June the company had the following transactions:

June 4	Issued credit memo to Fidelity, Inc., for inventory that Fidelity returned to us	$1,043
10	Received debit memo from B. R. Inman, who purchased merchandise from us on June 6. We shipped the wrong items, and Inman returned them to us	1,238
14	Issued debit memo for merchandise we purchased from Wyle Supply Company that was damaged in shipment. We returned the damaged inventory to Wyle	4,600
22	Received credit memo from Dietrich Distributing Co., from whom we purchased inventory on June 15. Dietrich discovered that they overcharged us	300

Required

Journalize the transactions in the general journal. Explanations are not required.

Exercise 6-11 *Identifying internal control strengths and weaknesses* **(L.O. 8)**

The following situations suggest either a strength or weakness in internal control. Identify each as *strength or weakness,* and give the reason for your answer.

a. The vice-president who signs checks assumes the accounting department has matched the invoice with other supporting documents and therefore does not examine the supporting documents.

b. Purchase invoices are recorded at net amount to highlight purchase discounts lost because of late payment.

c. The accounting department orders merchandise and approves invoices for payment.

d. The operator of the computer has no other accounting or cash-handling duties.

e. Cash received over the counter is controlled by the sales clerk, who rings up the sale and places the cash in the register. The sales clerk has access to the control tape stored in the register.

f. Cash received by mail goes straight to the accountant, who debits Cash and credits Accounts Receivable from the customer.

Exercise 6-12 *Identifying internal controls* (L.O. 8)

Identify the missing internal control characteristic in the following situations:

1. Business is slow at Malibu Theme Park on Tuesday, Wednesday, and Thursday nights. To reduce expenses the manager decides not to use a ticket taker on those nights. The ticket seller (cashier) is told to keep the tickets as a record of the number sold.
2. The manager of a discount store wants to speed the flow of customers through checkout. She decides to reduce the time spent by cashiers making change, so she prices merchandise at round dollar amounts—such as $8.00 and $15.00—instead of the customary amounts—$7.95 and $14.95.
3. Grocery stores such as Kroger and Winn Dixie purchase large quantities of their merchandise from a few suppliers. At another grocery store the manager decides to reduce paperwork. He eliminates the requirement that a receiving department employee prepare a receiving report, which lists the quantities of items received from the supplier.
4. When business is brisk, Seven-Eleven and many other retail stores deposit cash in the bank several times during the day. The manager at another convenience store wants to reduce the time spent by employees delivering cash to the bank, so he starts a new policy. Cash will build up over Saturdays and Sundays, and the total two-day amount will be deposited on Sunday evening.
5. In the course of auditing the records of a company, you find that the same employee orders merchandise and approves invoices for payment.

Problems *(Group A)*

Problem 6-1A *Features of an effective information system* (L.O. 1)

Chambers Corporation is revamping its information system. As the controller of the company, write a memo to make the president aware of the features of an effective information system. Write at least two sentences on each feature. Indicate which feature you believe is most important, and defend your position.

Problem 6-2A *Using the sales, cash receipts, and general journals* (L.O. 2,4,7)

The general ledger of Monterrey Telecommunications Company includes the following accounts:

Cash	111	Sales Revenue	411
Accounts Receivable	112	Sales Discounts	412
Notes Receivable	115	Sales Returns and Allowances	413
Equipment	141	Interest Revenue	417
Land	142	Gain on Sale of Land	418

All credit sales are on the company's standard terms of 2/10 n/30. Transactions in February that affected sales and cash receipts were as follows:

Feb. 1 Sold inventory on credit to G. M. Titcher, $900.
5 As an accommodation to another company, sold new equipment for its cost of $770, receiving cash in this amount.
6 Cash sales for the week totaled $2,107.
8 Sold merchandise on account to McNair Co., $2,830.
9 Sold land that cost $22,000 for cash of $40,000.

Feb. 11 Sold goods on account to Nickerson Builders, $6,099.

11 Received cash from G. M. Titcher in full settlement of her account receivable from February 1.

13 Cash sales for the week were $1,995.

15 Sold inventory on credit to Montez and Montez, a partnership, $800.

18 Issued credit memo to McNair Co. for $120 of merchandise returned to us by McNair. The goods we shipped were unsatisfactory.

19 Sold merchandise on account to Nickerson Builders, $3,900.

20 Cash sales for the week were $2,330.

21 Received $1,200 cash from McNair Co. in partial settlement of its account receivable. There was no discount.

22 Received cash from Montez and Montez for the account receivable from February 15.

22 Sold goods on account to Diamond Co., $2,022.

25 Collected $4,200 on a note receivable, of which $200 was interest.

27 Cash sales for the week totaled $2,970.

27 Sold inventory on account to Littleton Corporation, $2,290.

28 Issued credit memo to Diamond Co. for $680 for damaged goods it returned to us.

28 Received $1,510 cash on account from McNair Co. There was no discount.

Required

1. Use the appropriate journal to record the above transactions in a single-column sales journal (omit the Invoice No. column), a cash receipts journal, and a general journal. Carmel records sales returns and allowances in the general journal.

2. Total each column of the cash receipts journal. Determine that the total debits equal the total credits.

3. Show how postings would be made from the journals by writing the account numbers and check marks in the appropriate places in the journals.

Problem 6-3A *Correcting errors in the cash receipts journal* (L.O. 4)

The cash receipts journal below contains five entries. All five entries are for legitimate cash receipt transactions, but the journal contains some errors in recording the transactions. In fact, only one entry is correct, and each of the other four entries contains one error.

Cash Receipts Journal   Page 5

| | Debits | | Credits | | | | |
| | | | | | Other Accounts | | |
Date	Cash	Sales Discounts	Accounts Receivable	Sales Revenue	Account Title	P.R.	Amount
7/5	611	34	645		Meg Davis	✓	
9			346	346	Carl Ryther	✓	
10	8000			8000	Land	19	
19	73						
31	1060			1133			
	9744	34	991	9479	Totals		
	(11)	(42)	(12)	(41)			(✓)

Total Dr. = $9,778   Total Cr. = $10,470

Required

1. Identify the correct entry.
2. Identify the error in each of the other four entries.
3. Using the following format, prepare a corrected cash receipts journal.

Cash Receipts Journal Page 5

| | Debits | | Credits | | | | |
| | Cash | Sales Discounts | Accounts Receivable | Sales Revenue | Other Accounts | | |
Date					Account Title	P.R.	Amount
7/5					Meg Davis	✓	
9					Carl Ryther	✓	
10					Land	19	
19							
31							
	10090	34	991	1133	Totals		8000
	(11)	(42)	(12)	(41)			(✓)

Total Dr. = $10,124   Total Cr. = $10,124

Problem 6-4A *Using the purchases, cash disbursements, and general journals (L.O. 5,6,7)*

The general ledger of Greensboro Custom Frames includes the following accounts:

Cash	111	Purchase Discounts	512
Prepaid Insurance	116	Purchase Returns and	
Supplies	117	Allowances	513
Equipment	149	Rent Expense	562
Accounts Payable	211	Utilities Expense	265
Purchases	511		

Transactions in March that affected purchases and cash disbursements were as follows:

Mar. 1 Paid monthly rent, debiting Rent Expense for $1,150.

3 Purchased inventory on credit from Broussard Co., $4,600. Terms were 2/15 n/45.

4 Purchased supplies on credit terms of 2/10 n/30 from Harmon Sales, $800.

7 Paid gas and water bills, $406.

10 Purchased equipment on account from Lancer Co., $1,050. Payment terms were 2/10 n/30.

11 Returned the equipment to Lancer Co. It was defective. We issued a debit memo for $1,050 and mailed a copy to Lancer.

12 Paid Broussard Co. the amount owed on the purchase of March 3.

12 Purchased inventory on account from Lancer Co., $1,100. Terms were 2/10 n/30.

14 Purchased inventory for cash, $1,585.

Mar. 15 Paid an insurance premium, debiting Prepaid Insurance, $2,416.

16 Paid our account payable to Harmon Sales, less the discount, from March 6.

17 Paid electricity bill, $165.

20 Paid account payable to Lancer Co., less the discount, from March 12.

21 Purchased supplies on account from Master Supply, $754. Terms were net 30.

22 Purchased inventory on credit terms of 1/10 n/30 from Linz Brothers, $3,400.

26 Returned inventory purchased on March 22, to Linz Brothers, issuing a debit memo for $500.

31 Paid Linz Brothers the net amount owed from March 22, less the return on March 26.

Required

1. Use the appropriate journal to record the above transactions in a purchases journal, a cash disbursements journal (omit the Check No. column), and a general journal. Greensboro records purchase returns in the general journal.

2. Total each column of the special journals. Show that the total debits equal the total credits in each special journal.

3. Show how postings would be made from the journals by writing the account numbers and check marks in the appropriate places in the journals.

Problem 6-5A *Using the sales, cash receipts, and general journals; posting; and balancing the ledgers.* **(L.O. 2,3,4,7)**

During June, Boatright Custom Floors engaged in the following transactions:

June 1 Issued invoice no. 113 for credit sale to Aspen Co., $4,750. All credit sales are on the company's standard terms of 2/10 n/30.

3 Collected cash of $882 from Leah Burnet in payment of her account receivable within the discount period.

6 Cash sales for the week totaled $1,748.

7 Collected note receivable, $3,500, plus 10 percent interest.

9 Issued invoice no. 114 for sale on account to Wilder Co., $4,300.

11 Received cash from Aspen Co. in full settlement of its account receivable from the sale on June 1.

13 Cash sales for the week were $2,964.

14 Sold inventory on account to Goss Corp., issuing invoice no. 115 for $858.

15 Issued credit memo to Goss Corp. for $154 of merchandise returned to us by Goss. Part of the goods we shipped were defective.

19 Received cash from Wilder Co. in full settlement of its account receivable from June 9.

20 Cash sales for the week were $2,175.

22 Received cash of $2,904 from Goss Corp. on account from June 1.

24 Sold supplies to an employee for cash of $106, which was Boatright's cost.

27 Cash sales for the week totaled $1,650.

28 Issued invoice no. 116 to Thompson Co. for credit sale of inventory, $5,194.

June 29 Sold goods on credit to Leah Burnet, issuing invoice no. 117 for $3,819.

29 Issued credit memo to Leah Burnet for $1,397 of inventory she returned to us because it was unsatisfactory.

The general ledger of Boatright Custom Floors includes the following accounts and balances at June 1:

Account Number	Account Title	Balance	Account Number	Account Title	Balance
111	Cash.............	$4,217	411	Sales Revenue	
112	Accounts Receivable	3,804	412	Sales Discounts	
116	Supplies...........	1,290	413	Sales Returns and Allowances ..	
141	Notes Receivable ...	7,100	418	Interest Revenue ...	

Boatright's accounts receivable subsidiary ledger includes the following accounts and balances at June 1: Aspen Company, -0-; Leah Burnet, $900; Goss Corp., $2,904; Thompson Company, -0-; and Wilder Co., -0-.

Required

1. Open the general ledger and the accounts receivable subsidiary ledger accounts given, inserting their balances at June 1.
2. Record the above transactions on page 6 of a single-column sales journal, page 9 of a cash receipts journal, and page 5 of a general journal, as appropriate. Boatright records sales returns and allowances in the general journal.
3. Post daily to the accounts receivable subsidiary ledger. On June 30 post to the general ledger.
4. Total each column of the special journals. Show that the total debits equal the total credits in each special journal.
5. Balance the total of the customer account balances in the accounts receivable subsidiary ledger against the Accounts Receivable balance in the general ledger.

Problem 6-6A *Using the purchases, cash disbursements, and general journals; posting and balancing the ledgers* (L.O. 3,5,6,7)

De Gortari Company's September transactions affecting purchases and cash disbursements were as follows:

Sep. 1 Issued check no. 406 to pay AmeriCorp. in full on account. De Gortari received a 2 percent discount for prompt payment.

1 Issued check no. 407 to pay quarterly rent, debiting Prepaid Rent for $2,100.

2 Issued check no. 408 to pay net amount owed to Lynn Co., $1,455. De Gortari took a $45 discount.

5 Purchased supplies on credit terms of 2/10 n/30 from Westside Supply, $121.

7 Paid delivery expense, issuing check no. 409 for $739.

10 Purchased inventory on account from Hayden, Inc., $2,008. Payment terms were net 30.

11 Returned the inventory to Hayden, Inc., because it was defective. We issued a debit memo for $2,008 and mailed a copy to Hayden.

15 Issued check no. 410 for a cash purchase of inventory, $2,332.

Sep. 15 Paid semimonthly payroll with check no. 411, $1,224.

19 Issued check no. 412 to pay our account payable to Westside Supply from September 5. We did not earn the discount.

21 Purchased inventory on credit terms of 2/10 n/30 from Lynn Co., $4,150.

24 Purchased machinery on credit terms of 2/10 n/30 from AmeriCorp., $3,195.

26 Purchased supplies on account from Hayden, Inc., $467. Terms were net 30.

29 Issued check no. 413 to Lynn Co., paying the net amount owed from September 21.

30 Paid semimonthly payroll with check no. 414, $1,224.

The general ledger of De Gortari Company includes the following accounts and balances at September 1:

Account Number	Account Title	Balance	Account Number	Account Title	Balance
111	Cash.............	$15,996	511	Purchases.........	
115	Prepaid Rent......		512	Purchase Discounts	
116	Supplies..........	703	513	Purchase Returns	
151	Machinery........	21,800		and Allowances..	
211	Accounts Payable..	2,700	521	Salary Expense.....	
			551	Delivery Expense ..	

De Gortari's accounts payable subsidiary ledger includes the following balances at September 1: AmeriCorp., $1,200; Hayden, Inc., -0-; Lynn Company, $1,500; and Westside Supply, -0-.

Required

1. Open the general ledger and the accounts payable subsidiary ledger accounts, inserting their balances at September 1.

2. Record the above transactions on page 10 of a purchases journal, page 5 of a cash disbursements journal, and page 8 of a general journal, as appropriate. De Gortari records purchase returns in the general journal.

3. Post daily to the accounts payable subsidiary ledger. On September 30 post to the general ledger.

4. Total each column of the special journals. Determine that the total debits equal the total credits in each special journal.

5. Balance the total of the creditor account balances in the accounts payable subsidiary ledger against the balance of the Accounts Payable control account in the general ledger.

Problem 6-7A *Using all the journals, posting, and balancing the ledgers*
(L.O. 2,3,4,5,6,7)

Talbert Company completed the following transactions during July:

July 2 Issued invoice no. 913 for sale on account to N. J. Seiko, $4,100.

3 Purchased inventory on credit terms of 3/10 n/60 from Chicosky Co., $2,467.

5 Sold inventory for cash, $1,077.

5 Issued check no. 532 to purchase furniture for cash, $2,185.

8 Collected interest revenue of $1,775.

July 9 Issued invoice no. 914 for sale on account to Bell Co., $5,550.

10 Purchased inventory for cash, $1,143, issuing check no. 533.

12 Received cash from N. J. Seiko in full settlement of her account receivable, net of a 2 percent discount, from the sale on July 2.

13 Issued check no. 534 to pay Chicosky Co. the net amount owed from July 3.

13 Purchased supplies on account from Manley, Inc., $441. Terms were net end-of-month.

15 Sold inventory on account to M. O. Brown, issuing invoice no. 915 for $665.

17 Issued credit memo to M. O. Brown for $665 for defective merchandise returned to us by Brown.

18 Issued invoice no. 916 for credit sale to N. J. Seiko, $357.

19 Received $5,439 from Bell Co. in full settlement of its account receivable, $5,550, from July 9.

20 Purchased inventory on credit terms of net 30 from Sims Distributing, $2,047.

22 Purchased furniture on credit terms of 3/10 n/60 from Chicosky Co., $645.

22 Issued check no. 535 to pay for insurance coverage, debiting Prepaid Insurance for $1,000.

24 Sold supplies to an employee for cash of $54, which was Talbert's cost.

25 Issued check no. 536 to pay utilities, $453.

28 Purchased inventory on credit terms of 2/10 n/30 from Manley, Inc., $675.

29 Returned damaged inventory to Manley, Inc., issuing a debit memo for $675.

29 Sold goods on account to Bell Co., issuing invoice no. 917 for $496.

30 Issued check no. 537 to pay Manley, Inc., the amount owed from July 13.

31 Received $357 on account from N. J. Seiko on credit sale of July 18.

31 Issued check no. 538 to pay monthly salaries, $3,619.

Required

1. Open the following general ledger accounts using the account numbers given:

Cash	111	Sales Returns	
Accounts Receivable	112	and Allowances	413
Supplies	116	Interest Revenue	419
Prepaid Insurance	117	Purchases	511
Furniture	151	Purchase Discounts	512
Accounts Payable	211	Purchase Returns	
Sales Revenue	411	and Allowances	513
Sales Discounts	412	Salary Expense	531
		Utilities Expense	541

2. Open these accounts in the subsidiary ledgers:
   Accounts receivable subsidiary ledger: Bell Co., M. O. Brown, and N. J. Seiko.
   Accounts payable subsidiary ledger: Chicosky Co., Manley, Inc., and Sims Distributing.

3. Enter the transactions in a sales journal (page 7), a cash receipts journal (page 5), a purchases journal (page 10), a cash disbursements journal (page 8), and a general journal (page 6), as appropriate.

4. Post daily to the accounts receivable subsidiary ledger and the accounts payable subsidiary ledger. On July 31 post to the general ledger.

5. Total each column of the special journals. Show that the total debits equal the total credits in each special journal.

6. Balance the total of the customer account balances in the accounts receivable subsidiary ledger against Accounts Receivable in the general ledger. Do the same for the accounts payable subsidiary ledger and Accounts Payable in the general ledger.

Problem 6-8A *Identifying the characteristics of an effective internal control system*
(L.O. 8)

Nassar Real Estate Development Company prospered during the lengthy economic expansion of the 1980s. Business was so good that the company bothered with few internal controls. The recent decline in the local real estate market, however, has caused Nassar to experience a shortage of cash. Abraham Nassar, the company owner, is looking for ways to save money.

Required

As controller of the company, write a memorandum to convince Mr. Nassar of the company's need for a system of internal control. Be specific in telling him how an internal control system could possibly lead to saving money. Include the definition of internal control, and briefly discuss each characteristic beginning with competent and reliable personnel.

Problem 6-9A *Identifying internal control weaknesses* *(L.O. 8)*

Each of the following situations has an internal control weakness.

a. Jack Cassell owns a firm that performs engineering services. His staff consists of twelve professional engineers, and he manages the office. Often his work requires him to travel to meet with clients. During the past six months he has observed that when he returns from a business trip, the engineering jobs in the office have not progressed satisfactorily. He learns that when he is away several of his senior employees take over office management and neglect their engineering duties. One employee could manage the office.

b. Marta Frazier has been an employee of Griffith's Shoe Store for many years. Because the business is relatively small, Marta performs all accounting duties, including opening the mail, preparing the bank deposit, and preparing the bank reconciliation.

c. Most large companies have internal audit staffs that continuously evaluate the business's internal control. Part of the auditor's job is to evaluate how efficiently the company is running. For example, is the company purchasing inventory from the least expensive wholesaler? After a particularly bad year, Mason Tile Company eliminates its internal audit department to reduce expenses.

d. CPA firms, law firms, and other professional organizations use paraprofessional employees to do some of their routine tasks. For example, an accounting paraprofessional might examine documents to assist a CPA in conducting an audit. In the CPA firm of Grosso & Howe, Lou Grosso, the senior partner, turns over a significant portion of his high-level audit work to his paraprofessional staff.

e. In evaluating the internal control over cash disbursements, an auditor learns that the purchasing agent is responsible for purchasing diamonds for use in the company's manufacturing process, approving the invoices for payment, and signing the checks. No supervisor reviews the purchasing agent's work.

Required

1. Identify the missing internal control characteristic in each situation.
2. Identify the business's possible problem.
3. Propose a solution to the problem.

Problem 6-10A   *Identifying internal control weakness*   **(L.O. 8)**

Rocky Mountain Supply Co. makes all sales on credit. Cash receipts arrive by mail, usually within 30 days of the sale. Jan Sharp opens envelopes and separates the checks from the accompanying remittance advices. Sharp forwards the checks to another employee who makes the daily bank deposit but has no access to the accounting records. Sharp sends the remittance advices, which show the amount of cash received, to the accounting department for entry in the accounts. Sharp's only other duty is to grant sales allowances to customers. When she receives a customer check for less than the full amount of the invoice, she records the sales allowance and forwards the document to the accounting department.

Required

You are the outside auditor of Rocky Mountain Supply Co. Write a memo to the company president to identify the internal control weakness in his situation. State how to correct the weakness.

(Group B)

Problem 6-1B   *Components of a computer information system*   **(L.O. 1)**

St. Paul Corporation is installing a computer information system, and the board of directors is developing a broad policy statement to guide the design of the system. The board members seek your advice as a system designer. Write a memo to the board, detailing the interaction among the three components of a computer information system. Indicate which component is the most important in any information system—computer or manual—and defend your position.

Problem 6-2B   *Using the sales, cash receipts, and general journals*   **(L.O. 2,4,7)**

The general ledger of Fuselier, Inc., includes the following accounts, among others:

Cash	11	Sales Revenue	41
Accounts Receivable	12	Sales Discounts	42
Notes Receivable	15	Sales Returns and	
Supplies	16	Allowances	43
Land	18	Interest Revenue	47

All credit sales are on the company's standard terms of 2/10 n/30. Transactions in May that affected sales and cash receipts were as follows:

May 2 Sold inventory on credit to Dockery Co., $700.
   4 As an accommodation to a competitor, sold supplies at cost, $85, receiving cash.
   7 Cash sales for the week totaled $1,890.
   9 Sold merchandise on account to A. L. Prince, $7,320.

May 10 Sold land that cost $10,000 for cash of $10,000.
   11 Sold goods on account to Sloan Electric, $5,104.
   12 Received cash from Dockery Co. in full settlement of its account receivable from May 2.
   14 Cash sales for the week were $2,106.
   15 Sold inventory on credit to the partnership of Wilkie & Blinn, $3,650.
   18 Issued credit memo to A. L. Prince for $600 of merchandise returned to us by Prince. The goods shipped were unsatisfactory.
   20 Sold merchandise on account to Sloan Electric, $629.
   21 Cash sales for the week were $990.
   22 Received $4,000 cash from A. L. Prince in partial settlement of his account receivable.
   25 Received cash from Wilkie & Blinn for their account receivable from May 15.
   25 Sold goods on account to Olsen Co., $720.
   27 Collected $5,125 on a note receivable, of which $125 was interest.
   28 Cash sales for the week totaled $3,774.
   29 Sold inventory on account to R. O. Bankston, $242.
   30 Issued credit memo to Olsen Co. for $40 for inventory they returned to us because it was damaged in shipment.
   31 Received $2,720 cash on account from A. L. Prince.

Required

1. Fuselier records sales returns and allowances in the general journal. Use the appropriate journal to record the above transactions in a single-column sales journal (omit the Invoice No. column), a cash receipts journal, and a general journal.
2. Total each column of the cash receipts journal. Show that the total debits equal the total credits.
3. Show how postings would be made from the journals by writing the account numbers and check marks in the appropriate places in the journals.

Problem 6-3B *Correcting errors in the cash receipts journal* **(L.O. 4)**

The cash receipts journal below contains five entries. All five entries are for legitimate cash receipt transactions, but the journal contains some errors in recording the transactions. In fact, only one entry is correct, and each of the other four entries contains one error.

Cash Receipts Journal   Page 13

| | Debits | | Credits | | | | |
| | | | | | Other Accounts | | |
Date	Cash	Sales Discounts	Accounts Receivable	Sales Revenue	Account Title	P.R.	Amount
5/6		500		500			
7	429	22			Mike Harrison	✓	451
12	2160				Note Receivable	13	2000
					Interest Revenue	45	160
18				330			
24	1100		770				
	3689	522	770	830	Totals		2611
	(11)	(42)	(12)	(41)			(✓)

Total Dr. = $4,211   Total Cr. = $4,211

1. Identify the correct entry.
2. Identify the error in each of the other four entries.
3. Using the following format, prepare a corrected cash receipts journal.

Cash Receipts Journal

Page 13

	Debits		Credits				
					Other Accounts		
Date	**Cash**	**Sales Discounts**	**Accounts Receivable**	**Sales Revenue**	**Account Title**	**P.R.**	**Amount**
5/6							
7					Mike Harrison	✓	
12					Note Receivable	13	
					Interest Revenue	45	
18							
24							
	4189	22	1221	830	Totals		2160
	(11)	(42)	(12)	(41)			(✓)

Total Dr. = $4,211   Total Cr. = $4,211

Problem 6-4B *Using the purchases, cash disbursements, and general journals (L.O. 5,6,7)*

The general ledger of Schiffman, Inc., includes the following accounts:

Cash	11	Purchases	51
Prepaid Insurance	16	Purchase Discounts	52
Supplies	17	Purchase Returns and	
Furniture	19	Allowances	53
Accounts Payable	21	Rent Expense	56
		Utilities Expense	58

Transactions in August that affected purchases and cash disbursements were as follows:

Aug. 1 Purchased inventory on credit from Wood Co., $3,400. Terms were 2/10 n/30.

1 Paid monthly rent, debiting Rent Expense for $2,000.

5 Purchased supplies on credit terms of 2/10 n/30 from Ross Supply, $450.

8 Paid electricity bill, $588.

9 Purchased furniture on account from A-1 Office Supply, $4,100. Payment terms were net 30.

10 Returned the furniture to A-1 Office Supply. It was the wrong color. Issued a debit memo for $4,100, and mailed a copy to A-1 Office Supply.

11 Paid Wood Co. the amount owed on the purchase of August 1.

12 Purchased inventory on account from Wynne, Inc., $4,400. Terms were 3/10 n/30.

13 Purchased inventory for cash, $655.

Aug. 14 Paid a semiannual insurance premium, debiting Prepaid Insurance, $1,200.

15 Paid our account payable to Ross Supply from August 5.

18 Paid gas and water bills, $196.

21 Purchased inventory on credit terms of 1/10 n/45 from Software, Inc., $5,200.

21 Paid account payable to Wynne, Inc., from August 12.

22 Purchased supplies on account from Office Sales, Inc., $274. Terms were net 30.

25 Returned part of the inventory purchased on August 21 to Software, Inc., issuing a debit memo for $1,200.

31 Paid Software, Inc., the net amount owed from August 21, less the return, on August 25.

Required

1. Schiffman, Inc., records purchase returns in the general journal. Use the appropriate journal to record the above transactions in a purchase journal, a cash disbursements journal (omit the Check No. column), and a general journal.

2. Total each column of the special journals. Show that the total debits equal the total credits in each special journal.

3. Show how postings would be made from the journals by writing the account numbers and check marks in the appropriate places in the journals.

Problem 6-5B *Using the sales, cash receipts, and general journals, posting, and balancing the ledgers* **(L.O. 2,3,4,7)**

During April, Baldwin Wallace Company had these transactions:

Apr. 2 Issued invoice no. 436 for credit sale to Vail Co., $5,200. All credit sales are made on the company's standard terms of 2/10 n/30.

3 Collected cash from H. M. Burger in payment of his account receivable within the discount period.

5 Cash sales for the week totaled $2,057.

7 Collected note receivable, $2,000, plus interest of $210.

10 Issued invoice no. 437 for sale on account to Van Allen Co., $1,850.

11 Sold supplies to an employee for cash of $54, which was the cost.

12 Received $5,096 cash from Vail Co. in full settlement of their account receivable from the sale of April 2.

12 Cash sales for the week were $1,698.

14 Sold inventory on account to Electro, Inc., issuing invoice no. 438 for $2,000.

16 Issued credit memo to Electro, Inc., for $610 of merchandise returned to us by Electro. Some of the shipped goods were damaged.

19 Cash sales for the week were $3,130.

20 Received $1,813 from Van Allen Co. in full settlement of its account receivable, $1,850, from April 10.

25 Received cash of $7,455 from Electro, Inc., on account.

26 Cash sales for the week totaled $2,744.

27 Issued invoice no. 439 to Clay Co. for credit sales of inventory, $3,640.

Apr. 28 Sold goods on credit to H. M. Burger, issuing invoice no. 440 for $2,689.

30 Issued credit memo to H. M. Burger for $404 for inventory he returned to us because it was unsatisfactory.

The general ledger of Baldwin Wallace includes the following accounts and balances at April 1:

Account Number	Account Title	Balance	Account Number	Account Title	Balance
111	Cash	$ 3,579	411	Sales Revenue	
112	Accounts Receivable	10,555	412	Sales Discounts	
116	Supplies	1,756	413	Sales Returns and	
141	Notes Receivable . . .	5,000		Allowances	
			418	Interest Revenue . . .	

Baldwin Wallace's accounts receivable subsidiary ledger includes the following accounts and balances at April 1: H. M. Burger, $3,100; Clay Company, -0-; Electro, Inc., $7,455; Vail Company, -0-; and Van Allen Co., -0-.

Required

1. Open the general ledger and the accounts receivable subsidiary ledger accounts given, inserting their balances at April 1.
2. Record the transactions on page 4 of a single-column sales journal, page 13 of a cash receipts journal, and page 7 of a general journal, as appropriate. Baldwin Wallace records sales returns and allowances in the general journal.
3. Post daily to the accounts receivable subsidiary ledger, and on April 30 post to the general ledger.
4. Show that the total debits equal the total credits in each special journal.
5. Balance the total of the customer account balances in the accounts receivable subsidiary ledger against the Accounts Receivable balance in the general ledger.

Problem 6-6B *Using the purchases, cash disbursements; and general journals; posting and balancing the ledgers* **(L.O. 3,5,6,7)**

Noonan Company's November purchases and cash disbursement transactions are as follows:

Nov. 1 Issued check no. 346 to pay ENTEL Corp. in full on account. Noonan received a 2 percent discount for prompt payment.

1 Issued check no. 347 to pay quarterly rent, debiting Prepaid Rent for $2,400.

2 Issued check no. 348 to pay net amount owed to Arbor Machine Co. Noonan took a 2 percent discount.

5 Purchased supplies on credit terms of 1/10 n/30 from Chin Music Co., $264.

7 Paid delivery expense, issuing check no. 349 for $388.

10 Purchased inventory on account from W. A. Mozart, Inc., $1,681. Payment terms were net 30.

11 Returned the inventory to W. A. Mozart, Inc. It was defective. We issued a debit memo and mailed a copy to Mozart.

15 Issued check no. 350 for a cash purchase of inventory, $2,889.

15 Paid semimonthly payroll with check no. 351, $1,595.

Nov. 19 Issued check no. 352 to pay our account payable to Chin Music Co. from November 5.

21 Purchased inventory on credit terms of 2/10 n/30 from Arbor Machine Co., $3,250.

24 Purchased machinery on credit terms of 2/10 n/30 from ENTEL Corp., $1,558.

26 Purchased supplies on account from W. A. Mozart, Inc., $309. Terms were net 30.

29 Issued check no. 353 to Arbor Machine Co., paying the net amount owed from November 21.

30 Paid semimonthly payroll with check no. 354, $1,595.

The general ledger of Noonan Company includes the following accounts and balances at November 1:

Account Number	Account Title	Balance	Account Number	Account Title	Balance
111	Cash	$17,674	511	Purchases	
115	Prepaid Rent	800	512	Purchase Discounts	
116	Supplies.	884	513	Purchase Returns and Allowances . .	
151	Machinery	33,600			
211	Accounts Payable . .	3,750	521	Salary Expense	
			551	Delivery Expense . .	

Noonan's accounts payable subsidiary ledger includes the following balances at November 1: Arbor Machine Co., $650; Chin Music Co., -0-; ENTEL Corp., $3,100; and W. A. Mozart, Inc., -0-.

Required

1. Open the general ledger and the accounts payable subsidiary ledger accounts given, inserting their balances at November 1.
2. Record the above transactions on page 3 of a purchases journal, page 8 of a cash disbursements journal, and page 12 of a general journal, as appropriate. Noonan records purchase returns in the general journal.
3. Post daily to the accounts payable subsidiary ledger. Post to the general ledger on November 30.
4. Total each column of the special journals. Show that the total debits equal the total credits in each special journal.
5. Balance the total of the creditor account balances in the accounts payable subsidiary ledger against the balance of the Accounts Payable control account in the general ledger.

Problem 6-7B *Using all the journals, posting, and balancing the ledgers*
(L.O. 2,3,4,5,6,7)

Van Tright Sales Company had these transactions during January:

Jan. 2 Issued invoice no. 191 for sale on account to L. E. Wooten, $2,350.

3 Purchased inventory on credit terms of 3/10 n/60 from Delwood Plaza, $1,900.

4 Sold inventory for cash, $808.

5 Issued check no. 473 to purchase furniture for cash, $1,087.

8 Collected interest revenue of $440.

Jan. 9 Issued invoice no. 192 for sale on account to Cortez Co., $6,250.

10 Purchased inventory for cash, $776, issuing check no. 474.

12 Received cash from L. E. Wooten in full settlement of her account receivable, net of a 2 percent discount, from the sale of January 2.

13 Issued check no. 475 to pay Delwood Plaza net amount owed from January 3.

13 Purchased supplies on account from Havrilla Corp., $689. Terms were net end-of-month.

15 Sold inventory on account to J. R. Wakeland, issuing invoice no. 193 for $743.

17 Issued credit memo to J. R. Wakeland for $743 for defective merchandise returned to us by Wakeland.

18 Issued invoice no. 194 for credit sale to L. E. Wooten, $1,825.

19 Received cash from Cortez Co. in full settlement of its account receivable from January 9.

20 Purchased inventory on credit terms of net 30 from Jasper Sales, $2,150.

22 Purchased furniture on credit terms of 3/10 n/60 from Delwood Plaza, $775.

22 Issued check no. 476 to pay for insurance coverage, debiting Prepaid Insurance for $1,345.

24 Sold supplies to an employee for cash of $86, which was Van Tright's cost.

25 Issued check no. 477 to pay utilities, $388.

28 Purchased inventory on credit terms of 2/10 n/30 from Havrilla Corp., $421.

29 Returned damaged inventory to Havrilla Corp., issuing a debit memo for $421.

29 Sold goods on account to Cortez Co., issuing invoice no. 195 for $567.

30 Issued check no. 478 to pay Havrilla Corp. on account from January 13.

31 Received cash on account from L. E. Wooten on credit sale of January 18.

31 Issued check no. 479 to pay monthly salaries, $3,200.

Required

1. Open the following general ledger accounts using the account numbers given:

Cash	111	Sales Returns and Allowances	413
Accounts Receivable	112	Interest Revenue	419
Supplies	116	Purchases	511
Prepaid Insurance	117	Purchase Discounts	512
Furniture	151	Purchase Returns	
Accounts Payable	211	and Allowances	513
Sales Revenue	411	Salary Expense	531
Sales Discounts	412	Utilities Expense	541

2. Open these accounts receivable subsidiary ledgers.
   Accounts receivable subsidiary ledger: Cortez Co., J. R. Wakeland, and L. E. Wooten.
   Accounts payable subsidiary ledger: Delwood Plaza, Havrilla Corp., and Jasper Sales.

3. Enter the transactions in a sales journal (page 8), a cash receipts journal (page 3), a purchase journal (page 6), a cash disbursements journal (page 9), and a general journal (page 4), as appropriate.
4. Post daily to the accounts receivable subsidiary ledger and to the accounts payable subsidiary ledger. On January 31 post to the general ledger.
5. Total each column of the special journals. Show that the total debits equal the total credits in each special journal.
6. Balance the total of the customer account balances in the accounts receivable subsidiary ledger against Accounts Receivable in the general ledger. Do the same for the accounts payable subsidiary ledger and Accounts Payable in the general ledger.

Problem 6-8B   *Identifying the characteristics of an effective internal control system (L.O. 8)*

An employee of McNemar Aircraft Service Company recently stole thousands of dollars of the company's cash. The company has decided to install a new system of internal controls.

Required

As controller of McNemar Aircraft Service Company, write a memo to the president explaining how the separation of duties helps safeguard assets.

Problem 6-9B   *Identifying internal control weaknesses   (L.O. 8)*

Each of the following situations has an internal control weakness:

a. Discount stores such as Walmart and Meier's receive a large portion of their sales revenue in cash, with the remainder in credit-card sales. To reduce expenses, a store manager ceases purchasing fidelity bonds on the cashiers.

b. The office supply company from which Toland Sporting Goods purchases cash receipt forms recently notified Toland that the last shipped receipts were not prenumbered. Dick Toland, the owner, replied that he did not use the receipt numbers, so the omission is not important.

c. Lancer Computer Programs is a software company that specializes in computer programs with accounting applications. Their most popular program prepares the general journal, cash receipts journal, purchases journal, cash disbursements journal, accounts receivable subsidiary ledger, and general ledger. In the company's early days, the manager and eight employees wrote the computer programs, lined up manufacturers to produce the diskettes, sold the products to stores such as ComputerLand and ComputerCraft, and performed the general management and accounting of the company. As the company has grown, the number of employees has increased dramatically. Recently, the development of a new software program stopped while the programmers redesigned Lancer's accounting system. Lancer's own accountants could have performed this task.

d. Myra Jones, a widow with no known sources of outside income, has been a trusted employee of Stone Products Company for 15 years. She performs all cash handling and accounting duties, including opening the mail, preparing the bank deposit, accounting for all aspects of cash and accounts receivable, and preparing the bank reconciliation. She has just purchased a new Cadillac and a new home in an expensive suburb. Lou Stone, the owner of the company, wonders how she can afford these luxuries on her salary.

e. Linda Cyert employs three professional interior designers in her design studio. She is located in an area with a lot of new construction, and her business is booming. Ordinarily, Linda does all the purchasing of furniture, draperies, carpets, fabrics, sewing services, and other materials and labor needed to complete jobs. During the summer she takes a long vacation, and in her absence she allows each designer to purchase materials and labor. At her return, Cyert reviews operations and notes that expenses are much higher and net income much lower than in the past.

Required

1. Identify the missing internal control characteristic in each situation.
2. Identify the business's possible problem.
3. Propose a solution to the problem.

Problem 6-10B *Identifying internal control weakness* **(L.O. 8)**

Appalachian Dental Supply makes all sales on credit. Cash receipts arrive by mail, usually within 30 days of the sale. Brad Stokes opens envelopes and separates the checks from the accompanying remittance advices. Stokes forwards the checks to another employee who makes the daily bank deposit but has no access to the accounting records. Stokes sends the remittance advices, which show the amount of cash received, to the accounting department for entry in the accounts. Stokes's only other duty is to grant sales allowances to customers. When he receives a customer check for less than the full amount of the invoice, he records the sales allowance and forwards the document to the accounting department.

Required

You are the outside auditor of Appalachian Dental Supply. Write a memo to the company president to identify the internal control weakness in his situation. State how to correct the weakness.

Extending Your Knowledge

Decision Problems

1. Reconstructing Transactions from Amounts Posted to the Accounts Receivable Ledger (L.O. 2,3,4)

A fire destroyed some accounting records of Roemer Company. General Manager Charles Zhang asks for your help in reconstructing the records. *He needs to know the beginning and ending balances of Accounts Receivable and the credit sales and cash receipts on account from customers during March.* All Roemer Company's sales are on credit, with payment terms of 2/10 n/30. All cash receipts on account reached Roemer within the 10-day discount period, except as noted. The only accounting record preserved from the fire is the accounts receivable subsidiary ledger, which follows.

Grant Adams

Date	Item	Jrnl. Ref.	Debit	Credit	Balance
Mar. 8		S.6	2,178		2,178
16		S.6	903		3,081
18		CR.8		2,178	903
19		J.5		221	682
27		CR.8		682	-0-

Lou Gross

Date	Item	Jrnl. Ref.	Debit	Credit	Balance
Mar. 1	Balance				1,096
5		CR.8		1,096	-0-
11		S.6	396		396
21		CR.8		396	-0-
24		S.6	1,944		1,944

Norris Associates

Date	Item	Jrnl. Ref.	Debit	Credit	Balance
Mar. 1	Balance				883
15		S.6	2,635		3,518
29		CR.8		883*	2,635

*Cash receipt did not occur within the discount period.

Suzuki, Inc.

Date	Item	Jrnl. Ref.	Debit	Credit	Balance
Mar. 1	Balance				440
3		CR.8		440	-0-
25		S.6	3,655		3,655
29		S.6	1,123		4,778

2. Understanding an Accounting System   (L.O. 1,3,6)

The external auditor must ensure that the amounts shown on the balance sheet for Accounts Receivable represent actual amounts that customers owe the company. Each customer account in the accounts receivable subsidiary ledger must represent an actual credit sale to the person indicated, and the customer's balance must not have been collected. This auditing concept is called *validity* or *validating the accounts receivable.*

The auditor must also ensure that all amounts that the company owes are included in Accounts Payable and other liability accounts. For example, all credit purchases of inventory made by the company—and not yet paid—should be included in the balance of the Accounts Payable account. This auditing concept is called *completeness.*

Required

Suggest how an auditor might test a customer's account receivable balance for validity. Indicate how the auditor might test the balance of the Accounts Payable account for completeness.

Ethical Issue

On a recent trip to the Soviet Union, Randolph Buchholz, sales manager of Microelectronic Devices, took his wife at company expense. Melanie Johnson, vice-president of sales and Mr. Buchholz's boss, thought his travel and entertainment expenses looked excessive. However, Ms. Johnson approved the reimbursement because she owed Mr. Buchholz a favor. Ms. Johnson, well aware that the company president routinely reviews all expenses recorded in the cash disbursements journal, had the accountant record Mrs. Buchholz's expenses in the general journal as follows:

Sales Promotion Expense	3,500	
Cash		3,500

Required

1. Does recording the transaction in the general journal rather than in the cash disbursements journal affect the amounts of cash and total expenses reported in the financial statements?
2. Why did Ms. Johnson want this transaction recorded in the general journal?
3. What is the ethical issue in this situation? What role does accounting play in the ethical issue?

Chapter 7

Cash and Receivables

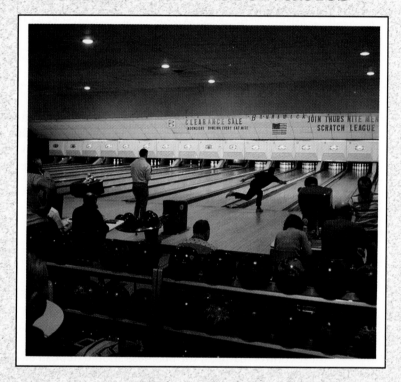

The U.S. bowling boom peaked three decades ago. But for Bowl America's Eddie Goldberg and his son, Les, business has never been better.

Bowl America's roots go back to an energetic young man named Edward Goldberg. During the Depression, Goldberg ran a luncheonette in Baltimore. In 1940 he and three backers put up $30,000 to open a bowling alley in Clarendon, Va., a few miles outside Washington.

Having weathered the *cash* crunch of the early Sixties, Bowl America has since chosen to steer clear of leverage [debt]. The company has less than $100,000 in long-term debt, and over $12 million . . . in *cash* and securities. Expansion, says Goldberg, will be paid for out of *cash flow*. This conservative approach has served Bowl America's investors well. [Emphasis added]

Source: Fleming Meeks, "Bowling for Dollars," *Forbes*, March 19, 1990, pp. 112, 114. Used with permission of Forbes, Inc.

Among all the receivables, payables, inventory, and plant assets, it is easy to lose sight of the basics of running a business. Cash is the most scarce asset, and having enough of it to weather hard times and expand is the secret of Bowl America's success and the success of most other companies. The first half of this chapter shows how to account for cash, with particular emphasis given to internal control over this most liquid of all assets. The second half of the chapter covers accounts and notes receivable.

The Bank Account as a Control Device

How does a business protect its cash and other assets? With a system of internal control. Keeping cash in a *bank account* is part of internal control because banks have established practices for safeguarding cash. Banks also provide depositors with detailed records of cash transactions. To take full advantage of these control features, the business should deposit all cash receipts in the bank account and make all cash payments through it (except petty cash disbursements, which we cover later). We now discuss banking records and documents.

For many businesses, cash is the most important asset. After all, cash is the most common means of exchange, and most transactions ultimately affect cash. Cash is the most tempting asset for theft. Consequently, internal controls for cash are more elaborate than for most other assets. We consider cash to be not just paper money and coins but also checks, money orders, and money kept in bank accounts. Cash includes neither stamps, because they are supplies, nor IOUs payable to the business, because they are receivables.

The documents used to control a bank account include the signature card, the deposit ticket, the check, the bank statement, and the bank reconciliation.

Signature Card.   Banks require each person authorized to transact business through an account in that bank to sign a signature card. The bank compares the signatures on documents against the *signature card* to protect the bank and the depositor against forgery.

Deposit Ticket.   Banks supply standard forms as *deposit tickets*. The customer fills in the dollar amount and the date of deposit. The customer retains either (1) a duplicate copy of the deposit ticket or (2) a deposit receipt, depending on the bank's practice, as proof of the transaction.

Check. To draw money from an account, the depositor writes a **check**, which is the document that instructs the bank to pay the designated person or business the specified amount of money. There are three parties to a check: the *maker*, who signs the check; the *payee*, to whose order the check is drawn; and the *bank* on which the check is drawn.

Most checks are serially numbered and preprinted with the name and address of the depositor and the bank. The checks have places for the date, the name of the payee, the signature of the maker, and the amount. The bank name and bank identification number and the depositor account number are usually imprinted in magnetic ink for machine processing.

Exhibit 7-1 shows a check drawn on the bank account of Business Research, Inc. The check has two parts, the check itself and the remittance advice. The *remittance advice*, an optional attachment, tells the payee the reason for the payment. The maker (Business Research) retains a carbon copy of the check for its recording in the check register (cash disbursements journal). Note that internal controls at Business Research require two signatures on checks.

Bank Statement. Most banks send monthly **bank statements** to their depositors. The statement shows the account's beginning and ending balance for the period and lists the month's transactions. Included with the statement are the maker's *canceled checks,* those checks that have been paid by the bank on behalf of the depositor. The bank statement also lists any other deposits and changes in the account. Deposits appear in chronological order, checks in a logical order, along with the date each check cleared the bank.

Exhibit 7-2 is the bank statement of Business Research, Inc., for the month ended January 31, 19X6. At many banks, some depositors receive their state-

EXHIBIT 7-1 *Check with Remittance Advice*

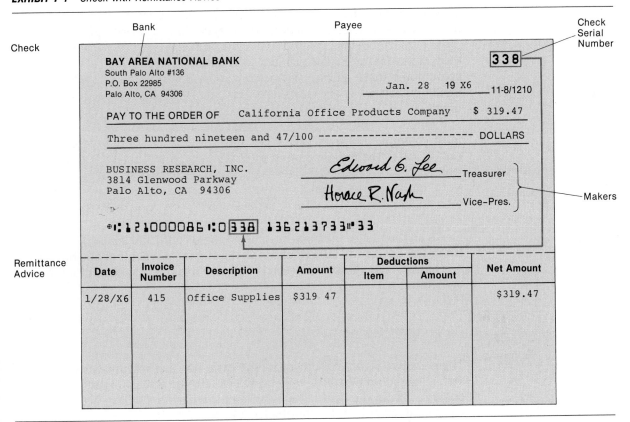

EXHIBIT 7-2 *Bank Statement*

BAY AREA NATIONAL BANK
South Palo Alto #136
P.O. Box 22985
Palo Alto, CA   94306

ACCOUNT STATEMENT

Business Research, Inc.
3814 Glenwood Parkway
Palo Alto, CA   94306

CHECKING ACCOUNT 136-213733

CHECKING ACCOUNT SUMMARY AS OF 01-31-X6

BEGINNING BALANCE	TOTAL DEPOSITS	TOTAL WITHDRAWALS	SERVICE CHARGES	ENDING BALANCE
6556.12	3448.61	4602.00	14.25	5388.48

──────── CHECKING ACCOUNT TRANSACTIONS ────────

DEPOSITS

DEPOSIT	01-04	1000.00
DEPOSIT	01-04	112.00
DEPOSIT	01-08	194.60
BANK COLLECTION	01-26	2114.00
INTEREST	01-31	28.01

CHARGES

SERVICE CHARGE	01-31	14.25

CHECKS:

CHECKS			CHECKS			BALANCES	
NUMBER	DATE	AMOUNT	NUMBER	DATE	AMOUNT	DATE	BALANCE
332	01-12	3000.00	334	01-10	100.00	12-31	6556.12
656	01-06	100.00	335	01-06	100.00	01-04	7616.12
333	01-12	150.00	336	01-31	1100.00	01-06	7416.12
						01-08	7610.72
						01-12	4360.72
						01-26	6474.12
						01-31	5388.48

OTHER CHARGES		DATE	AMOUNT
NSF		01-04	52.00

MONTHLY SUMMARY

7 WITHDRAWALS	4360 MINIMUM BALANCE	5812 AVERAGE BALANCE

ments on the first of the month, some on the second, and so on. This spacing eliminates the clerical burden of supplying all the statements at one time. Most businesses—like Business Research—receive their bank statement for the calendar month.

Bank Reconciliation

There are two records of the business's cash: its Cash account in its own general ledger and the bank statement, which tells the actual amount of cash the business has in the bank. The balance in the business's Cash account rarely equals the balance shown on the bank statement.

The books and the bank statement may show different amounts, but both be correct. The difference arises because of a time lag in recording certain transactions. When a firm writes a check, it immediately credits its Cash account. The bank, however, will not subtract the amount of the check until the check reaches it for payment. This may take days, even weeks if the payee waits to cash the check. Likewise, the business debits Cash for all cash receipts, and it may take a day or so for the bank to add this amount to the business's bank balance.

Good internal control means knowing where a company's money comes from, how it is spent, and the current cash balance. How else can the accountant keep the accurate records management needs to make informed decisions? The accountant must report the correct cash amount on the balance sheet. To ensure accuracy the accountant explains the reasons for the difference between the firm's records and the bank statement figures on a certain date. This process is called the **bank reconciliation.** Properly done, the bank reconciliation assures that all cash transactions have been accounted for and that the bank and book records of cash are correct.

Common items that cause differences between the bank balance and the book balance are

1. Items recorded by the company but not yet recorded by the *bank:*
   a. **Deposits in transit** (outstanding deposits). The company has recorded these deposits but the bank has not.
   b. **Outstanding checks.** These checks have been issued by the company and recorded on its books but have not yet been paid by its bank.

2. Items recorded by the bank but not yet recorded by the *company:*
   a. **Bank collections.** The bank sometimes collects money on behalf of depositors. Many businesses have their customers pay directly to the company bank account. This practice, called a lock-box system, reduces the possibility of theft and also places the business's cash in circulation faster than if the cash had to be collected and deposited by company personnel. An example is a bank's collecting cash on a note receivable and the related interest revenue for the depositor. The bank may notify the depositor of these bank collections on the bank statement.
   b. **Service charge.** This amount is the bank's fee for processing the depositor's transactions. Banks commonly base the service charge on the balance in the account. The depositor learns the amount of the service charge from the bank statement.
   c. *Interest revenue on checking account.* Many banks pay interest to depositors who keep a large enough balance of cash in the account. This is generally the case with business checking accounts. The bank notifies the depositor of this interest on the bank statement.
   d. **NSF (nonsufficient funds) checks** received from customers. To understand how to handle NSF checks, also called hot checks, you first need to know the route a check takes. The maker writes the check, credits Cash to record the payment on the books, and gives the check to the payee. On receiving the check, the payee debits Cash on his or her books and deposits the check in the bank. The payee's bank immediately adds the receipt amount to the payee's bank balance on the assumption that the check is good. The check is returned to the maker's bank, which then deducts the check amount from the maker's bank balance. If the maker's bank balance is insufficient to pay the check, the maker's bank refuses to pay the check, reverses this deduction, and sends an NSF notice back to the payee's bank. The payee bank subtracts the receipt amount from the payee's bank balance and notifies the

payee of this action. This process may take from three to seven days. The company may learn of NSF checks through the bank statement, which lists the NSF check as a charge (subtraction), as shown near the bottom of Exhibit 7-2.

   e. *Checks collected, deposited, and returned to payee by the bank for reasons other than NSF.* Banks return checks to the payee if (1) the maker's account has closed, (2) the date is stale (some checks state "void after 30 days"), (3) the signature is not authorized, (4) the check has been altered, or (5) the check form is improper. Accounting for all returned checks is the same as for NSF checks.

   f. *The cost of printed checks.* This charge against the company's bank account balance is handled like a service charge.

3. Errors by either the company or the bank. For example, a bank may improperly charge (decrease) the bank balance of Business Research, Inc., for a check drawn by another company, perhaps Business Research Associates. Or a company may miscompute its bank balance on its own books. Computational errors are becoming less frequent with widespread use of computers. Nevertheless, all errors must be corrected, and the corrections will be a part of the bank reconciliation.

Steps in Preparing the Bank Reconciliation

The steps in preparing the bank reconciliation are

1. Start with two figures, the balance shown on the bank statement (*balance per bank*) and the balance in the company's Cash account (*balance per books*), as in Exhibit 7-3, Panel B. These two amounts will probably disagree because of the timing differences discussed earlier.

OBJECTIVE 1

Prepare a bank reconciliation and related journal entries

2. Add to, or subtract from, the *bank* balance those items that appear on the books but not on the bank statement:

   a. Add *deposits in transit* to the bank balance. Deposits in transit are identified by comparing the deposits listed on the bank statement to the company list of cash receipts. They show up as cash receipts on the books but not as deposits on the bank statement. As a control measure, the accountant should also ensure that deposits in transit from the preceding month appear on the current month's bank statement. If they do not, the deposits may be lost.

   b. Subtract *outstanding* checks from the bank balance. Outstanding checks are identified by comparing the canceled checks returned with the bank statement to the company list of checks in the cash disbursements journal. They show up as cash payments on the books but not as paid checks on the bank statement. This comparison also verifies that all checks paid by the bank were valid company checks and were correctly recorded by the bank and by the company. Outstanding checks are usually the most numerous items on a bank reconciliation.

3. Add to, or subtract from, the *book* balance those items that appear on the bank statement but not on the company books:

   a. Add to the book balance (a) *bank collections* and (b) any *interest revenue* earned on the money in the bank. These items are identified by comparing the deposits listed on the bank statement to the company list of cash receipts. They show up as cash receipts on the bank statement but not on the books.

   b. Subtract from the book balance (a) *service charges,* (b) *cost of printed checks,* and (c) *other bank charges* (for example, charges for NSF or stale

EXHIBIT 7-3 *Bank Reconciliation*

Panel A—Reconciling Items:

1. Deposit in transit, $1,591.63.
2. Bank error; add $100 to bank balance.
3. Outstanding checks: no. 337, $286; no. 338, $319.47; no. 339, $83; no. 340, $203.14; no. 341, $458.53.

4. Bank collection, $2,114, including interest revenue of $214.
5. Interest earned on bank balance, $28.01.
6. Book error; add $360 to book balance.
7. Bank service charge, $14.25.
8. NSF check from L. Ross, $52.

Panel B—Bank Reconciliation:

Business Research, Inc.
Bank Reconciliation
January 31, 19X6

Bank:			Books:		
Balance, January 31		$5,388.48	Balance, January 31		$3,294.21
Add:			Add:		
1. Deposit of January 30 in transit		1,591.63	4. Bank collection of note receivable, including interest revenue of $214		2,114.00
2. Correction of bank error—Business Research Associates check erroneously charged against company account		100.00	5. Interest revenue earned on bank balance		28.01
		7,080.11	6. Correction of book error—Overstated amount of check no. 333		360.00
3. Less outstanding checks:					5,796.22
No. 337	$286.00		Less:		
No. 338	319.47		7. Service charge	$14.25	
No. 339	83.00		8. NSF check	52.00	(66.25)
No. 340	203.14				
No. 341	458.53	(1,350.14)			
Adjusted bank balance		$5,729.97	Adjusted book balance		$5,729.97

date checks). These items are identified by comparing the other charges listed on the bank statement to the cash disbursements recorded on the company books. They show up as subtractions on the bank statement but not as cash payments on the books.

4. Compute the *adjusted bank balance* and the *adjusted book balance*. The two adjusted balances should be equal.
5. Journalize each item in 3, that is, each item listed on the book portion of the bank reconciliation. These items must be recorded on the company books because they affect cash.
6. Correct all book errors and notify the bank of any errors it has made.

Bank Reconciliation Illustrated

The bank statement in Exhibit 7-2 indicates that the January 31 bank balance of Business Research, Inc., is $5,388.48. However, the company's Cash account has a balance of $3,294.21. In following the steps outlined above, the accountant finds these reconciling items:

1. The January 30 deposit of $1,591.63 does not appear on the bank statement.

2. The bank erroneously charged a $100 check—number 656—written by Business Research Associates against the Business Research, Inc., account.

3. Five company checks issued late in January and recorded in the cash disbursements journal have not been paid by the bank:

Check No.	Date	Amount
337	Jan. 27	$286.00
338	28	319.47
339	28	83.00
340	29	203.14
341	30	458.53

4. The bank collected on behalf of the company a note receivable, $2,114 (including interest revenue of $214). This cash receipt has not been recorded in the cash receipts journal.

5. The bank statement shows interest revenue of $28.01 that the bank has paid the company on its cash balance.

6. Check number 333 for $150 paid to Brown Company on account was recorded in the cash disbursements journal as a $510 amount, creating a $360 understatement of the Cash balance per books.

7. The bank service charge for the month was $14.25.

8. The bank statement shows an NSF check for $52, which was received from customer L. Ross.

Exhibit 7-3 is the bank reconciliation based on the above data. Panel A lists the reconciling items, which are keyed by number to the actual reconciliation in Panel B. Note that after the reconciliation, the adjusted bank balance equals the adjusted book balance. This equality is the accuracy check for the reconciliation.

Recording Entries from the Reconciliation

The bank reconciliation does not directly affect the journals or the ledgers. Like the work sheet, the reconciliation is an accountant's tool, separate from the company's books.

The bank reconciliation acts as a control device by signaling the company to record the transactions listed as reconciling items in the Books section because the company has not yet done so. For example, the bank collected the note receivable on behalf of the company, but the company has not yet recorded this cash receipt. In fact, the company learned of the cash receipt only when it received the bank statement.

Why does the company *not* need to record the reconciling items on the Bank side of the reconciliation? Those items have already been recorded on the company books.

Based on the reconciliation in Exhibit 7-3, Business Research, Inc., makes these entries. They are dated January 31 to bring the Cash account to the correct balance on that date:

Jan. 31	Cash	2,114.00	
	Notes Receivable		1,900.00
	Interest Revenue		214.00
	Note receivable collected by bank.		

Jan. 31	Cash	28.01	
	Interest Revenue		28.01
	Interest earned on bank balance.		

31	Cash	360.00	
	Accounts Payable—Brown Co.		360.00
	Correction of check register, check no. 333.		

31	Miscellaneous Expense	14.25	
	Cash		14.25
	Bank service charge.		

Note: Miscellaneous Expense is debited for the bank service charge because the service charge pertains to no particular expense category.

31	Accounts Receivable—L. Ross	52.00	
	Cash		52.00
	NSF check returned by bank.		

These entries bring the business's books up to date.

The entry for the NSF check needs explanation. Upon learning that L. Ross's $52 check was not good, Business Research credits Cash to bring the Cash account up-to-date. Since Business Research still has a receivable from Ross, it debits Accounts Receivable—L. Ross and pursues collection from him.

Reporting Cash

Cash is the first current asset listed on the balance sheet of most companies. Even small businesses have several bank accounts and one or more petty cash funds that are kept on hand for making small disbursements. However, companies usually combine all cash amounts into a single total for reporting on the balance sheet. They also include liquid assets like time deposits and certificates of deposit. These are interest-bearing accounts that can be withdrawn with no penalty after a short period of time. Although they are slightly less liquid than cash, they are sufficiently similar to be reported along with cash. For example, the balance sheet of Kraft, Inc., maker of Miracle Whip, Philadelphia Cream Cheese, Duracell batteries, and other well-known products, recently reported (in millions of dollars):

Assets:

Cash, time deposits, and certificates of deposit	$ 194.1
Temporary investments.....................	127.6
Accounts and notes receivable	941.7
Inventories	1,211.3
Total current assets	$2,474.7

It is important to perform the bank reconciliation on the balance sheet date in order to be assured of reporting the correct amount of cash.

Internal Control over Cash Receipts

Internal control over cash receipts ensures that all cash receipts are deposited in the bank and the company's accounting record is correct. Many businesses receive cash over the counter and through the mail. Each source of cash receipts calls for *security measures*.

The cash register offers management control over cash received in a store. First, the machine should be positioned so that customers can see the amounts the cashier enters into the register. No person willingly pays more than the marked price for an item, so the customer helps prevent the sales clerk from overcharging and pocketing the excess over actual prices. Also, company policy should require issuance of a receipt to make sure each sale is recorded in the register.

Second, the register's cash drawer opens only when the sales clerk enters an amount on the keys, and a roll of tape locked inside the machine records each amount. At the end of the day, a manager proves the cash by comparing the total amount in the cash drawer against the tape's total. This step helps prevent outright theft by the clerk. For security reasons, the clerk should not have access to the tape.

Third, pricing merchandise at "uneven" amounts—say, $3.95 instead of $4.00—means that the clerk generally must make change, which in turn means having to get into the cash drawer. This requires entering the amount of the sale on the keys and so onto the register tape.

At the end of the day, the cashier or other employee with cash-handling duties deposits the cash in the bank. The tape goes to the accounting department as the basis for an entry in the cash receipts journal. These security measures, coupled with periodic on-site inspection by a manager, discourage fraud.

All incoming mail should be opened by a mail-room employee. This person should compare the actual enclosed amount of cash or check with the attached remittance advice. If no advice was sent, the mail-room employee should prepare one and enter the amount of each receipt on a control tape. At the end of the day, this control tape is given to a responsible official, such as the controller, for verification. Cash receipts should be given to the cashier, who combines them with any cash received over the counter and prepares the bank deposit.

Having a mail-room employee be the first to handle postal cash receipts is just another application of a good internal control procedure—in this case, separation of duties. If the accountants opened postal cash receipts, they could easily hide a theft.

The mail-room employee forwards the remittance advices to the accounting department. They provide the data for entries in the cash receipts journal and postings to customers' accounts in the accounts receivable ledger. As a final step, the controller compares the three records of the day's cash receipts: (1) the control tape total from the mail room, (2) the bank deposit amount from the cashier, and (3) the debit to Cash from the accounting department.

An added measure used to control cash receipts is a *fidelity bond*, which is an insurance policy that the business buys to guard against theft. The fidelity bond helps in two ways. First, the insurance company that issues the policy investigates the backgrounds of the workers whose activities will be covered, such as the mail-room employees who handle incoming cash and the employees who handle inventory. Second, if the company suffers a loss due to the misconduct of a covered employee, the insurance company reimburses the business.

Cash Short and Over. A difference often exists between actual cash receipts and the day's record of cash received. Usually the difference is small and results from honest errors. Suppose the cash register tapes of a large department store indicate sales revenue of $25,000, but the cash received is $24,980. To record the day's sales, the store would make this entry:

Cash	24,980	
Cash Short and Over	20	
Sales Revenue		25,000
Daily cash sales.		

As the entry shows, Cash Short and Over is debited when sales revenue exceeds cash receipts. This account is credited when cash receipts exceed sales. A debit balance in the Cash Short and Over account appears on the income statement as Miscellaneous Expense, a credit balance as Other Revenue.

This account's balance should be small. The debits and credits for cash over and short collected over an accounting period tend to cancel each other out. A large balance signals the accountant to investigate. For example, too large a debit balance may mean an employee is stealing. Cash Short and Over, then, acts as an internal control device.

Internal Control Over Cash Disbursements

Payment by *check* is an important control over cash disbursements. First, the check acts as a source document. Second, to be valid the check must be signed by an authorized official, so each payment by check draws the attention of management. Before signing the check, the manager should study the invoice, the receiving report, the purchase order, and other supporting documents. (A discussion of these documents follows.) As further security and control over cash disbursements, many firms require two signatures on a check, as we saw in Exhibit 7-1. To avoid document alteration, some firms also use machines that indelibly stamp the amount on the check.

In very small businesses, the proprietor or partners may control cash disbursements by reviewing the supporting documents themselves and personally writing all checks. However, in larger businesses this is impractical, so the duties of approving invoices for payment and writing checks are performed by authorized employees. Strong internal control is achieved through clear-cut assignment of responsibility, proper authorization, and separation of duties.

Petty Cash Disbursements

It would be uneconomical for a business to write a separate check for an executive's taxi fare, a box of pencils needed right away, or the delivery of a special message across town. Therefore, companies keep a small amount of cash on hand to pay for such minor amounts. This fund is called **petty cash.**

Even though the individual amounts paid through the petty cash fund may be small, such expenses occur so often that the total amount over an accounting period may grow quite large. Thus the business needs to set up these controls over petty cash: (1) designate an employee to administer the fund as its custodian, (2) keep a specific amount of cash on hand, (3) support all fund disbursements with a petty cash ticket, and (4) replenish the fund through normal cash disbursement procedures.

OBJECTIVE 3
Account for petty cash transactions

To open the petty cash fund, a payment is approved for a predetermined amount and a check for this amount is issued to Petty Cash. Assume that on February 28 the business decides to establish a petty cash fund of $200. The custodian cashes the check and places the currency and coin in the fund, which may be a cash box, safe, or other device. The petty cash custodian is assigned the responsibility for controlling the fund. Starting the fund is recorded as follows:

Feb. 28	Petty Cash	200	
	Cash in Bank		200
	To open the petty cash fund.		

For each petty cash disbursement, the custodian prepares a *petty cash ticket* like the one illustrated in Exhibit 7-4.

Observe the signatures (or initials, for the custodian) that identify the recipient of petty cash and the fund custodian. Requiring both signatures reduces unauthorized cash disbursements. The custodian keeps all the petty cash tickets in the fund. The sum of the cash plus the total of the ticket amounts should equal the opening balance at all times—in this case, $200. Also, the Petty Cash account keeps its prescribed $200 balance at all times. Maintaining the Petty Cash account at this balance, supported by the fund (cash plus tickets totaling the same amount), is a characteristic of an imprest system. The control feature of an **imprest system** is that it clearly identifies the amount that the custodian is responsible for.

Disbursements reduce the amount of cash in the fund, so periodically the fund must be replenished. Suppose that on March 31 the fund has $118 in cash and $82 in tickets. A check for $82 is issued, made payable to Petty Cash. The fund custodian cashes this check for currency and coins and puts the money in the fund to return its actual cash to $200. The petty cash tickets identify the accounts to be debited: Office Supplies for $23, Delivery Expense for $17, and Miscellaneous Selling Expense for $42. The entry to record replenishment of the fund is

Mar. 31	Office Supplies	23	
	Delivery Expense	17	
	Miscellaneous Selling Expense	42	
	Cash in Bank		82
	To replenish the petty cash fund.		

If this cash payment exceeds the sum of the tickets—that is, if the fund comes up short, Cash Short and Over is debited for the missing amount. If the

EXHIBIT 7-4 *Petty Cash Ticket*

Petty Cash Ticket

PETTY CASH TICKET	
Date Mar. 25, 19X4	**No.** 45
Amount $23.00	
For Box of floppy diskettes	
Debit Office Supplies, Acct. No. 145	
Received by *Lewis Wright*	**Fund Custodian** WAR

sum of the tickets exceeds the payment, Cash Short and Over is credited. Note that replenishing the fund does *not* affect the Petty Cash account. Petty Cash keeps its $200 balance at all times.

Whenever petty cash runs low, the fund is replenished. It *must* be replenished on the balance sheet date. Otherwise, the reported balance for Petty Cash will be overstated by the amount of the tickets in the fund. The income statement will understate the expenses listed on these tickets.

Petty Cash is debited only when starting the fund (see the February 28 entry) or changing its amount. In our illustration, suppose the business decides to raise the fund amount from $200 to $250 because of increased demand for petty cash. This step would require a $50 debit to Petty Cash.

Summary Problem for Your Review

1. The Cash account of Bain Company at February 28, 19X3, follows.

Cash

Feb.	1	Balance 4,195	Feb.	3	400
	6	800		12	3,100
	15	1,800		19	1,100
	23	900		25	500
	28	2,400		27	900
Feb. 28		Balance 4,095			

2. Bain Company receives this bank statement on February 28, 19X3 (negative amounts appear in parentheses):

Bank Statement for February 19X3

Beginning balance		$4,195
Deposits:		
Feb. 7	$ 800	
15	1,800	
24	900	3,500
Checks (total per day):		
Feb. 8	$ 400	
16	3,100	
23	1,100	(4,600)
Other items:		
Service charge		(10)
NSF check from M. E. Crown		(700)
Bank collection of note receivable		
for the company		1,000*
Interest on account balance		15
Ending balance		$3,400

*Includes interest of $119.

Additional data:

Bain Company deposits all cash receipts in the bank and makes all cash disbursements by check.

Required:

1. Prepare the bank reconciliation of Bain Company at February 28, 19X3.
2. Record the entries based on the bank reconciliation.

SOLUTION TO REVIEW PROBLEM

Requirement 1

Bain Company
Bank Reconciliation
February 28, 19X3

Bank:

Balance, February 28, 19X3		$3,400
Add: Deposit of February 28 in transit.		2,400
		5,800
Less: Outstanding checks issued on Feb. 25		
($500) and Feb. 27 ($900)		(1,400)
Adjusted bank balance, February 28, 19X3		$4,400

Books:

Balance, February 28, 19X3		$4,095
Add: Bank collection of note receivable,		
including interest of $119		1,000
Interest earned on bank balance		15
		5,110
Less: Service charge	$ 10	
NSF check	700	(710)
Adjusted book balance, February 28, 19X3		$4,400

Requirement 2

Feb. 28	Cash		1,000	
	Note Receivable ($1,000 − $119)			881
	Interest Revenue			119
	Note receivable collected by bank.			
28	Cash		15	
	Interest Revenue			15
	Interest earned on bank balance.			
28	Miscellaneous Expense		10	
	Cash			10
	Bank service charge.			
28	Accounts receivable—M. E. Crown		700	
	Cash			700
	NSF check returned by bank.			

Accounts and Notes Receivable _____

From automobiles to houses to bicycles to dinners, people buy on credit every day. As high as annual credit sales for retailers are, credit sales are even higher for manufacturers and wholesalers. Clearly, credit sales lie at the heart of the United States economy, as they do in other developed countries.

Each credit transaction involves at least two parties—the **creditor,** who sells a service or merchandise and obtains a receivable, and the **debtor,** who makes the purchase and creates a payable. This section focuses on the creditor's accounting. The accounts that generally appear on a creditor's balance sheet are highlighted in Exhibit 7-5. We will discuss these accounts in our study of receivables.

Different Types of Receivables _____

A receivable arises when a business (or person) sells goods or services to a second business (or person) on credit. A receivable is the seller's claim against the buyer for the amount of the transaction.

Receivables are monetary claims against businesses and individuals. They are acquired mainly by selling goods and services and by lending money.

The two major types of receivables are accounts receivable and notes receivable. A business's *accounts receivable* are the amounts that its customers owe it.

EXHIBIT 7-5 *Balance Sheet*

Example Company **Balance Sheet** **Date**					
Assets			**Liabilities**		
Current:			Current:		
Cash		$X,XXX	Accounts payable		$X,XXX
Accounts receivable	**$X,XXX**		Notes payable, short-term		X,XXX
Less Allowance for			Accrued current liabilities		X,XXX
uncollectible accounts	**(XXX)**	X,XXX	Total current liabilities		X,XXX
Notes receivable, short-term		X,XXX			
Inventories		X,XXX			
Prepaid expenses		X,XXX			
Total		X,XXX	Long-term:		
			Notes payable, long-term		X,XXX
Investments and long-term receivables:			Total liabilities		X,XXX
Investments in other companies		X,XXX			
Notes receivable, long-term		X,XXX			
Other receivables		X,XXX			
Total		X,XXX	**Stockholders' Equity**		
Plant assets:			Stockholders' equity		X,XXX
Property, plant, and equipment		X,XXX	Total liabilities and		
Total assets		$X,XXX	stockholders' equity		$X,XXX

These accounts receivable are sometimes called *trade receivables*. They are current assets.

Accounts receivable should be distinguished from accruals, notes, and other assets not arising from everyday sales because accounts receivable pertain to the main thrust of the business's operations. Moreover, amounts included as accounts receivable should be collectible according to the business's normal receivables terms (such as net 30, or 2/10 n/30).

Notes receivable are more formal than accounts receivable. The debtor in a note receivable arrangement promises in writing to pay the creditor a definite sum at a definite future date. The terms of these notes usually extend for at least 60 days. A written document known as a *promissory note* serves as evidence of the receivable. A note may require the debtor to pledge *security* for the loan. This means that the borrower promises that the lender may claim certain assets if the borrower fails to pay the amount due at maturity.

Notes receivable due within one year or less are *current assets*. Those notes due beyond one year are *long-term assets*. Some notes receivable are collected in periodic installments. The portion due within one year is a current asset, with the remaining amount a long-term asset. GM may hold a $6,000 note receivable from you, but only the $1,500 you owe on it this year is a current asset to GM.

Other receivables is a miscellaneous category that includes loans to employees and branch companies. Usually these are long-term assets, but they are current if receivable within one year or less. Long-term notes receivable, and other receivables, are often reported on the balance sheet after current assets and before plant assets as shown in Exhibit 7-5.

Each type of receivable is a separate account in the general ledger and may be supported by a subsidiary ledger if needed.

The Credit Department

A customer who buys goods using a credit card is buying on account. This transaction creates a receivable for the store. Most companies with a high proportion of sales on account have a separate credit department. This department evaluates customers who apply for credit cards by using standard formulas—which include the applicant's income and credit history, among other factors—for deciding which customers the store will sell to on account. After approving a customer, the credit department monitors customer payment records. Customers with a history of paying on time may receive higher credit limits. Those who fail to pay on time have their limits reduced or eliminated. The credit department also assists the accounting department in measuring collection losses on customers who do not pay.

Uncollectible Accounts (Bad Debts)

Selling on credit creates both a benefit and a cost. Customers unwilling or unable immediately to pay cash may make a purchase on credit. Revenue and profit rise as sales increase. The cost to the seller of extending credit arises from the failure to collect from some credit customers. Accountants label this cost **uncollectible account expense, doubtful account expense,** or **bad debt expense.**

The extent of uncollectible account expense varies from company to company. It depends on the credit risks that managers are willing to accept. Many small retail businesses accept a higher level of risk than do large stores like Sears. Why? Small businesses often have personal ties to customers, which increases the likelihood that customers will pay their accounts.

Measuring Uncollectible Accounts

For a firm that sells on credit, uncollectible account expense is as much a part of doing business as salary expense and depreciation expense. Uncollectible Account Expense—an operating expense—must be measured, recorded, and reported. To do so, accountants use the allowance method or the direct write-off method.

Allowance Method. To present the most accurate financial statements possible, accountants in firms with large credit sales use the **allowance method** of measuring bad debts. This method records collection losses based on estimates prior to determine that the business will not collect from specific customers.

Smart managers know that not every customer will pay in full. But managers should not simply credit Accounts Receivable for the amount they believe will not be collected. That would cause the balance of Accounts Receivable to be less than the total of the individual accounts, and managers do not simply write off a customer's account on a hunch.

Rather than try to guess which accounts will go bad, managers, based on collection experience, estimate the total bad debt expense for the period. The business debits Uncollectible Account Expense (or Doubtful Account Expense) for the estimated amount and credits **Allowance for Uncollectible Accounts (or Allowance for Doubtful Accounts),** a contra account related to Accounts Receivable. This account shows the estimated amount of collection losses.

To properly match expense against revenue, the uncollectible account expense is estimated—based on past collection experience—and recorded when the sales are made. This expense entry has two effects: (1) it decreases net income by debiting an expense account, and (2) it decreases net accounts receivable by crediting the allowance account. (Allowance for Uncollectible Accounts, the contra account, is subtracted from Accounts Receivable to measure net accounts receivable.)

Assume the company's sales for 19X1 are $240,000 and that past collection experience suggests estimated bad debt expense of $3,100 for the year. The 19X1 journal entries are as follows, with accounts receivable from customers Rolf and Anderson separated for emphasis:

19X1	Accounts Receivable—Rolf	1,300	
	Accounts Receivable—Anderson	1,700	
	Accounts Receivable—Various Customers	237,000	
	Sales Revenue		240,000
	To record credit sales.		
19X1	Uncollectible Account Expense	3,100	
	Allowance for Uncollectible Accounts		3,100
	To record estimated bad debt expense, based on past collection experience.		

The account balances at December 31, 19X1, are as follows:

Accounts Receivable	Allowance for Uncollectible Accounts	Sales Revenue	Uncollectible Account Expense
240,000	3,100	240,000	3,100

Net accounts receivable
= $236,900

The 19X1 financial statements will report:

Income Statement:	19X1
Revenue:	
Sales revenue.....................................	$240,000
Expense:	
Uncollectible account expense.....................	3,100

Balance Sheet:	December 31, 19X1
Current assets:	
Accounts receivable	$240,000
Less: Allowance for uncollectible accounts.........	3,100
Net accounts receivable.........................	$236,900

Writing off Uncollectible Accounts

During 19X2 the company collects on most of the accounts receivable. How-ever, the credit department determines that customers Rolf and Anderson cannot pay the amounts they owe. The accountant writes off their receivables and makes the following entries:

19X2	Cash	235,000	
	Accounts Receivable—Various		
	Customers		235,000
	To record collections on account.		

19X2	Allowance for Uncollectible Accounts........	3,000	
	Accounts Receivable—Rolf		1,300
	Accounts Receivable—Anderson		1,700
	To write off uncollectible accounts.		

The write-off entry has no effect on net income because it includes no debit to an expense account. The entry also has no effect on *net* accounts receivable because both the Allowance account debited and the Accounts Receivable account credited are part of *net* accounts receivable. The account balances at December 31, 19X2, are as follows:

Accounts Receivable		Allowance for Uncollectible Accounts	
240,000	235,000	3,000	3,100
	1,300		
	1,700		100
2,000			

The financial statements for 19X1 and 19X2 will report the following. To highlight the matching of expense and revenue, we are assuming no sales are made in 19X2.

Income Statement:	19X1	19X2
Revenue:		
Sales revenue.............................	$240,000	$ 0
Expense:		
Uncollectible account expense.................	3,100	0

| | December 31, | |
Balance Sheet:	19X1	19X2
Current assets:		
Accounts receivable	$240,000	$ 2,000
Less: Allowance for uncollectible accounts......	3,100	100
Net accounts receivable......................	$236,900	$ 1,900

Bad Debt Write-Offs Rarely Equal the Allowance for Uncollectibles

Bad debt write-offs of customer accounts are actual amounts due from customers, but the allowance amount is based on estimates. Write-offs equal the allowance only if the estimate of bad debts is perfect—a rare occurrence. Usually the difference between write-offs and the allowance is small, as shown in the preceding example. If the allowance is too large for one period, the estimate of bad debts for the next period can be cut back. If the allowance is too low, an adjusting entry debiting Uncollectible Account Expense and crediting Allowance for Uncollectible Accounts can be made at the end of the period. This credit brings the Allowance account to a realistic balance. Estimating uncollectibles will be discussed shortly.

Recoveries of Uncollectible Accounts

When an account receivable is written off as uncollectible, the customer still has an obligation to pay. However, the likelihood of receiving cash is so low that the company ceases its collection effort and writes off the account. Such accounts are filed for use in future credit decisions. Some companies turn them over to an attorney for collection in the hope of recovering part of the receivable. To record a recovery, the accountant reverses the write-off and records the collection in the regular manner. The reversal of the write-off is needed to give the customer account receivable a debit balance.

Assume that the write-off of Rolf's account ($1,300) occurs in February 19X2. In August Rolf pays the account in full. The journal entries for this situation follow:

Feb. 19X2	To write off Rolf's account as uncollectible (same as above):		
	Allowance for Uncollectible Accounts	1,300	
	Accounts Receivable—Rolf..........		1,300
Aug. 19X2	To reinstate Rolf's account:		
	Accounts Receivable—Rolf	1,300	
	Allowance for Uncollectible Accounts		1,300

To record collection from Rolf:

Cash	1,300	
Accounts Receivable—Rolf		1,300

Estimating Uncollectibles

How are bad debt estimates made? The most logical way to estimate bad debts is to look at the business's past records. Both the percentage of sales method and the aging of accounts receivable method use the company's collection experience.

Percentage of Sales. A business may compute uncollectible account expense as a percentage of total credit sales (or total sales). Uncollectible account expense is recorded as an adjusting entry at the end of the period.

Basing its decision on figures from the last four periods, a business estimates that bad debt expense will be 2.5 percent of credit sales. If credit sales for 19X3 total $500,000, the adjusting entry to record bad debt expense for the year is

Adjusting Entries

Dec. 31	Uncollectible Account Expense ($500,000 × .025)	12,500	
	Allowance for Uncollectible Accounts ..		12,500

Under the percentage of sales method, the amount of this entry ignores the prior balance in Allowance for Uncollectible Accounts.

A business may change the percentage rate from year to year, depending on its collection experience. Suppose collections of accounts receivable in 19X4 are greater, and write-offs are less, than expected. The credit balance in Allowance for Uncollectible Accounts would be too large in relation to the debit balance of Accounts Receivable. How would the business change its bad debt percentage rate in this case? *Decreasing* the percentage rate would reduce the credit entry to the allowance account, and the allowance account balance would not grow too large.

New businesses, with no credit history on which to base their rates, may obtain estimated bad debt percentages from industry trade journals, government publications, and other sources of collection data.

Aging the Accounts. The second popular method of estimating bad debts is called **aging the accounts.** In this approach, individual accounts receivable are analyzed according to the length of time that they have been receivable from the customer. Performed manually, this is time-consuming. Computers greatly ease the burden. Schmidt Home Builders groups its accounts receivable into 30-day periods, as the accompanying table shows.

Schmidt bases the percentage figures on the company's collection experience. In the past, the business has collected all but 0.1 percent of accounts aged from 1 to 30 days, all but 1 percent of accounts aged 31 to 60 days, and so on.

The total amount receivable in each age group is multiplied by the appropriate percentage figure. For example, the $69,000 in accounts aged 1 to 30 days is multiplied by 0.1 percent (.001), which comes to $69. The total balance needed in the Allowance for Uncollectible Accounts—$3,769—is the sum of the amounts computed for the various groups ($69 + $250 + $750 + $2,700).

Customer Name	Age of Account				
	1–30 Days	31–60 Days	61–90 Days	Over 90 Days	Total Balance
Oxwall Tools Co. . . .	$20,000				$ 20,000
Chicago Pneumatic Parts.	10,000				10,000
Sarasota Pipe Corp. .		$13,000	$10,000		23,000
Seal Coatings, Inc. . .			3,000	$1,000	4,000
Other accounts*	39,000	12,000	2,000	2,000	55,000
Totals.	$69,000	$25,000	$15,000	$3,000	$112,000
Estimated percentage uncollectible	0.1%	1%	5%	90%	
Allowance for Uncollectible Accounts.	$69	$250	$750	$2,700	$3,769

* Each of the "Other accounts" would appear individually.

Suppose the Allowance account has a $2,100 credit balance from the previous period:

Allowance for Uncollectible Accounts

	Unadjusted balance 2,100

Under the aging method, the adjusting entry is designed to adjust this account balance from $2,100 to $3,769, the needed amount determined by the aging schedule. To bring the Allowance balance up to date, Schmidt makes this entry:

Adjusting Entries

Dec. 31	Uncollectible Account Expense	1,669
	Allowance for Uncollectible Accounts ($3,769 − $2,100)	1,669

Observe that under the aging method, the adjusting entry takes into account the prior balance in Allowance for Uncollectibles. Now the Allowance account has the correct balance:

Allowance for Uncollectible Accounts

	Unadjusted balance 2,100
	Adjustment amount 1,669
	Adjusted balance 3,769

It is possible that the allowance account might have a *debit* balance at year end prior to the adjusting entry. How can this occur? Bad debt write-offs during the year could have exceeded the allowance amount. Suppose the unadjusted balance in Allowance for Uncollectible Accounts is a *debit* amount of $1,500:

Allowance for Uncollectible Accounts

	Unadjusted balance 1,500

In this situation, the adjusting entry is

Adjusting Entries

Dec. 31	Uncollectible Account Expense		
	($3,769 + $1,500)	5,269	
	Allowance for Uncollectible Accounts		5,269

After posting, the allowance account is up to date:

Allowance for Uncollectible Accounts

		Unadjusted balance	1,500	Adjustment amount 5,269
				Adjusted balance 3,769

On the balance sheet, the $3,769 is subtracted from the Accounts Receivable figure—which the table on page 351 shows is $112,000—to report the expected realizable value of the accounts receivable—$108,231 ($112,000 − $3,769).

In addition to supplying the information needed for accurate financial reporting, the aging method directs management's attention to the accounts that should be pursued for payment.

Comparing the Percentage of Sales and the Aging Methods. In practice, many companies use both the percentage of sales and the aging of accounts methods. For interim statements (monthly or quarterly), companies use the percent of sales method because it is easier to apply. At the end of the year, these companies use the aging method to ensure that Accounts Receivable is reported at expected realizable value. For this reason, auditors usually require an aging of the accounts on the year-end date. The two methods work well together because the percent of sales approach focuses on measuring bad debt expense on the income statement, whereas the aging approach is designed to measure net accounts receivable on the balance sheet.

Direct Write-off Method. Under the **direct write-off method** of accounting for bad debts, the company waits until the credit department decides that a customer's account receivable is uncollectible. Then the accountant debits Uncollectible Account Expense and credits the customer's account receivable to write off the account.

Assume it is 19X2 and most credit customers have paid for their 19X1 purchases. At this point, the credit department believes that two customers— Garcia and Smith—will never pay. The department directs the accountant to write off Garcia and Smith as bad debts.

The following entries show the business's accounting for 19X1 credit sales and 19X2 collections and uncollectible accounts.

19X1	Accounts Receivable—Garcia	800	
	Accounts Receivable—Smith	1,200	
	Accounts Receivable—Various Customers	98,000	
	Sales Revenue		100,000
	To record credit sales of $100,000.		

19X2	Cash	97,000	
	Accounts Receivable—Various		
	Customers		97,000
	To record cash collections of $97,000.		

19X2	Uncollectible Account Expense	2,000	
	Accounts Receivable—Garcia		800
	Accounts Receivable—Smith		1,200
	To write off uncollectible accounts and record bad debt expense of $2,000.		

Of course, this company would continue making credit sales as an important part of doing business. But what we want to know right now is how the direct write-off method affects financial statements. To see its impact most clearly, let's assume that the company stopped making credit sales altogether in 19X2. Consider the following partial financial statements for 19Xl and 19X2, based on the above journal entries.

Income Statement:	**19X1**	**19X2**
Revenue:		
Sales revenue.....................................	$100,000	$ 0
Expense:		
Uncollectible account expense	0	2,000

	December 31,	
Balance Sheet:	**19X1**	**19X2**
Accounts receivable	$100,000	$1,000

Let's ask two important questions about this approach to accounting for bad debts.

1. How accurately does the direct write-off method measure income? As we have seen, following generally accepted accounting principles means matching an accounting period's expenses against its revenues. The goal is to provide the most accurate picture of income, which measures how well a business's operations are performing. But the direct write-off method does not match a period's bad debt expense against the same period's sales revenue. In our example, the full amount of sales revenue appears for 19Xl, but the expenses incurred to generate this revenue—the bad debts—appear in 19X2. This gives misleading income figures for both years, as would failing to report any other expense—salary, depreciation, and so on—in the correct period. The $2,000 bad debt expense should be matched against the $100,000 sales revenue.

2. How accurately does the direct write-off method value accounts receivable? The 19Xl balance sheet shows accounts receivable at the full $100,000 figure. But any businessperson knows that bad debts are unavoidable when selling on credit. No intelligent manager expects to collect the entire amount. Is the $100,000 figure, then, the expected realizable value of the accounts? No, showing the full $100,000 in the balance sheet falsely implies that these accounts receivable are worth their face value.

The direct write-off method is simple to use, and it causes no great error if collection losses are insignificant in amount. However, you see that the resulting accounting records are not as accurate as they could be. The allowance method is a better way to account for uncollectible account expense.

Credit Balances in Accounts Receivable

Occasionally, customers overpay their accounts or return merchandise for which they have already paid. The result is a credit balance in the customer's account receivable. Assume the company's subsidiary ledger contains 213 accounts, with balances as shown:

210 accounts with *debit* balances totaling	$185,000
3 accounts with *credit* balances totaling........	2,800
Net *debit* total of all balances	$182,200

The company should *not* report the asset Accounts Receivable at the net amount—$182,200. Why not? The credit balance—the $2,800—is a liability. Like any other liability, customer credit balances are debts of the business. A balance sheet that did not indicate to management or to other financial statement users that the company had this liability amount would be misleading if the $2,800 is material in relation to net income or total current assets. Therefore, the company would report on its balance sheet:

Assets		Liabilities	
Current:		Current:	
Accounts receivable ..	$185,000	Credit balances in customer accounts .	$2,800

Credit-Card Sales

Credit-card sales are common in retailing. American Express, Diners Club, Carte Blanche, VISA, and MasterCard are popular.

The customer presents the credit card as payment for a purchase. The seller prepares a sales invoice in triplicate. The customer and the seller keep copies as receipts. The third copy goes to the credit-card company, which then pays the seller the transaction amount and bills the customer.

Credit cards offer consumers the convenience of buying without having to pay the cash immediately. Also, consumers receive a monthly statement from the credit-card company, detailing each credit-card transaction. They can write a single check to cover the entire month's credit-card purchases.

Retailers also benefit from credit-card sales. They do not have to check a customer's credit rating. The company that issues the card has already done so. Retailers do not have to keep an accounts receivable subsidiary ledger account for each customer, and they do not have to collect cash from customers. The copy of the sale invoice that retailers send to the credit-card company signals the card issuer to pursue payment. Further, retailers receive cash more quickly from the credit-card companies than they would from the customers themselves. Of course, these services to the seller do not come free.

The seller receives less than 100 percent of the face value of the invoice. The credit-card company takes a 5 percent[1] discount on the sale to cover its services. The seller's entry to record a $100 Diners Club sale is

Accounts Receivable—Diners Club	100	
Sales Revenue		100

On collection of the discounted value, the seller records:

Cash	95	
Credit-Card Discount Expense	5	
Accounts Receivable—Diners Club		100

Internal Control over Collections of Accounts Receivable

Businesses that sell on credit receive most of their cash receipts by mail. Internal control over collections on account is an important part of the overall internal control system. The first part of this chapter detailed control procedures over cash receipts, but a critical element of internal control deserves emphasis here: the separation of cash-handling and cash-accounting duties. Consider the following case.

OBJECTIVE 5

Identify internal control weaknesses in accounts receivable

Butler Supply Co. is a small, family-owned business that takes pride in the loyalty of its workers. Most company employees have been with the Butlers for at least five years. The company makes 90 percent of its sales on account.

The office staff consists of a bookkeeper and a supervisor. The bookkeeper maintains the general ledger and the accounts receivable subsidiary ledger. He also makes the daily bank deposit. The supervisor prepares monthly financial statements and any special reports the Butlers require. She also takes sales orders from customers and serves as office manager.

Can you identify the internal control weakness? The bookkeeper has access to the general ledger, the accounts receivable subsidiary ledger, and the cash. The bookkeeper could take a customer check and write off the customer's account as uncollectible.[2] Unless the supervisor or some other manager reviews the bookkeeper's work regularly, the theft may go undetected. In small businesses like Butler Supply Co., such a review may not be routinely performed.

How can this control weakness be corrected? The supervisor could open incoming mail and make the daily bank deposit. The bookkeeper should not be allowed to handle cash. Only the remittance slips would be forwarded to the bookkeeper to indicate which customer accounts to credit. Removing cash-handling duties from the bookkeeper, along with keeping the accounts receivable subsidiary ledger away from the supervisor, separates duties and strengthens internal control. It reduces an employee's opportunity to steal cash and then cover it up with a false credit to a customer account.

Another step should be taken. The bookkeeper should total the amount posted as credits to customer accounts receivable each day. The manager

---

[1]The rate varies among companies and over time.
[2]The bookkeeper would need to forge the endorsements of the checks and deposit them in a bank account he controls. This is easier to do than you might imagine.

should then compare this total to the day's bank deposit slip. Agreement of the two records gives some assurance that customer accounts were posted correctly and helps avoid accounting errors. Also, the manager should prepare the bank reconciliation.

Notes Receivable

As we pointed out earlier in this chapter, notes receivable are more formal arrangements than accounts receivable. Often the debtor signs a promissory note, which serves as evidence of the debt. Let's take a moment to define the special terms used to discuss notes receivable.

Promissory note. A written promise to pay a specified amount of money at a particular future date.

Maker of a note. The person or business that signs the note and promises to pay the amount required by the note agreement. The maker is the debtor.

Payee of the note. The person or business to whom the maker promises future payment. The payee is the creditor.

Principal amount, or **principal.** The amount loaned out by the payee and borrowed by the maker of the note.

Interest. The revenue to the payee for loaning out the principal and the expense to the maker for borrowing the principal.

Interest period. The period of time during which interest is to be computed. It extends from the original date of the note to the maturity date.

Interest rate. The percentage rate that is multiplied by the principal amount to compute the amount of interest on the note.

Maturity date, or due date. The date on which final payment of the note is due.

Maturity value. The sum of principal and interest due at the maturity date of a note.

Note period or note term. Synonyms for the interest period.

Exhibit 7-6 illustrates a promissory note. Study it carefully, and identify each of the above items for the note agreement.

Identifying the Maturity Date of a Note

Some notes specify the maturity date of a note, as shown in Exhibit 7-6. Other notes state the period of the note, in days or months. When the period is given in months, the note's maturity date falls on the same day of the month as the date the note was issued. For example, a 6-month note dated February 16 matures on August 16.

When the period is given in days, the maturity date is determined by counting the days from date of issue. A 120-day note dated September 14, 19X2, matures on January 12, 19X3, as shown below:

Month	Number of Days	Cumulative Total
Sep. 19X2	16*	16
Oct. 19X2	31	47
Nov. 19X2	30	77
Dec. 19X2	31	108
Jan. 19X3	12	120

*30 − 14 = 16.

EXHIBIT 7-6 *A Promissory Note*

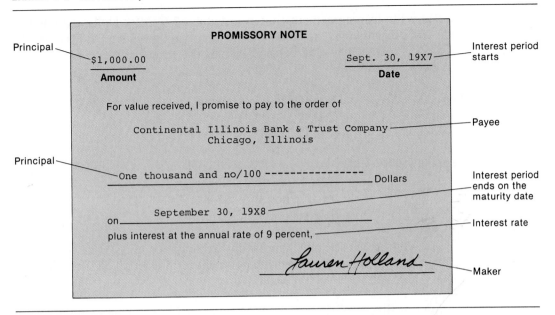

Computing Interest on a Note

The formula for computing interest is

$$\textbf{Principal} \times \textbf{Rate} \times \textbf{Time} = \textbf{Amount of Interest}$$

Using the data in Exhibit 7-6, Continental Bank computes its interest revenue for one year on its note receivable as:

Principal		Rate		Time		Interest
$1,000	×	.09	×	1 yr.	=	$90

The *maturity value* of the note is $1,090 ($1,000 principal + $90 interest). Note that the time element is one (1) because interest is computed over a 1-year period.

When the interest period of a note is stated in months, we compute the interest based on the 12-month year. Interest on a $2,000 note at 15 percent for 3 months is computed as:

Principal		Rate		Time		Interest
$2,000	×	.15	×	3/12	=	$75

When the interest period of a note is stated in days, we sometimes compute interest based on a 360-day year rather than a 365-day year. The interest on a $5,000 note at 12 percent for 60 days is computed as:

Principal		Rate		Time		Interest
$5,000	×	.12	×	60/360	=	$100

Recording Notes Receivable

OBJECTIVE 6

Account for notes receivable

Consider the loan agreement shown in Exhibit 7-6. After Holland signs the note and presents it to the bank, Continental Bank gives her $1,000 cash. At maturity, Holland pays the bank $1,090 ($1,000 principal plus $90 interest). The bank's entries are

Sep. 30, 19X7	Note Receivable—L. Holland	1,000	
	Cash		1,000
	To record the loan.		

Sep. 30, 19X8	Cash	1,090	
	Note Receivable—L. Holland		1,000
	Interest Revenue ($1,000 × .09 × 1).		90
	To record collection at maturity.		

Some companies sell merchandise in exchange for notes receivable. This arrangement occurs often when the payment term extends beyond the customary accounts receivable period, which generally ranges from 30 to 60 days.

Suppose that on October 20, 19X3, General Electric sells equipment for $15,000 to Dorman Builders. Dorman signs a 90-day promissory note at 10 percent annual interest. General Electric's entries to record the sale and collection from Dorman are

Oct. 20, 19X3	Note Receivable—Dorman Builders ...	15,000	
	Sales Revenue		15,000
	To record sale.		

Jan. 18, 19X4	Cash	15,375	
	Note Receivable—Dorman Builders.....................		15,000
	Interest Revenue ($15,000 × .10 × 90/360)		375
	To record collection at maturity.		

A company may accept a note receivable from a trade customer who fails to pay an account receivable within the customary 30 to 60 days. The customer signs a promissory note—that is, becomes the maker of the note—and gives it to the creditor, who becomes the payee.

Suppose Casa de Sanchez, Inc., sees that it will not be able to pay off its account payable to Hoffman Supply that is due in 15 days. Hoffman may accept a note receivable from Casa de Sanchez. Hoffman's entry is

May 3	Note Receivable—Casa de Sanchez, Inc........	2,400	
	Accounts Receivable—Casa de Sanchez, Inc.................		2,400
	To receive a note on account from a customer.		

Hoffman later records interest and collection as illustrated in the preceding examples.

Why does a company accept a note receivable instead of pressing its demand for payment of the account receivable? The company may pursue receipt but learn that its customer does not have the money. A note receivable gives the company written evidence of the maker's debt, which may aid any legal action for collection. Also, the note receivable may carry a pledge by the maker that gives the payee certain assets if cash is not received by the due date. The company's reward for its patience is the interest revenue that it earns on the note receivable.

Discounting a Note Receivable

A note receivable is a *negotiable instrument,* which means it is readily transferable from one business or person to another and may be sold for cash. To get cash quickly, payees sometimes sell a note receivable to another party before the note matures. The payee endorses the note and hands it over to the note purchaser—often a bank—who collects the maturity value of the note at the maturity date.

Selling a note receivable before maturity is called **discounting a note receivable** because the payee of the note receives less than its maturity value. This lower price decreases the amount of interest revenue the payee earns on the note. Giving up some of this interest is the price the payee is willing to pay for the convenience of receiving cash early.

Return to the preceding example with General Electric and Dorman Builders. Recall that the maturity date of the Dorman note is January 18, 19X4. Let's assume General Electric discounts the Dorman note at First City National Bank on December 9, 19X3. The discount period—which is the number of days from the date of discounting to the date of maturity (this is the period the bank will hold the note)—is 40 days; 22 days in December, and 18 days in January. Assume the bank applies a 12 percent annual interest rate in computing the discounted value of the note. The bank will want to use a discount rate that is higher than the interest rate on the note in order to increase its earnings. GE may be willing to accept this higher rate in order to get cash quickly. The discounted value, called the *proceeds,* is the amount that GE receives from the bank. The proceeds are computed as follows:

Principal amount	$15,000	
+ Interest ($15,000 × .10 × 90/360)	375	
= Maturity value	15,375	$170 $170
− Discount ($15,375 × .12 × 40/360)	(205)	
= Proceeds	$15,170	

At maturity the bank collects $15,375 from the maker of the note, earning $205 of interest revenue.

Observe two points in the above computation: (1) The discount is computed on the *maturity value* of the note (principal plus interest) rather than on the original principal amount, and (2) the discount period extends *backward* from the maturity date (January 18, 19X4) to the date of discounting (December 9, 19X3). Follow this diagram:

Oct. 20, 19X3   90 Days   Jan. 18, 19X4

/- - > - - - - - - - - - - - > - - - - - - - - - > - - - - - - - - > - - - -/\

Principal   +   Interest   =   Maturity
$15,000 $375 $15,375

                          Dec. 9, 19X3   40 Days   Jan. 18, 19X4
                          /- - - - < - - - - - - < - - - - - - < - - -/<

                          Proceeds   =   Discount   −   Maturity
                          $15,170 $205 $15,375

General Electric's entry to record discounting the note is

Dec. 9, 19X3   Cash   15,170
                     Note Receivable—Dorman Builders   15,000
                     Interest Revenue ($15,170 —
                          $15,000)   170
                To record discounting a note receivable.

When the proceeds from discounting a note receivable are less than the principal amount of the note, the payee records a debit to Interest Expense for the amount of the difference. For example, General Electric could discount the note receivable for cash proceeds of $14,980. The entry to record this transaction is

Dec. 9, 19X3   Cash   14,980
                Interest Expense   20
                     Note Receivable—Dorman Builders   15,000

The term *discount* has been used here to distinguish the interest earned by the payee of the note from the interest to be earned by the purchaser of the note. Fundamentally, the discount is interest.

Contingent Liabilities on Discounted Notes Receivable

Discounting a note receivable creates a **contingent**—that is, a potential—**liability** for the endorser. The contingent liability is this: If the maker of the note (Dorman, in our example) fails to pay the maturity value to the new payee (the bank), then the original payee (General Electric, the note's endorser) legally must pay the bank the amount due.[3] Now we see why the liability is "potential." If Dorman pays the bank, then General Electric can forget the note. But if Dorman dishonors the note—fails to pay it—General Electric has an actual liability.

This contingent liability of General Electric exists from the time of endorsement to the maturity date of the note. In our example, the contingent liability exists from December 9, 19X3—when General Electric endorsed the note—to the January 18, 19X4, maturity date.

Contingent liabilities are not reported with actual liabilities on the balance sheet. After all, they are not real debts. However, financial-statement users should be alerted that the business has *potential* debts. Many businesses report contingent liabilities in a footnote to the financial statements. General Electric's end-of-period balance sheet might carry this note:

> As of December 31, 19X3, the Company is contingently liable on notes receivable discounted in the amount of $15,000.

Dishonored Notes Receivable

If the maker of a note does not pay a note receivable at maturity, the maker is said to **dishonor,** or **default on,** the note. Because the term of the note has expired, the note agreement is no longer in force, nor is it negotiable. However, the payee still has a claim against the maker of the note and usually transfers the claim from the note receivable account to Accounts Receivable.

---

[3]The discounting agreement between the endorser and the purchaser may specify that the endorser has no liability if the note is dishonored at maturity.

The payee records interest revenue earned on the note and debits Accounts Receivable for the full maturity value of the note.

Suppose Rubinstein Jewelers has a six-month, 10 percent note receivable for $1,200 from D. Hatachi. On the February 3 maturity date, Hatachi defaults. Rubinstein Jewelers would record the default as follows:

Feb. 3 Accounts Receivable—D. Hatachi
   [$1,200 + ($1,200 × .10 × 6/12)] 1,260
       Note Receivable—D. Hatachi   1,200
       Interest Revenue ($1,200 × .10 × 6/12)   60
   To record dishonor of note receivable.

Rubinstein would pursue collection from Hatachi as a promissory note default. The company may treat accounts receivable such as this as a special category to highlight them for added collection efforts. If the account receivable later proves uncollectible, the account is written off against Allowance for Uncollectible Accounts in the manner previously discussed.

The maker may dishonor a note after it has been discounted by the original payee. For example, suppose Dorman Builders dishonors its note (maturity value, $15,375) to General Electric (GE) after GE has discounted the note to the bank. On dishonor, the bank adds a *protest fee* to cover the cost of a statement about the facts of the dishonor and requests payment from General Electric, which then becomes the holder of the dishonored note. Assume GE pays the maturity value of the note, plus the $25 protest fee, to the bank. This creates an obligation for Dorman to pay GE. GE then presents the statement to Dorman and makes the following entry on the maturity date of the note:

Jan. 18, 19X4 Accounts Receivable—Dorman Builders
    ($15,375 + $25) 15,400
        Cash   15,400
    To record payment of dishonored note
    receivable that has been discounted.

GE's collection of cash, or write-off of the uncollectible account receivable, would be recorded in the normal manner, depending on the ultimate outcome. If GE charges Dorman additional interest, GE's collection entry debits Cash and credits Accounts Receivable and Interest Revenue.

Accruing Interest Revenue

Notes receivable may be outstanding at the end of the accounting period. The interest revenue that was accrued on the note up to that point should be recorded as part of that period's earnings. Recall that interest revenue is earned over time, not just when cash is received.

Suppose First City Bank receives a one-year $1,000 note receivable, with 9 percent interest, on October 1, 19X7. The bank's accounting period ends December 31. How much of the total interest revenue does First City Bank earn in 19X7? How much in 19X8?

The bank will earn three months' interest in 19X7—for October, November, and December. In 19X8, the bank will earn nine months' interest—for January through September. Therefore, at December 31, 19X7, First City will make the following adjusting entry to accrue interest revenue:

Dec. 31, 19X7 Interest Receivable
     ($1,000 × .09 × 3/12) 22.50
         Interest Revenue 22.50
     To accrue interest revenue earned
     in 19X7 but not yet received.

Then, on the maturity date First City Bank may record collection of principal and interest as follows:

Sept. 30, 19X8   Cash [$1,000 + ($1,000 × .09)] 1,090.00
                      Note Receivable 1,000.00
                      Interest Receivable
                          ($1,000 × .09 × 3/12) 22.50
                      Interest Revenue
                          ($1,000 × .09 × 9/12) 67.50
                      To record collection of note receiv-
                      able on which interest has been pre-
                      viously accrued.

The entries to accrue interest revenue earned in 19X7 and to record collection in 19X8 assign the correct amount of interest to each year.

Reporting Receivables and Allowances: Actual Reports

Let's take a look at how some well-known companies report their receivables and related allowances for uncollectibles on the balance sheet. The terminology and setup vary, but you can understand these actual presentations based on what you have learned in this chapter.

Bobbie Brooks, a manufacturer of women's clothing, reported under Current Assets (in thousands):

> Accounts receivable, less allowance
>   for doubtful accounts of $602 ...... $35,873

To figure the total accounts receivable amount, add the allowance to the net accounts receivable amount: $602 + $35,873 = $36,475.

Premark International, Inc., which makes Tupperware plastic food-storage containers, combines accounts and notes receivable (amounts in millions):

> Accounts and notes receivable, less
>   allowances of $19.5 .... $309.9

General Electric Company reports a single amount for its current receivables in the body of the balance sheet and supplements it with a detailed note (amounts in millions):

> Current receivables (note 8) $4,872
>
> Note 8: Current Receivables
>   Customers' accounts and notes. $3,989
>   Associated companies   49
>   Nonconsolidated affiliates   21
>   Other   927
>   4,986
>   Less allowance for losses ......   (114)
> $4,872

Deere & Company, maker of farm machinery, lists more detail in the body of the balance sheet (amounts in thousands of dollars):

Trade receivables:
Dealer accounts and notes	$2,373,018
Retail notes	40,558
Total	2,413,576
Less allowances	39,183
Trade receivables, net	$2,374,393

Nashua Corporation, manufacturer of copying machines and paper products, reported approximately $70,000,000 in net accounts and notes receivable. In addition, the company disclosed a contingent liability for discounted accounts and notes receivable in its Notes to Financial Statements:

ACCOUNTS RECEIVABLE:

At December 31, 19X1 and 19X0, the company was contingently liable to third parties as a result of the sale of certain accounts and notes receivable of approximately $19,000,000 and $16,000,000, respectively.

The companies we have featured so far list receivables as *current assets.* National Can Corporation, however, had some long-term receivables that it reported as other assets (amounts in thousands of dollars).

OTHER ASSETS:

Notes and accounts receivable, less allowances $36,970

National Can also disclosed in a note entitled Notes and Accounts Receivable that:

Notes and accounts receivable included in other assets are net of allowances for doubtful accounts of $16,772.

OBJECTIVE 8
Use financial ratios to evaluate a company's position

Use of Accounting Information in Decision Making

In making decisions, owners and managers use some ratios based on the relative liquidity of assets. In Chapter 4, for example, we discussed the current ratio, which indicates the ability to pay current liabilities with current assets. A more stringent measure of the ability to pay current liabilities is the **acid-test** (or **quick**) ratio. The acid-test ratio assumes that all current liabilities are payable immediately and that the debtor will convert the most liquid assets to cash. The three most liquid asset categories are cash, short-term investments, and current receivables. Short-term investments (covered in Chapter 14) are the second most liquid assets because they are readily convertible to cash at the will of the owner. All the owner must do to generate cash is sell these investments. The acid-test ratio is computed as follows:

$$\text{Acid-test ratio} = \frac{\text{Cash} + \text{Short-term investments} + \text{Net current receivables}}{\text{Total current liabilities}}$$

The higher the acid-test ratio, the better off the business is. An increasing acid-test ratio over time usually indicates improving business operations.

Inventory is excluded from the acid-test ratio because it may not be easy to sell the goods. A company may have an acceptable current ratio (in which inventory is included) and a poor acid-test ratio because of a large amount of inventory.

Automobile dealers can operate smoothly with an acid-test ratio of .20. The average acid-test ratio for women's dress manufacturers is .90. Most department stores' ratio values cluster about .80, and travel agencies average 1.10. In general, an acid-test ratio of 1.00 is considered safe.

After a business makes a credit sale, the next critical event in the business cycle is collection of the receivable. Several financial ratios center on receivables. **Days' sales in receivables**, also called the *collection period,* indicates how many days it takes to collect the average level of receivables. The shorter the collection period, the more cash the organization has for operations. The longer the collection period, the less cash is available to pay bills and expand. Days' sales in receivables can be computed in two steps, as follows:

$$1. \quad \text{One day's sales} = \frac{\text{Net sales}}{365 \text{ days}}$$

$$2. \quad \begin{array}{l}\text{Days' sales in} \\ \text{average accounts} \\ \text{receivable}\end{array} = \frac{\text{Average net accounts receivable}}{\text{One day's sales}} = \frac{(\text{Beginning net receivables} + \text{Ending net receivables})/2}{\text{One day's sales}}$$

The length of the collection period depends on the credit terms of the company's sales. For example, sales on net 30 terms should be collected within approximately 30 days. When there is a discount, such as 2/10 net 30, the collection period may be shorter. Terms of net 45 or net 60 will result in longer collection periods. Whenever the collection period lengthens, the business must find other sources of financing, such as borrowing. During recessions, customers pay more slowly, and a longer collection period may be unavoidable.

Summary Problems for Your Review

Problem 1

CPC International, Inc., is the food-products company that produces Skippy peanut butter, Hellmann's mayonnaise, and Mazola corn oil. The company balance sheet at December 31, 19X7, reported:

	Millions
Notes and accounts receivable [total]	$549.9
Allowances for doubtful accounts	(12.5)

Required

1. How much of the December 31, 19X7, balance of notes and accounts receivable did CPC expect to collect? Stated differently, what was the

expected realizable value of these receivables?

2. Journalize, without explanations, 19X8 entries for CPC, assuming:
   a) Estimated Doubtful Account Expense of $19.2 million, based on the percentage of sales method.
   b) Write-offs of accounts receivable totaling $23.6 million.
   c) December 31, 19X8, aging of receivables, which indicates that $15.3 million of the total receivables of $582.7 million is uncollectible.

3. Show how CPC International's receivables and related allowance will appear on the December 31, 19X8, balance sheet.

4. What is the expected realizable value of receivables at December 31, 19X8? How much is doubtful account expense for 19X8?

Problem 2

Suppose Exxon, Inc., engaged in the following transactions:

19X4

Apr. 1   Loaned $8,000 to Bland Co., a service station. Received a one-year, 10 percent note.

June 1   Discounted the Bland note at the bank at a discount rate of 12 percent.

Nov. 30   Loaned $6,000 to Flores, Inc., a regional distributor of Exxon products, on a three-month, 11 percent note.

19X5

Feb. 28   Collected the Flores note at maturity.

Exxon's accounting period ends on December 31.

Required

Explanations are not needed.

1. Record the 19X4 transactions on April 1, June 1, and November 30 on Exxon's books.
2. Make any adjusting entries needed on December 31, 19X4.
3. Record the February 28, 19X5, collection of the Flores note.
4. Which transaction creates a contingent liability for Exxon? When does the contingency begin? When does it end?
5. Write a footnote that Exxon could use in its 19X4 financial statements to report the contingent liability.

SOLUTIONS TO REVIEW PROBLEMS

Problem 1

		Millions
1.	Expected realizable value of receivables ($549.9 − $12.5)	$537.4

		Millions	
2.	a) Doubtful Account Expense	19.2	
	Allowance for Doubtful Accounts		19.2
	b) Allowance for Doubtful Accounts	23.6	
	Accounts Receivable		23.6

Allowance for Doubtful Accounts

19X8 Write-offs	23.6	Dec. 31, 19X7	12.5
		19X8 Expense	19.2
		19X8 balance prior to December 31, 19X8	8.1

c) Doubtful Account Expense ($15.3 − $8.1) 7.2

       Allowance for Doubtful Accounts 7.2

	Millions
3. Notes and accounts receivable	$582.7
Allowance for doubtful accounts	(15.3)
4. Expected realizable value of receivables at December 31, 19X8 ($582.7 − $15.3)	$567.4
Doubtful account expense for 19X8 ($19.2 + $7.2)	26.4

Problem 2

19X4

1. Apr. 1   Note Receivable—Bland Co   8,000

              Cash   8,000

     June 1   Cash 7,920*

           Interest Expense   80

              Note Receivable—Bland Co   8,000

*Computation of proceeds:

Principal	$8,000
+ Interest ($8,000 × .10 × 12/12)	800
= Maturity value	8,800
− Discount ($8,800 × .12 × 10/12)	880
= Proceeds	$7,920

     Nov. 30   Note Receivable—Flores, Inc.   6,000

              Cash   6,000

2.   **Adjusting Entries**

19X4

Dec. 31   Interest Receivable ($6,000 × .11 × 1/12) .   55

             Interest Revenue   55

19X5

3. Feb. 28   Cash [$6,000 + ($6,000 × .11 × 3/12)]   6,165

              Note Receivable—Flores, Inc. . . . . : . . .   6,000

              Interest Receivable   55

              Interest Revenue ($6,000 × . 11 × 2/12)   110

4. Discounting the Bland note receivable creates a contingent liability for Exxon. The contingency exists from the date of discounting the note receivable (June 1) to the maturity date of the note (April 1, 19X5).

5. Note XX—Contingent liabilities: At December 31, 19X4, the Company is contingently liable on notes receivable discounted in the amount of $8,000.

ummary

he *bank account* helps to control and safeguard cash. Businesses use the *bank statement* and the *bank reconciliation* to account for banking transactions. An *iprest system* is used to control petty cash disbursements. Many companies record purchases at *net cost* in order to highlight the inefficiency of paying invoices late and thus losing purchase discounts.

Credit sales create receivables. Accounts receivable are usually current assets, and notes receivable may be current or long-term.

Uncollectible receivables are accounted for by the allowance method or the direct write-off method. The *allowance method* matches expenses to sales revenue and also results in a more realistic measure of net accounts receivable. The *percentage of sales method* and the *aging of accounts receivable method* are the two main approaches to estimating bad debts under the allowance method. The *direct write-off method* is easy to apply, but it fails to match the uncollectible account expense to the corresponding sales revenue. Also, accounts receivable are reported at their full amount, which misleadingly suggests that the company expects to collect all its accounts receivable.

In *credit-card* sales, the seller receives cash from the credit card company (American Express, for example), which bills the customer. For the convenience of receiving cash immediately, the seller pays a fee, which is a percentage of the sale.

Companies that sell on credit receive most customer collections in the mail. Good *internal control* over mailed-in cash receipts means separating cash-handling duties from cash-accounting duties.

Notes receivable are formal credit agreements. Interest earned by the creditor is computed by multiplying the note's principal amount by the interest rate times the length of the interest period.

Because notes receivable are negotiable, they may be sold. Selling a note receivable—called *discounting a note*—creates a *contingent (possible) liability* for the note's payee.

All accounts receivable, notes receivable, and allowance accounts appear in the balance sheet. However, companies use various formats and terms to report these assets.

The *acid-test ratio* measures ability to pay current liabilities from the most liquid current assets. *Days' sales in receivables* indicates how long it takes to collect receivables.

elf-Study Questions

est your understanding of the chapter by marking the best answer for each of ne following questions.

1. Which of the following items appears on the bank side of a bank reconciliation? *(pp. 336, 337)*
   a. Book error
   b. Outstanding check
   c. NSF check
   d. Interest revenue earned on bank balance

2. Which of the following reconciling items requires a journal entry on the books of the company? *(p. 337)*
   a. Book error
   b. Outstanding check
   c. NSF check
   d. Interest revenue earned on bank balance
   e. All of the above but b
   f. None of the above

3. What is the major internal control measure over the cash receipts of a K Mart store? *(p. 340)*
   a. Reporting the day's cash receipts to the controller
   b. Preparing a petty cash ticket for all disbursements from the fund

c. Pricing merchandise at uneven amounts, coupled with use of a cash register

d. Channeling all cash receipts through the mail room, whose employees have no cash-accounting responsibilities

4. Longview, Inc., made the following entry related to uncollectibles:

Uncollectible Account Expense.................... 1,900
    Allowance for Uncollectible Accounts.........   1,900

The purpose of this entry is to *(p. 347)*
a. Write off uncollectibles   c. Age the accounts receivable
b. Close the expense account   d. Record bad debt expense

5. Longview, Inc., also made this entry:

Allowance for Uncollectible Accounts 2,110
    Accounts Receivable (detailed)   2,110

The purpose of this entry is to *(p. 348)*
a. Write off uncollectibles   c. Age the accounts receivable
b. Close the expense account   d. Record bad debt expense

6. The credit balance in Allowance for Uncollectibles is $14,300 prior to the adjusting entries at the end of the period. The aging of accounts indicates that an allowance of $78,900 is needed. The amount of expense to record is *(p. 351)*
a. $14,300   c. $78,900
b. $64,600   d. $93,200

7. The most important internal control over cash receipts is *(p. 355)*
a. Assigning an honest employee the responsibility for handling cash
b. Separating the cash-handling and cash-accounting duties
c. Ensuring that cash is deposited in the bank daily
d. Centralizing the opening of incoming mail in a single location

8. A six-month, $30,000 note specifies interest of 9 percent. The full amount of interest on this note will be *(p. 357)*
a. $450   c. $1,350
b. $900   d. $2,700

9. The note in the preceding question was issued on August 31, and the company's accounting year ends on December 31. The year-end balance sheet will report interest receivable of *(p. 361)*
a. $450   c. $1,350
b. $900   d. $2,700

10. Discounting a note receivable creates a (an) *(p. 360)*
a. Cash disbursement   c. Protest fee
b. Interest expense   d. Contingent liability

Answers to the Self-Study Questions follow the Accounting Vocabulary.

Accounting Vocabulary

Acid-test ratio. Ratio of the sum of cash plus short-term investments plus net current receivables to current liabilities. Tells whether the entity could pay all its current liabilities if they came due immediately. Also called the Quick ratio *(p. 363)*.

Aging of accounts receivable. A way to estimate bad debts by analyzing individual accounts receivable according to the length of time they have been due *(p. 350)*.

Allowance for doubtful accounts. A contra account, related to accounts receivable, that holds the estimated amount of collection losses. Also called Allowance for uncollectible accounts *(p. 347)*.

Allowance for uncollectible accounts. Another name for Allowance for doubtful accounts *(p. 347)*.

Allowance method. A method of recording collection losses based on estimates prior to determining that the business will not collect from specific customers *(p. 347)*.

Bad debt expense. Another name for Uncollectible account expense *(p. 346)*.

Bank collection. Collection of money by the bank on behalf of a depositor *(p. 335)*.

Bank reconciliation. Process of explaining the reasons for the difference between a depositor's records and the bank's records about the depositor's bank account *(p. 335)*.

Bank statement. Document for a particular bank account showing its beginning and ending balances and listing the month's transactions that affected the account *(p. 333)*.

Check. Document that instructs the bank to pay the designated person or business the specified amount of money *(p. 333)*.

Contingent liability. A potential liability *(p. 360)*.

Creditor. The party to a credit transaction who sells a service or merchandise and obtains a receivable *(p. 345)*.

Days' sales in receivables. Ratio of average net accounts receivable to one day's sales. Tells how many days' sales remain in Accounts Receivable awaiting collection *(p. 364)*.

Debtor. The party to a credit transaction who makes a purchase and creates a payable *(p. 345)*.

Default on a note. Failure of the maker of a note to pay at maturity. Also called Dishonor of a note *(p. 360)*.

Deposit in transit. A deposit recorded by the company but not yet by its bank *(p. 335)*.

Direct write-off method. A method of accounting for bad debts by which the company waits until the credit department decides that a customer's account receivable is uncollectible and then records uncollectible account expense and credits the customer's account receivable *(p. 352)*.

Discounting a note receivable. Selling a note receivable before its maturity *(p. 359)*.

Dishonor of a note. Another name for Default on a note *(p. 360)*.

Doubtful account expense. Another name for Uncollectible account expense *(p. 346)*.

Imprest system. A way to account for petty cash by maintaining a constant balance in the petty cash account, supported by the fund (cash plus disbursement tickets) totaling the same amount *(p. 342)*.

Interest. The revenue to the payee for loaning out the principal, and the expense to the maker for borrowing the principal *(p. 356)*.

Interest period. The period of time during which interest is to be computed, extending from the original date of the note to the maturity date *(p. 356)*.

Interest rate. The percentage rate that is multiplied by the principal amount to compute the amount of interest on a note *(p. 356)*.

Maker of a note. The person or business that signs the note and promises to pay the amount required by the note agreement. The maker is the debtor *(p. 356)*.

Maturity date. The date on which the final payment of a note is due. Also called the Due date *(p. 356)*.

Maturity value. The sum of the principal and interest due at the maturity date of a note *(p. 356)*.

Nonsufficient funds (NSF) check. A "hot" check, one for which the payer's bank account has insufficient money to pay the check *(p. 335)*.

Other receivables. A miscellaneous category that includes loans to employees and branch companies— usually long-term assets reported on the balance sheet after current assets and before plant assets. *(p. 346)*.

Outstanding check. A check issued by the company and recorded on its books but not yet paid by its bank *(p. 335)*.

Payee of a note. The person or business to whom the maker of a note promises future payment. The payee is the creditor *(p. 356)*.

Petty cash. Fund containing a small amount of cash that is used to pay minor expenditures *(p. 341)*.

Principal amount. The amount loaned out by the payee and borrowed by the maker of a note *(p. 356)*.

Promissory note. A written promise to pay a specified amount of money at a particular future date *(p. 356).*

Quick ratio. Another name for the Acid-test ratio *(p. 363).*

Receivable. A monetary claim against a business or an individual, acquired mainly by selling goods and services and by lending money *(p. 345).*

Service charge. Bank's fee for processing a depositor's transactions *(p. 335).*

Uncollectible account expense. Cost to the seller of extending credit. Arises from the failure to collect from credit customers *(p. 346).*

Answers to Self-Study Questions

1. b	3. c	5. a	7. b	9. b
2. e	4. d	6. b	8. c	10. d

ASSIGNMENT MATERIAL

Questions

1. Briefly state how each of the following serves as an internal control measure over cash: bank account, signature card, deposit ticket, and bank statement.

2. Each of the items in the following list must be accounted for in the bank reconciliation. Next to each item, enter the appropriate letter from the following possible treatments: (a) bank side of reconciliation—add the item; (b) bank side of reconciliation—subtract the item; (c) book side of reconciliation—add the item; (d) book side of reconciliation—subtract the item.

   _____ Outstanding check
   _____ NSF check
   _____ Bank service charge
   _____ Cost of printed checks
   _____ Bank error that decreased bank balance

   _____ Deposit in transit
   _____ Bank collection
   _____ Customer check returned because of unauthorized signature
   _____ Book error that increased balance of Cash account

3. What purpose does a bank reconciliation serve?

4. Suppose a company has six bank accounts, two petty cash funds, and three certificates of deposit that can be withdrawn on demand. How many cash amounts would this company likely report on its balance sheet?

5. Describe internal control procedures for cash received by mail.

6. What balance does the Petty Cash account have at all times? Does this balance always equal the amount of cash in the fund? When are the two amounts equal? When are they unequal?

7. Name the two parties to a receivable/payable transaction. Which party has the receivable? Which party has the payable? Which party has the asset? Which party has the liability?

8. List three categories of receivables. State how each category is classified for reporting on the balance sheet.

9. Name the two methods of accounting for uncollectible receivables. Which method is easier to apply? Which method is consistent with generally accepted accounting principles?

10. Identify the accounts debited and credited to account for (a) the allowance method and (b) the direct write-off method.

11. Which entry decreases net income under the allowance method of accounting for uncollectibles: the entry to record uncollectible account expense or the entry to write off an uncollectible account receivable?

12. May a customer pay his or her account receivable after it has been written off? If not, why not? If so, what entries are made to account for reinstating the customer's account and for collecting cash from the customer?

13. Identify and briefly describe the two ways to estimate bad debt expense and uncollectible accounts.

14. Briefly describe how a company may use both the percentage of sales method and the aging method to account for uncollectibles.

15. How does a credit balance arise in a customer's account receivable? How does the company report this credit balance on its balance sheet?

16. Many businesses receive most of their cash on credit sales through the mail. Suppose you own a business so large that you must hire employees to handle cash receipts and perform the related accounting duties. What internal control feature should you use to ensure that the cash received from customers is not taken by a dishonest employee?

17. For each of the following notes receivable, compute the amount of interest revenue earned during 19X6:

	Principal	Interest Rate	Interest Period	Maturity Date
a. Note 1	$ 10,000	9%	90 days	11/30/19X6
b. Note 2	50,000	10%	6 months	9/30/19X6
c. Note 3	100,000	8%	5 years	12/31/19X7
d. Note 4	15,000	12%	60 days	1/15/19X7

18. Name three situations in which a company might receive a note receivable. For each situation, show the account debited and the account credited to record receipt of the note.

19. Suppose you hold a 180-day, $5,000 note receivable that specifies 10 percent interest. After 60 days you discount the note at 12 percent. How much cash do you receive?

20. How does a contingent liability differ from an ordinary liability? How does discounting a note receivable create a contingent liability? When does the contingency cease to exist?

21. Why does the payee of a note receivable usually need to make adjusting entries for interest at the end of the accounting period?

22. Recall the real-world disclosures of receivables the chapter presents. Show three ways to report Accounts Receivable of $100,000 and Allowance for Uncollectible Accounts of $2,800 on the balance sheet or in the related notes.

23. Why is the acid-test ratio a more stringent measure of the ability to pay current liabilities than is the current ratio?

Exercises

Exercise 7-1 *Bank reconciliation* *(L.O. 1)*

Betsy Willis's checkbook lists the following:

Date	Check No.	Item	Check	Deposit	Balance
9/1					$ 525
4	622	Apple Tree Gift Shop	$ 19		506
9		Dividends		$ 116	622
13	623	Bell Telephone Co.	43		579
14	624	Gulf Oil Co.	58		521
18	625	Cash	50		471
26	626	St. Alban's Episcopal Church	25		446
28	627	Bent Tree Apartments	275		171
30		Paycheck		1,000	1,171

The September bank statement shows:

```
Balance ....................................   $525
Add: Deposits ..............................    116
Deduct checks: No.                 Amount
                622  ...............  $19
                623  ...............   43
                624  ...............   68*
                625  ...............   50       (180)
Other charges:
     Printed checks ...................  $ 8
     Service charge ...................   12    (20)
Balance ....................................   $441
```
*This is the correct amount of check number 624.

Required:

Prepare Betsy's bank reconciliation at September 30.

Exercise 7-2   *Bank reconciliation*   **(L.O. 1)**

Mike Gilliam operates four EXXON stations. He has just received the monthly bank statement at October 31 from First National Bank, and the statement shows an ending balance of $3,940. Listed on the statement are a service charge of $12, two NSF checks totaling $74, and a $9 charge for printed checks. In reviewing his cash records, Gilliam identifies outstanding checks totaling $467 and an October 31 deposit of $788, which does not appear on the bank statement. During October he recorded a $190 check for the salary of a part-time employee by debiting Salary Expense and crediting Cash for $19. Gilliam's cash account shows an October 31 cash balance of $4,527.

Required

1. Prepare the bank reconciliation at October 31.
2. Record the entries that Gilliam should make in the general journal on October 31. Include an explanation for each entry.

Exercise 7-3   *Internal control over cash receipts*   **(L.O. 2)**

A cash register is located in each department of Kestner's Payless Discount Store. The register shows the amount of each sale, the cash received from the customer, and any change returned to the customer. The machine also produces a customer receipt but keeps no record of transactions. At the end of the day, the clerk counts the cash in the register and gives it to the cashier for deposit in the company bank account.

Required:

Write a memo to convince the store manager that there is an internal control weakness over cash receipts. Identify the weakness that gives an employee the best opportunity to steal cash, and state how to prevent this theft.

Exercise 7-4 *Accounting for petty cash* **(L.O. 3)**

Community Charities of Gatlinburg, Tennessee, created a $100 imprest petty cash fund. During the first month of use, the fund custodian authorized and signed petty cash tickets as follows:

Ticket No.	Item	Account Debited	Amount
1	Delivery of pledge cards to donors	Delivery Expense	$22.19
2	Mail package	Postage Expense	2.80
3	Newsletter	Supplies Expense	4.14
4	Key to closet	Miscellaneous Expense	.85
5	Waste basket	Miscellaneous Expense	3.78
6	Staples	Supplies Expense	5.37

Required:

1. Make general journal entries for creation of the petty cash fund and its replenishment. Include explanations.
2. Immediately prior to replenishment, describe the items in the fund.
3. Immediately after replenishment, describe the items in the fund.

Exercise 7-5 *Using the allowance and the direct write-off method for bad debts*
(L.O. 4)

On September 30, Trinity Fruit Supply had a $26,000 debit balance in Accounts Receivable and a $2,100 credit balance in Allowance for Uncollectible Accounts. During October the company had sales of $135,000, which included $88,000 in credit sales. Other data for October include:

Collections on accounts receivable, $91,000
Write-offs of uncollectible receivables, $1,070
Uncollectible account expense, estimated as 2 percent of credit sales

Required

1. Prepare journal entries to record sales, collections, uncollectible account expense by the allowance method, and write-offs of uncollectibles during October.
2. Show the ending balances in Accounts Receivable, Allowance for Uncollectible Accounts, and *net* accounts receivable at October 31. Does Trinity expect to collect the net amount of the receivable?
3. Suppose Trinity used the direct write-off method. Record uncollectible account expense for October by the direct write-off method. What amount of net accounts receivable would Trinity report on its October 31 balance sheet under the direct write-off method? Does Trinity expect to collect this much of the receivable? Give your reason.

Exercise 7-6 *Using the aging approach to estimate bad debts* **(L.O. 4)**

At December 31, 19X7, the accounts receivable balance of Wang, Limited, is $266,000. The allowance for doubtful accounts has a $3,910 credit balance.

Accountants for Wang, Limited, prepare the following aging schedule for its accounts receivable:

Total Balance	Age of Accounts			
	1–30 Days	31–60 Days	61–90 Days	Over 90 Days
$266,000	$104,000	$78,000	$69,000	$15,000
Estimated percentage uncollectible	.3%	1.2%	6.0%	50%

Journalize the adjusting entry for doubtful accounts based on the aging schedule. Show the T-account for the allowance.

Exercise 7-7   Controlling cash receipts from customers   (L.O. 5)

As a recent college graduate, you land your first job in the customer collections department of Coffey & Schwayze, a partnership. Lela Coffey, the president, has asked you to propose a system to ensure that cash received by mail from customers is properly handled. Draft a short memorandum identifying the essential element in your proposed plan, and state why this element is important.

Exercise 7-8   Recording a note receivable and accruing interest revenue   (L.O. 6)

Record the following transactions in the general journal.

Nov. 1 Loaned $30,000 cash to R. Milpas on a 1-year, 9% note.
Dec. 3 Sold goods to Lofland, Inc., receiving a 90-day, 12% note for $3,750.
     16 Received a $2,000, 6-month, 12% note on account from J. Baker.
     31 Accrued interest revenue on all notes receivable.

Exercise 7-9   Recording a note receivable and accruing interest revenue   (L.O. 6)

Record the following transactions in the general journal:

Apr. 1, 19X2 Loaned $6,000 to Bing Bingham on a 1-year, 9% note.
Dec. 31, 19X2 Accrued interest revenue on the Bingham note.
Dec. 31, 19X2 Closed the interest revenue account.
Apr. 1, 19X3 Received the maturity value of the note from Bing Bingham.

Exercise 7-10   Accounting for a dishonored note receivable   (L.O. 6)

Record the following transactions in the general journal, assuming the company uses the allowance method to account for uncollectibles:

May 18 Sold goods to Joliff Map Supply, receiving a 120-day, 12% note for $2,700.
Sep. 15 The note is dishonored.
Nov. 30 After pursuing collection from Joliff Map Supply, wrote off their account as uncollectible.

Exercise 7-11   Recording notes receivable, discounting a note, and reporting the contingent liability in a note   (L.O. 6,7)

Prepare general journal entries to record the following transactions:

Aug. 14 Sold goods on account to E. Pucci, $2,900.

Dec. 2 Received a $2,900, 180-day, 10% note from E. Pucci in satisfaction of his past-due account receivable.

30 Sold the Pucci note by discounting it to a bank at 15%. (Use a 360-day year, and round amounts to the nearest dollar.)

Write the note to disclose the contingent liability at December 31.

Exercise 7-12   *Recording bad debts by the allowance method*   **(L.O. 4,7)**

At December 31, 19X5, Glanville Contractors has an accounts receivable balance of $129,000. Sales revenue for 19X5 is $950,000, including credit sales of $600,000. For each of the following situations, prepare the year-end adjusting entry to record doubtful account expense. Show how the accounts receivable and the allowance for doubtful accounts are reported on the balance sheet.

a. Allowance for Doubtful Accounts has a credit balance before adjustment of $1,600. Glanville Contractors estimates that doubtful account expense for the year is ½ of 1% of credit sales.

b. Allowance for Doubtful Accounts has a debit balance before adjustment of $1,100. Glanville Contractors estimates that $4,600 of the accounts receivable will prove uncollectible.

Exercise 7-13   *Reporting receivables with credit balances*   **(L.O. 7)**

The accounts receivable subsidiary ledger includes the following summarized data:

83 accounts with debit balances totaling	$113,650
9 accounts with credit balances totaling	3,980
Net total of balances.	$109,670

The company accountant proposes to report only the net total of $109,670. Show how these data should be reported on the balance sheet.

Exercise 7-14   *Evaluating ratio data*   **(L.O. 8)**

McKaig & Laughlin, a department store, reported the following amounts in its 19X8 financial statements. The 19X7 figures are given for comparison.

	19X8		19X7	
Current assets:				
Cash		$ 12,000		$ 8,000
Short-term investments		13,000		11,000
Accounts receivable	$80,000		$74,000	
less Allowance for				
uncollectibles	7,000	73,000	6,000	68,000
Inventory		191,000		187,000
Prepaid insurance		2,000		2,000
Total current assets		291,000		276,000
Total current liabilities		114,000		107,000
Net sales		813,000		762,000

Required

1. Determine whether the acid-test ratio improved or deteriorated from 19X7 to 19X8. How does McKaig & Laughlin's acid-test ratio compare with the industry average of .80?
2. Compare the days' sales in receivables measure for 19X8 with the company's credit terms of net 30.

Problems   *(Group A)*

Problem 7-1A   *Bank reconciliation and related journal entries*   **(L.O. 1,2)**

The August 31 bank statement of Master Control Company has just arrived from United Bank. To prepare the Master Control bank reconciliation, you gather the following data:

1. Master Control's Cash account shows a balance of $5,616.14 on August 31.
2. The bank statement includes two charges for returned checks from customers. One is a $395.00 check received from Shoreline Express and deposited on August 20, returned by Shoreline's bank with the imprint "Unauthorized Signature." The other is an NSF check in the amount of $146.67 received from Lipsey, Inc. This check had been deposited on August 17.
3. The following Master Control checks are outstanding at August 31:

Check No.	Amount
237	$ 46.10
288	141.00
291	578.05
293	11.87
294	609.51
295	8.88
296	101.63

4. The bank statement includes a deposit of $1,191.17, collected by the bank on behalf of Master Control. Of the total, $1,011.81 is collection of a note receivable, and the remainder is interest revenue.
5. The bank statement shows that Master Control earned $38.19 of interest on its bank balance during August. This amount was added to Master Control's account by the bank.
6. The bank statement lists a $10.50 subtraction for the bank service charge.
7. On August 31 the Master Control treasurer deposited $306.15, but this deposit does not appear on the bank statement.
8. The bank statement includes a $300.00 deposit that Master Control did not make. The bank had erroneously credited the Master Control account for another bank customer's deposit.
9. The August 31 bank balance is $7,784.22.

Required

1. Prepare the bank reconciliation for Master Control Company at August 31.
2. Record in general journal form the entries necessary to bring the book balance of Cash into agreement with the adjusted book balance on the reconciliation. Include an explanation for each entry.

Problem 7-2A   *Bank reconciliation and related journal entries*   **(L.O. 1,2)**

Assume selected columns of the cash receipts journal and the check register of Hard Rock Cafe appear as follows at April 30, 19X4:

Cash Receipts Journal (Posting reference is CR)		Check Register (Posting reference is CD)	
Date	Cash Debit	Check No.	Cash Credit
Apr. 2	$ 4,174	3113	$ 991
8	407	3114	147
10	559	3115	1,930
16	2,187	3116	664
22	1,854	3117	1,472
29	1,060	3118	1,000
30	337	3119	632
Total	$10,578	3120	1,675
		3121	100
		3122	2,413
		Total	$11,024

Assume the Cash account of Hard Rock Cafe shows the following information at April 30, 19X4.

Cash

Date	Item	Jrnl. Ref.	Debit	Credit	Balance
Apr. 1	Balance				7,911
30		CR.6	10,578		18,489
30		CD.11		11,024	7,465

Hard Rock Cafe received the following bank statement on April 30, 19X4.

Bank Statement for April 19X4

Beginning balance		$ 7,911
Deposits and other Credits:		
Apr. 4	$4,174	
9	407	
12	559	
17	2,187	
22	1,368 BC	
23	1,854	10,549
Checks and other Debits:		
Apr. 7	$ 991	
13	1,390	
14	903 US	
15	147	
18	664	
26	1,472	
30	1,000	
30	20 SC	6,587
Ending Balance		$11,873

Explanation: BC-Bank Collection   US-Unauthorized Signature   SC-Service Charge

Additional data for the bank reconciliation include:

1. The unauthorized signature check was received from S. M. Holt.
2. The $1,368 bank collection of a note receivable on April 22 included $185 interest revenue.

3. The correct amount of check number 3115, a payment on account, is $1,390. (The Hard Rock Cafe accountant mistakenly recorded the check for $1,930.)

Required

1. Prepare the bank reconciliation of Hard Rock Cafe at April 30, 19X4.
2. Record the entries based on the bank reconciliation. Include explanations.

Problem 7-3A   *Accounting for petty cash transactions*   *(L.O. 2,3)*

Suppose that on June 1 Hitachi Electronics opens a district office in Little Rock and creates a petty cash fund with an imprest balance of $350. During June, Sharon Dietz, the fund custodian, signs the following petty cash tickets:

Ticket Number	Item	Amount
1	Postage for package received	$ 8.40
2	Decorations and refreshments for office party	13.19
3	Two boxes of floppy disks	16.82
4	Typewriter ribbons	27.13
5	Dinner money for sales manager entertaining a customer	50.00
6	Plane ticket for executive business trip to Memphis	69.00
7	Delivery of package across town	6.30

On June 30, prior to replenishment, the fund contains these tickets plus $173.51. The accounts affected by petty cash disbursements are Office Supplies Expense, Travel Expense, Delivery Expense, Entertainment Expense, and Postage Expense.

Required

1. Explain the characteristics and the internal control features of an imprest fund.
2. Make the general journal entries to create the fund and to replenish it. Include explanations. Also, briefly describe what the custodian does on these dates.
3. Make the entry on July 1 to increase the fund balance to $500. Include an explanation, and briefly describe what the custodian does.

Problem 7-4A   *Accounting for uncollectibles by the direct write-off and allowance methods   (L.O. 4,7)*

On May 31, Sironia, Inc. had a $216,000 debit balance in Accounts Receivable. During June the company had sales revenue of $788,000, which included $640,000 in credit sales. Other data for June include:

Collections on accounts receivable, $599,400
Write-offs of uncollectible receivables, $8,700

Required

1. Record uncollectible account expense for June by the *direct write-off* method. Show all June activity in Accounts Receivable and Uncollectible Account Expense.
2. Record uncollectible account expense and write-offs of customer accounts for June by the *allowance* method. Show all June activity in Accounts Receivable, Allowance for Uncollectible Accounts, and Uncollectible Account Expense. The May 31 unadjusted balance in Allowance for Uncol-

lectible Accounts was $2,200 (credit). Uncollectible Account expense was estimated at 2 percent of credit sales.

3. What amount of uncollectible account expense would Sironia, Inc. report on its June income statement under the two methods? Which amount better matches expense with revenue? Give your reason.

4. What amount of *net* accounts receivable would Sironia, Inc. report on its June 30 balance sheet under the two methods? Which amount is more realistic? Give your reason.

Problem 7-5A *Uncollectibles, notes receivable, discounting notes, dishonored notes, and accrued interest revenue* **(L.O. 4,6)**

Assume Ralston Purina, manufacturer of pet foods, completed the following selected transactions:

19X5

Nov. 1 Sold goods to Safeway, Inc., receiving a $22,000, 3-month, 12 percent note.

Dec. 31 Made an adjusting entry to accrue interest on the Safeway note.

31 Made an adjusting entry to record doubtful account expense based on an aging of accounts receivable. The aging analysis indicates that $197,400 of accounts receivable will not be collected. Prior to this adjustment, the credit balance in Allowance for Doubtful Accounts is $189,900.

19X6

Feb. 1 Collected the maturity value of the Safeway note.

23 Received a 90-day, 15 percent, $4,000 note from Bliss Company on account. (This year February has 28 days.)

Mar. 31 Discounted the Bliss Co. note to Lakewood Bank at 20 percent.

Apr. 23 Sold merchandise to Lear Corporation, receiving a 60-day, 10 percent note for $6,000.

June 22 Lear Corp. dishonored its note at maturity; converted the maturity value of the note to an account receivable.

July 15 Loaned $8,500 cash to McNeil, Inc., receiving a 30-day, 12 percent note.

17 Sold merchandise to Grant Corp., receiving a 3-month, 10 percent, $8,000 note.

Aug. 5 Collected $6,100 on account from Lear Corporation.

14 Collected the maturity value of the McNeil, Inc., note.

17 Discounted the Grant Corp. note to Lakewood Bank at 15 percent.

Oct. 17 Grant Corp. dishonored its note at maturity; paid Lakewood Bank the maturity value of the note plus a protest fee of $50 and debited an account receivable from Grant Corp.

Dec. 15 Wrote off as uncollectible the account receivable from Grant Corp.

Required

Record the transactions in the general journal. Explanations are not required.

Problem 7-6A *Using the percentage of sales and aging approaches for uncollectibles* **(L.O. 4,7)**

The December 31, 19X4, balance sheet of Brazos Rubber Products reports the following:

Accounts Receivable $141,000

Allowance for Doubtful Accounts (credit balance)   3,200

At the end of each quarter, Brazos estimates doubtful account expense to be 1½ percent of credit sales. At the end of the year, the company ages its accounts receivable and adjusts the balance in Allowance for Doubtful Accounts to correspond to the aging schedule. During 19X5 Brazos completes the following selected transactions:

Jan. 16   Wrote off as uncollectible the $403 account receivable from DePaul, Inc., and the $1,719 account receivable from Frank Shoe Company.

Mar. 31   Recorded doubtful account expense based on credit sales of $100,000.

Apr. 15   Received $300 from Frank Shoe Company after prolonged negotiations with Frank Shoe Company's attorney. Brazos has no hope of collecting the remainder.

May 13   Wrote off as uncollectible the $2,980 account receivable from M. E. Cate.

June 30   Recorded doubtful account expense based on credit sales of $114,000.

Aug. 9   Made a compound entry to write off the following uncollectible accounts: Clifford, Inc., $235; Matz Co., $188; and Lew Norris, $1,006.

Sep. 30   Recorded doubtful account expense based on credit sales of $130,000.

Oct. 18   Wrote off as uncollectible the $767 account receivable from Bliss Co. and the $430 account receivable from Micro Data.

Dec. 31   Recorded doubtful account expense based on the following summary of the aging of accounts receivable.

Total Balance	Age of Accounts			
	1–30 Days	31–60 Days	61–90 Days	Over 90 Days
$127,400	$74,600	$31,100	$12,000	$9,700
Estimated percentage uncollectible	0.1%	0.4%	5.0%	30.0%

Dec. 31   Made the closing entry for Doubtful Account Expense for the entire year.

Required

1. Record the transactions in the general journal.
2. Open the Allowance for Doubtful Accounts and post entries affecting that account. Keep a running balance.
3. Most companies report two-year comparative financial statements. If Brazos's Accounts Receivable balance is $127,400 at December 31, 19X5, show how the company would report its accounts receivable on a comparative balance sheet for 19X5 and 19X4, as follows:

	19X5	19X4
Accounts receivable	_____	_____
Less: Allowance for doubtful accounts	_____	_____
Net accounts receivable	_____	_____

Problem 7-7A *Controlling cash receipts from customers* **(L.O. 5)**

Medical Laboratory Service provides laboratory testing for samples that physicians send in. All work is performed on account, with regular monthly billing to participating doctors. Agnes Bisset, accountant for Medical Laboratory Service, receives and opens the mail. Company procedure requires her to separate customer checks from the remittance slips, which list the amounts she posts as credits to customer accounts receivable. Bisset deposits the checks in the bank. She computes each day's total amount posted to customer accounts and agrees this total to the bank deposit slip. This is intended to ensure that all receipts are deposited in the bank.

Required

As the auditor of Medical Laboratory Service, write a memo to management to evaluate the company's internal controls over cash receipts from customers. If the system is effective, identify its strong features. If the system has flaws, propose a way to strengthen the controls.

Problem 7-8A *Accounting for notes receivable, including discounting notes and accruing interest revenue* **(L.O. 6)**

A company received the following notes during 19X5. Notes (1), (2), and (3) were discounted on the dates and at the rates indicated.

Note	Date	Principal Amount	Interest Rate	Term	Date Discounted	Discount Rate
(1)	July 15	$ 6,000	8%	6 months	Oct. 15	12%
(2)	Aug. 19	11,000	12%	90 days	Aug. 30	15%
(3)	Sep. 1	16,000	15%	120 days	Nov. 2	20%
(4)	Oct. 30	7,000	12%	3 months	—	—
(5)	Nov. 19	15,000	10%	60 days	—	—
(6)	Dec. 1	12,000	9%	1 year	—	—

Required

As necessary in requirements 1 through 5, identify each note by number, compute interest using a 360-day year for those notes with terms specified in days or years, round all interest amounts to the nearest dollar, and present entries in general journal form. Explanations are not required.

1. Determine the due date and maturity value of each note.
2. For each discounted note, determine the discount and proceeds from sale of the note.
3. Journalize the discounting of notes (1) and (2).
4. Journalize a single adjusting entry at December 31, 19X5, to record accrued interest revenue on notes (4), (5), and (6).
5. Journalize the collection of principal and interest on note (4).

Problem 7-9A *Notes receivable, discounted notes, dishonored notes, and accrued interest revenue* **(L.O. 6)**

Record the following selected transactions in the general journal. Explanations are not required.

19X2
Dec. 21   Received a $10,800, 30-day, 10 percent note on account from Zettler Gas Service.

Dec. 31 Made an adjusting entry to accrue interest on the Zettler note.

31 Made an adjusting entry to record doubtful account expense in the amount of 2/3 of 1 percent on credit sales of $604,800.

31 Made a compound closing entry for the appropriate accounts.

19X3

Jan. 20 Collected the maturity value of the Zettler note.

Apr. 19 Sold merchandise to city of Denver, receiving $500 cash and a 120-day, 12 percent note for $5,000.

May 1 Discounted the city of Denver note to First National Bank at 15 percent.

Sep. 14 Loaned $6,000 cash to Allstate Investors, receiving a 3-month, 13 percent note.

30 Received a $1,675, 60-day, 16 percent note from Matt Kurtz on his past-due account receivable.

Nov. 29 Matt Kurtz dishonored his note at maturity. Because of Kurtz's failure to pay—first his account, and now the note—decided to accrue no interest revenue and wrote off the note as uncollectible.

Dec. 14 Collected the maturity value of the Allstate Investors note.

31 Wrote off as uncollectible the accounts receivable of Ty Larson, $330, and Terry Gee, $460.

Problem 7-10A   Using ratio data to evaluate a company's position   (L.O. 8)

The comparative financial statements of Associated Mills Corp. for 19X6, 19X5, and 19X4 included the following selected data:

	Millions		
Balance sheet:	19X6	19X5	19X4
Current assets:			
Cash	$ 49	$ 66	$ 51
Short-term investments	131	174	122
Receivables, net of allowance for doubtful accounts of $6, $6, and $5	237	265	218
Inventories	389	341	302
Prepaid expenses	61	27	46
Total current assets	$ 867	$ 873	$ 739
Total current liabilities	$ 482	$ 528	$ 403
Income statement:			
Sales revenue	$5,189	$4,995	$4,206
Cost of sales	2,834	2,636	2,418

Required

1. For 19X6 and 19X5 compute these ratios:
   a. Current ratio
   b. Acid-test ratio
   c. Inventory turnover
   d. Days' sales in average receivables

2. Explain for top management which ratio values showed improvement from 19X5 to 19X6 and which ratio values showed deterioration. Which item in the financial statements caused some ratio values to improve and others to deteriorate?

Problem 7-1B   *Bank reconciliation and related journal entries* **(L.O. 1,2)**

The May 31 bank statement of Pressler Institute has just arrived from Central Bank. To prepare the Pressler bank reconciliation, you gather the following data:

1. The May 31 bank balance is $4,330.82.
2. The bank statement includes two charges for returned checks from customers. One is an NSF check in the amount of $67.50 received from Harley Doherty, a customer, recorded on the books by a debit to Cash, and deposited on May 19. The other is a $195.03 check received from Maria Gucci and deposited on May 21. It was returned by Ms. Gucci's bank with the imprint "Unauthorized Signature."
3. The following Pressler checks are outstanding at May 31:

Check No.	Amount
616	$403.00
802	74.25
806	36.60
809	161.38
810	229.05
811	48.91

4. The bank statement includes two special deposits: $899.14, which is the amount of dividend revenue the bank collected from General Electric Company on behalf of Pressler; and $16.86, the interest revenue Pressler earned on its bank balance during May.
5. The bank statement lists a $6.25 subtraction for the bank service charge.
6. On May 31 the Pressler treasurer deposited $381.14, but this deposit does not appear on the bank statement.
7. The bank statement includes a $410.00 deduction for a check drawn by Marimont Freight Company. Pressler promptly notified the bank of its error.
8. Pressler's Cash account shows a balance of $3,521.55 on May 31.

Required

1. Prepare the bank reconciliation for Pressler Institute at May 31.
2. Record in general journal form the entries necessary to bring the book balance of Cash into agreement with the adjusted book balance on the reconciliation. Include an explanation for each entry.

Problem 7-2B   *Bank reconciliation and related journal entries* **(L.O. 1,2)**

Selected columns of the cash receipts journal and the check register of Gulf Resources appear as follows at March 31, 19X5:

Cash Receipts Journal (Posting reference is CR)		Check Register (Posting reference is CD)	
Date	Cash Debit	Check No.	Cash Credit
Mar. 4	$2,716	1413	$ 1,465
9	544	1414	1,004
11	1,655	1415	450
14	896	1416	8
17	367	1417	775
25	890	1418	88
31	2,038	1419	4,126
Total	$9,106	1420	930
		1421	200
		1422	2,267
		Total	$11,313

Assume the Cash account of Gulf Resources shows the following information on March 31, 19X5.

Cash

Date	Item	Jrnl. Ref.	Debit	Credit	Balance
Mar. 1	Balance				14,188
31		CR. 10	9,106		23,294
31		CD. 16		11,313	11,981

Gulf Resources received the following bank statement on March 31, 19X5.

Bank Statement for March 19X5

Beginning balance			$14,188
Deposits and other Credits:			
Mar. 5		$2,716	
10		544	
11		1,655	
15		896	
18		367	
25		890	
31		1,000 BC	8,068
Checks and other Debits:			
Mar. 8		$ 441 NSF	
9		1,465	
13		1,004	
14		450	
15		8	
22		775	
29		88	
31		4,216	
31		25 SC	8,472
Ending balance			$13,784

Explanation: BC-Bank Collection   NSF-Nonsufficient Fund Check
SC-Service Charge

Additional data for the bank reconciliation include:

1. The NSF check was received late in February from L. M. Arnett.
2. The $1,000 bank collection of a note receivable on March 31 included $122 interest revenue.
3. The correct amount of check number 1419, a payment on account, is $4,216. (The Gulf Resources accountant mistakenly recorded the check for $4,126.)

Required

1. Prepare the bank reconciliation of Gulf Resources at March 31, 19X5.
2. Record the entries based on the bank reconciliation. Include explanations.

Problem 7-3B   *Accounting for petty cash transactions* **(L.O. 2,3)**

Suppose that on April 1 IBM opens a regional office in Omaha and creates a petty cash fund with an imprest balance of $200. During April, Eleanor McGillicuddy, the fund custodian, signs the following petty cash tickets:

Ticket Number	Item	Amount
101	Pencils	$ 6.89
102	Cab fare for executive	25.00
103	Delivery of package across town	7.75
104	Dinner money for executives entertaining a customer	80.00
105	Postage for package received	10.00
106	Decorations for office party	18.22
107	Two boxes of floppy disks	14.37

On April 30, prior to replenishment, the fund contains these tickets plus $34.77. The accounts affected by petty cash disbursements are Office Supplies Expense, Travel Expense, Delivery Expense, Entertainment Expense, and Postage Expense.

Required

1. Explain the characteristics and the internal control features of an imprest fund.
2. Make the general journal entries to create the fund and to replenish it. Include explanations. Also, briefly describe what the custodian does on these dates.
3. Make the entry on May 1 to increase the fund balance to $300. Include an explanation, and briefly describe what the custodian does.

Problem 7-4B *Accounting for uncollectibles by the direct write-off and allowance methods* **(L.O. 4,7)**

On February 28 Centex Warehouse Co. had a $72,000 debit balance in Accounts Receivable. During March the company had sales revenue of $509,000, which included $443,000 in credit sales. Other data for March include:

Collections on accounts receivable, $451,600
Write-offs of uncollectible receivables, $3,300

Required

1. Record uncollectible account expense for March by the *direct write-off* method. Show all March activity in Accounts Receivable and Uncollectible Account Expense.
2. Record uncollectible account expense and write-offs of customer accounts for March by the *allowance* method. Show all March activity in Accounts Receivable, Allowance for Uncollectible Accounts, and Uncollectible Account Expense. The February 28 unadjusted balance in Allowance for Uncollectible Accounts was $800 (debit). Uncollectible account expense was estimated at 2 percent of credit sales.
3. What amount of uncollectible account expense would Centex Warehouse Co. report on its March income statement under the two methods? Which amount better matches expense with revenue? Give your reason.
4. What amount of *net* accounts receivable would Centex Warehouse Co. report on its March 31 balance sheet under the two methods? Which amount is more realistic? Give your reason.

Problem 7-5B *Uncollectibles, notes receivable, discounting notes, dishonored notes, and accrued interest revenue* **(L.O. 4,6)**

Assume the Sherwin-Williams Company, a major manufacturer of paint products, completed the following selected transactions:

19X4

Dec. 1   Sold goods to Central Paint Supply, receiving a $15,000, 3-month, 10 percent note.

31   Made an adjusting entry to accrue interest on the Central Paint Supply note.

31   Made an adjusting entry to record doubtful account expense based on an aging of accounts receivable. The aging analysis indicates that $355,800 of accounts receivable will not be collected. Prior to this adjustment, the credit balance in Allowance for Doubtful Accounts is $346,100.

19X5

Feb. 18   Received a 90-day, 10 percent, $5,000 note from Dilley, Inc., on account. (This year February has 28 days.)

Mar. 1   Collected the maturity value of the Central Paint Supply note.

8   Discounted the Dilley note to First State Bank at 16 percent.

Apr. 21   Sold merchandise to Brown Group, receiving a 60-day, 9 percent note for $4,000.

June 20   Brown Group dishonored its note at maturity and converted the maturity value of the note to an account receivable.

July 12   Loaned $60,000 cash to Consolidated Investments, receiving a 90-day, 13 percent note.

13   Sold merchandise to Pearson Paint Shop, receiving a 4-month, 12 percent, $2,500 note.

Aug. 2   Collected $4,060 on account from Brown Group.

Sep. 13   Discounted the Pearson Paint Shop note to First State Bank at 18 percent.

Oct. 10   Collected the maturity value of the Consolidated Investments note.

Nov. 13   Pearson Paint Shop dishonored its note at maturity; paid First State Bank the maturity value of the note plus a protest fee of $35 and debited an account receivable from Pearson Paint Shop.

Dec. 31   Wrote off as uncollectible the account receivable from Pearson Paint Shop.

Required

Record the transactions in the general journal. Explanations are not required.

Problem 7-6B *Using the percentage of sales and aging approaches for uncollectibles (L.O. 4,7)*

The December 31, 19X6, balance sheet of Safelite Auto Glass reports the following:

Accounts Receivable $256,000
Allowance for Doubtful Accounts (credit balance) 7,100

At the end of each quarter, Safelite Auto Glass estimates doubtful account expense to be 2 percent of credit sales. At the end of the year, the company ages its accounts receivable and adjusts the balance in Allowance for Doubtful Accounts to correspond to the aging schedule. During 19X7 Safelite completes the following selected transactions:

Jan. 31   Wrote off as uncollectible the $855 account receivable from Spinelli Company and the $3,287 account receivable from Leo Maltsburger.

Mar. 31 Recorded doubtful account expense based on credit sales of $120,000.

May 2 Received $1,000 from Leo Maltsberger after prolonged negotiations with Maltsberger's attorney. Safelite has no hope of collecting the remainder.

June 15 Wrote off as uncollectible the $1,120 account receivable from Lisa Brown.

June 30 Recorded doubtful account expense based on credit sales of $166,000.

July 14 Made a compound entry to write off the following uncollectible accounts: C. H. Harris, $766; Graphics Unlimited, $2,413; and Ben McQueen, $134.

Sep. 30 Recorded doubtful account expense based on credit sales of $141,400.

Nov. 22 Wrote off the following accounts receivable as uncollectible: Monet Corp., $1,345; Blocker, Inc., $2,109; and Main Street Plaza, $755.

Dec. 31 Recorded doubtful account expense based on the following summary of the aging of accounts receivable:

Total Balance	Age of Accounts			
	1–30 Days	31–60 Days	61–90 Days	Over 90 Days
$294,600	$161,500	$86,000	$32,000	$15,100
Estimated percentage uncollectible	0.2%	0.5%	4.0%	50.0%

Dec. 31 Made the closing entry for Doubtful Account Expense for the entire year.

Required

1. Record the transactions in the general journal.
2. Open the Allowance for Doubtful Accounts, and post entries affecting that account. Keep a running balance.
3. Most companies report two-year comparative financial statements. If Safelite's Accounts Receivable balance is $294,600 at December 31, 19X7, show how the company would report its accounts receivable in a comparative balance sheet for 19X7 and 19X6, as follows:

	19X7	19X6
Accounts receivable	_____	_____
Less: Allowance for doubtful accounts	_____	_____
Net accounts receivable	_____	_____

Problem 7-7B *Controlling cash receipts from customers* (L.O. 5)

Chavanne Sporting Goods distributes merchandise to sporting goods stores. All sales are on credit, so virtually all cash receipts arrive in the mail. Evelyn Hupp, the company president, has just returned from a trade association meeting with new ideas for the business. Among other things, Hupp plans to institute stronger internal controls over cash receipts from customers.

Required

Outline a set of procedures to ensure that all cash receipts are deposited in the bank and that the total amount of each day's cash receipts are posted as credits to customer accounts receivable.

Problem 7-8B
Accounting for notes receivable, including discounting notes and accruing interest revenue **(L.O. 6)**

A company received the following notes during 19X3. Notes (1), (2), and (3) were discounted on the dates and at the rates indicated.

Note	Date	Principal Amount	Interest Rate	Term	Date Discounted	Discount Rate
(1)	July 12	$12,000	10%	3 months	Aug. 12	15%
(2)	Aug. 4	6,000	11%	90 days	Sep. 30	13%
(3)	Oct. 21	5,000	15%	60 days	Nov. 3	18%
(4)	Nov. 30	12,000	12%	6 months	—	—
(5)	Dec. 7	9,000	10%	30 days	—	—
(6)	Dec. 23	15,000	9%	1 year	—	—

Required

As necessary in requirements 1 through 5, identify each note by number, compute interest using a 360-day year for those notes with terms specified in days or years, round all interest amounts to the nearest dollar, and present entries in general journal form. Explanations are not required.

1. Determine the due date and maturity value of each note.
2. For each discounted note, determine the discount and proceeds from sale of the note.
3. Journalize the discounting of notes (1) and (2).
4. Journalize a single adjusting entry at December 31, 19X3, to record accrued interest revenue on notes (4), (5), and (6).
5. Journalize the collection of principal and interest on note (5).

Problem 7-9B
Notes receivable, discounted notes, dishonored notes, and accrued interest revenue **(L.O. 6)**

Record the following selected transactions in the general journal. Explanations are not required.

19X6
Dec. 19   Received a $5,000, 60-day, 12 percent note on account from City Cablevision.

     31   Made an adjusting entry to accrue interest on the City Cablevision note.

     31   Made an adjusting entry to record doubtful account expense in the amount of 8/10 of 1 percent of credit sales of $474,500.

     31   Made a compound closing entry for the appropriate accounts.

19X7
Feb. 17   Collected the maturity value of the City Cablevision note.

Mar. 22   Sold merchandise to Idaho Power Co., receiving $1,400 cash and a 90-day, 10 percent note for $6,000.

May   3   Discounted the Idaho Power Co. note to First National Bank at 15 percent.

June   1   Loaned $10,000 cash to Linz Brothers, receiving a 6-month, 11 percent note.

Oct. 31   Received a $1,500, 60-day, 12 percent note from Ned Pierce on his past-due account receivable.

Dec. 1 Collected the maturity value of the Linz Brothers note.

30 Ned Pierce dishonored his note at maturity. Because of Pierce's failure to pay—first his account, and now the note—decided to accrue no interest revenue and wrote off the note receivable as uncollectible.

31 Wrote off as uncollectible the accounts receivable of Al Bynum, $435, and Ray Sharp, $276.

Problem 7-10B *Using ratio data to evaluate a company's position* (L.O. 8)

The comparative financial statements of Domingo Catalog Merchants for 19X4, 19X3, and 19X2 included the following selected data:

	Millions		
Balance sheet:	19X4	19X3	19X2
Current assets:			
Cash	$ 17	$ 28	$ 22
Short-term investments	73	101	69
Receivables, net of			
allowance for doubtful			
accounts of $7, $6, and $4	136	154	127
Inventories..........................	428	373	341
Prepaid expenses	42	31	25
Total current assets	$ 696	$ 687	$ 584
Total current liabilities	$ 430	$ 446	$ 388
Income statement:			
Sales revenue	$2,671	$2,505	$1,944
Cost of sales	1,180	1,160	963

Required

1. For 19X4 and 19X3 compute these ratios:
   a. Current ratio
   b. Acid-test ratio
   c. Inventory turnover
   d. Days' sales in average receivables
2. Explain for top management which ratio values showed improvement from 19X3 to 19X4 and which ratio values showed deterioration. Which item in the financial statements caused some ratio values to improve and others to deteriorate?

Extending Your Knowledge

Decision Problems

1. Using the Bank Reconciliation to Detect a Theft (L.O. 3)

Agricultural Equipment Company has poor internal control over its cash transactions. Recently Grace Goodrich, the controller, has suspected the cashier of stealing. Details of the business's cash position at September 30 follow.

1. The Cash account shows a balance of $19,502. This amount includes a September 30 deposit of $3,794 that does not appear on the September 30 bank statement.

2. The September 30 bank statement shows a balance of $16,424. The bank statement lists a $200 credit for a bank collection, an $8 debit for the service charge, and a $36 debit for an NSF check. The Agricultural Equipment accountant has not recorded any of these items on the books.

3. At September 30 the following checks are outstanding:

Check No.	Amount
154	$116
256	150
278	253
291	190
292	206
293	145

4. The cashier handles all incoming cash and makes bank deposits. He also reconciles the monthly bank statement. His September 30 reconciliation follows.

Balance per books, September 30		$19,502
Add: Outstanding checks		560
Bank collection		200
		20,262
Less: Deposits in transit	$3,794	
Service charge	8	
NSF check	36	3,838
Balance per bank, September 30		$16,424

Goodrich has requested that you determine whether the cashier has stolen cash from the business and, if so, how much. Goodrich also asks you to identify how the cashier has attempted to conceal the theft. To make this determination, you perform your own bank reconciliation using the format illustrated in the chapter. There are no bank or book errors. Goodrich also asks you to evaluate the internal controls and to recommend any changes needed to improve them.

2. Estimating the Collectibility of Accounts Receivable (L.O. 1,6,7)

Assume you work in the corporate loan department of Brunswick Bank. Maria Presti, owner of MP Manufacturing Inc., a manufacturer of wooden furniture, has come to you seeking a loan for $350,000 to buy new manufacturing equipment to expand her operations. She proposes to use her accounts receivable as collateral for the loan and has provided you with the following information from her most recent audited financial statements:

	(Thousands)		
	19X9	19X8	19X7
Sales	$1,475	$1,589	$1,502
Cost of goods sold	876	947	905
Gross profit	599	642	597
Other expenses	518	487	453
Net profit or (loss) before taxes	$ 81	$ 155	$ 144
Accounts receivable	$ 458	$ 387	$ 374
Allowance for doubtful accounts ...	23	31	29

Required

1. What analysis would you perform on the information Ms. Presti has provided? Would you grant the loan based on this information? Give your reason.
2. What additional information would you request from Ms. Presti? Give your reason.
3. Assume Ms. Presti provided you with the information requested in question 2. What would make you change the decision you made in question 1?

Ethical Issue

Goodwill Finance Company is in the consumer loan business. It borrows from banks and loans out the money at higher interest rates. Goodwill's bank requires Goodwill to submit quarterly financial statements in order to keep its line of credit. Goodwill's main asset is Notes Receivable. Therefore, Uncollectible Account Expense and Allowance for Uncollectible Accounts are important accounts.

Goodwill's owner, Jacob Marleybone, likes net income to increase in a smooth pattern rather than to increase in some periods and decrease in other periods. To report smoothly increasing net income, Marleybone underestimates Uncollectible Account Expense in some periods. In other periods, Marleybone overestimates the expense. He reasons that the income overstatements roughly offset the income understatements over time.

Required

Is Goodwill's practice of smoothing income ethical? Give your reasons.

Financial Statement Problems

1. Accounts Receivable and Related Uncollectibles (L.O. 1)
Use data from the Goodyear Tire & Rubber Company balance sheet and the related note titled Accounts and Notes Receivable, in Appendix C, to answer these questions. Show all amounts in millions, rounded to the nearest $100,000. For example, show $8,600,000 as $8.6 million.

1. How much did Goodyear's customers owe the company at December 31, 1990? Of this amount, how much did Goodyear expect to collect?
2. Journalize the following for the year ended December 31, 1991, using Goodyear's actual account titles. Explanations are not required.
   a. Net sales revenue of $10,906.8 million. Give one entry for the year's total, assuming all net sales revenue is earned on account.
   b. Doubtful account expense, estimated to equal 1 percent of net sales.
   c. Cash collections on account, $10,977.9 million.
   d. Write-offs of uncollectibles totaling $96.5 million.
3. Post to Accounts and Notes Receivable and Allowance for Doubtful Accounts, inserting these accounts' December 31, 1990, balances.
4. After posting, compare your account balances to those at December 31, 1991, in the Accounts and Notes Receivable note. Your figures should agree with the Goodyear actual amounts.
5. How much did Goodyear's customers owe the company at December 31, 1991? How much of this total did Goodyear expect to collect? Describe in words the amount reported for Accounts and Notes Receivable on Goodyear's December 31, 1991, balance sheet.

2. Accounts Receivable, Uncollectibles, and Notes Receivable (L.O. 1,5)
Obtain the annual report of an actual company of your choosing.

Required

1. How much did customers owe the company at the end of the current year? Of this amount how much did the company expect to collect? How much did the company expect *not* to collect?

2. Assume during the current year that the company recorded doubtful account expense equal to 1 percent of net sales. Starting with the beginning balance, analyze the Allowance for Doubtful Accounts to determine the amount of the receivable write-offs during the current year.

3. If the company does not have notes receivable, you may skip this requirement. If notes receivable are present at the end of the current year, assume their interest rate is 9 percent. Also assume that no new notes receivable arose during the following year. Journalize these transactions that took place during the following year:

   a. Received cash for 75 percent of the interest revenue earned during the year.

   b. Accrued the remaining portion of the interest revenue earned during the year.

   c. At year end collected one half of the notes receivable.

4. Suppose the company discounted a $500,000 note receivable. Under what heading in the annual report would the company report the discounting of a note receivable? Show how the company would disclose this fact.

Comprehensive Problem for Part Two

Complete Accounting Cycle for a Merchandising Entity;
Special Journals

J. T. McCord Company closes its books and prepares financial statements at the end of each month. The company completed the following transactions during August:

Aug. 1 Issued check no. 682 for August office rent of $2,000. (Debit Rent Expense.)

2 Issued check no. 683 to pay salaries of $1,240, which includes salary payable of $930 from July 31. McCord does *not* use reversing entries.

2 Issued invoice no. 503 for sale on account to R. T. Loeb, $600.

3 Purchased inventory on credit terms of 1/15 n/60 from Grant Publishers, $1,400.

4 Received net amount of cash on account from Fullam Company, $2,156, within the discount period.

4 Sold inventory for cash, $330.

5 Issued credit memo no. 267 to Park-Hee, Inc., for merchandise returned to McCord, $550.

5 Issued check no. 684 to purchase supplies for cash, $780.

6 Collected interest revenue of $1,100.

Aug. 7 Issued invoice no. 504 for sale on account to K. D. Skipper, $2,400.

8 Issued check no. 685 to pay Federal Company $2,600 of the amount owed at July 31. This payment occurred after the end of the discount period.

11 Issued check no. 686 to pay Grant Publishers the net amount owed from August 3.

12 Received cash from R. T. Loeb in full settlement of her account receivable from August 2.

16 Issued check no. 687 to pay salary expense of $1,240.

19 Purchased inventory for cash, $850, issuing check no. 688.

22 Purchased furniture on credit terms of 3/15 n/60 from Beaver Corporation, $510.

23 Sold inventory on account to Fullam Company, issuing invoice no. 505 for $9,966.

24 Received half the July 31 amount receivable from K. D. Skipper— after the end of the discount period.

25 Issued check no. 689 to pay utilities, $432.

26 Purchased supplies on credit terms of 2/10 n/30 from Federal Company, $180.

30 Returned damaged inventory to company from whom McCord made the cash purchase on August 19, receiving cash of $850.

30 Granted a sales allowance of $175 to K. D. Skipper, issuing credit memo no. 268.

31 Purchased inventory on credit terms of 1/10 n/30 from Suncrest Supply, $8,330.

31 Issued check no. 690 to J. T. McCord, owner of the business, for personal withdrawal, $1,700.

Required

1. Open these accounts with their account numbers and July 31 balances in the various ledgers.

General Ledger:

101	Cash	$ 4,490
102	Accounts Receivable	22,560
104	Interest Receivable	
105	Inventory	41,800
109	Supplies	1,340
117	Prepaid Insurance	2,200
140	Note Receivable, Long-term	11,000
160	Furniture	37,270
161	Accumulated Depreciation	10,550
201	Accounts Payable	12,600
204	Salary Payable	930
207	Interest Payable	320
208	Unearned Sales Revenue	
220	Note Payable, Long-term	42,000
301	Common Stock	25,000
302	Retained Earnings	29,260
303	Dividends	
400	Income Summary	
401	Sales Revenue	

402	Sales Discounts . . . .
403	Sales Returns and Allowances . . . .
410	Interest Revenue . . . .
501	Purchases. . . . .
502	Purchase Discounts . . . .
503	Purchase Returns and Allowances . . . .
510	Salary Expense . . . .
513	Rent Expense . . . .
514	Depreciation Expense . . . .
516	Insurance Expense. . . . .
517	Utilities Expense . . . .
519	Supplies Expense. . . . .
523	Interest Expense. . . . .

Accounts Receivable Subsidiary Ledger: Fullam Company, $2,200; R. T. Loeb; Park-Hee, Inc., $11,590; K. D. Skipper, $8,770.

Accounts Payable Subsidiary Ledger: Beaver Corporation; Federal Company, $12,600; Grant Publishers; Suncrest Supply.

2. Journalize the August transactions in a sales journal (page 4), a cash receipts journal (page 11), a purchases journal (page 8), a cash disbursements journal (page 5), and a general journal (page 9). Use the journals as illustrated in Chapter 6. McCord makes all credit sales on terms of 2/10 n/30.

3. Post daily to the accounts receivable subsidiary ledger and the accounts payable subsidiary ledger. On August 31, post to the general ledger.

4. Prepare a trial balance in the Trial Balance columns of a work sheet, and use the following information to complete the work sheet for the month ended August 31:

a. Accrued interest revenue, $100.
b. Supplies on hand, $990.
c. Prepaid insurance expired, $550.
d. Depreciation expense, $230.

e. Accrued salary expense, $1,030.
f. Accrued interest expense, $320.
g. Unearned sales revenue, $450.*
h. Inventory on hand, $47,700.

*On August 2, J. T. McCord Company sold inventory to R. T. Loeb and collected in full on August 12. Upon learning that the shipment to Loeb was incomplete, McCord plans to ship the goods to her during September. At August 31, $450 of unearned sales revenue needs to be recorded.

5. Prepare J. T. McCord Company's bank reconciliation at August 31. The bank statement shows a cash balance of $2,863 and lists all cash receipts for the month except the amount received on the 30th. Checks 689 and 690 did not clear the bank during August. The bank statement also reveals a bank error. The bank mistakenly deducted $870 for check number 684. J. T. McCord Company keeps just enough money on deposit to avoid service charges but earns no interest on the bank balance.

6. Prepare McCord's multiple-step income statement and statement of retained earnings for August. Prepare the balance sheet at August 31.

7. Journalize and post the adjusting and closing entries.

8. Prepare a postclosing trial balance at August 31. Also, balance the total of the customer accounts in the accounts receivable subsidiary ledger against the Accounts Receivable balance in the general ledger. Do the same for the accounts payable subsidiary ledger and Accounts Payable in the general ledger.

Chapter 8

Merchandise Inventory

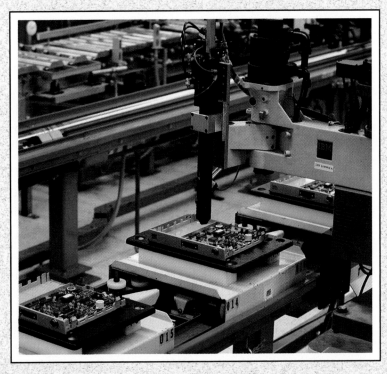

Whittaker Corporation, a manufacturer of precision tools, announced yesterday that it was slashing inventories in anticipation of slower sales during the third and fourth quarters of 1991. Analysts were caught off guard by the Whittaker announcement. As recently as June 30, Whittaker was expanding rapidly to take advantage of the new markets arising from the European business unification scheduled for 1992. Company plans called for opening an assembly plant in Belgium and also increasing the sales force by 30 percent. What caused operations to sour so suddenly?

Rafael Montalban, senior analyst at Piper & Jeffries in New York City, argues that Whittaker's slide began late last year. Mr. Montalban issued a blistering attack on Whittaker management in March, noting that the company's inventory was becoming obsolete. Unlike competitors, who were using electrically controlled robots in their manufacturing processes, Whittaker stuck to the hydraulic robots developed during the 1980s. The obsolete machinery produced inferior products that ceased to sell. Whittaker has a warehouse full of unsaleable inventory, which will pose a challenge for the company and its accountants.

Among other topics, this chapter discusses how to account for inventory that has lost some of its value.

Merchandise inventory is the largest *current asset* on the balance sheet of most businesses that manufacture or buy inventory for resale. Polaroid Corporation reported inventories of $412.7 million, compared with receivables of $289.5 million and cash of $187.0 million. Inventories are important to merchandisers of all sizes. Buying and selling inventory is the heart of wholesaling and retailing, whether the business is Sears, Safeway, or the corner hardware store.

Inventory is the major current asset of most merchandisers. What is their major expense? It is *cost of sales*, or *cost of goods sold* (COGS). For example, Westinghouse Electric Corporation reported its cost of sales at $7.1 billion compared with distribution, administrative, and general expenses of $1.5 billion. For Westinghouse and many other companies, cost of goods sold is greater than all other expenses combined.

Exhibit 8-1 traces the flow of inventory costs during the accounting period. The model presented in Exhibit 8-1 is fundamental to accounting for inventory.

The business starts each period with **beginning inventory,** the goods that are left over from the preceding period. During the period, the business purchases additional goods for resale. Together, beginning inventory and net purchases make up **goods available for sale.** Over the course of the period, the business sells some of the available goods. The cost of the inventory sold to customers is called the **cost of goods sold.** This cost is an expense because the inventory is no longer of use to the company. The goods still on hand at the end of the period are called **ending inventory.** Its cost is an asset because these goods are still available for sale.

EXHIBIT 8-1 *Flow of Inventory Costs*

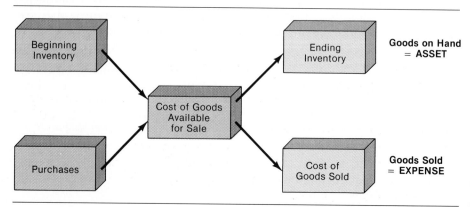

EXHIBIT 8-2 *Inventory and Cost of Goods Sold for Revco D.S., Inc.*

	(amounts in millions)
Beginning inventory	$ 276
+ Net purchases	1,348
= Cost of goods available for sale	1,624
− Ending inventory	317
= Cost of goods sold	$1,307

Exhibit 8-2 uses data from the financial statements of Revco D.S., Inc., a chain of discount drug stores concentrated in Ohio, Texas, and the Southeast, to present the flow of inventory costs in a format different from that shown in Exhibit 8-1. Notice that ending inventory is subtracted from cost of goods available for sale to figure the cost of goods sold. Throughout this chapter we ignore freight-in to avoid clutter.

The rest of this chapter fills in the details of our inventory cost flow model.

Figuring the Cost of Inventory

A necessary step in accounting for inventory is determining the cost of *ending inventory.* At the end of each period the *quantity* of inventory is multiplied by the *unit cost* of inventory to compute the cost of ending inventory.

Determining the Quantity of Inventory. Most businesses physically count their inventory at least once each year, often on the last day of the fiscal year. Inventory, an asset, must be reported accurately on the balance sheet.

You may have worked at a grocery store or some other type of retail business. If so, you will recall the process of "taking the inventory." Some entities shut the business down to get a good count of inventory on hand. Others count the goods on a weekend. Still others inventory the merchandise while business is being conducted. How is it done in a large organization?

Assume Revco Drug takes a complete physical inventory on its year-end date. Teams of counters in the company's approximately 1,700 stores record the quantities of each inventory item on hand. Each store forwards its total count to corporate headquarters, where home office employees determine the inventory grand total.

Complications may arise in determining the inventory quantity. Suppose the business has purchased some goods that are in transit when the inventory is counted. Even though these items are not physically present, they should be included in the inventory count if title to the goods has passed to the purchaser. When title passes from seller to purchaser, the purchaser becomes the legal owner of the goods.

The FOB—free on board—terms of the transaction govern when title passes from the seller to the purchaser. **FOB shipping point** indicates that title passes when the goods leave the seller's place of business. **FOB destination** means that title passes when the goods arrive at the purchaser's location. Therefore, goods in transit that are purchased FOB shipping point should be included in the purchaser's inventory. Goods in transit that are bought FOB destination should not be included.

Usually, the business has a purchase invoice, which lists the quantity of goods in transit and shows the FOB terms. Similarly, the business may have sold inventory that has not yet been shipped to the customer. If title has passed, these goods should be excluded from the seller's inventory, even though they may still be at the seller's place of business.

Another complication in counting inventory arises from consigned goods. In a **consignment** arrangement, the owner of the inventory (the consignor) transfers the goods to another business (the consignee). For a fee, the consignee sells the inventory on the owner's behalf. The consignee does *not* take title to the consigned goods and, therefore, should not include them in its own inventory. Consignments are common in retailing. Suppose Revco Drug is the consignee for some L'Eggs hosiery in its stores. Should Revco include this consigned merchandise in its inventory count? No, because Revco does not own the goods. Instead, the L'Eggs wholesaler—the consignor—includes the consigned goods in his or her inventory. A rule of thumb is to include in inventory only what the business owns.

Determining the Unit Cost of Inventory. Inventories are normally accounted for at historical cost, as the *cost principle* requires. **Inventory cost** is the price the business pays to acquire the inventory—not the selling price of the goods. Suppose a business purchases inventory for $10 and offers it for sale at $15. The inventory cost is reported at $10, not $15. Inventory cost includes its invoice price, less any purchase discount, plus sales tax, tariffs, transportation charges, insurance while in transit, and all other costs incurred to make the goods ready for sale.

The inventory quantity multiplied by the unit cost equals the cost of inventory. Thirty tape recorders at a cost of $100 each results in an inventory cost of $3,000.

<table>
<tr><td>OBJECTIVE 1
Apply four inventory
costing methods</td></tr>
</table>

Inventory Costing Methods

Determining the unit cost of inventory is easy when the unit cost remains constant during the period. However, the unit cost often changes. For example, during times of inflation, prices rise. The tape recorder model that cost the retailer $100 in January may cost $115 in June and $122 in October. Suppose the retailer sells 15 tape recorders in November. How many of them cost $100, how many cost $115, and how many cost $122? To compute the cost of goods sold and ending inventory amounts, the accountant must have some means of assigning the business's cost to each item sold. The four costing methods that GAAP allows are

1. Specific unit cost
2. Weighted-average cost
3. First-in, first-out (FIFO) cost
4. Last-in, first-out (LIFO) cost

A company can use any of these methods. Many companies use several methods—different methods for different categories of inventory.

Specific Unit Cost

Some businesses deal in inventory items that may be identified individually, like automobiles, jewels, and real estate. These businesses usually cost their inventory at the **specific cost** of the particular unit. For instance, a Chevrolet dealer may have two vehicles in the showroom—a "stripped-down" model that cost $14,000 and a "loaded" model that cost $17,000. If the dealer sells the loaded model for $19,700, cost of goods sold is $17,000, the cost of the specific unit. The gross margin on this sale is $2,700 ($19,700 − $17,000). If the stripped-down auto is the only unit left in inventory at the end of the period, ending inventory is $14,000, the cost to the retailer of the specific unit on hand.

The specific unit cost method is also called the *specific identification* method. This method is not practical for inventory items that have common characteristics, such as bushels of wheat, gallons of paint, or boxes of laundry detergent.

Weighted-Average Cost, FIFO Cost, and LIFO Cost

The weighted-average cost, first-in, first-out (FIFO), and last-in, first-out (LIFO) methods are fundamentally different from the specific unit cost method. These methods do not assign to inventory the specific cost of particular units. Instead, they assume different flows of costs into and out of inventory.

Weighted-Average Cost. The **weighted-average cost method,** often called the **average cost method,** is based on the weighted-average cost of inventory during the period. Average cost is determined by dividing the cost of goods available for sale (beginning inventory plus purchases) by the number of units available. Ending inventory and cost of goods sold are computed by multiplying the number of units by weighted-average cost per unit. Assume that cost of goods available for sale is $90, and 60 units are available. Weighted-average cost is $1.50 per unit ($90/60 = $1.50). Ending inventory of 20 units has an average cost of $30 (20 × $1.50 = $30). Cost of goods sold (40 units) is $60 (40 × $1.50). Panel A of Exhibit 8-3 gives the data in more detail. Panel B of the exhibit shows the weighted-average cost computations.

First-in, First-out (FIFO) Cost. Under the **first-in, first-out (FIFO) method,** the company must keep a record of the cost of each inventory unit purchased. The unit costs used in computing the ending inventory may be different from the unit costs used in computing the cost of goods sold. Under FIFO, the first costs into inventory are the first costs out to cost of goods sold— hence the name *first-in, first-out.* Ending inventory is based on the costs of the most recent purchases. In our example, the FIFO cost of ending inventory is $36. Cost of goods sold is $54. Panel A of Exhibit 8-3 gives the data, and Panel B shows the FIFO computations.

Last-in, First-out (LIFO) Cost. The **last-in, first-out (LIFO) method** also depends on the costs of particular inventory purchases. LIFO is the opposite of FIFO. Under LIFO, the last costs into inventory are the first costs out to cost of goods sold. This leaves the oldest costs—those of beginning inventory and the earliest purchases of the period—in ending inventory. In our example, the LIFO cost of ending inventory is $24. Cost of goods sold is $66. Panel A of Exhibit 8-3 gives the data, and Panel B shows the LIFO computations.

Panel A—Illustrative Data:

Beginning inventory (10 units @ $1 per unit)		$ 10
Purchases:		
No. 1 (25 units @ $1.40 per unit)	$ 35	
No. 2 (25 units @ $1.80 per unit)	45	
Total		80
Cost of goods available for sale (60 units)		90
Ending inventory (20 units @ $? per unit)		?
Cost of goods sold (40 units @ $? per unit)		$?

Panel B—Ending Inventory and Cost of Goods Sold:

Weighted-Average Cost Method:

Cost of goods available for sale—see Panel A (60 units @ average cost of $1.50* per unit)	$ 90
Ending inventory (20 units @ $1.50 per unit)	30
Cost of goods sold (40 units @ $1.50 per unit)	$ 60

*Cost of goods available for sale	$ 90
Number of units available for sale	÷60
Average cost per unit	$1.50

FIFO Cost Method:

Cost of goods available for sale (60 units—see Panel A)		$ 90
Ending inventory (cost of the *last* 20 units available:)		
20 units @ $1.80 per unit (from purchase no. 2)		36
Cost of goods sold (cost of the *first* 40 units available):		
10 units @ $1.00 per unit (all of beginning inventory)	$ 10	
25 units @ $1.40 per unit (all of purchase no. 1)	35	
5 units @ $1.80 per unit (from purchase no. 2)	9	
Total		$ 54

LIFO Cost Method:

Cost of goods available for sale (60 units—see Panel A)		$ 90
Ending inventory (cost of the *first* 20 units available):		
10 units @ $1.00 per unit (all of beginning inventory)	$ 10	
10 units @ $1.40 per unit (from purchase no. 1)	14	
Total		24
Cost of goods sold (cost of the *last* 40 units available):		
25 units @ $1.80 per unit (all of purchase no. 2)	45	
15 units @ $1.40 per unit (from purchase no. 1)	21	
Total		$ 66

Income Effects of FIFO, LIFO, and Weighted-Average Cost

In our discussion and examples, the cost of inventory rose during the accounting period. When prices change, different costing methods produce different cost of goods sold and ending inventory figures, as Exhibit 8-3 shows. When

EXHIBIT 8-4 Income Effects of FIFO, LIFO, and Weighted-Average Cost Inventory Methods

	FIFO		LIFO		Weighted-Average
Sales revenue (assumed)		$100,000		$100,000	$100,000
Costs of goods sold:					
Goods available for sale (assumed)	$ 90,000		$ 90,000		$ 90,000
Ending inventory..................	36,000		24,000		30,000
Cost of goods sold.................		54,000		66,000	60,000
Gross margin		$ 46,000		$ 34,000	$ 40,000

Summary of Income Effects—When Inventory Costs Are Increasing:

FIFO—Highest ending inventory	LIFO—Lowest ending inventory	Weighted-average—Results fall
Lowest cost of goods sold	Highest cost of goods sold	between the extremes
Highest gross margin	Lowest gross margin	of FIFO and LIFO

inventory costs are increasing, FIFO ending inventory is *highest* because it is priced at the most recent costs, which are the highest. LIFO ending inventory is *lowest* because it is priced at the oldest costs, which are the lowest. *Weighted-average* cost avoids the extremes of FIFO and LIFO. When inventory costs are decreasing, FIFO ending inventory is lowest, and LIFO is highest.

Exhibit 8-4 summarizes the income effects of the three inventory methods based on the data from Exhibit 8-3. Study the exhibit carefully, focusing on ending inventory, cost of goods sold, and gross margin.

The Income Tax Advantage of LIFO

When prices are rising, applying the LIFO method results in the *lowest taxable income* and thus the *lowest income taxes*. Let's use the gross margin data of Exhibit 8-4.

OBJECTIVE 2
Distinguish between the income effects and the tax effects of the inventory costing methods

	FIFO	LIFO	Weighted-Average
Gross margin.............................	$46,000	$34,000	$40,000
Operating expenses (assumed)	26,000	26,000	26,000
Income before income tax	$20,000	$ 8,000	$14,000
Income tax expense (40%)	$ 8,000	$ 3,200	$ 5,600

Income tax expense is lowest under LIFO ($3,200) and highest under FIFO ($8,000). The most attractive feature of LIFO is reduced income tax payments.

The Internal Revenue Service allows companies to use LIFO for tax purposes only if they use LIFO for financial reporting purposes. However, they may also report an alternative inventory amount in the notes to their financial statements. Federal-Mogul Corporation, a maker of industrial products, reported inventories at LIFO cost but also disclosed the FIFO cost of inventory in Note D, as follows. Observe that FIFO cost is higher than LIFO cost (amounts in millions).

	19X6	19X5
Inventories—Note D	$189	$148

Note D: *Inventories*
Inventories are stated at . . . last-in, first-out (LIFO) cost. . . . Use of the first-in, first-out (FIFO) cost method would have increased inventories by $95 million in 19X6 and $89 million in 19X5. . . .

Of what use is Federal-Mogul's disclosure of the alternative amounts under FIFO? An investor may be comparing Federal-Mogul with a company that uses FIFO. Federal-Mogul's inventory and cost of goods sold amounts under LIFO are not comparable with the other company's FIFO figures. To compare the two companies, the investor can convert Federal-Mogul's LIFO amounts to the FIFO basis. Simply substitute the FIFO amounts in place of those reported under LIFO. Here are the cost of goods sold figures (amounts in millions):

OBJECTIVE 3

Convert a company's cost of goods sold from the LIFO basis to the FIFO basis

	LIFO Amounts as Reported in the Income Statement			FIFO Amounts Based on Information in the Notes
Beginning inventory	$ 148	+ $89	=	$ 237
Net purchases	765			765
Cost of goods available for sale	913			1,002
Less: Ending inventory ...	189	+ $95	=	284
Cost of goods sold	$ 724			$ 718

Cost of goods sold under FIFO ($718 million) can now be used to compare the two companies. In the computation, notice that purchases are the same under FIFO and LIFO. Beginning FIFO inventory is the LIFO amount ($148 million) plus the increase to FIFO ($89 million), a total of $237 million. Ending FIFO inventory is the LIFO amount ($189 million) plus the increase ($95 million), a total of $284 million. These changes cause FIFO cost of goods sold to be less than the LIFO amount, which would cause income to be higher under FIFO. This is valuable information for an investor.

The 1970s and early 1980s were marked by high inflation, so many companies changed to LIFO for its tax advantage. Exhibit 8-5, based on an American Institute of Certified Public Accountants (AICPA) survey of 600 companies, indicates that LIFO and FIFO are the most popular inventory costing methods.

Generally Accepted Accounting Principles: A Comparison of the Inventory Methods

We may ask three questions to judge the three major inventory costing methods. (1) How well does each method match inventory expense—the cost of goods sold—to sales revenue on the income statement? (2) Which method reports the most up-to-date inventory amount on the balance sheet? (3) What effect do the methods have on income taxes? The weighted-average cost method produces amounts between the extremes of LIFO and FIFO.

LIFO better matches the current value of cost of goods sold with current revenue by assigning to this expense the most recent inventory costs. By con-

Exhibit 8-5 *Use of the Various Inventory Methods*

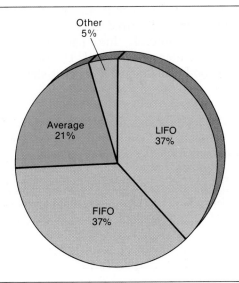

trast, FIFO matches the oldest inventory costs against the period's revenue—a poor matching of current expense with current revenue.

FIFO reports the most current inventory costs on the balance sheet. LIFO can result in absurd balance sheet valuations of inventories because the oldest prices are left in ending inventory.

As shown in the preceding section, LIFO results in the lowest income tax payments when prices are rising. Tax payments are highest under FIFO. When inventory prices are decreasing, tax payments are highest under LIFO and lowest under FIFO.

FIFO is criticized because it overstates income by so-called inventory profit during periods of inflation. Briefly, **inventory profit** is the difference between gross margin figured on the FIFO basis and gross margin figured on the LIFO basis. Exhibit 8-4 illustrates inventory profit. The $12,000 difference between FIFO and LIFO gross margins ($46,000 − $34,000 = $12,000) results from the difference in cost of goods sold. This $12,000 amount is called *FIFO inventory profit, phantom profit,* or *illusory profit.* Why? Because to stay in business the company must replace the inventory it has sold. The replacement cost of the merchandise is more closely approximated by the cost of goods sold under LIFO ($66,000) than the FIFO amount ($54,000).

LIFO is criticized because it allows managers to manipulate net income. Assume inventory prices are rising rapidly, and a company wants to show less income for the year (in order to pay less taxes). Managers can buy a large amount of inventory near the end of the year. Under LIFO these high inventory costs immediately become expense—as cost of goods sold. As a result, the income statement reports a lower net income. Conversely, if the business is having a bad year, management may wish to increase reported income. To do so, managers can delay a large purchase of high-cost inventory until the next period. This inventory is not expensed as cost of goods sold in the current year. Thus management avoids decreasing the current year's reported income.

A company may want to report the highest income, and FIFO meets this need when prices are rising. But the company must pay the highest income taxes under FIFO. When prices are falling, LIFO reports the highest income.

Which inventory method is better—LIFO or FIFO? There is no single answer to this question. Different companies have different motives for the inventory method they choose. Polaroid Corporation uses FIFO, J. C. Penney Company uses LIFO, and Motorola, Inc., uses weighted-average cost. Still other companies use more than one method. The Black and Decker Manufacturing Company uses both LIFO and FIFO, as it stated in an annual report (amounts in millions):

Inventories $390

NOTES TO CONSOLIDATED FINANCIAL STATEMENTS
Note 1: Summary of Accounting Policies
Inventories: The cost of United States inventories is based on the last-in, first-out (LIFO) method; all other inventories are based on the first-in, first-out (FIFO) method. The cost of . . . inventories stated under the LIFO method represents approximately 40% of the value of total inventories.

Consistency Principle

The **consistency principle** states that businesses should use the same accounting methods and procedures from period to period. Consistency makes it possible to compare a company's financial statements from one period to the next.

Suppose you are analyzing a company's net income pattern. The company has switched from LIFO to FIFO. Its net income has increased dramatically but only as a result of the change in inventory method. If you did not know of the change, you might believe that the company's increased income arose from improved operations, which is not the case.

The consistency principle does not require that all companies within an industry use the same accounting method. Nor does it mean that a company may *never* change its own accounting method. However, a company making an accounting change must disclose the effect of the change on net income, as shown below for Midland-Ross Corporation, a large company that makes electrical products, mechanical controls, foundry products, and thermal systems:

EXCERPT FROM NOTE A OF THE MIDLAND-ROSS FINANCIAL STATEMENTS
Inventories: The LIFO method of valuing inventories was extended to substantially all of the electrical and mechanical controls inventories. . . . The effect of the change was to reduce net income . . . by $4,638,000. . . .

Disclosure Principle

The **disclosure principle** holds that a company's financial statements should report enough information for outsiders to make knowledgeable decisions about the company. In short, the company should report *relevant, reliable,* and *comparable* information about its economic affairs. With respect to inventories, this means to disclose the method or methods in use. As we have seen, a company reports a different net income figure depending on whether it uses the LIFO, the FIFO, or the weighted-average cost method. Without knowledge of the inventory method, a banker could gain an unrealistic impression of a company and make an unwise lending decision. For example, suppose the banker is comparing two companies—one that uses LIFO and the other that uses FIFO. The FIFO company reports higher net income but only because it uses a particular inventory method. Without knowledge of the accounting methods the companies are using, the banker could loan money to the wrong business. Or he could refuse a loan to a promising customer.

In conjunction with the consistency principle, the disclosure principle requires companies to report the net income effect of a change in accounting method. For example, suppose you are considering an investment in Midland-Ross Corporation. In analyzing Midland-Ross you observe that net income increased very little from the preceding year. Would you be inclined to invest in the company? Probably not. However, the foregoing note explains that Midland-Ross's change to the LIFO method reduced net income by $4,638,000. If the company had not changed inventory methods, net income would have been $4,638,000 higher. This information casts a different light on Midland-Ross's operations and may influence your investment decision. This is the disclosure principle in action.

Materiality Concept

The materiality concept states that a company must perform strictly proper accounting only for items and transactions that are significant to the business's financial statements. Information is significant—what accountants call *material*—when its inclusion and correct presentation in the financial statement would cause a statement user to change a decision because of that information. Immaterial—insignificant—items justify less than perfect accounting. The inclusion and proper presentation of *immaterial* items would not affect a statement user's decision. The materiality concept frees accountants from having to compute and report every last item in strict accordance with GAAP. Thus the materiality concept reduces the cost of recording accounting information.

How does a business decide where to draw the line between what is material and what is immaterial? This decision rests to a great degree on how large the business is. Wendy's, for example, has close to $500 million in assets. Management would likely treat as immaterial a $100 cost of inventory. Suppose the cost should properly be debited to Inventory. However, the amount is immaterial to Wendy's total assets and net income, so company accountants may expense the cost immediately by debiting Cost of Goods Sold. Will this accounting treatment affect anyone's decision about Wendy's? Probably not, so it doesn't matter how the cost is accounted for.

Large companies may draw the materiality line at a figure as high as $10,000 and expense any smaller amount. Smaller firms may choose to expense only those items less than $50. Materiality varies from company to company. An amount that is material to the local service station may not be material to General Motors.

An item can be material even though its amount is small. For example, suppose Wendy's changes from the weighted-average cost method to the LIFO method. In the year of the change, the effect on net income may be immaterial. Wendy's will still disclose this accounting change, however, because in later years net income may be significantly higher or lower because of the accounting change. As we discussed under the disclosure principle, people need to know what accounting methods a company is using.

Summary Problem for Your Review

Suppose an IBM division that handles computer components has these inventory records for January 19X6:

Date	Item	Quantity	Unit Cost	Sale Price
Jan. 1	Beginning inventory	100 units	$ 8	
6	Purchase	60 units	9	
13	Sale	70 units		$ 20
21	Purchase	150 units	9	
24	Sale	210 units		22
27	Purchase	90 units	10	
30	Sale	30 units		25

Company accounting records reveal that related operating expense for January was $1,900.

Required

1. Prepare the January income statement, showing amounts for LIFO, FIFO, and weighted-average cost. Label the bottom line "Operating income." (Round figures to whole dollar amounts.)
2. Suppose you are the financial vice-president of IBM Corporation. Which inventory method would you use if your motive is to
   a. Minimize income taxes?
   b. Report the highest operating income?
   c. Report operating income between the extremes of FIFO and LIFO?
   d. Report inventory at the most current cost?
   e. Attain the best matching of current expense with current revenue?

State the reason for each of your answers.

SOLUTION TO REVIEW PROBLEM

Requirement 1

IBM Corporation
Income Statement for Components
Month Ended January 31, 19X6

	LIFO		FIFO		Weighted-Average
Sales revenue............		$6,770		$6,770	$6,770
Cost of goods sold:					
Beginning inventory....	$ 800		$ 800		$ 800
Net purchases.........	2,790		2,790		2,790
Cost of goods					
available for sale	3,590		3,590		3,590
Ending inventory	720		900		808
Cost of goods sold		2,870		2,690	2,782
Gross margin............		3,900		4,080	3,988
Operating expenses		1,900		1,900	1,900
Operating income........		$2,000		$2,180	$2,088

Computations:

Sales revenue: $(70 \times \$20) + (210 \times \$22) + (30 \times \$25) = \$6,770$

Beginning inventory: $100 \times \$8 = \$800$

Purchases: $(60 \times \$9) + (150 \times \$9) + (90 \times \$10) = \$2,790$

Ending inventory–LIFO: $90^* \times \$8 = \$720$

               FIFO: $90 \times \$10 = \$900$

      Weighted-average: $90 \times \$8.975^{**} = \$808$ (rounded from 807.75)

---

* Number of units in ending inventory $= 100 + 60 - 70 + 150 - 210 + 90 - 30 = 90$

**$\$3,590/400$ units $= \$8.975$ per unit

   Number of units available $= 100 + 60 + 150 + 90 = 400$

Requirement 2

a. Use LIFO to minimize income taxes. Operating income under LIFO is lowest when inventory unit costs are increasing, as they are in this case (from $8 to $10). (If inventory costs were decreasing, income under FIFO would be lowest.)

b. Use FIFO to report the highest operating income. Income under FIFO is highest when inventory unit costs are increasing, as in this situation.

c. Use weighted-average cost to report an operating income amount between the FIFO and LIFO extremes. This is true in this problem situation and in others whether inventory unit costs are increasing or decreasing.

d. Use FIFO to report inventory at the most current cost. The oldest inventory costs are expensed as cost of goods sold, leaving in ending inventory the most recent (most current) costs of the period.

e. Use LIFO to attain the best matching of current expense with current revenue. The most recent (most current) inventory costs are expensed as cost of goods sold.

Accounting Conservatism

Conservatism in accounting means to report items in the financial statements at amounts that lead to the gloomiest immediate financial results. Conservatism comes into play when there are alternative ways to account for the item. What advantage does conservatism give a business? Management often looks on the brighter side of operations and may overstate a company's income and asset values. Many accountants regard conservatism as a counterbalance to management's optimistic tendencies. The goal is for financial statements to present realistic figures.

Conservatism appears in accounting guidelines like "anticipate no gains, but provide for all probable losses" and "if in doubt, record an asset at the lowest reasonable amount and a liability at the highest reasonable amount."

Accountants generally regard the historical cost of acquiring an asset as its maximum value. Even if the current market value of the asset increases above its cost, businesses do not write up (that is, increase) the asset's accounting value. Assume that a company purchased land for $100,000, and its value increased to $300,000. Accounting conservatism dictates that the historical cost $100,000 be maintained as the accounting value of the land.

Conservatism also directs accountants to decrease the accounting value of an asset if it appears unrealistically high—even if no transaction occurs.

Assume that a company paid $35,000 for inventory that has become obsolete, and its current value is only $12,000. Conservatism dictates that the inventory be written down (that is, decreased) to $12,000.

The **lower-of-cost-or-market rule** (abbreviated as LCM) shows accounting conservatism in action. LCM requires that an asset be reported in the financial statements at the lower of its historical cost or its market value. Applied to inventories, *market value* generally means *current replacement cost* (that is, how much the business would have to pay in the market on that day to purchase the same amount of inventory that it has on hand). If the replacement cost of inventory falls below its historical cost, the business must write down the value of its goods. The business reports ending inventory at its LCM value on the balance sheet. In the chapter-opening vignette, Whittaker Corporation has a warehouse full of obsolete inventory. This inventory must be written down to market value. How is the write-down accomplished?

Suppose a business paid $3,000 for inventory on September 26. By December 31, its value has fallen. The inventory can now be replaced for $2,200. Market value is below cost, and the December 31 balance sheet reports this inventory at its LCM value of $2,200. Usually, the market value of inventory is higher than historical cost, so inventory's accounting value is cost for most companies. Exhibit 8-6 presents the effects of LCM on the income statement and the balance sheet. The point of the exhibit is to show that the lower of (a) cost or (b) market value—replacement cost—is the relevant amount for valuing inventory on the income statement and the balance sheet. Companies are not required to show both cost and market value amounts. However, they may report the higher amount in parentheses, as shown on the balance sheet in the exhibit.

EXHIBIT 8-6 *Lower-of-Cost-or-Market (LCM) Effects*

Income Statement:

Sales revenue		$20,000
Cost of goods sold:		
Beginning inventory (LCM = Cost)	$ 2,800	
Net purchases	11,000	
Cost of goods available for sale	13,800	
Ending inventory—		
Cost = $3,000		
Replacement cost (market value) = $2,200		
LCM = Market	2,200	
Cost of goods sold		11,600
Gross margin		$ 8,400

Balance Sheet:

Current assets:		
Cash	$	XXX
Short-term investments		XXX
Accounts receivable		XXX
Inventories, at market (which is lower than $3,000 cost)		2,200
Prepaid expenses		XXX
Total current assets		$ X,XXX

OBJECTIVE 4

Apply the lower-of-cost-or-market rule to inventory

LCM states that of the $3,000 cost of ending inventory in Exhibit 8-6, $800 is considered to have expired even though the inventory was not sold during the period. Its replacement cost is only $2,200, and that amount is carried forward to the next period as the cost of beginning inventory. Suppose during the next period the replacement cost of this inventory increases to $2,500. Accounting conservatism states that it would not be appropriate to write up the book value of inventory. The market value of inventory ($2,200 in this case) is used as its cost in future LCM determinations.

Examine the following income statement effect of LCM summarized from Exhibit 8-6. What expense absorbs the impact of the $800 inventory write down? Cost of goods sold is increased by $800 because ending inventory is $800 less at market ($2,200) than it would have been at cost ($3,000).

	Ending Inventory at		
	Cost	LCM	
Cost of goods available for sale	$13,800	$13,800	
Ending inventory:			
Cost.....	3,000		} $800 Lower
Replacement cost (market value)		2,200	at LCM
Cost of goods sold....	$10,800	$11,600	} $800 Higher at LCM

Exhibit 8-6 also reports the application of LCM for inventories in the body of the balance sheet. Companies often disclose LCM in notes to their financial statements, as shown below for CBS, Inc.:

NOTE 1: STATEMENT OF SIGNIFICANT ACCOUNTING POLICIES

Inventories. Inventories are stated at the *lower of cost* (principally based on average cost) *or market value*. [emphasis added]

Effect of Inventory Errors

OBJECTIVE 5
Explain why inventory errors counterbalance

Businesses determine inventory amounts at the end of the period. In the process of counting the items, applying unit costs, and computing amounts, errors may arise. As the period 1 segment of Exhibit 8-7 shows, an error in the ending inventory amount creates errors in the cost of goods sold and gross margin amounts. Compare period 1, when ending inventory is overstated, and cost of goods sold is understated, each by $5,000, with period 3, which is correct. Period 1 should look exactly like period 3.

Recall that one period's ending inventory is the next period's beginning inventory. Thus the error in ending inventory carries over into the next period: note the highlighted amounts in Exhibit 8-7.

Because the same ending inventory figure that is *subtracted* in computing cost of goods sold in one period is *added* as beginning inventory to compute cost of goods sold in the next period, the error's effect cancels out at the end of the second period. The overstatement of cost of goods sold in period 2 counterbalances the understatement in cost of goods sold in period 1. Thus the total gross margin amount for the two periods is the correct $100,000 figure whether or not an error entered into the computation.

However, inventory errors cannot be ignored simply because they counterbalance. Suppose you are analyzing trends in the business's operations. Exhibit 8-7 shows a drop in gross margin from period 1 to period 2, followed

EXHIBIT 8-7 *Effects of Inventory Errors*

	Period 1 Ending Inventory Overstated By $5,000		Period 2 Beginning Inventory Overstated By $5,000		Period 3 Correct	
Sales revenue		$100,000		$100,000		$100,000
Cost of goods sold:						
Beginning inventory	$10,000		**$15,000**		$10,000	
Net purchases	50,000		50,000		50,000	
Cost of goods available for sale .	60,000		65,000		60,000	
Ending inventory	**15,000**		10,000		10,000	
Cost of goods sold		45,000		55,000		50,000
Gross margin....................		$ 55,000		$ 45,000		$ 50,000
			$100,000			

The authors thank Carl High for this example.

by an increase in period 3. But that picture of operations is untrue because of the accounting error. Correct gross margin is $50,000 each period. To provide accurate information for decision making, all inventory errors should be corrected.

Methods of Estimating Inventory

OBJECTIVE 6

Estimate inventory by two methods

Often a business must *estimate* the value of its inventory. Because of cost and inconvenience, few companies physically count their inventories at the end of each month, yet they may need monthly financial statements. A fire or a flood may destroy inventory, and to file an insurance claim, the business must estimate the value of its loss. In both cases, the business needs to know the value of ending inventory without being able to count it. Two methods for estimating ending inventory are the *gross margin method* (or *gross profit method*) and the *retail method*. These methods are widely used in actual practice.

Gross Margin (Gross Profit) Method

The **gross margin method** is a way of estimating inventory based on the familiar cost-of-goods-sold model:

> **Beginning inventory**
> **+ Net purchases**
> ─────────────────────────
> **= Cost of goods available for sale**
> **− Ending inventory**
> ─────────────────────────
> **= Cost of goods sold**

Rearranging *ending inventory* and *cost of goods sold,* the model becomes useful for estimating ending inventory:

Beginning inventory		$14,000
Net purchases		66,000
Cost of goods available for sale		80,000
Cost of goods sold:		
Net sales revenue	$100,000	
Less estimated gross margin of 40%	40,000	
Estimated cost of goods sold		60,000
Estimated cost of *ending inventory*		$20,000

Beginning inventory
+ Net purchases
_____

= Cost of goods available for sale
− Cost of goods sold
_____

= Ending inventory

Suppose a fire destroys your business's inventory. To collect insurance, you must estimate the cost of the ending inventory. If the fire did not also destroy your accounting records, beginning inventory and net purchases amounts may be taken directly from the accounting records. The Sales Revenue, Sales Returns, and Sales Discounts accounts indicate net sales up to the date of the fire. Using the entity's normal *gross margin rate* (that is, gross margin divided by net sales revenue), the gross margin by multiplying net sales by the gross margin rate. Then subtract the gross margin from net sales. The last step is to subtract cost of goods sold from goods available to estimate ending inventory. Exhibit 8-8 illustrates the computations.

Accountants, managers, and auditors use the gross margin method to test the overall reasonableness of an ending inventory amount that has been determined by a physical count. This method helps to detect large errors.

Retail Method

Retail establishments (department stores, drug stores, hardware stores, and so on) use the **retail method** to estimate their inventory cost. The retail method, like the gross margin method, is based on the cost-of-goods-sold model. However, the retail method requires that the business record inventory purchases both at *cost*—as shown in the purchase records—and at *retail* (selling) price—as shown on the price tags. This is not a burden because price tags show the retail price of inventory, and most retailers set their retail prices by adding standard markups to their cost. For example, a department store may pay $6 for a man's belt, mark it up $4, and price the belt at $10 retail. In the retail method, the seller's inventory cost is determined by working backward from its retail value. Exhibit 8-9 illustrates the process.

In Exhibit 8-9 the accounting records show the goods available for sale at cost ($168,000) and at retail ($280,000). The cost ratio is .60 ($168,000/$280,000). For simplicity, we round all such percentages to two decimal places in this chapter. Subtracting *net sales revenue* (a retail amount) from *goods available for sale at retail* yields *ending inventory at retail* ($50,000). The business multiplies *ending inventory at retail* by the cost ratio to figure *ending inventory at cost* ($30,000).

EXHIBIT 8-9 *Retail Method of Estimating Inventory (amounts assumed)*

	Cost	Retail
Beginning inventory	$ 24,000	$ 40,000
Net purchases.................................	144,000	240,000
Goods available for sale	168,000	280,000
Cost ratio: $168,000/$280,000 = .60		
Less: Net sales revenue (which is stated at retail)		(230,000)
Ending inventory, at retail		$ 50,000
Ending inventory, at cost ($50,000 × .60)........	$ 30,000	

Suppose the retailer has four categories of inventory, each with a different cost ratio. How would the business use the retail method to estimate the overall cost of the ending inventory? Apply the retail method separately to each category of inventory, using its specific cost ratio, then add the costs of the four categories to determine the overall cost of inventory.

Even though the retail method is an estimation technique, some retailers use it to compute the inventory value for their financial statements. They make physical counts of inventory throughout the year to validate the retail-method amounts. For example, Marshall Field & Company, a department store chain headquartered in Chicago, uses the retail method, as disclosed in its annual report:

Merchandise inventories (note 1C) $179,007,250

Note 1C: Inventory Pricing
Substantially all merchandise inventories are valued by use of the *retail method.* [emphasis added]

Periodic and Perpetual Inventory Systems

Different businesses have different inventory information needs. We now look at the two main inventory systems: the *periodic system* and the *perpetual system.*

Periodic Inventory System

OBJECTIVE 7

Account for inventory by the periodic and perpetual systems

In the **periodic inventory system,** the business does not keep a continuous record of the inventory on hand. Instead, at the end of the period, the business makes a physical count of the inventory on hand and applies the appropriate unit costs to determine the cost of ending inventory. The business makes the standard end-of-period inventory entries, as discussed in Chapter 5 and shown in the example that follows. This system is also called the *physical system* because it relies on the actual physical count of inventory. The periodic system is used to account for inventory items that have a low unit cost. Low-cost items may not be valuable enough to warrant the cost of keeping a running record of the inventory on hand.

Entries under the Periodic System. In the periodic system, the business records purchases of inventory in the Purchases account (an expense account).

At the end of the period, the business removes the beginning balance from the Inventory account and enters the ending balance, as determined by the physical count. Assume the following data for a K Mart store's April transactions.

Beginning inventory	$ 80,000
Ending inventory	102,000
Credit purchases (net of discounts and returns)	600,000
Credit sales (net of discounts and returns)	900,000

Summary entries for April:

To record credit purchases:

Purchases	600,000	
Accounts Payable		600,000

To record credit sales:

Accounts Receivable	900,000	
Sales Revenue		900,000

Inventory entries at the end of the period:

Income Summary	80,000	
Inventory (beginning balance)		80,000
Inventory (ending balance)	102,000	
Income Summary		102,000

Reporting on the financial statements:

Balance sheet at April 30:

Inventory	$102,000

Income statement for April:

Sales revenue		$900,000
Cost of goods sold:		
Beginning inventory	$ 80,000	
Net purchases	600,000	
Cost of goods available	680,000	
Ending inventory	102,000	
Cost of goods sold		578,000
Gross margin		$322,000

Perpetual Inventory System

In the **perpetual inventory system,** the business keeps a continuous record for each inventory item. The records thus show the inventory on hand at all times. Perpetual records are useful in preparing monthly, quarterly, or other interim financial statements. The business can determine the cost of ending inventory and the cost of goods sold directly from the accounts without having to physically count the merchandise.

The perpetual system offers a higher degree of control than the periodic system because the inventory information is always up to date. Consequently businesses use the perpetual system for high-unit-cost inventories, such as gemstones and automobiles. Nevertheless, companies physically count their inventory at least once each year to check the accuracy of their perpetual records.

Perpetual inventory records can be computer listings of inventory items or inventory cards like the Computerworld record shown in Exhibit 8-10. The accountant adds information to the computer list or the card on a daily basis. A running balance conveniently shows the latest inventory value. The perpetual record serves as a subsidiary record to the inventory account in the general ledger.

The perpetual inventory record indicates that the business uses the FIFO basis, as shown by the November 30 sale. The cost of the first unit sold is the oldest unit cost on hand. Perpetual records may also be kept on the average cost basis. However, most companies that use the weighted-average cost method, and virtually all companies that use the LIFO method, keep their perpetual records either on the FIFO basis or stated in units only (not dollars). This is much easier computationally and minimizes bookkeeping costs. At the end of the period these companies convert ending inventory and cost of goods sold to the LIFO or weighted-average cost basis for the financial statements. Perpetual inventory records provide information such as the following:

1. When customers inquire about how soon they can get a home computer, the salesperson can answer the question after referring to the perpetual inventory record. On November 7 the salesperson would reply that the company's stock is low, and the customer may have to wait a few days. On November 26 the salesperson could offer immediate delivery.

2. The perpetual records alert the business to reorder when inventory becomes low. On November 7 the company would be wise to purchase inventory. Sales may be lost if the business cannot promise immediate delivery.

3. At November 30 the company prepares monthly financial statements. The perpetual inventory records show the company's ending inventory of home computers at $2,630, and its cost of goods sold for this product at $5,480.

EXHIBIT 8-10 *Perpetual Inventory Record—FIFO Basis*

Item   Home Computer Model RK-42

Date	Received Qty.	Received Unit Cost	Received Total	Sold Qty.	Sold Unit Cost	Sold Total	Balance Qty.	Balance Unit Cost	Balance Total
Nov. 1							14	$300	$4,200
5				4	$300	$1,200	10	300	3,000
7				9	300	2,700	1	300	300
12	5	$320	$1,600				1	300	300
							5	320	1,600
26	7	330	2,310				1	300	300
							5	320	1,600
							7	330	2,310
30				1	300	300	1	320	320
				4	320	1,280	7	330	2,310
Totals	12	—	$3,910	18	—	$5,480	8	—	$2,630

No physical count is necessary at this time. However, a physical inventory is needed once a year to verify the accuracy of the records.

Perpetual inventory systems are becoming increasingly sophisticated. *The Wall Street Journal* (June 11, 1990) carried a story about Frito-Lay's Decision Support System. It can tell the company president (and other managers) the weekly sales of Ruffles Light potato chips by each route salesman. In one case, Frito-Lay identified a drop in sales of tortilla chips by a particular chain of stores. Within two weeks, the company revised its marketing strategy and turned sales up again. Without the perpetual system, this would have taken three months.

Entries under the Perpetual System. In the perpetual system, the business records purchases of inventory by debiting the Inventory account. When the business makes a sale, two entries are necessary. The company records the sale in the usual manner—debits Cash or Accounts Receivable and credits Sales Revenue for the sale price of the goods. The company also debits Cost of Goods Sold and credits Inventory for cost. The debit to Inventory (for purchases) and the credit to Inventory (for sales) serve to keep an up-to-date record of inventory on hand. Therefore, no end-of-period adjusting entries are needed. The Inventory account already carries the correct ending balance.

In the perpetual system, Cost of Goods Sold is an account in the general ledger. By contrast, in the periodic system, cost of goods sold is simply a total on the income statement.

To illustrate the entries under the perpetual system, let's use the same data we used in discussing the periodic system, which follow.

Ending inventory	$102,000
Credit purchases (net of discounts and returns)	600,000
Credit sales (net of discounts and returns)	900,000
Cost of goods sold	578,000

Summary entries for April:

To record credit purchases:

Inventory	600,000	
Accounts Payable		600,000

To record credit sales:

Accounts Receivable	900,000	
Sales Revenue		900,000
Cost of Goods Sold	578,000	
Inventory		578,000

Reporting on the financial statements:

Balance sheet at April 30:

Inventory	$102,000

Income statement for April:

Sales revenue	$900,000
Cost of goods sold	578,000
Gross margin	$322,000

You should compare the entries and financial statement presentations under the *periodic* and the *perpetual* systems. Note that the entries to record purchases and sales differ under the two systems but that the financial statement amounts are the same.

Internal Control over Inventory _____

Internal control over inventory is important because inventory is the lifeblood of a merchandiser. Successful companies take great care to protect their inventory. Elements of good internal control over inventory include:

1. Physically counting inventory at least once each year no matter which system is used
2. Maintaining efficient purchasing, receiving, and shipping procedures
3. Storing inventory to protect it against theft, damage, and decay
4. Limiting access to inventory to personnel who do *not* have access to the accounting records
5. Keeping perpetual inventory records for high-unit-cost merchandise
6. Purchasing inventory in economical quantities
7. Keeping enough inventory on hand to prevent shortage situations, which lead to lost sales
8. Not keeping too large an inventory stockpiled, thus avoiding the expense of tying up money in unneeded items and avoiding obsolescense

The annual physical count of inventory (item 1) is necessary because the only way to be certain of the amount of inventory on hand is to count it. Errors arise in the best accounting systems, and the count is needed to establish the correct value of the inventory. When an error is detected, the records are brought into agreement with the physical count.

Keeping inventory handlers away from the accounting records (item 4) is an essential separation of duties, discussed in Chapter 6. An employee with access to inventory and the accounting records can steal the goods and make an entry to conceal the theft. For example, he could increase the amount of an inventory write-down to make it appear that goods decreased in value when in fact they were stolen.

Computerized Inventory Records _____

Computer systems have revolutionized accounting for inventory. Perpetual inventory systems are rapidly replacing periodic methods. Computerized systems can provide up-to-the-minute inventory data useful for managing the business. They help cut accounting cost by processing large numbers of transactions without computational error. Computer systems also enhance internal control. They increase efficiency because managers always know the quantity and cost of inventory on hand. Managers can make better decisions about quantities to buy, prices to pay for the inventory, prices to charge customers, and sale terms to offer. Knowing the quantity on hand helps to safeguard the inventory.

Computer inventory systems vary considerably. At one extreme are complex systems used by huge retailers like Sears, J. C. Penney, and K Mart. Purchases of inventory are recorded in perpetual records stored in a central computer. The inventory tags are coded electronically for updating the perpetual records when a sale is recorded on the cash register. Have you noticed sales clerks passing the inventory ticket over a particular area of the checkout counter? A sensing device in the counter reads the stock number, quantity, cost, and sale price of the item sold. In other systems, the sales clerk passes an electronic device over the inventory tag. The computer records the sale and updates the inventory records. In effect, a journal entry is recorded for each sale, a procedure that is not economical without a computer.

Small companies also use minicomputers and microcomputers to keep perpetual inventory records. These systems may be similar to the systems used by large companies. In less-sophisticated operations, a company may have sales clerks write inventory stock numbers on sales slips. The stock number identifies the particular item of inventory, such as men's shirts or children's shoes. The business may accumulate all sales slips for the week. If the company has its own computer system, an employee may type the sales information into the computer and store the perpetual records on a magnetic disk. To learn the quantity, cost, or other characteristic of a particular item of inventory, a manager can view the inventory record on the computer monitor. For broader-based decisions affecting the entire inventory, managers use printouts of all items in stock. Many small businesses hire outside computer service centers to do much of the accounting for inventory. Regardless of the arrangement, managers get periodic printouts showing inventory data needed for managing the business. Manual reporting of this information is more time consuming and expensive.

Summary Problems for Your Review

Problem 1

Centronics Data Computer Corporation reported a net loss for the year. In its financial statements, the company noted:

Balance Sheet:

Current assets:
  Inventories (notes 1C and 2) $48,051,000

> Note 1C: Inventories are stated at the lower of cost or market. Cost is determined on a first-in, first-out (FIFO) basis.
>
> Note 2: Declining . . . market conditions during [the] fiscal [year] adversely affected anticipated sales of the Company's older printer products; . . . Accordingly, the statement of loss . . . includes a [debit] of $9,600,000.

Required

1. At which amount did Centronics report its inventory, cost or market value? How can you tell?
2. If the reported inventory of $48,051,000 represents market value, what was the cost of the inventory?

Problem 2

American Hospital Supply Corporation reported using the LIFO inventory method. Its inventory amount was $490.5 million.

Required

1. Suppose that during the period covered by this report, the company made an error that understated its ending inventory by $15 million. What effect would this error have on *cost of goods sold* and *gross margin* of the period? On *cost of goods sold* and *gross margin* of the following period? On *total gross margin* of both periods combined?

2. When American Hospital Supply reported the above amount for inventory, prices were rising. Would FIFO or LIFO have shown a higher gross margin? Why?

SOLUTIONS TO REVIEW PROBLEMS

Problem 1

1. Centronics reported its inventory at *market value*, as indicated by (a) its valuing inventories at LCM and (b) the declining market conditions that caused the company to "include a [debit] of $9,600,000" in "the statement of loss." The company debited the $9,600,000 to a loss account or to cost of goods sold. The credit side of the entry was to Inventory—for a write down to market value.

2. The cost of inventory before the write down was $57,651,000 ($48,051,000 + $9,600,000). The $48,051,000 market value is what is left of the original cost. Thus the amount to be carried forward to future periods is $48,051,000.

Problem 2

1. Understating ending inventory by $15 million has the following effects on *cost of goods sold* and *gross margin*:

	Cost of Goods Sold	Gross Margin
Period during which error was made	OVERSTATED by $15 million	UNDERSTATED by $15 million
Following period	UNDERSTATED by $15 million	OVERSTATED by $15 million
Combined total	CORRECTLY STATED	CORRECTLY STATED

2. When prices are rising, FIFO results in higher gross margin than LIFO. FIFO matches against sales revenue the lower inventory costs of beginning inventory and purchases made during the early part of the period.

Summary

Accounting for inventory plays an important part in merchandisers' accounting systems because selling inventory is the heart of their business. Inventory is generally the largest current asset on their balance sheet, and inventory expense—called cost of goods sold—is usually the largest expense on the income statement.

Businesses multiply the quantity of inventory items by their unit cost to determine inventory cost. Inventory costing methods are *specific unit cost; weighted-average cost; first-in, first-out (FIFO) cost; and last-in, first-out* (LIFO) cost. Only businesses that sell unique items, like automobiles and jewels, use the specific identification method. Most other companies use the other methods.

FIFO reports ending inventory at the most current cost. LIFO reports cost of goods sold at the most current cost. When inventory costs increase, LIFO produces the highest cost of goods sold and the lowest income, thus minimizing income taxes. FIFO results in the highest income. The weighted-average cost method avoids the extremes of FIFO and LIFO.

The *consistency principle* demands that a business stick with the inventory method it chooses. The *disclosure principle* requires the reporting of comparable information. If a change in inventory method is warranted, the company must report the effect of the change on income. Under the *materiality concept*, a company must perform strictly proper accounting only for significant items. The *lower-of-cost-or-market rule*—an example of accounting *conservatism*—requires that businesses report inventory on the balance sheet at the lower of its cost or current replacement value.

The *gross profit method* and the *retail method* are two techniques for estimating the cost of inventory. These methods come in handy for preparing interim financial statements and for estimating the cost of inventory destroyed by fire and other casualties.

Merchandisers with high-price-tag items generally use the *perpetual inventory system*, which features a running inventory balance. In the past most merchandisers handling low-price-tag items used the *periodic system*. Recent advances in information technology have led to replacement of periodic inventory systems with perpetual systems. A physical count of inventory is needed in both systems for control purposes.

Self-Study Questions

Test your understanding of the chapter by marking the best answer to each of the following questions.

1. Which of the following items is the greatest in dollar amount? *(p. 397)*
   a. Beginning inventory   d. Ending inventory
   b. Purchases   e. Cost of goods sold
   c. Cost of goods available for sale

2. Sound Warehouse counts 15,000 compact disks, including 1,000 CDs held on consignment, in its Waco, Texas, store. The business has purchased an additional 2,000 units on FOB destination terms. These goods are still in transit. Each CD cost $3.40. The cost of the inventory to report on the balance sheet is *(p. 397)*
   a. $47,600   c. $54,400
   b. $51,000   d. $57,800

3. The inventory costing method that best matches current expense with current revenue is *(p. 402)*
   a. Specific unit cost   d. LIFO
   b. Weighted-average cost   e. FIFO or LIFO, depending on
   c. FIFO   whether inventory costs are increasing or decreasing

4. The consistency principle has the most direct impact on *(p. 404)*
   a. Whether to include or exclude an item in inventory
   b. Whether to change from one inventory method to another
   c. Whether to write inventory down to a market value below cost
   d. Whether to use the periodic or the perpetual inventory system

5. Application of the lower-of-cost-or-market rule often results in (p. 408)
   a. Higher ending inventory
   b. Lower ending inventory
   c. A counterbalancing error
   d. A change from one inventory method to another

6. An error understated ending inventory of 19X7. This error will (p. 410)
   a. Overstate 19X7 cost of sales
   b. Understate 19X8 cost of sales
   c. Not affect stockholders' equity at the end of 19X8
   d. All of the above

7. Beginning inventory was $35,000, purchases were $146,000, and sales totaled $240,000. With a normal gross margin rate of 35 percent, how much is ending inventory? (p. 411)
   a. $25,000
   b. $35,000
   c. $97,000
   d. $181,000

8. Beginning inventory was $20,000 at cost and $40,000 at retail. Purchases were $120,000 at cost and $210,000 at retail. Sales were $200,000. How much is ending inventory at cost? (p. 411)
   a. $22,000
   b. $26,000
   c. $28,000
   d. $50,000

9. The year-end entry to close beginning inventory in a perpetual inventory system is (p. 415)
   a. Income Summary XXX
        Inventory XXX
   b. Inventory XXX
        Income Summary XXX
   c. Either of the above, depending on whether inventory increased or decreased during the period
   d. Not needed

10. Which of the following statements is true? (p. 416)
    a. Separation of duties is not an important element of internal control for inventories.
    b. The perpetual system is used primarily for low-unit-cost inventory.
    c. An annual physical count of inventory is needed regardless of the type of inventory system used.
    d. All the above are true.

Answers to the Self-Study Questions follow the Accounting Vocabulary.

Accounting Vocabulary

Average cost method. Another name for the Weighted-average cost method (p. 399).

Beginning inventory. Goods left over from the preceding period (p. 396).

Conservatism. Concept that underlies presenting the gloomiest possible figures in the financial statements (p. 407).

Consignment. Transfer of goods by the owner (consignor) to another business (consignee) who, for a fee, sells the inventory on the owner's behalf. The consignee does not take title to the consigned goods (p. 398).

Consistency principle. A business must use the same accounting methods and procedures from period to period (p. 404).

Disclosure principle. Holds that a company's financial statements should report enough information for outsiders to make knowledgeable decisions about the company (p. 404).

Ending inventory. Goods still on hand at the end of the period (p. 396).

First-in, first-out (FIFO) method. Inventory costing method by which the first costs into inventory are the first costs out to cost of goods sold. Ending inventory is based on the costs of the most recent purchases (p. 399).

FOB destination. Terms of a transaction that govern when the title to the inventory passes from the seller to the purchaser—when the goods arrive at the purchaser's location *(p. 397).*

FOB shipping point. Terms of a transaction that govern when the title to the inventory passes from the seller to the purchaser—when the goods leave the seller's place of business *(p. 397).*

Goods available for sale. Beginning inventory plus net purchases *(p. 396).*

Gross margin method. A way to estimate inventory based on a rearrangement of the cost of goods sold model: Beginning inventory + Net purchases = Cost of goods available for sale. Cost of goods available for sale − Cost of goods sold = Ending inventory. Also called the Gross profit method *(p. 410).*

Inventory cost. Price paid to acquire inventory—not the selling price of the goods. Inventory cost includes its invoice price, less all discounts, plus sales tax, tariffs, transportation fees, insurance while in transit, and all other costs incurred to make the goods ready for sale *(p. 398).*

Inventory profit. Difference between gross margin figured on the FIFO basis and gross margin figured on the LIFO basis *(p. 403).*

Last-in, first-out (LIFO) method. Inventory costing method by which the last costs into inventory are the first costs out to cost of goods sold. This leaves the oldest costs—those of beginning inventory and the earliest purchases of the period—in ending inventory *(p. 399).*

Lower-of-cost-or-market (LCM) rule. Requires that an asset be reported in the financial statements at the lower of its historical cost or its market value (current replacement cost) *(p. 408).*

Materiality concept. States that a company must perform strictly proper accounting only for items and transactions that are significant to the business's financial statements *(p. 405).*

Periodic inventory system. The business does not keep a continuous record of the inventory on hand. Instead, at the end of the period the business makes a physical count of the on-hand inventory and applies the appropriate unit costs to determine the cost of the ending inventory *(p. 412).*

Perpetual inventory system. The business keeps a continuous record for each inventory item to show the inventory on hand at all times *(p. 413).*

Retail method. A way to estimate inventory cost based on the cost-of-goods-sold model. The retail method requires that the business record inventory purchases both at cost and at retail. Multiply ending inventory at retail by the cost ratio to estimate the ending inventory's cost *(p. 411).*

Specific unit cost method. Inventory cost method based on the specific cost of particular units of inventory *(p. 398).*

Weighted-average cost method. Inventory costing method based on the weighted average cost of inventory during the period. Weighted-average cost is determined by dividing the cost of goods available for sale by the number of units available. Also called the Average cost method *(p. 399).*

Answers to Self-Study Questions

1. c
2. a $(15,000 - 1,000) \times \$3.40 = \$47,600$
3. d
4. b
5. b
6. d
7. a $\$35,000 + \$146,000 = \$181,000$
   $\$240,000 - (.35 \times \$240,000) = \$156,000$
   $\$181,000 - \$156,000 = \$25,000$

	Cost	Retail	
8. c Beginning inventory	$ 20,000	$ 40,000	
Purchases....................	120,000	210,000	**Cost Ratio**
Goods available	140,000 ÷	250,000 =	.56
Sales		200,000	
Ending inventory—at retail		$ 50,000	
at cost ($50,000 × .56)	$ 28,000		

9. d

10. c

ASSIGNMENT MATERIAL _____

Questions

1. Why is merchandise inventory so important to a retailer or whole-saler?
2. If beginning inventory is $10,000, purchases total $85,000, and ending inventory is $12,700, how much is cost of goods sold?
3. If beginning inventory is $32,000, purchases total $119,000, and cost of goods sold is $127,000, how much is ending inventory?
4. What role does the cost principle play in accounting for inventory?
5. What two items determine the cost of ending inventory?
6. Briefly describe the four generally accepted inventory cost methods. During a period of rising prices, which method produces the highest reported income? Which produces the lowest reported income?
7. Which inventory costing method produces the ending inventory valued at the most current cost? Which method produces the cost-of-goods-sold amount valued at the most current cost?
8. What is the most attractive feature of LIFO? Does LIFO have this advantage during periods of increasing prices or during periods of decreasing prices? Why has LIFO had this advantage recently?
9. Which inventory costing methods are used the most in practice?
10. What is inventory profit? Which method produces it?
11. Identify the chief criticism of LIFO.
12. How does the consistency principle affect accounting for inventory?
13. Briefly state the disclosure principle.
14. What governs whether an item of information is material to an accountant? Contrast material information and immaterial information.
15. Briefly describe the influence that the concept of conservatism has on accounting for inventory.
16. Manley Company's inventory has a cost of $48,000 at the end of the year, and the current replacement cost of the inventory is $51,000. At which amount should the company report the inventory on its balance sheet? Suppose the current replacement cost of the inventory is $45,000 instead of $51,000. At which amount should Manley report the inventory? What rule governs your answers to these questions?
17. Gabriel Company accidentally overstated its ending inventory by $10,000 at the end of period 1. Is gross margin of period 1 overstated or understated? Is gross margin of period 2 overstated, understated, or unaffected by the period 1 error? Is total gross margin for the two periods overstated, understated, or correct? Give the reason for your answer.
18. Identify two methods of estimating inventory amounts. What familiar model underlies both estimation methods?

19. A fire destroyed the inventory of Olivera Company, but the accounting records were saved. The beginning inventory was $22,000, purchases for the period were $71,000, and sales were $140,000. Olivera's customary gross margin is 45 percent of sales. Use the gross margin method to estimate the cost of the inventory destroyed by the fire.

20. Suppose your company deals in expensive jewelry. Which inventory system should you use to achieve good internal control over the inventory? If your business is a hardware store that sells low-cost goods, which inventory system would you be likely to use? Why would you choose this system?

21. Identify the accounts debited and credited in the standard purchase and sale entries under (a) the periodic inventory system and (b) the perpetual inventory system.

22. What is the role of the physical count of inventory in (a) the periodic inventory system and (b) the perpetual inventory system?

23. True or false? A company that sells inventory of low unit cost needs no internal controls over the goods. Any inventory loss would probably be small.

Exercises

Exercise 8-1   Computing ending inventory by four methods   (L.O. 1)

Malzone Precision Instruments' inventory records for industrial switches indicate the following at October 31:

Oct.	1	Beginning inventory	10 units @ $130
	8	Purchase	4 units @ 140
	15	Purchase	11 units @ 150
	26	Purchase	5 units @ 156

The physical count of inventory at October 31 indicates that eight units are on hand, and the company owns them. Compute ending inventory and cost of goods sold using each of the following methods:

1. Specific unit cost, assuming five $150 units and three $130 units are on hand
2. Weighted-average cost
3. First in, first out
4. Last in, first out

Exercise 8-2   Recording periodic inventory transactions   (L.O. 1)

Use the data in Exercise 8-1 and the periodic inventory system to journalize:

1. Total October purchases in one summary entry. All purchases were on credit.
2. Total October sales in one summary entry. Assume the selling price was $300 per unit, and all sales were on credit.
3. October 31 entries for inventory. Malzone Precision Instruments uses LIFO.

Exercise 8-3   Computing the tax advantage of LIFO over FIFO   (L.O. 2)

Use the data in Exercise 8-1 to illustrate the income tax advantage of LIFO over FIFO, assuming sales revenue is $7,000, operating expenses are $1,100, and the income tax rate is 30 percent.

Exercise 8-4 *Converting LIFO financial statements to the FIFO basis* **(L.O. 2,3)**

Hennig Nursery reported:

Balance sheet:	19X5	19X4
Inventories—note 4	$ 65,800	$ 59,300
Income statement:		
Net purchases	404,100	372,700
Cost of goods sold	397,600	381,400

Note 4. The company determines inventory cost by the last-in, first-out method. If the first-in, first-out method were used, inventories would be $5,200 higher at year end 19X5 and $3,500 higher at year end 19X4.

Required

Show the cost-of-goods-sold computations for 19X5 under LIFO and FIFO. Which method would result in higher reported income? Show the amount of the difference.

Exercise 8-5 *Note disclosure of a change in inventory method* **(L.O. 2,3)**

CPC International, Inc., maker of Hellmann's mayonnaise, Mazola corn oil, and other foods, included the following in its annual report:

> *Inventories* are stated at the lower of cost or market. . . . Outside the United States, inventories generally are valued at average cost. In the United States, vegetable oils and corn are valued at cost on the last-in, first-out method. Other United States inventories are valued at cost on the first-in, first-out method. Had the first-in, first-out method been used for all United States inventories, the carrying value of these inventories would have increased by $20.3 million.

Suppose CPC International were to change to the FIFO method for all its inventories. Write the note to disclose this accounting change in the company's financial statements. Indicate the effect of the change on income before income tax.

Exercise 8-6 *The effect of lower-of-cost-or-market on the income statement* **(L.O. 4)**

From the following inventory records of DeGaulle Corporation for 19X7, prepare the company's income statement through gross margin. Apply the lower-of-cost-or-market rule.

Beginning inventory (average cost)	300 @ $41.33 =	$ 12,399
(replacement cost)	300 @ 41.91 =	12,573
Purchases during the year	2,600 @ 45.50 =	118,300
Ending inventory (average cost)	400 @ 45.07 =	18,028
(replacement cost)	400 @ 42.10 =	16,840
Sales during the year	2,500 @ 80.00*=	200,000

*Selling price per unit.

Exercise 8-7 *Applying the lower-of-cost-or-market rule* **(L.O. 4)**

Imhoff Company's income statement for March reported the following data:

Income Statement:

Sales revenue		$88,000
Cost of goods sold:		
Beginning inventory	$17,200	
Net purchases	51,700	
Cost of goods available for sale	68,900	
Ending inventory	22,800	
Cost of goods sold		46,100
Gross margin		$41,900

Prior to releasing the financial statements, it was discovered that the current replacement cost of ending inventory was $20,400. Correct the above data to include the lower-of-cost-or-market value of ending inventory. Also, show how inventory would be reported on the balance sheet.

Exercise 8-8   Correcting an inventory error   (L.O. 5)

Robinette Auto Supply reported the following comparative income statement for the years ended September 30, 19X5 and 19X4:

Robinette Auto Supply
Income Statements
For the Year Ended September 30,

	19X5		19X4	
Sales revenue		$132,300		$121,700
Cost of goods sold:				
Beginning inventory	$14,000		$12,800	
Net purchases	72,000		66,000	
Cost of goods available	86,000		78,800	
Ending inventory	16,600		14,000	
Cost of goods sold		69,400		64,800
Gross margin		62,900		56,900
Operating expenses		30,300		26,100
Net income		$ 32,600		$ 30,800

During 19X5 accountants for the company discovered that ending 19X4 inventory was understated by $1,500. Prepare the corrected comparative income statement for the two-year period. What was the effect of the error on net income for the two years combined? Explain your answer.

Exercise 8-9   Estimating inventory by the gross margin method   (L.O. 6)

Jansen Unpainted Furniture began April with inventory of $41,000. The business made net purchases of $37,600 and had net sales of $55,000 before a fire destroyed the company's inventory. For the past several years, Jansen's gross margin on sales has been 40 percent. Estimate the cost of the inventory destroyed by the fire.

Exercise 8-10   Estimating inventory by the retail method   (L.O. 6)

Assume the inventory records of Brewster's, a regional chain of stereo shops, revealed the following:

	At Cost	At Retail
Beginning inventory	$ 30,400	$ 48,000
Net purchases	113,000	191,000
Net sales		201,000

Use the retail inventory method to estimate the ending inventory of the business.

Exercise 8-11 *Recording perpetual inventory transactions* **(L.O. 7)**

Jerrel Bolton Chevrolet Company keeps perpetual inventory records for its automobile inventory. During May the company made credit purchases of inventory costing $93,300. Cash sales came to $63,100, credit sales on notes receivable totaled $85,400, and cost of goods sold reached $119,550. Record these summary transactions in the general journal.

Exercise 8-12 *Computing the ending amount of a perpetual inventory* **(L.O. 7)**

Piazza String World Music Center carries a large inventory of guitars, keyboards, and other musical instruments. Because each item is expensive, Piazza uses a perpetual inventory system. Company records indicate the following for a particular line of Casio keyboards:

Date	Item	Quantity	Unit Cost
May 1	Balance	5	$80
6	Sale	3	
8	Purchase	11	85
17	Sale	4	
30	Sale	3	

Compute ending inventory and cost of goods sold for keyboards by the FIFO method. Also show the computation of cost of goods sold by the standard formula: Beginning inventory + Purchases − Ending inventory = Cost of goods sold.

Problems (Group A)

Problem 8-1A *Computing inventory by three methods* **(L.O. 1)**

Emerson Electric Co. began the year with 73 units of inventory that cost $26 each. During the year Emerson made the following purchases:

Mar. 11	113 @ $27
May 2	81 @ 29
July 19	167 @ 32
Nov. 18	44 @ 36

The company uses the periodic inventory system, and the physical count at December 31 indicates that ending inventory consists of 91 units.

Required

Compute the ending inventory and cost of goods sold amounts under (1) weighted-average cost, (2) FIFO cost, and (3) LIFO cost. Round weighted-average cost per unit to the nearest cent, and round all other amounts to the nearest dollar.

Problem 8-2A *Computing inventory, cost of goods sold, and FIFO inventory profit* **(L.O. 1,2)**

Lincoln Beverage Distributors specializes in soft drinks. The business began operations on January 1, 19X1, with an inventory of 500 cases of drinks that cost $2.01 each. During the first month of operations the store purchased inventory as follows:

Purchase no. 1	60 @ $2.10	
Purchase no. 2	120 @ 2.35	
Purchase no. 3	600 @ 2.50	
Purchase no. 4	40 @ 2.75	

The ending inventory consists of 500 cases of drinks.

Required

1. Complete the following tabulation, rounding weighted-average cost to the nearest cent and all other amounts to the nearest dollar:

	Ending Inventory	Cost of Goods Sold
a. Weighted-average cost	———	———
b. FIFO cost	———	———
c. LIFO cost	———	———

2. Compute the amount of inventory profit under FIFO.
3. Which method produces the most current ending inventory cost? Which method produces the most current cost-of-goods-sold amount? Give the reason for your answers.

Problem 8-3A *Preparing an income statement directly from the accounts* **(L.O. 1,2)**

The records of Upjohn Healthcare Products include the following accounts for one of its products at December 31 of the current year:

Inventory

Jan. 1 Balance	{700 units @ $7.00}	4,900	

Purchases

Jan. 6	300 units @ $7.05	2,115	
Mar. 19	1,100 units @ 7.35	8,085	
June 22	8,400 units @ 7.50	63,000	
Oct. 4	500 units @ 8.80	4,400	
Dec. 31 Balance		77,600	

Sales Revenue

	Feb. 5	1,000 units @ $12.00	12,000
	Apr. 10	700 units @ 12.10	8,470
	July 31	1,800 units @ 13.25	23,850
	Sep. 4	3,500 units @ 13.50	47,250
	Nov. 27	3,100 units @ 15.00	46,500
	Dec. 31 Balance		138,070

Required

1. Compute the quantities of goods in (a) ending inventory and (b) cost of goods sold during the year.
2. Prepare a partial income statement through gross margin under the weighted-average cost, FIFO cost, and LIFO cost methods.

Problem 8-4A *Converting an actual company's reported income from the LIFO basis to the FIFO basis* **(L.O. 3)**

Colgate-Palmolive Company uses the LIFO method for inventories. In a recent annual report, Colgate-Palmolive reported these amounts on the balance sheet (in millions):

	December 31,	
	19X9	**19X8**
Inventories................	$591	$630

A note to the financial statements indicated that if current cost (assume FIFO) had been used, inventories would have been higher by $25 million at the end of 19X9 and higher by $21 million at the end of 19X8. The income statement reported sales revenue of $5,039 million and cost of goods sold of $2,843 million for 19X9.

Required

1. Show the computation of Colgate-Palmolive's cost of goods sold and gross margin for 19X9 by the LIFO method as actually reported.
2. Compute Colgate-Palmolive's cost of goods sold and gross margin for 19X9 by the FIFO method.
3. Which method makes the company look better in 19X9? Give your reason. What is the amount of inventory profit for 19X9?

Problem 8-5A *Applying the lower-of-cost-or-market rule* **(L.O. 4)**

The financial statements of Dubrovnik Business Systems were prepared on the cost basis without considering whether the replacement value of ending inventory was less than cost. Following are selected data from those statements:

From the income statement:

Sales revenue		$278,000
Cost of goods sold:		
Beginning inventory	$ 60,000	
Net purchases...................	122,000	
Cost of goods available for sale ...	182,000	
Ending inventory...............	53,000	
Cost of goods sold..............		129,000
Gross margin		$149,000

From the balance sheet:

Current assets:	
Inventory.........................	$ 53,000

The replacement costs were $68,000 for beginning inventory and $51,000 for ending inventory.

Required

1. Revise the data to include the appropriate lower-of-cost-or-market value of inventory.
2. How is the lower-of-cost-or-market rule conservative? How is conservatism shown in Dubrovnik's situation?

Problem 8-6A *Correcting inventory errors over a three-year period* **(L.O. 5)**

The accounting records of Elm Mott Custom Window Frames show these data (in millions):

	19X6	19X5	19X4
Net sales revenue	$350	$280	$240
Cost of goods sold:			
Beginning inventory	$ 65	$ 55	$ 70
Net purchases	195	135	130
Cost of goods available . . .	260	190	200
Less Ending inventory . . .	70	65	55
Cost of goods sold	190	125	145
Gross margin	160	155	95
Operating expenses	113	109	76
Net income.	$ 47	$ 46	$ 19

In early 19X7, a team of internal auditors discovered that the ending inventory of 19X4 had been overstated by $12 million. Also, the ending inventory for 19X6 had been understated by $8 million. The ending inventory at December 31, 19X5, was correct.

Required

1. Prepare corrected income statements for the three years.
2. State whether each year's net income and stockholders' equity amounts are understated or overstated. For each incorrect figure, indicate the amount of the understatement or overstatement.

Problem 8-7A *Estimating inventory by the gross margin method; preparing a multiple-step income statement* **(L.O. 6)**

Assume Baldwin Piano Company estimates its inventory by the gross margin method when preparing monthly financial statements. For the past two years, the gross margin has averaged 40 percent of net sales. Assume further that the company's inventory records for stores in the southwestern region reveal the following data:

Inventory, July 1	$ 267,000
Transactions during July:	
Purchases.	3,689,000
Purchase discounts	26,000
Purchase returns	12,000
Sales	6,230,000
Sales returns	22,000

Required

1. Estimate the July 31 inventory using the gross margin method.
2. Prepare the July income statement through gross margin for the Baldwin Piano Company stores in the southwestern region. Use the multiple-step format.

Problem 8-8A *Estimating inventory by the retail method; recording periodic inventory transactions* **(L.O. 6)**

The fiscal year of Dayton Hudson Corporation ends on January 31. Assume the following inventory data for the jewelry department of a Dayton Hudson Store:

	Cost	Retail
Inventory, Jan. 31, 19X3	$ 31,200	$ 63,300
Transactions during the year ended January 31, 19X4:		
Purchases	154,732	301,190
Purchase returns.	5,800	11,290
Sales.		314,600
Sales returns		18,190

Required

1. Use the retail method to estimate the cost of the store's ending inventory of jewelry at January 31, 19X4.
2. Assuming Dayton Hudson uses the periodic inventory system, prepare general journal entries to record:
   a. Inventory purchases and sales during fiscal year 19X4. Assume all purchases and one-half of company sales were on credit. All other sales were for cash.
   b. Inventory entries at January 31, 19X4. Closing entries for Purchases and Purchase Returns are not required.

Problem 8-9A *Using the perpetual inventory system; applying the lower-of-cost-or-market rule* **(L.O. 4,7)**

Midas is a popular brand of automobile mufflers. Assume the following data for a Midas Muffler store:

	Purchased	Sold	Balance
Dec. 31, 19X3			120 @ $6 = $720
Mar. 15, 19X4	50 @ $7 = $350		
Apr. 10		80	
May 29	100 @ 8 = 800		
Aug. 3		130	
Nov. 16	90 @ 9 = 810		
Dec. 12		70	

Required

1. Prepare a perpetual inventory record for Midas, using the FIFO method.
2. Assume Midas sold the 130 units on August 3 on account for $22 each. Record the sale and related cost of goods sold in the general journal under the FIFO method.
3. Suppose the current replacement cost of the ending inventory of this Midas store is $750 at December 31, 19X4. Use the answer to requirement 1 to compute the lower-of-cost-or-market (LCM) value of the ending inventory.

Problem 8-10A *Recording periodic and perpetual inventory transactions* **(L.O. 7)**

Yankee Sales Company records reveal the following at December 31 of the current year.

Inventory

Jan. 1 Balance	
900 units @ $7.00 6,300	

Purchases

Feb. 4 300 units @ $7.05 2,115	
Apr. 11 1,100 units @ 7.35 8,085	
June 22 8,400 units @ 7.50 63,000	
Aug. 19 500 units @ 8.80 4,400	
Dec. 31 Balance 77,600	

Sales Revenue

Mar. 8 1,000 units @ $12.00	12,000
May 24 700 units @ 12.10	8,470
Aug. 19 1,800 units @ 13.25	23,850
Oct. 4 3,500 units @ 13.50	47,250
Nov. 14 3,100 units @ 15.00	46,500
Dec. 31 Balance	138,070

Required

Make summary journal entries to record:

1. Purchases, sales, and end-of-period inventory entries, assuming Yankee Sales Company uses the periodic inventory system and the FIFO cost method. All purchases are on credit. Cash sales are $20,000, with the remaining sales on account.

2. Purchases, sales, and cost of goods sold, assuming Yankee Sales Company uses the perpetual inventory system and the FIFO cost method. All purchases are on credit. Cash sales are $20,000, with the remaining sales on account.

(Group B)

Problem 8-1B *Computing inventory by three methods* **(L.O. 1)**

Pearle Vision Center began the year with 140 units of inventory that cost $80 each. During the year Pearle made the following purchases:

Feb. 3	....	217 @ $81
Apr. 12	....	95 @ 82
Aug. 8	....	210 @ 84
Oct. 24	....	248 @ 88

The company uses the periodic inventory system, and the physical count at December 31 indicates that ending inventory consists of 229 units.

Required

Compute the ending inventory and cost of goods sold amounts under (1) weighted-average cost, (2) FIFO cost, and (3) LIFO cost. Round weighted-average cost per unit to the nearest cent, and round all other amounts to the nearest dollar.

Problem 8-2B *Computing inventory, cost of goods sold, and FIFO inventory profits* **(L.O. 1,2)**

Shellenberger's specializes in men's shirts. The store began operations on January 1, 19X1, with an inventory of 200 shirts that cost $13 each. During the year the store purchased inventory as follows:

Purchase no. 1	....	110 @ $14
Purchase no. 2	....	80 @ 15
Purchase no. 3	....	320 @ 15
Purchase no. 4	....	100 @ 18

The ending inventory consists of 150 shirts.

Required

1. Complete the following tabulation, rounding average cost to the nearest cent and all other amounts to the nearest dollar:

	Ending Inventory	Cost of Goods Sold
a. Weighted-average cost........	_____	_____
b. FIFO cost	_____	_____
c. LIFO cost	_____	_____

2. Compute the amount of inventory profit under FIFO.
3. Which method produces the most current ending inventory cost? Which method produces the most current cost-of-goods-sold amount? Give the reason for your answers.

Problem 8-3B *Preparing an income statement directly from the accounts* **(L.O. 1,2)**

The records of The Kitchen Cupboard include the following accounts for one of its products at December 31 of the current year:

Inventory

Jan. 1	Balance	{300 units @ $3.00} {100 units @ 3.10}	1,210

Purchases

Feb. 6	800 units @ $3.15	2,520
May 19	600 units @ 3.35	2,010
Aug. 12	460 units @ 3.50	1,610
Oct. 4	800 units @ 3.75	3,000
Dec. 31 Balance		9,140

Sales Revenue

	Mar. 12	500 units @ $4.00	2,000
	June 9	1,100 units @ 4.20	4,620
	Aug. 21	300 units @ 4.50	1,350
	Nov. 2	600 units @ 4.50	2,700
	Dec. 18	100 units @ 4.75	475
	Dec. 31 Balance		11,145

Required

1. Compute the quantities of goods in (a) ending inventory and (b) cost of goods sold during the year.
2. Prepare a partial income statement through gross margin under the weighted-average cost, FIFO cost, and LIFO cost methods. Round weighted-average cost to the nearest cent and all other amounts to the nearest dollar.

Problem 8-4B *Converting an actual company's reported income from the LIFO basis to the FIFO basis* **(L.O. 3)**

J. C. Penney, Inc., uses the LIFO method for inventories. In a recent annual report, Penney reported these amounts on the balance sheet (in millions):

| | End of Fiscal Year | |
	19X6	19X5
Merchandise inventories	$2,168	$2,298

A note to the financial statements indicated that if another method (assume FIFO) had been used, inventories would have been higher by $10 million at the end of fiscal year 19X6 and higher by $16 million at the end of 19X5. The income statement reported sales revenue of $14,740 million and cost of goods sold of $9,786 million for 19X6.

Required

1. Show the computation of Penney's cost of goods sold and gross margin for fiscal year 19X6 by the LIFO method as actually reported.
2. Compute Penney's cost of goods sold and gross margin for 19X6 by the FIFO method.
3. Which method makes the company look better in 19X6? Give your reason. Were inventory costs increasing or decreasing during 19X6? How can you tell?

Problem 8-5B *Applying the lower-of-cost-or-market rule* **(L.O. 4)**

Assume that accountants prepared the financial statements of Takamoto TV and Appliance on the cost basis without considering whether the replacement value of ending inventory was less than cost. Following are selected data from those statements:

From the income statement:

Sales revenue		$832,000
Cost of goods sold:		
Beginning inventory	$104,000	
Net purchases........................	493,000	
Cost of goods available for sale	597,000	
Ending inventory.....................	143,000	
Cost of goods sold....................		454,000
Gross margin		$378,000

From the balance sheet:

Current assets:		
Inventory............................		$143,000

The replacement costs were $107,000 for beginning inventory and $135,000 for ending inventory.

Required

1. Revise the data to include the appropriate lower-of-cost-or-market value of inventory.
2. How is the lower-of-cost-or-market rule conservative? How is conservatism shown in Takamoto's situation?

Problem 8-6B *Correcting inventory errors over a three-year period* **(L.O. 5)**

The accounting records of the Tanglewood Farms Restaurant chain show these data (in millions):

	19X3	19X2	19X1
Net sales revenue	$200	$160	$175
Cost of goods sold:			
Beginning inventory	$ 15	$ 25	$ 40
Net purchases	135	100	90
Cost of goods available	150	125	130
Less Ending inventory	30	15	25
Cost of goods sold	120	110	105
Gross margin	80	50	70
Operating expenses	74	38	46
Net income	$ 6	$ 12	$ 24

In early 19X4, a team of internal auditors discovered that the ending inventory of 19X1 had been understated by $8 million. Also, the ending inventory for 19X3 had been overstated by $5 million. The ending inventory at December 31, 19X2, was correct.

Required

1. Prepare corrected income statements for the three years.
2. State whether each year's net income as reported here and the related stockholders' equity amounts are understated or overstated. For each incorrect figure, indicate the amount of the understatement or overstatement.

Problem 8-7B *Estimating inventory by the gross margin method; preparing a multiple-step income statement* **(L.O. 6)**

Assume Taco Bell estimates its inventory by the gross margin method when preparing monthly financial statements. For the past two years, gross margin has averaged 25 percent of net sales. Assume further that the company's inventory records for stores in the southeastern region reveal the following data:

Inventory, March 1	$ 398,000
Transactions during March:	
Purchases.	6,585,000
Purchase discounts	149,000
Purchase returns	8,000
Sales	8,667,000
Sales returns	17,000

Required

1. Estimate the March 31 inventory using the gross margin method.
2. Prepare the March income statement through gross margin for the Taco Bell stores in the southeastern region. Use the multiple-step format.

Problem 8-8B *Estimating inventory by the retail method; recording periodic inventory transactions* **(L.O. 6)**

The fiscal year of F. W. Woolworth Co. (and many other retailers) ends on January 31. Assume the following inventory data for the housewares department of a Woolworth store:

	Cost	Retail
Inventory, Jan. 31, 19X5	$ 84,500	$153,636
Transactions during the year ended January 31, 19X6:		
Purchases	419,220	762,500
Purchase returns...........................	18,090	33,172
Sales......................................		690,300
Sales returns		15,140

Required

1. Use the retail method to estimate the cost of the store's ending inventory of housewares at January 31, 19X6. Round off the ratio to two decimal places.
2. Assuming Woolworth uses the periodic inventory system, prepare general journal entries to record:
   a. Inventory purchases and sales during fiscal year 19X6. Assume all purchases and 10 percent of company sales were on credit. All other sales were for cash.
   b. Inventory entries at January 31, 19X6. Closing entries for Purchases and Purchase Returns are not required.

Problem 8-9B *Using the perpetual inventory system; applying the lower-of-cost-or-market rule* **(L.O. 4,7)**

United Technologies manufactures high-technology products used in the aviation and other industries. Perhaps its most famous product is the Pratt & Whitney aircraft engine. Assume the following data for United Technologies' product SR450:

	Purchased	Sold	Balance
Dec. 31, 19X1			110 @ $5 = $550
Feb. 10, 19X2	80 @ $6 = $480		
Apr. 7		160	
May 29	110 @ 7 = 770		
July 13		120	
Oct. 4	100 @ 8 = 800		
Nov. 22		80	

Required

1. Prepare a perpetual inventory record for product SR450, using the FIFO method.
2. Assume United Technologies sold the 160 units on April 7 on account for $13 each. Record the sale and related cost of goods sold in the general journal under the FIFO method.
3. Suppose the current replacement cost of the ending inventory of product SR450 is $305 at December 31, 19X2. Use the answer to Requirement 1 to compute the lower-of-cost-or-market (LCM) value of the ending inventory.

Problem 8-10B *Recording periodic and perpetual inventory transactions* **(L.O. 7)**

Diego Associates records reveal the following at December 31 of the current year:

Inventory

Jan. 1	Balance ⎰400 units @ $3.00⎱	1,510	
	⎱100 units @ 3.10⎰		

Purchases

Jan. 22	800 units @ $3.15	2,520	
Apr. 8	600 units @ 3.35	2,010	
July 12	460 units @ 3.50	1,610	
Sep. 11	800 units @ 3.75	3,000	
Dec. 31 Balance		9,140	

Sales Revenue

		Feb. 8	500 units @ $4.00	2,000
		Apr. 22	1,100 units @ 4.20	4,620
		July 21	300 units @ 4.50	1,350
		Oct. 14	600 units @ 4.50	2,700
		Nov. 27	100 units @ 4.75	475
		Dec. 31 Balance		11,145

Required

Make summary journal entries to record:

1. Purchases, sales, and end-of-period inventory entries, assuming Diego Associates uses the periodic inventory system and the FIFO cost method. All purchases are on credit. Cash sales are $4,000, with the remaining sales on account.

2. Purchases, sales, and cost of goods sold, assuming Diego Associates uses the perpetual inventory system and the FIFO cost method. All purchases are on credit. Cash sales total $4,000, with the remainder on account.

Extending Your Knowledge

Decision Problems

1. Assessing the Impact of a Year-End Purchase of Inventory (L.O. 2)

Tailwind Cycling Center is nearing the end of its first year of operations. The company made the following inventory purchases:

January	1,000 units @	$100	=	$100,000
March	1,000	100		100,000
May	1,000	110		110,000
July	1,000	130		130,000
September	1,000	140		140,000
November	1,000	150		150,000
Totals	6,000			$730,000

Sales for the year will be 5,000 units for $1,200,000 revenue. Expenses other than cost of goods sold and income taxes will be $200,000. The president of the company is undecided about whether to adopt FIFO or LIFO.

The company has storage capacity for 5,000 additional units of inventory. Inventory prices are expected to stay at $150 per unit for the next few months. The president is considering purchasing 4,000 additional units of inventory at $150 each before the end of the year. He wishes to know how the purchase would affect net income under both FIFO and LIFO. The income tax rate is 40 percent, and income tax is an expense.

Required

1. To aid company decision making, prepare income statements under FIFO and under LIFO, both without and with the year-end purchase of 4,000 units of inventory at $150 per unit.
2. Compare net income under FIFO without and with the year-end purchase. Make the same comparison under LIFO. Under which method does the year-end purchase have the greater effect on net income?
3. Under which method can a year-end purchase be made in order to manipulate net income?

2. Assessing the Impact of the Inventory Costing Method on the Financial Statements (L.O. 2,3,4)

The inventory costing method chosen by a company can affect the financial statements and thus the decisions of the users of those statements.

Required

1. A leading accounting researcher stated that one inventory costing method reports the most recent costs in the income statement, while another method reports the most recent costs in the balance sheet. In this person's opinion, this results in one or the other of the statements being "inaccurate" when prices are rising. What did the researcher mean?
2. Conservatism is an accepted accounting concept. Would you want management to be conservative in accounting for inventory if you were (a) a shareholder and (b) a prospective shareholder? Give your reason.
3. Beechwood Ltd. follows conservative accounting and writes the value of its inventory of bicycles down to market, which has declined below cost. The following year, an unexpected cycling craze results in a demand for bicycles that far exceeds supply, and the market price increases above the previous cost. What effect will conservatism have on the income of Beechwood over the two years?

Ethical Issue

During 19X6, Crocker-Hinds Company changed to the LIFO method of accounting for inventory. Suppose that during 19X7 Crocker-Hinds changes back to the FIFO method, and the following year switches back to LIFO again.

Required

1. What would you think of a company's ethics if it changed accounting methods every year?
2. What accounting principle would changing methods every year violate?
3. Who can be harmed when a company changes its accounting methods too often? How?

Financial Statement Problems

1. Inventories   (L.O. 1,2)

The notes are an important part of a company's financial statements, giving valuable details that would clutter the tabular data presented in the statements. This problem will help you learn to use a company's inventory notes. Refer to the Goodyear Tire & Rubber Company statements and related notes in Appendix C. Answer the following questions.

1. How much were Goodyear's total inventories at December 31, 1991? The Inventories note lists three categories of inventories that are classified as current assets. Name these, and briefly explain what you think each category means.
2. How does Goodyear value its inventories? Which cost methods does the company use?
3. By rearranging the cost-of-goods-sold formula, you can solve for net purchases, which are not disclosed in Goodyear's statements. Show how to compute Goodyear's net purchases during 1991. For this computation you should use the beginning and ending balances of Finished product inventories.
4. Compute the amounts of cost of goods sold and gross margin that Goodyear would have reported for 1991 if the company had used the FIFO method for inventories. The Inventories note gives relevant information on the difference between LIFO and FIFO costs of beginning and ending inventories (the approximate current cost of inventories is the FIFO cost). Assume this difference applies exclusively to Finished product inventories. As a top manager of Goodyear, which inventory method would you select if your motive were to report the maximum acceptable gross margin? Which method would you select to minimize income tax?

2. Inventories   (L.O. 1,2)

Obtain the annual report of an actual company *that includes Inventories among its current assets.* Answer these questions about the company.

1. How much were the company's total inventories at the end of the current year? At the end of the preceding year?
2. How does the company value its inventories? Which cost method or methods does the company use?
3. Depending on the nature of the company's business, would you expect the company to use a periodic inventory system or a perpetual system? Give your reason.
4. By rearranging the cost-of-goods-sold formula, you can solve for net purchases, which are not disclosed. Show how to compute the company's net purchases during the current year. You should examine the company's note titled *Inventories, Merchandise inventories,* or a similar term. If the company discloses several categories of inventories, including a title similar to Finished Goods, use the beginning and ending balances of Finished Goods for the computation of net purchases. If only one category of Inventories is disclosed, use these beginning and ending balances.
5. If the company does not use the LIFO method for inventories, you can omit this requirement. If the company uses LIFO, convert gross margin from the LIFO basis, as reported, to the FIFO basis, which approximates current cost. For this computation, assume the entire amount of the excess of FIFO (or current) cost over LIFO cost applies to Finished Goods inventories. If your motive were to maximize reported income, would you prefer LIFO or FIFO? If your goal were to minimize income tax, which method is preferable?

Chapter 9

Plant Assets, Intangible Assets, and Related Expenses

Business assets are separated into current assets, those typically useful for one year or less, and long-lived assets, those useful for longer than a year. Count the references to long-lived assets in this excerpt from *The Wall Street Journal*, August 16, 1990, p. A1: Reprinted by permission of *The Wall Street Journal*, © 1990 Dow Jones & Company, Inc. All Rights Reserved Worldwide.

Iraq has just invaded Kuwait, and Larry Brady is thumbing through documents to gauge the effect on his company, a far-flung conglomerate called FMC Corp. Halfway through, he stops and looks up in horror. Five new FMC street-sweepers, worth $400,000, are on a *freighter* bound for Kuwait City—and they're just hours from their destination.

"Get that *ship* turned around!" Mr. Brady, the execu-

tive vice president, barks to Joe Murdock, international business manager at FMC's sweeper division in Pomona, Calif. "Saddam Hussein isn't getting his hands on those sweepers."

Mr. Murdock is already phoning the *freighter's* captain when Mr. Brady calls. Take a quick turn into Abu Dhabi, Mr. Murdock orders the captain, just in time.

It's crisis management time at FMC Corp., as at hundreds of businesses across the U.S. and the world. For the past two weeks, FMC executives have been meeting and moving nearly nonstop to prevent damage—for instance, by planning Middle East evacuation routes for employees—and to take advantage of opportunities, such as gearing up *factories* in Malaysia to speed production of *oil-field equipment*. [Emphasis added]

Long-lived assets used in the operation of the business and not held for sale as investments are further divided into plant assets and intangible assets. **Plant assets** are those long-lived assets that are tangible. Their physical form provides their usefulness, for instance, land, buildings, equipment, and coal and other minerals. Of the plant assets, land is unique. Its cost is *not* depreciated—expensed over time—because its usefulness does not decrease like that of other assets. Most companies report plant assets under the heading Property, Plant, and Equipment.

Intangible assets are useful not because of their physical characteristics but because of the special rights they carry. Patents, copyrights, and trademarks are intangible assets. Examples of famous patents are the recipe for Coca-Cola and the Dolby noise-reduction process. Accounting for intangibles is similar to accounting for plant assets.

This area has its own terminology. Different names apply to the expense for the cost of the various assets, as shown in Exhibit 9-1.

The first half of the chapter discusses and illustrates how to identify the cost of a plant asset and how to expense its cost. The second half considers disposing of plant assets and how to account for natural resources and intangible assets. Unless stated otherwise, we describe accounting in accordance with generally accepted accounting principles, as distinguished from reporting to the IRS for income tax purposes.

The Cost of a Plant Asset

The cost principle directs a business to carry an asset on the balance sheet at the amount paid for it. The **cost of a plant asset** is the purchase price, applicable taxes, purchase commissions, and all other amounts paid to acquire the

EXHIBIT 9-1 *Terminology Used in Accounting for Plant Assets and Intangible Assets*

Asset Account on the Balance Sheet	Related Expense Account on the Income Statement
Land	None
Buildings, Machinery and Equipment, Furniture and Fixtures, and Land Improvements	Depreciation
Natural Resources	Depletion
Intangibles	Amortization

asset and to ready it for its intended use. Because the types of costs differ for various categories of plant assets, we discuss the major groups individually.

Land

The cost of land includes its purchase price (cash plus any note payable given), brokerage commission, survey fees, legal fees, and any back property taxes that the purchaser pays. Land cost also includes any expenditures for grading and clearing the land and for demolishing or removing any unwanted buildings.

OBJECTIVE 1

Identify the elements of a plant asset's cost

The cost of land does *not* include the cost of fencing, paving, sprinkler systems, and lighting. These separate plant assets—called land improvements—are subject to depreciation.

Suppose you are a real estate developer, and you sign a $300,000 note payable to purchase 100 acres of land for subdivision into 5-acre lots. You also pay $10,000 in back property tax, $8,000 in transfer taxes, $5,000 for removal of an old building, a $1,000 survey fee, and $260,000 for the construction of fences, all in cash. What is the cost of this land?

Purchase price of land		$300,000
Add related costs:		
Back property tax	$10,000	
Transfer taxes	8,000	
Removal of building	5,000	
Survey fee	1,000	
Total incidental costs		24,000
Total cost of land		$324,000

The entry to record purchase of the land is

Land	324,000	
Note Payable		300,000
Cash		24,000

Buildings

The cost of constructing a building includes architectural fees, building permits, contractors' charges, and payments for materials, labor, and overhead. When an existing building (new or old) is purchased, its cost includes the purchase price, brokerage commission, sales and other taxes, and cash or credit expenditures for repairing and renovating the building for its intended purpose. The factories mentioned in the chapter-opening vignette would be classified as buildings.

Machinery and Equipment

The cost of machinery and equipment, such as the oil-field equipment mentioned in the vignette, includes its purchase price (less any discounts), transportation charges, insurance while in transit, sales and other taxes, purchase commission, installation costs, and any expenditures to test the asset before placing it in service. The freighters mentioned in the vignette are also equipment. Companies may carry a Ships account for ocean-going vessels.

Land Improvements

In the land example, the cost of the fences ($260,000) is not part of the cost of the land. Instead, the $260,000 would be recorded in a separate account entitled Land Improvements. This account includes costs for such other items as driveways, parking lots, and sprinkler systems. Although these assets are located on the land, they are subject to decay, and therefore their cost should be depreciated, as we discuss later in this chapter. Also, the cost of a new building constructed on the land is a debit to the asset account Building.

Group (or Basket) Purchases of Assets

Businesses often purchase several assets (as a group, or in a "basket") for a single amount. For example, a company may pay one price for land and an office building. The company must identify the cost of each asset. The total cost is divided between the assets according to their relative sales (or market) values. This allocation technique is called the **relative-sales-value method.**

Suppose Xerox Corporation purchases land and a building in Kansas City for a midwestern sales office. The building sits on two acres of land, and the combined purchase price of land and building is $2,800,000. An appraisal indicates that the land's market (sales) value is $300,000 and the building's market (sales) value is $2,700,000.

An accountant first figures the ratio of each asset's market price to the total market price. Total appraised value is $3,000,000. Thus land, valued at $300,000, is 10 percent of the total market value. Building's appraised value is 90 percent of the total.

Asset	Market (Sales) Value		Total Market Value		Percentage
Land	$ 300,000	÷	$3,000,000	=	10%
Building	2,700,000	÷	$3,000,000	=	90%
Total	$3,000,000				100%

The percentage for each asset is multiplied by the total purchase price to give its cost in the purchase.

Asset	Total Purchase Price		Percentage		Allocated Cost
Land	$2,800,000	×	.10	=	$ 280,000
Building	$2,800,000	×	.90	=	2,520,000
Total			1.00		$2,800,000

Assuming Xerox pays cash, the entry to record the purchase of the land and building is

Land	280,000	
Building	2,520,000	
Cash		2,800,000

Depreciation of Plant Assets

OBJECTIVE 2

Explain the concept of depreciation

The process of allocating a plant asset's cost to expense over the period the asset is used is called *depreciation*. This process is designed to match the asset's expense against the revenue generated over the asset's life, as the matching principle directs. The primary purpose of depreciation accounting is therefore to measure income. Of less importance is the need to account for the asset's decline in usefulness.

Suppose a bank buys a computer. The business believes the computer offers four years of service after which obsolescence will make it worthless. Using straight-line depreciation (which we discuss later in this chapter), the bank expenses one quarter of the asset's cost in each of its four years of use.

Let's contrast what depreciation accounting is with what it is *not*. (1) *Depreciation is not a process of valuation*. Businesses do not record depreciation based on appraisals of their plant assets made at the end of each period. Instead, businesses allocate the asset's cost to the periods of its useful life based on a specific depreciation method. (We discuss these methods in this chapter.) (2) *Depreciation does not mean that the business sets aside cash to replace assets as they become fully depreciated*. Establishing such a cash fund is a decision entirely separate from depreciation. *Accumulated depreciation* is that portion of the plant asset's cost that has already been recorded as expense. Accumulated depreciation does not represent a growing amount of cash.

Determining the Useful Life of a Plant Asset

No asset (other than land) offers an unlimited useful life. For some plant assets physical *wear and tear* from operations and the elements may be the important cause of depreciation. For example, physical deterioration takes its toll on the usefulness of trucks and furniture.

Assets like computers, other electronic equipment, and airplanes may become *obsolete* before they physically deteriorate. An asset is obsolete when another asset can do the job better or more efficiently. Thus an asset's useful life may be much shorter than its physical life. Accountants usually depreciate computers over a short period of time—perhaps four years—even though they know the computers will remain in working condition much longer. Whether wear and tear or obsolescence causes depreciation, the asset's cost is depreciated over its expected useful life.

Measuring Depreciation

To measure depreciation for a plant asset, we must know its *cost*, its *estimated useful life*, and its *estimated residual value*.

Cost is the purchase price of the asset. We discussed cost under the heading The Cost of a Plant Asset, beginning on page 440.

Estimated useful life is the length of the service the business expects to get from the asset. Useful life may be expressed in years (as we have seen so far), units of output, miles, or other measures. For example, the useful life of a building is stated in years. The useful life of a bookbinding machine may be stated as the number of books the machine is expected to bind—that is, its expected units of output. A reasonable measure of a delivery truck's useful life is the total number of miles the truck is expected to travel. Companies base such estimates on past experience and information from industry trade magazines and government publications.

Estimated residual value—also called *scrap value* and *salvage value*—is the expected cash value of the asset at the end of its useful life. For example, a business may believe that a machine's useful life will be seven years. After that time, the company expects to sell the machine as scrap metal. The amount the business believes it can get for the machine is the estimated residual value. In computing depreciation, estimated residual value is *not* depreciated because the business expects to receive this amount from disposing of the asset. The full cost of a plant asset is depreciated if the asset is expected to have no residual value. The plant asset's cost minus its estimated residual value is called the **depreciable cost**.

Of the factors entering the computation of depreciation, only one factor is known—cost. The other two factors—residual value and useful life—must be estimated. Depreciation, then, is an estimated amount.

OBJECTIVE 3

Account for depreciation by four methods

Depreciation Methods

Four basic methods exist for computing depreciation: straight-line, units-of-production, declining-balance, and sum-of-years-digits. These four methods allocate different amounts of depreciation expense to different periods. However, they all result in the same total amount of depreciation, the asset's depreciable cost over the life of the asset. Exhibit 9-2 presents the data used to illustrate depreciation computations by the four methods.

Straight-Line (SL) Method

In the **straight-line (SL)** method, an equal amount of depreciation expense is assigned to each year (or period) of asset use. Depreciable cost is divided by useful life in years to determine the annual depreciation expense. The equation for SL depreciation, applied to the limo data from Exhibit 9-2, is

$$\text{Straight-line depreciation per year} = \frac{\text{Cost} - \text{Residual value}}{\text{Useful life in years}}$$

$$= \frac{\$41,000 - \$1,000}{5}$$

$$= \$8,000$$

The entry to record this depreciation is

Depreciation Expense	8,000	
Accumulated Depreciation		8,000

EXHIBIT 9-2 *Data for Depreciation Computations*

Data Item	Amount
Cost of limousine............	$41,000
Estimated residual value	1,000
Depreciable cost	$40,000
Estimated useful life:	
Years......................	5 years
Units of production........	400,000 units

EXHIBIT 9-3 Straight-Line Depreciation Schedule

| Date | Asset Cost | Depreciation for the Year | | | | Accumulated Depreciation | Asset Book Value |
		Depreciation Rate	Depreciable Cost		Depreciation Amount		
1- 1-X1	$41,000						$41,000
12-31-X1		.20	× $40,000	=	$8,000	$ 8,000	33,000
12-31-X2		.20	× 40,000	=	8,000	16,000	25,000
12-31-X3		.20	× 40,000	=	8,000	24,000	17,000
12-31-X4		.20	× 40,000	=	8,000	32,000	9,000
12-31-X5		.20	× 40,000	=	8,000	40,000	1,000

Assume that the limo was purchased on January 1, 19X1, and the business's fiscal year ends on December 31. A *straight-line depreciation schedule* is presented in Exhibit 9-3.

The final column of Exhibit 9-3 shows the asset's *book value,* which is its cost less accumulated depreciation. Book value is also called carrying amount.

As an asset is used, accumulated depreciation increases, and the book value decreases. (Note the Accumulated Depreciation column and the Book Value column.) An asset's final book value is its *residual value* ($1,000 in the exhibit). At the end of its useful life, the asset is said to be fully depreciated.

Units-of-Production (UOP) Method

In the **units-of-production (UOP)** method, a fixed amount of depreciation is assigned to each unit of output produced by the plant asset. Depreciable cost is divided by useful life in units to determine this amount. This per-unit depreciation expense is multiplied by the number of units produced each period to compute depreciation for the period. The UOP depreciation equation for the limo data in Exhibit 9-2 is

$$\text{Units-of-production depreciation per unit of output} = \frac{\text{Cost} - \text{Residual value}}{\text{Useful life in units}}$$

$$= \frac{\$41,000 - \$1,000}{400,000 \text{ miles}}$$

$$= \$.10$$

EXHIBIT 9-4 Units-of-Production Depreciation Schedule

| Date | Asset Cost | Depreciation for the Year | | | | Accumulated Depreciation | Asset Book Value |
		Depreciation Per Unit	Number of Units		Depreciation Amount		
1- 1-19X1	$41,000						$41,000
12-31-19X1		$.10	× 90,000	=	$ 9,000	$ 9,000	32,000
12-31-19X2		.10	× 120,000	=	12,000	21,000	20,000
12-31-19X3		.10	× 100,000	=	10,000	31,000	10,000
12-31-19X4		.10	× 60,000	=	6,000	37,000	4,000
12-31-19X5		.10	× 30,000	=	3,000	40,000	1,000

Assume the limo is expected to be driven 90,000 miles (*miles* are the *units* in our example) during the first year, 120,000 during the second, 100,000 during the third, 60,000 during the fourth, and 30,000 during the fifth. The UOP depreciation schedule for this asset is shown in Exhibit 9-4.

The amount of UOP depreciation per period varies with the number of units the asset produces. Note that the total number of units produced is 400,000, the measure of this asset's useful life. Therefore, UOP depreciation does not depend directly on time as the other methods do.

Double-Declining-Balance (DDB) Method

Double-declining-balance (DDB) is one of the accelerated-depreciation methods. An **accelerated-depreciation** method writes off a relatively larger amount of the asset's cost nearer the start of its useful life than does straight-line. **DDB depreciation** computes annual depreciation by multiplying the asset's book value by a constant percentage, which is two times the straight-line depreciation rate. DDB amounts are computed as follows:

First, the straight-line depreciation rate per year is computed. For example, a 5-year limousine has a straight-line depreciation rate of 1/5, or 20 percent. A 10-year asset has a straight-line rate of 1/10, or 10 percent, and so on.

Second, the straight-line rate is multiplied by 2 to compute the DDB rate. The DDB rate for a 5-year asset is 40 percent ($20\% \times 2 = 40\%$). For a 10-year asset the DDB rate is 20 percent ($10\% \times 2 = 20\%$).

Third, The DDB rate is multiplied by the period's beginning asset book value (cost less accumulated depreciation). Residual value of the asset is ignored in computing depreciation by the DDB method, except during the last year.

The DDB rate for the limousine in Exhibit 9-2 is

$$\text{DDB rate per year} = \left(\frac{1}{\text{Useful life in years}} \times 2 \right) = \left(\frac{1}{5 \text{ years}} \times 2 \right)$$

$$= (20\% \times 2) = 40\%$$

Fourth, the final year's depreciation amount is the amount needed to reduce the asset's book value to its residual value. In the DDB depreciation schedule in Exhibit 9-5, the fifth and final year's depreciation is $4,314—the $5,314 book

EXHIBIT 9-5 *Double-Declining-Balance Depreciation Schedule*

Date	Asset Cost	DDB Rate		Asset Book Value		Depreciation Amount	Accumulated Depreciation	Asset Book Value
				Depreciation for the Year				
1- 1-19X1	$41,000							$41,000
12-31-19X1		.40	×	$41,000	=	$16,400	$16,400	24,600
12-31-19X2		.40	×	24,600	=	9,840	26,240	14,760
12-31-19X3		.40	×	14,760	=	5,904	32,144	8,856
12-31-19X4		.40	×	8,856	=	3,542	35,686	5,314
12-31-19X5						4,314*	40,000	1,000

*Last-year depreciation is the amount needed to reduce asset book value to the residual value ($5,314 − $1,000 = $4,314).

value less the $1,000 residual value. The residual value should not be depreciated but should remain on the books until the asset's disposal.

Many companies change to the straight-line method during the next-to-last year of the asset's life. Under this plan, annual depreciation for 19X4 and 19X5 is $3,928. Depreciable cost at the end of 19X3 is $7,856 (book value of $8,856 less residual value of $1,000). Depreciable cost can be spread evenly over the last two years of the asset's life ($7,856 ÷ 2 remaining years = $3,928 per year).

The DDB method differs from the other methods in two ways. (1) The asset's residual value is ignored initially. In the first year, depreciation is computed on the asset's full cost. (2) The final year's calculation is changed in order to bring the asset's book value to the residual value.

Sum-of-Years-Digits (SYD) Method

In the **sum-of-years-digits (SYD)** method—another accelerated method—depreciation is figured by multiplying the depreciable cost of the asset by a fraction. The *denominator* of the SYD fraction is the sum of the years' digits. For a 5-year asset, the years' digits are 1, 2, 3, 4, and 5, and their sum is 15 (1 + 2 + 3 + 4 + 5 = 15). For a 10-year asset, the denominator is 55. Adding the years for a very long-lived asset is tedious. Chances arise for error in the mathematics. Thus we have an easy formula for computing the sum of the years' digits:

Sum of the years' digits = N(N + 1)/2

where N is the useful life of the asset expressed in years. For example, when N equals 5, we have:

$$\frac{5(5 + 1)}{2} = \frac{30}{2} = 15$$

The *numerator* of the SYD fraction for the first year of a 5-year asset is 5. The numerator is 4 for the second year, 3 for the third year, 2 for the fourth year, and 1 for the fifth year.

The SYD depreciation equation for the limo in Exhibit 9-2 is

$$\text{SYD depreciation per year} = (\text{Cost} - \text{Residual value}) \times \frac{\text{Years' digits, largest first}}{\text{Sum of years' digits}}$$

$$= (\$41,000 - \$1,000) \times \frac{5^*}{1 + 2 + 3 + 4 + 5}$$

$$= \$40,000 \times \frac{5}{15} = \$13,333$$

---

*5 for first year; 4 for second year; 3 for third year; 2 for fourth year; 1 for fifth year.

Exhibit 9-6 is the SYD depreciation schedule based on our example data. Note that each year's fraction is multiplied by the depreciable cost ($40,000).

EXHIBIT 9-6 *Sum-of-Years-Digits Depreciation Schedule*

Date	Asset Cost	Depreciation for the Year			Accumulated Depreciation	Asset Book Value
		SYD Fraction	Depreciable Cost	Depreciation Amount		
1- 1-19X1	$41,000					$41,000
12-31-19X1		5/15 ×	$40,000 =	$13,333	$13,333	27,667
12-31-19X2		4/15 ×	40,000 =	10,667	24,000	17,000
12-31-19X3		3/15 ×	40,000 =	8,000	32,000	9,000
12-31-19X4		2/15 ×	40,000 =	5,333	37,333	3,667
12-31-19X5		1/15 ×	40,000 =	2,667	40,000	1,000

Comparison of the Depreciation Methods

Compare the four methods in terms of the yearly amount of depreciation:

Amount of Depreciation Per Year

			Accelerated Methods	
Year	Straight-Line	Units-of-Production	Double-Declining-Balance	Sum-of-Years-Digits
1	$ 8,000	$ 9,000	$16,400	$13,333
2	8,000	12,000	9,840	10,667
3	8,000	10,000	5,904	8,000
4	8,000	6,000	3,542	5,333
5	8,000	3,000	4,314	2,667
Total	$40,000	$40,000	$40,000	$40,000

The yearly amount of depreciation varies by method, but the total $40,000 depreciable cost systematically becomes expense under all four methods.

Generally accepted accounting principles (GAAP) direct a business to match the expense of an asset against the revenue that the asset produces. For a plant asset that generates revenue evenly over time, the straight-line method best meets the matching principle. During each period the asset is used, an equal amount of depreciation is recorded.

The units-of-production method best fits those assets that wear out because of physical use, not obsolescence. Depreciation is recorded only when the asset is used, and the more units the asset generates in a given year, the greater the depreciation expense.

The accelerated methods (DDB and SYD) apply best to those assets that generate greater revenue earlier in their useful lives. The greater expense recorded under the accelerated methods in the early periods is matched against those periods' greater revenue.

Exhibit 9-7 graphs the relationship between annual depreciation amounts for straight-line, units-of-production, and the accelerated depreciation methods.

The graph of straight-line depreciation is flat because annual depreciation is the same amount in each period. Units-of-production depreciation follows no particular pattern because annual depreciation depends on the use of the asset. The greater the use, the greater is the amount of depreciation. Accelerated depreciation is greatest in the asset's first year and less in the later years.

EXHIBIT 9-7 *Depreciation Patterns*

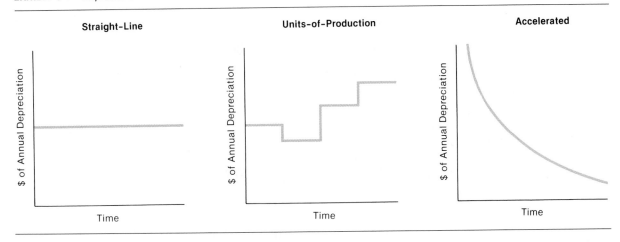

A recent survey indicated that over 70 percent of companies use the straight-line method, approximately 20 percent use an accelerated method, and the remainder use the units-of-production method. For example, Sears uses straight-line, Motorola uses double-declining-balance, Eastman Kodak uses sum-of-years-digits, and Gulf Oil uses units-of-production.

Summary Problem for Your Review

Hubbard Company purchased equipment on January 1, 19X5, for $44,000. The expected life of the equipment is 10 years, and its residual value is $4,000. Under three depreciation methods, the annual depreciation expense and the balance of accumulated depreciation at the end of 19X5 and 19X6 are

	Method A		Method B		Method C	
Year	Annual Depreciation Expense	Accumulated Depreciation	Annual Depreciation Expense	Accumulated Depreciation	Annual Depreciation Expense	Accumulated Depreciation
19X5	$4,000	$4,000	$7,273	$ 7,273	$8,800	$ 8,800
19X6	4,000	8,000	6,545	13,818	7,040	15,840

Required

1. Identify the depreciation method used in each instance, and show the equation and computation for each. (Round off to the nearest dollar.)
2. Assume continued use of the same method through year 19X7. Determine the annual depreciation expense, accumulated depreciation, and book value of the equipment for 19X5 through 19X7 under each method.

SOLUTION TO REVIEW PROBLEM

Requirement 1

Method A: Straight-line

Depreciable cost = $40,000 ($44,000 − $4,000)

Each year: $40,000/10 years = $4,000

Method B: Sum-of-years-digits

$$SYD = N(N + 1)/2 = 10(10 + 1)/2 = 55$$

$$\text{Depreciable cost} = \$40,000 \; (\$44,000 - \$4,000)$$

$$19X5: 10/55 \times \$40,000 = \$7,273$$

$$19X6: 9/55 \times \$40,000 = \$6,545$$

Method C: Double-declining-balance

$$\text{Rate} = \left(\frac{1}{10 \text{ years}} \times 2\right) = (10\% \times 2) = 20\%$$

$$19X5: .20 \times \$44,000 = \$8,800$$

$$19X6: .20 \times (\$44,000 - \$8,800) = \$7,040$$

Requirement 2

Year	Method A Straight-Line Annual Depreciation Expense	Accumulated Depreciation	Book Value	Method B Sum-of-Years-Digits Annual Depreciation Expense	Accumulated Depreciation	Book Value	Method C Double-Declining-Balance Annual Depreciation Expense	Accumulated Depreciation	Book Value
Start			$44,000			$44,000			$44,000
19X5	$4,000	$ 4,000	40,000	$7,273	$ 7,273	36,727	$8,800	$ 8,800	35,200
19X6	4,000	8,000	36,000	6,545	13,818	30,182	7,040	15,840	28,160
19X7	4,000	12,000	32,000	5,818	19,636	24,364	5,632	21,472	22,528

Computations for 19X7:

Straight-line:	$40,000/10 years = $4,000
Sum-of-years-digits:	8/55 × $40,000 = $5,818
Double-declining-balance:	.20 × $28,160 = $5,632

Depreciation and Income Taxes

The majority of companies use the straight-line depreciation method for reporting to their stockholders and creditors on their financial statements. Companies keep a separate set of depreciation records for computing their income taxes. For income tax purposes, most companies use an accelerated depreciation method.

Suppose you are a business manager. The IRS allows an accelerated depreciation method, which most managers choose in preference to straight-line depreciation. Why? Because it provides the most depreciation expense as quickly as possible, thus decreasing your immediate tax payments. The cash you save may be applied to best fit your business needs. This is the strategy most businesses follow.

To understand the relationships among cash flow (cash provided by operations), depreciation, and income tax, recall our earlier depreciation example:

First-year depreciation under straight-line is $8,000, and under double-declining-balance it is $16,400. For illustrative purposes here, assume that DDB is permitted for reporting to the income tax authorities. Assume that the business has $400,000 in cash sales and $300,000 in cash operating expenses during the asset's first year, and the income tax rate is 30 percent. The cash flow analysis appears in Exhibit 9-8.

OBJECTIVE 4

Identify the best depreciation method for income tax purposes

Exhibit 9-8 highlights several important business relationships. Compare the amount of cash provided by operations before income tax. Both columns show $100,000. If there were no income taxes, the total cash provided by operations would be the same regardless of the depreciation method used. Depreciation is a noncash expense and so does not affect cash from operations.

However, depreciation is a tax-deductible expense. The higher the depreciation expense, the lower the income before tax and thus the lower the income tax payment. Therefore, accelerated depreciation helps conserve cash for use in the business. Exhibit 9-8 indicates that the business will have $2,520 more cash at the end of the first year if it uses accelerated depreciation instead of SL ($74,920 against $72,400). Suppose the company invests this money to earn a return of 10 percent during the second year. Then the company will be better off by $252 ($2,520 × 10% = $252). The cash advantage of using the accelerated method is the $252 of additional revenue.

The Tax Reform Act of 1986 created a special depreciation method—used only for income tax purposes—called the Modified Accelerated Cost Recovery System (MACRS). Under this method, assets are grouped into one of eight classes, as shown in Exhibit 9-9. Depreciation for the first four classes is computed by the double-declining-balance method. Depreciation for 15-year assets and 20-year assets is computed by the 150-percent-declining-balance method. Under this method, the annual depreciation rate is computed by multiplying the straight-line rate by 1.50. For a 20-year asset, the straight-line

EXHIBIT 9-8 Cash Flow Advantage of Accelerated Depreciation over Straight-Line (SL) Depreciation for income Tax Purposes

	Income Tax Rate 30 percent	
	SL	Accelerated
Revenues	$400,000	$400,000
Cash operating expenses	300,000	300,000
Cash provided by operations before income tax	100,000	100,000
Depreciation expense (a noncash expense)	8,000	16,400
Income before income tax	92,000	83,600
Income tax expense (30%)	27,600	25,080
Net income	$ 64,400	$ 58,520
Supplementary cash flow analysis:		
Cash provided by operations before income tax	$100,000	$100,000
Income tax expense	27,600	25,080
Cash provided by operations	$ 72,400	$ 74,920
Extra cash available for investment if DDB is used ($74,920 − $72,400)		$ 2,520
Assumed earnings rate on investment of extra cash		×.10
Cash advantage of using DDB over SL		$ 252

Class Identified by Years of Asset Life	Representative Assets	Depreciation Method
3 years	Race horses	DDB
5 years	Automobiles, light trucks	DDB
7 years	Equipment	DDB
10 years	Equipment	DDB
15 years	Sewage treatment plants	150% DDB
20 years	Certain real estate	150% DDB
27 1/2 years	Residential rental property	Straight-line
31 1/2 years	Nonresidential rental property	Straight-line

rate is .05 (1/20 = .05), so the annual MACRS depreciation rate is .075 (.05 × 1.50 = .075). Most real estate is depreciated by the straight-line method.

Special Issues in Depreciation Accounting

Two special issues in depreciation accounting are (1) depreciation for partial years and (2) change in the useful life of a depreciable asset.

Depreciation for Partial Years

Companies purchase plant assets as needed. They do not wait until the beginning of a year or a month. Therefore, companies must develop policies to compute *depreciation for partial years*. Suppose a company purchases a building on April 1 for $500,000. The building's estimated life is 20 years, and its estimated residual value is $80,000. The company's fiscal year ends on December 31. Consider how the company computes depreciation for the year ended December 31.

Many companies compute partial-year depreciation by first computing a full year's depreciation. They then multiply this amount by the fraction of the year they held the asset. Assuming the straight-line method, the year's depreciation is $15,750, computed as follows:

$$\frac{(\$500,000 - \$80,000)}{20} = \$21,000 \text{ per year} \times \frac{9}{12} = \$15,750$$

What if the company bought the asset on April 18? A widely used policy directs businesses to record no depreciation on assets purchased after the fifteenth of the month and to record a full month's depreciation on an asset bought on or before the fifteenth. Thus the company would record no depreciation for April on an April 18 purchase. In this case, the year's depreciation would be $14,000 ($21,000 × 8/12).

How is partial-year depreciation computed under the other depreciation methods? Suppose this building is acquired on October 4 and the company uses the double-declining-balance method. For a 20-year asset, the DDB rate is 10 percent (1/20 = 5% × 2 = 10%). The annual depreciation computations for 19X1, 19X2, and 19X3 are as follows:

Date	Asset Cost	DDB Rate	Depreciation for the Year				Accumulated Depreciation	Asset Book Value
			Asset Book value	Fraction of the year	Depreciation Amount			
10- 4-19X1	$500,000							$500,000
12-31-19X1		1/20 × 2 = .10 × $500,000 ×		3/12	=	$12,500	$ 12,500	487,500
12-31-19X2		.10 × 487,500 ×		12/12	=	48,750	61,250	438,750
12-31-19X3		.10 × 438,750 ×		12/12	=	43,875	105,125	394,875

Partial-year depreciation under the sum-of-years-digits method is computed similarly, by taking the appropriate fraction of a full year's amount. Assuming the building is acquired on September 28, 19X1, depreciation for the remainder of 19X1 will cover three months. With a 20-year life, the sum of the years' digits is 210 [(20 × 21)/2], and the first-year fraction is 20/210. SYD depreciation, which is based on depreciable cost of $420,000 (cost of $500,000 less residual value of $80,000), is computed as follows for the remainder of 19X1, for 19X2, and for 19X3:

Period	SYD Depreciation Computations
April-December 19X1	($420,000 × 20/210 × 3/12) = $10,000
Calendar year 19X2	($420,000 × 20/210 × 9/12) + ($420,000 × 19/210 × 3/12) = $39,500
Calendar year 19X3	($420,000 × 19/210 × 9/12) + ($420,000 × 18/210 × 3/12) = $37,500

No special computation is needed for partial-year depreciation under the units-of-production method. Simply use the number of units produced, regardless of the time period the asset is held.

Change in the Useful Life of a Depreciable Asset

As previously discussed, a business must estimate the useful life of a plant asset to compute depreciation. This prediction is the most difficult part of accounting for depreciation. After the asset is put into use, the business is able to refine its estimate based on experience and new information. Such a change is called a *change in accounting estimate*. In an actual example, Walt Disney Productions included the following note in its financial statements:

Note 5

. . . [T]he Company extended the estimated useful lives of certain theme park ride and attraction assets based upon historical data and engineering studies. The effect of this change was to decrease depreciation by approximately $8 million (an increase in net income of approximately $4.2 million ...).

Such accounting changes are common because no business has perfect foresight. Generally accepted accounting principles require the business to report the nature, reason, and effect of the change on net income, as the Disney example shows. To *record* a change in accounting estimate, the remaining book value of the asset is spread over its adjusted remaining useful life. The adjusted useful life may be longer or shorter than the original useful life.

Assume that a Disney hot dog stand cost $40,000 and the company originally believed the asset had an 8-year useful life with no residual value. Using the straight-line method, the company would record $5,000 depreciation each year ($40,000/8 years = $5,000). Suppose Disney used the asset for 2 years. Accumulated depreciation reached $10,000, leaving a remaining depreciable book value (cost *less* accumulated depreciation *less* residual value) of $30,000 ($40,000 − $10,000). From its experience with the asset during the first 2 years, management believes the asset will remain useful for an additional 10 years. The company would compute a revised annual depreciation amount and record it as follows:

Asset's Remaining Depreciable Book Value	÷	(New) Estimated Useful Life Remaining	=	(New) Annual Depreciation Amount
$30,000	÷	10 years	=	$3,000

Yearly depreciation entry based on new estimated useful life:

Depreciation Expense-Hot Dog Stand	3,000	
Accumulated Depreciation-Hot Dog Stand		3,000

Using Fully Depreciated Assets

A fully depreciated asset is one that has reached the end of its *estimated* useful life. No more depreciation is recorded for the asset. If the asset is no longer suitable for its purpose, the asset is disposed of, as discussed in the next section. However, the company may be in a cash bind and unable to replace the asset. Or the asset's useful life may have been underestimated at the outset. Foresight is not perfect. In any event, companies sometimes continue using fully depreciated assets. The asset account and its related accumulated depreciation account remain in the ledger even though no additional depreciation is recorded for the asset.

Disposal of Plant Assets

OBJECTIVE 5

Account for disposal of plant assets

Eventually, a plant asset ceases to serve a company's needs. The asset may have become worn out, obsolete, or for some other reason no longer useful to the business. Generally, a company disposes of a plant asset by selling or exchanging it. If the asset cannot be sold or exchanged, then disposal takes the form of junking the asset. Whatever the method of disposal, the business should bring depreciation up to date to measure the asset's final book value properly.

To account for disposal, credit the asset account and debit its related accumulated depreciation account. Suppose the final year's depreciation expense has just been recorded for a machine that cost $6,000 and was estimated to have zero residual value. The machine's accumulated depreciation thus totals $6,000. Assuming this asset cannot be sold or exchanged, the entry to record its disposal is

Accumulated Depreciation—Machinery	6,000	
Machinery		6,000
To dispose of fully depreciated machine.		

If assets are junked prior to being fully depreciated, the company records a loss equal to the asset's book value. Suppose store fixtures that cost $4,000 are disposed of in this manner. Accumulated depreciation is $3,000, and book value is therefore $1,000. Disposal of these store fixtures is recorded as follows:

Accumulated Depreciation-Store Fixtures ...	3,000	
Loss on Disposal of Store Fixtures	1,000	
Store Fixtures		4,000
To dispose of store fixtures.		

Loss accounts such as Loss on Disposal of Store Fixtures decrease net income. Losses are reported on the income statement and closed to Income Summary along with expenses.

Selling a Plant Asset

Suppose the business sells furniture on September 30, 19X4, for $5,000 cash. The furniture cost $10,000 when purchased on January 1, 19X1, and has been depreciated on a straight-line basis. Managers estimated a 10-year useful life and no residual value. Prior to recording the sale of the furniture, accountants must update depreciation. Since the business uses the calendar year as its accounting period, partial depreciation must be recorded for the asset's expense from January 1, 19X4, to the sale date. The straight-line depreciation entry at September 30, 19X4, is

Sep. 30	Depreciation Expense ($10,000/10 years × 9/12)	750	
	Accumulated Depreciation—Furniture		750
	To update depreciation.		

After this entry is posted, the Furniture account and the Accumulated Depreciation—Furniture account appear as follows. The furniture book value is $6,250 ($10,000 − $3,750).

Furniture		Accumulated Depreciation—Furniture	
Jan. 1, 19X1 10,000		Dec. 31, 19X1 1,000	
		Dec. 31, 19X2 1,000	
		Dec. 31, 19X3 1,000	
		Sep. 30, 19X4 750	
		Balance 3,750	

The entry to record sale of the furniture for $5,000 cash is

Sep. 30	Cash	5,000	
	Accumulated Depreciation—Furniture	3,750	
	Loss on Sale of Furniture	1,250	
	Furniture		10,000
	To sell furniture.		

When recording the sale of a plant asset, the business must remove the balances in the asset account (Furniture, in this case) and its related accumulated depreciation account and also record a gain or a loss if the amount of cash received differs from the asset's book value. In our example, cash of $5,000 is less than the book value of the furniture, $6,250. The result is a loss of $1,250.

Suppose the sale price had been $7,000. The business would have had a gain of $750 (Cash, $7,000 − asset book value, $6,250).

The entry to record this transaction would be

Sep. 30	Cash	7,000	
	Accumulated Depreciation—Furniture	3,750	
	Furniture		10,000
	Gain on Sale of Furniture		750
	To sell furniture.		

A gain is recorded when an asset is sold for a price greater than the asset's book value. A loss is recorded when the sale price is less than book value. Gains increase net income. Gains are reported on the income statement and closed to Income Summary along with the revenues.

Exchanging Plant Assets

Businesses often exchange (trade in) their old plant assets for similar assets that are newer and more efficient. For example, a pizzeria may decide to trade in its five-year-old Nissan delivery car for a newer model. To record the exchange, the business must remove from the books the balances for the asset being exchanged and its related accumulated depreciation account.

Assume that the pizzeria's old delivery car cost $7,000 and has accumulated depreciation totaling $6,000. The book value, then, is $1,000. The cash price for a new delivery car is $9,000, and the auto dealer offers a $1,000 trade-in allowance. The pizzeria pays cash for the remaining $8,000. The trade-in is recorded with this entry:

Delivery Auto (new)	9,000	
Accumulated Depreciation (old)	6,000	
Delivery Auto (old)		7,000
Cash ($9,000 − $1,000)		8,000

In this example, the book value and the trade-in allowance are both $1,000, and so no gain or loss occurs on the exchange. Usually, however, an exchange results in a gain or a loss. If the trade-in allowance received is greater than the book value of the asset being given, the business has a gain. If the trade-in allowance received is less than the book value of the asset given, the business has a loss. Generally accepted accounting principles require that losses (but not gains) be recognized on the exchange of similar assets. We now turn to the entries for gains and losses on exchanges, continuing our delivery-car example and its data.[1]

Situation 1. Loss recognized on asset exchange:

Assume that the new Nissan has a cash price of $9,000 and the dealer gives a trade-in allowance of $600 on the old vehicle. The pizzeria pays the balance, $8,400, in cash. The loss on the exchange is $400 (book value of old asset given, $1,000, minus trade-in allowance received, $600). The account Loss on Exchange of Delivery Auto is debited for $400. The entry to record this exchange is

Delivery Auto (new)	9,000	
Accumulated Depreciation—Delivery Auto (old)	6,000	
Loss on Exchange of Delivery Auto...................	400	
Delivery Auto (old)............................		7,000
Cash ($9,000 − $600)		8,400

Situation 2. Gain *not* recognized on asset exchange:

Assume that the new Nissan's cash price is $9,000 and the seller gives a $1,300 trade-in allowance. The pizzeria pays the balance, $7,700, in cash. The gain is $300 (trade-in allowance received, $1,300, minus book value of old asset given, $1,000). However, the pizzeria does not recognize the gain. Instead, it reduces the cost of the new asset by the amount of the unrecognized gain.

Delivery Auto (new) ($9,000—gain of $300)	8,700	
Accumulated Depreciation—Delivery Auto (old)	6,000	
Delivery Auto (old)............................		7,000
Cash ($9,000 − $1,300)		7,700

Why are losses, and not gains, recognized? The Accounting Principles Board reasoned a company should not record a gain merely because it has substituted one plant asset for a similar plant asset. However, losses are recorded because conservatism favors the recognition of losses rather than gains.

Control of Plant Assets

Control of plant assets includes safeguarding them and having an adequate accounting system. To see the need for controlling plant assets, consider the following actual situation. The home office and top managers of the company are in New Jersey. The company manufactures gas pumps in Canada, which are sold in Europe. Top managers and owners of the company rarely see the manufacturing plant and therefore cannot control plant assets by on-the-spot management. What features does their internal control system need? Safeguarding plant assets includes:

1. Assigning responsibility for custody of the assets.
2. Separating custody of assets from accounting for the assets. (This is a cornerstone of internal control in almost every area.)
3. Setting up security measures, for instance, armed guards and restricted access to plant assets, to prevent theft.

---

[1]GAAP rules for exchanges may differ from income tax rules. In this discussion, we are concerned with the accounting rules.

4. Protecting assets from the elements (rain, snow, and so on).
5. Having adequate insurance against fire, storm, and other casualty losses.
6. Training operating personnel in the proper use of the asset.
7. Keeping a regular maintenance schedule.

Plant assets are controlled in much the same way that high-priced inventory is controlled—with the help of subsidiary records. For plant assets, companies use a plant asset ledger. Each plant asset is represented by a record describing the asset and listing its location and the employee responsible for it. These details aid in safeguarding the asset. The ledger record also shows the asset's cost, useful life, and other accounting data. Exhibit 9-10 is an example.

The ledger record provides the data for computing depreciation on the asset. It serves as a subsidiary record of accumulated depreciation. The asset balance ($190,000) and accumulated depreciation amount ($45,000) agree with the balances in the respective general ledger accounts (Store Fixtures and Accumulated Depreciation—Store Fixtures).

Accounting for Natural Resources and Depletion

OBJECTIVE 6

Account for natural resource assets and depletion

Natural resources such as iron ore, coal, oil, gas, and timber are plant assets of a special type. An investment in natural resources could be described as an investment in inventories in the ground (coal) or on top of the ground (timber). As plant assets (such as machines) are expensed through depreciation, so natural resource assets are expensed through depletion. **Depletion expense** is that portion of the cost of natural resources that is used up in a particular period. Depletion expense is computed in the same way as *units-of-production* depreciation.

An oil well may cost $100,000 and contain an estimated 10,000 barrels of oil. The depletion rate would be $10 per barrel ($100,000/10,000 barrels). If 3,000 barrels are extracted during the year, depletion expense is $30,000 (3,000 barrels X $10 per barrel). The depletion entry for the year is

Depletion Expense (3,000 barrels × $10)   30,000
      Accumulated Depletion—Oil   30,000

EXHIBIT 9-10 *Plant Asset Ledger Record*

Asset	Clothing racks		Location	Ladies better dresses		
Employee responsible for the asset	Department manager					

Cost	$190,000		**Purchased From**	Boone Supply Co.
Depreciation Method	SL			
Useful Life	10 years		**Residual Value**	$10,000
General Ledger Account	Store fixtures			

Date	Explanation	Asset			Accumulated Depreciation		
		Dr	Cr	Bal	Dr	Cr	Bal
Jul. 3, 19X4	Purchase	190,000		190,000			
Dec. 31, 19X4	Deprec.					9,000	9,000
Dec. 31, 19X5	Deprec.					18,000	27,000
Dec. 31, 19X6	Deprec.					18,000	45,000

If 4,500 barrels are removed the next year, that period's depletion is $45,000 (4,500 barrels X $10 per barrel). Accumulated Depletion is a contra account similar to Accumulated Depreciation.

Natural resource assets can be reported as follows:

Property, Plant, and Equipment:		
Land		$120,000
Buildings	$800,000	
Equipment	160,000	
	960,000	
Less: Accumulated depreciation	410,000	550,000
Oil	**$340,000**	
Less: Accumulated depletion	**90,000***	250,000
Total property, plant, and equipment		$920,000

*Includes the $30,000 recorded above.

Computers and Depreciation

A computer is invaluable in helping a company keep track of all plant asset transactions, from acquisition to depreciation to disposal. The general ledger account Machinery may have hundreds of subsidiary machine accounts, each with its own Accumulated Depreciation account.

Complications in tax law have resulted in complex depreciation calculations. The tax reforms of 1981 and on have brought about a material difference in depreciation amounts calculated using generally accepted accounting principles and those calculated under tax laws. Also, depreciation allowable under federal tax law can differ from depreciation permitted by state law. A company may, then, have to deal with three different depreciation systems at the same time. And suppose an asset is disposed of before it is fully depreciated. The calculations grow in complexity. Computers greatly ease the accounting burden.

Companies of all sizes may use depreciation modules that come with their computerized accounting packages. The computer performs its functions accurately, but an accountant with solid knowledge of tax law and depreciation must ensure that the calculations are reasonable. Auditors use spreadsheets to perform independent recalculations of depreciation.

Accounting for Intangible Assets and Amortization _____

Intangible assets are a class of long-lived assets that are not physical in nature. Instead, these assets are special rights to current and expected future benefits from patents, copyrights, trademarks, franchises, leaseholds, and goodwill.

The acquisition cost of an intangible asset is debited to an asset account. The intangible is expensed through **amortization,** the systematic reduction of a lump-sum amount. Amortization applies to intangible assets in the same way depreciation applies to plant assets and depletion applies to natural resources. All three methods of expensing assets are conceptually the same.

Amortization is generally computed on a straight-line basis over the asset's estimated useful life—up to a maximum of 40 years, according to GAAP. However, obsolescence often cuts an intangible asset's useful life shorter than its legal life. Amortization expense is written off directly against the asset

OBJECTIVE 7
Account for intangible assets and amortization

account rather than held in an accumulated amortization account. The residual value of most intangible assets is zero.

Assume that a business purchases a patent on a special manufacturing process. Legally, the patent may run for 17 years. However, the business realizes that new technologies will limit the patented process's life to 4 years. If the patent cost $80,000, each year's amortization expense is $20,000 ($80,000/4). The balance sheet reports the patent at its acquisition cost less amortization expense to date. After 1 year, the patent has a $60,000 balance ($80,000 − $20,000), after 2 years a $40,000 balance, and so on.

Patents are federal government grants giving a holder the exclusive right for 17 years to produce and sell an invention. Patented products include IBM computers and the recipe for Coca-Cola. Like any other asset, a patent may be purchased. Suppose a company pays $170,000 to acquire a patent and the business believes the expected useful life of the patent is only 5 years. Amortization expense is $34,000 per year ($170,000/5 years). The company's acquisition and amortization entries for this patent are

Jan. 1	Patents	170,000	
	Cash		170,000
	To acquire a patent.		
Dec. 31	Amortization Expense—Patents		
	($170,000/5)	34,000	
	Patents		34,000
	To amortize the cost of a patent.		

Copyrights are exclusive rights to reproduce and sell a book, musical composition, film, or other work of art. Issued by the federal government, copyrights extend 50 years beyond the author's (composer's, artist's) life. The cost of obtaining a copyright from the government is low, but a company may pay a large sum to purchase an existing copyright from the owner. For example, a publisher may pay the author of a popular novel $1 million or more for the book's copyright. The useful life of a copyright is usually no longer than 2 or 3 years, so each period's amortization amount is a high proportion of the copyright's cost.

Trademarks and **trade names** are distinctive identifications of products or services. The "eye" symbol that flashes across the television screen is a trademark that identifies the CBS television network. NBC uses the peacock as its trademark. Seven-Up, Pepsi, Egg McMuffin, and Rice-a-Roni are everyday trade names. Advertising slogans that are legally protected include United Airlines' "Fly the friendly skies" and Avis Rental Car's "We try harder."

The cost of a trademark or trade name is amortized over its useful life, not to exceed 40 years. The cost of advertising and promotions that use the trademark or trade name is not a part of the asset's cost but a debit to the advertising expense account.

Franchises and **licenses** are privileges granted by a private business or a government to sell a product or service in accordance with specified conditions. The Dallas Cowboys football organization is a franchise granted to its owner by the National Football League. McDonald's restaurants and Holiday Inns are popular franchises. Consolidated Edison Company (ConEd) holds a New York City franchise right to provide electricity to residents. The acquisition costs of franchises and licenses are amortized over their useful lives rather than over legal lives, subject to the 40-year maximum.

A **leasehold** is a prepayment that a lessee (renter) makes to secure the use of an asset from a lessor (landlord). Often leases require the lessee to make this prepayment in addition to monthly rental payments. The lessee debits the monthly lease payments to the Rent Expense account. The prepayment, however, is a debit to an intangible asset account entitled Leaseholds. This amount is amortized over the life of the lease by debiting Rent Expense and crediting Leaseholds. Some leases stipulate that the last year's rent must be paid in advance when the lease is signed. This prepayment is debited to Leaseholds and transferred to Rent Expense during the last year of the lease.

Sometimes lessees modify or improve the leased asset. For example, a lessee may construct a fence on leased land. The lessee debits the cost of the fence to a separate intangible asset account, Leasehold Improvements, and amortizes its cost over the term of the lease or the life of the asset, if shorter.

Goodwill in accounting is a more limited term than in everyday use, as in "goodwill among men." In accounting, **goodwill** is defined as the excess of the cost of an acquired company over the sum of the market values of its net assets (assets minus liabilities). Suppose Company A acquires Company B at a cost of $10 million. The sum of the market values of Company B's assets is $9 million, and its liabilities total $1 million. In this case, Company A paid $2 million for goodwill, computed as follows:

Purchase price paid for Company B.............		$10 million
Sum of the market values of Company B's assets.	$9 million	
Less: Company B's liabilities	1 million	
Market value of Company B's net assets.........		8 million
Excess is called *goodwill*		$ 2 million

Company A's entry to record the acquisition of Company B, including its goodwill, would be

Assets (Cash, Receivables, Inventories,		
Plant Assets, all at market value)	9,000,000	
Goodwill	2,000,000	
Liabilities		1,000,000
Cash		10,000,000

Goodwill has special features, which include the following points:

1. Goodwill is recorded, at its cost, only when it is purchased in the acquisition of another company. Even though a favorable location, a superior product, or an outstanding reputation may create goodwill for a company, it is never recorded by that entity. Instead, goodwill is recorded only by an acquiring company. A purchase transaction provides objective evidence of the value of the goodwill.

2. According to generally accepted accounting principles, goodwill is amortized over a period not to exceed 40 years. In reality, the goodwill of many entities increases in value. Nevertheless, the Accounting Principles Board specified in *Opinion No. 17* that the cost of all intangible assets must be amortized as expense. Some foreign countries do not require their companies to amortize goodwill. American companies complain of a competitive disadvantage because foreign companies omit this expense and, as a result, report higher net income. The *Opinion* prohibits a lump-sum write-off of the cost of goodwill upon acquisition.

Capital Expenditures versus Revenue Expenditures (Expenses)

OBJECTIVE 8

Distinguish capital expenditures from revenue expenditures

When a company makes a plant asset expenditure, it must decide whether to debit an asset account or an expense account. In this context, **expenditure** refers to either a cash or credit purchase of goods or services related to the asset. Examples of these expenditures range from replacing the windshield wipers on an automobile to adding a wing to a building.

Expenditures that increase the capacity or efficiency of the asset or extend its useful life are called **capital expenditures.** For example, the cost of a major overhaul that extends a taxi's useful life is a capital expenditure. Repair work that generates a capital expenditure is called an **extraordinary repair.** The amount of the capital expenditure, said to be capitalized, is a debit to an asset account. For an extraordinary repair on a taxi, we would debit the asset account Automobile.

Other expenditures do not extend the asset's capacity or efficiency. Expenditures that merely maintain the asset in its existing condition or restore the asset to good working order are called **revenue expenditures** because these costs are matched against revenue. Examples include the costs of repainting a taxi, repairing a dented fender, and replacing tires. The work that creates the revenue expenditure, said to be expensed, is a debit to an expense account. For the **ordinary repairs** on the taxi, we would debit Repair Expense.

Costs associated with intangible assets and natural resource assets also must be identified as either a capital expenditure or a revenue expenditure. For example, a license fee paid to the state of Arkansas to mine bauxite is a capital expenditure. This cost should be debited to the Bauxite Mineral Asset account. The cost of selling the ore—sales commissions paid to a broker, for example—is a revenue expenditure and should be debited to an expense account.

The distinction between capital and revenue expenditures is often a matter of opinion. Does the work extend the life of the asset, or does it only maintain the asset in good order? When doubt exists as to whether to debit an asset or an expense, companies tend to debit an expense for two reasons. First, many expenditures are minor in amount, and most companies have a policy of debiting expense for all expenditures below a specified minimum, such as $1,000. Second, the income tax motive favors debiting all borderline expenditures to expense in order to create an immediate tax deduction. Capital expenditures are not immediate tax deductions.

Exhibit 9-11 illustrates the distinction between capital expenditures and revenue expenditures (expense) for several delivery truck expenditures. Note also the difference between extraordinary and ordinary repairs.

Would additional costs for shipping, security, fuel, and communications that FMC incurred due to the Persian Gulf crisis be capital expenditures or operating expense? Operating expense, because those costs do not add to the lives or the usefulness of FMC's assets.

Treating a capital expenditure as a revenue expenditure, or vice versa, creates errors in the financial statements. Suppose a company makes an extraordinary repair to equipment and erroneously expenses this cost. It is a capital expenditure that should have been debited to an asset account. This accounting error overstates expenses and understates net income on the income statement. On the balance sheet, the equipment account is understated, and so is stockholders' equity. Capitalizing the cost of an ordinary repair creates the opposite error. Expenses are understated and net income is overstated on the income statement. The balance sheet reports overstated amounts for assets and stockholders' equity.

EXHIBIT 9-11 *Delivery Truck Expenditures*

Debit an Asset Account for Capital Expenditures	Debit Repair and Maintenance Expense for Revenue Expenditures
Extraordinary repairs: Major engine overhaul Modification of body for new use of truck Addition to storage capacity of truck	Ordinary repairs: Repair of transmission or other mechanism Oil change, lubrication, and so on Replacement tires, windshield, and the like Paint job

Summary Problems for Your Review

Problem 1

The figures that follow appear in the Solution to the Summary Problem, Requirement 2, on page 450.

	Method A Straight-Line			Method C Double-Declining-Balance		
Year	Annual Depreciation Expense	Accumulated Depreciation	Book Value	Annual Depreciation Expense	Accumulated Depreciation	Book Value
Start			$44,000			$44,000
19X5	$4,000	$ 4,000	40,000	$8,800	$ 8,800	35,200
19X6	4,000	8,000	36,000	7,040	15,840	28,160
19X7	4,000	12,000	32,000	5,632	21,472	22,528

Required

Suppose the income tax authorities permitted a choice between these two depreciation methods. Which method would you select for income tax purposes? Why?

Problem 2

A corporation purchased a building at a cost of $500,000 on January 1, 19X3. Management has depreciated the building by using the straight-line method, a 35-year life, and a residual value of $150,000. On July 1, 19X7, the company sold the building for $575,000 cash. The fiscal year of the corporation ends on December 31.

Required

Record depreciation for 19X7 and record the sale of the building on July 1, 19X7.

SOLUTIONS TO REVIEW PROBLEMS

Problem 1

For tax purposes, most companies select the accelerated method because it results in the most depreciation in the earliest years of the equipment's life. Accelerated depreciation minimizes taxable income and income tax payments in the early years of the asset's life, thereby maximizing the business's cash at the earliest possible time.

Problem 2

To record depreciation to date of sale and related sale of building:

19X7

July 1	Depreciation Expense—Building [($500,000 − $150,000)/35 years × ½ year]		5,000	
	Accumulated Depreciation— Building			5,000
	To update depreciation.			
July 1	Cash		575,000	
	Accumulated Depreciation—Building [($500,000 − $150,000)/35 years × 4 ½ years]		45,000	
	Building			500,000
	Gain on Sale of Building			120,000
	To record sale of building.			

Summary

Plant assets are long-lived assets that the business uses in its operation. These assets are not held for sale as inventory. The cost of all plant assets but land is expensed through *depreciation*. The cost of natural resources, a special category of long-lived assets, is expensed through *depletion*. Long-lived assets called *intangibles* are rights that have no physical form. The cost of intangibles is expensed through *amortization*. Depreciation, depletion, and amortization are identical in concept.

Businesses may compute the depreciation of plant assets by four methods: *straight-line*, *units-of-production*, and the *accelerated* methods: *double-declining-balance* and *sum-of-years-digits*. To measure depreciation, the accountant subtracts the asset's estimated residual value from its cost and divides that amount by the asset's estimated useful life. Most companies use the straight-line method for financial reporting purposes, and almost all companies use an accelerated method for income tax purposes. Accelerated depreciation results in greater tax deductions early in the asset's life. These deductions decrease income tax payments and conserve cash that the company can use in its business.

Before disposing of a plant asset, the business updates the asset's depreciation. Disposal is recorded by removing the book balances from both the asset account and its related accumulated depreciation account. Disposal often results in recognition of a gain or a loss.

Depletion of natural resources is computed on a units-of-production basis. *Amortization* of intangibles is computed on a straight-line basis over a maximum of 40 years. However, the useful lives of most intangibles are shorter than their legal lives.

Capital expenditures increase the capacity or the efficiency of an asset or extend its useful life. Accordingly, they are debited to an asset account. Revenue expenditures, on the other hand, merely maintain the asset's usefulness and are debited to an expense account.

Self-Study Questions

Test your understanding of the chapter by marking the best answer for each of the following questions.

1. Which of the following payments is *not* included in the cost of land? (p. 441)
   a. Removal of old building
   b. Legal fees
   c. Back property taxes paid at acquisition
   d. Cost of fencing and lighting

2. A business paid $120,000 for two machines valued at $90,000 and $60,000. The business will record these machines at (p. 442)
   a. $90,000 and $60,000
   b. $60,000 each
   c. $72,000 and $48,000
   d. $70,000 and $50,000

3. Which of the following definitions fits depreciation? (pp. 442)
   a. Allocation of the asset's market value to expense over its useful life
   b. Allocation of the asset's cost to expense over its useful life
   c. Decreases in the asset's market value over its useful life
   d. Increases in the fund set aside to replace the asset when it is worn out

4. Which depreciation method's amounts are not computed based on time? (p. 445)
   a. Straight-line
   b. Units-of-production
   c. Double-declining-balance
   d. Sum-of-years-digits

5. Which depreciation method gives the largest amount of expense in the early years of using the asset and therefore is best for income tax purposes? (p. 451)
   a. Straight-line
   b. Units-of-production
   c. Accelerated
   d. All are equal.

6. A company paid $450,000 for a building and was depreciating it by the straight-line method over a 40-year life with estimated residual value of $50,000. After 10 years, it became evident that the building's remaining useful life would be 40 years. Depreciation for the eleventh year is (p. 454)
   a. $7,500
   b. $8,750
   c. $10,000
   d. $12,500

7. Labrador, Inc., scrapped an automobile that cost $14,000 and had book value of $1,100. The entry to record this disposal is (p. 455)

   a. Loss on Disposal of Automobile 1,100
        Automobile   1,100
   b. Accumulated Depreciation 14,000
        Automobile   14,000
   c. Accumulated Depreciation 12,900
        Automobile   12,900
   d. Accumulated Depreciation 12,900
        Loss of Disposal of Automobile.............. 1,100
        Automobile   14,000

8. Depletion is computed in the same manner as which depreciation method? (p. 458)
   a. Straight-line
   b. Units-of-production
   c. Double-declining-balance
   d. Sum-of-years-digits

9. Lacy Corporation paid $550,000 to acquire Gentsch, Inc. Gentsch's assets had a market value of $900,000, and its liabilities were $400,000. In recording the acquisition, Lacy will record goodwill of *(p. 461)*
    a. $50,000
    b. $100,000
    c. $550,000
    d. $0

10. Which of the following items is a revenue expenditure? *(p. 462)*
    a. Property tax paid on land one year after it is acquired
    b. Survey fee paid during the acquisition of land
    c. Legal fee paid to acquire land
    d. Building permit paid to construct a warehouse on the land

Answers to the Self-Study Questions follow the Accounting Vocabulary.

Accounting Vocabulary

Accelerated depreciation. A type of depreciation method that writes off a relatively larger amount of the asset's cost nearer the start of its useful life than does the straight-line method *(p. 446)*.

Amortization. The systematic reduction of a lump-sum amount. Expense that applies to intangible assets in the same way depreciation applies to plant assets and depletion applies to natural resources *(p. 459)*.

Capital expenditure. Expenditure that increases the capacity or efficiency of an asset or extends its useful life. Capital expenditures are debited to an asset account *(p. 462)*.

Copyright. Exclusive right to reproduce and sell a book, musical composition, film, or other work of art. Issued by the federal government, copyrights extend 50 years beyond the author's life *(p. 460)*.

Cost of a plant asset. Purchase price, sales tax, purchase commission, and all other amounts paid to acquire the asset and to ready it for its intended use *(p. 440)*.

Depletion. That portion of a natural resource's cost that is used up in a particular period. Depletion expense is computed in the same way as units of production depreciation *(p. 458)*.

Depreciable cost. The cost of a plant asset minus its estimated residual value *(p. 444)*.

Double-declining-balance (DDB) method. An accelerated depreciation method that computes annual depreciation by multiplying the asset's decreasing book value by a constant percentage, which is two times the straight-line rate *(p. 446)*.

Estimated residual value. Expected cash value of an asset at the end of its useful life. Also called Residual value, Scrap value and Salvage value *(p. 443)*.

Estimated useful life. Length of the service that a business expects to get from an asset, may be expressed in years, units of output, miles, or other measures *(p. 443)*.

Expenditure. Either a cash or credit purchase of goods or services related to an asset *(p. 462)*.

Extraordinary repair. Repair work that generates a capital expenditure *(p. 462)*.

Franchises and licenses. Privileges granted by a private business or a government to sell a product or service in accordance with specified conditions *(p. 460)*.

Goodwill. Excess of the cost of an acquired company over the sum of the market values of its net assets (assets minus liabilities) *(p. 461)*.

Intangible asset. An asset with no physical form, a special right to current and expected future benefits *(p. 440)*.

Leasehold. Prepayment that a lessee (renter) makes to secure the use of an asset from a lessor (landlord) *(p. 461)*.

Ordinary repair. Repair work that creates a revenue expenditure, which is debited to an expense account *(p. 462)*.

Patent. A federal government grant giving the holder the exclusive right for 17 years to produce and sell an invention *(p. 460)*.

Plant asset. Long-lived assets, like land, buildings, and equipment, used in the operation of the business *(pp. 440)*.

Relative-sales-value method. Allocation technique for identifying the cost of each asset purchased in a group for a single amount *(p. 442)*.

Revenue expenditure. Expenditure that merely maintains an asset in its existing condition or restores the asset to good working order. Revenue expenditures are expensed (matched against revenue) *(p. 462)*.

Straight-line method. Depreciation method in which an equal amount of depreciation expense is assigned to each year (or period) of asset use *(p. 444)*.

Sum-of-years-digits (SYD) method. An accelerated depreciation method by which depreciation is figured by multiplying the depreciable cost of the asset by a fraction. The denominator of the SYD fraction is the sum of the years' digits of the asset's life. The numerator of the SYD fraction starts with the asset life in years and decreases by one each year thereafter *(p. 447)*.

Trademarks and trade names. Distinctive identifications of a product or service *(p. 460)*.

Units-of-production (UOP) method. Depreciation method by which a fixed amount of depreciation is assigned to each unit of output produced by the plant asset *(p. 445)*.

Answers to Self-Study Questions

1. d
2. c $90,000/($90,000 + $60,000) \times $120,000 = $72,000;
   $60,000/($90,000 + $60,000) \times $120,000 = $48,000
3. b
4. b
5. c
6. a Depreciable cost = $450,000 − $50,000 = $400,000
   $400,000/40 years = $10,000 per year
   $400,000 − ($10,000 × 10 years) = $300,000/40 years = $7,500
      per year
7. d
8. b
9. a $550,000 − ($900,000 − $400,000) = $50,000
10. a

ASSIGNMENT MATERIAL _____

Questions

1. To what types of long-lived assets do the following expenses apply: depreciation, depletion, and amortization?
2. Describe how to measure the cost of a plant asset. Would an ordinary cost of repairing the asset after it is placed in service be included in the asset's cost?
3. Suppose land is purchased for $100,000. How do you account for the $8,000 cost of removing an unwanted building?
4. When assets are purchased as a group for a single price and no individual asset cost is given, how is each asset's cost determined?
5. Define depreciation. Present the common misconceptions about depreciation.
6. Which depreciation method does each of the graphs on the next page characterize—straight-line, units-of-production, or accelerated?

7. Which of the four depreciation methods results in the most depreciation in the first year of the asset's life?

8. Explain the concept of accelerated depreciation. Which other depreciation method is used in the definition of declining-balance depreciation?

9. The level of business activity fluctuates widely for Harwood Delivery Service, reaching its peak around Christmas each year. At other times, business is slow. What depreciation method is most appropriate for the company's fleet of Chevy Luv trucks?

10. Oswalt Computer Service Center uses the most advanced computers available to keep a competitive edge over other service centers. To maintain this advantage, Oswalt usually replaces its computers before they are worn out. Describe the major factors affecting the useful life of a plant asset and indicate which seems more relevant to Oswalt's computers.

11. Estimated residual value is not considered in computing depreciation during the early years of the asset's life by one of the methods. Which method is it?

12. Which type of depreciation method is best from an income tax standpoint? Why?

13. How does depreciation affect income taxes? How does depreciation affect cash provided by operations?

14. Describe how to compute depreciation for less than a full year and how to account for depreciation for less than a full month.

15. Ragland Company paid $10,000 for office furniture. The company expected it to remain in service for 6 years and to have a $ 1,000 residual value. After 2 years' use, company accountants believe the furniture will last an additional 6 years. How much depreciation will Ragland record for each of these 6 years, assuming straight-line depreciation and no change in the estimated residual value?

16. When a company sells a plant asset before the year's end, what must it record before accounting for the sale?

17. Describe how to determine whether a company experiences a gain or a loss when an old plant asset is exchanged for a new one. Does generally accepted accounting favor the recognition of gains or losses? Which accounting concept underlies your answer?

18. Identify seven elements of internal control designed to safeguard plant assets.

19. What expense applies to natural resources? By which depreciation method is this expense computed?

20. How do intangible assets differ from most other assets? Why are they assets at all? What expense applies to intangible assets?

21. Why is the cost of patents and other intangible assets often expensed over a shorter period than the legal life of the asset?

22. Your company has just purchased another company for $400,000. The market value of the other company's net assets is $325,000. What is the $75,000 excess called? What type of asset is it? What is the maximum period over which its cost is amortized under generally accepted accounting principles?

23. IBM Corporation is recognized as a world leader in the manufacture and sale of computers. The company's success has created vast amounts of business goodwill. Would you expect to see *this* goodwill reported on IBM's financial statements? Why or why not?

24. Distinguish a capital expenditure from a revenue expenditure. The title "revenue expenditure" is curious in that a revenue expenditure is a debit to an expense account. Explain why revenue expenditures are so named.

25. Are ordinary repairs capital expenditures or revenue expenditures? Which type of expenditures are extraordinary repairs?

Exercises

Exercise 9-1   *Identifying the elements of a plant asset's cost*   **(L.O. 1)**

A company purchased land, paying $56,000 cash as a down payment and signing a $120,000 note payable for the balance. In addition, the company paid delinquent property tax of $2,000, a title fee of $500, and a $3,400 charge for leveling the land and removing an unwanted building. The company constructed an office building on the land at a cost of $410,000. It also paid $12,000 for a fence around the boundary of the property, $2,400 for the company sign near the entrance to the property, and $6,000 for special lighting of the grounds. Determine the cost of the company's land, land improvements, and building.

Exercise 9-2   *Allocating cost to assets acquired in a basket purchase*   **(L.O. 1)**

Faber Castell Company bought three used machines in a $20,000 purchase. An independent appraisal of the machines produced the following figures:

Machine No.	Appraised Value
1	$ 4,000
2	12,000
3	8,000

Assuming Faber Castell paid cash for the machines, record the purchase in the general journal, identifying each machine's individual cost in a separate Machine account.

Exercise 9-3   *Explaining the concept of depreciation*   **(L.O. 2)**

Greg Davenport has just slept through the class in which Professor Spyros explained the concept of depreciation. Because the next test is scheduled for Wednesday, Greg telephones Leah Gerbing to get her notes from the lecture. Leah's notes are concise: "Depreciation—Sounds like Greek to me." Greg next tries Ray Mellichamp, who says he thinks depreciation is what happens when an asset wears out. Peggy Bower is confident that depreciation is the process of building up a cash fund to replace an asset at the end of its useful life. Explain the concept of depreciation for Greg. Evaluate the explanations of Ray and Peggy. Be specific.

Exercise 9-4 *Computing depreciation by four methods* **(L.O. 3)**

A company delivery truck was acquired on January 2, 19X1, for $12,000. The truck was expected to remain in service for 4 years and last 88,000 miles. At the end of its useful life, company officials estimated that the truck's residual value would be $1,000. The truck traveled 24,000 miles in the first year, 28,000 in the second year, 21,000 in the third year, and 15,000 in the fourth year. Prepare a schedule of *depreciation expense* per year for the truck under the four depreciation methods. Show your computations.

Exercise 9-5 *Recording partial-year depreciation computed by two methods* **(L.O. 3)**

Situation 1. Baylor Corporation purchased office furniture on June 3, 19X4, for $2,600 cash. Anne Baylor expects it to remain useful for 8 years and to have a residual value of $200. Baylor uses the straight-line depreciation method. Record Baylor's depreciation on the furniture for the year ended December 31, 19X4.

Situation 2. Spain Company purchased equipment on October 19, 19X2, for $19,500, signing a note payable for that amount. Spain estimated that this equipment will be useful for 3 years and have a residual value of $1,500. Assuming Spain uses sum-of-years-digits depreciation, record Spain's depreciation on the machine for the year ended December 31, 19X2.

Exercise 9-6 *Journalizing a change in a plant asset's useful life* **(L.O. 3)**

A company purchased a building for $680,000 and depreciated it on a straight-line basis over a 30-year period. The estimated residual value was $80,000. After using the building for 15 years, the company realized that wear and tear on the building would force the company to replace it before 30 years. Starting with the 16th year, the company began depreciating the building over a revised total life of 20 years, retaining the $80,000 estimate of residual value. Record depreciation expense on the building for years 15 and 16.

Exercise 9-7 *Preparing a plant ledger card; units-of-production depreciation* **(L.O. 3)**

Citizens Wholesale Grocers uses a plant ledger card to account for its delivery vehicles, which are located at the company's service garage. The fleet of vehicles cost $96,000 when purchased from Ericksen Ford Company on September 1, 19X2. This cost is the debit balance in the Delivery Vehicles account in the general ledger. Citizens uses the units-of-production depreciation method and estimates a useful life of 480,000 miles and a $6,000 residual value for the trucks. The garage foreman is responsible for the vehicles. The company's fiscal year ends on December 31. Miles traveled were 30,000 in 19X2; 105,000 in 19X3; and 98,000 in 19X4. Complete a plant ledger card for these vehicles through December 31, 19X4, using a format similar to Exhibit 9-10.

Exercise 9-8 *Identifying depreciation methods for income tax and financial reporting purposes* **(L.O. 4)**

Using the data in Exercise 9-4, identify the depreciation method that would be most advantageous from an income tax perspective. Which depreciation method do most companies use for reporting to their stockholders and creditors on their financial statements?

Exercise 9-9 *Recording the sale of a plant asset* **(L.O. 5)**

On January 2, 19X1, Ribbon Paper Products purchased store fixtures for $7,700 cash, expecting the fixtures to remain in service for 10 years. Ribbon has depreciated the fixtures on a sum-of-years-digits basis, assuming no estimated residual value. On October 30, 19X8, Ribbon sold the fixtures for $850 cash. Record depreciation expense on the fixtures for the 10 months ended October 30, 19X8, and also record the sale of the fixtures.

Exercise 9-10 *Exchanging plant assets* **(L.O. 5)**

A machine cost $10,000. At the end of 4 years, its accumulated depreciation was $4,500. For each of the following situations, record the trade-in of this old machine for a new, similar machine.

Situation 1.   The new machine had a cash price of $12,400; the dealer allowed a trade-in allowance of $4,000 on the old machine, and you paid the $8,400 balance in cash.

Situation 2.   The new machine had a cash price of $13,000; the dealer allowed a trade-in allowance of $5,900 on the old machine; and you signed a note payable for the $7,100 balance.

Exercise 9-11 *Recording natural resource assets and depletion* **(L.O. 6)**

Yellowstone Mines paid $198,500 for the right to extract ore from a 200,000-ton mineral deposit. In addition to the purchase price, Yellowstone also paid a $500 filing fee and a $1,000 license fee to the state of Wyoming. Because Yellowstone purchased the rights to the minerals only, the company expected the asset to have zero residual value when fully depleted. During the first year of production, Yellowstone removed 35,000 tons of ore. Make general journal entries to record (a) purchase of the mineral rights (debit Mineral Asset), (b) payment of fees, and (c) depletion for first-year production.

Exercise 9-12 *Recording intangibles, amortization, and a change in the asset's useful life* **(L.O. 7)**

Part 1.   Ryther Corporation manufactures high-speed printers and has recently purchased for $3.52 million a patent for the design for a new laser printer. Although it gives legal protection for 17 years, the patent is expected to provide Ryther with a competitive advantage for only 8 years. Assuming the straight-line method of amortization, use general journal entries to record (a) the purchase of the patent and (b) amortization for 1 year.

Part 2.   After using the patent for 4 years, Ryther learns at an industry trade show that another company is designing a more efficient printer. Based on this new information, Ryther decides, starting with year 5, to amortize the remaining cost of the patent over 2 additional years, giving the patent a total useful life of 6 years. Record amortization for year 5.

Exercise 9-13 *Computing and recording goodwill* **(L.O. 7)**

Company Pratt purchased Saks Corporation, paying $1 million cash. The market value of Saks Corporation assets was $1.7 million, and Saks had liabilities of $1.1 million.

(a) Compute the cost of the goodwill purchased by Pratt Company.
(b) Record the purchase by Pratt Company.
(c) Record amortization of goodwill for year 1, assuming the straight-line method and a useful life of 10 years.

Exercise 9-14 *Distinguishing capital expenditures from revenue expenditures* **(L.O. 8)**

Classify each of the following expenditures as a capital expenditure or a revenue expenditure (expense) related to machinery: (a) purchase price, (b) sales tax paid on the purchase price, (c) transportation and insurance while machinery is in transport from seller to buyer, (d) installation, (e) training of personnel for initial operation of the machinery, (f) special reinforcement to the machinery platform, (g) income tax paid on income earned from the sale of products manufactured by the machinery, (h) major overhaul to extend useful life by three years, (i) ordinary recurring repairs to keep the machinery in good working order, (j) lubrication of the machinery before it is placed in service, (k) periodic lubrication after the machinery is placed in service.

Problems   *(Group A)*

Problem 9-1A *Identifying the elements of a plant asset's cost* (L.O. 1)

United America Insurance Company incurred the following costs in acquiring land, making land improvements, and constructing and furnishing an office building.

(a)	Purchase price of four acres of land, including an old building that will be used for storage (land market value is $380,000; building market value is $20,000)	$316,000
(b)	Landscaping (additional dirt and earth moving)	8,100
(c)	Fence around the boundary of the land	17,650
(d)	Attorney fee for title search on the land..................	600
(e)	Delinquent real estate taxes on the land to be paid by United America.......................................	5,900
(f)	Company signs at front of the company property	1,800
(g)	Building permit for the office building	350
(h)	Architect fee for the design of the office building	19,800
(i)	Masonry, carpentry, roofing, and other labor to construct office building	509,000
(j)	Concrete, wood, steel girders, and other materials used in the construction of the office building	214,000
(k)	Renovation of the storage building	41,800
(l)	Repair of storm damage to storage building during construction	2,200
(m)	Landscaping (trees and shrubs)	6,400
(n)	Parking lot and concrete walks on the property...........	19,750
(o)	Lights for the parking lot, walkways, and company signs .	7,300
(p)	Supervisory salary of construction supervisor (85 percent to office building, 9 percent to fencing, parking lot, and concrete walks, and 6 percent to storage building renovation) .	40,000
(q)	Office furniture for the office building	107,100
(r)	Transportation and installation of furniture..............	1,100

United America depreciates buildings over 40 years, land improvements over 20 years, and furniture over 8 years, all on a straight-line basis with zero residual value.

Required

1. Set up columns for Land, Land Improvements, Office Building, Storage Building, and Furniture. Show how to account for each of the foregoing costs by listing the cost under the correct column. Compute the total amount that would be debited to each account.

2. Assuming that all construction was complete and the assets were placed in service on May 4, record depreciation for the year ended December 31. Round off figures to the nearest dollar.

Problem 9-2A *Explaining the concept of depreciation* **(L.O. 2)**

The board of directors of Fort Worth Parking Lot Company is reviewing the 19X8 annual report. A new board member—a consulting psychologist with little business experience—questions the company accountant about the depreciation amounts. The psychologist wonders why depreciation expense has decreased from $20,000 in 19X6 to $18,400 in 19X7 to $17,200 in 19X8. She states that she could understand the decreasing annual amounts if the company had been disposing of properties each year, but that has not occurred. Further, she notes that growth in the city is increasing the values of company properties. Why is the company recording depreciation when the property values are increasing?

Required

Write a paragraph or two to explain the concept of depreciation to the psychologist and to answer that person's questions.

Problem 9-3A *Computing depreciation by four methods and the cash flow advantage of accelerated depreciation for tax purposes* **(L.O. 3,4)**

On January 9, 19X1, Ross, Inc., paid $92,000 for equipment used in manufacturing automotive supplies. In addition to the basic purchase price, the company paid $700 transportation charges, $100 insurance for the goods in transit, $4,100 sales tax, and $3,100 for a special platform on which to place the equipment in the plant. Ross management estimates that the equipment will remain in service for 5 years and have a residual value of $10,000. The equipment will produce 50,000 units in the first year, with annual production decreasing by 5,000 units during each of the next 4 years (that is, 45,000 units in year 2, 40,000 units in year 3, and so on). In trying to decide which depreciation method to use, Ross management has requested a depreciation schedule for each of the four generally accepted depreciation methods (straight-line, units-of-production, double-declining-balance, and sum-of-years-digits).

Required

1. For each of the four generally accepted depreciation methods, prepare a depreciation schedule showing asset cost, depreciation expense, accumulated depreciation, and asset book value. Use the format of Exhibits 9-3 through 9-6.
2. Ross reports to stockholders and creditors in the financial statements using the depreciation method that maximizes reported income in the early years of asset use. For income tax purposes, however, the company uses the depreciation method that minimizes income tax payments in those early years. Consider the first year Ross uses the equipment. Identify the depreciation methods that meet Ross's objectives, assuming the income tax authorities would permit the use of any of the methods.

3. Assume cash provided by operations before income tax is $120,000 for the equipment's first year. The income tax rate is 30 percent. For the two depreciation methods identified in Requirement 2, compare the net income and cash provided by operations (cash flow). Use the format of Exhibit 9-8 for your answer. Show which method gives the net-income advantage and which method gives the cash-flow advantage. Ignore the earnings rate in the cash-flow analysis.

Problem 9-4A *Journalizing and posting plant asset transactions; capital expenditures versus revenue expenditures (L.O. 1,3,5,8)*

Assume that an Eckerd drugstore completed the following transactions:

19X2
Jan.   6   Paid $9,000 cash for a used delivery truck.
          7   Paid $800 to have the truck engine overhauled.
          8   Paid $200 to have the truck modified for business use.
Aug. 21   Paid $156 for a minor tuneup.
Dec. 31   Recorded depreciation on the truck by the sum-of-years-digits method (assume a 4-year life and a $2,000 residual value).
         31   Closed the appropriate accounts.

19X3
Feb.   8   Traded in the delivery truck for a new truck costing $13,000. The dealer granted a $4,000 allowance on the old truck, and the store paid the balance in cash. Recorded 19X3 depreciation for the year to date and then recorded the exchange of trucks.
July   8   Repaired the new truck's damaged fender for $625 cash.
Dec. 31   Recorded depreciation on the new truck by the sum-of-years-digits method. (Assume a 4-year life and a residual value of $3,000.)
         31   Closed the appropriate accounts.

Required

1. Open the following accounts in the general ledger: Delivery Trucks; Accumulated Depreciation—Delivery Trucks; Truck Repair Expense; Depreciation Expense—Delivery Trucks; and Loss on Exchange of Delivery Trucks.
2. Record the transactions in the general journal, and post to the ledger accounts opened.

Problem 9-5A *Recording plant asset transactions; exchanges; changes in useful life (L.O. 1,3,5,8)*

Consolidated Freightways, Inc., provides nationwide general freight service. The company's balance sheet includes the following assets under Property, Plant, and Equipment: Land, Buildings, Motor Carrier Equipment, and Leasehold Improvements. Assume the company has a separate accumulated depreciation account for each of these assets except land and leasehold improvements. Amortization on leasehold improvements is credited directly to the Leasehold Improvements account rather than to Accumulated Amortization—Leasehold Improvements.

Assume that Consolidated Freightways completed the following transactions:

Jan.   5   Traded in motor-carrier equipment with book value of $47,000 (cost of $130,000) for similar new equipment with a cash cost of $176,000. Consolidated received a trade-in allowance of $50,000 on the old equipment and paid the remainder in cash.

Feb. 22 Purchased motor-carrier equipment for $136,000 plus 5 percent sales tax and $200 title fee. The company gave a 60-day, 12 percent note in payment.

Apr. 23 Paid the equipment note and related interest.

July 9 Sold a building that had cost $550,000 and had accumulated depreciation of $247,500 through December 31 of the preceding year. Depreciation is computed on a straight-line basis. The building has a 30-year useful life and a residual value of $55,000. Consolidated received $100,000 cash and a $600,000 note receivable.

Aug. 16 Paid cash to improve leased assets at a cost of $10,200.

Oct. 26 Purchased land and a building for a single price of $300,000. An independent appraisal valued the land at $115,000 and the building at $230,000.

Dec. 31 Recorded depreciation as follows:

Motor-carrier equipment has an expected useful life of 5 years and an estimated residual value of 5 percent of cost. Depreciation is computed on the sum-of-years-digits method. Make separate depreciation entries for equipment acquired on January 5 and February 22.

Amortization on leasehold improvements is computed on a straight-line basis over the life of the lease, which is 10 years, with zero residual value.

Depreciation on buildings is computed by the straight-line method. The company had assigned to its older buildings, which cost $200,000,000, an estimated useful life of 30 years with a residual value equal to 10 percent of the asset cost. However, management has come to believe that the buildings will remain useful for a total of 40 years. Residual value remains unchanged. The company has used all its buildings, except for the one purchased on October 26, for 10 years. The new building carries a 40-year useful life and a residual value equal to 10 percent of its cost. Make separate entries for depreciation on the building acquired on October 26 and the other buildings purchased in earlier years.

Required

Record the transactions in the general journal.

Problem 9-6A *Distinguishing capital expenditures from revenue expenditures; preparing a plant ledger record* **(L.O. 3,5,8)**

Suppose Consolidated Edison Co. uses plant ledger cards to control its service trucks, purchased from Bird-Kultgen Ford. The supervisor is responsible for the trucks, which are located at the company's service garage. The following transactions were completed during 19X3 and 19X4:

19X3
Jan. 6 Paid $10,420 cash for a used service truck (truck no. 501).
   7 Paid $2,500 to have the truck engine overhauled.
   8 Paid $180 to have the truck modified for business use.
Nov. 5 Paid $107 for replacement of one tire.
Dec. 31 Recorded depreciation on the truck by the double-declining-balance method, based on a 4-year useful life and a $1,100 residual value.

19X4
July 16 Repaired a damaged fender on truck no. 501 at a cash cost of $877.
Sep. 6 Traded in service truck no. 501 for a new one (truck no. 633) with a cash cost of $18,000. The dealer granted a $4,500 allowance on the

old truck, and Consolidated Edison paid the balance in cash. Recorded 19X4 depreciation for year to date and then recorded exchange of the trucks.

Dec. 31 Recorded depreciation on truck no. 633 by the double-declining-balance method, on a 4-year life and a $1,500 residual value.

Required

1. Identify the capital expenditures and the revenue expenditures in the transactions. Which expenditures are debited to an asset account? Which expenditures are debited to an expense account?
2. Prepare a separate plant ledger record for each of the trucks.

Problem 9-7A *Recording intangibles, natural resources, and the related expenses (L.O. 6,7)*

Part 1. Georgia-Pacific Corporation is one of the world's largest forest products companies. The company's balance sheet includes the assets Natural Gas, Oil, and Coal.

Suppose Georgia-Pacific paid $1.5 million cash for a lease giving the firm the right to work a mine that contained an estimated 125,000 tons of coal. Assume that the company paid $10,000 to remove unwanted buildings from the land and $45,000 to prepare the surface for mining. Further assume that Georgia-Pacific signed a $20,000 note payable to a landscaping company to return the land surface to its original condition after the lease ends. During the first year, Georgia-Pacific removed 35,000 tons of coal, which it sold on account for $17 per ton.

Required

Make general journal entries to record all transactions related to the coal, including depletion and sale of the first-year production.

Part 2. Collins Foods International, Inc., is the largest of the companies that operate Kentucky Fried Chicken franchised restaurants and is also the majority owner of Sizzler Restaurants. The company's balance sheet reports the asset Cost in Excess of Net Assets of Purchased Businesses. Assume that Collins purchased this asset as part of the acquisition of another company, which carried these figures:

Book value of assets	$2.4 million
Market value of assets	3.1 million
Liabilities	2.2 million

Required

1. What is another title for the asset Cost in Excess of Net Assets of Purchased Businesses?
2. Make the general journal entry to record Collins's purchase of the other company for $1.3 million cash.
3. Assuming Collins amortizes Cost in Excess of Net Assets of Purchased Businesses over 20 years, record the straight-line amortization for one year.

Part 3. Suppose Collins purchased a Kentucky Fried Chicken franchise license for $240,000. In addition to the basic purchase price, Collins also paid a lawyer $8,000 for assistance with the negotiations. Collins management believes the appropriate amortization period for its cost of the franchise license is 8 years.

Required

Make general journal entries to record the franchise transactions, including straight-line amortization for one year.

(Group B)

Problem 9-1B *Identifying the elements of a plant asset's cost* **(L.O. 1)**

Song Kim Company incurred the following costs in acquiring land and a garage, making land improvements, and constructing and furnishing a home office building.

Depr.–Land improv. $2,865
Home office bldg. $24,878
Garage $1,425
Furniture $11,644

(a)	Purchase price of 3 1/2 acres of land, including an old building that will be used as a garage for company vehicles (land market value is $600,000; building market value is $60,000)	$550,000
(b)	Delinquent real estate taxes on the land to be paid by Song Kim	3, 700
(c)	Landscaping (additional dirt and earth moving)	3,550
(d)	Title insurance on the land acquisition	1,000
(e)	Fence around the boundary of the land	14,100
(f)	Building permit for the home office building	200
(g)	Architect fee for the design of the home office building	25,000
(h)	Company signs near front and rear approaches to the company property	23,550
(i)	Renovation of the garage	23,800
(j)	Concrete, wood, steel girders, and other materials used in the construction of the home office building	514,000
(k)	Masonry, carpentry, roofing, and other labor to construct home office building	734,000
(l)	Repair of vandalism damage to home office building during construction	4,100
(m)	Parking lots and concrete walks on the property	17,450
(n)	Lights for the parking lot, walkways, and company signs	8,900
(o)	Supervisory salary of construction supervisor (90 percent to home office building, 6 percent to fencing, parking lot, and concrete walks, and 4 percent to garage renovation)	55,000
(p)	Office furniture for the home office building	123,500
(q)	Transportation of furniture from seller to the home office building	700
(r)	Landscaping (trees and shrubs)	9,100

Song Kim depreciates buildings over 40 years, land improvements over 20 years, and furniture over 8 years, all on a straight-line basis with zero residual value.

Required

1. Set up columns for Land, Land Improvements, Home Office Building, Garage, and Furniture. Show how to account for each of the foregoing costs by listing the cost under the correct account. Compute the total amount that would be debited to each account.

2. Assuming that all construction was complete and the assets were placed in service on March 19, record depreciation for the year ended December 31. Round figures to the nearest dollar.

Problem 9-2B *Explaining the concept of depreciation* *(L.O. 2)*

The board of directors of Sacramento Construction Company is having its regular quarterly meeting. Accounting policies are on the agenda, and depreciation is being discussed. A new board member, a physician, has some strong opinions about two aspects of depreciation policy. Dr. Johansson argues that depreciation must be coupled with a fund to replace company assets. Otherwise, there is no substance to depreciation, he argues. He also challenges the 5-year estimated life over which Sacramento is depreciating company computers. He notes that the computers will last much longer and should be depreciated over at least 10 years.

Required

Write a paragraph or two to explain the concept of depreciation to Dr. Johansson and to answer his arguments.

Problem 9-3B *Computing depreciation by four methods and the cash flow advantage of accelerated depreciation for tax purposes* *(L.O. 3,4)*

On January 2, 19X1, Industrial Products, Inc., purchased 3 used delivery trucks at a total cost of $53,000. Before placing the trucks in service, the company spent $1,200 painting them, $1,800 replacing their tires, and $4,000 overhauling their engines and reconditioning their bodies. Industrial Products management estimates that the trucks will remain in service for 6 years and have a residual value of $6,000. The trucks' combined annual mileage is expected to be 16,000 miles in each of the first 4 years and 18,000 miles in each of the next 2 years. In trying to decide which depreciation method to use, Ralph Winter, the general manager, requests a depreciation schedule for each of the four generally accepted depreciation methods (straight-line, units-of-production, double-declining-balance, and sum-of-years-digits).

Required

1. Assuming Industrial Products depreciates its delivery trucks as a unit, prepare a depreciation schedule for each of the four generally accepted depreciation methods, showing asset cost, depreciation expense, accumulated depreciation, and asset book value. Use the formats of Exhibits 9-3 through 9-6.
2. Industrial Products reports to stockholders and creditors in the financial statements using the depreciation method that maximizes reported income in the early years of asset use. For income tax purposes, however, the company uses the depreciation method that minimizes income tax payments in those early years. Consider the first year that Industrial Products uses the delivery trucks. Identify the depreciation methods that meet the general manager's objectives, assuming the income tax authorities would permit the use of any of the methods.
3. Assume cash provided by operations before income tax is $80,000 for the delivery trucks' first year. The income tax rate is 30 percent. For the two depreciation methods identified in Requirement 2, compare the net income and cash provided by operations (cash flow). Use the format of Exhibit 9-8 for your answer. Show which method gives the net-income advantage and which method gives the cash-flow advantage. Ignore the earnings rate in the cash-flow analysis.

Problem 9-4B *Journalizing and posting plant asset transactions; capital expenditures versus revenue expenditures* (L.O. 1,3,5,8)

Consumers Power Company provides electrical power to part of Michigan. Assume that the company completed the following transactions:

19X4
Jan. 3 Paid $22,000 cash for a used service truck.
      5 Paid $1,200 to have the truck engine overhauled.
      7 Paid $300 to have the truck modified for business use.
Oct. 3 Paid $930 for transmission repair and oil change.
Dec. 31 Used the double-declining-balance method to record depreciation on the truck. (Assume a 4-year life.)
     31 Closed the appropriate accounts.

19X5
Mar. 13 Replaced the truck's broken windshield for $275 cash.
June 26 Traded in the service truck for a new truck costing $27,000. The dealer granted an $8,000 allowance on the old truck, and Consumers Power paid the balance in cash. Recorded 19X5 depreciation for the year to date and then recorded the exchange of trucks.
Dec. 31 Used the double-declining-balance method to record depreciation on the new truck. (Assume a 4-year life.)
     31 Closed the appropriate accounts.

Required

1. Open the following accounts in the general ledger: Service Trucks; Accumulated Depreciation—Service Trucks; Truck Repair Expense; Depreciation Expense—Service Trucks; and Loss on Exchange of Service Trucks.
2. Record the transactions in the general journal and post to the ledger accounts opened.

Problem 9-5B *Recording plant asset transactions; exchanges; changes in useful life* (L.O. 1,3,5,8)

A. C. Nielsen Company surveys American viewing trends. Nielsen's balance sheet reports the following assets under Property and Equipment: Land, Buildings, Office Furniture, Communication Equipment, Televideo Equipment, and Leasehold Improvements. The company has a separate accumulated depreciation account for each of these assets except land and leasehold improvements. Amortization on leasehold improvements is credited directly to the Leasehold Improvements account rather than to Accumulated Depreciation—Leasehold Improvements.

Assume that Nielsen completed the following transactions:

Jan. 4 Traded in communication equipment with book value of $31,000 (cost of $66,000) for similar new equipment with a cash cost of $78,000. The seller gave Nielsen a trade-in allowance of $20,000 on the old equipment, and Nielsen paid the remainder in cash.
     19 Purchased office furniture for $45,000 plus 6 percent sales tax and $300 shipping charge. The company gave a 90-day, 10 percent note in payment.
Apr. 19 Paid the furniture note and related interest.
Aug. 29 Sold a building that had cost $475,000 and had accumulated depreciation of $353,500 through December 31 of the preceding year. Depreciation is computed on a straight-line basis. The building has a 30-year useful life and a residual value of $47,500. Nielsen received $250,000 cash and a $750,000 note receivable.

Sep. 6 Paid cash to improve leased assets at a cost of $26,000.

Nov. 10 Purchased used communication and televideo equipment from the Gallup polling organization. Total cost was $90,000 paid in cash. An independent appraisal valued the communication equipment at $65,000 and the televideo equipment at $35,000.

Dec. 31 Recorded depreciation as follows:

Equipment is depreciated by the double-declining-balance method over a 5-year life with zero residual value. Record depreciation on the equipment purchased on January 4 and on November 10 separately.

Office furniture has an expected useful life of 8 years with an estimated residual value of $5,000. Depreciation is computed by the sum-of-years-digits method.

Amortization on leasehold improvements is computed on a straight-line basis over the life of the lease, which is 6 years, with zero residual value.

Depreciation on buildings is computed by the straight-line method. The company had assigned buildings an estimated useful life of 30 years and a residual value that is 10 percent of cost. After using the buildings for 20 years, the company has come to believe that their total useful life will be 35 years. Residual value remains unchanged. The buildings cost $96,000,000.

Required

Record the transactions in the general journal.

Problem 9-6B *Distinguishing capital expenditures from revenue expenditures; preparing a plant ledger record* **(L.O. 3,5,8)**

Suppose Kraft, Inc., uses plant ledger cards to control its service trucks, purchased from Rountree Motors. The supervisor is responsible for the trucks, which are located at the company's service garage. The following transactions were completed during 19X6 and 19X7:

19X6

Jan. 10 Paid $14,000 cash for a used service truck (truck no. 214).

11 Paid $1,500 to have the truck engine overhauled.

12 Paid $250 to have the truck modified for business use.

Aug. 3 Paid $603 for transmission repair and oil change.

Dec. 31 Recorded depreciation on the truck by the double-declining-balance method, based on a 5-year life and a $1,500 residual value.

19X7

Mar. 13 Replaced a damaged bumper on truck no. 214 at a cash cost of $295.

May 12 Traded in service truck no. 214 for a new one (truck no. 267) with a cash cost of $23,500. The dealer granted a $9,000 allowance on the old truck, and Kraft paid the balance in cash. Recorded 19X7 depreciation for year to date and then recorded exchange of the trucks.

Dec. 31 Recorded depreciation on truck no. 267 by the double-declining-balance method, based on a 5-year life and a $2,000 residual value.

Required

1. Identify the capital expenditures and the revenue expenditures in the transactions. Which expenditures are debited to an asset account? Which expenditures are debited to an expense account?

2. Prepare a separate plant ledger record for each of the trucks.

Problem 9-7B *Recording intangibles, natural resources, and the related expenses*
(L.O. 6,7)

Part 1.   Transco Energy Company operates a pipeline that provides natural gas to Atlanta; Washington, D.C.; Philadelphia; and New York City. The company's balance sheet includes the asset Oil Properties.

Suppose Transco paid $6 million cash for an oil lease that contained an estimated reserve of 725,000 barrels of oil. Assume that the company paid $350,000 for additional geological tests of the property and $110,000 to prepare the surface for drilling. Prior to production, the company signed a $65,000 note payable to have a building constructed on the property. Because the building provides on-site headquarters for the drilling effort and will be abandoned when the oil is depleted, its cost is debited to the Oil Properties account and included in depletion charges. During the first year of production, Transco removed 82,000 barrels of oil, which it sold on credit for $19 per barrel.

Required

Make general journal entries to record all transactions related to the oil and gas property, including depletion and sale of the first-year production.

Part 2.   United Telecommunications, Inc., (United Telecom) provides communication services in Florida, North Carolina, New Jersey, Texas, and other states. The company's balance sheet reports the asset Cost of Acquisitions in Excess of the Fair Market Value of the Net Assets of Subsidiaries. Assume that United Telecom purchased this asset as part of the acquisition of another company, which carried these figures:

Book value of assets	$640,000
Market value of assets	920,000
Liabilities	405,000

Required

1. What is another title for the asset Cost of Acquisitions in Excess of the Fair Market Value of the Net Assets of Subsidiaries?
2. Make the general journal entry to record United Telecom's purchase of the other company for $600,000 cash.
3. Assuming United Telecom amortizes Cost of Acquisitions in Excess of the Fair Market Value of the Net Assets of Subsidiaries over 20 years, record the straight-line amortization for one year.

Part 3.   Suppose United Telecom purchased a patent for $190,000. Before using the patent, United incurred an additional cost of $25,000 for a lawsuit to defend the company's right to purchase it. Even though the patent gives United legal protection for 17 years, company management has decided to amortize its cost over a 5-year period because of the industry's fast-changing technologies.

Required

Make general journal entries to record the patent transactions, including straight-line amortization for 1 year.

Extending Your Knowledge

Decision Problems

1. Measuring Profitability Based on Different Inventory and Depreciation Methods (L.O. 3)

Suppose you are considering investing in two businesses, PanAm Industries and Lucerne Dairies. The two companies are virtually identical, and both began operations at the beginning of the current year. During the year, each company purchased inventory as follows:

Jan.	4	12,000 units at	$4 =	$ 48,000	
Apr.	6	5,000 units at	5 =	25,000	
Aug.	9	7,000 units at	6 =	42,000	
Nov.	27	10,000 units at	7 =	70,000	
Totals		34,000		$185,000	

During the first year, both companies sold 25,000 units of inventory.

In early January both companies purchased equipment costing $200,000 that had a 10-year estimated useful life and a $20,000 residual value. PanAm uses the first-in, first-out (FIFO) method for its inventory and straight-line depreciation for its equipment. Lucerne uses last-in, first-out (LIFO) and double-declining-balance depreciation. Both companies' trial balances at December 31 included the following:

Sales revenue.........................	$300,000
Purchases	185,000
Operating expenses	80,000

Required

1. Prepare both companies' income statements.
2. Prepare a schedule that shows why one company appears to be more profitable than the other. Explain the schedule and amounts in your own words. What accounts for the different amounts?
3. Is one company more profitable than the other? Give your reason.

2. Plant Assets and Intangible Assets (L.O. 7,8)

The following questions are unrelated except that they apply to fixed assets and intangible assets:

1. The manager of Meadowlake, Inc., regularly buys plant assets and debits the cost to Repairs and Maintenance Expense. Why would he do that, since he knows this action violates GAAP?
2. The manager of Spruce Lake Company regularly debits the cost of repairs and maintenance of plant assets to Plant and Equipment. Why would she do that, since she knows she is violating GAAP?
3. It has been suggested that, since many intangible assets have no value except to the company that owns them, they should be valued at $1.00 or zero on the balance sheet. Many accountants disagree with this view. Which view do you support? Why?

Ethical Issue

Champion Air Filters purchased land and a building for the lump sum of $3 million. To get the maximum tax deduction, Champion managers allocated 90 percent of the purchase price to the building and only 10 percent to the land. A more realistic allocation would have been 75 percent to the building and 25 percent to the land.

Required

1. Explain the tax advantage of allocating too much to the building and too little to the land.
2. Was Champion's allocation ethical? If so, state why. If not, why not? Identify who was harmed.

Financial Statement Problems

1. Plant Assets and Intangible Assets (L.O. 4,5,8)

Refer to the Goodyear Tire & Rubber Company financial statements in Appendix C, and answer the following questions.

1. Which depreciation method does Goodyear use for the purpose of reporting to stockholders and creditors in the financial statements? What type of depreciation method does the company use for income tax purposes? Why is this method preferable for income tax purposes?
2. Depreciation expense is embedded in the expense amounts listed on the income statement. The statement of cash flows gives the amount of depreciation. What was depreciation for 1991? Record depreciation expense for 1991.
3. The statement of cash flows also reports purchases of plant assets and the proceeds (sale prices) received on disposal of plant assets. How much were Goodyear's plant asset acquisitions during 1991? Journalize Goodyear's acquisition of plant assets.
4. How much did Goodyear receive on the sale of plant assets during 1991? Assume the plant assets that were sold had a cost of $55.0 million and accumulated depreciation of $43.1 million. Record the sale of these plant assets.
5. In what category on the income statement are revenue expenditures most likely included?

2. Plant Assets and Intangible Assets (L.O. 3,5,7)

Obtain the annual report of an actual company of your choosing. Annual reports are available in various forms including the original document in hard copy, microfiche, and computerized data bases such as that provided by Disclosure, Inc. Answer these questions about the company. Concentrate on the current year in the annual report you select.

1. Which depreciation method or methods does the company use for reporting to stockholders and creditors in the financial statements? Does the company disclose the estimated useful lives of plant assets for depreciation purposes? If so, identify the useful lives.
2. Depreciation and amortization expenses are often combined since they are similar. Many income statements embed depreciation and amortization in other expense amounts. To learn the amounts of these expenses, it often becomes necessary to examine the statement of cash flows. Where does your company report depreciation and amortization? What were these expenses for the current year? (Note: The company you selected may have only depreciation—no amortization.)
3. How much did the company spend to acquire plant assets during the current year? See the statement of cash flows. Journalize the acquisitions in a single entry.
4. How much did the company receive on the sale of plant assets? Assume a particular cost and accumulated depreciation of the plant assets sold. Journalize the sale of the assets, assuming the sale resulted in a $700,000 loss.
5. What categories of intangible assets does the company report? What is their reported amount?

Chapter 10

Current Liabilities
and Payroll Accounting

I n the annals of marketing devices run amok, few can compare to the airlines' wildly popular frequent flier plans. Early this year, when most carriers tripled the free mileage a suitcase-happy passenger can win, even they knew things had gone too far. "In the back of our minds," says Michael Gunn, head of marketing at American Airlines, "we were trying to figure out how to get out of this mess." With every day that passes, the airlines have fresh reasons to worry about what the giveaways are costing—and they are out to clip the programs' wings.

Up to now most airlines have not bothered to account for frequent flier liabilities on their balance sheets in any significant way. The reasoning has been that most free flights filled airline seats that otherwise would have been empty and that the programs were a minor addition to the cost of doing business. American, for instance, puts the cost of free tickets issued in 1987 at about 10% of their full value, or some $20 million.

Source: Thomas Moore, "Cutting Back on Fliers' Freebies," *Fortune*, June 6, 1988, pp. 149–50. Used with permission of *Fortune*. © 1989 The Time Inc. Magazine Company. All Rights Reserved.

This actual example illustrates the challenge of accounting for current liabilities. In this case the airlines have a liability for the cost of providing customers with free trips.

A *liability* is an obligation to transfer assets or to provide services in the future. The obligation may arise from a transaction with an outside party. For example, a business incurs a liability when it issues a note payable to buy equipment or to borrow money. Also, the obligation may arise in the absence of individual transactions. For example, interest expense accrues with the passage of time. Until this interest is paid it is a liability. Income tax, a liability of corporations, accrues as income is earned. Proper accounting for liabilities is as important as proper accounting for assets. The failure to record an accrued liability causes the balance sheet to understate the related expense and thus overstates owner's equity. An overly positive view of the business is the result.

Current liabilities are obligations due within one year or within the company's operating cycle if it is longer than one year. Obligations due beyond this period of time are classified as long-term liabilities. We discuss long-term liabilities in Chapter 11. We now turn to accounting for current liabilities, including those arising from payroll expenses.

Current Liabilities of Known Amount

Current liabilities fall into one of two categories: those of a known amount and those whose amount must be estimated. We look first at current liabilities of known amount.

OBJECTIVE 1
Account for current liabilities

Trade Accounts Payable

Amounts owed to suppliers for products or services that are purchased on open account are accounts payable. We have seen many accounts payable examples in previous chapters. For example, a business may purchase inventories and office supplies on an account payable.

Short-Term Notes Payable

Short-term notes payable, a common form of financing, are notes payable that are due within one year. Companies often issue short-term notes payable to borrow cash or to purchase inventory or plant assets. In addition to recording the note payable and its eventual payment, the business must also accrue interest expense and interest payable at the end of the period. The following entries are typical of this liability:

19X1

Sep. 30	Purchases		8,000	
		Note Payable, Short-Term		8,000
		Purchase of inventory by issuing a one-year 10-percent note payable.		

Dec. 31	Interest Expense ($8,000 × .10 × 3/12)		200	
		Interest Payable		200
		Adjusting entry to accrue interest expense at year end.		

The balance sheet at December 31, 19X1, will report the Note Payable of $8,000 and the related Interest Payable of $200 as current liabilities. The 19X1 income statement will report interest expense of $200.

The following entry records the note's payment:

19X2

Sep. 30	Note Payable, Short-Term	8,000	
	Interest Payable	200	
	Interest Expense ($8,000 × .10 × 9/12)	600	
	Cash [$8,000 + ($8,000 × .10)]		8,800
	Payment of a note payable and interest at maturity.		

The cash payment entry must split the total interest on the note between the portion accrued at the end of the previous period ($200) and the current period's expense ($600).

 ### Short-Term Notes Payable Issued at a Discount

In another common borrowing arrangement, a company may **discount a note payable** at the bank. Discounting means that the bank subtracts the interest amount from the note's face value. The borrower receives the net amount. In effect, the borrower prepays the interest, which is computed on the principal of the note.

Suppose Procter & Gamble discounts a $100,000, 60-day note payable to its bank at 12 percent. The company will receive $98,000—that is, the $100,000 face value less interest of $2,000 ($100,000 × .12 × 60/360). Assume this transaction occurs on November 25, 19X1. Procter & Gamble's entries to record discounting the note would be

19X1

Nov. 25	Cash ($100,000 − $2,000)		98,000	
	Discount on Note Payable ($100,000 x .12 × 60/360)		2,000	
		Note Payable, Short-Term		100,000
	Discounted a $100,000, 60-day, 12 percent note payable to borrow cash.			

Discount on Note Payable is a contra account to the liability Note Payable, Short-Term. A balance sheet prepared immediately after this transaction would report the note payable at its net amount of $98,000, as follows:

Current liabilities:

Note payable, short-term	$100,000
Less: Discount on note payable	(2,000)
Note payable, short-term, net	$ 98,000

The accrued interest at year end must still be recorded, as it would for any note payable. The adjusting entry at December 31 records interest for 36 days as follows:

19X1

Dec. 31   Interest Expense ($100,000 × .12 × 36/360)   1,200
          Discount on Note Payable   1,200
       Adjusting entry to accrue interest expense at year end.

This entry credits the Discount account instead of Interest Payable. Why? Because the Discount balance represents future interest expense, and the accrual of interest records the current-period portion of the expense. Furthermore, crediting the Discount reduces this contra account's balance and increases the net amount of the Note Payable. After the adjusting entry, only $800 of the Discount remains, and the carrying value of the Note Payable increases to $99,200, as follows:

Current liabilities:
     Note payable, short-term $100,000
         Less: Discount on note payable
            ($2,000 − $1,200) . . . .   (800)
     Note payable, short-term, net   . . . . $ 99,200

Finally, the business records the note's payment:

19X2

Jan. 24   Interest Expense ($100,000 × .12 × 24/360) .   800
          Discount on Note Payable   800
       To record interest expense.

       Note Payable, Short-Term   100,000
          Cash   100,000
       To pay note payable at maturity.

After these entries, the balances in the note payable account and the discount account are zero. Each period's income statement reports the appropriate amount of interest expense.

Sales Tax Payable

Most states levy a sales tax on retail sales. Retailers charge their customers the sales tax in addition to the price of the item sold. Because the retailers owe the state the sales tax collected, the account Sales Tax Payable is a current liability. For example, Pizza Time Theatre, Inc. (home of Chuck E. Cheese) reported sales tax payable of $737,712 as a current liability. States do not levy sales tax on the sales of manufacturers like Procter & Gamble and General Motors. Such companies sell their products to wholesalers and retailers rather than to final consumers. Therefore, they have no sales tax liability.

Suppose one Saturday's sales at a Pizza Time Theatre totaled $2,000. The business would have collected an additional 5 percent in sales tax, which would equal $100 ($2,000 × .05). The business would record that day's sales as follows:

Cash ($2,000 × 1.05)   2,100
       Sales Revenue   2,000
       Sales Tax Payable ($2,000 × .05)   100
To record cash sales of $2,000 subject to 5 percent sales tax.

Companies forward the collected sales tax to the taxing authority at regular intervals, at which time they debit Sales Tax Payable and credit Cash. Observe that Sales Tax Payable does *not* correspond to any sales tax expense that the business is incurring. Nor does this liability arise from the purchase of any asset. Rather, the obligation arises because the business is collecting for the government.

Many companies consider it inefficient to credit Sales Tax Payable when recording sales. They record the sale in an amount that includes the tax. Then prior to paying tax to the state, they make a single entry for the entire period's transactions to bring Sales Revenue and Sales Tax Payable to their correct balances.

Suppose a company made July sales of $100,000, subject to a tax of 6 percent. Its summary entry to record the month's sales could be

July 31	Cash ($100,000 × 1.06)	106,000	
	Sales Revenue		106,000
	To record sales for the month.		

The entry to adjust Sales Revenue and Sales Tax Payable to their correct balances is

July 31	Sales Revenue [$106,000 − ($106,000 ÷ 1.06)] ...	6,000	
	Sales Tax Payable		6,000
	To record sales tax.		

Companies that follow this procedure need to make an adjusting entry at the end of the period in order to report the correct amounts of revenue and sales tax liability on their financial statements.

Current Portion of Long-Term Debt

Some long-term notes payable and long-term bonds payable must be paid in installments. The **current portion of long-term debt,** or *current maturity,* is the amount of the principal that is payable within one year. This amount does not include the interest due. Of course, any liability for accrued interest payable must also be reported, but a separate account, Interest Payable, is used for that purpose.

H. J. Heinz Company, probably best known for its ketchup, owed almost $200 million on long-term debt at April 30, the end of its fiscal year. Nearly $14 million was a current liability because it was due within one year. The remaining $186 million was a long-term liability. Suppose the interest rate on the debt was 6 percent and that interest was last paid the preceding November 30. Heinz Company's April 30 balance sheet would report:

Current Liabilities (in part)	Millions
Portion of long-term debt due within one year	$ 14
Interest payable ($200 × .06 × 5/12)..............	5
Long-Term Debt and Other Liabilities (in part)	
Long-term debt	$186

Accrued Expenses

As shown in the Heinz Company presentation, *accrued expenses,* such as interest on the note, create current liabilities because the interest is due within the year. Therefore, the interest payable (accrued interest) is reported as a current liability. Other important liabilities for accrued expenses are payroll and the related payroll taxes, which we discuss in the second part of this chapter.

Unearned Revenues

Unearned revenues are also called *deferred revenues, revenues collected in advance,* and *customer prepayments.* Each account title indicates that the business has received cash from its customers before earning the revenue. The company has an obligation to provide goods or services to the customer.

The Dun & Bradstreet (D&B) Corporation provides credit evaluation services on a subscription basis. When finance companies pay in advance to have D&B investigate the credit histories of potential customers, D&B incurs a liability to provide future service. The liability account is called Unearned Subscription Revenue (which could also be titled Unearned Subscription Income).

Assume that Dun & Bradstreet charges $150 for a finance company's three-year subscription. Dun & Bradstreet's entries would be

19X1
Jan. 1 Cash	150	
Unearned Subscription Revenue		150
To record receipt of cash at start of the three-year subscription agreement.		

19X1, 19X2, 19X3
Dec. 31 Unearned Subscription Revenue	50	
Subscription Revenue ($150/3)		50
To record subscription revenue earned at the end of each of three years.		

Dun & Bradstreet's financial statements would report this sequence:

	December 31		
Balance Sheet	**Year 1**	**Year 2**	**Year 3**
Current liabilities			
Unearned subscription revenue ..	$100	$50	$-0-

Income Statement	**Year 1**	**Year 2**	**Year 3**
Revenues			
Subscription revenue	$ 50	$50	$50

Customer Deposits Payable

Some companies require cash deposits from customers as security on borrowed assets. These amounts are called Customer Deposits Payable because the company must refund the cash to the customer under certain conditions.

For example, telephone companies demand a cash deposit from a customer before installing a telephone. Utility companies and businesses that lend tools and appliances commonly demand a deposit as protection against damage and theft. When the customer ends service or returns the borrowed asset, the company refunds the cash deposit—if the customer has paid all the bills and has not damaged the company's property. Because the company generally must return the deposit, that obligation is a liability. The uncertainty of when the deposits will be refunded and their relatively small amounts cause many companies to classify Customer Deposits Payable as current liabilities. This is consistent with the concept of conservatism.

Certain manufacturers demand security deposits from the merchandisers who sell their products. Stanley Home Products, Inc., for example, demands a deposit from its dealers. The security deposits, called Dealers' Security Deposits, recently came to $4 million on Stanley's balance sheet, a small amount compared with its total current liabilities of over $62 million.

Current Liabilities That Must Be Estimated

A business may know that a liability exists but not know the exact amount. The liability may not simply be ignored. The unknown amount of a liability must be estimated for reporting on the balance sheet.

Estimated current liabilities vary among companies. As an example, let's look at Estimated Warranty Payable, a liability account common among merchandisers.

Estimated Warranty Payable

Many merchandising companies guarantee their products against defects under *warranty* agreements. The warranty period may extend for any length of time. Ninety-day warranties and one-year warranties are common.

Whatever the warranty's lifetime, the matching principle demands that the company record the *warranty expense* in the same period that the business recognizes sales revenue. After all, offering the warranty—and incurring any possible expense through the warranty agreement—is a part of generating revenue through sales. At the time of the sale, however, the company does not know which products are defective. The exact amount of warranty expense cannot be known with certainty, so the business must estimate its warranty expense and open the related liability account—Estimated Warranty Payable (also called Accrued Warranty Costs and Product Warranty Liability). Even though the warranty liability is a contingency, it is accounted for as an actual liability because the obligation for the warranty expense has occurred and its amount can be estimated.

Companies may make a reliable estimate of their warranty expense based on their experience. Assume a company made sales of $200,000, subject to product warranties. Company management, noting that in past years between 2 percent and 4 percent of products proved defective, estimates that 3 percent of the products will require repair or replacement during the one-year warranty period. The company records warranty expense of $6,000 ($200,000 × .03) for the period:

Warranty Expense...............................	6,000	
Estimated Warranty Payable................		6,000
To accrue warranty expense.		

Assume that defective merchandise totals $5,800. The company may either repair or replace it. Corresponding entries follow.

Estimated Warranty Payable....................	5,800	
Cash		5,800
To repair defective products sold under warranty.		

Estimated Warranty Payable......................	5,800	
Inventory.................................		5,800

To replace defective products sold under warranty.

Note that the expense is $6,000 on the income statement no matter what the cash payment or the cost of the replacement inventory. In future periods, the company may come to debit the liability Estimated Warranty Payable for the remaining $200. However, *when* the company repairs or replaces defective merchandise has no bearing on when the company records warranty expense. The business records warranty expense in the same period as the sale.

Other Estimated Current Liabilities

Estimated Vacation Pay Liability. Most companies grant paid vacations to their employees. The employees receive this benefit during the time they take their vacation, but they earn the compensation by working the other days of the year. Two-week vacations are common. To match expense with revenue properly, the company accrues the vacation pay expense and liability for each of the 50 workweeks of the year. Then, the company records payment during the two-week vacation period. Employee turnover, terminations, and ineligibility force companies to estimate the vacation pay liability.

Suppose a company's January payroll is $100,000 and vacation pay adds 4 percent (2 weeks of annual vacation divided by 50 workweeks each year). Experience indicates that only 80 percent of the vacations will be taken in any one month, so the January vacation pay estimate is $3,200 ($100,000 × .04 × .80). In January the company records vacation pay as follows:

Jan. 31	Vacation Pay Expense	3,200	
	Estimated Vacation Pay Liability		3,200

Each month thereafter, the company makes a similar entry for 4 percent of the payroll.

If an employee takes a vacation in August, his $2,000 monthly salary is recorded as follows:

Aug. 31	Estimated Vacation Pay Liability	2,000	
	Cash		2,000

Estimated Frequent Flier Liability of an Airline Company. The chapter-opening vignette describes airlines' frequent flier plans. In a typical arrangement, a passenger who travels a certain number of miles can take a free trip or upgrade her ticket from coach class to first class. The operating expense of providing this free service creates a liability for the airline. When should the expense and estimated frequent flier liability be recorded? As the airline earns revenue from its paying customers. Under the matching principle, a company should record expense when it earns the related revenue. Because the ultimate cost of providing the free transportation is uncertain, the airline must estimate this expense and the related liability. Suppose American Airlines records revenue of $1 million in February. Further, assume American estimates that this revenue-producing travel will give customers free trips that are estimated to cost American 3 percent of the revenue. American could record frequent flier expense and liability as follows:

Feb. 28	Frequent Flier Expense ($1,000,000 × .03)	30,000	
	Estimated Frequent Flier Liability		30,000

In July, when a frequent flier takes a free trip costing the airline $150, American could record the transaction as follows:[1]

July 8 Estimated Frequent Flier Liability   150
            Cash, Wages Payable, and other
                accounts   150

Contingent Liabilities

OBJECTIVE 2

Account for contingent liabilities

A *contingent liability* is not an actual liability. Instead, it is a potential liability that depends on a *future* event arising out of a past transaction. For example, a town government may sue the company that installed new street lights, claiming that the electrical wiring is faulty. The past transaction is the street-light installation. The future event is the court case that will decide the suit. The lighting company thus faces a contingent liability, which may or may not become an actual obligation.

It would be unethical for the company to withhold knowledge of the lawsuit from its creditors and from anyone considering investing in the business. A person or business could be misled into thinking the company is stronger financially than it really is. The disclosure principle of accounting requires a company to report any information deemed relevant to outsiders of the business. The goal is to arm people with relevant, reliable information for decision making.

Sometimes the contingent liability has a definite amount. From Chapter 8 recall that the payee of a discounted note has a contingent liability. If the maker of the note pays at maturity, the contingent liability ceases to exist. However, if the maker defaults, the payee, who sold the note, must pay its maturity value to the purchaser. In this case, the payee knows the note's maturity value, which is the amount of the contingent liability.

Another contingent liability of known amount arises from guaranteeing that another company will pay a note payable that the other company owes to a third party. This practice, called cosigning a note, obligates the guarantor to pay the note and interest if, and only if, the primary debtor fails to pay. Thus the guarantor has a contingent liability until the note becomes due. If the primary debtor pays off, the contingent liability ceases to exist. If the primary debtor fails to pay, the guarantor's liability becomes actual.

The amount of a contingent liability may be hard to determine. For example, companies face lawsuits, which may cause possible obligations of amounts to be determined by the courts.

Contingent liabilities may be reported in two ways. In what is called a **short presentation,** the contingent liability appears in the body of the balance sheet, after total liabilities, but with no amount given. Generally an explanatory note accompanies a short presentation. Sears, Roebuck and Company reported contingent liabilities this way:

	Millions
Total liabilities	$27,830.7
Contingent liabilities (note 10)	—

Note 10: Various legal actions and governmental proceedings are pending against Sears, Roebuck and Co. and its subsidiaries. . . . The consequences of these matters are not presently determinable but, in the opinion of management, the ultimate liability resulting, if any, will not have a material effect on the company.

[1]The credit side of this entry would depend on the airline's particular situation. Cash is credited for expenses paid currently, Wages Payable for the cost of ticketing passengers and baggage handling, and so on.

Contingent liabilities do not have to be mentioned in the body of the balance sheet. Many companies use a second method of reporting, presenting the footnote only. International Business Machines Corporation (IBM) mentions its contingent liabilities in a half-page supplementary note labeled *litigation*.

The line between a contingent liability and a real liability may be hard to draw. As a practical guide, the FASB says to record an actual liability if (1) it is probable that the business has suffered a loss and (2) its amount can be reasonably estimated. If both of these conditions are met, the FASB reasons that the obligation has passed from contingent to real, even if its amount must be estimated. Suppose that at the balance sheet date, a hospital has lost a court case for uninsured malpractice but the amount of damages is uncertain. The hospital estimates that the liability will fall between $1.0 and $2.5 million. In this case, the hospital must record a loss or expense and a liability for $1.0 million. The income statement will report the loss and the balance sheet the liability. Also, the hospital must disclose in a note the possibility of an additional $1.5 million loss.

Summary Problem for Your Review

This problem consists of three independent parts.

1. A Wendy's hamburger restaurant made cash sales of $4,000 subject to a 5 percent sales tax. Record the sales and the related sales tax. Also record Wendy's payment of the tax to the state government.
2. At April 30, 19X2, H. J. Heinz Company reported its 6 percent long-term debt:

Current Liabilities (in part)

Portion of long-term debt due within one year	$ 14,000,000
Interest payable ($200 × .06 × 5/12)	5,000,000

Long-Term Debt and Other Liabilities (in part)

Long-term debt	$186,000,000

The company pays interest on its long-term debt on November 30 each year.

Show how Heinz Company would report its liabilities on the year-end balance sheet at April 30, 19X3. Assume the current maturity of its long-term debt is $16 million.
3. What distinguishes a contingent liability from an actual liability?

SOLUTION TO REVIEW PROBLEM

1.

Cash ($4,000 × 1.05).............................	4,200	
Sales Revenue.................................		4,000
Sales Tax Payable ($4,000 × .05)		200
To record cash sales and related sales tax.		

Sales Tax Payable	....	200
Cash	....	200
To pay sales tax to the state government.		

2. H. J. Heinz Company balance sheet at April 30, 19X3:

Current Liabilities (in part)

Portion of long-term debt due within one year	$ 16,000,000
Interest payable ($186 × .06 × 5/12)	4,650,000

Long-Term Debt and Other Liabilities (in part)

Long-term debt	$170,000,000

3. A contingent liability is a *potential* liability, which may or may not become an actual liability.

Accounting for Payroll

Payroll, also called *employee compensation,* is a major expense of many businesses. For service organizations, such as CPA firms, real estate brokers, and travel agents, payroll is *the* major expense of conducting business. Service organizations sell their personnel's services, so employee compensation is their primary cost of doing business, just as cost of goods sold is the largest expense in merchandising.

Employee compensation takes different forms. Some employees collect a **salary,** which is income stated at a yearly, monthly, or weekly rate. Other employees work for **wages,** which is employee pay stated at an hourly figure. Sales employees often receive a **commission,** which is a percentage of the sales the employee has made. Some companies reward excellent performance with a **bonus,** an amount over and above regular compensation.

Businesses often pay employees at a base rate for a set number of hours—called straight time. For working any additional hours—called overtime—the employee receives a higher rate.

Assume that Lucy Childres is an accountant for an electronics company. Lucy earns $600 per week straight time. The company workweek runs 40 hours, so Lucy's hourly straight-time pay is $15 ($600/40). Her company pays her **time and a half** for overtime. That rate is 150 percent (1.5 times) the straight-time rate. Thus Lucy earns $22.50 for each hour of overtime she works ($15.00 × 1.5 = $22.50). For working 42 hours during a week, she earns $645, computed as follows:

Straight-time pay for 40 hours	....	$600
Overtime pay for 2 overtime hours:		
2 × $22.50	....	45
Total pay	....	$645

Gross Pay and Net Pay

Many years ago, employees brought home all that they had earned. For example, Lucy Childres would have taken home the full $645 total that she made. Payroll accounting was straightforward. Those days are long past.

The federal government, most state governments, and even some city governments demand that employers act as collection agents for employee taxes, which are deducted from employee checks. Insurance companies, labor unions, and other organizations may also receive pieces of employees' pay. Amounts withheld from an employee's check are called deductions.

Gross pay is the total amount of salary, wages, commissions, or any other employee compensation before taxes and other deductions are taken out. **Net pay**—the gross pay minus all deductions—is the amount that the employee actually takes home.

Many companies also pay employee **fringe benefits,** which are a form of employee compensation. Examples include health and life insurance paid directly to the insurance companies. Another example is retirement pay, which the employee does not receive immediately in cash. Payroll accounting has become quite complex. Let's turn now to a discussion of payroll deductions.

Payroll Deductions

Payroll deductions that are *withheld* from employees' pay fall into two categories: (1) *required deductions,* which include employee income tax and social security tax; and (2) *optional deductions,* which include union dues, insurance premiums, charitable contributions, and other amounts that are withheld at the employee's request. After they are withheld, payroll deductions become the liability of the employer, who assumes responsibility for paying the outside party. For example, the employer pays the government the employee income tax withheld and pays the union the employee union dues withheld.

Required Payroll Deductions

Employee Income Tax. The law requires most employers to withhold income tax from their employees' salaries and wages. The amount of income tax deducted from gross pay is called **withheld income tax.** For many employees, this deduction is the largest. The amount withheld depends on the employee's gross pay and on the number of withholding allowances the employee claims.

Each employee may claim himself or herself, his or her spouse, and each dependent as a withholding allowance. An unmarried taxpayer has one allowance, a married couple two allowances, a married couple with one child three allowances, and so on. Each allowance lowers the amount of tax withheld from the employee's paycheck. The employee files a Form W-4 with the employer to indicate the number of allowances claimed for withholding purposes. Exhibit 10-1 shows a W-4 for R. C. Dean, who claims four.

The employer sends its employees' withheld income tax to the government. The amount of the income tax withheld determines how often the employer submits tax payments. The employer must remit the taxes to the government

EXHIBIT 10-1   W-4 Form

```
---------------- Cut here and give the certificate to your employer. Keep the top portion for your records. -----------------
```

Form **W-4** Department of the Treasury Internal Revenue Service	**Employee's Withholding Allowance Certificate** ► For Privacy Act and Paperwork Reduction Act Notice, see reverse.		OMB No. 1545-0010 **19 91**
1 Type or print your first name and middle initial R.C.	Last name Dean		**2** Your social security number 344-86-4529

Home address (number and street or rural route) 4376 Palm Drive	**3** Marital status	☐ Single ☒ Married ☐ Married, but withhold at higher Single rate.
City or town, state, and ZIP code Fort Lauderdale, FL 33317		**Note:** If married, but legally separated, or spouse is a nonresident alien, check the Single box.

4 Total number of allowances you are claiming (from line G above or from the Worksheets on back if they apply) **4**

5 Additional amount, if any, you want deducted from each pay . . . . **5** $

6 I claim exemption from withholding and I certify that I meet ALL of the following conditions for exemption:
- Last year I had a right to a refund of **ALL** Federal income tax withheld because I had **NO** tax liability; **AND**
- This year I expect a refund of **ALL** Federal income tax withheld because I expect to have **NO** tax liability; **AND**
- This year if my income exceeds $550 and includes nonwage income, another person cannot claim me as a dependent.

If you meet all of the above conditions, enter the year effective and "EXEMPT" here ► **6** 19

7 Are you a full-time student? (**Note:** Full-time students are not automatically exempt.) . . . . **7** ☐ Yes ☒ No

Under penalties of perjury, I certify that I am entitled to the number of withholding allowances claimed on this certificate or entitled to claim exempt status.

Employee's signature ► *R.C. Dean*   Date ► 7-22 , 19 92

8 Employer's name and address (**Employer:** Complete 8 and 10 only if sending to IRS) Blumenthal's Crescent Square Shopping Center Fort Lauderdale, FL 33310	**9** Office code (optional) 14	**10** Employer identification number 83-19475

at least quarterly. Every business must account for payroll taxes on a calendar-year basis regardless of its fiscal year.

The employer accumulates taxes in the Employee Income Tax Payable account. The word *payable* indicates that the account is the employer's liability to the government, even though the employees are the people taxed.

Employee Social Security (FICA) Tax.   The *Federal Insurance Contributions Act (FICA)*, also known as the Social Security Act, created the Social Security Tax. The Social Security program provides retirement, disability, and medical benefits. The law requires employers to withhold Social Security (FICA) tax from employees' pay. The amount of tax withheld from employees' pay varies from year to year. Congress adjusts tax rates and the level of employee pay subject to the tax as shown in Exhibit 10-2 for the retirement benefit portion of the tax. The Medicare portion of the Social Security tax—also included in the 7.65 percent tax rate—applies to higher levels of employee earnings.

Because the FICA tax rate is approximately 8 percent of the first $50,000 that the employee earns in a year, we use these figures in our examples and in the assignment materials at the end of the chapter. For each employee who earns

EXHIBIT 10-2   Social Security Taxes

Year	Employee Earnings Subject to the Tax	Social Security (FICA) Tax Rate	Maximum Amount of Social Security (FICA) Tax Withheld from Employee Pay During the Year
1991	$53,400	.0765	$4,085
1992	*	.0765	*
⋮	⋮	⋮	⋮
1996	69,000†	.0765	5,279†

*Not set by Congress at the time of this writing.
†Estimated

$50,000 or more, the employer withholds $4,000 ($50,000 X .08) from the employee's pay and sends that amount to the federal government. The employer records this employee tax in the account FICA Tax Payable.

Assume that Rex Jennings, an employee, earned $48,500 prior to December. Jennings's salary for December is $3,500. How much FICA tax will be withheld from his December paycheck? The computation follows.

Employee earnings subject to the tax in one year	$50,000
Employee earnings prior to the current pay period	48,500
Current pay subject to FICA tax	$ 1,500
FICA tax rate	× .08
FICA tax to be withheld from current pay	$ 120

Optional Payroll Deductions

As a convenience to its employees, many companies make payroll deductions and disburse cash according to employee instructions. Union dues, insurance payments, payroll savings plans, and gifts to charities are examples. The account Employees' Union Dues Payable holds employee deductions for union membership.

Employer Payroll Taxes

Employers must bear the expense of at least three payroll taxes: (1) Social Security (FICA) tax, (2) state unemployment compensation tax, and (3) federal unemployment compensation tax.

Employer FICA Tax. In addition to the responsibility for handling the employee contribution to Social Security, the employer also must pay into the program. The employer's Social Security tax is the same as the amount withheld from employee pay. Thus the Social Security system is funded by equal contributions from employees and employers. Using our 8 percent and $50,000 annual pay figures, the maximum annual employer tax on each employee is $4,000 ($50,000 X .08). The liability account the employer uses for this payroll tax is the same FICA Tax Payable account used for the amount withheld from employee pay. The tax rate and the amount of earnings subject to the tax both change as Congress passes new legislation.

State and Federal Unemployment Compensation Taxes. These two payroll taxes are products of the Federal Unemployment Tax Act (FUTA). In recent years, employers have paid a combined tax of 6.2 percent on the first $7,000 of each employee's annual earnings. The proportion paid to the state is 5.4 percent, and 0.8 percent is paid to the federal government. The state government then uses the money to pay unemployment benefits to people who are out of work. The employer uses the accounts Federal Unemployment Tax Payable and State Unemployment Tax Payable. Exhibit 10-3 shows a typical disbursement of payroll costs by an employer company.

Payroll Entries

Exhibit 10-4 summarizes an employer's entries to record a monthly payroll of $10,000 (all amounts are assumed for illustration only).

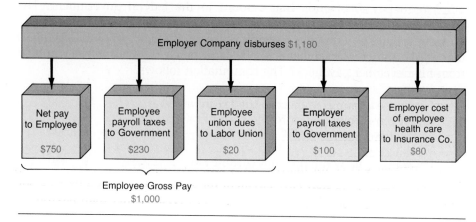

Employer Company disburses $1,180

Net pay to Employee	Employee payroll taxes to Government	Employee union dues to Labor Union	Employer payroll taxes to Government	Employer cost of employee health care to Insurance Co.
$750	$230	$20	$100	$80

Employee Gross Pay
$1,000

Entry A in Exhibit 10-4 records the employer's *salary expense*. The *gross salary* of all employees, $10,000, is their monthly pay before any deductions. The federal government imposes the two taxes. Most states and some cities also levy income taxes, which are accounted for in like manner. The union dues are optional. Employees' take-home (net) pay is $7,860. One important point about this payroll transaction is that the employees pay their own income and FICA taxes and union dues. The employer serves merely as a collecting agent and sends these amounts to the government and the union.

Entry B records the employer's *payroll taxes*. In addition to the employees' FICA tax ($800 in entry A), the employer must also pay the $800 FICA tax shown in entry B. The other two employer payroll taxes are state and federal unemployment taxes. Employees make no payments for unemployment taxes.

Entry C records employee *fringe benefits* paid by the employer. The company in the exhibit pays health and life insurance for its employees, a common

EXHIBIT 10-4 Payroll Accounting by the Employer

Objective 4

Make basic payroll entries

A.	Salary Expense (or Wage Expense or Commission Expense)	10,000	
	Employee Income Tax Payable		1,200
	FICA Tax Payable ($10,000 × .08)		800
	Employee Union Dues Payable.............		140
	Salary Payable to Employees (take-home pay)		7,860
	To record *salary expense*.		
B.	Payroll Tax Expense..............................	1,420	
	FICA Tax Payable ($10,000 × .08)		800
	State Unemployement Tax Payable ($10,000 × .054)		540
	Federal Unemployment Tax Payable ($10,000 × .008)		80
	To record employer's *payroll taxes*.		
C.	Health Insurance Expense for Employees	800	
	Life Insurance Expense for Employees	200	
	Pension Expense.................................	500	
	Employee Benefits Payable		1,500
	To record employee *fringe benefits* payable by employer.		

practice. Also, the employer funds pensions (that is, pays cash into a pension plan) for the benefit of employees when they retire. In the exhibit, the employer's pension expense for the month is $500, and the total employer expense for fringe benefits is $1,500. The total payroll expense of the employer in Exhibit 10-4 is $12,920 (gross salary of $10,000 + employer payroll taxes of $1,420 + fringe benefits of $1,500).

A company's payments to people who are not employees—outsiders called independent contractors—are *not* company payroll expenses. Consider two CPAs, Fermi and Scott. Fermi is a corporation's chief financial officer. Scott is the corporation's outside auditor. Fermi is an employee of the corporation and his compensation is a debit to Salary Expense. Scott, on the other hand, performs auditing service for many clients, and the corporation debits Auditing Expense when it pays her. Any payment for services performed by a person outside the company is a debit to an expense account other than payroll.

The Payroll System _____

Good business means paying employees accurately and paying them on time. Also, companies face the legal responsibility for handling employees' and their own payroll taxes, as we have seen. These demands require companies to process a great deal of payroll data. Efficient accounting is important. To make payroll accounting accurate and timely, accountants have developed the payroll system.

The components of the payroll system are a *payroll register*, a special *payroll bank account*, *payroll checks*, and an *earnings record* for each employee.

Payroll Register

Each pay period, the company organizes the payroll data in a special journal called the *payroll register*, or *payroll journal*. This register lists each employee and the figures the business needs to record payroll amounts. The payroll register, which resembles the cash disbursements journal, or check register, also serves as a check register by providing a column for recording each payroll check number.

The payroll register in Exhibit 10-5 includes sections for recording Gross Pay, Deductions, Net Pay, and Account Debited. *Gross Pay* has columns for straight-time pay, overtime pay, and total gross pay for each employee. Columns under the *Deductions* heading vary from company to company. Of course the employer must deduct federal income tax and FICA tax. (State income tax is left out for convenience.) Additional column headings depend on which optional deductions the business handles. In the exhibit, the employer deducts employee payroll taxes, union dues, and gifts to United Way and then sends the amounts to the proper parties. The business may add deduction columns as needed. The *Net Pay* section lists each employee's net (take-home) pay and the number of the check issued to him or her. The last two columns indicate the *Account Debited* for the employee's gross pay. (The company has office workers and salespeople.)

In the exhibit, W. L. Chen earned gross pay of $500. His net pay was $381.45, paid with check number 1621. Chen is an office worker, so his salary is debited to Office Salary Expense.

EXHIBIT 10-5 *Payroll Register*

Week ended December 27, 19X3

| | | a | b | c | d | e | f | g | h | i | j | k | l |
| | | **Gross Pay** | | | | **Deductions** | | | | **Net Pay** | | **Account Debited** | |
Employee Name	Hours	Straight-time	Overtime	Total	Federal Income Tax	FICA Tax	Union Dues	United Way Charities	Total	(c–h) Amount	Check No.	Office Salary Expense	Sales Salary Expense
Chen, W. L.	40	500.00		500.00	71.05	40.00	5.00	2.50	118.55	381.45	1621	500.00	
Dean, R. C.	46	400.00	90.00	490.00	59.94	39.20	5.00	2.00	101.14	388.86	1622		490.00
Ellis, M.	41	560.00	21.00	581.00	86.14	46.48	5.00		137.62	443.38	1623	581.00	
Trimble, E. A.	40	1,360.00		1,360.00	463.22			15.00	478.22	881.78	1641		1,360.00
Total		12,940.00	714.00	13,654.00	3,167.76	861.94	85.00	155.00	4,269.70	9,384.30		4,464.00	9,190.00

Note that the business deducted no FICA tax from E. A. Trimble. She has already earned more than $50,000. Any employee whose earnings exceed this annual maximum pays no additional FICA tax during that year.[2]

The payroll register in Exhibit 10-5 gives the employer the information needed to record salary expense for the pay period. Using the total amounts for columns *d* through *l*, the employer records total salary expense as follows:

Dec. 27	Office Salary Expense	4,464.00	
	Sales Salary Expense	9,190.00	
	Employee Income Tax Payable		3,167.76
	FICA Tax Payable		861.94
	Employee Union Dues Payable		85.00
	Employee United Way Payable		155.00
	Salary Payable to Employees		9,384.30

Payroll Bank Account

After recording the payroll, the company books include a credit balance in Salary Payable to Employees for net pay of $9,384.30. (See column i in Exhibit 10-5.) How the business pays this liability depends on its payroll system. Many companies disburse paychecks to employees from a special payroll bank account. The employer draws a check for net pay ($9,384.30 in our illustration) on its regular bank account and deposits this check in the special payroll bank account. Then the company writes paychecks to employees out of the payroll account. When the paychecks clear the bank, the payroll account has a zero balance, ready for the activity of the next pay period. Disbursing paychecks from a separate bank account isolates net pay for analysis and control, as discussed later in the chapter.

Other payroll disbursements—for withheld taxes, union dues, and so on—are neither as numerous nor as frequent as weekly or monthly paychecks. The employer pays taxes, union dues, and charities from its regular bank account.

Payroll Checks

Most companies pay employees by check. A *payroll check* is like any other check except that its perforated attachment lists the employee's gross pay, payroll deductions, and net pay. These amounts are taken from the payroll register. Exhibit 10-6 shows payroll check number 1622, issued to R. C. Dean for net pay of $388.86 earned during the week ended December 27, 19X3. To enhance your ability to use payroll data, trace all amounts on the check attachment to the payroll register in Exhibit 10-5.

Increasingly, companies are paying employees by automatic deposits to the employee's personal bank account. By a prearranged agreement, the employee can authorize the company to make the deposit directly to the bank. With no check to write and deliver to the employee, the company saves time and money. The employee avoids the trouble of receiving, endorsing, and depositing the paycheck.

---

[2]For clarity we ignore the additional tax for Medicare benefits.

Recording Cash Disbursements for Payroll _____

Most employers must make at least three entries to record payroll cash disbursements: net pay to employees, payroll taxes to the government and payroll deductions, and employee fringe benefits.

Net Pay to Employees. When the employer issues payroll checks to employees, the company debits Salary Payable to Employees and credits Cash.

Using the data in Exhibit 10-5, the company would make the following entry to record the cash payment (column i) for the December 27 weekly payroll:

Dec. 27	Salary Payable to Employees	9,384.30	
	Cash		9,384.30

Payroll Taxes to the Government and Payroll Deductions. The employer must send to the government two sets of payroll taxes: those withheld from employees' pay and those paid by the employer. Based on Exhibit 10-5, columns d through g, the business would record a series of cash payment entries summarized as follows (employer tax amounts are assumed):

Dec. 27	Employee Income Tax Payable	3,167.76	
	FICA Tax Payable ($861.94 × 2)	1,723.88	
	Employee Union Dues Payable	85.00	
	Employee United Way Payable	155.00	
	State Unemployment Tax Payable	104.62	
	Federal Unemployment Tax Payable	15.50	
	Cash		5,251.76

EXHIBIT 10-6 *Payroll Check*

Blumenthal's							1622

Payroll Account
Fort Lauderdale, FL

12-27 19 X3

Pay to the Order of ___ R.C. Dean _____ $ | 388.86

Three hundred eighty-eight & 86/100 . . . . Dollars

Republic Bank
Fort Lauderdale,
Florida 33310

Anna Figaro
Treasurer

⑆ ⑈1119000311⑈ 0787⑈ 500004154⑈

Pay			Deductions					Net Pay	Check No.
Straight-time	Over-time	Gross	Income Tax	FICA	Union Dues	United Way	Total		
400.00	90.00	490.00	59.94	39.20		2.00	101.14	388.86	1622

Fringe Benefits.   The employer might pay for employees' insurance coverage and pension plan. Assuming the total cash payment for these benefits is $1,927.14, this entry for payments to third parties would be

Dec. 27	Employee Benefits Payable..............	1,927.14	
	Cash.............................		1,927.14

Earnings Record

The employer must file payroll tax returns with the federal and state governments and must provide the employee with a wage and tax statement, Form W-2, at the end of the year. Therefore, employers maintain an earnings record for each employee. Exhibit 10-7 is a five-week excerpt from the earnings record of employee R. C. Dean.

The employee earnings record is not a journal or a ledger, and it is not required by law. It is an accounting tool—like the work sheet—that the employer uses to prepare payroll tax reports. Year-to-date earnings also indicate when an employee has earned $50,000, the point at which the employer can stop deducting FICA tax.

Exhibit 10-8 is the Wage and Tax Statement, Form W-2, for employee R. C. Dean. The employer prepares this statement and gives copies to the employee and to the Internal Revenue Service (IRS). Dean uses the W-2 to prepare his personal income tax return. The IRS uses the W-2 to ensure that Dean is paying income tax on all his income from that job. The IRS matches Dean's income as reported on his tax return with his earnings as reported on the W-2.

Internal Control over Payrolls _____

The internal controls over cash disbursements discussed in Chapter 6 apply to payroll. In addition, companies adopt special controls in payroll accounting. The large number of transactions and the many different parties involved increase the risk of a control failure. Accounting systems feature two types of special controls over payroll: controls for efficiency and controls for safeguarding cash.

Controls for Efficiency

For companies with many employees, reconciling the bank account can be time consuming because of the large number of outstanding payroll checks. For example, a March 30 payroll check would probably not have time to clear the bank before a bank statement on March 31. This check and others in a March 30 payroll would be outstanding. Identifying a large number of outstanding checks for the bank reconciliation increases accounting expense. To limit the number of outstanding checks, many companies use two payroll bank accounts. They make payroll disbursements from one payroll account one month and from the other payroll account the next month. By reconciling each account every other month, a March 30 paycheck has until April 30 to clear the bank before the account is reconciled. This essentially eliminates outstanding checks, cuts down the time it takes to prepare the bank reconciliation, and decreases accounting expense. Also, many companies' checks become void if not cashed within a certain period of time. This too limits the number of outstanding checks.

EXHIBIT 10-7 *Employee Earnings Record for 19X3*

Employee Name and Address:

Dean, R. C.
4376 Palm Drive
Fort Lauderdale, FL 33317

Social Security No.: 344-86-4529
Marital Status: Married
Withholding Exemptions: 4
Pay Rate: $400 per week
Job Title: Salesperson

| Week Ended | Hours | Gross Pay | | | | Deductions | | | | | Net Pay | |
		Straight-time	Overtime	Total	To Date	Federal Income Tax	FICA Tax	Union Dues	United Way Charities	Total	Amount	Check No.
Nov. 29	40	400.00		400.00	21,340.00	42.19	32.00		2.00	76.19	323.81	1525
Dec. 6	40	400.00		400.00	21,740.00	42.19	32.00		2.00	76.19	323.81	1548
Dec. 13	44	400.00	60.00	460.00	22,200.00	54.76	36.80		2.00	93.56	366.44	1574
Dec. 20	48	400.00	120.00	520.00	22,720.00	66.75	41.60		2.00	110.35	409.65	1598
Dec. 27	46	400.00	90.00	490.00	23,210.00	59.94	39.20		2.00	101.14	388.86	1622
Total		20,800.00	2,410.00	23,210.00		2,346.72	1,856.80		104.00	4,307.52	18,902.48	

EXHIBIT 10-8 *Employee Wage and Tax Statement, Form W-2*

1 Control number	2222	For Paperwork Reduction Act Notice, see separate instructions OMB No. 1545-0008	**For Official Use only** ▶		

2 Employer's name, address, and ZIP code	6 Statutory employee ☒ Deceased ☐ Pension plan ☐ Legal rep. ☐ 942 emp. ☐ Subtotal ☐ Deferred compensation ☐ Void ☐

Blumenthal's
Crescent Square Shopping Center
Fort Lauderdale, FL 33310

7 Allocated tips	8 Advance EIC payment
9 Federal income tax withheld 2,346.72	10 Wages, tips, other compensation 23,210.00

3 Employer's identification number 83-19475	4 Employer's state I.D. number	11 Social security tax withheld 1,856.80	12 Social security wages 23,210.00

5 Employee's social security number 344-86-4529		13 Social security tips	14 Nonqualified plans

19a Employee's name, address and ZIP code R.C. Dean	15 Dependent care benefits	16 Fringe benefits incl. in Box 10

4376 Palm Drive
Fort Lauderdale, FL 33310

	17 See instr. for Forms W-2/W-2P	18 Other

19b Employee's address and ZIP code

20	21	22	23

24 State income tax	25 State wages, tips, etc.	26 Name of state	27 Local income tax	28 Local wages, tips, etc.	29 Name of locality

Copy A For Social Security Administration   Dept. of the Treasury—Internal Revenue Service

Form **W-2 Wage and Tax Statement 1990**

Do NOT CUT or Separate Forms on This Page

1 Control number	2222	For Paperwork Reduction Act Notice, see separate instructions OMB No. 1545-0008	**For Official Use only** ▶		

2 Employer's name, address, and ZIP code	6 Statutory employee ☒ Deceased ☐ Pension plan ☐ Legal rep. ☐ 942 emp. ☐ Subtotal ☐ Deferred compensation ☐ Void ☐

Blumenthal's
Crescent Square Shopping Center
Fort Lauderdale, FL 33310

7 Allocated tips	8 Advance EIC payment
9 Federal income tax withheld 2,346.72	10 Wages, tips, other compensation 23,210.00

3 Employer's identification number 83-19475	4 Employer's state I.D. number	11 Social security tax withheld 1,856.80	12 Social security wages 23,210.00

5 Employee's social security number 344-86-4529		13 Social security tips	14 Nonqualified plans

19a Employee's name, address and ZIP code R.C. Dean	15 Dependent care benefits	16 Fringe benefits incl. in Box 10

4376 Palm Drive
Fort Lauderdale, FL 33310

	17 See instr. for Forms W-2/W-2P	18 Other

19b Employee's address and ZIP code

20	21	22	23

24 State income tax	25 State wages, tips, etc.	26 Name of state	27 Local income tax	28 Local wages, tips, etc.	29 Name of locality

Copy A For Social Security Administration   Dept. of the Treasury—Internal Revenue Service

Form **W-2 Wage and Tax Statement 1990**

Other payroll controls for efficiency include following established policies for hiring and firing employees and complying with government regulations. Hiring and firing policies provide guidelines for keeping a qualified, diligent work force dedicated to achieving the business's goals. Complying with government regulations avoids paying fines and penalties.

Controls for Safeguarding Cash

Owners and managers of small businesses can monitor their payroll disbursements by personal contact with their employees. Large corporations cannot do so. These businesses must establish controls to ensure that payroll disbursements are made only to legitimate employees and for the correct amounts. A particular danger is that payroll checks may be written to a fictitious employee and cashed by a dishonest employee. To guard against this crime and other possible breakdowns in internal control, large businesses adopt strict internal control policies.

The duties of hiring and firing employees should be separated from the duties of distributing paychecks. Otherwise, a dishonest supervisor, for example, could add a fictitious employee to the payroll. When paychecks are issued, the supervisor could simply pocket the nonexistent person's paycheck for his or her own use.

Requiring an identification badge bearing an employee's photograph helps internal control. Issuing paychecks only to employees with badges ensures that only actual employees receive pay.

On occasion management should instruct an employee from the home office, perhaps an internal auditor, to distribute checks in the branch office personally rather than have the payroll department mail the checks. No one will claim a paycheck that has been issued to a fictitious employee. Any check left over after the distribution signals that payroll fraud has been attempted. Management would pursue an investigation.

A time-keeping system helps ensure that employees have actually worked the number of hours claimed. Having employees punch time cards at the start and end of the workday proves their attendance—as long as management makes sure that no employee punches in and out for others too. Some companies have their workers fill in weekly or monthly time sheets.

Again we see that the key to good internal control is separation of duties. The responsibilities of the personnel department, the payroll department, the accounting department, time-card management, and paycheck distribution should be kept separate.

Reporting Payroll Expense and Liabilities _____

OBJECTIVE 6
Report current liabilities

At the end of its fiscal year, the company reports the amount of *payroll liability* owed to all parties—employees, state and federal governments, unions, and so forth. Payroll liability is *not* the payroll expense for the year. The liability at year end is the amount of the expense that is still unpaid. Payroll expense appears on the income statement, payroll liability on the balance sheet.

Unisys Corporation reported accrued payrolls and commissions of approximately $164 million as a current liability on its year-end balance sheet (see Exhibit 10-9). However, Unisys's payroll expense for the year far exceeded $164 million. (Exhibit 10-9 also presents the other current liabilities that we have discussed in this chapter.)

Exhibit 10-10 summarizes all the current liabilities that we have discussed in this chapter.

Computer Accounting Systems for Current Liabilities _____

Current liabilities arising from a high volume of similar transactions are well suited for computerized accounting. One of the most common transactions of a merchandiser is the credit purchase of inventory. It is efficient to integrate

EXHIBIT 10-9 *Partial Unisys Corporation Balance Sheet*

Current Liabilities	Millions
Notes payable within one year	$ 397
Current maturities of long-term debt	31
Accounts payable	397
Accrued payrolls and commissions	**164**
Accrued taxes other than income taxes	69
Customers' deposits and prepayments	155
Dividends payable to shareholders	28
Estimated income taxes	111
Total current liabilities	$1,352

the accounts payable and perpetual inventory systems. When merchandise dips below a predetermined level, the system automatically prepares a purchase request. After the order is placed and the goods are received, inventory and accounts payable data are entered on magnetic tape. The computer reads the tape, then debits Inventory and credits Accounts Payable to account for the purchase. For payments, the computer debits Accounts Payable and credits Cash. The program may also update account balances and print journals, ledger accounts, and the financial statements.

The face amount of notes payable and their interest rates and payment dates can be stored for electronic data processing. Computer programs calculate interest, print the interest checks, journalize the transactions, and update account balances.

Payroll transactions are also ideally suited for computer processing. Employee pay rates and withholding data are stored on magnetic tape. Each payroll period, computer operators enter the number of hours worked by each employee. The machine performs the calculations, prints the payroll register and paychecks, and updates the employee earnings records. The program also computes payroll taxes and prepares quarterly reports to government agencies. Expense and liability accounts are automatically updated for the payroll transactions.

EXHIBIT 10-10 *Categories of Current Liabilities*

Amount of Liability Known When Recorded	Amount of Liability Must Be Estimated When Recorded

Trade accounts payable
Short-term notes payable
Sales tax payable
Current portion of long-term debt
Accrued expenses payable:
  Interest payable
  Payroll liabilities (salary payable,
    wages payable, and commissions
    payable)
  Payroll taxes payable (employee and
    employer)
Unearned revenues (revenues collected
  in advance of being earned)
Customer deposits payable
	Warranty payable
	Income tax payable
	Vacation pay
	  liability

Summary Problem for Your Review

Beth Denius, Limited, a clothing store, employs one salesperson, Alan Kingsley. His straight-time pay is $360 per week. He earns time and a half for hours worked in excess of 40 per week. Denius withholds income tax (11.0 percent) and FICA tax (8.0 percent) from Kingsley's pay. She also pays the following employer payroll taxes: FICA (8.0 percent) and state and federal unemployment (5.4 percent and 0.8 percent, respectively). In addition, Denius contributes to a pension plan an amount equal to 10 percent of Kingsley's gross pay.

During the week ended December 26, 19X4, Kingsley worked 48 hours. Prior to this week Kingsley has earned $5,470.

Required

1. Compute Kingsley's gross pay and net pay for the week.
2. Record the following payroll entries that Denius would make:
   a. Expense for Kingsley's salary, including overtime pay
   b. Employer payroll taxes
   c. Expense for fringe benefits
   d. Payment of cash to Kingsley
   e. Payment of all payroll taxes
   f. Payment for fringe benefits
3. How much total payroll expense did Denius incur for the week? How much cash did the business spend on its payroll?

SOLUTION TO REVIEW PROBLEM

Requirement 1

Gross Pay:	Straight-time pay for 40 hours		$360.00
	Overtime pay:		
	Rate per hour ($360/40 × 1.5) .. $13.50		
	Hours (48 − 40) .... × 8	108.00	
	Total gross pay	$468.00	
Net Pay:	Gross pay		$468.00
	Less: Withheld income tax ($468 × .11) ...	$ 51.48	
	Withheld FICA tax ($468 × .08)	37.44	88.92
	Net pay		$379.08

Requirement 2

a.	Sales Salary Expense	468.00	
	Employee Income Tax Payable		51.48
	FICA Tax Payable		37.44
	Salary Payable to Employee		379.08
b.	Payroll Tax Expense	66.45	
	FICA Tax Payable ($468 × .08)		37.44
	State Unemployment Tax Payable ($468 × .054)..		25.27
	Federal Unemployment Tax Payable ($468 × .008)		3.74
c.	Pension Expense ($468 × .10)	46.80	
	Employee Benefits Payable....................		46.80
d.	Salary Payable to Employee	379.08	
	Cash..		379.08

e.	Employee Income Tax Payable	51.48	
	FICA Tax Payable ($37.44 × 2)	74.88	
	State Unemployment Tax Payable	25.27	
	Federal Unemployment Tax Payable	3.74	
	Cash		155.37
f.	Employee Benefits Payable	46.80	
	Cash		46.80

Requirement 3

Denius incurred *total payroll expense* of $581.25 (gross salary of $468.00 + payroll taxes of $66.45 + fringe benefits of $46.80). See entries *a–c*.

Denius *paid cash* of $581.25 on payroll (Kingsley's net pay of $379.08 + payroll taxes of $155.37 + fringe benefits of $46.80). See entries *d–f*.

Summary

Current liabilities may be divided into those of *known amount* and those that must be *estimated*. Trade accounts payable, short-term notes payable, and the related liability for accrued expenses are among current liabilities of known amount. Current liabilities that must be estimated are warranties payable and corporations' income tax payable.

Contingent liabilities are not actual liabilities but potential liabilities that may arise in the future. Contingent liabilities, like current liabilities, may be of known amount or an indefinite amount. A business that faces a lawsuit not yet decided in court has a contingent liability of indefinite amount.

Payroll accounting handles the expenses and liabilities arising from compensating employees. Employers must withhold income and FICA taxes from employees' pay and send these *employee payroll taxes* to the government. In addition, many employers allow their employees to pay for insurance and union dues and to make gifts to charities through payroll deductions. An employee's net pay is the gross pay less all payroll taxes and optional deductions.

An *employer's* payroll expenses include FICA and unemployment taxes, which are separate from the payroll taxes borne by the employees. Also, most employers provide their employees with fringe benefits, like insurance coverage and retirement pensions.

A *payroll system* consists of a payroll register, a payroll bank account, payroll checks, and an earnings record for each employee. Good *internal controls* over payroll disbursements help the business to conduct payroll accounting efficiently and to safeguard the company's cash. The cornerstone of internal controls is the separation of duties.

Current liabilities arising from a high volume of repetitive transactions are well suited for computer processing. Trade accounts payable, notes payable and the related interest, and payrolls are three examples.

Self-Study Questions

Test your understanding of the chapter by marking the best answer for each of the following questions.

1. A $10,000, 9 percent, one-year note payable was issued on July 31. The balance sheet at December 31 will report interest payable of *(p. 486)*
   a. $0 because the interest is not due yet
   b. $300
   c. $375
   d. $900

2. If the note payable in the preceding question had been discounted, the cash proceeds from issuance would have been (p. 486)
   a. $9,100
   b. $9,625
   c. $9,700
   d. $10,000

3. Which of the following liabilities creates *no* expense for the company? (p. 488)
   a. Interest
   b. Sales tax
   c. FICA tax
   d. Warranty

4. Suppose Unitex Tire Company estimates that warranty costs will equal 1 percent of tire sales. Assume that November sales totaled $900,000, and the company's outlay in tires and cash to satisfy warranty claims was $7,400. How much warranty expense should the November income statement report? (p. 490)
   a. $1,600
   b. $7,400
   c. $9,000
   d. $16,400

5. Apex Sporting Company is a defendant in a lawsuit that claims damages of $55,000. On the balance sheet date, it appears likely that the court will render a judgment against Apex. How should Apex report this event in its financial statements? (p. 493)
   a. Omit mention because no judgment has been rendered
   b. Disclose the contingent liability in a note
   c. Use a short presentation only
   d. Report the loss on the income statement and the liability on the balance sheet

6. Emilie Frontenac's weekly pay is $320, plus time and a half for overtime. The tax rates applicable to her earnings are 8 percent for income tax and 8 percent for FICA. What is Emilie's take-home pay for a week in which she works 50 hours? (pp. 495, 498)
   a. $369.60
   b. $392.00
   c. $404.80
   d. $440.00

7. Which payroll tax applies (or taxes apply) mainly to the employer? (p. 497)
   a. Withheld income tax
   b. FICA tax
   c. Unemployment compensation tax
   d. Both b and c

8. The main reason for using a separate payroll bank account is to (p. 501)
   a. Safeguard cash by avoiding writing payroll checks to fictitious employees
   b. Safeguard cash by limiting paychecks to amounts based on time cards
   c. Increase efficiency by isolating payroll disbursements for analysis and control
   d. All of the above

9. The key to good internal controls in the payroll area is (p. 506)
   a. Using a payroll bank account
   b. Separating payroll duties
   c. Using a payroll register
   d. Using time cards

10. Which of the following items is reported as a current liability on the balance sheet? (p. 507)
    a. Short-term notes payable
    b. Estimated warranties
    c. Accrued payroll taxes
    d. All of the above

Answers to the Self-Study Questions follow the Accounting Vocabulary.

Accounting Vocabulary

Bonus. Amount over and above regular compensation (p. 494).

Commission. Employee compensation computed as a percentage of the sales that the employee has made (p. 494).

Current portion of long-term debt. Amount of the principal that is payable within one year *(p. 488).*

Discounting a note payable. A borrowing arrangement in which the bank subtracts the interest amount from the note's face value. The borrower receives the net amount *(p. 486).*

FICA tax. Federal Insurance Contributions Act (FICA), or Social Security tax, which is withheld from employees' pay *(p. 496).*

Fringe benefits. Employee compensation, like health and life insurance and retirement pay, which the employee does not receive immediately in cash *(p. 495).*

Gross pay. Total amount of salary, wages, commissions, or any other employee compensation before taxes and other deductions are taken out *(p. 495).*

Net pay. Gross pay minus all deductions, the amount of employee compensation that the employee actually takes home *(p. 495).*

Payroll. Employee compensation, a major expense of many businesses *(p. 494).*

Salary. Employee compensation stated at a yearly, monthly, or weekly rate *(p. 494).*

Short presentation. A way to report contingent liabilities in the body of the balance sheet, after total liabilities but with no amount given *(p. 492).*

Short-term note payable. Note payable due within one year, a common form of financing *(p. 485).*

Social Security tax. Another name for FICA tax *(p. 496).*

Time and a half. Overtime pay computed as 150 percent (1.5 times) the straight-time rate *(p. 494).*

Unemployment compensation tax. Payroll tax paid by employers to the government, which uses the money to pay unemployment benefits to people who are out of work *(p. 497).*

Wages. Employee pay stated at an hourly figure *(p. 494).*

Withheld income tax. Income tax deducted from employees' gross pay *(p. 495).*

Answers to Self-Study Questions

1. c $10,000 \times .09 \times 5/12 = $375
2. a $10,000 - ($10,000 \times .09) = $9,100
3. b
4. c $900,000 \times .01 = $9,000
5. d
6. a Overtime pay: $320/40 = $8 \times 1.5 = $12 per hour $\times$ 10 hours = $120
   Gross pay = $320 + $120 = $440
   Deductions = $440 \times (.08 + .08) = $70.40
   Take-home pay = $440 - $70.40 = $369.60

7. c
8. c
9. b
10. d

ASSIGNMENT MATERIAL _____

Questions

1. Give a more descriptive account title for each of the following current liabilities: Accrued Interest, Accrued Salaries, Accrued Income Tax.
2. What distinguishes a current liability from a long-term liability? What distinguishes a contingent liability from an actual liability?
3. A company purchases a machine by signing a $21,000, 10 percent, one-year note payable on July 31. Interest is to be paid at maturity. What two current liabilities related to this purchase does the company report on its December 31 balance sheet? What is the amount of each liability?

4. A company borrowed cash by discounting a $15,000, 8 percent, six-month note payable to the bank, receiving cash of $14,400. (a) Show how the amount of cash was computed. Also, identify (b) the total amount of interest expense to be recognized on this note and (c) the amount of the borrower's cash payment at maturity.

5. Explain how sales tax that is paid by consumers is a liability of the store that sold the merchandise.

6. What is meant by the term *current portion of long-term debt,* and how is this item reported in the financial statements?

7. At the beginning of the school term, what type of account is the tuition that your college or university collects from students? What type of account is the tuition at the end of the school term?

8. Why is a customer deposit a liability? Give an example.

9. Patton Company warrants its products against defects for three years from date of sale. During the current year, the company made sales of $300,000. Store management estimates warranty costs on those sales will total $18,000 over the three-year warranty period. Ultimately, the company paid $22,000 cash on warranties. What is the company's warranty expense for the year? What accounting principle governs this answer?

10. Identify two contingent liabilities of a definite amount and two contingent liabilities of an indefinite amount.

11. Describe two ways to report contingent liabilities.

12. Why is payroll expense relatively more important to a service business such as a CPA firm than it is to a merchandising company?

13. Two persons are studying Allen Company's manufacturing process. One person is Allen's factory supervisor, and the other person is an outside consultant who is an expert in the industry. Which person's salary is the payroll expense of Allen Company? Identify the expense account that Allen would debit to record the pay of each person.

14. What are two elements of an employer's payroll expense in addition to salaries, wages, commissions, and overtime pay?

15. What determines the amount of income tax that is withheld from employee paychecks?

16. What are FICA taxes? Who pays them? What are the funds used for?

17. Identify two required deductions and four optional deductions from employee paychecks.

18. Identify three employer payroll taxes.

19. Who pays state and federal unemployment taxes? What are these funds used for?

20. Briefly describe a payroll accounting system's components and their functions.

21. How much Social Security tax has been withheld from the pay of an employee who has earned $52,288 during the current year? How much Social Security tax must the employer pay for this employee?

22. Briefly describe the two principal categories of internal controls over payroll.

23. Why do some companies use two special payroll bank accounts?

24. Identify three internal controls designed to safeguard payroll cash.

Exercises

Exercise 10-1   *Recording sales tax two ways* (L.O. 1)

Make general journal entries to record the following transactions of Meridian Golf Company for a two-month period. Explanations are not required.

March 31   Recorded cash sales of $83,600 for the month, plus sales tax of 7 percent collected on behalf of the state of Idaho. Record sales tax in a separate account.

April   6   Sent March sales tax to the state.

Journalize these transactions a second time. Record the sales tax initially in the Sales Revenue account.

Exercise 10-2   *Accounting for warranty expense and the related liability*   *(L.O. 1)*

The accounting records of Nathan Cook, Inc., included the following balances at the end of the period:

Estimated Warranty Payable	Sales Revenue	Warranty Expense
Beg. bal. 4,100	141,000	

In the past, Cook's warranty expense has been 7 percent of sales. During the current period, Cook paid $9,430 to satisfy the warranty claims of customers.

Required

1. Record Cook's warranty expense for the period and the company's cash payments during the period to satisfy warranty claims. Explanations are not required.
2. What ending balance of Estimated Warranty Payable will Cook report on its balance sheet?

Exercise 10-3   *Recording note payable transactions*   *(L.O. 1)*

Record the following note payable transactions of Toronto Development, Inc., in the company's general journal. Explanations are not required.

19X2
May   1   Purchased equipment costing $6,000 by issuing a one-year, 10 percent note payable.

Dec. 31   Accrued interest on the note payable.

19X3
May   1   Paid the note payable at maturity.

Exercise 10-4   *Discounting a note payable*   *(L.O. 1)*

On November 1, 19X4, Budget Counseling Center discounted a six-month, $12,000 note payable to the bank at 12 percent.

Required

1. Prepare general journal entries to record (a) issuance of the note, (b) accrual of interest at December 31, and (c) payment of the note at maturity in 19X5. Explanations are not required.
2. Show how the Budget Counseling Center would report the note on the December 31, 19X4, balance sheet.

Exercise 10-5   *Reporting a contingent liability*   *(L.O. 2)*

National Instrument Control is a defendant in lawsuits brought against the marketing and distribution of its products. Damages of $1.8 million are claimed against National, but the company denies the charges and is vigorously defending itself. In a recent talk-show interview, the president of the company stated that he could not predict the outcome of the lawsuits. Nevertheless, he said, management does not believe that any actual liabilities resulting from the lawsuits will significantly affect the company's financial position.

Required

Prepare a partial balance sheet to show how National Instrument Control would report this contingent liability in a short presentation. Total actual liabilities are $4.7 million. Also, write the disclosure note to describe the contingency.

Exercise 10-6   *Accruing a contingency*   **(L.O. 2)**

Refer to the National Instrument Control situation in the preceding exercise. Suppose National's attorneys believe it is probable that a judgment of $500,000 will be rendered against the company.

Required

Describe how to report this situation in the National Instrument Control financial statements. Journalize any entry required under GAAP. Explanations are not required.

Exercise 10-7   *Computing net pay*   **(L.O. 3)**

Hatch Bailey is a salesman in the men's department of Rich's Department Store in Atlanta. He earns a base monthly salary of $550 plus an 8 percent commission on his sales. Through payroll deductions, Hatch donates $5 per month to a charitable organization, and he authorizes Rich's to deduct $12.50 monthly for health insurance on his family. Tax rates on Hatch's earnings are 9 percent for income tax and 8 percent for FICA, subject to the maximum. During the first 11 months of the year, he earned $47,140. Compute Hatch's gross pay and net pay for December, assuming his sales for the month are $61,300.

Exercise 10-8   *Computing and recording gross pay and net pay*   **(L.O. 3,4)**

Sandy Jastremsky works for a Seven-Eleven store for straight-time earnings of $6 per hour, with time-and-a-half compensation for hours in excess of 40 per week. Sandy's payroll deductions include withheld income tax of 10 percent of total earnings, FICA tax of 8 percent of total earnings, and a weekly deduction of $5 for a charitable contribution to United Fund. Assuming Sandy worked 43 hours during the week, (a) compute her gross pay and net pay for the week, and (b) make a general journal entry to record the store's wage expense for Sandy's work, including her payroll deductions. Explanations are not required. Round all amounts to the nearest cent.

Exercise 10-9   *Recording a payroll*   **(L.O. 3,4)**

Famous & Barr Department Store incurred salary expense of $42,000 for December. The store's payroll expense includes employer FICA tax of 8 percent in addition to state unemployment tax of 5.4 percent and federal unemployment tax of 0.8 percent. Of the total salaries, $38,400 is subject to FICA tax, and $9,100 is subject to unemployment tax. Also, the store provides the following fringe benefits for employees: health insurance (cost to the store, $1,062.15); life insurance (cost to the store, $351.07); and pension benefits (cost to the store, $707.60). Record Famous & Barr's payroll taxes and its expenses for employee fringe benefits. Explanations are not required.

Exercise 10-10 *Reporting current and long-term liabilities* **(L.O. 6)**

Suppose Jack in the Box borrowed $500,000 on December 31, 19X0, by issuing 9 percent long-term debt that must be paid in annual installments of $100,000 plus interest each January 2. By inserting appropriate amounts in the following excerpts from the company's partial balance sheet, show how Jack in the Box would report its long-term debt.

	December 31,				
	19X1	19X2	19X3	19X4	19X5
Current liabilities:					
Current portion of long-term debt .	$___	$___	$___	$___	$___
Interest payable	___	___	___	___	___
Long-term liabilities:					
Long-term debt..................	___	___	___	___	___

Exercise 10-11 *Reporting current and long-term liabilities* **(L.O. 6)**

Assume Wilson Sporting Goods completed these selected transactions during December 19X6:

1. Sport Spectrum, a chain of sporting goods stores, ordered $60,000 of baseball and golf equipment. With its order, Sport Spectrum sent a check for $60,000. Wilson will ship the goods on January 3, 19X7.
2. The December payroll of $295,000 is subject to employee withheld income tax of 9 percent, FICA tax of 8 percent (employee and employer), state unemployment tax of 5.4 percent, and federal unemployment tax of 0.8 percent. On December 31, Wilson pays employees but accrues all tax amounts.
3. Sales of $2,000,000 are subject to estimated warranty cost of 1.4 percent.
4. On December 2, Wilson signed a $100,000 note payable that requires annual payments of $20,000 plus 9 percent interest on the unpaid balance each December 2.

Required

Report these items on Wilson's balance sheet at December 31, 19X6.

Problems   *(Group A)*

Problem 10-1A *Journalizing liability-related transactions* **(L.O. 1)**

The following transactions of University Cooperative occurred during 19X2 and 19X3. Record the transactions in the company's general journal. Explanations are not required.

19X2
Feb. 3 Purchased a machine for $4,200, signing a six-month, 11 percent note payable.
     28 Recorded the week's sales of $27,000, one-third for cash, and two-thirds on credit. All sales amounts are subject to a 5 percent state sales tax.
Mar. 7 Sent the last week's sales tax to the state.

Apr. 30 Borrowed $100,000 on a 9 percent note payable that calls for annual installment payments of $25,000 principal plus interest.

May 10 Received $1,125 in security deposits from customers. University Cooperative refunds most deposits within three months.

Aug. 3 Paid the six-month, 11 percent note at maturity.

10 Refunded security deposits of $1,125 to customers.

Sep. 14 Discounted a $6,000, 12 percent, 60-day note payable to the bank, receiving cash for the net amount after interest was deducted from the note's maturity value.

Nov. 13 Recognized interest on the 12 percent discounted note and paid off the note at maturity.

30 Purchased inventory at a cost of $7,200, signing a 10 percent, three-month note payable for that amount.

Dec. 31 Accrued warranty expense, which is estimated at 3 percent of sales of $145,000.

31 Accrued interest on all outstanding notes payable. Make a separate interest accrual entry for each note payable.

19X3

Feb. 28 Paid off the 10 percent inventory note, plus interest, at maturity.

Apr. 30 Paid the first installment and interest for one year on the long-term note payable.

Problem 10-2A *Identifying contingent liabilities (L.O. 2)*

Hunting Horn Farm provides riding lessons for girls ages 8 through 15. Most students are beginners, and none of the girls owns her own horse. Janet Christie, the owner of Hunting Horn, uses horses stabled at her farm and owned by the Averys. Most of the horses are for sale, but the economy has been bad for several years and horse sales have been slow. The Averys are happy that Janet uses their horses in exchange for rooming and boarding them. Because of a recent financial setback, Janet cannot afford insurance. She seeks your advice about her business exposure to liabilities.

Required

Write a memorandum to inform Janet of specific contingent liabilities arising from the business. It will be necessary to define a contingent liability because she is a professional horse trainer, not a businessperson. Propose a way for Janet to limit her exposure to these liabilities.

Problem 10-3A *Computing and recording payroll amounts (L.O. 3,4)*

The partial monthly records of Yokohama Company show the following figures.

Employee Earnings:

(1) Straight-time earnings	$?	(7) Medical insurance	$ 1,373
(2) Overtime pay	5,109	(8) Total deductions	?
(3) Total employee earnings	?	(9) Net pay	58,813

Deductions and Net Pay: **Accounts Debited:**

(4) Withheld income tax ..	9,293	(10) Salary Expense	31,278
(5) FICA tax.............	8,052	(11) Wage Expense	?
(6) Charitable contributions	885	(12) Sales Commission Expense	27,931

Required

1. Determine the missing amounts on lines (1), (3), (8), and (11).
2. Prepare the general journal entry to record Yokohama's payroll for the month. Credit Payrolls Payable for net pay. No explanation is required.

Problem 10-4A   *Computing and recording payroll amounts*   **(L.O. 3,4)**

Assume that Margo Benson is a commercial lender in Chase Manhattan Bank's mortgage banking department in New York City. During 19X2 she worked for the bank all year at a $4,195 monthly salary. She also earned a year-end bonus equal to 12 percent of her salary

Benson's federal income tax withheld during 19X2 was $822 per month. Also, there was a one-time withholding of $2,487 on her bonus check. State income tax withheld came to $61 per month, and the city of New York withheld income tax of $21 per month. In addition, there were one-time withholdings of $64 (state) and $19 (city) on the bonus. The FICA tax withheld was 8 percent of the first $50,000 in annual earnings. Benson authorized the following payroll deductions: United Fund contribution of 1 percent of total earnings, and life insurance of $17 per month

Chase Manhattan Bank incurred payroll tax expense on Benson for FICA tax of 8 percent of the first $50,000 in annual earnings. The bank also paid state unemployment tax of 5.4 percent, and federal unemployment tax of 0.8 percent on the first $7,000 in annual earnings. The bank also provided Benson with the following fringe benefits: health insurance at a cost of $48 per month, and pension benefits to be paid to Benson during her retirement. During 19X2 Chase Manhattan's cost of Benson's pension program was $8,083.

Required

1. Compute Benson's gross pay, payroll deductions, and net pay for the full year of 19X2. Round all amounts to the nearest dollar.
2. Compute Chase Manhattan Bank's total 19X2 payroll cost for Benson.
3. Prepare Chase Manhattan Bank's summary general journal entries to record its expense for
   a. Benson's total earnings for the year, her payroll deductions, and her net pay. Debit Salary Expense and Executive Bonus Compensation as appropriate. Credit liability accounts for the payroll deductions and Cash for net pay.
   b. Employer payroll taxes for Benson. Credit liability accounts.
   c. Fringe benefits provided to Benson. Credit a liability account.

   Explanations are not required.

Problem 10-5A   *Selecting the correct data to record a payroll*   **(L.O. 4)**

Assume the following payroll information appeared in the records of a small plant operated by Sharp Electronics:

Required

1. Prepare the general journal entry to record the payroll for the week ended July 31, including payroll taxes and fringe benefits.
2. Prepare the general journal entry to record the payment of the week's salaries to employees on July 31.
3. Assume that Sharp pays all its liabilities to the federal government in a single monthly amount. Prepare the general journal entry to record the July 31, 19X4, payment of federal taxes. (Liabilities to the federal government include FICA taxes and those items with *federal* and *U.S.* in the account title.)

4. Assume that Sharp pays all other payroll liabilities shortly after the end of the month. Prepare a single general journal entry to record the August 3 payment for these July liabilities.

Explanations are not required for journal entries.

	Payroll for Week Ended Friday July 31, 19X4	Payroll for Month of July 19X4
Salaries:		
Supervisor salaries	$42,375	$162,639
Office salaries	9,088	37,261
Deductions:		
Employee federal income tax	5,960	23,182
FICA tax	3,266	13,392
Employee health insurance	922	3,780
Employee union dues	708	2,903
Employee U.S. savings bonds..........	665	2,727
Net pay................................	39,942	153,916
Employer payroll taxes:		
FICA tax	3,266	13,392
State unemployment tax	2,119	10,793
Federal unemployment tax	314	1,599
Employer cost of fringe benefits for employees:		
Health insurance	2,034	7,904
Life insurance	1,053	4,096
Pension.............................	1,667	6,835

Problem 10-6A   *Journalizing, posting, and reporting liabilities*   (L.O. 1,2,4,6)

The TU Electric Company general ledger at September 30, 19X7, the end of the company's fiscal year, includes the following account balances before adjusting entries. Parentheses indicate a debit balance.

Notes Payable, Short-Term	$29,000	Employer Payroll		
Discount on Notes Payable	(2,100)	Taxes Payable	$	____
Accounts Payable	88,240	Employee Benefits Payable		____
Current Portion of Long-Term Debt Payable	____	Estimated Vacation Pay Liability		2,105
Interest Payable	____	Sales Tax Payable		372
Salary Payable............	____	Property Tax Payable		1,433
Employee Payroll Taxes Payable	____	Unearned Rent Revenue ..		3,900
		Long-Term Debt Payable ..		220,000
		Contingent Liabilities		____

The additional data needed to develop the adjusting entries at September 30 are as follows:

a. The $29,000 balance in Notes Payable, Short-Term consists of two notes. The first note, with a principal amount of $21,000, was issued on August 31, matures one year from date of issuance, and was discounted at 10 percent. The second note, with a principal amount of $8,000, was issued on September 2 for a term of 90 days and bears interest at 9 percent. It was not discounted.

b. The long-term debt is payable in annual installments of $55,000, with the next installment due on January 31, 19X8. On that date, TU Electric will also pay one year's interest at 10.5 percent. Interest was last paid on January 31. To shift the current installment of the long-term debt to a current liability, debit Long-Term Debt Payable and credit Current Portion of Long-Term Debt Payable.

c. Gross salaries for the last payroll of the fiscal year were $4,319. Of this amount, employee payroll taxes payable were $958, and salary payable was $3,361.

d. Employer payroll taxes payable were $755, and TU Electric's liability for employee life insurance was $1,004.

e. TU Electric estimates that vacation pay is 4 percent of gross salaries.

f. On August 1 the company collected six months' rent of $3,900 in advance.

g. At September 30 TU Electric is the defendant in a $200,000 lawsuit, which the company expects to win. However, the outcome is uncertain. TU Electric reports contingent liabilities "short," with an explanatory note.

Required

1. Open the listed accounts, inserting their unadjusted September 30 balances.

2. Journalize and post the September 30 adjusting entries to the accounts opened. Key adjusting entries by letter.

3. Prepare the liability section of TU Electric's balance sheet at September 30.

Problem 10-7A *Using a payroll register; recording a payroll* **(L.O. 5)**

Assume that payroll records of a district sales office of General Mills, Inc., provided the following information for the weekly pay period ended December 18, 19X3:

Employee	Hours Worked	Weekly Earnings Rate	Federal Income Tax	Health Insurance	United Way Contribution	Earnings through Previous Week
Ginny Akin	43	$400	$ 94	$9	$7	$17,060
Leroy Dixon	46	480	121	5	5	22,365
Karol Stastny	47	800	219	6	—	49,247
David Trent	40	240	32	4	2	3,413

Ginny Akin and David Trent work in the office, and Leroy Dixon and Karol Stastny work in sales. All employees are paid time and a half for hours worked in excess of 40 per week. For convenience, round all amounts to the nearest dollar. Show computations. Explanations are not required for journal entries.

Required

1. Enter the appropriate information in a payroll register similar to Exhibit 10-5. In addition to the deductions listed, the employer also takes out FICA tax: 8 percent of the first $50,000 of each employee's annual earnings.

2. Record the payroll information in the general journal.

3. Assume that the first payroll check is number 178, paid to Ginny Akin. Record the check numbers in the payroll register. Also, prepare the general journal entry to record payment of net pay to the employees.

4. The employer's payroll taxes include FICA of 8 percent of the first $50,000 of each employee's annual earnings. The employer also pays unemployment taxes of 6.2 percent (5.4 percent for the state and 0.8 percent for the

federal government) on the first $7,000 of each employee's annual earnings. Record the employer's payroll taxes in the general journal.

Problem 10-8A *Reporting current liabilities* *(L.O. 6)*

Following are six pertinent facts about events during the current year at Alliance Rubber Company.

1. On August 31, Alliance signed a six-month, 12 percent note payable to purchase a machine costing $31,000. The note requires payment of principal and interest at maturity.
2. On October 31, Alliance received rent of $2,000 in advance for a lease on a building. This rent will be earned evenly over four months.
3. On November 30, Alliance discounted a $10,000 note payable to InterBank Savings. The interest rate on the one-year note is 12 percent.
4. December sales totaled $104,000 and Alliance collected sales tax of 9 percent. This amount will be sent to the state of Tennessee early in January.
5. Alliance owes $75,000 on a long-term note payable. At December 31, $25,000 of this principal plus $900 of accrued interest are payable within one year.
6. Sales of $909,000 were covered by Alliance's product warranty. At January 1 estimated warranty payable was $11,300. During the year Alliance recorded warranty expense of $27,900 and paid warranty claims of $30,100.

Required

For each item, indicate the account and the related amount to be reported as a current liability on Alliance's December 31 balance sheet.

(Group B)

Problem 10-1B *Journalizing liability-related transactions* *(L.O. 1)*

The following transactions of Munoz, Inc., occurred during 19X4 and 19X5. Record the transactions in the company's general journal. Explanations are not required.

19X4
Jan. 9 Purchased a machine at a cost of $5,000, signing a 12 percent, six-month note payable for that amount.
   29 Recorded the week's sales of $22,200, three-fourths on credit, and one-fourth for cash. Sales amounts are subject to an additional 6 percent state sales tax.
Feb. 5 Sent the last week's sales tax to the state.
   28 Borrowed $300,000 on a 10 percent note payable that calls for annual installment payments of $50,000 principal plus interest.
Apr. 8 Received $778 in deposits from distributors of company products. Munoz refunds the deposits after six months.
July 9 Paid the six-month, 12 percent note at maturity.
Oct. 8 Refunded security deposits of $778 to distributors.
   22 Discounted a $5,000, 10 percent, 90-day note payable to the bank, receiving cash for the net amount after interest was deducted from the note's maturity value.
Nov. 30 Purchased inventory for $3,100, signing a six-month, 8 percent note payable.

Dec. 31   Accrued warranty expense, which is estimated at 2 1/2 percent of sales of $650,000.

31   Accrued interest on all outstanding notes payable. Make a separate interest accrual entry for each note payable.

19X5

Jan. 20   Paid off the 10 percent discounted note payable. Made a separate entry for the interest.

Feb. 28   Paid the first installment and interest for one year on the long-term note payable.

May 31   Paid off the 8 percent note plus interest at maturity.

Problem 10-2B   *Identifying contingent liabilities*   **(L.O. 2)**

Covert Buick Company is the only Buick dealer in Austin, Texas, and one of the largest Buick dealers in the southwestern United States. The dealership sells new and used cars and operates a body shop and a service department. Duke Covert, the general manager, is considering changing insurance companies because of a disagreement with Doug Stillwell, Austin agent for the Travelers Insurance Company. Travelers is doubling Covert's liability insurance cost for the next year. In discussing insurance coverage with you, a trusted business associate, Stillwell brings up the subject of contingent liabilities.

Required

Write a memorandum to inform Covert Buick Company of specific contingent liabilities arising from the business. In your discussion, define a contingent liability.

Problem 10-3B   *Computing and recording payroll amounts*   **(L.O. 3,4)**

The partial monthly records of The Art Center show the following figures:

Employee Earnings:

(1) Straight-time employee earnings .	$16,431	(7) Medical insurance	$	668
(2) Overtime pay	?	(8) Total deductions		3,409
(3) Total employee earnings	?	(9) Net pay		15,936

Deductions and Net Pay: **Accounts Debited:**

(4) Withheld income tax .	1,403	(10) Salary Expense	?
(5) FICA tax	?	(11) Wage Expense	4,573
(6) Charitable contributions	340	(12) Sales Commission Expense	5,077

Required

1. Determine the missing amounts on lines (2), (3), (5), and (10).
2. Prepare the general journal entry to record The Art Center's payroll for the month. Credit Payrolls Payable for net pay. No explanation is required.

Problem 10-4B   *Computing and recording payroll amounts*   **(L.O. 3,4)**

Assume that Seth Reichlin is a vice-president of Bank of America's leasing operations in San Francisco. During 19X6 he worked for the company all year at a $3,625 monthly salary. He also earned a year-end bonus equal to 10 percent of his salary.

Reichlin's federal income tax withheld during 19X6 was $537 per month. Also, there was a one-time federal withholding tax of $1,007 on his bonus check. State income tax withheld came to $43 per month, and there was a one-time state withholding tax of $27 on the bonus. The FICA tax withheld was 8.0 percent of the first $50,000 in annual earnings. Reichlin authorized the following payroll deductions: United Fund contribution of 1 percent of total earnings, and life insurance of $19 per month.

Bank of America incurred payroll tax expense on Reichlin for FICA tax of 8 percent of the first $50,000 in annual earnings. The bank also paid state unemployment tax of 5.4 percent and federal unemployment tax of 0.8 percent on the first $7,000 in annual earnings. In addition, the bank provides Reichlin with health insurance at a cost of $35 per month and pension benefits. During 19X6 Bank of America paid $7,178 into Reichlin's pension program.

Required

1. Compute Reichlin's gross pay, payroll deductions, and net pay for the full year 19X6. Round all amounts to the nearest dollar.
2. Compute Bank of America's total 19X6 payroll cost for Reichlin.
3. Prepare Bank of America's summary general journal entries to record its expense for
   a. Reichlin's total earnings for the year, his payroll deductions, and his net pay. Debit Salary Expense and Executive Bonus Compensation as appropriate. Credit liability accounts for the payroll deductions and Cash for net pay.
   b. Employer payroll taxes on Reichlin. Credit liability accounts.
   c. Fringe benefit provided to Reichlin. Credit a liability account.
   Explanations are not required.

Problem 10-5B   *Selecting the correct data to record a payroll*   **(L.O. 4)**

Assume that the accompanying payroll information appeared in the records of *Car and Driver* magazine.

	Payroll for Week Ended Friday March 31, 19X9	Payroll for Month of March 19X9
Salaries:		
Editorial salaries	$6,203	$27,178
Warehousing salaries	3,118	13,128
Deductions:		
Employee federal income tax	1,115	5,612
FICA tax	641	2,699
Employee health insurance	481	2,025
Employee contributions to United Fund	367	1,545
Employee U.S. savings bonds	288	1,213
Net pay	6,429	27,212
Employer payroll taxes:		
FICA tax	641	2,699
State unemployment tax	520	2,160
Federal unemployment tax	77	320
Employer cost of fringe benefits for employees:		
Health insurance	663	2,458
Life insurance	324	1,368
Pensions	451	1,899

Required

1. Prepare the general journal entries to record the payroll for the week ended March 31, including payroll taxes and fringe benefits.

2. Prepare the general journal entry to record the payment of the week's salaries to employees on March 31.

3. Assume that *Car and Driver* pays all its liabilities to the federal government in a single monthly amount. Prepare the general journal entry to record the April 1, 19X9, payment of federal taxes. (Liabilities to the federal government include FICA taxes and those items with *federal* and *U.S.* in the account title.)

4. Assume that *Car and Driver* pays all other payroll liabilities shortly after the end of the month. Prepare a single general journal entry to record the April 4 payment for these March liabilities.

Explanations are not required for journal entries.

Problem 10-6B *Journalizing, posting, and reporting liabilities* (L.O. 1,2,4,6)

The general ledger of Tea Rose, Inc., at June 30, 19X3, end of the company's fiscal year, includes the following account balances before adjusting entries. Parentheses indicate a debit balance.

Notes Payable, Short-Term	$ 25,000	Employee Benefits Payable	$ _____
Discount on Notes Payable	(900)	Estimated Vacation Pay	
Accounts Payable	105,520	Liability	7,620
Current Portion of Long-		Sales Tax Payable	738
Term Debt Payable	_____	Customer Deposits	
Interest Payable	_____	Payable	6,950
Salary Payable	_____	Unearned Rent Revenue . .	4,800
Employee Payroll		Long-Term Debt Payable . .	120,000
Taxes Payable	_____	Contingent Liabilities	_____
Employer Payroll			
Taxes Payable	_____		

The additional data needed to develop the adjusting entries at June 30 are as follows:

a. The $25,000 balance in Notes Payable, Short-Term consists of two notes. The first note, with a principal amount of $15,000, was issued on January 31. It matures six months from date of issuance and was discounted at 12 percent. The second note, with a principal amount of $10,000, was issued on April 22 for a term of 90 days. It bears interest at 10 percent. It was not discounted. Interest on this note will be paid at maturity.

b. The long-term debt is payable in annual installments of $40,000 with the next installment due on July 31. On that date, Tea Rose will also pay one year's interest at 9 percent. Interest was last paid on July 31 of the preceding year. To shift the current installment of the long-term debt to a current liability, debit Long-Term Debt Payable and credit Current Portion of Long-Term Debt Payable.

c. Gross salaries for the last payroll of the fiscal year were $5,044. Of this amount, employee payroll taxes payable were $1,088, and salary payable was $3,956.

d. Employer payroll taxes payable were $876, and Tea Rose's liability for employee health insurance was $1,046.

e. Tea Rose estimates that vacation pay expense is 4 percent of gross salaries.

f. On February 1 the company collected one year's rent of $4,800 in advance.

g. At June 30 Tea Rose is the defendant in a $500,000 lawsuit, which the company expects to win. However, the outcome is uncertain. Tea Rose reports contingent liabilities short, with an explanatory note.

Required

1. Open the listed accounts, inserting their unadjusted June 30 balances.
2. Journalize and post the June 30 adjusting entries to the accounts opened. Key adjusting entries by letter.
3. Prepare the liability section of the balance sheet at June 30.

Problem 10-7B *Using payroll register; recording a payroll* *(L.O. 5)*

Assume that the payroll records of a district sales office of Liquid Paper Corporation provided the following information for the weekly pay period ended December 21, 19X5:

Employee	Hours Worked	Hourly Earnings Rate	Federal Income Tax	Union Dues	United Way Contributions	Earnings Through Previous Week
Lance Blanks	42	$18	$153	$6	$5	$52,474
James English	47	8	56	4	4	23,154
Louise French	40	11	72	—	4	4,880
Roberto Garza	41	22	188	6	8	49,600

James English and Louise French work in the office, and Lance Blanks and Roberto Garza work in sales. All employees are paid time and a half for hours worked in excess of 40 per week. For convenience, round all amounts to the nearest dollar. Show computations. Explanations are not required for journal entries.

Required

1. Enter the appropriate information in a payroll register similar to Exhibit 10-5. In addition to the deductions listed, the employer also takes out FICA tax: 8 percent of the first $50,000 of each employee's annual earnings.
2. Record the payroll information in the general journal.
3. Assume that the first payroll check is number 319, paid to Lance Blanks. Record the check numbers in the payroll register. Also, prepare the general journal entry to record payment of net pay to the employees.
4. The employer's payroll taxes include FICA tax of 8 percent of the first $50,000 of each employee's earnings. The employer also pays unemployment taxes of 6.2 percent (5.4 percent for the state and 0.8 percent for the federal government on the first $7,000 of each employee's annual earnings). Record the employer's payroll taxes in the general journal.

Problem 10-8B *Reporting current liabilities* *(L.O. 6)*

Following are six pertinent facts about events during the current year at Herbissimo Fragrances.

1. On September 30, Herbissimo signed a six-month, 9 percent note payable to purchase inventory costing $30,000. The note requires payment of principal and interest at maturity.
2. On October 31, Herbissimo discounted a $50,000 note payable to Lake Air National Bank. The interest rate on the one-year note is 10 percent.
3. On November 30, Herbissimo received rent of $4,200 in advance for a lease on a building. This rent will be earned evenly over three months.

4. December sales totaled $38,000 and Herbissimo collected an additional state sales tax of 7 percent. This amount will be sent to the state of Arizona early in January.

5. Herbissimo owes $100,000 on a long-term note payable. At December 31, $20,000 of this principal plus $2,100 of accrued interest are payable within one year.

6. Sales of $430,000 were covered by Herbissimo's product warranty. At January 1, estimated warranty payable was $8,100. During the year Herbissimo recorded warranty expense of $22,300 and paid warranty claims of $23,600.

Required

For each item, indicate the account and the related amount to be reported as a current liability on Herbissimo's December 31 balance sheet.

Extending Your Knowledge

Decision Problems

1. Identifying Internal Control Weaknesses and their Solution   (L.O. 5)

Hall Custom Homes is a large home-building business in Phoenix, Arizona. The owner and manager is Lawrence Hall, who oversees all company operations. He employs 15 work crews, each made up of 6 to 10 members. Construction supervisors, who report directly to Hall, lead the crews. Most supervisors are longtime employees, so Hall trusts them greatly. Hall's office staff consists of an accountant and an office manager.

Because employee turnover is rapid in the construction industry, supervisors hire and terminate their own crew members. Supervisors notify the office of all personnel changes. Also, supervisors forward to the office the employee W-4 forms, which the crew members fill out to claim tax-withholding exemptions. Each Thursday the supervisors submit weekly time sheets for their crews, and the accountant prepares the payroll. At noon on Friday the supervisors come to the office to get paychecks for distribution to the workers at 5 P.M.

Hall's accountant prepares the payroll, including the payroll checks, which are written on a single payroll bank account. Hall signs all payroll checks after matching the employee name to the time sheets submitted by the foremen. Often the construction workers wait several days to cash their paychecks. To verify that each construction worker is a bona-fide employee, the accountant matches the employee's endorsement signature on the back of the canceled payroll check with the signature on that employee's W-4 form.

Required

1. List one *efficiency* weakness in Hall's payroll accounting system. How can Hall correct this weakness?
2. Identify one way that a supervisor can defraud Hall under the present system.
3. Discuss a control feature Hall can use to *safeguard* against the fraud you identified in Requirement 2.

2. Questions About Liabilities (L.O. 1,2)

The following questions are not related.

a. A friend comments that he thought liabilities represented amounts owed by a company and asks why unearned revenues are shown as a current liability. How would you respond?

b. A warranty is like a contingent liability in that the amount to be paid is not known at year end. Why are warranties payable shown as a current liability while contingent liabilities are reported in the notes to the financial statements?

c. Auditors have procedures for determining whether they have discovered all of a company's contingent liabilities. These procedures differ from the procedures used for determining that accounts payable are correctly stated. If you were an auditor, how would you go about identifying a client's contingent liabilities?

Ethical Issue

IBM is the defendant in numerous lawsuits claiming unfair trade practices. IBM has strong incentives not to disclose these contingent liabilities. However, generally accepted accounting principles require companies to report their contingent liabilities.

Required

1. State why a company would prefer not to disclose its contingent liabilities.
2. Describe how a bank could be harmed if a company seeking a loan did not disclose its contingent liabilities.
3. What is the ethical tightrope that a company must walk in reporting its contingent liabilities?

Financial Statement Problems

1. Current and Contingent Liabilities and Payroll (L.O. 1,2,6)

Details about a company's current and contingent liabilities and payroll costs appear in a number of places in the annual report. Use the Goodyear Tire & Rubber Company financial statements to answer these questions.

1. Give the breakdown of Goodyear's current liabilities at December 31, 1991. Give the 1992 entry to record the payment of December 31, 1991, accounts payable.
2. How much of Goodyear's long-term debt at December 31, 1991, was due within one year? In the Credit Arrangements note, which liabilities were obviously included in the portion due within one year?
3. Does Goodyear use a short presentation for contingent liabilities? Where does the company report contingencies? What is the Goodyear management opinion as to the ultimate effect of lawsuits pending against the company?
4. The balance sheet lists a $352.8 million liability for "Accrued payrolls and other compensation." Was compensation expense for the year equal to, less than, or greater than this amount? Give your reason.

2. Current and Contingent Liabilities and Payroll (L.O. 1,2,6)

Obtain the annual report of an actual company of your choosing. Details about the company's current and contingent liabilities and payroll costs may appear in a number of places in the annual report. Use the statements of the company you select to answer these questions. Concentrate on the current year in the annual report.

1. Give the breakdown of the company's current liabilities at the end of the current year. Journalize the payment in the following year of Accounts Payable reported on the balance sheet.
2. How much of the company's long-term debt at the end of the current year was reported as a current liability? Do the notes to the financial statements identify the specific items of long-term debt coming due within the next year? If so, identify the specific liabilities.
3. Identify the payroll-related current liability at the end of the current year. Give its amount, and record its payment in the next year.
4. Does the company report any unearned revenue? If so, identify the item and give its amount.
5. Where does the company report contingent liabilities—on the face of the balance sheet or in a note? Give important details about the company's contingent liabilities at the end of the current year.

Comprehensive Problem for Part Three

Comparing Two Businesses

At age 25, you invented a mechanical pencil that is now being sold worldwide. After laboring diligently for several years, you have recently sold the business to a large company. Now you are ready to invest in a small resort property located where the golf is great and your family and friends will enjoy visiting. Several locations fit this description: Jekyll Island, Georgia; Lakeway, Texas; and La Jolla, California. Each place has its appeal, but Lakeway finally wins out. The main allure is that prices there are low, so a dollar will stretch further. Two small resorts are available, both with access to a golf course designed by Jack Nicklaus. The property owners provide the following data:

	Lakeway Resort	Texas Hideaway
Cash	$ 44,100	$ 63,800
Accounts receivable	20,500	18,300
Inventory	74,200	68,400
Land	270,600	269,200
Buildings	1,880,000	1,960,000
Accumulated depreciation	(350,000)	(822,600)
Furniture and fixtures	740,000	933,000
Accumulated depreciation	(207,000)	416,300)
Total assets	$2,472,400	$2,073,800
Total liabilities	$1,124,300	$1,008,500
Owner equity	1,348,100	1,065,300
Total liabilities and owner equity	$2,472,400	$2,073,800

Income statements for the last three years report total net income of $441,000 for Lakeway Resorts and $283,000 for Texas Hideaway.

Inventories.   Lakeway Resorts uses the FIFO inventory method, and Texas Hideaway uses the LIFO method. If Lakeway had used LIFO, its reported inventory would have been $7,000 lower. If Texas Hideaway had used FIFO, its reported inventory would have been $6,000 higher. Three years ago there was little difference between LIFO and FIFO amounts for either company.

Plant Assets.   Lakeway uses the straight-line depreciation method and an estimated useful life of 40 years for buildings and 10 years for furniture and fixtures. Estimated residual values are $480,000 for buildings and $50,000 for furniture and fixtures. Lakeway's buildings are 10 years old, and the furniture and fixtures have been used for 3 years.

Texas Hideaway uses the sum-of-years-digits method and depreciates buildings over 30 years with an estimated residual value of $460,000. The furniture and fixtures, now 3 years old, are being depreciated over 10 years with an estimated residual value of $85,000.

Accounts Receivable.   Lakeway Resort uses the direct write-off method for uncollectibles. Texas Hideaway uses the allowance method. The Lakeway owner estimates that $2,000 of Lakeway's receivables are doubtful. Prior to the current year, uncollectibles were insignificant. Texas Hideaway's receivables are already reported at net realizable value.

Required

1. Puzzled at first by how to compare the two resorts, you decide to convert Lakeway Resort's balance sheet to the accounting methods and the estimated useful lives used by Texas Hideaway. Round all depreciation amounts to the nearest $100. The necessary revisions will not affect Lakeway's total liabilities.
2. Convert Lakeway's total net income for the last three years to reflect the accounting methods used by Texas Hideaway. Round all depreciation amounts to the nearest $100.
3. Compare the pictures of the two resorts after revising Lakeway's figures with the pictures of the two resorts beforehand. Which resort looked better at the outset? Which resort looks better when they are placed on equal footing?

Chapter 11

Long-Term Liabilities

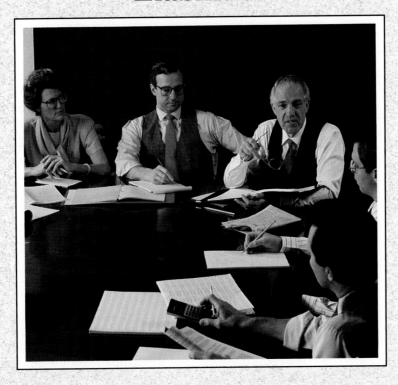

The tension was easily felt . . . when the top financial executives from IBM met with investment advisers from the brokerage firms of Merrill Lynch and Salomon Brothers. The purpose of their meeting was to price the largest public debt offering in U.S. corporate history.

Those attending the meeting were well aware of the numerous economic shocks that had recently hit the financial world: rapidly rising interest rates, falling stock and bond prices, gold and silver selling at record high prices, and the U.S. dollar sinking in value in foreign exchange markets. In the midst of this, the world's largest computer and business equipment company was going to the public debt market for the first time in its corporate history in an effort to borrow $1 billion. The public offering by IBM was to consist of $500 million in 7-year notes and $500 million in 25-year debentures. Because of the rapidly changing economic environment, the small group of executives and investment bankers felt a need to act quickly on the deal.

Source: Kenneth R. Ferris, *Financial Accounting and Corporate Reporting: A Casebook*, 2nd ed. (Homewood, IL: BPI, 1989), p. 184. Used with permission of the author.

Corporations may finance—that is, raise money for—their operations in different ways. They may issue stock to their owners, and they may reinvest assets earned by profitable operations, as we have seen. This chapter discusses the third way of financing operations, **long-term liabilities.**

Two common long-term liabilities are notes payable and bonds payable. A note payable, which we studied in Chapter 10, is a promissory note issued by the company to borrow money from a single lender, like a bank or an insurance company. **Bonds payable** are groups of notes payable issued to multiple lenders, called bondholders. This chapter also discusses accounting for lease liabilities and pension liabilities.

The Nature of Bonds

A company needing millions of dollars may be unable to borrow so large an amount from a single lender. To gain access to more investors, the company may issue bonds. Each bond is, in effect, a long-term note payable that bears interest. Bonds are debts of the company for the amounts borrowed from the investors.

Purchasers of bonds receive a bond certificate, which carries the issuing company's name. The certificate also states the *principal,* which is the amount that the company has borrowed from the bondholder. This figure, typically stated in units of $1,000, is also called the bond's face value, maturity value, or par value. The bond obligates the issuing company to pay the holder the principal amount at a specific future date, called the maturity date, which also appears on the certificate.

Bondholders loan their money to companies for a price: interest on the principal. The bond certificate states the interest rate that the issuer will pay the holder and the dates that the interest payments are due (generally twice a year). Some bond certificates name the bondholder (the investor). When the company pays back the principal, the holder returns the certificate, which the company retires (or cancels). Exhibit 11-1 shows an actual bond certificate, with the various features highlighted.

The board of directors may authorize a bond issue. In some companies the stockholders—as owners—may also have to vote their approval.

Issuing bonds usually requires the services of a securities firm, like Merrill Lynch, to act as the *underwriter* of the bond issue. The **underwriter** purchases the bonds from the issuing company and resells them to its clients, or it may sell the bonds for a commission from the issuer, agreeing to buy all unsold bonds.

EXHIBIT 11-1 *Bond (Note) Certificate*

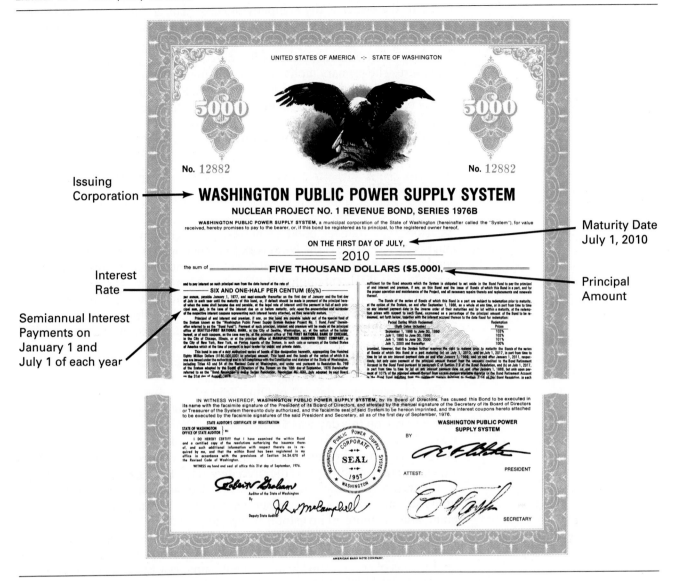

Issuing Corporation → **WASHINGTON PUBLIC POWER SUPPLY SYSTEM**

Maturity Date July 1, 2010

Principal Amount

Interest Rate → SIX AND ONE-HALF PER CENTUM (6½%)

Semiannual Interest Payments on January 1 and July 1 of each year

Types of Bonds

Bonds may be *registered* bonds or *coupon* bonds. The owner of a **registered bond** receives interest checks from the issuing company, which keeps a listing of the names and addresses of the bondholders. Owners of **coupon bonds** receive interest by detaching a perforated coupon—which states the interest due and the date of payment—from the bond and depositing it in a bank for collection. A company with coupon bonds needs no registry of bondholders. The responsibility for cashing coupons rests with the bondholders. Most bonds issued today are registered.

All the bonds in a particular issue may mature at the same time (**term bonds**), or they may mature in installments over a period of time (**serial bonds**). By issuing serial bonds, the company spreads its principal payments over time and avoids paying the entire principal at one time. Serial bonds are like installment notes payable.

assets that used for specific fees security

Secured, or mortgage, bonds give the bondholder the right to take specified assets of the issuer if the company defaults, that is, fails to pay interest or principal. Unsecured bonds, called **debentures,** are backed only by the good faith of the borrower.

A secured bond is not necessarily more attractive to an investor than is a debenture. The primary motive of a person investing in bonds is to receive the interest amounts and the bonds' maturity value on time. Thus a debenture from a business with an excellent record in meeting obligations may be more attractive to an investor than a secured bond from a business that has just been started or that has a bad credit record.

Bond Prices

Investors may transfer bond ownership through bond markets. The most famous bond market is the New York Exchange, which lists several thousand bonds. Bond prices are quoted at a percentage of their maturity value. For example, a $1,000 bond quoted at 100 is bought or sold for $1,000, which is 100 percent of its par value. The same bond quoted at 101½ has a market price of $1,015 (101.5 percent of par value, or $1,000 × 1.015). Prices are quoted to the 8th of 1 percent. A $1,000 bond quoted at 88⅜ is priced at $883.75 ($1,000 × .88375).

Exhibit 11-2 contains actual price information for the bonds of Ohio Edison Company, taken from *The Wall Street Journal.*

On this particular day, 12 of Ohio Edison's 9½ percent, $1,000 par value bonds maturing in the year 2006 (indicated by 06) were traded. The bonds' highest price on this day was $795 ($1,000 × .795). The lowest price of the day was $785 ($1,000 × .785). The closing price (last sale of the day) was $795. This price was 2 points higher than the closing price of the preceding day. What was the bonds' closing price the preceding day? It was 77½ (79½ − 2).

The factors that affect the market price of a bond include the length of time until the bond matures. The sooner the maturity date, the more attractive the bond, and the more an investor is willing to pay for it. Also, the bonds issued by a company with a proven ability to meet all payments commands a higher price than an issue from a company with a poor record. Bond price hinges too on the rates of other available investment plans. Is a 12 percent bond the best way to invest $1,000, or does another investment strategy pay a higher rate? Of course, the higher the percentage rate, the higher the market price. Buying a 13 percent bond will cost you more than buying an 8 percent bond, given that both issues have the same maturity date and have been issued by equally sound businesses.

A bond issued at a price above its maturity (par) value is said to be issued at a **premium,** and a bond issued at a price below maturity (par) value has a **discount.** As a bond nears maturity, its market price moves toward par value. On the maturity date the market value of a bond exactly equals its par value because the company that issued the bond pays that amount to retire the bond.

EXHIBIT 11-2   *Bond Price Information*

Bonds	Volume	High	Low	Close	Net Change
OhEd 9½ 06	12	79½	78½	79½	+2

Present Value

A dollar received today is worth more than a dollar received in the future. You may invest today's dollar and earn income from it. Likewise, deferring any payment gives your money a longer period to grow. Money earns income over time, a fact called the *time value of money*. Let's examine how the time value of money affects the pricing of bonds.

Assume a bond with a face value of $1,000 reaches maturity three years from today and carries no interest. Would you pay $1,000 to purchase the bond? No, because the payment of $1,000 today to receive the same amount in the future provides you with no income on the investment. You would not be taking advantage of the time value of money. Just how much would you pay today in order to receive $1,000 at the end of three years? The answer is some amount *less* than $1,000. Let's suppose that you feel $750 is a good price. By investing $750 now to receive $1,000 later, you earn $250 interest revenue over the three years. The issuing company sees the transaction this way: It pays you $250 interest for the use of your $750 for three years.

The amount that a person would invest *at the present time* to receive a greater amount at a future date is called the **present value** of a future amount. In our example, $750 is the present value of the $1,000 amount to be received three years later.

Our $750 bond price is a reasonable estimate. The exact present value of any future amount depends on (1) the amount of the future payment (or receipt), (2) the length of time from the investment to the date when the future amount is to be received (or paid), and (3) the interest rate during the period. Present value is always less than the future amount. We discuss the method of computing present value in Appendix A. We need to be aware of the present-value concept, however, in the discussion of bond prices that follows.

Bond Interest Rates

Bonds are sold at market price, which is the amount that investors are willing to pay at any given time. Market price is the bond's present value, which equals the present value of the principal payment plus the present value of the cash interest payments (which are made semiannually, annually, or quarterly over the term of the bond).

Two interest rates work to set the price of a bond. The **contract interest rate,** or **stated rate,** is the interest rate that determines the amount of cash interest the borrower pays—and the investor receives—each year. For example, Chrysler's 8 percent bonds have a contract interest rate of 8 percent. Thus Chrysler pays $8,000 of interest annually on each $100,000 bond. Each semi-annual interest payment is $4,000 ($100,000 × .08 × ½).

The **market interest rate,** or **effective rate,** is the rate that investors demand for loaning their money. The market rate varies, sometimes daily. A company may issue bonds with a contract interest rate that differs from the prevailing market interest rate. Chrysler may issue its 8 percent bonds when the market rate has risen to 9 percent. Will the Chrysler bonds attract investors in this market? No, because investors can earn 9 percent on other bonds of similar risk. Therefore, investors will purchase Chrysler bonds only at a price less than par value. The difference between the lower price and face value is a *discount.* Conversely, if the market interest rate is 7 percent, Chrysler's 8 percent bonds will be so attractive that investors will pay more than face value for them. The difference between the higher price and face value is a *premium.*

Issuing Bonds Payable

Suppose Chrysler Corporation has $50 million in 8 percent bonds that mature in 10 years. Assume that Chrysler issues these bonds at par on January 1, 1992. The issuance entry is

1992
Jan. 1 Cash 50,000,000
                 Bonds Payable   50,000,000
           To issue 8%, 10-year bonds at par.

The corporation that is borrowing money makes a one-time entry similar to this to record the receipt of cash and the issuance of bonds. Afterward, investors buy and sell the bonds through the bond markets. The buy-and-sell transactions between investors do not involve the corporation that issued the bonds. It keeps no records of these transactions, except for the names and addresses of the bondholders. This information is needed for mailing the interest and principal payments.

Interest payments occur each January 1 and July 1. Chrysler's entry to record the first semiannual interest payment is

1992
July 1 Interest Expense ($50,000,000 × .08 × 6/12) 2,000,000
                 Cash   2,000,000
           To pay semiannual interest on bonds payable.

At maturity, Chrysler will record payment of the bonds as follows:

2002
Jan. 1 Bonds Payable 50,000,000
                 Cash   50,000,000
           To pay bonds payable at maturity.

Issuing Bonds Payable between Interest Dates

The foregoing entries to record Chrysler's bond transactions are straightforward because the company issued the bonds on an interest payment date (January 1). However, corporations often issue bonds between interest dates.

Suppose Cincinnati Milacron, Inc., issues $75 million of 12 percent debentures due June 15, 2012. These bonds are dated June 15, 1992, and carry the price "100 plus accrued interest from date of original issue." An investor purchasing the bonds after the bond date must pay market value *plus accrued interest.* The issuing company will pay the full semiannual interest amount to the bondholder at the next interest payment date. Companies do not split semiannual interest payments among two or more investors who happen to hold the bonds during a particular six-month interest period.

Assume that Cincinnati Milacron sells $100,000 of its bonds on July 15, 1992, one month after the date of original issue on June 15. Also assume that the market price of the bonds on July 15 is the face value. The company receives one month's accrued interest in addition to the bond's face value. Cincinnati's entry to record issuance of the bonds payable is

1992

July 15	Cash	101,000	
	Bonds Payable		100,000
	Interest Payable ($100,000 × .12 ×$1/12$) .		1,000
	To issue 12%, 20-year bonds at par, one month after the original issue date.		

Cincinnati's entry to record the first semiannual interest payment is

1992

Dec. 15	Interest Expense ($100,000 × .12 × $5/12$)	5,000	
	Interest Payable	1,000	
	Cash ($100,000 × .12 × $6/12$)..........		6,000
	To pay semiannual interest on bonds payable.		

The debit to Interest Payable eliminates the credit balance in that account (from July 15). Cincinnati has now paid off that liability.

Note that Cincinnati Milacron pays a full six months' interest on December 15. After subtracting the one month's accrued interest received at the time of issuing the bond, Cincinnati has recorded interest expense for five months ($5,000). This interest expense is the correct amount for the five months that the bonds have been outstanding.

Selling bonds between interest dates at market value plus accrued interest simplifies the borrower's bookkeeping. The business pays the same amount of interest on each bond regardless of the length of time the person has held the bond. The business need not compute each bondholder's interest payment on an individual basis. Imagine the paperwork necessary to keep track of the interest due hundreds of bondholders who each bought bonds on a different date.

When an investor sells bonds to another investor, the price is always "plus accrued interest." Suppose you hold bonds as an investment for two months of a semiannual interest period and sell the bonds to another investor before receiving your interest. The person who buys the bonds will receive your two months of interest on the next specified interest date. Business practice dictates that you must collect your share of the interest from the buyer when you sell the bonds. For this reason, all bond transactions are "plus accrued interest."

Issuing Bonds Payable at a Discount

We know that market conditions may force the issuing corporation to accept a discount price for its bonds. Suppose Chrysler issues $100,000 of its 8 percent, 10-year bonds when the market interest rate is slightly above 8 percent. The market price of the bonds drops to 98, which means 98 percent of par value. Chrysler receives $98,000 ($100,000 × .98) at issuance. The entry is

1992

Jan. 1	Cash ($100,000 × .98)	98,000	
	Discount on Bonds Payable	2,000	
	Bonds Payable		100,000
	To issue 8%, 10-year bonds at a discount.		

After posting, the bond accounts have the following balances:

Bonds Payable	Discount on Bonds Payable
100,000	2,000

Chrysler's balance sheet immediately after issuance of the bonds reports:

Long-term liabilities:
Bonds payable, 8%, due 2002. . . . . $100,000
Less: Discount on bonds payable 2,000 $98,000

Discount on Bonds Payable is a contra account to Bonds Payable. Subtracting its balance from Bonds Payable yields the book value, or carrying amount, of the bonds. The relationship between Bonds Payable and the Discount account is similar to the relationships between Equipment and Accumulated Depreciation and between Accounts Receivable and Allowance for Uncollectible Accounts. Thus Chrysler's liability is $98,000, which is the amount the company borrowed. If Chrysler were to pay off the bonds immediately (an unlikely occurrence), Chrysler's required outlay would be $98,000 because the market price of the bonds is $98,000.

Interest Expense on Bonds Issued at a Discount. We earlier discussed the difference between the contract interest rate and the market interest rate. Suppose the market rate is 8¼ percent when Chrysler issues its 8 percent bonds. The ¼ percent interest rate difference creates the $2,000 discount on the bonds. Chrysler borrows $98,000 cash but must pay $100,000 cash when the bonds mature, 10 years later. What happens to the $2,000 balance of the discount account over the life of the bond issue?

The $2,000 discount is really an additional interest expense to the issuing company. That amount is a cost—beyond the stated interest rate—that the business pays for borrowing the investors' money.

The discount amount is an interest expense not paid until the bond matures. However, the borrower—the bond issuer—benefits from the use of the investors' money each accounting period over the full term of the bond issue. The matching principle directs the business to match expense against its revenues on a period-by-period basis. The discount is allocated to interest expense through amortization each accounting period over the life of the bonds.

STRAIGHT-LINE AMORTIZATION OF DISCOUNT. We may amortize bond discount by dividing it into equal amounts for each interest period. This method is called straight-line amortization. In our example, the beginning discount is $2,000, and there are 20 semiannual interest periods during the bonds' 10-year life. Therefore, ¹⁄₂₀ of the $2,000 ($100) of bond discount is amortized each interest period. Chrysler's semiannual interest entry on July 1, 1992, is

OBJECTIVE 1

Account for basic bonds payable transactions using the straight-line amortization method

1992
July 1 Interest Expense   4,100
                  Cash ($100,000 × .08 × ⁶⁄₁₂)   4,000
                  Discount on Bonds Payable ($2,000/20)   100
          To pay semiannual interest and amortize
          discount on bonds payable.

Interest expense of $4,100 is the sum of the contract interest ($4,000, which is paid in cash) plus the amount of discount amortized ($100). Discount on Bonds Payable is credited to amortize (reduce) the account's debit balance.

Because Discount on Bonds Payable is a contra account, each reduction in its balance increases the book value of Bonds Payable. Twenty amortization entries will decrease the discount balance to zero, which means that the carrying amount of Bonds Payable will have increased by $2,000 up to its face value of $100,000. The entry to pay off the bonds at maturity is

2002

Jan. 1	Bonds Payable............................	100,000	
	Cash..................................		100,000
	To pay bonds payable at maturity.		

Issuing Bonds Payable at a Premium

To illustrate issuing bonds at a premium, let's change the Chrysler example. Assume that the market interest rate is 7½ percent when the company issues its 8 percent, 10-year bonds. Because 8 percent bonds are attractive in this market, investors pay a premium price to acquire them. If the bonds are priced at 103½ (103.5 percent of par value), Chrysler receives $103,500 cash upon issuance. The entry is

1992

Jan. 1	Cash ($100,000 × 1.035)	103,500	
	Bonds Payable		100,000
	Premium on Bonds Payable		3,500
	To issue 8%, 10-year bonds at a premium.		

After posting, the bond accounts have the following balances:

Bonds Payable	Premium on Bonds Payable
100,000	3,500

Chrysler's balance sheet immediately after issuance of the bonds reports:

Long-term liabilities:		
Bonds payable, 8%, due 2002........	$100,000	
Premium on bonds payable	3,500	$103,500

Premium on Bonds Payable is added to Bonds Payable to show the book value, or carrying amount, of the bonds. Chrysler's liability is $103,500, which is the amount that the company borrowed. Immediate payment of the bonds would require an outlay of $103,500 because the market price of the bonds at issuance is $103,500. The investors would be unwilling to give up the bonds for less than their market value.

Interest Expense on Bonds Issued at a Premium. The ½ percent difference between the 8 percent contract rate on the bonds and the 7½ percent market interest rate creates the $3,500 premium. Chrysler borrows $103,500 cash but must pay only $100,000 cash at maturity. We treat the premium as a savings of interest expense to Chrysler. The premium cuts Chrysler's cost of borrowing the money. We account for the premium much as we handled the discount. We amortize the bond premium as a decrease in interest expense over the life of the bonds.

STRAIGHT-LINE AMORTIZATION OF PREMIUM. In our example, the beginning premium is $3,500, and there are 20 semiannual interest periods during the bonds' 10-year life. Therefore, 1/20 of the $3,500 ($175) of bond premium is amortized each interest period. Chrysler's semiannual interest entry on July 1, 1992, is

```
1992
July 1   Interest Expense ...........................   3,825
            Premium on Bonds Payable ($3,500/20) ........     175
               Cash ($100,000 × .08 × 6/12) .............           4,000
         To pay semiannual interest and amortize
         premium on bonds payable.
```

Interest expense of $3,825 is the remainder of the contract cash interest ($4,000) less the amount of premium amortized ($175). The debit to Premium on Bonds Payable reduces its credit balance.

Reporting Bonds Payable

Bonds payable are reported on the balance sheet at their maturity amount plus any unamortized premium or minus any unamortized discount. For example, at December 31, Chrysler in the preceding example would have amortized Premium on Bonds Payable for two semiannual periods ($175 × 2 = $350). The Chrysler balance sheet would show these bonds payable as follows:

```
Long-term liabilities:
   Bonds payable, 8%, due 2002 ...................   $100,000
   Premium on bonds payable [$3,500 − (2 × $175)] ..      3,150   $103,150
```

Over the life of the bonds, twenty amortization entries will decrease the premium balance to zero. The payment at maturity will debit Bonds Payable and credit cash for $100,000.

Adjusting Entries for Interest Expense _____

Companies issue bonds when they need cash. The interest payments seldom occur on December 31 (or the end of the fiscal year). Nevertheless, interest expense must be accrued at the end of the period to measure income accurately. The accrual entry may often be complicated by the need to amortize a discount or a premium for only a partial interest period.

Suppose Xenon, Inc., issues $100,000 of its 8 percent, 10-year bonds at a $2,000 discount on October 1, 1992. Assume that interest payments occur on March 31 and September 30 each year. On December 31 Xenon records interest for the three-month period (October, November, and December) as follows:

```
1992
Dec. 31   Interest Expense ..................................   2,050
             Interest Payable ($100,000 × .08 × 3/12) .........         2,000
             Discount on Bonds Payable ($2,000/10 × 3/12) ....            50
          To accrue three months' interest and amortize
          discount on bonds payable for three months.
```

Interest Payable is credited for the three months of cash interest that have accrued since September 30. Discount on Bonds Payable is credited for three months of amortization.

The balance sheet at December 31, 1992, reports Interest Payable of $2,000 as a current liability. Bonds Payable appears as a long-term liability, presented as follows:

Long-term liabilities:
Bonds payable, 8%, due 2002 . . . . $100,000
Less: Discount on bonds payable ($2,000 − $50) . . <u>1,950</u> $98,050

Observe that the balance of Discount on Bonds Payable decreases by $50. The bonds' carrying amount also increases by $50. The bonds' carrying amount continues to increase over its 10-year life, reaching $100,000 at maturity, when the discount will be fully amortized.

The next semiannual interest payment occurs on March 31, 1993:

1993
Mar. 31 Interest Expense 2,050
          Interest Payable 2,000
              Cash ($100,000 × .08 × 6/12) 4,000
              Discount on Bonds Payable ($2,000/10 × 3/12) 50
          To pay semiannual interest, part of which was
          accrued, and amortize three months' discount on
          bonds payable.

Amortization of a premium over a partial interest period is similar except that Premium on Bonds Payable is debited.

Summary Problem for Your Review

Assume that Alabama Power Company has outstanding an issue of 9 percent bonds that mature on May 1, 2013. Further, assume that the bonds are dated May 1, 1993, and Alabama Power pays interest each April 30 and October 31.

Required

1. Will the bonds be issued at par, at a premium, or at a discount if the market interest rate is 8 percent at date of issuance? if the market interest rate is 10 percent?
2. Assume Alabama Power issued $1,000,000 of the bonds at 104 on May 1, 1993.
   a. Record issuance of the bonds.
   b. Record the interest payment and amortization of premium or discount on October 31, 1993.
   c. Accrue interest and amortize premium or discount on December 31, 1993.
   d. Show how the company would report the bonds on the balance sheet at December 31, 1993.
   e. Record the interest payment on April 30, 1994.

SOLUTION TO REVIEW PROBLEM

Requirement 1.   If the market interest rate is 8 percent, 9 percent bonds will be issued at a *premium*. If the market rate is 10 percent, the 9 percent bonds will be issued at a *discount*.

Requirement 2

```
        1993
a. May   1   Cash ($1,000,000 × 1.04) . . . . . . . . . . . . . .   1,040,000
                 Bonds Payable . . . . . . . . . . . . . . . . .                  1,000,000
                 Premium on Bonds Payable . . . . . . .                             40,000
             To issue 9%, 20-year bonds at a premium.

b. Oct. 31   Interest Expense . . . . . . . . . . . . . . . . . . . . . .   44,000
             Premium on Bonds Payable ($40,000/40) .    1,000
                 Cash ($1,000,000 × .09 × ⁶⁄₁₂) . . . . .                           45,000
             To pay semiannual interest and amortize
             premium on bonds payable.

c. Dec. 31   Interest Expense . . . . . . . . . . . . . . . . . . . . . .   14,667
             Premium on Bonds Payable
             ($40,000/40 × ²⁄₆) . . . . . . . . . . . . . . . . . . . . .      333
                 Interest Payable
                 ($1,000,000 × .09 × ²⁄₁₂) . . . . . . . . . . .                    15,000
             To accrue interest and amortize bond
             premium for two months.

d. Long-term liabilities:
             Bonds payable, 9%, due 2013 . . .    $1,000,000
             Premium on bonds payable
                 ($40,000 − $1,000 − $333) . . . .       38,667    $1,038,667
        1994
e. Apr. 30   Interest Expense . . . . . . . . . . . . . . . . . . . . . .   29,333
             Interest Payable . . . . . . . . . . . . . . . . . . . . . .   15,000
             Premium on Bonds Payable
             ($40,000/40 × ⁴⁄₆) . . . . . . . . . . . . . . . . . . . . .      667
                 Cash ($1,000,000 × .09 × ⁶⁄₁₂) . . . . .                           45,000
             To pay semiannual interest, part of which
             was accrued, and amortize four months'
             premium on bonds payable.
```

SUPPLEMENT TO SUMMARY PROBLEM SOLUTION

Bond problems include many details. You may find it helpful to check your work. We verify the answers to the Summary Problem in this supplement.

On April 30, 1994, the bonds have been outstanding for one year. After the entries have been recorded, the account balances should show the results of one year's cash interest payments and one year's bond premium amortization.

Fact 1:   Cash interest payments should be $90,000 ($1,000,000 × .09).

Accuracy check: Two credits to Cash of $45,000 each = $90,000. Cash payments are correct.

Fact 2:	Premium amortization should be $2,000 ($40,000/40 semian-nual periods × 2 semiannual periods in 1 year).
Accuracy check:	Three debits to Premium on Bonds Payable ($1,000 + $333 + $667) = $2,000. Premium amortization is correct.
Fact 3:	Also we can check the accuracy of interest expense recorded during the year ended December 31, 1993.
	The bonds in this problem will be outstanding for a total of 20 years, or 240 (that is, 20 × 12) months. During 1993 the bonds are outstanding for 8 months (May through December).
	Interest expense for 8 months *equals* payment of cash interest for 8 months minus premium amortization for 8 months. Interest expense should therefore be ($1,000,000 × .09 × $8/12$ = $60,000) minus [($40,000/240) × 8 = $1,333] or ($60,000 − $1,333 = $58,667).
Accuracy check:	Two debits to Interest Expense ($44,000 + $14,667) = $58,667. Interest expense for 1993 is correct.

Effective-Interest Method of Amortization

The straight-line amortization method has a theoretical weakness. Each period's amortization amount for a premium or discount is the same dollar amount over the life of the bonds. However, over that time the bonds' carrying amount continues to increase (with a discount) or decrease (with a premium). Thus the fixed dollar amount of amortization changes as a percentage of the bonds' carrying amount, making it appear that the bond issuer's interest rate changes over time. This appearance misleads because in fact the issuer locked in a fixed interest rate when the bonds were issued. The interest rate on the bonds does not change.

GAAP *(Accounting Principles Board Opinion No. 21)* specifies that discounts and premiums be amortized using the effective-interest method unless the difference between the straight-line method and the effective-interest method is immaterial. In that case, either method is permitted. We will see how the effective-interest method keeps each interest expense amount at the same percentage of the bonds' carrying amount for every interest payment over the bonds' life. The total amount amortized over the life of the bonds is the same under both methods.

Effective-Interest Method of Amortizing Discount

OBJECTIVE 2
Amortize bond discount and premium by the effective-interest method

Assume that Bethlehem Steel Corporation issues $100,000 of its 9 percent bonds at a time when the market rate of interest is 10 percent. Also assume that these bonds mature in five years and pay interest semiannually, so there are 10 semiannual interest payments. The issue price of the bonds is $96,149.[2] The discount on these bonds is $3,851 ($100,000 − $96,149).

Exhibit 11-3 illustrates amortization of the discount by the effective-interest method.

---

[2] We compute this present value using the tables that appear in Appendix A.

EXHIBIT 11-3 *Effective-Interest Method of Amortizing Bond Discount*

Panel A—Bond Data

Maturity value—$100,000

Contract interest rate—9%

Interest paid—4½% semiannually, $4,500 ($100,000 × .045)

Market interest rate at time of issue—10% annually, 5% semiannually

Issue price—$96,149

Panel B—Amortization Table

	A	B	C	D	E
Semiannual Interest Period	Interest Payment (4½% of Maturity Value)	Interest Expense (5% of Preceding Bond Carrying Amount)	Discount Amortization (B − A)	Discount Account Balance (D − C)	Bond Carrying Amount ($100,000 − D)
Issue Date				$3,851	$ 96,149
1	$4,500	$4,807	$307	3,544	96,456
2	4,500	4,823	323	3,221	96,779
3	4,500	4,839	339	2,882	97,118
4	4,500	4,856	356	2,526	97,474
5	4,500	4,874	374	2,152	97,848
6	4,500	4,892	392	1,760	98,240
7	4,500	4,912	412	1,348	98,652
8	4,500	4,933	433	915	99,085
9	4,500	4,954	454	461	99,539
10	4,500	4,961*	461	-0-	100,000

* Adjusted for effect of rounding.

The exhibit reveals the following important facts about effective interest method amortization of bond discount:

Column A. The semiannual interest payments are constant because they are governed by the contract interest rate and the bonds' maturity value.

Column B. The interest expense each period is computed by multiplying the preceding bond carrying amount by the market interest rate (5 percent semiannually). This rate is the *effective interest rate* because its effect determines the interest expense each period. The amount of interest each period increases as the effective interest rate, a constant, is applied to the increasing bond carrying amount (column E).

Column C. The excess of each interest expense amount (column B) over each interest payment amount (column A) is the discount amortization for the period.

Column D. The discount balance decreases by the amount of amortization for the period (column C). The discount decreases from $3,851 at the bonds' issue date to zero at their maturity. The balance of the discount plus the bonds' carrying amount equal the bonds' maturity value.

Column E.   The bonds' carrying amount increases from $96,149 at issuance to $100,000 at maturity.

Recall that we want to present interest expense amounts over the full life of the bonds at a fixed percentage of the bonds' carrying amount. The 5 percent rate—the effective interest rate—*is* that percentage. We have figured the cost of the money borrowed by the bond issuer—the interest expense—as a constant percentage of the carrying amount of the bonds. The dollar *amount* of interest expense varies from period to period but not the interest percentage *rate.*

The accounts debited and credited under the effective interest amortization method and the straight-line method are the same. Only the amounts differ. We may take the amortization amounts directly from the table in the exhibit. We assume that the first interest payment occurs on July 1 and use the appropriate amounts from Exhibit 11-3, reading across the line for the first interest payment date:

July 1	Interest Expense (column B)	4,807	
	Discount on Bonds Payable (column C)		307
	Cash (column A)........................		4,500
	To pay semiannual interest and amortize discount on bonds payable.		

Effective-Interest Method of Amortizing Premium

Let's modify the Bethlehem Steel example to illustrate the interest method of amortizing bond premium. Assume that Bethlehem Steel issues $100,000 of five-year, 9 percent bonds that pay interest semiannually. If the bonds are issued when the market interest rate is 8 percent, their issue price is $104,100.[3] The premium on these bonds is $4,100, and Exhibit 11-4 illustrates amortization of the premium by the interest method.

Exhibit 11-4 reveals the following important facts about the effective-interest method of amortizing bond premium:

Column A.   The semiannual interest payments are a constant amount fixed by the contract interest rate and the bonds' maturity value.

Column B.   The interest expense each period is computed by multiplying the preceding bond carrying amount by the effective interest rate (4 percent semiannually). Observe that the amount of interest decreases each period as the bond carrying amount decreases.

Column C.   The excess of each interest payment (column A) over the period's interest expense (column B) is the premium amortization for the period.

Column D.   The premium balance decreases by the amount of amortization for the period (column C) from $4,100 at issuance to zero at maturity. The bonds' carrying amount minus the premium balance equals the bonds' maturity value.

Column E.   The bonds' carrying amount decreases from $104,100 at issuance to $100,000 at maturity.

Assuming that the first interest payment occurs on October 31, we read across the line for the first interest payment date and pick up the appropriate amounts.

---

[3] Again, we compute the present value of the bonds using the tables in Appendix A.

EXHIBIT 11-4 *Effective-Interest Method of Amortizing Bond Premium*

Panel A—Bond Data

Maturity value—$100,000
Contract interest rate—9%
Interest paid—4½% semiannually, $4,500 ($100,000 × .045)
Market interest rate at time of issue—8% annually, 4% semiannually
Issue price—$104,100

Panel B—Amortization Table

Semiannual Interest Period	A Interest Payment (4½% of Maturity Value)	B Interest Expense (4% of Preceding Bond Carrying Amount)	C Premium Amortization (A − B)	D Premium Account Balance (D − C)	E Bond Carrying Amount ($100,000 + D)
Issue Date				$4,100	$104,100
1	$4,500	$4,164	$336	3,764	103,764
2	4,500	4,151	349	3,415	103,415
3	4,500	4,137	363	3,052	103,052
4	4,500	4,122	378	2,674	102,674
5	4,500	4,107	393	2,281	102,281
6	4,500	4,091	409	1,872	101,872
7	4,500	4,075	425	1,447	101,447
8	4,500	4,058	442	1,005	101,005
9	4,500	4,040	460	545	100,545
10	4,500	3,955*	545	-0-	100,000

* Adjusted for effect of rounding.

Oct. 31	Interest Expense (column B)	4,164	
	Premium on Bonds Payable (column C)	336	
	Cash (column A)		4,500
	To pay semiannual interest and amortize premium on bonds payable.		

At year end it is necessary to make an adjusting entry for accrued interest and amortization of the bond premium for a partial period. In our example, the last interest payment occurred on October 31. The adjustment for November and December must cover two months, or one-third of a semiannual period. The entry, with amounts drawn from Exhibit 11-4, line 2, is

Dec. 31	Interest Expense ($4,151 × ⅓)	1,384	
	Premium on Bonds Payable ($349 × ⅓)	116	
	Interest Payable ($4,500 × ⅓)		1,500
	To accrue two months' interest and amortize premium on bonds payable for two months.		

The second interest payment occurs on April 30 of the following year. The payment of $4,500 includes interest expense for four months (January through April), the interest payable at December 31, and premium amortization for four months. The payment entry is

Apr. 30	Interest Expense ($4,151 × ⅔)	2,767	
	Interest Payable	1,500	
	Premium on Bonds Payable ($349 × ⅔)	233	
	Cash		4,500
	To pay semiannual interest, some of which was accrued, and amortize premium on bonds payable for four months.		

If these bonds had been issued at a discount, procedures for these interest entries would be the same, except that Discount on Bonds Payable would be credited.

Bond Sinking Fund

Bond indentures—the contracts under which bonds are issued—often require the borrower to make regular periodic payments to a *bond sinking fund*. A fund is a group of assets that are segregated for a particular purpose. A **bond sinking fund** is used to retire bonds payable at maturity. A trustee manages this fund for the issuer, investing the company's payments in income-earning assets. The company's payments into the fund and the interest revenue—which the trustee reinvests in the fund—accumulate. The target amount of the sinking fund is the face value of the bond issue at maturity. When the bonds come due, the trustee sells the sinking-fund assets and uses the cash proceeds to pay off the bonds. The bond sinking fund provides security of payment to investors in unsecured bonds.

Most companies report sinking funds under the heading Investments, a separate asset category between current assets and plant assets on the balance sheet. A bond sinking fund is not a current asset because it may not be used to pay current liabilities. Accounting for the interest, dividends, and other earnings on the bond sinking fund requires use of the accounts Sinking Fund and Sinking-Fund Revenue.

Sperry Corporation has outstanding $40 million of 8.2 percent sinking-fund debentures. The company must make annual sinking-fund payments. The entry to deposit $2 million with the trustee is

Jan. 5	Sinking Fund	2,000,000	
	Cash		2,000,000
	To make annual sinking-fund deposit.		

If the trustee invests the cash and reports annual sinking-fund revenue of $150,000, the fund grows by this amount, and Sperry makes the following entry at year end:

Dec. 31	Sinking Fund	150,000	
	Sinking-Fund Revenue		150,000
	To record sinking-fund earnings.		

Assume that Sperry has made the required sinking-fund payments over a period of years and that these payments plus the fund earnings have accumulated a cash balance of $40.2 million at maturity. The trustee pays off the bonds and returns the excess cash to Sperry, which makes the following entry:

```
Jan. 4    Cash .............................    200,000
          Bonds Payable.....................  40,000,000
                Sinking Fund .................              40,200,000
          To record payment of bonds payable
          and receipt of excess sinking-fund cash
          at maturity.
```

If the fund balance is less than the bonds' maturity value, the entry is similar to the foregoing entry. However, the company pays the extra amount and credits Cash.

Retirement of Bonds Payable

OBJECTIVE 3

Account for retirement
of bonds payable

Normally companies wait until maturity to pay off, or retire, their bonds payable. All bond discount or premium has been amortized, and the retirement entry debits Bonds Payable and credits Cash for the bonds' maturity value.

Companies sometimes retire their bonds payable prior to maturity. The main reason for retiring bonds early is to relieve the pressure of making interest payments. Interest rates fluctuate. The company may be able to borrow at a lower interest rate and use the proceeds from new bonds to pay off the old bonds, which bear a higher rate.

Some bonds are **callable,** which means that the issuer may *call,* or pay off, the bonds at a specified price whenever the issuer wants. The call price is usually a few percent above par, perhaps 104 or 105. Callable bonds give the issuer the benefit of being able to take advantage of low interest rates by paying off the bonds at the most favorable time. An alternative to calling the bonds is to purchase them in the open market at their current market price. Whether the bonds are called or purchased in the open market, the journal entry is the same.

Air Products and Chemicals, Inc., has $70,000,000 of debentures outstanding with unamortized discount of $350,000. Lower interest rates in the market may convince management to pay off these bonds now. Assume that the bonds are callable at 103. If the market price of the bonds is 99¼ will Air Products call the bonds or purchase them in the open market? The market price is lower than the call price, so market price is the better choice. Retiring the bonds at 99¼ results in a gain of $175,000, computed as follows:

```
Par value of bonds being retired ......   $70,000,000
Unamortized discount ...............          350,000
Book value.........................        69,650,000
Market price ($70,000,000 × .9925) ....    69,475,000
Gain on retirement .................     $    175,000
```

The entry to record retirement of the bonds, immediately after an interest date, is

```
June 30   Bonds Payable.....................  70,000,000
                Discount on Bonds Payable ....                  350,000
                Cash ($70,000,000 × .9925).....              69,475,000
                Extraordinary Gain on
                     Retirement of Bonds Payable .                175,000
          To retire bonds payable before maturity.
```

The entry removes the bonds payable and the related discount from the accounts and records a gain on retirement. Of course, any existing premium would be removed with a debit. If Air Products and Chemicals had retired only half of these bonds, the accountant would remove half of the discount or premium. Likewise, if the price paid to retire the bonds exceeds their carrying amount, the retirement entry would record a loss with a debit to the account Extraordinary Loss on Retirement of Bonds. GAAP identifies gains and losses on early retirement of debt as *extraordinary*, and they are reported separately on the income statement, net of tax. Chapter 13 discusses extraordinary items in more detail.

Convertible Bonds and Notes

Many corporate bonds and notes payable may be converted into the common stock of the issuing company at the option of the investor. These bonds and notes, called **convertible bonds** (or **notes**), combine the safety of assured interest receipts and receipt of principal on the bonds with the opportunity for large gains on the stock. The conversion feature is so attractive that investors usually accept a lower contract, or stated, interest rate than they would on nonconvertible bonds. The lower cash interest payments benefit the issuer. Convertible bonds are recorded like any other debt at issuance.

OBJECTIVE 4
Account for conversion of bonds payable

If the market price of the issuing company's stock gets high enough, the bondholders will convert the bonds into stock. The corporation records conversion by debiting the bond accounts and crediting the stockholders' equity accounts. The carrying amount of the bonds becomes the book value of the newly issued stock. No gain or loss is recorded.

Prime Western, Inc., had convertible *notes* outstanding carried on the books at $12.5 million. Assume that the maturity value of the notes was $13 million. Also assume that Prime Western's stock rose significantly so that noteholders converted the notes into 400,000 shares of the company's $1 par common stock. Prime Western's entry to record conversion is

May 14	Notes Payable	13,000,000	
	Discount on Notes Payable		500,000
	Common Stock (400,000 × $1) . .		400,000
	Paid-in Capital in Excess of Par—Common		12,100,000
	To record conversion of notes payable.		

Observe that the carrying amount of the notes ($13,000,000 − $500,000) becomes the amount of increase in stockholders' equity ($400,000 + $12,100,000). The entry closes the notes (or bonds) payable account and its related discount or premium account. Common Stock is credited for its par value, and Paid-in Capital in Excess of Par is credited for the remaining amount.

Current Portion of Long-Term Debt

Serial bonds and serial notes are payable in serials, or installments. The portion payable within one year is a current liability, and the remaining debt is long-term. At June 30, 1990, Birmingham Steel Corporation, had $30,961,000 of long-term debt maturing in various annual amounts from 1994 through 2001.

The portion payable in 1991 was $3,809,000. Therefore, $3,809,000 was a current liability at June 30, 1990, and $27,152,000 was a long-term liability. Birmingham Steel reported the following among its liabilities at June 30, 1990:

	$ Millions
Current liabilities:	
Current portion of long-term debt	$ 3,809
Long-term debt less current portion	27,152

Mortgage Notes Payable

You have probably heard of mortgage payments. Many notes payable are mortgage notes, which actually contain two agreements. The *note* is the borrower's promise to pay the lender the amount of the debt. The **mortgage**—a security agreement related to the note—is the borrower's promise to transfer the legal title to certain assets to the lender if the debt is not paid on schedule. The borrower is said to pledge these assets as security for the note. Often the asset that is pledged was acquired with the borrowed money. For example, most homeowners sign mortgage notes to purchase their residence, pledging that property as security for the loan. Businesses sign mortgage notes to acquire buildings, equipment, and other long-term assets. Mortgage notes are usually serial notes that require monthly or quarterly payments.

Advantage of Financing Operations with Debt versus Stock

OBJECTIVE 5

Explain the advantages and disadvantages of borrowing

Businesses have different ways to acquire assets. Management may decide to purchase or to lease equipment. The money to finance the asset may come from the business's retained earnings, a note payable, a stock issue, or a bond issue. Each financing strategy has its advantages and disadvantages. Let's examine how issuing stock compares with issuing bonds.

Bonds differ from stocks in important ways. Stock shares give the holder part ownership of the corporation and a voice in management. Bonds merely give the holder a creditor's claim to the debtor's assets. Bond certificates carry dates for maturity and interest payments, unlike stock, which does not come due at any specific time. Companies are not obligated to declare dividends on stock.

Issuing stock raises capital without incurring the liabilities and interest expense that accompany bonds. However, by issuing stock the business spreads the ownership, control, and income of the corporation among more shares. Management may wish to avoid this dilution of its ownership. Borrowing money through bonds raises liabilities and interest expense, which the corporation must pay whether or not it earns a profit. But borrowing does not affect stockholder control: bondholders are creditors with no voice in management. Borrowing also provides a tax advantage in that interest expense is tax-deductible. Dividends paid to stockholders are not tax-deductible because they are not an expense.

Exhibit 11-5 illustrates the earnings-per-share (EPS) advantage of borrowing. Suppose a corporation with 100,000 shares of common stock outstanding needs $500,000 for expansion. Management is considering two financing

EXHIBIT 11-5 *Earnings-Per-Share Advantage of Borrowing*

	Plan 1 Borrow $500,000 at 10%	Plan 2 Issue $500,000 of Common Stock
Income before interest and income tax....	$200,000	$200,000
Less interest expense ($500,000 × .10)	50,000	-0-
Income before income tax	150,000	200,000
Less income tax expense (40%)	60,000	80,000
Net income	$ 90,000	$120,000
Earnings per share on new project:		
Plan 1 ($90,000/100,000 shares).........	$ .90	
Plan 2 ($120,000/150,000 shares)........		$ .80

plans. Plan 1 is to issue $500,000 of 10 percent bonds payable, and plan 2 is to issue 50,000 shares of common stock for $500,000. Management believes the new cash can be invested in operations to earn income of $200,000 before interest and taxes.

The earnings-per-share amount is higher if the company borrows. The business earns more on the investment ($90,000) than the interest it pays on the bonds ($50,000). Earning more income on borrowed money than the related interest expense increases the earnings for common stockholders and is called **trading on the equity.** It is widely used in business to increase earnings per share of common stock.

Dividend payments to the new stockholders under plan 2 would also make borrowing more attractive than issuing stock. Assume that net income generates an increase in cash of the same amount. If under plan 2 the company were to pay dividends of $50,000—the same as the interest expense under plan 1—its net cash inflow would be $70,000 ($120,000 − $50,000), compared with $90,000 under plan 1.

Borrowing has its disadvantages. Interest expense may be high enough to eliminate net income and lead to a cash crisis and even bankruptcy. Also, borrowing creates liabilities that accrue during bad years as well as during good years. In contrast, a company that issues stock can omit its dividends during a bad year.

The following quotation from *Business Week* (July 2, 1990, p. 38) describes how a major company overextended its financial capabilities. A *leveraged buyout* is a debt-financed acquisition of another company, often with so-called junk bonds. These bonds bear high interest rates because their probability of repayment is relatively low.

> Was it only last year that financier Henry Kravis and his partners borrowed a whopping $28 billion to buy RJR Nabisco in the biggest leveraged buyout in history? It seems like an age—namely, the age of excessive debt. Now, only 17 months later, the landscape is littered with casualties of overborrowing—Robert Campeau, Merv Griffin, Donald Trump. Kravis, whose name became synonymous with leveraged buyouts in the go-go 1980s, seems determined to avoid the same fate. Adapting to the pay-as-you-go 1990s, Kohlberg Kravis Roberts is planning to put RJR on a sounder financial footing. The firm indicated that it would plow $1.7 billion of new equity into the food and tobacco giant and retire some $4 billion of high-yield junk bonds. Said a Shearson Lehman Hutton trader, "It's the official end of the junk-bond era."

Lease Liabilities

A **lease** is a rental agreement in which the tenant **(lessee)** agrees to make rent payments to the property owner **(lessor)** in exchange for the use of the asset. Leasing allows the lessee to acquire the use of a needed asset without having to make the large initial cash down payment that purchase agreements require. Accountants divide leases into two types: operating and capital.

Operating Leases

You are already familiar with **operating leases**, which are usually short-term or cancelable. Many apartment leases and most car-rental agreements are for a year or less. These operating leases give the lessee the right to use the asset but provide the lessee with no continuing rights to the asset. The lessor retains the usual risks and rewards of owning the leased asset. To account for an operating lease, the lessee debits Rent Expense (or Lease Expense) and credits Cash for the amount of the lease payment. The lessee's books do not report the leased asset or any lease liability (except perhaps a prepaid rent amount or a rent accrual at the end of the period).

Capital Leases

More and more businesses nationwide are turning to capital leasing to finance the acquisition of assets. A *capital lease* is long-term and noncancelable. Accounting for a capital lease is much like accounting for a purchase. The lessor removes the asset from her books. The lessee enters the asset into his accounts and records a lease liability at the beginning of the lease term.

Most companies lease some of their plant assets rather than buy them. *A recent survey of 600 companies indicates that they have more leases than any other type of long-term debt.*

Southland Corporation owns 7-Eleven convenience stores. Suppose the company leases a building, agreeing to pay $10,000 annually for a 20-year period, with the first payment due immediately. This arrangement is similar to purchasing the building on an installment plan. In an installment purchase, Southland would debit Building and credit Cash and Installment Note Payable. The company would then pay interest and principal on the note payable and record depreciation on the building. Accounting for a capital lease follows this pattern.

Southland records the building at cost, which is the sum of the $10,000 initial payment plus the present value of the 19 future lease payments of $10,000 each. The company credits Cash for the initial payment and credits Lease Liability for the present value of the future lease payments. Assume the interest rate on Southland's lease is 10 percent and the present value (PV) of the future lease payments is $83,650. At the beginning of the lease term, Southland makes the following entry:

19X1		
Jan. 2 Building ($10,000 + $83,650)	93,650	
Cash		10,000
Lease Liability (PV of future lease payments). . .		83,650

To acquire a building and make the first annual lease payment on a capital lease.

Because Southland has capitalized the building, the company records depreciation. Assume the building has an expected life of 25 years. It is depreciated over the lease term of 20 years because the lessee has the use of the building only for that period. No residual value enters into the depreciation computation because the lessee will have no residual asset when the building is returned to the lessor at the expiration of the lease. Therefore, the annual depreciation entry is

19X1			
Dec. 31	Depreciation Expense ($93,650/20)................	4,683	
	Accumulated Depreciation—Building		4,683
	To record depreciation on leased building.		

At year end Southland must also accrue interest on the lease liability. Interest expense is computed by multiplying the lease liability by the interest rate on the lease. The following entry credits Lease Liability (not Interest Payable) for this interest accrual:

19X1			
Dec. 31	Interest Expense ($83,650 × .10)	8,365	
	Lease Liability		8,365
	To accrue interest on the lease liability.		

The balance sheet at December 31, 19X1 reports:

Assets

Plant assets:		
Building	$93,650	
Less Accumulated depreciation....................	4,683	$88,967

Liabilities

Current liabilities:	
Lease liability (next payment due on Jan. 2, 19X2).............	$10,000
Long-term liabilities:	
Lease liability [beginning balance ($83,650) + interest accrual ($8,365) − current portion ($10,000)]	82,015

The lease liability is split into current and long-term portions because the next payment ($10,000) is a current liability and the remainder is long-term.

The January 2, 19X2, lease payment is recorded as follows:

19X2			
Jan. 2	Lease Liability	10,000	
	Cash.......................................		10,000
	To make second annual lease payment on building.		

Distinguishing a Capital Lease from an Operating Lease. How would you distinguish a capital lease from an operating lease? *FASB Statement No. 13* provides the guidelines. To be classified as a **capital lease,** a particular lease agreement must meet any *one* of the following criteria:

1. The lease transfers title of the leased asset to the lessee at the end of the lease term. Thus the lessee becomes the legal owner of the leased asset.

2. The lease contains a *bargain purchase option*. The lessee can be expected to purchase the leased asset and become its legal owner.
3. The lease term is 75 percent or more of the estimated useful life of the leased asset. The lessee uses up most of the leased asset's service potential.
4. The present value of the lease payments is 90 percent or more of the market value of the leased asset. In effect, the lease payments operate as installment payments for the leased asset.

Only those leases that fail to meet *all* of these criteria may be accounted for as operating leases.

Off-Balance-Sheet Financing

An important part of business is obtaining the funds needed to acquire assets. To finance operations a company may issue stock, borrow money, or retain earnings in the business. Notice that all three of these financing plans affect the right-hand side of the balance sheet. Issuing stock affects the stock account. Borrowing creates notes or bonds payable. Internal funds come from retained earnings.

Off-balance-sheet financing is the acquisition of assets or services with debt that is not reported on the balance sheet. A prime example is an operating lease. The lessee has the use of the leased asset, but neither the asset nor any lease liability is reported on the balance sheet. Off-balance-sheet financing keeps the reported amount of debt, and the debt ratio, lower than if the liability were reported on the balance sheet.

In the past, most leases were accounted for by the operating method. However, *FASB Statement No. 13* has required businesses to account for an increasing number of leases by the capital lease method. Also, *FASB Statement No. 13* has brought about detailed reporting of operating lease payments in the notes to the financial statements. The inclusion of more lease information—be they capital or operating leases—makes the accounting information for decision making more complete.

Pension Liabilities

Most companies have a pension plan for their employees. A **pension** is employee compensation that will be received during retirement. Employees earn the pensions by their service, so the company records pension expense as employees work for the company. *FASB Statement No. 87* gives the rules for measuring pension expense. To record the company's payment into a pension plan, the company debits Pension Expense and credits Cash. Insurance companies and pension trusts manage pension plans. They receive the employer payments and any employee contributions, then invest these amounts for the future benefit of the employees. The goal is to have the funds available to meet any obligations to retirees, much as a bond sinking fund is designed to retire bonds payable at maturity.

Pensions are perhaps the most complex area of accounting. As employees earn their pensions and the company pays into the pension plan, the assets of the plan grow. The obligation for future pension payments to employees also accumulates. At the end of each period, the company compares the fair market value of the assets in the pension plan—cash and investments—with the accumulated benefit obligation of the pension plan. The *accumulated benefit obligation* is the present value of promised future pension payments to retirees. If the plan assets exceed the accumulated benefit obligation, the plan is said to be overfunded. In this case, the asset and obligation amounts need be reported only in the notes to the financial statements. However, if the accumulated benefit obligation exceeds plan assets, the company must report the excess liability amount as a long-term pension liability in the balance sheet.

The pension plan of Mainstream Manufacturing & Sales, Inc., has assets with a fair market value of $3 million on December 31, 19X0. On this date the accumulated pension benefit obligation to employees is $4 million. Mainstream's balance sheet will report Long-Term Pension Liability of $1 million. This liability will be listed, in no particular order, along with Bonds Payable, Long-Term Notes Payable, Lease Liabilities, and other long-term liabilities.

FASB Statement No. 87 started requiring companies to report pension liabilities in this manner in 1987. Before that date, pensions were another example of off-balance-sheet financing. Companies received the benefit of their employees' service but could avoid reporting pension liabilities on the balance sheet.

Computers and Corporate Financial Planning _____

Corporations, large and small, deal with complex financial planning issues. A large corporation such as Tenneco, a major manufacturer of petrochemicals, might consider how to finance a new project. Suppose Tenneco wants to build a new refinery and expects total costs of $75,000,000. How does Tenneco find the best way to raise the needed funds? The company may consider the financing alternatives: issue common stock, preferred stock, bonds, or different combinations of stocks and bonds. Financial-modeling techniques on microcomputers can help answer these questions thanks to spreadsheet capabilities. This assessment is often called "what if" analysis—that is, "what if" we finance with common stock, "what if" we finance with new bonds, and so on.

The answers to these "what if" questions appear on a spreadsheet template that projects the company's financial statements for, say, the next five years. A preferred stock issue would probably mean higher annual dividend payments than would a common stock issue. The financial statements would show this higher payment. Likewise, long-term borrowing would involve interest expense, but these charges are tax-deductible, unlike dividend payments to stockholders. The spreadsheet could show the consequences of financing through stock and through bonds, with a summary such as Exhibit 11-5. By studying the projected financial statements, management can select the most favorable path.

Nonmonetary considerations cannot be modelled so easily on a spreadsheet. For example, is the company willing to dilute the control of the shareholders by issuing more stock? If the company borrows the needed funds, will the rating of its existing bonds suffer? Computers are not as well suited to answering qualitative questions such as these.

Summary Problem for Your Review

The Cessna Aircraft Company has outstanding an issue of 8 percent convertible bonds that mature in 2012. Suppose the bonds were dated October 1, 1992, and pay interest each April 1 and October 1.

Required

1. Complete the following effective interest amortization table through October 1, 1994.

   Bond Data:

   Maturity value—$100,000
   Contract interest rate—8%
   Interest paid—4% semiannually, $4,000 ($100,000 × .04)

   Market interest rate at time of issue—9% annually, 4½% semiannually
   Issue price—90¾

   Amortization Table:

Semiannual Interest Date	A Interest Payment (4% of Maturity Amount)	B Interest Expense (4½% of Preceding Bond Carrying Amount)	C Discount Amortization (B − A)	D Discount Account Balance (D − C)	E Bond Carrying Amount ($100,000 − D)
10-1-92					
4-1-93					
10-1-93					
4-1-94					
10-1-94					

2. Using the amortization table, record the following transactions:
   a. Issuance of the bonds on October 1, 1992.
   b. Accrual of interest and amortization of discount on December 31, 1992.
   c. Payment of interest and amortization of discount on April 1, 1993.
   d. Conversion of one-third of the bonds payable into no-par stock on October 2, 1994.
   e. Retirement of two-thirds of the bonds payable on October 2, 1994. Purchase price of the bonds was 102.

SOLUTION TO REVIEW PROBLEM

Requirement 1.   (Amortization Table)

Semiannual Interest Date	A Interest Payment (4% of Maturity Amount)	B Interest Expense (4½% of Preceding Bond Carrying Amount)	C Discount Amortization (B − A)	D Discount Account Balance (D − C)	E Bond Carrying Amount ($100,000 − D)
10-1-92				$9,250	$ 90,750
4-1-93	$4,000	$4,084	$84	9,166	90,834
10-1-93	4,000	4,088	88	9,078	90,922
4-1-94	4,000	4,091	91	8,987	91,013
10-1-94	4,000	4,096	96	8,891	91,109

Requirement 2.

1992

a. Oct. 1 Cash ($100,000 × .9075) 90,750
              Discount on Bonds Payable 9,250
                 Bonds Payable   100,000
              To issue 8%, 20-year bonds at a discount.

b. Dec. 31 Interest Expense ($4,084 × ³⁄₆) 2,042
              Discount on Bonds Payable
                 ($84 × ³⁄₆)   42
              Interest Payable ($4,000 × ³⁄₆).   2,000
              To accrue interest and amortize bond
              discount for three months.

1993

c. Apr. 1 Interest Expense 2,042
              Interest Payable 2,000
                 Discount on Bonds Payable ($84 × ³⁄₆)   42
                 Cash   4,000
              To pay semiannual interest, part of which was
              accrued, and amortize three months' discount
              on bonds payable.

1994

d. Oct. 2 Bonds Payable ($100,000 × ⅓) 33,333
                 Discount on Bonds Payable ($8,891 × ⅓)   2,964
                 Common Stock ($91,109 × ⅓)   30,369
              To record conversion of bonds payable.

e. Oct. 2 Bonds Payable ($100,000 × ⅔) 66,667
              Extraordinary Loss on Retirement of Bonds   7,260
                 Discount on Bonds Payable ($8,891 × ⅔)   5,927
                 Cash ($100,000 × ⅔ × 1.02)   68,000
              To retire bonds payable before maturity.

Summary

A corporation may borrow money by issuing bonds and long-term notes payable. A bond contract, called an *indenture*, specifies the maturity value of the bonds, the contract interest rate, and the dates for paying interest and principal. The owner of *registered* bonds receives an interest check from the company. The owner of *coupon* bonds deposits an interest coupon in the bank. Bonds may be secured (*mortgage* bonds) or unsecured (*debenture* bonds).

Bonds are traded through organized markets, like the New York Exchange. Bonds are typically divided into $1,000 units. Their prices are quoted at a percentage of face value.

Market interest rates fluctuate and may differ from the contract rate on a bond. If a bond's contract rate exceeds the market rate, the bond sells at a *premium*. A bond with a contract rate below the market rate sells at a *discount*.

Money earns income over time, a fact that gives rise to the *present-value concept*. An investor will pay a price for a bond equal to the present value of the bond principal plus the present value of the bond interest.

Straight-line amortization allocates an equal amount of premium or discount to each interest period. In the *effective-interest method* of amortization, the market rate at the time of issuance is multiplied by the bonds' carrying amount to determine the interest expense each period and to compute the amount of discount or premium amortization.

A *bond sinking fund* accumulates the money to pay the bonds' face value at maturity. Companies may retire their bonds payable before maturity. *Callable* bonds give the borrower the right to pay off the bonds at a specified call price, or the company may purchase the bonds in the open market. Any gain or loss on early extinguishment of debt is classified as *extraordinary*.

Convertible bonds and notes give the investor the privilege of trading the bonds in for stock of the issuing corporation. The carrying amount of the bonds becomes the book value of the newly issued stock.

A lease is a rental agreement between the *lessee* and the *lessor*. In an *operating lease* the lessor retains the usual risks and rights of owning the asset. The lessee debits Rent Expense and credits Cash when making lease payments. A *capital lease* is long-term, noncancelable, and similar to an installment purchase of the leased asset. In a capital lease, the lessee capitalizes the leased asset and reports a lease liability.

Companies also report a *pension liability* on the balance sheet if the accumulated benefit obligation exceeds the market value of pension plan assets.

Self-Study Questions

Test your understanding of the chapter by marking the best answer for each of the following questions.

1. An unsecured bond is called a *(p. 532)*
    a. Serial bond
    b. Registered bond
    c. Debenture bond
    d. Mortgage bond

2. How much will an investor pay for a $100,000 bond priced at 101⅞, plus a brokerage commission of $1,100? *(p. 532)*
    a. $100,000
    b. $101,100
    c. $101,875
    d. $102,975

3. A bond with a stated interest rate of 9½ percent is issued when the market interest rate is 9¾ percent. This bond will sell at *(p. 532)*
    a. Par value
    b. A discount
    c. A premium
    d. A price minus accrued interest

4. Ten-year, 11 percent bonds payable of $500,000 were issued for $532,000. Assume the straight-line amortization method is appropriate. The total annual interest expense on these bonds is *(pp. 538, 539)*
    a. $51,800
    b. $55,000
    c. $58,200
    d. A different amount each year because the bonds' book value decreases as the premium is amortized

5. Use the facts in the preceding question but assume the effective interest method of amortization is used. Total annual interest expense on the bonds is *(p. 544)*
    a. $51,800
    b. $55,000
    c. $58,200
    d. A decreasing amount each year because the bonds' book value decreases as the premium is amortized

6. Bonds payable with face value of $300,000 and carrying amount of $288,000 are retired before their scheduled maturity with a cash outlay of $292,000. Which of the following entries correctly records this bond retirement? *(p. 546)*

a. Bonds Payable.......................... 300,000
   Discount on Bonds Payable............... 12,000
      Cash 292,000
      Extraordinary Gain...................... 20,000
b. Bonds Payable.......................... 300,000
   Extraordinary Loss 4,000
      Discount on Bonds Payable............. 12,000
      Cash 292,000
c. Bonds Payable.......................... 300,000
      Discount on Bonds Payable............. 6,000
      Cash 292,000
      Extraordinary Gain...................... 2,000
d. Bonds Payable.......................... 288,000
   Discount on Bonds Payable............... 12,000
      Extraordinary Gain...................... 8,000
      Cash 292,000

7. An advantage of financing operations with debt versus stock is *(pp. 548– 549)*
   a. The tax-deductibility of interest expense on debt
   b. The legal requirement to pay interest and principal
   c. Lower interest payments compared with dividend payments
   d. All of the above

8. In a capital lease, the lessee records *(pp. 550–551)*
   a. A leased asset and a lease liability   c. Interest on the lease liability
   b. Depreciation on the leased asset   d. All of the above

9. Which of the following is an example of off-balance-sheet financing? *(p. 552)*
   a. Operating lease   c. Debenture bonds
   b. Current portion of long-term debt   d. Convertible bonds

10. A corporation's pension plan has accumulated benefit obligations of $830,000 and assets that are worth $790,000. What will this company report for its pension plan? *(p. 553)*
    a. Accumulated benefit obligation of $830,000
    b. Note disclosure of the $40,000 excess of accumulated benefit obligation over plan assets
    c. Long-term pension liability of $40,000
    d. Nothing

Answers to the Self-Study Questions follow the Accounting Vocabulary.

Accounting Vocabulary

Bond discount. Excess of a bond's maturity (par) value over its issue price *(p. 532)*.

Bond indenture. Contract under which bonds are issued *(p. 545)*.

Bond premium. Excess of a bond's issue price over its maturity (par) value *(p. 532)*.

Bond sinking fund. Group of assets segregated for the purpose of retiring bonds payable at maturity *(p. 545)*.

Bonds payable. Groups of notes payable (bonds) issued to multiple lenders called bondholders *(p. 530)*.

Callable bonds. Bonds that the issuer may call or pay off at a specified price whenever the issuer wants *(p. 546)*.

Capital lease. Lease agreement that meets any one of four criteria: (1) The lease transfers title of the leased asset to the lessee. (2) The lease contains a bargain purchase option. (3) The lease term is 75 percent or more of the estimated useful life of the leased asset. (4) The present value of the lease payments is 90 percent or more of the market value of the leased asset (p. 551).

Contract interest rate. Interest rate that determines the amount of cash interest the borrower pays and the investor receives each year. Also called the Stated interest rate (p. 533).

Convertible bonds. Bonds that may be converted into the common stock of the issuing company at the option of the investor (p. 547).

Coupon bonds. Bonds for which the owners receive interest by detaching a perforated coupon (which states the interest due and the date of payment) from the bond and depositing it in a bank for collection (p. 531).

Debentures. Unsecured bonds, backed only by the good faith of the borrower (p. 532).

Effective interest rate. Another name for Market interest rate (p. 533).

Lease. Rental agreement in which the tenant (lessee) agrees to make rent payments to the property owner (lessor) in exchange for the use of the asset (p. 550).

Lessee. Tenant in a lease agreement (p. 550).

Lessor. Property owner in a lease agreement (p. 550).

Market interest rate. Interest rate that investors demand in order to loan their money. Also called the Effective interest rate (p. 533).

Mortgage. Borrower's promise to transfer the legal title to certain assets to the lender if the debt is not paid on schedule (p. 548).

Off-balance-sheet financing. Acquisition of assets or services with debt that is not reported on the balance sheet (p. 552).

Operating lease. Usually a short-term or cancelable rental agreement (p. 550).

Pension. Employee compensation that will be received during retirement (p. 552).

Present value. Amount a person would invest now to receive a greater amount at a future date (p. 533).

Registered bonds. Bonds for which the owners receive interest checks from the issuing company (p. 531).

Serial bonds. Bonds that mature in installments over a period of time (p. 531).

Stated interest rate. Another name for the Contract interest rate (p. 533).

Term bonds. Bonds that all mature at the same time for a particular issue (p. 531).

Trading on the equity. Earning more income on borrowed money than the related interest expense, which increases the earnings for the owners of the business. (p. 549),

Underwriter. Organization that purchases the bonds from an issuing company and resells them to its clients, or sells the bonds for a commission, agreeing to buy all unsold bonds (p. 530).

Answers to Self-Study Questions

1. c
2. d [($100,000 × 1.01875) + $1,100 = $102,975]
3. b
4. a [($500,000 × .11) − ($32,000/10) = $51,800]
5. d
6. b
7. a
8. d
9. a
10. c

ASSIGNMENT MATERIAL

Questions

1. Identify three ways to finance the operations of a corporation.
2. How do bonds payable differ from a note payable?
3. How does an underwriter assist with the issuance of bonds?
4. Why would an investor require the borrower to set up a sinking fund?

5. Compute the price to the nearest dollar for the following bonds with a face value of $10,000:

 a. 93 b. 88¾ c. 101⅜ d. 122½ e. 100

6. In which of the following situations will bonds sell at par? at a premium? at a discount?

 a. 9% bonds sold when the market rate is 9%

 b. 9% bonds sold when the market rate is 10%

 c. 9% bonds sold when the market rate is 8%

7. Identify the accounts to debit and credit for transactions (a) to issue bonds at *par,* (b) to pay interest, (c) to accrue interest at year end, and (d) to pay off bonds at maturity.

8. Identify the accounts to debit and credit for transactions (a) to issue bonds at a *discount,* (b) to pay interest, (c) to accrue interest at year end, and (d) to pay off bonds at maturity.

9. Identify the accounts to debit and credit for transactions (a) to issue bonds at a *premium,* (b) to pay interest, (c) to accrue interest at year end, and (d) to pay off bonds at maturity.

10. Why are bonds sold for a price "plus accrued interest"? What happens to accrued interest when bonds are sold by an individual?

11. How does the straight-line method of amortizing bond discount (or premium) differ from the effective-interest method?

12. A company retires ten-year bonds payable of $100,000 after five years. The business issued the bonds at 104 and called them at 103. Compute the amount of gain or loss on retirement. How is this gain or loss reported on the income statement?

13. Bonds payable with a maturity value of $100,000 are callable at 102½. Their market price is 101¼. If you are the issuer of these bonds, how much will you pay to retire them before maturity?

14. Why are convertible bonds attractive to investors? Why are they popular with borrowers?

15. Describe how to report serial bonds payable on the balance sheet.

16. Contrast the effects on a company of issuing bonds versus issuing stock.

17. Identify the accounts a lessee debits and credits when making operating lease payments.

18. What characteristics distinguish a capital lease from an operating lease?

19. A business signs a capital lease for the use of a building. What accounts are debited and credited (a) to begin the lease term and make the first lease payment, (b) to record depreciation, (c) to accrue interest on the lease liability, and (d) to make the second lease payment?

20. Show how a lessee reports on the balance sheet any leased equipment and the related lease liability under a capital lease.

21. What is off-balance-sheet financing? Give two examples.

22. Distinguish an overfunded pension plan from an underfunded plan. Which situation requires the company to report a pension liability on the balance sheet? How is this liability computed?

Exercises

Exercise 11-1 *Issuing bonds payable and paying interest (L.O. 1)*

Malachite, Inc., issues $300,000 of 10 percent, 20-year bonds payable that are dated April 30. Record (a) issuance of bonds at par on May 31 and (b) the next semiannual interest payment on October 31.

Exercise 11-2 *Issuing bonds payable, paying and accruing interest, and amortizing discount by the straight-line method* **(L.O. 1)**

On February 1 Truly Fine Corp. issues 20-year, 10 percent bonds payable with a face value of $1,000,000. The bonds sell at 98 and pay interest on January 31 and July 31. Truly Fine amortizes bond discount by the straight-line method. Record (a) issuance of the bonds on February 1, (b) the semiannual interest payment on July 31, and (c) the interest accrual on December 31.

Exercise 11-3 *Issuing bonds payable, paying and accruing interest, and amortizing premium by the straight-line method* **(L.O. 1)**

A. V. Cross Corporation issues 30-year, 8 percent bonds payable with a face value of $5,000,000 on March 31. The bonds sell at 101½ and pay interest on March 31 and September 30. Assume Cross amortizes bond premium by the straight-line method. Record (a) issuance of the bonds on March 31, (b) payment of interest on September 30, and (c) accrual of interest on December 31.

Exercise 11-4 *Preparing an effective-interest amortization table; recording interest payments and the related discount amortization* **(L.O. 2)**

Southwest Mortgage Co. is authorized to issue $500,000 of 11 percent, 10-year bonds payable. On January 2, when the market interest rate is 12 percent, the company issues $400,000 of the bonds and receives cash of $377,060. Southwest amortizes bond discount by the effective-interest method.

Required

1. Prepare an amortization table for the first four semiannual interest periods. Follow the format of Exhibit 11-3, Panel B.
2. Record the first semiannual interest payment on June 30 and the second payment on December 31.

Exercise 11-5 *Preparing an effective-interest amortization table; recording interest accrual and payment and the related premium amortization* **(L.O. 2)**

On September 30, 1992, the market interest rate is 11 percent. Auto Power, Inc., issues $300,000 of 12 percent, 20-year sinking-fund bonds payable at 108. The bonds pay interest on March 31 and September 30. Auto Power amortizes bond premium by the effective-interest method.

Required

1. Prepare an amortization table for the first four semiannual interest periods. Follow the format of Exhibit 11-4, Panel B.
2. Record issuance of the bonds on September 30, 1992, the accrual of interest at December 31, 1992, and the semiannual interest payment on March 31, 1993.

Exercise 11-6 *Journalizing sinking fund transactions* **(L.O. 2)**

Auto Power established a sinking fund for the bond issue in Exercise 11-5. Record payment of $8,000 into the sinking fund on March 31, 1993. Also record sinking-fund revenue of $900 on December 31, 1993, and the payment of the bonds at maturity on September 30, 2012. At maturity date the sinking-fund balance was $296,000.

Exercise 11-7 *Recording retirement of bonds payable* **(L.O. 3)**

Alliance Corp. issued $500,000 of 9 percent bonds payable at 97 on October 1, 19X0. These bonds mature on October 1, 19X8, and are callable at 101. Allied pays interest each April 1 and October 1. On October 1, 19X5, when the bonds' market price is 104, Allied retires the bonds in the most economical way available. Record the payment of interest and amortization of bond discount at October 1, 19X5, and the retirement of the bonds on that date. Alliance uses the straight-line amortization method.

Exercise 11-8 *Recording conversion of bonds payable* **(L.O. 4)**

Mending Tape Company issued $400,000 of 8½ percent bonds payable on July 1, 19X4, at a price of 101½. After 5 years the bonds may be converted into the company's common stock. Each $1,000 face amount of bonds is convertible into 40 shares of $20 par stock. The bonds' term to maturity is 15 years. On December 31, 19X9, bondholders exercised their right to convert the bonds into common stock.

Required

1. What would cause the bondholders to convert their bonds into common stock?
2. Without making journal entries, compute the carrying amount of the bonds payable at December 31, 19X9. Mending Tape Company uses the straight-line method to amortize bond premium and discount.
3. All amortization has been recorded properly. Journalize the conversion transaction at December 31, 19X9.

Exercise 11-9 *Recording early retirement and conversion of bonds payable* **(L.O. 3,4)**

Monolithic Industries reported the following at September 30:

Long-term liabilities:
Convertible bonds payable, 9%, 8 years to maturity $200,000
Discount on bonds payable 6,000 $194,000

Required

1. Record retirement of one half of the bonds on October 1 at the call price of 101.
2. Record conversion of one fourth of the bonds into 4,000 shares of Monolithic's $5 par common stock on October 1.

Exercise 11-10 *Reporting long-term debt and pension liability on the balance sheet* **(L.O. 5)**

a. A note to the financial statements of Mapco, Inc., reported (in thousands):

Note 5: Long-Term Debt
Total $537,888
Less—Current portion   22,085
        Unamortized discount   1,391
Long-term debt $514,412

Assume that none of the unamortized discount relates to the current portion of long-term debt. Show how Mapco's balance sheet would report these liabilities.

b. El Campo Incorporated's pension plan has assets with a market value of $720,000. The plan's accumulated benefit obligation is $840,000. What amount of long-term pension liability, if any, will El Campo report on its balance sheet?

Exercise 11-11 *Analyzing alternative plans for raising money* **(L.O. 5)**

Link Inc. is considering two plans for raising $1,000,000 to expand operations. Plan A is to borrow at 10 percent, and plan B is to issue 200,000 shares of common stock. Before any new financing, Link has 200,000 shares of common stock outstanding. Management believes the company can use the new funds to earn income of $420,000 before interest and taxes. The income tax rate is 40 percent.

Required

Prepare an analysis like Exhibit 11-5 to determine which plan will result in higher earnings per share.

Exercise 11-12   *Journalizing capital lease and operating lease transactions* **(L.O. 6)**

A capital lease agreement for equipment requires 10 annual payments of $8,000, with the first payment due on January 2, 19X5. The present value of the nine future lease payments at 12 percent is $42,624.

a. Journalize the following lessee transactions:

19X5
Jan. 2   Beginning of lease term and first annual payment.
Dec. 31 Depreciation of equipment.
    31   Interest expense on lease liability.
19X6
Jan. 2   Second annual lease payment.

b. Journalize the January 2, 19X5, lease payment if this is an operating lease.

Problems   *(Group A)*

Problem 11-1A   *Journalizing bond transactions (at par) and reporting bonds payable on the balance sheet* **(L.O. 1)**

The board of directors of Sabatini Carbonic Company authorizes the issue of $2 million of 8 percent, 20-year bonds payable. The semiannual interest dates are February 28 and August 31. The bonds are issued through an underwriter on April 30, 19X7, at par plus accrued interest.

Required

1. Journalize the following transactions:
   a. Issuance of the bonds on April 30, 19X7.
   b. Payment of interest on August 31, 19X7.
   c. Accrual of interest on December 31, 19X7.
   d. Payment of interest on February 28, 19X8.
2. Check your recorded interest expense for 19X7, using as a model the supplement to the summary problem on page 540.
3. Report interest payable and bonds payable as they would appear on the Sabatini Carbonic Company balance sheet at December 31, 19X7.

Problem 11-2A   *Issuing notes at a premium, amortizing by the straight-line method, and reporting notes payable on the balance sheet* **(L.O. 1,2)**

On March 1, 19X6, Leviton Laboratories issues 9¼ percent, 10-year notes payable with a face value of $300,000. The notes pay interest on February 28 and August 31, and Leviton amortizes premium and discount by the straight-line method.

Required

1. If the market interest rate is 10½ percent when Leviton issues its notes, will the notes be priced at par, at a premium, or at a discount? Explain.

2. If the market interest rate is 8⅝ percent when Leviton issues its notes, will the notes be priced at par, at a premium, or at a discount? Explain.

3. Assume the issue price of the notes is 103. Journalize the following note payable transactions:
   a. Issuance of the notes on March 1, 19X6.
   b. Payment of interest and amortization of premium on August 31, 19X6.
   c. Accrual of interest and amortization of premium on December 31, 19X6.
   d. Payment of interest and amortization of premium on February 28, 19X7.

4. Check your recorded interest expense for the year ended February 28, 19X7, using as a model the supplement to the summary problem on page 540.

5. Report interest payable and notes payable as they would appear on the Leviton balance sheet at December 31, 19X6.

Problem 11-3A *Analyzing a company's long-term debt, journalizing its transactions, and reporting the long-term debt on the balance sheet* **(L.O. 2)**

Assume that the notes to Popeye's Fried Chicken's financial statements reported the following data on September 30, Year 1 (the end of the fiscal year):

NOTE E—LONG-TERM DEBT

7% debentures due Year 20, net of unamortized discount of $71,645,000 (effective interest rate of 11%)	$159,855,000
Notes payable, interest of 8.67%, due in annual amounts of $22,840,000 in Years 5 through 16	274,080,000

Assume Popeye's amortizes discount by the effective interest method.

Required

1. Answer the following questions about Popeye's long-term liabilities:
   a. What is the maturity value of the 7% debenture bonds?
   b. What are Popeye's annual cash interest payments on the 7% debenture bonds?
   c. What is the carrying amount of the 7% debenture bonds at September 30, Year 1?

2. Prepare an amortization table through September 30, Year 4, for the 7% debenture bonds. Round all amounts to the nearest thousand dollars and assume Popeye's pays interest annually on September 30. Use the following format for the amortization table:

End of Annual Interest Period	A Interest Payment (7% of Maturity Value)	B Interest Expense (11% of Preceding Bond Carrying Amount)	C Discount Amortization (B − A)	D Discount Balance (D − C)	E Bond Carrying Amount ($231,500 − D)
Sep. 30, Yr. 1					
Sep. 30, Yr. 2					
Sep. 30, Yr. 3					
Sep. 30, Yr. 4					

3. Record the September 30, Year 3 and Year 4, interest payments on the 7% debenture bonds.

4. There is no premium or discount on the notes payable. Assuming annual interest is paid on September 30 each year, record Popeye's September 30, Year 2, interest payment on the notes payable. Round interest to the nearest thousand dollars.

5. Show how Popeye's would report the debenture bonds payable and notes payable at September 30, Year 4.

Problem 11-4A *Issuing convertible bonds at a discount, amortizing by the effective-interest method, retiring bonds early, converting bonds, and reporting the bonds payable on the balance sheet* **(L.O. 2,3,4)**

On December 31, 19X1, Herrera, Inc., issues 11 percent, 10-year convertible bonds with a maturity value of $500,000. The semiannual interest dates are June 30 and December 31. The market interest rate is 13 percent, and the issue price of the bonds is 89. Herrera amortizes bond premium and discount by the effective-interest method.

Required

1. Prepare an effective-interest method amortization table like Exhibit 11-3 for the first four semiannual interest periods.
2. Journalize the following transactions:
   a. Issuance of the bonds on December 31, 19X1. Credit Convertible Bonds Payable.
   b. Payment of interest on June 30, 19X2.
   c. Payment of interest on December 31, 19X2.
   d. Retirement of bonds with face value of $100,000 on July 1, 19X3. Herrera purchases the bonds at 94 in the open market.
   e. Conversion by the bondholders on July 1, 19X3, of bonds with face value of $200,000 into 50,000 shares of Herrera $1 par common stock.
3. Prepare the balance sheet presentation of the bonds payable that are outstanding at December 31, 19X3.

Problem 11-5A *Journalizing bonds payable and capital lease transactions* **(L.O. 1,6)**

Journalize the following transactions of Republic Iron Works:

19X1
Jan. 1 Issued $2,000,000 of 9 percent, 10-year bonds payable at 97.
   1 Signed a 5-year capital lease on machinery. The agreement requires annual lease payments of $16,000, with the first payment due immediately. At 12 percent, the present value of the four future lease payments is $48,590.
July 1 Paid semiannual interest and amortized discount by the straight-line method on our 9 percent bonds payable.
   1 Made the $100,000 sinking-fund payment required by the indenture on our 9 percent bonds payable.
Dec. 31 Accrued semiannual interest expense and amortized discount by the straight-line method on our 9 percent bonds payable.
   31 Recorded depreciation on leased machinery.
   31 Accrued interest expense on the lease liability.
   31 Recorded bond sinking-fund earnings of $5,500.
19X11
Jan. 1 Paid the 9 percent bonds at maturity from the sinking fund ($1,993,000) and the remainder from company cash.

Problem 11-6A *Financing operations with debt or with stock* **(L.O. 5)**

Marketing studies have shown that consumers prefer upscale stores, and recent trends in industry sales have supported the research. To capitalize on this trend, Modern Views, Inc., is embarking on a massive expansion. Plans call for opening 100 new stores within the next 18 months. Each store is scheduled to be 50 percent larger than the company's existing stores, furnished more elaborately, and stocked with more expensive merchandise. Management estimates that company operations will provide $8 million of the cash needed for expansion. Modern Views must raise the remaining $5.5 million from outsiders. The board of directors is considering obtaining the $5.5 million either through borrowing or by issuing common stock.

Required

Discuss for company management the advantages and the disadvantages of borrowing and of issuing common stock to raise the needed cash. Which method of raising the funds would you recommend?

Problem 11-7A   *Reporting liabilities on the balance sheet (L.O. 6)*

The Naval Salvage Supply Corp. accounting records include these items:

Bonds payable, current portion	$ 75,000	Mortgage note payable, long-term	$ 82,000
Capital lease liability, long-term	81,000	Accumulated depreciation, equipment	46,000
Discount on bonds payable	7,000	Bond sinking fund	119,000
Interest revenue	5,000	Capital lease liability, current	18,000
Equipment acquired under capital lease	113,000	Mortgage note payable, current	23,000
Pension plan assets (market value)	116,000	Accumulated pension benefit obligation	124,000
Interest payable	13,000	Bonds payable, long-term	400,000
Interest expense	57,000		

Required

Show how these items would be reported on the Naval Salvage Supply balance sheet, including headings for current liabilities, long-term liabilities, and so on. Note disclosures are not required.

(Group B)

Problem 11-1B   *Journalizing bond transactions (at par) and reporting bonds payable on the balance sheet (L.O. 1)*

The board of directors of Hunt Boston Corp. authorizes the issue of $3 million of 9 percent, 10-year bonds payable. The semiannual interest dates are May 31 and November 30. The bonds are issued through an underwriter on June 30, 19X5, at par plus accrued interest.

Required

1. Journalize the following transactions:
   a. Issuance of the bonds on June 30, 19X5.
   b. Payment of interest on November 30, 19X5.
   c. Accrual of interest on December 31, 19X5.
   d. Payment of interest on May 31, 19X6.
2. Check your recorded interest expense for 19X5, using as a model the supplement to the summary problem on page 540.
3. Report interest payable and bonds payable as they would appear on the Hunt Boston Corp. balance sheet at December 31, 19X5.

Problem 11-2B   *Issuing bonds at a discount, amortizing by the straight-line method, and reporting bonds payable on the balance sheet* **(L.O. 1,2)**

On March 1, 19X4, Garth Corp. issues 10½ percent, 20-year bonds payable with a face value of $500,000. The bonds pay interest on February 28 and August 31. Garth amortizes premium and discount by the straight-line method.

Required

1. If the market interest rate is 9⅜ percent when Garth issues its bonds, will the bonds be priced at par, at a premium, or at a discount? Explain.
2. If the market interest rate is 10⅞ percent when Garth issues its bonds, will the bonds be priced at par, at a premium, or at a discount? Explain.
3. Assume the issue price of the bonds is 96. Journalize the following bond transactions:
   a. Issuance of the bonds on March 1, 19X4.
   b. Payment of interest and amortization of discount on August 31, 19X4.
   c. Accrual of interest and amortization of discount on December 31, 19X4.
   d. Payment of interest and amortization of discount on February 28, 19X5.
4. Check your recorded interest expense for the year ended February 28, 19X5, using as a model the supplement to the summary problem on page 540.
5. Report interest payable and bonds payable as they would appear on the Garth balance sheet at December 31, 19X4.

Problem 11-3B   *Analyzing an actual company's long-term debt, journalizing its transactions, and reporting the long-term debt on the balance sheet* **(L.O. 2)**

The notes to Baker International's financial statements recently reported the following data on September 30, Year 1 (the end of the fiscal year):

> **NOTE 4. INDEBTEDNESS**
>
> Long-Term debt at September 30, Year 1, included the following:
>
> | | |
> |---|---:|
> | 6.00% debentures due Year 20 with an effective interest rate of 14.66%, net of unamortized discount of $123,152,000 .... | $101,848,000 |
> | Other indebtedness with an interest rate of 10.30%, due $12,108,000 in Year 5 and $19,257,000 in Year 6 ..... | 31,365,000 |

Assume Baker amortizes discount by the effective-interest method.

Required

1. Answer the following questions about Baker's long-term liabilities:
   a. What is the maturity value of the 6.00% debenture bonds?
   b. What are Baker's annual cash interest payments on the 6.00% debenture bonds?
   c. What is the carrying amount of the 6.00% debenture bonds at September 30, Year 1?
2. Prepare an amortization table through September 30, Year 4, for the 6.00% debenture bonds. Round all amounts to the nearest thousand dollars, and assume Baker pays interest annually on September 30. Use the following format for the amortization table:

End of Annual Interest Period	A Interest Payment (6% of Maturity Value)	B Interest Expense (14.66% of Preceding Bond Carrying Amount)	C Discount Amortization (B − A)	D Discount Balance (D − C)	E Bond Carrying Amount ($225,000 − D)
Sep. 30, Yr. 1					
Sep. 30, Yr. 2					
Sep. 30, Yr. 3					
Sep. 30, Yr. 4					

3. Record the September 30, Year 3 and Year 4, interest payments on the 6.00% debenture bonds.

4. There is no premium or discount on the other indebtedness. Assuming annual interest is paid on September 30 each year, record Baker's September 30, Year 2, interest payment on the other indebtedness. Round interest to the nearest thousand dollars.

5. Show how Baker would report the debenture bonds payable and other indebtedness of September 30, Year 4.

Problem 11-4B *Issuing convertible bonds at a premium, amortizing by the effective-interest method, retiring bonds early, converting bonds, and reporting the bonds payable on the balance sheet* **(L.O. 2,3,4)**

On December 31, 19X1, Ernst, Inc., issues 12 percent, 10-year convertible bonds with a maturity value of $300,000. The semiannual interest dates are June 30 and December 31. The market interest rate is 11 percent, and the issue price of the bonds is 106. Ernst amortizes bond premium and discount by the effective-interest method.

Required

1. Prepare an effective-interest method amortization table like Exhibit 11-4 for the first four semiannual interest periods.
2. Journalize the following transactions:
   a. Issuance of the bonds on December 31, 19X1. Credit Convertible Bonds Payable.
   b. Payment of interest on June 30, 19X2.
   c. Payment of interest on December 31, 19X2.
   d. Retirement of bonds with face value of $100,000 on July 1, 19X3. Ernst pays the call price of 102.
   e. Conversion by the bondholders on July 1, 19X3, of bonds with face value of $150,000 into 10,000 shares of Ernst's $10 par common stock.
3. Prepare the balance sheet presentation of the bonds payable that are outstanding at December 31, 19X3.

Problem 11-5B *Journalizing bonds payable and capital lease transactions* **(L.O. 1,6)**

Journalize the following transactions of Evergreen Products, Inc.:

19X1
Jan. 1 Issued $500,000 of 8 percent, 10-year bonds payable at 93.
     1 Signed a 5-year capital lease on equipment. The agreement requires annual lease payments of $20,000, with the first payment due immediately. At 12 percent, the present value of the four future lease payments is $60,750.
July 1 Paid semiannual interest and amortized discount by the straight-line method on our 8 percent bonds payable.

July   1   Made the $25,000 sinking-fund payment required by the indenture on our 8 percent bonds payable.

Dec. 31   Accrued semiannual interest expense, and amortized discount by the straight-line method on our 8 percent bonds payable.

31   Recorded depreciation on leased equipment.

31   Accrued interest expense on the lease liability.

31   Recorded bond sinking-fund earnings of $1,000.

19X11

Jan.   1   Paid the 8 percent bonds at maturity from the sinking fund and received excess cash of $7,800.

Problem 11-6B   *Financing operations with debt instead of with stock*   (L.O. 5)

Two businesses must consider how to raise $10 million.

Minneapolis Corporation is in the midst of its most successful period since it began operations in 1960. For each of the past 10 years, net income and earnings per share have increased by 15 percent. The outlook for the future is equally bright, with new markets opening up and competitors unable to manufacture products of Minneapolis's quality. Minneapolis Corporation is planning a large-scale expansion.

St. Paul Company has fallen on hard times. Net income has remained flat for five of the last six years, even falling by 10 percent from last year's level of profits. Top management has experienced unusual turnover, and the company lacks strong leadership. To become competitive again, St. Paul Company desperately needs $10 million for expansion.

Required

Propose a plan for each company to raise the needed cash. Which company should borrow? Which company should issue stock? Consider the advantages and the disadvantages of raising money by borrowing and by issuing stock, and discuss them in your answer.

Problem 11-7B   *Reporting liabilities on the balance sheet*   (L.O. 6)

The accounting records of Pantel Corp. include the following items:

Bond sinking fund	$ 80,000	Mortgage note payable, long-term	$ 67,000
Accumulated pension benefit obligation	210,000	Building acquired under capital lease	190,000
Bonds payable, long-term	180,000	Interest expense	47,000
Premium on bonds payable	13,000	Pension plan assets (market value)	190,000
Interest payable	9,200		
Interest revenue	5,300	Bonds payable, current portion	60,000
Capital lease liability, long-term	73,000	Accumulated depreciation, building	108,000

Required

Show how these items would be reported on the Pantel balance sheet, including headings for current liabilities, long-term liabilities, and so on. Note disclosures are not required.

Extending Your Knowledge

Decision Problems

1. Analyzing Alternative Ways of Raising $5 Million   (L.O. 6)

Business is going well for MicroCraft of Vermont, Inc. The board of directors of this family-owned company believes that MicroCraft could earn an additional $2,000,000 in income before interest and taxes by expanding into new markets. However, the $5,000,000 that the business needs for growth cannot be raised within the family. The directors, who strongly wish to retain family control of MicroCraft, must consider issuing securities to outsiders. They are considering three financing plans.

Plan A is to borrow at 9 percent. Plan B is to issue 200,000 shares of common stock. Plan C is to issue 100,000 shares of nonvoting, $3.75 preferred stock. ($3.75 is the annual dividend per share of preferred stock.) MicroCraft presently has 500,000 shares of common stock outstanding. The income tax rate is 40 percent.

Required

1. Prepare an analysis similar to Exhibit 11-5 to determine which plan will result in the highest earnings per share of common stock.
2. Recommend one plan to the board of directors. Give your reasons.

2. Questions about Long-Term Debt   (L.O. 6 and Appendix A)

The following questions are not related.

a. Why do you think corporations prefer operating leases over capital leases? How do you think a wise shareholder would view an operating lease?
b. Companies like to borrow for longer terms when interest rates are low and for shorter terms when interest rates are high? Why is this statement true?
c. If you were to win $2,000,000 from a Canadian lottery, you would receive the $2,000,000, whereas if you win $2,000,000 in one of the big U.S. lotteries, you would receive 20 annual payments of $100,000. Are the prizes equivalent? If not, why not?

Ethical Issue

Ling-Temco-Vought, Inc. (LTV), manufacturer of aircraft and related electronic devices, borrowed heavily during the 1960s to exploit the advantage of financing operations with debt. At first, LTV was able to earn operating income much higher than its interest expense and was therefore quite profitable. However, when the business cycle turned down, LTV's debt burden pushed the company to the brink of bankruptcy. Operating income was less than interest expense.

Required

Is it unethical for managers to saddle a company with a high level of debt? Or is it just risky? Who could be hurt by a company's taking on too much debt? Discuss.

1. Long-Term Debt *(L.O. 2,3)*

The Goodyear Tire & Rubber Company's balance sheet, statement of cash flow, and note titled "Credit Arrangements"—all given in Appendix C—provide details about the company's long-term debt. Use those data to answer the following questions.

1. How much long-term debt did Goodyear pay off during 1991? How much new long-term debt did the company incur during 1991? Journalize these transactions using Goodyear's actual account titles.
2. Prepare a T-account for the sum of current "Notes Payable to Banks and Overdrafts" and "Long-Term Debt and Capital Leases" to show the beginning and ending balances and all activity in the account during 1991. Note: There is a $2.6 million inconsistency in the account that the authors are unable to explain! Insert the $2.6 million inconsistency in the appropriate place.
3. Journalize, in a single entry, Goodyear's interest expense for 1991, assuming amortization of Discount on Long-Term Debt was $7.3 million for the year.
4. In what foreign currencies is some of Goodyear's long-term debt stated?
5. Study the Credit Arrangements Note. At December 31, 1991, how much additional long-term debt had Goodyear already lined up for use as needed?

2. Long-Term Debt *(L.O. 2,3)*

Obtain the annual report of an actual company of your choosing. Answer these questions about the company. Concentrate on the current year in the annual report you select.

1. Examine the statement of cash flows. How much long-term debt did the company pay off during the current year? How much new long-term debt did the company incur during the year? Journalize these transactions using the company's actual account balances.
2. Prepare a T-account for the Long-Term Debt account to show the beginning and ending balances and all activity in the account during the year. If there is a discrepancy, insert this amount in the appropriate place. Note: Even the authors cannot explain all details in actual financial statements!
3. Study the notes to the financial statements. Is any of the company's retained earnings balance restricted as a result of borrowings? If so, indicate the amount of the retained earnings balance that is restricted and the amount that is unrestricted. How will the restriction affect the company's dividend payments in the future?
4. Journalize the company's interest expense for the current year in a single entry. If the company discloses the amount of amortization of premium or discount on long-term debt, use the actual figures. If not, assume the amortization of discount totaled $700,000 for the year.

Chapter *12*

Corporate Organization,
Paid-In Capital,
and the Balance Sheet

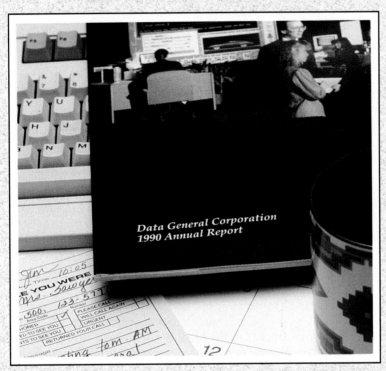

Data General Corporation
1990 Annual Report

What highflying computer stock has risen 300 percent since January 1? Apple Computer? Sun Microsystems? Or maybe Microsoft?

Wrong. It's Data General, the aging maker of minicomputers for corporate and industrial use. This stock was almost given up for dead by traders who watched its relentless slide from . . . 38 in 1987 to 4½ as this year began. But Data General *shares* have since quadrupled. Now analysts who practically ignored the *stock* are looking at it again and, in some cases, boosting their earnings forecasts.

Yesterday, the Westborough, Mass., computer maker continued its startling comeback, reporting its second consecutive profitable quarter on a narrow 1.8 percent revenue increase from a year earlier. The stock jumped 1½ to 18 on the New York *Stock* Exchange. . . . [emphasis added]

Source: William M. Bulkalay, "Data General's Stock Rises from Ashes," *The Wall Street Journal* (April 26, 1991), p. C1. Reprinted by permission of *The Wall Street Journal*, © 1991 Dow Jones & Company, Inc. All Rights Reserved Worldwide.

The period surrounding the date of this article's publication would be a good time for Data General to raise money by issuing new stock. Profits are up, the outlook for the company is bright, and Data General's stock price is higher than it has been in the recent past. Issuing stock, as we will see in this chapter, is an important way for a corporation to finance its operations.

The corporation is the dominant form of business organization in the United States. Data General is a prime example, with operations around the world. Although proprietorships and partnerships are more numerous, corporations transact more business and are larger in terms of total assets, sales revenue, and number of employees. Most well-known companies, such as Data General, CBS, General Motors, IBM, and Boeing, are corporations. Their full names include *Corporation* or *Incorporated* (abbreviated *Corp.* and *Inc.*) to indicate that they are corporations—for example, CBS, Inc. and General Motors Corporation. This chapter and the next two chapters discuss various aspects of corporations.

Capital Stock

A corporation issues stock certificates to its owners in exchange for their investments in the business. The basic unit of capital stock is called a *share*. A corporation may issue a stock certificate for any number of shares it wishes—one share, one hundred shares, or any other number. Exhibit 12-1 depicts an actual stock certificate for one share of IBM stock. The certificate shows the company name, the stockholder name, the number of shares, and the par value of the stock (which we discuss later).

Stock in the hands of a stockholder is said to be **outstanding.** The total number of shares of stock outstanding at any time represents 100 percent ownership of the corporation. Because stock represents the corporation's capital, it is often called capital stock.

Stockholder Rights

The ownership of stock entitles stockholders to four basic rights, unless specific rights are withheld by agreement with the stockholders.

1. The right to participate in management by voting on matters that come before the stockholders. This is the stockholder's sole right to a voice in the management of the corporation. Each share of stock entitles the owner to one vote.

2. The right to receive a proportionate part of any dividend. Each share of stock in a particular class receives an equal dividend.

EXHIBIT 12-1   *Stock Certificate*

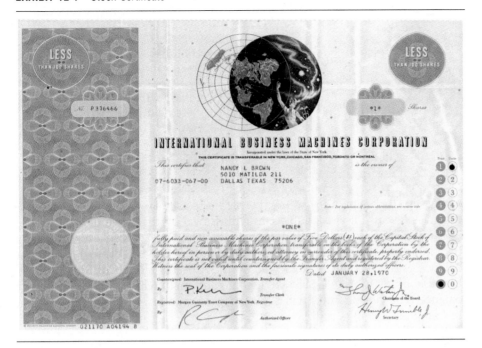

3. The right to receive a proportionate share (based on number of shares held) of any assets remaining after the corporation pays its liabilities in liquidation.

4. The right to maintain one's proportionate ownership in the corporation. Suppose you own 5 percent of a corporation's stock. If the corporation issues 100,000 new shares of stock, it must offer you the opportunity to buy 5 percent (5,000) of the new shares. This right, called the **preemptive right,** is usually withheld from the stockholders.

Stockholders' Equity

Recall that a corporation is a creature of the state and that stockholders have limited personal liability for corporate debts. Without safeguards, a corporation could borrow money, use the cash to pay huge cash dividends, and declare bankruptcy. States therefore consider it necessary to protect creditors from dishonest corporate managers. Many states limit a corporation's dividend payments to the balance of its retained earnings. In effect, the corporation cannot use paid-in capital as the basis for declaring cash dividends. Consequently, state laws require corporations to report the sources of their capital: paid-in capital (contributed capital), and retained earnings. Exhibit 12-2 outlines a simplified corporation balance sheet to distinguish these categories of stockholders' equity.

An investment of cash or any other asset in a corporation increases its assets and stockholders' equity. The corporation's entry for receipt of a $20,000 stockholder investment in the business is

Oct. 20	Cash	20,000	
	Capital Stock		20,000
	Investment by stockholders.		

EXHIBIT 12-2 *Simplified Corporation Balance Sheet*

Assets	$600,000	Liabilities	$240,000
		Stockholders' Equity	
		Paid-in capital:	
		Capital stock	**200,000**
		Retained earnings . .	**160,000**
		Total stockholders'	
		equity	**360,000**
		Total liabilities and	
Total assets	$600,000	stockholders' equity .	$600,000

Capital stock is paid-in capital. It is regarded as the permanent capital of the business because it is *not* subject to withdrawal by the stockholders.

Profitable operations produce income, which increases stockholders' equity through an account called Retained Earnings. At the end of the year, the balance of the Income Summary account is closed to Retained Earnings. For example, if net income is $95,000, Income Summary will have a $95,000 credit balance. The closing entry will debit Income Summary to transfer net income to Retained Earnings as follows:

Dec. 31	Income Summary	95,000	
	Retained Earnings		95,000
	To close Income Summary by transferring net *income* to Retained Earnings.		

If operations produce a net *loss* rather than net income, the Income Summary account will have a debit balance. Income Summary must be credited to close it. With a $60,000 loss, the closing entry is:

Dec. 31	Retained Earnings	60,000	
	Income Summary		60,000
	To close Income Summary by transferring net *loss* to Retained Earnings.		

A large loss may cause a debit balance in the Retained Earnings account. This condition—called a Retained Earnings **deficit**, or accumulated deficit—is reported on the balance sheet as a negative amount in stockholders' equity. Assume a $50,000 deficit:

Stockholders' Equity

Paid-in capital:	
Capital stock	$200,000
Deficit	(50,000)
Total stockholders' equity	$150,000

If the corporation has been profitable and has sufficient cash, a distribution of cash may be made to the stockholders. Such distributions—called dividends—decrease both the assets and the retained earnings of the business. The balance of the Retained Earnings account at any time is the sum of earnings accumulated since incorporation, minus any losses, and minus all dividends distributed to stockholders. Retained Earnings is entirely separate from the paid-in capital invested in the business by the stockholders.

Some people think of Retained Earnings as a fund of cash. It is not, because Retained Earnings is an element of stockholders' equity, representing a claim against all assets resulting from cumulative earnings minus cumulative dividends since the corporation's beginning.

Classes of Stock

Corporations issue different types of stock to appeal to a wide variety of investors. The stock of a corporation may be either common or preferred and either par or no-par.

Common and Preferred Stock

Every corporation issues **common stock**, the most basic form of capital stock. Unless designated otherwise, the word *stock* is understood to mean "common stock." Common stockholders have the four basic rights of stock ownership, unless a right is specifically withheld. For example, some companies issue Class A common stock, which usually carries the right to vote, and Class B common stock, which may be nonvoting. (Classes of common stock may also be designated Series A, Series B, and so on.) The general ledger has a separate account for each class of common stock. In describing a corporation, we would say the common stockholders are the owners of the business.

Owners of **preferred stock** also have the four basic stockholder rights, unless a right is specifically denied. Often the right to vote is withheld from preferred stockholders. Preferred stock gives its owners certain advantages over common stockholders. These benefits include the priority to receive dividends before the common stockholders and the priority to receive assets before the common stockholders if the corporation liquidates. Because of the preferred stockholders' priorities, we see that common stock represents the residual ownership in the corporation's assets after subtracting the liabilities and the claims of preferred stockholders. Companies may issue different classes of preferred stock (Class A and Class B or Series A and Series B, for example). Each class is recorded in a separate account.

Par Value and No-Par Stock

legal minimum amount

Stock may be par value stock or no-par stock. **Par value** is an arbitrary amount assigned to a share of stock. Most companies set the par value of their common stock quite low. J. C. Penney's common stock par value is 50¢ per share, Bethlehem Steel's common stock par value is $8 per share, and Ralston Purina's common stock par value is 41 $\frac{2}{3}$¢ per share. Par value of preferred stock is often higher; $100 per share is typical, but some preferred stocks have par values of $25 and $10. Par value is used to compute dividends on preferred stock, as we shall see. **No-par** stock does not have par value, but some no-par stock has a *stated value*, which makes it similar to par value stock. The stated value is also an arbitrary amount that accountants treat as though it were par value.

Issuing Stock

Large corporations such as PepsiCo, Xerox, and British Petroleum need huge quantities of money to operate. They cannot expect to finance all their operations through borrowing. They need capital that they raise by issuing stock.

The charter that the incorporators receive from the state includes an **authorization** for the business to issue—that is, to sell—a certain number of shares of stock. Corporations may sell the stock directly to the stockholders or they may use the service of an *underwriter*, such as the brokerage firms Merrill Lynch and Dean Witter. An underwriter agrees to buy all the stock it cannot sell to its clients.

The corporation need not issue all the stock that the state allows. Management may hold some stock back and issue it later if the need for additional capital arises. The stock that the corporation does issue to stockholders is called issued stock. Only by issuing stock—not by receiving authorization—does the corporation increase the asset and stockholders' equity amounts on its balance sheet.

The price that the stockholder pays to acquire stock from the corporation is called the *issue price*. Often the issue price far exceeds the stock's par value because the par value was intentionally set quite low. A combination of market factors, including the company's comparative earnings record, financial position, prospects for success, and general business conditions, determines issue price. Investors will not pay more than market value for the stock. The following sections show how to account for the issuance of stock.

Issuing Common Stock

Issuing Common Stock at Par. Suppose Medina Corporation issues 500 shares of its $10 par common stock for cash equal to its par value. The stock issuance entry is

OBJECTIVE 1

Record the issuance of stock

Jan. 8	Cash (500 × $10)	5,000	
	Common Stock		5,000
	To issue common stock at par.		

The amount invested in the corporation, $5,000 in this case, is called paid-in capital or contributed capital. The credit to Common Stock records an increase in the paid-in capital of the corporation.

Issuing Common Stock at a Premium. A corporation usually issues its common stock for a price above par value. The excess amount above par is called a **premium.** Assume Medina issues $10 par common stock for a price of $25. The $15 difference is a premium. This sale of stock increases the corporation's paid-in capital by $25, the total issue price of the stock. Both the par value of the stock and the premium are part of paid-in capital. A premium on the sale of stock is not gain, income, or profit to the corporation, because the entity is dealing with its own stockholders. This illustrates one of the fundamentals of accounting: a company cannot earn a profit, nor can it incur a loss, when it sells its stock to, or buys its stock from, its own stockholders.

Suppose Medina Corporation issues 4,000 shares of its $10 par common stock for $25 per share—a total of $100,000 (4,000 × $25). The premium per share is $15 ($25 − $10), and the entry to record the issuance of the stock is

Jan. 23	Cash (4,000 × $25)........................	100,000	
	Common Stock (4,000 × $10)		40,000
	Paid-in Capital in Excess of Par—		
	Common (4,000 × $15)		60,000
	To issue common stock at a premium.		

Account titles that could be used in place of Paid-in Capital in Excess of Par—Common are Additional Paid-in Capital—Common, and Premium on Common Stock. Since both par value and premium amounts increase the corporation's capital, they appear in the stockholders' equity section of the balance sheet.

At the end of the first year, Medina Corporation would report stockholders' equity on its balance sheet as follows, assuming the corporate charter authorizes 20,000 shares of common stock and retained earnings is $85,000:

Stockholders' Equity

Paid-in capital:	
Common stock, $10 par, 20,000 shares authorized, 4,500 shares issued	$ 45,000
Paid-in capital in excess of par	60,000
Total paid-in capital	105,000
Retained earnings	85,000
Total stockholders' equity	$190,000

We determine the dollar amount reported for common stock by multiplying the total number of shares *issued* (500 + 4,000) by the par value per share. The *authorization* reports the maximum number of shares the company may issue under its charter.

Issuing Common Stock at a Discount.   Stock issued at a price below par is said to be issued at a **discount.** For example, the issuance of $5 par common stock for $3 creates a $2 discount per share. The entry to record 1,000 shares of $5 par common stock issued for $3 per share is

Feb. 18	Cash (1,000 × $3)	3,000	
	Discount on Common Stock (1,000 × $2)	2,000	
	Common Stock (1,000 × $5)		5,000
	To issue common stock at a discount.		

What is the paid-in capital in this case? It is $3,000, the amount invested by the stockholders. The discount is reported in the stockholders' equity section of the balance sheet immediately after the stock account (as just shown for reporting a premium). However, the discount account—because it has a debit balance—is subtracted from the credit-balance par value of the stock issued to figure the capital amount.

The issuance of stock at a discount is rare. In fact, it is illegal in most states. When stock is sold at a discount, the stockholder has a *contingent liability* for the discount amount. If the corporation later liquidates, its creditors can require the original stockholder to pay the discount amount. Many companies set the par value of their common stock very low to avoid this contingent liability. A company is not likely to issue its stock at a price below an already low par value.

Issuing No-Par Common Stock.   The contingent liability on common stock issued at a discount may explain why some state laws allow companies to issue no-par stock. If the stock has no par value, there can be no discount and thus no contingent liability. A recent survey of 600 companies revealed that they had 108 issues of no-par stock.

When no-par stock is issued, the asset received is debited and the stock account is credited. Glenwood Corporation issues 300 shares of no-par common stock for $20 per share. The stock issuance entry is

Aug. 14   Cash (300 × $20) 6,000
           Common Stock   6,000
         To issue no-par common stock.

Regardless of the stock's price, Cash is debited and Common Stock is credited for the amount of cash received. There is no Paid-in Capital in Excess of Par for true no-par stock.

Assume that the charter authorizes Glenwood to issue 5,000 shares of no-par stock and the company has $3,000 in retained earnings. The corporation would report stockholders' equity as follows:

Stockholders' Equity

Paid-in capital:
    Common stock, no-par, 5,000 shares
        authorized, 300 shares issued $6,000
    Retained earnings...................   3,000
    Total stockholders' equity........... $9,000

Issuing No-Par Common Stock with a Stated Value.   Accounting for no-par stock with a stated value is identical to accounting for par value stock. The premium account for no-par common is entitled Paid-in Capital in Excess of Stated Value—Common.

Issuing Common Stock for Assets Other Than Cash.   When a corporation issues stock in exchange for assets other than cash, it debits the assets received for their current market value and credits the capital accounts accordingly. The assets' prior book value does not matter because the stockholder will demand stock equal to the market value of the asset given. Assume Kahn Corporation issues 15,000 shares of its $1 par common stock for equipment worth $4,000 and a building worth $120,000. The entry is

Nov. 12   Equipment 4,000
         Building 120,000
           Common Stock (15,000 × $1)   15,000
           Paid-in Capital in Excess of Par—
             Common ($124,000 − $15,000)   109,000
         To issue common stock in exchange for equipment and a building.

Paid-in capital increases by the amount of the assets' current market value, $124,000 in this case.

Issuing Common Stock through Subscriptions.   Established companies usually issue stock and receive the full price in a single transaction. New corporations, to gauge their ability to raise capital, often take subscriptions for their stock. A **stock subscription** is a contract that obligates an investor to purchase the corporation's stock at a later date. Because a contract exists between the two parties, the corporation acquires an asset, Subscription Receivable, when it receives the subscription. The investor gains an equity in the corporation by promising to pay the subscription amount. Depending on the subscription agreement, the subscriber may pay the subscription in a lump sum or in installments.

Assume Medina Corporation receives a subscription on May 31 for 1,000 shares of $10 par common stock. The subscription price is $22 per share. The subscriber makes a down payment of $6,000 and agrees to pay the $16,000 balance in two monthly installments of $8,000 each. Medina Corporation will issue the stock when the subscriber pays in full. The entry to record receipt of the subscription is

May 31	Cash	6,000	
	Subscription Receivable—Common		
	($22,000 − $6,000)	16,000	
	Common Stock Subscribed		
	(1,000 × $10)		10,000
	Paid-in Capital in Excess of Par—		
	Common (1,000 × $12)		12,000
	To receive common stock subscription at $22 per share.		

Subscription Receivable—Common is a current asset if collection is expected within one year. Otherwise it is long-term and is reported in the Other Assets category on the balance sheet. Common Stock Subscribed is an element of stockholders' equity, reported immediately beneath Common Stock (and above Paid-in Capital in Excess of Par—Common) on the balance sheet. The "Subscribed" label will be dropped when the subscription is paid off and the stock is issued. Paid-in Capital in Excess of Par—Common is the same premium account that is credited when stock is sold for cash at a price in excess of par. The entries to record receipt of the two installments and issuance of the stock are

June 30	Cash ($16,000 × ½)	8,000	
	Subscription Receivable—Common		8,000
	To collect first installment on common stock subscription.		
July 31	Cash ($16,000 × ½)	8,000	
	Subscription Receivable—Common		8,000
	To collect second installment on common stock subscription.		
31	Common Stock Subscribed	10,000	
	Common Stock		10,000
	To issue common stock under subscription agreement.		

The last entry is needed to transfer the par value of the stock from the Subscribed account to Common Stock.

Because the subscription is a legally binding contract, subscribers must pay their subscriptions in full. If they fail to do so, state laws govern the settlement between the corporation and the defaulting subscriber.

Issuing Preferred Stock

Not all corporations issue preferred stock. A recent survey of 600 companies indicated that only 213 had preferred stock outstanding. Accounting for preferred stock follows the pattern illustrated for common stock. Assume the Medina Corporation charter authorizes issuance of 5,000 shares of 5 percent, $100 par preferred stock. On July 31 the company issues 400 shares at a price of $110. (Preferred stock usually sells at its par value or at a premium.) The issuance entry is

```
July 31   Cash (400 × $110) .........................   44,000
               Preferred Stock (400 × $100) ............            40,000
               Paid-in Capital in Excess of Par—Preferred
                    (400 × $10) .........................             4,000
          To issue preferred stock at a premium.
```

Observe that the Paid-in Capital in Excess of Par account title includes the word Preferred. A corporation lists separate accounts for Paid-in Capital in Excess of Par on Preferred Stock and on Common Stock to differentiate the two classes of equity.

Accounting for *no-par preferred stock* follows the pattern illustrated for no-par common stock.

Donated Capital

Corporations occasionally receive gifts, or donations. For example, city council members may offer a company free land to encourage it to locate in their city. Cities in the southern United States have lured some companies away from the North using this offer. The free land is called a donation. Also, a stockholder may make a donation to the corporation in the form of cash, land, or other assets or stock that the corporation can resell.

A donation is a gift that increases the assets of the corporation. However, the donor (giver) receives no ownership interest in the company in return. A transaction to receive a donation does not increase the corporation's revenue, and thus it does not affect income. Instead, the donation creates a special category of stockholders' equity called **donated capital.** The corporation records a donation by debiting the asset received at its current market value, and by crediting Donated Capital, a stockholders' equity account.

Suppose Burlington Industries receives 100 acres of land as a donation from the city of Raleigh, North Carolina. The current market value of the land is $150,000. Burlington records receipt of the donation as follows:

```
Apr. 18   Land ..................................   150,000
               Donated Capital ...................             150,000
          To receive land as a donation from the city.
```

Donated capital is reported on the balance sheet after the stock accounts in the paid-in capital section of stockholders' equity.

Incorporation of a Going Business

OBJECTIVE 2

Account for the
incorporation of
a going business

You may dream of having your own business someday, or you may currently be a business proprietor or partner. Businesses that begin as a proprietorship or a partnership often incorporate at a later date. By incorporating a going business, the proprietor or partners avoid the unlimited liability for business debts. And, as discussed, incorporating also makes it easier to raise capital.

To account for the incorporation of a going business, we close the owner equity accounts of the prior entity and set up the stockholder equity accounts of the corporation. Suppose Santa Fe Travel Associates is a partnership owned by Joe Brown and Monica Lee. The partnership balance sheet, after all adjustments and closing entries, reports Joe Brown, Capital, of $50,000, and Monica Lee, Capital, of $70,000. They incorporate the travel agency as Santa Fe Travel

Company, Inc., with an authorization to issue 200,000 shares of $1 par common stock. Joe and Monica agree to receive common stock equal in par value to their partnership owner equity balances. The entry to record the incorporation of the business is

Feb. 1	Joe Brown, Capital	50,000	
	Monica Lee, Capital	70,000	
	Common Stock		120,000
	To incorporate the business, close the capital accounts of the partnership, and issue common stock to the incorporators.		

Let's review the first half of this chapter by showing the stockholders' equity section of Medina Corporation's balance sheet. (Assume that all figures, which are arbitrary, are correct.) Note the two sections of stockholders' equity: paid-in capital and retained earnings. Also observe the order of the equity accounts: preferred stock at par value, paid-in capital in excess of par on preferred stock, common stock at par value, common stock subscribed, and paid-in capital in excess of par on common stock. If Medina had a Preferred Stock Subscribed account, it would appear after Preferred Stock and before Paid-in Capital in Excess of Par—Preferred (corresponding to the order illustrated for the common stock accounts).

Stockholders' Equity

Paid-in capital:	
Preferred stock, 5%, $100 par, 5,000 shares authorized, 400 shares issued	$ 40,000
Paid-in capital in excess of par—preferred	4,000
Common stock, $10 par, 20,000 shares authorized, 4,500 shares issued	45,000
Common stock subscribed, 1,000 shares	10,000
Paid-in capital in excess of par—common	72,000
Donated capital	60,000
Total paid-in capital	231,000
Retained earnings	85,000
Total stockholders' equity	$316,000

OBJECTIVE 3

Prepare the stockholders' equity section of a corporation balance sheet

Summary Problems for Your Review

Problem 1

Test your understanding of the first half of this chapter by answering whether each of the following statements is true or false.

_____ a. The owner of 100 shares of preferred stock has greater voting rights than the owner of 100 shares of common stock.

_____ b. Par value stock is worth more than no-par stock.

_____ c. Issuance of 1,000 shares of $5 par value stock at $12 increases contributed capital by $12,000.

_____ d. The issuance of stock at a discount occurs less frequently than issuance of stock at a premium.

_____ e. The issuance of no-par stock with a stated value is fundamentally different from issuing par value stock.

_____ f. A corporation issues its preferred stock in exchange for land and a building with a combined market value of $200,000. This transaction increases the corporation's stockholders' equity by $200,000 regardless of the assets' prior book value.

_____ g. Receipt of a subscription contract does not increase the stockholders' equity of the corporation unless the subscriber makes a down payment.

_____ h. Common Stock Subscribed is a part of stockholders' equity.

Problem 2

Adolph Coors Company is a leading brewery. The company has two classes of common stock. Note that only the Class A common stockholders are entitled to vote. Coors's balance sheet included the following presentation:

Shareholders' Equity

Capital stock	
Class A common stock, voting, $1 par value, authorized and issued 1,260,000 shares	$ 1,260,000
Class B common stock, non-voting, no-par value, authorized and issued 46,200,000 shares	11,000,000
	12,260,000
Additional paid-in capital..........................	2,011,000
Retained earnings	872,403,000
	$886,674,000

Required

a. Record the issuance of the Class A common stock. Assume the additional paid-in capital amount relates to the Class A common stock. Use the Coors account titles.

b. Record the issuance of the Class B common stock. Use the Coors account titles.

c. Rearrange the Coors stockholders' equity section to correspond to the following format:

Shareholders' Equity

Paid-in capital:	
Class A common stock	$
Paid-in capital in excess of par—Class A common stock	
Class B common stock	
Total paid-in capital	_____
Retained earnings................................	
Total shareholders' equity	$_____

d. What is the total paid-in capital of the company?

e. How did Coors withhold the voting privilege from their Class B common stockholders?

Problem 1

a.	False	b.	False	c.	True	d.	True
e.	False	f.	True	g.	False	h.	True

Problem 2

a.

Cash............................	3,271,000	
Class A Common Stock........		1,260,000
Additional Paid-in Capital.....		2,011,000
To record issuance of Class A com- mon stock at a premium.		

b.

Cash............................	11,000,000	
Class B Common Stock........		11,000,000
To record issuance of Class B common stock.		

c. Shareholders' Equity

Paid-in Capital:

Class A common stock, voting, $1 par value, authorized and issued 1,260,000 shares	$ 1,260,000
Paid-in capital in excess of par—Class A com- mon stock...............................	2,011,000

Class B common stock, nonvoting, no par
    value, authorized and issued 46,200,000
    shares ....
	11,000,000

Total paid-in capital	14,271,000
Retained earnings.........................	872,403,000
Total shareholders' equity	$886,674,000

d. Total paid-in capital is $14,271,000, as shown in the answer to *c*.

e. The voting privilege was withheld from stockholders by specific agreement with them.

Organization Cost

The costs of organizing a corporation include legal fees, taxes and fees paid to the state, and charges by promoters for selling the stock. These costs are grouped in an account titled Organization Cost, which is an asset because these costs contribute to a business's start-up. Suppose Mary Kay Cosmetics, Inc., pays legal fees of $15,000 and the state of Texas incorporation fee of $500 to organize the corporation. In addition, a promoter charges a fee of $24,000 for selling the stock and receives the corporation's no-par stock as payment. Mary Kay's journal entries to record these organization costs are

Mar. 31	Organization Cost ($15,000 + $500)	15,500	
	Cash		15,500
	Legal fees and state incorporation fee to organize the corporation.		
Apr. 3	Organization Cost........................	24,000	
	Common Stock		24,000
	Promoter fee for selling stock in organization.		

Organization cost is an *intangible asset,* reported on the balance sheet along with patents, trademarks, goodwill, and any other intangibles. We know that an intangible asset should be amortized over its useful life, and organization costs will benefit the corporation for as long as the corporation operates. But how long will that be? We cannot know in advance, but we still must expense these costs over some period of time. The Internal Revenue Service tax laws allow corporations to use a minimum 5-year useful life for amortization. GAAP allows a maximum 40-year useful life. Companies therefore amortize organization costs over a period between 5 and 40 years. Assume a 10-year life, and the preceding organization cost of $39,500 ($15,500 + $24,000) would be amortized by a debit to Amortization Expense and a credit to Organization Cost for $3,950 ($39,500/10) each year.

Dividend Dates

A corporation must declare a dividend before paying it. The board of directors alone has the authority to declare a dividend. The corporation has no obligation to pay a dividend until the board declares one, but once declared, the dividend becomes a legal liability of the corporation. Three relevant dates for dividends are

1. **Declaration date.** On the declaration date, the board of directors announces the intention to pay the dividend. The declaration creates a liability for the corporation. Declaration is recorded by debiting Retained Earnings and crediting Dividends Payable.
2. **Date of record.** The people who own the stock on the date of record receive the dividend. The corporation announces the record date, which follows the declaration date by a few weeks, as part of the declaration. The corporation makes no journal entry on the date of record because no transaction occurs. Nevertheless, much work takes place behind the scenes to properly identify the stockholders of record on this date because the stock is being traded continuously.
3. **Payment date.** Payment of the dividend usually follows the record date by two to four weeks. Payment is recorded by debiting Dividends Payable and crediting Cash. *check actually goes out*

Dividends on Preferred and Common Stock

Declaration of a cash dividend is recorded by debiting Retained Earnings and crediting Dividends Payable as follows:

June 19	Retained Earnings	XXX	
	Dividends Payable		XXX
	To declare a cash dividend.		

Payment of the dividend, which usually follows declaration by a few weeks, is recorded by debiting Dividends Payable and crediting Cash:

July 2	Dividends Payable	XXX	
	Cash		XXX
	To pay a cash dividend.		

Dividends Payable is a current liability. When a company has issued both preferred and common stock, the preferred stockholders receive their dividends first. The common stockholders receive dividends only if the total declared dividend is large enough to pay the preferred shareholders first.

Pine Industries, Inc., in addition to its common stock, has 9,000 shares of preferred stock outstanding. Preferred dividends are paid at the annual rate of $1.75 per share. Assume Pine declares an annual dividend of $150,000. The allocation to preferred and common stockholders is

	Total Dividend of $150,000
Preferred dividend (9,000 shares × $1.75 per share)	$ 15,750
Common dividend (remainder: $150,000 − $15,750)	134,250
Total dividend	$150,000

OBJECTIVE 4

Allocate dividends to preferred and common stock

If Pine declares only a $20,000 dividend, preferred stockholders receive $15,750, and the common stockholders receive $4,250 ($20,000 − $15,750).

This example illustrates an important relationship between preferred stock and common stock. To an investor, the preferred stock is safer because it receives dividends first. For example, if Pine Industries earns only enough net income to pay the preferred stockholders' dividends, the owners of common stock receive no dividends at all. However, the earnings potential from an investment in common stock is much greater than from an investment in preferred stock. Preferred dividends are usually limited to the specified amount, but there is no upper limit on the amount of common dividends.

We noted that preferred stockholders enjoy the advantage of priority over common stockholders in receiving dividends. The dividend preference is stated as a percentage rate or a dollar amount. For example, preferred stock may be "6 percent preferred," which means that owners of the preferred stock receive an annual dividend of 6 percent of the par value of the stock. If par value is $100 per share, preferred stockholders receive an annual cash dividend of $6 per share (6 percent of $100). The preferred stock may be "$3 preferred," which means that stockholders receive an annual dividend of $3 per share regardless of the preferred stock's par value. The dividend rate on no-par preferred stock is stated in a dollar amount per share.

Cumulative and Noncumulative Preferred Stock

The allocation of dividends may be complex if the preferred stock is *cumulative*. Corporations sometimes fail to pay a dividend to their preferred stockholders. This occurrence is called *passing the dividend,* and the passed dividends are said to be **in arrears.** The owners of **cumulative preferred stock** must receive all dividends in arrears before the corporation pays dividends to the common stockholders.

The preferred stock of Pine Industries is cumulative. Suppose the company passed the 19X4 preferred dividend of $15,750. Before paying dividends to its common stockholders in 19X5, the company must first pay preferred dividends of $15,750 for both 19X4 and 19X5, a total of $31,500. *Preferred stock is cumulative in the eyes of the law unless it is specifically labeled as noncumulative.*

Assume that Pine Industries passes its 19X4 preferred dividend. In 19X5 the company declares a $50,000 dividend. The entry to record the declaration is

Sep. 6	Retained Earnings 50,000		
	Dividends Payable, Preferred ($15,750 × 2).		31,500
	Dividends Payable, Common		
	($50,000 − $31,500)		18,500
	To declare a cash dividend.		

If the preferred stock is **noncumulative,** the corporation is not obligated to pay dividends in arrears. Suppose that the Pine Industries preferred stock was noncumulative, and the company passed the 19X4 preferred dividend of $15,750. The preferred stockholders would lose the 19X4 dividend forever. Of course, the common stockholders would not receive a 19X4 dividend either. Before paying any common dividends in 19X5, the company would have to pay the 19X5 preferred dividend of $15,750.

Having dividends in arrears on cumulative preferred stock is *not* a liability to the corporation. (A liability for dividends arises only after the board of directors declares the dividend.) Nevertheless, a corporation must report cumulative preferred dividends in arrears. This information alerts common stockholders as to how much in cumulative preferred dividends must be paid before any dividends will be paid on the common stock. This gives the common stockholders an idea about the likelihood of receiving dividends and satisfies the disclosure principle.

Dividends in arrears are often disclosed in notes, as follows (all dates and amounts assumed). Observe the two references to Note 3 in this section of the balance sheet. The "6 percent" after "Preferred stock" is the dividend rate.

Preferred stock, 6 percent, par $50, 2,000 shares issued (Note 3) . $100,000
Retained earnings (Note 3)   414,000

Note 3—Cumulative preferred dividends in arrears. At December 31, 19X2, dividends on the company's 6 percent preferred stock were in arrears for 19X1 and 19X2, in the amount of $12,000 (6% × $100,000 × 2 years).

Participating and Nonparticipating Preferred Stock

The owners of **participating preferred stock** may receive—that is, *participate in*—dividends beyond the stated amount or stated percentage. Assume that the corporation declares a dividend. First, the preferred stockholders receive their dividends. If the corporation has declared a large enough dividend, then the common stockholders receive their dividends. If an additional dividend amount remains to be distributed, common stockholders and participating preferred stockholders share it. For example, the owners of a $4 preferred stock must receive the specified annual dividend of $4 per share before the common stockholders receive any dividends. Then a $4 dividend is paid on each common share. The participation feature takes effect only after the preferred and common stockholders have received the specified $4 rate. Payment of an extra *common* dividend of, say, $1.50 is accompanied by a $1.50 dividend on each preferred share.

Participating preferred stock is rare. In fact, preferred stock is nonparticipating unless it is specifically described as participating on the stock certificate and in the financial statements. Therefore, if the preferred stock in our example is nonparticipating (the usual case), the largest annual dividend that a preferred stockholder will receive is $4.

Convertible Preferred Stock

Convertible preferred stock may be exchanged by the preferred stockholders, if they choose, for another class of stock in the corporation. For example, the Pine Industries preferred stock may be converted into the company's common stock. A note to Pine's balance sheet describes the conversion terms as follows:

> The ... preferred stock is convertible at the rate of 6.51 shares of common stock for each share of preferred stock outstanding.

If you owned 100 shares of Pine's convertible preferred stock, you could convert it into 651 (100 × 6.51) shares of Pine common stock. Under what condition would you exercise the conversion privilege? You would do so if the market value of the common stock that you could receive from conversion exceeded the market value of the preferred stock that you presently held. This way, you as an investor could increase your personal wealth.

Pine Industries preferred stock has par value of $100 per share, and the par value of the common stock is $1. The company would record conversion of 100 shares of preferred stock, issued previously at par, into 651 shares of common stock as follows:

Mar. 7	Preferred Stock (100 × $100)	10,000	
	Common Stock (651 × $1)		651
	Paid-in Capital in Excess of Par—		
	Common		9,349
	Conversion of preferred stock into common.		

If the preferred stock was issued at a premium, Paid-in Capital in Excess of Par—Preferred must also be debited to remove its balance from the books.

Preferred stock, we see, offers alternative features not available to common stock. Preferred stock is cumulative or noncumulative, participating or nonparticipating, and convertible or not convertible.

Rate of Return on Total Assets and Rate of Return on Stockholders' Equity

Investors and creditors are constantly evaluating the ability of managers to earn profits. Investors search for companies whose stocks are likely to increase in value. Creditors are interested in profitable companies that can pay their debts. Investment and credit decisions often include a comparison of companies. But a comparison of IBM's net income to the net income of a new company in the computer industry simply is not meaningful. IBM's profits may run into the billions of dollars, which far exceed a new company's net income. Does that automatically make IBM a better investment? Not necessarily. To make relevant comparisons between companies different in size, scope of operations, or any other measure, investors, creditors, and managers use some standard profitability measures, including rate of return on total assets and rate of return on stockholders' equity.

The **rate of return on total assets,** or simply **return on assets,** measures a company's success in using its assets to earn income for the persons who are financing the business. Creditors have loaned money to the corporation and earn interest. Stockholders have invested in the corporation's stock and expect the company to earn net income. The sum of interest expense and net income is the return to the two groups that have financed the corporation's activities, and this is the numerator of the return on assets ratio. The denominator is average total assets. Return on assets is computed as follows, using actual data

OBJECTIVE 5
Compute two profitability measures

from the 1990 annual report of Birmingham Steel Corporation (amounts in thousands of dollars):

$$\begin{array}{c}\text{Rate of} \\ \text{return} \\ \text{on total} \\ \text{assets}\end{array} = \frac{\text{Net income} + \text{interest expense}}{\text{Average total assets}} = \frac{\$16,306 + \$8,376}{(\$300,752 + \$314,405)/2} = \frac{\$24,682}{\$307,579} = .080$$

Net income and interest expense are taken from the income statement. Average total assets is computed from the beginning and ending balance sheets. How is this profitability measure used in decision making? To compare companies. By relating the sum of net income and interest expense to average total assets, we have a standard measure that describes the profitability of all types of companies. Brokerage companies such as Merrill Lynch and Kidder Peabody often single out particular industries as good investments. For example, brokerage analysts may believe that the steel industry is in a growth phase. These analysts would identify specific steel companies whose profitabilities are likely to lead the industry and so be sound investments. Return on assets is one measure of profitability.

What is a good rate of return on total assets? There is no single answer to this question because rates of return vary widely by industry. For example, high-technology companies earn much higher returns than do utility companies, groceries, and manufacturers of consumer goods such as toothpaste.

Rate of return on stockholders' equity, often called **return on equity,** shows the relationship between net income and average common stockholders' equity. The numerator is net income minus preferred dividends, information taken from the income statement. The denominator is average common stockholders' equity—total stockholders' equity minus preferred equity. Birmingham Steel Corporation's rate of return on common stockholders' equity for 1990 is computed as follows (amounts in thousands of dollars):

$$\begin{array}{c}\text{Rate of} \\ \text{return} \\ \text{on common} \\ \text{stock-} \\ \text{holders'} \\ \text{equity}\end{array} = \frac{\text{Net income} - \text{preferred dividends}}{\begin{array}{c}\text{Average} \\ \text{common} \\ \text{stockholders'} \\ \text{equity}\end{array}} = \frac{\$16,306 - \$0}{(\$145,044 + \$150,782)/2} = \frac{\$16,306}{\$147,913} = .110$$

Birmingham Steel has no preferred stock, so preferred dividends are zero. With no preferred stock outstanding, average *common* stockholders' equity is the same as average *total* equity—the average of the beginning and ending amounts.

Observe that return on equity (11 percent) is higher than return on assets (8 percent). This difference results from the interest expense component of return on assets. Companies such as Birmingham Steel borrow at one rate, say 7 percent, and invest the funds to earn a higher rate, say 10 percent. The company's creditors are guaranteed a fixed rate of return on their loans. The stockholders, conversely, have no guarantee that the corporation will earn net income, so their investments are more risky. Consequently, stockholders demand a higher rate of return than do creditors, and this explains why return on equity should exceed return on assets. If return on assets is higher, the company is in trouble.

Investors and creditors use return on common stockholders' equity in much the same way as they use return on total assets—to compare companies. The higher the rate of return, the more successful the company. A 15-percent return on common stockholders' equity is considered quite good in most industries. Investors also compare a company's return on stockholders' equity to interest rates available in the market. If interest rates are almost as high as return on equity, many investors will lend their money to earn interest. They choose to forgo the extra risk of investing in stock when the rate of return on equity is too low.

Different Values of Stock

The business community refers to several different *stock values* in addition to par value. These values include market value, redemption value, liquidation value, and book value.

Market Value

A stock's **market value** is the price for which a person could buy or sell a share of the stock. The issuing corporation's net income, financial position, its future prospects, and the general economic conditions determine market value (also called market price). Daily newspapers report the market price of many stocks. Corporate financial statements report the high and the low market values of the company's common stock for each quarter of the year. *In almost all cases, stockholders are more concerned about the market value of a stock than any of the other values discussed below.* A stock listed at (an alternative term is *quoted at*) 29¼ sells for, or may be bought for, $29.25 per share. The purchase of 100 shares of this stock would cost $2,925 ($29.25 × 100), plus a commission. If you were selling 100 shares of this stock, you would receive cash of $2,925 less a commission. The commission is the fee an investor pays to a stockbroker for buying or selling the stock.

Redemption Value

Preferred stock's fixed dividend rate makes it somewhat like debt. However, companies do not get a tax deduction for preferred dividend payments. Thus they may wish to buy back, or redeem, their preferred stock to avoid paying the dividends. Preferred stock that provides for redemption at a set price is called redeemable preferred stock. In some cases, the company has the *option* of redeeming its preferred stock at a set price. In other cases, the company is *obligated* to redeem the preferred stock. The price the corporation agrees to pay for the stock, which is set when the stock is issued, is called **redemption value.**

The preferred stock of Pine Industries, Inc., is "redeemable at the option of the Company at $25 per share." Beginning in 1992, Pine is "required to redeem annually 6,765 shares of the preferred stock ($169,125 annually)." Pine's annual redemption payment to the preferred stockholders will include this redemption value plus any dividends in arrears.

Liquidation Value

Liquidation value, which applies only to preferred stock, is the amount the corporation agrees to pay the preferred stockholder per share if the company liquidates. Great Northern Nekoosa Corporation, a large paper company, has preferred stock with "a preference of $50 in liquidation." Dividends in arrears are added to liquidation value in determining the payment to the preferred stockholders if the company liquidates.

Book Value

The **book value** of a stock is the amount of owners' equity on the company's books for each share of its stock. Corporations often report this amount in their annual reports. If the company has only common stock outstanding, its book value is computed by dividing total stockholders' equity by the number of shares outstanding. A company with stockholders' equity of $180,000 and 5,000 shares of common stock outstanding has book value of $36 per share ($180,000/5,000 shares).

If the company has both preferred and common stock outstanding, the preferred stockholders have the first claim to owners' equity. Ordinarily, preferred stock has a specified liquidation or redemption value. The book value of preferred is its redemption value plus any cumulative dividends in arrears on the stock. Its book value *per share* equals the sum of redemption value and any cumulative dividends in arrears divided by the number of preferred shares outstanding. After the corporation figures the preferred shares' book value, it computes the common stock book value per share. The corporation divides the common equity (total stockholders' equity minus preferred equity) by the number of common shares outstanding.

Assume that the company balance sheet reports the following amounts:

Stockholders' Equity

Paid-in capital:	
Preferred stock, 6%, $100 par, 5,000 shares authorized,	
400 shares issued	$ 40,000
Paid-in capital in excess of par—preferred	4,000
Common stock, $10 par, 20,000 shares authorized,	
4,500 shares issued	45,000
Common stock subscribed, 1,000 shares	10,000
Paid-in capital in excess of par—common	72,000
Total paid-in capital	171,000
Retained earnings	85,000
Total stockholders' equity	$256,000

Suppose that four years (including the current year) of cumulative preferred dividends are in arrears and preferred stock has a redemption value of $130 per share.

Book value computations treat subscribed stock as though it were issued stock. The book-value-per-share computations for this corporation follow.

Preferred:	
Redemption value (400 shares × $130)	$ 52,000
Cumulative dividends ($40,000 × .06 × 4)	9,600
Stockholders' equity allocated to preferred	$ 61,600
Book value per share ($61,600/400 shares)	$ 154.00
Common:	
Total stockholders' equity	$256,000
Less stockholders' equity allocated to preferred	61,600
Stockholders' equity allocated to common	$194,400
Book value per share [$194,400/(4,500 shares + 1,000 shares)]	$35.35

How is book value per share used in decision making? Companies negotiating the purchase of a corporation may wish to know the book value of its stock. The book value of stockholders' equity may figure into the negotiated purchase price. Corporations—especially those whose stock is not publicly traded—may buy out a retiring executive, agreeing to pay the book value of the person's stock in the company. In general, however, book value is virtually meaningless to an outside investor when book value is not directly related to the market value of stock.

Accounting for Income Taxes by Corporations _____

Income Tax Expense is based on *pretax accounting income* from the income statement. Income Tax Payable is based on *taxable income* from the income tax return filed with the Internal Revenue Service. Pretax accounting income and taxable income are rarely the same amount.

INCOME TAX EXPENSE equals PRETAX ACCOUNTING INCOME from Income Statement multiplied by INCOME TAX RATE	INCOME TAX PAYABLE equals TAXABLE INCOME from Tax Return multiplied by INCOME TAX RATE

The authors are indebted to Jean Marie Hudson for this presentation.

Some revenues and expenses enter the determination of accounting income in periods different from the periods in which they enter the determination of taxable income. Over a period of several years, total pretax accounting income may equal total taxable income, but for any one year the two income amounts are likely to differ.

The most important difference between pretax accounting income and taxable income occurs when a corporation uses the straight-line method to compute depreciation for the financial statements and a special tax depreciation method for the tax return and the payment of taxes. The tax depreciation method is called the **modified accelerated cost recovery system,** abbreviated as MACRS. For any one year, MACRS depreciation listed on the tax return may differ from accounting depreciation on the income statement.

Suppose Krieg Corporation has income before income tax (also called pretax accounting income) of $500,000 in each of two years. The accounting issue is, What is the correct amount of income tax expense for the two years? By answering this question, we can complete Krieg's income statement:

Income Statement (partial)

	19X1	19X2
Income before income tax	$500,000	$500,000
Income tax expense	?	?
Net income	$?	$?

Suppose Krieg uses straight-line depreciation to compute income for the income statement. On the tax return, Krieg uses MACRS depreciation, and so the tax returns report taxable income of $400,000 in 19X1 and $600,000 in 19X2. Total taxable income for the two years combined—$1 million—is the same as total pretax accounting income. However, each year shows a difference between the two income measures. With a 34 percent tax rate, income tax payable to the government is $136,000 ($400,000 × .34) in 19X1 and $204,000 ($600,000 × .34) in 19X2. Should Krieg report these amounts as income tax expense on the income statement? No, because this would amount to using the cash basis to account for income taxes. For reporting to shareholders and creditors, corporations must treat income as if it were all taxed currently even though the company may pay the tax in earlier or later years.

Generally accepted accounting principles do not permit accounting for income tax expense using the cash basis. GAAP requires use of the accrual basis of accounting. Corporations account for income tax expense and all other expenses based on when the expense occurs, not on when it is paid. The process of accruing income taxes during the period that the related income occurs is called **income tax allocation.** The goal of income tax allocation is to match the period's expenses against its revenues. In this case, Krieg Corporation will record the same amount of income tax expense in both years because pretax accounting income is the same.

Corporations generally record Income Tax Expense based on the amount of *pretax accounting income* multiplied by the tax rate. Income Tax Payable is credited for an amount equal to *taxable income* multiplied by the tax rate. When these two amounts differ, a new account, Deferred Income Tax, is credited or debited to balance the entry. In Exhibit 12-3, Deferred Income Tax is credited in 19X1 because pretax accounting income ($500,000) exceeds taxable income ($400,000). The reverse is true in 19X2, and Deferred Income Tax is debited. The 19X2 entry eliminates the preceding credit balance in Deferred Income Tax.

For other corporations, the 19X1 entry may include a debit to Deferred Income Tax. This occurs if taxable income exceeds pretax accounting income. In that case, the credit to Income Tax Payable is greater than the debit to Income Tax Expense, and the balancing amount is a debit to Deferred Income Tax. Entries in later years will include credits to eliminate the debit balance in Deferred Income Tax. Here is a way to remember whether to debit or credit Deferred Income Tax:

Debit: Income Tax Expense for the amount equal to pretax accounting income multiplied by the income tax rate.
Credit: Income Tax Payable for the amount equal to taxable income multiplied by the income tax rate.
Debit or
Credit: Deferred Income Tax for the amount needed to balance the entry.

Exhibit 12-4 shows Krieg's comparative income statement for 19X1 and 19X2. Income Tax Expense comes directly from the entries recorded in Exhibit 12-3.

Net income is the same both years because pretax income is the same. Tax allocation thus matches income tax expense against income in accordance with the matching principle and the accrual basis of accounting. Income Tax Payable and Deferred Income Tax are reported on the balance sheet. Accounting for income tax by corporations is a controversial area that has received much FASB attention.

EXHIBIT 12-3   *Income Tax Entries for a Corporation*

19X1	Income Tax Expense ($500,000 × .34)	170,000	
	Income Tax Payable ($400,000 × .34) . . .		136,000
	Deferred Income Tax ($100,000 × .34) . .		34,000
19X2	Income Tax Expense ($500,000 × .34)	170,000	
	Deferred Income Tax ($100,000 × .34)	34,000	
	Income Tax Payable ($600,000 × .34) . . .		204,000

EXHIBIT 12-4 *Income Tax on a Corporation Income Statement*

Krieg Corporation Partial Income Statement For the years Ended December 31, 19X1 and 19X2		
	19X1	**19X2**
Income before income tax	$500,000	$500,000
Income tax expense ($500,000 × .34 both years) . .	170,000	170,000
Net income	$330,000	$330,000

Summary Problems for Your Review

Problem 1

Use the following accounts and related balances to prepare the classified balance sheet of Whitehall, Inc., at September 30, 19X4. Use the account format of the balance sheet.

Common stock, $1 par, 50,000 shares authorized, 20,000 shares issued	$ 20,000	Long-term note payable .	$ 74,000
		Inventory	85,000
		Property, plant, and equipment, net	225,000
Dividends payable	4,000	Donated capital	18,000
Cash	9,000	Accounts receivable, net .	23,000
Accounts payable	28,000	Preferred stock, $3.75, no-par, 10,000 shares, authorized, 2,000 shares issued	24,000
Stock subscription receivable—common . .	2,000		
Retained earnings	56,000		
Paid-in capital in excess of par—common	115,000	Common stock sub-scribed 3,000 shares . . .	3,000
Organization cost, net . . .	1,000	Income tax payable	3,000

Problem 2

The balance sheet of Trendline Corporation reported the following at March 31, 19X6, end of its fiscal year. Note that Trendline reports paid-in capital in excess of par or stated value after the stock accounts.

Stockholders' Equity

Preferred stock, 4%, $10 par, 10,000 shares authorized (redemption value, $110,000)	$100,000
Common stock, no-par, $5 stated value, 100,000 shares authorized	250,000
Common stock subscribed	17,500
Paid-in capital in excess of par or stated value:	
Common stock	214,000
Donated capital	65,000
Retained earnings	330,000
Total stockholders' equity	$976,500

Required

a. Is the preferred stock cumulative or noncumulative? Is it participating or nonparticipating? How can you tell?

b. What is the total amount of the annual preferred dividend?

c. How many shares of preferred and common stock has the company issued?

d. How many shares of common stock are subscribed?

e. What was the market value of the assets donated to the corporation?

f. Compute the book value per share of the preferred stock and the common stock. No prior year preferred dividends are in arrears, but Trendline has not declared the current-year dividend.

SOLUTIONS TO REVIEW PROBLEMS

Problem 1

Whitehall, Inc.
Balance Sheet
September 30, 19X4

Assets			Liabilities		
Current:			**Current:**		
Cash		$ 9,000	Accounts payable		$ 28,000
Accounts receivable, net		23,000	Dividends payable		4,000
Stock subscription receivable—			Income tax payable		3,000
common		2,000	Total current liabilities		35,000
Inventory		85,000	Long-term note payable		74,000
Total current assets		119,000	Total liabilities		109,000
Property, plant, and equipment, net		225,000			
Intangible assets:			**Stockholders' Equity**		
Organization cost, net		1,000	Paid-in capital:		
			Preferred stock, $3.75, no-par,		
			10,000 shares authorized,		
			2,000 shares issued	$ 24,000	
			Common stock, $1 par,		
			50,000 shares authorized,		
			20,000 shares issued	20,000	
			Common stock subscribed,		
			3,000 shares	3,000	
			Paid-in capital in excess of		
			par—common	115,000	
			Donated capital	18,000	
			Total paid-in capital	180,000	
			Retained earnings	56,000	
			Total stockholders' equity		236,000
			Total liabilities and		
Total assets		$345,000	stockholders' equity		$345,000

Problem 2

a. The preferred stock is *cumulative* and *nonparticipating* because it is not specifically labeled otherwise.

b. Total annual preferred dividend: $4,000 ($100,000 × .04)

c. Preferred stock issued: 10,000 shares
   Common stock issued: 50,000 shares ($250,000/$5 stated value)

d. Common stock subscribed: 3,500 shares ($17,500/$5 stated value)

e. Market value of donated assets: $55,000

f. Book values per share of preferred and common stock:

Preferred:
Redemption value	$110,000
Cumulative dividend for current year ($100,000 × .04)	4,000
Stockholders' equity allocated to preferred	$114,000
Book value per share ($114,000/10,000 shares)	$11.40

Common:
Total stockholders' equity..................................	$976,500
Less stockholders' equity allocated to preferred	114,000
Stockholders' equity allocated to common	$862,500
Book value per share [$862,500/(53,500 shares = 50,000 shares issued + 3,500 shares subscribed)]........................	$16.12

Summary

A corporation is a separate legal and business entity. Corporations may issue different classes of stock: *par value, no-par value, common,* and *preferred.* Stock is usually issued at a *premium*—an amount above par value. Also, corporations may issue stock under a *subscription* agreement. The balance sheet carries the capital raised through stock issuance under the heading Paid-in Capital or Contributed Capital in the stockholders' equity section.

Corporations may receive *donations* from outsiders or from stockholders. Donated Capital is a stockholders' equity account.

Only when the board of directors declares a *dividend* does the corporation incur the liability to pay dividends. Preferred stock has priority over common stock as to dividends, which may be stated as a percentage of par value or as a dollar amount per share. In addition, preferred stock has a claim to dividends in arrears if it is *cumulative* and a claim to further dividends if it is *participating.* *Convertible* preferred stock may be exchanged for the corporation's common stock.

Return on assets and *return on stockholders' equity* are two standard measures of profitability. A healthy company's return on equity should exceed its return on assets.

A stock's *market value* is the price for which a share may be bought or sold. *Redemption value, liquidation value,* and *book value*—the amount of owners' equity per share of company stock—are other values that may apply to stock.

Income tax expense of a corporation is based on pretax accounting income. *Income tax payable* is based on taxable income. A difference between the expense and the payable creates a debit or a credit to the Deferred Income Tax account.

Self-Study Questions

Test your understanding of the chapter by marking the best answer for each of the following questions.

1. The arbitrary value assigned to a share of stock is called *(p. 575)*
   a. Market value
   b. Liquidation value
   c. Book value
   d. Par value

2. Which is the most widely held class of stock? *(p. 575)*
   a. Par value common stock
   b. No-par common stock
   c. Par value preferred stock
   d. No-par preferred stock

3. An asset received by a corporation in exchange for the corporation's stock should be recorded at *(p. 578)*
   a. The asset's book value
   b. The asset's market value
   c. The stock's par value
   d. An amount set by the board of directors

4. Mangum Corporation receives a subscription for 1,000 shares of $100 par preferred stock at $104 per share. This transaction increases Mangum's paid-in capital by *(p. 579)*
   a. $0 because the corporation received no cash
   b. $4,000
   c. $100,000
   d. $104,000

5. Organization cost is classified as a (an) *(p. 584)*
   a. Operating expense
   b. Current asset
   c. Contra item in stockholders' equity
   d. None of the above

6. Trade Days, Inc., has 10,000 shares of $3.50, $50 par preferred stock, and 100,000 of $4 par common stock outstanding. Two years' preferred dividends are in arrears. Trade Days declares a cash dividend large enough to pay the preferred dividends in arrears, the preferred dividend for the current period, and a $1.50 dividend to common. What is the total amount of the dividend? *(p. 585)*
   a. $255,000
   b. $220,000
   c. $150,000
   d. $105,000

7. The preferred stock of Trade Days, Inc., in the preceding question was issued at $55 per share. Each preferred share can be converted into 10 common shares. The entry to record the conversion of this preferred stock into common is *(p. 587)*

   a. Cash 550,000
          Preferred Stock   500,000
          Paid-in Capital in Excess of Par—Preferred   50,000

   b. Preferred Stock 500,000
          Paid-in Capital in Excess of Par—Preferred . .   50,000
          Common Stock   550,000

   c. Preferred Stock 500,000
          Paid-in Capital in Excess of Par—Preferred . .   50,000
          Common Stock   400,000
          Paid-in Capital in Excess of Par—Common   150,000

   d. Preferred Stock 550,000
          Common Stock   400,000
          Paid-in Capital in Excess of Par—Common   150,000

8. Which profitability measure should be higher for a successful corporation? *(p. 588)*
   a. Return on assets
   b. Return on stockholders' equity

9. When an investor is buying stock as an investment, the value of most direct concern is *(pp. 586, 587)*
   a. Par value
   b. Market value
   c. Liquidation value
   d. Book value

10. Pretax accounting income is $200,000. Taxable income is $180,000, and the income tax rate is 30 percent. The balance sheet will report *(p. 592)*
    a. Income tax expense of $54,000
    b. Income tax payable of $60,000
    c. Deferred income tax of $6,000
    d. All of the above

Answers to the Self-Study Questions follow the Accounting Vocabulary.

Accounting Vocabulary

Additional paid-in capital. Another name for Paid-in capital in excess of par *(p. 577)*.

Authorization of stock. Provision in a corporate charter that gives the state's permission for the corporation to issue—that is, to sell—a certain number of shares of stock (p. 576).

Book value of stock. Amount of stockholders' equity on the company's books for each share of its stock (p. 590).

Common stock. The most basic form of capital stock. In describing a corporation, the common stockholders are the owners of the business (p. 575).

Contributed capital. Another name for Paid-in capital (p. 576).

Convertible preferred stock. Preferred stock that may be exchanged by the preferred stockholders, if they choose, for another class of stock in the corporation (p. 586).

Cumulative preferred stock. Preferred stock whose owners must receive all dividends in arrears before the corporation pays dividends to the common stockholders (p. 585).

Date of record. Date on which the owners of stock to receive a dividend are identified (p. 584).

Declaration date. Date on which the board of directors announce the intention to pay a dividend. The declaration creates a liability for the corporation (p. 584).

Deficit. Debit balance in the retained earnings account (p. 574).

Discount on stock. Excess of the par value of stock over its issue price (p. 577).

Dividends in arrears. Cumulative preferred dividends that the corporation has failed to pay (p. 585).

Donated capital. Special category of stockholders' equity created when a corporation receives a donation (gift) from a donor who receives no ownership interest in the company (p. 580).

Income tax allocation. Process of accruing income taxes during the period that the related income occurs, with the goal of matching the period's expenses—including income tax expense—against the period's revenues, regardless of when the income tax is paid (p. 592).

Liquidation value of stock. Amount a corporation agrees to pay a preferred stockholder per share if the company liquidates (p. 589).

Market value of stock. Price for which a person could buy or sell a share of stock (p. 589).

Modified Accelerated Cost Recovery System (MACRS). Special tax depreciation method (p. 591).

Organization cost. The costs of organizing a corporation, including legal fees, taxes and fees paid to the state, and charges by promoters for selling the stock. Organization cost is an intangible asset (p. 583).

Outstanding stock. Stock in the hands of stockholders. (p. 572).

Par value. Arbitrary amount assigned to a share of stock (p. 575).

Participating preferred stock. Preferred stock whose owners may receive—that is, participate in—dividends beyond the stated amount or stated percentage (p. 586).

Payment date. Payment of the dividend usually follows the record date by two to four weeks. (p. 584).

Preemptive right. A stockholder's right to maintain a proportionate ownership in a corporation (p. 573).

Preferred stock. Stock that gives its owners certain advantages over common stockholders, such as the priority to receive dividends before the common stockholders and the priority to receive assets before the common stockholders if the corporation liquidates (p. 575).

Premium on stock. Excess of the issue price of stock over its par value (p. 576)

Rate of return on total assets. The sum of net income plus interest expense divided by average total assets. This ratio measures the success a company has in using its assets to earn income for the persons who finance the business. Also called Return on assets (p. 587).

Rate of return on common stockholders' equity. Net income minus preferred dividends, divided by average common stockholders' equity. A measure of profitability. Also called Return on common stockholders' equity (p. 588).

Redemption value of stock. Price a corporation agrees to pay for stock, which is set when the stock is issued (p. 589).

Return on assets. Another name for Rate of return on total assets *(p. 587)*.

Return on common stockholders' equity. Another name for Rate of return on common stockholders' equity *(p. 588)*.

Stock subscription. Contract that obligates an investor to purchase the corporation's stock at a later date *(p. 578)*.

Answers to Self-Study Questions

1. d
3. b
5. d Intangible asset

2. a
4. d (1,000 shares × $104 = $104,000)
6. a [(10,000 × $3.50 × 3 = $105,000)
    + (100,000 × $1.50
    = $150,000) = $255,000]

7. c
9. b

8. b
10. c

ASSIGNMENT MATERIAL _____

Questions

1. Name the four rights of a stockholder. Is preferred stock automatically nonvoting? Explain how a right may be withheld from a stockholder.
2. Dividends on preferred stock may be stated as a percentage rate or a dollar amount. What is the annual dividend on these preferred stocks: 4 percent, $100 par; $3.50, $20 par; and 6 percent, no-par with $50 stated value?
3. Which event increases the assets of the corporation: authorization of stock or issuance of stock? Explain.
4. Suppose H. J. Heinz Company issued 1,000 shares of its 3.65 percent, $100 par preferred stock for $120. How much would this transaction increase the company's paid-in capital? How much would it increase Heinz's retained earnings? How much would it increase Heinz's annual cash dividend payments?
5. Give two alternative account titles for Paid-in Capital in Excess of Par— Common Stock.
6. Explain the contingent liability created by issuance of stock at a discount.
7. How does issuance of 1,000 shares of no-par stock for land and a building, together worth $150,000, affect paid-in capital?
8. Why does receipt of a stock subscription increase the corporation's assets and owners' equity?
9. Give an example of a transaction that creates donated capital for a corporation.
10. Journalize the incorporation of the Barnes & Connally partnership. The partners' capital account balances exceed the par value of the new corporation's common stock. (Omit amounts.)
11. Rank the following accounts in the order they would appear on the balance sheet: Common Stock, Organization Cost, Donated Capital, Preferred Stock, Common Stock Subscribed, Stock Subscription Receivable (due within six months), Retained Earnings, Dividends Payable. Also, give each account's balance sheet classification.
12. What type of account is Organization Cost? Briefly describe how to account for organization cost.
13. Briefly discuss the three important dates for a dividend.

14. Mancini Inc. has 3,000 shares of its $2.50, $10 par preferred stock outstanding. Dividends for 19X1 and 19X2 are in arrears, and the company has declared no dividends on preferred stock for the current year, 19X3. Assume that Mancini declares total dividends of $35,000 at the end of 19X3. Show how to allocate the dividends to preferred and common (a) if preferred is cumulative and (b) if preferred is noncumulative.

15. As a preferred stockholder, would you rather own cumulative or noncumulative preferred? If all other factors are the same, would the corporation rather the preferred stock be cumulative or noncumulative? Give your reason.

16. How are cumulative preferred dividends in arrears reported in the financial statements? When do dividends become a liability of the corporation?

17. Distinguish between the market value of stock and the book value of stock. Which is more important to investors?

18. How is book value per share of common stock computed when the company has both preferred stock and common stock outstanding?

19. Why should a healthy company's rate of return on stockholders' equity exceed its rate of return on total assets?

20. Briefly describe how to account for the income tax of a corporation. State how an entry to Deferred Income Tax arises.

Exercises

Exercise 12-1 _Issuing Stock_ **(L.O. 1)**

Journalize the following stock issuance transactions of Adams Corporation. Explanations are not required.

Feb. 19 Issued 1,000 shares of $1.50 par common stock for cash of $12.50 per share

Mar. 3 Sold 300 shares of $4.50, no-par Class A preferred stock for $12,000 cash.

11 Received inventory valued at $25,000 and equipment with market value of $16,000 for 3,300 shares of the $1.50 par common stock.

15 Issued 1,000 shares of 5 percent, no-par Class B preferred stock with stated value of $50 per share. The issue price was cash of $60 per share.

Exercise 12-2 _Stock subscriptions_ **(L.O. 1)**

Betsy Ross Corporation has just been organized and is selling its stock through stock subscriptions. Record the following selected transactions that occurred during June 19X6.

June 3 Received a subscription to 500 shares of $1 par common stock at the subscription price of $20 per share. The subscriber paid one-fourth of the subscription amount as a down payment. The corporation will issue the stock when it is fully paid.

18 Collected one-half of the amount receivable from the subscriber.

July 3 Collected the remainder from the subscriber and issued the stock.

Exercise 12-3 _Recording issuance of stock_ **(L.O. 1)**

The actual balance sheet of Gulf Resources & Chemical Corporation, as adapted, reported the following stockholders' equity. Note that Gulf has two separate classes of preferred stock, labeled as Series A and Series B. All dollar amounts, except for per-share amounts, are given in thousands.

Stockholders' Investment
(same as stockholders' equity)

Preferred stock, $1 par, authorized 4,000,000 shares (Note 7)

Series A..	$ 58
Series B..	376
Common stock, $.10 par, authorized 20,000,000, [issued and] outstanding 9,130,000 shares............................	913
Capital in excess of par....................................	75,542

Note 7. Preferred Stock:	Shares [Issued and] Outstanding
Series A..........	58,000
Series B..........	376,000

Required

Assume that the Series A preferred stock was issued for $3 cash per share, the Series B preferred was issued for $20 cash per share, and the common was issued for cash of $69,195. Make the summary journal entries to record issuance of all the Gulf Resources stock. Explanations are not required.

Exercise 12-4 *Recording issuance of no-par stock (L.O. 1)*

Alexanians, located in Lansing, Michigan, is an importer of European furniture and Oriental rugs. The corporation issues 10,000 shares of no-par common stock for $50 per share. Record issuance of the stock (a) if the stock is true no-par stock and (b) if the stock has stated value of $5 per share.

Exercise 12-5 *Incorporating a partnership (L.O. 2)*

The Podunk Jaybirds are a semiprofessional baseball team that has been operated as a partnership by D. Robertson and G. Childres. In addition to their management responsibilities, Robertson also plays second base and Childres sells hot dogs. Journalize the following transactions in the first month of operation as a corporation:

May 14   The incorporators paid legal fees of $990 and state taxes and fees of $500 to obtain a corporate charter.

14   Issued 2,500 shares of $5 par common stock to Robertson and 1,000 shares to Childres. Robertson's capital balance on the partnership books was $20,000, and Childres's capital balance was $8,000.

18   The city of Podunk donated 20 acres of land to the corporation for a stadium site. The land's market value was $40,000.

Exercise 12-6 *Stockholders' equity section of a balance sheet (L.O. 3)*

The charter of Majorex Corporation authorizes the issuance of 5,000 shares of Class A preferred stock, 1,000 shares of Class B preferred stock, and 10,000 shares of common stock. During a two-month period, Majorex completed these stock-issuance transactions:

June 23   Issued 1,000 shares of $1 par common stock for cash of $12.50 per share.

July   2   Sold 300 shares of $4.50, no-par Class A preferred stock for $20,000 cash.

12   Received inventory valued at $25,000 and equipment with market value of $16,000 for 3,300 shares of the $1 par common stock.

17 Issued 1,000 shares of 5 percent, no-par Class B preferred stock with stated value of $50 per share. The issue price was cash of $60 per share.

Prepare the stockholders' equity section of the Majorex balance sheet for the transactions given in this exercise. Retained Earnings has a balance of $63,000.

Exercise 12-7 *Paid-in capital for a corporation* (*L.O. 3*)

Flavan Corp. has recently organized. The company issued common stock to an attorney who gave Flavan legal services of $6,200 to help in organizing the corporation. It issued common stock to another person in exchange for his patent with a market value of $40,000. In addition, Flavan received cash both for 2,000 shares of its preferred stock at $110 per share and for 26,000 shares of its common stock at $15 per share. The city of Fond du Lac donated 50 acres of land to the company as a plant site. The market value of the land was $300,000, Without making journal entries, determine the total paid-in capital created by these transactions.

Exercise 12-8 *Stockholders' equity section of a balance sheet* (*L.O. 3*)

Mexico Lindo, Inc., has the following selected account balances at June 30, 19X7. Prepare the stockholders' equity section of the company's balance sheet.

Common stock, no-par with $5 stated value, 500,000 shares authorized, 120,000 shares issued	$600,000	Preferred stock subscribed, 1,000 shares	$ 20,000
Donated capital	103,000	Inventory	112,000
Accumulated depreciation— machinery and equipment	62,000	Machinery and equipment	109,000
Retained earnings	119,000	Preferred stock subscription receivable	8,000
Paid-in capital in excess of par—preferred	88,000	Preferred stock, 5%, $20 par, 20,000 shares authorized, 10,000 shares issued	200,000
		Organization cost, net	3,000

Exercise 12-9 *Computing dividends on preferred and common stock* (*L.O. 4*)

The following elements of stockholders' equity are adapted from the balance sheet of Gulf Resources & Chemical Corporation. All dollar amounts, except the dividends per share, are given in thousands.

Stockholders' Equity

Preferred stock, cumulative and nonparticipating, $1 par (Note 7)

Series A, 58,000 shares issued	$ 58
Series B, 376,000 shares issued	376
Common stock, $.10 par, 9,130,000 shares issued	913

Note 7. Preferred Stock:

	Designated Annual Cash Dividend Per Share
Series A	$ .20
Series B	1.30

Assume that the Series A preferred has preference over the Series B preferred and the company has paid all preferred dividends through 19X4.

Compute the dividends to both series of preferred and to common for 19X5 and 19X6 if total dividends are $0 in 19X5 and $1,200,000 in 19X6. Round to the nearest dollar.

Exercise 12-10 *Evaluating profitability* (*L.O. 5*)

Kelly Services, Inc., reported these figures for 19X7 and 19X6:

	19X7	19X6
Income statement:		
Interest expense	$ 7,400,000	7,100,000
Net income	24,000,000	21,700,000
Balance sheet:		
Total assets	351,000,000	317,000,000
Preferred stock, $1.30, no-par, 100,000 shares issued and outstanding	2,500,000	2,500,000
Common stockholders' equity	164,000,000	151,000,000
Total stockholders' equity	166,500,000	153,500,000

Compute rate of return on total assets and rate of return on common stockholders' equity for 19X7. Do these rates of return suggest strength or weakness? Give your reason.

Exercise 12-11 *Book value per share of preferred and common stock* (*L.O. 6*)

The balance sheet of International Graphics Corporation reported the following, with all amounts, including shares, in thousands:

Redeemable preferred stock; redemption value $5,103	$ 4,860
Common stockholders' equity 8,120 shares issued and outstanding	216,788
Total stockholders' equity	$221,648

Assume that International has paid preferred dividends for the current year and all prior years (no dividends in arrears), and the company has 100 shares of preferred stock outstanding. Compute the book value per share of the preferred stock and the common stock.

Exercise 12-12 *Book value per share of preferred and common stock; preferred dividends in arrears* (*L.O. 4,6*)

Refer to Exercise 12-11. Compute the book value per share of the preferred stock and the common stock, assuming that three years' preferred dividends (including dividends for the current year) are in arrears. Assume the preferred stock is cumulative and its dividend rate is 6 percent.

Exercise 12-13 *Recording a corporation's income tax* (*L.O. 7*)

BiSports Corp. has pretax accounting income of $690,000 in 19X5 and $660,000 in 19X6. Taxable income is $680,000 in 19X5 and $670,000 in 19X6. Record the corporation's income taxes for both years. The tax rate is 34 percent. What is the balance in the Deferred Income Tax account at the end of each year?

Problems

(Group A)

Problem 12-1A *Organizing a corporation* (*L.O. 1*)

Marla Fredricks and Allison LaChapelle are opening a Sav-On office supply store in a shopping center in Hagerstown, Maryland. The area is growing, and no competitors are located in the immediate vicinity. Their most fundamental decision is how to organize the business. Marla thinks the partnership form is best. Allison favors the corporate form of organization. They seek your advice.

Required

Discuss the advantages and the disadvantages of organizing the business as a corporation. Refer back to Chapter 1 if necessary.

Problem 12-2A *Journalizing corporation transactions and preparing the stockholders' equity section of the balance sheet* **(L.O. 1,3)**

Lanz Corporation received a charter from the state of New Jersey. The company is authorized to issue 20,000 shares of 5 percent, $50 par preferred stock and 300,000 shares of no-par common stock. During its start-up phase, the company completed the following transactions:

Oct. 2 Paid fees of $4,000 and incorporation taxes of $3,000 to the state of New Jersey to obtain the charter and file the required documents for incorporation.

 4 Issued 900 shares of common stock to the promoters who organized the corporation. Their fee was $45,000.

 5 Accepted subscriptions for 1,000 shares of common stock at $50 per share and received a down payment of one-fourth of the subscription amount.

 9 Issued 2,000 shares of common stock in exchange for equipment valued at $100,000.

 14 Issued 600 shares of preferred stock for cash of $54 per share.

 30 Collected one-third of the stock subscription receivable.

 31 Earned a small profit for October and closed the $12,600 credit balance of Income Summary into Retained Earnings.

Required

1. Record the transactions in the general journal.
2. Prepare the stockholders' equity section of the Lanz balance sheet at October 31.

Problem 12-3A *Journalizing corporation transactions and preparing the stockholders' equity section of the balance sheet* **(L.O. 1,2,3)**

The partners who owned Horner & Roads wished to avoid the unlimited personal liability of the partnership form of business, so they incorporated the partnership as Penrod Drilling, Inc. The charter from the state of Texas authorizes the corporation to issue 10,000 shares of 6 percent, $100 par preferred stock and 250,000 shares of no-par common stock with a stated value of $5 per share. In its first month, Penrod Drilling completed the following transactions:

Dec. 1 Paid incorporation taxes of $1,500 and a charter fee of $2,000 to the state of Texas and paid legal fees of $1,900 to organize as a corporation.

 3 Issued 750 shares of common stock to the promoter for assistance with issuance of the common stock. The promotion fee was $7,500.

 3 Issued 5,100 shares of common stock to Horner and 3,800 shares to Roads in return for the net assets of the partnership. Horner's capital balance on the partnership books was $51,000, and Roads's capital balance was $38,000.

5   Accepted subscriptions for 5,000 shares of common stock at $10 per share and received a down payment of 25 percent of the subscription amount.

7   Received a small parcel of land valued at $84,000 as a donation from the city of Midland.

12   Issued 1,000 shares of preferred stock to acquire a patent with a market value of $110,000.

22   Issued 1,500 shares of common stock for $10 cash per share.

28   Collected 20 percent of the stock subscription receivable.

Required

1.   Record the transactions in the general journal.
2.   Prepare the stockholders' equity section of the Penrod Drilling balance sheet at December 31. Retained Earnings balance is $91,300.

Problem 12-4A   *Stockholders' equity section of the balance sheet* **(L.O. 3)**

Stockholders' equity information is given for Advantage Consultants, Inc., and Vanguard Corporation. The two companies are independent.

Advantage Consultants, Inc.   Advantage Consultants, Inc., is authorized to issue 50,000 shares of $5 par common stock. All the stock was issued at $8 per share. The company incurred a net loss of $12,000 in 19X1. It earned net income of $60,000 in 19X2 and $130,000 in 19X3. The company declared no dividends during the three-year period.

Vanguard Corporation.   Vanguard's charter authorizes the company to issue 10,000 shares of $2.50 preferred stock with par value of $100 and 120,000 shares of no-par common stock. Vanguard issued 1,000 shares of the preferred stock at $110 per share. It issued 40,000 shares of the common stock for a total of $320,000. The company's retained earnings balance at the beginning of 19X3 was $72,000, and net income for the year was $90,000. During 19X3 the company declared the specified dividend on preferred and a $.50 per share dividend on common. Preferred dividends for 19X2 were in arrears.

Required

For each company, prepare the stockholders' equity section of its balance sheet at December 31, 19X3. Show the computation of all amounts. Entries are not required.

Problem 12-5A   *Analyzing the stockholders' equity of an actual corporation* **(L.O. 1,3,4)**

The purpose of this problem is to familiarize you with the financial statement information of a real company, U and I Group. U and I, which makes food products and livestock feeds, included the following stockholders' equity on its year-end balance sheet at February 28:

Stockholders' Equity	($ Thousands)
Voting Preferred Stock, 5.5% cumulative—par value $23 per share; authorized 100,000 shares in each class:	
Class A—issued 75,473 shares	$ 1,736
Class B—issued 92,172 shares	2,120
Common stock—par value $5 per share; authorized 5,000,000 shares; issued 2,870,950 shares	14,355
[Additional] Paid-in Capital	5,548
Retained earnings	8,336
	$32,095

Required

1. Identify the different issues of stock U and I has outstanding.
2. Is the preferred stock participating or nonparticipating? How can you tell?
3. Give the summary entries to record issuance of all the U and I stock. Assume that all the stock was issued for cash and that the additional paid-in capital applies to the common stock. Explanations are not required.
4. Rearrange the U and I stockholders' equity section to correspond, as appropriate, to the format and terminology illustrated on page 596. Assume the total stockholders' equity of $32,095,000 is correct.
5. Suppose U and I passed its preferred dividends for one year. Would the company have to pay these dividends in arrears before paying dividends to the common stockholders? Give your reason.
6. What amount of preferred dividends must U and I declare and pay each year to avoid having preferred dividends in arrears?
7. Assume preferred dividends are in arrears for 19X8.
   a. Write Note 5 of the February 28, 19X8, financial statements to disclose the dividends in arrears.
   b. Record the declaration of a $500,000 dividend in the year ended February 28, 19X9. An explanation is not required.

Problem 12-6A *Preparing a corporation balance sheet; measuring profitability (L.O. 3,5)*

The following accounts and related balances of Gillen Art Associates, Inc., are arranged in no particular order. Use them to prepare the company's classified balance sheet in the account format at June 30, 19X2. Also compute rate of return on total assets and rate of return on common stockholders' equity for the year ended June 30, 19X2. Do these rates of return suggest strength or weakness? Give your reason.

Trademark, net	$ 9,000	Common stockholders'	
Organization cost, net	14,000	equity, June 30, 19X1	$322,000
Preferred stock, $.20,		Net income	31,000
no-par, 10,000 shares		Total assets, June 30,	
authorized and issued	27,000	19X1	504,000
Stock subscription		Interest expense	6,100
receivable—common	12,000	Property, plant, and	
Cash	19,000	equipment, net	267,000
Accounts receivable, net	34,000	Common stock, $1 par,	
Paid-in capital in excess		500,000 shares	
of par—common	19,000	authorized, 214,000	
Income tax payable	26,000	shares issued	214,000
Long-term note payable	72,000	Prepaid expenses	10,000
Inventory	148,000	Common stock	
Dividends payable	9,000	subscribed, 22,000	
Retained earnings	?	shares	22,000
Accounts payable	31,000	Donated capital	6,000

Problem 12-7A *Computing dividends on preferred and common stock (L.O. 4)*

Whitehead Institute, Inc., has 10,000 shares of $3.50, no-par preferred stock and 50,000 shares of no-par common stock outstanding. Whitehead declared and paid the following dividends during a three-year period: 19X1, $20,000; 19X2, $90,000; and 19X3, $265,000.

Required

1. Compute the total dividends to preferred stock and common stock for each of the three years if
   a. Preferred is noncumulative and nonparticipating
   b. Preferred is cumulative and nonparticipating.
2. For case *1b,* record the declaration of the 19X3 dividends on December 28, 19X3, and the payment of the dividends on January 17, 19X4.

Problem 12-8A *Analyzing the stockholders' equity of an actual corporation* *(L.O. 4,6)*

The balance sheet of Elsimate, Inc., reported the following:

Shareholders' Investment
(same as stockholders' equity)

Redeemable non-voting preferred stock, no-par (Redemption value $358,000)	$320,000
Common stock, $1.50 par value, authorized 75,000 shares; issued 36,000 shares.....................	54,000
[Additional] paid-in capital........................	231,000
Retained earnings	119,000
Total shareholders' investment	$724,000

Notes to the financial statements indicate that 8,000 shares of $2.60 preferred stock with a stated value of $40 per share were issued and outstanding. Preferred dividends are in arrears for three years, including the current year. The additional paid-in capital was contributed by the common stockholders. On the balance sheet date, the market value of the Elsimate common stock was $7.50 per share.

Required

1. Is the preferred stock cumulative or noncumulative, participating or non-participating? How can you tell?
2. What is the amount of the annual preferred dividend?
3. Which class of stockholders controls the company? Give your reason.
4. What is the total paid-in capital of the company?
5. What was the total market value of the common stock?
6. Compute the book value per share of the preferred stock and the common stock.

Problem 12-9A *Computing and recording a corporation's income tax* *(L.O. 7)*

The accounting (not the income tax) records of Jones Corporation provide the comparative income statement for 19X7 and 19X8:

	19X7	19X8
Total revenue.....................................	$930,000	$990,000
Expenses:		
Cost of goods sold	430,000	460,000
Operating expenses	270,000	280,000
Total expenses before tax	700,000	740,000
Pretax accounting income........................	$230,000	$250,000

Total revenue of 19X8 includes rent revenue of $15,000 that was received late in 19X7. This rent revenue is included in 19X8 total revenue because it was earned in 19X8. However, revenue that is collected in advance is included in the taxable income of the year when the cash is received.

Also, the operating expenses of each year include depreciation of $50,000 computed on the straight-line method. In calculating taxable income on the tax return, Jones Corporation uses the Modified Accelerated Cost Recovery System (MACRS). MACRS depreciation was $80,000 for 19X7 and $20,000 for 19X8.

Required

(Assume a corporate income tax rate of 34 percent.)

1. Compute taxable income for each year.
2. Journalize the corporation's income taxes for each year.
3. Prepare the corporation's single-step income statement for each year.

(Group B)

Problem 12-1B   *Organizing a corporation*   **(L.O. 1)**

Patrick Ledoux and Michael Suttle are opening a Big Boy Restaurant in a growing section of Seattle. There are no competing family restaurants in the immediate vicinity. Their most fundamental decision is how to organize the business. Patrick thinks the partnership form is best for their business. Michael favors the corporate form of organization. They seek your advice.

Required

Discuss the advantages and the disadvantages of organizing the business as a corporation. Refer back to Chapter 1 if necessary.

Problem 12-2B   *Journalizing corporation transactions and preparing the stockholders'*
equity section of the balance sheet   **(L.O. 1,3)**

Metzger Brothers Corporation was organized under the laws of the state of Vermont. The charter authorizes Metzger to issue 100,000 shares of $3, no-par preferred stock and 500,000 shares of common stock with $1 par value. During its start-up phase, the company completed the following transactions:

July 5   Paid fees and incorporation taxes of $12,000 to the state of Vermont to obtain the charter and file the required documents for incorporation.

6   Issued 500 shares of common stock to the promoters who organized the corporation. Their fee was $20,000.

7   Accepted subscriptions for 1,000 shares of common stock at $30 per share and received a down payment of one-third of the subscription amount.

12   Issued 300 shares of preferred stock for cash of $20,000.

14   Issued 800 shares of common stock in exchange for land valued at $24,000.

31   Collected one-half of the stock subscription receivable.

31   Earned a small profit for July and closed the $21,000 credit balance of Income Summary into the Retained Earnings account.

Required

1. Record the transactions in the general journal.
2. Prepare the stockholders' equity section of the Metzger balance sheet at July 31.

Problem 12-3B *Journalizing corporation transactions and preparing the stockholders' equity section of the balance sheet (L.O. 1,2,3)*

The partnership of Endicott and Barbisch needed additional capital to expand into new markets, so the business incorporated as Salinas, Inc. The charter from the state of Arizona authorizes Salinas to issue 50,000 shares of 6 percent, $100 par preferred stock and 100,000 shares of no-par common stock with a stated value of $5 per share. In its first month, Salinas completed the following transactions:

Dec. 1 Paid a charter fee of $500 and incorporation taxes of $2,100 to the state of Arizona and paid legal fees of $1,000 to organize as a corporation.

2 Issued 300 shares of common stock to the promoter for assistance with issuance of the common stock. The promotional fee was $1,800.

2 Issued 9,000 shares of common stock to Endicott and 12,000 shares to Barbisch in return for the net assets of the partnership. Endicott's capital balance on the partnership books was $54,000, and Barbisch's capital balance was $72,000.

4 Accepted subscriptions for 4,000 shares of common stock at $6 per share and received a down payment of 20 percent of the subscription amount.

8 Received a small parcel of land valued at $80,000 as a donation from the city of Phoenix.

10 Issued 400 shares of preferred stock to acquire a patent with a market value of $50,000.

16 Issued 600 shares of common stock for cash of $3,600.

30 Collected one-third of the stock subscription receivable.

Required

1. Record the transactions in the general journal.
2. Prepare the stockholders' equity section of the Salinas, Inc., balance sheet at December 31. Retained Earnings' balance is $42,100.

Problem 12-4B *Stockholders' equity section of the balance sheet (L.O. 3)*

The following summaries for Navarro Corp. and Action Manpower, Inc., provide the information needed to prepare the stockholders' equity section of the company balance sheet. The two companies are independent.

Navarro Corp.   Navarro Corp. is authorized to issue 50,000 shares of $1 par common stock. All the stock was issued at $6 per share. The company incurred net losses of $30,000 in 19X1 and $14,000 in 19X2. It earned net incomes of $23,000 in 19X3 and $52,000 in 19X4. The company declared no dividends during the four-year period.

Action Manpower, Inc.   Action's charter authorizes the company to issue 5,000 shares of 5 percent, $100 par preferred stock and 500,000 shares of no-par common stock. Action issued 1,000 shares of the preferred stock at $105 per share. It issued 100,000 shares of the common stock for $150,000. The company's retained earnings balance at the beginning of 19X4 was $120,000. Net income for 19X4 was $80,000, and the company declared a 5 percent preferred dividend for 19X4. Preferred dividends for 19X3 were in arrears.

Required

For each company, prepare the stockholders' equity section of its balance sheet at December 31, 19X4. Show the computation of all amounts. Entries are not required.

Problem 12-5B *Analyzing the stockholders' equity of an actual corporation* **(L.O. 3,4)**

The purpose of this problem is to familiarize you with the financial statement information of a real company. Bethlehem Steel Corporation is one of the nation's largest steel companies. Bethlehem included the following stockholders' equity on its balance sheet:

Stockholders' Equity	($ Millions)
Preferred stock—	
Authorized 20,000,000 shares in each class; issued:	
$5.00 Cumulative Convertible Preferred Stock, at $50.00	
stated value, 2,500,000 shares	$ 125
$2.50 Cumulative Convertible Preferred Stock, at $25.00	
stated value, 4,000,000 shares	100
Common stock—$8 par value—	
Authorized 80,000,000 shares; issued 48,308,516 shares	621
Retained earnings	529
	$1,375

Observe that Bethlehem reports no Paid-in Capital in Excess of Par or Stated Value. Instead, the company reports these items in the stock accounts.

Required

1. Identify the different issues of stock Bethlehem has outstanding.
2. Is the preferred stock participating or nonparticipating? How can you tell?
3. Which class of stock did Bethlehem issue at par or stated value, and which class did it issue above par or stated value?
4. Rearrange the Bethlehem Steel stockholders' equity section to correspond, as appropriate, to the terminology and format illustrated on page 596. Assume Bethlehem is authorized to issue 20,000,000 shares of the $5 preferred stock and an additional 20,000,000 shares of the $2.50 preferred. Assume the total stockholders' equity of $1,375 million is correct. Report dollar amounts in millions, as Bethlehem does.
5. Suppose Bethlehem passed its preferred dividends for one year. Would the company have to pay these dividends in arrears before paying dividends to the common stockholders? Give your reason.
6. What amount of preferred dividends must Bethlehem declare and pay each year to avoid having preferred dividends in arrears?
7. Assume preferred dividends are in arrears for 19X5.
   a. Write Note 6 of the December 31, 19X5, financial statements to disclose the dividends in arrears.
   b. Journalize the declaration of a $60 million dividend for 19X6. An explanation is not required.

Problem 12-6B *Preparing a corporation balance sheet; measuring profitability* **(L.O. 3,5)**

The following accounts and related balances of McIntosh Products, Inc., are arranged in no particular order. Use them to prepare the company's classified balance sheet in the account format at November 30, 19X7. Also compute rate of return on total assets and rate of return on common stockholders' equity for the year ended November 30, 19X7. Do these rates of return suggest strength or weakness? Give your reason.

Accounts payable	$ 31,000	Income tax payable	$ 17,000
Stock subscription receivable, preferred ..	1,000	Long-term note payable .	104,000
		Accounts receivable, net .	101,000
Retained earnings	?	Preferred stock, 4%, $10 par, 25,000 shares authorized, 3,000 shares issued	30,000
Common stock, $5 par, 100,000 shares authorized, 42,000 shares issued	210,000		
		Cash..................	41,000
Dividends payable	3,000	Inventory	226,000
Total assets, November 30, 19X6	781,000	Property, plant, and equipment, net	378,000
Net income............	36,200	Organization cost, net ...	6,000
Common stockholders' equity, November 30, 19X6	483,000	Prepaid expenses	13,000
		Preferred stock subscribed 700 shares .	7,000
Interest expense	12,800	Patent, net	31,000
Donated capital	109,000	Additional paid-in capital—common	85,000

Problem 12-7B *Computing dividends on preferred and common stock* (*L.O. 4*)

Hankamer Corporation has 5,000 shares of 5 percent, $10 par value preferred stock and 100,000 shares of $1.50 par common stock outstanding. During a three-year period Hankamer declared and paid cash dividends as follows: 19X1, $0; 19X2, $10,000; and 19X3, $27,000.

Required

1. Compute the total dividends to preferred stock and common stock for each of the three years if
   a. Preferred is noncumulative and nonparticipating.
   b. Preferred is cumulative and nonparticipating.
2. For case *1b*, record the declaration of the 19X3 dividends on December 22, 19X3, and the payment of the dividends on January 14, 19X4.

Problem 12-8B *Analyzing the stockholders' equity of an actual corporation* (*L.O. 4,6*)

The balance sheet of Oak Manufacturing, Inc., reported the following:

Stockholders' Investment (same as stockholders' equity)	($ Thousands)
Cumulative convertible preferred stock	$ 45
Common stock, $1 par value, authorized 40,000,000 shares; issued 16,000,000 shares	16,000
[Additional] paid-in capital	176,000
Retained earnings	(77,165)
Total stockholders' investment	$114,880

Notes to the financial statements indicate that 9,000 shares of $1.60 preferred stock with a stated value of $5 per share were issued and outstanding. The preferred stock has a redemption value of $25 per share, and preferred dividends are in arrears for two years, including the current year. The additional paid-in capital was contributed by the common stockholders. On the balance sheet date, the market value of the Oak Manufacturing common stock was $7.50 per share.

Required

1. Is the preferred stock cumulative or noncumulative, participating or nonparticipating? How can you tell?
2. What is the amount of the annual preferred dividend?
3. What is the total paid-in capital of the company?
4. What was the total market value of the common stock?
5. Compute the book value per share of the preferred stock and the common stock.

Problem 12-9B *Computing and recording a corporation's income tax* **(L.O. 7)**

The accounting (not the income tax) records of Waterhouse Microfilms, Inc., provide the comparative income statement for 19X3 and 19X4:

	19X3	19X4
Total revenue..................................	$680,000	$720,000
Expenses:		
Cost of goods sold	290,000	310,000
Operating expenses	180,000	190,000
Total expenses before tax	470,000	500,000
Pretax accounting income.........................	$210,000	$220,000

Total revenue of 19X4 includes rent of $10,000 that was received late in 19X3. This rent is included in 19X4 total revenue because the rent was earned in 19X4. However, rent revenue that is collected in advance is included in taxable income when the cash is received. In calculating taxable income on the tax return, this rent revenue belongs in 19X3.

Also, the operating expenses of each year include depreciation of $40,000 computed under the straight-line method. In calculating taxable income on the tax return, Waterhouse Corporation uses the Modified Accelerated Cost Recovery System (MACRS). MACRS depreciation was $60,000 for 19X3 and $20,000 for 19X4.

Required

(Assume a corporate income tax rate of 34 percent.)

1. Compute taxable income for each year.
2. Journalize the corporation's income taxes for each year.
3. Prepare the corporation's single-step income statement for each year.

Extending Your Knowledge

Decision Problems

1. Evaluating Alternative Ways of Raising Capital   (L.O. 1,3)

R. Atari and G. Stacey have written a computer program for a video game that they believe will rival Nintendo. They need additional capital to market the product, and they plan to incorporate their partnership. They are considering alternative capital structures for the corporation. Their primary goal is to raise as much capital as possible without giving up control of the business. The partners plan to receive 170,000 shares of the corporation's common stock in return for the net assets of the partnership. After the partnership books are closed and the assets adjusted to current market value, Atari's capital balance is $90,000 and Stacey's balance is $80,000.

The corporation's plans for a charter include an authorization to issue 5,000 shares of preferred stock and 500,000 shares of $1 par common stock. Atari and Stacey are uncertain about the most desirable features for the preferred stock. Prior to incorporating, the partners have discussed their plans with two investment groups. The corporation can obtain capital from outside investors under either of the following plans:

Plan 1. Group 1 will invest $105,000 to acquire 1,000 shares of $5, no-par preferred stock and $130,000 to acquire 130,000 shares of common stock. Each preferred share receives 50 votes on matters that come before the stockholders. The investors in Group 1 would attempt to control the corporation if they have the majority of the corporate votes.

Plan 2. Group 2 will invest $220,000 to acquire 2,000 shares of 6 percent, $100 par nonvoting, noncumulative, participating preferred stock.

Required

Assume the corporation is chartered.

1. Journalize the issuance of common stock to Atari and Stacey.
2. Journalize the issuance of stock to the outsiders under both plans.
3. Assume net income for the first year is $130,000 and total dividends of $19,800 are properly subtracted from retained earnings. Prepare the stockholders' equity section of the corporation balance sheet under both plans.
4. Recommend one of the plans to Atari and Stacey. Give your reasons.

2. Questions About Corporations (L.O. 1,3,6)

1. Why do you think capital stock and retained earnings are shown separately in the shareholders' equity section?
2. Mary Reznick, major shareholder of M-R Inc., proposes to sell some land she owns to the company for common shares in M-R. What problem does M-R, Inc. face in recording the transaction?
3. Preferred shares generally are preferred with respect to dividends and on liquidation. Why would investors buy common stock when preferred stock is available?
4. What does it mean if the liquidation value of a company's preferred stock is greater than its market value.
5. If you owned 100 shares of stock in Magna Corporation and someone offered to buy the stock for its book value, would you accept their offer? Why or why not?

Ethical Issue

George Campbell paid $50,000 for a franchise that entitled him to market Success Associates software programs in the countries of the European Common Market. Campbell intended to sell individual franchises for the major language groups of western Europe—German, French, English, Spanish, and

Italian. Naturally, investors considering buying a franchise from Campbell asked to see the financial statements of his business.

Believing the value of the franchise to be greater than $50,000, Campbell sought to capitalize his own franchise at $500,000. The law firm of McDonald & LaDue helped Campbell form a corporation chartered to issue 500,000 shares of common stock with par value of $1 per share. Attorneys suggested the following chain of transactions:

1. A third party borrows $500,000 and purchases the franchise from Campbell.
2. Campbell pays the corporation $500,000 to acquire all its stock.
3. The corporation buys the franchise from the third party, who repays the loan.

In the final analysis, the third party is debt-free and out of the picture. Campbell owns all the corporation's stock, and the corporation owns the franchise. The corporation balance sheet lists a franchise acquired at a cost of $500,000. This balance sheet is Campbell's most valuable marketing tool.

Required

1. What is unethical about this situation?
2. Who can be harmed? How can they be harmed? What role does accounting play?

Financial Statement Problems

1. Stockholders' Equity   (L.O. 1,3,6)

The Goodyear Tire & Rubber Company financial statements appear in Appendix C. Answer these questions about the company's common stock.

1. What classes of stock does the balance sheet report? What is the par value? How many shares are authorized? How many shares were outstanding at December 31, 1991?
2. For issuances of stock, Goodyear obviously credited the Common Stock account for a specific amount per share. What was the amount? What was the average issue price per share?
3. The Quarterly Data and Market Price Information note, near the end of Goodyear's annual report, indicates that during 1991, the company's common stock was priced in the $16–$54 range. Based on this fact, does Goodyear's balance sheet suggest that the company issued its common stock recently or in the distant past? How can you tell?
4. Like most other corporations, Goodyear allows its stockholders and employees to purchase the company's stock through dividend reinvestment and stock purchase plans. These are mentioned in the statement of stockholders' equity. Record Goodyear's issuance of stock under these plans during 1991, assuming the company received cash.

2. Stockholders' Equity   (L.O. 1,3,6)

Obtain the annual report of an actual company of your choosing. Annual reports are available in various forms including the original document in hard copy, microfiche, and computerized data bases such as that provided by Disclosure, Inc.

Answer these questions about the company. Concentrate on the current year in the annual report you select.

1. What classes of stock does the company have outstanding? What is its par value? How many shares are authorized? How many shares were outstanding on the most current balance sheet date?

2. Under what title does the company report additional paid-in capital?

3. How much is total stockholders' equity? If the total is not labeled, compute total stockholders' equity.

4. Using the company's terminology, journalize the issuance of 100,000 shares of the company's common stock at $55 per share. Recompute all account balances to include the effect of this transaction.

5. Compute the average amount paid in per share of the company's common stock. Then examine the recent market prices of the company's stock in the multiyear summary of financial data. Compare the average amount paid in per share with recent market prices to determine whether the bulk of the company's stock was issued within the recent past. Give the reason for your answer.

Chapter *13*

Retained Earnings, Dividends, Treasury Stock, and the Income Statement

In the 1991 annual report, the following footnote appeared:

Unusual Losses and Events

In February 1991, it came to the attention of Magid Corp. directors that certain officers of its Milwaukee-based mail order operations had engaged in unauthorized accounting procedures and computer manipulations in the areas of accounts receivable and accounts payable. The adjustments necessary to restate accounts re-ceivable resulted in losses of approximately $8.6 million, and the adjustments to correct accounts payable resulted in losses of approximately $3.1 million.

Company executives believe that the overstate-ment of accounts receivable and the understatement of liabilities occurred prior to 1991. However, mainly because of the absence of the related accounting records and other data, accountants have been unable to identify the periods in which the unauthorized pro-cedures and manipulations occurred.

Clearly the losses resulting from the computer manipulations fall outside the major ongoing operations of the corporation. It would be inappropriate to report the losses as though they resulted from the sale of inventory or from any other ongoing operation. The section of this chapter on the corporation income statement discusses how to report special gains and losses.

Retained Earnings and Dividends

We have seen that the equity section on the corporation balance sheet is called stockholders' equity or shareholders' equity. The paid-in capital accounts and retained earnings make up the stockholders' equity section.

Retained Earnings is the corporation account that carries the balance of the business's net income less its net losses from operations and less any declared dividends accumulated over the corporation's lifetime. *Retained* means "held on to." Retained Earnings is accumulated income to cover dividends and any future losses. Because Retained Earnings is an owners' equity account, it normally has a credit balance. Corporations may use other labels for Retained Earnings, among them Earnings Reinvested in the Business and Retained Income.

A debit balance in Retained Earnings, which arises when a corporation's expenses exceed its revenues, is called a *deficit*. This amount is subtracted from the sum of the credit balances in the other equity accounts on the balance sheet to determine total stockholders' equity. In a recent survey, 37 of 600 companies (6.2 percent) had a retained earnings deficit.

At the end of each accounting period, the Income Summary account—which carries the balance of net income for the period—is closed to the Retained Earnings account. Assume the following amounts are drawn from a corporation's temporary accounts.

Income Summary

Dec. 31, 19X1	Expenses	750,000	Dec. 31, 19X1	Revenues	850,000
			Dec. 31, 19X1	Bal.	100,000

This final closing entry transfers net income from Income Summary to Retained Earnings:

19X1			
Dec. 31	Income Summary	100,000	
	Retained Earnings		100,000
	To close net income to Retained Earnings.		

If 19X1 was the corporation's first year of operations, the Retained Earnings account now has an ending balance of $100,000:

Retained Earnings

	Jan. 1, 19X1	Bal.	-0-
	Dec. 31, 19X1	Net inc.	100,000
	Dec. 31, 19X1	Bal.	100,000

A $60,000 net loss for the year would produce this debit balance in Income Summary:

Income Summary

Dec. 31, 19X3	Expenses	470,000	Dec. 31, 19X3	Revenues	410,000
Dec. 31, 19X3	Bal.	60,000			

To close a $60,000 loss, we would credit Income Summary and debit Retained Earnings, as follows:

Dec. 31	Retained Earnings	60,000	
	Income Summary		60,000
	To close net loss to Retained Earnings.		

After posting, Income Summary's balance is zero, and the Retained Earnings balance is decreased by $60,000.

Remember that the account title includes the word *earnings. Credits to the Retained Earnings account arise only from net income.* When we examine a corporation's financial statements and want to learn how much net income the corporation has earned and retained in the business, we turn to Retained Earnings.

After the corporation has earned net income, its board of directors may declare and pay a cash dividend to the stockholders. The entry on January 15, 19X2, to record the declaration of a $35,000 dividend is

Jan. 15	Retained Earnings	35,000	
	Dividends Payable		35,000
	To declare a cash dividend.		

After the dividend declaration is posted, the Retained Earnings account has a $65,000 credit balance:

Retained Earnings

Jan. 15, 19X2	Dividend	35,000	Jan. 1, 19X2	Bal.	100,000
			Jan. 15, 19X2	Bal.	65,000

The Retained Earnings account is not a reservoir of cash waiting for the board of directors to pay dividends to the stockholders. Instead, Retained Earnings is an owners' equity account representing a claim on all assets in general and not on any asset in particular. Its balance is the cumulative, lifetime earnings of the company less its cumulative losses and dividends. In fact, the corporation may have a large balance in Retained Earnings but not have the cash to pay a dividend. Why? Because the company purchased a building. The company may have abundant cash from borrowing but very little retained earnings. To *declare* a dividend, the company must have an adequate balance in Retained Earnings. To *pay* the dividend, it must have the cash. Cash and Retained Earnings are two entirely separate accounts having no necessary relationship.

Stock Dividends

A **stock dividend** is a proportional distribution by a corporation of its own stock to its stockholders. Stock dividends are fundamentally different from cash dividends because stock dividends do not transfer the assets of the corporation to the stockholders. Cash dividends are distributions of the asset cash, but stock dividends cause changes *only* in the stockholders' equity of the corporation. The effect of a stock dividend is an increase in the stock account and a decrease in Retained Earnings. Because both of these accounts are elements of stockholders' equity, total stockholders' equity is unchanged. There is merely a transfer from one stockholders' equity account to another, and no asset or liability is affected by a stock dividend.

The corporation distributes stock dividends to stockholders in proportion to the number of shares they already own. For example, suppose you owned 300 shares of Xerox Corporation common stock. If Xerox distributed a 10 percent common stock dividend, you would receive 30 (300 × .10) additional shares. You would now own 330 shares of the stock. All other Xerox stockholders would receive additional shares equal to 10 percent of their prior holdings. You would all be in the same relative position after the dividend as you were before.

In distributing a stock dividend, the corporation gives up no assets. Why, then, do companies issue stock dividends?

Reasons for Stock Dividends

A corporation may choose to distribute stock dividends for these reasons:

1. To continue dividends but conserve cash. A company may want to keep cash in the business in order to expand, buy inventory, pay off debts, and so on. Yet the company may wish to continue dividends in some form. To do so, the corporation may distribute a stock dividend. The debit to Retained Earnings indirectly conserves cash by decreasing the Retained Earnings available for the declaration of future cash dividends. Stockholders pay tax on cash dividends but not on stock dividends.

2. To reduce the market price per share of its stock. Many companies pay low cash dividends and grow by reinvesting their earnings in operations. As they grow, the company's stock price increases. If the price gets high enough, eventually some potential investors may be prevented from purchasing the stock. Distribution of a stock dividend may cause the market price of a share of the company's stock to decrease because of the increased supply of the stock.

Suppose the market price of a share of stock is $50. If the corporation doubles the number of shares of its stock outstanding by issuing a stock dividend, the market price of the stock would drop by approximately one-half, to $25 per share. The objective is to make the stock less expensive and thus attractive to a wider range of investors.

Entries for Stock Dividends

The board of directors announces stock dividends on the declaration date. The date of record and the distribution date follow. (This is the same sequence of dates used for a cash dividend.) The declaration of a stock dividend does *not* create a liability because the corporation is not obligated to pay assets. (Recall that a liability is a claim on *assets*.) Instead, the corporation has declared its intention to distribute its stock. Assume General Lumber Corporation has the following stockholders' equity prior to the dividend:

OBJECTIVE 1
Account for stock dividends

Stockholders' Equity

Paid-in capital:
Common stock, $10 par, 50,000 shares authorized, 20,000 shares issued	$200,000
Paid-in capital in excess of par—common	70,000
Total paid-in capital	270,000
Retained earnings	85,000
Total stockholders' equity	$355,000

The entry to record a stock dividend depends on the size of the dividend. Generally accepted accounting principles (GAAP) distinguish between **small stock dividends** (less than 25 percent of the corporation's issued stock) and **large stock dividends** (25 percent or more of issued stock). Stock dividends between 20 percent and 25 percent are rare.

Assume General Lumber Corporation declares a 10 percent (small) common stock dividend on November 17. The company will distribute 2,000 (20,000 × .10) shares in the dividend. On November 17 the market value of its common stock is $16 per share. GAAP requires small stock dividends to be accounted for at market value. Therefore, Retained Earnings is debited for the market value of the 2,000 dividend shares. Common Stock Dividend Distributable is credited for par value, and Paid-in Capital in Excess of Par is credited for the remainder. General Lumber makes the following entry on the declaration date:[1]

Nov. 17	Retained Earnings (20,000 × .10 × $16)	32,000	
	Common Stock Dividend Distributable (20,000 × .10 × $10)		20,000
	Paid-in Capital in Excess of Par—Common		12,000
	To declare a 10 percent common stock dividend.		

On the distribution (payment) date, the company records issuance of the dividend shares as follows:

Dec. 12	Common Stock Dividend Distributable	20,000	
	Common Stock		20,000
	To issue common stock in a stock dividend.		

Common Stock Dividend Distributable is an owner's equity account. (It is *not* a liability because the corporation has no obligation to pay assets.) If the

---

[1]Committee on Accounting Procedure, "Accounting Research Bulletin No. 43," *Restatement and Revision of Accounting Research Bulletins* (New York: AICPA, 1961), Chap. 7, Sec. B, pars. 10–14.

company prepares financial statements after the declaration of the stock dividend but before issuing it, Common Stock Dividend Distributable is reported in the stockholders' equity section of the balance sheet immediately after Common Stock and Common Stock Subscribed and before Paid-in Capital in Excess of Par—Common. However, this account holds the par value of the dividend shares only from the declaration date to the date of distribution.

The following tabulation shows the changes in stockholders' equity caused by the stock dividend:

Stockholders' Equity	Before the Dividend	After the Dividend	Change
Paid-in capital:			
Common stock, $10 par, 50,000 shares authorized, 20,000 shares issued	$200,000		
22,000 shares issued		$220,000	**Up by $20,000**
Paid-in capital in excess of par—common............	70,000	82,000	**Up by $12,000**
Total paid-in capital.......	270,000	302,000	**Up by $32,000**
Retained earnings	85,000	53,000	**Down by $32,000**
Total stockholders' equity .	$355,000	$355,000	**Unchanged**

Compare stockholders' equity before and after the stock dividend. Observe the increase in the balances of Common Stock and Paid-in Capital in Excess of Par—Common and the decrease in Retained Earnings. Also observe that total stockholders' equity is unchanged from $355,000.

Amount of Retained Earnings Transferred in a Stock Dividend. Stock dividends are said to be *capitalized retained earnings* because they transfer an amount from retained earnings to paid-in capital. The paid-in capital accounts are more permanent than retained earnings because they are not subject to dividends. As we saw in the preceding illustration, the amount transferred from Retained Earnings in a *small* stock dividend is the market value of the dividend shares because the effect on the market price of each share of the company's stock is likely to be small. Therefore, many stockholders view small stock dividends as distributions little different from cash dividends.

A *large* stock dividend, though, significantly increases the number of shares available in the market and so is likely to decrease the stock price significantly. Because of the drop in market price per share, a large stock dividend is not likely to be perceived as a dividend. GAAP does not require that large stock dividends be accounted for at a specific amount. A common practice is to use the par value of the dividend shares.

Suppose General Lumber declared a 50 percent common stock dividend. The declaration entry is

Dec. 7	Retained Earnings (20,000 × .50 × $10 par) .	100,000	
	Common Stock Dividend Distributable.		100,000
	To declare a 50 percent common stock dividend.		

Issuance of the dividend shares on the payment date is recorded by this entry:

Dec. 22	Common Stock Dividend Distributable	100,000	
	Common Stock.....................		100,000
	To issue common stock in a stock dividend.		

Once again, total stockholders' equity is unchanged. For a large stock dividend, the increase in Common Stock is exactly offset by the decrease in Retained Earnings.

Stock Splits

A large stock *dividend* may decrease the market price of the stock. The stock then becomes attractive to more people. A stock *split* also decreases the market price of stock—with the intention of making the stock more attractive. A **stock split** is an increase in the number of authorized, issued, and outstanding shares of stock coupled with a proportionate reduction in the par value of the stock. For example, if the company splits its stock 2 for 1, the number of outstanding shares is doubled and each share's par value is halved. Most leading companies in the United States—IBM, Ford Motor Company, Borg-Warner Corporation, Giant Food, Inc., and others—have split their stock.

Assume that the market price of a share of IBM common stock is $120 and that the company wishes to decrease the market price to approximately $30. IBM decides to split the common stock 4 for 1 in order to reduce the stock's market price from $120 to $30. A 4-for-1 stock split means that the company would have four times as many shares of stock outstanding after the split as it had before and that each share's par value would be quartered. Assume IBM had 150 million shares of $5 par common stock issued and outstanding before the split.

Stockholders' Equity	($ Millions)
Paid-in capital:	
Common stock, **$5 par**, 900 million shares authorized,	
150 million shares issued	$ 750
Paid-in capital in excess of par—common	5,200
Total paid-in capital	5,950
Retained earnings	20,000
Total stockholders' equity	$25,950

After the 4-for-1 stock split, IBM would have 3,600 million shares authorized and 600 million shares (150 million shares × 4) of $1.25 par ($5/4) common stock issued and outstanding. Total stockholders' equity would be exactly as before the stock split. Indeed, the balance in the Common Stock account does not even change. Only the par value of the stock and the number of shares authorized and issued change. Compare the highlighted figures in the two stockholders' equity presentations.

Stockholders' Equity	($ Millions)
Paid-in capital:	
Common stock, **$1.25 par**, 3,600 million shares authorized,	
600 million shares issued	$ 750
Paid-in capital in excess of par—common	5,200
Total paid-in capital	5,950
Retained earnings	20,000
Total stockholders' equity	$25,950

Because the stock split affects no account balances, no formal journal entry is necessary. Instead, the split is recorded in a memorandum entry such as the following:

Aug. 19   Called in the outstanding $5 par common stock and distributed four shares of $1.25 par common stock for each old share previously outstanding.

A company may engage in a reverse split to decrease the number of shares of stock outstanding. For example, IBM could split its stock 1 for 4. After the split, par value would be $20 ($5 × 4), shares authorized would be 225 million (900 million/4), and shares issued and outstanding would be 37.5 million (150 million/4). Reverse splits are rare.

Stock Dividends and Stock Splits

A stock dividend and a stock split both increase the number of shares of stock owned per stockholder. Also, neither a stock dividend nor a stock split changes the investor's total cost of the stock owned. For example, assume you paid $3,000 to acquire 150 shares of Avon Products common stock. If Avon distributes a 100 percent stock dividend, your 150 shares increase to 300, but your total cost is still $3,000. Likewise, if Avon distributes a 2-for-1 stock split, your shares increase in number to 300, but your total cost is unchanged. Neither type of stock action is taxable income to the investor.

Both a stock dividend and a stock split increase the corporation's number of shares outstanding. For example, a 100 percent stock dividend and a 2-for-1 stock split both double the outstanding shares and cut the stock's market price per share in half. They differ in that a stock *dividend* shifts an amount from retained earnings to paid-in capital, leaving par value per share unchanged. A stock *split* affects no account balances whatsoever but instead changes the par value of the stock. It also increases the number of shares authorized.

Exhibit 13-1 summarizes the effects of dividends and stock splits on total stockholders' equity.

OBJECTIVE 2
Distinguish stock splits from stock dividends

EXHIBIT 13-1   *Effects of Dividends and Stock Splits on Total Stockholders' Equity*

	Declaration	Payment of Cash or Distribution of Stock
Cash dividend	Decrease	None
Stock dividend	None	None
Stock split	None	None

Source: Adapted from Beverly Terry.

Treasury Stock

Corporations may purchase their own stock from their shareholders for several reasons. (1) The company may have issued all its authorized stock and need the stock for distributions to officers and employees under bonus plans or stock purchase plans. (2) The purchase may help support the stock's current market price by decreasing the supply of stock available to the public. (3) The business may be trying to increase net assets by buying its shares low and hoping to sell them for a higher price later. (4) Management may gather in the stock to avoid a takeover by an outside party.

A corporation's own stock that it has issued and later reacquired is called **treasury stock.**[2] (In effect, the corporation holds the stock in its treasury.) For

---

[2]In this book we illustrate the *cost* method of accounting for treasury stock because it is used most widely. Alternative methods are presented in intermediate accounting courses.

practical purposes, treasury stock is like unissued stock: neither category of stock is outstanding in the hands of shareholders. The company does not receive cash dividends on its treasury stock, and treasury stock does not entitle the company to vote or to receive assets in liquidation. The difference between unissued stock and treasury stock is that treasury stock has been issued and bought back.

The purchase of treasury stock decreases the company's assets and its stockholders' equity. The size of the company literally decreases, as shown on the balance sheet. The Treasury Stock account has a debit balance, which is the opposite of the other owners' equity accounts. Therefore, Treasury Stock is a contra stockholders' equity account.

Purchase of Treasury Stock

We record the purchase of treasury stock by debiting Treasury Stock and crediting the asset given in exchange—usually Cash. Suppose that Southwest Drilling Company had the following stockholders' equity before purchasing treasury stock:

Stockholders' Equity

Paid-in capital:	
Common stock, $1 par, 10,000 shares authorized,	
8,000 shares issued	$ 8,000
Paid-in capital in excess of par—common	12,000
Total paid-in capital	20,000
Retained earnings	14,600
Total stockholders' equity	$34,600

On November 22 Southwest purchases 1,000 shares of its $1 par common as treasury stock, paying cash of $7.50 per share. Southwest records the purchase as follows:

Nov. 22	Treasury Stock, Common (1,000 × $7.50)	7,500	
	Cash		7,500
	Purchased 1,000 shares of treasury stock at		
	$7.50 per share.		

OBJECTIVE 3

Account for treasury stock

Treasury stock is recorded at cost, without reference to the par value of the stock. The Treasury Stock account appears beneath retained earnings on the balance sheet, and its balance is subtracted from the sum of total paid-in capital and retained earnings, as follows:

Stockholders' Equity

Paid-in capital:	
Common stock, $1 par, 10,000 shares authorized,	
8,000 shares issued	$ 8,000
Paid-in capital in excess of par—common	12,000
Total paid-in capital	20,000
Retained earnings	14,600
Subtotal	34,600
Less Treasury stock (1,000 shares at cost)	**(7,500)**
Total stockholders' equity	$27,100

Observe that the purchase of treasury stock does not decrease the number of shares issued. The Common Stock, Paid-in Capital in Excess of Par, and

Retained Earnings accounts remain unchanged. However, total stockholders' equity decreases by the cost of the treasury stock. Also, shares of stock *outstanding* decrease from 8,000 to 7,000. To compute the number of outstanding shares, subtract the treasury shares (1,000) from the shares issued (8,000). Although the number of outstanding shares is not required to be reported on the balance sheet, this figure is important. Only outstanding shares have a vote, receive cash dividends, and share in assets if the corporation liquidates.

Sale of Treasury Stock

Sale of Treasury Stock at Cost.   Treasury stock may be sold at any price agreeable to the corporation and the purchaser. If the stock is sold for the same price that the corporation paid to reacquire it, the entry is a debit to Cash and a credit to Treasury Stock for the same amount.

Sale of Treasury Stock above Cost.   If the sale price is greater than reacquisition cost, the difference is credited to the account Paid-in Capital from Treasury Stock Transactions. Suppose Southwest Drilling Company resold 200 of its treasury shares for $9 per share. The entry is

Dec. 7	Cash (200 × $9)	1,800	
	Treasury Stock, Common (200 × $7.50—the purchase cost per share)		1,500
	Paid-in Capital from Treasury Stock Transactions .		300
	To sell 200 shares of treasury stock at $9 per share.		

Paid-in Capital from Treasury Stock Transactions is reported with the other paid-in capital accounts on the balance sheet, beneath the Common Stock and Capital in Excess of Par accounts.

Sale of Treasury Stock below Cost.   At times the resale price is less than cost. The difference between these two amounts is debited to Paid-in Capital from Treasury Stock Transactions if this account has a credit balance, as in our example. If the difference between resale price and cost is greater than the credit balance in Paid-in Capital from Treasury Stock Transactions, or if Paid-in Capital from Treasury Stock Transactions has a zero balance, then the company debits Retained Earnings for the remaining amount. For example, Southwest Drilling records the sale of 400 shares of treasury stock at $5 per share in the following entry:

Dec. 23	Cash (400 × $5)	2,000	
	Paid-in Capital from Treasury Stock Transactions	300	
	Retained Earnings	700	
	Treasury Stock, Common (400 × $7.50—the purchase cost per share)		3,000
	To sell 400 shares of treasury stock at $5 per share.		

Paid-in Capital from Treasury Stock Transactions receives only a $300 debit because that is the extent of this account's credit balance. (See the preceding example illustrating the sale of treasury stock above cost.) The remaining $700 is debited to Retained Earnings.

No Gain or Loss from Treasury Stock Transactions

The purchase and sale of treasury stock do not affect net income. Sale of treasury stock above cost is an increase in paid-in capital, not income. Likewise, sale of treasury stock below cost is a decrease in paid-in capital or

Retained Earnings, not a loss. Treasury stock transactions take place between the business and its owners, the stockholders. Because a company cannot earn a profit in dealing in its own stock with its owners, we credit Paid-in Capital from Treasury Stock Transactions for sale above cost and debit that account (and, if necessary, Retained Earnings) for a sale below cost. These accounts appear on the balance sheet, not on the income statement.

Does this mean that a company cannot increase its net assets by buying treasury stock low and selling it high? Not at all. Management often buys treasury stock because it believes the market price of its stock is too low. For example, a company may buy 500 shares of its stock at $10 per share. Suppose it holds the stock as the market price rises and resells the stock at $14 per share. The net assets of the company increase by $2,000 [500 shares × ($14 − $10 = $4 difference per share)]. This increase is reported as paid-in capital and not as income.

Summary Problem for Your Review

Simplicity Pattern Co., Inc., reported the following stockholders' equity:

Shareholders' Equity	($ Thousands)
Preferred stock, $1.00 par value	
Authorized − 10,000,000 shares	
Issued − None	$ —
Common stock, 8 ⅓ cents par value	
Authorized, 30,000,000 shares	
Issued 13,733,229 shares	1,144
Capital in excess of par value	48,122
Earnings retained in business	89,320
	138,586
Less treasury stock, at cost (1,919,000 common shares)	14,742
	$123,844

Required

1. What was the average issue price per share of the common stock?
2. Journalize the issuance of 1,200 shares of common stock at $4 per share. Use Simplicity's account titles.
3. How many shares of Simplicity's common stock are outstanding?
4. How many shares of common stock would be outstanding after Simplicity split its common stock 3 for 1?
5. Using Simplicity account titles, journalize the declaration of a stock dividend when the market price of Simplicity common stock is $3 per share. Consider each of the following stock dividends independently:
   a. Simplicity declares a 10 percent common stock dividend on the shares outstanding, computed in 3.
   b. Simplicity declares a 100 percent common stock dividend on the shares outstanding, computed in 3.
6. Journalize the following treasury stock transactions, assuming they occur in the order given:
   a. Simplicity purchases 500 shares of treasury stock at $8 per share.
   b. Simplicity sells 100 shares of treasury stock for $9 per share.
   c. Simplicity sells 100 shares of treasury stock for $5 per share.

SOLUTION TO SUMMARY PROBLEM

1. Average issue price of the common stock was $3.59 per share [($1,144,000 + $48,122,000)/13,733,229 shares = $3.59].

2. Cash (1,200 × $4) 4,800
      Common Stock (1,200 × $.08 1/3) 100
      Capital in Excess of Par Value 4,700
   To issue common stock at a premium.

3. Shares outstanding = 11,814,229 (13,733,229 shares issued minus 1,919,000 shares of treasury stock)

4. Shares outstanding after a 3-for-1 stock split = 35,442,687 (11,814,229 shares outstanding × 3)

5a. Earnings Retained in Business
      (11,814,229 × .10 × $3) 3,544,269
      Common Stock Dividend Distributable
        (11,814,229 × .10 × $.08 ⅓) 98,452
      Capital in Excess of Par Value 3,445,817
   To declare a 10 percent common stock dividend.

b. Earnings Retained in Business
      (11,814,229 × $.08 ⅓) 984,519
      Common Stock Dividend Distributable 984,519
   To declare a 100 percent common stock dividend.

6a. Treasury Stock (500 × $8) 4,000
      Cash 4,000
   To purchase 500 shares of treasury stock at $8 per share.

b. Cash (100 × $9) 900
      Treasury Stock (100 × $8) 800
      Paid-in Capital from Treasury Stock
        Transactions 100
   To sell 100 shares of treasury stock at $9 per share.

c. Cash (100 × $5) 500
   Paid-in Capital from Treasury Stock
      Transactions (balance from answer 6b) ... 100
   Earnings Retained in Business 200
      Treasury Stock (100 × $8) 800
   To sell 100 shares of treasury stock at $5 per share.

Retirement of Stock

A corporation may purchase its own common stock or preferred stock and retire it by canceling the stock certificates. The retired stock cannot be reissued. Companies usually retire their stock in order to replace it with another issue of stock or to liquidate shares when they go out of business. Retiring stock, like purchasing treasury stock, decreases the outstanding stock of the corporation. Unlike a treasury stock purchase, stock retirement decreases the number of shares issued. Assets are decreased by the amount paid to buy the shares being retired. In retiring stock, the corporation removes the balances from all paid-in capital amounts related to the retired shares, like Capital in Excess of Par.

A corporation may repurchase shares for retirement for a price that is below the stock's issue price (par value plus any capital in excess of par). This difference between purchase price and issue price is a credit to Paid-in Capital from Retirement of Common Stock (or Preferred Stock).

Assume that a corporation issued its $10 par common stock for $14, a $4 premium per share. If the company later purchases 500 shares of the stock for retirement at $13 per share, the retirement entry is

May 22	Common Stock (500 × $10)	5,000	
	Paid-in Capital in Excess of Par—Common (500 × $4).	2,000	
	Cash (500 × $13)		6,500
	Paid-in Capital from Retirement of Common Stock...........................		500
	To purchase and retire common stock.		

Paid-in Capital from Retirement of Common Stock is reported after Capital in Excess of Par—Common, along with any other paid-in capital accounts related to the common.

If the corporation must pay more for the stock than its issue price, the excess is debited to Retained Earnings. Assume the corporation paid $16 per share to purchase the stock for retirement. The entry is

May 22	Common Stock (500 × $10)	5,000	
	Paid-in Capital in Excess of Par—Common (500 × $4).	2,000	
	Retained Earnings	1,000	
	Cash (500 × $16)		8,000
	To purchase and retire common stock.		

Retiring stock, like purchasing stock, is a transaction that does not affect net income. No gain or loss arises from stock retirement because the company is doing business with its owners. The entries we presented in illustrating stock retirement affect *balance sheet accounts*, not income statement accounts.

Restrictions on Retained Earnings

Dividends, purchases of treasury stock, and retirements of stock require payments by the corporation to its stockholders. In fact, treasury stock purchases and stock retirements are returns of paid-in capital to the stockholders. These outlays decrease the corporation's assets, so fewer assets are available to pay liabilities. Therefore, its creditors seek to restrict a corporation's dividend payments and treasury stock purchases. For example, a bank may agree to loan $500,000 only if the borrowing corporation limits dividend payments and purchases of its stock.

To ensure that corporations maintain a minimum level of stockholders' equity for the protection of creditors, state laws restrict the amount of its own stock that a corporation may purchase. The maximum amount a corporation can pay its stockholders without decreasing paid-in capital is its balance of retained earnings. Therefore, restrictions on dividends and stock purchases focus on the balance of retained earnings.

Companies usually report their retained earnings restrictions in notes to the financial statements. The following actual disclosure by RTE Corporation, a manufacturer of electronic transformers, is typical:

NOTES TO CONSOLIDATED FINANCIAL STATEMENTS
NOTE F—LONG-TERM DEBT

The . . . loan agreements . . . restrict cash dividends and similar payments to shareholders. Under the most restrictive of these provisions, retained earnings of $4,300,000 were unrestricted as of December 31, 19X3.

In another actual example, Chromalloy American Corporation could not declare dividends, purchase treasury stock, or purchase stock for retirement, as indicated by its Note 8:

NOTES TO CONSOLIDATED FINANCIAL STATEMENTS
8: LONG-TERM DEBT

The Company's loan agreements contain covenants which restrict the declaration or payment of cash dividends and the purchase . . . or retirement of capital stock. At December 31, 19X3, . . . all of the Company's [retained] earnings were restricted due to these covenants.

Appropriations of Retained Earnings

Appropriations are restrictions of Retained Earnings that are recorded by formal journal entries. A corporation may appropriate—segregate in a separate account—a portion of Retained Earnings for a specific use. For example, the board of directors may appropriate part of Retained Earnings for building a new manufacturing plant, for meeting possible future liabilities, or for other reasons. A debit to Retained Earnings and a credit to a separate account—Retained Earnings Appropriated for Plant Expansion—records the appropriation. This appropriated retained earnings account appears directly above the regular Retained Earnings account on the balance sheet.

An appropriation does *not* decrease total retained earnings. Any appropriated amount is simply a portion of retained earnings that is earmarked for a particular purpose. When the need for the appropriation no longer exists, an entry debits the Retained Earnings Appropriated account and credits Retained Earnings. This entry closes the Appropriation account and returns its amount back to the regular Retained Earnings account.

Retained earnings appropriations are rare. Corporations generally disclose any retained earnings restrictions in the notes to the financial statements as illustrated in the preceding section. The notes give the corporation more room to describe the nature and amounts of any restrictions. Thus corporations satisfy the requirement for adequate disclosure.

Disclosing any restriction on retained earnings is important to stockholders and possible investors because the restricted amounts may not be used for dividends. A corporation with a $100,000 balance in Retained Earnings and a $60,000 restriction may declare a maximum dividend of $40,000—if the cash is available and the board of directors so decides.

Variations in Reporting Stockholders' Equity

Real-world accounting and business practices may use terminology and formats in reporting stockholders' equity that differ from our general examples. We use a more detailed format in this book to help you learn the components of the stockholders' equity section. Companies assume that readers of their statements already understand the omitted details.

One of the most important skills you will learn in this course is the ability to understand the financial statements of actual companies. Thus we present in Exhibit 13-2 a side-by-side comparison of our general teaching format and the format that you are more likely to encounter in real-world balance sheets. Note the following points in the real-world format:

1. The heading Paid-in Capital does not appear. It is commonly understood that Preferred Stock, Common Stock, and Additional Paid-in Capital are elements of paid-in capital.

2. Preferred stock is often reported in a single amount that combines its par value and premium.

3. For presentation in the financial statements, all additional paid-in capital—from capital in excess of par on common stock, treasury stock transactions, stock retirement, and donated capital—appears as a single amount labeled Additional Paid-in Capital. Additional Paid-in Capital belongs to the common stockholders, and so it follows Common Stock in the real-world format.

4. Often, total stockholders' equity ($4,053,000 in the exhibit) is not specifically labeled.

EXHIBIT 13-2 *Formats for Reporting Stockholders' Equity*

General Teaching Format		Real-World Format	
Stockholders' equity		**Stockholders' equity**	
Paid-in capital:		Preferred stock, 8%, $10 par, 30,000 shares authorized and issued	$ 310,000
Preferred stock, 8%, $10 par, 30,000 shares authorized and issued	$300,000		
Paid-in capital in excess of par—preferred	10,000	Common stock, $1 par, 100,000 shares authorized, 60,000 shares issued	60,000
Common stock, $1 par, 100,000 shares authorized, 60,000 shares issued	60,000	Additional paid-in capital	2,160,000
		Retained earnings (Note 7)	1,565,000
Paid-in capital in excess of par—common	1,940,000	Less treasury stock, common (1,400 shares at cost)	(42,000)
Paid-in capital from treasury stock transactions—common	9,000		$4,053,000
Paid-in capital from retirement of preferred stock	11,000		
Donated capital—plant site	200,000	*Note 7—Restriction on retained earnings.*	
Total paid-in capital	2,530,000	At December 31, 19XX, $400,000 of retained earnings is restricted by the company's board of directors to absorb the effect of any contingencies that may arise. Accordingly, possible dividend declarations are restricted to a maximum of $1,165,000 ($1,565,000 − $400,000).	
Retained earnings appropriated for contingencies	400,000		
Retained earnings-unappropriated	1,165,000		
Total retained earnings	1,565,000		
Subtotal	4,095,000		
Less treasury stock, common (1,400 shares at cost)	(42,000)		
Total stockholders' equity	$4,053,000		

Corporation Income Statement _____

A corporation's net income receives more attention than any other item in the financial statements. Net income measures the business's ability to earn a profit and answers the question of how successfully the company has managed its operations. To stockholders, the larger the corporation's profit, the greater the likelihood of dividends. To creditors, the larger the corporation's profit, the better able it is to pay its debts. Net income builds up a company's assets and owners' equity. It also helps to attract capital from new investors who hope to receive dividends from future successful operations.

Suppose you are considering investing in the stock of two manufacturing companies. In reading their annual reports and examining their past records, you learn that the companies showed the same net income figure for last year and that each company has increased its net income by 15 percent annually over the last five years. You observe, however, that the two companies have generated income in different ways.

Company A's income has resulted from the successful management of its central operations (manufacturing). Company B's manufacturing operations have been flat for two years. Its growth in net income has resulted from selling off segments of its business at a profit. Which company would you invest in?

Company A holds the promise of better future earnings. This corporation earns profits from continuing operations. We may reasonably expect the business to match its past earnings in the future. Company B shows no growth from operations. Its net income results from one-time transactions, the selling off of its operating assets. Sooner or later, Company B will have sold off the last of its assets used in operations. When that occurs, the business will have no means of generating income. Based on this reasoning, your decision is to invest in the stock of Company A.

This example points to two important investment considerations: the *trend* of a company's earnings and the *makeup* of its net income. More intelligent investment decisions are likely if the income statement separates the results of central, continuing operations from special, one-time gains and losses. We now discuss the components of the corporation income statement. We will see how the income statement reports the results of operations in a manner that allows statement users to get a good look at the business's operations. Exhibit 13-3 will be used throughout these discussions. The items of primary interest are highlighted for emphasis.

Continuing Operations

We have seen that income from a business's continuing operations helps financial statement users make predictions about the business's future earnings. In the income statement of Exhibit 13-3, the topmost section reports income from continuing operations. This part of the business is expected to continue from period to period. We may use this information to predict that Electronics Corporation will earn income of approximately $54,000 next year.

Note that income tax expense has been deducted in arriving at income from continuing operations. The tax that corporations pay on their income is a significant expense. The federal income tax rate for corporations varies from time to time, and the current maximum rate is 34 percent. For computational ease, let's use an income tax rate of 40 percent in our illustrations. This is a reasonable estimate of combined federal and state income taxes. The $36,000 income tax expense in Exhibit 13-3 equals the pretax income from continuing operations multiplied by the tax rate ($90,000 × .40 = $36,000).

Discontinued Operations

Most large corporations engage in several lines of business. For example, General Mills, Inc., best known for its food products, also has retailing and restaurant operations. Sears, Roebuck & Co., in addition to its retail stores, has a real estate subsidiary, an insurance company, and a savings and loan enterprise. We call each significant part of a company a **segment of the business.**

A company may sell a segment of its business. Such a sale is not a regular source of income because a company cannot keep on selling its segments indefinitely. The sale of a business segment is viewed as a one-time transaction. The income statement carries information on the segment that has been disposed of under the heading Discontinued Operations. This section of the income statement is divided into two components: (1) operating income or (loss) on the segment disposed of and (2) any gain (or loss) on the disposal.

EXHIBIT 13-3   Corporation Income Statement

Electronics Corporation Income Statement For the Year Ended December 31, 19X5		
Sales revenue		$500,000
Cost of goods sold		240,000
Gross margin		260,000
Operating expenses (detailed)		181,000
Operating income		79,000
Other gains (losses)		
Gain on sale of machinery		11,000
Income from continuing operations before income tax		90,000
Income tax expense		36,000
Income from continuing operations		54,000
Discontinued operations:		
Operating income, $30,000,		
less income tax of $12,000	$18,000	
Gain on disposal, $5,000,		
less income tax of $2,000	3,000	21,000
Income before extraordinary item and cumulative		
effect of change in depreciation method		75,000
Extraordinary flood loss, $20,000,		
less income tax saving of $8,000		(12,000)
Cumulative effect of change in depreciation		
method, $10,000, less income tax of $4,000		6,000
Net income		$ 69,000
Earnings per share of common stock (20,000 shares outstanding):		
Income from continuing operations		$2.70
Income from discontinued operations		1.05
Income before extraordinary item and cumulative		
effect of change in depreciation method		3.75
Extraordinary loss		(.60)
Cumulative effect of change in depreciation method		.30
Net income		$3.45

OBJECTIVE 5

Identify the elements of a corporation income statement

Income and gain are taxed at the 40 percent rate and reported as follows:

Discontinued operations:
Operating income, $30,000, less income tax,
$12,000 . . . . $18,000
Gain on disposal, $5,000, less income tax, $2,000 .   3,000
$21,000

Trace this presentation to Exhibit 13-3.

It is necessary to separate discontinued operations into these two components because the company may operate the discontinued segment for part of the year. This is the operating income (or loss) component. Then, usually a gain (or loss) on the disposal of the segment occurs.

Discontinued operations are common in business. The Black and Decker Manufacturing Company disposed of its gasoline chain saw business. Purolator, Inc., sold its armored-car segment, and RJR Nabisco disposed of its fast-food business, including Kentucky Fried Chicken. Each of these items was disclosed as discontinued operations in the company's income statement.

Extraordinary Gains and Losses

Extraordinary gains and losses, also called extraordinary items, are both unusual for the company and infrequent. Losses from natural disasters (like earthquakes, floods, and tornadoes), and the taking of company assets by a foreign government (expropriation), are extraordinary.

Extraordinary items are reported along with their income tax effect. Assume Electronics Corporation lost $20,000 of inventory in a flood. This flood loss, which reduces income, also reduces the company's income tax. The tax effect of the loss is computed by multiplying the amount of the loss by the tax rate. The tax effect decreases the net amount of the loss in the same way that the tax effect of income reduces the amount of net income. An extraordinary loss can be reported along with its tax effect as follows:

Extraordinary flood loss . . . . $(20,000)
Less income tax saving . . . .   8,000 $(12,000)

Trace this item to the income statement in Exhibit 13-3. An extraordinary gain is reported the same way, net of the income tax on the gain.

Gains and losses due to employee strikes, the settlement of lawsuits, discontinued operations, and the sale of plant assets are *not* extraordinary items. They are considered normal business occurrences. However, because they are outside the business's central operations, they are reported on the income statement as other gains and losses. An example is the gain on sale of machinery in Exhibit 13-3.

Cumulative Effect of a Change in Accounting Principle

Companies sometimes change from one accounting method to another, such as from double-declining-balance (DDB) to straight-line depreciation, or from FIFO to weighted-average cost for inventory. An accounting change makes it difficult to compare one period's financial statements with the statements of preceding periods. Without detailed information, investors and creditors can be led to believe the current year is better or worse than the preceding year when in fact the only difference is a change in accounting method. To help investors separate the effects of business operations from those effects generated by a change in accounting method, companies report the effect of the accounting change in a special section of the income statement. The section usually appears after extraordinary items.

A relevant aspect of the accounting change is the cumulative effect on net income of prior years. GAAP requires companies that change accounting methods to disclose the difference between net income actually reported under the old method being discontinued and the net income that the company would have experienced if it had used the new method all along.

Suppose Electronics Corporation changed from DDB to straight-line depreciation at the beginning of 19X5. How will this affect the 19X5 financial statements? The change in depreciation method will have two consequences. The first consequence affects income from continuing operations, which will include the effect of 19X5 depreciation expense by the new method, straight-line. The second consequence affects cumulative amounts from previous years. If the company had been using straight-line depreciation every year, net income would have been $6,000 higher ($10,000 less the additional income tax of $4,000). In this case the cumulative effect of the change increases net income. A change from straight-line to double-declining-balance would usually produce a negative cumulative effect.

Changes in inventory methods and changes in revenue methods are also generally reported in this manner. Numerous exceptions make changes in accounting principle—usually a change in accounting method—a complicated area. Details are covered in later accounting courses.

Earnings Per Share (EPS) _a calculate_

The final segment of a corporation income statement presents the company's earnings per share, abbreviated as EPS. In fact, GAAP requires that corporations disclose EPS figures on the income statement.

Earnings per share is the amount of a company's net income per share of its outstanding common stock. EPS is a key measure of a business's success. Consider a corporation with net income of $200,000 and 100,000 shares of common stock outstanding. Its EPS is $2 ($200,000/100,000). A second corporation may also have net income of $200,000 but only 50,000 shares of common stock outstanding. Its EPS is $4 ($200,000/50,000).

Just as the corporation lists separately its different sources of income—from continuing operations, discontinued operations, and so on—it lists separately the EPS figure based on different income sources. Consider that Electronics Corporation had $54,000 in income from continuing operations, $21,000 in income from discontinued operations, an extraordinary loss of $12,000, and a $6,000 cumulative effect of an accounting change. Net income was $69,000 ($54,000 + $21,000 − $12,000 + $6,000). Electronics had 20,000 common shares outstanding for the entire accounting period. The company's EPS is reported on the income statement as follows:

Earnings per share of common stock (20,000 shares outstanding):

Income from continuing operations ($54,000/20,000)	$2.70
Income from discontinued operations ($21,000/20,000)	1.05
Income before extraordinary item and cumulative effect of	
change in depreciation method ($75,000/20,000)	3.75
Extraordinary loss ($12,000/20,000)	(.60)
Cumulative effect of change in depreciation method	
($6,000/20,000)	.30
Net income ($69,000/20,000)	$3.45

The income statement user can understand the nature of the business's EPS amounts when presented in this detail.

Exhibit 13-3 presents the detailed income statement of Electronics Corporation for the year ended December 31, 19X5. The income statement is in multiple-step format.

Weighted Average Number of Shares of Common Stock Outstanding. Computing EPS is straightforward if the number of common shares outstanding does not change over the entire accounting period. For many corporations, however, this figure varies over the course of the year. Consider a corporation that had 100,000 shares outstanding from January through November, then purchased 60,000 shares as treasury stock. This company's EPS would be misleadingly high if computed using 40,000 (100,000 − 60,000) shares. To make EPS as meaningful as possible, corporations use the weighted average number of common shares outstanding during the period.

Let's assume the following figures for Diskette Demo Corporation. From January through May the company had 240,000 shares of common stock outstanding; from June through August, 200,000 shares; and from September through December, 210,000 shares. We compute the weighted average by considering the outstanding shares per month as a fraction of the year:

Number of Common Shares Outstanding		Fraction of Year			Weighted Average Number of Common Shares Outstanding
240,000	×	5/12	(January through May)	=	100,000
200,000	×	3/12	(June through August)	=	50,000
210,000	×	4/12	(September through December)	=	70,000
			Weighted average number of common shares outstanding during the year		220,000

The 220,000 weighted average would be divided into net income to compute the corporation's EPS.

Preferred Dividends. Throughout the EPS discussion we have used only the number of shares of common stock outstanding. Holders of preferred stock have no claim to the business's income beyond the stated preferred dividend. However, preferred dividends do affect the EPS figure. Recall that EPS is earnings per share of *common* stock. Also recall that dividends on preferred stock are paid first. Therefore, preferred dividends must be subtracted from income subtotals (income from continuing operations, income before extraordinary items, and net income) in the computation of EPS. Preferred dividends are not subtracted from income or loss from discontinued operations, and they are not subtracted from extraordinary gains and losses.

If Electronics Corp. had 10,000 shares of preferred stock outstanding, each with a $1.50 dividend, the annual preferred dividend would be $15,000 (10,000 × $1.50). The $15,000 would be subtracted from each of the different income subtotals, resulting in the following EPS computations for the company:

Earnings per share of common stock (20,000 shares outstanding):

Income from continuing operations ($54,000 − $15,000)/20,000	$1.95
Income from discontinued operations ($21,000/20,000)	1.05
Income before extraordinary item and cumulative effect of change in depreciation method ($75,000 − $15,000)/20,000.......	3.00
Extraordinary loss ($12,000/20,000)	(.60)
Cumulative effect of change in depreciation method ($6,000/20,000)	.30
Net income ($69,000 − $15,000)/20,000	$2.70

Dilution.   Some corporations make their preferred stock more attractive to investors by offering convertible preferred stock. Holders of convertible preferred may exchange the preferred stock for common stock. If in fact the preferred stock is converted to common stock, then the EPS will be *diluted*—reduced—because more common stock shares are divided into net income. Because convertible preferred can be traded in for common stock, the common stockholders want to know the amount of the decrease in EPS if the preferred stock is converted into common. To provide this information, corporations present two sets of EPS amounts: EPS based on outstanding common shares (primary EPS), and EPS based on outstanding common shares plus the number of additional common shares that would arise from conversion of the preferred stock into common (diluted EPS). Other types of securities can also cause dilution of EPS amounts.

EPS is the most widely used accounting figure. Many income statement users place top priority on EPS. Also, a stock's market price is related to the company's EPS. By dividing the market price of a company's stock by its EPS, we compute a statistic called the price-to-earnings ratio. *The Wall Street Journal* reports the price-to-earnings ratios (listed as P/E) daily for more than 3,000 companies.

Statement of Retained Earnings

Retained earnings may be a significant portion of a corporation's owners' equity. The year's income increases the retained earnings balance, and dividends decrease it. Retained earnings are so important that corporations prepare a financial statement to report the major changes in this equity account. The statement of retained earnings for Electronics Corporation appears in Exhibit 13-4. Some companies report income and retained earnings on a single statement. Exhibit 13-5 illustrates how Electronics would combine its income statement and its statement of retained earnings.

Prior Period Adjustments

OBJECTIVE 6
Account for prior period adjustments

What happens when a company makes an error in recording revenues or expenses? Detecting the error in the period in which it occurs allows the company to make a correction before preparing that period's financial statements.

EXHIBIT 13-4   *Statement of Retained Earnings*

Electronics Corporation Statement of Retained Earnings For the Year Ended December 31, 19X5	
Retained earnings balance, December 31, 19X4	$130,000
Net income for 19X5	69,000
	199,000
Dividends for 19X5	(21,000)
Retained earnings balance, December 31, 19X5	$178,000

EXHIBIT 13-5 *Statement of Income and Retained Earnings*

Electronics Corporation
Statement of Income and Retained Earnings
For the Year Ended December 31, 19X5

Sales revenue	$500,000
Cost of goods sold	240,000

Net income for 19X5	69,000
Retained earnings, December 31, 19X4	130,000
	199,000
Dividends for 19X5	(21,000)
Retained earnings, December 31, 19X5	$178,000

Earnings per share of common stock (20,000 shares outstanding):

Income from continuing operations	$2.70
Income from discontinued operations	1.05
Income before extraordinary item and cumulative effect of change in depreciation method	3.75
Extraordinary loss	(.60)
Cumulative effect of change in depreciation method	.30
Net income	$3.45

But failure to detect the error until a later period means that the business will have reported an incorrect amount of income on its income statement. After closing the revenue and expense accounts, the Retained Earnings account will absorb the effect of the error, and its balance will be wrong until the error is corrected.

Corrections to the beginning balance of Retained Earnings for errors of an earlier period are called **prior period adjustments.** The correcting entry includes a debit or credit to Retained Earnings for the error amount and a debit or credit to the asset or liability account that was misstated. The prior period adjustment appears on the corporation's statement of retained earnings to indicate to readers the amount and the nature of the change in the Retained Earnings balance.

Assume that De Graff Corporation recorded income tax expense for 19X4 as $30,000. The correct amount was $40,000. This error resulted in understating 19X4 expenses by $10,000 and overstating net income by $10,000. A bill from the government in 19X5 for the additional $10,000 in taxes alerts the De Graff management to the mistake. The entry to record this prior period adjustment in 19X5 is

19X5			
June 19	Retained Earnings	10,000	
	Income Tax Payable		10,000
	Prior period adjustment to correct error in recording income tax expense of 19X4.		

The debit to Retained Earnings keeps the error correction from being reported on the income statement of 19X5. Recall the matching principle. If Income Tax Expense is debited when the prior period adjustment is recorded in 19X5, then this $10,000 in taxes would appear on the 19X5 income statement. This would not be proper, since the expense arose from 19X4 operations.

This prior period adjustment would appear on the statement of retained earnings, as follows:

De Graff Corporation Statement of Retained Earnings For the Year Ended December 31, 19X5	
Retained earnings balance, December 31, 19X4, **as originally reported**	$390,000
Prior period adjustment—**debit to correct error in recording income tax expense of 19X4**	(10,000)
Retained earnings balance, December 31, 19X4, **as adjusted**	380,000
Net income for 19X5	114,000
	494,000
Dividends for 19X5	(41,000)
Retained earnings balance, December 31, 19X5	$453,000

Our example shows a prior period adjustment for additional expense. To make a prior period adjustment for additional income, Retained Earnings is credited and the misstated asset or liability is debited.

Summary Problem for Your Review

The following information was taken from the ledger of Kraft Corporation:

Loss on sale of discontinued operations	$ 5,000	Selling expenses	$ 78,000
Prior period adjustment—credit to Retained Earnings	5,000	Common stock, no-par, 45,000 shares issued	180,000
		Sales revenue	620,000
Gain on sale of plant assets	21,000	Interest expense	30,000
		Extraordinary gain	26,000
Cost of goods sold	380,000	Operating income, discontinued operations	25,000
Income tax expense (saving):		Loss due to lawsuit	11,000
Continuing operations	32,000	General expenses	62,000
Discontinued operations:		Preferred stock, 8%, $100 par, 500 shares issued	50,000
Operating income	10,000		
Loss on sale	(2,000)	Paid-in capital in excess of par—preferred	7,000
Extraordinary gain	10,000		
Cumulative effect of change in inventory method	(4,000)	Retained earnings, beginning, as originally reported	103,000
Treasury stock, common (5,000 shares at cost)	25,000	Cumulative effect of change in inventory method	(10,000)
Dividends	16,000		

Required

Prepare a single-step income statement and a statement of retained earnings for Kraft Corporation for the current year ended December 31. Include the earnings per share presentation and show computations. Assume no changes in the stock accounts during the year.

SOLUTION TO SUMMARY PROBLEM

Kraft Corporation
Income Statement
For the Year Ended December 31, 19XX

Revenue and gains:		
Sales revenue		$620,000
Gain on sale of plant assets		21,000
Total revenues and gains		641,000
Expenses and losses:		
Cost of goods sold	$380,000	
Selling expenses	78,000	
General expenses	62,000	
Interest expense	30,000	
Loss due to lawsuit	11,000	
Income tax expense	32,000	
Total expenses and losses		593,000
Income from continuing operations		48,000
Discontinued operations:		
Operating income, $25,000, less income tax, $10,000	15,000	
Loss on sale of discontinued operations, $5,000, less income tax saving, $2,000	(3,000)	12,000
Income before extraordinary item and cumulative effect of change in inventory method		60,000
Extraordinary gain, $26,000, less income tax, $10,000		16,000
Cumulative effect of change in inventory method, $10,000, less income tax saving, $4,000		(6,000)
Net income		$ 70,000

Earnings per share:	
Income from continuing operations [($48,000 − $4,000)/40,000 shares]	$1.10
Income from discontinued operations ($12,000/40,000 shares)	.30
Income before extraordinary item and cumulative effect of change in inventory method [($60,000 − $4,000)/40,000 shares]	1.40
Extraordinary gain ($16,000/40,000 shares)	.40
Cumulative effect of change in inventory method ($6,000/40,000)	(.15)
Net income [($70,000 − $4,000)/40,000 shares]	$1.65

Computations:

$$\text{EPS} = \frac{\text{Income} - \text{Preferred dividends}}{\text{Common shares outstanding}}$$

Preferred dividends: $50,000 × .08 = $4,000

Common shares outstanding: 45,000 shares issued − 5,000 treasury shares = 40,000 shares outstanding

Kraft Corporation
Statement of Retained Earnings
For the Year Ended December 31, 19XX

Retained earnings balance, beginning, as originally reported ...	$103,000
Prior period adjustment—credit	5,000
Retained earnings balance, beginning, as adjusted.............	108,000
Net income for current year	70,000
	178,000
Dividends for current year	(16,000)
Retained earnings balance, ending	$162,000

Summary

Retained Earnings carries the balance of the business's net income accumulated over its lifetime, less its declared dividends and any net losses. *Cash dividends* are distributions of corporate assets made possible by earnings. *Stock dividends* are distributions of the corporation's own stock to its stockholders. Stock dividends and *stock splits* increase the number of shares outstanding and lower the market price per share of stock.

Treasury stock is the corporation's own stock that has been issued and reacquired and is currently held by the company. The corporation may sell treasury stock for its cost or for more or less than cost. *Retirement* of stock cancels the designated shares, which cannot then be reissued.

Retained earnings may be *restricted* by law or contract or by the corporation itself. An *appropriation* is a restriction of retained earnings that is recorded by formal journal entries.

The corporate *income statement* lists separately the various sources of income—*continuing operations,* which include other gains and losses, *discontinued operations,* and *extraordinary gains and losses.* The bottom line of the income statement reports *net income* or *net loss* for the period. *Income tax expense* and *earnings-per-share* figures also appear on the income statement, likewise divided into different categories based on the nature of income. The *statement of retained earnings* reports the causes for changes in the Retained Earnings account. This statement may be combined with the income statement.

Self-Study Questions

Test your understanding of the chapter by marking the best answer for each of the following questions.

1. A corporation has total stockholders' equity of $100,000, including retained earnings of $19,000. The cash balance is $35,000. The maximum cash dividend the company can declare and pay is *(p. 618)*
   a. $19,000
   b. $35,000
   c. $65,000
   d. $100,000 .

2. A stock dividend *(p. 618)*
   a. Decreases stockholders' equity
   b. Decreases assets
   c. Leaves total stockholders' equity unchanged
   d. None of the above

3. Meyer's Thrifty Acres has 100,000 shares of $20 par common stock outstanding. The stock's market value is $37 per share. Meyer's board of directors declares and distributes a 1 percent common stock dividend. Which of the following entries shows the full effect of declaring and distributing the dividend? *(p. 619)*

a. Retained Earnings 37,000
     Common Stock Dividend Distributable   20,000
     Paid-in Capital in Excess of Par—Common   17,000

b. Retained Earnings 20,000
     Common Stock   20,000

c. Retained Earnings 17,000
     Paid-in Capital in Excess of Par—Common   17,000

d. Retained Earnings 37,000
     Common Stock   20,000
     Paid-in Capital in Excess of Par—Common   17,000

4. Lang Real Estate Investment Corporation declared and distributed a 50 percent stock dividend. Which of the following stock splits would have the same effect on the number of Lang shares outstanding? *(p. 622)*
   a. 2 for 1   c. 4 for 3
   b. 3 for 2   d. 5 for 4

5. A company purchased 10,000 of its $1.50 par common stock as treasury stock, paying $6 per share. This transaction *(p. 623)*
   a. Has no effect on company   c. Decreases owners' equity by
      assets $15,000
   b. Has no effect on owners' equity   d. Decreases owners' equity by
                                           $60,000

6. A restriction of retained earnings *(pp. 627, 628)*
   a. Has no effect on total retained earnings
   b. Reduces retained earnings available for the declaration of dividends
   c. Can be reported by a note or by appropriation of retained earnings, or both
   d. All of the above

7. Which of the following items is not reported on the income statement? *(p. 631)*
   a. Premium on stock   c. Income tax expense
   b. Extraordinary gains and losses   d. Earnings per share

8. The income statement item that is likely to be most useful for predicting income from year to year is *(p. 634)*
   a. Extraordinary items   c. Income from continuing
   b. Discontinued operations   operations
                                        d. Net income

9. In computing earnings per share (EPS), dividends on preferred stock are *(p. 634)*
   a. Added because they represent earnings to the preferred stockholders
   b. Subtracted because they represent earnings to the preferred stockholders
   c. Ignored because they do not pertain to the common stock
   d. Reported separately on the income statement

10. A corporation accidentally overlooked an accrual of property tax expense at December 31, 19X4. Accountants for the company detect the error early in 19X5 before the expense is paid. The entry to record this prior period adjustment is *(p. 636)*

a. Retained Earnings .   XXX   c. Retained Earnings .   XXX
     Property Tax   Property Tax
     Expense   XXX   Payable   XXX

b. Property Tax
   Expense XXX
       Property Tax
       Payable   XXX

d. Property Tax
   Payable XXX
       Property Tax
       Expense   XXX

Answers to the Self-Study Questions follow the Accounting Vocabulary.

Accounting Vocabulary

Appropriation of retained earnings. Restriction of retained earnings that is recorded by a formal journal entry *(p. 628)*.

Earnings per share (EPS). Amount of a company's net income per share of its outstanding common stock *(p. 633)*.

Extraordinary item. A gain or loss that is both unusual for the company and infrequent *(p. 632)*.

Large stock dividend. A stock dividend of 25 percent or more of the corporation's issued stock *(p. 619)*.

Prior period adjustment. Correction to retained earnings for an error of an earlier period is a prior period adjustment *(p. 636)*.

Segment of a business. A significant part of a company *(p. 631)*.

Small stock dividend. A stock dividend of less than 25 percent of the corporation's issued stock *(p. 619)*.

Stock dividend. A proportional distribution by a corporation of its own stock to its stockholders *(p. 618)*.

Stock split. An increase in the number of outstanding shares of stock coupled with a proportionate reduction in the par value of the stock *(p. 621)*.

Treasury stock. A corporation's own stock that it has issued and later reacquired *(p. 622)*.

Answers to Self-Study Questions

1. a	3. d	5. d	7. a	9. b
2. c	4. b	6. d	8. c	10. c

ASSIGNMENT MATERIAL

Questions

1. Identify the two main parts of stockholders' equity.
2. Identify the account debited and the account credited from the last closing entry a corporation makes each year. What is the purpose of this entry?
3. Ametek, Inc., reported a cash balance of $73 million and a retained earnings balance of $162.5 million. Explain how Ametek can have so much more retained earnings than cash. In your answer, identify the nature of retained earnings and state how it ties to cash.
4. A friend of yours receives a stock dividend on an investment. He believes stock dividends are the same as cash dividends. Explain why this is not true.
5. Give two reasons for a corporation to distribute a stock dividend.
6. A corporation declares a stock dividend on December 21 and reports Stock Dividend Payable as a liability on the December 31 balance sheet. Is this correct? Give your reason.

7. What percentage distinguishes a small stock dividend from a large stock dividend? What is the main difference in accounting for small and large stock dividends?

8. To an investor, a stock split and a stock dividend have essentially the same effect. Explain the similarity and difference to the corporation between a 100 percent stock dividend and a 2-for-1 stock split.

9. Give four reasons why a corporation may purchase treasury stock.

10. What effect does the purchase of treasury stock have on the (a) assets, (b) issued stock, and (c) outstanding stock of the corporation?

11. What is the normal balance of the Treasury Stock account? What type of account is Treasury Stock? Where is Treasury Stock reported on the balance sheet?

12. Revell Inc. purchased treasury stock for $25,000. If Revell sells half the treasury stock for $15,000, what account should it credit for the $2,500 difference? If Revell later sells the remaining half of the treasury stock for $9,000, what accounts should be debited for the $3,500 difference?

13. What effect does the purchase and retirement of common stock have on the (a) assets, (b) issued stock, and (c) outstanding stock of the corporation?

14. Why do creditors wish to restrict a corporation's payment of cash dividends and purchases of treasury stock?

15. What are two ways to report a retained earnings restriction? Which way is more common?

16. Identify three items on the income statement that generate income tax expense. What is an income tax saving, and how does it arise?

17. Why is it important for a corporation to report income from continuing operations separately from discontinued operations and extraordinary items?

18. Give two examples of extraordinary gains and losses and four examples of gains and losses that are *not* extraordinary.

19. What is the most widely used of all accounting statistics? What is the price-to-earnings ratio? Compute the price-to-earnings ratio for a company with EPS of $2 and market price of $12 per share of common stock.

20. What is the earnings per share of a company with net income of $5,500, issued common stock of 12,000 shares, and treasury common stock of 1,000 shares.

21. What account do all prior period adjustments affect? On what financial statement are prior period adjustments reported?

Exercises

Exercise 13-1 *Journalizing dividends and reporting stockholders' equity* **(L.O. 1)**

Bremond, Inc., is authorized to issue 100,000 shares of $1 par common stock. The company issued 50,000 shares at $6 per share, and all 50,000 shares are outstanding. When the retained earnings balance was $300,000, Bremond declared and distributed a 50 percent stock dividend. Later, Bremond declared and paid a $.20 per share cash dividend.

Required

1. Journalize the declaration and distribution of the stock dividend.
2. Journalize the declaration and payment of the cash dividend.
3. Prepare the stockholders' equity section of the balance sheet after both dividends.

Exercise 13-2 *Journalizing a stock dividend and reporting stockholders' equity* **(L.O. 1)**

The stockholders' equity for Taps Jewelry Corporation on September 30, 19X4—end of the company's fiscal year—follows.

Stockholders' Equity

Common stock, $10 par, 100,000 shares authorized, 50,000 shares issued	$500,000
Paid-in capital in excess of par— common	50,000
Retained earnings	280,000
Total stockholders' equity	$830,000

On November 16 the market price of Taps's common stock was $12 per share and the company declared a 10 percent stock dividend. Taps issued the dividend shares on November 30.

Required

1. Journalize the declaration and distribution of the stock dividend.
2. Prepare the stockholders' equity section of the balance sheet after the stock dividend.

Exercise 13-3 *Reporting stockholders' equity after a stock split* **(L.O. 2)**

McMillan Enterprises had the following stockholders' equity at May 31:

Common stock, $10 par, 200,000 shares authorized, 50,000 shares issued	$500,000
Paid-in capital in excess of par	180,000
Retained earnings	210,000
Total stockholders' equity	$890,000

On June 7, McMillan split its $10 par common stock 4 for 1. Make the memorandum entry to record the stock split, and prepare the stockholders' equity section of the balance sheet immediately after the split.

Exercise 13-4 *Journalizing treasury stock transactions* **(L.O. 3)**

Journalize the following transactions of The Cobbler, Inc., a national chain of shoe repair shops:

May 19 Issued 10,000 shares of no-par common stock at $12 per share.
Aug. 22 Purchased 900 shares of treasury stock at $14 per share.
Nov. 11 Sold 200 shares of treasury stock at $15 per share.
Dec. 28 Sold 100 shares of treasury stock at $11 per share.

Exercise 13-5 *Journalizing treasury stock transactions and reporting stockholders' equity* **(L.O. 3)**

Varsity Guild, Inc., had the following stockholders' equity on November 30:

Common stock, $5 par, 500,000 shares authorized, 50,000 shares issued	$250,000
Paid-in capital in excess of par	150,000
Retained earnings	220,000
Total stockholders' equity	$620,000

On December 19 the company purchased 2,000 shares of treasury stock at $7 per share. Journalize the purchase of the treasury stock and prepare the stockholders' equity section of the balance sheet at December 31.

Exercise 13-6 *Reporting a retained earnings restriction* (L.O. 4)

The agreement under which Reicher Corporation issued its long-term debt requires the restriction of $250,000 of the company's retained earnings balance. Total retained earnings is $470,000, and total paid-in capital is $820,000.

Required

Show how to report stockholders' equity (including retained earnings) on Reicher's balance sheet, assuming:

a. Reicher discloses the restriction in a note. Write the note.
b. Reicher appropriates retained earnings in the amount of the restriction and includes no note in its statements.

Exercise 13-7 *Preparing a multiple-step income statement* (L.O. 5)

The ledger of Innsbruck Corporation contains the following information for 19X7 operations:

Cost of goods sold	$45,000	Income tax saving—loss on discontinued operations	$ 20,000
Loss on discontinued operations	50,000	Extraordinary gain	12,000
Income tax expense— extraordinary gain	4,800	Sales revenue	130,000
Income tax expense— cumulative effect of change in depreciation method	2,000	Operating expenses (including income tax) .. Cumulative effect of change in depreciation method	60,000 6,000

Required

Prepare a multiple-step income statement for 19X7. Omit earnings per share. Was 19X7 a good year or a bad year for Innsbruck Corporation? Explain your answer in terms of the outlook for 19X8.

Exercise 13-8 *Computing earnings per share* (L.O. 5)

Fenner Corporation earned net income of $56,000 for the second quarter of 19X6. The ledger reveals the following figures:

Preferred stock, $1.75 per year, no-par, 1,600 shares issued and outstanding	$ 70,000
Common stock, $10 par, 42,000 shares issued.................	420,000
Treasury stock, common, 2,000 shares at cost.................	36,000

Required

Compute EPS for the quarter, assuming no changes in the stock accounts during the quarter.

Exercise 13-9 *Computing earnings per share* **(L.O. 5)**

Massachusetts Supply had 40,000 shares of common stock and 10,000 shares of $10 par, 5 percent preferred stock outstanding on December 31, 19X8. On April 30, 19X9, the company issued 9,000 additional common shares and ended 19X9 with 49,000 shares of common stock outstanding. Income from continuing operations of 19X9 was $115,400, and loss on discontinued operations (net of income tax) was $8,280. The company had an extraordinary gain (net of tax) of $55,200.

Required

Compute Massachusetts Supply's EPS amounts for 19X9, starting with income from continuing operations.

Exercise 13-10 *Preparing a statement of retained earnings with a prior period adjustment* **(L.O. 6)**

Big Red, Inc., a soft-drink company, reported a prior period adjustment in 19X9. An accounting error caused net income of prior years to be understated by $3.8 million. Retained earnings at January 1, 19X9, as previously reported, stood at $395.3 million. Net income for 19X9 was $92.1 million, and dividends were $39.8 million. Prepare the company's statement of retained earnings for the year ended December 31, 19X9.

Exercise 13-11 *Preparing a combined statement of income and retained earnings* **(L.O. 5,6)**

The Kroger Company, a large grocery company, had retained earnings of $792.6 million at the beginning of 19X7. The company showed these figures at December 31, 19X7:

	($ Millions)
Increases in retained earnings:	
Net income	$127.1
Decreases in retained earnings:	
Cash dividends—preferred	2.3
common	85.2
Debit to retained earnings due to purchase of preferred stock .	11.3

Required

Beginning with net income, prepare a combined statement of income and retained earnings for The Kroger Company for 19X7. The debit to Retained Earnings was caused by Kroger's paying $11.3 more to retire its preferred stock than the original issue price of the stock.

Problems   *(Group A)*

Problem 13-1A *Journalizing stockholders' equity transactions* **(L.O. 1,3)**

Feather, Inc., completed the following selected transactions during 19X6:

Jan. 13 Discovered that income tax expense of 19X5 was overstated by $9,000. Recorded a prior period adjustment to correct the error.

21 Split common stock 3 for 1 by calling in the 10,000 shares of $15 par common and issuing 30,000 shares of $5 par common.

Feb. 6 Declared a cash dividend on the 4,000 shares of $2.25, no-par preferred stock. Declared a $.20 per share dividend on the common stock outstanding. The date of record was February 27, and the payment date was March 20.

Mar. 20 Paid the cash dividends.

Apr. 18 Declared a 50 percent stock dividend on the common stock to holders of record April 30, with distribution set for May 30. The market value of the common stock was $8 per share.

May 30 Issued the stock dividend shares.

June 18 Purchased 2,000 shares of the company's own common stock at $12 per share.

Nov. 14 Sold 800 shares of treasury common stock for $10 per share.

Dec. 22 Sold 700 shares of treasury common stock for $16 per share.

Required

Record the transactions in the general journal.

Problem 13-2A *Journalizing dividend and treasury stock transactions and reporting stockholders' equity (L.O. 1,2,3)*

The balance sheet of Best of New Mexico, Inc., at December 31, 19X7, reported 10,000 shares of $.50, no-par preferred stock authorized and outstanding. The preferred was issued in 19X1 at $8 per share. Best of New Mexico also had 500,000 shares of $1 par common stock authorized with 100,000 shares issued. Paid-in Capital in Excess of Par—Common had a balance of $300,000. Retained Earnings had a balance of $18,000, and the preferred dividend for 19X7 was in arrears. During the two-year period ended December 31, 19X9, the company completed the following selected transactions:

19X8

Feb. 15 Purchased 5,000 shares of the company's own common stock for the treasury at $6 per share.

Apr. 2 Declared the cash dividend on the preferred stock in arrears for 19X7 and the current cash dividend on preferred. The date of record was April 16, and the payment date was May 1.

May 1 Paid the cash dividends.

May 2 Purchased and retired all the preferred stock at $7.50 per share.

Dec. 31 Earned net income of $55,000 for the year.

19X9

Mar. 8 Sold 2,000 shares of treasury common stock for $7 per share.

Sep. 28 Declared a 10 percent stock dividend on the *outstanding* common stock to holders of record October 15, with distribution set for October 31. The market value of Best of New Mexico common stock was $5 per share.

Oct. 31 Issued the stock dividend shares.

Nov. 5 Split the common stock 2 for 1 by calling in the 109,700 shares of old $1 par common stock and issuing twice as many shares of $.50 par common. (Stock splits affect all issued stock, including treasury stock and stock that is outstanding.)

Dec. 31 Earned net income of $73,000 during the year.

Required

1. Record the transactions in the general journal. Explanations are not required.

2. Prepare the stockholders' equity section of the balance sheet at two dates: December 31, 19X8, and December 31, 19X9.

Problem 13-3A *Using actual-company data to record transactions and report earnings per share* **(L.O. 1,3,5)**

The following items were taken from actual financial statements that reported amounts in millions, rounded to the nearest $100,000.

Hampton Industries, Inc., declared and paid cash dividends of $.1 million to preferred stockholders and also declared and issued a 10 percent stock dividend on its 2.0 million common shares outstanding. The par value of Hampton's common stock was $1.00 per share, and the market value of the stock at the time of the stock dividend was $6.50 per share.

Required

1. Journalize the declaration and payment of the cash dividend.
2. Journalize the declaration and issuance of the stock dividend.

At the beginning of the period, the Louisiana Land and Exploration Company had a treasury stock balance of $1.2 million. During the period, Louisiana paid $212.8 million to purchase treasury stock, and the company also sold treasury stock for $.6 million. The cost of the treasury stock was $.5 million.

Required

3. Journalize the purchase and the sale of treasury stock.
4. Compute the ending balance of the Treasury Stock account.

Crown Cork & Seal Company, Inc., purchased and retired 800,000 shares of its common stock at a cost of $40 per share. Assume that par value was $1 per share and that the common stock was issued for $9 per share.

Required

5. Journalize the purchase and retirement of the common stock.

G. C. Murphy Company reported a $1.3 million extraordinary gain on the issuance of treasury stock, which cost $3.4 million, to pay off long-term debt of $4.7 million. Murphy's income before extraordinary item was $17.0 million, and the company had 4.1 million shares of common stock outstanding.

Required

6. Journalize the transaction.
7. Show how Murphy reported earnings per share for the year.

Problem 13-4A *Purchasing treasury stock to fight off a takeover of the corporation* **(L.O. 3)**

Cinquante Corporation is positioned ideally in its industry. Located in Nogales, Arizona, Cinquante is the only company between Texas and California with reliable sources for its imported gifts. The company does a brisk business with specialty stores such as Pier 1 Imports. Cinquante's recent success has made the company a prime target for a takeover. An investment group from Minneapolis is attempting to buy 51 percent of Cinquante's outstanding stock against the wishes of Cinquante's board of directors. Board members are convinced that the Minneapolis investors would sell off the most desirable pieces of the business and leave little of value.

At the most recent board meeting, several suggestions were advanced to fight off the hostile takeover bid. The suggestion with the most promise is to purchase a huge quantity of treasury stock. Cinquante has the cash to carry out this plan.

Required

1. As a significant stockholder of Cinquante, write a memorandum to explain for the board how the purchase of treasury stock would make it more difficult for the Minneapolis group to take over Cinquante. Include in your memo a discussion of the effect that purchasing treasury stock would have on stock outstanding and on the size of the corporation.
2. Suppose Cinquante management is successful in fighting off the takeover bid and later sells the treasury stock at prices greater than the purchase price. Explain what effect these sales will have on assets, stockholders' equity, and net income.

Problem 13-5A *Journalizing prior period adjustments and dividend and treasury stock transactions; reporting retained earnings and stockholders' equity (L.O. 1,3,6)*

The balance sheet of Topeka Corporation at December 31, 19X3, presented the following stockholders' equity:

Paid-in capital:
Common stock, $1 par, 250,000 shares authorized, 50,000 shares issued	$ 50,000
Paid-in capital in excess of par—common	350,000
Total paid-in capital	400,000
Retained earnings	110,000
Total stockholders' equity	$510,000

During 19X4, Topeka completed the following selected transactions:

Jan. 7 Discovered that income tax expense of 19X3 was understated by $4,000. Recorded a prior period adjustment to correct the error.

Mar. 29 Declared a 50 percent stock dividend on the common stock. The market value of Topeka common stock was $7 per share. The record date was April 19, with distribution set for May 19.

May 19 Issued the stock dividend shares.

July 13 Purchased 2,000 shares of the company's own common stock at $6 per share.

Oct. 4 Sold 600 shares of treasury common stock for $8 per share.

Dec. 27 Declared a $.20 per share dividend on the common stock outstanding. The date of record was January 17, 19X5, and the payment date was January 31.

31 Closed the $62,000 credit balance of Income Summary to Retained Earnings.

Required

1. Record the transactions in the general journal.
2. Prepare the retained earnings statement at December 31, 19X4.
3. Prepare the stockholders' equity section of the balance sheet at December 31, 19X4.

Problem 13-6A *Preparing a single-step income statement and a statement of retained earnings and reporting stockholders' equity on the balance sheet (L.O. 5,6)*

The following information was taken from the ledger and other records of California Sales Corporation at June 30, 19X5:

Interest expense	$ 23,000	Dividends on common	
Gain on settlement of		stock	$ 12,000
lawsuit	8,000	Sales revenue	589,000
Sales returns	15,000	Retained earnings,	
Paid-in capital from		beginning, as	
retirement of preferred		originally reported	63,000
stock	16,000	Selling expenses	87,000
Interest revenue	5,000	Common stock, no-par,	
Treasury stock, common		22,000 shares autho-	
(2,000 shares at cost) . .	28,000	rized and issued	350,000
General expenses	71,000	Sales discounts	7,000
Loss on sale of		Extraordinary gain	27,000
discontinued segment .	8,000	Operating loss, discon-	
Prior period		tinued segment	9,000
adjustment-debit to		Loss on sale of plant	
Retained Earnings	4,000	assets	10,000
Cost of goods sold	319,000	Dividends on preferred	
Income tax expense		stock	?
(saving):		Preferred stock, 6%, $25	
Continuing operations	28,000	par, 20,000 shares au-	
Discontinued segment:		thorized, 4,000 shares	
Operating loss	(3,600)	issued	100,000
Loss on sale	(3,200)	Cumulative effect of	
Extraordinary gain	10,800	change in depreciation	
Cumulative effect of		method	7,000
change in depreci-			
ation method	3,000		

Required

1. Prepare a single-step income statement, including earnings per share, for California Sales Corporation for the fiscal year ended June 30, 19X5. Evaluate income for the year ended June 30, 19X5, in terms of the outlook for 19X6. Assume 19X5 was a typical year and that California Sales managers hoped to earn income from continuing operations equal to 8 percent of net sales.

2. Prepare the statement of retained earnings for the year ended June 30, 19X5.

3. Prepare the stockholders' equity section of the balance sheet at that date.

Problem 13-7A *Preparing a corrected combined statement of income and retained earnings* **(L.O. 5,6)**

Susan Clay, accountant for Verbatim, Inc., was injured in a sailing accident. Another employee prepared the income statement shown at the top of the next page for the fiscal year ended June 30, 19X4. The individual amounts listed on the income statement are correct. However, some accounts are reported incorrectly, and others do not belong on the income statement at all. Also, income tax (40 percent) has not been applied to all appropriate figures. Verbatim issued 24,000 shares of common stock in 19X1 and held 4,000 shares as treasury stock during the fiscal year 19X4. The retained earnings balance, as originally reported at June 30, 19X3, was $63,000.

Required

Prepare a corrected combined statement of income and retained earnings for fiscal year 19X4. Prepare the income statement in single-step format.

Verbatim, Inc.
Income Statement
June 30, 19X4

Revenues and gains:		
Sales		$533,000
Gain on retirement of preferred stock (issued for		
$70,000; purchased for $59,000)		11,000
Paid-in capital in excess of par—common		100,000
Total revenues and gains		644,000
Expenses and losses:		
Cost of goods sold	$233,000	
Selling expenses	103,000	
General expenses	74,000	
Sales returns	22,000	
Prior period adjustment—debit	4,000	
Dividends	15,000	
Sales discounts	10,000	
Income tax expense	32,000	
Total expenses and losses		493,000
Income from operations		151,000
Other gains and losses:		
Extraordinary gain	30,000	
Operating income on discontinued segment......	25,000	
Loss on sale of discontinued operations	(40,000)	
Total other gains		15,000
Net income		$166,000
Earnings per share............................		$7.30

Problem 13-8A   *Computing earnings per share and reporting a retained earnings restriction* (L.O. 4,5,6)

Augustine Construction's capital structure at December 31, 19X2, included 5,000 shares of $2.50 preferred stock and 130,000 shares of common stock. Common shares outstanding during 19X3 were 130,000 January through February; 119,000 during March; 121,000 April through October; and 128,000 during November and December. Income from continuing operations during 19X3 was $371,885. The company discontinued a segment of the business at a gain of $69,160, and an extraordinary item generated a loss of $49,510. The board of directors of Augustine has restricted $440,000 of retained earnings for expansion of the company's office facilities.

Required

1. Compute Augustine's earnings per share. Start with income from continuing operations. Income and loss amounts are net of income tax.
2. Show two ways of reporting Augustine's retained earnings restriction. Retained earnings at December 31, 19X2, was $439,800, and total paid-in capital at December 31, 19X3, is $947,610. Augustine declared no dividends during 19X3.

(Group B)

Problem 13-1B   *Journalizing stockholders' equity transactions* (L.O. 1,3)

Littlepage, Inc., completed the following selected transactions during the current year:

Jan. 9 Discovered that income tax expense of the preceding year was understated by $5,000. Recorded a prior period adjustment to correct the error.

Feb. 10 Split common stock 2 for 1 by calling in the 20,000 shares of $10 par common and issuing 40,000 shares of $5 par common.

Mar. 18 Declared a cash dividend on the 5 percent, $100 par preferred stock (1,000 shares outstanding). Declared a $.20 per share dividend on the common stock outstanding. The date of record was April 2, and the payment date was April 23.

Apr. 23 Paid the cash dividends.

July 30 Declared a 10 percent stock dividend on the common stock to holders of record August 21, with distribution set for September 11. The market value of the common stock was $15 per share.

Sep. 11 Issued the stock dividend shares.

    26 Purchased 2,000 shares of the company's own common stock at $16 per share.

Nov. 8 Sold 1,000 shares of treasury common stock for $20 per share.

Dec. 13 Sold 500 shares of treasury common stock for $14 per share.

Required

Record the transactions in the general journal.

Problem 13-2B *Journalizing dividend and treasury stock transactions and reporting stockholders' equity* **(L.O. 1,2,3)**

The balance sheet of Benton Harbor Manufacturing Company at December 31, 19X5, reported 100,000 shares of no-par common stock authorized, with 30,000 shares issued and a Common Stock balance of $180,000. Benton Harbor Manufacturing also had 5,000 shares of 6 percent, $10 par preferred stock authorized and outstanding. The preferred stock was issued in 19X1 at par. Retained Earnings had a credit balance of $104,000. During the two-year period ended December 31, 19X7, the company completed the following selected transactions:

19X6

Mar. 15 Purchased 1,000 shares of the company's own common stock for the treasury at $5 per share.

July 2 Declared the annual 6 percent cash dividend on the preferred stock and a $.75-per-share cash dividend on the common stock. The date of record was July 16, and the payment date was July 31.

July 31 Paid the cash dividends.

Nov. 30 Declared a 20 percent stock dividend on the *outstanding* common stock to holders of record December 21, with distribution set for January 11, 19X7. The market value of Benton Harbor common stock was $10 per share.

Dec. 31 Earned net income of $70,000 for the year.

19X7

Jan. 11 Issued the stock dividend shares.

June 30 Declared the annual 6 percent cash dividend on the preferred stock. The date of record was July 14, and the payment date was July 29.

July 29 Paid the cash dividends.

Aug. 2 Purchased and retired all the preferred stock at $14 per share.

Oct. 8 Sold 800 shares of treasury common stock for $12 per share.

Dec. 19 Split the no-par common stock 2 for 1 by issuing two new no-par shares for each old no-par share previously issued. Prior to the split, the corporation had issued 35,800 shares. Stock splits affect all issued stock, including treasury stock as well as stock that is outstanding.

31 Earned net income of $81,000 during the year.

Required

1. Record the transactions in the general journal. Explanations are not required.
2. Prepare the stockholders' equity section of the balance sheet at two dates: December 31, 19X6, and December 31, 19X7.

Problem 13-3B *Using actual-company data to record transactions and report earnings per share* **(L.O. 1,3,5)**

The following items were taken from the financial statements of actual companies that showed amounts in millions and rounded to the nearest $100,000.

The General Tire & Rubber Company declared and paid cash dividends of $35.2 million to its common stockholders and also declared and issued a 2 percent stock dividend on its 23.6 million common shares outstanding. The par value of General's common stock was $.30 per share, and the market value of the stock at the time of the stock dividend was $60 per share.

Required

1. Journalize the declaration and payment of the cash dividend.
2. Journalize the declaration and issuance of the stock dividend.

At the beginning of the year, IU International Corporation had a treasury stock balance of $288.3 million. During the year, IU paid $2.2 million to purchase treasury stock. The company also sold treasury stock for $79.9 million. The cost of the treasury stock sold was $68.3 million. In addition, IU paid $19.6 million to purchase and retire preferred stock with par value of $18.8 million. The preferred stock had been issued at par in previous years.

Required

3. Journalize the purchase and the sale of treasury stock.
4. Compute the ending balance of the Treasury Stock account.
5. Journalize the purchase and retirement of preferred stock.

Chesapeake Corporation of Virginia, a paper company, reported a $4.0 million extraordinary gain that resulted from issuing 200,000 shares of its $5 par common stock and giving $4.5 million in cash to pay off long-term debt of $16.5 million. Chesapeake's income before the extraordinary item was $8.5 million, and the company had 6.4 million shares of common stock outstanding.

Required

6. Journalize the transaction.
7. Show how Chesapeake reported earnings per share for the year.

Problem 13-4B *Increasing dividends to fight off a takeover of the corporation* **(L.O. 1)**

Simon Corporation is positioned ideally in the clothing business. Located in Syracuse, New York, Simon is the only company with a distribution network for its imported goods. The company does a brisk business with specialty stores such as Bloomingdale's, I. Magnin, and Bonwit Teller. Simon's recent success has made the company a prime target for a takeover. Against the wishes of Simon's board of directors, an investment group from Kansas City is attempting to buy 51 percent of Simon's outstanding stock. Board members are convinced that the Kansas City investors would sell off the most desirable pieces of the business and leave little of value.

At the most recent board meeting, several suggestions were advanced to fight off the hostile takeover bid. One suggestion is to increase the stock outstanding by distributing a 100 percent stock dividend.

Required

As a significant stockholder of Simon Corporation, write a short memo to explain to the board whether distributing the stock dividend would make it more difficult for the investor group to take over Simon Corporation. Include in your memo a discussion of the effect that the stock dividend would have on assets, liabilities, and total stockholders' equity—that is, the dividend's effect on the size of the corporation.

Problem 13-5B *Journalizing prior period adjustments and dividend and treasury stock transactions; reporting retained earnings and stockholders' equity (L.O. 1,3,6)*

The balance sheet of Mendoza Corporation at December 31, 19X1, reported the following stockholders' equity:

Paid-in capital:	
Common stock, $10 par, 100,000 shares	
authorized, 20,000 shares issued	$200,000
Paid-in capital in excess of par-common	300,000
Total paid-in capital.....................	500,000
Retained earnings	190,000
Total stockholders' equity	$690,000

During 19X2 Mendoza completed the following selected transactions:

Jan. 11 Discovered that income tax expense of 19X1 was overstated by $19,000. Recorded a prior period adjustment to correct the error.

Apr. 30 Declared a 10 percent stock dividend on the common stock. The market value of Mendoza common stock was $24 per share. The record date was May 21, with distribution set for June 5.

June 5 Issued the stock dividend shares.

July 29 Purchased 2,000 shares of the company's own common stock at $21 per share.

Nov. 13 Sold 1,000 shares of treasury common stock for $22 per share.

27 Declared a $.30 per share dividend on the common stock outstanding. The date of record was December 17, and the payment date was January 7, 19X3.

Dec. 31 Closed the $80,000 credit balance of Income Summary to Retained Earnings.

Required

1. Record the transactions in the general journal.
2. Prepare a retained earnings statement at December 31, 19X2.
3. Prepare the stockholders' equity section of the balance sheet at December 31, 19X2.

Problem 13-6B

Preparing a single-step income statement and a statement of retained earnings; reporting stockholders' equity on the balance sheet (L.O. 5,6)

The following information was taken from the ledger and other records of Yoshima, Inc., at September 30, 19X6.

Gain on sale of discontinued segment	$ 20,000	Sales revenue		$860,000
Prior period adjustment—credit to Retained Earnings	6,000	Treasury stock, common (1,000 shares at cost) .		11,000
		Dividends		35,000
		Interest revenue		4,000
Contributed capital from treasury stock transactions	7,000	Extraordinary loss		30,000
		Operating loss, discontinued segment		15,000
Sales discounts	18,000	Loss on insurance settlement		12,000
Interest expense	11,000	General expenses		113,000
Cost of goods sold	364,000	Preferred stock, $3, no-par 10,000 shares authorized, 5,000 shares issued		200,000
Cumulative effect of change in depreciation method	(3,000)			
Loss on sale of plant assets	8,000	Paid-in capital in excess of par-common		20,000
Sales returns	9,000	Retained earnings, beginning, as originally reported ...		88,000
Income tax expense (saving):				
Continuing operations	72,000	Selling expenses		136,000
Discontinued segment:		Common stock, $10 par, 25,000 shares authorized and issued		250,000
Operating loss	(6,000)			
Gain on sale	8,000			
Extraordinary loss	(12,000)			
Cumulative effect of change in depreciation method	(1,000)			

Required

1. Prepare a single-step income statement, including earnings per share, for Yoshima, Inc., for the fiscal year ended September 30, 19X6. Evaluate income for the year ended September 30, 19X6, in terms of the outlook for 19X7. Assume 19X6 was a typical year and that Yoshima managers hoped to earn income from continuing operations equal to 14 percent of net sales.
2. Prepare the statement of retained earnings for the year ended September 30, 19X6.
3. Prepare the stockholders' equity section of the balance sheet at that date.

Problem 13-7B

Preparing a corrected combined statement of income and retained earnings (L.O. 5,6)

Andie Beck, accountant for Cambridge Book Distributors, was injured in a skiing accident. Another employee prepared the accompanying income statement for the fiscal year ended December 31, 19X3.

The individual amounts listed on the income statement are correct. However, some accounts are reported incorrectly, and others do not belong on the income statement at all. Also, income tax (40 percent) has not been applied to all appropriate figures. Cambridge issued 52,000 shares of common stock in 19X1 and held 2,000 shares as treasury stock during 19X3. The retained earnings balance, as originally reported at December 31, 19X2, was $111,000.

Required

Prepare a corrected combined statement of income and retained earnings for 19X3. Prepare the income statement in single-step format.

Cambridge Book Distributors
Income Statement
19X3

Revenue and gains:		
Sales		$362,000
Prior period adjustment—credit		14,000
Gain on retirement of preferred stock (issued for		
$81,000; purchased for $71,000)		10,000
Paid-in capital in excess of par—common		80,000
Total revenues and gains		466,000
Expenses and losses:		
Cost of goods sold	$145,000	
Selling expenses	76,000	
General expenses	61,000	
Sales returns..............................	11,000	
Dividends	7,000	
Sales discounts............................	6,000	
Income tax expense	20,000	
Total expenses and losses		326,000
Income from operations......................		140,000
Other gains and losses:		
Gain on sale of discontinued operations	10,000	
Extraordinary flood loss.....................	(20,000)	
Operating loss on discontinued segment	(15,000)	
Total other losses		(25,000)
Net income		$115,000
Earnings per share		$2.30

Problem 13-8B *Computing earnings per share and reporting a retained earnings restriction* **(L.O. 4,5,6)**

The capital structure of Magna Entertainment Center, Inc., at December 31, 19X6, included 20,000 shares of $1.25 preferred stock and 44,000 shares of common stock. Common shares outstanding during 19X7 were 44,000 January through May, 50,000 June through August, and 60,500 September through December. Income from continuing operations during 19X7 was $81,100. The company discontinued a segment of the business at a loss of $6,630, and an extraordinary item generated a gain of $33,660. Magna's board of directors restricts $135,000 of retained earnings for contingencies.

Required

1. Compute Magna's earnings per share. Start with income from continuing operations. Income and loss amounts are net of income tax.
2. Show two ways of reporting Magna's retained earnings restriction. Retained earnings at December 31, 19X6, was $190,000, and total paid-in capital at December 31, 19X7, is $230,000. Magna declared no dividends during 19X7.

Extending Your Knowledge

Decision Problems

1. Analyzing Cash Dividends and Stock Dividends   (L.O. 1)

Pacific Union Corporation had the following stockholders' equity on June 30 of the current year:

Common stock, no-par, 100,000 shares issued	$ 750,000
Retained earnings	830,000
Total stockholders' equity	$1,580,000

In the past, Pacific Union has paid an annual cash dividend of $1.50 per share. Despite the large retained earnings balance, the board of directors wished to conserve cash for expansion. The board delayed the payment of cash dividends by one month and in the meantime distributed a 20 percent stock dividend. During the following year, the company's cash position improved. The board declared and paid a cash dividend of $1.25 per share.

Suppose you own 4,000 shares of Pacific Union common stock, acquired three years ago. The market price of the stock was $30 per share before any of the above dividends.

Required

1. How does the stock dividend affect your proportionate ownership in the company? Explain.
2. What amount of cash dividends did you receive last year? What amount of cash dividends will you receive after the above dividend action?
3. Immediately after the stock dividend was distributed, the market value of Pacific Union stock decreased from $30 per share to $25 per share. Does this represent a loss to you? Explain.
4. Suppose Pacific Union announces at the time of the stock dividend that the company will continue to pay the annual $1.50 cash dividend per share, even after the stock dividend. Would you expect the market price of the stock to decrease to $25 per share as in 3 above? Explain.

2. Earnings and Dividends   (L.O. 1,3,5)

a. An investor noted that the market price of stocks seemed to decline after the date of record. Why do you think that would be the case?
b. The treasurer of Miske Brewing Corp. wanted to disclose a large loss as an extraordinary item because Miske produced too much product just prior to a very cool summer. Why do you think the treasurer wanted to use that particular disclosure? Would such disclosure be acceptable?
c. Corporations sometimes purchase their own stock. When asked why they do so, management often respond that they feel the stock is undervalued. What advantage would the company gain by buying and selling its own stock under these circumstances?
d. Carter Inc. earned a significant profit in the year ended November 30, 19X2 because land it held was expropriated for a new highway. The company proposes to treat the sale of land to the government as other revenue. Why do you think Carter is proposing such treatment? Is this disclosure appropriate?

Ethical Issue

Oklatex Corporation is an independent oil producer in Odessa, Texas. In February, company geologists discovered a pool of oil that tripled the company's proven reserves. Prior to disclosing the new oil to the public, top managers of the company quietly bought most of Oklatex stock for themselves personally. After the discovery announcement, Oklatex stock price increased from $13 to $40.

Required

1. Did Oklatex managers behave ethically? Explain your answer.
2. Identify the accounting principle relevant to this situation.
3. Who was helped and who was harmed by management's action?

Financial Statement Problems

1. Treasury Stock, Retained Earnings, and Earnings per Share   (L.O. 3,5)

Use the Goodyear Tire & Rubber Company financial statements in Appendix C to answer these questions.

1. Goodyear reports stock *outstanding* on the balance sheet and gives details in the statement of shareholders' equity. At December 31, 1991, how many shares of Goodyear common stock were outstanding? How many shares were in the treasury? How many shares had Goodyear issued through December 31, 1991?
2. Goodyear uses a method of accounting for treasury stock that is different from the method discussed in this chapter. You can determine from the Statement of Changes in Shareholders' Equity the number of shares of treasury stock purchased during 1991. What was this amount?
3. Prepare a T-account for Retained Earnings to show the beginning and ending balances and all activity in the account during 1991.
4. Show how to compute all three earnings *per share* amounts for 1991.

2. Treasury Stock, Retained Earnings, and Earnings Per Share   (L.O. 3,5)

Obtain the annual report of an actual company of your choosing. Answer these questions about the company. Concentrate on the current year in the annual report you select.

1. How many shares of common stock did the company have outstanding at the end of the current year? How many shares were in the treasury? How many shares had the company issued through the date of the current balance sheet?
2. Compute average cost per share of treasury stock (common). Compare this figure to book value per share of common stock. Does it appear that the company was able to purchase treasury stock at book value?

   Note: This question can be answered only if the company reports the cost of treasury stock.
3. Prepare a T-account for Retained Earnings to show the beginning and ending balances and all activity in the account during the current year.
4. Did the company have any prior period adjustments during any year reported in the annual report? How can you tell?
5. Show how to compute all earnings (losses) *per share* amounts for the current year.

Chapter *14*

Investments
and Accounting for
International Operations

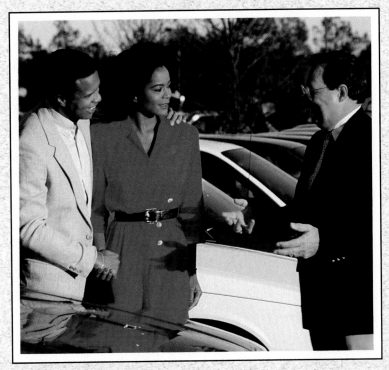

orporations do not always greet FASB statements with enthusiasm. Consider this complaint about an FASB rule.

Did you know that General Electric's assets have ballooned to $110 billion as of Dec. 31, up from $40 billion at the end of 1987? Or that General Motors' debt is now 47 percent of [stockholders' equity], up from 10 percent at the end of 1987?

No, these blue chips have not turned into [high-risk investments]. What's going on is just the sort of nonsense that the critics predicted from the Financial Accounting Standards Board rule on consolidation. Under this rule . . . all majority-owned subsidiaries must be [included in] the parent [company]'s financial statements, no matter what business the [subsidiary

companies] are in. Before the rule took effect with 1988 annual reports, companies with subsidiaries outside their core business . . . were not forced to fold the subs' assets and liabilities into the parent's consolidated balance sheet. . . .

Justification for the [new] rule was that [formerly] companies could bury liabilities in their subsidiaries. But the cure is worse than the disease. "Now GM looks like a finance company with a car division," quips Norman Strauss, a partner at [CPA firm] Ernst & Young.

Source: Dana Wechsler, "Mishmash Accounting," *Forbes*, November 27, 1989, p. 192. Used with permission of Forbes, Inc.

Prior to the new accounting rule, General Motors Corporation reported its financing company, GMAC, separately. A major impact of the new rule is that parent companies such as General Motors and Sears must now include the financial statements of subsidiaries such as GMAC and Allstate in the parent's consolidated financial statements. This gives the parent company's balance sheet and income statement a new look that some accountants find strange. In this chapter, we discuss how to account for investments in stocks—including consolidation accounting—and bonds. We also consider the challenging area of accounting for international operations.

Accounting for Investments

Stock Prices

Investors buy more stocks in transactions among themselves than in purchases directly from the issuing company. Each share of stock is issued only once, but it may be traded among investors many times thereafter. People and businesses buy and sell stocks from each other in markets, such as the New York Stock Exchange and the American Stock Exchange. Recall that stock ownership is transferable. Investors trade millions of stock shares each day. Brokers like Merrill Lynch and Prudential Bache handle stock transactions for a commission.

A broker may "quote you a stock price," which means to state the current market price per share. The financial community quotes stock prices in dollars and one-eighth fractions. A stock selling at 32⅛ costs $32.125 per share. A stock listed at 55¾ sells at $55.75. Financial publications and many newspapers carry daily information on the stock issues of thousands of corporations. These one-line summaries carry information as of the close of trading the previous day.

Exhibit 14-1 presents information for the common stock of the Boeing Company, a large aircraft manufacturer, just as this information appears in the newspaper listings.

During the previous 52 weeks, Boeing common stock reached a high of $64.875 and a low of $43.75. The annual cash dividend is $1.40 per share. During the previous day 678,800 (6,788 X 100) shares of Boeing common stock were traded. The prices of these transactions ranged from a high of $46.50 to a

EXHIBIT 14-1 *Stock Price Information*

52 Weeks		Stock	Dividend	Sales 100s	High	Low	Close	Net Change
High	Low							
64⅞	43¾	Boeing	1.40	6788	46½	45½	46⅛	+⅝

low of $45.50 per share. The day's closing price of $46.125 was $.625 (⅝ of one dollar) higher than the closing price of the preceding day.

What causes a change in a stock's price? The company's net income trend, the development of new products, court rulings, new legislation, business success, and upward market trends drive a stock's price up, and business failures and bad economic news pull it down. The market sets the price at which a stock changes hands.

Investments in Stock

To begin the discussion of investments in stock, we need to define two key terms. The person or company that owns stock in a corporation is the *investor*. The corporation that issued the stock is the *investee*. If you own shares of Boeing common stock, you are an investor and Boeing is the investee.

A business may purchase another corporation's stock simply to put extra cash to work in the hope of earning dividends and gains on the sale of the stock. Alternatively, the business may make the investment to gain a degree of control over the investee's operation. After all, stock is ownership. An investor holding 25 percent of the outstanding stock of the investee owns one-fourth of the business. This one-quarter voice in electing the directors of the corporation is likely to give the investor a lot of say in how the investee conducts its business. An investor holding more than 50 percent of the outstanding shares controls the investee.

Let's consider why one corporation might want to gain a say in another corporation's business. The investor may want to exert some control over the level of dividends paid by the investee. Or perhaps the investee has a line of products closely linked to the investor's own sales items. By influencing the investee's business, the investor may be able to exert some control on product distribution, product-line improvements, pricing strategies, and other important business considerations. A swimming-pool manufacturer might want to purchase stock in a diving-board company, a swimsuit maker, or some other corporation with related business.

Why doesn't the investor simply diversify its own operations, expanding into diving boards, swimsuits, and other related products? The cost may be too great. Also, the investor may not have experience with these other products. Why challenge a successful business in the marketplace when the investor can "buy into" a successful corporation's existing operations? The reasons for investing in a corporation in order to affect its operations to some degree make corporate investments attractive to many businesses.

Investments are not without risk. To offset the ill effects of a sudden downturn in the operations of any one investee, smart investors hold a portfolio of stocks. The portfolio holds investments in different companies. By diversifying its holdings, the investor gains protection from losing too much if any one investee runs into problems and its stock price plummets.

EXHIBIT 14-2   *Reporting Investments on the Balance Sheet*

Current Assets
   Cash... $X
   Short-term investments X
   Accounts receivable X
   Inventories.. X
   Prepaid expenses X
      Total current assets .... $X
Long-term investments (or simply Investments) X
Property, plant, and equipment X
Intangible assets X
Other assets X

Classifying Stock Investments

Investments in stock are assets to the investor. The investments may be short-term or long-term. **Short-term investments** are current assets. To be listed on the balance sheet as short-term, investments must be liquid (readily convertible to cash). Also, the investor must intend either to convert the investments to cash within one year or to use them to pay a current liability. Some companies report short-term investments under the heading **marketable securities**. Investments not meeting these two requirements are classified on the balance sheet as **long-term investments.**

Short-term investments include certificates of deposit, and stocks and bonds of other companies. *Long-term investments* include bond sinking funds and stocks and bonds that the investor expects to hold longer than one year or that are not readily marketable, for instance, real estate not used in the operations of the business. Exhibit 14-2 shows the positions of short-term and long-term investments on the balance sheet.

Observe that we report assets in the order of their liquidity. Cash is the most liquid asset, followed by Short-Term Investments, Accounts Receivable, and so on. Long-Term Investments are less liquid than Current Assets but more liquid than Property, Plant, and Equipment.

Accounting for Stock Investments

Accounting for stock investments varies with the nature and extent of the investment. The specific accounting method that GAAP directs us to follow depends first on whether the investment is short-term or long-term and second on the percentage of the investee's voting stock that the investor holds.

Short-Term Investments—The Cost Method (with LCM)

The **cost method** (with lower of cost or market) is used to account for short-term investments in stock. *Cost* is used as the initial amount for recording investments and as the basis for measuring gains and losses on their sale. These investments are reported on the balance sheet at the *lower of their cost or market* value. Therefore, we refer to the overall method as cost (with lower of cost or market).

All investments, including short-term investments, are recorded initially at cost. Cost is the price paid for the stock plus the brokerage commission. Accountants use no separate account for the brokerage commission paid. At purchase, the commission increases the cost of the investment. When the investment is sold, the sale commission decreases the amount of cash received. Suppose that Dade, Inc., purchases 1,000 shares of Hewlett-Packard Company common stock at the market price of 35¾ and pays a $550 commission. Dade intends to sell this investment within one year or less and, therefore, classifies it as short-term. Dade's entry to record the investment is

July 23	Short-Term Investment in Hewlett-Packard		
	Common Stock [(1,000 × $35.75) + $550]	36,300	
	Cash		36,300
	Purchased 1,000 shares of Hewlett-Packard		
	common stock at $35.75 plus commission of $550.		

OBJECTIVE 1
Account for investments in stock by the cost (LCM) method

Assume Dade receives a $.22 per share cash dividend on the Hewlett-Packard stock. Dade's entry to record receipt of the dividends is

Oct. 14	Cash (1,000 × $.22)	220	
	Dividend Revenue..........................		220
	Received $.22 per share cash dividend on Hewlett-		
	Packard common stock.		

Dividends do not accrue with the passage of time (as interest does). The investee has no liability for dividends until the dividends are declared. An investor makes no accrual entry for dividend revenue at year end in anticipation of a dividend declaration.

However, if a dividend declaration *does* occur before year end—say, on December 28—the investor debits Dividend Receivable and credits Dividend Revenue on that date. The investor reports this receivable and the revenue in the December 31 financial statements. Receipt of the cash dividend in January is recorded by a debit to Cash and a credit to Dividend Receivable.

Receipt of a *stock* dividend is *not* income to the investor, and no formal journal entry is needed. As we have seen, a stock dividend increases the number of shares held by the investor but does not affect the total cost of the investment. The *cost per share* of the stock investment therefore decreases. The investor usually makes a memorandum entry of the number of dividend shares received and the new cost per share. Assume that Dade, Inc., receives a 10 percent stock dividend on its 1,000-share investment in Hewlett-Packard Company, which cost $36,300. Dade would make a memorandum entry along this line:

Nov. 22	Received 100 shares of Hewlett-Packard common stock in 10 percent stock dividend. New cost per share is $33.00 ($36,300/1,100 shares).

Any gain or loss on the sale of the investment is the difference between the sale proceeds and the cost of the investment. Assume that Dade sells 400 shares of Hewlett-Packard stock for $35 per share, less a $280 commission. The entry to record the sale is

Dec. 18	Cash [(400 × $35) − $280]	13,720	
	Short-Term Investment in Hewlett-		
	Packard Common Stock (400 × $33.00) .		13,200
	Gain on Sale of Investment		520
	Sold 400 shares of investment in Hewlett-		
	Packard common stock.		

Observe that the cost per share of the investment ($33.00) is based on the total number of shares held, including those received as a dividend.

Reporting Short-Term Investments at Lower of Cost or Market (LCM)

Because of accounting conservatism, short-term investments in stock are reported at the lower of their cost or market (LCM) value. LCM is based on the view that losses, but not gains, should be recorded prior to the sale of the asset. LCM is applied to the *entire* short-term investment portfolio, not to individual stocks in the portfolio. On the balance sheet date, the investor computes the total cost and the total market value of the short-term investment portfolio and reports the investments at the lower amount. Assume Dade, Inc., owns three short-term investments—including the Hewlett-Packard common stock from the preceding example—with the following costs and market values. Also assume Dade purchased all the investments during the current year.

Short-term Investment Portfolio

Stock	Cost	Current Market Value
Ford Motor Co	$122,000	$128,000
Hewlett-Packard Company (cost: $36,300 − $13,200)	23,100	22,000
Kellogg	160,000	142,000
Total	$305,100	$292,000

Because the total market value of the investment portfolio ($292,000) is less than cost ($305,100), the investor's balance sheet will report short-term investments at market value of $292,000. However, the Short-Term Investments account carries a balance equal to the investments' cost, $305,100. The following entry is needed to bring the investments to the LCM value of $292,000:

Dec. 31	Unrealized Loss on Short-Term Investments ($305,100 − $292,000)	13,100	
	Allowance to Reduce Short-Term Investments to Market Value		13,100
	Wrote short-term investments down to market value.		

Unrealized Loss on Short-Term Investments is reported on the income statement among the Other Expenses and Losses. The Allowance account is reported contra to Short-Term Investments on the balance sheet as follows:

Current Assets

Cash..		$ XXX
Short-term investments, at cost	$305,100	
Less: Allowance to reduce short-term investments to market value	13,100	
Short-term investments, at market value............		292,000
Accounts receivable, net of allowance of $XXX.......		XXX

An alternative and more-often-used way to report these investments is to show the LCM value on the balance sheet and the higher amount in a note, as follows:

Current Assets

Cash	$	XXX
Short-term investments, at market value (Note 4)		292,000
Accounts receivable, net of allowance of $XXX		XXX

NOTE 4—SHORT-TERM INVESTMENTS:

Short-term investments are reported at the lower of their cost or market value. At December 31, 19XX, cost was $305,100.

If the portfolio cost is lower than market value, the investor reports short-term investments at cost and discloses market value in the note.

Long-Term Investments Accounted for by the Cost Method (with LCM)

An investor may own numerous investments, some short-term and others long-term. For accounting purposes, the two investment portfolios are *not* mixed. They are reported separately on the balance sheet, as shown in Exhibit 14-2. *Long-term* is seldom used in the account title. An investment is understood to be long-term unless specifically labeled as short-term.

Accounting for long-term investments in which the investor holds less than 20 percent of the investee's voting stock follows the procedures outlined for short-term investments. The beginning accounting value is cost, which is debited to an Investments account at the date of purchase. Gains and losses are recorded on sales. Long-term investments are reported on the balance sheet at the lower of total portfolio cost or market value. The main difference in accounting for long-term investments is that the debit balance of Unrealized Loss on Long-Term Investments is reported as a contra item in the stockholders' equity section of the balance sheet. As a practical matter, long-term investments accounted for by the cost method are rare. Most companies that purchase long-term investments in stock are seeking some measure of control. Thus, they use either the equity method or the consolidation method.

Long-Term Investments Accounted for by the Equity Method

The *cost* method (with LCM) of accounting for long-term investments applies when an investor holds less than 20 percent of the investee's voting stock. Such an investor usually plays no important role in the investee's operations. However, an investor with a larger stock holding—between 20 percent and 50 percent of the investee's voting stock—may *significantly influence* how the investee operates the business. Such an investor can likely affect the investee's decisions on dividend policy, product lines, sources of supply, and other important matters. For example, General Motors owns 34 percent of Isuzu, and Toyota owns part of 23 key suppliers. Because the investor has a voice in shaping business policy and operations, accountants believe that some measure of the investee's success and failure should be included in accounting for the investment. We use the **equity method** to account for investments in which the investor can significantly influence the decisions of the investee.

Investments accounted for by the equity method are recorded initially at cost. Suppose Phillips Petroleum Company pays $400,000 for 30 percent of the common stock of White Rock Corporation. Phillips's entry to record the purchase of this investment is

Jan. 6	Investment in White Rock Common Stock . .	400,000	
	Cash		400,000
	To purchase 30% investment in White Rock common stock.		

OBJECTIVE 2

Use the equity method for stock investments

Under the equity method, Phillips, as the investor, applies its percentage of ownership—30 percent, in our example—in recording its share of the investee's net income and dividends. If White Rock reports net income of $250,000 for the year, Phillips records 30 percent of this amount as an increase in the investment account and as equity-method investment revenue, as follows:

Dec. 31   Investment in White Rock Common Stock
            ($250,000 × .30)   75,000
                   Equity-Method Investment Revenue ..   75,000
        To record 30% of White Rock net income.

The Investment Revenue account carries the Equity-Method label to identify its source. This labeling is similar to distinguishing Sales Revenue from Service Revenue.

The investor increases the Investment account and records Investment Revenue when the investee reports income because of the close relationship between the two companies. As the investee's owner equity increases, so does the Investment account on the books of the investor.

Phillips records its proportionate part of cash dividends received from White Rock. Assuming White Rock declares and pays a cash dividend of $100,000, Phillips receives 30 percent of this dividend, recording it as follows:

Jan. 17   Cash ($100,000 × .30)   30,000
             Investment in White Rock
                Common Stock....................   30,000
        To record receipt of 30% of White Rock cash dividend.

Observe that the Investment account is credited for the receipt of a dividend on an equity-method investment. Why? Because the dividend decreases the investee's owner equity and so it also reduces the investor's investment. The investor received cash for this portion of the investment and reduced the investor's claim against the investee.

After the above entries are posted, Phillips's Investment account reflects its equity in the net assets of White Rock:

Investment in White Rock Common Stock

19X1			19X2		
Jan. 6	Purchase	400,000	Jan. 17	Dividends	30,000
Dec. 31	Net income	75,000			
19X2					
Jan. 17	Balance	445,000			

Gain or loss on the sale of an equity-method investment is measured as the difference between the sale proceeds and the carrying amount of the investment. For example, sale of one-tenth of the White Rock common stock for $41,000 would be recorded as follows:

Feb. 13   Cash   41,000
             Loss on Sale of Investment   3,500
               Investment in White Rock Common Stock
                 ($445,000 × 1/10)   44,500
        Sold one-tenth of investment in White Rock
        common stock.

Companies with investments accounted for by the equity method often refer to the investee as an *affiliated company*. The account title Investments in Affiliated Companies refers to investments that are accounted for by the equity method.

Consolidation Method

Most large corporations own controlling interests in other corporations. A **controlling** (or **majority**) **interest** is the ownership of more than 50 percent of the investee's voting stock. Such an investment enables the investor to elect a majority of the investee's board of directors and so control the investee. The investor is called the **parent company,** and the investee company is called the **subsidiary.** For example, Saturn Corporation, the auto maker, is a subsidiary of General Motors Corporation, the parent. The stockholders of General Motors control GM, and because GM owns Saturn Corporation, the GM stockholders also control Saturn.

Why have subsidiaries? Why not have the corporation take the form of a single legal entity? Subsidiaries may enable the parent to save on income taxes, may limit the parent's liabilities in a risky venture, and may ease expansion into foreign countries. For example, IBM may find it more feasible to operate in France through a French-based subsidiary company than through the American parent company.

Consolidation accounting is a method of combining the financial statements of two or more companies that are controlled by the same owners. This method implements the entity concept by reporting a single set of financial statements for the consolidated entity, which carries the name of the parent company.

Consolidated statements combine the balance sheets, income statements, and other financial statements of the parent company with those of majority-owned subsidiaries into an overall set as if the parents and its subsidiaries were a single entity. The goal is to provide a better perspective on total operations than could be obtained by examining the separate reports of each of the individual companies. The assets, liabilities, revenues, and expenses of each subsidiary are added to the parent's accounts. The consolidated financial statements present the combined account balances. For example, the balance in the Cash account of Saturn Corporation is added to the balance in the GM Cash account, and the sum of the two amounts is presented as a single amount in the consolidated balance sheet of General Motors. Each account balance of a subsidiary loses its identity in the consolidated statements. GM's financial statements are entitled "General Motors Corporation and Consolidated Subsidiaries." Saturn Corporation and the names of all other GM subsidiaries do not appear in the statement titles. But the names of the subsidiary companies may be listed in the parent company's annual report. A reader of corporate annual reports cannot hope to understand them without knowing how consolidated statements are prepared. Exhibit 14-3 diagrams a corporate structure whose parent corporation owns controlling interests in five subsidiary companies and an equity-method investment in another investee company.

> **OBJECTIVE 3**
> Consolidate parent and subsidiary balance sheets

Consolidated Balance Sheet—Parent Corporation Owns All of Subsidiary's Stock. Suppose that Parent Corporation has purchased all the outstanding common stock of Subsidiary Corporation at its book value of $150,000. In addition, Parent Corporation loaned Subsidiary Corporation $80,000. Note that the $150,000 is paid to the *former owners* of Subsidiary Corporation as private investors. The $150,000 is *not* an addition to the existing assets and stockholders' equity of Subsidiary Corporation. *That is, the books of Subsidiary*

EXHIBIT 14-3 *Parent Company with Consolidated Subsidiaries and an Equity-Method Investment*

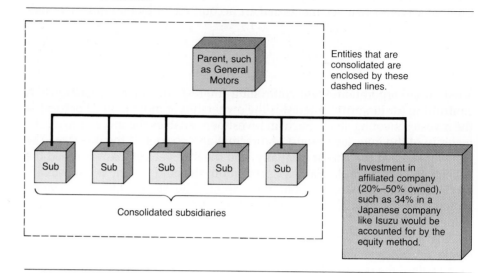

Corporation are completely unaffected by Parent Corporation's initial investment and Parent's subsequent accounting for that investment. Subsidiary Corporation is not dissolved. It lives on as a separate legal entity but with a new owner, Parent Corporation.

Parent Books¹			Subsidiary Books		
Investment in Subsidiary					
Corporation	150,000		No entry		
Cash		150,000			
Note Receivable from			Cash	80,000	
Subsidiary	80,000		Note Payable		
Cash		80,000	to Parent ...		80,000

Each legal entity has its individual set of books. The consolidated entity does not keep a separate set of books. Instead, a work sheet is used to prepare the consolidated statements. A major concern in consolidation accounting is this: *Do not double-count.*

Companies may prepare a consolidated balance sheet immediately after the acquisition. The consolidated balance sheet shows all the assets and liabilities of both the parent and the subsidiary. The Investment in Subsidiary account on the parent's books represents all the assets and liabilities of Subsidiary. The consolidated statements cannot show both the investment amount *plus* the amounts for the subsidiary's assets and liabilities. That would count the same resources twice. In fact, intercompany accounts—those that appear in both the parent's books and the subsidiary's books—should not be included in the consolidated statements at all. To avoid this double-counting we eliminate (a) the $150,000 Investment in Subsidiary on the parent's books and (b) the $150,000 stockholders' equity on the subsidiary's books ($100,000 Common Stock and $50,000 Retained Earnings).

---

¹The parent company may use either the cost method or the equity method for work sheet entries to the Investment account. Regardless of the method used, the consolidated statements are the same. Advanced accounting courses deal with this topic.

Explanation of Elimination Entry (a). Exhibit 14-4 shows the work sheet for consolidating the balance sheet. Consider the elimination entry for the parent-subsidiary ownership accounts, which are intercompany accounts. Entry (*a*) credits the parent Investment account to eliminate its debit balance. It also eliminates the subsidiary stockholders' equity accounts by debiting Common Stock for $100,000 and Retained Earnings for $50,000. The resulting consolidated balance sheet reports no Investment in Subsidiary account, and the Common Stock and Retained Earnings are those of Parent Corporation only. The consolidated balance sheet amounts are in the final column of the consolidation work sheet.

In summary, if the intercompany accounts were not eliminated, there would be a double-counting in the consolidated statement. The following chart summarizes the parent-subsidiary relationship:

Entity	Types of Records
Parent Corporation	Parent books
+ Subsidiary Corporation	Subsidiary books
= Preliminary consolidated balance sheet	No separate books, but periodically Parent and Subsidiary assets and liabilities are added together in a work sheet
− Eliminating entries	Intercompany accounts offset against each other to eliminate double-counting
= Consolidated balance sheet to outside investors	The report of the overall economic entity

Explanation of Elimination Entry (b). Parent Corporation loaned $80,000 to Subsidiary Corporation, and Subsidiary signed a note payable to Parent. Therefore, Parent's balance sheet includes an $80,000 note receivable and Subsidiary's balance sheet reports a note payable for this amount. This loan was entirely within the consolidated entity and so must be eliminated. Entry (*b*) accomplishes this. The $80,000 credit in the elimination column of the work sheet offsets Parent's debit balance in Notes Receivable from Subsidiary. After

EXHIBIT 14-4 *Work Sheet for Consolidated Balance Sheet—Parent Corporation Owns All of Subsidiary's Stock*

Assets	Parent Corporation	Subsidiary Corporation	Eliminations Debit	Eliminations Credit	Consolidated Amounts
Cash	12,000	18,000			30,000
Notes receivable from Subsidiary	80,000	—		(b) 80,000	—
Inventory	104,000	91,000			195,000
Investment in Subsidiary	150,000	—		(a) 150,000	—
Other assets	218,000	138,000			356,000
Total	564,000	247,000			581,000
Liabilities and Stockholders' Equity					
Accounts payable	43,000	17,000			60,000
Notes payable	190,000	80,000	(b) 80,000		190,000
Common stock	176,000	100,000	(a) 100,000		176,000
Retained earnings	155,000	50,000	(a) 50,000		155,000
Total	564,000	247,000	230,000	230,000	581,000

this work sheet entry, the consolidated amount for notes receivable is zero. The $80,000 debit in the elimination column offsets the credit balance of Subsidiary's notes payable, and the resulting consolidated amount for notes payable is the amount owed to those outside the consolidated entity.

Parent Corporation Buys Subsidiary's Stock at a Price above Book Value.[2]

A company may acquire a controlling interest in a subsidiary by paying a price above the book value of the subsidiary's owner equity. The excess of the price paid by the parent over the market value of the subsidiary's net assets (assets minus liabilities) is *goodwill*. What drives a company's market value up? The company may create goodwill through its superior products, service, or location. Goodwill is discussed in Chapter 9.

The subsidiary does not record goodwill. Doing so would violate the reliability principle. Goodwill is recorded only when a company purchases it as part of the acquisition of another company, that is, when a parent company purchases a subsidiary. The goodwill is recorded in the process of consolidating the parent and subsidiary financial statements.

Suppose Parent Corporation paid $450,000 to acquire 100 percent of the common stock of Subsidiary Corporation, which had Common Stock of $200,000 and Retained Earnings of $180,000. Parent's payment included $70,000 for goodwill ($450,000 − $200,000 − $180,000 = $70,000). The entry to eliminate Parent's Investment account against Subsidiary's equity accounts is

Dec. 31	Common Stock, Subsidiary	200,000	
	Retained Earnings, Subsidiary	180,000	
	Goodwill	70,000	
	Investment in Subsidiary		450,000
	To eliminate cost of investment in subsidiary against Subsidiary's equity balances and to recognize Subsidiary's unrecorded goodwill.		

In actual practice, this entry would be made only on the consolidation work sheet. Here we show it in general journal form for instructional purposes.

The asset goodwill is reported on the consolidated balance sheet among the intangible assets, after plant assets. Goodwill is amortized to expense over its useful life.

Consolidated Balance Sheet—Parent Company Owns Less Than 100 Percent of Subsidiary's Stock.

When a parent company owns more than 50 percent (a majority) of the subsidiary's stock but less than 100 percent of it, a new category of owners' equity, called *minority interest*, must appear on the balance sheet. Suppose Parent buys 75 percent of Subsidiary's common stock. The minority interest is the remaining 25 percent of Subsidiary's equity. Thus **minority interest** is the subsidiary's equity that is held by stockholders other than the parent company. Most companies report minority interest as a liability, while a few show it as a separate element of stockholders' equity. In this book, we list minority interest as a liability to be consistent with actual practice. Exhibit 14-5 is the consolidation work sheet. Again, focus on the Eliminations columns and the Consolidated Amounts.

---

[2]For simplicity, we are assuming that the fair market value of the subsidiary's net assets (assets minus liabilities) equals the book value of the company's owner equity. Advanced courses consider other situations.

Assets	P Company	S Company	Eliminations Debit	Eliminations Credit	Consolidated Amounts
Cash	33,000	18,000			51,000
Note receivable from P............	—	50,000		(b) 50,000	—
Accounts receivable, net	54,000	39,000			93,000
Inventory	92,000	66,000			158,000
Investment in S	120,000	—		(a) 120,000	—
Plant and equipment, net	230,000	123,000			353,000
Total	529,000	296,000			655,000
Liabilities and Stockholders' Equity					
Accounts payable.................	141,000	94,000			235,000
Notes payable...................	50,000	42,000	(b) 50,000		42,000
Minority interest	—	—		(a) 40,000	40,000
Common stock	170,000	100,000	(a) 100,000		170,000
Retained earnings	168,000	60,000	(a) 60,000		168,000
Total	529,000	296,000	210,000	210,000	655,000

Entry (a) eliminates P Company's Investment balance of $120,000 against the $160,000 owners' equity of S Company. Observe that all of S's equity is eliminated even though P holds only 75 percent of S's stock. The outside 25 percent interest in S's equity is credited to Minority Interest ($160,000 × .25 = $40,000). Thus entry *(a)* reclassifies 25 percent of S Company's equity as minority interest.

Entry (b) in Exhibit 14-5 eliminates S Company's $50,000 note receivable against P's note payable of the same amount. The consolidated amount of notes payable ($42,000) is the amount that S Company owes to outsiders.

The consolidated balance sheet of P Company, below, is based on the work sheet of Exhibit 14-5.

P Company and Consolidated Subsidiary
Consolidated Balance Sheet
December 31, 19XX

Assets

Cash....................................	$ 51,000
Accounts receivable, net.................	93,000
Inventory	158,000
Plant and equipment, net................	353,000
Total assets........................	$655,000

Liabilities and Stockholders' Equity

Accounts payable	$235,000
Notes payable	42,000
Minority interest.......................	40,000
Common stock	170,000
Retained earnings......................	168,000
Total liabilities and stockholders' equity	$655,000

The consolidated balance sheet reveals that ownership of P Company and its consolidated subsidiary is divided between P's stockholders (common stock and retained earnings totaling $338,000) and the minority interest of S Company ($40,000).

Income of a Consolidated Entity. The income of a consolidated entity is the net income of the parent plus the parent's proportion of the subsidiaries' net income. Suppose Parent Company owns all the stock of Subsidiary S-1 and 60 percent of the stock of Subsidiary S-2. During the year just ended, Parent earned net income of $330,000, S-1 earned $150,000, and S-2 had a net loss of $100,000. Parent Company would report net income of $420,000, computed as follows:

	Net Income (Net Loss)	Parent Stockholders' Ownership	Parent Net Income (Net Loss)
Parent Company	$330,000	100%	$330,000
Subsidiary S-1	150,000	100	150,000
Subsidiary S-2	(100,000)	60	(60,000)
Consolidated net income			$420,000

The parent's net income is the same amount that would be recorded under the equity method. However, the equity method stops short of reporting the investees' assets and liabilities on the parent balance sheet because with an investment in the range of 20–50 percent, the investor owns less than a controlling interest in the investee company.

The procedures for preparation of a consolidated income statement parallel those outlined above for the balance sheet. The consolidated income statement is discussed in an advanced course.

Investments in Bonds and Notes

Industrial and commercial companies invest far more in stock than they invest in bonds. The major investors in bonds are financial institutions, such as pension plans, bank trust departments, and insurance companies. For every issuer of bonds payable, at least one investor owns the bonds. The relationship between the issuer and the investor may be diagrammed as follows:

OBJECTIVE 5

Account for investments in bonds

Issuing Corporation   *Investor (Bondholder)*

Bonds payable ⟷ Investment in bonds

Interest expense ⟵——⟶ Interest revenue

The dollar amount of a bond transaction is the same for issuer and investor, but the accounts debited and credited differ. However, the accounts are parallel. For example, the issuer's interest expense is the investor's interest revenue.

An investment in bonds is classified either as short-term (a current asset) or as long-term. An investment is a current asset if (1) the investment is liquid (can readily be sold for cash) and (2) the owner intends to convert it to cash within one year or to use it to pay a current liability. An investment that is intended to be held longer than a year is classified as long-term.

Bond investments are recorded at cost, which includes the purchase price and any brokerage fees. Amortization of bond premium or discount is *not* recorded on short-term investments because the investor plans to hold the bonds for so short a period that any amortization would be immaterial. Investors hold long-term investments for a significant period and therefore amortize any premium or discount on the bonds.

Let's look at accounting for a *short-term* bond investment. Suppose that an investor purchases $10,000 of bonds on August 1, 19X2, paying 93 plus accrued interest and a brokerage commission of $250. The annual contract interest rate is 12 percent, paid semiannually on April 1 and October 1. The cost of the bonds is $9,550 [($10,000 × .93) + $250]. In addition, the investor pays accrued interest for the four months (April through July) since the last interest payment. The investor records the purchase on August 1 as follows:

Aug. 1 Short-Term Investment in Bonds
         [($10,000 × .93) + $250] 9,550
         Interest Receivable ($10,000 × .12 × 4/12) 400
              Cash.................................... 9,950
         To purchase short-term bond investment.

Accrued interest is *not* included in the cost of the investment but is debited to Interest Receivable.

The investor's entry for receipt of the first semiannual interest amount on October 1 is

Oct. 1 Cash ($10,000 × .12 × 6/12).................... 600
              Interest Receivable 400
              Interest Revenue ($10,000 × .12 × 2/12) 200
         To receive semiannual interest, part of which was accrued.

At October 1 the investor has held the bonds for two months. The entry correctly credits Interest Revenue for two months' interest. This entry does not include discount amortization on the bonds because the investment is short-term.

At December 31 the investor accrues interest revenue for three months (October, November, and December), debiting Interest Receivable and crediting Interest Revenue for $300 ($10,000 × .12 × 3/12). The investor's December 31 balance sheet reports the following information (we assume that the market price of the bonds is 96):

         Current assets:
              Short-term investment in bonds (Note 4) $9,550
              Interest receivable 300

Note 4: Short-term investments:
At December 31 the current market value of short-term investments in bonds was $9,600.

Observe that the investment is reported at cost, with the current market value disclosed in a note. The market value may also be reported parenthetically.

Current assets:
     Short-term investment in bonds (Current market value, $9,600) . $9,550
     Interest receivable 300

The investor measures any gain or loss on sale as the difference between the sale price (less any broker's commission) and the cost of the investment. For example, sale of the bonds for $9,700 will result in a gain of $150. This gain is reported as Other Revenue on a multiple-step income statement or beneath

Sales Revenue among the revenues and gains on a single-step statement. A loss would be reported as Other Expense on a multiple-step statement or among the expenses on a single-step statement.

Accounting for *long-term* investments in bonds follows the general pattern illustrated for short-term investments. For long-term investments, however, discount or premium is amortized to account more precisely for interest revenue. This additional step is needed because the bond investment will be held for longer than a year and, therefore, the amortization amount is likely to be material. The amortization of discount or premium on a bond investment affects Interest Revenue in the same way that the amortization affects Interest Expense for the company that issued the bonds.

The accountant records amortization on the cash interest dates and at year end, along with the accrual of interest receivable. Accountants rarely use separate discount and premium accounts for investments. Amortization of a discount is recorded by directly debiting the Long-Term Investment in Bonds account and crediting Interest Revenue. Amortization of a premium is credited directly to the Long-Term Investment account. This entry debits Interest Revenue. These entries bring the investment balance to the bonds' face value on the maturity date and record the correct amount of interest revenue each period.

Suppose the $10,000 of 12 percent bonds in the preceding illustration were purchased on August 1, 19X2, as a long-term investment. Interest dates are April 1 and October 1. These bonds mature on October 1, 19X6, so they will be outstanding for 50 months. Assume amortization of the discount by the straight-line method. The following entries for a long-term investment highlight the differences between accounting for a short-term bond investment and for a long-term bond investment:

Aug.	1	**Long-Term Investment in Bonds**		
		[($10,000 × .93) + $250]	9,550	
		Interest Receivable ($10,000 × .12 × 4/12)	400	
		Cash		9,950
		To purchase long-term bond investment.		
Oct.	1	Cash ($10,000 × .12 × 6/12)	600	
		Interest Receivable		400
		Interest Revenue ($10,000 × .12 × 2/12)		200
		To receive semiannual interest, part of which was accrued.		
Oct.	1	**Long-Term Investment in Bonds**		
		[($10,000 − $9,550)/50 × 2]	**18**	
		Interest Revenue		**18**
		To amortize discount on bond investment for two months.		
Dec. 31		Interest Receivable ($10,000 × .12 × 3/12)	300	
		Interest Revenue		300
		To accrue interest revenue for three months.		
Dec. 31		**Long-Term Investment in Bonds**		
		[($10,000 − $9,550)/50 × 3]	**27**	
		Interest Revenue		**27**
		To amortize discount on bond investment for three months.		

The financial statements at December 31, 19X2, report the following effects of this long-term investment in bonds (assume the bonds' market price is 102):

Balance sheet at December 31, 19X2:
  Current assets:
    Interest receivable .... $ 300
    Total current assets ....   X,XXX
  Long-term investments in bonds ($9,550 + $18 + $27)—Note 6   9,595
  Property, plant, and equipment ....   X,XXX

    Note 6: Long-term investments:
    At December 31, 19X2, the market value of long-term investments in bonds was $10,200.

Income statement (multiple-step) for the year ended December 31, 19X2:
  Other revenues:
    Interest revenue ($200 + $18 + $300 + $27) .... $ 545

In particular, note that the long-term investments in bonds are reported by the *amortized cost* method.

The amortization entry for a premium debits Interest Revenue and credits Long-Term Investment in Bonds. Where discount or premium is amortized by the effective-interest method, accounting for long-term investments follows the pattern illustrated here. Effective-interest amortization amounts are computed as shown for bonds payable in Chapter 11.

Exhibit 14-6 summarizes the accounting methods for investments.

EXHIBIT 14-6 *Accounting Methods for Investments*

Type of Investments	Accounting Method
Short-term investment in stock	Cost (lower of cost or market)
Long-term investment in stock:	
Investor owns less than 20 percent of investee stock	Cost (lower of cost or market)
Investor owns between 20 and 50 percent of investee stock	Equity
Investor owns greater than 50 percent of investee stock	Consolidation
Short-term investment in bonds	Cost
Long-term investment in bonds	Amortized cost

Summary Problem for Your Review

This problem consists of four independent items.

1. Identify the appropriate accounting method for each of the following situations:
   (a) Investment in 25 percent of investee's stock
   (b) Short-term investment in stock
   (c) Investment in more than 50 percent of investee's stock

2. At what amount should the following long-term investment portfolio be reported on the December 31 balance sheet? All the investments are less than 5 percent of the investee's stock and were purchased during the current year.

Stock	Investment Cost	Current Market Value
Eastman Kodak	$ 5,000	$ 5,500
Exxon	61,200	53,000
General Motors	3,680	6,230

Journalize any adjusting entry required by these data.

3. Investor paid $67,900 to acquire a 40 percent equity-method investment in the common stock of Investee. At the end of the first year, Investee's net income was $80,000, and Investee declared and paid cash dividends of $55,000. Journalize Investor's (a) purchase of the investment, (b) share of Investee's net income, (c) receipt of dividends from Investee, and (d) sale of Investee stock for $80,100.

4. Parent Company paid $100,000 for all the common stock of Subsidiary Company, and Parent owes Subsidiary $20,000 on a note payable. Complete the following consolidation work sheet:

Assets	Parent Company	Subsidiary Company	Eliminations Debit	Eliminations Credit	Consolidated Amounts
Cash	7,000	4,000			
Note receivable from Parent.	—	20,000			
Investment in Subsidiary	100,000	—			
Goodwill	—	—			
Other assets	108,000	99,000			
Total	215,000	123,000			

Liabilities and Stockholders' Equity

Accounts payable	15,000	8,000			
Notes payable	20,000	30,000			
Common stock	135,000	60,000			
Retained earnings	45,000	25,000			
Total	215,000	123,000			

SOLUTION TO SUMMARY PROBLEM

1. (a) Equity   (b) Cost (LCM)   (c) Consolidation

2. Report the investments at market value, $64,730, because market value is less than cost.

Stock	Investment Cost	Current Market Value
Eastman Kodak	$ 5,000	$ 5,500
Exxon	61,200	53,000
General Motors	3,680	6,230
Totals	$69,880	$64,730

Adjusting entry:
Unrealized Loss on Long-Term Investments
($69,880 − $64,730) 5,150
   Allowance to Reduce Long-Term Investments
   to Market Value 5,150
To write investments down to market value.

3. a. Investment in Investee Common Stock 67,900
      Cash 67,900
  To purchase 40% investment in Investee common stock.
b. Investment in Investee Common Stock
   ($80,000 × .40) 32,000
      Equity-Method Investment Revenue 32,000
  To record 40% of Investee net income.
c. Cash ($55,000 × .40) 22,000
      Investment in Investee Common Stock ... 22,000
  To record receipt of 40% of Investee cash dividend.
d. Cash 80,100
      Investment in Investee Common Stock
      ($67,900 + $32,000 − $22,000).......... 77,900
      Gain on Sale of Investment 2,200
  Sold investment in Investee common stock.

4. Consolidation work sheet:

Assets	Parent Company	Subsidiary Company	Eliminations Debit	Eliminations Credit	Consolidated Amounts
Cash	7,000	4,000			11,000
Note receivable from Parent	—	20,000		(a) 20,000	—
Investment in Subsidiary	100,000	—		(b) 100,000	—
Goodwill...........................	—	—	(b) 15,000		15,000
Other assets.......................	108,000	99,000			207,000
Total	215,000	123,000			233,000

Liabilities and Stockholders' Equity					
Accounts payable	15,000	8,000			23,000
Notes payable	20,000	30,000	(a) 20,000		30,000
Common stock	135,000	60,000	(b) 60,000		135,000
Retained earnings...................	45,000	25,000	(b) 25,000		45,000
Total	215,000	123,000	120,000	120,000	233,000

Accounting for International Operations

Did you know that Exxon and Bank of America earn most of their revenue outside the United States? It is common for American companies to do a large part of their business abroad. IBM, Ford, Coca-Cola, Boeing, and Kraft (Foods), among many others, are very active in other countries.

Accounting for business activities across national boundaries makes up the field of *international accounting*. As communications and transportation improve and trade barriers fall, global integration makes international accounting more important.

Economic Structures and Their Impact on International Accounting

The business environment varies widely across the globe. New York reflec the diversity of the market-driven economy of the United States. Japan's eco omy is similar to ours, although Japanese business activity focuses more imports and exports. The central government has controlled the economy Czechoslovakia and other Eastern-bloc countries, so private business dec sions are only beginning to take root there. In Brazil, extremely high rates inflation have made historical-cost amounts meaningless. Accountants mu continually adjust the price levels because of the rapid change in the value the cruzeiro, Brazil's monetary unit. International accounting deals with thes and other differences in economic structures.

Foreign Currencies and Foreign-Currency Exchange Rates

Each country uses its own national currency. Assume Boeing, a United State company, sells a 747 jet to Air France. Will Boeing receive United States dollar or French francs? If the transaction takes place in dollars, Air France mus exchange its francs for dollars in order to pay Boeing in U.S. currency. If th transaction takes place in francs, Boeing will receive francs, which it mus exchange for dollars. In either case, a step has been added to the transactior one company must convert domestic currency into foreign currency, or th other company must convert foreign currency into domestic currency.

The price of one nation's currency may be stated in terms of another coun try's monetary unit. This measure of one currency against another currency i called the **foreign-currency exchange rate**. In Exhibit 14-7, the dollar value of French franc is $.20. This means that one French franc could be bought fo twenty cents. Other currencies, such as the pound and the yen (also listed i Exhibit 14-7), are similarly bought and sold.

We use the exchange rate to convert the cost of an item given in one cur rency to its cost in a second currency. We call this conversion a *translatior* Suppose an item costs two hundred French francs. To compute its cost ir dollars, we multiply the amount in francs by the conversion rate: 200 Frencl francs × $.20 = $40.

EXHIBIT 14-7 *Foreign-Currency Exchange Rates*

Country	Monetary Unit	Dollar Value	Country	Monetary Unit	Dollar Value
Canada	Dollar	$ .87	Great Britain	Pound	$1.95
European Common Market	European Currency Unit	1.37	Italy	Lira	.0009
France	Franc	.20	Japan	Yen	.0075
Germany	Mark	.67	Mexico	Peso	.0003

Source: *The Wall Street Journal,* January 4, 1991, p. C10.

To aid the flow of international business, a market exists for foreign currencies. Traders buy and sell U.S. dollars, French francs, and other currencies in the same way that they buy and sell other commodities like beef, cotton, and automobiles. And just as supply and demand cause the prices of these other commodities to shift, so supply and demand for a particular currency cause exchange rates to fluctuate daily. When the demand for a nation's currency exceeds the supply of that currency, its exchange rate rises. When supply exceeds demand, the currency's exchange rate falls.

Two main factors determine the supply and demand for a particular currency: (1) the ratio of a country's imports to its exports, and (2) the rate of return available in the country's capital markets.

The Import/Export Ratio. Japanese exports far surpass Japan's imports. Customers of Japanese companies must buy yen (Japan's unit of currency) in the international currency market to pay for their purchases. This strong demand drives up the price—the foreign exchange rate—of the yen. France, in contrast, imports more goods than it exports. French businesses must sell francs in order to buy the foreign currencies needed to acquire the foreign goods. This increases the supply of the French franc and so decreases its price.

The Rate of Return. The rate of return available in a country's capital markets affects the amount of investment funds flowing into the country. When rates of return are high in a politically stable country such as the United States, international investors buy stocks, bonds, and real estate in that country. This increases the demand for the nation's currency and drives up its exchange rate.

Currencies are often described in the financial press as "strong" or "weak." What do these terms mean? The exchange rate of a **strong currency** is rising relative to other nations' currencies. The exchange rate of a **weak currency** is falling relative to other currencies.

Suppose on January 5 *The Wall Street Journal* listed the exchange rate for the British pound as $1.95. On January 6 that rate has changed to $1.93. We would say that the dollar has risen against the British pound—the dollar is stronger than the pound—because the pound has become less expensive, and so the dollar now buys more pounds. A stronger dollar would make travel to England more attractive to Americans.

Assume that *The Wall Street Journal* reports a rise in the exchange rate of the Japanese yen from $.0075 to $.0076. This indicates that the yen is stronger than the dollar. Japanese automobiles, cameras, and electronic products are more expensive because each dollar buys fewer yen.

In our example situation—in which the pound has dropped relative to the dollar and the yen has risen relative to the dollar—we would describe the yen as the strongest currency, the pound as the weakest currency, and the dollar as somewhere between the other two currencies.

Accounting for International Transactions

When an American company transacts business with a foreign company, the transaction price can be stated either in dollars or in the national currency of the other company. If the price is stated in dollars, the American company has no special accounting difficulties. The transaction is recorded and reported in dollars exactly as though the other company were also American.

OBJECTIVE 6

Account for transactions stated in a foreign currency

Purchases on Account

If the transaction price is stated in units of the foreign currency, the American company encounters two accounting steps. First, the transaction price must be translated into dollars for recording in the accounting records. Second, credit transactions (the most common international transaction) usually cause the American company to experience a **foreign-currency transaction gain** or **loss.** This type of gain or loss occurs when the exchange rate changes between the date of the purchase on account and the date of the subsequent payment of cash.

The credit purchase creates an Account Payable that is recorded at the prevailing exchange rate. Later, when the buyer pays cash, the exchange rate has almost certainly changed. Accounts Payable is debited for the amount recorded earlier, and Cash is credited for the amount paid at the current exchange rate. A debit difference is a loss, and a credit difference is a gain.

Suppose on April 1, Macy's Department Store imports Shalimar perfume from a French supplier at a price of 200,000 francs. The exchange rate is $.19 per French franc. Macy's records this credit purchase as follows:

Apr. 1	Purchases	38,000	
	Accounts Payable (200,000 × $.19)		38,000

Macy's translates the French franc price of the merchandise (200,000 Fr) into dollars ($38,000) for recording the purchase and the related account payable.

If Macy's were to pay this account immediately—which is unlikely in international commerce—Macy's would debit Accounts Payable and credit Cash for $38,000. Suppose, however, that the credit terms specify payment within 60 days. On May 20, when Macy's pays this debt, the exchange rate has fallen to $.18 per French franc. Macy's payment entry is

May 20	Accounts Payable	38,000	
	Cash (200,000 × $.18)		36,000
	Foreign-Currency Transaction Gain		2,000

Macy's has a gain because the company has settled the debt with fewer dollars than the amount of the original account payable. If on the payment date the exchange rate of the French franc had exceeded $.19, Macy's would have paid more dollars than the original $38,000. The company would have recorded a loss on the transaction as a debit to Foreign-Currency Transaction Loss.

Sales on Account

International sales on account also may be measured in foreign currency. Suppose IBM sells a small computer to the German government on December 9. The price of the computer is 140,000 German marks, and the exchange rate is $.64 per German mark. IBM's sale entry is

Dec. 9	Accounts Receivable (140,000 × $.64)	89,600	
	Sales Revenue		89,600

Assume IBM collects from Germany on December 30, when the exchange rate has fallen to $.63 per German mark. IBM receives fewer dollars than the recorded amount of the receivable and so experiences a foreign-currency transaction loss. The collection entry is

Dec. 30	Cash (140,000 × $.63)	88,200	
	Foreign-Currency Transaction Loss	1,400	
	Accounts Receivable		89,600

Foreign-Currency Transaction Gains and Losses are combined for each accounting period. The net amount of gain or loss can be reported as Other Revenue and Expense on the income statement.

Unrealized Foreign-Currency Transaction Gains and Losses. Foreign-currency transaction gains and losses are *realized* when cash is paid or received. In the illustrations thus far, cash receipts and cash payments occurred in the same period as the related sale or purchase. This will not always be the case. For example, in the preceding example, suppose IBM collects from the German government during January. At December 31, the German mark is worth only $.63. This is $.01 less than the exchange rate at which IBM recorded the receivable. In this case IBM will record a foreign-currency transaction loss for the decrease in the dollar value of the account receivable. The adjusting entry is

Dec. 31	Foreign-Currency Transaction Loss		
	[140,000 × ($.64 − $.63)]	1,400	
	Accounts Receivable		1,400

This loss is *unrealized* in the sense that IBM has not yet received cash from the customer. Suppose IBM collects on January 9, when the exchange rate is $.62 per mark. The cash receipt entry records a further loss as follows:

Jan. 9	Cash (140,000 × $.62)	86,800	
	Foreign-Currency Transaction Loss		
	[140,000 × ($.63 − $.62)]	1,400	
	Accounts Receivable ($89,600 − $1,400)		88,200

IBM would have recorded a foreign-currency transaction gain on January 9 if the exchange rate had exceeded $.63 per mark. In that case the cash collection would have been greater than the carrying amount of Accounts Receivable.

Hedging—A Strategy to Avoid Foreign-Currency Transaction Losses

One approach to avoiding foreign-currency transaction losses is to insist that international transactions be settled in dollars, which puts the burden of currency translation on the foreign party. However, that strategy may alienate customers and result in lost sales, or it may cause suppliers to demand unreasonable credit terms. Another way for a company to insulate itself from the effects of fluctuating foreign-currency exchange rates is called hedging.

Hedging means to protect oneself from losing by engaging in a counterbalancing transaction. An American company selling goods measured in Mexican pesos expects to receive a fixed number of pesos in the future. If the peso is weak, the American company would expect the pesos to be worth fewer dollars than the amount of the receivable—an expected loss situation.

The American company may have accumulated payables stated in Mexican pesos in the normal course of its business. Losses on the receipt of pesos would be approximately offset by gains on the payment of pesos to Mexican suppliers. Most companies do not have equal amounts of receivables and payables in the same foreign currency. However, buying futures contracts in the foreign currency effectively creates a payable to offset a receivable and vice versa. Many companies that do business internationally use hedging techniques.

Consolidation of Foreign Subsidiaries

An American company with a foreign subsidiary must consolidate the subsidiary's financial statements into its own statements for reporting to the public. The consolidation of a foreign subsidiary poses two special challenges. Many countries outside the United States specify accounting treatments that differ from American accounting principles. For the purpose of reporting to the American public, accountants for the parent company must first bring the subsidiary's statements into conformity with American GAAP.

The second accounting challenge arises when the subsidiary statements are expressed in a foreign currency. A preliminary step in the consolidation process is to translate the subsidiary statements into dollars. Then the dollar-value statements of the subsidiary can be combined with the parent statements in the usual manner, as illustrated in the first half of this chapter.

The process of translating a foreign subsidiary's financial statements into dollars may create a *foreign-currency translation adjustment*. This item appears in the financial statements of most multinational companies and is reported as part of stockholders' equity on the consolidated balance sheet.

A translation adjustment arises because of changes in the foreign exchange rate over time. In general, *assets* and *liabilities* in the foreign subsidiaries' financial statements are translated into dollars at the exchange rate in effect on the date of the statements. However, *stockholders' equity* is translated into dollars at older, historical exchange rates. This difference in exchange rates creates an out-of-balance condition on the balance sheet. The translation adjustment amount brings the balance sheet back into balance.

Suppose U.S. Express Corporation owns Mexican Imports, Inc., whose financial statements are expressed in pesos. U.S. Express wants to consolidate the Mexican subsidiary's financial statements into its own financial statements. When U.S. Express acquired Mexican Imports in 19X1, a peso was worth $.00040. When Mexican Imports earned its retained income during 19X1 through 19X6, the average exchange rate was $.00037. On the balance sheet

EXHIBIT 14-8 *Translation of a Foreign-Currency Balance Sheet into Dollars*

Mexican Imports Amounts	Pesos	Exchange Rate	Dollars
Assets	80,000,000	$.00030	$240,000
Liabilities	50,000,000	.00030	$150,000
Stockholders' equity:			
Common stock	10,000,000	.00040	40,000
Retained earnings	20,000,000	.00037	74,000
Translation adjustment	—		(24,000)
	80,000,000		$240,000

date in 19X6, a peso is worth only $.00030. Exhibit 14-8 shows how to translate Mexican Imports' balance sheet into dollars and illustrates how the translation adjustment arises.

The **foreign-currency translation adjustment** is the balancing amount that brings the dollar amount of the total liabilities and stockholders' equity of a foreign subsidiary into agreement with the dollar amount of its total assets ($240,000). Only after the translation adjustment do total liabilities and stockholders' equity equal total assets stated in dollars. In this case the translation adjustment is negative, and total stockholders' equity becomes $90,000 ($40,000 + $74,000 − $24,000).

OBJECTIVE 7

Compute a foreign-currency translation adjustment

What in the economic environment caused the negative translation adjustment? A weakening of the peso since the acquisition of Mexican Imports brought about the need for this adjustment. When U.S. Express acquired the foreign subsidiary in 19X1, a peso was worth $.00040. When Mexican Imports earned its retained income during 19X1 through 19X6, the average exchange rate was $.00037. On the balance sheet date in 19X6, a peso is worth only $.00030, so Mexican Imports' net assets (assets minus liabilities) are translated into only $90,000 ($240,000 − $150,000).

To bring stockholders' equity to $90,000 requires a $24,000 negative amount. In a sense, a negative translation adjustment is like a loss. But it is reported as a contra item in the stockholders' equity section of the balance sheet, not on the income statement. The Mexican Imports dollar figures in Exhibit 14-8 are the amounts that U.S. Express Corporation would include in its consolidated balance sheet.

The translation adjustment can be positive—a gain—as well as negative, *elimination entry*
depending on the movement of foreign currency exchange rates. The following excerpt from IBM's actual balance sheet shows a positive translation adjustment:

Stockholders' Equity:	Dollars in millions
Capital stock, par value $1.25 per share	$ 6,442
Shares authorized: 750,000,000	
Issued: 1988—590,037,328	
Retained earnings	31,186
Translation adjustments	1,917
	39,545
Less: Treasury stock, at cost (Shares: 19X8—296,820)	36
	$39,509

International Accounting Standards

For the most part, accounting principles are similar from country to country. However, some important differences exist. For example, some countries, such as Italy, require financial statements to conform closely to income tax laws. In other countries, such as Brazil and Argentina, high inflation rates dictate that companies make price-level adjustments to report amounts in units of common purchasing power. Neither practice is followed as closely in the United States.

Several organizations are working to achieve worldwide harmony of accounting standards. Chief among these is the International Accounting Standards Committee (IASC). Headquartered in London, the IASC operates much as the Financial Accounting Standards Board in the United States. It has the support of the accounting professions in the United States, most of the British Commonwealth countries, Japan, France, Germany, the Netherlands, and Mexico. However, the IASC has no authority to require compliance with its accounting standards. It must rely on cooperation by the various national accounting professions. Since its creation in 1973, the IASC has succeeded in narrowing some differences in international accounting standards.

Computers and Consolidations

Consider a large consolidated entity like W. R. Grace & Co., a company with widely diversified operations and perhaps 40 subsidiary firms included in its consolidated financial statements. Accountants performing Grace's consolidations face several problems. One, the 40 firms may not all use the same accounting system and classifications. Two, finding intercompany receivables and payables may be difficult. A computer search for each of the 40 companies may be necessary to bring to light all intercompany items (there are 40×39, which comes to 1,560 different possibilities!).

Large consolidated firms may custom design their own software to prepare consolidated financial statements. Alternatively, or in connection with custom-designed software, these businesses may use linked electronic spreadsheets (also called linked spreadsheets). With a linked spreadsheet, a value entered on one company's spreadsheet is automatically transmitted to other companies' spreadsheets as appropriate, a decision the computer makes based on account classification. Eliminations too can be entered on the consolidating spreadsheet. The amounts for the consolidated financial statements are drawn from this spreadsheet.

Windows offer computer users access to multiple spreadsheets, or parts of spreadsheets, on screen at the same time. Consider the benefit of entering a change in the spreadsheet of a subsidiary and seeing immediately on screen its effect on the parent company.

Summary Problems for Your Review

Problem 1

Journalize the following transactions of American Corp.:

19X5

Nov. 16   Purchased equipment on account for 40,000 Swiss francs when the exchange rate was $.63 per Swiss franc.

27   Sold merchandise on account to a Belgian company for 700,000 Belgian francs. Each franc is worth $.0305.

Dec. 22   Paid the Swiss company; the franc's exchange rate was $.625.

31   Adjusted for the change in the exchange rate of the Belgian franc. Its current exchange rate is $.0301.

19X6

Jan. 4   Collected from the Belgian company. The exchange rate is $.0307.

Problem 2

Translate the balance sheet of the Spanish subsidiary of American Corp. into dollars. When American acquired this subsidiary, the exchange rate of the peseta was $.0101. The average exchange rate applicable to retained earnings is $.0108. The peseta's current exchange rate is $.0111.

Before performing the translation, predict whether the translation adjustment will be positive or negative. Does this situation generate a translation gain or a translation loss? Give your reasons.

	Pesetas
Assets	200,000,000
Liabilities	110,000,000
Stockholders' equity:	
Common stock	20,000,000
Retained earnings........	70,000,000
	200,000,000

SOLUTION TO REVIEW PROBLEM

Problem 1

Entries for transactions stated in foreign currencies:

19X5			
Nov. 16	Equipment (40,000 × $.63)	25,200	
	Accounts Payable		25,200
27	Accounts Receivable (700,000 × $.0305)	21,350	
	Sales Revenue		21,350
Dec. 22	Accounts Payable	25,200	
	Cash (40,000 × $.625)		25,000
	Foreign-Currency Transaction Gain		200
31	Foreign-Currency Transaction Loss		
	[700,000 × ($.0305 − $.0301)]	280	
	Accounts Receivable		280
19X6			
Jan. 4	Cash (700,000 × $.0307)....................	21,490	
	Accounts Receivable		
	($21,350 − $280)....................		21,070
	Foreign-Currency Transaction Gain		420

Problem 2

This situation will generate a *positive* translation adjustment, which is like a gain. The gain occurs because the peseta's current exchange rate, which is used to translate net assets (assets minus liabilities), exceeds the historical exchange rates used for stockholders' equity. The translation of the balance sheet is as follows:

	Pesetas	Exchange Rate	Dollars
Assets	200,000,000	$.0111	$2,220,000
Liabilities......................	110,000,000	.0111	$1,221,000
Stockholders' equity:			
Common stock	20,000,000	.0101	202,000
Retained earnings	70,000,000	.0108	756,000
Translation adjustment	—		41,000
	200,000,000		$2,220,000

Summary

Investments are classified as short-term or long-term. *Short-term investments* are liquid, and the investor intends to convert them to cash within one year or less or to use them to pay a current liability. All other investments are *long-term*.

Different methods are used to account for stock investments, depending on the investor's degree of influence over the investee. All investments are recorded initially at *cost*. Short-term investments and long-term investments of less than 20 percent of the investee's stock are accounted for by the cost method (with lower-of-cost-or-market). These investments are reported on the balance sheet at the lower of their cost or current market (LCM) value. Separate LCM determinations apply to the short-term investment portfolio and the long-term portfolio.

The *equity* method is used to account for investments of between 20 and 50 percent of the investee company's stock. Such an investment enables the investor to significantly influence the investee's activities. Investee income is recorded by the investor by debiting the Investment account and crediting an account entitled Equity-Method Investment Revenue. The investor records receipt of dividends from the investee by crediting the Investment account.

Ownership of more than 50 percent of the voting stock creates a parent-subsidiary relationship, and the *consolidation* method must be used. Because the parent has control over the subsidiary, the subsidiary's financial statements are included in the consolidated statements of the parent company. Two features of consolidation accounting are (1) addition of the parent and subsidiary accounts to prepare the parent's consolidated statements and (2) elimination of intercompany items. When a parent owns less than 100 percent of the subsidiary's stock, the portion owned by outside investors is called *minority interest*. Purchase of a controlling interest at a cost greater than the market value of the subsidiary creates an intangible asset called *goodwill*. A consolidation work sheet is used to prepare the consolidated financial statements.

International accounting deals with accounting for business activities across national boundaries. A key issue is the translation of foreign-currency amounts into dollars, accomplished through a *foreign-currency exchange rate*. Changes in exchange rates cause companies to experience *foreign-currency transaction gains and losses* on credit transactions.

Consolidation of a foreign subsidiary's financial statements into the parent-company statements requires adjusting the subsidiary statements to American accounting principles and then translating the foreign-company statements into dollars. The translation process creates a *translation adjustment* that is reported in stockholders' equity. The International Accounting Standards Committee is working to harmonize accounting principles worldwide.

Self-Study Questions

Test your understanding of the chapter by marking the best answer for each of the following questions.

1. Short-term investments are reported on the balance sheet *(p. 662)*
   - a. Immediately after cash
   - b. Immediately after accounts receivable
   - c. Immediately after inventory
   - d. Immediately after current assets

2. Byforth, Inc., distributes a 10 percent stock dividend. An investor who owns Byforth stock should *(p. 663)*
   - a. Debit Investment and credit Dividend Revenue for the par value of the stock received in the dividend distribution

b. Debit Investment and credit Dividend Revenue for the market value of the stock received in the dividend distribution

c. Debit Cash and credit Investment for the market value of the stock received in the dividend distribution

d. Make a memorandum entry to record the new cost per share of Byforth stock held

3. Short-term investments are reported at the *(p. 664)*
   a. Total cost of the portfolio
   b. Total market value of the portfolio
   c. Lower of total cost or total market value of the portfolio
   d. Total equity value of the portfolio

4. Putsch Corporation owns 30 percent of the voting stock of Mazelli, Inc. Mazelli reports net income of $100,000 and declares and pays cash dividends of $40,000. Which method should Putsch use to account for this investment? *(p. 665)*
   a. Cost (with LCM)   c. Equity
   b. Market value   d. Consolidation

5. Refer to the facts of the preceding question. What effect do Mazelli's income and dividends have on Putsch's net income? *(p. 666)*
   a. Increase of $12,000   c. Increase of $30,000
   b. Increase of $18,000   d. Increase of $42,000

6. In applying the consolidation method, elimination entries are *(p. 669)*
   a. Necessary
   b. Required only when the parent has a receivable from, or a payable to, the subsidiary
   c. Required only when there is a minority interest
   d. Required only for the preparation of the consolidated balance sheet

7. Parent Company has separate net income of $155,000. Subsidiary A, of which Parent owns 90 percent, reports net income of $60,000, and Subsidiary B, of which Parent owns 60 percent, reports net income of $80,000. What is Parent Company's consolidated net income? *(p. 672)*
   a. $155,000   c. $263,000
   b. $257,000   d. $295,000

8. On May 16, the exchange rate of a German mark was $.58. On May 20, the exchange rate is $.57. Which of the following statements is true? *(p. 679)*
   a. The dollar has risen against the mark.
   b. The dollar has fallen against the mark.
   c. The dollar is weaker than the mark.
   d. The dollar and the mark are equally strong.

9. A strong dollar encourages *(p. 679)*
   a. Travel to the United States by foreigners
   b. Purchase of American goods by foreigners
   c. Americans to travel abroad
   d. Americans to save dollars

10. Ford Motor Company purchased auto accessories from an English supplier at a price of 500,000 British pounds. On the date of the credit purchase the exchange rate of the British pound was $1.80. On the payment date the exchange rate of the pound is $1.82. If payment is in pounds, Ford experiences *(p. 680)*
    a. A foreign-currency transaction gain of $10,000
    b. A foreign-currency transaction loss of $10,000
    c. Neither a transaction gain nor a loss because the debt is paid in dollars
    d. A translation adjustment to stockholders' equity

Answers to the Self-Study Questions follow the Accounting Vocabulary.

Accounting Vocabulary

Consolidated statements. Financial statements of the parent company plus those of majority-owned subsidiaries as if the combination were a single legal entity (p. 667).

Consolidation method for investments. A way to combine the financial statements of two or more companies that are controlled by the same owners (p. 667).

Controlling (majority) interest. Ownership of more than 50 percent of an investee company's voting stock (p. 667).

Cost method for investments. The method used to account for short-term investments in stock and for long-term investments when the investor holds less than 20 percent of the investee's voting stock. Under the cost method, investments are recorded at cost and reported at the lower of their cost or market value (p. 662).

Equity method for investments. The method used to account for investments in which the investor can significantly influence the decisions of the investee. Under the equity method, investments are recorded initially at cost. The investment account is debited (increased) for ownership in the investee's net income and credited (decreased) for ownership in the investee's dividends (p. 665).

Foreign-currency exchange rate. The measure of one currency against another currency (p. 678).

Foreign-currency transaction gain or loss. A gain or loss that occurs when the exchange rate changes between the date of a purchase or sale on account and the subsequent payment or receipt of cash (p. 680).

Foreign-currency translation adjustment. The balancing figure that brings the dollar amount of the total liabilities and stockholders' equity of a foreign subsidiary into agreement with the dollar amount of its total assets (p. 682).

Hedging. Protecting oneself from losing money in one transaction by engaging in a counterbalancing transaction (p. 681).

Long-term investment. Separate asset category reported on the balance sheet between current assets and plant assets (p. 662).

Marketable security. Another name for Short-term investment, one that may be sold any time the investor wishes (p. 662).

Minority interest. A subsidiary company's equity that is held by stockholders other than the parent company (p. 670).

Parent company. An investor company that owns more than 50 percent of the voting stock of a subsidiary company (p. 667).

Short-term investment. Investment that is readily convertible to cash and that the investor intends either to convert to cash within one year or to use to pay a current liability. Also called a Marketable security, a current asset (p. 662).

Strong currency. A currency that is rising relative to other nations' currencies (p. 679).

Subsidiary company. An investee company in which a parent company owns more than 50 percent of the voting stock (p. 667).

Weak currency. A currency that is falling relative to other nations' currencies (p. 679).

Answers to Self-Study Questions

1. a
2. d
3. c
4. c
5. c ($100,000 × .30 = $30,000; dividends have *no* effect on investor net income under the equity method)
6. a

7. b [$155,000 + ($60,000 × .90) + ($80,000 × .60) = $257,000]
8. a
9. c
10. b [500,000 × ($1.82 − $1.80)]

ASSIGNMENT MATERIAL _____

Questions

1. How are stock prices quoted in the securities market? What is the investor's cost of 1,000 shares of Ford Motor Company stock at 55¾, with a brokerage commission of $1,350?

2. What distinguishes a short-term investment from a long-term investment?

3. Show the positions of short-term investments and long-term investments on the balance sheet.

4. Outline the accounting methods for the different types of investment.

5. How does an investor record the receipt of a cash dividend on an investment accounted for by the cost method? How does this investor record receipt of a stock dividend?

6. An investor paid $11,000 for 1,000 shares of stock and later received a 10 percent stock dividend. Compute the gain or loss on sale of 300 shares of the stock for $2,600.

7. At what amount are short-term investments reported on the balance sheet? Are the short-term and long-term investment portfolios mixed, or are they kept separate?

8. When is an investment accounted for by the equity method? Outline how to apply the equity method. Include in your answer how to record the purchase of the investment, the investor's proportion of the investee's net income, and receipt of a cash dividend from the investee. Describe how to measure gain or loss on sale of this investment.

9. Identify three transactions that cause debits or credits to an equity-method investment account.

10. What are two special features of the consolidation method for investments?

11. Why are intercompany items eliminated from consolidated financial statements? Name two intercompany items that are eliminated.

12. Name the account that expresses the excess of cost of an investment over the market value of the subsidiary's owner equity. What type of account is this, and where in the financial statements is it reported?

13. When a parent company buys less than 100 percent of a subsidiary's stock, a certain account is created. What is it called and how do most companies report it?

14. How would you measure the net income of a parent company with three subsidiaries? Assume that two subsidiaries are wholly (100 percent) owned and that the parent owns 60 percent of the third subsidiary.

15. What is the difference between accounting for a short-term bond investment and a long-term bond investment?

16. Explain the difference between a foreign-currency transaction gain or loss and a translation adjustment. Indicate the specific location in the financial statements where each item is reported.

17. Which situation results in a foreign-currency transaction gain for an American business? Which situation results in a loss?
    a. Credit purchase denominated in pesos, followed by weakness in the peso

b. Credit purchase denominated in pesos, followed by weakness in the dollar

c. Credit sale denominated in pesos, followed by weakness in the peso

d. Credit sale denominated in pesos, followed by weakness in the dollar

18. Explain the concept of hedging against foreign-currency transaction losses.

19. What is the difference between a realized foreign-currency transaction gain and an unrealized foreign-currency transaction gain?

20. McVey, Inc., acquired a foreign subsidiary when the foreign-currency's exchange rate was $.32. Over the years the foreign currency has steadily risen against the dollar. Will McVey's balance sheet report a positive or a negative translation adjustment?

21. Describe the computation of a foreign-currency translation adjustment.

Exercises

Exercises 14-1 *Journalizing transactions under the cost method* **(L.O. 1)**

Journalize the following investment transactions of August Bush, Inc.:

1. Purchased 400 shares (8 percent) of Advanced Corporation common stock at $44 per share, with brokerage commission of $300.

2. Received cash dividend of $1 per share on the Advanced Corporation investment.

3. Received 200 shares of Advanced Corporation common stock in a 50 percent stock dividend.

4. Sold 200 shares of Advanced Corporation stock for $29 per share, less brokerage commission of $270.

Exercise 14-2 *Reporting investments at the lower of cost or material* **(L.O. 1)**

Colgate-Palmolive Company recently reported the following information (not including the question mark) on its balance sheet:

Current Assets	(Dollars in millions)
Cash and cash equivalents	$ 398
Marketable securities [short-term investments], at lower of cost or market	?

Assume that the cost of Colgate-Palmolive's short-term investments is $130 million and that current market value is $126 million.

Required

Apply the lower-of-cost-or-market method to Colgate-Palmolive's short-term investments by inserting the appropriate amount in place of the question mark. Write a note to identify the method used to report short-term investments and to disclose cost and market value. Journalize any needed adjustment, assuming the marketable securities were purchased during the current year.

Exercise 14-3 *Journalizing transactions under the equity method* **(L.O. 2)**

Sears, Roebuck and Co. owns equity-method investments in several companies. Suppose Sears paid $200,000 to acquire a 25 percent investment in All-Star Company. Further, assume All-Star Company reported net income of $140,000 for the first year and declared and paid cash dividends of $70,000.

Record the following in Sears's general journal: (a) purchase of the investment, (b) Sears's proportion of All-Star's net income, and (c) receipt of the cash dividends.

Exercise 14-4 *Recording equity-method transactions directly in the accounts* *(L.O. 2)*

Without making journal entries, record the transactions of Exercise 16-3 directly in the Investment in All-Star Company Common Stock account. Assume that after all the above transactions took place, Sears sold its entire investment in All-Star common stock for cash of $240,000. Journalize the sale of the investment.

Exercise 14-5 *Comparing the cost and equity methods* *(L.O. 1,2)*

Electrix Corporation paid $160,000 for a 25 percent investment in the common stock of Bluebonnet, Inc. For the first year, Bluebonnet reported net income of $84,000 and at year end declared and paid cash dividends of $16,000. On the balance sheet date the market value of Electrix's investment in Bluebonnet stock was $153,000.

Required

1. On Electrix's books, journalize the purchase of the investment, recognition of Electrix's portion of Bluebonnet's net income, and receipt of dividends from Bluebonnet under the equity method, which is appropriate for these circumstances.
2. Repeat Requirement 1 but follow the cost method for comparison purposes only.
3. Show the amount that Electrix would report for the investment on its year-end balance sheet under the two methods.

Exercise 14-6 *Completing a consolidation work sheet with minority interest* *(L.O. 3,4)*

Liquid Gas Corp. owns an 80 percent interest in Nino, Inc. Complete the following consolidation work sheet.

Assets	Liquid Gas Corp.	Nino, Inc.
Cash	$ 19,000	$ 14,000
Accounts receivable, net	82,000	53,000
Note receivable from Liquid Gas	—	12,000
Inventory	114,000	77,000
Investment in Nino	80,000	—
Plant assets, net	186,000	129,000
Other assets	22,000	8,000
Total	$503,000	$293,000
Liabilities and Stockholders' Equity		
Accounts payable	$ 44,000	$ 26,000
Notes payable	47,000	36,000
Other liabilities	52,000	131,000
Minority interest	—	—
Common stock	200,000	80,000
Retained earnings	160,000	20,000
Total	$503,000	$293,000

Exercise 14-7 *Elimination entries under the consolidation method* *(L.O. 4)*

Assume on December 31 that Shearson Financial Consultants, a 100 percent-owned subsidiary of American Express Company, had the following owners' equity:

Common Stock	$200,000
Retained Earnings	160,000

Assume further that American Express's cost of its investment in Shearson was $360,000 and that Shearson owed American Express $45,000 on a note.

Required

Give the work sheet entry in general journal form to eliminate (a) the investment of American Express and the stockholders' equity of Shearson and (b) the note receivable of American Express and note payable of Shearson.

Exercise 14-8 *Recording short-term bond investment transactions* *(L.O. 5)*

On June 30 Statistical Research, Inc., paid 92¼ for 8 percent bonds of Erdman Company as a short-term investment. The maturity value of the bonds is $20,000, and they pay interest on March 31 and September 30. Record Statistical Research's purchase of the bond investment, the receipt of semiannual interest on September 30, and the accrual of interest revenue on December 31.

Exercise 14-9 *Recording long-term bond investment transactions* *(L.O. 5)*

Assume the Erdman Company bonds in the preceding exercise are purchased as a long-term investment on June 30, 19X3. The bonds mature on September 30, 19X7.

Required

a. Using the straight-line method of amortizing the discount, journalize all transactions on the bonds for 19X3.
b. How much more interest revenue would the investor record in 19X3 for a long-term investment than for a short-term investment in these bonds? What accounts for this difference?

Exercise 14-10 *Journalizing foreign-currency transactions* *(L.O. 6)*

Journalize the following foreign-currency transactions:

Nov. 17 Purchased goods on account from a Japanese company. The price was 200,000 yen, and the exchange rate of the yen was $.0080.
Dec. 16 Paid the Japanese supplier when the exchange rate was $.0081.
    19 Sold merchandise on account to a French company at a price of 60,000 French francs. The exchange rate was $.16.
    31 Adjusted for the decrease in the value of the franc, which had an exchange rate of $.155.
Jan. 14 Collected from the French company. The exchange rate was $.17.

Exercise 14-11 *Translating a foreign-currency balance sheet into dollars* *(L.O. 7)*

Translate the balance sheet of Munson, Inc.'s Italian subsidiary into dollars. When Munson acquired the foreign subsidiary, an Italian lira was worth $.00090. The current exchange rate is $.00085. During the period when retained earnings were earned, the average exchange rate was $.00088.

Before performing the translation operation, predict whether the translation adjustment will be positive (a gain) or negative (a loss). Explain your answer.

	Lire
Assets	500,000,000
Liabilities	300,000,000
Stockholders' equity:	
Common stock	100,000,000
Retained earnings	100,000,000
	500,000,000

Problems

Problem 14-1A *Journalizing transactions under the cost and equity methods* **(L.O. 1,2)**

Iowa Beef Packers owns numerous investments in the stock of other companies. Assume Iowa Beef Packers completed the following investment transactions:

19X6

Jan. 2 Purchased 24,000 shares, which exceeds 20 percent, of the common stock of Agribusiness, Inc., at total cost of $810,000.

Mar. 16 Purchased 800 shares of Apex Company common stock as a short-term investment, paying 41½ per share plus brokerage commission of $800.

July 1 Purchased 8,000 additional shares of Agribusiness common stock at cost of $300,000.

Aug. 9 Received annual cash dividend of $.90 per share (total of $28,800) on the Agribusiness investment.

30 Received semiannual cash dividend of $.60 per share on the Apex investment.

Sep. 14 Received 200 shares of Apex common stock in a 25 percent stock dividend.

Oct. 22 Sold 400 shares of Apex stock for 30¼ per share less brokerage commission of $450.

Dec. 31 Received annual report from Agribusiness, Inc. Net income for the year was $440,000. Of this amount, Iowa Beef Packers' proportion is 35 percent.

19X7

Jan. 14 Sold 4,000 shares of Agribusiness stock for net cash of $141,000.

Required

Record the transactions in the general journal of Iowa Beef Packers.

Problem 14-2A *Applying the cost method (with LCM) and the equity method* **(L.O. 1,2)**

The beginning balance sheet of Ranco Incorporated recently included:

Investments in Affiliates $10,984,000

Investments in Affiliates refers to investments accounted for by the equity method. Ranco included its short-term investments among the current assets. Assume the company completed the following investment transactions during the year:

Jan. 2 Purchased 2,000 shares of common stock as a short-term investment, paying 12¼ per share plus brokerage commission of $1,000.

Jan. 5 Purchased new long-term investment in affiliate at cost of $540,000. Debit Investments in Affiliates.

Apr. 21 Received semiannual cash dividend of $.75 per share on the short-term investment purchased January 2.

May 17 Received cash dividend of $47,000 from affiliated company.

July 16 Sold 1,600 shares of the short-term investment (purchased on January 2) for 10⅛ per share less brokerage commission of $720.

Sep. 8 Sold other short-term investments for $136,000 less brokerage commission of $5,100. Cost of these investments was $120,600.

Nov. 17 Received cash dividend of $49,000 from affiliated company.

Dec. 31 Received annual reports from affiliated companies. Their total net income for the year was $550,000. Of this amount, Ranco's proportion is 22 percent.

Required

1. Record the transactions in the general journal of Ranco Incorporated.
2. Post entries to the Investments in Affiliates T-account and determine its balance at December 31.
3. Assume the beginning balance of Short-Term Investments was cost of $293,600. Post entries to the Short-Term Investments T-account and determine its balance at December 31.
4. Assuming the market value of the short-term investment portfolio is $190,300 at December 31, show how Ranco would report short-term investments and investments in affiliates on the ending balance sheet. Use the following format:

Cash .... $XXX
Short-term investments, at lower of cost or market (__?__, $__) ..
Accounts receivable XXX

Total current assets XXX
Investments in affiliates ....

Problem 14-3A *Preparing a consolidated balance sheet; no minority interest* **(L.O. 3,4)**

Bethlehem Corp. paid $166,000 to acquire all the common stock of Massada, Inc., and Massada owes Bethlehem $81,000 on a note payable. Immediately after the purchase on June 30, 19X3, the two companies' balance sheets were as follows:

Assets	Bethlehem Corp.	Massada, Inc.
Cash	$ 21,000	$ 20,000
Accounts receivable, net	91,000	42,000
Note receivable from Massada	81,000	—
Inventory	145,000	114,000
Investment in Massada	166,000	—
Plant assets, net	178,000	219,000
Total	$682,000	$395,000

Liabilities and Stockholders' Equity		
Accounts payable	$ 54,000	$ 49,000
Notes payable	177,000	149,000
Other liabilities	29,000	31,000
Common stock	274,000	118,000
Retained earnings...............	148,000	48,000
Total	$682,000	$395,000

. Prepare a consolidation work sheet.

. Prepare the consolidated balance sheet on June 30, 19X3. Show total assets, total liabilities, and total stockholders' equity. It is not necessary to classify assets and liabilities as current and long-term.

roblem 14-4A   *Preparing a consolidated balance sheet with minority interest*   (L.O. 3,4)

On March 22, 19X4, Titanium Corporation paid $180,000 to purchase 80 per-ent of the common stock of Millbank Company, and Millbank owes Titanium 67,000 on a note payable. Immediately after the purchase, the two compa-ies' balance sheets were as follows:

Assets	Titanium Corporation	Millbank Company
Cash	$ 41,000	$ 43,000
Accounts receivable, net..........	86,000	75,000
Note receivable from Millbank	67,000	—
Inventory	128,000	81,000
Investment in Millbank...........	180,000	—
Plant assets, net	277,000	168,000
Total	$779,000	$367,000

Liabilities and Stockholders' Equity		
Accounts payable	$ 72,000	$ 65,000
Notes payable	301,000	67,000
Other liabilities	11,000	10,000
Minority interest................	—	—
Common stock	141,000	160,000
Retained earnings...............	254,000	65,000
Total	$779,000	$367,000

Required

1. Prepare a consolidation work sheet.

2. Prepare the consolidated balance sheet on March 22, 19X4. Show total assets, total liabilities, and total stockholders' equity. It is not necessary to classify assets and liabilities as current and long-term.

Problem 14-5A   *Accounting for a long-term bond investment purchased at a premium* (L.O. 5)

Financial institutions such as insurance companies and pension plans hold Large quantities of bond investments. Suppose Southwestern Mutual Life pur-chases $600,000 of 9 percent bonds of Texell Corporation for 101 on July 1, 19X1. These bonds pay interest on March 1 and September 1 each year. They mature on March 1, 19X8.

Required

1. Journalize Southwestern Mutual's purchase of the bonds as a long-term investment on July 1, 19X1, receipt of cash interest and amortization of premium on September 1, 19X1, and accrual of interest revenue and amor-tization of premium at December 31, 19X1. Assume the amortization amounts are immaterial, so the straight-line method is appropriate for amortizing premium.

2. Show all financial statement effects of this long-term bond investment at December 31, 19X1. Assume a multiple-step income statement.

3. Repeat Requirement 2 under the assumption that Southwestern Mutual purchased these bonds as a short-term investment.

Note: Problem 14-6A is based on Appendix A.

Problem 14-6A *Computing the cost of a bond investment and journalizing its transactions* **(L.O. 5)**

On December 31, 19X1, when the market interest rate is 12 percent, an investor purchases $500,000 of Advanced Systems 6-year, 11.4 percent bonds at issuance. Determine the cost (present value) of this long-term bond investment. Journalize the purchase on December 31, 19X1, the first semiannual interest receipt on June 30, 19X2, and the year-end interest receipt on December 31, 19X2. The investor uses the effective-interest amortization method. Prepare a schedule for amortizing the discount on bond investment through December 31, 19X2. If necessary, refer to Chapter 11 and Appendix A.

Problem 14-7A *Journalizing foreign-currency transactions and reporting the transaction gain or loss; translating a foreign currency balance sheet* **(L.O. 6,7)**

Part A. Suppose Coca-Cola Company completed the following transactions.

Dec. 4 Sold soft-drink syrup on account to a Mexican company for $36,000. The exchange rate of the Mexican peso is $.0004, and the customer agrees to pay in dollars.

13 Purchased inventory on account from a Canadian company at a price of Canadian $100,000. The exchange rate of the Canadian dollar is $.80, and payment will be in Canadian dollars.

20 Sold goods on account to an English firm for 70,000 British pounds. Payment will be in pounds, and the exchange rate of the pound is $1.80.

27 Collected from the Mexican company.

31 Adjusted the accounts for changes in foreign-currency exchange rates. Current rates: Canadian dollar, $.81; English pound, $1.79.

Jan. 21 Paid the Canadian company. The exchange rate of the Canadian dollar is $.78.

Feb. 17 Collected from the English firm. The exchange rate of the British pound is $1.77.

Record these transactions in Coca-Cola's general journal, and show how to report the transaction gain or loss on the income statement.

Part B. Translate the foreign-currency balance sheet of the Japanese subsidiary of Rotan Mosby, Inc., into dollars. When Rotan Mosby acquired this subsidiary, the Japanese yen was worth $.0064. The current exchange rate is $.0073. During the period when the subsidiary earned its income, the average exchange rate was $.0069 per yen.

Before performing the translation calculations, indicate whether Rotan Mosby has experienced a positive or a negative translation adjustment. State whether the adjustment is a gain or a loss, and show where it is reported in the financial statements.

	Yen
Assets	300,000,000
Liabilities	80,000,000
Stockholders' equity:	
Common stock	20,000,000
Retained earnings	200,000,000
	300,000,000

Problem 14-1B   *Journalizing transactions under the cost and equity methods*   **(L.O. 1,2)**

Ford Motor Company owns numerous investments in the stock of other companies. Assume Ford completed the following investment transactions:

19X4

Mar. 19   Purchased 1,000 shares of ROX Corporation common stock as a short-term investment, paying 22½ per share plus brokerage commission of $700.

Apr. 1   Purchased 8,000 shares, which exceeds 20 percent, of the common stock of MIC Company at total cost of $720,000.

July 1   Purchased 1,600 additional shares of MIC Company common stock at cost of $140,000.

Aug. 14   Received semiannual cash dividend of $.75 per share on the ROX investment.

Sep. 15   Received semiannual cash dividend of $1.40 per share on the MIC investment.

Oct. 12   Received ROX common stock in a 10 percent stock dividend. Round the new cost per share to the nearest cent.

Nov. 9   Sold 200 shares of ROX stock for 28¼ per share, less brokerage commission of $175.

Dec. 31   Received annual report from MIC Company. Net income for the year was $350,000. Of this amount, Ford's proportion is 21.25 percent

19X5

Feb. 6   Sold 1,920 shares of MIC stock for net cash of $189,700.

Required

Record the transactions in the general journal of Ford Motor Company.

Problem 14-2B   *Applying the cost method (with LCM) and the equity method*   **(L.O. 1,2)**

The beginning balance sheet of Fairchild Industries, Inc., recently included:

Investments in Affiliates $84,057,000

Investments in Affiliates refers to investments accounted for by the equity method. Fairchild included its short-term investments among the current assets. Assume the company completed the following investment transactions during the year:

Jan. 3   Purchased 5,000 shares of common stock as a short-term investment, paying 9¼ per share plus brokerage commission of $1,350.

4   Purchased new long-term investment in affiliate at cost of $408,000. Debit Investments in Affiliates.

May 14   Received semiannual cash dividend of $.82 per share on the short-term investment purchased January 3.

June 15   Received cash dividend of $27,000 from affiliated company.

Aug. 28   Sold 1,000 shares of the short-term investment (purchased on January 3) for 10½ per share, less brokerage commission of $750.

Oct. 24   Sold other short-term investments for $226,000, less brokerage commission of $11,400. Cost of these investments was $243,100.

Dec. 15   Received cash dividend of $29,000 from affiliated company.

31   Received annual reports from affiliated companies. Their total net income for the year was $620,000. Of this amount, Fairchild's proportion is 30 percent.

Required

1. Record the transactions in the general journal of Fairchild Industries.
2. Post entries to the Investments in Affiliates T-account, and determine its balance at December 31.
3. Assume the beginning balance of Short-Term Investments was cost of $356,400. Post entries to the Short-Term Investments T-account and determine its balance at December 31.
4. Assuming the market value of the short-term investment portfolio is $142,600 at December 31, show how Fairchild Industries would report short-term investments and investments in affiliates on the ending balance sheet. Use the following format:

Cash	$XXX
Short-term investments, at lower of cost or market (? , $_) ..	_____
Accounts receivable.......................................	XXX
⌇	⌇
Total current assets	XXX
Investments in affiliates	_____

Problem 14-3B *Preparing a consolidated balance sheet; no minority interest* **(L.O. 3,4)**

Polski Corporation paid $179,000 to acquire all the common stock of Smackover, Inc., and Smackover owes Polski $55,000 on a note payable. Immediately after the purchase on May 31, 19X7, the two companies' balance sheets were as follows:

Assets	Polski Corporation	Smackover, Inc.
Cash	$ 18,000	$ 32,000
Accounts receivable, net	64,000	43,000
Note receivable from Smackover ..	55,000	—
Inventory	171,000	153,000
Investment in Smackover	179,000	—
Plant assets, net	205,000	138,000
Total	$692,000	$366,000

Liabilities and Stockholders' Equity		
Accounts payable	$ 76,000	$ 37,000
Notes payable	196,000	123,000
Other liabilities	44,000	27,000
Common stock	282,000	90,000
Retained earnings...............	94,000	89,000
Total	$692,000	$366,000

Required

1. Prepare a consolidation work sheet.
2. Prepare the consolidated balance sheet on May 31, 19X7. Show total assets, total liabilities, and total stockholders' equity. It is not necessary to classify assets and liabilities as current and long-term.

Problem 14-4B *Preparing a consolidated balance sheet with goodwill* **(L.O. 3,4)**

On August 17, 19X8, Concrete Products Corp. paid $229,000 to purchase all the common stock of Travelers, Inc., and Travelers owes Concrete Products $42,000 on a note payable. Immediately after the purchase, the two companies' balance sheets were as follows:

Assets	Concrete Products Corp.	Travelers, Inc.
Cash	$ 23,000	$ 37,000
Accounts receivable, net	104,000	54,000
Note receivable from Travelers	42,000	—
Inventory	213,000	170,000
Investment in Travelers	229,000	—
Plant assets, net	197,000	175,000
Goodwill........................	—	—
Total	$808,000	$436,000
Liabilities and Stockholders' Equity		
Accounts payable	$119,000	$ 77,000
Notes payable	223,000	71,000
Other liabilities	33,000	88,000
Common stock	219,000	113,000
Retained earnings...............	214,000	87,000
Total	$808,000	$436,000

Required

1. Prepare a consolidation work sheet.
2. Prepare the consolidated balance sheet on August 17, 19X8. Show total assets, total liabilities, and total stockholders' equity. It is not necessary to classify assets and liabilities as current and long-term.

Problem 14-5B *Accounting for a long-term bond investment purchased at a discount* *(L.O. 5)*

Financial institutions such as insurance companies and pension plans hold large quantities of bond investments. Suppose Aetna Life Insurance Company of New York purchases $500,000 of 8 percent bonds of General Motors Corporation for 97 on March 31, 19X0. These bonds pay interest on January 31 and July 31 each year. They mature on July 31, 19X8.

Required

1. Journalize Aetna's purchase of the bonds as a long-term investment on March 31, 19X0, receipt of cash interest and amortization of discount on July 31, 19X0, and accrual of interest revenue and amortization of discount at December 31, 19X0. Assume the amortization amounts are immaterial, so the straight-line method is appropriate for amortizing discount.
2. Show all financial statement effects of this long-term bond investment at December 31, 19X0. Assume a multiple-step income statement.
3. Repeat Requirement 2 under the assumption that Aetna purchased these bonds as a short-term investment.

Note: Problem 14-6B is based on Appendix A.

Problem 14-6B *Computing the cost of a bond investment and journalizing its transactions* **(L.O. 5)**

On December 31, 19X1, when the market interest rate is 10 percent, an investor purchases $400,000 of Jax Gold 10-year, 12.5 percent bonds at issuance. Determine the cost (present value) of the bond investment. Assume that the investment is long-term. Journalize the purchase on December 31, 19X1, the first seminannual interest receipt on June 30, 19X2, and the year-end interest receipt on December 31, 19X2. The investor uses the effective-interest amortization method. Prepare a schedule for amortizing the premium on the bond investment through December 31, 19X2. If necessary, refer to Chapter 11 and Appendix A.

Problem 14-7B *Journalizing foreign-currency transactions and reportig ther transaction gain or loss; translating a foreign-currency balance sheet* **(L.O. 6,7)**

Part A. Suppose Xerox Corporation completed the following transactions.

Dec. 1 Sold a photocopy machine on account to Pirelli Tire Company for $70,000. The exchange rate of the Italian lira is $.0007, and Pirelli agrees to pay in dollars.

10 Purchased supplies on account from a Canadian company at a price of Canadian $50,000. The exchange rate of the Canadian dollar is $.80, and payment will be in Canadian dollars.

17 Sold a photocopy machine on account to an English firm for 100,000 British pounds. Payment will be in pounds, and the exchange rate of the pound is $1.80.

22 Collected from Pirelli.

31 Adjusted the accounts for changes in foreign-currency exchange rates. Current rates: Canadian dollar, $.82; English pound, $1.78.

Jan. 18 Paid the Canadian company. The exchange rate of the Canadian dollar is $.77.

24 Collected from the English firm. The exchange rate of the British pound is $1.79.

Record these transactions in Xerox's general journal, and show how to report the transaction gain or loss on the income statement.

Part B. Translate the foreign-currency balance sheet of the Danish subsidiary of Millbank, Inc., into dollars. When Millbank acquired this subsidiary, the Danish krone was worth $.17. The current exchange rate is $.16. During the period when the subsidiary earned its income, the average exchange rate was $.18 per krone.

Before performing the translation calculations, indicate whether Millbank has experienced a positive or a negative translation adjustment. State whether the adjustment is a gain or a loss. Explain your answer.

	Krone
Assets	3,000,000
Liabilities	1,000,000
Stockholders' equity:	
Common stock	1,000,000
Retained earnings	1,000,000
	3,000,000

Extending Your Knowledge

Decision Problems

1. Understanding the Cost and Equity Methods of Accounting for Investments (L.O. 1,2)

Bruce Joyce is the accountant for Dunrobin Inc. whose year end is December 31. The company made two investments during the first week of January 19X7. Both investments are to be held for at least five years. Information about the investments follows:

a.   Dunrobin purchased forty percent of the common stock of Lonesome Dove, Inc., for its book value of $200,000. During the year ended December 31, 19X7, Lonesome Dove earned $85,000 and paid a total dividend of $30,000.

b.   Ten percent of the common stock of M-J Western Music Inc. was purchased for its book value of $50,000. During the year ended December 31, 19X7, M-J paid Dunrobin a dividend of $3,000. M-J earned a profit of $85,000 for that period.

Bruce has come to you as his auditor to ask how to account for the investments. Dunrobin has never had such investments before. You attempt to explain the proper accounting to him by indicating that different accounting methods apply to different situations.

Required

Help Bruce understand by:

1.   Describing the methods of accounting applicable to these investments.
2.   Identifying which method should be used to account for the investments in Lonesome Dove and M-J Western Music.

2. Understanding the Consolidation Method for Investments and Accounting for International Operations   (L.O. 3,4,7)

Srikant Datar inherited some investments, and he has received the annual reports of the companies in which the funds are invested. The financial statements of the companies are puzzling to Srikant, and he asks you the following questions:

1.   The companies label their financial statements as *consolidated* balance sheet, *consolidated* income statement, and so on. What are consolidated financial statements?
2.   Notes to the statements indicate that "certain intercompany transactions, loans, and other accounts have been eliminated in preparing the consolidated financial statements." Why does a company eliminate transactions, loans, and accounts? Srikant states that he thought a transaction was a transaction and that a loan obligated a company to pay real money. He wonders if the company is juggling the books to defraud the IRS.
3.   The balance sheet lists the asset Goodwill. What is Goodwill? Does this mean that the company's stock has increased in value?
4.   The stockholders' equity section of the balance sheet reports Translation Adjustments. Srikant asks what is being translated and why this item is negative.

Respond to each of Srikant's questions.

Ethical Issue

Montpelier Company owns 18 percent of the voting stock of Nashua Corporation. The remainder of the Nashua stock is held by numerous investors with small holdings. Ralph Knox, president of Montpelier and a member of Nashua's board of directors, heavily influences Nashua's policies.

Under the cost method of accounting for investments, Montpelier's net income increases as it receives dividends from Nashua. Montpelier pays President Knox a bonus computed as a percentage of Montpelier's net income. Therefore, Knox can control his personal bonus to a certain extent by influencing Nashua's dividends.

A recession occurs in 19X0, and corporate income is low. Knox uses his power to have Nashua Corporation pay a large cash dividend. This action requires Nashua to borrow so heavily that it may lead to financial difficulty.

Required

1. In getting Nashua to pay the large cash dividend, is Knox acting within his authority as a member of the Nashua board of directors? Are Knox's actions ethical? Whom can his actions harm?
2. Discuss how using the equity method of accounting for investments would decrease Knox's potential for manipulating his bonus.

Financial Statement Problems

1. Investments in Stock (L.O. 1,2,3)

The Goodyear Tire & Rubber Company financial statements and related notes in Appendix C describe some of the company's investment activity. The balance sheet reveals that Goodyear's equity-method investment account is titled Investment in Affiliates, at Equity. The equity-method investment revenue could be included as part of Other Income.

Required

1. Journalize the following assumed transactions of 1991. Use Goodyear account titles, and show amounts in millions rounded to the nearest $100,000 (for example, $101.4 million).
   a. Equity-method investment revenue of $41.4 million. Label this account Equity in Earnings of Affiliates.
   b. Receipt of cash dividends of $45.9 million from affiliated companies. Insert the December 31, 1990, balance in Investment in Affiliates, and post the entries to this account. Compare its balance to the amount shown on the balance sheet at December 31, 1991.
2. What were Goodyear's balances of short-term investments (short-term securities) at December 31, 1990, and December 31, 1991? What method is used to account for these investments? Make a single journal entry for 1991 to account for the change in this account's balance from the beginning to the end of the year.
3. What is the only word appearing in the title of *all* the Goodyear financial statements? What does this word indicate?

4. Goodyear's financial statements indicate whether the company owns 100 percent or less of its consolidated subsidiaries. Which is it, and what is the evidence supporting your answer?

2. Investments in Stock (L.O. 1,2,3)

Obtain the annual report of an actual company of your choosing. Answer these questions about the company. Concentrate on the current year in the annual report you select.

1. Many companies refer to other companies in which they own equity-method investments as *affiliated companies*. This signifies the close relationship between the two entities even though the investor does not own a controlling interest.

   Does the company have equity-method investments? Cite the evidence. If present, what were the balances in the investment account at the beginning and the end of the current year? If the company had no equity-method investments, skip the next question, and go to number 3.

2. Scan the income statement. If equity-method investments are present, what amount of revenue (or income) did the company earn on the investments during the current year? Scan the statement of cash flows. What amount of dividends did the company receive during the current year from companies in which it held equity-method investments? Note: The amount of dividends received may not be disclosed. If not, you can still compute the amount of dividends received—from the following T-account.

Investments, at Equity

Beg. bal. (from balance sheet)	W		
Equity-method revenue (from income statement)	X	**Dividends received (unknown; must compute)**	**Y**
End. bal. (from balance sheet)	Z		

3. The company probably owns some consolidated subsidiaries. You can tell whether the parent company owns 100 percent or less of the subsidiaries. Examine the income statement and the balance sheet to determine whether there are any minority interests. If so, what does that fact indicate?

4. The stockholders' equity section of most balance sheets lists Foreign Currency Translation Adjustment or a similar account title. A positive amount signifies a gain, and a negative amount indicates a loss. The change in this account balance from the beginning of the year to the end of the year signals whether the U.S. dollar was strong or weak during the year in comparison to the foreign currencies. For the company you are analyzing, was the dollar strong or weak during the current year?

Comprehensive Problem for Part Four

Accounting for Corporate Transactions

North American Industries' corporate charter authorizes the company to issue 500,000 shares of $1 par value common stock and 100,000 shares of 5 percent, $10 par value preferred stock. During the first quarter of operations, North American completed the following selected transactions:

Oct. 1 Issued 75,000 shares of common stock for cash of $6 per share.

2 Signed a capital lease for equipment. The lease requires a down payment of $50,000, plus 20 quarterly lease payments of $10,000. Present value of the future lease payments is $135,900 at an annual interest rate of 16 percent.

5 Issued 2,000 shares of preferred stock to attorneys who helped organize the corporation. Their bill listed legal services of $22,000.

22 Received land from the county as an incentive for locating in Nashville. Fair market value of the land was $150,000.

30 Purchased 5,000 shares (20 percent) of the outstanding common stock of Newbold Corp. as a long-term investment, $85,000.

Nov. 1 Issued $200,000 of 9 percent, 10-year bonds payable at 94.

14 Purchased short-term investments in the common stocks of Coca-Cola, $22,000, and Goodyear Tire, $31,000.

19 Experienced an extraordinary flood loss of inventory that cost $21,000. Cash received from the insurance company was $8,000.

20 Purchased 2,000 shares of the company's common stock for the treasury. Cost was $5 per share.

Dec. 1 Received cash dividends of $1,100 on the Coca-Cola investment.

16 Sold 1,000 shares of the treasury stock for cash of $6.25 per share.

29 Received a report from Newbold Corp. indicating that net income for November and December was $70,000.

30 Sold merchandise on account, $716,000. Cost of the goods was $439,000. Operating expenses totaled $174,000, with $166,000 of this amount paid in cash. North American uses a perpetual inventory system.

31 Accrued interest and amortized discount (straight-line method) on the bonds payable.

31 Accrued interest on the capital lease liability.

31 Depreciated the equipment acquired by the capital lease. The company uses the double-declining-balance method.

31 Market values of short-term investments: Coca-Cola stock, $24,000, and the Goodyear stock, $30,000.

31 Accrued income tax expense of $20,000.

31 Closed all revenues, expenses, and losses to Retained Earnings in a single closing entry.

31 Declared a quarterly cash dividend of $.125 per share on the preferred stock. Record date is January 11, with payment scheduled for January 19.

Required

1. Record these transactions in the general journal. Explanations are not required.

2. Prepare a single-step income statement for the quarter ended December 31, including earnings per share. Income tax expense of $20,000 should be reported as follows: Income tax expense of $24,000 is used in arriving at income before extraordinary items. The tax effect of the extraordinary loss is an income tax saving of $4,000.

3. Report the liabilities and the stockholders' equity as they would appear on the balance sheet at December 31.

Chapter *15*

Statement of Cash Flows

For decades we've made the most fundamental and far-reaching economic decisions on the basis of that supposedly magic number, the bottom line.

As investors, we buy and sell stocks depending on whether a company's earnings are growing or shrinking. As managers, we decide what investments to make based largely on what earnings the projects will yield.

We're making a big mistake. Reported earnings have become virtually worthless in terms of their ability to tell us what's really going on at a company.

Take Prime Motor Inns, until a few months ago the world's second-largest hotel operator. Last year Prime reported a healthy net income of $77 million—18 percent of revenues—up nearly 15 percent from the year before. In September Prime filed for Chapter 11 bankruptcy.

What happened? Could the bankruptcy filing have been foreseen? Prime's problem was that it didn't have enough cash coming in. . . . According to banking consultants Financial Proformas, Inc., Prime had a $15 million cash *outflow* from operations in 1989—the year it reported a $77 million profit—compared with a positive cash flow of $58 million the year before.

Source: Dana Wechsler Linden, *Forbes*, November 12, 1990, p. 106. Used with permission of Forbes, Inc.

Income statements and balance sheets are anchored to the accrual basis of accounting for measuring performance and financial position. Another major statement, the statement of cash flows, is required by GAAP to complete the picture of performance and position.

Consider some common questions asked by managers, investors, and creditors. What were the company's sources of cash during the period? Did operations—buying and selling the company's major products—generate the bulk of its cash receipts, or did the business have to sell off plant assets to keep the cash balance at an acceptable level? Did the company have to borrow heavily during the period? How did the entity spend its cash? Was it busy paying off debts, or were cash disbursements devoted to expanding the business? This chapter discusses the statement of cash flows. As its title implies, the statement of cash flows helps explain a company's performance in generating cash.

Cash flows are cash receipts and cash payments (disbursements). The **statement of cash flows** reports cash receipts and cash disbursements classified according to the entity's major activities: operating, investing, and financing. The statement reports a net cash inflow or a net cash outflow for each activity and for the overall business.

Purposes of the Statement of Cash Flows

The statement of cash flows is designed to fulfill the following purposes:

1. *To predict future cash flows.* Cash, not reported accounting income, pays the bills. In many cases, a business's sources and uses of cash do not change dramatically from year to year. If so, past cash receipts and disbursements are a reasonably good predictor of future cash receipts and disbursements.

2. *To evaluate management decisions.* If managers make wise investment decisions, their businesses prosper. If they make unwise decisions, the businesses suffer. The statement of cash flows reports the company's investment in plant and equipment and thus gives investors and creditors cash-flow information for evaluating managers' decisions. A classic example is Montgomery Ward's decision shortly after World War II *not* to expand the business. Ward's top management expected a recession and decided to play it safe until the United States economy settled down after the war. Sears, Roebuck, on the other hand, predicted a strong economy and went full speed ahead. Sears's decision proved better, and Montgomery Ward fell significantly behind Sears.

3. *To determine the ability to pay dividends to stockholders and interest and principal to creditors.* Stockholders are interested in receiving dividends on their investments in the company's stock. Creditors want to receive their interest and principal amounts on time. The statement of cash flows helps investors and creditors predict whether the business can make these payments.

4. *To show the relationship of net income to changes in the business's cash.* Usually, cash and net income move together. High levels of income tend to lead to increases in cash, and vice versa. However, a company's cash balance can decrease when net income is high, and cash can increase when income is low. The failures of companies such as Prime Motor Inns, which was earning net income but had insufficient cash, have pointed to the need for cash flow information.

Basic Concept of the Statement of Cash Flows _____

The balance sheet reports the cash balance at the end of the period. By examining two consecutive balance sheets, you can tell whether cash increased or decreased during the period. However, the balance sheet does not indicate *why* the cash balance changed. The income statement reports revenues, expenses, and net income—clues about the sources and uses of cash—but it still does not tell *why* cash increased or decreased.

The statement of cash flows reports the entity's cash receipts and cash payments during the period—where cash came from and how it was spent. It explains the *causes* for the change in the cash balance. This information cannot be learned solely from the other financial statements.

The balance sheet is the only financial statement that is dated as of the end of the period. The income statement and the statement of retained earnings cover the period from beginning to end. The statement of cash flows also covers the entire period and therefore is dated "For the Year Ended XXX" or "For the Month Ended XXX." Its timing and its position among the statements is shown in this diagram:

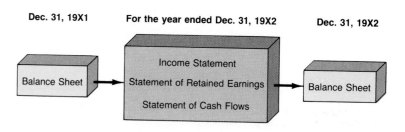

Operating, Investing, and Financing Activities _____

A good way to evaluate a business is based on three types of business activities. After the business is up and running, operations are the most important activity, followed by investing activities and financing activities. The statement of cash flows in Exhibit 15-1 shows how cash receipts and disbursements are divided into operating activities, investing activities, and financing activities. As Exhibit 15-1 illustrates, each set of activities (operating, investing, and financing) includes both cash inflows—receipts—and cash outflows—payments. Outflows are shown in parentheses to indicate that payments must be

EXHIBIT 15-1   Statement of Cash Flows

Anchor Corporation
Statement of Cash Flows
For the Year Ended December 31, 19X2
Increase (Decrease) in Cash and Cash Equivalents
(amounts in thousands)

Cash flows from operating activities:
Receipts:
Collections from customers .... $ 271
Interest received on notes receivable 10
Dividends received on investments in stock 9
   Total cash receipts .... $ 290
Payments:
To suppliers .... $(133)
To employees .... (58)
For interest..................................... (16)
For income tax .... (15)
   Total cash payments .... (222)
   Net cash inflow from operating activities....... 68
Cash flows from investing activities:
Acquisition of plant assets .... $(306)
Loan to another company .... (11)
Proceeds from sale of plant assets 62
   Net cash outflow from investing activities ...... (255)
Cash flows from financing activities:
Proceeds from issuance of common stock .... $ 101
Proceeds from issuance of long-term debt 94
Payment of long-term debt .... (11)
Payment of dividends .... (17)
   Net cash inflow from financing activities 167
Net decrease in cash .... $ (20)
Cash balance, December 31, 19X1 42
Cash balance, December 31, 19X2 .... $ 22

subtracted. Each section of the statement reports a net cash inflow or a net cash outflow.

Operating activities create revenues and expenses in the entity's major line of business. Therefore, operating activities affect the income statement, which reports the accrual-basis effects of operating activities. The statement of cash flows reports their impact on cash. The largest cash inflow from operations is the collection of cash from customers. Less important inflows are receipts of interest on loans and dividends on stock investments. The operating cash outflows include payments to suppliers and to employees and payments for interest and taxes. Anchor's net cash inflow from operating activities is $68,000. A large positive operating cash flow is a good sign about a company. In the long run operations must be the main source of a business's cash.

Investing activities increase and decrease the assets that the business has to work with. A purchase or sale of a plant asset like land, a building, or equipment is an investing activity, as is the purchase or sale of an investment in stock or bonds of another company. On the statement of cash flows, investing activities include more than the buying and selling of assets that are classified

OBJECTIVE 2
Distinguish among operating, investing, and financing activities

as investments on the balance sheet. Making a loan—an investing activity because the loan creates a receivable for the lender—and collecting on the loan are also reported as investing activities on the statement of cash flows. The acquisition of plant assets dominates the company's investing activities, which produce a net cash outflow of $255,000.

Investments in plant assets lay the foundation for future operations. A company that invests in plant and equipment appears stronger than one that is selling off its plant assets. Why? The latter company may have to sell income-producing assets in order to pay the bills. Its outlook is bleak.

Financing activities obtain the cash from investors and creditors needed to launch and sustain the business. Financing activities include issuing stock, borrowing money by issuing notes and bonds payable, selling treasury stock, and making payments to the stockholders—dividends and purchases of treasury stock. Payments to the creditors include principal payments only. The payment of interest is an operating activity. Financing activities brought in net cash of $167,000. One thing to watch among financing activities is whether the business is borrowing heavily. Excessive borrowing has been the downfall of many companies.

Overall, cash decreased by $20,000 during 19X2. The company began the year with cash of $42,000 and ended with $22,000.

Each of these categories of activities includes both cash receipts and cash disbursements, as shown in Exhibit 15-2. The exhibit lists the more common cash receipts and cash disbursements that appear on the statement of cash flows.

EXHIBIT 15-2 *Cash Receipts and Disbursements Reported on the Statement of Cash Flows*

Operating Activities	
Cash Receipts	**Cash Disbursements**
Collections from customers	Payments to suppliers
Receipts of interest and dividends on investments	Payments to employees
	Payments of interest and income tax
Other operating receipts	Other operating disbursements

Investing Activities	
Cash Receipts	**Cash Disbursements**
Sale of plant assets	Acquisition of plant assets
Sale of investments that are not cash equivalents	Acquisition of investments that are not cash equivalents
Cash receipts on loans receivable	Making loans

Financing Activities	
Cash Receipts	**Cash Disbursements**
Issuing stock	Purchase of treasury stock
Selling treasury stock	Payment of dividends
Borrowing money	Paying principal amounts of debts

Cash and Cash Equivalents _____

On a statement of cash flows, *Cash* has a broader meaning than just cash on hand and cash in the bank. It includes **cash equivalents,** which are highly liquid short-term investments that can be converted into cash with little delay. Because one reason for holding these investments is their liquidity, they are treated as cash. Examples include money market investments and investments in U.S. Government Treasury bills. Businesses invest their extra cash in these types of liquid assets rather than let it remain idle. Throughout this chapter, the term *cash* refers to cash and cash equivalents.

Interest and Dividends _____

You may be puzzled by the listing of receipts of interest and dividends as operating activities. After all, these cash receipts result from investing activities. Interest comes from investments in loans, and dividends come from investments in stock. Equally puzzling is listing the payment of interest as part of operations. Interest expense results from borrowing money—a financing activity. After much debate, the FASB decided to include these items as part of operations. Why? Mainly because they affect the computation of net income. Interest revenue and dividend revenue increase net income, and interest expense decreases income. Therefore, cash receipts of interest and dividends and cash payments of interest are reported as operating activities on the cash flow statement.

In contrast, notice that dividend payments are not listed among the operating activities of Exhibit 15-2. Why? Because they do not enter the computation of income. Dividend payments are reported in the financing activities section of the cash flow statement because they go to the entity's owners, who finance the business by holding its stock.

Preparing the Statement of Cash Flows: The Direct Method _____

There are two basic ways to present the statement of cash flows. Both methods arrive at the same subtotals for operating activities, investing activities, financing activities, and the net change in cash for the period. They differ only in the manner of showing the cash flows from operating activities. The **direct method**, which the FASB prefers, lists the major categories of operating cash receipts and cash disbursements as shown in Exhibit 15-1. We discuss the indirect method later in the chapter.

> **OBJECTIVE 3**
>
> Prepare a statement of cash flows using the direct method

Illustrative Problem

Let's see how to prepare the statement of cash flows by the direct method in Exhibit 15-1. Suppose Anchor Corporation accountants have assembled the following summary of 19X2 transactions. Those transactions with cash effects are denoted by an asterisk.

Summary of 19X2 Transactions

Operating Activities:

1. Sales on credit, $284,000
*2. Collections from customers, $271,000
3. Interest revenue on notes receivable, $12,000
*4. Collection of interest receivable, $10,000
*5. Cash receipt of dividend revenue on investments in stock, $9,000
6. Cost of goods sold, $150,000
7. Purchases of inventory on credit, $147,000
*8. Payments to suppliers, $133,000
9. Salary and wage expense, $56,000
*10. Payments of salaries and wages, $58,000
11. Depreciation expense, $18,000
12. Other operating expense, $17,000
*13. Interest expense and payments, $16,000
*14. Income tax expense and payments, $15,000

Investing Activities:

*15. Cash payments to acquire plant assets, $306,000
*16. Loan to another company, $11,000
*17. Proceeds from sale of plant assets, $62,000, including $8,000 gain

Financing Activities:

*18. Proceeds from issuance of common stock, $101,000
*19. Proceeds from issuance of long-term debt, $94,000
*20. Payment of long-term debt, $11,000
*21. Declaration and payment of cash dividends, $17,000

These summary transactions give the data for both the income statement and the statement of cash flows. Some transactions affect one statement, some the other. Sales, for example, are reported on the income statement, but cash collections appear on the cash flow statement. Other transactions, such as the cash receipt of dividend revenue, affect both statements. *The statement of cash flows reports only those transactions with cash effects.*

Preparation of the statement of cash flows follows these steps: (1) identify the activities that increased cash and decreased cash—those items with asterisks in the Summary of 19X2 Transactions above; (2) classify each cash increase and each cash decrease as an operating activity, an investing activity, or a financing activity; and (3) identify the cash effect of each transaction. Preparing the statement is discussed in the next section.

Cash Flows from Operating Activities.   Operating cash flows are listed first because they are the largest and most important source of cash for most businesses. The failure of a company's operations to generate the bulk of its cash inflows for an extended period may signal trouble. This is not true of Anchor Corporation in Exhibit 15-1. Its operating activities were the largest source of cash receipts, $290,000.

CASH COLLECTIONS FROM CUSTOMERS. Cash sales bring in cash immediately. Credit sales, however, increase Accounts Receivable but not Cash. Receipts of cash on account are a separate transaction, and only cash receipts are reported on the statement of cash flows. "Collections from customers" on the statement include both cash sales and collections of accounts receivable from credit sales.

Collections from customers are Anchor's major operating source of cash—$271,000—in Exhibit 15-1.

CASH RECEIPTS OF INTEREST. Interest revenue is earned on notes receivable. The income statement reports interest revenue. As the clock ticks, interest accrues, but cash interest is received only on specified dates. Only the cash receipts of interest appear on the statement of cash flows—$10,000 in Exhibit 15-1.

CASH RECEIPTS OF DIVIDENDS. Dividends are earned on investments in stock. Dividend revenue is ordinarily recorded as an income statement item when cash is received. This cash receipt is reported on the statement of cash flows—$9,000 in Exhibit 15-1. (Note that dividends *received* are part of operating activities, but dividends *paid* are a financing activity.)

PAYMENTS TO SUPPLIERS. Payments to suppliers include all cash disbursements for inventory and operating expenses except employee compensation, interest, and income taxes. Suppliers are those entities that provide the business with its inventory and essential services. For example, a clothing store's payments to Levi Strauss, Liz Claiborne, and Reebok are listed as payments to suppliers. A grocery store makes payments to suppliers like Nabisco, Campbell's, and Coca-Cola. Other suppliers provide advertising, utility, and other services that are classified as operating expenses. This category *excludes* payments to employees, payments for interest, and payments for income taxes because these are separate categories of operating cash payments. In Exhibit 15-1, Anchor Corporation reports payments to suppliers of $133,000.

PAYMENTS TO EMPLOYEES. This category includes disbursements for salaries, wages, commissions, and other forms of employee compensation. Accrued amounts are excluded because they have not yet been paid. The income statement reports the expense, including accrued amounts. The statement of cash flows reports only the payments ($58,000) in Exhibit 15-1.

PAYMENTS FOR INTEREST EXPENSE AND INCOME TAX EXPENSE. These cash payments are reported separately from the other expenses. Interest payments show the cash cost of borrowing money. Excessive borrowing can lead to a large amount of interest payments resulting in financial trouble. Donald Trump's casinos and Macy's are examples of businesses that have faced problems because of too much borrowing. Income tax payments also deserve emphasis because of their significant amount. In the Anchor Corporation illustration, these expenses equal the cash payments. Therefore, the same amount appears on the income statement and the statement of cash flows. In actual practice, this is rarely the case. Year-end accruals and other transactions usually cause the expense and cash payment amounts to differ. The cash flow statement reports the cash payments for interest ($16,000) and income tax ($15,000).

DEPRECIATION, DEPLETION, AND AMORTIZATION EXPENSES. These expenses are *not* listed on the statement of cash flows in Exhibit 15-1 because they do not affect cash. For example, depreciation is recorded by debiting the expense and crediting Accumulated Depreciation. No debit or credit to the Cash account occurs.

Cash Flows from Investing Activities. Many analysts regard investing as a critical activity because a company's investments determine its future course. Large purchases of plant assets signal expansion, which is usually a good sign about the company. Low levels of investing activities over a lengthy period mean the business is not replenishing its capital assets. Knowing these cash flows helps investors and creditors evaluate the direction that managers are charting for the business.

CASH PAYMENTS TO ACQUIRE PLANT ASSETS AND INVESTMENTS, AND LOANS TO OTHER COMPANIES. These cash payments are similar because they acquire a noncash asset. The first transaction purchases plant assets, such as land, buildings, and equipment ($306,000) in Exhibit 15-1. In the second transaction, Anchor Corporation makes an $11,000 loan and obtains a note receivable. These are investing activities because the company is investing in assets for use in the business rather than for resale. These transactions have no effect on revenues or expenses and thus are not reported on the income statement. Another transaction in this category—not shown in Exhibit 15-1—is a purchase of an investment in the stocks or bonds of another company.

PROCEEDS FROM THE SALES OF PLANT ASSETS AND INVESTMENTS, AND COLLECTIONS OF LOANS. These transactions are the opposites of acquisitions of plant assets and investments, and making loans. They are cash receipts from investment transactions.

The sale of the plant assets needs explanation. The statement of cash flows reports that Anchor Corporation received $62,000 cash on the sale of plant assets. The income statement shows an $8,000 gain on this transaction. What is the appropriate amount to show on the cash flow statement? It is $62,000, the cash proceeds from the sale. Assuming Anchor sold equipment that cost $64,000 and had accumulated depreciation of $10,000, the journal entry to record this sale is

Cash	62,000	
Accumulated Depreciation....................	10,000	
Equipment		64,000
Gain on Sale of Plant Assets		
(from income statement)		8,000

The analysis indicates that the book value of the equipment was $54,000 ($64,000 − $10,000). However, the book value of the asset sold is not reported on the statement of cash flows. Only the cash proceeds of $62,000 are reported on the statement. For the income statement, only the gain is reported. Since a gain occurred, you may wonder why this cash receipt is not reported as part of operations. Operations consist of buying and selling merchandise or rendering services to earn revenue. Investing activities are the acquisition and disposition of assets used in operations. Therefore, the FASB views the sale of plant assets and the sale of investments as cash inflows from investing activities.

Investors and creditors are often critical of a company that sells large amounts of its plant assets. Such sales may signal an emergency. In other situations, selling off fixed assets may be good news about the company if it is getting rid of an unprofitable division. Whether sales of plant assets are good news or bad news should be evaluated in light of a company's operating and financing characteristics.

Cash Flows from Financing Activities. Cash flows from financing activities include the following:

PROCEEDS FROM ISSUANCE OF STOCK AND DEBT. Readers of the financial statements want to know how the entity obtains its financing. Issuing stock (preferred and common) and debt are two common ways to finance operations. In Exhibit 15-1, Anchor Corporation issued common stock of $101,000 and long-term debt of $94,000.

PAYMENT OF DEBT AND PURCHASES OF THE COMPANY'S OWN STOCK. The payment of debt decreases Cash, which is the opposite of borrowing money. Anchor Corporation reports debt payments of $11,000. Other transactions in this category are purchases of treasury stock and payments to retire the company's stock.

PAYMENT OF CASH DIVIDENDS. The payment of cash dividends decreases Cash and is therefore reported as a cash payment, as illustrated by Anchor's $17,000 payment in Exhibit 15-1. A dividend in another form—a stock dividend, for example—has no effect on Cash and is *not* reported on the cash flow statement.

Focus of the Statement of Cash Flows

The statement of cash flows focuses on the increase or decrease in cash during the period (highlighted in Exhibit 15-1 for emphasis). This check figure is taken from the comparative balance sheet that shows the beginning and ending balances. The cash flow statement, which adds up to the change in cash, shows the reasons why cash changed.

Exhibit 15-1 illustrates how the cash-balance information may be shown at the bottom of a statement of cash flows, a common format. However, the FASB does not require that the beginning and ending cash balances appear on the statement. Because the balance sheet reports these amounts, it is sufficient to show on the statement of cash flows only the change that occurred during the period.

EXHIBIT 15-3 *Income Statement*

Anchor Corporation		
Income Statement		
For the Year Ended December 31, 19X2		
(amounts in thousands)		
Revenues and gains:		
Sales revenue	$284	
Interest revenue	12	
Dividend revenue	9	
Gain on sale of plant assets	8	
Total revenues and gains		$313
Expenses:		
Cost of goods sold	$150	
Salary and wage expense	56	
Depreciation expense	18	
Other operating expense	17	
Interest expense	16	
Income tax expense	15	
Total expenses		272
Net income		$ 41

In our example, cash decreased by $20,000. Readers of the annual report might wonder why cash decreased during a good year. After all, Exhibit 15-3, Anchor's income statement, reports net income of $41,000. When a business is expanding, its cash often declines. Why? Because cash is invested in plant assets, such as land, buildings, and equipment, as reported in the cash flow statement. Conversely, cash may increase in a year when income is low—if the company borrows heavily. The statement of cash flows gives its readers a direct picture of where cash came from (cash inflows) and how cash was spent (cash outflows).

Summary Problem for Your Review

Drexel Corporation accounting records include the following information for the year ended June 30, 19X8:

1. Salary expense, $104,000
2. Interest revenue, $8,000
3. Proceeds from issuance of common stock, $31,000
4. Declaration and payment of cash dividends, $22,000
5. Collection of interest receivable, $7,000
6. Payments of salaries, $110,000
7. Credit sales, $358,000
8. Loan to another company, $42,000
9. Proceeds from sale of plant assets, $18,000, including $1,000 loss
10. Collections from customers, $369,000
11. Cash receipt of dividend revenue on stock investments, $3,000
12. Payments to suppliers, $319,000
13. Cash sales, $92,000
14. Depreciation expense, $32,000
15. Proceeds from issuance of short-term debt, $38,000
16. Payments of long-term debt, $57,000
17. Interest expense and payments, $11,000
18. Loan collections, $51,000
19. Proceeds from sale of investments, $22,000, including $13,000 gain
20. Amortization expense, $5,000
21. Purchases of inventory on credit, $297,000
22. Income tax expense and payments, $16,000
23. Cash payments to acquire plant assets, $83,000
24. Cost of goods sold, $284,000
25. Cash balance: June 30, 19X7—$83,000
               June 30, 19X8—$54,000

Required

Prepare Drexel Corporation's statement of cash flows and income statement for the year ended June 30, 19X8. Follow the formats of Exhibits 15-1 and 15-3.

Drexel Corporation
Statement of Cash Flows
For the Year Ended June 30, 19X8
Increase (Decrease) in Cash and Cash Equivalents
(amounts in thousands)

Item No. (Reference Only)			
	Cash flows from operating activities:		
	Receipts:		
10, 13	Collections from customers ($369 + $92)	$ 461	
5	Interest received on notes receivable	7	
11	Dividends received on investments in stock	3	
	Total cash receipts		471
	Payments:		
12	To suppliers	$(319)	
6	To employees	(110)	
17	For interest	(11)	
22	For income tax	(16)	
	Total cash payments		(456)
	Net cash inflow from operating activities		15
	Cash flows from investing activities:		
23	Acquisition of plant assets	$ (83)	
8	Loan to another company	(42)	
19	Proceeds from sale of investments	22	
9	Proceeds from sale of plant assets	18	
18	Collection of loans	51	
	Net cash outflow from investing activities		(34)
	Cash flows from financing activities:		
15	Proceeds from issuance of short-term debt	$ 38	
3	Proceeds from issuance of common stock	31	
16	Payments of long-term debt	(57)	
4	Dividends declared and paid	(22)	
	Net cash outflow from financing activities		(10)
	Net decrease in cash		$ (29)
25	Cash balance, June 30, 19X7		83
25	Cash balance, June 30, 19X8		$ 54

Drexel Corporation
Income Statement
For the Year Ended June 30, 19X8
(amounts in thousands)

Revenue and gains:		
Sales revenue ($358 + $92)	$450	
Gain on sale of investments	13	
Interest revenue	8	
Dividend revenue	3	
Total revenues and gains		$474
Expenses and losses:		
Cost of goods sold	$284	
Salary expense	104	
Depreciation expense	32	
Income tax expense	16	
Interest expense	11	
Amortization expense	5	
Loss on sale of plant assets	1	
Total expenses		453
Net income		$ 21

Computing Individual Amounts for the Statement of Cash Flows

How do accountants compute the amounts for the statement of cash flows? Many accountants prepare the statement of cash flows using the income statement amounts and *changes* in the related balance sheet accounts. Accountants label this the T-account approach.[1] Learning to analyze T-accounts in this manner is one of the most useful skills you will acquire from accounting. It will enable you to identify the cash effects of a wide variety of transactions. The following discussions use Anchor Corporation's comparative balance sheet in Exhibit 15-4 and income statement in Exhibit 15-3. For continuity, trace the $22,000 and $42,000 cash amounts on the balance sheet in Exhibit 15-4 to the bottom part of the cash flow statement in Exhibit 15-1, page 709.

Computing the Cash Amounts of Operating Activities

Computing Cash Collections from Customers. Collections can be computed by converting sales revenue (an accrual-basis amount) to the cash basis. A decrease in the balance of Accounts Receivable during the period indicates

EXHIBIT 15-4 *Comparative Balance Sheet*

Anchor Corporation Comparative Balance Sheet December 31, 19X2 and 19X1 (amounts in thousands)			
Assets	**19X2**	**19X1**	**Increase (Decrease)**
Current:			
Cash..................................	$ 22	$ 42	$(20)
Accounts receivable	93	80	13
Interest receivable........................	3	1	2
Inventory	135	138	(3)
Prepaid expenses	8	7	1
Long-term receivable from another company .	11	—	11
Plant assets, net	453	219	234
Total.....................................	$725	$487	$238
Liabilities			
Current:			
Accounts payable	$ 91	$ 57	$ 34
Salary and wage payable	4	6	(2)
Accrued liabilities	1	3	(2)
Long-term debt	160	77	83
Stockholders' Equity			
Common stock	359	258	101
Retained earnings........................	110	86	24
Total.....................................	$725	$487	$238

---

[1]The chapter appendix covers the work-sheet approach to preparation of the statement of cash flows.

that cash collections exceeded sales revenue. Therefore, we add the decrease to sales revenue to compute collections. An increase in Accounts Receivable means that sales exceeded cash receipts. This amount is subtracted from sales to compute collections. These relationships suggest the following computation for collections from customers:

$$\text{Collections from customers} = \text{Sales Revenue} \begin{cases} + \text{ Decrease in Accounts Receivable} \\ \text{or} \\ - \text{ Increase in Accounts Receivable} \end{cases}$$

Anchor Corporation's income statement (Exhibit 15-3 page 715) reports sales of $284,000. Exhibit 15-4 shows that Accounts Receivable increased from $80,000 at the beginning of the year to $93,000 at year end, a $13,000 increase. Based on these amounts, Collections equal $271,000: Sales Revenue, $284,000 minus the $13,000 increase in Accounts Receivable. Posting these amounts directly to Accounts Receivable highlights the Collections amount, $271,000.

Accounts Receivable

Beginning balance	80,000		
Sales	284,000	Collections	271,000
Ending balance	93,000		

We see that this computation required the income statement amount of Sales Revenue and the *change* in the related balance sheet account, Accounts Receivable. The amount of cash collections from customers is derived from these accounts. Cash collections—and the other amounts reported on the cash flow statement—are *not* the balances of separate ledger accounts. Instead, the cash flow amounts must be computed by analysis of related income statement and balance sheet accounts, as illustrated in this section.

All collections of receivables can be computed in the same way. For example, the illustrative problem indicates that Anchor Corporation received cash interest. To compute this operating cash receipt, note that the income statement, Exhibit 15-3, page 715, reports interest revenue of $12,000. Interest Receivable's balance in Exhibit 15-4 increased by $2,000. Cash receipts of interest must be $10,000 (Interest Revenue of $12,000 minus the $2,000 increase in Accounts Receivable).

Computing Payments to Suppliers. This computation includes two parts, payments for inventory and payments for expenses other than interest and income tax.

Payments for inventory are computed by converting cost of goods sold to the cash basis. We accomplish this by analyzing Cost of Goods Sold and Accounts Payable. Many companies also purchase inventory on short-term notes payable. In that case, we would analyze Short-Term Notes Payable in the same manner as Accounts Payable. The computation of cash payments for inventory is

$$\text{Payments for inventory} = \text{Cost of goods sold} \begin{cases} + \text{ Increase in Inventory} \\ \text{or} \\ - \text{ Decrease in Inventory} \end{cases} \text{and} \begin{cases} + \text{ Decrease in Accounts Payable*} \\ \text{or} \\ - \text{ Increase in Accounts Payable*} \end{cases}$$

*+ Decrease (or − Increase) in Short-term Notes Payable for inventory purchases

The logic behind this computation is that an increase in inventory leads to an increase in accounts payable that finds its way into a cash payment. A decrease in accounts payable can occur only if cash was paid. By contrast, an increase in accounts payable indicates that cash was *not* paid. A detailed analysis will show the validity of this computation.

Anchor Corporation reports cost of goods sold of $150,000. The balance sheet shows that Inventory decreased by $3,000. Accounts Payable increased by $34,000. These amounts combine to compute payments for inventory of $113,000: Cost of Goods Sold, $150,000, minus the decrease in Inventory, $3,000, minus the increase in Accounts Payable, $34,000—a total of $113,000.

The T-account analysis also indicates payments of $113,000 (with Purchases inserted for completeness):

Cost of Goods Sold

Beginning inventory	138,000	Ending inventory	135,000
Purchases	147,000		
Cost of goods sold	150,000		

Accounts Payable

		Beginning balance	57,000
Payments for inventory ..	**113,000**	Purchases	147,000
		Ending balance	91,000

Payments to suppliers ($133,000 in Exhibit 15-1) equal the sum of payments for inventory ($113,000) plus payments for operating expenses ($20,000), as explained next.

Computing Payments for Operating Expenses. Payments for operating expenses other than interest and income tax can be computed by analyzing Prepaid Expenses and Other Accrued Liabilities, as follows:

$$\text{Payments for operating expenses} = \begin{array}{c}\text{Operating expenses other than salaries, wages, and depreciation}\end{array} \begin{cases}+ \text{ Increase in Prepaid Expenses} \\ \text{or} \\ - \text{ Decrease in Prepaid Expenses}\end{cases} \text{ and } \begin{cases}+ \text{ Decrease in Accrued Liabili} \\ \text{or} \\ - \text{ Increase in Accrued Liabili}\end{cases}$$

Increases in prepaid expenses require cash payments, and decreases indicate that payments were less than expenses. Decreases in accrued liabilities can occur only from cash payments, and increases mean that cash was *not* paid.

Anchor's income statement reports operating expenses—other than salaries, wages, and depreciation—of $17,000. The balance sheet shows that prepaid expenses increased by $1,000, and accrued liabilities decreased by $2,000. Based on these data, payments for operating expenses total $20,000 ($17,000 + $1,000 + $2,000). This result is confirmed by the T-account analysis, as shown at the top of the next page.

Computing Payments to Employees. The company may have separate accounts for salaries, wages, and other forms of cash compensation to employees. To compute payments to employees, it is convenient to combine them into one account. Anchor's calculation begins with Salary and Wage Expense

Prepaid Expenses

Beginning balance	7,000	Expiration of prepaid	
Payments	**8,000**	expense	7,000←
Ending balance	8,000		

Accrued Liabilities

Payment of beginning		Beginning balance.........	3,000
balance	3,000	Accrual of expense at year	
		end	1,000←
		Ending balance	1,000

Operating Expenses (other than Salaries, Wages, and Depreciation)

↳Expiration of prepaid	
expense	7,000
→Accrual of expense at year	
end	1,000
Payments	**9,000**
Ending balance	17,000

Total payments = $20,000 ($8,000 + $3,000 + $9,000)

(an income statement account) and adjusts for the change in Salary and Wage Payable (a balance sheet account). The computation follows:

$$\begin{matrix} \text{Payments} \\ \text{to} \\ \text{employees} \end{matrix} = \begin{matrix} \text{Salary} \\ \text{and Wage} \\ \text{Expense} \end{matrix} \left\{ \begin{matrix} \textbf{+ Decrease in Salary and Wage Payable} \\ \textbf{or} \\ \textbf{- Increase in Salary and Wage Payable} \end{matrix} \right.$$

A decrease in the liability is added because it requires a cash payment. An increase in the liability indicates that the expense exceeds cash payments, so the increase is subtracted. Anchor's salary and wage expense is $56,000. The balance sheet in Exhibit 15-4 reports a $2,000 decrease in the liability. Thus cash payments to employees are $58,000 ($56,000 + $2,000). This is confirmed by analysis of the Salary and Wage Payable account:

Salary and Wage Payable

		Beginning balance........	6,000
Payments	**58,000**	Salary and wage expense ..	56,000
		Ending balance	4,000

Computing Payments of Interest and Income Taxes. In our illustrative problem, the expense and payment amount is the same for each of these expenses. Therefore, no analysis is required to determine the payment amount. If the expense and the payment differ, the payment can be computed by analyzing the related liability account. The payment computation follows the pattern illustrated for payments to employees.

Computing the Cash Amounts of Investing Activities

Investing activities affect asset accounts, such as Plant Assets, Investments, and Notes Receivable. The cash amounts of investing activities can be identified by analyzing these accounts. Most data for the computations are taken directly from the income statement and the beginning and ending balance sheets. Other amounts come from analysis of accounts in the ledger.

Computing Acquisitions and Sales of Plant Assets. Most companies have separate accounts for Land, Buildings, Equipment, and other plant assets. It is helpful to combine these accounts into a single summary for computing the cash flows from acquisitions and sales of these assets. Also, we subtract accumulated depreciation from the assets' cost and work with a net figure for plant assets. This allows us to work with a single plant asset account as opposed to a large number of plant asset and related accumulated depreciation accounts.

To illustrate, observe that Anchor Corporation's balance sheet (Exhibit 15-4) reports beginning plant assets, net of depreciation, of $219,000 and an ending net amount of $453,000. The income statement shows depreciation of $18,000 and an $8,000 gain on sale of plant assets. Assume the acquisitions total $306,000. How much are the proceeds from the sale of plant assets? First, we must determine their book value, computed as follows:

$$
\begin{array}{c}
\text{Beginning} \\
\text{Plant Asset} \\
\text{balance (net)}
\end{array} + \text{Acquisitions} - \text{Depreciation} - \begin{array}{c}
\text{Book value} \\
\text{of plant} \\
\text{assets sold}
\end{array} = \begin{array}{c}
\text{Ending} \\
\text{Plant Asset} \\
\text{balance (net)}
\end{array}
$$

$$
\$219{,}000 \ + \ \$306{,}000 \ - \ \$18{,}000 \ - \ \begin{array}{c}\text{Book} \\ \text{value} \\ \text{sold}\end{array} = \ \$453{,}000
$$

Isolating book value sold on the left-hand side rearranges the equation as follows:

$$- \text{Book value sold} = \$453{,}000 - \$219{,}000 - \$306{,}000 + \$18{,}000$$

$$\text{Book value sold} = \$54{,}000$$

Now we can compute the sale proceeds as follows:

$$\text{Sale proceeds} = \text{Book value sold, } \$54{,}000 + \text{Gain, } \$8{,}000 - \text{Loss, } \$0$$

$$= \$62{,}000$$

Trace the sale proceeds of $62,000 to the statement of cash flows in Exhibit 15-1. If the sale resulted in a loss of $3,000, the sale proceeds would be $51,000 ($54,000 − $3,000), and the statement would report $51,000 as a cash receipt from this investing activity.

The book value of plant assets sold can also be computed by analysis of the Plant Assets T-account:

Plant Assets (net)

Beginning balance	219,000	Depreciation	18,000
Acquisitions	306,000	**Book value of assets sold .**	**54,000**
Ending balance...........	453,000		

Computing Acquisitions and Sales of Assets Classified as Investments, and Loans and Their Collections. Accountants use a separate category of assets for investments in stocks, bonds, and other types of assets. The cash amounts of transactions involving these assets can be computed in the manner illustrated for plant assets. Investments are easier to analyze, however, because there is no depreciation to account for, as shown in the following T-account:

Investments

Beginning balance	XXX		
Purchases..................	**XXX**	Cost of investments sold	XXX
Ending balance.............	XXX		

Loan transactions follow the pattern illustrated on pages 718 and 719 for collections from customers. New loans cause a debit to a receivable and an outflow of cash. Collections increase cash and cause a credit to the receivable, as this T-account illustrates:

Loans and Notes Receivable

Beginning balance	XXX		
New loans made	**XXX**	Collections	**XXX**
Ending balance.............	XXX		

Computing the Cash Amounts of Financing Activities

Financing activities affect liability and stockholders' equity accounts, such as Notes Payable, Bonds Payable, Long-term Debt, Common Stock, Paid-in Capital in Excess of Par, and Retained Earnings. The cash amounts of financing activities can be computed by analyzing these accounts.

Computing Issuances and Payments of Long-term Debt. The beginning and ending balances of Long-term Debt, Notes Payable, or Bonds Payable are taken from the balance sheet. If either the amount of new issuances or the amount of the payments is known, the other amount can be computed. New debt issuances total $94,000. The computation of debt payments follows, using balances from Exhibit 15-4:

Beginning					**Ending**
Long-term Debt	**+ Issuance of new debt**	**− Payments**	**=**	**Long-term Debt**	
balance				**balance**	
$77,000	+	$94,000	− Payments =	$160,000	

Rearranging this equation results in the following:

$$- \text{Payments} = \$160,000 - \$77,000 - \$94,000$$

$$\text{Payments} = \$11,000$$

This computation arises from analysis of the Long-term Debt account:

Long-term Debt

		Beginning balance	77,000
Payments...............	11,000	Issuance of new debt	94,000
		Ending balance..........	160,000

Alternatively, the amount of payments can be inserted in the account to solve for the amount of new debt issued.

Computing Issuances and Retirements of Stock and Purchases and Sales of Treasury Stock. The cash effects of these financing activities can be determined by analyzing the various stock accounts. For example, the amount of a new issuance of common stock is determined by combining the Common Stock and any related Capital in Excess of Par account. It is convenient to work with a single summary account for stock as we do for plant assets. Using Exhibit 15-4 data, we have:

$$\begin{array}{c}\text{Beginning}\\\text{Stock}\\\text{balance}\end{array} + \text{Issuance of new stock} - \text{Retirements} = \begin{array}{c}\text{Ending}\\\text{Stock}\\\text{balance}\end{array}$$

$$\$258,000 + \quad\text{New Stock}\quad - \quad\$0\quad = \$359,000$$

Isolating new stock gives the final equation:

$$\textbf{Issuance of new stock} = \$359,000 - \$258,000 = \$101,000$$

The Common Stock T-account shows these amounts:

Common Stock		
	Beginning balance	258,000
Retirements of stock 0	**Issuance of new stock**	**101,000**
	Ending balance	359,000

Cash flows affecting Treasury Stock, a debit balance account, can be analyzed using the following equation:

$$\begin{array}{c}\text{Beginning}\\\text{Treasury Stock}\\\text{balance}\end{array} + \text{Purchases} - \text{Cost of treasury stock sold} = \begin{array}{c}\text{Ending}\\\text{Treasury Stock}\\\text{balance}\end{array}$$

Transaction amounts can also be computed by analyzing the Treasury Stock T-account:

Treasury Stock		
Beginning balance XXX		
Purchases of treasury stock . XXX	Cost of treasury stock sold ..	XXX
Ending balance XXX		

If either the purchase amount or the cost of treasury stock sold is known, the other amount can be computed. For a sale of treasury stock, the amount to report on the cash flow statement is the sale proceeds. Suppose a sale brought in cash that was $2,000 less than the $14,000 cost of the treasury stock sold. In this case, the statement of cash flows would report a cash receipt of $12,000 ($14,000 − $2,000).

Computing Dividend Payments. If the amount of the dividends is not given elsewhere (for example, in a statement of retained earnings), it can be computed by analyzing the Retained Earnings account. Beginning and ending amounts come from the balance sheet, and the income statement reports net income. Dividend declarations can be computed as shown here, using net income from Exhibit 15-3 and Retained Earnings balances from Exhibit 15-4. We assume Anchor Corporation had no stock dividends or other transactions that affected Retained Earnings during the year. If, for example, a stock dividend and a cash dividend occurred during the year, total dividends must be separated into stock dividends and cash dividends because stock dividends do not affect cash.

$$\begin{array}{c}\text{Beginning} \\ \text{Retained Earnings} \\ \text{balance}\end{array} + \text{Net income} - \begin{array}{c}\text{Dividend} \\ \text{declarations}\end{array} = \begin{array}{c}\text{Ending} \\ \text{Retained Earnings} \\ \text{balance}\end{array}$$

$$\$86{,}000 \quad + \quad \$41{,}000 \quad - \quad \text{Dividends} = \quad \$110{,}000$$

Keeping dividends on the left-hand side produces the following equation:

$$- \text{Dividends} = \$110{,}000 - \$86{,}000 - \$41{,}000$$

$$\text{Dividends} = -\$110{,}000 + \$86{,}000 + \$41{,}000$$

$$\text{Dividends} = \$17{,}000$$

Analysis of the Retained Earnings T-account illustrates the equation approach:

Retained Earnings

		Beginning balance........	86,000
Dividend declarations	17,000	Net income	41,000
		Ending balance	110,000

A change in the Dividends Payable account means that dividend payments differ from the amount declared. In this case, dividend payments are determined by first computing dividends declared as shown here. Then add the amount of any decrease in the balance of Dividends Payable or subtract the amount of any increase in that account balance. The result is the dividend payments figure. The Dividends Payable account illustrates the analysis:

Dividends Payable

		Beginning balance..........	XXX
Dividend payments	XXX	Dividend declarations	XXX
		Ending balance	XXX

Noncash Investing and Financing Activities

Companies make investments that do not require cash. They also obtain financing other than cash. Our illustrative problem included none of these transactions.

Suppose Anchor Corporation issued no-par common stock valued at $320,000 to acquire a warehouse. Anchor would journalize this transaction as follows:

Warehouse Building	320,000	
Common Stock		320,000

This transaction would not be reported on the cash flow statement because Anchor paid no cash. But the importance of the investment in the warehouse and the financing aspect of issuing stock require that the transaction be reported. Noncash investing and financing activities like this transaction are reported in a separate schedule that accompanies the statement of cash flows. Exhibit 15-5 illustrates how to report noncash investing and financing activities (all amounts are assumed). This information can be included in a schedule immediately following the cash flow statement or in a note.

OBJECTIVE 5

Prepare a statement of cash flows using the indirect method

Preparing the Statement of Cash Flows: The Indirect Method

An alternative way to compute cash flows from *operating* activities is the **indirect method.** This method, also called the **reconciliation method,** starts with net income and shows the reconciliation from net income to operating cash flows. It shows the link between net income and cash flow from operations better than the direct method. The main drawback of the indirect method is that it does not report the detailed operating cash flows—collections from customers and other cash receipts, payments to suppliers, payments to employees, and payments for interest and taxes.

The indirect method and the direct method are both permitted by the FASB. *These methods of preparing the cash flow statement affect only the operating activities section of the statement.* No difference exists in the reporting of investing activities or financing activities.

Exhibit 15-6 is Anchor Corporation's statement prepared by the indirect method. You will see that only the operating section of the statement differs from the direct method format in Exhibit 15-1.

Logic Behind the Indirect Method

The operating section of the statement begins with net income, taken directly from the income statement. A series of additions and subtractions follows. These are labeled "Add (subtract) items that affect net income and cash flow differently." In this section, we discuss those items.

Depreciation, Depletion, and Amortization Expenses. These expenses are added back in going from net income to cash flow from operations. Let's see why.

EXHIBIT 15-5 *Noncash Investing and Financing Activities (amounts in thousands)*

Acquisition of building by issuing common stock	$320
Acquisition of land by issuing note payable	72
Payment of long-term debt by transferring investment assets to the creditor	104
Acquisition of equipment by issuing short-term note payable	37
Total noncash investing and financing activities	$533

EXHIBIT 15-6 *Statement of Cash Flows*

Anchor Corporation
Statement of Cash Flows—Indirect Method for Operating Activities
For the Year Ended December 31, 19X2
Increase (Decrease) in Cash and Cash Equivalents
(amounts in thousands)

Cash flows from operating activities:			
Net income			$ 41
Add (subtract) items that affect net income			
and cash flow differently:			
Depreciation		$ 18	
Gain on sale of plant assets		(8)	
Increase in accounts receivable		(13)	
Increase in interest receivable		(2)	
Decrease in inventory		3	
Increase in prepaid expenses		(1)	
Increase in accounts payable		34	
Decrease in salary and wage payable		(2)	
Decrease in accrued liabilities		(2)	27
Net cash inflow from operating activities			68
Cash flows from investing activities:			
Acquisition of plant assets		$(306)	
Loan to another company		(11)	
Proceeds from sale of plant assets		62	
Net cash outflow from investing activities			(255)
Cash flows from financing activities:			
Proceeds from issuance of common stock		$ 101	
Proceeds from issuance of long-term debt		94	
Payment of long-term debt		(11)	
Payment of dividends		(17)	
Net cash inflow from financing activities			167
Net decrease in cash			$ (20)
Cash balance, December 31, 19X1			42
Cash balance, December 31, 19X2			$ 22

Depreciation is recorded as follows:

Depreciation Expense	18,000	
Accumulated Depreciation		18,000

This entry contains no debit or credit to Cash, so depreciation expense has no cash effect. However, depreciation is deducted from revenues in the computation of income. Therefore, in going from net income to cash flow from operations, we add depreciation back to net income. The addback simply cancels the earlier deduction. The following example should help: Suppose a company had only two transactions during the period, a $1,000 cash sale and depreciation expense of $300. Net income is $700 ($1,000 − $300). Cash flow from operations is $1,000. To show how net income ($700) relates to cash flow ($1,000), we must add the depreciation amount of $300.

All expenses with no cash effects are added back to net income on the cash flow statement. Depletion and amortization are two other examples. Likewise, revenues that do not provide cash are subtracted from net income. An example is equity-method investment revenue, which increases the Investment account, not Cash.

Gains and Losses on the Sale of Assets.   Sales of plant assets are investing activities on the cash flow statement. A gain or loss on the sale is an adjustment to income. Exhibit 15-6 includes an adjustment for a gain. Recall that equipment with a book value of $54,000 was sold for $62,000, producing a gain of $8,000. The way to learn how to treat an item on the cash flow statement is to examine the journal entry that recorded it, as shown on page 714.

The $8,000 gain is reported on the income statement and, therefore, is included in net income. However, the cash receipt from the sale is $62,000, which includes the gain. To avoid counting the gain twice, we need to remove its effect from income and report the cash receipt of $62,000 in the investing-activities section of the statement. Starting with net income, we subtract the gain. This deduction removes the gain's earlier effect on income. The sale of plant assets is reported as a $62,000 cash receipt from an investing activity, as shown in Exhibits 15-1 and 15-6.

A loss on the sale of plant assets is also an adjustment to net income on the statement of cash flows. However, a loss is added back to income to compute cash flow from operations. The proceeds from selling the plant assets are reported under investing activities.

Changes in the Current Asset and Current Liability Accounts.   Most current assets and current liabilities result from operating activities. Accounts receivable result from sales, inventory generates revenues, and prepaid expenses are used up in operations. On the liability side, accounts payable and short-term notes payable are ordinarily incurred to buy inventory, and accrued liabilities relate to salaries, utilities, and other expenses. Changes in these current accounts are reported as adjustments to net income on the cash flow statement. The following rules apply:

1. An *increase* in a current asset other than cash is subtracted from net income to compute cash flow from operations. Suppose a company makes a sale. Income is increased by the sale amount. However, collection of less than the full amount leaves Accounts Receivable with an increase. To compute the impact of revenue on the cash flow amount, it is necessary to subtract the $13,000 increase in Accounts Receivable from net income in Exhibit 15-6. The same logic applies to the other current assets. If they increase during the period, subtract the increase from net income.

2. A *decrease* in a current asset other than cash is added to net income. For example, suppose Accounts Receivable's balance decreased by $4,000 during the period. Cash receipts cause the Accounts Receivable balance to decrease, so decreases in Accounts Receivable and the other current assets are added to net income.

3. A *decrease* in a current liability is subtracted from net income. The payment of a current liability causes it to decrease, so decreases in current liabilities are subtracted from net income. For example, in Exhibit 15-6, the $2,000 decrease in Accrued Liabilities is subtracted from net income to compute net cash inflow from operating activities.

4. An *increase* in a current liability is added to net income. Suppose Accrued Liabilities increased during the year. This can occur only if cash is not spent to pay this liability, which means that cash payments are less than the related expense. Thus increases in current liabilities are added to net income.

Exhibit 15-7 summarizes these adjustments to convert net income to net cash inflow (or net cash outflow) from operating activities.

The computation of net cash inflow or net cash outflow from *operating* activities by the indirect method takes a path that is very different from the com-

Exhibit 15-7 *Relationship Between Net Income and Net Cash Flow from Operating Activities—*
Indirect Method

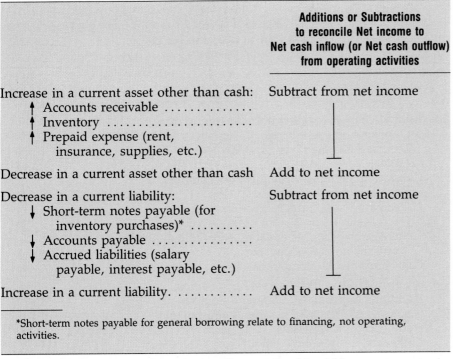

	Additions or Subtractions to reconcile Net income to Net cash inflow (or Net cash outflow) from operating activities
Increase in a current asset other than cash: ↑ Accounts receivable .... ↑ Inventory .... ↑ Prepaid expense (rent, insurance, supplies, etc.)	Subtract from net income
Decrease in a current asset other than cash	Add to net income

Decrease in a current liability:
↓ Short-term notes payable (for
    inventory purchases)* ....
↓ Accounts payable ....
↓ Accrued liabilities (salary
    payable, interest payable, etc.)
	Subtract from net income

Increase in a current liability.	Add to net income

*Short-term notes payable for general borrowing relate to financing, not operating, activities.

Authors' note: We thank Jean Marie Hudson for suggesting this exhibit.

putation by the direct method. However, the two methods arrive at the same amount of net cash flow. This is shown in Exhibits 15-1 and 15-6, which report a net cash inflow of $68,000.

Supplementary Disclosures

The company that uses the direct method for reporting operating activities on the cash flow statement must, according to *FASB Statement No. 95,* also report the reconciliation of net income to cash flow from operations. A format similar to the operating section under the indirect method (Exhibit 15-6) is suitable. The company that uses the indirect method may report the components of operating cash flows in a way similar to that used in the direct method. These supplementary disclosures can appear in notes to the statement or immediately beneath the statement near the noncash investing and financing activities. The goal is to give readers of the financial statements the information they need to make informed decisions about the company.

Exhibit 15-8 is the cash flow statement of Nike, Inc., maker of athletic shoes and clothing. Notice that Nike uses the indirect method to report cash flows from operating activities. Most companies use this format. Most of the items in Exhibit 15-8 have been discussed earlier, but three are new. First, deferred income taxes are added back to net income in the operating section. These taxes do not require current cash payments and are, therefore, similar to accrued liabilities. Second, financing activities include proceeds from exercise of options. This is the amount of cash received from issuance of stock to executives. Third, changes in exchange rates show the cash effect of fluctuations in foreign currencies, a topic that is beyond the scope of this course. Nike's reporting of this item agrees with GAAP.

Nike, Inc.
Statement of Cash Flows
For the Year Ended May 31, 19X7
(in thousands)

Cash provided (used) by operations:	
Net income	$ 35,879
Income charges (credits) not affecting cash:	
Depreciation	12,078
Deferred income taxes	8,486
Other	2,494
Changes in certain working capital components:	
Decrease in inventory	59,542
Decrease in accounts receivable	1,174
Decrease in other current assets	4,331
Increase in accounts payable, accrued liabilities, and income taxes payable	8,462
Cash provided by operations	132,446
Cash provided (used) by investing activities:	
Additions to property, plant and equipment	(11,874)
Disposals of property, plant and equipment	1,728
Additions to other assets	(930)
Cash used by investing activities	(11,076)
Cash provided (used) by financing activities:	
Additions to long-term debt	30,332
Reductions in long-term debt including current portion	(10,678)
Decrease in notes payable to banks	(18,489)
Proceeds from exercise of options	1,911
Dividends—common and preferred	(15,188)
Cash used by financing activities	(12,112)
Effect of exchange rate changes on cash	(529)
Net increase (decrease) in cash	108,729
Cash and equivalents, beginning of year	18,138
Cash and equivalents, end of year	$126,867

Computers and the Statement of Cash Flows

When the statement of cash flows became a required financial statement, computerized accounting systems were changed so that they could generate this statement as easily as they do the balance sheet and the income statement. Consider the direct method for preparing the statement of cash flows (see Exhibit 15-2). To get the amounts for the operating section, cash inflows and outflows (grouped by the related revenue and expense category) can be drawn from the posted files generated from cash receipts and cash payment records. Specifically, the cash receipts postings to Accounts Receivable provide the information necessary to show Cash Receipts from Customers. The computer adds the monthly postings to reach the yearly total. All other cash flows for operating activities, as well as cash flows for financing and investing activities, are handled similarly.

The computer can generate the statement of cash flows using the indirect method with equal ease. The only additional information needed, noncash income statement flows and changes in noncash current assets and current liabilities, comes from the computer general ledger files.

Do not be misled into believing that the statement of cash flows created from a computer's general ledger files is automatically correct from a generally accepted accounting principles point of view. For example, noncash financing and investing activities of a large corporation, such as Abbott Laboratories, a manufacturer of pharmaceuticals, might be incorrectly combined with the company's cash flows. The computerized system must be sophisticated enough to distinguish among the various categories of cash activities. Most important, accountants must analyze the information fed into the computer and check that its output adheres to generally accepted accounting principles. Revisions to a company's computer accounting system are common.

Summary Problem for Your Review

Prepare the 19X3 statement of cash flows for Robins Corporation, using the indirect method to report cash flows from operating activities. In a separate schedule, report Robins's noncash investing and financing activities.

	December 31,	
	19X3	**19X2**
Current assets:		
Cash and cash equivalents	$19,000	$ 3,000
Accounts receivable	22,000	23,000
Inventories	34,000	31,000
Prepaid expenses	1,000	3,000
Current liabilities:		
Notes payable (for inventory purchases)	$11,000	$ 7,000
Accounts payable	24,000	19,000
Accrued liabilities	7,000	9,000
Income tax payable	10,000	10,000

Transaction data for 19X3:

Purchase of equipment ...	$98,000	Depreciation expense.....	$ 7,000
Payment of cash		Issuance of long-term note	
dividends	18,000	payable to borrow cash .	7,000
Net income.............	26,000	Issuance of common stock	
Issuance of common stock		for cash	19,000
to retire bonds payable .	13,000	Sale of building	74,000
Purchase of long-term		Amortization expense	3,000
investment	8,000	Purchase of treasury stock	5,000
Issuance of long-term note		Loss on sale of building ..	2,000
payable to purchase			
patent	37,000		

SOLUTION TO REVIEW PROBLEM

Robins Corporation
Statement of Cash Flows
Year Ended December 31, 19X3
increase (Decrease) in Cash and Cash Equivalents

Cash flows from operating activities:		
Net income		$26,000
Add (subtract) items that affect net income and		
cash flow differently:		
Depreciation	$ 7,000	
Amortization	3,000	
Loss on sale of building......................	2,000	
Decrease in accounts receivable...............	1,000	
Increase in inventories.......................	(3,000)	
Decrease in prepaid expenses	2,000	
Increase in notes payable, short-term	4,000	
Increase in accounts payable	5,000	
Decrease in accrued liabilities.................	(2,000)	19,000
Net cash inflow from operating activities		45,000
Cash flows from investing activities:		
Purchase of equipment	$(98,000)	
Sale of building	74,000	
Purchase of long-term investment	(8,000)	
Net cash outflow from investing activities		(32,000)
Cash flows from financing activities:		
Issuance of common stock	$ 19,000	
Payment of cash dividends.....................	(18,000)	
Issuance of long-term note payable	7,000	
Purchase of treasury stock	(5,000)	
Net cash inflow from financing activities		3,000
Net increase in cash and cash equivalents		$16,000
Noncash investing and financing activities:		
Issuance of long-term note payable		
to purchase patent		$37,000
Issuance of common stock to retire bonds payable .		13,000
Total noncash investing and financing		
activities....................................		$50,000

Summary

The *statement of cash flows* reports a business's cash receipts, cash disburse-ments, and net change in cash for the accounting period. It shows *why* cash increased or decreased during the period. A required financial statement, it gives a different view of the business from the accrual-basis statements. The cash flow statement helps financial statement users predict the future cash flows of the entity. Cash includes cash on hand, cash in bank, and *cash equiv-alents* such as liquid, short-term investments.

The statement is divided into *operating activities, investing activities,* and *financing activities.* Operating activities create revenues and expenses; invest-ing activities affect long-term assets; and financing activities obtain the cash needed to launch and sustain the business. Each section of the statement includes cash receipts and cash payments and concludes with a net cash increase or decrease. In addition, *noncash investing and financing activities* are reported in an accompanying schedule.

Two formats are used to report operating activities. The *direct method* lists the major sources of cash receipts and disbursements—for example, cash collections from customers and cash payments to suppliers and to employees. The *indirect method* shows the reconciliation from net income to cash flow from operations. The FASB permits both methods but prefers the direct method. However, the indirect method is more widely used in practice.

Self-Study Questions

Test your understanding of the chapter by marking the best answer for each of the following questions.

1. The income statement and the balance sheet *(p. 707)*
   a. Report the cash effects of transactions
   b. Fail to report why cash changed during the period
   c. Report the sources and uses of cash during the period
   d. Are divided into operating, investing, and financing activities

2. The purpose of the statement of cash flows is to *(pp. 707, 708)*
   a. Predict future cash flows
   b. Evaluate management decisions
   c. Determine the ability to pay dividends and interest
   d. All of the above

3. A successful company's major source of cash should be *(pp. 709, 712)*
   a. Operating activities   c. Financing activities
   b. Investing activities   d. A combination of the above

4. Dividends paid to stockholders are reported on the statement of cash flows as a (an) *(pp. 709, 715)*
   a. Operating activity   c. Financing activity
   b. Investing activity   d. Combination of the above

5. Which of the following items appears on a cash flow statement prepared by the direct method? *(p. 709)*
   a. Depreciation expense   c. Loss on sale of plant assets
   b. Decrease in accounts receivable   d. Cash payments to suppliers

6. Interest Receivable's beginning balance is $18,000, and its ending amount is $14,000. Interest revenue earned during the year is $43,000. How much cash interest was received? *(p. 719)*
   a. $39,000   c. $45,000
   b. $43,000   d. $47,000

7. McGrath Company sold an investment at a gain of $22,000. The Investment account reports a beginning balance of $104,000 and an ending balance of $91,000. During the year, McGrath purchased new investments costing $31,000. What were the proceeds from the sale of investments? *(p. 723)*.
   a. $22,000   c. $66,000
   b. $44,000   d. $186,000

8. Noncash investing and financing activities *(p. 726)*
   a. Are reported in the main body of the cash flow statement
   b. Are reported in a separate schedule that accompanies the cash flow statement
   c. Are reported on the income statement
   d. Are not reported in the financial statements

9. The indirect method does a better job than the direct method at *(p. 726)*

a. Reporting the cash effects of financing activities
b. Reporting why the cash balance changed
c. Showing the link between net income and cash flow from operations
d. Reporting the separate components of operating cash flows such as collections from customers and payments to suppliers and employees

10. Net income is $17,000, depreciation is $9,000, and amortization is $3,000. In addition, the sale of a plant asset generated a $4,000 gain. Current assets other than cash increased by $6,000, and current liabilities increased by $8,000. What was the amount of cash flow from operations? (pp. 728, 729)

a. $23,000   c. $31,000
b. $27,000   d. $35,000

Answers to the Self-Study Questions follow the Accounting Vocabulary.

Accounting Vocabulary

Cash equivalents. Highly liquid short-term investments that can be converted into cash with little delay (p. 711).

Cash flows. Cash receipts and cash payments (disbursements) (p. 727).

Direct method. Format of the operating activities section of the statement of cash flows that lists the major categories of operating cash receipts (collections from customers and receipts of interest and dividends) and cash disbursements (payments to suppliers, to employees, for interest and income taxes) (p. 711).

Financing activities. Activity that obtains the funds from investors and creditors needed to launch and sustain the business. A section of the statement of cash flows (p. 730).

Indirect method. Format of the operating activities section of statement of cash flows that starts

with net income and shows the reconciliation from net income to operating cash flows. Also called the Reconciliation method (p. 726).

Investing activities. Activity that increases and decreases the assets that the business has to work with. A section of the statement of cash flows (p. 709).

Operating activities. Activity that creates revenue or expense in the entity's major line of business. Operating activities affect the income statement. A section of the statement of cash flows (p. 709).

Reconciliation method. Another name for the Indirect method of formatting the operating activities section of the statement of cash flows (p. 726).

Statement of cash flows. Reports cash receipts and cash disbursements classified according to the entity's major activities: operating, investing, and financing (p. 727).

Answer to Self-Study Questions

1. b
2. d
3. a
4. c
5. d
6. d ($43,000 + $4,000 decrease in Interest Receivable = $47,000)
7. c ($104,000 + $31,000 − Cost of investment sold = $91,000; Cost = $44,000; Proceeds = Cost, $44,000 + Gain, $22,000 = $66,000)
8. b
9. c
10. b ($17,000 + $9,000 + $3,000 − $4,000 − $6,000 + $8,000 = $27,000)

ASSIGNMENT MATERIAL _____

Questions

1. What information does the statement of cash flows report that is not shown on the balance sheet, the income statement, or the statement of retained earnings?

2. Identify four purposes of the statement of cash flows.

3. Identify and briefly describe the three types of activities that are reported on the statement of cash flows.

4. How is the statement of cash flows dated and why?

5. What is the check figure for the statement of cash flows, where is it obtained, and how is it used?

6. What is the most important source of cash for most successful companies?

7. How can cash decrease during a year when income is high? How can cash increase during a year when income is low? How can investors and creditors learn these facts about the company?

8. DeBerg, Inc., prepares its statement of cash flows using the *direct* method for operating activities. Identify the section of DeBerg's statement of cash flows where each of the following transactions will appear. If the transaction does not appear on the cash flow statement, give the reason.

a.	Cash..	14,000	
	Note Payable, Long-Term...............		14,000
b.	Salary Expense	7,300	
	Cash......................................		7,300
c.	Cash	28,400	
	Sales Revenue		28,400
d.	Amortization Expense.....................	6,500	
	Goodwill		6,500
e.	Accounts Payable	1,400	
	Cash......................................		1,400

9. Why are depreciation, depletion, and amortization expenses *not* reported on a cash flow statement that reports operating activities by the direct method? Why and how are these expenses reported on a statement prepared by the indirect method?

10. Mainline Distributing Company collected cash of $92,000 from customers and $6,000 interest on notes receivable. Cash payments included $24,000 to employees, $13,000 to suppliers, $6,000 as dividends to stockholders, and $5,000 as a loan to another company. How much was Mainline's net cash inflow from operating activities?

11. Summarize the major cash receipts and cash disbursements in the three categories of activities that appear on the cash flow statement.

12. Kirchner, Inc., recorded salary expense of $51,000 during a year when the balance of Salary Payable decreased from $10,000 to $2,000. How much cash did Kirchner pay to employees during the year? Where on the statement of cash flows should Kirchner report this item?

13. Marshall Corporation's beginning plant asset balance, net of accumulated depreciation, was $193,000, and the ending amount was $176,000. Marshall recorded depreciation of $37,000 and sold plant assets with a book value of $9,000. How much cash did Marshall pay to purchase plant assets during the period? Where on the statement of cash flows should Marshall report this item?

14. How should issuance of a note payable to purchase land be reported in the financial statements? Identify three other transactions that fall in this same category.

15. Which format of the cash flow statement gives a clearer description of the individual cash flows from operating activities? Which format better shows the relationship between net income and operating cash flow?

16. An investment that cost $65,000 was sold for $80,000, resulting in a $15,000 gain. Show how to report this transaction on a statement of cash flows prepared by the indirect method.

17. Identify the cash effects of increases and decreases in current assets other than cash. What are the cash effects of increases and decreases in current liabilities?

18. Milano Corporation earned net income of $38,000 and had depreciation expense of $22,000. Also, noncash current assets decreased $13,000, and current liabilities decreased $9,000. What was Milano's net cash flow from operating activities?

19. What is the difference between the direct method and the indirect method of reporting investing activities and financing activities?

20. Milgrom Company reports operating activities by the direct method. Does this method show the relationship between net income and cash flow from operations? If so, state how. If not, how can Milgrom satisfy this purpose of the cash flow statement?

Exercises

Exercise 15-1 *Identifying the purposes of the statement of cash flows* **(L.O. 1)**

Monterrey Western, a real estate partnership, has experienced an unbroken string of 10 years of growth in net income. Nevertheless, the business is facing bankruptcy! Creditors are calling all of Monterrey Western's outstanding loans for immediate payment, and the cash is simply not available. In trying to explain where Monterrey Western went wrong, it becomes clear that managers placed undue emphasis on net income and gave too little attention to cash flows.

Required

Write a brief memo, in your own words, to explain for Monterrey Western managers the purposes of the statement of cash flows.

Exercise 15-2 *Identifying activities for the statement of cash flows* **(L.O. 2)**

Identify each of the following transactions as an operating activity (O), an investing activity (I), a financing activity (F), a noncash investing and financing activity (NIF), or a transaction that is not reported on the statement of cash flows (N). Assume the direct method is used to report cash flows from operating activities.

_____ a. Purchase of long-term investment
_____ b. Payment of wages to employees
_____ c. Collection of cash interest
_____ d. Cash sale of land
_____ e. Distribution of stock dividend
_____ f. Acquisition of equipment by issuance of note payable
_____ g. Payment of long-term debt
_____ h. Acquisition of building by issuance of common stock
_____ i. Accrual of salary expense

_____ j. Payment of account payable
_____ k. Issuance of preferred stock for cash
_____ l. Payment of cash dividend
_____ m. Sale of long-term investment
_____ n. Amortization of bond discount
_____ o. Collection of account receivable
_____ p. Issuance of long-term note payable to borrow cash
_____ q. Depreciation of equipment
_____ r. Purchase of treasury stock
_____ s. Issuance of common stock for cash

Exercise 15-3 *Classifying transactions for the statement of cash flows* **(L.O. 2)**

Indicate where, if at all, each of the following transactions would be reported on a statement of cash flows prepared by the *direct* method and the accompanying schedule of noncash investing and financing activities.

a.	Accounts Payable	8,300	
	Cash		8,300
b.	Cash	81,000	
	Common Stock		12,000
	Paid-in Capital in Excess of Par—Common		69,000
c.	Treasury Stock	13,000	
	Cash		13,000
d.	Retained Earnings	36,000	
	Common Stock		36,000
e.	Cash	2,000	
	Interest Revenue		2,000
f.	Land	87,700	
	Cash		87,700
g.	Salary Expense	4,300	
	Cash		4,300
h.	Equipment	18,000	
	Cash		18,000
i.	Cash	7,200	
	Long-Term Investment		7,200
j.	Bonds Payable	45,000	
	Cash		45,000
k.	Building	164,000	
	Note Payable, Long-term		164,000
l.	Cash	1,400	
	Accounts Receivable		1,400
m.	Dividends Payable	16,500	
	Cash		16,500
n.	Furniture and Fixtures	22,100	
	Note Payable, Short-term		22,100

Exercise 15-4 *Computing cash flows from operating activities—direct method* **(L.O. 3)**

Analysis of the accounting records of Manufacturers Co–op reveals:

Collection of dividend revenue	$ 7,000	Depreciation	$12,000
Payment of interest	16,000	Decrease in current liabilities	20,000

Cash sales	12,000
Loss on sale of land	5,000
Acquisition of land	37,000
Payment of accounts payable	45,000
Net income	24,000
Payment of income tax	13,000
Increase in current assets other than cash	17,000
Payment of dividends	7,000
Collection of accounts receivable	93,000
Payment of salaries and wages	34,000

Compute cash flows from operating activities by the direct method. Use the format of the operating section of Exhibit 15-1.

Exercise 15-5 *Identifying items for the statement of cash flows—direct method* **(L.O. 3)**

Selected accounts of Quartz Products Corporation show:

Interest Receivable

Beginning balance	16,000	Cash receipts of interest	40,000
Interest revenue	40,000		
Ending balance	16,000		

Investments in Stock

Beginning balance	0	Cost of investments sold	9,000
Acquisitions	27,000		
Ending balance	18,000		

Long-Term Debt

Payments	69,000	Beginning balance	134,000
		Issuance of debt for cash	83,000
		Ending balance	148,000

For each account, identify the item or items that should appear on a statement of cash flows prepared by the direct method. State where to report the item.

Exercise 15-6 *Preparing the statement of cash flows—direct method* **(L.O. 3)**

The income statement and additional data of Illini Paper Company follow.

Illini Paper Company
Income Statement
Year Ended September 30, 19X2

Revenues:		
Sales revenue	$339,000	
Dividend revenue	8,000	$347,000
Expenses:		
Cost of goods sold	163,000	
Salary expense	85,000	
Depreciation expense	29,000	
Advertising expense	19,000	
Interest expense	2,000	
Income tax expense	9,000	307,000
Net income		$ 40,000

Additional data:

a. Collections from customers are $7,000 more than sales.

b. Payments to suppliers are $9,000 less than the sum of cost of goods sold plus advertising expense.

c. Payments to employees are $1,000 more than salary expense.

d. Dividend revenue, interest expense, and income tax expense equal their cash amounts.

e. Acquisition of plant assets is $116,000. Of this amount, $91,000 is paid in cash, $25,000 by signing a note payable.

f. Proceeds from sale of land, $19,000.

g. Proceeds from issuance of common stock, $30,000.

h. Payment of long-term note payable, $15,000.

i. Payment of dividends, $11,000.

j. Increase in cash balance, $?

Prepare Illini Paper Company's statement of cash flows and accompanying schedule of noncash investing and financing activities. Report operating activities by the *direct* method.

Exercise 15-7 *Computing amounts for the statement of cash flows* **(L.O. 4)**

Compute the following items for the statement of cash flows:

a. Beginning and ending Accounts Receivable are $26,000 and $22,000, respectively. Credit sales for the period total $81,000. How much are cash collections?

b. Cost of goods sold is $71,000. Beginning Inventory balance is $25,000, and ending Inventory balance is $21,000. Beginning and ending Accounts Payable are $11,000 and $8,000, respectively. How much are cash payments for inventory?

Exercise 15-8 *Computing amounts for the statement of cash flows* **(L.O. 4)**

Compute the following items for the statement of cash flows:

a. Beginning and ending Plant Assets, net, are $103,000 and $107,000, respectively. Depreciation for the period is $16,000, and acquisitions of new plant assets are $27,000. Plant assets were sold at a $1,000 loss. What were the cash proceeds of the sale?

b. Beginning and ending Retained Earnings are $45,000 and $73,000, respectively. Net income for the period is $62,000, and stock dividends are $12,000. How much are cash dividend payments?

Exercise 15-9 *Computing cash flows from operating activities—indirect method* **(L.O. 5)**

The accounting records of Manufacturers Co–op reveal the following:

Collection of dividend revenue	$ 7,000	Depreciation	$12,000
Payment of interest	16,000	Decrease in current liabilities	20,000
Cash sales	12,000	Increase in current assets other than cash	17,000
Loss on sale of land	5,000		
Acquisition of land	37,000	Payment of dividends	7,000
Payment of accounts payable	45,000	Collection of accounts receivable	93,000
Net income	24,000	Payment of salaries and wages	34,000
Payment of income tax	13,000		

Compute cash flows from operating activities by the indirect method. Use the format of the operating section of Exhibit 15-6.

Exercise 15-10 *Classifying transactions for the statement of cash flows* **(L.O. 3,5)**

Two transactions of Hoffman Banana Co. are recorded as follows:

a. Cash.. 9,000
    Accumulated Depreciation 83,000
    Loss on Sale of Equipment...................... 43,000
        Equipment 135,000
b. Land... 230,000
       Cash 130,000
       Note Payable 100,000

Required

1. Indicate where, how, and in what amount to report these transactions on the statement of cash flows and accompanying schedule of noncash investing and financing activities. Hoffman reports cash flows from operating activities by the *direct* method.
2. Repeat Requirement 1, assuming Hoffman reports cash flows from operating activities by the *indirect* method.

Exercise 15-11 *Preparing the statement of cash flows by the indirect method* **(L.O. 5)**

Use the income statement of Illini Paper Company in Exercise 15-6, plus these additional data:

a. Collections from customers are $7,000 more than sales.
b. Payments to suppliers are $9,000 less than the sum of cost of goods sold plus advertising expense.
c. Payments to employees are $1,000 more than salary expense.
d. Dividend revenue, interest expense, and income tax expense equal their cash amounts.
e. Acquisition of plant assets is $116,000. Of this amount, $91,000 is paid in cash, $25,000 by signing a note payable.
f. Proceeds from sale of land, $19,000.
g. Proceeds from issuance of common stock, $30,000.
h. Payment of long-term note payable, $15,000.
i. Payment of dividends, $11,000.
j. Increase in cash balance, $?
k. From the balance sheet:

	September 30,	
	19X2	**19X1**
Current Assets:		
Accounts receivable	$51,000	$58,000
Inventory	83,000	77,000
Prepaid expenses	9,000	8,000
Current Liabilities:		
Notes payable (for inventory purchases)	$20,000	$20,000
Accounts payable	35,000	22,000
Accrued liabilities	23,000	21,000

Prepare Illini Paper Company's statement of cash flows for the year ended September 30, 19X2, using the indirect method.

Problem 15-1A   *Using cash-flow information to evaluate performance*   **(L.O. 1)**

Top managers of Quest Programs, Inc., are reviewing company performance for 19X7. The income statement reports a 20 percent increase in net income over 19X6. However, most of the increase resulted from an extraordinary gain on insurance proceeds covering fire damage to the manufacturing plant. The balance sheet shows large increases in receivables and inventory. The cash flow statement, in summarized form, reports the following:

Net cash outflow from operating activities	$(80,000)
Net cash inflow from investing activities	40,000
Net cash inflow from financing activities	50,000
Increase in cash during 19X7	$ 10,000

Required

Write a memo to give Quest managers your assessment of 19X7 operations and your outlook for the future. Focus on the information content of the cash flow data.

Problem 15-2A   *Preparing the statement of cash flows—direct method*   **(L.O. 2,3)**

Texana Corporation accountants have developed the following data from the company's accounting records for the year ended April 30, 19X5:

1. Cash payments to acquire plant assets, $59,400
2. Cost of goods sold, $382,600
3. Proceeds from issuance of common stock, $8,000
4. Payment of cash dividends, $48,400
5. Collection of interest, $4,400
6. Acquisition of equipment by issuing short-term note payable, $16,400
7. Payments of salaries, $93,600
8. Credit sales, $583,900
9. Loan to another company, $12,500
10. Proceeds from sale of plant assets, $22,400, including $6,800 loss
11. Collections on accounts receivable, $562,600
12. Interest revenue, $3,800
13. Cash receipt of dividend revenue on stock investments, $4,100
14. Payments to suppliers, $478,500
15. Cash sales, $171,900
16. Depreciation expense, $59,900
17. Proceeds from issuance of short-term debt, $19,600
18. Payments of long-term debt, $50,000
19. Interest expense and payments, $13,300
20. Salary expense, $95,300
21. Loan collections, $12,800
22. Proceeds from sale of investments, $9,100, including $2,000 gain
23. Payment of short-term note payable by issuing common stock, $31,000
24. Amortization expense, $2,900
25. Income tax expense and payments, $37,900
26. Cash balance: April 30, 19X4—$39,300
                   April 30, 19X5—$?

Required

Prepare Texana Corporation's statement of cash flows for the year ended April 30, 19X5. Follow the format of Exhibit 15–1, but do *not* show amounts in thousands. Include an accompanying schedule of noncash investing and financing activities. Evaluate 19X5 from a cash-flow standpoint. Give your reasons.

Problem 15-3A *Preparing the statement of cash flows—direct method* **(L.O. 2,3,4)**

The 19X5 comparative balance sheet and income statement of Palo Duro Corp. follow.

Comparative Balance Sheet

	19X5	19X4	Increase (Decrease)
Current assets:			
Cash and cash equivalents	$ 15,400	$ 5,300	$10,100
Accounts receivable	28,600	26,900	1,700
Interest receivable	1,900	700	1,200
Inventories	83,600	87,200	(3,600)
Prepaid expenses....................	2,500	1,900	600
Plant assets:			
Land	89,000	60,000	29,000
Equipment, net	53,500	49,400	4,100
Total assets	$274,500	$231,400	$43,100
Current liabilities:			
Accounts payable	$ 31,400	$ 28,800	$ 2,600
Interest payable	4,400	4,900	(500)
Salary payable	3,100	6,600	(3,500)
Other accrued liabilities	13,700	16,000	(2,300)
Income tax payable	8,900	7,700	1,200
Long-term liabilities:			
Notes payable	75,000	100,000	(25,000)
Stockholders' equity:			
Common stock, no-par	88,300	64,700	23,600
Retained earnings	49,700	2,700	47,000
Total liabilities and stockholders' equity ..	$274,500	$231,400	$43,100

Income Statement for 19X5

Revenues:		
Sales revenue		$243,000
Interest revenue		8,600
Total revenues		251,600
Expenses:		
Cost of goods sold	$92,400	
Salary expense	27,800	
Depreciation expense	4,000	
Other operating expense	10,500	
Interest expense	11,600	
Income tax expense	29,100	
Total expenses		175,400
Net income		$ 76,200

Palo Duro had no noncash investing and financing transactions during 19X5. During the year there were no sales of land or equipment, no issuances of notes payable, no retirements of stock, and no treasury stock transactions.

Required

Prepare the 19X5 statement of cash flows, formatting operating activities by the direct method.

Problem 15-4A *Preparing the statement of cash flows—indirect method* **(L.O. 2,3,5)**

Required

Using the Palo Duro Corp. data from the preceding problem, prepare the 19X5 statement of cash flows by the indirect method. If your instructor also assigned Problem 15-3A, prepare only the operating activities section of the statement.

Problem 15-5A *Preparing the statement of cash flows—indirect method* **(L.O. 2,5)**

Plywood Products Corporation of America accountants have assembled the following data for the year ended December 31, 19X7:

	December 31,	
	19X7	**19X6**
Current accounts (all result from operations):		
Current assets:		
Cash and cash equivalents............	$85,700	$22,700
Accounts receivable..................	59,700	64,200
Inventories..........................	88,600	83,000
Prepaid expenses	5,300	4,100
Current liabilities:		
Notes payable (for inventory purchases)	$22,600	$18,300
Accounts payable....................	52,900	55,800
Income tax payable	18,600	16,700
Accrued liabilities..................	25,500	27,200

Transaction data for 19X7:

Acquisition of long-term		Sale of equipment	$58,000
investment............	$ 31,600	Amortization expense....	5,300
Acquisition of land by		Purchase of treasury stock	14,300
issuing long-term note		Loss on sale of equipment	11,700
payable..............	113,000	Payment of cash	
Stock dividends	31,800	dividends.............	18,300
Collection of loan........	8,700	Issuance of long-term	
Depreciation expense	26,800	note payable to borrow	
Acquisition of building...	125,300	cash.................	34,400
Retirement of bonds		Net income	67,100
payable by issuing		Issuance of common stock	
common stock	65,000	for cash	41,200

Required

Prepare Plywood Products' statement of cash flows, using the *indirect* method to report operating activities. Include an accompanying schedule of noncash investing and financing activities.

Problem 15-6A *Preparing the statement of cash flows—indirect method* **(L.O. 2,5)**

The comparative balance sheet of Oefinger, Inc., at March 31, 19X7, reported the following:

	March 31,	
	19X7	19X6

Current assets:

Cash and cash equivalents	$ 9,100	$ 4,000
Accounts receivable	19,400	21,700
Inventories	63,200	60,600
Prepaid expenses	1,900	1,700

Current liabilities:

Notes payable (for inventory purchases)	$ 4,000	$ 4,000
Accounts payable	30,300	27,600
Accrued liabilities	10,700	11,100
Income tax payable.............	8,000	4,700

Oefinger's transactions during the year ended March 31, 19X7, included the following:

Payment of cash dividend..	$30,000	Cash acquisition of building	$47,000
Cash acquisition of equipment.............	78,700	Net income	70,000
		Issuance of common stock	
Issuance of long-term note payable to borrow cash ..	50,000	for cash	11,000
		Stock dividend	18,000
Acquisition of land by issuing note payable.....	62,000	Sale of long-term investment	13,700
Amortization expense	2,000	Depreciation expense	9,000

Required

Prepare Oefinger's statement of cash flows for the year ended March 31, 19X7, using the *indirect* method to report cash flows from operating activities. Report noncash investing and financing activities in an accompanying schedule. All current account balances resulted from operating transactions.

Problem 15-7A *Preparing the statement of cash flows—direct and indirect methods* (L.O. 3,5)

To prepare the statement of cash flows, accountants for The Inn of Charleston, Inc., have summarized 19X3 activity in two accounts as follows:

Cash

Beginning balance	53,600	Payments on accounts payable	399,100
Collection of loan	13,000	Payments of dividends ...	27,200
Sale of investment	8,200	Payments of salaries	
Receipts of interest.......	12,600	and wages	143,800
Collections from		Payments of interest	26,900
customers	706,700	Purchase of equipment ...	31,400
Issuance of common stock	19,300	Payments of operating	
Receipts of dividends	4,500	expenses	34,300
		Payment of long-term debt	41,300
		Purchase of treasury stock	26,400
		Payment of income tax ...	18,900
Ending balance	68,600		

Common Stock

Beginning balance	84,400
Issuance for cash	19,300
Issuance to acquire land ..	80,100
Issuance to retire long-term debt	19,000
Ending balance	202,800

Required

1. Prepare The Inn of Charleston's statement of cash flows for the year ended December 31, 19X3, using the *direct* method to report operating activities. Also prepare the accompanying schedule of noncash investing and financing activities.

The Inn of Charleston's 19X3 income statement and selected balance sheet data follow.

The Inn of Charleston, Inc.
Income Statement
For the Year Ended December 31, 19X3

Revenues:		
Sales revenue		$734,300
Interest revenue		12,600
Dividend revenue		4,500
Total revenues		751,400
Expenses and losses:		
Cost of goods sold	$402,600	
Salary and wage expense	150,800	
Depreciation expense	24,300	
Other operating expense	44,100	
Interest expense	28,800	
Income tax expense	16,200	
Loss on sale of investments	1,100	
Total expenses		667,900
Net income		$ 83,500

The Inn of Charleston, Inc. Balance Sheet Data	Increase (Decrease)
Current assets:	
Cash and cash equivalents.................	$?
Accounts receivable	27,600
Inventories..............................	(11,800)
Prepaid expenses	600
Current liabilities:	
Accounts payable	$ (8,300)
Interest payable	1,900
Salary payable...........................	7,000
Other accrued liabilities	10,400
Income tax payable	(2,700)

Required

2. Use these data to prepare a supplementary schedule showing cash flows from operating activities by the *indirect* method. All activity in the current accounts results from operations.

Problem 15-8A *Preparing the statement of cash flows—indirect and direct methods*
(L.O. 3,4,5)

The comparative balance sheet of Paper Clips, Inc., at June 30, 19X7, included the following balances:

Paper Clips, Inc.
Partial Balance Sheet
June 30, 19X7 and 19X6

	19X7	19X6	Increase (Decrease)
Current assets:			
Cash	$21,300	$ 8,600	$12,700
Accounts receivable	45,900	48,300	(2,400)
Interest receivable	2,900	3,600	(700)
Inventories	68,600	60,200	8,400
Prepaid expenses.....................	3,700	2,800	900
Current liabilities:			
Notes payable, short-term			
(for general borrowing)	$13,400	$18,100	$(4,700)
Accounts payable	42,400	40,300	2,100
Income tax payable	13,800	14,500	(700)
Accrued liabilities	8,200	9,700	(1,500)
Interest payable	3,700	2,900	800
Salary payable	900	2,600	(1,700)

Transaction data for the year ended June 30, 19X7:

a. Net income, $56,200.
b. Depreciation expense on equipment, $10,200.
c. Purchased long-term investment, $4,900.
d. Sold land for $46,900, including $6,700 loss.
e. Acquired equipment by issuing long-term note payable, $14,300.
f. Paid long-term note payable, $61,000.
g. Received cash for issuance of common stock, $3,900.
h. Paid cash dividends, $38,100.
i. Paid short-term note payable by issuing common stock, $4,700.

Required

1. Prepare the statement of cash flows of Paper Clips, Inc., for the year ended June 30, 19X7, using the *indirect* method to report operating activities. Also prepare the accompanying schedule of noncash investing and financing activities. All current accounts except short-term notes payable result from operating transactions.

2. Prepare a supplementary schedule showing cash flows from operations by the *direct* method. The income statement reports the following: sales, $237,300; interest revenue, $10,600; cost of goods sold, $82,800; salary

expense, $38,800; other operating expenses, $37,200; depreciation expense, $10,200; income tax expense, $9,900; loss on sale of land, $6,700; interest expense, $6,100.

(Group B)

Problem 15-1B   Using cash-flow information to evaluate performance   (L.O. 1)

Top managers of Leadership Dynamics, Inc., are reviewing company performance for 19X4. The income statement reports a 12 percent increase in net income, the fifth consecutive year with an income increase above 10 percent. The income statement includes a nonrecurring loss without which net income would have increased by 16 percent. The balance sheet shows modest increases in assets, liabilities, and stockholders' equity. The assets posting the largest increases are plant and equipment because the company is halfway through a five-year expansion program. No other assets and no liabilities are increasing dramatically. A summarized version of the cash flow statement reports the following:

Net cash inflow from operating activities .	$120,000
Net cash outflow from investing activities	(90,000)
Net cash inflow from financing activities .	10,000
Increase in cash during 19X4	$ 40,000

Required

Write a memo to give top managers of Leadership Dynamics your assessment of 19X4 and your outlook for the future. Focus on the information content of the cash flow data.

Problem 15-2B   Preparing the statement of cash flows—direct method   (L.O. 1,3)

Oakland Bay Corporation accountants have developed the following data from the company's accounting records for the year ended July 31, 19X9:

1. Proceeds from issuance of short-term debt, $44,100
2. Payments of long-term debt, $18,800
3. Proceeds from sale of plant assets, $49,700, including $10,600 gain
4. Interest revenue, $12,100
5. Cash receipt of dividend revenue on stock investments, $5,700
6. Payments to suppliers, $683,300
7. Interest expense and payments, $37,800
8. Salary expense, $105,300
9. Cash payments to purchase plant assets, $181,000
10. Cost of goods sold, $481,100
11. Collection of interest revenue, $11,700
12. Acquisition of equipment by issuing short-term note payable, $35,500
13. Payments of salaries, $104,000
14. Credit sales, $608,100
15. Loan to another company, $35,000
16. Income tax expense and payments, $56,400
17. Depreciation expense, $27,700
18. Collections on accounts receivable, $673,100
19. Loan collections, $74,400
20. Proceeds from sale of investments, $34,700, including $3,800 loss
21. Payment of long-term debt by issuing preferred stock, $107,300
22. Amortization expense, $23,900

23. Cash sales, $146,000
24. Proceeds from issuance of common stock, $116,900
25. Payment of cash dividends, $50,500
26. Cash balance: July 31, 19X8—$53,800
       July 31, 19X9—$?

Required

Prepare Oakland Bay Corporation's statement of cash flows for the year ended July 31, 19X9. Follow the format of Exhibit 15-1, but do *not* show amounts in thousands. Include an accompanying schedule of noncash investing and financing activities. Evaluate 19X9 from a cash-flow standpoint. Give your reasons.

Problem 15-3B *Preparing the statement of cash flows—direct method* **(L.O. 2,3,4)**

The 19X3 comparative balance sheet and income statement of Gold Imari, Inc., follow:

Comparative Balance Sheet

	19X3	19X2	Increase (Decrease)
Current assets:			
Cash and cash equivalents	$ 37,500	$ 15,600	$ 21,900
Accounts receivable	41,500	43,100	(1,600)
Interest receivable	600	900	(300)
Inventories	94,300	89,900	4,400
Prepaid expenses	1,700	2,200	(500)
Plant assets:			
Land......................	35,100	10,000	25,100
Equipment, net	100,900	93,700	7,200
Total assets........................	$311,600	$255,400	$ 56,200
Current liabilities:			
Accounts payable	$ 16,400	$ 17,900	$ (1,500)
Interest payable....................	6,300	6,700	(400)
Salary payable	2,100	1,400	700
Other accrued liabilities..............	18,100	18,700	(600)
Income tax payable..................	6,300	3,800	2,500
Long-term liabilities:			
Notes payable	55,000	65,000	(10,000)
Stockholders' equity:			
Common stock, no-par	131,100	122,300	8,800
Retained earnings	76,300	19,600	56,700
Total liabilities and stockholders' equity ..	$311,600	$255,400	$ 56,200

Income Statement for 19X3

Revenues:		
Sales revenue		$461,800
Interest revenue		11,700
Total revenues		473,500
Expenses:		
Cost of goods sold	$205,200	
Salary expense	76,400	
Depreciation expense	15,300	
Other operating expense	49,700	
Interest expense	24,600	
Income tax expense	16,900	
Total expenses		388,100
Net income		$ 85,400

Gold Imari had no noncash investing and financing transactions during 19X3. During the year there were no sales of land or equipment, no issuances of notes payable, no retirements of stock, and no treasury stock transactions.

Required

Prepare the 19X3 statement of cash flows, formatting operating activities by the direct method.

Problem 15-4B *Preparing the statement of cash flows—indirect method* (*L.O. 2,3,5*)

Required

Using the Gold Imari data from the preceding problem, prepare the 19X3 statement of cash flows by the indirect method. If your instructor also assigned Problem 14-3B, prepare only the operating activities section.

Problem 15-5B *Preparing the statement of cash flows—indirect method* (*L.O. 2,5*)

Accountants for Creve Coeur Manufacturing have assembled the following data for the year ended December 31, 19X4:

	December 31,	
	19X4	**19X3**
Current accounts (all result from operations):		
Current assets:		
Cash and cash equivalents	$30,600	$34,800
Accounts receivable	70,100	73,700
Inventories	90,600	96,500
Prepaid expenses	3,200	2,100
Current liabilities:		
Notes payable (for inventory purchases)	$36,300	$36,800
Accounts payable	72,100	67,500
Income tax payable............	5,900	6,800
Accrued liabilities	28,300	23,200

Transaction data for 19X4:

Acquisition of long-term investment	$ 44,800	Sale of long-term investment	$12,200
Acquisition of building by issuing long-term note payable	162,000	Amortization expense	1,100
		Payment of long-term debt	47,800
		Gain on sale of investment	3,500
Stock dividends	12,600	Payment of cash dividends	48,300
Collection of loan	10,300	Issuance of long-term debt to borrow cash	21,000
Depreciation expense	19,200		
Acquisition of equipment .	69,000	Net income	92,500
Payment of long-term debt by issuing common stock	89,400	Issuance of preferred stock for cash	36,200

Required

Prepare Creve Coeur Manufacturing's statement of cash flows, using the *indirect* method to report operating activities. Include an accompanying schedule of noncash investing and financing activities.

Problem 15-6B *Preparing the statement of cash flows—indirect method* **(L.O. 2,5)**

The comparative balance sheet of Gold's Gym, Inc., at December 31, 19X5, reported the following:

	December 31,	
	19X5	**19X4**
Current assets:		
Cash and cash equivalents	$10,600	$ 2,500
Accounts receivable	28,600	29,300
Inventories	51,600	53,000
Prepaid expenses	4,200	3,700
Current liabilities:		
Notes payable		
(for inventory purchases)	$ 9,200	$ -0-
Accounts payable	21,900	28,000
Accrued liabilities	14,300	16,800
Income tax payable.............	11,000	14,300

Gold's transactions during 19X5 included the following:

Retirement of bonds payable by issuing common stock	$40,000	Sale of long-term investment	$ 6,000
Amortization expense	5,000	Depreciation expense	15,000
Payment of cash dividends	17,000	Cash acquisition of building	104,000
Cash acquisition of equipment............	55,000	Net income	21,600
Issuance of long-term note payable to borrow cash .	32,000	Issuance of common stock for cash	105,600
		Stock dividend	13,000

Required

Prepare Gold's Gym's statement of cash flows for the year ended December 31, 19X5. Use the *indirect* method to report cash flows from operating activities. Report noncash investing and financing activities in an accompanying schedule. All current account balances result from operating transactions.

Problem 15-7B *Preparing the statement of cash flows—direct and indirect methods* **(L.O. 3,5)**

To prepare the statement of cash flows, accountants for Republic Publishing Company have summarized 19X8 activity in two accounts as follows:

Cash

Beginning balance	87,100	Payments of operating expenses	46,100
Issuance of common stock	34,600	Payment of long-term debt......................	78,900
Receipts of dividends	1,900		
Collection of loan	18,500	Purchase of treasury stock	10,400
Sale of investments	9,900	Payment of income tax	8,000
Receipts of interest....................	12,200		
Collections from customers	268,100	Payments on accounts payable............................	101,600
Sale of treasury stock	26,200	Payments of dividends	1,800
		Payments of salaries and wages.........................	67,500
		Payments of interest	21,800
		Purchase of equipment	79,900
Ending balance	42,500		

Common Stock

Beginning balance	103,500
Issuance for cash	34,600
Issuance to acquire land	62,100
Issuance to retire long-term debt	21,100
Ending balance	221,300

Required

1. Prepare Republic's statement of cash flows for the year ended December 31, 19X8, using the *direct* method to report operating activities. Also prepare the accompanying schedule of noncash investing and financing activities.

Republic's 19X8 income statement and selected balance sheet data follow.

Republic Publishing Company
Income Statement
For the Year Ended December 31, 19X8

Revenues and gains:		
Sales revenue		$251,800
Interest revenue		12,200
Dividend revenue		1,900
Gain on sale of investments		700
Total revenues and gains		266,600
Expenses:		
Cost of goods sold	$103,600	
Salary and wage expense	66,800	
Depreciation expense............	10,900	
Other operating expense.........	44,700	
Interest expense	24,100	
Income tax expense	2,600	
Total expenses		252,700
Net income		$ 13,900

Republic Publishing Company
Balance Sheet Data

	Increase (Decrease)
Current assets:	
Cash and cash equivalents.................	$?
Accounts receivable	(16,300)
Inventories.............................	5,700
Prepaid expenses	(1,900)
Current liabilities:	
Accounts payable.......................	$ 7,700
Interest payable	2,300
Salary payable.........................	(700)
Other accrued liabilities	(3,300)
Income tax payable	(5,400)

Required

2. Use these data to prepare a supplementary schedule showing cash flows from operating activities by the *indirect* method. All activity in the current accounts results from operations.

Problem 15-8B *Preparing the statement of cash flows—indirect and direct methods* **(L.O. 3,4,5)**

Longenecker-Scott Corporation's comparative balance sheet at September 30, 19X4, included the following balances:

	19X4	19X3	Increase (Decrease)
Longenecker-Scott Corporation			
Partial Balance Sheet			
September 30, 19X4 and 19X3			
Current assets:			
Cash	$ 69,700	$ 17,600	$ 52,100
Accounts receivable	41,900	44,000	(2,100)
Interest receivable	4,100	2,800	1,300
Inventories	121,700	116,900	4,800
Prepaid expenses	8,600	9,300	(700)
Current liabilities:			
Notes payable, short-term	$ 22,000	$ -0-	$ 22,000
Accounts payable	61,800	70,300	(8,500)
Income tax payable	21,800	24,600	(2,800)
Accrued liabilities	17,900	29,100	(11,200)
Interest payable	4,500	3,200	1,300
Salary payable	1,500	1,100	400

Transaction data for the year ended September 30, 19X4:

a. Net income, $114,900.
b. Depreciation expense on equipment, $8,500.
c. Acquired long-term investments, $37,300.
d. Sold land for $38,100, including $10,900 gain.
e. Acquired equipment by issuing long-term note payable,$26,300.
f. Paid long-term note payable, $24,700.
g. Received cash of $51,900 for issuance of common stock.
h. Paid cash dividends, $64,300.
i. Acquired equipment by issuing short-term note payable, $22,000.

Required

1. Prepare Longenecker-Scott's statement of cash flows for the year ended September 30, 19X4, using the *indirect* method to report operating activities. Also prepare the accompanying schedule of noncash investing and financing activities. All current accounts except short-term notes payable result from operating transactions.

2. Prepare a supplementary schedule showing cash flows from operations by the *direct* method. The income statement reports the following: sales, $391,600; gain on sale of land, $10,900; interest revenue, $7,300; cost of goods sold, $161,500; salary expense, $63,400; other operating expenses, $29,600; income tax expense, $18,400; interest expense, $13,500; depreciation expense, $8,500.

Extending Your Knowledge

Decision Problems

1. Using the Statement of Cash Flows to Evaluate a Company's Operations (L.O. 1)

The statement of changes in financial position, forerunner of the statement of cash flows, included information in only two categories: sources of funds and uses of funds. *Funds* were usually defined as working capital (current assets minus current liabilities). The earlier statement permitted the information to report changes in working capital while today's statement of cash flows reports information about flows in cash and cash equivalents.

Required

a. Explain why you think the present day statement of cash flows, with its disclosure of the three different kinds of activities, is or is not an improvement over the earlier statement format that showed only sources and uses of funds.

b. Is information about cash flows more informative to users than information about working capital flows?

c. Briefly explain why comparative balance sheets and a statement of cash flows are more informative than just comparative balance sheets.

2. Preparing and Using the Statement of Cash Flows to Evaluate Operations (L.O. 4,5)

The 19X6 comparative income statement and the 19X6 comparative balance sheet of Towers & Foster, Inc., have just been distributed at a meeting of the company's board of directors.

Towers & Foster, Inc.
Comparative Income Statement
Years Ended December 31, 19X6 and 19X5
(amounts in thousands)

	19X6	19X5
Revenues and gains:		
Sales revenue	$484	$310
Gain on sale of equipment (sale price, $33)	—	18
Totals	$484	$328
Expenses and losses:		
Cost of goods sold	$221	$162
Salary expense	48	28
Depreciation expense	46	22
Interest expense	13	20
Amortization expense on patent	11	11
Loss on sale of land (sale price, $61)	—	35
Totals	339	278
Net income	$145	$ 50

Towers & Foster, Inc.
Comparative Balance Sheet
December 31, 19X6 and 19X5
(amounts in thousands)

Assets	19X6	19X5
Cash	$ 23	$ 63
Accounts receivable, net	72	61
Inventories	194	181
Long-term investments	31	-0-
Property, plant, and equipment	401	259
Accumulated depreciation	(244)	(198)
Patents	177	188
Totals	$654	$554

Liabilities and Owners' Equity

	19X6	19X5
Notes payable, short-term (for general borrowing)	$ 32	$101
Accounts payable	63	56
Accrued liabilities	12	17
Notes payable, long-term	147	163
Common stock, no-par	139	61
Retained earnings	261	156
Totals	$654	$554

In discussing the company's results of operations and year-end financial position, the members of the board of directors raise a fundamental question: Why is the cash balance so low? This question is especially troublesome to the board members because 19X6 showed record profits. As the controller of the company, you must answer the question.

Required

1. Prepare a statement of cash flows for 19X6 in the format that best shows the relationship between net income and operating cash flow. The company sold no plant assets or long-term investments and issued no notes payable during 19X6. The changes in all current accounts except short-term notes payable arose from operations. There were *no* noncash investing and financing transactions during the year. Show all amounts in thousands.

2. Answer the board members' question: Why is the cash balance so low? In explaining the business's cash flows, identify two significant cash receipts that occurred during 19X5 but not in 19X6. Also point out the two largest cash disbursements during 19X6.

3. Considering net income and the company's cash flows during 19X6, was it a good year or a bad year? Give your reasons.

Ethical Issue

FASB Statement No. 95 requires companies to report the statement of cash flows. Prior to 1988, companies disclosed similar information in the statement of changes in financial position (SCFP). The SCFP started with net income and made certain adjustments similar to the indirect method for reporting cash flows from operating activities.

Statement No. 95 states the FASB's preference for the direct method of reporting cash flows from operating activities. In public hearings, however, companies have argued that it would be expensive to assemble the data required by the direct method. Therefore, *FASB Statement No. 95* permits the indirect method. Most companies follow the indirect-method format.

Required

1. Which method of reporting cash flows from operating activities is easier for you to understand—the direct method (page 711) or the indirect method (page 726)? Give your reason.
2. Consider the computations of operating cash flows outlined on pages 718 to 726. Do the direct-method computations require many new data? Do the computations appear to be as expensive as companies have claimed?
3. Why do you think companies have resisted reporting operating cash flows by the direct method? Is this resistance in any way unethical? Give your reasons.

Financial Statement Problems

1. Using the Statement of Cash Flows   (L.O. 1,2,3,4,5)

The Goodyear Tire & Rubber Company statement of cash flows appears in Appendix C. Use this statement along with the company's other financial statements to answer the following questions.

1. By which method does Goodyear report net cash flows from *operating* activities? How can you tell?
2. Suppose Goodyear reported net cash flows from operating activities by the direct method. Compute these amounts for 1991:
   a. Collections from customers.
   b. Payments to employees. Assume Salary Expense, Wage Expense, and other payroll expenses totaled $850.0 million for the year.
   c. Payments for income tax.
3. Evaluate 1991 in terms of net income, cash flows, balance sheet position, and overall results. Be specific.

2. Computing Cash Flow Amounts and Using Cash Flow Data for Analysis (L.O. 1,2,3,4,5)

Obtain the annual report of an actual company of your choosing. Annual reports are available in various forms including the original document in hard copy, microfiche, and computerized data bases such as that provided by Disclosure, Inc.

Answer these questions about the company. Concentrate on the current year in the annual report you select.

1. By which method does the company report net cash flows from *operating activities?* How can you tell?
2. Suppose the company reported net cash flows from operating activities by the direct method. Compute these amounts for the current year:
   a. Collections from customers.
   b. Payments to employees. Assume that the sum of Salary Expense, Wage Expense, and other payroll expenses for the current year make up 60 percent of Selling, General, and Administrative Expenses (or expense of similar title).
   c. Payments for income tax.
3. Evaluate the current year in terms of net income (or net loss), cash flows, balance sheet position, and overall results. Be specific.

Appendix:

The Work-Sheet Approach to Preparing the Statement of Cash Flows

The main body of the chapter discusses the use of the statement of cash flows in decision making and shows how to prepare the statement using T-accounts. The T-account approach works well as a learning device, especially for simple situations. In actual practice, however, most companies face complex situations. In these cases, a work sheet can help accountants prepare the statement of cash flows. This appendix shows how to prepare the statement of cash flows using a specially designed work sheet.

The basic task in preparing the statement of cash flows is to account for all the cash effects of transactions that took the business from its beginning financial position to its ending financial position. Like the T-account approach, the work sheet approach helps the accountant identify the cash effects of all transactions of the period. The work sheet starts with the beginning balance sheet and concludes with the ending balance sheet. Two middle columns—one for debit amounts and the other for credit amounts—complete the work sheet. These columns, labeled Transaction Analysis, contain the data for the statement of cash flows. Exhibit 15A-1 presents the basic framework of the work sheet. Accountants can prepare the statement directly from the lower part of the work sheet (Panel B in Exhibit 15A-1). The advantage of the work sheet approach is that it organizes in one place all relevant data for the statement's preparation. Exhibit 15A-1 and the other exhibits in this appendix are based on the Anchor Coporation data in the chapter.

The work sheet can be used with either the direct method or the indirect method for operating activities. As with the T-account approach, cash flows from investing activities and cash flows from financing activities are unaffected by the method used for operating activities.

EXHIBIT 15A-1

	Balances Dec. 31, 19X1	Transaction Analysis Debit	Transaction Analysis Credit	Balances Dec. 31, 19X2
Anchor Corporation Work Sheet for Statement of Cash Flows For the Year Ended December 31, 19X2				
Panel A—Account Titles				
Cash				
Accounts receivable . .				
Retained earnings				
Panel B—Statement of Cash Flows				
Cash flows from operating activities: . . .				
Cash flows from investing activities: . . .				
Cash flows from financing activities: . . .				
Net increase (decrease) in cash				

Preparing the Work Sheet—Direct Method for Operating Activities

The direct method separates operating activities into cash receipts and cash payments. Exhibit 15A-2 is the work sheet for preparing the statement of cash flows by the direct method. The work sheet can be prepared by following these steps:

Step 1. In Panel A, insert the beginning and ending balances for Cash, Accounts Receivable, and all other balance sheet accounts through Retained Earnings. The amounts are taken directly from the beginning and ending balance sheets in Exhibit 15-4, page 718.

Step 2. In Panel B, lay out the framework of the statement of cash flows as shown in Exhibit 15A-1—that is, enter the headings for cash flows from operating activities, investing activities, and financing activities. Exhibit 15A-2 is based on the direct method and splits operating activities into Receipts and Payments.

Step 3. At the bottom of the work sheet, write Net Increase in Cash or Net Decrease in Cash, as the case may be. This final amount on the work sheet is the difference between ending cash and beginning cash, as reported on the balance sheet. Fundamentally, the statement of cash flows is designed to explain *why* this change in cash occurred during the period.

Step 4. Analyze the period's transactions in the middle columns of the work sheet. Transaction analysis is the most challenging part of preparing the work sheet. The remainder of this appendix explains this crucial step.

Step 5. Prepare the statement of cash flows directly from Panel B of the work sheet.

Transaction Analysis on the Work Sheet

For your convenience, we repeat the Anchor Corporation transaction data from page 712. Transactions with cash effects are denoted by an asterisk.

Operating Activities:

   a. Sales on credit, $284,000
 * b. Collections from customers, $271,000
   c. Interest revenue earned, $12,000
 * d. Collection of interest receivable, $10,000
 * e. Cash receipt of dividend revenue, $9,000
   f. Cost of goods sold, $150,000
   g. Purchases of inventory on credit, $147,000
 * h. Payments to suppliers, $133,000
   i. Salary and wage expense, $56,000
 * j. Payments of salaries and wages, $58,000
   k. Depreciation expense, $18,000
   l. Other operating expense, $17,000
 * m. Interest expense and payments, $16,000
 * n. Income tax expense and payments, $15,000

Anchor Corporation
Work Sheet for Statement of Cash Flows (Direct Method)
For the Year Ended December 31, 19X2

Panel A—Account Titles	Balances Dec. 31, 19X1	Transaction Analysis Debit		Transaction Analysis Credit		Balances Dec. 31, 19X2
Cash	42			(v)	20	22
Accounts receivable	80	(a)	284	(b)	271	93
Interest receivable	1	(c)	12	(d)	10	3
Inventory	138	(g)	147	(f)	150	135
Prepaid expenses	7	(h3)	1			8
Long-term receivable from another company	—	(p)	11			11
Plant assets, net	219	(o)	306	(k)	18	
				(q)	54	453
Totals	487					725
Accounts payable	57	(h1)	113	(g)	147	91
Salary and wage payable	6	(j)	58	(i)	56	4
Accrued liabilities	3	(h2)	19	(l)	17	1
Long-term debt	77	(t)	11	(s)	94	160
Common stock	258			(r)	101	359
Retained earnings	86	(f)	150	(a)	284	110
		(l)	17	(c)	12	
		(i)	56	(e)	9	
		(k)	18	(q)	8	
		(m)	16			
		(n)	15			
		(u)	17			
Totals	487		1,251		1,251	725

Panel B—Statement of Cash Flows

Cash flows from operating activites:				
Receipts:				
Collections from customers	(b)	271		
Interest received	(d)	10		
Dividends received	(e)	9		
Payments:				
To suppliers			(h1)	113
			(h2)	19
			(h3)	1
To employees			(j)	58
For interest			(m)	16
For income tax			(n)	15
Cash flows from investing activities:				
Acquisition of plant assets			(o)	306
Proceeds from sale of plant assets	(q)	62		
Loan to another company			(p)	11
Cash flows from financing activities:				
Proceeds from issuance of common stock	(r)	101		
Proceeds from issuance of long-term debt	(s)	94		
Payment of long-term debt			(t)	11
Payment of dividends			(u)	17
		547		567
Net decrease in cash	(v)	20		
Totals		567		567

Investing Activities:

* o. Cash payments to acquire plant assets, $306,000
* p. Loan to another company, $11,000
* q. Proceeds from sale of plant assets, $62,000, including $8,000 gain

Financing Activities:

* r. Proceeds from issuance of common stock, $101,000
* s. Proceeds from issuance of long-term debt, $94,000
* t. Payments of long-term debt, $11,000
* u. Declaration and payment of cash dividends, $17,000

Operating Activities. The transaction analysis on the work sheet appears in the form of journal entries. Observe that only balance sheet accounts appear on the work sheet. There are no income statement accounts. Therefore, revenue transactions are entered on the work sheet as credits to Retained Earnings. For example, in transaction *a*, sales on account are entered on the work sheet by debiting Accounts Receivable and crediting Retained Earnings. Cash is neither debited nor credited because credit sales do not affect cash. Nevertheless, this transaction and all other transactions should be entered on the work sheet in order to identify all the cash effects of the period's transactions. In transaction *c*, the earning of interest revenue is entered by debiting Interest Receivable and crediting Retained Earnings.

The revenue transactions that generate cash are also recorded by crediting Retained Earnings. For example, transaction *e* is a cash receipt of dividend revenue. The work sheet entry credits Retained Earnings and debits Dividends Received as a cash receipt from operating activities. Transaction *d* is a collection of interest receivable. The work sheet entry debits Interest Received—a cash receipt from operating activities—and credits Interest Receivable.

Expense transactions are entered on the work sheet as debits to Retained Earnings. In transaction *f*, cost of goods sold is entered by debiting Retained Earnings and crediting Inventory. Transaction *i* for salary and wage expense is entered by debiting Retained Earnings and crediting Salary and Wage Payable. In transaction *k*, depreciation is entered by debiting Retained Earnings and crediting Plant Assets, Net (this work sheet uses no Accumulated Depreciation account). In transaction *l*, other operating expense is entered by debiting Retained Earnings and crediting Accrued Liabilities. These transactions should be entered on the work sheet even though they have no direct effect on cash.

Transaction *m* is a cash payment of interest expense. The work sheet entry debits Retained Earnings and credits Payments for Interest under operating activities. Transaction *n* is a cash payment for income tax.

Transaction *h* deserves special emphasis. The Payment to Suppliers of $133,000 includes three individual amounts: payments of accounts payable, $113,000; payments of accrued liabilities, $19,000; and payments of prepaid expenses, $1,000. How were these three amounts computed? These amounts are the differences needed to reconcile each account's beginning balance to its ending balance. For example, Prepaid Expenses increased from a beginning balance of $7,000 to an ending amount of $8,000. This increase must occur through a cash payment of $1,000 (transaction *h3*). Payments of prepaid expenses are labeled as Payments to Suppliers on the statement of cash flows when operating activities are reported by the direct method. The $113,000 debit to Accounts Payable (transaction *h1*) is computed as the amount needed to complete the reconciliation from the beginning balance ($57,000) to the ending amount ($91,000), taking into consideration the $147,000 credit purchase of inventory in transaction *g* ($57,000 + $147,000 − $91,000 = $113,000). The

$19,000 debit to Accrued Liabilities (transaction $h2$) is the amount needed to reconcile the beginning balance to the ending balance after considering the $17,000 credit amount in transaction l.

Investing Activities. The first investing activity listed in Panel B of the work sheet is transaction o, the $306,000 cash payment to acquire plant assets. This transaction is entered on the work sheet by debiting Plant Assets, Net and crediting Acquisition of Plant Assets under cash flows from operating activities. Transaction q is a cash receipt from an investing activity. The cash proceeds of $62,000 from sale of plant assets are entered as a cash receipt under investing activities. The $8,000 gain is credited to Retained Earnings, with the remaining $54,000—the asset's book value—credited to Plant Assets, Net. The last investing transaction (transaction p) is a loan to another company, entered on the work sheet by debiting Long-term Receivable from Another Company and crediting Loan to Another Company under investing activities.

Financing Activities. The issuance of common stock for $101,000 cash (transaction r) is entered on the work sheet by debiting Proceeds from Issuance of Common Stock under financing activities and crediting Common Stock. The $94,000 issuance of long-term debt (transaction s) is entered in a similar manner but with a credit to Long-term Debt. The payment of long-term debt (transaction t) debits Long-Term Debt and credits Payment of Long-term Debt under financing activities. The payment of dividends (transaction u) debits Retained Earnings and credits Payment of Dividends as a financing cash payment.

Net Increase (Decrease) in Cash. The net increase or net decrease in cash or the period is the balancing amount needed to equate the total debits and total credits ($567,000) on the statement of cash flows. In Exhibit 15A-2, Anchor Corporation experienced a $20,000 decrease in cash. This amount is entered as a credit to Cash (transaction v) at the top of the work sheet and a debit to Net Decrease in Cash at the bottom. Totaling the columns completes the work sheet.

Preparing the Statement of Cash Flows from the Work Sheet

To prepare the statement of cash flows, which appears as Exhibit 15-1, page 709 of the text, the accountant has only to rewrite Panel B of the work sheet and add subtotals for the three categories of activities. In Exhibit 15A-2, net cash *inflows* from operating activities total $68,000 [receipts of $290,000 ($271,000 + $10,000 + $9,000) minus payments of $222,000 ($113,000 + $19,000 + $1,000 + $58,000 + $16,000 + $15,000)]. Net cash *outflows* from investing activities are $255,000 ($306,000 + $11,000 − $62,000). Net cash *inflows* from financing activities equal $167,000 ($101,000 + $94,000 − $11,000 − $17,000). Altogether, these three subtotals explain why cash decreased by $20,000 ($68,000 − $255,000 + $167,000 = −$20,000).

Preparing the Work Sheet—Indirect Method for Operating Activities

The indirect method shows the reconciliation from net income to net cash inflow (or net cash outflow) from operating activities. Exhibit 15A-3 is the work sheet for preparing the statement of cash flows by the indirect method.

Anchor Corporation
Work Sheet for Statement of Cash Flows (Indirect Method)
For the Year Ended December 31, 19X2

Panel A—Account Titles	Balances Dec. 31, 19X1	Transaction Analysis Debit		Transaction Analysis Credit		Balances Dec. 31, 19X2
			(Amounts in thousands)			
Cash	42			(q)	20	22
Accounts receivable	80	(d)	13			93
Interest receivable	1	(e)	2			3
Inventory	138			(f)	3	135
Prepaid expenses	7	(g)	1			8
Long-term receivable from another company	—	(l)	11			11
Plant assets, net	219	(k)	306	(b)	18	
				(c)	54	453
Totals	487					725
Accounts payable	57			(h)	34	91
Salary and wage payable	6	(i)	2			4
Accrued liabilities	3	(j)	2			1
Long-term debt	77	(o)	11	(n)	94	160
Common stock	258			(m)	101	359
Retained earnings	86	(p)	17	(a)	41	110
Totals	487		365		365	725

Panel B—Statement of Cash Flows

		Debit		Credit	
Cash flows from operating activities:					
Net income	(a)	41			
Add (subtract) items that affect net income and cash flow differently:					
Depreciation	(b)	18			
Gain on sale of plant assets				(c)	8
Increase in accounts receivable				(d)	13
Increase in interest receivable				(e)	2
Decrease in inventory	(f)	3			
Increase in prepaid expenses				(g)	1
Increase in accounts payable	(h)	34			
Decrease in salary and wage payable				(i)	2
Decrease in accrued liabilities				(j)	2
Cash flows from investing activities:					
Acquisition of plant assets				(k)	306
Proceeds from sale of plant assets	(c)	62			
Loan to another company				(l)	11
Cash flows from financing activities:					
Proceeds from issuance of common stock	(m)	101			
Proceeds from issuance of long-term debt	(n)	94			
Payment of long-term debt				(o)	11
Payment of dividends				(p)	17
		353			373
Net decrease in cash	(q)	20			
Totals		373			373

The steps in completing the work sheet using the indirect method are the same as those taken using the direct method. However, the data for the operating cash flows come from different sources. Net income, depreciation, depletion and amortization, and gains and losses on disposals of plant assets come from the income statement. The changes in noncash current asset accounts (Receivables, Inventory, and Prepaid Expenses for Anchor Corporation) and the current liability accounts (Accounts Payable, Salary and Wage Payable, and Accrued Liabilities) are taken directly from the comparative balance sheet.

The analysis of investing activities and financing activities uses the information presented on page 712 and repeated on pages 757 and 759 of this appendix. As mentioned previously, there is no difference for investing activities or financing activities between the direct-method work sheet and the indirect-method work sheet. Therefore, the analysis that follows focuses on cash flows from operating activities. The Anchor Corporation data come from the income statement (Exhibit 15-3, page 715) and the comparative balance sheet (Exhibit 15-4, page 718).

Transaction Analysis Under the Indirect Method

Net income (transaction a) is the first operating cash inflow. Net income is entered on the work sheet as a debit to Net Income under cash flows from operating activities and a credit to Retained Earnings. Next come the additions to, and subtractions from, net income, starting with depreciation (transaction b), which is debited to Depreciation on the work sheet and credited to Plant Assets, Net. Transaction c is the sale of plant assets. The $8,000 gain on the sale is entered as a credit to Gain on Sale of Plant Assets under operating cash flows—a subtraction from net income. This credit removes the $8,000 amount of the gain from cash flow from operations because the cash proceeds from the sale were not $8,000. The cash proceeds were $62,000, so this amount is entered on the work sheet as a debit under investing activities. To complete entry c, the plant assets' book value of $54,000 ($62,000 − $8,000) is credited to the Plant Assets, Net account.

Entries d through j reconcile net income to cash flows from operations for increases and decreases in the current assets other than Cash and for increases and decreases in the current liabilities. Entry d debits Accounts Receivable for its $13,000 increase during the year. This decrease in cash flows is credited to Increase in Accounts Receivable under operating cash flows. Entries e and g are similar for Interest Receivable and Prepaid Expenses.

During the year, Inventory decreased by $3,000. This increase in cash is credited to Inventory in work sheet entry f, with the debit to Decrease in Inventory under operating activities.

Entry h records the $34,000 increase in Accounts Payable by crediting this account. The resulting increase in cash is debited to Increase in Accounts Payable under operating cash flows. Entry i debits Salary and Wage Payable for its $2,000 decrease, with the offsetting credit to Decrease in Salary and Wage Payable. Entry j for Accrued Liabilities is similar.

Do not be confused by the different keying of investing transactions and financing transactions in Exhibits 15A-2 and 15A-3. Except for the letters used to key transactions, the entries are identical. For example, the $306,000 acquisition of plant assets is transaction o in Exhibit 15A-2 and transaction k in Exhibit 15A-3. In each exhibit, we maintain a continuous listing of transactions starting with the letter a. The two exhibits simply have different keyed letters because of the number of transactions.

The final item in Exhibit 15A-3 is the Net Decrease in Cash—transaction q on the work sheet—a credit to Cash and a debit to Net Decrease in Cash, exactly as in Exhibit 15A-2.

To prepare the statement of cash flows from the work sheet, the accountant merely rewrites Panel B of the statement, adding subtotals for the three categories of activities. In Exhibit 14A-3, net cash inflow from operating activities is $68,000 ($41,000 + $18,000 + $3,000 + $34,000 − $8,000 − $13,000 − $2,000 − $1,000 − $2,000 − $2,000). Of course, this is the same amount of net cash inflow from operating activities computed under the direct method from Exhibit 15A-2. The indirect-method statement of cash flows appears in Exhibit 15-6, page 727 of the text.

Noncash Investing and Financing Activities on the Work Sheet. Noncash investing and financing activities can also be analyzed on the work sheet. Because this type of transaction includes both an investing activity and a financing activity, it requires two work sheet entries. For example, suppose Anchor Corporation purchased a building by issuing common stock of $320,000. Exhibit 15A-4 illustrates the transaction analysis of this noncash investing and financing activity. Observe that Cash is unaffected.

Work sheet entry t1 records the purchase of the building, and entry *t2* records the issuance of the stock. The order of these entries is unimportant.

EXHIBIT 15A-4   *Noncash Investing and Financing Activities on the Work Sheet*

Anchor Corporation
Work Sheet for Statement of Cash Flows
For the Year Ended December 31, 19X2

	Balances Dec. 31, 19X1	Transaction Analysis Debit	Transaction Analysis Credit	Balances Dec. 31, 19X2
Panel A—Account Titles				
Cash.........................				
Accounts receivable				
Building ≧≦...................	650,000	(t1) 320,000		970,000
Common Stock	890,000		(t2) 320,000	1,210,000
Retained earnings..............				
Panel B—Statement of Cash Flows				
Cash flows from operating activities:				
Net increase ≧≦ (decrease) in cash				
Noncash investing and financing transactions:				
Purchase of building by issuance of common stock		(t2) 320,000	(t1) 320,000	

ASSIGNMENT MATERIAL

Problem 15A-1   *Preparing the work sheet for the statement of cash flows—direct method*

The 19X3 comparative balance sheet and income statement of Gold Imari, Inc., follow:

Comparative Balance Sheet

	19X3	19X2	Increase (Decrease)
Current assets:			
Cash and cash equivalents	$ 37,500	$ 15,600	$21,900
Accounts receivable...........................	41,500	43,100	(1,600)
Interest receivable	600	900	(300)
Inventories...................................	94,300	89,900	4,400
Prepaid expenses	1,700	2,200	(500)
Plant assets:			
Land	35,100	10,000	25,100
Equipment, net...............................	100,900	93,700	7,200
Total assets...................................	$311,600	$255,400	$56,200
Current liabilities:			
Accounts payable.............................	$ 16,400	$ 17,900	$ (1,500)
Interest payable	6,300	6,700	(400)
Salary payable................................	2,100	1,400	700
Other accrued liabilities	18,100	18,700	(600)
Income tax payable	6,300	3,800	2,500
Long-term liabilities:			
Notes payable.................................	55,000	65,000	(10,000)
Stockholders' equity:			
Common stock, no-par.........................	131,100	122,300	8,800
Retained earnings	76,300	19,600	56,700
Total liabilities and stockholders' equity	$311,600	$255,400	$56,200

Income Statement for 19X3

Revenues:		
Sales revenue		$461,800
Interest revenue		11,700
Total revenues		473,500
Expenses:		
Cost of goods sold	$205,200	
Salary expense	76,400	
Depreciation expense	15,300	
Other operating expense	49,700	
Interest expense	24,600	
Income tax expense	16,900	
Total expenses		388,100
Net income...........................		$ 85,400

Gold Imari had no noncash investing and financing transactions during 19X3.

Required

Prepare the work sheet for the 19X3 statement of cash flows. Format cash flows from operating activities by the *direct* method.

Problem 15A-2 *Preparing the work sheet for the statement of cash flows—indirect method*

Using the Gold Imari, Inc., data from the preceding problem, prepare the work sheet for the 19X3 statement of cash flows. Format cash flows from operating activities by the *indirect* method.

Problem 15A-3 *Preparing the work sheet for the statement of cash flows—indirect method*

Longenecker-Scott Corporation's comparative balance sheet at September 30, 19X4, follows.

Longenecker-Scott Corporation
Partial Balance Sheet
September 30, 19X4 and 19X3

	19X4	19X3	Increase (Decrease)
Current assets:			
Cash...	$ 69,700	$ 17,600	$ 52,100
Accounts receivable	41,900	44,000	(2,100)
Interest receivable..........................	4,100	2,800	1,300
Inventories	121,700	116,900	4,800
Prepaid expenses	8,600	9,300	(700)
Long-term investments	55,400	18,100	37,300
Plant assets:			
Land	65,800	93,000	(27,200)
Equipment, net	89,500	49,700	39,800
Total assets..................................	$456,700	$351,400	$105,300
Current liabilities:			
Notes payable, short-term	$ 22,000	$ -0-	$ 22,000
Accounts payable	61,800	70,300	(8,500)
Income tax payable	21,800	24,600	(2,800)
Accrued liabilities	17,900	29,100	(11,200)
Interest payable.............................	4,500	3,200	1,300
Salary payable	1,500	1,100	400
Note payable, long-term	62,900	61,300	1,600
Stockholders' equity:			
Common stock	142,100	90,200	51,900
Retained earnings...........................	122,200	71,600	50,600
Total liabilities and stockholders' equity	$456,700	$351,400	$105,300

Transaction data for the year ended September 30, 19X4:

a. Net income, $114,900.

b. Depreciation expense on equipment, $8,500.

c. Acquired long-term investments, $37,300.

d. Sold land for $38,100, including $10,900 gain.

e. Acquired equipment by issuing long-term note payable, $26,300.

f. Paid long-term note payable, $24,700.

g. Received cash of $51,900 for issuance of common stock.

h. Paid cash dividends, $64,300.

i. Acquired equipment by issuing short-term note payable, $22,000.

Required

Prepare Longenecker-Scott's work sheet for the statement of cash flows for the year ended September 30, 19X4, using the *indirect* method to report operating activities. Include on the work sheet the noncash investing and financing activities.

Problem 15A-4   *Preparing the work sheet for the statement of cash flows—direct method*

Refer to the data of Problem 15A-3.

Required

Prepare Longenecker-Scott's work sheet for the statement of cash flows for the year ended September 30, 19X4, using the *direct* method for operating activities. The income statement reports the following: sales, $391,600; gain on sale of land, $10,900; interest revenue, $7,300; cost of goods sold, $161,500; salary expense, $63,400; other operating expenses, $29,600; income tax expense, $18,400; interest expense, $13,500; depreciation expense, $8,500. Include on the work sheet the noncash investing and financing activities.

DISTINCTIONS BETWEEN FINANCIAL AND MANAGEMENT ACCOUNTING

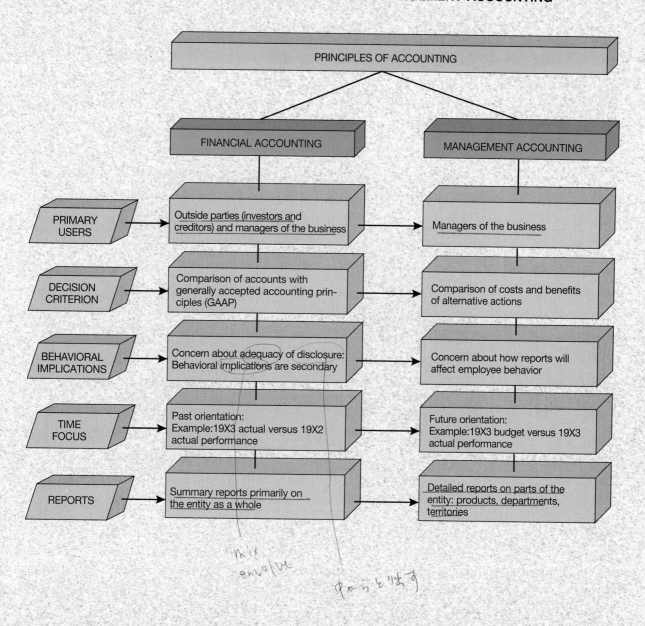

Chapter 16

Introduction to Management Accounting: The Master Budget

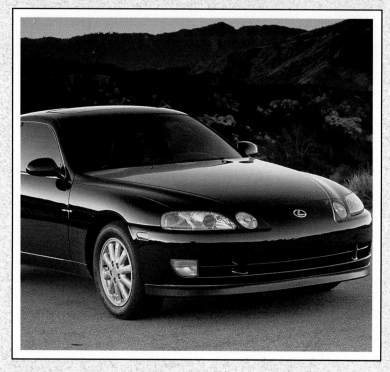

The automobile industry has changed dramatically. Cadillac and Lincoln buyers, who provide huge amounts of the profits of General Motors and Ford, respectively, are facing the challenge of new upper-end cars such as Toyota's Lexus and Nissan's Infiniti, which are selling extremely well.

Before introducing the Lexus and the Infiniti in the U.S. market, top managers of Toyota and Nissan had clearly defined goals. Their budgets called for U.S. dealers to sell specified numbers of Lexus and In-

finiti automobiles. Revenues come at a cost, so Toyota and Nissan managers also budgeted expenses—cost of goods sold, shipping expenses, sales commissions, and so on.

Did the Lexus and the Infiniti reach their sales and income targets? We may never know because these figures on specific products are buried in overall amounts reported to the public. But one point is certain: Top managers of Toyota and Nissan know exactly how the actual figures stacked up against the budget. That's how they run their business.

Our study of accounting has focused on gathering, processing, and reporting information for decision makers outside the business: investors, creditors, and government agencies. Thus far we have looked through their eyes at a business's past performance and financial position. The income statement tells users the results of the company's operations. The statement of cash flows reports where cash came from and how it was spent. The balance sheet shows the company's financial position. Accounting that reports to parties outside the business is called financial accounting.

We now shift our focus. We turn to a discussion of how accounting information helps shape the business's future, and we do this through the eyes of the people who run the business. The decision makers inside the company are called managers, and accounting designed to meet their information needs is called *management accounting*. The opening vignette illustrates this shift in focus. As you were reading it, did you notice the emphasis on goals, targets, and budgets? The final paragraph of the vignette underscores the role of budgeting in managing a business. Exhibit 16-1 summarizes the distinctions between management accounting and financial accounting.

Chapter 16 begins our study of management accounting by showing how budgets are prepared. We deal with the familiar financial statements: income statements and balance sheets. Our statements, however, will compile planned figures, not past figures, and we will evaluate performance by comparing actual results with budgeted amounts. Chapter 17 introduces a model of cost-volume-profit relationships, a favorite planning tool of managers, and Chapter 18 explores the effect of management policy on cost behavior.

Our first three chapters on management accounting are confined to nonmanufacturing organizations. In this way, we can explore two major tools (budgets and the cost-volume-profit model) without contending with the many new terms associated with manufacturing organizations. The latter appear in Chapters 19 and 20, which describe manufacturing accounting systems. Chapters 21 and 22 pursue management accounting tools in more depth. Chapter 23 highlights manufacturing costs and terms and recent developments such as activity-based costing and just-in-time manufacturing, while Chapters 24–27 focus on using accounting information to make business and special decisions. Above all, recognize that management accounting applies to all kinds of organizations, not just manufacturing companies.

Two Themes in Management Accounting

Two themes of management accounting are (1) the cost-benefit criterion and (2) behavioral implications. The *cost-benefit criterion* is a means for choosing among alternative accounting systems or methods—how well they help achieve management goals in relation to their costs. We use this common-

EXHIBIT 16-1 *Distinctions Between Management Accounting and Financial Accounting*

	Management Accounting	Financial Accounting
1. Primary users	Managers of the business	Outside parties (investors and creditors) and managers of the business
2. Decision criterion	Comparison of costs and benefits of proposed action	Comparison of accounts with generally accepted accounting principles (GAAP)
3. Behavioral implications	Concern about how reports will affect employee behavior	Concern about adequacy of disclosure. Behavioral implications are secondary
4. Time focus	Future orientation: Example: 19X3 **budget** versus 19X3 **actual** performance	Past orientation: Example: 19X3 **actual** versus 19X2 **actual** performance
5. Reports	Detailed reports on parts of the entity: products, departments, territories	Summary reports primarily on the entity as a whole

sense technique every day. For example, suppose you are asked whether you want cheese on your hamburger for an extra 25 cents. You weigh the benefit of adding the cheese against the cost. If the benefit exceeds the cost, you order cheese. If the benefit is less than 25 cents, you forgo the cheese.

A business application of the cost-benefit criterion is the installation of a budgeting system. A major benefit is to compel managers to plan and thus make different decisions than would have occurred from using only a historical system. Is an accounting system a good buy? The answer depends on managers' weighing perceived benefits against additional costs.

The *behavioral implications* of a course of action are also critical. Managers consider the effect of the action on people's behavior. Suppose the company in our example tries to increase sales by pressuring its sales staff to meet quotas. If a salesperson fails to meet quota for three consecutive months, he is fired. Depending on the personalities of the people involved, such a policy may lead to increased sales. But it may also create fear and cause a decline in sales. Effective management accounting systems apply the cost-benefit criterion in light of the behavioral implications of proposed action.

The Role of Management

How do managers use accounting information? Managers determine the company's goals and then plan and control its operations to reach those goals. They set long-range targets by asking questions such as: What will the company's total assets be in 5 years? By how much can the business increase sales over the next 10 years? Should the company spend $5 million on research to develop a new product line? Will it be profitable to introduce Lexus automobiles in the United States market? The most successful executives are able to consider a wide range of possible courses of action for their company. They answer these types of long-range questions by developing concrete plans of action.

Business must operate day by day also. Managers set short-range targets and communicate these goals to subordinates. To increase profits, suppose a business must increase production to 35,000 units next month. Similarly, cash inflow from operations must be $600,000 during December. Short-range goals like these must fit within the company's long-range strategy.

What features must an accounting system have to best meet management's information needs? What data help managers to plan and control business operations? How are decisions made by managers? This chapter and the next several answer these questions. We begin our discussion of management accounting by studying a manager's most valuable accounting tool: the budget.

The Budgeting System

A well-designed budgeting system includes the budget, the budget committee, and the budget period.

The Budget

The **budget** is management's quantitative expression of a plan of action and an aid to coordination and implementation. Budgets include quantities of products to be sold and their expected selling prices, numbers of employees and their pay, and a host of other amounts that are ultimately expressed in dollars. The budget summarizes the planning decisions of the business. A company may use a single budget to control all its operations or a separate budget for each subunit. This choice depends on the plans of the particular company's management. Our discussion will center on a company that uses an overall master budget to guide its operations. The **master budget** is the set of major financial statements and supporting schedules for the entire organization.

The Budget Committee

In many small businesses, the budgeting process is rather informal, with the owner and the employees deciding on goals for the future. In most medium-size-to-large organizations the **budget committee** oversees the preparation of the master budget. Because the master budget is the overall financial plan for the entire company, the budget committee includes representatives from all departments. Working together, they develop budget estimates "from the bottom up." Employees at the lowest level provide budget estimates to their supervisors, who make adjustments and forward the budget to middle managers, and so on up the line. For example, the vice-president of sales has each salesperson set a goal for the next period. The vice-president considers the goals of each salesperson and prepares an overall budget for the sales department. With sales personnel at all levels participating in the budget process, they are likely to work harder to achieve the budget than if it is handed down by top management. All other departments likewise collect budget information and forward it to the budget committee.

The committee coordinates the budget for the company as a whole. Without this coordination, the cost-of-goods-sold budget or the operating expense budget may be out of line with the sales budget, and vice versa.

Although top management has the final say in establishing the budget, it is best when many employees contribute to the overall process. An ideal budget results in all employees striving for excellence by trying to meet a clear-cut, coordinated set of goals.

The Budget Period

Budgets may cover any time period. Many companies use monthly, weekly, and daily cash budgets to ensure that they have enough cash on hand to meet immediate needs. Sales and expense budgets usually cover the accounting period, which may be a month, a quarter, or a year. Aligning the budget period with the accounting period makes the comparison of budgeted amounts and actual amounts easy. Most long-range budgets cover a five-year period. However, spans of 2, 3, or even 10 years are used.

Benefits of a Budget _____

The budgeting process offers these advantages:

1. *Provides direction.* The budgeting system forces managers to set realistic goals for the future. Without a formal plan, managers lack direction. This lack of planning filters throughout the company. The budget guides managers and department employees toward the achievement of specific goals. Toyota had clear goals in mind before investing so heavily in the marketing of Lexus automobiles.

2. *Motivates employees.* The budget motivates employees at all levels to meet the business's goals. Their work in preparing the budget makes it their personal target. This motivational aspect of budgeting underscores how budgeting affects employee behavior. Budgets can have negative effects on employee morale if used improperly. For example, some top managers simply impose the budget on their employees and hold employees responsible for its achievement. In this case, the budgeting system may demoralize workers and actually result in lower, rather than higher, profits.

3. *Coordinates activities.* The budget coordinates the activities of the entire organization. Coordination is crucial because the budget for one department affects other departments. For example, the company may be able to sell 50,000 units to earn its target net income. But the manufacturing plant may be able to produce only 40,000 units. The budget thus helps top managers identify the need to expand the plant by purchasing additional equipment. In turn managers may identify the need for additional sales personnel, office workers, delivery vehicles, and so on.

4. *Helps performance evaluation.* A budgeting system aids performance evaluation. The comparison of budgeted and actual amounts highlights areas that are performing according to plan and areas that need improvement. Actual cost of goods sold in excess of the budgeted amount may lead the business to start buying from a new supplier, or it may lead top management to fire the purchasing manager responsible for paying too high a price for inventory.

EXHIBIT 16-2 *Management Use of Budgeting and Accounting*

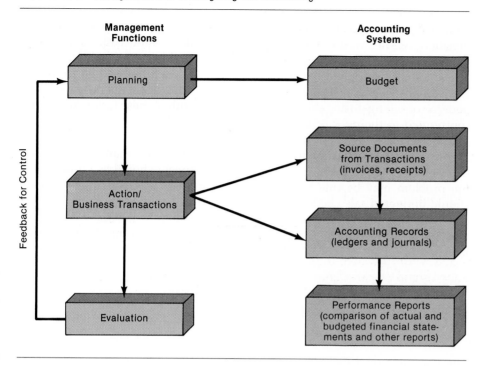

Without the budget, the top management may not even know the company is spending too much on inventory.

Exhibit 16-2 diagrams how managers use budgeting. Management planning (see the upper-left corner of the exhibit) leads to the budget. During the period, the business takes action by engaging in transactions—buying and selling. These transactions produce source documents, accounting records, and in turn performance reports. The performance reports are evaluated by managers whose feedback helps to control the organization. Managers then make new plans. Thus begins a new cycle of management planning and control.

The Performance Report

The comparison of budgeted goals with actual results is a key element in evaluating operations, identifying the need for corrective action, and preparing next period's budget. This point deserves a closer look. The performance report in Exhibit 16-3 serves as the basis for our discussion.

OBJECTIVE 1
Use a performance report

EXHIBIT 16-3 *Summarized Income Statement Performance Report for 19X7—*
Used for Control by Management

	Actual	Budget	Actual–Budget
Sales revenue	$550,000	$600,000	($50,000)
Total expenses ...	510,000	520,000	(10,000)
Net income	$ 40,000	$ 80,000	($40,000)

Actual 19X7 sales in Exhibit 16-3 were $550,000, which is $50,000 less than budgeted sales. The low sales level reduced actual net income to half the budgeted amount. Top managers would ask what went wrong. The vice-president of sales would have to explain why sales revenue was so far below the budgeted goal. The vice-president, in turn, would meet with the sales staff to learn why they failed to meet the budget. At least one of two problems exists in this example: (1) the budget was unrealistic, or (2) the business did a poor job of selling during the period. Of course, both of these factors may have contributed to the poor results.

Managers also use performance reports like this one to identify corrective action. The sales department did not perform well, and management must decide what to do about it. Perhaps the sales manager should be replaced. Or the problem may be due to our selling an inferior product. In any event, should budgeted sales be lowered for the next period? The answers to these questions will affect next period's budget. This example illustrates how managers use a budget to plan operations and to control the company in its drive for success.

Components of the Master Budget

The master budget includes the operating budget, the capital expenditures budget, and the financial budget. The **operating budget** sets the target revenues and expenses—and thus net income—for the period. The **capital expenditures budget** presents the company's plan for purchases of property, plant, and equipment and other assets that management uses to produce revenues over a long time. The **financial budget** projects the means of raising money from stockholders and creditors and plans cash management. This chapter discusses components of the operating budget and the financial budget. Chapter 25 covers budgeting for capital expenditures.

We summarize the components of the master budget as follows:

A. Operating budget
   1. Sales or revenue budget
   2. Purchases, cost of goods sold, and inventory budget
   3. Operating expense budget
   4. Budgeted income statement
B. Capital expenditures budget
C. Financial budget
   1. Cash budget: Statement of budgeted cash receipts and disbursements
   2. Budgeted balance sheet

The capstone of the operating budget is the budgeted income statement, which shows target revenues, expenses, and net income for the period. The financial budget results in the budgeted balance sheet, which gives budgeted amounts for each asset, liability, and owner equity. The budgeted financial statements look exactly like ordinary statements. The only difference is that they list budgeted rather than actual figures.

Exhibit 16-4 diagrams the various sections of the master budget for a non-manufacturing company, like K Mart, Safeway, or a wholesaler of auto parts. In addition to the components of the master budget in the preceding list, the

EXHIBIT 16-4 *Master Budget for a Nonmanufacturing Company*

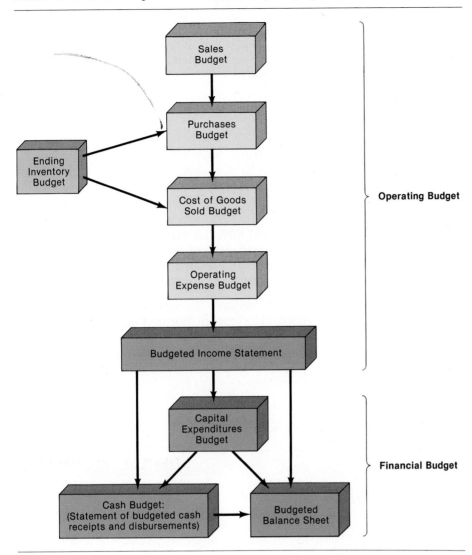

diagram includes ending inventory, which is directly related to sales, purchases, and cost of goods sold. Without a budget for inventory, the company could accidentally end the period with too much or too little inventory, and either event would be unwelcome. Too much inventory is expensive to keep in stock, and too little inventory risks losing a customer who needs the goods immediately.

Sales—the cornerstone of the master budget—is usually budgeted first because inventory levels, purchases, cost of goods sold, and operating expenses depend on sales activity. Sales revenue is the major measure of business activity. After sales and expenses are projected, the budgeted income statement can be prepared.

The capital expenditures budget, the income statement, and the plans for raising cash and paying debts provide information for the cash budget, which feeds into the budgeted balance sheet. Preparing the budgeted balance sheet is usually the last step in the process. We use Exhibit 16-4 as the framework for the remainder of the chapter.

Preparing the Master Budget

To learn how to apply the concepts and methods of budgeting, you should prepare a master budget. The following problem and solutions provide an illustration of the budgeting process.

Facts for Illustration

1. Suppose you manage Whitewater Sporting Goods Store number 18, which carries a complete line of canoeing, hiking, and other outdoor recreation gear. You know the merchandising end of the business but little about accounting and finance. Top management wants your input in the budgeting process. You are to prepare the master budget for your store for April, May, June, and July, the main selling season for these sporting goods. The division manager and the assistant controller (head of the accounting department) of the company will be here from headquarters next week to review the budget with you.

2. Cash collections follow sales because the company sells on account. When extra cash is needed, the company borrows on six-month installment notes payable.

3. The balance sheet of your store at March 31, 19X5, beginning of the budget period, follows.

Whitewater Sporting Goods Store No. 18
Balance Sheet
March 31, 19X5

Assets		Liabilities	
Current assets:		**Current liabilities:**	
Cash	$ 15,000	Accounts payable ...	$ 16,800
Accounts receivable,		Wages and commis-	
net	16,000	sions payable	4,250
Inventory	48,000	Total liabilities	21,050
Prepaid insurance	1,800		
	80,800	**Owners' Equity**	
Plant assets:		Owners' equity	78,950
Equipment and			
fixtures	32,000		
Accumulated			
depreciation	(12,800)		
	19,200	Total liabilities	
Total assets	$100,000	and owners' equity	$100,000

4. Sales in March were $40,000. Monthly sales are projected by sales personnel as follows:

April	$50,000
May	80,000
June	60,000
July	50,000

Sales are 60 percent cash and 40 percent on credit. All accounts receivable amounts are collected in the month following sale. The $16,000 of accounts receivable at March 31 arose from credit sales made in March (40 percent of $40,000). Uncollectible accounts are insignificant, so you can ignore them.

5. Whitewater wishes to maintain inventory equal to $20,000 plus 80 percent of the budgeted cost of goods sold for the following month. (All these percentages are drawn from the business's past experience.) Cost of goods sold averages 70 percent of sales. These data explain why the inventory on March 31 is $48,000, computed as follows:

$$\text{March 31 inventory} = \$20,000 \; + .80 \times (.70 \times \text{April sales of } \$50,000)$$

$$= \$20,000 \; + (.80 \times \$35,000)$$
$$= \$20,000 \; + \$28,000$$
$$= \$48,000$$

Whitewater pays for inventory as follows: 50 percent during the month of purchase and 50 percent during the next month. Accounts payable consist of inventory purchases only.

6. Monthly payroll consists of two parts: fixed wages of $2,500 plus sales commissions equal to 15 percent of sales. The company pays half of this amount during the month and half early in the following month. Therefore, at the end of each month Whitewater reports wages and commissions payable equal to half the month's payroll. This is why the $4,250 liability appears on the March 31 balance sheet—half the March payroll of $8,500:

$$\text{March payroll} = \text{Fixed wages of } \$2,500 + \text{Sales commissions of } \$6,000 \;(.15 \times \$40,000)$$

$$= \$8,500$$

$$\text{March 31 wages and commissions payable} = .50 \times \$8,500$$

$$= \$4,250$$

7. Other monthly expenses are

Rent expense . . . . $2,000, paid as incurred
Depreciation expense,
   including truck   500
Insurance expense . . . .   200 expiration of prepaid amount
Miscellaneous expense . . . . . .   5% of sales, paid as incurred

8. A used delivery truck will be purchased in April for $3,000 cash.

9. The company wishes to maintain a minimum cash balance of $10,000 at the end of each month. If necessary, the business can borrow the money on notes payable of $1,000 each at an annual interest rate of 12 percent. Management borrows no more money than the amount needed to maintain the $10,000 minimum cash balance. Notes payable require six equal monthly payments consisting of principal plus monthly interest on the entire unpaid principal. Borrowing and all principal and interest payments occur at the end of the month.

10. Income taxes are the responsibility of corporate headquarters, so you can ignore tax for budgeting purposes.

Assume you have studied the company guidelines on how to prepare a budget. The directions instruct you to prepare the following detailed schedules:

Schedule

A	Sales budget
B	Purchases, cost of goods sold, and inventory budget
C	Operating expense budget
D	Budgeted cash collections from customers
E	Budgeted cash disbursements for purchases
F	Budgeted cash disbursements for operating expenses

After compiling the schedules, you must prepare the following statements:

Exhibit

20-5	Budgeted income statement for the four months ended July 31, 19X5
20-6	Statement of budgeted cash receipts and disbursements by month for the four months ended July 31, 19X5
20-7	Budgeted balance sheet at July 31, 19X5

Preparing the Operating Budget

OBJECTIVE 2

Budget the components of the income statement

As you work through the preparation of this budget, keep in mind that you are developing the company's operating and financial plan for the next four months. The steps in this process may seem mechanical, but remember that budgeting stimulates thoughts about pricing, product lines, job assignments, needs for additional equipment, and negotiations of loans with banks. Preparation of the budget leads to decisions that affect the future course of the business. The operating budget—consisting of the sales budget, the purchases, cost of goods sold, and inventory budget, and the operating expense budget—results in the budgeted income statement.

Preparing the Budgeted Income Statement. *Step 1.* Sales—Schedule A—is the start of the budget effort. The budgeted sales amount for each product is determined by multiplying its sale price by the predicted unit sales. The overall sales budget is the sum of the budgets for individual products.

Schedule A—Sales Budget
    (Fact 4, pages 776–77)

	April	May	June	July	April-July Total
Cash sales, 60%	$30,000	$48,000	$36,000	$30,000	
Credit sales, 40%	20,000	32,000	24,000	20,000	
Total sales, 100%	$50,000	$80,000	$60,000	$50,000	$240,000

Trace the April-July total sales—$240,000—to the budgeted income statement in Exhibit 16-5.

EXHIBIT 16-5 *Budgeted Income Statement*

Whitewater Sporting Goods Store No. 18
Budgeted Income Statement
Four Months Ending July 31, 19X5

	Amount	Source
Sales	$240,000	Schedule A
Cost of goods sold	168,000	Schedule B
Gross margin	72,000	
Operating expenses:		
Wages and commissions $46,000		Schedule C
Rent 8,000		
Depreciation 2,000		
Insurance 800		
Miscellaneous 12,000	68,800	—
Income from operations	3,200	
Interest expense	225	Exhibit 20-6
Net income	$ 2,975	

Step 2. After budgeting sales, prepare the purchases, cost of goods sold, and inventory budget, which is Schedule B. This schedule determines cost of goods sold for the budgeted income statement, ending inventory for the budgeted balance sheet, and purchases for the cash budget. The relationship among these items is given by the cost-of-goods-sold computation:

Beginning Inventory + Purchases − Ending Inventory = Cost of Goods Sold

Beginning inventory is known, budgeted cost of goods is a fixed percentage of sales, and budgeted ending inventory is a specified amount. Therefore, you must solve for the budgeted purchases figure. By moving beginning inventory and ending inventory to the right side of the equation, isolate Purchases on the left side:

Purchases = Cost of Goods Sold + Ending Inventory − Beginning Inventory

Schedule B—Purchases, Cost of Goods Sold, and Inventory Budget
(Fact 5, page 777)

	April	May	June	July	April-July Total
Cost of goods sold (.70 × sales, from Schedule A)	$35,000	$56,000	$42,000	$35,000	$168,000
+ Desired ending inventory ($20,000 + .80 × Cost of goods sold for next month) . . .	64,800*	53,600	48,000	42,400‡	
= Total needs	99,800	109,600	90,000	77,400	
− Beginning inventory	(48,000)†	(64,800)	(53,600)	(48,000)	
= Purchases	$51,800	$44,800	$36,400	$29,400	

* 20,000 + (.80 × $56,000) = $64,800   ‡ Assumed for illustrative purposes.
† Balance at March 31 (Fact 3, page 776)

Schedule C—Operating Expenses Budget
(Facts 6 and 7, page 777)

	April	May	June	July	April-July Total
Wages, fixed amount	$ 2,500	$ 2,500	$ 2,500	$ 2,500	
Commission, 15% of sales from Schedule A	7,500	12,000	9,000	7,500	
Total wages and commissions	10,000	14,500	11,500	10,000	$46,000
Rent, fixed amount	2,000	2,000	2,000	2,000	8,000
Depreciation, fixed amount....................	500	500	500	500	2,000
Insurance, fixed amount	200	200	200	200	800
Miscellaneous, 5% of sales	2,500	4,000	3,000	2,500	12,000
Total operating expenses	$15,200	$21,200	$17,200	$15,200	$68,800

Since Schedule B is a forecast, you cannot know the *actual* ending inventory amount. You must include the desired ending inventory figure in the computation of projected purchases.

To solidify your understanding of how this information fits into the master budget, trace the total budgeted cost of goods sold ($168,000) to the income statement in Exhibit 16-5. We will be using the budgeted inventory and purchases amounts later.

Step 3. Some budgeted operating expenses, like sales commissions and delivery expenses, fluctuate and thus vary with changing sales. Other expenses, like rent, depreciation, and insurance, are the same each month (fixed) and do not vary with sales. Schedule C is the operating expense budget.

Trace the April-July totals (wages and commissions of $46,000, rent of $8,000, and so on) to the budgeted income statement in Exhibit 16-5.

Step 4. Steps 1 through 3 provide the information to determine income from operations on the budgeted income statement in Exhibit 16-5. (We explain computation of the interest expense as part of the cash budget.)

Preparing the Financial Budget

The second major section of the master budget is the financial budget, which consists of the budgeted statement of cash receipts and disbursements (cash budget) and the budgeted balance sheet.

Preparing the Cash Budget (Statement of Budgeted Cash Receipts and Disbursements). The **cash budget,** or **statement of budgeted cash receipts and disbursements,** details how the business intends to go from the beginning cash balance to the desired ending balance. Cash receipts and disbursements depend in part on revenues and expenses, which appear in the budgeted income statement. The cash budget, then, is usually prepared after the budgeted income statement.

The cash budget has the following major parts: cash collections from customers (Schedule D), cash disbursements for purchases (Schedule E), cash disbursements for operating expenses (Schedule F), and capital expenditures.

Schedule D—Budgeted Cash Collections from Customers

	April	May	June	July
Cash sales from Schedule A	$30,000	$48,000	$36,000	$30,000
Collection of last month's credit sales from Schedule A (Fact 4, pages 776–77)	16,000*	20,000	32,000	24,000
Total collections	$46,000	$68,000	$68,000	$54,000

*March 31 accounts receivable

Schedule E—Budgeted Cash Disbursements for Purchases

	April	May	June	July
50% of last month's purchases, from Schedule B	$16,800*	$25,900	$22,400	$18,200
50% of this month's purchases, from Schedule B	25,900	22,400	18,200	14,700
Total disbursements for purchases	$42,700	$48,300	$40,600	$32,900

*.50 × March purchases of $33,600 (amount assumed)

Schedule F—Budgeted Cash Disbursements for Operating Expenses

	April	May	June	July
Expense amounts from Schedule C:				
Wages and commissions:				
50% of last month's expenses from Schedule C (Fact 6, page 777)	$ 4,250*	$ 5,000	$ 7,250	$ 5,750
50% of this month's expenses from Schedule C	5,000	7,250	5,750	5,000
Total wages and commissions	9,250	12,250	13,000	10,750
Rent (Fact 7, page 777)	2,000	2,000	2,000	2,000
Miscellaneous (5% of sales, Schedule A)	2,500	4,000	3,000	2,500
Total disbursements for operating expenses	$13,750	$18,250	$18,000	$15,250

*March 31 wages and commissions payable

The cash receipt and disbursement data in Schedules D, E, and F and the $3,000 capital expenditure to acquire the truck appear in the cash budget, Exhibit 16-6. Acquisitions of long-term assets like the truck are based on a decision process called *capital budgeting*. We cover this management tool in Chapter 25.

In preparing the cash budget (Exhibit 16-6) you must first determine the cash available before financing. (This amount is $61,000 for April.) Add total disbursements ($59,450) to the minimum desired cash balance ($10,000) to find the total cash needed during April—$69,450. If cash available exceeds cash needed, an excess occurs. If cash needed is greater, a deficiency results. During April, you budget an $8,450 deficiency. The company then borrows $9,000 on a six-month note payable. (The loan exceeds the deficiency because Whitewater borrows in even $1,000 amounts.) Compute the budgeted cash balance

OBJECTIVE 4

Prepare a cash budget

EXHIBIT 16-6 *Cash Budget*

Whitewater Sporting Goods Store No. 18
Statement of Budgeted Cash Receipts and Disbursements
Four Months Ending July 31, 19X5

	April	May	June	July
Beginning cash balance	$15,000	$10,550	$10,410	$18,235
Cash receipts, collections from customers				
(Schedule D)	46,000	68,000	68,000	54,000
Cash available before financing	$61,000	$78,550	$78,410	$72,235
Cash disbursements:				
Purchases of inventory (Schedule E)	$42,700	$48,300	$40,600	$32,900
Operating expenses (Schedule F)	13,750	18,250	18,000	15,250
Purchase of truck (Fact 8, page 777)	3,000	—	—	—
Total disbursements	59,450	66,550	58,600	48,150
(1) Ending cash balance before financing	1,550	12,000	19,810	24,085
Minimum cash balance desired	10,000	10,000	10,000	10,000
Cash excess (deficiency).	$(8,450)	$ 2,000	$ 9,810	$14,085
Financing of cash deficiency (See Notes b–d below):				
Borrowing (at end of month)	$ 9,000			
Principal payments (at end of month)		$(1,500)	$(1,500)	$(1,500)
Interest expense (at 12% annually)		(90)	(75)	(60)
(2) Total effects of financing	9,000	(1,590)	(1,575)	(1,560)
Ending cash balance (1) + (2)	$10,550	$10,410	$18,235	$22,525

Notes: a. Insurance expense is the expiration of prepaid insurance, and depreciation is the expensing of the cost of a plant asset. Therefore, these expenses do not require cash outlays in the current accounting period.

b. Borrowing occurs in multiples of $1,000 and only for the amount needed to maintain a minimum cash balance of $10,000.

c. Monthly principal payments: $9,000/6 = $1,500.

d. Interest expense: May: $9,000 × (.12 × $\frac{1}{12}$) = $90.
June: ($9,000 − $1,500) × (.12 × $\frac{1}{12}$) = $75.
July: ($9,000 − $1,500 − $1,500) × (.12 × $\frac{1}{12}$) = $60.
Total: $90 + $75 + $60 = $225.

at the end of each month by subtracting total disbursements from the cash available before financing and then adding the total projected effects of financing.[1] Exhibit 16-6 shows that Whitewater expects to end April with $10,550 of cash. The exhibit also shows the budgeted cash balance at the end of May, June, and July.

Interest expense for the four months totals $225 ($90 + $75 + $60). This item is listed on the budgeted income statement in Exhibit 16-5.

Preparing the Budgeted Balance Sheet. The final step in preparing the master budget is to complete the balance sheet. You project each asset, liability, and owner equity account based on the plans outlined in the previous schedules and exhibits. Exhibit 16-7 presents the budgeted balance sheet. If desired, you can prepare separate schedules to show the computations of accounts receivable, plant assets, and so on.

The *master budget* has now been completed. It consists of the budgeted financial statements and all supporting schedules.

OBJECTIVE 5

Prepare a budgeted balance sheet

[1] In the case of loan payments, you will be adding a negative amount.

EXHIBIT 16-7 *Budgeted Balance Sheet*

Whitewater Sporting Goods Store No. 18
Budgeted Balance Sheet
July 31, 19X5

Assets

Current assets:

Cash (Exhibit 16-6)	$ 22,525	
Accounts receivable, net (.40 × July sales of $50,000; Schedule A)	20,000	
Inventory (Schedule B)	42,400	
Prepaid insurance (beginning balance of $1,800 − $800 for four months' expiration; fact 7 on page 777)	1,000	$ 85,925

Plant assets:

Equipment and fixtures (beginning balance of $32,000 + $3,000 truck acquisition; fact 8 on page 777)	35,000	
Accumulated depreciation (beginning balance of $12,800 + $500 depreciation for each of four months; fact 7 on page 777)	(14,800)	20,200
Total assets		$106,125

Liabilities

Current liabilities:

Short-term note payable ($9,000 − $4,500 paid back; Exhibit 16-6)	$ 4,500	
Accounts payable (.50 × July purchases of $29,400; Schedule B)	14,700	
Wages and commissions payable (.50 × July expense of $10,000; Schedule C)	5,000	
Total liabilities		$ 24,200

Owners' Equity

Owners' equity (beginning balance of $78,950 + $2,975 net income; Exhibit 16-5)		81,925
Total liabilities and owners' equity		$106,125

Summary of Budgeting Procedures

The most important budget documents are the budgeted income statement (Exhibit 16-5), the budgeted statement of cash receipts and disbursements (Exhibit 16-6), and the budgeted balance sheet (Exhibit 16-7). Top management analyzes these statements to ensure that all the budgeted figures are consistent with company goals. As the business strives to reach these goals, management controls operations by comparing actual results with the forecasted performance (as shown in Exhibit 16-3, the performance report).

Importance of Sales Forecasting _____

The Whitewater Sporting Goods illustration began with the sales budget, which is the foundation of a master budget. Managers—under the direction of the top marketing executive—invest ample resources in accurately forecasting sales. Factors considered in projecting sales include:

1. *Patterns of past sales.* By learning from past sales activity, a company can fine-tune its sales budget. This includes subdividing sales by product line,

geographical region, and salesperson. The more detailed the budget, the more helpful it is likely to be.

2. *Predictions of marketing personnel.* These people are calling on customers on a regular basis and can provide the most reliable, current information for forecasting sales. They conduct market research to learn which customers prefer certain products.

3. *Analysis of general and industry economic conditions.* In an economic recession, consumers usually delay expenditures on leisure-time products like Whitewater's sporting goods. What is the outlook for the economy next year?

4. *Strength of competitors.* A business must stay informed about what competitors are doing. For example, an effective advertising campaign by Chrysler can lure customers away from Ford and General Motors and decrease Ford and GM profits. An effective budget must consider the activity of competitors.

5. *Future changes in prices.* Budgeted sales equal the budgeted quantity multiplied by the expected future selling price. Any changes in prices affect the sales budget.

6. *Development of new product lines and phasing out of old product lines.* The budget must include the sales of new products expected to be introduced and eliminate old products that will be phased out. This ensures that the budget is based on an up-to-date product line.

7. *Plans for advertising and sales promotion.* Advertising stimulates sales, so plans for upcoming promotional efforts will affect the budgeted level of sales.

The importance of the sales forecast is not limited to profit-seeking organizations. For example, the revenue forecast is critical to hospitals, churches and synagogues, universities, cities, and states. Unless these organizations budget revenues accurately, they risk spending too much and running out of money just like profit-seeking businesses. All types of organizations base their budgets on general economic and industry data plus information that is specific to the entity. An entire industry exists to provide economic forecasting data. All types of organizations subscribe to forecasting newsletters, primarily to aid their budgeting efforts.

Budgeting and Short-Term Financing

The cash budget in Exhibit 16-6 illustrates the usual pattern of **short-term, self-liquidating financing.** This term refers to debt incurred to buy inventories that will be sold on credit. Cash collections are used to pay the debt.

The diagram below shows the financing plan budgeted in Exhibit 16-6. Whitewater had a temporary need for $9,000. The company borrowed this amount and paid it back from cash generated by operations.

Many companies have seasonal peaks of high sales volume and valleys of low activity. For example, retailers like Sears, J. C. Penney, and K Mart make most of their sales during November, December, and January. June, July, and August are slow months. Companies use the slow months to stock up on inventory for the rush near the end of the year and to remodel stores and make repairs. By increasing a store's attractiveness and efficiency, the company can attract more customers and increase sales.

When monthly sales fluctuate seasonally, companies often borrow on short-term, self-liquidating loans. A cash budget can help managers avoid a cash shortage. By planning ahead, the manager can shop around for the best interest rate on a short-term loan. Then, if a cash shortage looms in some months, the company is prepared. A carefully mapped budget keeps the cash balance well matched to cash needs.

Continuous (Rolling) Budgets

A **continuous**, or **rolling, budget** systematically adds a month as the month just ended is deleted. This budget keeps managers thinking ahead, with a steady planning horizon. Suppose Whitewater Sporting Goods prepared the following six-month sales budget:

OBJECTIVE 6
Use a continuous budget

	March	April	May	June	July	August
Budgeted sales ...	$40,000	$50,000	$80,000	$60,000	$50,000	$40,000

The first budget covers March through August. Roll 1 deletes March and adds September; roll 2 then deletes April and adds October; and so on.

Roll 1:	March	April	May	June	July	August	September	October
Budgeted sales ...	—	$50,000	$80,000	$60,000	$50,000	$40,000	$25,000	—

Roll 2:								
Budgeted sales ...	—	—	$80,000	$60,000	$50,000	$40,000	$25,000	$20,000

When managers desire, the sales budgets for individual months can be combined into quarterly or semiannual totals.

Budget Models, What-If Questions, and Microcomputer Applications

The master budget models the entire organization's objectives, inputs, and outputs. When we combine the budget's broad coverage with the speed and ease of microcomputers, we have a powerful tool for management analysis, planning, and control.

Many software programs allow preparation of the master budget on an electronic spreadsheet. The manager or the accountant can then ask "what-if" questions by changing any figure. *What* net income can we expect *if* we increase advertising by 20 percent? *What* will the cash balance be *if* we prepay the full cost of the advertising campaign at the beginning of the next period?

When the accountant changes one amount, the computer prepares a new budget that includes all the effects of that change. Computers make possible this nearly instant analysis of changes in the company's forecast. Managers can then study the answers to these questions.

The spreadsheet that displays these changes to "what-if" questions may be linked to increasingly detailed subsets of information. For example, assume that General Motors (GM) wants to examine "what-if" questions regarding possible car sales for February. The results of this investigation lead to changes in GM's net sales, required purchases, and projected cash receipts, not just for February but also for one or two subsequent months.

The first draft of a budget is seldom the final draft. Answers to what-if questions can provide revenue, expense, and income data on a wide range of possible sales levels. Managers can then respond to changes in the business with information rather than hunches. Suppose the budget—based on the best possible forecast—shows a poor year ahead. Managers can examine various patterns of sales and net income, and cash receipts and disbursements. They can study ways to cut costs and develop marketing strategies to increase demand for the company's products. The master budget may then be revised. Chapter 21 examines flexible budgets—those based on various levels of activity—in greater detail.

The computer's speed also enables managers to react promptly to new and unexpected situations as they arise. For example, an executive of a New Jersey utility, Public Service Electric and Gas Company, has commented on the company's plans if an oil embargo were announced tomorrow. Within 24 hours management would know from the master budget the major financial effects of the embargo. Without having to wait for monthly or quarterly financial statements, they could begin reacting to its effects immediately. Microcomputers and user-friendly software give these capabilities to many employees who are not expert computer programmers. Knowing what to expect is a result of a successful budgeting system.

Summary Problem for Your Review

Review the Whitewater Sporting Goods illustration in the chapter. Suppose you think that July sales might be $40,000 instead of the projected $50,000 in Schedule A, page 778. You draw up a new budget to learn what effect the change in the sales amount will have on the store.

Required

1. Revise schedules A, B, and C. Prepare a revised budgeted income statement for the four months ended July 31, 19X5.
2. Revise schedules D, E, and F. Prepare a revised cash budget for July and a revised budgeted balance sheet at July 31, 19X5.

   Note: You need not repeat the parts of the revised schedules that do not change.

Note: Although not required, for completeness this solution repeats the budgeted amounts for April, May, and June Revised figures appear in boldface for emphasis.

Requirement 1

Revised Schedule A—Sales Budget

	April	May	June	July	April–July Total
Cash sales, 60%	$30,000	$48,000	$36,000	**$24,000**	
Credit sales, 40%	20,000	32,000	24,000	**16,000**	
Total sales, 100%	$50,000	$80,000	$60,000	**$40,000**	$230,000

Revised Schedule B—Purchases, Cost of Goods Sold, and Inventory Budget

	April	May	June	July	April–July Total
Cost of goods sold (.70 × sales from Revised Schedule A)	$ 35,000	$ 56,000	$ 42,000	**$ 28,000**	**$161,000**
+ Desired ending inventory ($20,000 + .80 × cost of goods sold for next month) ..	64,800	53,600	**42,400**	**42,400**	
= Total needs............................	99,800	109,600	**84,400**	**70,400**	
− Beginning inventory	(48,000)	(64,800)	**(53,600)**	**(42,400)**	
= Purchases	$ 51,800	$ 44,800	**$ 30,800**	**$ 28,000**	

Revised Schedule C—Operating Expenses Budget

	April	May	June	July	April–July Total
Wages, fixed amount	$ 2,500	$ 2,500	$ 2,500	**$ 2,500**	
Commission, 15% of sales from Revised Schedule A	7,500	12,000	9,000	**6,000**	
Total wages and commissions	10,000	14,500	11,500	**8,500**	$44,500
Rent, fixed amount	2,000	2,000	2,000	**2,000**	8,000
Depreciation, fixed amount	500	500	500	**500**	2,000
Insurance, fixed amount	200	200	200	**200**	800
Miscellaneous, 5% of sales	2,500	4,000	3,000	**2,000**	11,500
Total operating expenses	$15,200	$21,200	$17,200	**$13,200**	$66,800

Whitewater Sporting Goods Store No. 18
Budgeted Income Statement
Four Months Ending July 31, 19X5

	Amount	Source
Sales...	$230,000	Revised Schedule A
Cost of goods sold	161,000	Revised Schedule B
Gross margin	69,000	
Operating expenses:		
Wages and commissions $44,500		Revised Schedule C
Rent 8,000		Revised Schedule C
Depreciation............................... 2,000		Revised Schedule C
Insurance 800		Revised Schedule C
Miscellaneous 11,500	66,800	Revised Schedule C
Income from operations	2,200	
Interest expense	225	Revised Exhibit 16-6
Net income......................................	$ 1,975	

Requirement 2

Revised Schedule D—Budgeted Cash Collections from Customers

	April	May	June	July
Cash sales from Revised Schedule A.......................	$30,000	$48,000	$36,000	**$24,000**
Collection of last month's credit sales,				
from Revised Schedule A	16,000*	20,000	32,000	24,000
Total collections	$46,000	$68,000	$68,000	**$48,000**

*March 31 accounts receivable

Revised Schedule E—Budgeted Disbursements for Purchases

	April	May	June	July
50% of last month's purchases, from Revised Schedule B	$16,800*	$25,900	$22,400	**$15,400**
50% of this month's purchases, from Revised Schedule B	25,900	22,400	**15,400**	**14,000**
Total disbursements for purchases........................	$42,700	$48,300	**$37,800**	**$29,400**

*Amount assumed for illustration

Revised Schedule F—Budgeted Disbursements for Operating Expenses

Expense amounts from Revised Schedule C:	April	May	June	July
Wages and commissions:				
50% of last month's expenses from Revised Schedule C .	$ 4,250*	$ 5,000	$ 7,250	**$ 5,750**
50% of this month's expenses from Revised Schedule C .	5,000	7,250	5,750	**4,250**
Total wages and commissions	9,250	12,250	13,000	**10,000**
Rent	2,000	2,000	2,000	2,000
Miscellaneous	2,500	4,000	3,000	2,000
Total disbursements for operating expenses	$13,750	$18,250	$18,000	**$14,000**

*March 31 wages and commissions payable

REVISED EXHIBIT 16-6 *Cash Budget*

Whitewater Sporting Goods Store No. 18
Statement of Budgeted Cash Receipts and Disbursements
Four Months Ending July 31, 19X5

	April	May	June	July
Beginning cash balance	$15,000	$10,550	$10,410	**$21,035**
Cash receipts, collections from customers (Revised Schedule D)	46,000	68,000	68,000	48,000
Cash available before financing	$61,000	$78,550	$78,410	$69,035
Cash disbursements:				
Purchases of inventory (Revised Schedule E)	$42,700	$48,300	**$37,800**	**$29,400**
Operating expenses (Revised Schedule F)	13,750	18,250	18,000	14,000
Purchase of truck	3,000	—	—	—
Total disbursements	59,450	66,550	55,800	43,400
(1) Ending cash balance before financing	1,550	12,000	22,610	25,635
Minimum cash balance desired	10,000	10,000	10,000	10,000
Cash excess (deficiency)	$(8,450)	$ 2,000	**$12,610**	**$15,635**
Financing of cash deficiency:				
Borrowing (at end of month)	$ 9,000			
Principal payments (at end of month)		$(1,500)	$(1,500)	$(1,500)
Interest expense (at 12% annually)		(90)*	(75)*	(60)*
(2) Total effects of financing	9,000	(1,590)	(1,575)	(1,560)
Ending cash balance (1) + (2)	$10,550	$10,410	**$21,035**	**$24,075**

*Interest expense: $90 + $75 + $60 = $225

REVISED EXHIBIT 16-7 *Budgeted Balance Sheet*

Whitewater Sporting Goods Store No. 18
Budgeted Balance Sheet
July 31, 19X5

Assets

Current assets:		
Cash (Revised Exhibit 16-6)	$ 24,075	
Accounts receivable, net (.40 X July sales of $40,000; Revised Schedule A)	16,000	
Inventory (Revised Schedule B)	42,400	
Prepaid insurance	1,000	$ 83,475
Plant assets:		
Equipment and fixtures	35,000	
Accumulated depreciation	(14,800)	20,200
Total assets		$103,675

Liabilities

Current liabilities:		
Short-term note payable	$ 4,500	
Accounts payable (.50 X July purchases of **$28,000**; Revised Schedule B)	14,000	
Wages and commissions payable (.50 X July expense of $8,500; Revised Schedule C)	4,250	
Total liabilities		$ 22,750

Owners' Equity

Owners' equity (beginning balance of $78,950 + **$1,975** net income; Revised Exhibit 16-5)		80,925
Total liabilities and owners' equity		$103,675

SUMMARY

Management accounting helps managers plan and control the operations of their organizations. A major element of the management plan is the *budget*, which expresses the business's goals for earning income and for asset, liability, and owner equity position. The master budget consists of the budgeted financial statements and supporting schedules.

The budget forces managers to set specific goals. Such goals provide direction for the organization and meaning to the work of individual employees. The budget coordinates the various activities of the organization and aids performance evaluation. Comparisons of budgeted and actual amounts reveal areas of the business that need improvement.

Many organizations have a *budget committee*, which includes representatives of all departments, to prepare the budget. The *budget period* usually coincides with the accounting period to ease the comparison of actual and budgeted amounts.

The components of the master budget that cover operations include *sales, purchases, cost of goods sold, inventory,* and *operating expenses*. These budgets are usually prepared in this order and are combined into the *budgeted income statement*. Sales comes first because most expenses, assets, and liabilities depend on sales volume. A second component of the master budget is the *capital expenditures budget*, which includes plans for purchasing long-term capital assets. The third main component is the financial budget, consisting of the *cash budget*, which is a statement of budgeted cash receipts and disbursements, and the *budgeted balance sheet*.

Many companies use *continuous*, or *rolling, budgets* that systematically add a future month as the month just ended is deleted. Continuous budgets keep managers thinking ahead with a steady planning horizon.

Microcomputers and electronic spreadsheets are ideally suited for use in budgeting because they allow managers to answer what-if questions. Analyzing data over a wide range of outcomes enables managers to meet the challenges brought about by changes in the business.

Self-Study Questions

Test your understanding of the chapter by marking the best answer for each of the following questions.

1. The budget is *(p. 771)*
   a. A general, not specific, statement of the business's goals
   b. Not used by most successful businesses
   c. A major tool of financial, rather than management, accounting
   d. None of the above

2. For the budget to be most effective, it should be prepared *(pp. 771, 772)*
   a. From the bottom up, with participation from employees at all levels
   b. From the top down, with managers developing goals based on their own experience
   c. Without reference to results obtained in past periods
   d. None of the above

3. Which of the following is *not* a benefit of a budgeting system? *(pp. 772, 773)*
   a. Coordinates activities
   b. Automatically fires under-achieving employees
   c. Aids performance evaluation
   d. Provides direction to the business

4. Chewning Corporation's actual revenues are $90,000, and expenses are $50,000. Budgeted revenues were $86,000, and budgeted expenses were

$51,000. What is the relationship between actual net income and budgeted net income? *(p. 773)*

a. Actual exceeds budget by $40,000

b. Budget exceeds actual by $35,000

c. Actual exceeds budget by $5,000

d. Budget exceeds actual by $5,000

5. The master budget starts with *(p. 774)*

a. Cash

b. Owners' equity

c. Sales

d. Inventory

6. The operating budget ends with *(pp. 774, 775)*

a. Budgeted sales

b. The budgeted income statement

c. The cash budget

d. The budgeted balance sheet

7. The most complex single part of the master budget is preparation of *(p. 781)*

a. Budgeted sales

b. The budgeted income statement

c. The cash budget

d. The budgeted balance sheet

8. The master budget usually ends with *(p. 782)*

a. Budgeted sales

b. The budgeted income statement

c. The cash budget

d. The budgeted balance sheet

9. A continuous (rolling) budget *(p. 785)*

a. Adds a month and deletes the month just ended

b. Keeps managers thinking ahead

c. Maintains a steady planning horizon

d. All of the above

10. Managers can use a microcomputer along with a master budget to *(pp. 785, 786)*

a. Develop strategies for dealing with a variety of possible situations

b. Eliminate all the uncertainty of the business environment

c. Prepare the budget correctly on the first attempt

d. Set near-perfect goals for the company

Answers to the Self-Study Questions follow the Accounting Vocabulary.

Accounting Vocabulary

Budget. Management's quantitative expression of a plan of action and an aid to coordination and implementation *(p. 771)*.

Budget committee. Group that prepares the master budget; includes representatives from all departments of the business *(p. 771)*.

Capital expenditures budget. Plan for purchases of property, plant, and equipment and other assets that management uses over a long time *(p. 774)*.

Cash budget. Details the way a business intends to go from the beginning cash balance to the desired ending balance. Also called the Statement of budgeted cash receipts and disbursements *(p. 780)*.

Continuous budget. Systematically adds a month or a quarter as the month or quarter just ended is deleted. Also called a Rolling budget *(p. 785)*.

Financial budget. Projects the means of raising money from stockholders and creditors and plans cash management *(p. 774)*.

Master budget. Budget that includes the major financial statements and supporting schedules. The master budget can be divided into the operating budget, the capital expenditures budget, and the financial budget *(p. 771)*.

Operating budget. Sets the target revenues and expenses, and thus net income, for the period *(p. 774)*.

Rolling budget. Another name for a Continuous budget *(p. 785).*

Short-term, self-liquidating financing. Debt incurred to buy inventories that will be sold and with the related cash collections used to pay the debt *(p. 784).*

Statement of budgeted cash receipts and disbursements. Another name for the Cash budget *(p. 780)*

Answers to Self-Study Questions

1. d
2. a
3. b
4. c   Actual: $90,000 − $50,000 = $40,000
    Budget: 86,000 − 51,000 = 35,000
    Actual over budget: $ 5,000
5. c

6. b
7. c
8. d
9. d

10. a

ASSIGNMENT MATERIAL _____

Questions

1. How does management accounting differ from financial accounting?
2. Identify two types of goals set by managers.
3. Briefly discuss three components of a budgeting system.
4. What are four benefits of using a budgeting system?
5. Draw a diagram that shows how managers use a budgeting system.
6. How does a manager use a performance report?
7. List the components of a master budget.
8. A Ford dealer sets a goal of selling more Ford automobiles than any other dealer in the city. Does this goal represent a budget? Give your reason.
9. Taft Corporation installs a budgeting system in which the president sets all the goals for the company. The vice-president checks up on all 90 employees to ensure that they are meeting top management's budget goals. What is the weakness in this budgeting system? How can the system be improved?
10. In most successful budgeting systems, who or what group in the organization prepares the budget? What makes this approach successful?
11. Why should the capital expenditures budget be prepared before the cash budget and the budgeted balance sheet?
12. How does a company budget inventory purchases? In your answer, show the relationships among purchases, cost of goods sold, and inventories.
13. What is the first step in preparing the master budget? Why does this step come first?
14. Outline the four steps in preparing an operating budget.
15. Identify the last item (prior to net income) to compute for the budgeted income statement. Where is this item computed initially, and why does it come last?
16. What is another name for the cash budget? Identify six subtotals or totals listed on the cash budget.
17. What is the last document to prepare for the master budget? Why does it come last?

18. Is sales forecasting important only to a profit-seeking business, or is it used by nonprofit organizations like hospitals and colleges? Give your reason.

19. Suppose you are the marketing vice-president of a company. What factors would you consider in forecasting the company's sales for the coming year?

20. Describe how short-term, self-liquidating financing works.

21. Tick-Tock Clocks is a chain of specialty shops operating in resort areas. During some periods, the managers of the company's 42 stores budget for the coming quarter, and during other periods they budget for the coming year. What type of budget should top management use to keep store managers looking ahead with a steady planning horizon? How does this budget work?

22. Why are microcomputers and electronic spreadsheets well suited for budgeting?

Exercises

Exercise 16-1 Preparing a performance report (L.O. 1)

During August Chez Bon, Inc.'s actual revenues were $131,000 compared with budgeted revenues of $142,000. August operating expenses were $122,000, and budgeted operating expenses were $137,000. The company also incurred interest expense, a nonoperating expense, of $5,000, which was not included in the budget because it arose from unexpected borrowing.

Prepare a performance report for Chez Bon to show the differences between actual income and budgeted income for August. What caused August results to turn out as they did? Comment on results as measured by operating income.

Exercise 16-2 Budgeting sales, cost of goods sold, and gross profit (L.O. 2)

Lisa Gatti operates a boutique called The Second Edition. She expects cash sales of $3,000 for October and a $500 monthly increase during November and December. Credit-card sales of $1,000 during October should be followed by 20 percent increases during November and December. Sales returns can be ignored. Credit card-companies like VISA, MasterCard, and American Express charge 5 percent on credit-card sales, so The Second Edition will net 95 percent. Cost of goods sold averages 60 percent of net sales.

Lisa asks you to prepare a schedule of budgeted sales, cost of goods sold, and gross profit for each month of the last quarter of 19X3. Also show totals for the quarter.

Exercise 16-3 Budgeting purchases, cost of goods sold, and inventory (L.O. 2)

The sales budget of Whitehouse Corp. for the nine months ended September 30 follows.

	Quarter Ended			
	March 31	June 30	Sep. 30	Nine-Month Total
Cash sales, 30%	$27,000	$ 42,000	$ 31,500	$100,500
Credit sales, 70%	63,000	98,000	73,500	234,500
Total sales, 100%	$90,000	$140,000	$105,000	$335,000

In the past, cost of goods sold has been 65 percent of total sales. The director of marketing, the production manager, and the financial vice-president agree that ending inventory should not go below $20,000 plus 10 percent of cost of goods sold for the following quarter. Whitehouse expects sales of $100,000 during the fourth quarter. The January 1 inventory was $22,000.

Required

Prepare a purchases, cost of goods sold, and inventory budget for each of the first three quarters of the year. Compute the cost of goods sold for the entire nine-month period. (Use Schedule B, page 779, as a model.)

Exercise 16-4 *Identifying amounts of purchases, inventory, and cost of goods sold* **(L.O. 2)**

Compute the missing amount for each of the independent situations below:

	A	B	C	D	E
Beginning inventory ...	$14,000	$?	$ 24,800	$11,100	$?
Purchases.............	?	86,200	?	45,300	77,900
Available	73,000	118,800	103,100	?	?
Ending inventory......	11,000	?	?	13,700	22,600
Cost of goods sold.....	$?	$ 87,700	$ 75,300	$?	$70,000

Exercise 16-5 *Budgeting quarterly income for a year* **(L.O. 3)**

Century 21 is a nationwide real estate firm. Suppose a suburban St. Louis office of the firm projects that year 2 quarterly sales will increase by 3 percent in quarter one, 3 percent in quarter two, 5 percent in quarter three, and 5 percent in quarter four. Management expects total operating expenses to be 85 percent of revenues during each of the first two quarters, 86 percent of revenues during the third quarter, and 81 percent during the fourth. The office manager expects to borrow $100,000 on July 1, with quarterly principal payments of $10,000 beginning on September 30 and interest paid at the annual rate of 12 percent. Year 1 last quarter sales were $520,000.

Required

Prepare a budgeted income statement for each of the four quarters of year 2 and for the entire year. Present the year 2 budget as follows:

Quarter 1	Quarter 2	Quarter 3	Quarter 4	Full Year

Exercise 16-6 *Identifying amounts in a cash budget* **(L.O. 4)**

Cablevision, Inc., has completed its cash budget for May and June. The budget is presented with missing amounts identified by a question mark (?). Cablevision's plan for eliminating any cash deficiency is to borrow the exact amount needed from its bank. The current annual interest rate is 12 percent. Cablevision pays back all borrowed amounts within one month to the extent cash is available without going below the desired minimum balance.

Required

Fill in each amount identified by a question mark.

Cablevision, Inc.
Cash Budget
May and June

	May	June
Beginning cash balance	$10,900	$?
Cash collections from customers	65,700	74,800
Sale of plant assets		900
Cash available before financing	$88,800	$?
Cash disbursements:		
Purchases of inventory	$52,400	$41,100
Operating expenses	31,900	30,500
Total disbursements	84,300	71,600
(1) Ending cash balance before financing	?	?
Minimum cash balance desired	10,000	10,000
Cash excess (deficiency)	$(5,500)	$?
Financing of cash deficiency:		
Borrowing (at end of month)	$?	
Principal payments (at end of month)		$?
Interest expense (at .010 monthly)		?
(2) Total effects of financing	?	?
Ending cash balance (1) + (2)	$?	$?
Interest expense: June: ?		

Exercise 16-7 *Computing cash receipts and disbursements* *(L.O. 4)*

For each of the items *a* through *d*, compute the amount of cash receipts or disbursements Gulf States Company would budget for December. A solution to one item may depend on the answer to an earlier item.

a. Management expects to sell 4,000 units in November and 4,200 in December. Each unit sells for $6. Cash sales average 30 percent of the total sales, and credit sales make up the rest. Two-thirds of credit sales are collected in the month of sale, with the balance collected the following month.

b. Management has budgeted inventory purchases of $30,000 for November and $25,000 for December. Gulf States Company pays for 50 percent of its inventory at the time of purchase in order to get a 2 percent discount. The business pays the balance the following month, with no further discount.

c. Management expects to sell equipment that cost $14,100 at a gain of $2,000. Accumulated depreciation on this equipment is $6,000.

d. The company pays rent and property taxes of $6,000 each month. Commissions and other selling expenses average 20 percent of sales. Gulf States Company pays two-thirds of these costs in the month incurred, with the balance paid in the following month.

Exercise 16-8 *Preparing a cash budget* *(L.O. 4)*

Waxman's, a family-owned furniture store, began October with $5,400 cash. Management forecasts that collections from credit customers will be $9,000 in October and $12,200 in November. The store is scheduled to receive $5,000 cash on a business note receivable in November. Projected cash disbursements include inventory purchases ($10,200 in October and $12,100 in November) and operating expenses ($3,000 each month).

Waxman's bank requires a $7,500 minimum balance in the store's checking account. At the end of any month when the account balance goes below $7,500, the bank automatically extends credit to the store in multiples of $1,000. Waxman's borrows as little as possible and pays back these loans in monthly installments of $1,000 plus 1.5 percent monthly interest on the entire unpaid principal. The first payment occurs at the end of the month following the loan.

Required

Prepare the store's cash budget for October and November.

Exercise 16-9 *Preparing a budgeted balance sheet* (L.O. 5)

Use the following information to prepare a budgeted balance sheet for Little Einstein's Book Store at July 31, 19X6. Show computations for cash and owners' equity amounts.

a. July 31 inventory balance, $16,000.
b. July payments for inventory, $5,900.
c. July payments of June 30 accounts payable and accrued liabilities, $6,100.
d. July 31 accounts payable balance, $4,900.
e. June 30 furnitures and fixtures balance, $34,800; accumulated depreciation balance, $27,700.
f. July capital expenditures of $3,200 budgeted for cash purchase of furniture.
g. July operating expenses, including income tax, total $4,200, half of which will be paid during July and half accrued at July 31.
h. July depreciation, $300.
i. Cost of goods sold, 50 percent of sales.
j. June 30 owners' equity, $25,700.
k. June 30 cash balance, $10,300.
l. July budgeted sales, $12,400.
m. July 31 accounts receivable balance, one-fourth of July sales.
n. July cash receipts, $12,300.

Exercise 16-10 *Preparing a rolling budget for the income statement* (L.O. 6)

El Conquistador, Inc., budgets the following total revenues, total expenses, and net income for the last four months of the year:

	September	October	November	December
Budgeted total revenues	$175,000	$160,000	$170,000	$189,000
Budgeted total expenses	93,000	87,000	89,000	97,000
Budgeted net income	$ 82,000	$ 73,000	$ 81,000	$ 92,000

Prepare El Conquistador's rolling monthly income statement budget for the quarters ending on November 30 and December 31.

Problem 16-1A *Budgeting income and evaluating income with a performance report*
(L.O. 1, 2, 3)

The Northeastern district office of Impala Fan Company divides its annual budget into semiannual periods. The district manager forecast that sales would increase during the first half of the current year by 8.1 percent over the first half of the preceding year. The manager also believed that second-half sales of the current year would exceed second-half sales of the preceding year by 4.5 percent. Cost of goods sold was budgeted at 43 percent of budgeted sales. Total operating expenses, including income taxes, were expected to be 36 percent of revenues during the first six-month period and 34 percent during the second period.

Actual sales, operating expenses, and net income for the four most recent semiannual periods follow.

| | Preceding Year | | Current Year | |
| | Semiannual Period | | Semiannual Period | |
	1	2	1	2
Sales	$113,000	$145,000	$124,000	$165,000
Cost of goods sold	40,000	63,000	66,000	81,000
Gross margin	73,000	82,000	58,000	84,000
Operating expenses...........	52,000	49,000	39,000	47,000
Net income (loss)	$ 21,000	$ 33,000	$ 19,000	$ 37,000

Required

1. Prepare a budgeted income statement for each semiannual period of the current year. Round all amounts to the nearest $1,000.

2. Prepare a summarized income statement performance report for the same period. Present the actual and budgeted income statements side by side. Show the differences between them. Round all amounts to the nearest $1,000.

3. Have operations been more or less successful in the current semiannual period compared with the preceding period? What aspects of operations have improved? What aspects have deteriorated?

Problem 16-2A *Budgeting income for three months* *(L.O. 2, 3)*

The budget committee of Altenau & Company has assembled the following data. You are the business manager, and you must prepare the budgeted income statements for April, May, and June 19X3.

1. Sales in March were $31,300. You forecast that monthly sales will increase 1.3 percent in April and May and 1.8 percent in June.

2. The company tries to maintain inventory of $8,000 plus 20 percent of sales budgeted for the following month. Monthly purchases average 55 percent of sales. Actual inventory on March 31 is $12,000. Sales budgeted for July are $30,600.

3. Monthly salaries amount to $3,000. Sales commissions equal 5 percent of sales. Combine salaries and commissions as a single figure.

4. Other monthly expenses are

Rent expense	$2,700, paid as incurred
Depreciation expense.........	500
Insurance expense	100, expiration of prepaid amount
Miscellaneous expense	3% of sales
Income tax	20% of income from operations

Required

Prepare Altenau's budgeted income statements for April, May, and June. Show cost of goods sold computations. Round *all* amounts to the nearest $100. For example, budgeted April sales are $31,700 ($31,300 × 1.013), May sales are $32,100 ($31,700 × 1.013), and June sales are $32,700 ($32,100 × 1.018).

Note: Problem 16-3A is designed to be completed using a computer spread-sheet model, although it can also be solved manually.

Problem 16-3A   *Preparing a budgeted income statement*   *(L.O. 2, 3)*

Hulme TV Appliances is budgeting net income for the six months ended June 30, 19X4. Fred Hulme, the owner, expects January sales of $50,000 for TVs and $10,000 for VCRs. He is hoping for 1 percent monthly sales growth for TVs and 3 percent for VCRs. Cost of goods sold is 70 percent of sales for TVs and 60 percent for VCRs. Hulme budgets monthly expenses as follows:

Salaries	$14,000 per month
Rent	2,000 per month
Depreciation	1,000 per month
Insurance	500 per month
Travel	750 per quarter (in January and April only)
Utilities	500 per month
Income tax rate	40%

Required

Create a spreadsheet model to prepare Hulme's budgeted income statement for the six months ended June 30, 19X4. Show each expense, total operating expenses, income from operations, income tax expense, and net income. Format the statement as follows:

	A	B	C	D	E	F	G	H
1				Hulme TV Appliances				
2				Budgeted Income Statement				
3				For the Six Months Ended June 30, 19X4				
4								
5		JAN	FEB	MAR	APR	MAY	JUN	TOTAL
6	Sales							
7	TVS							
8	VCRs							
9								
10	Total Sales							
11								
12	COGS							
13	TVs							
14	VCRs							
15								
16	Total COGS							
17								
18	Gross Pft							
19	TVs							
20	VCRs							
21								
22	Total GP							
23								
24	Oper exp							
25								

Problem 16-4A *Preparing a cash budget for three months* **(L.O. 4)**

Genie Products, Inc., is considering opening a sales office in a suburb of Charlotte, North Carolina, during May of the current year. The business estimates the office opening will cost $92,000. To finance start-up, Interstate Bank has agreed to loan Genie, in multiples of $10,000, the amount needed to keep Genie's cash balance above $5,000. The loan begins on the last day of any month in which Genie's cash balance goes below $5,000. The company will repay the loan in monthly installments of $10,000 each, beginning one month after the loan starts. Genie will also pay monthly interest of 1.5 percent on the entire unpaid balance until the loan is fully repaid.

Management expects Genie's operations to generate the following:

	May	June	July
Sales	$63,000	$71,000	$74,000
Cost of goods sold	45,000	51,000	52,000
Cash operating expenses......	6,000	9,000	9,000

On May 1 Genie expects to have $9,000 cash and $36,000 of inventory. Inventory is expected to decrease by $4,000 each month. Monthly cash receipts average 95 percent of sales. The company purchases inventory through cash disbursements.

Required

Prepare Genie's cash budgets for the months of May, June, and July.

Problem 16-5A *Preparing a budgeted balance sheet* **(L.O. 5)**

Boyd Motor Company has applied for a loan. Alliance Bank has requested a budgeted balance sheet at April 30, 19X8. As the controller (chief accounting officer) of Boyd, you have assembled the following information:

a. March 31 equipment balance, $35,200; accumulated depreciation, $22,800.

b. April capital expenditures of $41,700 budgeted for cash purchase of equipment.

c. April operating expenses, including income tax, total $13,600, 25 percent of which will be paid in cash and the remainder accrued at April 30.

d. April depreciation, $700.

e. Cost of goods sold, 60 percent of sales.

f. March 31 owners' equity, $74,900.

g. March 31 cash balance, $26,200.

h. April budgeted sales, $70,000, 60 percent of which is for cash sales. Of the remaining 40 percent, half will be collected in April and half in May.

i. April cash collections on March sales, $31,200.

j. April cash payments of March 31 liabilities, $17,300.

k. March 31 inventory balance, $22,400.

l. April purchases of inventory, $9,000 for cash and $40,600 on credit. Half of the credit purchases will be paid in April and half in May.

Required

Prepare the budgeted balance sheet of Boyd Motor Company at April 30, 19X8. Show separate computations for cash, inventory, and owners' equity balances.

Problem 16-6A   *Preparing a rolling budget for the income statement*   **(L.O. 6)**

The budgeted income statements of Buzze Music Company for the six most recent quarters follow.

Buzze Music Company
Budgeted Income Statements
For the Quarters Ended September 30, 19X2, through December 31, 19X3

	19X2		19X3			
	Sep. 30	Dec. 31	Mar. 31	June 30	Sep. 30	Dec. 31
Sales	$20,000	$70,000	$50,000	$60,000	$30,000	$80,000
Cost of goods sold	8,000	30,000	22,000	23,000	11,000	30,000
Gross margin ..	12,000	40,000	28,000	37,000	19,000	50,000
Operating expenses	5,000	16,000	12,000	17,000	10,000	22,000
Net income	$ 7,000	$24,000	$16,000	$20,000	$ 9,000	$28,000

Required

1. Combine the quarterly totals necessary to prepare Buzze's rolling budgeted income statement for the last semiannual period in 19X2 and for the four semiannual periods ending in 19X3. (The first semiannual period in 19X3 ends March 31, the second June 30, and so on.)
2. Based on the comparison of the last half of 19X2 with the last half of 19X3, does Buzze management appear to expect increasing or decreasing sales and net income for 19X3?

Problem 16-7A   *Preparing all the components of a master budget*   **(L.O. 2, 3, 4, 5)**

Grant-Pfizer's balance sheet at September 30, 19X4, follows.

Grant-Pfizer Limited
Balance Sheet
September 30, 19X4

Assets		Liabilities	
Current assets:		**Current liabilities:**	
Cash	$ 11,000	Accounts payable................	$ 40,000
Accounts receivable, net	45,000	Salaries and commissions payable .	10,000
Inventory	62,000	Total liabilities.....................	50,000
Prepaid insurance	4,000		
	122,000	**Owners' Equity**	
Plant assets:		Owners' equity....................	140,000
Furniture and fixtures............	96,000		
Accumulated depreciation	(28,000)		
	68,000	Total liabilities	
Total assets	$190,000	and owners' equity	$190,000

Additional budget information follows.

a. Sales in September were $90,000. Management projects these monthly sales: October $80,000; November $70,000; December $80,000; January $60,000.

    Sales are half for cash and half on credit. All accounts receivable are collected in the month following sale. Uncollectible accounts are insignificant and can be ignored.

b. For the new budget period management wishes to maintain inventory of $22,000 plus 75 percent of the cost of goods to be sold in the following month. Cost of goods sold averages 60 percent of sales. Grant-Pfizer pays for inventory as follows: 20 percent in the month of purchase and 80 percent in the next month.

c. Payroll is made up of fixed salaries of $1,000 and sales commissions equal to 10 percent of sales. The monthly payroll is accrued at the end of the month and paid early the next month.

d. Other monthly expenses are

Advertising expense	$3,600, paid as incurred
Rent expense	1,300, paid as incurred
Depreciation expense	1,000
Insurance expense	400, expiration of prepaid amount
Miscellaneous expense	2% of sales, paid as incurred

e. Management has budgeted $26,000 cash for the acquisition of furniture in October.

f. The company is required by its bank to maintain a minimum cash balance of $8,000 at the end of each month. Money can be borrowed in multiples of $1,000. Management borrows no more than what is needed to maintain the $8,000 minimum balance and pays back all debts less than $5,000 at the end of the next month. Short-term notes payable greater than $5,000 are paid back in three equal monthly principal payments. The monthly interest rate on all notes payable is 1 percent on the entire unpaid principal. Borrowing and all principal and interest payments occur at the end of the month.

g. In September purchases were $50,000, and salaries and commissions were $10,000.

h. The business is a partnership. The partners, therefore, pay personal income tax on their earnings. The business itself incurs no income tax liability, so income taxes do not enter into the computations.

Required

Prepare Grant-Pfizer's master budget for the fourth quarter of 19X4. Include the following statements and schedules:

Statements:
Budgeted income statement for the quarter ending December 31, 19X4
Statement of budgeted cash receipts and disbursements for the quarter ending December 31, 19X4
Budgeted balance sheet at December 31, 19X4

Schedules:
Sales
Purchases, cost of goods sold, and inventory
Operating expenses
Cash collections from customers
Cash disbursements for purchases
Cash disbursements for operating expenses

Problem 16-1B *Budgeting income and evaluating income with a performance report (L.O. 1, 2, 3)*

The Indiana office of Precision Instruments divides its annual budget into semiannual periods. The regional manager forecast that sales would increase during the first half of the current year by 2.5 percent over the first half of the preceding year. The manager also believed that second-half sales of the current year would exceed second-half sales of the preceding year by 8 percent. Cost of goods sold was budgeted at 56 percent of budgeted sales. Total operating expenses, including income taxes, were expected to be 30 percent of revenues during the first six-month period and 32 percent during the second period.

Actual sales, operating expenses, and net income for the four most recent semiannual periods follow.

	Preceding Year Semiannual Period 1	Preceding Year Semiannual Period 2	Current Year Semiannual Period 1	Current Year Semiannual Period 2
Sales	$32,000	$30,000	$34,000	$36,000
Cost of goods sold	19,000	14,000	16,000	17,000
Gross margin	13,000	16,000	18,000	19,000
Operating expenses	10,000	11,000	11,000	13,000
Net income (loss)	$ 3,000	$ 5,000	$ 7,000	$ 6,000

Required

1. Prepare a budgeted income statement for each semiannual period of the current year. Round all amounts to the nearest $1,000.
2. Prepare a summarized income statement performance report for the same period. Present the actual and the budgeted income statement side by side. Show the differences between them. Round all amounts to the nearest $1,000.
3. Identify the aspects of operations that are performing most successfully and the aspects that are performing least successfully. Comment on the relative success of overall operations.

Problem 16-2B *Budgeting income for three months (L.O. 2, 3)*

Representatives of the various departments of Tallahassee Construction Co. have assembled the following data. You are the business manager, and you must prepare the budgeted income statements for July, August, and September 19X6.

1. Sales in June were $18,400. You forecast that monthly sales will increase 2 percent in July, 2 percent in August, and 3 percent in September.
2. Tallahassee tries to maintain inventory of $5,000 plus 20 percent of sales budgeted for the following month. Monthly purchases average 65 percent of sales. Actual inventory on June 30 is $8,000. Sales budgeted for October are $20,500.
3. Monthly salaries amount to $1,200. Sales commissions equal 6 percent of sales. Combine salaries and commissions as a single figure on the income statements.
4. Other monthly expenses are

Rent expense	$1,200, paid as incurred
Depreciation expense	300
Insurance expense	100, expiration of prepaid amount
Miscellaneous expense	5% of sales
Income tax	20% of income from operations

Required

Prepare Tallahassee's budgeted income statements for July, August, and September. Show cost of goods sold computations. Round *all* amounts to the nearest $100. For example, budgeted July sales are $18,800 ($18,400 × 1.02), August sales are $19,200 ($18,800 × 1.02), and September sales are $19,800 ($19,200 × 1.03).

Note: Problem 16-3B is designed to be completed using a computer spreadsheet model, although it can also be solved manually.

Problem 16-3B   *Preparing a budgeted income statement*   (L.O. 2, 3)

Advanced Information Systems, Inc., is budgeting gross profit (gross margin) for the six months ended June 30, 19X5. Lynn Bradshaw, the owner, expects January sales of $70,000 for computer hardware and $25,000 for software. She is hoping for 2 percent monthly sales growth for hardware and 4 percent for software. Cost of goods sold is 70 percent of sales for hardware and 50 percent for software. The business budgets expenses as follows:

Salaries	$20,000 per month
Rent	2,500 per month
Depreciation	2,000 per month
Insurance	1,500 per month
Travel..........................	900 per quarter (in January and April only)
Utilities	650 per month
Income tax rate	40%

Required

Create a spreadsheet model to prepare the Advanced Information Systems income statement for the six months ended June 30, 19X5. Show each expense, total operating expenses, income from operations, income tax expense, and net income. Format the statement as follows:

	A	B	C	D	E	F	G	H
			Advanced Information Systems, Inc.					
1			Advanced Information Systems, Inc.					
2			Budgeted Income Statement					
3			For the Six Months Ended June 30, 19X4					
4								
5		JAN	FEB	MAR	APR	MAY	JUN	TOTAL
6	Sales							
7	Hardware							
8	Software							
9								
10	Total Sales							
11								
12	COGS							
13	Hardware							
14	Software							
15								
16	Total COGS							
17								
18	Gross Pft							
19	Hardware							
20	Software							
21								
22	Total GP							
23								
24	Oper exp							

Problem 16-4B *Preparing a cash budget for three months* (L.O. 4)

Midlantic Development Company is considering opening an office in a suburb of Chesapeake County, Virginia, during September of the current year. The business estimates that the office opening will cost $17,000. To finance start-up, Guaranty Bank has agreed to loan Midlantic, in multiples of $1,000, the amount needed to keep Midlantic's cash balance above $10,000. The loan begins on the last day of any month in which Midlantic's cash balance goes below $10,000. The company will repay the loan in monthly installments of $1,000 each, beginning two months after the loan starts. Midlantic will also pay monthly interest of 1 percent on the entire unpaid balance until the loan is repaid.

Management expects Midlantic's operations to generate the following:

	August	September	October
Sales	$41,000	$44,000	$52,000
Cost of goods sold	17,000	21,000	26,000
Cash operating expenses	19,000	22,000	24,000
Collection of note receivable		25,000	

On August 1 Midlantic expects to have $7,000 cash and $7,000 of inventory. Inventory is expected to increase by $3,000 each month. Monthly cash receipts average 95 percent of sales. The company purchases inventory through cash disbursements.

Required

Prepare Midlantic's cash budgets for the months of August, September, and October.

Problem 16-5B *Preparing a budgeted balance sheet* (L.O. 5)

Kluzewski Supply has applied for a loan. The bank, Master Bank, has requested a budgeted balance sheet at June 30, 19X4. As the controller (chief accounting officer) of Kluzewski, you have assembled the following information:

a. May 31 equipment balance, $60,600; accumulated depreciation, $11,700.
b. June capital expenditures of $15,800 budgeted for cash purchase of equipment.
c. June operating expenses, including income tax, total $38,800, 75 percent of which will be paid in cash and the remainder accrued at June 30.
d. June depreciation, $400.
e. Cost of goods sold, 45 percent of sales.
f. May 31 owners' equity, $97,400.
g. May 31 cash balance, $33,900.
h. June budgeted sales, $50,000, 40 percent of which is for cash. Of the remaining 60 percent, half will be collected in June and half in July.
i. June cash collections on May sales, $14,900.
j. June cash payments of May 31 liabilities, $10,700.
k. May 31 inventory balance, $10,400.
l. June purchases of inventory, $11,000 for cash and $27,400 on credit. Half of the credit purchases will be paid in June and half in July.

Required

Prepare the budgeted balance sheet of Kluzewski Supply at June 30, 19X4. Show separate computations for cash, inventory, and owners' equity balances.

Problem 16-6B *Preparing a rolling budget for the income statement* **(L.O. 6)**

The budgeted income statements of Niagara Corp. for the six most recent quarters follow.

Niagara Corp.
Budgeted Income Statements
For the Quarters Ended September 30, 19X5, through December 31, 19X6

	19X5		19X6			
	Sep. 30	Dec. 31	Mar. 31	June 30	Sep. 30	Dec. 31
Sales........	$50,000	$90,000	$60,000	$80,000	$ 40,000	$120,000
Cost of goods sold	25,000	50,000	35,000	50,000	25,000	75,000
Gross margin	25,000	40,000	25,000	30,000	15,000	45,000
Operating expenses ..	22,000	20,000	22,000	23,000	25,000	24,000
Net income (loss)	$ 3,000	$20,000	$ 3,000	$ 7,000	$(10,000)	$ 21,000

Required

1. Combine the quarterly totals necessary to prepare Niagara's rolling budgeted income statement for the last semiannual period in 19X5 and for the four semiannual periods ending in 19X6. (The first semiannual period in 19X6 ends March 31, the second June 30, and so on.)
2. Based on the comparison of the last half of 19X6 with the last half of 19X5, does management appear to expect increasing or decreasing sales and net income for 19X6?

Problem 16-7B *Preparing all the components of a master budget* **(L.O. 2, 3, 4, 5)**

Fitness Associates' balance sheet at September 30, 19X4, follows.

Fitness Associates
Balance Sheet
September 30, 19X4

Assets		Liabilities	
Current assets:		Current liabilities:	
Cash	$ 7,000	Accounts payable	$ 32,000
Accounts receivable, net	25,000	Salaries and commissions payable .	8,000
Inventory.......................	67,000	Total liabilities	40,000
Prepaid insurance	2,000		
	101,000	**Owners' Equity**	
Plant assets:			
Furniture and fixtures	48,000	Owners' equity	90,000
Accumulated depreciation.........	(19,000)		
	29,000	Total liabilities	
Total assets	$130,000	and owners' equity	$130,000

Additional budget information follows.

a. Sales in September were $50,000. Management projects these monthly sales: October $60,000; November $70,000; December $80,000; January $80,000.

   Sales are half for cash and half on credit. All accounts receivable are collected in the month following sale. Uncollectible accounts are insignificant and can be ignored.

b. Management wishes to maintain inventory of $40,000 plus 75 percent of the cost of goods sold in the following month. Cost of goods sold averages 60 percent of sales. Fitness Associates pays for inventory as follows: 20 percent of each month's purchases in the month of purchase and the remaining 80 percent in the next month.

c. Payroll is made up of fixed salaries of $3,000 and sales commissions equal to 10 percent of sales. The monthly payroll is accrued at the end of the month and paid early the following month.

d. Other monthly expenses are

Advertising expense.........	$1,500, paid as incurred
Rent expense	900, paid as incurred
Depreciation expense........	600
Insurance expense	200, expiration of prepaid amount
Miscellaneous expense	2% of sales, paid as incurred

e. Management has budgeted $8,000 cash for the acquisition of furniture in October.

f. The company keeps a minimum cash balance of $5,000 at the end of each month. The company may borrow on short-term notes payable in multiples of $1,000. Management borrows no more than necessary. The company repays the notes in three equal monthly installments that begin one month after the company borrows. The notes also carry monthly interest of 1 percent on the entire unpaid principal. Borrowing and all principal and interest payments occur at the end of the month.

g. In September purchases were $40,000, and salaries and commissions were $8,000.

h. The business is a partnership. The partners, therefore, pay personal income tax on their earnings. The business itself incurs no income tax liability, so income taxes do not enter into the computations.

Required

Prepare Fitness Associates' master budget for the fourth quarter of 19X4. Include the following statements and schedules:

Statements:
Budgeted income statement for the quarter ending December 31, 19X4
Statement of budgeted cash receipts and disbursements for the quarter ending December 31, 19X4
Budgeted balance sheet at December 31, 19X4

Schedules:
Sales
Purchases, cost of goods sold, and inventory
Operating expenses
Cash collections from customers
Cash disbursements for purchases
Cash disbursements for operating expenses

Extending Your Knowledge

Decision Problems

1. Preparing a Cash Budget to Analyze a Loan Request   (L.O. 4)

Billy Disch Marine Co., a boat dealer, is requesting a $40,000 loan to finance the remodeling of its store. The bank requires a statement of budgeted cash receipts and disbursements to support the loan application.

The Disch Marine cash balance at February 28 is $5,100. During March the business expects to collect $3,900 from sales made in January and February. Also, in February the store sold an old display case for $700, and the owners expect to receive that amount during March. During March the business will pay off accounts payable of $2,100 and a note payable of $6,000 plus $540 interest.

The business expects monthly sales of $9,500 for March, April, and May. Experience indicates that Disch will collect 60 percent of sales in the month of sale, 30 percent in the month following sale, and 7 percent in the second month after sale. The remaining 3 percent is uncollectible.

The February 28 inventory is $37,800. Purchases average one-half of sales. Billy Disch pays all accounts payable arising from inventory purchases in time to receive a 2 percent discount, 80 percent in the month of purchase and 20 percent the next month.

Budgeted operating expenses for March are rent (8 percent of sales), advertising ($500), utilities ($330), depreciation ($240), and insurance ($120). Depreciation and insurance are recorded as the assets expire. Half of the advertising expense is paid as incurred, and half is accrued at the end of the month. During March Disch Marine will pay advertising of $160 that was accrued at February 28.

In order to make the loan, the bank requires that Disch Marine's cash balance be at least $2,000 before any effects of financing.

Required

Prepare a cash budget (a statement of budgeted cash receipts and disbursements) for Billy Disch Marine Co. for March. As the bank loan officer, decide if the business qualifies for the loan.

2. Projecting Cash Flow and Financial Statements to Analyze Alternatives (L.O. 2,3,4,5)

Jacky Carleton is a librarian in the business library of Canada Trust. Each autumn, as a hobby, Jacky weaves cotton placemats for sale through a local craft shop. The shop charges 10% commission and remits the net proceeds to Jacky at the end of December. The mats sell in the shop for $20 per set of four; the cost of the cotton is $7 per set. Jacky has woven and sold 25 sets each year for the past two years. Each December 31st, Jacky has always paid for the cotton and repaid $200 of the principal, along with accrued interest at 9%, on the loan she received on September 1, 19X1 for her four-harness loom. This was also the day the loom was purchased.

Jacky's weaving is very professional. She is considering buying an eight-harness loom immediately so she can weave more intricate placemats in linen. She estimates that each set would sell for $50, and the cost of the linen would be $18 per set. She can weave 15 sets in time for the Christmas rush. Jacky's supplier will sell her linen on credit until December 31. The new loom would cost $1,000. The bank has agreed to lend her the money at 12% per annum, with $200 principal plus accrued interest payable each December 31. Jacky plans to keep her original loom. She could make 25 sets of cotton placemats with her newly-purchased supply of cotton. The old loom is depreciated at $10 per month; monthly depreciation on the new loom would be $20. The balance sheet for Jacky's weaving at August 31, 19X3 follows:

Jacky Carleton, Weaver
Balance Sheet
August 31, 19X3

Current assets:			Current liabilities:		
Cash		$ 15	Bank loan payable		$100
Inventory of cotton		175	Accounts payable		74
		190	Interest payable		6
Fixed assets:					180
Loom		500			
Accumulated			Owner's equity		270
depreciation		(240)			
		260	Total liabilities		
Total assets		$ 450	and owner's equity		$450

Required

Prepare a statement of budgeted cash receipts and disbursements for the four months ended December 31, 19X3 for two alternatives: weaving the placemats in cotton and weaving the placemats in linen. For each alternative, prepare a budgeted income statement for the four months ended December 31, 19X3, and a budgeted balance sheet at December 31, 19X3. Which alternative would you recommend for Jacky? Give your reason.

Ethical Issue

Maxim Gorky, Inc., practices top-down budgeting. Top managers set targets for sales managers, who then develop goals for individual salespersons. Grace Faile, manager for the western district, uses her contacts and interpersonal skills to raise money for the Republican party. Randall Van Houten, president of Maxim Gorky, is a prominent Democrat. He suspects that Ms. Faile is using too much time for fund-raising and shirking her duty to the company. For 1994, Mr. Van Houten sets Ms. Faile's sales goal 40 percent above actual amounts for 1993. The increases expected of other sales managers average 25 percent. Van Houten justifies Faile's sales budget on the grounds that the western district has experienced the greatest growth and that Ms. Faile is extremely talented.

Required

1. What is the preferred model for establishing a budget—top-down or bottom-up? Give your reason.
2. Is Mr. Van Houten's treatment of Ms. Faile ethical? Explain.

Chapter 17

Cost-Volume-Profit Relationships and the Contribution Margin Approach to Decision Making

His big sin, Mr. Iacocca says, was trying to diversify. His decision put the company into the aerospace and defense businesses, but siphoned management attention and money from the crucial task of producing new vehicles. Now Chrysler has sold, or is trying to sell, those businesses. . . .

Along with diversification came a top-heavy . . . company structure that sent Chrysler's costs soaring. The company must now sell 1.9 million cars and trucks a year just to *break even*. That's far above the *break-even point* of 1.1 million vehicles in 1985 and a much bigger increase than can be justified by Chrysler's 1987 purchase of American Motors Corp.

"If I made a mistake, it was following other companies, and maybe those were grandiose schemes," says Mr. Iacocca. "We didn't need a [new] company [structure]. That's what made us top-heavy." [Emphasis added]

SOURCE: Adapted from Paul Ingrassia and Bradley A. Stertz, "With Chrysler Ailing, Lee Iacocca Concedes Mistakes in Managing," *The Wall Street Journal*, September 17, 1990, p. A1. Reprinted by permission of *The Wall Street Journal*, © 1990 Dow Jones & Company, Inc. All Rights Reserved Worldwide. Photo courtesy of Chrysler Corporation.

How much additional income does Chrysler Corporation earn when it sells 5,000 more Dodge Caravans? How much in additional expense does the sale of these 5,000 cars cost Chrysler? How many Caravans must the company sell for the Dodge Division to break even—earn zero profit?

Many questions in business—on the number of cars sold, the number of passengers transported by an airline, and so on—boil down to this general question: *What effects does a change in volume have on profits?* To answer these questions, managers study the links among cost, volume, and profit.

Cost-volume-profit (CVP) analysis helps managers to predict the outcome of their decisions by expressing the relationships among a business's costs, volume, and profit or loss. It is an important part of the budgeting system. We begin our discussion of this valuable decision-making tool by looking at costs.

Types of Costs

A **cost driver** is any factor whose change makes a difference in a related total cost. There are many possible cost drivers. The most prominent driver is volume, which is often expressed in physical *units* sold or produced or in total sales *dollars*. For example, the more T-shirts a company produces—that is, the greater the T-shirt volume—the greater the costs the company incurs. Non-volume factors also act as cost drivers. An example is weight, which may affect freight costs. To emphasize basic concepts in this chapter, we focus on volume as the cost driver.

Cost behavior describes how costs change—indeed, if they change—in response to a shift in a cost driver. We examine three basic types of costs: variable, fixed, and mixed. A **variable cost (variable expense)** is a cost that changes in total in direct proportion to a change in volume. For example, sales commissions are variable costs; the higher the sales, the higher the sales commissions. Variable costs also include cost of goods sold and delivery expense. Each of these costs rises or falls directly with any increase or decrease in sales volume.

Exhibit 17-1 shows the graphs of three different variable costs. The first graph presents the cost behavior of a product that costs $2 an item. The sloped line in the first graph indicates the 3,000 T-shirts cost $6,000 (3,000 × $2). We see that 4,500 T-shirts cost $9,000 (4,500 × $2).

The higher the cost of an item, the steeper the graph of its variable cost. For example, the second graph in Exhibit 17-1 is based on each item costing $3. Study this graph to confirm that 2,000 T-shirts cost $6,000 (2,000 × $3) and that

OBJECTIVE 1

Identify different cost behavior patterns

EXHIBIT 17-1 *Variable Cost Pattern*

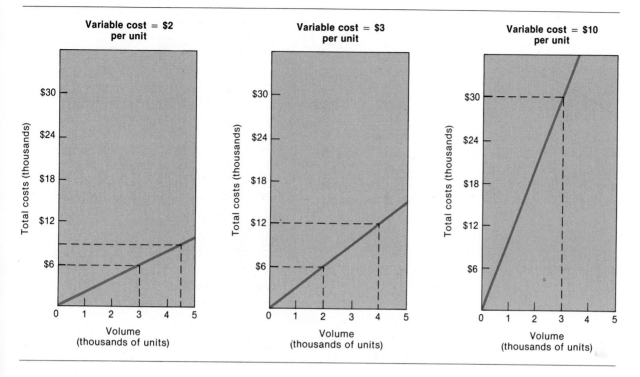

4,000 T-shirts cost $12,000 (4,000 × $3). The third variable cost graph, showing the cost behavior of designer T-shirts that cost $10 each, is steeper yet.

A variable cost graph always passes through the origin (where the cost and volume axes intersect) because at zero volume, the variable cost is zero. As volume increases, variable cost increases in a straight line that leads out from the origin. The steepness of the graph's slope depends on the variable cost per unit. A higher variable unit cost results in a steeper slope. A lower variable unit cost has a lower slope.

A **fixed cost (fixed expense)** is a cost that does not change in total despite changes in volume. For example, office rent does not usually change with the volume of business. A company must still pay its monthly rent regardless of whether sales volume rises, falls, or stays steady. Other examples of fixed costs are depreciation, property taxes, and many executive salaries. These costs occur even if the company makes no sales, for this is the nature of a fixed cost. Exhibit 17-2 graphs a fixed cost, which is always a horizontal line intersecting the cost axis at the level of the fixed cost. In the graph, fixed cost is $12,000, not changing with any shift in the volume.

A **mixed cost (mixed expense)** is part variable and part fixed. It is also called a semivariable cost. Consider a utility expense like electricity, for example. The company must pay a minimum charge regardless of how much electricity it used. In our illustrations, this fixed cost is $6,000. In addition, the company must pay a variable cost of $3 for every product sold. Exhibit 17-3 shows this mixed cost graph.

In a mixed cost graph, total cost is the sum of fixed cost plus the variable cost. At sales volume of 2,000 units, total cost is $12,000 [fixed cost of $6,000 + variable cost of $6,000 (2,000 × $3)]. At volume of 4,000 units, total cost is $18,000 [fixed cost of $6,000 + variable cost of $12,000 (4,000 × $3)]. All graphs of mixed costs show the same pattern. They intersect the cost axis at the fixed cost point, and the slope of the graph is the variable cost per unit.

EXHIBIT 17-2 *Fixed Cost Pattern*

Fixed Cost = $12,000

Synonyms abound in accounting. In cost-volume-profit analysis the following synonyms are widely used:

sales and *revenue*
variable cost and *variable expense*
fixed cost and *fixed expense*
income from operations and *operating income*
net income and *net profit*

Because you will encounter these synonyms in actual practice, we will use them freely in this chapter. To underscore basic relationships, income tax is assumed to be included among the expenses.

EXHIBIT 17-3 *Mixed Cost Pattern*

Fixed Cost = $6,000;
Variable Cost = $3 Per Unit

Contribution Margin Approach to Decision Making _____

An income statement can be prepared using two fundamentally different approaches. The early part of this book focused on accounting from the perspective of external users of the financial statements. That emphasis leads to the conventional income statement.

The present focus on management's use of accounting information calls for a different format for the income statement. In the management focus, the nature of an expense is important. Whether a cost is variable or fixed affects management decisions. Managers, then, want an income statement format that identifies the different types of costs. The contribution margin income statement provides this information.

The **contribution margin income statement** separates expenses into variable costs and fixed costs and highlights the **contribution margin**, which is the excess of sales over variable expenses. Exhibit 17-4 presents a contribution margin income statement alongside a conventional income statement for comparison.

Income from operations is the same on both income statements. However, the contribution margin of $9,000 differs from the gross margin of $16,000. The primary categories of expenses on the contribution margin statement are variable expenses and fixed expenses. By contrast, the conventional income statement contains no such distinctions. Instead, its primary categories of expenses are cost of goods sold and operating expenses.

The contribution margin receives its name because the excess of revenues over variable expenses "contributes" to the payment of fixed expenses. The amount of revenues left over "contributes" to profit. Management's goal, of course, is to make the contribution margin as large as possible.

Suppose that Reynolds Company managers are trying to predict the impact on operating income if sales increase by $4,000 (10 percent), from $40,000 to $44,000. Management, in drawing up the company budget, must know the impact of this possible sales increase on income from operations. If sales increase by 10 percent, variable expenses can be expected to increase by the same percentage. Fixed expenses will remain at $3,000.

> **OBJECTIVE 2**
> Use a contribution margin income statement to make business decisions

EXHIBIT 17-4 *Contribution Margin Income Statement*

Reynolds Company Conventional Income Statement Month Ended December 31, 19XX		
Sales revenue		$40,000
Cost of goods sold		24,000
Gross margin		**16,000**
Operating expenses:		
Selling	$6,000	
General and administrative	4,000	10,000
Income from operations		$ 6,000

Reynolds Company Contribution Margin Income Statement Month Ended December 31, 19XX		
Sales revenue		$40,000
Variable expenses:		
Cost of goods sold	$24,000	
Selling	4,000	
General and administrative	3,000	31,000
Contribution margin		**9,000**
Fixed expenses:		
Selling	2,000	
General and administrative	1,000	3,000
Income from operations		$ 6,000

We compute the income from operations resulting from the sales increase as follows:

Increase in sales revenue	$4,000
Increase in expenses:	
Fixed expenses	-0-
Variable expenses:	

$$\frac{\text{Increase in sales}}{\text{Current sales}} \times \text{Current variable expenses}$$

$\dfrac{\$4,000}{\$40,000}$	$\times$	$31,000	3,100

Increase in contribution margin	**900**
Income from operations before sales increase	6,000
Income from operations after sales increase	$6,900

Management can use this information to decide whether to expand operations. If the $900 increase in contribution margin is considered adequate, Reynolds will expand the business. If $900 is considered inadequate, then Reynolds will come up with another plan.

Important points about the analysis are that (1) fixed expenses do not change and (2) variable expenses increase proportionately with sales. That is, sales are expected to increase by 10 percent ($4,000/$40,000 = .10), and so variable expenses and the contribution margin also increase by 10 percent.

Similar analysis using the conventional income statement is not possible. Managers cannot use the conventional income statement to accurately predict the change in income from an increase in sales because this statement does not show which expenses are variable and which are fixed.

Relevant Range

A **relevant range** is the band of volume in which a specific relationship between cost and volume is valid. A fixed cost is fixed only in relation to a given relevant range (usually large) and a given time span (usually a particular budget period). Exhibit 17-5 shows a fixed cost level of $50,000 for the volume range of 0 to 10,000 units. Between 10,000 and 20,000 units, fixed expenses may be $80,000, and they may increase to $120,000 for volume above 20,000 units.

Companies use the relevant range concept in budgeting their costs. Suppose the business in Exhibit 17-5 expects sales volume of 12,000 during the year. For this period the relevant range is between 10,000 and 20,000 units, and managers would budget fixed expenses of $80,000. If actual sales for the year exceed 20,000 units, the company will consider hiring additional employees and perhaps open a new store, increasing rent expense. Fixed expenses will increase as the relevant range shifts to a new band of volume.

Fixed costs change from year to year, and so does the relevant range. Expecting sales of only 8,000 units next year, the business would budget fixed expenses in a lower relevant range. The company may have to shut down a sales office, lay off employees, and eliminate other fixed expenses.

The relevant range concept also applies to variable costs. Some variable expenses may behave differently at different levels of volume. For example, utility expenses for water and electricity often cost less per unit as usage increases. Also, a company may pay higher sales commission rates for higher levels of sales to encourage extra selling effort. Therefore, businesses should

EXHIBIT 17-5 *Relevant Range*

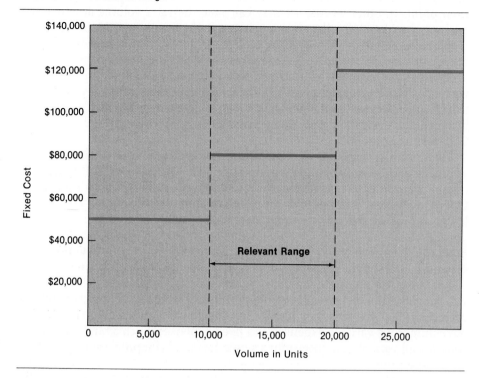

consider cost behavior—how both fixed and variable expenses change—over the full range of sales volumes that are likely to occur during the budget period.

Cost behavior is one of the most challenging aspects of budgeting. After managers set the business's sales goal for the next period, accountants estimate costs. The behavior of various costs affects the expense budget. If budgeted expenses are too high, top managers may revise budgets for sales or expenses before finally setting the profit goal for the period.

In cost-volume-profit analysis, which we discuss next, we begin by classifying each cost as either variable or fixed. Later in this chapter, we show how to separate a mixed cost into its variable and fixed components.

Cost-Volume-Profit Analysis

The easiest way to learn cost-volume-profit analysis is with an example. Suppose Maria Martinez is considering renting a booth at a county fair. Maria plans to sell travel posters for $3.50 each. She can purchase the posters for $2.10 each and can return all unsold items for a full refund. Rent for the booth will cost $700. Using this information, let's answer six questions about Maria's business.

Question 1: What Is Maria's Break-Even Sales Level?

The study of cost-volume-profit analysis is often called **break-even analysis.** Why? CVP analysis allows us to compute an amount in unit sales or dollar sales at which revenue equals expenses. This sales level is called the **break-even point.** In other words, we may calculate the sales volume at which the business breaks even. Revenue must reach the break-even point to cover costs. Sales below the break-even point mean a loss. Sales above break-even bring a profit. CVP, or break-even, analysis answers the questions, How many units must the business sell to cover expenses? and How much in sales must we reach before we earn a profit? The break-even point is often only incidental to managers because their focus is on the sales level needed to earn a target net income. However, the break-even point is a useful place to start the analysis of CVP relationships.

Two popular methods in cost-volume-profit analysis are the equation approach and the contribution margin approach. The focus in CVP analysis is often on *operating income* (income from operations) rather than on *net income*. Operating income is easier to predict because it omits extraordinary gains and losses and other special items that affect net income.

OBJECTIVE 3
Compute break-even sales

Equation Approach. In the equation approach, we start by dividing total expenses into variable expenses and fixed expenses.

For Maria Martinez, the variable cost is her cost of goods sold. This expense will equal the number of posters sold multiplied by her $2.10 cost to purchase each item. Her fixed cost is the $700 rent expense. A large company would have numerous variable expenses and fixed expenses. Such a business would combine all variable expenses into a single total and compute a single total for fixed expenses.

Our next step is to express income in equation form:

Sales − Variable expenses − Fixed expenses = Operating income

We find it useful to rearrange the equation to place the variables on the left-hand side and the dollar amounts on the right:

Sales − Variable expenses = Fixed expenses + Operating income

At the break-even point, income equals expenses, so net income is zero. Sales equals the unit selling price multiplied by the number of units sold. Variable expenses equals variable cost per unit times the number of units sold. We substitute these terms into the equation and enter the dollar amounts that we have:

Sales −	Variable expenses	= Fixed expenses + Operating income
$\left(\begin{array}{c}\text{Unit}\\\text{sale} \times \text{Units sold}\\\text{price}\end{array}\right)$ −	$\left(\begin{array}{c}\text{Unit}\\\text{variable} \times \text{Units sold}\\\text{cost}\end{array}\right)$	= Fixed expenses + Operating income
($3.50 × Units sold) −	($2.10 × Units sold) =	$700 + $0
($3.50 −	$2.10) × Units sold =	$700 + $0
	$1.40 × Units sold =	$700
	Units sold =	$700/$1.40
	Break-even sales in units =	500 units

Maria must sell 500 units to break even. Her break-even sales in dollars is the 500 units times their selling price of $3.50. Break-even dollar sales are $1,750 (500 units × $3.50).

Another form of the equation approach determines dollar sales first and unit sales second. We divide the variable expense per unit $2.10, by the selling price, $3.50, to determine the ratio of the variable expense to the selling price:

$$\frac{\text{Variable expense}}{\text{Selling price}} = \frac{\$2.10}{\$3.50} = .60$$

We use this ratio in the equation, as follows:

Sales − Variable expense	=	Fixed expenses + Operating income
Sales − (.60 × Sales)	=	$700 + $0
Sales − (.60 × Sales)	=	$700
.40 × Sales	=	$700
Sales	=	$700/.40
Break-even sales in dollars	=	**$1,750**
Break-even sales in units	=	**500 ($1,750/$3.50)**

Contribution Margin Approach. A second way to do CVP analysis is the contribution margin approach. Each unit sold has a *contribution margin,* which is the excess of the sale price over variable expenses. The contribution margin can be expressed per unit, as a percentage, or as a ratio. Sales revenue "contributes" this excess, so to speak, to the recovery of fixed costs, with any remaining excess going to operating income, as follows for Maria Martinez's business:

	Per Unit	Percent	Ratio
Sale price	$ 3.50	100%	1.00
Variable expense	−2.10	−60	−.60
Contribution margin	$ 1.40	40%	.40

In percentage terms, sales of 100 percent minus the variable expense percentage equals the **contribution margin percentage.** Likewise, 100 percent minus the contribution margin percentage equals the variable expense percentage. These relationships can be diagrammed:

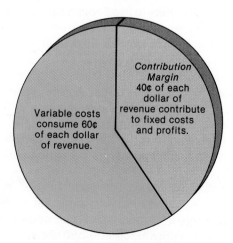

Breakdown of $1 of Revenue

In our illustration, the contribution margin *per unit* is $1.40 ($3.50 − $2.10). To compute break-even sales in units sold, divide fixed expenses by the contribution margin per unit:

$$\text{Break-even sales in units} = \frac{\text{Fixed expenses}}{\text{Contribution margin per unit}}$$

$$= \frac{\$700}{\$1.40}$$

$$= 500 \text{ units}$$

We may use percentages in the contribution margin approach. In our example, the contribution margin percentage is $1.40/$3.50, or 40 percent. Earlier we subtracted the variable cost percentage (60 percent) from sales (100 percent) to compute the 40 percent contribution margin percentage. The contribution margin percentage equals the contribution margin divided by the sale price.

We may use the sale price and variable cost of a single item, or we may use the total sales figure and the total variable cost amount of the entire product line in our computations. For example, consider the figures that arise from Maria's selling 500 items. Total sales equals $1,750 ($3.50 × 500), and the total contribution margin is $700 ($1.40 × 500). We see that $700/$1,750 equals .40, or 40 percent. Break-even sales in dollars can be computed as follows by the contribution margin approach:

$$\text{Break-even sales in dollars} = \frac{\text{Fixed expenses}}{\text{Contribution margin ratio}}$$

$$= \frac{\$700}{.40}$$

$$= \$1,750$$

If unit variable costs rise, then the amount needed to reach break-even sales increases. Why? A higher unit variable cost lowers the contribution margin. In contrast, a lower unit variable cost means a higher contribution margin, which leads to lower break-even sales.

If sales increase, so does net income. To find the increase in operating income, we can multiply the increase in sales by the contribution margin ratio. For example, Maria's contribution margin ratio is .40. If sales increase by $1,000, for example, then operating income grows by $400.

The business press often refers to break-even sales, or break-even revenues. For example, a news story such as the chapter-opening vignette might report that "the Big Three auto makers have slashed their sales break-even point in North America from 12.2 million cars and trucks to only 9.1 million this year." The companies could accomplish this by decreasing fixed expenses, which is the numerator of the break-even formula. As the numerator decreases, the break-even amount decreases too. Similarly, increasing the contribution margin per unit—the denominator in the formula—will also decrease the break-even amount. For example, a reduction in variable expenses like tires or radiators will increase the contribution margin per automobile and so reduce the break-even amount.

Should you use the equation approach or the contribution margin approach? Use either, depending on your personal preference. You should know both approaches, however, because certain decision situations may give the information in one form or the other—but not both.

We return to questions about Maria's business.

Question 2. If a Fixed Cost (Such as Rent Expense) Is Changed, What Would Break-Even Sales Be?

Suppose the rental on the booth were $1,050 instead of $700. What is Maria's break-even point in units sold and dollar sales?

Use the formula discussed in the contribution margin approach:

$$\textbf{Break-even sales in units} = \frac{\textbf{Fixed expenses}}{\textbf{Contribution margin per unit}}$$

$$= \frac{\$1,050}{\$1.40}$$

$$= \textbf{750 units}$$

$$\textbf{Break-even sales in dollars} = \frac{\textbf{Fixed expenses}}{\textbf{Contribution margin ratio}}$$

$$= \frac{\$1,050}{.40}$$

$$= \textbf{\$2,625}$$

The $1,050 in fixed expenses is an increase of $350, or 50 percent, in excess of $700. Note that the break-even point also rises by 50 percent, from 500 to 750 units. This match in percentage between the increase in fixed expenses and the increase in the break-even point always exists (if other factors are held constant). Maria must sell more posters to cover the higher fixed costs. Similarly, a decrease in fixed expenses means that she can sell less and still cover these costs.

Question 3. If the Sale Price Is Changed, What Would Break-Even Sales Be?

Suppose the sale price per poster is $3.85 rather than $3.50. Variable expense per unit remains at $2.10, and fixed expenses stay at $700. What are Maria's revised break-even sales in units and in dollars? The unit contribution margin becomes $1.75 ($3.85 − $2.10) and the new contribution margin ratio is .4545 ($1.75/ $3.85).

Compute break-even in units and in dollars as follows:

$$\textbf{Break-even sales in units} = \frac{\textbf{Fixed expenses}}{\textbf{Contribution margin per unit}}$$

$$= \frac{\$700}{\$1.75}$$

$$= \textbf{400 units}$$

$$\textbf{Break-even sales in dollars} = \frac{\textbf{Fixed expenses}}{\textbf{Contribution margin ratio}}$$

$$= \frac{\$700}{.4545}$$

$$= \textbf{\$1,540}$$

Note that an increase in sale price reduces break-even sales, in units and in dollars. This occurs because the contribution margin per unit increases. Consequently, it takes fewer sales at the higher price to break even. Conversely, a reduction in sale price would decrease the contribution margin and force Maria to increase sales just to break even.

Question 4. If a Variable Cost Is Changed, What Would Break-Even Sales Be?

Suppose variable cost per unit is $2.38 instead of $2.10. The unit sale price remains $3.50, and fixed costs stay at $700. Compute break-even sales in units and in dollars.

The new unit contribution margin is $1.12 ($3.50 − $2.38), and the new contribution margin ratio is .32 ($1.12/$3.50). Break-even sales are

$$\text{Break-even sales in units} = \frac{\text{Fixed expenses}}{\text{Contribution margin per unit}}$$

$$= \frac{\$700}{\$1.12}$$

$$= 625 \text{ units}$$

$$\text{Break-even sales in dollars} = \frac{\text{Fixed expenses}}{\text{Contribution margin ratio}}$$

$$= \frac{\$700}{.32}$$

$$= \$2,187.50$$

An increase in variable cost per unit decreases the contribution margin and means that Maria must increase sales in units and in dollars to break even. A decrease in variable cost per unit would lower the break-even point.

Question 5. How Many Units Must Be Sold to Earn a Target Operating Income?

Suppose Maria would be content with operating income of $490 for a week's work in the booth. Assuming a unit sale price of $3.50, variable expense of $2.10 per unit, and fixed expenses of $700, how many posters must Maria sell to earn a profit of $490?

Until now, we have concentrated on break-even sales, the point where operating income is zero. How should we consider a target operating income greater than zero? The contribution margin must be sufficient to cover the fixed expenses plus the target operating income. Our contribution margin approach is basically unchanged. However, the numerator now contains both fixed expenses and the target operating income.

OBJECTIVE 4

Compute the sales level needed to earn a target operating income

$$\text{Target sales in units} = \frac{\text{Fixed expenses} + \text{Target operating income}}{\text{Contribution margin per unit}}$$

$$= \frac{\$700 + \$490}{\$1.40}$$

$$= \frac{\$1,190}{\$1.40}$$

$$= 850 \text{ units}$$

$$\text{Target sales in dollars} = \frac{\text{Fixed expenses + Target operating income}}{\text{Contribution margin ratio}}$$

$$= \frac{\$700 + \$490}{.40}$$

$$= \frac{\$1,190}{.40}$$

$$= \$2,975$$

The minimum level needed to earn operating income of $490 is 850 units, or $2,975 (850 × $3.50).

Question 6. What Operating Income Is Expected at Various Sales Levels?

A convenient way to answer this question is to graph the cost-volume-profit relationships, as shown in Exhibit 17-6.

To set up the graph, we place units on the horizontal axis and dollars on the vertical axis. We label each axis appropriately. (We have chosen to place labels every 100 units and every $500. These labels offer enough detail for ease in understanding the graph but do not clutter it. Labels on the graphs depend on the data in the problem. The labels should be helpful but not crowd the information.) We use Maria Martinez's data (as originally given) and follow five steps:

Step 1. Choose a relevant sales volume, such as 1,000 units. Plot the point for sales dollars at that volume: 1,000 units × $3.50 per unit = sales of $3,500. Draw the *sales line* from the origin through the $3,500 point.

EXHIBIT 17-6 *Cost-Volume-Profit Graph*

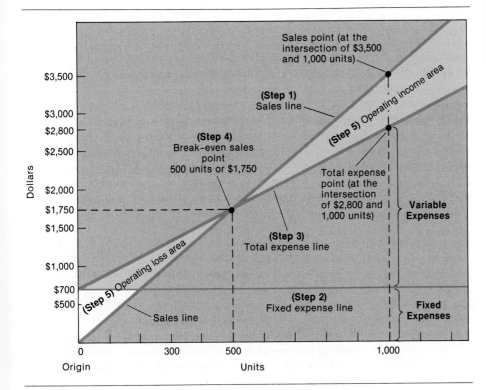

OBJECTIVE 5

Graph a set of cost-volume-profit relationships

Step 2. Draw the *fixed expense line,* which intersects the dollar amount axis at $700 and runs across the graph horizontally.

Step 3. Compute variable expense at a relevant sales volume, such as 1,000 units: 1,000 units × $2.10 per unit = variable expense of $2,100. Add variable expense to fixed expense: $2,100 + $700 = $2,800. Plot the total expense point ($2,800) for 1,000 units. Then draw a line through this point from the $700 fixed expenses intercept on the dollar amount axis. This is the *total expense line.*

Step 4. Identify the *break-even point.* The break-even point is the spot where the sales line intersects the total expense line. The equations we used earlier told us that Maria's break-even point was 500 units, or $1,750 in sales. The graph gives us the same information visually.

Step 5. Mark the *operating income* and the *operating loss* areas on the graph. To the left of the break-even point, expenses exceed sales. Consider unit sales of 300, which provide dollar sales of $1,050 (300 × $3.50). Total expenses are $1,330 [(300 × $2.10) + $700]. Therefore, the graph point for sales of 300 units lies in the operating loss area. The vertical distance between the total expense line and the sales line equals the operating loss. For sales of 300 units, the loss is $280 (sales of $1,050 minus total expenses of $1,330).

To the right of the break-even point, Maria earns a profit. The vertical distance between the sales line and the total expense line equals the amount of operating income.

We can tell from the graph whether operating loss, break-even, or operating income results from a given sales figure. We can also see the amount of any operating loss or operating income. By contrast, the equation approach indicates income or loss for a single sales amount. Many computer programs display graphs for CVP analysis. The CVP graph is a valuable budgeting tool because it can show expected operating income or operating loss for all sales levels, from zero units to the company's upper limit.

Summary Problem for Your Review

Grady Nutt is considering opening a small booth at the county fair. Grady's rent expense will be $600. He plans to sell souvenirs, which cost $.95 each, at an average selling price of $1.75.

Required

1. Use the contribution margin approach to compute Grady's break-even sales in units and in dollars. Round the contribution margin ratio to three decimal places.
2. How many units must he sell to earn operating income of $720? What are dollar sales at this level? Round to the nearest dollar.
3. Prepare a graphic solution to the break-even problem, showing operating income and operating loss areas from 0 to 2,000 units. Mark the break-even sales level and the sales level needed to earn operating income of $720.

Requirement 1

The unit contribution margin is $.80 ($1.75 − $.95). The contribution margin ratio is .457 ($.80/$1.75)

$$\text{Break-even sales in units} = \frac{\text{Fixed expenses}}{\text{Contribution margin per unit}} = \frac{\$600}{\$.80} = 750 \text{ units}$$

$$\text{Break-even sales in dollars} = \frac{\text{Fixed expenses}}{\text{Contribution margin ratio}} = \frac{\$600}{.457} = \$1,313$$

Requirement 2

$$\text{Target sales in units} = \frac{\text{Fixed expenses} + \text{Operating income}}{\text{Contribution margin per unit}}$$

$$= \frac{\$600 + \$720}{\$.80} = \frac{\$1,320}{\$.80} = 1,650 \text{ units}$$

Target sales in dollars = $2,888 (1,650 units × $1.75)

Requirement 3

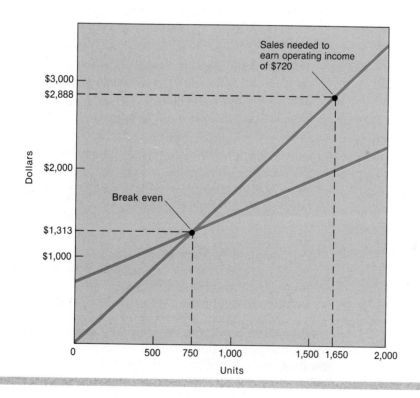

Margin of Safety

The **margin of safety** is the excess of expected sales over break-even sales. In other words, the margin of safety is the drop in sales dollars that the company can absorb before incurring an operating loss. A high margin of safety serves as a cushion. A low margin of safety is a warning. Managers use the margin of safety to evaluate current operations or to measure the risk of a new business plan. The lower the margin, the higher the risk. The higher the margin, the lower the risk.

Suppose the break-even point is 375 units and the company expects to sell 825 units during the period. Assuming a sale price of $3.50 per unit, we compute the margin of safety as follows:

OBJECTIVE 6
Compute a margin of safety

$$\text{Margin of safety in units} = \text{Expected sales in units} - \text{Break-even sales in units}$$
$$= 825 - 375 = 450$$

$$\text{Margin of safety in dollars} = \text{Margin of safety in units} \times \text{Sale price per unit}$$
$$= 450 \text{ units} \times \$3.50 = \$1,575$$

Sales can drop by 450 units, or $1,575, before the company incurs a loss.

For any level of sales, managers can compute the margin of safety as a percentage. We divide the margin of safety in units (450) by sales in units (825), which equals 55 percent. We reach the same percentage by dividing the margin of safety in dollars ($1,575) by sales in dollars (825 units × $3.50 = $2,888).

Assumptions Underlying CVP Analysis

Cost-volume-profit analysis is based on the following assumptions:

1. The cost-volume-profit relationships are linear over a wide range of production and sales. Linear relationships can be graphed as straight lines (like all the lines in Exhibit 17-6).
2. Expenses can be classified as either variable or fixed (we discuss mixed costs later in this chapter).
3. Sale prices, unit variable costs, and total fixed expenses will be unchanged during the period under consideration.
4. Volume is the sole cost driver. The influences of other possible cost drivers (such as weight or size) are held constant or regarded as insignificant.
5. The relevant range of volume is specified.
6. The sales mix of products will be unchanged during the period under consideration. **Sales mix** is the combination of products that make up total sales. For example, the sales mix of a furniture store may be 70 percent household furniture and 30 percent office furniture. We discuss sales mix in the next section.

When these conditions are met, CVP analysis is precise. Most actual business conditions do not perfectly correspond to these assumptions, and the resulting analysis becomes an approximation. The next two sections discuss how to deal with these real-world situations.

Sales Mix

Our illustrations thus far have focused on a single product, travel posters. Most companies sell more than one product, so sales mix must be considered in figuring CVP relationships. Sales mix has an important effect on profits. For example, the business earns more income selling high-margin products than by selling an equal number of low-margin items.

Management's discussion of income statements often refers to sales mix. For example, an annual report of Deere and Company, a manufacturer of farm equipment, stated that profits decreased because of "a less favorable mix of products sold." What is a "less favorable mix of products"? It is the selling of items with relatively low contribution margins.

We may perform CVP analysis for a company that sells more than one product by using the same equations that we have discussed in analyzing a company selling a single product. *However, we must first express the number of units in terms of a single product.*

Let's return to the Maria Martinez example. Suppose Maria plans to sell two types of posters instead of one. Recall that the basic poster costs $2.10 and sells for $3.50. The second, larger, poster costs $3.92 and will sell for $6.00.

An ongoing business uses its experience to compute its sales mix. Maria, however, is starting a new venture. Suppose she estimates that she will sell 500 large posters and 400 regular posters. To compute break-even sales in units, Maria arranges the data as follows:

	Regular Posters	Large Posters	Total
Sale price per unit	$3.50	$6.00	
Variable expense per unit	2.10	3.92	
Contribution margin per unit	$1.40	$2.08	
Estimated sales in units	×400	×500	900
Estimated contribution margin	$ 560 +	$1,040 =	$1,600
Weighted-average contribution margin per unit ($1,600/900 units)— rounded to three decimal places			$1.778

$$\text{Break-even sales in total units} = \frac{\text{Fixed expenses}}{\text{Weighted-average contribution margin per unit}} = \frac{\$700}{\$1.778} = \underline{\underline{394 \text{ units}}}$$

Break-even sales of regular posters $\left(394 \times \dfrac{400}{900}\right)$ .... $\underline{175 \text{ units}}$

Break-even sales of large posters $\left(394 \times \dfrac{500}{900}\right)$ .... $\underline{219 \text{ units}}$

The overall break-even point in dollar sales is $1,927: 175 regular posters (175 × $3.50 = $613) plus 219 large posters (219 × $6 = $1,314). At break-even, Maria's net income can be computed:

	Regular	Large	Total
Sales:			
Regular (175 units × $3.50)	$613		
Large (219 units × $6.00)		$1,314	$1,927
Variable expenses:			
Regular (175 units × $2.10)	368		
Large (219 units × $3.92)		859	1,227
Contribution margin	$245	$ 455	$ 700
Fixed expenses			700
Operating income			$ -0-

Let's review our approach. First, we computed the weighted-average contribution margin per unit. This figure expresses both types of posters in terms of a single hypothetical product that has a contribution margin of $1.778. From here on, the contribution margin approach follows the usual pattern. Divide fixed expenses by contribution margin per unit to determine break-even sales in total units. The last step is to separate total units (394) into regular posters (175) and large posters (219).

After performing a CVP analysis, prepare an income statement as a check on your analysis. If the CVP analysis focuses on breaking even, as in the preceding example, the income statement should show operating income of zero. If the CVP analysis shows the sales level needed to earn a target operating income, the income statement should report that income amount.

If Maria's sales mix changes, planned operating income will differ from these estimates. For example, if she sells a higher proportion of large posters, she stands a chance of earning more money because the large posters generate a higher contribution margin.

CVP sales-mix analysis enters the budgeting system. Suppose a company's profits have decreased. Analysis of the sales mix in the past may indicate that this decrease resulted from concentrating on low-margin products. This information can be used to budget a campaign to try to sell products with a higher contribution margin.

Computer Spreadsheet Analysis of CVP Relationships

OBJECTIVE 7

Separate a mixed cost into its variable and fixed components

Computer spreadsheets are ideally suited for cost-volume-profit analysis because computers can be programmed to show income for any number of sales levels. Spreadsheet programs answer as many "what-if" questions as managers wish to ask: What will variable expenses be if sales rise by a certain amount? By a certain number of units? What if sales fall? If we cut fixed expenses, how many units of each product must we sell to reach a certain level of profits? Computer spreadsheet programs allow managers to analyze the results of any one change or the results of many changes in the business's figures.

Suppose Hyden Company wishes to expand its operations by opening two new stores. The business has received two bids from outside contractors for the construction job. The first bid is $100,000, and the second bid is $140,000. Variable expenses fluctuate between 40 percent and 50 percent of its sales. Fixed costs are expected to be from $280,000 to $420,000. Managers need to know the sales level that the business must reach to earn operating income of $100,000, operating income of $150,000, and operating income of $200,000. A computer spreadsheet program provides the answers to these questions, as shown in Exhibit 17-7, which helps management make an informed decision.

The person who writes the spreadsheet program uses a single formula based on the CVP relationships. The computer places the varying input amounts in the formula and computes the 27 amounts that appear in the exhibit. The computer handles this job in seconds and figures the amounts without computational error.

Managers can insert new figures for fixed expenses, variable expenses, operating income—whatever they wish to change—in order to evaluate the financial results of the various situations. Managers use the computer output—which covers the wide range of cost, volume, and profit patterns—to plan their best course of action. As discussed in the preceding chapter, the spreadsheet is a valuable budgeting tool.

EXHIBIT 17-7   Spreadsheet Analysis of CVP Relationships

```
D8: [W13] ^$716,667                                        READY

           A              B              C         D         E
                    Sales Required to Earn Annual Operating Income of
1
2          -----------------------------------------------------------
3                                    $100,000   $150,000   $200,000
4     Fixed         Variable         --------   --------   --------
5     Expenses      Expenses
6     --------      --------
7
8     $280,000      40% of Sales     $633,333   $716,667   $800,000
9                   45% of Sales      690,909    781,818    872,727
10                  50% of Sales      760,000    860,000    960,000
11
12
13    $350,000      40% of Sales      750,000    833,333    916,667
14                  45% of Sales      818,818    909,091  1,000,000
15                  50% of Sales      900,000  1,000,000  1,100,000
16
17
18    $420,000      40% of Sales      866,667    950,000  1,033,333
19                  45% of Sales      945,455  1,036,364  1,127,273
20                  50% of Sales    1,040,000  1,140,000  1,240,000
17-Jul-91   11:29 AM                                        NUM
```

Summary Problem for Your Review

Part A.   Chambers Company sells T-shirts for $8. Management expects October sales to be between 12,000 units and 20,000 units. The business will incur fixed expenses of $10,000 and variable expenses of 50 percent of sales.

Required

1. Use both the equation approach and the contribution margin approach to compute the company's break-even monthly sales in units and in dollars.
2. Compute the monthly sales level needed to earn operating income of $14,000. Use either the equation approach or the contribution margin approach.

Part B.   Chambers's sales reach 18,000 units during October. Cost of goods sold makes up 60 percent of variable expenses. Operating expenses are the other 40 percent of variable expenses and all of fixed expenses.

Required

1. Prepare a contribution margin income statement for Chambers for the month of October.
2. Compute income from operations if sales decrease by 10 percent.

SOLUTION TO SUMMARY PROBLEM

Part A—Requirement 1

Equation approach:

$$\text{Sales} - \text{Variable expenses} = \text{Fixed expenses} + \text{Operating income}$$

$$\left(\begin{matrix}\text{Unit} \\ \text{sale} \\ \text{price}\end{matrix} \times \text{Units sold}\right) - \left(\begin{matrix}\text{Unit} \\ \text{variable} \\ \text{cost}\end{matrix} \times \text{Units sold}\right) = \text{Fixed expenses} + \text{Operating income}$$

$$(\$8 \times \text{ Units sold}) - (\$8 \times .50) \times \text{Units sold} = \$10,000 + \$0$$

$$(\$8 - \$4) \times \text{Units sold} = \$10,000 + \$0$$

$$\$4 \times \text{Units sold} = \$10,000$$

$$\text{Units sold} = \$10,000/\$4$$

$$\text{Break-even sales in units} = 2,500 \text{ units}$$

$$\text{Break-even sales in dollars} = 2,500 \text{ units} \times \$8 = \$20,000$$

Contribution margin approach:

$$\text{Break-even sales in units} = \frac{\text{Fixed expenses} + \text{Target operating income}}{\text{Contribution margin per unit}}$$

$$= \frac{(\$10,000 + \$0)}{(\$8 - \$4)}$$

$$= \frac{\$10,000}{\$4}$$

$$= 2,500 \text{ units}$$

$$\text{Break-even sales in dollars} = 2,500 \text{ units} \times \$8 = \$20,000$$

Requirement 2

Equation approach:

$$\left(\begin{matrix}\text{Unit} \\ \text{sale} \\ \text{price}\end{matrix} \times \text{Units sold}\right) - \left(\begin{matrix}\text{Unit} \\ \text{variable} \\ \text{cost}\end{matrix} \times \text{Units sold}\right) = \text{Fixed expenses} + \begin{matrix}\text{Target} \\ \text{operating income}\end{matrix}$$

$$(\$8 \times \text{Units sold}) - (\$8 \times .50) \times \text{Units sold} = \$10,000 + \$14,000$$

$$(\$8 - \$4) \times \text{Units sold} = \$10,000 + \$14,000$$

$$\$4 \times \text{Units sold} = \$24,000$$

$$\text{Units sold} = \$24,000/\$4$$

$$\text{Target sales in units} = 6,000 \text{ units}$$

$$\text{Target sales in dollars} = 6,000 \text{ units} \times \$8 = \$48,000$$

Contribution margin approach:

$$\text{Target sales in units} = \frac{\text{Fixed expenses} + \text{Target operating income}}{\text{Contribution margin per unit}}$$

$$= \frac{(\$10,000 + \$14,000)}{(\$8 - \$4)}$$

$$= \frac{\$24,000}{\$4}$$

$$= 6,000 \text{ units}$$

$$\text{Target sales in dollars} = 6,000 \text{ units} \times \$8 = \$48,000$$

Part B—Requirement 1

Chambers Company
Contribution Margin Income Statement
Month of October 19XX

Sales revenue (18,000 × $8)		$144,000
Variable expenses:		
Cost of goods sold ($144,000 × .50 × .60)	$43,200	
Operating expenses ($144,000 × .50 × .40)	28,800	72,000
Contribution margin		72,000
Fixed expenses:		
Operating expenses		10,000
Income from operations		$ 62,000

Requirement 2

Decrease in sales revenue ($144,000 × .10)	$14,440
Decrease in expenses:	
Fixed expenses	$ -0-
Variable expenses ($72,000 × .10)	7,200
Decrease in contribution margin	(7,200)
Income from operations before sales decrease	62,000
Income from operations after sales decrease	$54,800

Summary

Cost-volume-profit (CVP) analysis examines the relationships among a company's expenses, revenues, and income. These relationships depend on cost behavior. We classify costs as *fixed, variable,* or *mixed.*

Two popular ways to use cost-volume-profit analysis are the *equation approach* and the *contribution margin approach.* The contribution margin is the excess of sale price over total variable expenses. The contribution margin ratio is the contribution margin divided by the sale price.

CVP analysis yields an amount in unit sales or in dollar sales at which operating income equals expenses, which is the *break-even point.* Management can also project target sales using CVP analysis. *Graphic* displays of CVP relationships present information over a wide range of sales levels, not just at the break-even point. CVP analysis is widely used in budgeting.

The *margin of safety* is the excess of actual or expected sales over the sales figure at break-even. The larger the margin, the lower the risk of a given plan.

CVP analysis has certain limitations. For example, we must restrict analysis to the span of volume over which fixed costs remain unchanged, which we call the *relevant range*.

The *contribution margin income statement* reports variable expenses and fixed expenses separately. This format allows management to analyze costs. Computer spreadsheet programs can be programmed to measure CVP relationships across a wide range of conditions.

Self-Study Questions

Test your understanding of the chapter by marking the best answer for each of the following questions.

1. Cost-volume-profit analysis is most directly useful to *(p. 810)*
   a. Managers for predicting the outcome of their decisions
   b. Investors for deciding how much to pay for a company's stock
   c. Lenders for analyzing a loan request
   d. Tax authorities for setting income tax rates

2. The graph of a mixed cost *(p. 812)*
   a. Passes through the origin and slopes upward
   b. Is horizontal from the point marking the level of fixed costs
   c. Has a steeper slope than the graph of a fixed cost or a variable cost
   d. Slopes upward from the point marking the level of fixed costs

3. Refer to Exhibit 17-4, page 813. What will income from operations be if sales increase by 25 percent? *(pp. 813, 814)*
   a. $7,500   c. $10,000
   b. $8,250   d. $12,750

4. Refer to Exhibit 17-5, page 815. If sales are 21,000 units, the business can expect fixed expenses of *(pp. 814, 815)*
   a. $50,000   c. $120,000
   b. $80,000   d. Cannot be determined from the information given

5. At the break-even point *(p. 816)*
   a. Sales equal fixed expenses   c. Sales equal total expenses
   b. Sales equal variable expenses   d. Sales exactly equal operating income

6. Variable expenses consume 70 percent of sales, and fixed expenses total $420,000. The break-even point in dollars is *(p. 817)*
   a. $140,000   c. $1,260,000
   b. $600,000   d. $1,400,000

7. What happens to the break-even point if both variable expenses and fixed expenses increase? *(pp. 819, 820)*
   a. Break-even sales increase
   b. Break-even sales decrease
   c. Break-even sales are unchanged because the two changes offset each other
   d. The effect on break-even cannot be determined from the information given

8. Refer to Exhibit 17-6, page 821. At sales of 900 units, the company will earn operating income of
   a. $560   c. $2,800
   b. $1,260   d. $3,150

9. William Thomas Corporation's monthly sales have averaged $480,000 for the past year. The monthly break-even point is $400,000. The company's margin of safety percentage is (p. 824)
   a. 16⅔%   c. 62½%
   b. 20%   d. 100%

10. Raj Mujadeen sells handmade Oriental rugs for $1,000 each and machine-made rugs for $300 each. Customers buy five times as many machine-made rugs as handmade rugs. Variable expenses consume 80 percent of sales, and monthly fixed expenses total $2,000. How many of each type of rug must Raj sell to earn monthly operating income of $3,000? (p. 825)
    a. 8 handmade and 40 machine-made   c. 12 handmade and 60 machine-made
    b. 10 handmade and 50 machine-made   d. 20 handmade and 100 machine-made

Answers to the Self-Study Questions follow the Accounting Vocabulary.

Accounting Vocabulary

Break-even analysis. Another name for Cost-volume-profit analysis (p. 815).

Break-even point. Amount of unit sales or dollar sales at which revenue equals expenses (p. 818).

Contribution margin. Excess of sale price over total variable expenses (p. 813).

Contribution margin income statement. Separates expenses into variable costs and fixed costs and highlights the contribution margin, which is the excess of sales over total variable expenses (p. 813).

Contribution margin percentage. Sales of 100 percent minus the variable expense percentage (p. 817).

Cost behavior. Description of how costs change in response to a shift in a cost driver (p. 810).

Cost driver. Any factor whose change causes a change in a related total cost (p. 810).

Cost-volume-profit (CVP) analysis. Expresses the relationships among costs, volume, and profit or loss. An important part of a budgeting system

that helps managers predict the outcome of their decisions (p. 810).

Fixed cost. Cost that does not change in total as volume changes (p. 811).

Fixed expense. Expense that does not change in total as volume changes (p. 811).

Margin of safety. Excess of expected sales over break-even sales (p. 823).

Mixed cost. Cost that is part variable and part fixed (p. 811).

Mixed expense. Expense that is part variable and part fixed (p. 811).

Relevant range. Band of activity or volume in which actual operations are likely to occur. Within this range, a particular relationship exists between revenue and expenses (p. 814).

Sales mix. Combination of products that make up total sales (p. 824).

Variable cost. Cost that changes in total in direct proportion with changes in volume or activity (p. 810).

Variable expense. Expense that changes in total in direct proportion with changes in volume or activity (p. 810)

Answers to Self-Study Questions

1. a
2. d

3. b Increase in contribution margin ($9,000 × .25) $2,250
Income from operations before sales increase 6,000
Income from operations after sales increase $8,250

4. c

5. c

6. d Sales − .70 Sales = $420,000; .30 Sales = $420,000;
Break-even sales = $420,000/.30 = $1,400,000

7. a

8. a Draw a vertical line up from 900 units on the horizontal axis, inter-secting both the sales line and the total expense line. Using the ver-tical axis to the left, measure the vertical distance between the sales line and the total expense line. This dollar amount of operating income is $560.

9. a Margin of safety in dollars = $80,000 ($480,000 − $400,000)
Margin of safety as a percentage = 16⅔% ($80,000/$480,000)

10. b

	Handmade	Machine-Made	Total
Sale price per unit	$1,000	$300	
Variable expense per unit (80%)	800	240	
Contribution margin per unit	$ 200	$ 60	
Estimated sales in units	× 1	× 5	6
Estimated contribution margin	$ 200	+ $300 = $ 500	
Weighted-average contribution margin per unit ($500/6 units)			$83.333

$$\text{Target sales in total units} = \frac{\text{Fixed expenses + Target operating income}}{\text{Weighted-average contribution margin per unit}} = \frac{\$2,000 + \$3,000}{\$83.333} = 60 \text{ units}$$

Target sales of handmade rugs (60 units × ⅙) .... 10 units
Target sales of machine-made rugs (60 units × ⅚) .... 50 units

ASSIGNMENT MATERIAL

Questions

1. How is cost-volume-profit analysis used in budgeting?
2. Define the three types of cost behavior patterns.
3. Draw graphs of the three types of costs.
4. What are six questions cost-volume-profit analysis can answer?
5. How does a contribution margin income statement differ from a conven-tional income statement? Which income statement is more useful for pre-dicting the income effect of a change in sales? Why?
6. Why is the concept of the relevant range important to cost-volume-profit analysis?
7. Draw a graph of fixed expenses from 0 to 50,000 units. The relevant range lies between 20,000 and 35,000 units, where fixed expenses are $300,000. Below the relevant range, fixed expenses are $200,000. Above the rele-vant range, fixed expenses are $400,000.
8. What is the break-even point? What is its significance to a business?
9. Give the contribution margin formulas for break-even sales in units and in dollars.

10. How does an increase in fixed expenses affect the break-even point? How does a decrease in fixed expenses affect break-even sales? Give the reason for each answer.

11. How does an increase in variable expenses affect the break-even point? How does a decrease in variable expenses affect break-even sales? Give the reason for each answer.

12. How does an increase in selling price affect the break-even point? How does a decrease in selling price affect break-even sales? Give the reason for each answer.

13. Briefly outline two ways to compute the target sales in dollars needed to earn a given operating income.

14. Give the contribution margin formula for target sales in units needed to earn a given operating income. Do the same for target sales in dollars.

15. Identify the steps in the preparation of a cost-volume-profit graph.

16. What advantages does a CVP graph have over the equation approach and the contribution margin approach?

17. How does the margin of safety serve as a measure of risk?

18. Give the assumptions underlying cost-volume-profit analysis.

19. Briefly describe how to perform CVP analysis when a company sells more than one product.

20. Why are computer spreadsheets useful for CVP analysis?

Exercises

Exercise 17-1   *Graphing cost behaviors*   **(L.O. 1)**

Graph each of the following cost behavior patterns over a relevant range from 0 to 10,000 units:

a. Fixed expenses of $25,000.

b. Mixed expenses made up of fixed costs of $10,000 and variable costs of $3 per unit.

c. Variable expenses of $5 per unit.

Exercise 17-2   *Preparing a contribution margin income statement*   **(L.O. 2, 3)**

Vela Shirtmakers's April income statement appears on the next page.

Vela accounting records indicate that cost of goods sold is a variable expense and that selling expense is 20 percent fixed and 80 percent variable. General and administrative expense is half fixed and half variable.

Vela Shirtmakers Income Statement April 19XX		
Sales revenue.....................................		$637,000
Cost of goods sold		448,000
Gross margin.....................................		189,000
Operating expenses:		
Selling	$72,000	
General and administrative (including income tax) ..	42,000	114,000
Income from operations		$ 75,000

Required

Prepare Vela's contribution margin income statement for April. Compute the expected increase in operating income to the nearest $1,000 if sales increase by $100,000. Round decimals to three places.

Exercise 17-3 *Using a contribution margin income statement* *(L.O. 2, 3)*

For its top managers, Sun Refining Corp. formats its income statement as follows:

Sun Refining Corp.	
Contribution Margin Income Statement	
Three Months Ended March 31, 19X3	
Sales revenue..........................	$385,000
Variable expenses	154,000
Contribution margin	231,000
Fixed expenses	196,000
Income from operations	$ 35,000

Sun's relevant range is between sales of $310,000 and $430,000. Prepare contribution margin income statements at those volume levels. Also compute break-even sales in dollars.

Exercise 17-4 *Computing break-even sales by the contribution margin approach (L.O. 3)*

NMNB of Santa Fe has fixed expenses of $50,000 and variable expenses of $3 per unit of its product, which it sells for $5.50 per unit.

Required

1. Compute the company's contribution margin per unit and its contribution margin ratio to six decimal places.
2. Determine the break-even point in units and in dollars, using the contribution margin approach.

Exercise 17-5 *Computing break-even sales under different CVP relationships* *(L.O. 3)*

For several years, Schlotzsky's Restaurant has offered a lunch special for $4.50. Monthly fixed expenses have been $4,500. The variable cost of a meal has been $1.50. Rudy Valero, the owner, believes that by remodeling the restaurant and upgrading the food services, he can increase the price of the lunch special to $5.25. Monthly fixed expenses would increase to $6,300, and the variable expenses would increase to $1.75 per meal.

Required

Use the equation approach to compute Schlotzsky's monthly break-even sales in dollars before and after remodeling.

Exercise 17-6 *Computing break-even sales and operating income or loss under different conditions* **(L.O. 3,4)**

Red Ball Motor Freight delivers freight through Iowa, Nebraska, and Kansas. The company has monthly fixed expenses of $420,000 and a contribution margin of 70 percent of revenues.

Required

1. Compute Red Ball's monthly break-even sales in dollars. Use the contribution margin approach.
2. Compute Red Ball's monthly operating income or operating loss if revenues are $500,000 and if they are $700,000.

Exercise 17-7 *Computing break-even sales and sales needed to earn a given operating income; sales-mix considerations* **(L.O. 3,4)**

A. Dale's Auto Supply has fixed monthly expenses of $3,900 and a contribution margin ratio of 30 percent. What must monthly sales be for the business to break even? to earn operating income of $3,300?

B. Barb's Boutique sells two product lines, one with a contribution margin ratio of 50 percent, the other with a contribution margin ratio of 60 percent. Each product line makes up one half of sales. If monthly fixed expenses are $3,850, what must monthly sales be for the business to break even? to earn operating income of $4,950?

Exercise 17-8 *Cost-volume-profit analysis with a sales mix* **(L.O. 3,4)**

Three college friends open an off-campus shop named Wild Eyes T-Shirts. They plan to sell a standard T-shirt for $6 and a fancier version for $7.50. The $6 shirt costs them $3, and the $7.50 shirt costs them $3.50. The friends expect to sell two fancy T-shirts for each standard T-shirt. Their monthly fixed expenses are $1,870. How many of each type of T-shirt must they sell monthly to break even? to earn $1,210? Round decimals to three places.

Exercise 17-9 *Graphing cost-volume-profit relationships* **(L.O. 5)**

Suppose that Wrigley Field, the home field for the Chicago Cubs baseball team, earns total revenue that averages $9 for every ticket sold. Assume that annual fixed expenses are $8 million and that variable expenses are $1 per ticket.

Required

Prepare the ballpark's cost-volume-profit graph under these assumptions. Show the break-even point in dollars and in tickets. Label fixed expenses, variable expenses, operating loss area, and operating income area on the graph.

Exercise 17-10 *Analyzing a cost-volume-profit graph* **(L.O. 5)**

The top managers of Burdick Hunter, Inc., are planning the budget for 19X6. The accountant who prepared the accompanying cost-volume-profit graph forgot to label the lines.

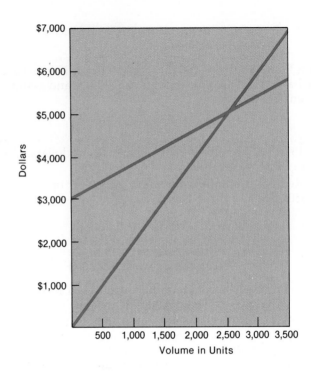

Required

Answer the following questions asked by the managers:

1. What do the lines mean?
2. Where is the operating income area? The operating loss area?
3. What is break-even sales in units and in dollars?
4. What will operating income (or operating loss) be if sales are 1,700 units?
5. What sales level in dollars is needed to earn operating income of $1,000?

Exercise 17-11 *Computing a margin of safety (L.O. 6)*

Pink Panther convenience store has a monthly operating profit goal of $5,000. Variable expenses are 60 percent of sales, and fixed monthly expenses are $7,000. Compute the monthly margin of safety in dollars if the store achieves its profit goal. Express Pink Panther's margin of safety as a percent of target sales.

Problems   *(Group A)*

Problem 17-1A *Explaining the effects of different cost behavior patterns on the break-even point and on likely profits (L.O. 1)*

Saffron Restaurant Supply is opening early next year. The owner is considering two plans for obtaining the plant assets and employee labor needed for operations. Plan 1 calls for purchasing all equipment outright and paying employees straight salaries. Under plan 2, Saffron would lease equipment month by month and pay employees low salaries but give them a big part of their pay in commissions on sales.

Required

Discuss the effects of the two plans on variable expenses, fixed expenses, break-even sales, and likely profits for a new business in the start-up stage. Indicate which plan you favor for Saffron.

Problem 17-2A *Analyzing cost behavior; computing break-even sales and operating income under different CVP relationships; preparing a contribution margin income statement* **(L.O. 1, 2, 3)**

The accounting records of Bergdorf, Inc., summarize the fiscal year ended February 28, 19X3:

Quarter ended	Sales	Total expenses
May 31, 19X2	$230,500	$210,000
Aug. 31, 19X2	185,000	186,500
Nov. 30, 19X2	199,500	187,000
Feb. 28, 19X3	265,000	218,500

Required

1. Categorize total expenses as fixed, variable, or mixed. Give your reasoning.
2. Bergdorf's cost analysts determine that variable expenses consume 40 percent of sales and fixed annual expenses total $450,000. Compute break-even sales in dollars for the year. Use the contribution margin approach.
3. Prepare Bergdorf's contribution margin income statement at the break-even point for the year ended February 28, 19X3. Cost of goods sold is 83 percent of total variable expenses. The remainder of variable expenses is 11 percent selling and 6 percent general. Fixed expenses are 40 percent selling and 60 percent general.
4. Compute income from operations if sales increase by $150,000 above the break-even point.

Problem 17-3A *Contribution margin and break-even analysis* **(L.O. 2, 3)**

The accounting records of four different companies yield the information given in the following table.

Required

Fill in the blanks for each company. Show your work, and round contribution margin ratios to three decimal places. By just looking over the data, which company do you think has the lowest break-even point? Which company actually does have the lowest break-even point? What causes the low break-even point?

	A	B	C	D
Target sales	$560,000	$280,000	$248,000	$ _____
Variable expenses			132,000	130,000
Fixed expenses	312,000	120,000		
Income (loss) from operations	$ _____	$ _____	$ 7,000	$160,000
Units sold	112,000	11,000		8,000
Unit contribution margin		$12	$4	$40
Contribution margin ratio	.30			

Problem 17-4A

Computing break-even revenue and the revenue needed to earn a target operating income; preparing a contribution margin income statement (L.O. 2, 3, 4)

Windjammer Cruises sails a schooner from Miami. The average cruise has 80 tourists on board. Each person pays $75 for a day sail in the Caribbean. The ship sails 100 days each year.

The schooner has a crew of 12. Each member earns an average of $85 per cruise. The crew is paid only when the ship sails. Other variable expenses are for refreshments, which average $14 per passenger per cruise. Fixed annual expenses total $115,800.

Required

1. Compute revenue and variable expenses for each cruise.
2. Use the equation approach to compute the number of cruises needed annually to break even.
3. Use the contribution margin approach to compute the number of cruises needed annually to earn $200,000. Is this profit goal realistic? Give the reason.
4. Prepare Windjammer's contribution margin income statement for 100 cruises each year. Report only two categories of expenses: variable and fixed.

Problem 17-5A

CVP analysis under different conditions (L.O. 2, 3, 4)

Suppose Tynes Advertising Associates imprints calendars with company names. The company has fixed expenses of $480,000 each month plus variable expense of $2 per carton of calendars. For each carton of calendars sold, Tynes earns revenue of $3.20.

Required

1. Use the equation approach to compute the number of cartons of calendars Tynes must sell each month to break even.
2. Use the contribution margin approach to compute the dollar amount of monthly sales Tynes needs in order to earn $60,000 in operating income.
3. Prepare Tynes's contribution margin income statement for June for sales of 450,000 cartons of calendars. Cost of goods sold is 70 percent of variable expenses. Operating expenses make up the rest of variable and all of fixed expenses.
4. The company is considering an expansion that will increase fixed expenses by 40 percent and variable expenses by 10 percent. Compute the new break-even point in units and in dollars. Use either the equation approach or the contribution margin approach. Compute the contribution margin ratio to four decimal places.

Problem 17-6A

Using a contribution margin income statement for break-even analysis; sales mix, margin of safety, and changes in the CVP relationship (L.O. 2, 3, 6)

The contribution margin income statement of The Right Stuff Men's Store for November 19X5 is as follows:

The Right Stuff Men's Store
Contribution Margin Income Statement
November 19X5

Sales revenue		$60,000
Variable expenses:		
Cost of goods sold	$22,000	
Selling	13,000	
General and administrative	7,000	42,000
Contribution margin		18,000
Fixed expenses:		
Selling	11,000	
General and administrative	1,000	12,000
Income from operations		$ 6,000

The Right Stuff sells two ties for every belt. The ties sell for $7, with variable expense of $4.90 per unit. The belts sell for $6, with variable unit cost of $4.20.

Required

1. Determine The Right Stuff's monthly break-even point in the numbers of ties and belts. Prove the correctness of your computation by preparing a summary contribution income statement at break even. You need show only two categories of expenses: variable and fixed.
2. Compute The Right Stuff's margin of safety in dollars.
3. Suppose The Right Stuff increases monthly sales by 15 percent above $60,000. Compute income from operations.
4. The Right Stuff may expand the store and increase monthly fixed expenses by $4,800. Use the contribution margin approach to determine the new break-even sales in dollars.

Problem 17-7A *Computing break-even sales and sales needed to earn a given operating income; graphing cost-volume-profit relationships* **(L.O. 3, 4, 5)**

Mission Viejo Travel is opening an office in San Diego. Fixed monthly expenses are office rent ($3,400), depreciation of office furniture ($190), utilities ($140), a special telephone line ($390), a connection with the airlines' computerized reservation service ($480), and the salary of a travel agent ($1,800). Variable expenses are utilities (3 percent of sales), incentive compensation of the employee (6 percent of sales), advertising (6 percent of sales), supplies and postage (1 percent of sales), and a usage fee for the telephone line and computerized reservation service (4 percent of sales). The business is a partnership, so it pays no business income tax.

Required

1. Use the contribution margin approach to compute the travel agency's break-even sales in dollars. If the average sale is a $400 plane ticket, how many units does it take to break even?
2. Use the equation approach to compute dollar sales needed to earn monthly operating income of $3,500.
3. Graph the travel agency's cost-volume-profit relationships. Assume an average sale is a $400 plane ticket. Show the break-even point, fixed expenses, variable expenses, operating loss area, operating income area, and the sales in units and dollars where monthly operating income of $3,500 is earned. The graph should range from 0 to 40 units.

4. Assume that the average sale price increases to $600. Use the contribution margin approach to compute the new break-even point in units. What is the effect of the sale price increase on the break-even point?

(Group B)

Problem 17-1B *Explaining the contribution margin approach and the margin of safety to decision makers (L.O. 2, 6)*

Huntington Clothiers is managed as traditionally as the button-down shirts that have made it famous. Arch Huntington founded the business in 1952 and has directed operations "by the seat of his pants" ever since. Approaching retirement, he must turn the business over to his son, Ralph. Recently Mr. Huntington and Ralph had this conversation:

Ralph: Dad, I am convinced that we can increase sales by advertising. With our contribution margin, I think we can spend $500 monthly on advertising and increase monthly sales by $6,000. Net income should increase by $3,100.

Mr. Huntington: You know how I feel about advertising. We've never needed it in the past. Why now?

Ralph: Two new shops have opened near us this year, and those guys are getting lots of business. I've noticed our profit margin slipping as the year has unfolded. Our margin of safety is at its lowest point ever.

Mr. Huntington: Profit margin I understand, but what is the contribution margin that you mentioned? And what is this margin of safety?

Required

Explain for Mr. Huntington the contribution margin approach to decision making. Show how Ralph computed the $3,100. (Treat advertising as a fixed cost.) Also, describe what Ralph means by the margin of safety, and explain why the business's situation is critical.

Problem 17-2B *Analyzing cost behavior; computing break-even sales and operating income under different CVP relationships; preparing a contribution margin income statement (L.O. 1, 2, 3)*

Federal Trading Company accounting records summarize the fiscal year ended November 30, 19X2:

Quarter ended	Sales	Total expenses
Feb. 28, 19X2	$161,000	$115,000
May 31, 19X2	138,000	109,000
Aug. 31, 19X2	111,000	93,000
Nov. 30, 19X2	119,000	101,000

Required

1. Categorize total expenses as fixed, variable, or mixed. Give your reasoning.
2. Federal's cost analysts determine that variable expenses consume 44 percent of sales and fixed annual expenses total $176,640. Compute break-even sales in dollars for the year. Use the contribution margin approach.
3. Prepare Federal's contribution margin income statement at the break-even point for the year ended November 30, 19X2. Cost of goods sold is 71 percent of total variable expenses. The remainder of variable expenses is 19 percent selling and 10 percent general. Fixed expenses are evenly divided between selling and general.

4. Compute income from operations if sales increase by $30,000 above the break-even point.

Problem 17-3B   *Contribution margin and break-even analysis*   **(L.O. 2, 3)**

The accounting records of four different companies yield the following information:

	A	B	C	D
Target sales	$_____	$290,000	$_____	$500,000
Variable expenses	100,000	120,000	104,000	_____
Fixed expenses	80,000	138,000		_____
Income (loss) from operations	$_____	$_____	$ 35,000	$ 60,000
Units sold	5,000			100,000
Unit contribution margin		$100	$6	$2
Contribution margin ratio	.200		.600	

Required

Fill in the blanks for each company. Show your work, and round contribution margin ratios to three decimal places. By just looking over the data, which company do you think has the lowest break-even point? Which company actually does have the lowest break-even point? What causes the low break-even point?

Problem 17-4B   *Computing break-even revenue and the revenue needed to earn a target operating income; preparing a contribution margin income statement*   **(L.O. 2, 3, 4)**

The Mystic Clipper is a schooner that sails from Annapolis, Maryland, during the spring and fall. During the summer the ship leaves from Mystic, Connecticut. The average cruise has 45 tourists on board, and each person pays $50 for a day sail. The ship sails 80 days each year.

The Clipper has a crew of 8. Each member earns an average of $100 per cruise. The crew is paid only when the ship sails. The other variable expenses are for refreshments, which average $10 per passenger per cruise. Fixed annual expenses total $51,000.

Required

1. Compute revenue and variable expenses for each cruise.
2. Use the equation approach to compute the number of cruises the Clipper must take each year to break even.
3. Use the contribution margin approach to compute the number of cruises needed each year to earn $70,000. Is this profit goal realistic? Give your reason.
4. Prepare the Clipper's contribution margin income statement for 80 cruises for the year. Report only two categories of expenses: variable and fixed.

Problem 17-5B   *CVP analysis under different conditions*   **(L.O. 2, 3, 4)**

Suppose Toledo Ballpoints imprints ballpoint pens with company logos. The company has fixed expenses of $331,500 each month plus variable expenses of $1.60 per box of pens. For each box of pens sold, the company earns revenue of $2.90.

Required

1. Use the equation approach to compute the number of boxes of pens Toledo must sell each month to break even.

2. Use the contribution margin approach to compute the dollar amount of monthly sales Toledo needs in order to earn $25,500 in operating income. Round the contribution margin ratio to six decimal places.

3. Prepare Toledo's contribution margin income statement for August for sales of 240,000 boxes of pens. Cost of goods sold is 80 percent of variable expenses. Operating expenses make up the rest of variable expenses and all of fixed expenses.

4. The company is considering an expansion that will increase fixed expenses by 30 percent and variable expenses by 10 cents per box of pens. Compute the new break-even point in units and in dollars. Use either the equation approach or the contribution margin approach. (Round the contribution margin ratio to six decimal places.)

Problem 17-6B *Using a contribution margin income statement for break-even analysis; sales mix, margin of safety, and changes in the CVP relationship* **(L.O. 2, 3, 6)**

The contribution margin income statement of Gino's Trattoria for May 19X6 is as follows:

Gino's Trattoria		
Contribution Margin Income Statement		
May 19X6		

Sales revenue		$160,000
Variable expenses:		
Cost of goods sold	$32,000	
Selling	25,000	
General and administrative........	3,000	60,000
Contribution margin...............		100,000
Fixed expenses:		
Selling	27,000	
General and administrative........	9,000	36,000
Income from operations.............		$ 64,000

Gino's sells three small pizzas for every large pizza. A small pizza sells for $10, with variable expense of $4.25. A large pizza sells for $20, with variable expense of $6.

Required

1. Determine Gino's monthly break-even point in the numbers of small pizzas and large pizzas. Prove the correctness of your computation by preparing a summary contribution margin income statement at break-even. You need show only two categories of expenses: variable and fixed.

2. Compute Gino's margin of safety in dollars.

3. If Gino's can increase monthly sales by 15 percent above $160,000, what will income from operations be?

4. Gino's hopes to decrease monthly fixed expenses by $10,000 to scale back operations. Use the contribution margin approach to determine the new break-even sales in dollars.

Problem 17-7B *Computing break-even sales and sales needed to earn a given operating income; graphing cost-volume-profit relationships* **(L.O. 3, 4, 5)**

Water Oaks Travel is opening an office in Oklahoma City. Fixed monthly expenses are office rent ($3,000), depreciation of office furniture ($200), utilities ($110), a special telephone line ($520), a connection with the airlines' computerized reservation service ($380), and the salary of a travel agent ($1,400). Variable expenses are utilities (2 percent of sales), incentive compensation for the employee (5 percent of sales), advertising (4 percent of sales), supplies and postage (1 percent of sales), and a usage fee for the telephone line and computerized reservation service (3 percent of sales). The business is a proprietorship, so it pays no business income tax.

Required

1. Use the contribution margin approach to compute Water Oaks' break-even sales in dollars. If the average sale is a $300 plane ticket, how many units does it take to break even?
2. Use the equation approach to compute dollar sales needed to earn monthly operating income of $4,000.
3. Graph the travel agency's cost-volume-profit relationships. Assume an average sale is a $300 plane ticket. Show the break-even point, fixed expenses, variable expenses, operating loss area, operating income area, and the sales in units and dollars where monthly operating income of $4,000 is earned. The graph should range from 0 to 50 units.
4. Assume that the average sale price increases to $440. Use the contribution margin approach to compute the new break-even point in units. What is the effect of the sale price increase on the break-even point?

Extending Your Knowledge

Decision Problems

1. Using Cost-Volume-Profit Analysis to Make Business Decisions
(L.O. 1,3,4)

William and Roberta Higgins live in Calgary, Alberta. Their daughter, Celine, is now six months old, and Roberta is considering going back to work. Roberta's mother lives in Calgary and would be delighted to babysit her new granddaughter.

Two years ago, William and Roberta spent their vacation in Thailand. Both of them enjoyed the Thai food. Roberta is a professional chef and was impressed with the cooking methods and the spices used. Calgary has no Thai restaurant, and the Higgins are contemplating opening one. Roberta would supervise the cooking, and William would leave his current job with an oil company to be the maitre'd. The restaurant would serve dinner Tuesday through Saturday, 6 p.m. to midnight.

Calgary is one of the fastest growing cities in Canada. International companies have established offices in the city, and services, including retailers of high-quality merchandise, have quickly expanded. People eat dinner out two or three nights a week. Business entertaining is also frequent.

William has noticed a restaurant for lease a short drive from the Higgins' home. The seating capacity is seven tables, each of which can seat four. Tables could be moved together for a large party. Roberta is planning two seatings per evening.

William and Roberta have drawn up the following estimates:

Average revenue, including drinks and dessert	$40 per meal
Average cost of the food, including preparation	$12 per meal
Chef and dishwasher's salaries	$50,000 per year
Rent (premises, equipment)	$3,000 per month
Cleaning (linen and premises)	$500 per month
Replacement of dishes, cutlery, glasses	$300 per month
Utilities, advertising, telephone	$1,400 per month

Required

Compute break-even revenue for the restaurant. Also compute the amount of revenue needed to earn net income of $80,000 for the year. Is this target net income realistic? Give your reason.

2. Using a Contribution Margin Income Statement to Make Business Decisions   (L.O. 2,3)

Humpty Dumpty Toy Company markets three lines of toys. Each line is manufactured by a different company, and each line has a different set of cost-volume-profit relationships.

	Newborns	Toddlers	Preschoolers
Sales	$320,000	$150,000	$270,000
Variable expenses	64,000	75,000	108,000
Contribution margin	256,000	75,000	162,000
Fixed expenses	188,000	120,000	126,000
Income (loss) from operations	$ 68,000	$(45,000)	$ 36,000

Average sale prices are $2 for toys for newborns, $3 for toys for toddlers, and $5 for preschoolers' toys.

Required

1. Which product line is the least profitable?
2. Compute break-even sales in units for the company as a whole. Carry the weighted average contribution margin per unit to four decimal places.
3. Prepare a contribution margin income statement—for each product line—at the break-even point.
4. Prepare a contribution margin income statement assuming that sales of toddler toys are eliminated altogether.
5. Would it be wise to drop the toddler toy line? What would explain the overall operating loss that would result if the company did drop the toddler toy line?

Ethical Issue

In recent years, professional sports teams have shifted from paying stars straight salaries to paying them lower salaries but adding a bonus that depends on team revenues. In this way a star is more motivated to play harder. The more the team wins, the greater the team revenues as more and more fans flock to the stadium and as television companies increase payments for the rights to broadcast the games. If the star has a bad year, the team may lose more and revenue could drop, which would lower the star's compensation. By shifting player compensation from straight salary to a bonus based on team revenues, these player contracts increase the team's percentage of variable costs and decrease its percentage of fixed costs.

Required

1. Why would team owners favor these contracts?
2. Are team owners taking advantage of stars? Are these contracts ethical?

Chapter 18

Cost Behavior Analysis

Companies are making planning and control decisions that significantly affect their employees. "Re-engineering," which includes organizing employees into work teams and retraining workers to do multiple jobs, allows companies to dramatically increase productivity. According to Al Ehrbar of *The Wall Street Journal*, "Companies like Motorola Inc., Xerox Corp., Ford Motor Co. and Banc One Corp. have already achieved stunning productivity gains through re-engineering, and thousands of others are scrambling to copy their successes."

What are the accounting implications for companies that re-engineer their operations? These companies are decreasing labor costs dramatically, often substituting the fixed costs of machines in place of the variable expense of workers' hourly pay. In many companies, fixed costs are increasing while variable expenses are decreasing.

This trend may be good for the "bottom line" of companies that re-engineer their operations, but there is a significant drawback for the United States' work force. Re-engineering may result in the loss of as many as 25 million jobs, with no indication that new jobs will be created elsewhere in the economy to offset the loss.

Source: Al Ehrbar, "'Re-Engineering' Gives Firms New Efficiency, Workers the Pink Slip," *The Wall Street Journal*, March 16, 1993, p. A1.

How much will Banc One's profit increase if the company replaces 200 clerical workers with optical scanners to process checks? What will happen to American Airlines' maintenance costs if three Boeing 757s are added to its fleet? By how much will Sears' warranty expense decrease if manufacturing is re-engineered to reduce lawnmower defects by 50%? Managers face questions like these every day. They can make better planning and control decisions if they understand how costs behave, that is, how business activities, or drivers, affect costs.

The previous chapter considered one cost driver—total volume of activity—and introduced the two basic cost behavior patterns—fixed and variable. In this chapter we examine how another factor, management policy, affects costs. We also show how managers analyze cost behavior. Knowledge of cost behavior is essential, particularly for budgeting and evaluating performance. We begin by looking at committed fixed costs.

Fixed Costs

Fixed costs, defined and graphed in Chapter 17, also are called *capacity costs*. They give businesses the capability to operate at planned levels for activities such as manufacturing, sales, administration, and research. Long-run sales forecasts, available technology, and management strategies affect the amounts of fixed costs managers are willing to incur. In the short-run, these costs usually are unaffected by differences between planned and actual volumes of activity. For planning and control, fixed costs may be categorized as either committed or discretionary.

Committed Fixed Costs

Committed fixed costs are the costs that result from having property, plant, equipment, and key managerial personnel. In the short run, managers can do little to change their amounts. Examples include depreciation, property taxes, insurance, and long-term lease amounts. Motorola, Ford, and Banc One in the chapter-opening vignette are increasing committed fixed costs to remain competitive.

Committed fixed costs usually are incurred in large, indivisible "chunks." Consider machines that mount tires onto wheels in an automobile assembly

OBJECTIVE 1
Identify types of fixed costs

plant. Workers may mount 50,000 tires per month on each machine. If a Ford Motor Company plant needs an additional 30,000 units of tire-mounting capacity, its manager cannot go out and buy 60% (30,000/50,000) of a machine. He can buy one machine, which would yield 20,000 more units of capacity than needed. By contrast, the manager can purchase exactly 30,000 more tires or wheels.

The amount of a company's committed fixed cost is approximately what it would incur even if a strike, shortage of materials, or other problem temporarily stopped production and sales activity. These costs of plant and basic organization cannot be reduced without hurting the company's ability to meet long-term goals. Indeed, many committed fixed costs cannot be altered in response to month-to-month or even year-to-year volume changes. For example, a cancer-treatment hospital must have the sophisticated equipment needed to treat patients regardless of whether 5 or 50 people are admitted in any particular month.

OBJECTIVE 2

Use cost behavior analysis to make business decisions

Effects on Decisions. Should Procter and Gamble build a new plant to meet budgeted increases in demand for its soap products? Should the size of a new audio-video store in a mall be 40,000 or 80,000 square feet? To answer these and other capacity-related questions, managers take a long-term view. The goal is to tailor capacity to expected demand in order to maximize operating income over a number of years. Such decisions require trade-offs between operating results in individual years.

Mary Harmon is considering two store sites for her deli restaurant and take-out business. Each of the stores must be leased for two years. Harmon's decision depends of forecasted demand for her restaurant's food. Exhibit 18-1 gives the data for the site-selection decision. Exhibit 18-2 shows forecasted contribution-margin income statements, based on predicted demand levels, for both the smaller and larger stores.

For 19X1 only, Mary Harmon would be better off with the smaller store. The additional 25,000 (50,000 − 25,000) orders of sales capacity of the larger store is not needed that year; the smaller store has enough capacity to satisfy predicted demand. The excess capacity of the large store thus provides no usable benefit in 19X1, but costs $20,000 ($60,000 − $40,000) in additional rent. This cost accounts for the $20,000 ($50,000 − $30,000) difference in income from operations.

For 19X2 considered alone, Harmon would be worse off with the smaller store. Its lower capacity of 25,000 orders restricts sales to that number despite

EXHIBIT 18-1 *Data for Selection of Restaurant Site*

Panel A—Product-Related Data:

Average revenue per order	$ 7
Average variable cost per order	3
Average contribution margin per order	$ 4
Predicted demand for orders, 19X1	25,000
Predicted demand for orders, 19X2	40,000

Panel B—Store-Related Data:

	Smaller Store	Larger Store
Capacity in orders served	25,000	50,000
Annual rent expense	$40,000	$60,000
Annual other fixed expenses	$10,000	$10,000

Smaller Store

	19X1		19X2
Sales revenue (25,000 × $7)	$175,000	(25,000 × $7)	$175,000
Variable expenses (25,000 × $3)	75,000	(25,000 × $3)	75,000
Contribution margin	100,000		100,000
Fixed expenses:			
Rent	$40,000		$40,000
Other	10,000 50,000		10,000 50,000
Income from operations	$50,000		$50,000

Two-year total
$100,000

Larger Store

	19X1		19X2
Sales revenue (25,000 × $7)	$175,000	(40,000 × $7)	$280,000
Variable expenses (25,000 × $3)	75,000	(40,000 × $3)	120,000
Contribution margin	100,000		160,000
Fixed expenses:			
Rent	$60,000		$60,000
Other	10,000 70,000		10,000 70,000
Income from operations	$30,000		$90,000

Two-year total
$120,000

higher demand in the marketplace. Revenues, expenses, and income from operations therefore are the same as in 19X1. On the other hand, for 19X2 the larger store's capacity allows Harmon to satisfy all 40,000 units of predicted demand. The net benefit of the additional units of capacity is $40,000, computed as follows:

$$\begin{matrix} \text{Additional} \\ \text{contribution} \\ \text{margin} \end{matrix} \quad - \quad \begin{matrix} \text{Additional} \\ \text{fixed} \\ \text{expense} \end{matrix} \quad = \quad \begin{matrix} \text{Additional} \\ \text{operating} \\ \text{income} \end{matrix}$$

$$\begin{matrix} \text{Additional} \\ \text{sales units} \end{matrix} \times \left(\begin{matrix} \text{unit} \\ \text{sale} \\ \text{price} \end{matrix} - \begin{matrix} \text{unit} \\ \text{variable} \\ \text{cost} \end{matrix} \right) - \begin{matrix} \text{Additional} \\ \text{fixed expense} \end{matrix} = \begin{matrix} \text{Additional} \\ \text{operating} \\ \text{income} \end{matrix}$$

(40,000 − 25,000) ×	($7 − $3)	− ($60,000 − $40,000) =	
15,000 ×	($4)	− $20,000	=
	$60,000	− $20,000	= $40,000

This $40,000 of additional income appears in Exhibit 18-2 as the difference between the larger store's 19X2 income of $90,000 and the smaller store's $50,000.

To decide which store to lease, Mary Harmon must consider both years together. On the basis of her demand predictions, she should lease the larger store. Although she incurs a $20,000 cost of idle capacity in 19X1, the total expected operating income over the two-year period with the larger store ($120,000) is $20,000 more than the total with the smaller store.

Many managers would take this analysis one step further. They would consider the possibility that actual demand for food may differ from the initial,

		Low Demand 32,000 orders		High Demand 48,000 orders
Sales revenue (32,000 × $7)		$224,000	(48,000 × $7)	$336,000
Variable expenses (32,000 × $3)		96,000	(48,000 × $3)	144,000
Contribution margin...............		128,000		192,000
Fixed expenses:				
Rent................	$60,000		$60,000	
Other	10,000	70,000	10,000	70,000
Income from operations		$58,000		$122,000

"most likely," predictions. Suppose Harmon believes her restaurant's success in 19X1 may encourage someone to open a competing business nearby, resulting in 19X2 demand of only 32,000 orders. Conversely, the restaurant could be more successful than predicted. Customers may demand as many as 48,000 orders the second year. In either case, 19X2 operating income for the smaller store would remain $50,000 (Exhibit 18-2) because both the low number of 32,000 orders and the high number of 48,000 are above that store's 25,000-order capacity. Exhibit 18-3 shows expected operating incomes for the larger store for both the lower and the higher levels of demand.

Effects of Varying Predictions.   Exhibits 18-2 and 18-3 together demonstrate why accurate demand predictions are critical for determining the appropriate amount of capacity to buy or lease. If 19X2 demand is only 32,000 orders, Mary Harmon would be better off leasing the smaller store. Its two-year total operating income of $100,000 in Exhibit 18-2 is $12,000 more than the $88,000 ($30,000 + $58,000) total for the larger store. The larger store allows her to fill 7,000 (32,000 − 25,000) more orders in the second year, but the $28,000 (7,000 × $4) contribution margin on those orders is insufficient to offset the extra two-year rent expense of $40,000. If 19X2 demand turns out to be 48,000 orders, the larger store would be even more attractive than the initial computations indicate. This store allows Harmon to meet the additional 8,000 (48,000 − 40,000) units of 19X2 demand, adding $32,000 (8,000 × $4) to the initial $20,000 difference in total operating incomes. The two-year income for the larger store increases to $152,000 ($30,000 + $122,000), but the total for the smaller store remains $100,000.

Which store size should Mary Harmon choose? Her decision is affected by her attitudes toward risk. Because of its lower fixed cost, the smaller store has a lower breakeven point in units and a higher margin of safety each year. It also provides more operating income at lower volume levels, including 25,000 orders. The smaller store is the more conservative choice.

The larger store requires a higher sales volume to break even, but it provides additional capacity that could lead to higher incomes at higher volume levels, including the owner's initial, most-likely predictions. Regardless of the decision, Harmon's objective from a control standpoint will be to use as much of the leased capacity as possible. For a given committed fixed cost that provides a specific amount of capacity, increased usage usually leads to increased operating income.

Discretionary Fixed Costs

Discretionary, or **managed, fixed costs** (1) arise from periodic (usually yearly) budget decisions that reflect top-management policies, and (2) have no clear relationship between inputs and outputs. Examples include advertising, public relations, employee training programs, management salaries, and research.

For many costs there is a measurable relationship between *inputs*, represented by the costs, and *outputs*, represented by production, sales, or service activity. For example, a construction contractor may specify that five gallons of paint should be used to finish the inside of a house. He may then calculate the cost. In contrast, the proper amount to spend on an advertising campaign to sell the house is not so easy to determine. As a department store executive said, "Fifty percent of my advertising is a total waste. The trouble is, I don't know which 50% is wasted."

The "correct" amount to spend for advertising, research, police protection, and education programs cannot be measured precisely. For this reason, at the beginning of each budget period managers and their supervisors budget discretionary costs on the basis of traditions, rules of thumb, industry customs, and the anticipated behavior of targeted competitors.

The resources acquired with discretionary budget expenditures must be carefully planned and used to produce the desired effects. Consider an employee training program. The full amount authorized for the program may be spent for first-rate seminars, and all targeted employees may attend the presentations. The setup is perfect, but the program will have little effect on operations if the attendees are indifferent or if the seminar materials are designed for a different industry.

In addition to one-year versus multiple-year planning horizons, there is another difference between discretionary fixed costs and committed fixed costs. It is more difficult to determine whether resources acquired with discretionary costs are used effectively. Why? The results of advertising, research, and training programs are much harder to measure than the results of using plant and equipment to make products such as automobiles. Mary Harmon, for example, may be convinced that her employees would benefit from a one-day seminar on sexual-harassment awareness. But imagine how difficult it would be for her to measure the long-term effects, both financial and interpersonal, of such a program!

There is another key difference between discretionary and committed fixed costs. Under temporarily difficult circumstances, some discretionary expenditures can be reduced for short time periods with little damage to the organization's ability to meet long-range goals. During a year of operating losses, a company that had been spending $100,000 on labor relations programs may cut back those expenditures. The unfavorable effects of this discretionary cutback may be far less severe than the effects of selling a plant, which is a committed cost.

Engineered and Discretionary Variable Costs _____

In Chapter 17 we saw that a variable cost changes in direct proportion to changes in activity volume. Variable costs may be classified as either engineered or discretionary.

Engineered variable costs result from measurable, often observable, cause-and-effect relationships between inputs (the costs) and outputs. These costs are most frequently found in manufacturing and distribution businesses. Examples of input-output relationships include one pound of potatoes per 8-ounce bag of potato chips, two fan belts per automobile, and one square foot of shrink-wrap material per package of bacon. Other examples are 4 hours to stain and varnish a piece of furniture, 3 minutes to sew a shirt, and 10 seconds

EXHIBIT 18-4 *Variable Cost Behavior Patterns*

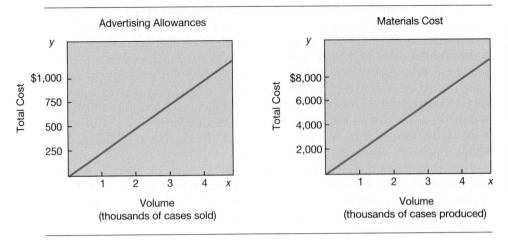

to mount a tire onto a wheel. The efficiency of these costs can be measured by relating the quantity of inputs used to the quantity of outputs achieved.

Most variable costs are engineered, but some are discretionary. **Discretionary variable costs** change with sales or production volume simply because management has decided to spend a certain percentage of each sales dollar, or a certain dollar amount for each unit sold, for such items as research and advertising. A change in the behavior of these costs indicates a change in management's authorization to spend, which is discretionary. By contrast, a change in cause-and-effect relationships brought about by either new technology or different methods of performing tasks is engineered, not discretionary.

Discretionary variable costs have graphical patterns similar to those of engineered material and labor costs, but for different reasons. Consider advertising allowances. Manufacturers such as Coca-Cola and Pepsi stimulate sales by giving their retailers an advertising allowance per unit sold. In turn, the retailers are supposed to spend the money for local advertising and sales promotions.

Suppose the costs of the Coca-Cola Company include an advertising allowance to retailers of $0.25 per case of drinks sold, and materials are used at the rate of $2 per case produced. Exhibit 18-4 graphs the costs of these advertising allowances and materials in relation to volume. The two graphs look identical, but in reality no clear cause-and-effect relationship exists between cases sold and advertising allowances in the first graph. Coca-Cola's top management easily could decide to pay the retailers a lump-sum amount (fixed cost) or both a lump-sum and a per-case allowance (mixed cost) next year. In the second graph, the cost of materials varies directly with the number of cases produced. The cause-and-effect nature of this variable cost, which is engineered, is much more likely to continue from year to year than is that of discretionary advertising allowances to retailers.

Using Cost Behavior Analysis to Budget and Control Operating Expenses

If they understand how costs behave, managers are better able to prepare useful budgets and to analyze results. Managers' approaches to budgeting depend on the traditions and management styles of their organizations. Consider a travel agency. How many agents should be employed? What should be the budgeted monthly compensation cost? Two basic budgeting approaches are available to answer these questions: the discretionary-fixed-cost approach and the engineered-variable-cost approach.

Discretionary-Fixed-Cost Approach

Most businesses manage operating labor costs as discretionary fixed costs. They tend to rely on department managers to judge the size of the necessary work force. Managers are reluctant to overhire because of the danger of having too many employees if the workload decreases. Consequently, short busy periods cause overtime or the hiring of temporary workers.

OBJECTIVE 3
Identify two approaches for controlling operating labor costs

The **discretionary-fixed-cost approach** to managing relies on personal supervision for controlling costs. Managers control both by in-person oversight and by analyzing records of physical quantities (for example, tours booked, flights ticketed). Budgeted costs and consequent actual costs usually are very close, so variances are small. A **variance** is the difference between an actual amount and the corresponding budgeted amount.

Engineered-Variable-Cost Approach

A second approach to managing operating labor costs is to treat them as engineered variable costs. Use of the term *engineered* implies measurement. **Work measurement** is the careful analysis of a task: its size, the methods used, and its efficiency. Managers measure the workload in an operation or process in order to determine the number of employees needed to perform the work. To evaluate and improve performance, they need to quantify both inputs and outputs.

The work that is measured often is expressed in terms of cost drivers. Budgets are set for the units of cost-driver activity that occur in a given time span; for example, orders packed per hour, credit applications processed per day, and phone calls answered per shift.

The engineered-variable-cost approach to managing applies formal work measurement to the budgeting process. Assume that 12 travel agents are employed by All Seasons Travel Agency of New York City. Each agent earns $2,400 per month. Careful analysis reveals that an agent should be able to book 24 trips in an eight-hour workday. Every agent works 20 days per month, yielding a monthly capacity of 5,760 (24 × 20 × 12) bookings.[1]

The engineered-cost approach is to develop a budget formula keyed to the unit cost of the individual trip booked. This cost may be computed as follows:

$$\text{Unit cost} = \frac{\text{Monthly salary}}{\text{Trips booked per month}}$$

$$= \frac{\$2,400}{(24 \text{ trips} \times 20 \text{ days})}$$

$$= \frac{\$2,400}{480} = \$5 \text{ per trip booked}$$

---

[1]This number is the approximate average or "normal" workload.

EXHIBIT 18-5   *Approaches to Budgeting Operating Labor Costs*

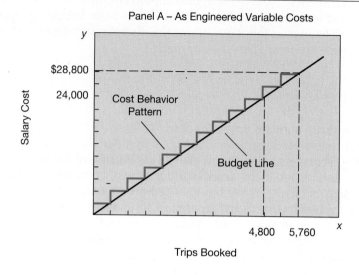

Panel A – As Engineered Variable Costs

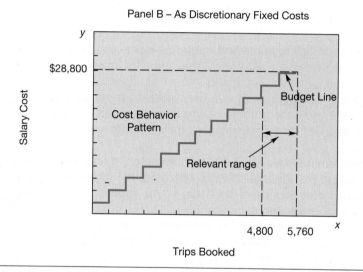

Panel B – As Discretionary Fixed Costs

Exhibit 18-5, Panel A, shows how the engineered-variable-cost approach plots the cost of each agent employed, step by step. The budget line is drawn at the end of each step to underscore the idea that each person should be working at full capacity. This tough-minded approach treats humans like water that can be turned on and off at a faucet. By contrast, Panel B of the exhibit shows how the discretionary-fixed-cost approach plots a horizontal line for a relevant range of workload. The individuals employed would be treated as a stable work force that is expected to have occasional idle time.

Performance Reports

In our example, managers using the engineered-variable-cost approach would prepare the following performance report for a month in which 5,088 trips were booked:

	Budget as an Engineered Variable Cost	Actual Cost	Variance	
			Amount	Equivalent Persons
Agents' salaries	$25,440*	$28,800[†]	$3,360[u]	1.4[‡]

The $3,360 unfavorable variance, which is equivalent to the salaries of 1.4 agents, is the price that management paid for one or both of the following:

1. inefficient productivity by the agents
2. overstaffing in relation to the actual workload

The agents' capacity was 5,760 bookings, not 5,088. If every customer who called or came through the door was served, management paid (consciously or unconsciously) $3,360 during the month to maintain a stable work force geared to "normal" needs. The alternative is to hire and lay-off agents monthly, according to expected workload.

For comparison, consider a performance report prepared by users of the discretionary-fixed-cost approach:

	Budget as a Discretionary Fixed Cost	Actual Cost	Variance
Agents' salaries	$28,800[§]	$28,800[§]	0

The budget in this report is not based on formal work measurements. Instead, agency managers used judgment to determine the appropriate number of agents to employ.

Opponents of the engineered-variable-cost approach argue that it is too harsh and sometimes infeasible, because labor unions or laws restrict managements' ability to continually hire and lay-off workers. Those who favor the approach insist that even in these cases, consistently large variances can spur action. For example, managers may go to the bargaining table with a union to change work rules. Similarly, they may lobby legislators to change laws that hurt an industry's competitive position. Evidence from work measurement helps managers to be more persuasive.

Trade-Offs between Fixed and Variable Costs _____

Management strategies often include trade-offs between fixed and variable costs. In the auto industry, for example, increased expenditures for robotic equipment (a fixed cost) have decreased labor and other variable costs. This type of computer-controlled production equipment also has greatly improved the quality of automobiles. Higher quality means less cost incurred to repair defects. Similarly, banks, hospitals, and other service organizations are re-engineering their work. Machines are processing checks, running lab tests, and typing envelopes, tasks that people once performed.

---

*5,088 trips × $5
[†]12 agents × $2,400
[u] = Unfavorable (actual costs exceeded budgeted costs)
[‡]$3,360/$2,400 = 1.4 salaries.
[§]12 agents × $2,400.

In general, when committed fixed costs increase relative to variable costs, managers lose some of their ability to respond to changes in short-term conditions. For example, consider that mail volume in the U.S. Postal Service fluctuates from month to month. It is much easier for the postmaster to adjust employee work schedules than to buy and sell mail-sorting machines. On the other hand, companies must be willing to invest in fixed-cost resources to take advantage of market opportunities.

In some cases, investments may be necessary just to survive. Companies are re-engineering their manufacturing processes in order to reduce the time it takes to make their products. If a manufacturer can ship goods to customers within one or two weeks and competitors are quoting two-to-three month deliveries, the company can charge higher prices or capture a greater market share, or both. As long as the new technology is not too expensive, the manufacturer should be able to increase profits.

Sometimes managers choose between discretionary fixed and variable costs in order to maximize short-run income. Consider Sullivan Software Company, a new company about to launch its only product, Megaworks. President Frank Sullivan is considering two plans for paying salespeople. Plan one is a salary of $30,000 plus a commission of $40 for each item sold. Plan two is a straight commission of $80 per item. The average contribution margin of the company's software is $200 per unit sold, not including sales commission.

Exhibit 18-6 graphs the cost behavior patterns for one salesperson under each plan. Sullivan wants the plan that will maximize operating income. Other factors being equal, the plan that will minimize total compensation, and thereby maximize operating income, depends on the number of items each employee sells. Below 750 items, the variable-cost plan minimizes cost; the fixed salary saved is greater than the additional commission expense from the higher rate paid per item.

At volume levels above 750, the mixed-cost plan is better because its savings in variable commissions exceed the fixed salary that must be paid. The point of

OBJECTIVE 4

Compute the equal-cost volume of two cost behavior patterns

EXHIBIT 18-6   *Alternative Sales Force Compensation Plans*

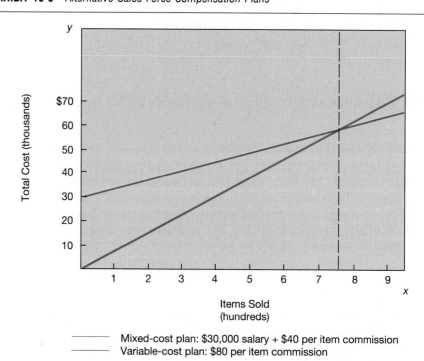

Mixed-cost plan: $30,000 salary + $40 per item commission
Variable-cost plan: $80 per item commission

indifference between the plans, where operating incomes are equal, is found by equating the total costs under the two plans:

$$\text{Mixed-plan total cost} = \text{Variable-plan total cost}$$

$$\$30{,}000 + (\$40 \times \text{items sold}) = (\$80 \times \text{items sold})$$

$$\$30{,}000 = (\$80 - \$40) \times \text{items sold}$$

$$\$30{,}000 = \$40 \times \text{items sold}$$

$$\frac{\$30{,}000}{\$40} = \text{items sold}$$

$$750 = \text{items sold}$$

The variable-cost plan may give salespeople the incentive to work harder and sell more software items than the mixed-cost plan. In making his selection, Sullivan would consider these incentive effects in relation to the higher total cost at volume levels above 750 items. He would have to balance his desire to control costs with the need to keep his sales staff highly motivated.

Summary Problem for Your Review

Part A.   Colores de Garcia makes and sells industrial paints in Monterrey, Mexico. Eduardo Garcia, the owner, is considering two alternatives for paying his four salespersons next year (19X5). Plan A is a straight commission of $0.40 per gallon sold. Plan B is a salary of $20,000 each plus a commission of $0.20 per gallon.

Required

1. Graph the cost behavior patterns of both plans.
2. Determine both graphically and with equations the number of gallons all four salespersons together would have to sell for Garcia to pay the same total compensation under both plans.

Part B.   In 19X4, Garcia operated at full capacity of 400,000 gallons. Each salesperson was paid according to plan A above. The average sale price was $10 per gallon, and the average variable cost (excluding commission) was $6 per gallon. Fixed expenses totaled $1,000,000.
   Garcia believes his sales force can sell 500,000 gallons in 19X5 and every year thereafter if his company can produce them. He estimates an additional committed fixed cost of $200,000 would be required to provide the additional capacity.

Required

1. Compute 19X5 operating income on a contribution-margin income statement if Garcia acquires the additional capacity and produces and sells 500,000 gallons. Assume Garcia switches to plan B (a salary of $20,000 each and commission of $0.20 per gallon) to pay salespersons.

2. Repeat Requirement 1 assuming Garcia continues to pay compensation according to plan A (a straight commission of $0.40 per gallon).
3. At production and sales volume of 500,000 gallons per year, which employee compensation plan should Garcia use? Why?

SOLUTION TO REVIEW PROBLEM

Part A—Requirement 1

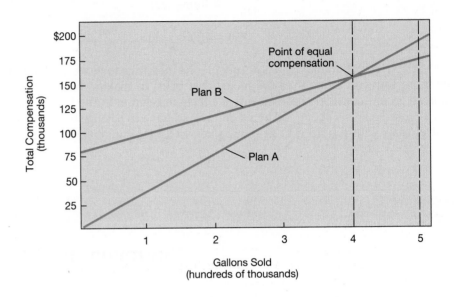

Part A—Requirement 2

Plan A total compensation = Plan B total compensation
$0.40 × gallons sold = $20,000 × 4 salespersons + ($0.20 × gallons s
($0.40 − $0.20) × gallons sold = $80,000
$0.20 × gallons sold = $80,000
gallons sold = $\dfrac{\$80,000}{\$0.20}$
gallons sold = 400,000

Part B—Requirements 1 and 2

	Plan B Salary Plus Commission		Plan A Commission Only
Sales revenue (500,000 × $10).........	$5,000,000		$5,000,000
Sales commissions (500,000 × $0.20)...	100,000	(500,000 × $0.40)	200,000
Other variable expense..............	3,000,000		3,000,000
Contribution margin	1,900,000		1,800,000
Sales salary expense	80,000		—
Other fixed expense	1,200,000		1,200,000
Operating income	$ 620,000		$ 600,000

Part B—Requirement 3   At production and sales volume of 500,000 gallons, Garcia should select plan B because operating income is higher.

Determining How Costs Behave _____

To budget and control costs, managers need to know how cost drivers affect costs. For many costs, a single cost driver can explain cost behavior. That driver is usually some measure of volume of activity. For example, the number of items sold is adequate to explain the total sales commission expense of Sullivan Software Company. By contrast, several cost drivers may be necessary to predict other costs. For example, materials-handling costs in a warehouse might be affected by the size of materials handled, their weight, and also by the number of individual pieces. These three drivers together can provide a better understanding of cost behavior than any single driver by itself.

The Cost Function

A **cost function** is a mathematical statement of the relationship between a cost and one or more cost drivers. To see how cost functions may be determined, consider a cost (airplane engine repairs) with a single cost driver (number of hours flown). The cost to be predicted is usually denoted as y, and the cost driver as x. In a cost function, the cost is called the **dependent variable**, y, because its value depends on the value of the **independent variable**, x. The analyst faces the problem of **cost estimation,** or **cost approximation**, which is the determination of the underlying relationship between x and y over a specified relevant range of x. After estimating the cost function, a manager may use it to answer a question such as, How much repair cost will we incur if our airplanes operate for 15,000 hours in May?

Major Assumptions

In practice, cost approximations are often based on two major assumptions:

1. Cost behavior can be explained adequately by one cost driver instead of two or more.
2. The cost function is linear over the relevant range. That is, the function can be graphed as a straight line, with the cost on the y-axis and the cost driver on the x-axis.

In many cases, these assumptions produce only rough approximations of costs. Most costs are affected by more than one cost driver. Also, many costs, because of such factors as employee learning and discounts for high-volume purchases of goods or services, are nonlinear. These two assumptions illustrate the cost-benefit criterion discussed in Chapter 16. Managers tend to rely on the rough approximations because the costs of developing and using more complex and precise estimation methods exceed their benefits (through better decisions).

An example of a nonlinear cost is shown in Exhibit 18-7. The total cost y is packing labor, purchased at a rate of $15 per hour. The cost driver x is customer orders packed. Each worker can pack 10 orders per hour. Packing labor is an example of a **step-function variable cost,** which is purchased in whole quantities (hours) but used in fractional quantities (tenths of hours per order). Because the steps are small, this step-function cost can be budgeted as a linear variable cost with little loss of accuracy.

EXHIBIT 18-7 *Step-Function Variable Cost*

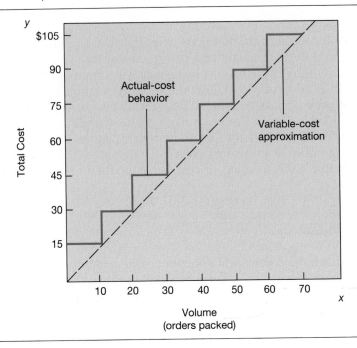

If there is a single cost driver and the cost function is linear, each cost has a behavior pattern whose expected value, E(*y*), is

$$E(y) = A + Bx$$

where *A* and *B* are parameters of the relationship. (A **parameter** is a constant, such as *A*, or a coefficient, such as *B*, in a model or system of equations.) In cost-function models, *A* represents total fixed cost and *B* represents variable cost per unit of *x*. Use caution in interpreting *A*. It is not the fixed cost at zero volume. Instead, *A* is the *portion* of total cost that does not vary with the level of the cost driver *within the relevant range*. If the fixed cost is discretionary, at least some of it probably can be avoided if production or sales activity completely shuts down.

The job of the cost analyst in the cost-estimation process is to estimate *a* and *b*, which are linear approximations of *A* and *B*, respectively. These approximations are used to predict total cost *y*:

$$y' = a + bx$$

where *y'* is the predicted or estimated cost for a specified level of the cost driver, *x*. For example, if the total fixed cost *a* is $40,000 and variable unit cost *b* is $10 per machine-hour, the cost-estimation equation is

Total repair cost = $40,000 + ($10 × machine-hours worked)

The analyst can then predict total repair cost *y* to be $60,000 for *x* = 2,000 machine-hours ($40,000 + [$10 × 2,000]) and $70,000 for *x* = 3,000 machine-hours ($40,000 + [$10 × 3,000]). Actual expenditures for repairs might differ from these predicted amounts for any of four reasons: (1) The relationship between variable repair costs and machine-hours worked may not be perfectly linear; (2) *a* and *b* are only approximations of *A* and *B*, (3) other cost drivers may affect repair costs; and (4) random, unpredictable factors may affect repair costs.

Types of Cost Functions

The three major types of cost functions—variable, fixed, and mixed—are variations of the basic cost estimation formula: $y' = a + bx$. The functions are graphed in Exhibit 18-8.

Panel A shows a variable cost, one that changes in total in direct proportion to changes in the volume of cost driver x. When volume is zero, total cost is zero. Consider a company that sells luxury yachts, each of which costs $100,000. If the company has no sales during a particular month, the total cost of goods sold for the month is zero. If the company sells four yachts, its cost of goods sold will be twice the amount for sales of two yachts. Cost of goods sold for four yachts is $400,000 ($100,000 × 4), and for two yachts, $200,000 ($100,000 × 2). In this case b is $100,000.

Panel B graphs a fixed cost, one that does not change in total despite changes in the volume of activity. As we have discussed, this cost behavior pattern usually is related to a specified relevant range of activity. Suppose a manager who is paid $75,000 per year can supervise the production of any number of yachts, up to 20. The manager's fixed salary cost, a, is $75,000. If the company produces between 21 and 40 yachts in a one-year period, two supervisors will be needed. Then, a jumps up to $150,000.

EXHIBIT 18-8   *Types of Cost Functions*

Panel A – Variable Cost

$y' = bx$, because $a = 0$

Panel B – Fixed Cost

$y' = a$, because $b = 0$

Panel C – Mixed Cost

$y' = a + bx$

A mixed cost, which is a combination of variable and fixed elements, is graphed in Panel C. Total cost y changes as x changes within the relevant range, but not in direct proportion. Consider a color copy machine that rents for $500 per month plus $0.10 per copy produced ($a$ = $500 and b = $0.10). Here, the cost-function graph originates at the fixed cost of $500 and rises according to the volume. If 2,000 copies are made in a month, the total cost is $700 ($500 + [$0.10 × 2,000]). If twice as many copies are made, the total cost is $900 ($500 + [$0.10 × 4,000]). The total cost at the 4,000-copy volume level is less than twice the total cost at the 2,000-copy level because the fixed cost is the same.

Ideally, for planning and control purposes, mixed costs would be subdivided into two accounts: one account for the fixed component and a separate account for the variable component. This action would call attention to the two different cost behavior patterns. In practice, however, mixed costs rarely are subdivided. Costs such as electrical power, equipment repairs, and shop maintenance generally are accounted for in total. Why? Even if individual invoices could be separated into their fixed and variable amounts, the benefits of doing so are not likely to outweigh the clerical cost.

Accountants and managers rely on experience to identify mixed-cost accounts. They use past data to develop cost functions for predicting future costs. The analysis we discuss next can be used to separate mixed costs into fixed and variable components, which then may be budgeted separately.

Estimating Mixed Cost Functions

Steps in Estimation

To determine a linear mixed-cost function, an analyst must first identify the total cost to be predicted. Then, he or she must proceed as follows: (1) choose the cost driver, (2) collect a sample of data on the cost and the cost driver, (3) plot the data, and (4) estimate the cost function. The analyst then evaluates the function, that is, decides whether it is reliable for predicting the cost. Sometimes the analyst performs these steps several times before settling on an acceptable function.

Step 1: Choose the cost driver. Exhibit 18-9 gives examples of cost drivers in several business function areas. The cost function should be based on a theory that explains the relationship between the cost and the cost driver. When variables tend to move together, they are said to be highly correlated. However, no theory exists to explain a high correlation between, for example, sunspot activity and Eastman Kodak's research and development costs. On the other hand, if a study were to show a high correlation between the cost of conducting research and the number of research projects, the number of research projects is a good cost driver.

Step 2: Collect a sample of data on the cost and the cost driver. An ideal sample consists of numerous data *observations* for a company with stable operating methods and technology. The time period used to measure the cost and the driver should be the same. For example, the number of customer orders processed in a month could be used to predict monthly, not quarterly or yearly, order-processing costs. One observation, or sample point, might be $4,500 of order-processing cost and 1,200 orders processed in December 19X3.

Business Function	Examples of Cost Drivers
Research and development	Number of projects
	Length of projects
	Number of personnel
Manufacturing	Materials costs
	Materials size or weight
	Labor hours or costs
	Number of parts
	Number of items produced
Distribution	Dollar value of items distributed
	Size of items distributed
	Weight of items distributed
	Number of items distributed
Marketing	Number of advertisements
	Number of marketing personnel
Customer service	Number of service calls
	Number of products serviced

Step 3: Plot the data. A plot of the sample points reveals the general relationship between the cost and the cost driver. It also highlights extreme observations that do not represent the normal relationship between the two variables. Extreme points may result from errors in recording the data or from an unusual event, such as a labor strike. Plotting the data also helps the analyst determine the relevant range of the cost function. Different behavior patterns may exist at different levels of volume.

Panel A of Exhibit 18-10 shows a linear relationship between marketing expense and number of advertisements. If a straight line were drawn through the middle of the points from lower left to upper right, the points would cluster around the line. (See Exhibit 18-13 for examples of these lines.) No extreme observations are apparent. The relevant range of a cost function developed from these sample points would be from the lowest to the highest values of x.

Panel B reveals that no linear relationship exists between marketing expense and units of product sold. The points are scattered randomly instead of arranged in a generally linear pattern. Analysts therefore would conclude that units of product sold do not "drive" marketing expense and would be an inappropriate independent variable for the cost function.

Step 4: Estimate the cost function. The analyst's task is to separate mixed costs into their fixed and variable components. We illustrate three methods of estimating mixed-cost functions: the high-low method, the visual-fit method, and the least-squares regression method. All three illustrations are based on the following data.

The Boeing Company, located in Seattle, Washington, is a leading manufacturer of commercial aircraft. Boeing uses sophisticated equipment that must be maintained to serve its intended purpose. For manufacturers such as Boeing, maintenance is a major expense, and maintenance employees are highly-respected within the company.

EXHIBIT 18-10 *Plots of Sample Data Points for Predicting Marketing Expense*

Panel A – Cost Driver Is Number of Advertisements

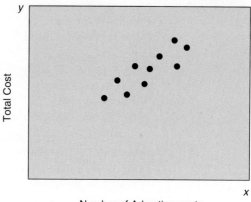

Number of Advertisements

Panel B – Cost Driver Is Units of Product Sold

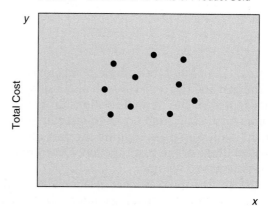

Units of Product Sold

EXHIBIT 18-11 *Data for Cost Function Estimation Procedures*

Month	Cost Driver: Number of Machine-Hours (x)	Cost: Maintenance Costs Incurred (y)
January	210	$2,300
February	220	2,700
March	110	1,800
April	180	2,100
May	150	2,100
June	80	1,400
July	100	1,800
August	130	1,700
September	100	1,500

EXHIBIT 18-12   *Plot of Sample Data*

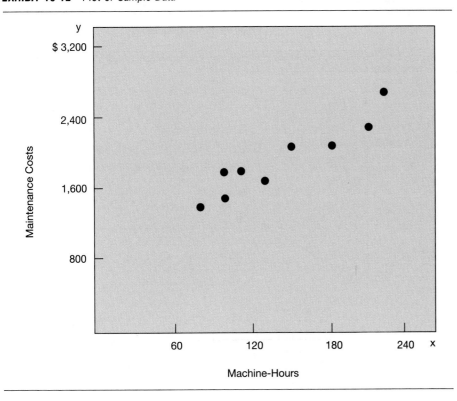

Suppose Boeing accountants have observed the machinery maintenance costs listed in Exhibit 18-11 for a recent nine-month period. They believe machine-hours are the primary cost drivers of variable maintenance cost. The exhibit shows nine pairs of (cost driver, cost) observations within the relevant range of 80 to 220 machine-hours. The plot of the points, Exhibit 18-12, reveals a strong linear relationship between machine-hours and maintenance costs. Therefore, a linear cost function should describe the relationship.

The High-Low Method

The **high-low method** estimates a cost function on the basis of only the highest-volume and the lowest-volume points (values of the independent variable) within the relevant range of the sample. If one of these points is an unrepresentative extreme value, or *outlier*, that has been caused by a strike, fire, or other unusual event, it is discarded. The next-highest-volume (or next-lowest-volume) point is used in its place. This action is taken because the points used in the computation of parameters a and b in the cost-estimation formula $y' = a + bx$, must represent the normal relationship between the cost and cost driver. Otherwise, the cost function is useless.

After selecting the high and low points, the analyst connects them with a line and extends it back to the vertical axis, as in Exhibit 18-13, panel A. The intercept becomes a, the fixed portion of total cost, and the slope of the line becomes b, the variable cost per machine hour.

OBJECTIVE 6

Use three methods to estimate mixed-cost functions

EXHIBIT 18-13 *Cost Function Estimations*

Panel A – High-Low Method

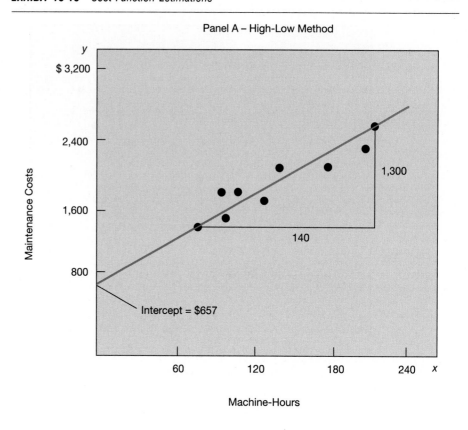

Machine-Hours

Panel B – Visual-Fit Method

Machine-Hours

EXHIBIT 18-13   *(continued)*

Panel C – Least-Squares Regression Method

The first step in computing the values of these parameters is determining the differences between the high and low values of x and y:

	Number of Machine-Hours (x)	Maintenance Costs (y)
High	220	$2,700
Low	80	1,400
Difference	140	$1,300

With these results, the value of the variable cost per machine hour, b, now can be computed:

$$\text{Variable rate} = \frac{\text{Change in costs}}{\text{Change in volume}} = \frac{\$2,700 - \$1,400}{220 - 80} = \frac{\$1,300}{140}$$

$$= \$9.286 \text{ per machine-hour}$$

The value of a can then be found as follows:

Fixed component = Total mixed cost less variable component
At high point = $2,700 − (220 × $9.286)
= $2,700 − $2,043 = $657

At low point = $1,400 − (80 × $9.286)
= $1,400 − $743 = $657

Therefore, the high-low method results in the following cost function:

$$y' = a + bx$$

Total maintenance cost = \$657 per month plus \$9.286 per machine-hour

The high-low method is easy to use, but it has a major defect. It uses only two data observations, regardless of the number of observations available. Because these two points may not represent the normal relationship between the cost and the cost driver, and because better estimation methods are available, the high-low method is only recommended when very few observations of past results are available.

The Visual-Fit Method

The simplest method of cost estimation that uses all available data is the **visual-fit method**. The analyst visually fits a line to the points, trying to come close to as many points as possible. Because the line represents all data points (except outliers), visual-fit usually results in approximately equal numbers of points falling above and below the line, as in Exhibit 18-13, panel B. Inspection of the line in relation to the points gives the analyst a better understanding of the relationship than a view of the data plot only (Exhibit 18-12).

The intercept a of the visual-fit line is \$800, taken directly from the graph. The slope can be computed from the line. For example, the line passes through \$2,500 on the vertical (y) axis at a volume level of 213 on the horizontal (x) axis. The point ($x = 213$, $y = \$2,500$) can be used with the y-intercept point ($x = 0$, $y = \$800$) to determine the variable portion of the cost function formula:

$$\text{Variable rate} = \frac{\text{Change in costs}}{\text{Change in volume}} = \frac{\$2,500 - \$800}{213 - 0} = \frac{\$1,700}{213}$$

$$= \$7.981 \text{ per machine-hour}$$

The cost function is therefore:

Total maintenance cost = \$800 per month plus \$7.981 per machine-hour

The visual-fit method is better than the high-low method, but visual-fit is very subjective. Two people could draw "best-fitting" lines through the same points with different intercepts and slopes. Also, this method provides no measure of how closely the line "fits" the plotted points. In general, the closer the sample points are to the cost function line, the more accurate the estimation of the cost function. The next method addresses these weaknesses of the visual-fit approach.

The Least-Squares Regression Method

The **least-squares regression method**, or simply **regression analysis**, is a formal model that measures the average amount of change in the dependent variable y (maintenance cost) that is associated with a one-unit change in the independent variable, or cost driver, x (machine-hours). If the relationship is linear, regression analysis is the most accurate way to determine the cost behavior of a mixed cost from a sample of past observations. The regression equation is the formula for *the* best-fitting straight line through the plot of sample points. The formula's parameters can be computed by hand, but nearly all regression analysis is performed using computers. Regression software programs are widely available and inexpensive.

The line in Exhibit 18-13, panel C was fitted by a least-squares regression program. The data in Exhibit 18-11 were used as program inputs. In addition to the panel C graph, the program provided the following formula:

$$y' = a + bx$$
$$y' = \$862 + \$7.532x$$

What does this equation tell Boeing Company managers? For the nine months ended September 30, maintenance costs over the relevant range of 80 to 220 machine-hours averaged $862 per month plus $7.532 per machine-hour. Boeing accountants can use the equation to help managers accurately predict maintenance costs. These predictions may translate into higher profits for the company.

In Exhibit 18-13, panel C, notice that none of the points lies on the regression line. The vertical difference between each point and the line is called a *deviation*. Each deviation is the difference between an actual amount of maintenance cost and the predicted cost (on the line) for the associated number of machine-hours. The least-squares method is so-named because the sum of the squared values of all such deviations is the smallest for any line fitted to the data.

Consider the month of May, when $2,100 of maintenance cost was observed at a volume of 150 machine-hours (Exhibit 18-11). The predicted maintenance cost for 150 machine-hours is

$$y' = \$862 + \$7.532x$$
$$y' = \$862 + \$7.532(150)$$
$$y' = \$862 + \$1,130$$
$$y' = \$1,992$$

The deviation for May is $108 ($2,100 − $1,992). If accountants had used the formula to predict maintenance cost that month, the actual cost, $2,100, would have been 5.4% ($108 ÷ $1,992) more than the predicted cost. This amount of error in cost estimation is widely regarded as acceptable.

Comparison of Methods

The three methods used to estimate fixed and variable costs produced different results:

	Total Fixed Cost	Variable Cost Rate
High-low method	$657	$9.286
Visual-fit	800	7.981
Least-squares regression	862	7.532

Because the parameter values are different, predictions based on the three cost function formulas will differ. Suppose Boeing accountants want to predict maintenance costs for volume levels of 100, 150, and 200 machine-hours. The predictions are shown in the following table.

Method	Machine-Hours		
	100	**150**	**200**
High-low	$657 + $9.286(100) = $1,586	$657 + $9.286(150) = $2,050	$657 + $9.286(200) = $2,514
Visual fit	$800 + $7.981(100) = $1,598	$800 + $7.981(150) = $1,997	$800 + $7.981(200) = $2,396
Regression	$862 + $7.532(100) = $1,615	$862 + $7.532(150) = $1,992	$862 + $7.532(200) = $2,368

In this sample, the high-low method generates the lowest estimate of fixed cost ($657). Therefore, at low volume levels (100 hours), high-low produces lower total-cost predictions than regression analysis. But the high-low method has a higher estimate of variable cost per machine-hour. Thus at high volume levels (200 hours), high-low predicts greater total cost because the variable portion is a larger component of total cost. The visual-fit method produces cost estimates between the other two.

These results apply to this sample only, but serve to illustrate that the methods produce different predictions. The relationships among costs predicted by the three methods depend upon (1) the locations of the high and low points in relation to the regression line and (2) the skill of the analyst in the visual-fit procedure. Regression analysis is the best method because it uses all available data points, is the most objective, and shows exactly how well the estimated cost function fits the data. Companies such as Motorola, Xerox, Ford, and Banc One would prefer the regression method in deciding whether to re-engineer their operations.

Evaluating Cost Functions

OBJECTIVE 7

Evaluate a mixed-cost function

Regardless of which estimation method is used, the resulting cost function should be evaluated both at the time it is determined and then periodically as it is being used. Two important criteria for the initial evaluation are economic plausibility and goodness of fit.

Economic plausibility means that the relationship must be credible. Suppose that a regression equation for predicting equipment maintenance costs, using number of machine-hours as the independent variable, has a negative slope coefficient b. Such a result suggests that maintenance costs would go down as the number of machine-hours increases! Logic tells us the opposite is true—maintenance should increase as production activity increases.

What could cause such a backward-looking result? It may be that maintenance is performed on machines when production activity is low because that is the best time to take the machines out of service. The observed relationship between maintenance costs (recorded as incurred) and machine-hours would be due to the discretionary timing of maintenance activity and not to the underlying cause-and-effect relationship. If an unreasonable pattern emerges from a regression, accountants should rethink their assumptions. They may need to select a different cost driver. On the other hand, they simply may need to refine the way they collect their sample data.

Goodness of fit means that the relationship must explain past costs well. In effect, the regression line must come close to the plotted sample data points. Regression analysis software programs give the analyst a goodness-of-fit statistic known as r^2, the **coefficient of determination**. It tells the percentage of variation in total cost (y) that is explained by changes in the cost driver (x). If in our example $r^2 = 0.80$, that means that 80% of the fluctuation in maintenance costs is explained by the volume of machine-hours. A manager can use r^2 to determine how much confidence to put in regression analysis predictions.

After the cost function has been used for several periods, predicted costs should be compared with actual costs. Large differences might be due to errors in the sample data that were used to determine the function. New technology may have changed the relationship between the cost and the cost driver, or current activity volumes may fall outside the relevant range of the function. Whatever the reason, the equation should be used only as long as it provides reliable estimates.

Summary Problem for Your Review

Elizabeth Gray, purchasing manager of High-Value Stores, needs a cost function to predict purchasing department costs. She believes the primary cost driver is the number of purchase orders placed. Gray collected the following observations for the most-recent six quarters of activity:

Quarter	No. of Purchase Orders	Total Cost (thousands)
1	1,875	$312
2	1,500	225
3	3,800	380
4	2,300	275
5	3,500	312
6	2,700	325

Required

1. Plot the data observations, with total purchasing department cost as the dependent variable (y) and number of purchase orders as the independent variable (x).

2. Regression analysis reveals that the equation of the best-fitting straight line through the sample points is:

$$\text{Total cost} = \$183{,}160 + \$46.57 \text{ per purchase order}$$

Draw the regression analysis line on the graph.

3. Use the high-low method to estimate the cost function. Draw the high-low line on the graph, and compare the high-low equation with the regression analysis equation.

4. Use both the high-low and regression analysis cost functions to predict purchasing department cost for a quarter in which Gray places 3,000 purchase orders with suppliers.

SOLUTION TO REVIEW PROBLEM

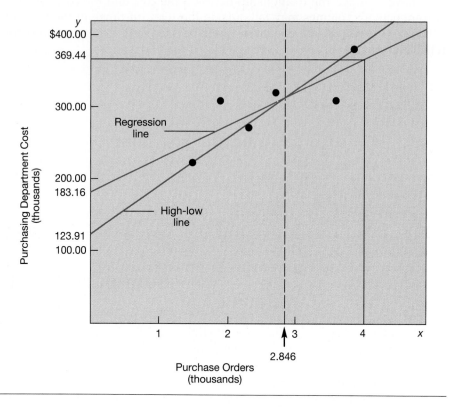

Requirement 3

$$\text{Variable rate} = \frac{\text{Change in costs}}{\text{Change in volume}} = \frac{\$380,000 - \$225,000}{3,800 - 1,500} = \frac{\$155,000}{2,300}$$

$$= \$67.391 \text{ per purchase order}$$

Fixed component = Total mixed cost less variable component
At high point   = $380,000 − ($67.391 × 3,800)
             = $380,000 − $256,086
             = $123,914

At low point   = $225,000 − ($67.391 × 1,500)
             = $225,000 − $101,086
             = $123,914

Because the high point of the sample falls above the regression line and the low point is below it, the high-low cost function has a steeper slope ($67.391 versus $46.57) and a smaller fixed-cost component ($123,914 versus $183,160). The high-low equation predicts less costs at low volume levels (below 2,846 purchase orders) and more cost at high volume levels.

Requirement 4
High-low prediction:

$$\text{Total cost} = \$123,914 + (\$67.391 \times 3,000)$$
$$= \$123,914 + \$202,173$$
$$= \$326,087$$

Regression analysis prediction:

$$\text{Total cost} = \$183{,}160 + (\$46.57 \times 3{,}000)$$
$$= \$183{,}160 + \$139{,}710$$
$$= \$322{,}870$$

Summary

Cost behavior analysis examines the relationships between costs and the activities, or drivers, that cause them. Knowledge of these relationships, which are called *cost behavior patterns,* is essential for evaluating operations and predicting future costs. We classify costs as fixed, variable, or mixed.

Fixed, or capacity, costs may be categorized as either committed or discretionary. *Committed fixed costs* are costs caused primarily by having property, plant, equipment, and key managerial personnel. They cannot be changed much by month-to-month or even year-to-year management decisions. Accurate predictions of future activity levels are crucial for management to determine the amounts of these fixed costs to incur.

Discretionary fixed costs (1) arise from periodic (usually yearly) budget decisions that reflect top-management policies, and (2) have no clear relationship between inputs and outputs. The appropriate amounts of these costs are difficult to determine with precision, so budgeted amounts often are based on traditions, rules of thumb, or industry customs. In many cases, discretionary-fixed-cost expenditures may be temporarily cut back without damaging a company's ability to meet long-term goals.

Fixed costs provide the capacity to operate at a particular activity level, and variable costs result from using available capacity. *Engineered variable costs* result from measurable, often observable, cause-and-effect relationships between inputs (the costs) and outputs. Their efficiency may be measured by relating the quantity of inputs used to the quantity of outputs achieved. By contrast, *discretionary variable costs* change with production or sales activity simply because management has decided to incur the costs on a percentage or a per-unit basis.

Managers use one of two methods to budget and control the costs of operating labor. The *discretionary-fixed-cost* approach relies on management's judgment to determine the size of the work force. The *engineered-variable-cost approach* uses *work measurement* to calibrate the workload in a process or operation in order to determine the number of employees needed to perform the work.

Managers make decision trade-offs between fixed and variable costs. For example, they may increase spending on robotic equipment in order to save labor costs. Fixed-cost expenditures for state-of-the-art technology may be needed to remain competitive, but these inflexible costs restrict management's ability to respond to changes in short-run conditions. Mixed costs have both fixed and variable components that usually are not identified separately.

To predict and control a cost, managers need to know how the cost behaves. They develop a *cost function,* which expresses the mathematical relationship between the cost and its cost driver.

Three methods are widely used to separate mixed costs into their fixed and variable elements on the basis of samples of past data. The *high-low method* uses only the highest-volume and lowest-volume points of the sample. Because these two points may not represent normal relationships, this method is not recommended unless very few observations of past results are available.

The *visual-fit method* relies on the ability of the analyst to visually fit a line to the plot of sample points. It is better than the high-low method because it uses all sample points, but it is subjective and does not provide a measure of how well the line fits the points.

The most accurate method to determine the behavior pattern of a mixed cost is *least-squares regression*. Regression software programs graph the sample points and give the formula of the straight line that best fits the points. The *coefficient of determination, r^2*, tells the percentage of variation in the cost that is explained by changes in the cost driver. The r^2 measure helps the analyst determine how much confidence to put in specific cost function predictions.

Self-Study Questions

1. Costs caused primarily from having property, plant, equipment, and key managerial personnel are called *(p. 847)*
    a. Committed fixed costs
    b. Discretionary fixed costs
    c. Mixed costs
    d. Step-function variable costs

2. Refer to Exhibit 18-1 *(p. 848)*. If demand for orders in 19X1 is 20,000, operating income for the larger store would be (Exhibit 18-2) *(p. 849)*
    a. $30,000
    b. $80,000
    c. $10,000
    d. $70,000

3. Holmes Co. pays one salesperson a salary of $70,000 and another a salary of $40,000 plus a commission of $50 per item sold. At what sales level will the two salesperson's earnings be equal? *(pp. 856–57)*
    a. 2,200
    b. 600
    c. 1,400
    d. Cannot be determined from the information given.

4. If a cost function is linear *(p. 859)*
    a. It can be graphed as a straight line
    b. It is either variable or fixed, but not mixed
    c. When the volume of the cost driver doubles, the amount of the cost doubles
    d. The slope coefficient of the independent variable is negative

5. For a particular cost driver activity level, a difference between an actual cost incurred and the cost predicted by a linear equation may be caused by *(p. 860)*
    a. Nonlinearity in the relationship between the cost and the cost driver
    b. The effect of other cost drivers on the cost
    c. Unpredictable factors that affect the cost
    d. All of the above

6. Plotting a sample of (cost driver, cost) observations helps the analyst *(p. 863)*
    a. Determine the general relationship between the cost and the cost driver
    b. Identify extreme observations that do not represent the normal relationship between the cost and the cost driver
    c. Prove cause-and-effect relationships between the cost and the cost driver
    d. a and b

7. The high-low method of mixed-cost estimation uses only the highest and lowest observations of the *(p. 865)*
    a. Fixed-cost component
    b. Slope coefficient
    c. Independent variable (cost driver)
    d. Dependent variable (total cost)

8. The most accurate method of cost function approximation is called the *(p. 868)*
    a. High-low method

b. Visual-fit method

c. Least-squares regression method

d. Mixed-cost-formula method

9. The coefficient of determination (r^2) tells *(p. 870)*

a. The average change in a cost function's dependent variable for each one-unit change in the independent variable

b. The percentage of variation in total cost explained by changes in the cost driver

c. The proportion of fixed cost to total cost at the average volume level of the relevant range

d. The sum of the squares of deviations between observed data points and the least-squares regression line

10. If every point in a plotted sample of data observations lies very close to the least-squares regression line, we say that the cost function passes the *(p. 870)*

a. Goodness-of-fit test

b. Cause-and-effect test

c. Economic-plausibility test

d. All of the above

Answers to the Self-Study Questions follow the Accounting Vocabulary.

Accounting Vocabulary

Coefficient of determination (r^2). The statistic that tells the percentage of variation in a cost that is explained by changes in the cost driver *(p. 870)*.

Committed fixed costs. Fixed costs that result from having property, plant, equipment, and key managerial personnel *(p. 847)*.

Cost estimation (cost approximation). Determination of the underlying relationship between a cost and its cost driver over a specified relevant range of the cost driver *(p. 859)*.

Cost function. A mathematical statement of the relationship between a cost and one or more cost drivers *(p. 859)*.

Dependent variable. The cost to be predicted in a cost function *(p. 859)*.

Discretionary (managed) fixed costs. Fixed costs that (1) arise from periodic (usually yearly) budget decisions that reflect top-management policies, and (2) have no clear relationship between inputs and outputs *(p. 850)*.

Discretionary-fixed-cost approach. An approach to managing operating labor costs that relies on personal supervision by managers *(p. 853)*.

Discretionary variable costs. Variable costs that change with sales or production volume simply because

management has decided to spend a certain percentage of each sales dollar, or a certain dollar amount for each unit sold *(p. 852)*.

Economic plausibility. A cost function evaluation criterion that means that the relationship between the cost and the cost driver must be credible *(p. 870)*.

Engineered variable costs. Variable costs that result from measurable, often observable, cause-and-effect relationships between inputs (the costs) and outputs *(p. 851)*.

Engineered-variable-cost approach. An approach to managing operating labor costs that applies formal work measurement to the budgeting process *(p. 853)*.

Goodness of fit. A cost function evaluation criterion that means that the relationship between the cost and the cost driver must explain past costs well *(p. 870)*.

High-low method. A way of estimating a cost function that uses only the highest-volume and lowest-volume points within the relevant range of a sample *(p. 865)*.

Independent variable. The cost driver in a cost function *(p. 859)*.

Least-squares regression method (regression analysis). A formal model that measures the average amount of change in the dependent variable that is associated with a one-unit change in the independent variable *(p. 868)*.

Parameter. A constant or coefficient in a model or system of equations *(p. 860)*.

Step-function variable cost. A variable cost that is purchased in whole quantities (e.g., hours) but used in fractional quantities (e.g., tenths of hours) *(p. 859)*.

Variance. The difference between an actual amount and the corresponding budgeted amount *(p. 853)*.

Visual-fit method. A cost function estimation method in which the analyst visually fits a line to the plot of all sample data points *(p. 868)*.

Work measurement. The careful analysis of a task—its size, the methods used, and its efficiency *(p. 853)*.

Answers to Self-Study Questions

1. a
2. c (20,000 × contribution margin of $4 per order) − fixed expenses of $70,000 = $80,000 − $70,000 = $10,000
3 b. $70,000 = $40,000 + $50 per item sold
     $30,000 = $50 per item sold
     $\dfrac{\$30,000}{\$50}$ = items sold = 600

4. a
5. d
6. c
7. c
8. d
9. b
10. a

ASSIGNMENT MATERIAL ————————————————————

Questions

1. Why are fixed costs also called capacity costs?
2. How do committed costs differ from discretionary costs?
3. What determines the level of committed costs? Of discretionary costs?
4. What is a cost driver? Give three examples of cost drivers.
5. How do step-function variable costs differ from strictly variable costs that change in direct proportion to changes in activity volume?
6. Give two ways committed-fixed-cost expenditures for automated equipment are helping companies compete in the marketplace.
7. What two assumptions frequently are made when estimating a cost function?
8. "Ideally, there should be no accounts for mixed costs." Explain.
9. Describe how mixed costs are budgeted.
10. The general form of a cost estimation equation is $y' = a + bx$. What does each of the four variables represent?
11. Why is the concept of the relevant range important in mixed-cost estimation?
12. Power cost for the Wertheim Company is $2,000 per month plus $1.00 per machine-hour. In January, 8,000 machine-hours were worked. What was the average unit cost (fixed plus variable) per machine-hour? What would be the average unit cost at a volume of 16,000 hours in February?
13. List the four steps in estimating a cost function on the basis of past cost relationships.
14. Why is a plot of the sample data observations important when using the high-low method?

15. Why is least-squares regression analysis usually preferred over the high-low method? Over the visual-fit method?

16. "The high-low-method cost function always predicts higher cost at high volume levels than the regression-analysis cost function." Do you agree or disagree? Explain.

17. What two criteria are important in evaluating cost functions? Which criterion can be checked with a plot of sample data?

18. Is a high coefficient of determination (close to 1.00) better than or worse than a low coefficient of determination (close to zero)? Explain.

19. Two years ago, Mahon Company accountants developed a cost function to predict machinery maintenance cost on the basis of machine-hours (the independent variable). What might cause the function to be inaccurate today? What would indicate the need for a new function?

Exercises

Exercise 18-1 *Identifying cost behavior patterns* **(L.O. 1)**

Ann Bolger, a hospital administrator, heard a lecture on different kinds of cost behavior. Afterward, she identified several hospital costs and presented you with the following list:

1. Leasing cost of X-ray equipment ($10,000 per year plus $0.50 per film)
2. Training costs of an administrative resident
3. Straight-line depreciation on operating-room equipment
4. Costs incurred by Dr. Milotte in cancer research
5. Repairs to hospital furniture
6. Electricity costs
7. Nursing wages per patient (one nurse is added to a shift for every five patients)

Required

Classify each cost item on the list as one of the following: committed fixed, discretionary fixed, strictly variable, step-function variable, or mixed.

Exercise 18-2 *Graphing cost behavior patterns* **(L.O. 2,5)**

Rod Holmes is considering the following three plans for paying his salespeople next year:

Discretionary-fixed-cost plan: a salary of $70,000
Discretionary-variable-cost plan: a commission of $175 per item sold
Mixed-cost plan: a salary of $40,000 plus a commission of $50 per item sold

Required

1. Graph the cost behavior pattern of each plan on a single graph.
2. From the graph, determine which plan would result in the lowest total cost to Holmes at a volume level of 500 items sold by each salesperson.

Exercise 18-3 *Computing equal-cost volume of different cost behavior patterns*
　　　　　　　　(L.O. 2,4)

(Refer to Exercise 18-2).　　Now assume that Holmes is uncomfortable with graphical solutions. He much prefers to make business decisions on the basis of algebraic computations.

Required

1. Compute the point of indifference, in terms of items sold, between the discretionary-fixed-cost plan and the mixed-cost plan. If the volume level is above the point of indifference, which plan results in the lower total cost? Why?
2. Compute the point of indifference between the discretionary-variable-cost plan and the mixed-cost plan. If the volume level is above the point of indifference, which plan yields the lower cost? Why?

Exercise 18-4 *Analyzing capacity costs to make business decisions* *(L.O. 1,2)*

A. Jimmy Warren has decided to rent a store to sell T-shirts, sweatshirts, and other college souvenir items. He will pay $25,000 to rent the space for one year. The average selling price for each item sold is $15; the average variable cost per item is $5. How many items must Warren sell to break even?
B. Now assume Warren has two alternative store sites to consider. He believes he can sell 10,000 items each year if he rents the larger store for $45,000. Alternatively, expected demand with the smaller store is 8,000 items. It rents for $20,000 annually. Which store should Warren rent?

Exercise 18-5 *Analyzing cost behavior by the high-low method* *(L.O. 6)*

Maxine Baylor has been hired as a cost analyst by the plaintiff in a predatory pricing suit. She needs to estimate the behavior pattern of the defendant's utility costs. All she has to go on are the following sparse data:

Monthly Activity in Machine-Hours	Monthly Utility Costs Incurred
600	$3,700
1,000	4,500

Required

1. Use the high-low method to estimate the monthly fixed utility cost and the variable utility cost per machine-hour. Express the cost function in the form $y' = a + bx$.
2. What total utility expense would you expect at an activity level of 800 machine-hours? At 1,800 machine-hours?

Exercise 18-6 *Analyzing cost behavior by the visual-fit method* *(L.O. 6)*

Robert Keyes, president of his own trucking company, believes that total annual operating costs are a function of gross ton-miles of work. Past records show (in thousands):

	Year			
	19X1	19X2	19X3	19X4
Gross ton-miles	800	1,200	400	1,600
Total operating costs	$350	$350	$150	$550

Required

1. Plot the four data points.
2. Visually fit your "best-fitting" line to the points.
3. Using the graph, estimate the cost function for total operating costs.

Exercise 18-7 *Comparing the high-low and visual-fit methods of cost function estimation* **(L.O. 6)**

(Refer to Exercise 18-6.) Robert Keyes has just remembered a major drawback of the visual-fit method—its subjectivity. It relies on the skill of the analyst to draw a representative "best-fitting" line. Keyes decides to check his visual-fit estimates of fixed operating cost and variable cost per ton-mile with the high-low method. "At least it's objective," he thinks.

Required

1. Using the high-low method, estimate the cost function for Keyes Trucking Company.
2. Explain why differences exist between the visual-fit parameters and the high-low parameters you computed.
3. What step in the high-low method is not entirely objective?

Exercise 18-8 *Evaluating a cost function at the time of estimation* **(L.O. 7)**

Angus McLeod had difficulty budgeting machinery maintenance costs for the highly automated plant he manages. At a seminar on regression analysis, he became convinced that this "most accurate" method of cost-function estimation was the answer to his problem. After returning to work, he asked a cost analyst to run two regressions, one using production labor-hours as the independent variable and one using machine-hours. The computer software program the analyst used revealed the following:

Regression Analysis Cost Function	Coefficient of Determination (r^2)
Total maintenance cost = $1,000 per month + $2 per labor-hour	0.15
Total maintenance cost = $800 per month − $0.75 per machine-hour	.55

Required

1. Which, if either, cost function should McLeod use to predict future machinery maintenance costs?
2. If your answer to Requirement 1 was "neither," what should McLeod do?

Exercise 18-9 *Evaluating a cost function during use* **(L.0.7)**

Ed Timmerman of Timmerman Appliance Repair Co. has been using the following cost prediction equation for three years to predict the total cost of service calls each month: Total cost = $1,500 + $20 per service call. Timmerman was very pleased with the equation when it was estimated. Its coefficient of determination (r^2) was calculated to be 0.80, and he was convinced that the number of service calls was the most important driver of the variable portion of service cost.

During the last six months, the following data were recorded:

	January	February	March	April	May	June
Service calls	120	80	100	110	85	110
Total cost	$4,500	$3,650	$3,800	$4,450	$3,450	$4,150

Required

1. Is the cost function providing reliable estimates of total service costs?

2. What might cause a once-accurate cost function to lose accuracy over time?

Exercise 18-10 _Evaluating performance of clerical labor_ **(L.O.3)**

All-America Insurance Co. employs 10 clerks to process insurance claims. Each clerk works 20 eight-hour days per month and is paid a monthly salary of $2,560. On the basis of a work-measurement study, All-America's senior management budgeted the efficiency of each clerk as the processing of four claims per hour. In April, 19X3, the 10 clerks processed a total of 6,000 claims.

Required

1. Prepare a performance report for April using the engineered-variable-cost approach. What does the report tell management about the clerks' performance during the month?
2. Prepare a performance report using the discretionary-fixed-cost approach. Compare the variance with the one produced by the report in Requirement 1.

Problems

(Group A)

Problem 18-1A _Analyzing capacity costs to make business decisions: two-year time period_ **(L.O. 1,2)**

Julie Massey has decided to sell gourmet hamburgers in her hometown of Abilene, Texas. She predicts that the average sales price and variable cost of her burgers will be $3.00 and $1.25, respectively. A major decision that she must make is whether to open at one location on the north side of town or at two locations—one on the north side and one on the south side. Massey has located two vacant stores that would serve her purposes well. Each would rent for $30,000 per year, and each would require a two-year lease. She predicts that other fixed costs would total $5,000 per store per year.

Massey believes that 30,000 hamburgers will be demanded on each side of town in 19X4 and that demand will grow to 50,000 per side in 19X5. She also predicts that one-half of the potential customers on the south side of town would drive to the north side if she opens only one store. The expected number of hamburgers sold each year under each alternative course of action is therefore:

	One Store	Two Stores
19X4	45,000	60,000
19X5	75,000	100,000

Required

1. Prepare contribution-margin income statements to determine expected operating income for 19X4 for both the one-store alternative and the two-store alternative.
2. Repeat Requirement 1 for 19X5.
3. Which course of action results in the greater expected operating income for the two-year period? Should Julie Massey rent one store or two?

Problem 18-2A _Using knowledge of cost behavior patterns to evaluate different payment plans_ **(L.O. 2,4)**

Walter Templin owns Western Motors, a used-car sales company. Western Motors has lots in five different cities. For many years, Templin has paid his salespeople a monthly salary plus a bonus for each car sold. In March 19X4, the monthly salary was $1,600 and the bonus was $25 per car sold.

In April 19X4, Templin received information that J. D. Harrington, one of his best salespersons, was about to resign and join the sales staff at Royal Motors. When questioned by Templin, Harrington responded, "It's nothing personal. Royal simply offered me a better deal." Salespeople at Royal Motors receive a base monthly salary of $1,200 plus 6% of the gross margin on each car. The gross margin is computed as sales price less purchase cost and other costs incurred on a car before it is sold.

Prompted by this discussion, Templin gathered the following data on (1) Harrington and (2) the average for all 48 sales personnel of Western Motors for March 19X4:

	J. D. Harrington	Average for 48 Salespeople
Cars sold	37	21
Average gross margin	$1,100	$450

Required

1. Compute the March 19X4 compensation paid by Western Motors to J. D. Harrington and to the average salesperson. Also compute the total compensation Western Motors paid.
2. Compute the March 19X4 compensation that Western Motors would have paid to Harrington and to the average salesperson if it had used the Royal Motors payment plan. Compute the total compensation Western Motors would have paid.
3. Given an average gross margin per car of $450, at what volume level in cars sold would the Western Motors and Royal Motors plans result in the same compensation paid to each salesperson?
4. Compare and contrast the two compensation plans. Which plan would be better for Western Motors?

Problem 18-3A   *Using the high-low method of cost-function estimation*   **(L.O. 6)**

Like many private schools, Stanford University tries to recover about one-third of its total costs from tuition revenue. The remainder is recovered through endowment income and charitable donations. Stanford is preparing a budgeted income statement for the coming fiscal year, which will end August 31, 19X4. Tuition revenue for 19X3 was $54 million; and for 19X2, $48 million. Total expenses for 19X3 were $165.6 million; and for 19X2, $153.6 million. No tuition rate changes occurred in either 19X2 or 19X3. The tuition rate is not expected to change in 19X4, and tuition revenue is expected to be $60 million.

Required

1. Using tuition revenue as the cost driver (independent variable), compute Stanford's total-expense cost function as implied by the observations in 19X2 and 19X3.
2. On the basis of the cost function estimated in Requirement 1, what total expense should Stanford expect in 19X4?
3. Is tuition revenue the best independent variable for predicting total expenses? As financial vice-president of the university, what two alternative independent variables would you want to investigate?

Problems 18-4A   *Computing cost functions with the high-low, visual-fit, and regression analysis methods*   **(L.O. 6)**

Casey Pacioli, financial analyst at Central Railroad, is analyzing the behavior of monthly operating costs for budgeting purposes. Operating costs include such items as fuel and labor but not the costs of maintaining engines and track. Pacioli has collected a sample of monthly operating costs and track miles hauled (miles clocked by engines that pull railroad cars) for the most recent year, as follows:

Month	Operating Cost	Track Miles Hauled
January	$47,100	3,420
February	50,400	5,310
March	60,900	5,410
April	69,000	8,440
May	74,200	9,320
June	77,400	8,910
July	78,400	8,870
August	98,600	10,980
September	89,500	4,980
October	65,100	5,220
November	48,100	4,480
December	38,600	2,980

Required

1. Plot the data observations, with operating cost as the dependent variable and track miles hauled as the independent variable.
2. Does there appear to be an outlier point? If so, what should Pacioli do with the observation?
3. Visually fit a line to the points. Using the graph, estimate the cost function for total operating cost.
4. Using the high-low method, compute the equation of the line relating operating costs and track miles hauled.
5. The least-squares regression method results in the following cost function: Total operating cost = $30,919 + ($5.40 × track miles hauled). Use the least-squares, visual-fit, and high-low methods to predict total operating cost at a volume of 8,910 track miles hauled. Which is the best prediction?

Problem 18-5A *Interpreting a least-squares regression cost function* *(L.O. 6,7)*

Elliot Bay Tarp and Tent (EBTT) Company has difficulty controlling its use of heavy-duty eyelets, nylon thread, glue, and other low-cost materials. These materials are called "supplies." The company traditionally has regarded supplies as variable costs.

Over the last several months, every time production volume was above average, EBTT incurred a total supplies cost that was less than the budgeted amount. When volume was below average, the cost incurred was greater than budgeted. This pattern led Judy Fouhy, the new accountant, to suspect that part of the supplies cost was fixed. EBTT uses square feet of products (tarps and tents) as its production volume measure.

Fouhy decided to use least-squares regression analysis to explore this issue. She obtained the following regression results with supplies cost as the dependent variable and square feet of products as the independent variable:

$$y \text{ intercept } (a): \$1,800$$
$$\text{Slope coefficient } (b): \ 0.072$$
$$\text{Coefficient of determination } (r^2): \ \ 0.58$$

Required

1. Suppose 100,000 square feet of products are produced in an average

month. What percentage of supplies cost is variable in an average month? What percentage is fixed?

2. Are fluctuations in supplies cost caused by anything other than square feet of products produced? What percentage of the fluctuations are not explained by square feet of products?

3. Assuming that both volume levels are within the relevant range of the cost function, what supplies cost would you predict in a month when 75,000 square feet of products are produced? In a month when 150,000 are produced?

4. In addition to budget versus actual cost comparisons, what else would indicate that supplies is actually a mixed cost?

Problem 18-6A   *Evaluating a mixed-cost function* **(L.O. 7)**

The head of the Consumer Products Manufacturing Department of the Petty Company was concerned about some cost behavior data given to him by the new cost analyst. The analyst's first assignment was to apply regression analysis to various costs in the department.

One regression on monthly data was run with building maintenance cost as the dependent variable and production labor hours as the independent variable. Production workers have two primary responsibilities: operate production machinery and maintain the factory buildings. The cost function and coefficient of determination (r^2) were computed to be:

$$y = \$7,542 - \$0.54x \qquad r^2 = 0.89$$

The cost analyst remarked to his boss, "I suggest that we use the building as intensively as possible to keep maintenance costs down."
Required

1. Compute the building maintenance costs for two months—one in which 4,000 labor-hours are worked, and one in which 6,000 hours are worked. Comment on the results.

2. Is it logical that increased use of the building causes decreased maintenance costs? What mistake did the cost analyst make in evaluating the cost funtion?

3. What could the analyst have done differently to avoid his mistake?

(Group B)

Problem 18-1B   *Analyzing capacity costs to make business decisions: two-year time period* **(L.O. 1,2)**

Harold Read has decided to sell pizza in his home state of Rhode Island. He predicts that the average sales price and variable cost of his pizza will be $5 and $2, respectively. A major decision that he must make is whether to open at one location, in the town of Barrington, or at two—one in Barrington and one in nearby Bristol. Read has located two vacant stores that would serve his purposes well. Each would rent for $25,000 per year, and each would require a two-year lease. He predicts that other fixed costs would total $8,000 per store per year.

Read believes that more pizzas will be demanded each year if he opens two stores. However, he does not expect the two-store demand to be twice the one-store demand, because some customers will drive from Bristol to Barrington if he opens only one store. The predicted number of pizzas sold each year under each alternative course of action is:

	One Store	Two Stores
19X4	33,000	40,000
19X5	46,000	60,000

Required

1. Prepare contribution-margin income statements to determine expected operating income for 19X4 for both the one-store alternative and the two-store alternative.
2. Repeat Requirement 1 for 19X5.
3. Which course of action results in the greater expected operating income for the two-year period? Should Harold Read rent one store or two?

Problem 18-2B *Using knowledge of cost behavior patterns to evaluate different payment plans (L.O. 2,4)*

Grant Newton owns West Coast Marine, a power boat sales company. West Coast Marine has stores in five different cities. For many years, Newton has paid his salespeople a monthly salary plus a bonus for each boat sold. In May 19X4, the monthly salary was $2,000 and the bonus was $100 per boat sold.

In June 19X4, Newton received information that Richard Hughes, one of his best salespersons, was about to resign and join the sales staff at Pacific Marine. When questioned by Newton, Hughes responded, "Pacific simply offered me a better deal." Salespeople at Pacific Marine receive a base monthly salary of $1,000 plus 10% of the contribution margin on each boat (exclusive of bonus).

Prompted by this discussion, Newton gathered the following data on (1) Hughes and (2) the average for all 10 sales personnel of West Coast Marine for May 19X4:

	Richard Hughes	Average for 10 Salespeople
Boats sold	30	20
Average contribution margin	$2,500	$1,500

Required

1. Compute the May 19X4 compensation paid by West Coast Marine to Richard Hughes and to the average salesperson. Also compute the total compensation West Coast Marine paid.
2. Compute the May 19X4 compensation that West Coast Marine would have paid to Hughes and to the average salesperson if it had used the Pacific Marine payment plan. Compute the total compensation West Coast Marine would have paid.
3. Given an average contribution margin per boat of $1,500, at what volume level in boats sold would the West Coast Marine and Pacific Marine plans result in the same compensation paid to each salesperson?
4. Compare and contrast the two compensation plans. Which plan would be better for West Coast Marine?

Problem 18-3B *Using the high-low method of cost-function estimation (L.O. 6)*

The Helping Hand builds houses and sells them at heavily discounted prices to low-income families. The organization tries to recover about 60% of the cost of each house from the buyer. The remainder is provided by private donors.

Helping Hand is preparing a budget for the coming fiscal year, 19X5. Donations for 19X4 totaled $4 million; and for 19X3, $3.2 million. Total expenses for 19X4 were $9.8 million; and for 19X3, $8.2 million. Donations of $5 million are expected in 19X5.

Required

1. Using donations as the cost driver (independent variable), compute Helping Hand's total-expense cost function as implied by the observations in 19X3 and 19X4.
2. On the basis of the cost function estimated in Requirement 1, what total expense should Helping Hand expect in 19X5?
3. Is donations the best independent variable for predicting total expenses? As treasurer of the organization, what alternative independent variables would you want to investigate?

Problem 18-4B *Computing cost functions with the high-low, visual-fit, and regression analysis methods* **(L.O. 6)**

The Brittish Look manufactures and sells a line of sports coats. Michael Bond, the company's cost accountant, is analyzing the behavior of monthly production costs for budgeting purposes. Bond has collected a sample of monthly production costs and coats produced for the most recent year, as follows:

Month	Production Cost	Coats Produced
January	$66,200	342
February	69,500	531
March	80,000	541
April	88,100	844
May	93,300	932
June	96,500	891
July	97,500	887
August	117,700	1,098
September	108,600	498
October	84,200	522
November	67,200	448
December	57,700	298

Required

1. Plot the data observations, with production cost as the dependent variable and costs produced as the independent variable.
2. Does there appear to be an outlier point? If so, what should Bond do with the observation?
3. Visually fit a line to the points. Using the graph, estimate the cost function for total production cost.
4. Using the high-low method, compute the equation of the line relating production costs and coats produced.
5. The least-squares regression method results in the following cost function: Total production cost = $50,019 + ($54 × coats produced). Use the least-squares, visual-fit, and high-low methods to predict total operating cost at a volume of 750 coats. Which is the best prediction?

Problem 18-5B *Interpreting a least-squares regression cost function* **(L.O. 6,7)**

Space Manufacturing Company has been having difficulty budgeting its electricity costs. The company traditionally has regarded these costs as variable, but Dean Haun, the cost accountant, suspects that part of the cost is fixed. In recent months, whenever production volume was above average, electricity cost was less than the budgeted amount. Conversely, when volume was below average, the cost incurred was greater than budgeted.

Haun decided to use least-squares regression analysis to explore this issue. He obtained the following regression results with electricity cost as the dependent variable and tools produced as the independent variable:

$$y \text{ intercept } (a): \$2,000$$
$$\text{Slope coefficient } (b): \quad 0.05$$
$$\text{Coefficient of determination } (r^2): \quad 0.70$$

Required

1. Suppose 50,000 tools are produced in an average month. What percentage of electricity cost is variable in an average month? What percentage is fixed?

2. Are fluctuations in electricity costs caused by anything other than the number of tools produced? What percentage of the fluctuations are not explained by number of tools?

3. Assuming that both volume levels are within the relevant range of the cost function, what electricity cost would you predict in a month when 40,000 tools are produced? In a month when 80,000 are produced?

4. In addition to budget versus actual cost comparisons, what else would indicate that electricity is actually a mixed cost?

Problem 18-6B   *Evaluating a mixed-cost function*   *(L.O. 7)*

Benny Carle, head of the customer-service department of the Corral Electronics Company, is concerned about some cost behavior data given to him by the new cost analyst. The analyst's first assignment was to use regression analysis to develop a cost function for predicting total service department cost. The service department repairs defective products when customers return them. Returns often take place four to five months after sale, and sales volume fluctuates widely from month to month.

The analyst ran a regression with total cost as the dependent variable and number of electronics products sold as the independent variable. The cost function and coefficient of determination (r^2) were computed to be:

$$y = \$6,000 - \$20x \qquad r^2 = 0.75$$

The analyst remarked to Carle, "It looks like the only way to reduce our costs is to sell more products!"

Required

1. Compute total service department cost for two months—one in which 200 products are sold and one in which 250 products are sold. Comment on the results.

2. Is it logical that selling more products causes service department costs to go down? What mistake did the cost analyst make in evaluating the cost function?

3. What could the analyst have done differently to avoid her mistake?

Extending Your Knowledge

Decision Problem

Using Knowledge of Cost Behavior to Make Business Decisions; Trade-offs between Variable and Fixed Costs (L.O. 1,2,4)

Juan Bermudez started Bermudez Marine several years ago to make specialized 21-foot sailboats. These boats have become very popular, and Bermudez sees an opportunity to expand. He is evaluating two courses of action. He could hire additional workers and keep his operations labor-intensive. Alternatively, he could invest in machinery to automate many processes, making operations more capital-intensive.

Bermudez predicts he could sell 400 boats in 19X5 and each year thereafter if he can produce that many. Annual fixed costs for the current capacity of 200 boats per year are $300,000. Variable costs are $7,500 per boat. At a sales price of $10,000 per boat, Bermudez Marine will make $200,000 operating income on revenue of $2,000,000 and expenses of $1,800,000 in 19X4.

To make 400 boats, Bermudez could purchase robotic machines to automate several processes, increasing annual fixed costs to $2,000,000 and reducing variable costs to $4,000 per boat. Alternatively, he could double current operations, leaving variable costs at $7,500 per boat and increasing fixed costs to only $600,000.

Required

1. Calculate the predicted operating income for 19X5 for each alternative course of action under three different predictions of production and sales volume: 300 boats, 400 boats, and 500 boats.
2. Calculate the production and sales volume at which the two alternatives would yield an equal operating income.
3. Comment on how Bermudez's confidence in his prediction of annual sales of 400 boats might affect his decision.

Ethical Issue

Southwestern Bell Telephone Company (SWBT) serves over nine million customers in the five-state region of Texas, Oklahoma, Missouri, Kansas, and Arkansas. The company processes millions of customer receipts (remittances) each month with a system designed both to minimize processing cost and maximize cash flow. To accomplish these objectives, the SWBT centers must quickly pick up, open, extract, sort, prepare, and deposit customer checks several times each day, as they become available at local post offices. Even very short delays can result in sizable increases in the company's banking costs.

Customer envelopes are opened by high-speed machines. They are then sorted manually for appropriate treatment—either standard or some category of "special handling." Suppose that a new machine can automatically extract and sort checks. Each machine costs $90,000 and lasts five years. One machine would be needed for each of SWBT's several processing centers, and each would replace 12 workers.

Required

1. What factors would remittance-processing managers consider in evaluating these machines?
2. Is replacement of human workers with machines ethical? Is replacement of thousands of workers by automated equipment different from replacement of a few dozen?

Chapter 19

Manufacturing Accounting and Job Order Costing

Competition between U.S. manufacturers and their Japanese counterparts continues in many industries, including electronics, robotics, and automobile production. For example, Japan currently enjoys a sizable share of the U.S. auto market, and the Japanese auto manufacturer Toyota forges into the 1990s with visions for improving operations through robotics.

The man behind Toyota's automation drive is Tadaaki Jagawa, the 54-year-old director in charge of production engineering. He has high hopes for what robots and computers can do. By [next year], he wants 85% of the work in Toyota's engine assembly plants to be mechanized, up from 73% now. And he says automated design and manufacturing could cut to 22 months from 24 the time it takes to translate a car from concept sketch to start of production.

SOURCE: Joseph B. White and Clay Chandler, "Pressed by All Sides, Hard-Driving Toyota Trims Back Its Goals," *The Wall Street Journal*, May 19, 1992, p. A8.

This chapter shifts gears to focus on an important sector of business: manufacturing. Previous chapters dealt with merchandisers that acquired their inventory through purchases. This chapter and the next show how manufacturers account for the cost of the goods they produce. Consider the distinction between an automobile dealer and Toyota, which manufacturers the autos.

An automobile dealer sells the cars to the public. Like all merchandisers, the auto dealer buys its inventory ready for resale to customers. Determining the cost of each automobile is relatively easy. Cost is the price that the dealer pays for the cars plus the freight and insurance charges incurred in transporting them to the dealership.

How do we account for the companies—Toyota, General Motors, Ford, and others—that make the autos the dealers sell? Manufacturers use their labor force and factory assets to shape raw materials into finished products. Their manufacturing processes begin with materials—metal, plastics, and related items. These materials are molded, cut, and riveted into automobiles. The process of converting these materials into finished products makes it more difficult to measure a manufacturer's inventory cost than that of a merchandiser.

In this and the next chapter we turn our attention to manufacturers, with emphasis on their cost accounting systems. The first part of this chapter introduces manufacturing accounting. The second part discusses a particular system for controlling and determining a manufacturer's costs—job order costing.

Manufacturing and the Value Chain

Before proceeding, let us regard manufacturing in perspective. Consider a company like Apple Computer. Many people would describe Apple (or IBM or Hewlett-Packard) as a manufacturing company. More accurately, Apple may be described as a company that does manufacturing. Why? Because manufacturing is only one of its major business functions. Indeed, Apple's marketing costs exceed its manufacturing costs. Companies that do manufacturing also do many other things, as illustrated by the value chain shown on page 890.

In talking about the value chain, managers sometimes use the image of a river to describe the flow of value. Research, development, and product design are "upstream." That is, they occur prior to manufacturing. Similarly, marketing, distribution, and customer service are "downstream" in the sense that they follow manufacturing.

Considered in relationship to one another, the two upstream functions, manufacturing, and the three downstream functions form a chain. A **value chain** is the sequence of all business functions in which value is added to a firm's products or services.

Modern companies are concerned about the value chain taken as a whole. They aim to control the total costs of the entire chain. For example, companies may willingly spend more in manufacturing to enhance product quality and therefore reduce the customer service costs of honoring product warranties later on. Even though the manufacturing costs are higher then, the total costs of the product—as measured by the entire value chain—may be lower.

Traditionally, cost accounting has been associated with manufacturing. Why? Because manufacturers must determine the costs of the products they make, and accountants can measure these costs. Nevertheless, the basic concepts of how to plan and control costs and how to compute the costs of products and services are applicable to the entire value chain.

Many companies commonly regarded as manufacturers do little if any manufacturing themselves. Instead, they subcontract manufacturing to suppliers. Examples are shoe companies like Nike or Reebok. Almost all their shoes are manufactured by low-wage factories in places like Taiwan and South Korea. Nike and Reebok are intermediaries between the manufacturer and the consumer. Nike's and Reebok's principal functions are product design and marketing.

Objectives of a Cost System

Companies that do manufacturing have developed cost accounting systems to serve more than one purpose simultaneously:

Cost control—to help plan and control the manufacturing function

Product costing—to compute manufacturing product costs for financial statements

Product costing—to compute manufacturing product costs for pricing and product-mix decisions. The full cost of a product extends beyond manufacturing and encompasses all the upstream and downstream business functions in the value chain.

Exhibit 19-1 illustrates the dual objectives of *cost control* and *product costing* for an auto manufacturer like Toyota.

An important focus of cost accounting is the control of cost. Businesses achieve cost control through the evaluation of management performance. Managers strive for the maximum output of finished products at the minimum total cost to the company—not only of manufacturing but of all the functions in the value chain. The company's actual manufacturing product cost and

EXHIBIT 19-1   *Dual Objectives of a Manufacturing Cost Accounting System*

output provide the information the company needs to measure manufacturing performance—how well a manager succeeds in controlling costs while manufacturing goods.

Product costing—determining the cost to the company of each of its products—is a primary objective in manufacturing cost accounting. The company must know its product costs in order to measure inventory values (and so the cost of goods sold) and profitability (revenues minus expenses, which include the cost of goods sold).

Product costs for the entire value chain frequently help managers decide on pricing: How much does the manufacturer charge the merchandiser for its goods? The answer depends in large part on how much it costs to manufacture and market these goods. Also, managers must determine which products to emphasize. For example, General Motors managers may learn that the company is losing money on commercial vehicles, and this information may lead the company to drop that product line. This decision depends on accurate product cost data for each product.

Our discussion in this chapter centers on product costing. Chapter 21 focuses on cost control. We will now take a closer look at manufacturing inventory.

Manufacturing Accounts

Inventory Accounts—Materials, Work in Process, and Finished Goods

Inventory considerations differ between merchandiser and manufacturer. Merchandisers need only one category of inventory for the finished goods they buy and sell. By contrast, manufacturers have three inventory accounts, as we discuss in a moment. Exhibit 19-2 compares the inventory accounts of a manufacturing company and a merchandising company. *Note that the two types of business have identical balance sheets except for the inventory accounts.*

OBJECTIVE 1

Prepare the financial statements of a manufacturing company

Manufacturing Firm			Merchandising Firm		
Current assets:			Current assets:		
Cash		$ X,XXX	Cash		$ X,XXX
Short-term			Short-term		
investments ...		X,XXX	investments ...		X,XXX
Receivables......		X,XXX	Receivables......		X,XXX
Inventories:			**Inventories......**		**13,000**
Materials	$1,000		Prepaid expenses		X,XXX
Work in					
process	4,000				
Finished goods	8,000				
Total					
inventories...		13,000			
Prepaid expenses		X,XXX			
Total current			Total current		
assets.........		$XX,XXX	assets.........		$XX,XXX

The **Materials Inventory,** also called **Raw Materials Inventory,** account holds the cost of materials on hand and intended for use in the manufacturing process. An auto manufacturer's materials include metal, plastics, glass, and fabric. Raw materials for Bethlehem Steel include iron ore, coal, and chemicals. Materials—kept in vats, bins, or other storage areas—are collectively called *stores.*

The **Work in Process Inventory** account gives the cost of the goods that are in the manufacturing process and not yet complete. For an auto manufacturer, partially completed cars and trucks make up its work in process inventory. For a petroleum refiner, work in process is the crude oil being distilled into gasoline, different grade oils, and other products. Work in process inventory is also called *work in progress* and *goods in process.*

The cost of completed goods that have not yet been sold makes up the **Finished Goods Inventory** account. Manufacturers store finished goods in warehouses, tanks, on parking lots, or whatever storage facility is appropriate to the particular type of inventory. Finished goods are what the manufacturer sells to a merchandising business. For example, Procter & Gamble manufactures Tide soap and Crest toothpaste, which it sells to Safeway, K mart, and other stores. The Finished Goods account of a manufacturer, then, becomes the Inventory account of a merchandiser.

Materials, work in process, and finished goods are assets to the manufacturer and so are reported as current assets on the balance sheet, as Exhibit 19-2 shows. Our goal is to take the information in these inventory accounts to compute the cost of goods manufactured.

Cost of Goods Manufactured

You know the merchandiser's computation of cost of goods sold: beginning inventory + purchases − ending inventory = cost of goods sold. All of a merchandiser's inventory is finished goods. The merchandiser has no materials or work in process inventory. A manufacturer, however, produces its own inventory. **Cost of goods manufactured** is the manufacturer's counterpart to the merchandiser's Purchases account. Therefore, cost of goods manufactured

EXHIBIT 19-3 *Cost of Goods Manufactured on the Income Statement*

Manufacturing Firm		Merchandising Firm	
Sales revenue	$XX,XXX	Sales revenue	$XX,XXX
Cost of goods sold:		Cost of goods sold:	
Beginning finished		Beginning	
goods inventory .	$ 6,000	inventory	$ 6,000
Cost of goods		**Purchases**	**42,000**
manufactured ...	**42,000**	Goods available	
Goods available		for sale	48,000
for sale	48,000	Ending inventory ..	(8,000)
Ending finished		Cost of goods sold .	40,000
goods inventory .	(8,000)	Gross margin........	X,XXX
Cost of goods sold .	40,000	Operating expenses:	
Gross margin........	X,XXX	Marketing.........	X,XXX
Operating expenses:		General	X,XXX
Marketing.........	X,XXX	Total operating	
General	X,XXX	expenses........	X,XXX
Total operating		Net income	$ X,XXX
expenses........	X,XXX		
Net income	$ X,XXX		

represents the cost of *finished* goods that the business has produced. Exhibit 19-3 shows that Cost of Goods Manufactured takes the place of Purchases in computing cost of goods sold. *Otherwise, a manufacturer's income statement is identical to the income statement of a merchandiser.*

Purchases, for a merchandiser, is simply the total cost of all goods bought for resale during the current period. Cost of goods manufactured is more complex. Before we illustrate how to compute this amount, we must introduce some new terms.

Definitions of Key Manufacturing Terms

Direct Materials.   To be considered **direct materials,** materials must meet two requirements: (1) the materials must become a physical part of the finished product, and (2) the cost of the materials must be separately and conveniently traceable through the manufacturing process to finished goods. Consider again an automobile manufacturer. The body frames, the side moldings, glass, and interior fabrics are among the direct materials. We can trace them directly to the finished automobile. Also, we can follow their costs from the purchase of raw materials through work in process to finished goods.

Direct Labor.   **Direct labor** is the compensation of the employees who physically convert materials into the company's products. For Toyota, direct labor is the pay of employees who work on production lines manufacturing automobiles. For a shoe manufacturer, direct labor includes the wages of the machine operators and the persons who actually assemble the shoes. The efforts of these persons can be traced *directly* to finished goods.

Factory Overhead.   **Factory overhead** includes all manufacturing costs other than direct materials and direct labor. Examples include indirect materials, indirect labor, and other costs, such as factory utilities, repairs, maintenance, rent, insurance, and property taxes and depreciation on the factory building and equipment. Factory overhead is also called *manufacturing overhead* and, more accurately, *indirect manufacturing cost.*

Indirect Materials. The nuts, bolts, and lubricants used in the manufacture of cars and trucks are also materials that become physical parts of the finished product. However, compared with the cost of the body frames and side moldings, the costs of nuts, bolts, and lubricants are minor. Measuring the cost of these low-priced materials is difficult for a single automobile. How would a supervisor figure the cost of a squirt of lubricant? Of the silicone sealer around the windshield? And how useful would this detailed information be? We call the material whose cost cannot conveniently be traced directly to particular finished products **indirect material.** Indirect materials are accounted for as part of factory overhead cost.

Indirect Labor. Other factory labor costs are classified as **indirect labor.** These costs are difficult to trace to specific products. Examples include the pay of forklift operators, janitors, and plant guards. Forklift operators move a wide variety of materials and finished goods around the factory. Plant guards provide security for the entire building. Indirect labor, like indirect materials, is a part of factory overhead.

Two of the major cost elements are sometimes combined in cost terminology as follows. **Prime costs** consist of direct materials plus direct labor. **Conversion costs** consist of direct labor plus factory overhead.

OBJECTIVE 2

Compute cost of goods manufactured

EXHIBIT 19-4 *Statement of Cost of Goods Manufactured*

Autos Unlimited Statement of Cost of Goods Manufactured Month Ended December 31, 19X3			
			(Thousands)
Beginning work in process inventory			$ 5,000
Add: Direct materials used:			
Beginning inventory	$ 9,000		
Purchases of materials	27,000		
Available for use	36,000		
Ending inventory	(22,000)		
Direct materials used		$14,000	
Direct labor		19,000	
Factory overhead:			
Indirect materials	$ 1,500		
Indirect labor	3,500		
Depreciation—factory building	2,000		
Depreciation—factory equipment	1,000		
Utilities	2,500		
Insurance	1,000		
Property tax	500	12,000	
Total manufacturing costs incurred during the month			45,000
Total manufacturing costs to account for			50,000
Less: ending work in process inventory			(4,000)
Cost of goods manufactured			$46,000

$$\text{Prime costs} \begin{cases} \text{Direct materials} \\ \text{Direct labor} \\ \text{Factory overhead} \end{cases} \Big\} \text{Conversion costs}$$

Exhibit 19-4 shows the computation of cost of goods manufactured. This statement of cost of goods manufactured is an internal statement, prepared by cost accountants for the business's managers.

Computation of cost of goods manufactured starts with the work in process inventory ($5,000) at the beginning of the period. These goods become complete in the manufacturing process during the current period, so their cost becomes part of cost of goods manufactured. To this amount we add the three components of manufacturing cost: direct materials used ($14,000), direct labor ($19,000), and factory overhead cost ($12,000). Exhibit 19-4 looks closely at direct materials used. Direct labor is simply the total direct labor cost incurred during the period. Factory overhead is the sum of various costs. Direct materials used, direct labor, and factory overhead total $45,000, which is the **total manufacturing cost** incurred during the period. We subtract ending work in process inventory—because cost of goods manufactured refers to the cost of *finished goods* manufactured—to get $46,000.

Exhibit 19-5 diagrams the flow of costs through a manufacturing system. It reveals a similar computational format at all three stages—direct materials, work in process, and finished goods. The cost of direct materials used is beginning direct materials plus purchases minus the ending balance. Observe that the final amount at each stage flows into the next stage. Thus, the cost of direct materials used becomes part of cost of goods manufactured, which in turn is included in cost of goods sold. Trace the direct materials and work in process portions of the exhibit in Exhibit 19-4, which gives more details for computing costs of goods manufactured.

EXHIBIT 19-5   *Flow of Costs Through a Manufacturing Company—Three Similar Computations*

Direct Materials	Work in Process	Finished Goods
Beginning inventory + Purchases	Beginning inventory + Direct materials used Direct labor Factory overhead	Beginning inventory + Cost of goods manufactured
= Direct materials available for use − Ending inventory	= Subtotal − Ending inventory	= Goods available for sale − Ending inventory
= Direct materials used	= Cost of goods manufactured	= Cost of goods sold

The authors are indebted to Judith Cassidy for this presentation.

Inventoriable Costs and Period Costs

The rules of financial accounting have a major influence on accounting for manufacturing costs. For example, the manufacturing costs are **inventoriable costs**, which are all costs of a product regarded as an asset for financial reporting under generally accepted accounting principles. Inventoriable costs become expenses (in the form of cost of goods sold) only when the units in inventory are sold. Of course, the sales may occur in the same accounting period as manufacture or in a subsequent period. Manufacturing costs are regarded as inventoriable because direct materials, direct labor, and factory overhead costs are necessary to obtain the physical products in inventory.

All costs other than manufacturing costs are regarded as immediate expenses. These costs are often called **period costs** because they are expensed in the period in which they are incurred. They are never traced through the inventory accounts. Examples are research, marketing, and distribution expenses.

The distinction between inventoriable costs and period costs is illustrated as follows:

The boxes also help distinguish between companies that do manufacturing and those that do not. For example, a retailer or wholesaler buys goods for resale without changing their basic form. The *only* inventoriable cost is the cost of merchandise. All labor, depreciation, insurance, utilities, and other operating costs are period costs. In contrast, any of these costs that are related to the manufacturing effort are inventoriable for companies that do manufacturing.

Note that a manufacturing company may classify some labor, depreciation, utilities, and other operating costs as inventoriable costs and some as period costs. All such costs identified with the manufacturing function are inventoriable costs. Those costs identified with marketing or other functions in the value chain are period costs.

Various Meanings of Product Costs

Accountants frequently use the term *product costs* to describe those costs allocated to units of product. **Product cost** is a general term that denotes different costs allocated to products for different purposes. As Exhibit 19-6 shows, accountants should use *manufacturing product costs* to denote *inventoriable costs*.

The term *full product costs* denotes a set of complete product costs encompassing the entire value chain. For decisions regarding choices and pricing of products, managers want the cost of products to include all (or nearly all) the costs of the entire business.

Perpetual and Periodic Inventory Systems _____

Chapter 8 compared the accounting for inventories under the periodic system and the perpetual system. Most manufacturers use the perpetual system because they need a continuous record of materials, work in process, and

EXHIBIT 19-6 *Different Meanings of the Term "Product Costs" and Their Relations to the Value Chain*

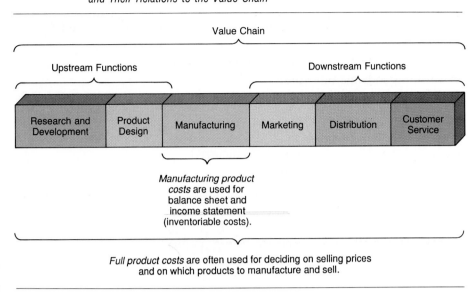

finished goods on hand. The perpetual records help managers control operations and also provide the data for interim financial statements. Physical counts of inventories are taken at least annually to check the accuracy of the records.

Manufacturers that use a periodic inventory system follow the general accounting procedures that merchandisers use, as discussed in Chapter 8. In this chapter we concentrate on the perpetual system because it is more commonly used by manufacturers.

Summary Questions for Your Review

1. What inventory accounts does a manufacturer have that a merchandising entity does not need?
2. What is the manufacturer's counterpart to a merchandiser's Purchases account?
3. Show how to compute cost of goods manufactured. Use the following amounts: direct materials used ($24,000), direct labor ($9,000), factory overhead ($17,000), and work in process, beginning ($5,000) and ending ($4,000).
4. Diagram the flow of costs through a manufacturing company.
5. Identify the following as either an inventoriable cost or a period cost:
   a. Depreciation on factory equipment
   b. Depreciation on salespersons' automobiles
   c. Insurance on factory building
   d. Factory manager's salary
   e. Marketing manager's salary

1. Materials Inventory, Work in Process Inventory, and Finished Goods Inventory

2. Cost of goods manufactured

3. Cost of goods manufactured:

Beginning work in process inventory		$ 5,000
Add: Direct materials used...................	$24,000	
Direct labor	9,000	
Factory overhead	17,000	
Total manufacturing costs incurred during the period		50,000
Total manufacturing costs to account for		55,000
Less: Ending work in process inventory		(4,000)
Cost of goods manufactured		$51,000

4. Flow of costs through a manufacturing company:

Direct Materials	Work in Process	Finished Goods
Beginning inventory + Purchases	Beginning inventory + Direct materials used Direct labor Factory overhead	Beginning inventory + Cost of goods manufactured
= Direct materials available for use − Ending inventory	= Subtotal − Ending inventory	= Goods available for sale − Ending inventory
= Direct materials used	= Cost of goods manufactured	= Cost of goods sold

5. a. Inventoriable cost; b. Period cost; c. Inventoriable cost; d. Inventoriable cost; e. Period cost

Job Order Costing

There are two main types of accounting systems for product costing: *job order costing* and *process costing*. This chapter discusses job order costing, and the next chapter covers process costing. Because these chapters deal primarily with inventory costs, our discussions emphasize inventoriable costs, not period costs. *Manufacturers account for and control period costs the same way that merchandisers do.*

Job order costing is an accounting system used by companies that manufacture products (1) as individual units or (2) in distinct batches that receive varying degrees of attention and skill. Industries using job order costing include aircraft, furniture, construction, and machinery. Their inventory items are unique or few of a kind, differing from the identical products that roll off a production line, such as tubes of toothpaste, boxes of cereal, and rolls of carpet. Mass-produced inventories are accounted for by the process costing system, discussed in the next chapter.

The essential feature of job order costing (often shortened to *job costing*) is the allocation of costs to a specific job. (The job may be a production order, work order, project, or batch.) The job may consist of a single unit, like a bridge built by a construction contractor, or a group of similar units in a distinct batch, like 10 recliner chairs built by a furniture manufacturer. We illustrate job order costing for a manufacturing situation, but the system applies to other types of business, such as an auto-repair shop (the job is one automobile needing repair), a research organization (the job is a research project), and an accounting firm (the job is a tax return).

In a job cost system, the job is the focus, so the manufacturer accumulates materials, labor, and overhead costs by job. Cost control is the key to earning a profit on each job. If cost is too high, profit is reduced or eliminated. Managers monitor each job to help ensure that its cost stays within the budgeted limits.

Job Costing Illustrated

Consider the Ramirez Furniture Company, which has a job order costing system with the following inventories on December 31, 19X4:

<table>
<tr><td>Materials inventory (many kinds)</td><td>$20,000</td></tr>
<tr><td>Work in process inventory (5 jobs)</td><td>29,000</td></tr>
<tr><td>Finished goods inventory (unsold units from 2 jobs)</td><td>12,000</td></tr>
</table>

OBJECTIVE 3
Use job order costing information

The following is a summary of relevant transactions for the year 19X5:

<table>
<tr><td>1.</td><td>Materials purchased on account</td><td>$320,000</td></tr>
<tr><td>2.</td><td>Direct materials requisitioned for manufacturing</td><td>285,000</td></tr>
<tr><td></td><td>Indirect materials requisitioned for manufacturing</td><td>40,000</td></tr>
<tr><td>3.</td><td>Factory wages incurred</td><td>335,000</td></tr>
<tr><td>4.</td><td>Direct labor on jobs</td><td>250,000</td></tr>
<tr><td></td><td>Indirect labor to support factory activities</td><td>85,000</td></tr>
<tr><td>5.</td><td>Factory overhead (depreciation on plant and equipment)</td><td>50,000</td></tr>
<tr><td>6.</td><td>Factory overhead (factory utilities)</td><td>20,000</td></tr>
<tr><td>7.</td><td>Factory overhead (factory insurance)</td><td>5,000</td></tr>
<tr><td>8.</td><td>Factory overhead (property taxes—factory)</td><td>10,000</td></tr>
<tr><td>9.</td><td>Factory overhead applied to jobs</td><td>200,000</td></tr>
<tr><td>10.</td><td>Cost of goods completed and transferred to finished goods inventory</td><td>740,000</td></tr>
<tr><td>11.</td><td>Sales on account</td><td>996,000</td></tr>
<tr><td></td><td>Cost of goods sold</td><td>734,000</td></tr>
</table>

The accounting for these transactions will now be explained, step by step.

Job Cost Record

The bulk of the work in cost accounting is a detailed recording and summarization of source documents such as requisitions, time tickets, and invoices. The document used to accumulate and control cost in a job order system is a **job cost record**. This cost record lists the materials, labor, and overhead costs charged to the job. It is the basic internal document used by management to control the manufacturing costs of products in this system. Exhibit 19-7 illustrates a job cost record. It includes sections for direct materials, direct labor, and overhead costs.

EXHIBIT 19-7 *Job Cost Record*

Job Cost Record

Job No.   293

Customer Name and Address   Macy's New York City

Job Description   10 recliner chairs

Date	Direct Materials		Direct Labor		Factory Overhead Costs		
	Requisition Numbers	Amount	Time Ticket Numbers	Amount	Date	Rate	Amount
Date Promised 7–31			Date Started 7–24		Date Completed 7–29		
19X5 7-24	334	$ 90	236,251,258	$150	7-29	120% of Direct labor	$480
25	338	180	264,269,273,291	200			
28	347	230	305	50			

Overall Cost Summary

Direct materials . . . . . $ 500
Direct labor   400
Factory overhead   480

| Totals | | $500 | | $400 | Total Job Cost . . . . . . | | $1,380 |

This cost record shows that for Job 293, the direct materials cost $500, direct labor cost $400, and factory overhead cost $480, for a total of $1,380. Each chair cost the manufacturer $138 ($1,380/10). Managers would use this information by comparing these actual costs with budgeted amounts. Suppose the direct materials budget for this job was $470. The $500 actual cost of direct materials exceeds budget, so managers would determine the reason for the cost overrun and seek to improve future performance. The remainder of the chapter discusses how to account for the direct materials, direct labor, and factory overhead costs.

The job cost record in Exhibit 19-7 is the basic record for product costing. A file of current job cost records is the subsidiary ledger for the general ledger account, Work in Process Inventory. As each job begins, a job cost record is prepared. As units are worked on, costs are applied to the products. When the job is completed, its cost is transferred to Finished Goods Inventory. We now illustrate these accounting procedures.

Accounting for Materials in a Job Cost System

OBJECTIVE 4

Account for materials in a job order costing system

Manufacturing companies that use job order costing tend to have relatively low inventories. Only when they receive an order do they acquire the added materials needed to fill the order, produce the goods, and deliver the merchandise. Suppose Ramirez, our furniture manufacturer, receives an order for 10 recliner chairs. The company may need to buy additional lumber, so Ramirez sends a *purchase order* to a lumber supplier.

In practice, general ledger entries are made monthly. To offer a sweeping overview, however, we use a summary entry for the entire year 19X5. Our first entry is for purchases of materials (data from page 899):

1. Materials Inventory 320,000

     Accounts Payable   320,000

Ramirez receives the lumber and stores it. Control over materials in storage is established with a subsidiary materials ledger. This ledger holds perpetual inventory records, which list the quantity and the cost of manufacturing materials received and used. They show the cost of materials on hand at all times. Exhibit 19-8 shows a materials ledger record for the lumber (only) that goes into the manufacture of chairs.

Materials received are logged in by receiving report number (abbreviated as *Rec. Report No.* in Exhibit 19-8). Materials used in the product are recorded by materials requisition number (*Mat. Req. No.*). Management can use these underlying data to follow the flow of materials through the production process and so control operations on a day-to-day basis.

EXHIBIT 19-8 *Materials Ledger Record*

Materials Ledger Record

Item No.   B-220   Description   Lumber/Recliner chairs

	Received				Used				Balance		
Date	Rec. Report No.	Units	Price	Total Price	Mat. Req. No.	Units	Price	Total Price	Units	Price	Total Price
19X5 7-20									30	$9.00	$270
7-23	678	20	$9.00	$180					50	9.00	450
7-24					334	10	$9.00	$90	40	9.00	360

The general ledger has a Materials Inventory account. This account is supported by a subsidiary ledger—the materials ledger—that includes a separate record for each raw material. Exhibit 19-9 illustrates the general ledger account and the materials ledger for Ramirez. The balance of Materials Inventory in the general ledger equals the sum of the balances in the materials ledger.

After materials are purchased and stored, the manufacturing process is set in motion by a document called a **materials requisition,** the formal title for a request prepared by manufacturing personnel. In effect, they ask that the lumber be moved from storage to the factory so work can begin. Exhibit 19-10 illustrates a materials requisition for the lumber needed to manufacture the 10 recliner chairs that make up job 293. (See the job description in Exhibit 19-7 and the "Used" section in Exhibit 19-8.) The details in materials requisitions are posted to job cost records.

Direct and Indirect Materials.   To introduce the main points of manufacturing accounting, the first half of this chapter omitted some of the detailed procedures. One such step is the way to account for *direct* materials separately

EXHIBIT 19-9 *Materials Inventory Accounts*

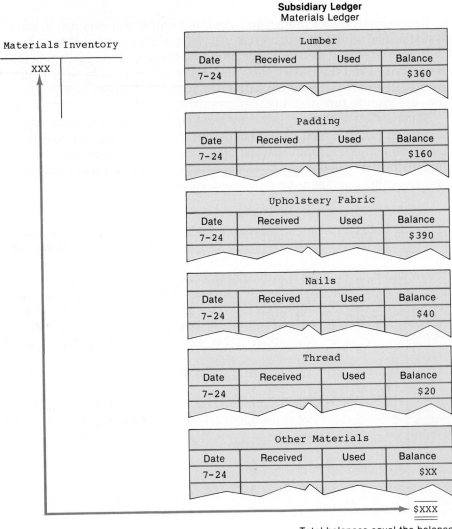

Subsidiary Ledger
Materials Ledger

Materials Inventory

XXX

Lumber			
Date	Received	Used	Balance
7-24			$360

Padding			
Date	Received	Used	Balance
7-24			$160

Upholstery Fabric			
Date	Received	Used	Balance
7-24			$390

Nails			
Date	Received	Used	Balance
7-24			$40

Thread			
Date	Received	Used	Balance
7-24			$20

Other Materials			
Date	Received	Used	Balance
7-24			$XX

$XXX

Total balances equal the balance
in the general ledger account.

from *indirect* materials. Recall that the cost of indirect materials is part of Factory Overhead. The flow of materials costs is diagrammed as (data from page 899):

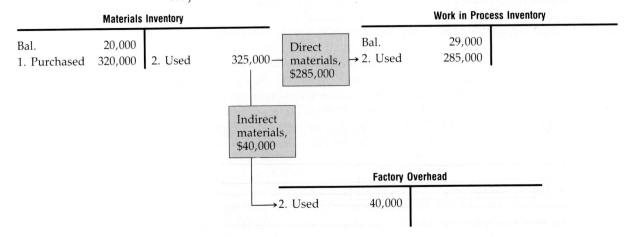

Materials Inventory

Bal.	20,000		
1. Purchased	320,000	2. Used	325,000

Direct materials, $285,000

Indirect materials, $40,000

Work in Process Inventory

Bal.	29,000		
2. Used	285,000		

Factory Overhead

2. Used	40,000

EXHIBIT 19-10 *Materials Requisition*

Materials Requisition No. 334				
Date 7-24-X5			Job No. 293	
Item No.	Item	Quantity	Unit Price	Amount
B-220	Lumber/Recliner chairs	10	$9.00	$90

Materials Inventory is debited for the cost of all materials purchased, direct *and* indirect. Observe that the Materials Inventory account in Exhibit 19-9 includes the cost of direct materials—lumber, padding, and upholstery fabric—and the cost of indirect materials—nails and thread. When either type of materials is used in production, Materials Inventory is credited. For direct materials, the debit is made directly to Work in Process Inventory. For indirect materials, the debit is made to Factory Overhead. (Recall that factory overhead includes all manufacturing costs other than direct materials and direct labor.)

Of course, the furniture manufacturer will work on many jobs over the course of the accounting period. At regular intervals (commonly a month but for our illustration a year), accountants collect the data from the materials requisitions to make a single journal entry, like the following 19X5 entry for Ramirez:

2.	Work in Process Inventory	285,000	
	Factory Overhead	40,000	
	Materials Inventory		325,000

As Exhibit 19-10 indicates, $90 of the direct materials relates to job 293. The Ramirez computer would enter the $90 on the job cost record.

Job Cost Record

Job. No.   293

Customer Name and Address   Macy's New York City

Job Description   10 recliner chairs

Date Promised 7-31		Date Started 7-24		Date Completed		
Date	Direct Materials		Direct Labor		Factory Overhead Costs		
	Requisition Numbers	Amount	Time Ticket Numbers	Amount	Date	Rate	Amount
19X5							
7-24	334	$90					

Overall Cost Summary

Direct materials . . . . . . $
Direct labor . . . .
Factory overhead . . . . .

Total Job Cost . . . . $

Totals

Accounting for Labor in a Job Cost System

OBJECTIVE 5

Account for labor in a job order costing system

Control over labor cost in a job cost system is established through time tickets and payroll registers, as discussed in Chapter 10. Exhibit 19-11 illustrates a time ticket used in a job cost system. Managers use its data to charge labor cost to a particular job.

The **labor time ticket** identifies the employee, the hours spent on a particular job, and the labor cost charged to the job. Time tickets are accumulated by job to determine the labor cost to be allocated to each job.

The company's entry for 19X5 for all factory wages for all jobs is

3. Factory Wages..................................... 335,000
      Wages Payable 335,000

This entry records the actual labor cost incurred. The separation of direct labor and indirect labor is accomplished as shown in the accompanying diagram.

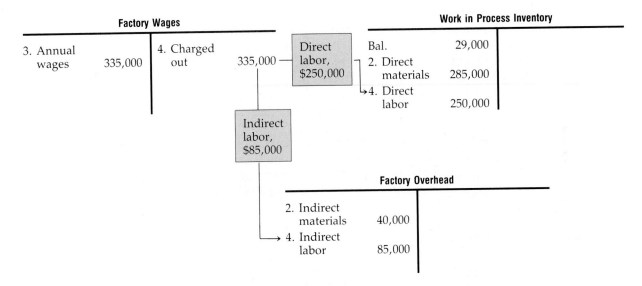

Direct and Indirect Labor.   After the factory wages have been recorded, direct labor is debited directly to Work in Process Inventory. Indirect labor

EXHIBIT 19-11   *Labor Time Ticket*

	Labor Time Ticket	No. 251
EMPLOYEE Jay Barlow		Date 7-24
JOB 293		

Time:		Rate $8.00
Started	1:00	Cost of labor
Stopped	8:30	charged to job $60.00
Elapsed	7:30	

Employee   *Jay Barlow*

Supervisor   *G. Dean Childres*

passes through the Factory Overhead account en route to Work in Process Inventory. The transfer of labor cost to production results in a credit to the Factory Wages account. The following entry allocates factory wages to Work in Process Inventory and Factory Overhead:

4. Work in Process Inventory 250,000
   Factory Overhead............................ 85,000
        Factory Wages 335,000

This entry brings the balance in Factory Wages to zero, its transferred balance now allocated between Work in Process Inventory (direct labor) and Factory Overhead (indirect labor).

Assume that $150 of the direct labor cost relates to Job 293. The Ramirez computer would enter Job 293's direct labor on the job cost record. The $150 amount in the accompanying job cost record includes Jay Barlow's wages of $60 (ticket 251, Exhibit 19-11) and the labor costs entered onto time tickets 236 and 258.

Job Cost Record							

Job No. ___293___

Customer Name and Address   Macy's, New York City

Job Description   10 recliner chairs

Date Promised 7-31		Date Started 7-24		Date Completed			
Date	**Direct Materials**		**Direct Labor**		**Factory Overhead Costs**		
	Requisition Numbers	Amount	Time Ticket Numbers	Amount	Date	Rate	Amount
19X5 7-24	334	$ 90	236,251,258	$150			
					Overall Cost Summary		
					Direct materials..... $		
					Direct labor........		
					Factory overhead....		
Totals					Total Job Cost...... $		

The Work in Process Inventory account now contains the cost of direct materials and direct labor charged to Job 293—and the costs of many other jobs as well. Work in Process Inventory serves as a control account, with the job cost records giving the supporting details for each job. The balance in Work in Process Inventory should equal the total of the individual job costs, in the same manner illustrated for Materials Inventory in Exhibit 19-9. The job cost records thus serve as a subsidiary ledger for the general ledger balance in Work in Process Inventory.

We summarize the accounting for materials and labor just illustrated:

Work in process inventory	=	**General ledger (usually monthly totals only)**
↑		↑
Job cost records	=	**Subsidiary ledger (perhaps daily summaries)**
↑		↑
Material requisitions and time tickets	=	**Source documents (minute-to-minute, hour-to-hour records)**

We see that accounting data are most condensed in the general ledger and most detailed in the source documents.

In practice, the daily accounting duties are carried out using source documents and subsidiary ledgers. Copies of the source documents are independently summarized and are usually journalized and posted to the general ledger only once a month.

Accounting for Factory Overhead in a Job Cost System

Materials requisitions and labor time tickets make it easy to identify direct materials and direct labor with a specific job. Factory overhead, on the other hand, includes a variety of costs that cannot be linked to a particular job. How do we allocate overhead cost to jobs?

Overhead costs are recorded as incurred. The following entries—depreciation on plant and equipment, factory utilities, insurance, and property taxes—are typical. Note that all these overhead costs are debited to a single account—Factory Overhead in the general ledger. The account titles in parentheses in the following entries indicate the subsidiary accounts that are debited in an overhead subsidiary ledger. Budgeting these individual items and then keeping track of their actual amounts help managers control overhead costs.

5. Factory Overhead (Depreciation—Plant and
   Equipment) 50,000
       Accumulated Depreciation—Plant and
       Equipment 50,000

6. Factory Overhead (Factory Utilities) 20,000
       Cash..................................... 20,000

7. Factory Overhead (Factory Insurance) 5,000
       Prepaid Insurance—Factory 5,000

8. Factory Overhead (Property Taxes—Factory) 10,000
       Property Tax Payable..................... 10,000

The Factory Overhead account now contains all the overhead costs of the period:

Factory Overhead		
2. Indirect materials	40,000	
4. Indirect labor	85,000	
5. Depreciation—plant and equipment	50,000	
6. Factory utilities	20,000	
7. Factory insurance	5,000	
8. Property taxes—factory	10,000	
Total actual overhead cost	210,000	

It would be virtually impossible to say that a specific amount of overhead (for example, the cost of heating the factory) was incurred on any particular job. Yet factory overhead costs certainly add to the costs of producing goods. We now discuss how accountants apply overhead in job costing.

Management wants to tie overhead cost to the costs of manufacturing the business's different products. After all, indirect materials, indirect labor, and all the other individual accounts that make up factory overhead contribute to product costs. And if product costs are to help management in product pricing, income determination, and inventory valuation, they must be timely as well as accurate.

The most accurate application of overhead could be made only at the end of the year, after actual results are determined. However, this timing would be too late. Managers want product-cost information throughout the year, not only at the end of the period. To meet these needs, accountants usually budget overhead application rates—that is, they compute a rate in advance of production. The usual steps in applying factory overhead using an annual averaging process follow.

1. Select a **cost application base,** which is a common denominator linking costs among all products. Ideally, this application base should be the primary cost driver, the best available measure of the cause-and-effect relationship between overhead costs and production volume. In many companies direct labor costs rise and fall proportionately with changes in production volume, and direct labor dollars or direct labor hours are chosen as the cost application base. In companies with highly automated production processes, labor is less important, and the cost allocation base is often machine hours.

2. Prepare a budget for the planning period, ordinarily a year. The two key items are (a) budgeted total overhead and (b) budgeted total volume of the cost application base, which is direct labor cost in our Ramirez illustration.

3. Compute the **budgeted factory overhead rate** by dividing the total budgeted overhead by the cost application base.

4. Obtain the actual application base data (such as direct labor cost or machine hours) as the year unfolds.

5. Apply the budgeted overhead to the jobs by multiplying the budgeted rate times the actual application base data for each job.

6. At the end of the year, account for any differences between the amount of overhead actually incurred and the amount of overhead applied to products.

The Ramirez forecast is based on a volume of activity expressed in direct labor cost. Assume detailed forecasts predict total overhead of $212,000 for the next year at an anticipated $265,000 direct-labor-cost level of activity. The budgeted factory overhead rate is computed as follows:

$$\text{Budgeted factory overhead rate} = \frac{\text{Total budgeted overhead}}{\text{Total budgeted direct labor cost}} = \frac{\$212,000}{\$265,000} = .80 \text{ or } 80\%$$

The 80 percent rate would be used for applying overhead cost to jobs.

To *apply overhead* means to debit Work in Process Inventory for the cost of overhead and to credit the Factory Overhead account. The overhead application rate is used to compute the amount of overhead to apply to a specific job. In our example, for each dollar of direct labor debited to Work in Process Inventory, 80 cents in overhead cost is also debited to that account. If the actual direct labor cost of a job is $800 (see Step 4), 80 percent of that amount, or $640, is debited to Work in Process Inventory as factory overhead (see Step 5 above).

The budgeted factory overhead rate is applied to all jobs uniformly throughout the year. After the direct materials and direct labor costs have been applied to a job, the overhead is applied, as shown in the accompanying record for Job 293. Recall that total direct labor cost for the job is $400. With an overhead application rate of 80 percent of direct labor, the amount of overhead to charge to Job 293 is $320 ($400 × .80).

Job Cost Record

Job No.   293

Customer Name and Address   Macy's, New York City

Job Description   10 recliner chairs

Date Promised 7-31	Date Started 7-24	Date Completed 7-29

Date	Direct Materials		Direct Labor		Factory Overhead Costs		
	Requisition Numbers	Amount	Time Ticket Numbers	Amount	Date	Rate	Amount
19X5							
7-24	334	$ 90	236,251,258	$150	7-29	120% of Direct labor	$480
25	338	180	264,269,273,291	200			
28	347	230	305	50			
					Overall Cost Summary		
					Direct materials.....	$ 500	
					Direct labor........	400	
					Factory overhead....	480	
Totals		$500		$400	Total Job Cost......	$ 1,380	

The job cost record for job 293 is complete. It provides the detailed subsidiary ledger support for the debits to the general ledger account, Work in Process Inventory.

Of course, similar applications of overhead have been made for other jobs in 19X5. The total overhead applied to all jobs worked on during 19X5 was 80 percent of $250,000 direct labor, .80 X $250,000 = $200,000. The journal entry to apply overhead to production is

9. Work in Process Inventory 200,000
       Factory Overhead 200,000

Trace this application of Factory Overhead to Work in Process Inventory.

Factory Overhead			Work in Process Inventory	
2.	40,000	9. Applied 200,000	Bal.	29,000
4.	85,000		2.	285,000
5.	50,000	Factory	4.	250,000
6.	20,000	Overhead → 9.		200,000
7.	5,000	Applied		
8.	10,000			
Actual costs	210,000			
Bal.	10,000			

An additional detail exists in accounting for overhead cost. First, however, we need to discuss accounting for finished goods and the sale of inventory.

Accounting for Finished Goods, Sales, and Cost of Goods Sold

As each job is completed, its cost is transferred from Work in Process Inventory to Finished Goods Inventory. The completion date is written on the job cost record, which is compared with the budget and filed away. Then, sales of finished goods are recorded as they occur.

A summary entry for goods completed in 19X5 follows:

10.	Finished Goods Inventory	740,000	
	Work in Process Inventory		740,000

In turn, familiar entries would be made for sales and cost of goods sold.

11.	Accounts Receivable	996,000	
	Sales Revenue		996,000
	Cost of Goods Sold	734,000	
	Finished Goods Inventory		734,000

The second entry is needed to maintain the perpetual inventory record. (Only the first entry is needed as sales are made in a periodic inventory system.)

The key accounts for product costs now show:

Work in Process Inventory					Finished Goods Inventory				Cost of Goods Sold	
Bal.	29,000	10.	740,000	Bal.	12,000	11.	734,000	11.	734,000	
2.	285,000			10.	740,000					
4.	250,000									
9.	200,000			Bal.	18,000					
Bal.	24,000									

Disposing of Overapplied and Underapplied Overhead

The application of factory overhead cost to production will usually not bring to zero the balance in the Factory Overhead account. This account is debited for *actual cost* and credited for *applied amounts*—equal to the budgeted factory overhead rate multiplied by the actual direct labor cost.

The total debits to Factory Overhead for the year may not equal the total credits to the account. A *debit* balance remaining in the Factory Overhead account is called **underapplied overhead.** In our illustration, actual overhead ($210,000 debited to the account) exceeded the amount applied to jobs ($200,000 credited to the account) during the period, which resulted in $10,000 in underapplied overhead. Conversely, a *credit* balance, called **overapplied overhead,** results when applied overhead exceeds the actual amount. Accountants usually ignore over- and underapplied overhead during the year and dispose of it at year end. The entry to close the Factory Overhead account adjusts the records to account for the actual overhead cost incurred during the year. The more accurate the budgeted overhead rate, the less the difference between actual and applied amounts of factory overhead for the year.

If the amount of over- or underapplied overhead is *significant,* it often is allocated to Work in Process, Finished Goods, and Cost of Goods Sold based on their relative balances before the allocation. For example, suppose 15 percent of the year's production is still in process, 25 percent is finished but unsold, and the remaining 60 percent has been sold. If *overapplied* overhead at the end of the period is $50,000—a significant amount in relation to total factory overhead, cost of goods sold, or another appropriate benchmark—the Factory Overhead Account will have a $50,000 credit balance. The entry to dispose of this credit balance debits Factory Overhead as follows:

Dec. 31	Factory Overhead	50,000	
	Work in Process Inventory ($50,000 × .15)		7,500
	Finished Goods Inventory ($50,000 × .25)		12,500
	Cost of Goods Sold ($50,000 × .60)		30,000

This entry removes the $50,000 credit balance from Factory Overhead. It also adjusts Work in Process, Finished Goods, and Cost of Goods Sold to actual costs.

If the over- or underapplied amount is *insignificant,* it can be closed to Cost of Goods Sold without seriously affecting the financial statements. This is an application of the *materiality concept.* Suppose actual overhead cost exceeded the amount of overhead applied to jobs. In our illustration the year's production resulted in the following summary activity in the Factory Overhead account:

Factory Overhead

Actual	210,000	Applied	200,000
Balance—Underapplied	10,000		

The $10,000 is minor relative to the $210,000 of actual overhead cost for the year. Moreover, the Cost of Goods Sold balance ($734,000) dwarfs the balances of Work in Process Inventory and Finished Goods Inventory ($24,000 and $18,000, respectively). This means that an allocation of $10,000 to the three accounts would have tiny effects on the balances in ending work in process and finished goods. Therefore, we may close this underapplied overhead to Cost of Goods Sold as follows:

Dec. 31	Cost of Goods Sold	10,000	
(Entry 12)	Factory Overhead		10,000

Posting this entry brings the Factory Overhead account to a zero balance and completes the job order cost accounting example.

Overview of Illustration

Exhibit 19-12 provides an overview of the Ramirez job order costing illustration. The key inventory accounts and Cost of Goods Sold are displayed at the top. Accounts for Factory Wages and Factory Overhead also are shown. The relationships of subsidiary material records to Materials Inventory and of subsidiary job cost records to Work in Process Inventory are also illustrated.

As Exhibit 19-12 makes clear, the ending balance sheet accounts would be

Materials Inventory	$15,000
Work in Process Inventory	24,000
Finished Goods Inventory	18,000

EXHIBIT 19-12 *Job Order Costing, General Flow of Costs (in thousands)*

The condensed income statement for 19X5 would report the following through gross margin:

Sales	$996,000
Cost of goods sold	734,000
Gross margin (or gross profit)	$262,000

As mentioned previously, the remainder of the manufacturer's income statement (operating expenses, other revenue and expense, and net income) is the same as for a merchandising entity.

Computers and Manufacturing Accounting

Managers need a tremendous amount of information to plan manufacturing operations and to keep costs under control. A company manufacturing hundreds of items may have a materials subledger running to perhaps thousands of accounts. Little wonder then that so many manufacturers have turned to computerized accounting.

Also, during periods of high customer demand, a manufacturer will focus on meeting production schedules, and important accounting controls may be relaxed. As peak production season winds down, managers may find it difficult to bring the accounting information up to date. A computerized system is easier to keep current throughout the entire year.

Computer software for manufacturers may integrate all facets of cost accounting, from materials purchases to overhead application. Assume management wants to manufacture a range of products within a certain time frame. The computer can access engineering specifications for the product, calculate materials and time requirements, coordinate deadlines with limited production capacity, and issue a series of purchase orders and work orders consistent with management plans.

A computerized accounting package can generate a broad variety of management reports. These reports are available at critical points in the production process, giving management the opportunity to monitor progress and make improvements on the spot.

Collecting certain data for a computerized system is straightforward. For example, a number of computer terminals may be set up on the production floor. At various stages in the manufacturing process, an employee inserts his magnetically imprinted identification card into the terminal. The system thus captures direct labor time and cost without detailed labor records.

Summary Problem for Your Review

Hillis Incorporated had the following inventories at the end of 19X4:

Materials	$20,000
Work in Process	17,000
Finished Goods	11,000

During January 19X5 Hillis completed the following transactions:

1. Purchased materials on account, $31,000.
2. Requisitioned (placed into production) direct materials, $39,000.
3. Factory payroll incurred, $40,000.
4. Allocated factory labor as follows: direct labor, 90 percent; indirect labor, 10 percent.
5. Requisitioned (placed into production) indirect materials, $3,000.
6. Incurred other factory overhead, $13,000 (credit Accounts Payable).
7. Applied factory overhead to production at 50 percent of direct labor.
8. Completed production, $99,000.
9. Sold goods on account, $172,000; cost of goods sold, $91,400.
10. Closed ending balance of Factory Overhead to Cost of Goods Sold.

Required

1. Record the transactions in the general journal.
2. Determine the ending balances in the three inventory accounts and Cost of Goods Sold.

SOLUTION TO REVIEW PROBLEM

Requirement 1 (Journal entries)

1.	Materials Inventory	31,000	
	Accounts Payable		31,000
2.	Work in Process Inventory	39,000	
	Materials Inventory		39,000
3.	Factory Wages	40,000	
	Wages Payable		40,000
4.	Work in Process Inventory ($40,000 × .90)	36,000	
	Factory Overhead ($40,000 × .10)	4,000	
	Factory Wages		40,000
5.	Factory Overhead	3,000	
	Materials Inventory		3,000
6.	Factory Overhead	13,000	
	Accounts Payable		13,000
7.	Work in Process Inventory ($36,000 × .50)	18,000	
	Factory Overhead		18,000
8.	Finished Goods Inventory	99,000	
	Work in Process Inventory		99,000
9.	Accounts Receivable	172,000	
	Sales Revenue		172,000
	Cost of Goods Sold	91,400	
	Finished Goods Inventory		91,400
10.	Cost of Goods Sold	2,000	
	Factory Overhead		2,000

Balance in Factory Overhead for entry 10:

Factory Overhead

(4)	4,000	(7)	18,000
(5)	3,000		
(6)	13,000		
Bal.	2,000		

Requirement 2 (Ending balances)

Materials Inventory

Bal.	20,000	(2)	39,000
(1)	31,000	(5)	3,000
Bal.	9,000		

Work in Process Inventory

Bal.	17,000	(8)	99,000
(2)	39,000		
(4)	36,000		
(7)	18,000		
Bal.	11,000		

Finished Goods Inventory

Bal.	11,000	(9)	91,400
(8)	99,000		
Bal.	18,600		

Cost of Goods Sold

(9)	91,400		
(10)	2,000		
Bal.	93,400		

Summary

Manufacturing companies use cost accounting systems to help plan and control the manufacturing function and to compute manufacturing product costs for the financial statements and for pricing and product mix decisions. They use separate inventory accounts for raw materials, work in process, and finished goods. The *Materials Inventory* account carries the cost of direct and indirect materials that are held for use in production. The *Work in Process Inventory* account shows the cost of goods that are still in the manufacturing process and not yet complete. *Finished Goods Inventory* represents completed goods that have not yet been sold. This account corresponds to the single inventory account of a merchandising business.

A manufacturer obtains inventory for resale by producing the goods. The manufacturer's *cost of goods manufactured* replaces the purchases account of a merchandiser. Otherwise, a manufacturer's income statement resembles the income statement of a merchandiser.

Direct materials include all the important materials used to make the product. *Direct labor* is the cost of employing people who physically produce the company's product. These two costs are traced directly to finished goods. *Factory overhead* includes all other manufacturing costs, including *indirect materials* and *indirect labor*.

Manufacturers keep inventory costs separate from all the other costs of running the business. *Inventoriable costs* are those identified with inventory. *Period costs* are accounted for as operating expenses and are never traced through the inventory accounts.

In a *job order costing system*—designed to account for products manufactured as individual units or in batches—costs are accumulated for specific jobs. A *job cost record* lists the materials, labor, and overhead costs of completing the job. In a job cost system this document is the basic internal management device for accumulating and controlling costs. It serves as the subsidiary record for Work in Process Inventory. The cost of materials is traced via materials ledger cards. Labor costs are traced by time tickets.

The Factory Overhead account, which includes many different costs, is debited for actual costs incurred. Overhead cost is applied to product at a budgeted rate usually stated as a percentage of direct labor cost. At the end of the period, any *underapplied* or *overapplied overhead* is closed,

Self-Study Questions

Test your understanding of the chapter by marking the best answer for each of the following questions.

1. Which of the following is an inventory account of a manufacturer but not of a merchandiser? *(p. 892)*
   a. Cost of goods manufactured
   b. Merchandise inventory
   c. Work in process
   d. Direct labor

2. Cost of goods manufactured is used to compute *(p. 893)*
   a. Cost of goods sold
   b. Factory overhead applied
   c. Direct materials used
   d. Finished goods inventory

3. Beginning work in process inventory is $35,000; manufacturing costs for the period total $140,000; and ending work in process inventory is $20,000. What is the cost of goods manufactured? *(pp. 893–4)*
   a. $125,000
   b. $155,000
   c. $175,000
   d. $195,000

4. Which of the following is a period cost? *(p. 896)*
   a. Materials inventory
   b. Direct labor
   c. Factory overhead
   d. Selling expense

5. Job order costing would be an appropriate system to account for the manufacture of *(p. 898)*
   a. Aircraft
   b. Matches
   c. Zippers
   d. Cardboard boxes

6. What purpose does a job cost record serve? *(pp. 899–900)*
   a. Lists total materials, labor, and overhead costs charged to a job
   b. Is management's basic internal document that helps to control cost in a job cost system
   c. Both of the above
   d. Neither of the above

7. Using direct materials in production and charging direct labor costs to a job result in a debit to *(pp. 903, 905)*
   a. Direct materials and direct labor
   b. Work in process inventory
   c. Finished goods inventory
   d. Materials inventory and factory wages

8. Which documents serve as a subsidiary ledger for the general ledger balance of Work in Process Inventory? *(pp. 899, 905)*
   a. Job cost records
   b. Materials requisitions
   c. Labor time tickets
   d. Materials ledger accounts

9. Why is direct labor often used as a basis for applying overhead cost to jobs? *(p. 907)*
   a. Overhead is very similar to direct labor
   b. Overhead includes direct labor
   c. Overhead occurs before direct labor is charged to a job
   d. Overhead occurs in relation to the incurrence of direct labor cost

10. At the end of the period, after overhead has been applied to all jobs, Factory Overhead has a credit balance of $900. We would say that overhead has been *(p. 909)*

a. Misstated   c. Overapplied

b. Incorrectly applied   d. Underapplied

Answers to the Self-Study Questions follow the Accounting Vocabulary.

Accounting Vocabulary

Budgeted factory overhead rate. Budgeted total overhead cost divided by the budgeted rate base *(p. 907)*.

Conversion costs. Direct labor plus overhead *(p. 894)*.

Cost application base. A common denominator linking costs among all products. Ideally the best available measure of the cause-and-effect relationship between overhead costs and production volume *(p. 907)*.

Cost of goods manufactured. Manufacturers' counterpart to the Purchases account. Cost of goods manufactured takes the place of purchases in the computation of cost of goods sold *(p. 892)*.

Direct labor. Cost of salaries and wages for the employees who physically convert materials into the company's products; labor costs that are conveniently traceable to finished goods *(p. 893)*.

Direct material. Material that becomes a physical part of a finished product and whose cost is separately and conveniently traceable through the manufacturing process to finished goods *(p. 893)*.

Factory overhead. All manufacturing costs other than direct materials and direct labor *(p. 893)*.

Finished goods inventory. Completed goods that have not yet been sold *(p. 892)*.

Indirect labor. Factory labor costs other than direct labor. Indirect labor costs, which are difficult to trace to specific products, include the pay of forklift operators, janitors, and plant guards *(p. 894)*.

Indirect materials. Manufacturing materials whose cost cannot easily be traced directly to particular finished products *(p. 894)*.

Inventoriable cost. A cost of a product regarded as an asset under GAAP *(p. 895)*.

Job cost record. Document used to accumulate and control cost in a job order system *(p. 899)*.

Job order costing. Accounting system used by companies that manufacture products as individual units or in batches, each of which receives varying degrees of attention and skill *(p. 898)*.

Labor time ticket. Document that identifies an employee, the amount of time the employee spent on a particular job, and the employee's labor cost charged to the job *(p. 904)*.

Materials inventory. Materials on hand and intended for use in the manufacturing process. Also called Raw materials inventory *(p. 892)*.

Materials requisition. Request for materials prepared by manufacturing personnel, the document that sets a manufacturing process in motion *(p. 901)*.

Overapplied overhead. Credit balance in the Factory Overhead account; results when applied overhead exceeds the actual overhead cost *(p. 909)*.

Period cost. Operating expenses that are never traced through the inventory accounts *(p. 896)*.

Prime costs. Direct materials plus direct labor *(p. 894)*.

Product cost. General term that denotes different costs allocated to products for different purposes *(p. 897)*.

Raw materials inventory. Another name for Materials inventory *(p. 892)*.

Total manufacturing cost. Sum of direct materials used, direct labor, and factory overhead. Total manufacturing cost is used to compute cost of goods manufactured, which is part of cost of goods sold *(p. 895)*.

Underapplied overhead. Debit balance remaining in the Factory Overhead account after overhead is applied; means that actual overhead cost exceeded the amount applied to jobs *(p. 909).*

Value chain. Sequence of all business functions in which value is added to a firm's products or services *(p. 888).*

Work in process inventory. Cost of the goods that are in the manufacturing process and not yet complete *(p. 890).*

Answers to Self-Study Questions

1. c
2. a
3. b ($35,000 + $140,000 − $20,000 = $155,000)
4. d

5. a
6. c
7. b

8. a
9. d
10. c

ASSIGNMENT MATERIAL _____

Questions

1. How do manufacturing companies differ from merchandisers? What inventory accounts does a manufacturer use that a merchandiser does not need?

2. Identify the various business functions in the value chain of a manufacturing company. Separate the upstream functions from the downstream functions. To which functions is cost accounting relevant?

3. What are the purposes of the cost accounting systems of a manufacturer?

4. What is the manufacturer's counterpart to the Purchases account of a merchandiser?

5. Distinguish direct materials from indirect materials and direct labor from indirect labor. Direct materials and direct labor are debited directly to what inventory account when placed in production? What account do indirect materials and indirect labor pass through en route to this inventory account?

6. Give examples of direct material and indirect material for a home builder.

7. Identify six or more components of factory overhead. Is overhead an asset or an expense account to a manufacturer?

8. Outline the flow of inventory costs through a manufacturing company's accounting system.

9. Distinguish between inventoriable costs and period costs. Which represents an asset, and which is used to account for expenses?

10. What costs should managers consider in deciding on the selling price of a product: inventoriable costs or full product costs? Give your reason.

11. Name two benefits of a perpetual inventory system.

12. What do the terms "charged to a job" and "applied to jobs" mean? What account is debited when a cost is applied to a job?

13. What is the essential nature of a job order costing system? How can companies that use a job cost system operate with low levels of inventories?

14. What document is used to control costs in a job cost system? Identify the three categories of costs listed on this document.

15. Name three documents or records used to account for raw materials, control them, and move them through the production process. Give the function served by each document.

16. Use T-accounts to outline how the costs of materials and labor are transferred to Work in Process Inventory. Include both direct and indirect materials and direct and indirect labor.

17. What document is used to charge labor cost to specific jobs? Briefly describe how the document is used.

18. Is factory overhead cost applied to jobs by a precise identification of the overhead cost of each job or by an estimation process? Briefly discuss the process.

19. Is Factory Overhead debited for actual overhead cost or the amount of overhead applied to product? Which amount is credited to Factory Overhead?

20. How can factory overhead be underapplied? How can it be overapplied?

21. Insignificant amounts of over- or underapplied overhead are closed to what account? Significant amounts are closed to what three accounts?

22. Which of the following accounts have their balances brought to zero at the end of the period? Which keep their ending balances to start the next period—Materials Inventory, Factory Overhead, Finished Goods Inventory, Factory Wages?

23. What three categories of manufacturing costs are listed on a statement of cost of goods manufactured?

24. Summarize the computation of cost of goods manufactured. You can use your own dollar amounts.

Exercises

Exercise 19-1 *Reporting current assets of a manufacturer* **(L.O. 1)**

Consider the following selected accounts of Frostex Foods:

Cost of goods sold	$101,000	Prepaid expenses	$ 5,000
Direct labor	47,000	Marketing expense	39,000
Direct materials	25,000	Work in process inventory	42,000
Accounts receivable	73,000	Factory overhead	26,000
Cash	9,000	Finished goods inventory	68,000
Cost of goods manufactured	94,000	Materials inventory	21,000

Required

Show how Frostex would report current assets on the balance sheet. Not all accounts are used.

Exercise 19-2 *Computing cost of goods manufactured* **(L.O. 2)**

Compute cost of goods manufactured from the following account balances:

	Beginning of Year	End of Year
Materials inventory	$22,000	$26,000
Work in process inventory	36,000	30,000
Finished goods inventory	18,000	23,000
Purchases of raw materials		75,000
Direct labor		82,000
Indirect labor		15,000
Factory insurance		9,000
Depreciation—factory building and equipment		11,000
Repairs and maintenance—factory		4,000
Marketing expenses		63,000
General and administrative expenses		29,000
Income tax expense		30,000

Exercise 19-3 — Preparing a manufacturer's income statement (L.O. 1, 2)

Prepare an income statement for the company in Exercise 19-2, assuming it sold 27,000 units of its product at a price of $14 during the current year.

Exercise 19-4 — Computing cost of goods manufactured and cost of goods sold (L.O. 2)

Compute cost of goods manufactured and cost of goods sold for the following situation:

Direct materials used	$53,000
Ending finished goods inventory	34,000
Depreciation of factory equipment	11,000
Factory repairs and maintenance	16,000
Beginning work in process inventory	19,000
Direct labor	59,000
Indirect labor	23,000
Indirect materials	13,000
Miscellaneous factory overhead	4,000
Property tax on factory building	3,000
Marketing expenses	37,000
Beginning finished goods inventory	27,000
Factory utilities	17,000
Ending work in process inventory	26,000
Depreciation of factory building	9,000
Nonfactory administrative expenses	43,000

Exercise 19-5 — Computing gross margin for a manufacturer (L.O. 2)

Supply the missing amounts from the following computation of gross margin:

Sales revenue			$483,000
Cost of goods sold:			
Beginning finished goods inventory		$ 91,000	
Cost of goods manufactured:			
Beginning work in process inventory		$ 57,000	
Direct materials used	$84,000		
Direct labor	X		
Factory overhead	51,000		
Total manufacturing costs incurred during the period		231,000	
Total manufacturing costs to account for		X	
Ending work in process inventory		(40,000)	
Cost of goods manufactured		X	
Goods available for sale		X	
Ending finished goods inventory		(107,000)	
Cost of goods sold			X
Gross margin			$ X

Exercise 19-6 — Analyzing job cost data (L.O. 3)

Bancroft Publishing Company job cost records yielded the following information:

| Job | Dates | | | Total Cost of Job at July 31 |
No.	Started	Finished	Sold	
1	June 19	July 14	July 15	$ 1,700
2	June 29	July 21	July 26	17,000
3	July 3	Aug. 11	Aug. 13	6,500
4	July 7	July 29	Aug. 1	6,200
5	July 9	July 30	Aug. 2	2,700
6	July 22	Aug. 11	Aug. 13	1,300
7	July 23	July 27	July 29	1,300

Compute Bancroft's cost of (a) work in process inventory at July 31, (b) finished goods inventory at July 31, and (c) cost of goods sold for July.

Exercise 19-7 *Journalizing manufacturing transactions* (*L.O. 4, 5, 6*)

Record the following transactions in the general journal:

a. Purchased materials on account, $11,100.
b. Paid factory wages, $14,000.
c. Used in production: direct materials, $9,000; and indirect materials, $2,000.
d. Applied factory labor to jobs: direct labor, 80 percent; indirect labor, 20 percent.
e. Recorded factory overhead: depreciation, $13,000; insurance, $1,700; property tax, $4,200 (credit Property Tax Payable).
f. Applied factory overhead to jobs, 150% percent of direct labor.
g. Completed production, $27,000.
h. Sold inventory on account, $22,000; cost of goods sold, $14,000.
i. Paid marketing expenses, $2,000.

Exercise 19-8 *Identifying manufacturing transactions* (*L.O. 4, 5, 6*)

Describe the transactions indicated by the letters in the following manufacturing accounts:

Materials Inventory	
(a)	(b)
	(e)

Work in Process Inventory	
(b)	(h)
(d)	(j)
(g)	

Finished Goods Inventory	
(h)	(i)
	(j)

Factory Wages	
(c)	(d)

Factory Overhead	
(d)	(g)
(e)	
(f)	
(j)	

Cost of Goods Sold	
(i)	(j)

Exercise 19-9 *Using the Work in Process Inventory account* (*L.O. 4, 5, 6*)

August production generated the following activity in the Work in Process Inventory account of Swingline Manufacturing Company:

Work in Process Inventory	
August 1 Bal.	10,000
Direct materials used	23,000
Direct labor charged to jobs	31,000
Factory overhead applied to jobs	11,000

Completed production, not yet recorded, consists of Jobs B-78, G-65, and Y-11, with total costs of $14,000, $19,000, and $33,000, respectively.

Required

1. Compute the cost of work in process at August 31.
2. Journalize completed production for August.
3. Journalize the credit sale of Job G-65 for $41,000. Also make the cost-of-goods-sold entry.

Exercise 19-10   *Accounting for overhead cost*   *(L.O. 6)*

Selected cost data for Maness & Shrake are presented below:

Budgeted factory overhead cost for the year	$105,000
Budgeted direct labor cost for the year	84,000
Actual factory overhead cost for the year	100,600
Actual direct labor cost for the year	80,000

Required

1. Compute the budgeted factory overhead rate.
2. Journalize the application of overhead cost for the year.
3. By what amount is factory overhead over- or underapplied? Is this amount significant or insignificant?
4. Based on your answer to (3), journalize disposition of the overhead balance.

Problems   *(Group A)*

Problem 19-1A   *Completing a manufacturer's income statement*   *(L.O. 1, 2)*

Certain item descriptions and amounts are missing from the income statement of Medco Systems.

Medco Systems
Income Statement
For the Month Ended March 31, 19X6

Sales revenue				$231,000
Cost of goods sold:				
Beginning _____ inventory			$ X	
Cost of goods _____:				
Beginning _____ inventory		$ X		
Direct _____:				
Beginning materials inventory	$34,000			
Purchases of materials	70,000			
Available for use	X			
Ending materials inventory	(26,000)			
Direct _____		$ X		
Direct _____		83,000		
_____		19,000		
Total _____ costs _____			X	
Total _____ costs _____			X	
Ending _____ inventory			(49,000)	
Cost of goods _____			163,000	
Goods available for sale			192,000	
Ending _____ inventory			(54,000)	
Cost of goods _____				X
Gross margin				93,000
Operating expenses:				
Marketing			23,000	
General			26,000	
Total operating expense				X
Income before income tax				X
Income tax expense (30%)				X
Net income				$ X

Required

Supply the missing item descriptions (————) and the missing amounts (X).

Problem 19-2A   *Analyzing job cost data* **(L.O. 3)**

Pacific Irrigation Company job cost records yielded the following information. The company has a perpetual inventory system.

Job No.	Dates Started	Dates Finished	Dates Sold	Total Cost of Job at March 31	Total Manufacturing Cost Added In April
1	2/26	3/7	3/9	$2,200	
2	2/3	3/12	3/13	1,100	
3	3/29	3/31	4/3	300	
4	3/31	4/1	4/1	400	$ 400
5	3/17	4/24	4/27	1,400	2,200
6	4/8	4/12	4/14		700
7	4/23	5/6	5/9		1,200
8	4/30	5/22	5/26		600

Required

1. Compute Pacific's cost of (a) work in process inventory at March 31 and April 30, (b) finished goods inventory at March 31 and April 30, and (c) cost of goods sold for March and April.
2. Make summary journal entries to record the transfer of completed units from work in process to finished goods for March and April.
3. Record the sale of Job 5 for $7,000.

Problem 19-3A   *Computing manufacturing cost amounts for the financial statements* **(L.O. 2, 4, 5, 6)**

Assume Levi Strauss & Company accounting records include the following cost information on jobs for the manufacture of a line of jeans. During the most recent year Levi Strauss incurred total manufacturing cost of $163.2 million on materials, labor, and factory overhead, of which $28.2 million represented direct materials used. Beginning balances for the year were materials inventory, $3.4 million; work in process inventory, $2.6 million; and finished goods inventory, $7.4 million. The company applies overhead to work in process (and finished goods) based on the relationship between overhead and direct labor costs. At year end the inventory accounts showed these balances (millions):

	Materials	Direct Labor	Factory Overhead
Materials inventory	$0.9	$-0-	$-0-
Work in process inventory	1.5	2.0	2.5
Finished goods inventory	2.4	3.2	4.0

Required

1. Prepare Levi Strauss's statement of cost of goods manufactured for the line of jeans.
2. Compute cost of goods sold for the product.
3. Record the transfer from Work in Process Inventory to Finished Goods Inventory and the transfer from Finished Goods Inventory to Cost of Goods Sold during the year.

Problem 19-4A   *Accounting for manufacturing transactions*   (L.O. 3, 4, 5, 6)

Doyle Wilson Homes builds prefabricated houses in a factory. The company uses a perpetual inventory system and a job cost system in which each house represents a job. The following transactions and events were completed during May:

(a) Purchases of materials on account, $204,900.
(b) Requisitions of direct materials and direct labor used in manufacturing:

	Direct Materials	Direct Labor
House #613	$26,100	$11,600
House #614	41,700	22,500
House #615	31,000	14,700
House #616	54,000	23,800
House #617	43,900	20,700
House #618	32,800	14,600

(c) Depreciation of factory equipment used on different houses, $14,300.
(d) Other overhead costs incurred on houses #613–#618:

Factory wages	$21,600
Equipment rentals paid	6,000
Liability insurance expired	3,900

(e) Applied overhead to jobs at the budgeted overhead rate of 30 percent of direct labor.
(f) Houses completed: #613, #615, #616.
(g) Houses sold: #615 for $59,900; #616 for $103,900.

Required

1. Record the foregoing transactions and events in the general journal.
2. Open T-accounts for Work in Process Inventory and Finished Goods Inventory. Post the appropriate entries to these accounts, identifying the entry by letter. Determine the ending account balances assuming the beginning balances were zero.
3. List the costs of unfinished houses, and show that this total amount equals the ending balance in the Work in Process Inventory account.
4. List the costs of completed houses that have not yet been sold, and show that this total amount equals the ending balance in the Finished Goods Inventory account.

Problem 19-5A   *Preparing and using a job cost record*   (L.O. 4, 5, 6)

D. E. Shipp Company produces conveyor belts used by other companies in their manufacturing processes. Shipp has a job cost system and a perpetual inventory system.

On September 22 Shipp received an order for 50 industrial-grade belts from Ogden Jones Corporation at a price of $56 each. The job, assigned number 449, was promised for October 15. After purchasing the materials, Shipp began production on September 30 and incurred the following costs in completing the order:

Date	Materials Requisition No.	Description	Amount
9-30	593	20 lbs. rubber @ $9	$180
10-2	598	30 meters polyester fabric @ $7	210
10-3	622	12 meters steel cord @ $12	144

Date	Time Ticket No.	Description	Amount
9-30	1754	8 hours @ $9	$ 72
10-3	1805	31 hours @ $8	248

Shipp charges overhead to jobs based on the relationship between estimated overhead ($375,000) and estimated direct labor ($250,000). The job was completed on October 3 and shipped to Ogden Jones on October 5.

Required

1. Prepare a job cost record similar to Exhibit 19-7.
2. Journalize in summary form the requisition of direct materials and the application of direct labor and factory overhead to Job 449.
3. Journalize completion of the job and sale of the goods.

Problem 19-6A *Comprehensive accounting treatment of manufacturing transactions (L.O. 1, 3, 4, 5, 6)*

Consumers Electric Company manufactures specialized parts used in the generation of power. Initially, the company manufactured the parts for its own use, but it gradually began selling them to other public utilities as well. The trial balance of Consumer Electric's manufacturing operation on January 1 of the current year follows.

Consumers Electric Company—Manufacturing Operations
Trial Balance
January 1, 19XX

Cash	$ 32,740	
Accounts receivable	65,860	
Inventories:		
Materials	18,910	
Work in process	43,350	
Finished goods	78,550	
Plant assets	342,860	
Accumulated depreciation		$145,960
Accounts payable		88,650
Wages payable		5,700
Common stock		200,000
Retained earnings		141,960
Sales revenue		—
Cost of goods sold	—	
Factory wages	—	
Factory overhead	—	
Marketing and general expenses	—	
	$582,270	$582,270

January 1 balances in the subsidiary ledgers:

Materials ledger: Steel, $4,730; Petrochemicals, $5,280; Electronic parts, $7,800; Indirect materials, $1,100.

Work in process ledger: Job 86, $43,350.

Finished goods ledger: Transformers, $35,770; Transmission lines, $21,910; Switches, $20,870.

January transactions are summarized as follows:

(a) Materials purchased on credit: Steel, $12,660; Petrochemicals, $19,570; Electronic parts, $28,360; Indirect materials, $6,130.

(b) Materials used in production (requisitioned):
Job 86: Steel, $1,580, Petrochemicals, $3,400.
Job 87: Steel, $10,580, Petrochemicals, $9,870; Electronic parts, $4,690.
Job 88: Steel, $2,930, Petrochemicals, $7,680; Electronic parts, $29,920.
Indirect materials, $4,760.

(c) Factory wages incurred during January, $51,730, of which $49,560 was paid. Wages payable at December 31 were paid during January, $5,700.

(d) Labor time tickets for the month: Job 86, $3,650; Job 87, $19,880; Job 88, $16,560; Indirect labor, $11,640.

(e) Factory overhead incurred on account, $27,660.

(f) Depreciation recorded on factory plant and equipment, $6,710.

(g) Payments on account, $79,330.

(h) Factory overhead applied at the budgeted rate of 120 percent of direct labor.

(i) Jobs completed during the month: Job 86, one transformer at total cost of $56,360; Job 87, 620 switches at total cost of $68,876.

(j) Marketing and general expenses paid, $21,660.

(k) Credit sales on account: All of Job 86 for $91,490 (cost $56,360); Job 87, 480 switches for $88,030 (cost, $53,323).

(l) Collections on account, $177,880.

Required

1. Open T-accounts for the general ledger, the materials ledger, the work in process ledger, and the finished goods ledger. Insert each account balance as given, and use the reference *Bal.*

2. Record the January transactions directly in the accounts, using the letters as references. Consumers Electric has a perpetual inventory system.

3. Prepare a trial balance at January 31 of the current year.

4. Prepare a multiple-step income statement through income from operations for January of the current year, assuming any balance in Factory Overhead is insignificant. Take amounts directly from the trial balance, and report cost of goods sold as a single amount.

Problem 19-7A *Using a manufacturing system to account for overhead cost*
(L.O. 4, 5, 6)

Selected accounts of Zettler Coating Contractors follow.

Accounts Receivable

| Aug. 1 | Balance | 122,400 | Aug.31 | Collections | 365,900 |
| 31 | Sales | (1) | | | |

Materials Inventory

| Aug. 1 | Balance | 31,500 | Aug.31 | Requisitions | (2) |
| 31 | Purchases | 54,600 | | | |

Work in Process Inventory

Aug. 1	Balance	73,200	Aug.31	Jobs completed	(5)
31	Direct materials	(3)			
31	Direct labor	104,000			
31	Factory overhead	(4)			

Finished Goods Inventory

| Aug. 1 | Balance | 59,500 | Aug.31 | Jobs sold | (7) |
| 31 | Jobs completed | (6) | | | |

Factory Overhead

Aug. 1	Balance	800	Aug.31	Applied at rate of 80% of direct labor cost	(8)
31	Costs incurred: indirect materials of $31,400, indirect labor, etc.				
	Total amount	81,900			

Cost of Goods Sold

| Aug.31 | Jobs sold | (9) | | | |

Sales Revenue

| | | | Aug.31 | Sales | (10) |

Selected balances at August 31 are

Accounts receivable.................	$103,700
Materials inventory	28,400
Work in process inventory	43,700
Finished goods inventory	72,900

Required

1. Determine the amounts of the numbered items in the accounts.
2. a. Was factory overhead under- or overapplied at August 1?
   b. What is the August 31 balance in Factory Overhead? Is factory overhead under- or overapplied at August 31?
   c. Assume August 31 is the end of the company's fiscal year. Give the year-end entry to close the Factory Overhead account, depending on whether the August 31 balance is significant or insignificant. You must make this judgment.

Problem 19-1B *Completing a manufacturer's income statement* **(L.O. 1, 2)**

Certain item descriptions and amounts are missing from the income statement
of Hoppe Manufacturing Company.

Hoppe Manufacturing Company
Income Statement
For the Year Ended June 30, 19X9

Sales revenue			$ X
Cost of goods sold:			
Beginning _____ inventory		$ 101,000	
Cost of goods _____.			
Beginning _____ inventory	$ 28,000		
Direct _____:			
Beginning materials inventory	$ X		
Purchases of materials	62,000		
Available for use	79,000		
Ending materials inventory	(23,000)		
Direct _____		$ X	
Direct _____		X	
_____		38,000	
Total _____ costs _____	166,000		
Total _____ costs _____	X		
Ending _____ inventory	(31,000)		
Cost of goods _____		163,000	
Goods available for sale		X	
Ending _____ inventory		(X)	
Cost of goods _____			168,000
Gross margin			234,000
Operating expenses:			
Marketing		99,000	
General		X	
Total operating expense			144,000
Income before income tax			X
Income tax expense (40%)			X
Net income			$ ×

Required

Supply the missing item descriptions _____ and the missing amounts (X).

Problem 19-2B *Analyzing job cost data* **(L.O. 3)**

Trujillo Manufacturing Company job cost records yielded the following information. The company has a perpetual inventory system.

Job No.	Dates Started	Dates Finished	Sold	Total Cost of Job at June 30	Total Manufacturing Costs Added in July
1	5/26	6/7	6/9	$ 700	
2	6/3	6/12	6/13	1,700	
3	6/3	6/30	7/1	2,400	
4	6/17	7/24	7/27	100	$ 500
5	6/29	7/29	8/3	400	1,600
6	7/8	7/12	7/14		800
7	7/23	8/6	8/9		300
8	7/30	8/22	8/26		2,900

Required

1. Compute Trujillo's cost of (a) work in process inventory at June 30 and
   July 31, (b) finished goods inventory at June 30 and July 31, and (c) cost of
   goods sold for June and July.

2. Make summary journal entries to record the transfer of completed units from work in process to finished goods for June and July.
3. Record the sale of Job 4 for $850.

Problem 19-3B Computing manufacturing cost amounts for the financial statements (L.O. 2, 4, 5, 6)

Stride-Rite Shoe Company makes the Sperry Top-Sider deck shoe. Assume Stride-Rite accounting records include the following cost information on jobs for the manufacture of the basic brown leather Top-Sider.

During the most recent year Stride-Rite incurred total manufacturing cost of $21.4 million on materials, labor, and factory overhead, of which $4.6 million represented overhead applied. Beginning balances for the year were materials inventory, $500,000; work in process inventory, $700,000; and finished goods inventory, $400,000. The company applies overhead to work in process (and finished goods) based on the relationship between overhead and direct labor costs. At year end the inventory accounts showed these balances:

	Materials	Direct Labor	Factory Overhead
Materials inventory	$600,000	$ -0-	$ -0-
Work in process inventory........	300,000	450,000	150,000
Finished goods inventory.........	100,000	150,000	50,000

Required

1. Prepare Stride-Rite's statement of cost of goods manufactured for the brown leather Top-Sider shoe.
2. Compute cost of goods sold for the Top-Sider product.
3. Compute the cost of materials purchased during the year.

Problem 19-4B Accounting for manufacturing transactions (L.O. 3, 4, 5, 6)

Centennial Homes, Inc., is a home builder in Dallas, Texas. Assume Centennial uses a perpetual inventory system and a job cost system in which each house represents a job. Because it constructs houses on-site rather than in a factory, the company uses accounts titled Construction Wages (not Factory Wages), Overhead (not Factory Overhead), and Supervisory Salaries for indirect labor. The following transactions and events were completed during August:

(a) Purchases of materials on account, $385,600.
(b) Requisitions of direct materials and direct labor used in manufacturing:

	Direct Materials	Direct Labor
House #302	$36,800	$19,100
House #303	39,100	17,400
House #304	45,600	20,500
House #305	22,400	11,000
House #306	63,900	33,700
House #307	52,800	27,500

(c) Depreciation of equipment used in construction, $5,800.
(d) Other overhead costs incurred on houses #302–#307:

Supervisory salaries	$17,000
Equipment rentals paid	7,300
Liability insurance expired	5,100

(e) Applied overhead to jobs at the budgeted overhead rate of 30% of direct labor excluding supervision.

(f) Houses completed: #302, #304, #305, #307.

(g) Houses sold: #305 for $41,500; #307 for $115,000.

Required

1. Record the foregoing transactions and events in the general journal.
2. Open T-accounts for Work in Process Inventory and Finished Goods Inventory. Post the appropriate entries to these accounts, identifying the entry by letter. Determine the ending account balances assuming the beginning balances were zero.
3. List the costs of unfinished houses, and show that this total amount equals the ending balance in the Work in Process Inventory account.
4. List the costs of completed houses that have not yet been sold, and show that this total amount equals the ending balance in the Finished Goods Inventory account.

Problem 19-5B *Preparing and using a job cost record* **(L.O. 4, 5, 6)**

Maxell Magnetic Tape Company manufactures diskettes for use in reproducing sound. Maxell has a job cost system and a perpetual inventory system.

On November 2 Maxell began production of 10,000 diskettes, assigned job number 378, to be sold to music stores for $1.25 each. The company incurred the following costs in completing the job:

Date	Materials Requisition No.	Description	Amount
11-2	36	31 lbs. polypropylene @ $8	$248
11-2	37	68 lbs. magnetic filament @ $13	884
11-3	42	7 lbs. bucylic acid @ $48	336

Date	Time Ticket No.	Description	Amount
11-2	556	12 hours @ $10	$120
11-3	557	24.5 hours @ $8	196

Maxell charges overhead to jobs based on the relationship between estimated overhead ($560,000) and estimated direct labor ($448,000). The job was completed on November 3 and shipped to music stores when ordered.

Required

1. Prepare a job cost record similar to Exhibit 19-7.
2. Journalize in summary form the requisition of direct materials and the application of direct labor and factory overhead to job 378.
3. Journalize completion of the job and sale of 500 diskettes.

Problem 19-6B *Comprehensive accounting treatment of manufacturing transactions* **(L.O. 1, 3, 4, 5, 6)**

Monarch Accessories manufactures specialized parts used in its business. Initially, the company manufactured the parts for its own use, but it gradually began selling them to other companies as well. Monarch's trial balance on April 1, the beginning of the current fiscal year, follows.

April 1 balances in the subsidiary ledgers:

Materials ledger: Steel, $1,580; Petrochemicals, $2,810; Electronic parts, $1,960; Indirect materials, $430.

Work in process ledger: Job 145, $35,880.

Finished goods ledger: Transformers, $5,310; Transmission lines, $4,780; Switches, $8,870.

Monarch Accessories
Trial Balance
April 1, 19XX

Cash	$ 19,160	
Accounts receivable	74,290	
Inventories:		
Materials	6,780	
Work in process.................	35,880	
Finished goods..................	18,960	
Plant assets	244,570	
Accumulated depreciation..........		$103,680
Accounts payable		26,770
Wages payable		3,670
Common stock....................		120,000
Retained earnings		145,520
Sales revenue		—
Cost of goods sold	—	
Factory wages	—	
Factory overhead..................	—	
Marketing and general expenses	—	
	$399,640	$399,640

April transactions are summarized as follows:

(a) Materials purchased on credit: Steel, $5,540; Petrochemicals, $9,690; Electronic parts, $15,830; Indirect materials, $3,590.

(b) Materials used in production (requisitioned):
Job 145: Steel, $340, Petrochemicals, $1,770.
Job 146: Steel, $3,570, Petrochemicals, $5,720; Electronic parts, $3,980.
Job 147: Steel, $1,970, Petrochemicals, $3,610; Electronic parts, $3,730.
Indirect materials, $2,380.

(c) Factory wages incurred during April, $31,930, of which $30,520 was paid. Wages payable at March 31 were paid during April, $3,670.

(d) Labor time tickets for the month: Job 145, $3,000; Job 146, $12,050; Job 147, $9,940; Indirect labor, $6,940.

(e) Factory overhead incurred on account, $4,630.

(f) Depreciation recorded on factory plant and equipment, $3,450.

(g) Payments on account, $36,040.

(h) Factory overhead applied at the budgeted rate of 70 percent of direct labor.

(i) Jobs completed during the month: Job 145, two transformers at total cost of $43,090; Job 146, 200 switches at total cost of $33,755.

(j) Marketing and general expenses paid, $27,470.

(k) Credit sales on account: All of Job 145 for $97,640 (cost $43,090); Job 146, 120 switches for $35,100 (cost, $20,253).

(l) Collections on account, $127,470.

Required

1. Open T-accounts for the general ledger, the materials ledger, the work in process ledger, and the finished goods ledger. Insert each account balance as given, and use the reference *Bal.*

2. Record the April transactions directly in the accounts, using the letters as references. Monarch has a perpetual inventory system.

3. Prepare a trial balance at April 30 of the current year.

4. Prepare a multiple-step income statement through income from operations for April of the current year, assuming any balance in Factory Overhead is insignificant. Take amounts directly from the trial balance, and report cost of goods sold as a single amount.

Problem 19-7B Using a manufacturing system to account for overhead cost
(L.O. 4, 5, 6)

Selected accounts of Waltham Quartz Products follow.

Accounts Receivable

Nov. 1	Balance	28,900	Nov. 30	Collections	254,600
30	Sales	(1)			

Materials Inventory

Nov. 1	Balance	8,400	Nov. 30	Requisitions	(2)
30	Purchases	41,700			

Work in Process Inventory

Nov. 1	Balance	24,600	Nov. 30	Jobs completed	(5)
30	Direct materials	(3)			
30	Direct labor	68,000			
30	Factory overhead	(4)			

Finished Goods Inventory

Nov. 1	Balance	101,200	Nov. 30	Jobs sold	(7)
30	Jobs completed	(6)			

Factory Overhead

Nov. 30	Costs incurred: indirect materials of $9,000, indirect labor, etc. Total amount	75,200	Nov. 1	Balance	1,100
			30	Applied at rate of 110% of direct labor cost	(8)

Cost of Goods Sold

Nov. 30	Jobs sold	(9)	

Sales Revenue

		Nov. 30	Sales	(10)

Selected balances at Nov. 30 are

Accounts receivable...................	$31,400
Materials inventory	10,100
Work in process inventory	21,900
Finished goods inventory	89,800

Required

1. Determine the amounts of the numbered items in the accounts.
2. a. Was factory overhead under- or overapplied at November 1?
   b. What is the November 30 balance in Factory Overhead? Is factory overhead under- or overapplied at November 30?
   c. Assume November 30 is the end of the company's fiscal year. Give the year-end entry to close the Factory Overhead account depending on whether the November 30 balance is significant or insignificant. You must make this judgment.

Extending Your Knowledge

Decision Problems

1. Costing and Pricing for Identical Orders   (L.O. 3, 4, 5, 6)

Davison Chocolate Ltd. is located in Indianapolis. The company prepares gift boxes of chocolates as favors for private parties and corporate promotions. Each order contains a selection of chocolates determined by the customer, and the box is designed according to the customer's specifications.

One of Davison's largest customers is the Andrews and Ng law firm. This organization sends chocolates to its clients each Christmas and also provides them at firm gatherings. The law firm's managing partner, Peter Andrews, placed the client gift order in September for 500 boxes of cream-filled dark chocolates. However, Andrews and Ng did not organize its December staff party until the last week of November. This order for an additional 100 boxes is identical to the ones to be distributed to the clients.

The cost per box for the original 500-box order was estimated as follows:

Chocolate, filling, wrappers, box	$14.00
Employee time to fill and wrap the box (10 min.)	1.00
Factory overhead	.50
Total manufacturing cost	$15.50

Because Andrews and Ng is such a good customer, Joan Davison, the president of Davison Chocolate Ltd., priced the order at $17.00 per box.

In the past few months Davison Chocolate Ltd. has experienced price increases for both dark chocolate and employee time. All other costs have remained the same. The cost per box for the second order is estimated to be

Chocolate, filling, wrappers, box	$15.00
Employee time to fill and wrap the box (10 min.)	1.10
Factory overhead	.55
Total manufacturing cost	$16.65

Required

1. Do you agree with the cost analysis for the second order? Explain your answer.
2. Should the two orders be accounted for as one job or two in Davison Chocolate Ltd.'s system?
3. What selling price per box should Joan Davison set for the second order? What are the advantages and disadvantages of this price?

2. Using Cost Data to Price a New Product (L.O. 4, 5, 6)

Interstate Communication, Inc., is experimenting with a new process for manufacturing special telephone equipment in an attempt to lower the cost and sale price of its products. The goal is to capture a larger share of the telephone equipment market. The new process uses laser technology that decreases the amount of raw material needed to make a telephone. The *current* manufacturing process requires the following inputs per 1,000 telephones:

Direct materials:		
Material A	20 lbs. @	$ 11
Material B....................	130 lbs. @	9
Material C	8 lbs. @	106
Direct labor:		
Fabricating	80 hrs. @	$ 10
Assembling	20 hrs. @	12
Testing	50 hrs. @	13
Factory overhead @ 150% of direct labor cost		

The *new technology* would decrease the amounts of material A by 20 percent and of material C by 40 percent. It would also require three pounds of material D, which costs $22 per pound. Fabricating and testing would require 10 percent less time, but purchase of the laser machine would increase overhead to 175 percent of direct labor cost.

Interstate sells its products for 60 percent above cost but would need to increase this margin to 65 percent for telephone equipment manufactured by the new process to compensate for the lower selling price. Market analysis shows that customer demand for telephones is extremely sensitive to price. Interstate personnel believe any sale price reduction more than 50 cents per telephone will increase sales volume enough to warrant using the new production process.

Required

Compute the current selling price of a telephone and the price of a telephone using the laser technology to decide whether to proceed with the new process. Make a recommendation to the company.

Ethical Issue

North Carolina has the greatest concentration of furniture manufacturers in the United States. These companies dominate furniture sales in the southeastern United States. To break into this market, Ramirez Furniture Company is considering several options. Under one plan, Ramirez would charge no overhead cost to products destined for the southeastern market. This would enable Ramirez to offer its furniture at lower prices than its competitors charge.

Required

1. Is Ramirez's pricing strategy ethical? Discuss.
2. Can Ramirez expect to follow this strategy indefinitely? Give your reason.

Chapter 20

Process Costing

Acme Metals Inc. (until recently Acme Steel) is the nation's smallest fully integrated steel producer and, perhaps not coincidentally, one of the more resourceful. . . .

Based in the Chicago suburb of Riverdale, Acme produces around 1 million tons of raw steel a year, not much compared with USX's 11 million tons last year. But far more important than its capacity is its ability to produce steel [. . .] to suit many different customers' specialized needs. . . .

Acme thus tends to serve manufacturers that need steel but don't need a great deal of it—for products like cutlery, shovels and lawn mower blades. Take the steel used in retractable tape measures. It must be lightweight, flexible enough to roll up, stiff enough to extend 6 feet and smooth enough to take paint and delicate markings. . . .

Acme's Riverdale mill is pretty old-fashioned. Its molten steel is still poured into ingot molds—that's the way that allows the company the most flexibility in producing . . . designer steel. [The company] has spent $80 million since 1987 on things like modernizing the finishing process in the cold-rolling mill, thereby increasing labor productivity by 25%.

Job order costing and process costing are the two major accounting systems for determining the costs of products. Chapter 19 discussed job order costing. This chapter explains process costing, which applies to products such as those manufactured by Acme Metals Inc.

SOURCE: Adapted from Christopher Palmeri, "Designer Steel," *Forbes,* June 8, 1992, p. 67.

Process Costing: An Overview

The major difference between job order product costing described in the preceding chapter and process product costing is the type of products that are the objects of costing. Job order costing and process costing are the ends of a spectrum.

For specific units or small batches of custom-made products

For mass production of like units

Job order product costing systems

Process product costing systems

Exhibit 20-1 compares job order costing and process costing. **Process costing** is a system for assigning costs to goods that are mass-produced in a continuous sequence of steps called *processes*. Companies in manufacturing industries—steel, chemicals, petroleum, cosmetics, food, and beverages, for example—use process costing systems. Each of several departments is responsible for one specific process, although a single department may perform more than one process.

In the manufacturing process, the physical form of the product often changes as it passes from one process to another (and so from one department to another). For example, corn flake cereal starts as raw corn. The corn is cleaned and cooked before being packaged as corn flakes and shipped for sale to consumers. A company that produces corn flakes—like Kellogg's or General Mills—may have one department for cleaning, one department for cooking, and one department for packaging.

A mass-production manufacturing process produces large numbers of identical units—rods of steel, boxes of cereal, gallons of paint, and cases of Coca-Cola. In contrast, a job system produces custom goods. In a process system the flow of goods through the factory is continuous and repetitive. Job cost records are not used. Instead, cost is accumulated in each department for a week or a month. At the end of the period, total manufacturing cost is the sum of the costs added in the processing departments. Unit cost is computed by dividing total manufacturing cost by the number of units produced. For example, if it cost $600,000 to produce 150,000 units during July, unit cost is $4.00 ($600,000/150,000 units).

EXHIBIT 20-1 *Comparison of Process Costing and Job Order Costing*

Job Order Costing: Examples include aircraft, construction, auditing, repairing, and jewelry

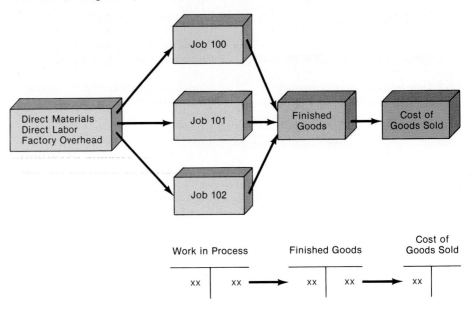

Process Costing: Examples include flour, glass, paint, paper, and silicon wafers

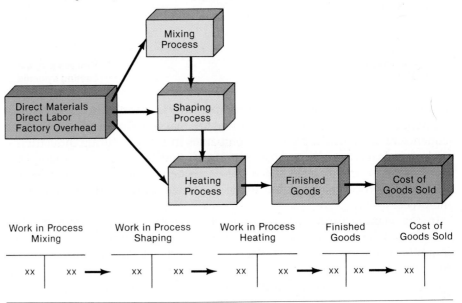

Consider a manufacturing company that produces its goods in three steps. The business mixes materials to produce ceramic blocks, shapes the blocks into figurines, and heats the statues for hardness. The company has a Mixing Department, a Shaping Department, and a Heating Department. To account for the costs that make up the finished products, accountants use three work in process inventory accounts—one for mixing, one for shaping, and one for heating. Exhibit 20-1 shows the flow of costs in this three-step process.

Note in the exhibit that mixing costs accumulate in the Work in Process Inventory—Mixing account. After mixing is completed, the blocks are transferred to the Shaping Department, and so are the costs. When shaping has been completed, product costs flow to Work in Process—Heating and then on to Finished Goods Inventory. When the figurines are sold, the cost of the inventory is transferred into Cost of Goods Sold. For comparison, the exhibit also diagrams the flow of costs through a job order costing system, which has only one Work in Process Inventory account.

Exhibit 20-2 uses dollar amounts to illustrate costs flowing through a process system. Each Work in Process account lists direct materials, direct labor, and factory overhead.

You will notice that each of the Work in Process accounts has a nonzero ending balance. Why? Because the manufacturing process is ongoing. No department ever sits idle. At any time, the Mixing Department will be carrying on its function while the Shaping Department and the Heating Department are handling their tasks. Before the Mixing Department ships off the most recent batch of ceramic blocks, it has already begun preparing the next batch. In Exhibit 20-2, we see that the Mixing Department has forwarded goods costing $10,000 to the Shaping Department. At the start of the next period, the Mixing Department is working on goods costing $2,000, which are left over from the preceding period.

EXHIBIT 20-2 Flow of Costs through a Process Costing System (amounts in thousands)

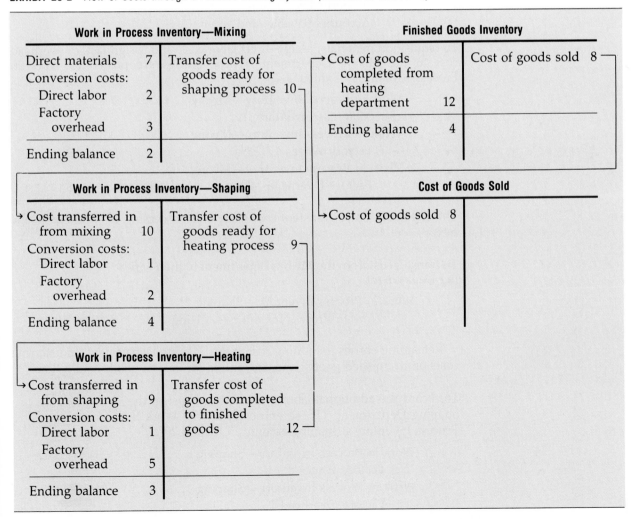

Likewise, as the Shaping Department is completing one batch of figurines, it may be starting to shape a second batch. Since any department at any time will be engaged in the manufacturing process, its Work in Process Inventory account will carry a nonzero balance.

Recording Costs

The journal entries for a process cost accounting system are like those for a job order costing system. That is, direct materials, direct labor, and factory overhead are recorded as follows (all amounts are in thousands and assumed for illustrative purposes):

To purchase materials and incur direct labor and factory overhead:

Materials Inventory	11	
Accounts Payable		11
Factory Wages	3	
Wages Payable		3
Factory Overhead	5	
Accumulated Depreciation		1
Property Tax Payable		1
Accounts Payable, and so on		3

To requisition materials, assign direct labor cost, and assign factory overhead cost to the Mixing Department. (These entries are posted to Work in Process—Mixing in Exhibit 20-2):

Work in Process Inventory—Mixing	7	
Materials Inventory		7
Work in Process Inventory—Mixing	2	
Factory Wages		2
Work in Process Inventory—Mixing	3	
Factory Overhead		3

The following entry transfers cost from one processing department to the next:

To transfer cost from the Mixing Department to the Shaping Department:

Work in Process Inventory—Shaping	10	
Work in Process Inventory—Mixing		10

Remaining entries for adding cost in the Shaping Department, transferring costs on to finished goods, and accounting for cost of goods sold follow.

To record the additional labor and overhead cost of the Shaping Department. (These entries affect the Work in Process Inventory—Shaping account in Exhibit 20-2.)

Work in Process Inventory—Shaping	1	
Factory Wages		1
Work in Process Inventory—Shaping	2	
Factory Overhead		2

Entries for the Heating Department parallel those for the Shaping Department.

To transfer cost of goods completed from the Heating Department to Finished Goods:

Finished Goods Inventory	12	
Work in Process Inventory—Heating		12

To account for the cost of goods sold:

Cost of Goods Sold	8	
Finished Goods Inventory		8

Unlike a job order costing system, a process costing system is likely to have a separate work in process account for each processing department. In a job order system the work in process account is supported by job cost records for the various jobs.

Conversion Costs

Conversion costs are all manufacturing costs other than direct materials costs. The preceding chapter provided the usual major distinctions among manufacturing costs: the threefold category of direct materials, direct labor, and indirect manufacturing costs (factory overhead). This time-honored threefold category still dominates practice, but not as much as it once did. Why? Because many companies, particularly those using process costing and automation, have seen direct labor costs become less and less important in relation to total manufacturing costs. A twofold category is often used:

> Direct materials
> Conversion costs

In many companies direct labor has vanished as a major cost category. It has become merely an element of conversion costs. This reduces accounting expense by eliminating the elaborate tracking of labor cost.

Tracing the Flow of Costs

In process costing, the accounting task is to trace the flow of costs through the production process. This task has two parts. First, we must account for the cost of goods that have been completed in one department and sent to the second department. Second, we must account for the cost of incomplete units, which remain within a department.

Let's look at a sports company that manufactures swim masks. This company's Shaping Department shapes the body of the swim masks. The direct material is the plastic that is formed into the masks. The partially completed masks then move to the Finishing Department, where the clear faceplate is inserted in the body and sealed in place.

Assume that during October, the Shaping Department incurs the following costs in processing 50,000 masks:

Direct materials		$140,000
Conversion costs:		
Direct labor	$21,250	
Factory overhead	46,750	68,000
Costs to account for		$208,000

If the shaping process is complete for all 50,000 masks, the costs to be transferred to Work in Process Inventory—Finishing are the full $208,000. The unit cost is $4.16 ($208,000/50,000 units). But suppose that shaping is complete for only 40,000 units. At October 31 the Shaping Department still has 10,000 masks in process. How do we compute unit cost when the total cost applies to finished units *and* unfinished units? Accountants answer this question by using the concept of *equivalent units of production.*

Equivalent Units of Production

OBJECTIVE 2

Compute equivalent units of production

Equivalent units of production—often called simply equivalent units—is a measure of the number of complete units that *could* have been manufactured from start to finish using the costs incurred during the period.

Let's assume that the 10,000 unfinished units still in the Shaping Department are one-quarter complete. The number of equivalent units equals the number of partially complete units times the percentage of completion: 10,000 units × 25% complete = 2,500 units regarding conversion costs. The number 2,500 tells us how many whole units are represented by the partially complete units. We add the 2,500 units to the number of finished units—40,000—to arrive at the period's equivalent units of production regarding conversion costs: 42,500.

The idea of equivalent units is not confined to manufacturing situations. It is a basic common denominator for measuring activities, output, and workload. For example, colleges and universities measure student enrollments in "full-time equivalents." Suppose a full-time class load is 12 hours per term. Assume 1,000 students are taking a full load and an additional 1,000 students are taking an average of 6 hours in classes. This school has a full-time equivalent enrollment of 1,500 students [1,000 + (1,000 × 6/12)].

Steps in Process Cost Accounting

Using the data from the swim mask example, we will discuss the five-step application of process costing.

Step 1: Summarize the Flow of Production in Physical Units

The left part of Exhibit 20-3 tabulates the movement of swim masks into and out of the Shaping Department. We assume for clarity that work began October 1, so the Work in Process account had no balance at September 30.

Step 2: Compute Output in Terms of Equivalent Units of Production

Cost accountants compute equivalent units separately for the two types of costs incurred in manufacturing: direct materials and conversion costs. The Shaping Department has 10,000 units unfinished at October 31. We assume that all direct materials have been added (the chemicals have been added to begin shaping the bodies of the swimming masks) but that three-quarters of the conversion costs (direct labor and factory overhead) remain to be applied. Thus all 50,000 units are finished in terms of direct material. We must compute equivalent units for the conversion costs. Since 25 percent of conversion costs

Shaping Department
For the Month Ended October 31, 19XX

| | Step 1 | Step 2 Equivalent Units of Production | |
| | Flow of | | |
Flow of Production	Physical Units	Direct Materials	Conversion Costs
Units to account for:			
Work in process, September 30........................	—		
Started production during October	50,000		
Total physical units to account for	50,000		
Units accounted for:			
Completed and transferred out during October	40,000	40,000	40,000
Work in process, October 31	10,000	10,000	2,500*
Total physical units accounted for	50,000		
Equivalent units of production		50,000	42,500

*10,000 units each 25% complete = 2,500 equivalent units

have already been added, we multiply the 10,000 unfinished units by .25, which gives us 2,500 units. Added to the 40,000 finished units, the equivalent units for conversion costs come to 42,500.

Exhibit 20-3 combines the data for Step 1 and Step 2. Note that the number of equivalent units for direct materials and conversion costs are different. This is often the case.

Step 3: Summarize Total Costs to Account For

Exhibit 20-4 summarizes the total costs to account for in the Shaping Department (cost data are assumed). These costs are the total debits in Work in Process Inventory—Shaping, including any beginning balance. The Shaping Department has 50,000 units and $208,000 of costs to account for.

EXHIBIT 20-4 *Step 3: Summary of Total Costs to Account For*

Shaping Department
For the Month Ended October 31, 19XX

Work in Process—Shaping

	Physical Units	Dollars		Physical Units	Dollars
Inventory, September 30	-0-	$ -0-	Transferred out	40,000	$?
Production started:	50,000		Ending inventory	10,000	?
Direct materials		140,000	Total accounted for	50,000	
Conversion costs:					
Direct labor		21,250			
Factory overhead		46,750			
Total to account for	50,000	$208,000			

Step 4: Compute Equivalent-Unit Costs

In Step 2 we computed the number of equivalent units for direct materials (50,000) and conversion costs (42,500). Because their equivalent units differ, a separate cost per unit must be computed for materials cost and for conversion costs. Exhibit 20-4 provides the data. The direct materials cost is $140,000. Conversion costs are $68,000, the sum of direct labor ($21,250) and factory overhead ($46,750).

We now have all the data needed to apply process costing in this example. We divide the direct materials cost by the equivalent units for direct materials: $140,000/50,000 = $2.80. The $2.80 is the unit price for direct materials. We compute unit price for conversion cost in a similar manner: $68,000/42,500 = $1.60. Exhibit 20-5 shows the computation of equivalent-unit costs.

Step 5: Apply Total Cost to Units Completed and to Units in Ending Work in Process Inventory

OBJECTIVE 3

Apply total cost to units completed and units in ending work in process inventory

OBJECTIVE 4

Record process costing transactions

Exhibit 20-6 shows how the unit costs computed in Step 4 are applied to units completed and to units in ending work in process. With Step 5 we account for the cost of the shaping process during the period.

The 40,000 units completed and transferred out of the shaping department bear a unit cost of $4.40 (direct materials of $2.80 + conversion cost of $1.60). The 10,000 units still in process at the end of the period have 10,000 equivalent units of *direct materials* (at $2.80 per unit) and 2,500 equivalent units of *conversion cost* (at $1.60 per unit). Observe that the sum of these two unit costs ($2.80 and $1.60) is the same as total unit cost of the completed units ($4.40), from Step 4. Also, total cost accounted for ($208,000) must agree with the total from Step 3.

October production in the Shaping Department would be recorded thus:

To requisition materials and apply labor and overhead cost to the Shaping Department. (Exhibit 20-4)

Work in Process Inventory—Shaping	140,000	
Materials Inventory		140,000
Work in Process Inventory—Shaping	21,250	
Factory Wages		21,250
Work in Process Inventory—Shaping	46,750	
Factory Overhead		46,750

The entry to transfer the cost of completed units from the Shaping Department to the Finishing Department is given below Exhibit 20-6.

EXHIBIT 20-5 *Step 4: Computation of Equivalent-Unit Costs*

Shaping Department For the Month Ended October 31, 19XX			
	Direct Materials	Conversion Costs	Total
Work in process, September 30	$ -0-	$ -0-	$ -0-
Costs added during October	$140,000	$ 68,000	$208,000
Divide by equivalent units of production . .	÷50,000	÷42,500	
Cost per equivalent unit	$ 2.80 +	$ 1.60	= $ 4.40

EXHIBIT 20-6 Step 5: Application of Total Cost to Units Completed and to Units in Ending Work in Process Inventory

Shaping Department
For the Month Ended October 31, 19XX

	Direct Materials	Conversion Costs	Total
Units completed and transferred out (40,000)	40,000 × $4.40		= $176,000
Units in ending work in process inventory (10,000):			
Direct materials	10,000 × $2.80		= 28,000
Conversion costs		2,500 × $1.60 =	4,000
Total cost of work in process			32,000
Total cost accounted for			$208,000

Work in Process Inventory—Finishing	176,000	
Work in Process Inventory—Shaping		176,000

After these entries are posted, the Work in Process Inventory—Shaping account appears as follows:

Work in Process Inventory—Shaping

Balance, September 30	—	Transferred to Finishing	176,000
Direct materials	140,000		
Direct labor	21,250		
Factory overhead	46,750		
Balance, October 31	32,000		

With Shaping Department costs accounted for, we proceed to the Finishing Department. First, however, let's reinforce what you have learned with a Summary Problem for Your Review.

Summary Problem for Your Review

Identify the missing amounts X and Y in the following production cost report prepared by Jacobs-Webster, Inc., for May:

Assembly Department
Production Cost Report
For the Month Ended May 31, 19XX

	Physical Units	Total Costs
Work in process, April 30	—	$ —
Started in production during May	20,000	43,200*
Total to account for	20,000	$43,200
Completed and transferred to Finishing Department during May	16,000	$ X
Work in process, May 31 (25% complete as to direct materials, 55% complete as to conversion cost)	4,000	Y
Total accounted for	20,000	$43,200

*Includes direct materials of $6,800 and conversion costs of $36,400.

SOLUTION TO REVIEW PROBLEM

Step 1: Flow of Production in Physical Units;
Step 2: Equivalent Units of Production

Assembly Department
For the Month Ended May 31, 19XX

Flow of Production	Step 1 Flow of Physical Units	Step 2 Equivalent Units of Production	
		Direct Materials	Conversion Costs
Units to account for:			
Work in process, April 30......................	—		
Started production during May...................	20,000		
Total physical units to account for	20,000		
Units accounted for:			
Completed and transferred out during May	16,000	16,000	16,000
Work in process, May 31	4,000	1,000*	2,200*
Total physical units accounted for	20,000		
Equivalent units of production		17,000	18,200

*Direct materials: 4,000 units each 25% complete = 1,000 equivalent units
Conversion costs: 4,000 units each 55% complete = 2,200 equivalent units

Step 3: Summary of Total Costs to Account For

Assembly Department
For the Month Ended May 31, 19XX

Work in Process—Assembly

	Physical Units	Dollars
Inventory, April 30	-0-	$ -0-
Production started:	20,000	
Direct materials		6,800
Conversion costs		36,400
Total to account for	20,000	$43,200

Step 4: Computation of Equivalent-Unit Costs

Assembly Department
For the Month Ended May 31, 19XX

	Direct Materials	Conversion Costs	Total
Work in process, April 30..............	$ -0-	$ -0-	$ -0-
Costs added during May...............	$ 6,800	$ 36,400	43,200
Divide by equivalent units of production	÷17,000	÷18,200	
Cost per equivalent unit	$.40 +	$2.00 =	$2.40

Assembly Department
For the Month Ended May 31, 19XX

	Direct Materials	Conversion Costs	Total
X Units completed and transferred out (16,000)		16,000 × $2.40	= $38,400
Units in ending work in process inventory (4,000):			
Direct materials	1,000 × $.40		= 400
Conversion costs		2,200 × $2.00	= 4,400
Y Total cost of work in process			4,800
Total cost accounted for............................			$43,200

Process Costing Extended to a Second Department

Most manufacturing systems have multiple processing steps. In this section, we introduce a second department to complete the picture of process costing. We also introduce beginning inventories of work in process, a complicating factor that was not present in our examples up to this point.

As in many areas of accounting, there are alternative methods of accounting for process costs. We discuss two: the first-in, first-out (FIFO) method and the weighted-average method. A third method, standard costing, is covered in cost and advanced managerial accounting texts. FIFO and weighted-average differ in their treatment of beginning work in process inventory; when there is no beginning inventory, the two methods are identical. The alternatives are equally applicable to a first process, such as swim mask shaping, and later processes, such as finishing.

The Finishing Department adds the faceplates and sealant to the shaped swim masks. The faceplate is the direct material added in the finishing process. It is important to keep in mind that *direct materials* in the Finishing Department refer to the faceplates added *in that department* and not to the materials (the plastic) added in the previous Shaping Department. Likewise, *conversion cost* in the Finishing Department refers to all manufacturing costs (other than direct materials) of that department only.

We assume 5,000 units were in process in the Finishing Department on October 1. These units were 60 percent complete as to Finishing Department conversion costs but 0 percent complete as to direct materials because the faceplates are added near the end of the finishing process. These facts, used throughout discussion of the accounting for the Finishing Department, are summarized in Exhibit 20-7. (Refer to Exhibit 20-7, page 946.)

Equivalent Units in a Second Department—FIFO Method

The major accounting task in dealing with a second department is the computation of equivalent units. Exhibit 20-8 summarizes the flow of physical units (Step 1) in order to compute the equivalent units of production (Step 2) for the Finishing Department. Note that there are three categories of equiva-

EXHIBIT 20-7 Finishing Department Facts for October

Units:

Work in process, September 30 (0% complete as to direct materials, 60% complete as to conversion costs) .... 5,000 units

Transferred in from Shaping Department during October .... 40,000 units

Completed during October .... 38,000 units

Work in process, October 31 (0% complete as to direct materials, 30% complete as to conversion costs) .. 7,000 units

Costs:

Work in process, September 30 .... $ 24,000
(Transferred-in cost $22,900;
Conversion costs, $1,100)

Transferred in from Shaping Department during October 176,000

Direct materials added during October 19,000

Conversion costs added during October:

Direct labor	$ 3,710	
Factory overhead	11,130	14,840

lent units. In addition to equivalent units for *direct materials* and *conversion costs* added in the Finishing Department, we must also compute equivalent units for those units that were *transferred in* from the preceding department. Whenever there is a second department, it will always have units and costs transferred in from the preceding department. In our illustration, 40,000 units were transferred into the Finishing Department during October. Of these transferred-in units, 33,000 units were completed, and 7,000 units remained in ending inventory. For transferred-in costs, equivalent units include the full total (33,000 + 7,000 = 40,000).

The **first-in, first-out (FIFO)** method of process costing is used in Exhibit 20-8 (as well as Exhibits 20-9 through 20-12). With FIFO, the focus is on the current period—October in this example. The computation of equivalent units in Exhibit 20-8 is confined to work done in the current period. Likewise, the computation of costs per equivalent unit in Exhibit 20-9 uses only costs incurred in the current period. In Step 5, Exhibit 20-10, the current month equivalent units are costed with the current month unit costs. A major advantage of the FIFO method is that with these October amounts, the efficiency of production in the month can be judged independently of production efficiency in other months. Current month data are important for planning and control purposes as well as for FIFO inventory valuation.

Under FIFO, equivalent units of direct materials have three components: beginning work in process inventory, units both transferred in and completed during the month, and ending work in process inventory. Exhibit 20-7 indicates that the beginning inventory contained 5,000 units that had no direct materials (faceplates) on October 1. During October, these units were completed first; the Finishing Department added the faceplates to complete them. Then faceplates were added to the 33,000 units that were both transferred in and completed. Ending inventory has no faceplates on October 31. Consequently, there are no equivalent units in ending inventory. Altogether, equivalent unit production for direct materials is 38,000. These amounts are shown in Exhibit 20-8 in the middle column under Step 2.

Equivalent units of *conversion costs* also have three components: beginning work in process inventory, units transferred in and completed during the

	Finishing Department For the Month Ended October 31, 19XX			
	Step 1	**Step 2** Equivalent Units of Production		
Flow of Production	**Flow of Physical Units**	**Transferred In**	**Direct Materials**	**Conversion Costs**
Units to account for:				
Work in process, September 30	5,000			
Transferred in during October	40,000			
Total physical units to account for	45,000			
Units accounted for:				
Completed and transferred out during October:				
From beginning inventory	5,000	—	5,000*	2,000*
Transferred in and completed during October				
(38,000 − 5,000)	33,000	33,000	33,000	33,000
Work in process, October 31	7,000	7,000	— †	2,100†
Total physical units accounted for	45,000			
Equivalent units of production		40,000	38,000	37,100

*Direct materials: 5,000 units each 100% completed in Finishing Department during October = 5,000 equivalent units.
 Conversion costs: 5,000 units each 40% completed in Finishing Department during October = 2,000 equivalent units.
†Direct materials: 7,000 units each 0% completed in Finishing Department during October = 0 equivalent units.
 Conversion costs: 7,000 units each 30% completed in Finishing Department during October = 2,100 equivalent units.

month, and ending work in process inventory. The Finishing Department's beginning inventory of 5,000 units was 60 percent complete as to conversion costs when the last period ended. During October the Finishing Department completed these 5,000 units by adding the remaining 40 percent of conversion costs. For beginning inventory, equivalent production is 2,000 units (5,000 × .40). Units transferred in and completed during the month (33,000 units) are the second component of equivalent production. Ending inventory is the third component. At October 31 the inventory of 7,000 units still in process in the Finishing Department is 30 percent complete as to conversion costs, so equivalent production includes 2,100 units (7,000 × .30). Altogether, equivalent production for conversion costs totals 37,100 units (2,000 + 33,000 + 2,100). Exhibit 20-8 summarizes the equivalent-unit computations for the Finishing Department.

Equivalent-Unit Costs in a Second Department—FIFO Method

The October costs of the Finishing Department are accumulated as shown in Exhibit 20-9. The exhibit shows how equivalent units are used to compute the equivalent-unit costs in the Finishing Department process. Note that the $24,000 beginning balance of work in process is kept separate from the costs incurred during the current period. That is, the $24,000 is not included in the computation of equivalent-unit costs for work done in October. The work in process beginning balance is the cost incurred in *September* on the 5,000 physical units in process on October 1. Under FIFO, each *October* cost per equivalent unit is computed by dividing an October cost by an October number of equivalent units of work.

Finishing Department
For the Month Ended October 31, 19XX

	Transferred-In Costs	Direct Materials	Conversion Costs	Total
Work in process, September 30 (from Exhibit 20-7)	Work done before October			$ 24,000
Costs added during October (from Exhibit 20-7) ...	$176,000	$ 19,000	$ 14,840	209,840
Divide by equivalent units (from Exhibit 20-8)	÷40,000	÷38,000	÷37,100	
Cost per equivalent unit	$4.40	$.50	$.40	
Total costs to account for........................				$233,840

Application of Total Cost in a Second Department—FIFO Method

Exhibit 20-10 shows how to apply total cost of the Finishing Department to units completed and transferred to finished goods and to units still in process at the end of the period.

The entries for the Shaping Department were recorded on page 943. The following entries record Finishing Department activity during October.

EXHIBIT 20-10 FIFO Method
Step 5: Application of Total Cost to Units Completed
and Units in Ending Work in Process Inventory

Finishing Department
For the Month Ended October 31, 19XX

	Transferred-In Costs	Direct Materials	Conversion Costs	Total
Units completed and transferred out to Finished Goods Inventory:				
From work in process, September 30:.............				$ 24,000
Costs added during October:				
Direct materials.............................	—	5,000 × $.50		2,500
Conversion costs	—		2,000 × $.40	800
Total completed from September 30 inventory ..				27,300
Units transferred in and completed during October..	33,000 × ($4.40 + $.50 + $.40)			174,900
Total costs transferred out				202,200
Work in process, October 31:				
Transferred-in costs............................	7,000 × $4.40			30,800
Direct materials...............................		—		—
Conversion costs			2,100 × $.40	840
Total work in process, October 31				31,640
Total cost accounted for				$233,840

To transfer in cost of completed units from the Shaping Department:

Work in Process Inventory—Finishing.............	176,000	
Work in Process Inventory—Shaping..........		176,000

To requisition materials and apply conversion costs to the Finishing Department (amounts from Exhibit 20-7):

Work in Process Inventory—Finishing.............	19,000	
Materials Inventory		19,000
Work in Process Inventory—Finishing.............	3,710	
Factory Wages...............................		3,710
Work in Process Inventory—Finishing.............	11,130	
Factory Overhead............................		11,130

The entry to transfer the cost of completed units from the Finishing Department to finished goods is based on the dollar amount taken from Exhibit 20-10:

Finished Goods Inventory	202,200	
Work in Process Inventory—Finishing.........		202,200

After posting, the key accounts appear as follows. Observe the accumulation of costs as debits to Work in Process and the transfer of costs from one account to the next.

Work in Process Inventory—Shaping

(Exhibit 20-4)		(Exhibit 20-6)	
Balance, September 30	—	Transferred to Finishing	176,000
Direct materials	140,000		
Direct labor	21,250		
Factory overhead	46,750		
Balance, October 31	32,000		

Work in Process Inventory—Finishing

(Exhibit 20-7)		(Exhibit 20-10)	
Balance, September 30	24,000	Transferred to finished goods	202,200
Transferred from Shaping	176,000		
Direct materials	19,000		
Direct labor	3,710		
Factory overhead	11,130		
Balance, October 31	31,640		

Finished Goods Inventory

Balance, September 30	—		
Transferred from Finishing	202,200		

Production Cost Report

A **production cost report** summarizes the operations of a processing department for the period. Exhibit 20-11 is a production cost report for the Finishing Department for October. It shows the department's beginning inventory (5,000 units; cost $24,000), the number of units and the cost transferred in during the month (40,000 units; cost $176,000), and the costs added. These amounts make up the totals to account for. The production cost report also shows the units completed (38,000), the costs transferred out of the department ($202,200), and the ending inventory (7,000 units; cost $31,640).

These reports vary from company to company, depending on the level of detail desired by the managers. If managers want more detail, some or all of the additional information in Exhibits 20-8, 20-9, and 20-10 can be included. For example, Exhibit 20-12 provides more detail than Exhibit 20-11.

How is the production report used for decision making? Managers compare direct materials and conversion costs—particularly the unit costs in Exhibit 20-12—with budgeted amounts for the department. If these costs are too high, corrective action is taken. If costs are below budget, the employees responsible may receive incentive awards.

Managers also compare the number of units produced with budgeted production. Production that is too low can be investigated and corrected. If production in excess of budget is welcomed, such performance may lead to various rewards for responsible employees.

Process Costing in a Second Department—Weighted-Average Method

OBJECTIVE 6

Account for process costing in a second department using the weighted-average method

We now rework our swim mask Finishing Department example to demonstrate the second process costing method, weighted-average. The FIFO meth-

EXHIBIT 20-11 FIFO Method
Production Cost Report

Finishing Department
Production Cost Report
For the Month Ended October 31, 19XX

	Physical Units	Total Costs
Work in process, September 30	5,000	$ 24,000
Transferred in from Shaping Department during October	40,000	176,000
Cost added in Finishing Department during October:		
Direct materials.....................................	—	19,000
Conversion costs ($3,710 + $11,130)	—	14,840
Total to account for	45,000	$233,840
Completed and transferred to finished goods		
during October	38,000	$202,200
Work in process, October 31	7,000	31,640
Total accounted for	45,000	$233,840

EXHIBIT 20-12 *FIFO Method*
Production Cost Report (Expanded)

Finishing Department
Production Cost Report (Expanded)
For the Month Ended October 31, 19XX

		Transferred-in Costs	Direct Materials	Conversion Costs	Total
	Work in process, September 30				$ 24,000
	Cost added during October	$176,000	$ 19,000	$ 14,840	209,840
(Step 3)	Total cost to account for				$233,840
	Equivalent units for work during October				
	(Steps 1 and 2 in Exhibit 20–8)	÷40,000	÷38,000	÷37,100	
(Step 4)	Cost per equivalent unit	$ 4.40	$ .50	$ .40	
(Step 5)	Application of total costs:				
	From work in process, September 30				$ 24,000
	Costs added during October		5,000 × $.50 = $2,500	2,000 × $.40 = $800	3,300
	Total completed from September 30 inventory				27,300
	Units transferred in and completed during October	33,000 × ($4.40 + $.50 + $.40)			174,900
					202,200
	Work in process, October 31:				
	Transferred-in costs	7,000 × $4.40			30,800
	Direct materials		—		—
	Conversion costs			2,100 × $.40	840
	Total work in process, October 31				31,640
	Total costs accounted for				$233,840

od costs (1) physical units completed and transferred out and (2) work in process ending inventory by costing equivalent units of work done *in the current month* with current month unit costs. By contrast, the **weighted-average method** costs these two categories of physical units by costing work done *by the end of the current month* with unit costs that are weighted averages of current month and prior month unit costs. Weighted-average Exhibits 20-13 through 20-17 correspond to FIFO Exhibits 20-8 through 20-12, respectively. Both methods use the same five general steps.

Steps 1 and 2: Summarize the Flow of Physical Units and Compute Equivalent Units of Production

Exhibit 20-13 shows that 38,000 units were completed and transferred out of the Finishing Department in October. The full 38,000 equivalent units of production are assigned to these physical units in each Step 2 category. Why? Because by October 31, all these units had been transferred into Finishing from Shaping, faceplates had been added to all of them, and all the finishing conversion work had been done. In short, they had been completed. The equivalent units for ending inventory of work in process are the same for the weighted-average method as for FIFO. All the Finishing Department work done on these 7,000 units by October 31 was done in October, because they were among the 40,000 units transferred in from Shaping during the month.

Finishing Department
For the Month Ended October 31, 19XX

| | Step 1 | Step 2 Equivalent Units of Production | | |
| | Flow of | | | |
Flow of Production	Physical Units	Transferred In	Direct Materials	Conversion Costs
Units to account for:				
Work in process, September 30	5,000			
Transferred in during October	40,000			
Total physical units to account for................	45,000			
Units accounted for:				
Completed and transferred out during October.	38,000	38,000	38,000*	38,000*
Work in process, October 31	7,000	7,000	—†	2,100†
Total physical units accounted for	45,000			
Equivalent units of production		45,000	38,000	40,100

*Direct materials: 38,000 units each 100% completed in Finishing Department by October 31 = 38,000 equivalent units.
 Conversion costs: 38,000 units each 100% completed in Finishing Department by October 31 = 38,000 equivalent units.
†Direct materials: 7,000 units each 0% completed in Finishing Department by October 31 = 0 equivalent units.
 Conversion costs: 7,000 units each 30% completed in Finishing Department by October 31 = 2,100 equivalent units.

Step 3: Summarize Total Costs to Account For

The total cost to account for (Exhibit 20-14) is the sum of work in process beginning inventory cost ($24,000) and the costs added to the work in process account during October ($209,840). The total is $233,840.

Step 4: Compute Equivalent Unit Costs

The numerators and denominators of the weighted-average unit cost calculations include both current month amounts and amounts from October's beginning work in process inventory. In our example, the resulting unit costs are

Finishing Department
For the Month Ended October 31, 19XX

	Transferred-In Costs	Direct Materials	Conversion Costs	Total
Work in process, September 30	$ 22,900	—	$ 1,100	$ 24,000
Costs added during October (from Exhibit 20-7) ...	176,000	$19,000	14,840	209,840
Total cost	$198,900	$19,000	$15,940	
Divide by equivalent units (from Exhibit 20-13)	÷45,000	÷38,000	÷40,100	
Cost per equivalent unit	$4.42	$.50	$.3975	
Total costs to account for				$233,840

EXHIBIT 20-15 *Weighted-Average Method*
Step 5: Application of Total Cost to Units Completed
and Units in Ending Work in Process Inventory

Finishing Department
For the Month Ended October 31, 19XX

	Transferred-In Costs	Direct Materials	Conversion Costs	Total
Units completed and transferred out to Finished Goods Inventory	38,000 × ($4.42 + $.50 + $.3975)			$202,065
Work in process, October 31:				
Transferred-in costs...........................	7,000 × $4.42			30,940
Direct materials		—		—
Conversion costs			2,100 × $.3975	835
Total work in process, October 31				31,775
Total cost accounted for.......................				$233,840

weighted averages of September unit costs and October unit costs. The computations are shown in Exhibit 20-14. Consider conversion costs. The $1,100 cost of the 3,000 equivalent units (5,000 × .60, Exhibit 20-7) for conversion costs in October 1 work in process inventory is added to the $14,840 cost of the 37,100 (Exhibit 20-8) equivalent units of conversion in October. The sum, $15,940, is then divided by the sum of the equivalent units, 40,100 (3,000 + 37,100). The resulting cost of $.3975 is a weighted average of September's unit cost of $.3667 ($1,100 ÷ 3,000) and October's unit cost of $.40 ($14,840 ÷ 37,100).

EXHIBIT 20-16 *Weighted-Average Method*
Production Cost Report

Finishing Department
Production Cost Report
For the Month Ended October 31, 19XX

	Physical Units	Total Costs
Work in process, September 30	5,000	$ 24,000
Transferred in from Shaping Department during October....................	40,000	176,000
Costs added in Finishing Department during October:		
Direct materials...	—	19,000
Conversion costs ($3,710 + $11,130)	—	14,840
Total to account for	45,000	$233,840
Completed and transferred to finished goods.............................		
during October	38,000	$202,065
Work in process, October 31	7,000	31,775
Total accounted for	45,000	$233,840

EXHIBIT 20-17 *Weighted-Average Method Production Cost Report (Expanded)*

Finishing Department
Production Cost Report (Expanded)
For the Month Ended October 31, 19XX

		Transferred-in Costs	Direct Materials	Conversion Costs	Total
	Work in process, September 30	$ 22,900	—	$ 1,100	$ 24,000
	Cost added during October	176,000	$ 19,000	14,840	209,840
(Step 3)	Total costs to account for	$198,900	$ 19,000	$15,940	$233,840
	Equivalent units for work during October				
	(Steps 1 and 2 in Exhibit 20–13)	÷45,000	÷38,000	÷40,100	
(Step 4)	Cost per equivalent unit	$ 4.42	$ .50	$.3975	
(Step 5)	Application of total costs:				
	Units completed during October	38,000 × ($4.42 + $.50 + $.3975)			$202,065
	Work in process, October 31:				
	Transferred-in costs	7,000 × $4.42			30,940
	Direct materials		—		—
	Conversion costs			2,100 × $.3975	835
	Total work in process, October 31:				31,775
	Total costs accounted for				$233,840

Step 5: Apply Total Cost to Units Completed and to Units in Ending Work in Process Inventory

With the weighted-average method, the 38,000 physical units completed and transferred out of Finishing during October are costed in one step. Because 38,000 equivalent units in each input category were assigned to these units (Exhibit 20-13), the total cost is 38,000 multiplied by the full equivalent unit cost of $5.3175 ($4.42 + $.50 + $.3975). The result is $202,065 (Exhibit 20-15). Equivalent units in October 31 work in process inventory also are costed at the appropriate unit amounts.

The weighted-average production cost reports in Exhibits 20-16 and 20-17 are similar to their FIFO counterparts. They too may signal the need for action if actual costs or production quantities differ materially from budgeted amounts. However, their reported unit costs are not as useful for evaluating the efficiency of October production because they are affected by the costs incurred in September. But managers may choose to use the weighted-average method because (1) the computations required to cost physical units are simpler than those of the FIFO method and (2) the differences in costs assigned to units are often immaterial.

Summary Problem for Your Review

This problem extends the Summary Problem for Your Review on page 943 to a second processing department. Jacobs-Webster, Inc., had the following activity in its Finishing Department during May.

Finishing Department Facts for May

Units:
Work in process, April 30 (20% complete as to direct materials, 70% complete as to conversion costs) .... 4,000 units
Transferred in from Assembly Department during May .... 16,000 units
Completed during May .... 15,000 units
Work in process, May 31 (36% complete as to direct materials, 80% complete as to conversion costs) .... 5,000 units
Costs:
Work in process, April 30 .... $18,000
(Transferred-in costs, $11,982; direct materials costs, $488; conversion costs, $5,530)
Transferred in from Assembly Department during May 38,400
Direct materials added during May...................................... 6,400
Conversion costs added during May 24,300

Required

Show the allocation of total cost to units completed and units in ending work in process inventory in the Finishing Department during May. Use

1. The FIFO method.
2. The weighted-average method.

SOLUTION TO REVIEW PROBLEM

1. The FIFO method.

Step 1: Flow of Production in Physical Units;
Step 2: Equivalent Units of Production

Finishing Department
For the Month Ended May 31, 19XX

Flow of Production	Step 1 Flow of Physical Units	Step 2 Equivalent Units of Production Transferred In	Direct Materials	Conversion Costs
Units to account for:				
Work in process, April 30	4,000			
Transferred in during May	16,000			
Total physical units to account for......................	20,000			
Units accounted for:				
Completed and transferred out during May:				
From beginning inventory	4,000	—	3,200*	1,200*
Transferred in and completed during May (16,000 − 5,000)	11,000	11,000	11,000	11,000
Work in process, May 31	5,000	5,000	1,800†	4,000†
Total physical units accounted for	20,000			
Equivalent units of production		16,000	16,000	16,200

* Direct materials: 4,000 units each 80% completed = 3,200 equivalent units.
  Conversion costs: 4,000 units each 30% completed = 1,200 equivalent units.
† Direct materials: 5,000 units each 36% completed = 1,800 equivalent units.
  Conversion costs: 5,000 units each 80% completed = 4,000 equivalent units.

Finishing Department
For the Month Ended May 31, 19XX

	Transferred-In Costs	Direct Materials	Conversion Costs	Total
Work in process, April 30 ..	Work done before May			$18,000
Costs added during May . . .	$38,400	$ 6,400	$24,300	69,100
Divide by equivalent units . .	÷16,000	÷16,000	÷16,200	
Cost per equivalent unit	$2.40	$.40	$1.50	
Total cost to account for				$87,100

Step 5: Application of Total Cost to Units Completed
and Units in Ending Work in Process Inventory

Finishing Department
For the Month Ended October 31, 19XX

	Transferred-In Costs	Direct Materials	Conversion Costs	Total
Units completed and transferred out to Finished Goods Inventory:				
From work in process, April 30				$18,000
Costs added during May:				
Direct materials	—	3,200 × $.40		1,280
Conversion costs	—		1,200 × $1.50	1,800
Total completed from April 30 inventory				21,080
Units transferred in and completed during May. . . .	11,000 × ($2.40 + $.40 + $1.50)			47,300
Total costs transferred out ..				68,380
Work in process, May 31:				
Transferred-in costs	5,000 × $2.40			12,000
Direct materials		1,800 × $.40		720
Conversion costs			4,000 × $1.50	6,000
Total work in process, May 31				18,720
Total cost accounted for				$87,100

2. *The weighted-average method.*

Step 1: Flow of Production in Physical Units;
Step 2: Equivalent Units of Production

Finishing Department
For the Month Ended May 31, 19XX

Flow of Production	Step 1 Flow of Physical Units	Step 2 Equivalent Units of Production		
		Transferred In	Direct Materials	Conversion Costs
Units to account for:				
Work in process, April 30	4,000			
Transferred in during May	16,000			
Total physical units to account for...............	20,000			
Units accounted for:				
Completed and transferred out during May	15,000	15,000	15,000	15,000
Work in process, May 31	5,000	5,000	1,800*	4,000*
Total physical units accounted for	20,000			
Equivalent units of production		20,000	16,800	19,000

*Direct materials: 5,000 units each 36% completed = 1,800 equivalent units.
Conversion costs: 5,000 units each 80% completed = 4,000 equivalent units.

Steps 3 and 4: Computation of Equivalent-Unit Costs

Finishing Department
For the Month Ended May 31, 19XX

	Transferred-In Costs	Direct Materials	Conversion Costs	Total
Work in process, April 30	$11,982	$ 488	$ 5,530	$18,000
Costs added during May	38,400	6,400	24,300	69,100
Total cost.....................................	$50,382	$ 6,888	$29,830	
Divide by equivalent units	÷20,000	÷16,800	÷19,000	
Cost per equivalent unit	$2.52	$.41	$1.57	
Total cost accounted for				$87,100

Step 5: Application of Total Cost to Units Completed and Units in Ending Work in Process Inventory

Finishing Department
For the Month Ended October 31, 19XX

	Transferred-In Costs	Direct Materials	Conversion Costs	Total
Units completed and transferred out to Finished Goods Inventory	38,000 × ($4.42 + $.50 + $.3975)			$202,065
Work in process, October 31:				
Transferred-in costs...........................	7,000 × $4.42			30,940
Direct materials		—		—
Conversion costs			2,100 × $.3975	835
Total work in process, October 31				31,775
Total cost accounted for.......................				$233,840

Summary

Process costing is a system for assigning costs to products that are mass-produced in continuous fashion through a sequence of production steps, or processes. In a process costing system, costs are accumulated by processes and flow from one process to another until the product is completed.

The main accounting problem in process costing is determining, for each process, the costs assigned to (1) units of product completed and transferred out during a production period (either into another process for further processing or into finished goods inventory) and (2) ending inventory of work in process. A complication arises because goods in process may be in various stages of completion. Cost accountants compute the number of equivalent units of production that could have been manufactured from start to finish with the costs that were incurred in each department during the period. Equivalent units of work in each input category are computed for physical (output) units both completed and in process.

Two methods are widely used for process costing: FIFO and weighted-average. FIFO focuses on current period work. With this method, equivalent units of work performed in the current month are costed at current month unit costs. By contrast, the weighted-average method costs all work to account for each month—work in process at the beginning of the month and current month work—with unit costs that are a weighted average of current and prior month's costs. With both methods, accountants follow a five-step procedure for each process.

First, the flow of production in physical units is determined. Second, equivalent units of production are computed for physical units completed and transferred out and for ending work in process inventory. Third, the total cost to account for is calculated by adding the beginning balance of work in process to current costs added to the account. Fourth, unit costs are computed for each input category: materials transferred in from the previous process (if any), materials added from direct materials inventory, and conversion costs. Finally, physical units are costed by multiplying equivalent units from Step 2 by equivalent-unit costs from Step 4.

The operations of processing departments are summarized in monthly production cost reports. Managers compare costs in the reports with budgeted costs in order to evaluate processing performance.

Self-Study Questions

Test your understanding of the chapter by marking the best answer to each of the following questions.

1. For which of the following products is a process costing system most appropriate? *(p. 935)*
   a. Breakfast cereal
   b. Automobiles
   c. Houses
   d. Furniture

2. A key difference between job order costing and process costing is that *(p. 936)*
   a. Costs are assigned to direct materials in job costing and to indirect materials in process costing
   b. Job costing uses a single work in process account and process costing uses a separate work in process account for each department
   c. Job order costing, but not process costing, uses conversion costs
   d. Factory overhead is used in process costing but not in job order costing

3. During August the Assembly Department of Fisk Manufacturing Company completed and transferred 20,000 intercom units to the Finishing Department. The Assembly Department's August 31 inventory included

6,000 units, 90 percent complete as to direct materials and 75 percent complete as to conversion costs. Under FIFO, August equivalent units of the Assembly Department total *(p. 940)*

a. 20,000

b. 24,500

c. 25,400

d. 25,400 as to direct materials and 24,500 as to conversion costs

4. The concept of equivalent units is useful for *(p. 942)*

a. Measuring the cost of direct materials and conversion costs incurred in a processing department

b. Measuring the unit costs of direct materials and conversion costs to compute the cost of goods transferred from one processing department to the next

c. Separating the cost of a manufacturing *process* from the cost of a manufacturing *activity*

d. Dividing ending inventory between finished goods and work in process

5. The entry to record the transfer of goods from the Heating Department to the Drying Department is *(p. 943)*

a. Finished Goods XXX
   Work in Process—Drying XXX

b. Work in Process—Heating XXX
   Work in Process—Drying XXX

c. Work in Process—Heating XXX
   Finished Goods XXX

d. Work in Process—Drying XXX
   Work in Process—Heating XXX

6. The costs to account for in a second processing department include those associted with *(p. 945)*

a. Beginning work in process and goods transferred in during the period

b. Beginning work in process and costs added during the period

c. Beginning work in process, goods transferred in, and costs added during the period

d. Beginning work in process and ending work in process

7. Refer to the production cost report in Exhibit 20-11, page 914. The unit cost of goods completed and transferred to finished goods during October was *(p. 950)*

a. $4.40   c. $4.90

b. $4.80   d. $5.32

8. If you already know equivalent units for transferred-in costs, direct materials costs, and conversion costs under FIFO, what is the easiest way to compute equivalent units under the weighted-average method? *(p. 952)*

a. Add the equivalent units in beginning work in process inventory to the FIFO equivalent units.

b. Subtract the equivalent units in beginning work in process inventory from the FIFO equivalent units.

c. Add the equivalent units in ending work in process inventory to the FIFO equivalent units.

d. Subtract the equivalent units in ending work in process inventory from the FIFO equivalent units.

9. If direct materials are added at the beginning of a second processing department, direct materials equivalent units for that department are *(p. 946)*

a. Less than transferred-in equivalent units

b. Equal to transferred-in equivalent units

  c. Greater than transferred-in equivalent units

  d. Always equal to the number of physical units transferred in currently, regardless of whether FIFO or weighted-average is used

10. An advantage of the FIFO method over the weighted-average method is that *(p. 954)*

  a. It is simpler in its computations

  b. It is more useful for income determination

  c. It is more useful for inventory valuation

  d. It is more useful for manufacturing performance evaluation

Answers to the Self-Study Questions follow the Accounting Vocabulary.

Accounting Vocabulary

Conversion costs. All manufacturing costs other than direct materials costs *(p. 939)*.

Equivalent units. Measure of the number of complete units that could have been manufactured from start to finish using the costs incurred during the period *(p. 940)*.

FIFO method. First-in, first-out; a process costing method that costs each period's equivalent units of work with that period's average cost per equivalent unit *(p. 946)*.

Process costing. System for assigning costs to goods that are mass-produced in a continuous sequence of steps *(p. 935)*.

Production cost report. Summary of the activity in a processing department for a period *(p. 950)*.

Weighted-average method. A process costing method that costs all equivalent units of work to account for each period with a weighted average of that period's and the previous period's average cost per equivalent unit *(p. 951)*.

Answers to Self-Study Questions

1. a
2. b
3. d Direct materials: 20,000 + (6,000 × .90) = 25,400
   Conversion costs: 20,000 + (6,000 × .75) = 24,500
4. b
5. d
6. c
7. d $202,200/38,000 = $5.32
8. a
9. b
10. d

ASSIGNMENT MATERIAL _____

Questions

1. Distinguish a process cost accounting system from a job order system.
2. Which type of costing system—job order or process costing—would be better suited to account for manufacture of each of the following products: (a) chemicals, (b) automobiles, (c) lumber, (d) hand-held calculators, (e) custom lampshades?

3. Why does a process costing system use multiple work in process accounts but a job order system use only one such account?

4. Give the entries (accounts only) to record the following: (a) purchase of materials; (b) incurrence of labor; (c) overhead cost; (d) requisition of materials and application of labor and overhead to Work in Process Inventory—Department 1 (combine in one entry); (e) transfer of cost of work in process inventory from Department 1 to Department 2; (f) transfer of cost of completed units to finished goods; (g) cost of goods sold.

5. What is an equivalent unit of production? Give an example of equivalent units.

6. Montague Manufacturing Company completed and transferred 35,000 units of its product to a second department during the period. At the end of the period, another 10,000 units were in work in process inventory, 20 percent complete. How many equivalent units did Montague produce during the period?

7. Outline the five steps to account for a process costing system.

8. How are equivalent units used in Exhibits 20-5 and 20-6?

9. Why might a company have different numbers of equivalent units for direct materials and conversion costs?

10. What information does a production cost report give? Why does the format of the report differ from company to company?

11. What is the major accounting challenge in a process costing system that has more than one processing department? Why is this such a challenge?

12. Using the FIFO method, compute the equivalent units of production for Department 2 during July:

Units:
Work in process, June 30 (10% complete as to direct materials, 40% complete as to conversion costs). . . .	1,000 units
Transferred in from Department 1 during July	25,000 units
Completed during July	22,000 units
Work in process, July 31 (20% complete as to direct materials, 70% complete as to conversion costs). . . .	4,000 units

13. Repeat Question 12, using the weighted-average method.

14. Under what condition are FIFO equivalent-unit costs equal to weighted-average equivalent-unit costs?

15. "Unit costs in process costing are averages, but that is not true in job order costing." Do you agree or disagree? Explain.

Exercises

Exercise 20-1 *Diagramming flows through a process costing system* **(L.O. 1)**

Vines & Crocker manufactures furniture in a three-stage process that includes milling, assembling, and finishing, in that order. Direct materials are added in the milling and finishing departments, and direct labor and overhead are applied in all three departments. The company's general ledger includes the following accounts:

Work in Process Inventory—Finishing	Factory Wages
Raw Materials Inventory	Work in Process Inventory—
Finished Goods Inventory	Milling
Factory Overhead	Work in Process Inventory—
Cost of Goods Sold	Assembling

Required

Outline the flow of costs through the company's accounts. Include a T-account for each account title given.

Exercise 20-2 *Computing equivalent units in a single department* **(L.O. 2)**

Insert the missing values:

Flow of Production	Flow of Physical Units	Equivalent Units of Production	
		Direct Materials	Conversion Costs
Units to account for:			
Work in process, November 30	12,000		
Started production during December	X		
Total physical units to account for	67,000		
Units accounted for:			
Completed and transferred out during December:			
ª From beginning inventory	12,000	X*	X*
Started and completed during December	47,000	X	X
ª Work in process, December 31	X	X†	X†
Total physical units accounted for	67,000		
Equivalent units of production		X	X

> * Direct materials: 40% completed during December
>   Conversion costs: 50% completed during December
> † Direct materials: 20% completed during December
>   Conversion costs: 30% completed during December

Exercise 20-3 *Computing equivalent units and applying cost to completed units and work in process* **(L.O. 2, 3, 5)**

Gray Matter, Inc., experienced the following activity in its Finishing Department during December.

Units:	
Work in process, November 30 (60% complete as to direct materials, 80% complete as to conversion costs).	8,000 units
Transferred in from Heating Department during December	31,000 units
Completed during December	26,000 units
Work in process, December 31 (60% complete as to direct materials, 80% complete as to conversion costs).	13,000 units
Costs:	
Work in process, November 30.......................	$ 59,000
Transferred in from Heating Department during December	108,500
Direct materials added during December	72,500
Conversion costs added during December..............	102,000

Required

1. Compute the number of equivalent units produced by the Finishing Department during December. Use the FIFO method.
2. Compute unit costs, and apply total cost to (a) units completed and transferred to finished goods and (b) units in December 31 work in process inventory.

Exercise 20-4 *Computing equivalent units and applying cost to completed units and work in process* **(L.O. 2, 3, 6)**

Repeat Exercise 20-3, using the weighted-average method. Assume that the November 30 balance of Work in Process—Finishing Department ($59,000) comprises the following amounts: transferred-in costs, $26,050; direct materials costs, $12,676; and conversion costs, $20,274.

Exercise 20-5 *Transferring costs between processing departments* **(L.O. 2, 3, 4)**

The Mixing Department of a chemical company began February with no work in process inventory. During the month, production that cost $37,500 (direct materials, $9,500, and conversion costs, $28,000) was started on 21,000 units. A total of 17,000 units were completed and transferred to the Heating Department. The ending work in process inventory was 50 percent complete as to direct materials and 75 percent complete as to conversion costs.

Required

1. Journalize the transfer of cost from the Mixing Department to the Heating Department.
2. What is the balance in Work in Process—Mixing on February 28?
3. Account for the total cost incurred during February.

Exercise 20-6 *Computing processing costs and journalizing cost transfers* **(L.O. 2, 4)**

The following information was taken from the ledger of Vanderpool Products. Ending inventory is 70 percent complete as to direct materials but only 40 percent complete as to conversion costs.

Work in Process—Forming

	Physical Units	Dollars		Physical Units	Dollars
Inventory, November 30	-0-	$ -0-	Transferred to Painting	72,000	?
Production started:	80,000				
1. Direct materials		271,600			
2. Conversion costs		225,600			
Ending inventory	8,000	?			

Required

Journalize the transfer of cost to the Painting Department.

Exercise 20-7 *Computing equivalent units in two departments* (L.O. 2, 5)

Selected production and cost data of Cordoba, Inc., follow for May 19X5.

| | Flow of Physical Units | |
Flow of Production	Sanding Department	Finishing Department
Units to account for:		
Work in process, April 30	20,000	6,000
Transferred in during May	70,000	75,000
Total physical units to account for	90,000	81,000
Units accounted for:		
Completed and transferred out during May:		
From beginning inventory................	20,000*	6,000‡
Transferred in and completed during May .	55,000	70,000
Work in process, May 31..................	15,000†	5,000§
Total physical units accounted for.............	90,000	81,000

  * Direct materials: 20 percent completed during May
    Conversion costs: 30 percent completed during May
  † Direct materials: 50 percent completed during May
    Conversion costs: 40 percent completed during May
  ‡ Direct materials: ⅔ completed during May
    Conversion costs: 40 percent completed during May
  § Direct materials: 50 percent completed during May
    Conversion costs: 60 percent completed during May

Required

Compute equivalent units for goods transferred in, direct materials, and conversion costs for each department. Use the FIFO method.

Exercise 20-8 *Computing equivalent units in a second department* (L.O. 2, 6)

Repeat Exercise 20-7 for the Finishing Department, using the weighted-average method.

Exercise 20-9 *Journalizing process costing transactions* (L.O. 4)

Record the following selected process cost accounting transactions in the general journal:

a. Purchase of raw materials on account, $4,200.

b. Requisition of direct materials to Processing Department 1, $1,800.

c. Payment of factory labor, $11,000.

d. Incurrence of factory overhead costs: depreciation, $600; insurance, $500; utilities paid, $900.

e. Application of conversion costs to Processing Department 1: direct labor, $1,900; factory overhead, $2,850.

f. Transfer of cost from Processing Department 1 to Department 2, $5,300.

g. Application of conversion costs to Processing Department 2: direct labor, $700; factory overhead, $1,050.

h. Transfer of cost from Processing Department 2 to finished goods, $5,200.

Exercise 20-10 *Using a production cost report* (L.O. 4)

Cost accountants for South Fork Manufacturing prepared the following production cost report for February:

Finishing Department
Production Cost Report
For the Month Ended February 28, 19XX

	Physical Units	Total Costs
Work in process, January 31	14,000	$ 82,000
Transferred in from Grinding Department during February	90,000	392,000
Cost added in Finishing Department during February:		
Direct materials..................................	—	58,000
Conversion costs:		
Direct labor	—	84,000
Factory overhead	—	83,000
Total to account for	104,000	$699,000
Completed and transferred to finished goods during February	95,000	$650,000
Work in process, February 28	9,000	49,000
Total accounted for	104,000	$699,000

Required

Journalize all February activity in the Finishing Department.

Problems

(Group A)

Problem 20-1A *Computing equivalent units and applying cost to completed units and work in process; no beginning inventory or cost transferred in* **(L.O. 2, 3)**

Suruga Bay, Inc., produces component parts that are used in hand-held calculators. One part, a diode generator, is manufactured in a single processing department. No diode generators were in process on May 31, and Suruga started production on 12,000 units during June. Completed production for June totaled 9,900 units. The June 30 work in process was 20 percent complete as to direct materials and 30 percent complete as to conversion costs. Direct materials costing $6,192 were placed in production during June, and direct labor of $5,100 and factory overhead of $2,271 were applied to the manufacture of diode generators.

Required

1. Compute the number of equivalent units of production and the unit costs for June.
2. Show the application of total cost to (a) units completed and transferred to finished goods, and (b) units still in process at June 30.
3. Prepare a T-account for Work in Process Inventory to show its activity during June, including the June 30 balance.

Problem 20-2A *Computing equivalent units, applying cost to completed units and work in process, and journalizing transactions; no beginning inventory or cost transferred in* **(L.O. 2, 3, 4)**

Santa Fe Sheep & Wool Company produces wool fabric by a three-stage process: cleaning, spinning, and weaving, in that order. Costs incurred in the Cleaning Department during September are summarized as follows:

Work in Process Inventory—Cleaning

Direct materials	70,400
Direct labor	2,580
Factory overhead	8,700

September activity in the Cleaning Department included completion of 17,000 pounds of wool, which were transferred to the Spinning Department. Also, work on 3,000 pounds began, which on September 30 was 20 percent complete with respect to direct materials and 60 percent complete with respect to conversion costs.

Required

1. Compute the equivalent units of production and unit costs in the Cleaning Department for September.
2. Prove that the sum of (a) cost of goods transferred out of the Cleaning Department and (b) ending Work in Process Inventory—Cleaning equals the total cost accumulated in the department during September.
3. Journalize all transactions affecting the company's cleaning process during September, including those already posted.

Problem 20-3A *Computing equivalent units for a second department with beginning inventory; applying cost to completed units and work in process; FIFO Method* **(L.O. 2, 3, 5)**

Motor Parts Corporation manufactures auto bumpers in a two-stage process that includes shaping and plating. Steel alloy is the basic raw material of the shaping process. The steel is molded according to the design specifications of the automobile manufacturers (Chrysler, Ford, and General Motors). The Plating Department then adds a finish plate of chrome to give the new bumper a shiny appearance.

At March 31, before recording the transfer of cost from the Plating Department to Finished Goods Inventory, the Motor Parts general ledger included the following account:

Work in Process Inventory—Plating

Feb. 28 Balance	24,600
Transferred in from Shaping	30,000
Direct materials	27,060
Direct labor	17,100
Factory overhead	37,620

Work in process of the Plating Department on February 28 consisted of 600 bumpers that were 50 percent complete as to direct materials and conversion costs. During March 3,000 bumpers were transferred in from the Shaping Department. The Plating Department transferred 2,200 bumpers to finished goods in March, and 1,400 bumpers were still in process on March 31. This ending inventory was 40 percent complete as to direct materials and 70 percent complete as to conversion costs.

Required

1. Compute the equivalent units of production, unit costs, and total cost to account for in the Plating Department for March. Use the FIFO method.
2. Show the application of total Plating Department cost for March to (a) cost of goods transferred out of the Plating Department and (b) cost of ending Work in Process Inventory—Plating on March 31.

Problem 20-4A *Preparing a production cost report and recording transactions based on the report's information* **(L.O. 4)**

Required

1. Prepare the March production cost report for the Plating Department in Problem 20-3A.
2. Journalize all transactions affecting the Plating Department during March, including those entries that have already been posted.

Problem 20-5A *Computing equivalent units for a second department with beginning inventory and applying cost to completed units and work in process; FIFO method* **(L.O. 2, 3, 5)**

The manufacture of hand tools, such as pliers and screwdrivers, occurs in four departments and also includes two additional operations. Consider screwdrivers with plastic handles. Manufacture of the handles includes mixing and heating the raw materials, shaping the mix by pouring it into molds, and drying. Production of the screwdrivers is then completed in two operations: assembling the handles and shanks, and packaging for shipment to retail outlets such as K Mart, Target, and True Value hardware stores.

Process costing information for the Drying Department of Master Craft Company for a period follows. No direct materials are required.

Units:
Work in process, beginning (30% complete as to conversion costs)	7,000 units
Transferred in from the Molding Department during the period	32,000 units
Completed during the period	16,000 units
Work in process, ending (20% complete as to conversion costs)	23,000 units

Costs:
Work in process, beginning	$ 1,190
Transferred in from the Molding Department during the period	3,840
Conversion costs added during the period	1,295

The cost of direct materials in the assembling and packaging phases includes the cost of the plastic handles transferred out of the Drying Department plus the cost of the metal shanks, which is $1,493. The assembling and packaging operations are entirely automated. Assembling occurs at the rate of 4,000 units per hour and packaging at 2,000 per hour. Conversion cost is allocated to the assembling operation at the predetermined rate of $25.00 per machine hour and to packaging at the rate of $27.50 per machine hour. There is only one work order for the screwdrivers.

Required

1. Compute the number of equivalent units (screwdrivers) produced by the Drying Department during the period, unit costs, and total cost to account for. Use the FIFO method.
2. Show the application of total cost to (a) units completed and transferred to the assembly operation and (b) units in ending work in process inventory.
3. Compute the total manufacturing cost of the 16,000 screwdrivers completed and transferred to finished goods. Also compute the unit cost of each complete screwdriver to the nearest cent.

Problem 20-6A *Computing equivalent units for a second department with beginning inventory and applying cost to completed units and work in process;weighted-average method* **(L.O. 2, 3, 6)**

Repeat Problem 20-5A, using the weighted-average method. Assume the $1,190 balance of Work in Process—Drying Department at the beginning of the period comprises $645 of transferred-in cost and $545 of conversion cost.

(Group B)

Problem 20-1B *Computing equivalent units and applying cost to completed units and work in process; no beginning inventory or cost transferred in* **(L.O. 2, 3)**

Southwest Custom Specialties engraves and prints specialty books on wildlife. Production occurs in three processes: engraving, printing, and binding. The Engraving Department was empty on May 31. In mid-June Southwest started production on 65,000 books. Of this number, 52,600 books were engraved during June. The June 30 work in process in the Engraving Department was 20 percent complete as to direct materials and 50 percent complete as to conversion costs. Direct materials costing $137,700 were placed in production in the Engraving Department during June, and direct labor of $43,140 and factory overhead of $62,700 were applied in this department.

Required

1. Compute the number of equivalent units of production and unit costs in the Engraving Department for June.
2. Show the application of total cost in the Engraving Department to (a) units completed and transferred to Printing during June and (b) units still in process at June 30.
3. Prepare a T-account for Work in Process Inventory—Engraving to show its activity during June, including the June 30 balance.

Problem 20-2B *Computing equivalent units, applying cost to completed units and work in process, and journalizing transactions; no beginning inventory or cost transferred in* **(L.O. 2, 3, 4)**

Bellmead Newsprint, Inc., manufactures newsprint (the paper stock on which newspapers are printed) by a four-stage process that includes mixing, cooking, rolling, and cutting. In the Mixing Department, wood pulp and chemicals, the basic raw materials, are blended. The resulting mix is heated in the Cooking Department in much the same way food is prepared. Then the cooked mix is rolled to produce sheets. The final process, cutting, divides the sheets into large rolled units for shipment to newspaper companies.

Cost accumulation in the Mixing Department during August is summarized in the following account:

Work in Process Inventory—Mixing		
Direct materials	24,700	
Direct labor	7,400	
Factory overhead	13,500	

August activity in the Mixing Department consisted of completion of the mixing process for 1,800 rolls of newsprint plus partial completion of 300 additional rolls. These in-process units were 33⅓ percent complete with respect to direct materials and conversion costs.

Required

1. Compute the equivalent units of production and unit costs in the Mixing Department for August.
2. Prove that the sum of (a) cost of goods transferred out of the Mixing Department and (b) ending Work in Process Inventory—Mixing equals the total cost accumulated in the department during August.
3. Journalize all transactions affecting the company's mixing process during August, including those already posted.

Problem 20-3B *Computing equivalent units for a second department with beginning inventory; applying cost to completed units and work in process; FIFO method* **(L.O. 2, 3, 5)**

Basset & Ames manufactures broadloom carpet in seven processes: spinning, dyeing, plying, spooling, tufting, latexing, and shearing.

First, fluff nylon purchased from a company such as DuPont or Monsanto is spun into yarn that is dyed the desired color. Then two or more threads of the yarn are joined together, or plied, for added strength. The plied yarn is spooled for use in the actual carpet making. Tufting is the process by which yarn is added to burlap backing. After the backing is latexed to hold it together and make it skid resistant, the carpet is sheared to give it an even appearance and feel.

At March 31, before recording the transfer of cost from department to department, the Basset & Ames general ledger included the following account for one of its lines of carpet:

Work in Process Inventory—Dyeing

Feb. 28 Balance	10,900
Transferred in from Spinning	21,280
Direct materials	12,390
Direct labor	7,207
Factory overhead	42,900

Work in process inventory of the Dyeing Department on February 28 consisted of 75 rolls that were 60 percent complete as to direct materials and conversion costs. During March 560 rolls were transferred in from the Spinning Department. The Dyeing Department completed 500 rolls of the carpet in March, and 135 rolls were still in process on March 31. This ending inventory was 100 percent complete as to direct materials and 80 percent complete as to conversion costs.

Required

1. Compute the equivalent units of production, unit costs, and total cost to account for in the Dyeing Department for March. Use the FIFO method.
2. Show the application of total Dyeing Department cost for March to (a) cost of goods transferred from Dyeing to Plying and (b) cost of ending Work in Process Inventory—Dyeing on March 31.

Problem 20-4B *Preparing a production cost report and recording transactions based on the information in the report* **(L.O. 4)**

Required

1. Prepare the March production cost report for the Dyeing Department in Problem 20-3B.
2. Journalize all transactions affecting the Dyeing Department during March, including those entries that have already been posted.

Problem 20-5B *Computing equivalent units for a second department with beginning inventory and applying cost to completed units and work in process; FIFO method* **(L.O. 2, 3, 5)**

The manufacture of lawn mowers includes two processes: forming the blade housing from steel and assembling the parts of the mower. Two additional operations, lubricating the moving parts and testing the completed mowers, complete their manufacture. The completed mowers are transferred to finished goods prior to shipment to Sears, Montgomery Ward, Penney's, and other department stores.

Process costing information for the Assembling Department of Lawn Genie, Inc., for a period follows. No direct materials are required.

Units:
Work in process, beginning (60% complete as to conversion costs)	2,000 units
Transferred in from the Forming Department during the period	9,000 units
Completed during the period	6,000 units
Work in process, ending (70% complete as to conversion costs)	5,000 units

Costs:
Work in process, beginning	$ 92,000
Transferred in from the Forming Department during the period	333,000
Conversion costs added during the period	66,400

The cost of direct materials in the lubricating and testing phases is the cost of the mowers transferred out of the Assembling Department. The lubricating operation is entirely automated and takes 30 seconds per mower. Testing each completed mower requires an average of five minutes of a technician's time. Conversion costs are $30 per machine hour for lubricating and $50 per man hour for testing. There is only one work order for the mowers in each production run.

Required

1. Compute the number of equivalent units (mowers) produced by the Assembling Department during the period, unit costs, and total cost to account for. Use the FIFO method.
2. Show the application of total cost to (a) units completed and transferred to the lubricating operation and (b) units in ending work in process inventory.
3. Compute the total manufacturing cost of the 6,000 mowers completed and transferred to finished goods. Also compute the unit cost of each complete mower (to the nearest cent).

Problem 20-6B *Computing equivalent units for a second department with beginning inventory and applying cost to completed units and work in process; weighted-average method* **(L.O. 2, 3, 6)**

Repeat Problem 20-5B, using the weighted-average method. Assume the $92,000 balance of Work in Process—Assembling Department at the beginning of the period comprises $71,250 of transferred in cost and $20,750 of conversion cost.

Extending Your Knowledge

Decision Problems

1. Preparing a Production Cost Report and Identifying Decisions That Would Be Based on the Information (L.O. 5)

Fort Bend Manufacturing Company makes automobile parts. The following cost data for the company's Finishing Department are available for October.

Equivalent units of production:

Flow of Production	Flow of Physical Units	Equivalent Units of Production		
		Transferred In	Direct Materials	Conversion Costs
Units to account for:				
Beginning work in process inventory	12,000			
Transferred in during October	28,000			
Total units to account for	40,000			
Units accounted for:				
Completed and transferred out to finished goods during October:				
From beginning inventory	12,000	—	7,200	6,000
Transferred in from Molding and completed during October	24,000	24,000	24,000	24,000
Work in process, October 31	4,000	4,000	800	1,200
Total physical units accounted for	40,000			
Equivalent units of production		28,000	32,000	31,200

Unit costs:	Transferred-In Costs	Direct Materials	Conversion Costs	Total
Work in process, September 30	Work done before October			$ 59,000
Costs added during October	$ 64,400	$ 35,200	$ 49,920	149,520
Divide by equivalent units	÷28,000	÷32,000	÷31,200	
Cost per equivalent unit	$ 2.30	$ 1.10	$ 1.60	
Total cost to account for				$208,520

Allocation of total cost:	Transferred-In Costs	Direct Materials	Conversion Costs	Total
Units completed and transferred out to finished goods:				
From work in process, September 30 ..				$ 59,000
Costs added during October:				
Direct materials.................	—	7,200 × $1.10		7,920
Conversion costs	—		6,000 × $1.60	9,600
Total completed from September 30 inventory				76,520
Units transferred in from Molding and completed during October......	24,000 × ($2.30 + $1.10 + $1.60)			120,000
Total costs transferred out				196,520
Work in process, October 31:				
Transferred-in costs.................	4,000 × $2.30			9,200
Direct materials.....................		800 × $1.10		880
Conversion costs			1,200 × $1.60	1,920
Total work in process, October 31				12,000
Total cost accounted for				$208,520

Required

1. Prepare a production cost report for the Finishing Department for the month of October.
2. Discuss specific decisions that would be based on the information in the report.

2. Process Costing in the Same Department for Two Consecutive Months (L.O. 2, 3)

Waterford Pottery makes ceramic bowls. The bowls are made, fired, and dried in the Forming Department. Then they are transferred to the Finishing Department to be painted and shipped to retail outlets. No bowls are broken at any point in the procedure. The following information is available for the Forming Department for January and February 19X5:

Forming Department

Units:

Work in process, January 1 (50% complete as to direct materials, 25% complete as to conversion costs)........	100 bowls
Production started during January	800 bowls
Work in process, January 31 (40% complete as to direct materials, 20% complete as to conversion costs)........	300 bowls
Production started during February	900 bowls
Work in process, February 28 (70% complete as to direct materials, 50% complete as to conversion costs)........	600 bowls

Costs:

Work in process, January 1	$ 200
Costs added during January:	
Direct materials	1,005
Conversion costs.....................................	635
Costs added during February:	
Direct materials	1,440
Conversion costs.....................................	840

Required

1. Compute the equivalent units of production, unit costs and total cost to account for in the Forming Department for January. Show the application of total Forming Department cost for January to (a) cost of goods transferred from Forming to Finishing and (b) cost of ending Work in Process Inventory—Forming at January 31, 19X5.
2. Compute the equivalent units of production, equivalent-unit costs, and total cost to account for in the Forming Department for February. Show the application of total Forming Department cost for February to (a) cost of goods transferred from Forming to Finishing and (b) cost of ending Work in Process Inventory—Forming at February 28, 19X5.
3. Prepare the January and February (individually by month) production cost reports for the Forming Department.

Ethical Issue

Hutch Manufacturing produces component parts for laser optic equipment. Customers include civilian companies and the U.S. government. Under most government contracts Hutch receives reimbursement for its manufacturing costs plus a specified profit margin. For most civilian contracts Hutch bids a fixed price and either earns a profit or incurs a loss, depending on how well the company controls costs. For both government and civilian jobs, top Hutch managers allocate to the government contracts any overhead whose proper allocation to a particular product is less than certain.

Required

1. Is Hutch's overhead allocation practice ethical? Give your reason.
2. Who benefits and who is harmed by the Hutch practice?

Chapter 21

Flexible Budgets and Standard Costs

During a meeting at a manufacturing plant, you overhear the following remarks being made by company employees [of Springfield Remanufacturing Corporation, an engine remanufacturer headquartered in Springfield, Mo.]:

"Cash flow is projected to increase by $20,000 this month."

"The overhead variance for last week was $6,000 unfavorable, but I project it will be zero next week."

"Our labor figures are right on target!"

"Operating income for the month was $88,000, which represents a 3.4% return on sales!"

"If we watch our material usage variance we could very well end the month making a profit large enough to qualify everyone for a bonus!"

In the great game of business, employees who lack an understanding of the "rules of the game" are unable to perform effectively for the business team and may even hinder opportunities for it to succeed.

At Springfield Remanufacturing all employees—not just the accountants—receive formal training in understanding financial data. This training helps manufacturing personnel control costs and contribute to company profits and to their own personal bonuses. One aspect of the training includes an understanding of cost variances for materials, labor, and overhead. This chapter explains these management tools in the section on standard costing.

SOURCE: Adapted from Olen L. Green, Stevan K. Olson, and Marty Callison, "Understanding the Numbers," *Management Accounting*, May 1992, pp. 39–40.

Chapter 16 introduced management accounting by emphasizing that budgets are the main tool for planning and control. Chapter 17 showed how to budget profit levels by analyzing cost-volume-profit relationships. Chapters 19 and 20 explored accounting for manufacturing companies. In this chapter we now explore budgeting in more depth. The first half of the chapter covers flexible budgets, and the second half discusses standard costs, which are an outgrowth of the flexible budget. We begin by reviewing the cost behavior patterns and the relevant range, which were introduced in Chapter 17.

Cost Behavior Patterns

Accountants define cost as resources given up to achieve a specific objective. For now, consider costs as dollars paid for goods and services. Examples are the costs of materials, factory wages, sales commissions, utilities, and interest expense. Distinctions among these categories of costs are important in many accounting situations. In budgeting, however, they can be treated similarly.

Cost behavior is the movement of a cost in response to a measure of volume such as sales. Two extreme types of cost behavior are variable and fixed. Variable costs are those whose total amount changes in direct proportion with changes in volume or activity. Fixed costs are costs whose total amount does not change during a given time period over a wide range of volume. Examples include depreciation, property taxes, insurance, and executive salaries.

Throughout this chapter, we assume that each cost is either variable or fixed or that it can be divided into variable and fixed portions. A mixed cost has both variable and fixed components. The compensation of a salesperson who is paid a flat monthly salary plus a commission based on his or her sales is a mixed cost. Water expense computed as a fixed monthly amount plus a unit cost per 100 gallons used is also a mixed cost.

Note that the "variable" and "fixed" characteristics of a cost relate to its *total* amount, not its *per-unit* amount. A variable cost is variable with respect to its *total* amount. A fixed cost is fixed with respect to its *total* amount. The behavior of variable and fixed costs with respect to per-unit sales is different, as the following table shows.

	If Volume Increases (Decreases)	
Type of Cost	**Total Cost**	**Cost Per Unit**
Variable cost (example: sales commission)	Increases (decreases)	No change
Fixed cost (example: monthly rent)	No change	Decreases (increases)

Illustrations will clarify the difference between the total and the unit amounts of variable cost and fixed cost. Suppose a sales clerk in the shoe department of a J. C. Penney store is paid a sales commission of $2 per pair of shoes sold, which is a variable cost. Weekly sales of 200 pairs generates total sales commission expense of $400. Unit selling cost—the commission—remains $2 per pair of shoes.

Now consider the fixed monthly rent of a cookie store in a shopping mall. Total monthly rent expense of $2,000 does not change in response to changes in volume. If the store sells 20,000 cookies each month, the rent expense per unit is $.10 ($2,000 rent/20,000 cookies). But if the store sells 40,000 cookies monthly, the unit cost of rent is only $.05 ($2,000/40,000). In either case, the total monthly rent is fixed at $2,000.

Relevant Range

The definition of a *fixed cost* has two underlying assumptions.

1. The total cost will not change for a given time period, which is the *budget period*. Fixed costs may change from budget year to budget year because of changes in salary levels, number of workers, rent levels, and property tax levels. But fixed costs are not expected to change within a given budget period.
2. The total cost will not change over a wide range of volume, which is the *relevant range*.

Fixed costs are based on an expected band of volume. For example, a toy manufacturer may have monthly fixed costs of $200,000 when it is producing 16,000 to 24,000 units per month. However, after the Christmas rush, sales fall below 16,000 units, and fixed costs decrease to $175,000. So "fixed" is a useful concept, but "fixed" does not mean forever or under all operating conditions. Instead, it relates to a relevant range of volume, as shown by the following graph of cost behavior:

Having reviewed the necessary concepts and terms, let's turn to flexible budgets and their role in management decision making.

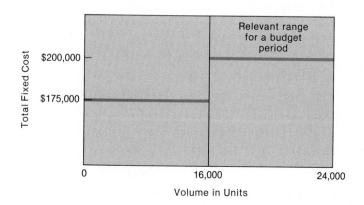

Flexible Budgets

The master budget in Chapter 16 is a **static budget,** which is prepared for only one level of volume. It is not altered after it is drawn up, regardless of changes in volume, cost drivers, or other conditions during the budget period. Consider a master budget based on a single target sales volume of 200,000 units. Assume actual volume turns out to be 180,000 units. The comparison of actual and budgeted results, which is an example of a **performance report,** follows (amounts assumed).

	Actual Results	Static (Master) Budget	Variance
Units sold	180,000	200,000	20,000 U
Sales	$540,000	$600,000	$60,000 U
Expenses	500,000	525,000	25,000 F
Operating income	$ 40,000	$ 75,000	$35,000 U

Variance is the difference between an actual amount and the corresponding budgeted amount. Throughout U = unfavorable variance and F = favorable variance.

This performance report is difficult to analyze because the budget is based on 200,000 units, but only 180,000 units were sold. Note the $25,000 expense variance. Why did it occur? Because of efficient cost control? Because of a lower sales volume? We are unsure. This performance report, based on a static budget, simply does not provide enough detail to answer these important management questions.

For a detailed analysis of performance, managers often use a **flexible budget,** which is a set of budgets covering a range of volume rather than a single level of volume. Flexible budgets are also called *variable budgets* because they present budgeted amounts for different levels of volume. Managers find flexible budgets helpful for studying the behavior of expenses as volume fluctuates. Microcomputers and electronic spreadsheets have placed this budgeting tool at the disposal of most middle and top managers in the United States.

Exhibit 21-1 shows a condensed flexible budget for Bellmead Pools & Supply, which installs swimming pools. Throughout this illustration we assume that all pools are sold and installed in the same month. Therefore, we use the terms *pool sales* and *pool installations* interchangeably.

In this example, the total variable cost of installing a $12,000 swimming pool is $8,000. A more detailed budget would list the individual variable costs, such as direct materials and direct labor. It might also detail the various fixed expenses, including depreciation on equipment, insurance, and administrative overhead. Total monthly fixed expenses are $20,000.

Flexible budgets are useful both before and after a budget period. As a planning tool, they can help managers identify the level of volume that will serve as the business's target level for the coming period. As a control device, they help managers analyze actual results.

The **budget formula**—the heart of the flexible budget—shows how to compute the budget amounts:

$$\text{Revenues} - \text{Variable expenses} - \text{Fixed expenses} = \text{Operating income (loss)}$$

$$\left(\begin{array}{c}\text{Number of units sold} \\ \times \text{ Unit sale price}\end{array}\right) - \left(\begin{array}{c}\text{Number of units sold} \\ \times \text{ Variable cost per unit}\end{array}\right) - \text{Fixed expenses} = \text{Operating income (loss)}$$

EXHIBIT 21-1   *Flexible Budget*

Bellmead Pools & Supply
Flexible Budget
Each Month of the Period April–August 19X5

	Budget Formula per Unit	Various Levels of Volume		
Units.....................	—	6	8	10
Sales	$12,000	$72,000	$96,000	$120,000
Variable expenses	8,000	48,000	64,000	80,000
Fixed expenses............	(see Note)	20,000	20,000	20,000
Total expenses		68,000	84,000	100,000
Operating income (loss)....		$ 4,000	$12,000	$ 20,000

Note: Fixed expenses are given as a total amount rather than as a cost per unit.

In this illustration, Bellmead Pools' cost behavior is fixed expenses of $20,000 per month plus variable expenses of $8,000 per pool sold and installed. Exhibit 21-1 shows the expected results for three operating levels. Other volume levels could be added for 7, 9, or any other number of pools per month, as the situation warrants. Keep in mind that a flexible budget relates to a specific relevant range only. Expenses are unlikely to behave according to a set formula outside some volume range. For example, a volume of 15 pools per month may not fall within the relevant range. In such cases, managers must develop a new budget formula.

Graphing the Budget Expense Formula

Another budgeting tool is a graph of the expense formula. With such a graph, the accountant can provide a budget customized to any volume level. The graph in Exhibit 21-2 shows total expenses for Bellmead Pools & Supply for all volume levels from 0 to 11 pools sold per month. Let us assume this span of volume is the relevant range. Also, we assume that management based the master budget—the static budget—on a projected sales volume of 8 pools per month.

The graph displays an overall picture of the direct materials, direct labor, and all other expenses that must be planned at various volume levels. When the company plans to build 8 pools, the total expense level ($84,000) for this volume is highlighted (as Exhibit 21-2 shows).

A budget graph also helps analyze actual results. Exhibit 21-3 is the graph of actual versus budgeted results for the peak season of 19X5. The graph shows that actual expenses exceeded budgeted expenses during April, June, and August. Actual expenses were less than budget for May and July. Overall, the budget and actual figures are close.

EXHIBIT 21-2 *Bellmead Pools & Supply*
Graph of Monthly Flexible Expense Budget

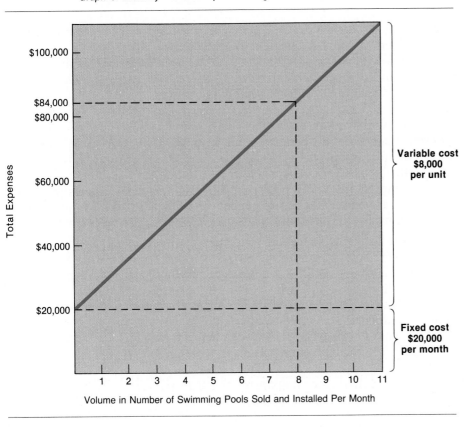

Variable cost
$8,000
per unit

Fixed cost
$20,000
per month

Total Expenses

Volume in Number of Swimming Pools Sold and Installed Per Month

EXHIBIT 21-3 *Bellmead Pools & Supply*
Graph of Actual and Budgeted Monthly Total Expenses

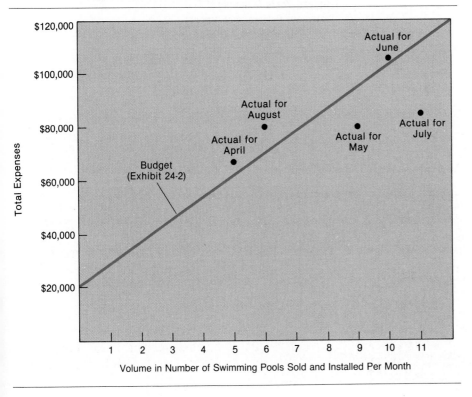

Actual for
June

Actual for
August

Actual for
April

Actual for
May

Actual for
July

Budget
(Exhibit 24-2)

Total Expenses

Volume in Number of Swimming Pools Sold and Installed Per Month

Analyzing the Results

Managers usually have a cycle of planning and control. They (1) prepare a master budget, (2) transact business to achieve their goals, and (3) compare actual results with the master budget. The flexible budget helps managers analyze variances from planned results, which fall into two major categories: sales volume variances and flexible budget variances.

1. **Sales volume variances** are those differences between the amounts in the flexible budget and the corresponding amounts in the static (master) budget. For example, assume Bellmead Pools & Supply set a goal of selling 8 pools each month during April–August 19X5 and budgeted accordingly. During June the company installs 10 pools. Exhibit 21-4, column 4, shows that the sales volume variance is the difference between the flexible budget for actual volume achieved (column 3) and the static (master) budget (column 5).

2. **Flexible budget variances** are differences between actual results and the flexible budget. This category of variances is based on the actual sales level achieved. For example, Bellmead Pools & Supply budgeted total expenses of $100,000 for the sale of 10 pools. In June the company sells and installs 10 pools, but total expenses exceed budget. This can be seen in Exhibit 21-3, where total expenses for June lie above the budget line. Exhibit 21-4 shows how to compute a flexible budget variance: actual results (column 1) minus the flexible budget for actual volume achieved (column 3).

OBJECTIVE 2

Prepare an income statement performance report

We have seen that mere comparison of a *static (master)* budget with *actual* results does not explain much, because the actual sales level may differ from

EXHIBIT 21-4 *Income Statement Performance Report*

Bellmead Pools & Supply
Income Statement Performance Report
For the Month Ended June 30, 19X5

	(1) Actual Results at Actual Prices	(2) (1)–(3) Flexible Budget Variances	(3) Flexible Budget for Actual Volume Achieved*	(4) (3)–(5) Sales Volume Variances	(5) Static (Master) Budget*
Units	10	-0-	10	2 F	8
Sales	$120,000	$ -0-	$120,000	$24,000 F	$96,000
Variable expenses	83,000	3,000 U	80,000	16,000 U	64,000
Fixed expenses............	22,000	2,000 U	20,000	-0-	20,000
Total expenses	105,000	5,000 U	100,000	16,000 U	84,000
Operating income	$ 15,000	$5,000 U	$ 20,000	$ 8,000 F	$12,000

Flexible budget variance, $5,000 U   Sales volume variance, $8,000 F

Total variance from static budget, $3,000 F

U = unfavorable variance; F = favorable variance
*Amounts from Exhibit 21-1

the level that was used in preparing the master budget. But a flexible budget does provide the information needed to understand why actual revenues, expenses, and income differ from budgeted amounts. Exhibit 21-4 is an income statement performance report based on a flexible budget. Study it carefully, especially the two variance columns.

In Exhibit 21-4, column 3 information is taken from Exhibit 21-1. For the flexible budget amounts we match units sold to actual sales in units, which in this case is 10. Use of a flexible budget allows us to analyze results over a range of activity levels within the scope of the relevant range. Had actual sales been 6 units, we could have made the comparison based on 6 units by drawing the necessary data from Exhibit 21-1.

Exhibit 21-4 shows that actual operating income ($15,000 in column 1) exceeded the static (master) budget amount ($12,000 in column 5) by $3,000. This difference is explained by an $8,000 favorable sales volume variance (column 4) and a $5,000 unfavorable flexible budget variance (column 2). Stated differently, strong sales caused actual income to exceed budget by $8,000. However, the company failed to control expenses as well as expected, resulting in an unfavorable flexible budget variance of $5,000.

How would the owners of the company use this information? Perhaps they would reward the sales staff, and they would certainly determine why expenses were too high. Our analysis of the performance report shows the unfavorable $5,000 variance, but it does not identify why expenses exceeded budget, nor does it identify the cure. Those answers depend on the specific situation. For example, Bellmead's higher-than-expected expenses might have resulted from an increase in the cost of gunite, the concrete derivative used to construct swimming pools. Such an increase might be unavoidable. However, the expense level might have resulted from wasting materials or mismanaging employees. If so, the owner would take corrective action. Variance information can direct a manager to areas of the business deserving praise or needing improvement.

Managers can of course analyze expenses in a more detailed manner—by listing each expense separately. Also, the flexible budget variances can be analyzed further, as the next major section of the chapter explains. First, however, test your understanding of the coverage thus far by working the summary problem for review.

Summary Problem for Your Review

Exhibit 21-4 indicates that Bellmead Pools & Supply sold and installed 10 swimming pools during June. Suppose June sales were 7 pools instead of 10. Suppose further that the price of each pool was $12,500 instead of the budgeted $12,000. Actual variable expenses were $57,400, and actual fixed expenses were $19,000.

Required

1. Given these new assumptions, prepare a revised income statement performance report like Exhibit 21-4.
2. Show that the flexible budget variances and the sales volume variances in operating income account for the difference between actual operating income and the static (master) budgeted income.

3. As the company owner, what specific employees would you praise or criticize after you analyze this performance report?

SOLUTION TO REVIEW PROBLEM

Requirement 1

Bellmead Pools & Supply
Income Statement Performance Report—Revised
For the Month Ended June 30, 19X5

	(1) Actual Results at Actual Prices	(2) (1) – (3) Flexible Budget Variances	(3) Flexible Budget for Actual Volume Achieved	(4) (3) – (5) Sales Volume Variances	(5) Static (Master) Budget
Units sold	7	-0-	7	1 U	8
Sales	$87,500	$3,500 F	$84,000	$12,000 U	$96,000
Variable expenses	57,400	1,400 U	56,000	8,000 F	64,000
Fixed expenses	19,000	1,000 F	20,000	—	20,000
Total expenses	76,400	400 U	76,000	8,000 F	84,000
Operating income	$11,100	$3,100 F	$ 8,000	$ 4,000 U	$12,000

     Flexible budget variance,   Sales volume variance,
       $3,100 F $4,000 U

         Total variance from static budget,
             $900 U

U = unfavorable variance; F = favorable variance

Requirement 2

Static (master) budget operating income ...	$12,000	
Actual operating income at actual prices ...	11,100	
Total difference to account for	$ 900	U
Sales volume variance....................	$ 4,000	U
Flexible budget variance.................	3,100	F
Total variance	$ 900	U

Requirement 3

After investigation, management may praise the salespersons who sold pools more expensive than the budgeted sale price of $12,000 and the employees responsible for cutting fixed cost by $1,000.

 Management may criticize the sales staff for not meeting the goal of selling 8 pools during the month. Also, construction or purchasing personnel were responsible for spending $1,400 more in variable costs than budget to construct the 7 pools. Of course, managers must shoulder some of the blame. They control the use of company resources hour-by-hour and day-by-day. These performance report figures summarize the overall effects of control efforts.

Standard Costing

A **standard cost** is a carefully predetermined cost that is usually expressed on a per-unit basis. It is a target cost, a cost that should be attained. Standard costs are budgeted costs for a single unit of output. **Standard cost systems** help to build budgets, gauge performance, obtain product costs, and save bookkeeping costs. Such systems help managers analyze the relationships between what should have occurred (standard costs) and what did occur (actual costs). In the chapter-opening vignette, employees are hoping the actual costs of materials and overhead for the month will be less than the standard (budgeted) costs.

Standard costs are used by a wide variety of organizations and in conjunction with any kind of product costing—job order, process, or a hybrid system. A construction company that builds tract houses uses a job cost system to accumulate the cost of each house. To measure performance, the company may compare actual cost for each house with the standard cost. Companies like General Mills use a process cost system for many of the foods they manufacture. To remain competitive, General Mills helps control costs by developing standard costs. Standard costing provides a concrete goal for manufacturing personnel. They strive to produce the product at standard cost or less. The difference between profits and losses often depends on controlling each activity that affects product cost.

Variances between actual and standard costs are divided into price and efficiency effects for direct materials and direct labor. A *price variance* measures how well a business keeps the unit prices of materials and labor within standards. An *efficiency variance* measures whether the quantity of materials or labor used to make a product is within the budget. By pinpointing price and efficiency effects, standard costing helps managers find ways of reducing costs. This is the purpose of the standard cost system of Springfield Remanufacturing Corporation in the opening vignette. It also identifies those employees who deserve praise for controlling costs. Over which type of variance—price or efficiency—would manufacturing personnel seem to have more control? The efficiency variance, because they manage the plant, which uses materials. Springfield Remanufacturing probably has a purchasing department that is responsible for the prices paid for materials.

At first glance, standard cost systems might appear to be more costly to operate than other systems. Obviously, a start-up investment is necessary to develop the standards. But the ongoing data-processing costs can be less than so-called actual cost systems. For example, it is more economical simply to carry all inventories at standard unit prices. In this way, the system avoids the extra data-collection costs and possible confusion of making cost flow assumptions such as first-in, first-out or last-in, first-out.

This section of the chapter explains how standard costing divides flexible budget variances—explained in the first half of the chapter—into price and efficiency effects. We continue using the Bellmead Pools & Supply example.

Relationship Between Standard Costs and Flexible Budgets

What standard of performance should be used? *Currently attainable standards* are the most popular. They are standards that can be achieved but with difficulty. Standard costs are set low enough that employees view their fulfillment as possible, though perhaps not probable. Variances tend to be unfavorable, but managers accept the standards as reasonable goals.

Does a standard cost differ from a budgeted cost? No, if the standards are attainable. However, the term *standard cost* usually refers to a unit cost, whereas *budgeted cost* refers to a total cost. For example, suppose the budgeted variable expenses in Exhibit 21-4 included direct materials as follows:

	Budget Formula Per Unit	Flexible Budget for Various Levels of Volume		
Swimming pools installed	1	6	8	10
Direct materials	$2,000	$12,000	$16,000	$20,000

The standard cost of direct materials is $2,000 *per unit.* Budgeted cost is the total cost for the installation of all pools sold during the period. For 8 pools, budgeted cost is $16,000. For 10 pools, budgeted cost is $20,000. But standard cost of direct materials remains $2,000 per unit regardless of changes in total outlays because of differences in sales volume. *Think of a standard variable cost as a budget for a single unit.*

Illustration of Standard Costing

Let's return to our Bellmead Pools example. Recall that 10 swimming pools were sold and installed during June and that the static (master) budget had been prepared for 8 pools per month. Exhibit 21-5 provides the cost data to be used throughout our discussion of standard costing applications.

To focus on the main points of standard costing, we assume the standard cost system applies to materials, labor, and production overhead, but not to selling and administrative expenses. We also assume purchases of direct materials equals materials used.

Direct Material and Direct Labor Variances

Flexible budget variances for direct material and direct labor are often subdivided into price and efficiency variances.

The **price variance** is the difference between the actual unit prices of inputs and their standard unit prices, multiplied by the number of *actual inputs used:*

$$\text{Price variance} = \begin{array}{c}\text{Difference between}\\ \text{actual and budgeted}\\ \text{unit prices of inputs}\end{array} \times \text{Actual inputs used}$$

The **efficiency variance**—also called the **usage variance** and the **quantity variance**—is the difference between the quantity of inputs actually used and the quantity that should have been used (the flexible budget) for the actual output achieved, multiplied by the *standard unit price:*

$$\text{Efficiency variance} = \left(\begin{array}{c}\text{Inputs}\\ \text{actually}\\ \text{used}\end{array} - \begin{array}{c}\text{Inputs that should}\\ \text{have been used}\\ \text{for actual output}\end{array}\right) \times \begin{array}{c}\text{Standard}\\ \text{unit price}\\ \text{of input}\end{array}$$

EXHIBIT 21-5 *Facts for Illustration of Standard Costing*

Bellmead Pools & Supply
Facts for Illustration of Standard Costing
Month of June

Panel A—Comparison of Actual Results with Flexible Budget:
  Installed 10 Swimming Pools:

	Actual Results at Actual Prices	Flexible Budget	Flexible Budget Variances
Variable expenses:			
Direct materials	$ 23,100[a]	$ 20,000[c]	$3,100 U
Direct labor	41,800[b]	42,000[c]	200 F
Variable production overhead	9,000	8,000[d]	1,000 U
Selling and administrative expenses. .	9,100	10,000	900 F
Total variable expenses	83,000	80,000	3,000 U
Fixed expenses:			
Fixed production overhead	12,300	12,000[e]	300 U
Selling and administrative expenses. .	9,700	8,000	1,700 U
Total fixed expenses	22,000	20,000	2,000 U
Total expenses	$105,000	$100,000	$5,000 U

[a] $23,100 = 11,969 cubic yards at actual price of $1.93 per cubic yard.
[b] $41,800 = 3,800 hours at actual price of $11.00 per hour.
[c] See Panel B.
[d] Variable production overhead was budgeted at $2.00 per direct labor hour:
   $8,000 = 4,000 direct labor hours (10 pools × 400 direct labor hours) × $2.00.
[e] Fixed production overhead was budgeted at $12,000 per month.

Panel B—Standards for Direct Material and Direct Labor Flexible Budget:
  10 Swimming Pools:

	(1) Standard Inputs Budgeted for 10 Finished Units (Swimming Pools Installed)	(2) Standard Price per Unit of Input	(1) × (2) Flexible Budget for 10 Finished Units of Output
Direct materials	1,000 cubic yards per pool × 10 pools = 10,000 cubic yards	$ 2.00	$20,000
Direct labor	400 hours per pool × 10 pools = 4,000 hours	10.50	42,000

Price variances are computed not only for their own sake but also to give managers a sharper focus on efficiency. In this way, efficiency can be measured by holding unit prices constant. Thus managers' judgments about efficiency are unaffected by price changes. Efficiency variances have an important underlying assumption: All unit prices are *standard* prices.

Direct Materials Variances.   The relevant data for computing Bellmead Pools' direct materials variances are on the next page.

	Actual Cost	Flexible Budget Standard Cost	Flexible Budget Variance
Cubic yards	11,969	10,000	
Unit price	× $1.93	× $2.00	
Total	$23,100	$20,000	$3,100 U

Managers seek to gain further insight by dividing this flexible budget variance into price and efficiency variances.

OBJECTIVE 3

Compute direct materials cost variances

$$\text{Price variance} = \begin{array}{c}\textbf{Difference between}\\ \textbf{actual and budgeted}\\ \textbf{unit prices of inputs}\end{array} \times \textbf{Actual inputs used}$$

$$\text{Price variance} = (\$1.93 - \$2.00) \times 11,969 \text{ cubic yards}$$

$$= \$838 \text{ F}$$

$$\text{Efficiency variance} = \left(\begin{array}{c}\textbf{Actual}\\ \textbf{inputs}\\ \textbf{used}\end{array} - \begin{array}{c}\textbf{Inputs that should}\\ \textbf{have been used}\\ \textbf{for actual output}\end{array}\right) \times \begin{array}{c}\textbf{Standard}\\ \textbf{unit price}\\ \textbf{of input}\end{array}$$

$$\text{Efficiency variance} = \left(\begin{array}{c}\textbf{11,969}\\ \textbf{cubic yards}\end{array} - \begin{array}{c}\textbf{10,000}\\ \textbf{cubic yards}\end{array}\right) \times \begin{array}{c}\textbf{\$2.00 per}\\ \textbf{cubic yard}\end{array}$$

$$= (11,969 - 10,000) \times \$2.00$$

$$= \$3,938 \text{ U}$$

The direct materials variances—from the beginning of this section—can be explained as follows:

Price variance	$ 838	F
Efficiency variance	3,938	U
Total flexible budget variance	$3,100	U

EXHIBIT 21-6 *Bellmead Pools & Supply*
Direct Materials Variance Computations

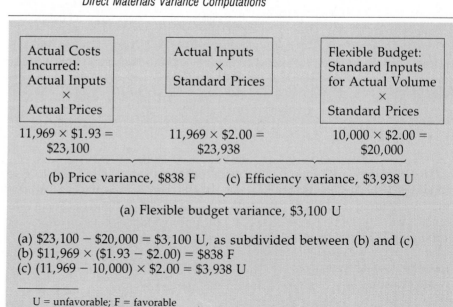

(a) $23,100 − $20,000 = $3,100 U, as subdivided between (b) and (c)
(b) $11,969 × ($1.93 − $2.00) = $838 F
(c) (11,969 − 10,000) × $2.00 = $3,938 U

U = unfavorable; F = favorable

Exhibit 21-6 summarizes the direct materials cost variance computations. Variance analysis begins with a total variance to be explained—in this example, the $3,100 flexible budget variance.

Direct Labor Variances. The relevant data for computing Bellmead Pools' direct labor variances are

	Actual Cost	Flexible Budget Standard Cost	Flexible Budget Variance
Hours	3,800	4,000	
Hourly rate	× $11.00	× $10.50	
Total	$41,800	$42,000	$200 F

Price variance = $\dfrac{\text{Difference between actual and budgeted unit prices of inputs}}{} \times \text{Actual inputs used}$

Price variance = ($11.00 − $10.50) × 3,800 hours

= $1,900 U

OBJECTIVE 4
Compute direct labor cost variances

This variance is also called the *direct labor rate variance.*

Efficiency variance = $\left(\begin{array}{c}\text{Actual inputs used}\end{array} - \begin{array}{c}\text{Inputs that should have been used for actual output}\end{array}\right) \times \begin{array}{c}\text{Standard unit price of input}\end{array}$

Efficiency variance = (3,800 hours − 4,000 hours) × $10.50 per hour

= $2,100 F

The direct labor variances—from the beginning of this section—can be explained as follows:

Price variance	$1,900 U
Efficiency variance	2,100 F
Total flexible budget variance	$ 200 F

To relate standard costing to the overall budget, trace these total flexible budget variances to Exhibit 21-5. In addition, Exhibit 21-7 summarizes the direct labor variance computations, providing an overall picture to aid your study.

Management Use of Variance Information

Variances do not identify problems or their solutions. But they often raise questions that deserve attention. For example, an unfavorable materials price variance may point to the need to shop around for a new supplier of raw materials. *Price* effects, though, may depend on market factors, which are hard or sometimes impossible to control. An unfavorable labor efficiency variance, however, may spur management to examine employee performance. The company certainly has greater control over its own people than it has over outside markets.

EXHIBIT 21-7 *Bellmead Pools & Supply*
Direct Labor Variance Computations

Actual Costs Incurred: Actual Inputs × Actual Prices	Actual Inputs × Standard Prices	Flexible Budget: Standard Inputs for Actual Volume × Standard Prices
$3,800 \times \$11.00 =$ $\$41,800$	$3,800 \times \$10.50 =$ $\$39,900$	$4,000 \times \$10.50 =$ $\$42,000$

(b) Price variance, $1,900 U   (c) Efficiency variance, $2,100 F

(a) Flexible budget variance, $200 F

(a) $41,800 - $42,000 = $200 F, as subdivided between (b) and (c)
(b) $3,800 \times (\$11.00 - \$10.50) = \$1,900$ U
(c) $(3,800 - 4,000) \times \$10.50 = \$2,100$ F

U = unfavorable; F = favorable

Managers sometimes trade off price and efficiency effects, accepting an unfavorable variance in one area in order to achieve a favorable variance in the other. In our example, Bellmead's favorable materials price variance may have resulted from using cheaper material. The unfavorable materials efficiency variance may have arisen because employees had to use more material than standard, perhaps because of its inferior quality. Thus the company's strategy failed. The overall materials cost variance was unfavorable by $3,100.

In another trade-off between price and efficiency, Bellmead used more expensive labor than standard. But the company gained greater efficiency, and the company achieved a net labor cost saving of $200.

When should a variance be investigated? If significant variances are likely, hour-to-hour and day-to-day monitoring of quantities of materials and direct labor hours is desirable. When and how to investigate is often based on personal judgment. For example, a manager may believe that a 5 percent variance in a $1 million materials cost deserves more attention than a 20 percent variance in a $10,000 budget. Rules of thumb—such as "Investigate all variances above $5,000" and "Investigate all variances 25 percent or more above standard cost"—are also common in practice.

Production Overhead Variances

Ideally, production overhead cost variances should be computed and monitored for individual overhead costs like property taxes, utilities, and insurance, but many companies compute variances on total overhead. Many companies split production overhead variances into two parts: a *flexible budget variance* and a *production volume variance*.

The *flexible budget variance* for production overhead shows whether managers are keeping total overhead cost within the budgeted amount for the actual production of the period. The *production volume variance* arises when actual production differs from the level in the static (master) budget. The two variances combine to explain the difference between actual overhead cost and standard overhead cost that has been applied to production. Before discussing the computation of overhead variances, let's review how overhead cost is applied to production.

Applying Overhead to Production. In a system that uses standard costs, overhead is applied to production at a budgeted rate, as discussed in the two preceding chapters. Companies develop overhead standards based on past experience and budgets that reflect the business's goals. Suppose Exhibit 21-8 is Bellmead Pools' flexible overhead budget, which shows activity levels for 6, 8, 9, and 10 pools per month. We have highlighted the static (master) budget level of 8 pools and the actual production level of 10 pools because these levels are useful for computing the overhead variances.

Exhibit 21-8 indicates that Bellmead applies $5.75 of overhead cost to production for each direct labor hour spent installing a swimming pool. Of this amount, $2.00 is for variable overhead, and $3.75 is for fixed overhead. These standards can be based on any level of production that is consistent with company goals. In this case, Bellmead's goal is static (master) budget volume of 8 pools per month.

Bellmead accountants assemble the data in Exhibit 21-9 for computing the overhead cost variances associated with actual production of 10 pools.

The total production overhead cost variance is the difference between actual cost and standard overhead applied to production. For Bellmead Pools & Supply, the total overhead cost variance is favorable by $1,700 ($21,300 − $23,000). Accountants break the total variance down further for management use.

Flexible Budget (Controllable) Production Overhead Variance. The **flexible budget production overhead variance** is the difference between total actual overhead—fixed and variable—and the flexible budget amount for actual production volume. Bellmead Pools' flexible budget variance for June is computed as follows (data from Exhibit 21-9):

OBJECTIVE 5
Compute production overhead cost variances

Total actual overhead cost	$21,300
Flexible budget overhead for actual production	20,000
Flexible budget variance	$ 1,300 U

EXHIBIT 21-8   *Flexible Monthly Production Overhead Cost Budget*

Bellmead Pools & Supply
Flexible Monthly Production Overhead Cost Budget

	Static (Master) Budget			Flexible Budget for Actual Production
Number of pools installed per month	6	8	9	10
Standard direct labor hours	2,400	3,200	3,600	4,000
Budgeted production overhead cost:				
Variable	$ 4,800	$ 6,400	$ 7,200	$ 8,000
Fixed	12,000	12,000	12,000	12,000
Total.	$16,800	$18,400	$19,200	$20,000
Standard variable overhead rate per direct labor hour	$6,400/3,200 = $2.00			
Standard fixed overhead rate per direct labor hour . .	$12,000/3,200 = $3.75			
Standard total overhead rate per direct labor hour . .	$18,400/3,200 = $5.75			

EXHIBIT 21-9 *Data for Computing Production Overhead Cost Variances Two-Variance Analysis*

Bellmead Pools & Supply
Data for Computing Production Overhead Cost Variances

	Actual Cost (Exhibit 21-5)	Flexible Budget for Actual Production (Exhibit 21-8)	Standard Overhead Applied to Production (Exhibit 21-8)
Variable overhead	$ 9,000	$ 8,000	4,000 direct labor hours × $2.00 = $ 8,000
Fixed overhead ..	12,300	12,000	4,000 direct labor hours × $3.75 = 15,000
Total overhead ..	$21,300	$20,000	4,000 direct labor hours × $5.75 = $23,000

Total production overhead cost variance
$1,700 F

Total June overhead was $21,300, compared with the flexible budget amount of $20,000. The unfavorable variance raises questions regarding managers' control of costs. Often this variance is due more to variable costs than to fixed costs, and production managers exercise considerable control over variable overhead. Therefore, many accountants call this the **controllable overhead variance.** Because control often is not clear-cut, we prefer to label it simply as the flexible budget variance.

Production Volume Overhead Variance. The **production volume overhead variance** is the difference between the flexible budget for actual production and standard overhead applied to production (data from Exhibit 21-9):

Flexible budget overhead for actual production	$20,000
Standard overhead applied to production	23,000
Production volume variance	$ 3,000 F

When the overhead flexible budget amount is less than the standard overhead applied to production, the variance is favorable, as shown for Bellmead Pools. The increase in volume from 8 pools to 10 pools was favorable because productive capacity was more fully utilized than expected. Had the flexible budget amount exceeded the standard overhead applied to production, the variance would have been unfavorable because less than the expected amount of the company's productive capacity was used.

Exhibit 21-9 reveals that variable overhead is (always) the same for the flexible budget and the amount applied to production. Therefore, the production volume variance must be due solely to fixed cost effects. An alternative computation of this variance clarifies this point (all data from Exhibit 21-8):

Standard direct labor hours for actual production	4,000
Standard direct labor hours for static (master) budget	3,200
Actual production in excess of static budget	800
Standard *fixed* overhead rate per direct labor hour . . .	×$3.75
Production volume variance	$ 3,000 F

The production volume variance is favorable because Bellmead installed more pools than the static budget called for. The sum of the two overhead variances explains the total favorable production overhead variance of $1,700:

Flexible budget (controllable) variance	$1,300 U
Production volume variance	3,000 F
Total overhead cost variance explained	$1,700 F

Exhibit 21-10 summarizes the computation of overhead cost variances for a two-variance analysis. Amounts shown are for Bellmead Pools & Supply.

Three-Variance Overhead Analysis

The two-variance analysis just described is common in practice. Some companies, however, perform a three-variance analysis that splits the flexible budget variance into spending and efficiency effects. This split helps managers explain *why* the actual overhead cost incurred differed from the flexible budget overhead for actual production.

Production Overhead Efficiency Variance. The **production overhead efficiency variance** is the difference between the flexible budget for actual production and the flexible budget for the actual units of the overhead cost application base (direct labor hours for Bellmead Pools). From Exhibit 21-11:

Flexible budget overhead for actual production	$20,000
Flexible budget overhead for actual direct labor hours	19,600
Production overhead efficiency variance	$ 400 F

The efficiency variance for production overhead measures the extra variable overhead cost incurred (or saved) because the number of cost driver units

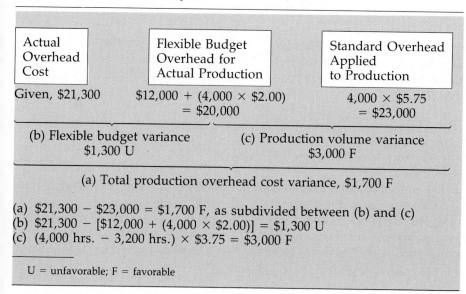

EXHIBIT 21-10 *Bellmead Pools & Supply*
Production Overhead Variance Computations
Two-Variance Analysis

Actual Overhead Cost	Flexible Budget Overhead for Actual Production	Standard Overhead Applied to Production
Given, $21,300	$12,000 + (4,000 × $2.00) = $20,000	4,000 × $5.75 = $23,000

(b) Flexible budget variance
$1,300 U

(c) Production volume variance
$3,000 F

(a) Total production overhead cost variance, $1,700 F

(a) $21,300 − $23,000 = $1,700 F, as subdivided between (b) and (c)
(b) $21,300 − [$12,000 + (4,000 × $2.00)] = $1,300 U
(c) (4,000 hrs. − 3,200 hrs.) × $3.75 = $3,000 F

U = unfavorable; F = favorable

	Actual Cost (Exhibit 21-5)	Flexible Budget for Actual Direct Labor Hours Worked	Flexible Budget for Actual Production (Exhibit 21-8)
		3,800 direct labor hours	4,000 direct labor hours
Variable overhead	$ 9,000	× $2.00 = $7,600	× $2.00 = $8,000
Fixed overhead	12,300	12,000	12,000
Total overhead	$21,300	$19,600	$20,000

actually used differed from the standard number. Bellmead Pools accountants
chose direct labor hours to apply variable overhead to pools installed because
these labor hours are the drivers of their variable overhead costs. If the number
of hours worked is greater than (less than) the 4,000 that should have been
worked to install 10 pools, we expect this *variable* cost to be greater than (less
than) the $8,000 that should have been incurred.

Why is the efficiency variance due solely to variable cost effects? Because
fixed overhead cost does not vary with direct labor hours worked within the
relevant range of production. Exhibit 21-8 shows that this range includes, at a
minimum, 2,400 to 4,000 hours. In our example month, we would not expect
any less depreciation expense or management salary cost, for example,
because company employees worked only 3,800 hours instead of the expected
4,000.

An alternative computation of the efficiency variance reinforces this
point:

Standard direct labor hours for actual production	4,000
Actual direct labor hours worked	3,800
Actual hours less than standard hours	200
Standard variable overhead rate per direct labor hour	×$2.00
Production overhead efficiency variance	$400 F

Production Overhead Spending Variance.   The **production overhead
spending variance** is the difference between the flexible budget for the actual
units of the cost application base and the total actual overhead cost (data from
Exhibit 21-11):

Flexible budget overhead for actual direct labor hours	$19,600
Total actual overhead cost	21,300
Production overhead spending variance	$ 1,700 U

The production overhead spending variance is the part of the flexible budget variance that is not explained by the relationship of variable overhead to
direct labor hours (or other cost driver). That is, it is the flexible budget variance minus the efficiency variance. The variance is called a *spending* variance
rather than a *price* variance because it is caused by both price and quantity

effects. Consider solvents used to clean decorative tiles installed in pool surfaces. If the price per gallon of solvents unexpectedly increases, an unfavorable spending variance results. But an unfavorable spending variance also arises if employees use more solvent per direct labor hour than expected. Thus, the *inefficient* use of supplies contributes to what is labeled a *spending* variance.

Notice that the flexible budget variance includes both variable and fixed overhead effects. The efficiency variance—one of the two variances that make up the flexible budget variance—is due solely to variable overhead. The spending variance, therefore, includes the entire fixed overhead flexible budget variance.

Exhibit 21-12 summarizes the computation of the two components of the flexible budget production overhead variance. The third variance in a three-variance analysis is the production volume variance. For Bellmead Pools, this variance is shown in Exhibit 21-10.

Standard Costs in the Accounts

Some companies use standard costing for control purposes without entering the standards in the accounts. Others make special standard cost entries.

Accounting systems differ among those companies that do record standard costs in the accounts. For example, one practice is to debit actual costs to Materials Inventory and Production Wages. When materials are used, or when labor is applied to production, these accounts are credited for *actual* cost. However, Work in Process Inventory is debited for *standard* cost. Differences in these entries reveal the cost variances. In our Bellmead Pools illustration, the Materials Inventory, Production Wages, and Production Overhead accounts have been debited for actual costs incurred. The resulting account balances before applying costs to production and before introducing standard costs follow.

EXHIBIT 21-12 *Bellmead Pools & Supply Production Overhead Variance Computations*
Three-Variance Analysis

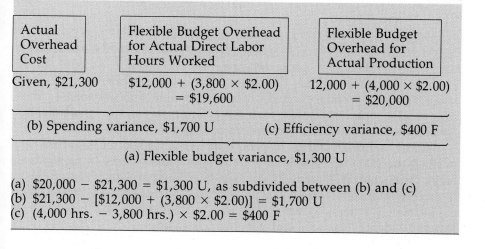

Actual Overhead Cost	Flexible Budget Overhead for Actual Direct Labor Hours Worked	Flexible Budget Overhead for Actual Production
Given, $21,300	$12,000 + (3,800 × $2.00) = $19,600	12,000 + (4,000 × $2.00) = $20,000

(b) Spending variance, $1,700 U   (c) Efficiency variance, $400 F

(a) Flexible budget variance, $1,300 U

(a) $20,000 − $21,300 = $1,300 U, as subdivided between (b) and (c)
(b) $21,300 − [$12,000 + (3,800 × $2.00)] = $1,700 U
(c) (4,000 hrs. − 3,800 hrs.) × $2.00 = $400 F

Materials Inventory	Production Wages	Production Overhead
Actual cost (assumed amount) 29,000	Actual cost 41,800	Actual cost 21,300

OBJECTIVE 6

Record transactions at standard cost

The entries to apply direct materials, direct labor, and production overhead to production and to record the cost variances from our two-variance analysis are:

Work in Process Inventory (standard cost)	20,000	
Direct Materials Efficiency Variance	3,938	
Direct Materials Price Variance		838
Materials Inventory (actual cost)		23,100
Direct materials used in production.		

Work in Process Inventory (standard cost)	42,000	
Direct Labor Price Variance	1,900	
Direct Labor Efficiency Variance		2,100
Production Wages (actual cost)		41,800
Direct labor applied to production.		

Work in Process Inventory (standard cost)	23,000	
Production Overhead Flexible Budget Variance	1,300	
Production Overhead Production Volume Variance		3,000
Production Overhead (actual cost)		21,300
Production overhead applied to production.		

After posting, the direct labor variance accounts appear as follows:

Direct Labor Price Variance	
Unfavorable variance 1,900	

Direct Labor Efficiency Variance	
	Favorable variance 2,100

A debit balance in a variance account is treated as expense, and a credit balance is handled as a contra expense, or a reduction in expense. In this example, Direct Labor Price Variance's debit balance is expense, and Direct Labor Efficiency Variance's credit balance is a reduction in expense. These variance accounts are closed to Income Summary in the usual manner. Accounting for materials and overhead parallel these entries for labor.

Assume Bellmead sold all 10 pools that were installed during June. After posting, the Materials Inventory account shows the balance of materials on hand. Production Wages and Production Overhead have zero balances. Work in Process Inventory is stated at standard cost. The differences between actual costs credited to the accounts and standard costs debited to Work in Process Inventory identify the total cost variances, as follows:

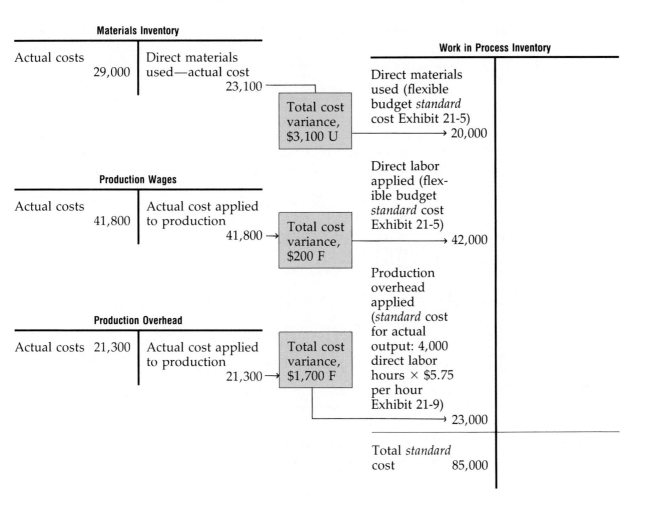

Materials Inventory

| Actual costs 29,000 | Direct materials used—actual cost 23,100 |

Production Wages

| Actual costs 41,800 | Actual cost applied to production 41,800 |

Production Overhead

| Actual costs 21,300 | Actual cost applied to production 21,300 |

Total cost variance, $3,100 U

Total cost variance, $200 F

Total cost variance, $1,700 F

Work in Process Inventory

Direct materials used (flexible budget *standard* cost Exhibit 21-5) → 20,000

Direct labor applied (flexible budget *standard* cost Exhibit 21-5) → 42,000

Production overhead applied (*standard* cost for actual output: 4,000 direct labor hours × $5.75 per hour Exhibit 21-9) → 23,000

Total *standard* cost 85,000

As goods are sold, standard costs flow through the accounts in the usual manner:

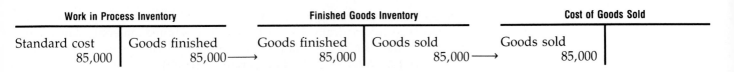

Work in Process Inventory

| Standard cost 85,000 | Goods finished 85,000 |

Finished Goods Inventory

| Goods finished 85,000 | Goods sold 85,000 |

Cost of Goods Sold

| Goods sold 85,000 | |

Standard Cost Income Statement for Management

Standard costing is a management tool, so the company does not usually report variance information to investors, creditors, and other outsiders. Managers, however, are vitally interested in the cost variances. Exhibit 21-13 illustrates an income statement the Bellmead president might use for planning and control purposes. We assume that Bellmead's sales for June were the 10 pools installed during the month.

EXHIBIT 21-13 *Income Statement*

Bellmead Pools & Supply
Income Statement
For the Month Ended June 30, 19X5

		Unfavorable	Favorable			
Sales revenue (Exhibit 21-4: 10 pools at $12,000)						$120,000
Cost of goods sold at standard cost						
(preceding section)				$85,000		
Cost variances:*		Unfavorable	Favorable			
Direct materials..........................		$3,100				
Direct labor			$ 200			
Production overhead		_____	1,700			
		3,100	1,900	1,200 U		
Cost of goods sold at actual cost						86,200
Gross margin................................						33,800
Selling and administrative expenses						
(variable, $9,100; fixed, $9,700—Exhibit 21-5)						18,800
Operating income						$ 15,000

*Cost variance detail:		Unfavorable	Favorable	Total	
Direct materials—	price		$ 838		
(Exhibit 21-6)	efficiency	$3,938		$3,100 U	
Direct labor—	price	1,900			
(Exhibit 21-7)	efficiency		2,100	200 F	
Production overhead—					
(Exhibit 21-10)	flexible budget	1,300			
	production volume		3,000	1,700 F	
Total				$1,200 U	

OBJECTIVE 7

Prepare a standard cost income statement for management

Computers and Standard Costs

This chapter links together the master budget, flexible budgets, and standard costs. As the swimming pool example indicates, many calculations are needed to maintain the standard cost system. The advantages of a computer are obvious—especially if you want daily or weekly reports on operations.

The computer can help set the standard costs. A job order begins the process. The product's identification number and the quantity desired are entered into the computer. The computer then accesses the engineering specifications for that particular product to find out what materials are needed. It multiplies the needed materials by the quantity ordered. By repeating this process over a large number of similar jobs, management can develop the historical data for calculating standard costs.

In some manufacturing environments, the job order may trigger the computer to issue automatically the exact amount of required materials. Any materials not used on the job are shipped back to storage, with the unused quantity credited to the Materials Efficiency Variance account.

Summary Problem for Your Review

Exhibit 21-5 indicates that Bellmead Pools & Supply installed 10 swimming pools during June. Suppose that June installations and sales were 7 pools instead of 10 and that actual expenses for the month were as follows:

Direct materials	7,400 cubic yards @ $2.00 per cubic yard
Direct labor	2,740 hours @ $10.00 per hour
Variable production overhead ..	$5,400
Fixed production overhead	$11,900

Required

1. Given these new data, prepare two exhibits, similar to Exhibits 21-5 and 21-8. Ignore selling and administrative expenses in your first exhibit, and show budgeted overhead cost only for 7 and 8 pools per month in your second exhibit.

2. Compute direct materials and direct labor price and efficiency variances.

3. Compute the total variance, the flexible budget variance, and the production volume variance for overhead. Divide the flexible budget variance into its two components, the spending variance and the efficiency variance.

4. Prepare a June income statement through operating income for the president of Bellmead Pools & Supply. Report all cost variances, and assume selling and administrative expenses for the month were $17,700.

SOLUTION TO REVIEW PROBLEM

Requirement 1

Bellmead Pools & Supply
Facts for Illustration of Standard Costing
Month of June

Panel A—Comparison of Actual Results with Flexible Budget: Installed 7 Swimming Pools

	Actual Results at Actual Prices	Flexible Budget	Flexible Budget Variances
Variable expenses:			
Direct materials......................	$14,800[a]	$14,000[c]	$ 800 U
Direct labor	27,400[b]	29,400[c]	2,000 F
Variable production overhead........	5,400	5,600[d]	200 F
Total variable expenses............	47,600	49,000	1,400 F
Fixed expenses:			
Fixed production overhead	11,900	12,000[e]	100 F
Total expenses	$59,500	$61,000	$1,500 F

[a] $14,800 = 7,400 cubic yards at actual price of $2.00 per cubic yard.
[b] $27,400 = 2,740 hours at actual price of $10.00 per hour.
[c] See Panel B.
[d] Variable production overhead was budgeted at $2.00 per direct labor hour: $5,600 = 2,800 direct labor hours (7 pools × 400 direct labor hours) × $2.00.
[e] Fixed production overhead was budgeted at $12,000 per month.

Panel B—Standards for Direct Material and Direct Labor Flexible Budget: 7 Swimming Pools

	(1) Standard Inputs Budgeted for 7 Finished Units (Swimming Pools Installed)	(2) Standard Price per Unit of Input	(1) × (2) Flexible Budget for 7 Finished Units of Output
Direct materials	1,000 cubic yards × 7	$ 2.00	$14,000
Direct labor	400 hours × 7	10.50	29,400

Bellmead Pools & Supply
Flexible Monthly Production Overhead Cost Budget

Number of pools installed per month	7	8
Standard direct labor hours......................	2,800	3,200
Budgeted production overhead cost:		
Variable	$ 5,600	$ 6,400
Fixed	12,000	12,000
Total	$17,600	$18,400

Standard variable overhead rate per direct labor
  hour .... $6,400/3,200 = $2.00

Standard fixed overhead rate per direct labor
  hour .... $12,000/3,200 = $3.75

Standard total overhead rate per direct labor hour $18,400/3,200 = $5.75

Requirement 2

$$\text{Price variance} = \begin{array}{c}\textbf{Difference between}\\ \textbf{actual and budgeted}\\ \textbf{unit prices of inputs}\end{array} \times \text{Actual inputs used}$$

Direct materials:

$$\text{Price variance} = (\$2.00 - \$2.00) \times 7{,}400 \text{ cubic yards}$$
$$= \$\text{-0-}$$

Direct labor:

$$\text{Price variance} = (\$10.00 - \$10.50) \times 2{,}740 \text{ hours}$$
$$= \$1{,}370 \text{ F}$$

$$\text{Efficiency variance} = \left(\begin{array}{c}\text{Actual}\\ \text{inputs}\\ \text{used}\end{array} - \begin{array}{c}\text{Inputs that should}\\ \text{have been used}\\ \text{for actual output}\end{array}\right) \begin{array}{c}\text{Standard}\\ \times \text{ unit price}\\ \text{of input}\end{array}$$

$$= \left(\begin{array}{c}\text{Actual cubic}\\ \text{yards or}\\ \text{hours used}\end{array} - \begin{array}{c}\text{Standard number of cubic}\\ \text{yards or hours allowed}\\ \text{for actual output}\end{array}\right) \begin{array}{c}\text{Standard}\\ \times \text{ unit price}\\ \text{of input}\end{array}$$

Direct materials:

$$\text{Efficiency variance} = \left(\begin{array}{c}7{,}400\\ \text{cubic}\\ \text{yards}\end{array} - \begin{array}{c}1{,}000 \text{ cubic yards}\\ \times 7\\ \text{swimming pools}\end{array}\right) \times \begin{array}{c}\$2.00\\ \text{per}\\ \text{cubic yard}\end{array}$$

$$= (7{,}400 - 7{,}000) \times \$2.00$$

$$= \$800 \text{ U}$$

Direct labor:

$$\text{Efficiency variance} = \left(\begin{array}{c}2{,}740\\ \text{hours}\\ \text{used}\end{array} - \begin{array}{c}400 \text{ hours}\\ \times 7 \text{ swimming}\\ \text{pools installed}\end{array}\right) \times \begin{array}{c}\$10.50\\ \text{per}\\ \text{hour}\end{array}$$

$$= (2{,}740 - 2{,}800) \times \$10.50$$

$$= \$630 \text{ F}$$

Requirement 3

Total actual overhead cost (variable, $5,400 + fixed, $11,900)	$17,300
Standard total overhead cost applied to production, 7 pools	
(2,800 direct labor hours × $5.75)	16,100
Total overhead cost variance	$ 1,200 U

Flexible Budget Variance:

Total actual overhead cost ($5,400 + $11,900)	$17,300
Flexible budget overhead for actual production	
($5,600 + $12,000)	17,600
Flexible budget variance	$ 300 F

Spending Variance:

Flexible budget overhead for actual direct labor hours worked	
[(2,740 direct labor hours × $2.00) + $12,000]	$17,480
Total actual overhead cost ($5,400 + $11,900)	17,300
Spending variance	$ 180 F

Efficiency Variance:

Flexible budget overhead for actual production (Requirement 1:	
variable, $5,600 + fixed, $12,000)	$17,600
Flexible budget overhead for actual direct labor hours worked	
[(2,740 direct labor hours × $2.00) + $12,000]	17,480
Efficiency variance	$ 120 F

Production Volume Variance:

Flexible budget overhead for actual production	
(Requirement 1: variable, $5,600 + fixed, $12,000)	$17,600
Standard overhead applied to production	
(Requirement 1: 2,800 direct labor hours × $5.75)	16,100
Production volume variance	$ 1,500 U

or

Standard direct labor hours for static (master) budget	
(Requirement 1: Master Budget)	3,200
Standard direct labor hours for actual production	
(Requirement 1: Flexible Budget)	2,800
Difference in direct labor hours between flexible budget	
and master budget	400
Standard fixed overhead rate per direct labor hour	
(Requirement 1: Master Budget)	×$3.75
Production volume variance	$ 1,500 U

Requirement 4

Bellmead Pools & Supply
Income Statement
For the Month Ended June 30, 19X5

Sales revenue (7 pools at $12,000)			$84,000
Cost of goods sold at standard cost (direct materials,			
$14,000 + direct labor, $29,400 + overhead, $16,100) .		$59,500	

Cost variances:*	Unfavorable	Favorable		
Direct materials	$ 800			
Direct labor		$2,000		
Overhead	1,200			
	$2,000	$2,000		
Net cost variance			-0-	
Cost of goods sold at actual cost				59,500
Gross margin				24,500
Selling and administrative expenses				17,700
Operating income				$ 6,800

*Cost variance detail:

	Unfavorable	Favorable	Total
Direct materials—price	$ -0-	$ -0-	
—efficiency	800		
Direct labor—price		1,370	
—efficiency		630	
Overhead—flexible budget		300	
—production volume . .	1,500		

Summary

A *static budget* is prepared for only one level of activity, usually the volume level that management expects for the period. A *flexible budget* is a set of budgets covering a range of volume. *Performance reports* compare actual and budgeted results for the sales volume achieved. Differences between actual and budgeted revenues and expenses are called *variances*. A variance is *favorable* if actual revenue exceeds budgeted revenue, or if actual expense is less than budgeted expense. An *unfavorable* variance occurs when actual revenue is less than budget, or actual expense exceeds budget.

Costs are classified as *variable, fixed,* or *mixed.* The total amount of a variable cost fluctuates in direct proportion to changes in volume. By contrast, the total amount of a fixed cost does not change during a given period over a wide range of volume. A mixed cost has both variable and fixed components. These distinctions are important to flexible budgeting, which identifies costs and income for different levels of volume.

The heart of a flexible budget is the *budget formula,* which expresses the behavior of costs. A *flexible budget graph* provides a customized budget for any volume level.

Standard costs are the predetermined costs that managers believe the business should incur in producing an item. The standards are set low enough to spur employees to improve their performance but not so low as to discourage workers. *Standard cost systems* are designed to control cost by analyzing differences between actual and standard costs. *Cost variances* are differences between actual cost and standard cost. In general, cost variances are divided into price and efficiency effects.

The *price variance* measures the effect price changes have on the cost of materials and labor. The *efficiency variance* gauges manager efficiency in using materials and labor.

Production overhead may be analyzed in two- or three-variance systems. The *flexible budget variance* is the difference between actual overhead cost and the flexible budget for actual output. It measures whether the company achieved its budgeted cost for the actual volume level achieved. The flexible budget variance may be subdivided into *spending* and *efficiency variances.* The *production volume variance* arises when actual production differs from the level in the static (master) budget.

Some companies use standard costing for control purposes without recording standard costs in the accounts. Others journalize the standards and the related cost variances. The variance information is helpful in planning and control. It does not automatically identify problems or cures, but it points to areas of the business needing correction.

Self-Study Questions

Test your understanding of the chapter by marking the best answer for each of the following questions.

1. A flexible budget shows *(p. 977)*
    a. Expected results over a range of volume levels
    b. A single target level of volume
    c. Price variances
    d. Volume variances

2. Which is the most useful formula for budgeting expenses? *(p. 977)*
   a. Expenses = Sales − Income
   b. Expenses = Fixed + Variable
   c. Expenses = Fixed + (Variable × Number of Units)
   d. Expenses = Standard + Variances

3. Flexible budget variances are differences between *(p. 980)*
   a. Actual results and the static (master) budget
   b. Actual results and the flexible budget
   c. The static (master) budget and the flexible budget
   d. None of the above

4. Standard cost variances help managers identify *(p. 983)*
   a. Ways of reducing cost   c. Both of the above
   b. Employees who control cost   d. None of the above

5. Cost variances for direct materials and direct labor are divided into *(p. 984)*
   a. Flexible budget effects and production volume effects
   b. Efficiency effects and flexible budget effects
   c. Controllable effects and master budget effects
   d. Price effects and efficiency effects

6. Krakow, Inc., paid $3 per pound for 10,000 pounds of direct materials purchased and used. Standard cost was $2.80 per pound, and standard usage for actual production was 11,000 pounds. How much is the price variance? *(p. 986)*
   a. $800 favorable   c. $2,800 favorable
   b. $2,000 unfavorable   d. $3,000 favorable

7. How much is the efficiency variance in the preceding question? *(p. 986)*
   a. $800 favorable   c. $2,800 favorable
   b. $2,000 unfavorable   d. $3,000 favorable

8. Cost variances for production overhead may be divided into *(p. 988)*
   a. Flexible budget effects and production volume effects
   b. Efficiency effects and flexible budget effects
   c. Controllable effects and master budget effects
   d. Price effects and efficiency effects

9. Actual overhead of Milstead Supply Company is $540,000. Overhead for static (master) budget volume is $500,000, and flexible budget overhead for actual production is $510,000. The production volume variance is *(p. 990)*
   a. $10,000 unfavorable   c. $40,000 unfavorable
   b. $30,000 unfavorable   d. Not determinable from the information given. Reason?

10. If direct labor hours are used to apply overhead to output produced, the sign (favorable or unfavorable) of the production overhead efficiency variance is the same as the sign of the *(p. 987, 992)*
    a. Direct materials efficiency variance
    b. Direct labor efficiency variance
    c. Production overhead spending variance
    d. Flexible budget production overhead variance

11. Gonzalez Manufacturing made the following entry for the use of direct materials in production:

Work in Process	380,000	
Direct Materials Efficiency Variance	35,000	
Direct Materials Price Variance		6,000
Materials Inventory.......................		409,000

Which of the following statements is true? *(p. 986)*

a. The price variance is unfavorable and the efficiency variance is favorable
b. The price variance is favorable and the efficiency variance is unfavorable
c. Both variances are favorable
d. Both variances are unfavorable

Answers to the Self-Study Questions follow the Accounting Vocabulary.

Accounting Vocabulary

Budget formula. The heart of a flexible budget; shows how to compute the budget amounts *(p. 977)*.

Controllable overhead variance. Another name for the Flexible budget overhead variance *(p. 990)*.

Efficiency variance. Difference between the quantity of inputs actually used and the quantity that should have been used for the actual output achieved, multiplied by the standard unit price of the input. Also called the Usage variance and the Quantity variance *(p. 984)*.

Flexible budget. Set of budgets covering a range of volume rather than a single level of volume *(p. 977)*.

Flexible budget overhead variance. Difference between total actual overhead (fixed and variable) and the flexible budget amount for actual production volume. Also called the Controllable variance *(p. 989)*.

Flexible budget variance. Difference between an amount in the flexible budget and the actual results for the corresponding item *(p. 980)*.

Performance report. Report that compares actual and budgeted results *(p. 977)*.

Price variance. Difference between the actual unit price of an input and a standard unit price, multiplied by the actual quantitiy of inputs used *(p. 984)*.

Production overhead efficiency variance. The difference between the flexible budget for actual production and the flexible budget for the actual units of the overhead cost application base *(p. 991)*.

Production volume overhead variance. Difference between the flexible budget for actual production and standard overhead applied to production *(p. 990)*.

Quantity variance. Another name for the Efficiency variance used to control materials and labor costs in a standard cost system *(p. 984)*.

Sales volume variance. Difference between a revenue, expense, or operating income amount in the flexible budget and the corresponding amount in the static (master) budget *(p. 980)*.

Spending variance. Difference between the flexible budget for the actual units of the cost application base and the total actual overhead cost *(p. 992)*.

Standard cost. Predetermined cost that management believes the business should incur in producing an item *(p. 983)*.

Standard cost system. Designed to control costs by analyzing the relationship between actual costs and standard costs *(p. 983)*.

Static budget. A budget prepared for only one level of activity *(p. 977)*.

Usage variance. Another name for the Efficiency variance used to control materials and labor costs in a standard cost system *(p. 983)*.

Variance. Difference between an actual amount and the corresponding budget amount *(p. 977)*.

1. a
2. c
3. b
4. c
5. d

6. b ($3.00 − $2.80) × 10,000 = $2,000 U
7. c (11,000 − 10,000) × $2.80 = $2,800 F
8. a
9. d Standard overhead applied to production is missing
10. b
11. b

ASSIGNMENT MATERIAL _____

Questions

1. Which costs in total amount move in direct proportion to changes in volume? Which costs do not fluctuate in total amount with volume changes? How do total and unit amounts behave for these two categories of costs?

2. What is the relevant range, and why must it be considered in preparing a flexible budget?

3. How does a static budget differ from a flexible budget?

4. Identify how managers use variance information from a performance report.

5. McLaren, Inc., prepared its static (master) budget for a sales level of 35,000 for the month. Actual sales totaled 46,000. Describe the problem of using the master budget to evaluate company performance for the month. Propose a better way to evaluate McLaren's performance for the period.

6. What advantage does a flexible expense budget graph offer over a flexible expense budget that shows four levels of volume?

7. What do the sales volume variance and the flexible budget variance measure?

8. Describe the purpose of a standard cost system.

9. What two general categories of cost variances do most standard cost systems provide?

10. Identify the similarities and differences between a standard cost and a budgeted cost.

11. Suppose your company is installing a standard cost system. What sort of standard cost is most popular? For employees, what purpose does a standard cost fulfill?

12. What does a price variance measure? How is it computed?

13. What does an efficiency variance measure? How is it computed?

14. Consider price variance and efficiency variance. How do they relate to the total variance between actual and budgeted cost for direct materials and direct labor?

15. Describe a trade-off that a manager might make for labor cost.

16. When should a cost variance be investigated?

17. What causes a flexible budget overhead variance? What information does this variance provide?

18. What information is provided by the overhead production volume variance? How is this variance computed?

19. Scott & White, Inc., enters standard costs in the company accounts. The actual cost of direct materials used to manufacture inventory was $21,600. The direct materials price variance was $2,000 favorable, and the efficiency variance was $1,400 unfavorable. Make the journal entry to charge materials to production.

20. How does a standard cost income statement for management differ from an income statement reported to the public?

Exercises

Exercise 21-1 *Preparing a flexible budget for the income statement* *(L.O. 1)*

Jaymar Production Company sells its main product for $6 per unit, and variable cost is $1.40 per unit. Fixed expenses are $180,000 per month for volumes up to 55,000 units of output. Above 55,000 units, monthly fixed expenses are $240,000.

Required

Prepare a monthly flexible budget for the product, showing sales, variable expenses, fixed expenses, and operating income or loss for volume levels of 40,000, 50,000, and 60,000 units.

Exercise 21-2 *Graphing expense behavior* *(L.O. 1)*

Graph the expense behavior of Jaymar Production Company in Exercise 21-1. Show total expenses for volume levels of 40,000, 50,000, 55,000, and 60,000 units.

Exercise 21-3 *Completing a performance report* *(L.O. 2)*

Erie, Inc., management received the following incomplete performance report:

Erie, Inc.
Income Statement Performance Report
For the Year Ended April 30, 19X3

	Actual Results at Actual Prices	Flexible Budget Variances	Flexible Budget for Actual Volume Achieved	Sales Volume Variances	Static (Master) Budget
Units	24,000	___	24,000	___	22,000
Sales	$192,000	___	$192,000		$176,000
Variable expenses	76,000		72,000		66,000
Fixed expenses	104,000		100,000		100,000
Total expenses	180,000		172,000		166,000
Operating income	$ 12,000	___	$ 20,000	___	$ 10,000

Required

Complete the performance report. Identify the employee group that should be praised and the group that may be subject to criticism. Give your reasons.

Exercise 21-4 *Preparing an income statement performance report* (L.O. 2)

Top managers of North Country Provision Co. estimated 19X6 sales of 150,000 units of its product at a unit price of $6. Actual sales for the year were 140,000 units at $6.50. Variable expenses were budgeted at $2.20 per unit, and actual variable expenses were $2.15 per unit. Actual fixed expenses of $428,000 exceeded budgeted fixed expenses of $410,000.

Required

Prepare North Country's income statement performance report in a format similar to Exhibit 21-4. The bracketed amounts at the bottom are not required. What variance contributed the most to the year's favorable results? Explain what probably caused this variance.

Exercise 21-5 *Computing price and efficiency variances for direct materials* (L.O. 3)

The following direct materials variance computations are incomplete:

$$\text{Price variance} = (\$7 - \$?) \times 3,560 \text{ pounds} = \$1,780 \text{ U}$$
$$\text{Efficiency variance} = (? - 3,600 \text{ pounds}) \times ? = ? \text{ F}$$
$$\text{Total materials cost variance} = \$?$$

Required

Fill in the missing values and identify the total variance as favorable or unfavorable.

Exercise 21-6 *Computing price and efficiency cost variances for materials and labor* (L.O. 3, 4)

Lear-Wright Corp., which uses a standard cost accounting system, manufactured 350,000 picture frames during the year, using 724,000 board feet of lumber purchased earlier in the year at actual unit cost of $1.22. Production required 6,700 direct labor hours that cost $8.10 per hour. The materials standard was two board feet of lumber per frame, at standard cost of $1.30 per foot. The labor standard was .019 direct labor hour per frame, at standard cost of $8.00 per hour.

Required

Compute the price and efficiency variances for direct materials and direct labor.

Exercise 21-7 *Journalizing standard costing transactions* (L.O. 6)

Make the journal entries to charge direct materials and direct labor to production in Exercise 21-6.

Exercise 21-8 *Explaining cost variances* (L.O. 3, 4, 5)

Diamond Point Corporation managers are seeking explanations for the variances in the following report:

Diamond Point Corporation
Income Statement for Managers
Year Ended December 31, 19X2

Sales revenue		$541,000
Cost of goods sold—standard	$310,000	
Cost variances:		
Materials: price	4,000 F	
efficiency	6,000 U	
Labor: price	8,000 U	
efficiency	3,000 F	
Overhead: flexible budget	9,000 U	
production volume	10,000 U	
Net cost variance	26,000 U	
Cost of goods sold—actual		336,000
Gross profit		205,000
Selling and administrative expenses		181,000
Operating income		$ 24,000

Required

Explain the meaning of each of Diamond Point Corporation's labor variances and each of the overhead variances.

Exercise 21-9   *Computing overhead cost variances*   **(L.O. 5)**

Great Pacific Coffee Company charges the following standard unit cost to production, based on master budget volume of 30,000 units per month:

Direct materials	$3.20
Direct labor	4.10
Overhead	1.00
Standard unit cost	$8.30

Great Pacific used the following flexible overhead cost budget:

	Monthly Volume		
Number of units	27,000	30,000	33,000
Standard direct labor hours	2,700	3,000	3,300
Budgeted overhead cost:			
Variable	$13,500	$15,000	$16,500
Fixed	15,000	15,000	15,000

Actual monthly production was 27,000 units. Actual overhead cost was variable, $14,700, and fixed, $15,200. Actual direct labor hours worked were 2,650.

Required

Compute the total overhead cost variance, the flexible budget variance, and the production volume variance for overhead cost. Also compute the overhead spending and efficiency variances.

Exercise 21-10   *Preparing a standard cost income statement for management*   **(L.O. 7)**

Keystone Manufacturing Co. revenue and expense information for the month of May follows.

	Revenue or Expense	
	Actual	Standard
Sales revenue	$160,000	$160,000
Cost of goods sold	?	91,000
Information regarding:		
Direct materials price variance	20,000	19,100
Direct materials efficiency variance	19,000	20,600
Direct labor price variance	42,000	43,400
Direct labor efficiency variance	44,000	42,300
Overhead flexible budget variance	15,000	15,900
Overhead production volume variance ...	15,900	15,600

Required

Prepare a standard cost income statement through gross profit. Report all cost variances for use by management.

Problems

(Group A)

Problem 21-1A *Preparing a flexible budget income statement and graphing cost behavior (L.O. 1)*

Bioseptic, Inc., produces and sells prepackaged tests for certain infectious diseases. The company's master budget income statement for 19X7 follows, based on expected sales volume of 110,000 units:

Bioseptic, Inc.
Master Budget Income Statement
Year 19X7

Sales	$440,000
Variable expenses:	
Cost of goods sold	$121,000
Sales commissions	33,000
Shipping	24,200
Utilities	11,000
Fixed expenses:	
Salaries	73,000
Depreciation	48,000
Rent	23,000
Insurance	17,700
Utilities	12,400
Total operating expenses	363,300
Income before income tax	76,700
Income tax expense (30%)	23,010
Net income	$ 53,690

Bioseptic's plant capacity is 125,000 units, so if actual volume exceeds 125,000 units, it will be necessary to expand the plant. In that case, salaries will increase by 10 percent, depreciation by 20 percent, rent by $11,000, and insurance by $2,800. Fixed utilities will be unchanged by the volume increase.

Required

1. Prepare a flexible budget income statement for the company, showing volume levels of 100,000, 110,000, 120,000, and 130,000 units.

2. Graph the total operating expense behavior of the company. Cost of goods sold is included.

Problem 21-2A *Preparing an income statement performance report* **(L.O. 2)**

Refer to the Bioseptic, Inc., situation of Problem 21-1A. The company sold 120,000 units during 19X7, and its actual income statement was as follows:

Bioseptic, Inc.	
Income Statement	
Year 19X7	
Sales	$487,000
Variable expenses:	
Cost of goods sold	$133,000
Sales commissions	39,000
Shipping	27,000
Utilities	12,000
Fixed expenses:	
Salaries	76,000
Depreciation	48,000
Rent	19,000
Insurance	15,000
Utilities	14,000
Total operating expenses	383,000
Income before income tax	104,000
Income tax expense (30%)	31,200
Net income	$ 72,800

Required

Prepare an income statement performance report for 19X7.

Problem 21-3A *Preparing a flexible budget and computing cost variances* **(L.O. 1, 3, 4, 5)**

Hi-Fidelity, Inc., manufactures compact disk players and uses flexible budgeting and a standard cost system. The company's performance report includes the selected data that follow:

Required

1. Prepare a flexible budget based on actual volume.
2. Compute the price variance and the efficiency variance for direct materials and direct labor. Compute the total variance, the flexible budget variance, and the production volume variance for overhead.
3. Show that the sum of the price variance plus the efficiency variance equals the total cost variance for direct materials and for direct labor. Use Exhibit 21-6 as a guide.

	Master Budget 12,000 Units	Actual Results 13,300 Units
Sales	$744,000	$811,300
Variable expenses:		
Cost of goods sold:		
Direct materials (18,000 lb. @ $7.00)	$126,000	
(17,800 lb. @ $7.07)		$125,846
Direct labor (24,000 hr. @ $6.20)	148,800	
(27,700 hr. @ $6.15)....................		170,355
Variable overhead (24,000 hr. @ $2.10) ...	50,400	
(27,700 hr. @ $2.22)....................		61,494
Fixed expenses:		
Cost of goods sold:		
Fixed overhead	93,600	104,000
Total cost of goods sold	418,800	461,695
Gross profit	$325,200	$349,605

Problem 21-4A *Using incomplete cost and variance information to determine the number of direct labor hours worked* **(L.O. 4)**

The city of Mobile has a shop that manufactures street signs. The manager of the shop uses standard costs to judge performance. Recently a clerk mistakenly threw away some of the records, and the manager has only partial data for July. He knows that the total direct labor variance for the month was $680—unfavorable, and that the standard labor price was $6.70 per hour. A recent pay raise caused an unfavorable labor price variance of $.30 per hour. The standard direct labor hours for actual July output were 2,500.

Required

1. Find the actual number of direct labor hours worked during July. First, find the actual direct labor price per hour. Then, determine the actual number of direct labor hours by setting up the computation of the total direct labor cost variance of $680.
2. Compute the direct labor price and efficiency variances.

Problem 21-5A *Computing and journalizing cost variances* **(L.O. 3, 4, 5, 6)**

Lumberjack Supply Co. manufactures hiking boots. The company prepares flexible budgets and uses a standard cost system to control manufacturing cost. The following standard unit cost of a pair of high-top boots is based on master budget volume of 14,000 pairs per month:

Direct materials (2.3 sq. yd. @ $2.10 per sq. yd.) ...		$ 4.83
Direct labor (2 hours @ $9.25 per hour)		18.50
Overhead:		
Variable	$1.22	
Fixed (2 hours @ $2.06 per hour)	4.12	5.34
Total unit cost..................................		$28.67

Transactions during November of the current year included these:

a. Actual production was 11,400 units.
b. Actual direct materials usage was 2.24 square yards per pair at actual cost of $2.17 per square yard.
c. Actual direct labor usage of 22,600 hours cost $208,372.
d. Total actual overhead cost was $58,310.

Required

1. Compute the price and efficiency variances for direct materials and direct labor. Carry amounts to two decimal places.
2. Journalize the usage of direct material and the application of direct labor, including the related cost variances.
3. Compute the total variance, the flexible budget variance, and the production volume variance for overhead. Also compute the overhead spending and efficiency variances for a three-variance overhead analysis.
4. Lumberjack management intentionally purchased superior materials for November production. How did this decision affect the other cost variances? Overall, was the decision wise?

Problem 21-6A *Computing cost variances and reporting to management (L.O. 3, 4, 5, 7)*

Lennox Manufacturing produces industrial plastics used in a variety of products. During April the company produced and sold 21,000 sheets of plastic and accumulated the following cost data:

	Standard Unit Cost	Total Actual Cost
Direct materials:		
Standard (3 lb. @ $1.22 per lb.)	$3.66	
Actual (67,200 lb. @ $1.18 per lb.)		$ 79,296
Direct labor:		
Standard (.1 hr. @ $7.00 per hr.)	.70	
Actual (2,200 hr. @ $6.90 per hr.)		15,180
Overhead: *favolable*		
Standard:		
Variable ($12.00 per direct labor hour) . . . $1.20		
Fixed ($32,000 for master budget volume of 20,000 units and 2,000 direct labor hours) 1.60	2.80	
Actual		59,340
Total	$7.16	$153,816

Required

1. Compute the price and efficiency variances for direct materials and direct labor.
2. Compute the total variance, the flexible budget variance, and the production volume variance for overhead.
3. Prepare a standard cost income statement through gross profit to report all variances to management. Sale price of the plastic was $10.90 per sheet.
4. Lennox intentionally purchased cheaper materials during April. Was the decision wise? Discuss the trade-off between the two materials cost variances.

(Group B)

Problem 21-1B *Preparing a flexible budget income statement and graphing cost behavior (L.O. 1)*

Columbia Pneumatic Tool Company manufactures solenoids for electronically controlled lawn sprinkler systems. The company's master budget income statement for 19X3 follows, based on expected sales volume of 36,000 units.

Columbia's plant capacity is 38,000 units, so if actual volume exceeds 38,000 units it will be necessary to rent additional space. In that case, salaries will increase by 10 percent, rent will double, and insurance expense will increase by $2,000. Depreciation and fixed utilities will be unaffected by the increase in volume.

Columbia Pneumatic Tool Company
Master Budget Income Statement
Year 19X3

Sales		$756,000
Variable expenses:		
Cost of goods sold	$288,000	
Sales commissions	37,800	
Shipping	18,000	
Utilities	14,400	
Fixed expenses:		
Salaries	110,000	
Depreciation	53,000	
Rent	45,000	
Insurance	11,000	
Utilities	9,000	
Total operating expenses		586,200
Income before income tax		169,800
Income tax expense (25%)		42,450
Net income		$127,350

Required

1. Prepare a flexible budget income statement for the company, showing volume levels of 30,000, 36,000, 40,000, and 44,000 units.
2. Graph the total operating expense behavior of the company. Cost of goods sold is included.

Problem 21-2B   *Preparing an income statement performance report*   *(L.O. 2)*

Refer to the Columbia Pneumatic Tool Company situation of Problem 21-1B. The company sold 44,000 units during 19X3, and its actual income statement was as reported below.

Required

Prepare an income statement performance report for 19X3.

Columbia Pneumatic Tool Company
Income Statement
Year 19X3

Sales		$928,000
Variable expenses:		
Cost of goods sold	$361,000	
Sales commissions	45,000	
Shipping	27,000	
Utilities	18,000	
Fixed expenses:		
Salaries	127,000	
Depreciation	66,000	
Rent	72,000	
Insurance	14,000	
Utilities	8,000	
Total operating expenses		738,000
Income before income tax		190,000
Income tax expense (25%)		47,500
Net income		$142,500

Problem 21-3B *Preparing a flexible budget and computing cost variances (L.O. 1, 3, 4, 5)*

Lands End Fabricating Company manufactures office furniture and uses flexible budgeting and a standard cost system. The company's performance report includes the following selected data:

	Master Budget 4,000 Units	Actual Results 3,800 Units
Sales	$800,000	$729,600
Variable expenses:		
Cost of goods sold:		
Direct materials (160,000 lb. @ $.80)	$128,000	
(164,000 lb. @ $.78)		$127,920
Direct labor (20,000 hr. @ $6.00)	120,000	
(19,300 hr. @ $6.03)		116,379
Variable overhead (20,000 hr. @ $4.00)	80,000	
(20,300 hr. @ $5.22)		105,966
Fixed expenses:		
Cost of goods sold:		
Fixed overhead	112,000	94,000
Total cost of goods sold	440,000	444,265
Gross profit	$360,000	$285,335

Required

1. Prepare a flexible budget based on actual volume.
2. Compute the price variance and the efficiency variance for direct materials and direct labor. Compute the total variance, the flexible budget variance, and the production volume variance for overhead.
3. Show that the sum of the price variance plus the efficiency variance equals the total cost variance for direct materials and for direct labor. Use Exhibit 21-6 as a guide.

Problem 21-4B *Using incomplete cost and variance information to determine the number of direct labor hours worked (L.O. 4)*

The state of Kentucky has a shop that manufactures road signs used throughout the state. The manager of the shop uses standard costs to judge performance. Recently a clerk mistakenly threw away some of the records, and the manager has only partial data for April. She knows that the total direct labor variance for the month was $900—favorable and that the standard labor price was $6 per hour. A recent pay raise caused an unfavorable labor price variance of $.25 per hour. The standard direct labor hours for actual April output were 2,900.

Required

1. Find the actual number of direct labor hours worked during April. First, find the actual direct labor price per hour. Then determine the actual number of direct labor hours by setting up the computation of the total direct labor cost variance of $900.
2. Compute the direct labor price and efficiency variances.

Problem 21-5B *Computing and journalizing cost variances (L.O. 3, 4, 5, 6)*

Consolidated Enterprises manufactures T-shirts that it sells to other companies for customizing with their own logos. Consolidated prepares flexible budgets and uses a standard cost system to control manufacturing cost. The standard unit cost of a basic white T-shirt given at the top of the next page is based on master budget volume of 20,000 T-shirts per month.

Direct materials (3 sq. yd. @ $.15 per sq. yd.) ...		$ .45
Direct labor (3 minutes @ $.20 per minute)		.60
Overhead:		
Variable	$.12	
Fixed (3 minutes @ $.1067 per minute)........	.32	.44
Total unit cost		$1.49

Transactions during May of the current year included the following:

a. Actual production and sales were 22,700 units.
b. Actual direct materials usage was 2.75 square yards per unit at actual cost of $.14 per square yard.
c. Actual direct labor usage of 69,200 minutes cost $14,532.
d. Total actual overhead cost was $10,107.

Required

1. Compute the price and efficiency variances for direct materials and direct labor. Carry amounts to two decimal places.
2. Journalize the usage of direct material and the application of direct labor, including the related cost variances.
3. Compute the total variance, the flexible budget variance, and the production volume variance for overhead. Then compute the overhead spending and efficiency variances.
4. Evaluate the performance of the plant manager in controlling overhead cost in May.

Problem 21-6B   *Computing cost variances and reporting to management (L.O. 3,4,5,7)*

Champion Academic Supplier manufactures ring binders used by college students. During August the company produced and sold 78,000 binders and accumulated the following cost data:

		Standard Unit Cost	Total Actual Cost
Direct materials:			
Standard (1 lb. @ $.15 per lb.)		$.15	
Actual (74,900 lb. @ $.16 per lb.)			$11,984
Direct labor:			
Standard (.02 hr. @ $5.00 per hr.)		.10	
Actual (1,600 hr. @ $5.05 per hr.)			8,080
Overhead:			
Standard:			
Variable ($6.00 per direct labor hour)	$.12		
Fixed ($12,000 for master budget			
volume of 80,000 units and 1,600			
direct labor hours)	.15	.27	
Actual			21,440
Total		$.52	$41,504

Required

1. Compute the price and efficiency variances for direct materials and direct labor.
2. Compute the total variance, the flexible budget variance, and the production volume variance for overhead.
3. Prepare a standard cost income statement through gross profit to report all variances to management. Sale price of the binders to college bookstores was $1.25 each.
4. Champion management purchased superior materials during August. Discuss the trade-off between the two materials' cost variances.

Extending Your Knowledge

Decision Problems

1. Preparing a Performance Report and Using It to Evaluate Company Performance (L.O. 2)

The board of directors of X-Out, Inc., is meeting to evaluate the company's performance for the year just ended. Suppose the accompanying report, which applies to X-Out's basic line of golf clubs, has been prepared for use at the meeting.

The directors are disappointed at the net income results. They ask if the company maintained the price of its golf clubs at budgeted sale price of $120, and they are told yes. Moreover, the levels of beginning and ending inventories were unchanged.

Required

1. Use the above information to prepare a more informative performance report.
2. A downturn in the economy was responsible for the company's inability to sell more golf clubs. How would you view company performance in light of this additional information? Would you decide to overhaul operations or keep the business operating on its present course?

X-Out, Inc.
Performance Report
Year Ended June 30, 19X7

	Actual Results	Master Budget	Variance
Sales	$2,655,000	$3,240,000	$585,000 U
Variable expenses:			
Cost of goods sold	$1,189,000	$1,546,000	$357,000 F
Promotion expense	126,800	110,000	16,800 U
Sales commissions	116,900	166,000	49,100 F
Shipping	64,000	87,000	23,000 F
Utilities	13,000	14,000	1,000 F
Fixed expenses:			
Salaries	341,600	439,000	97,400 F
Depreciation	306,000	313,000	7,000 F
Rent	143,500	171,000	27,500 F
Utilities	11,200	13,000	1,800 F
Total operating expenses	2,312,000	2,859,000	547,000 F
Income before income tax	343,000	381,000	38,000 U
Income tax expense (30%)	102,900	114,300	11,400 F
Net income	$ 240,100	$ 266,700	$ 26,600 U

2. Variance Analysis and Reporting in a Non-profit Organization (L.O. 1, 2)

St. Margaret's Church is a small congregation in Altamont, Oregon. At the end of 1992, the church membership was 87 families. Each family donated an average of $400 per year to the church's operating fund and $100 per year to the mission and service fund.

At the beginning of 1993, the Church's Stewardship, Mission and Service Committee estimated that, due to the building of a new factory ten miles outside Altamont, the church membership would grow by eleven families. In addition, the committee planned a stewardship campaign for 1993 with the aim of increasing average donations to $450 for the operating fund and $125 for mission and service.

During 1993, seven new families became members at St. Margaret's; no families left the congregation. The 1993 receipts amounted to $42,864 for operations, and $10,152 for mission and service.

Required

1. Assume that you were the Chairman of St. Margaret's Church's 1993 Stewardship Committee. Prepare an analysis for the Stewardship, Mission and Service Committee of the 1993 fund-raising efforts.

2. Write a one-paragraph report to summarize the results of the fund-raising campaign for the church's board of trustees.

Ethical Issue

Jurgens Products, Inc., budgets from the bottom up. Production workers prepare departmental goals, which are coordinated by supervisors. Top managers combine the departmental budgets into the company's overall flexible budget. Standard costs developed from the budget amounts are used for the full year.

Production workers have observed that the standard costs correspond closely to their own budget amounts. Accordingly, they have built a cushion for themselves by overestimating the quantities of materials and labor needed to manufacture a product.

Required

1. Are Jurgens's cost variances likely to be favorable or unfavorable? Why is this outcome likely to occur?

2. Whose behavior is unethical, and whose behavior is lax?

3. If this situation persists over several years, what is the likely outcome?

Chapter 22

Responsibility Accounting

In the early 1980s, a multibillion dollar conglomerate, doing business in more than 60 countries around the world, had five *operating divisions* in the United States employing about 7,000 people.

The most significant *operating divisions* were in the petroleum services business employing approximately 5,000 people, predominantly in the Southwest. With the collapse of energy prices, exploration activities within the United States were slashed, resulting in a large number of personnel being laid off.

Each segment (division) of a business is expected to pull its own weight. In this case a petroleum services company closed several operating divisions because they were losing money.

SOURCE: James A. Heely and Roy L. Nersesian, "Ethis Case Study: A Taxing Situation," *Management Accounting*, June 1992, p. 17.

What's the key concept in the chapter-opening vignette? Each division of the company is responsible for generating its own revenues and profits. This chapter shows how companies organize operations to place responsibility on managers. This area of analysis is called responsibility accounting.

Responsibility Accounting

Most businesses must divide the responsibility of management. Some companies are so geographically dispersed that one person cannot adequately oversee the entire operation. Other companies may have too many operations or too many employees for one person to handle all executive duties. To get the work done, executives must delegate authority over particular areas to middle-level managers. Depending on how complex or on how large the company is, the mid-level manager may in turn delegate authority to other employees to handle certain areas of operations under her responsibility. And so the responsibility chain grows.

How does the business measure each manager's performance? **Responsibility accounting** is a system for classifying financial data by defined areas in an organization in order to evaluate the performance of managers for activities under their supervision. Responsibility accounting is a key tool in managing all but single-person businesses. For example, automobile dealerships use responsibility accounting for separately measuring the performance of various activities such as new car sales, used car sales, parts sales, and the service department.

The basic unit in a responsibility accounting system is called a **responsibility center**, which is a part, segment, or subunit of an organization whose managers are accountable for specified activities. A center can be any subunit of an organization needing control. Each center works from a budget tailored to its particular activities. The three common types of responsibility centers are the cost center, the profit center, and the investment center.

1. Cost center. Responsibility center in which a manager is accountable for costs (expenses) only. Examples include a personnel department and a shipping department. It is important for these departments to control costs; they are not responsible for generating revenue. Consequently, only costs are reported for their activities. A shipping department manager is judged, for example, on the cost of shipping a certain volume of merchandise.

2. Profit center. Responsibility center in which a manager is accountable for

OBJECTIVE 1

Identify different types of responsibility centers, and specify the information they report revenues and costs (expenses). Examples are a McDonald's restaurant and a jewelry department in a Macy's store. In the chapter-opening vignette, the energy service divisions of the company are profit centers. Managers of these subunits are responsible for generating income (revenues minus expenses). Both revenues and expenses are reported to show the income of a profit center.

3. *Investment center.* Responsibility center in which a manager is accountable for investments, revenues, and costs (expenses). Examples are a Hilton hotel and an Exxon exploration division. Investment in the business is reported in addition to revenues and expenses so that return on investment (income divided by investment) can be computed. Top managers, as well as investors, evaluate projects by comparing their returns on investment.

Illustration of Responsibility Accounting

The simplified organization chart in Exhibit 22-1 illustrates how companies may use responsibility accounting in the fast-food industry. At the top level, a district manager oversees the branch managers, who supervise the managers of the individual restaurants (called stores). Store managers have limited freedom to make operating decisions. They may decide on how to handle local advertising, the number of employees and their schedules, and the store hours. Branch managers oversee several stores, evaluate store managers' performance, and set store managers' compensation levels. In turn, district managers oversee several branches, evaluate branch managers' performance and compensation, and decide on district prices and sales promotions. District managers are accountable to regional managers, who answer to home-office vice-presidents.

Exhibit 22-2 provides a more detailed view of how responsibility accounting is used to evaluate profit centers. Examine the lowest level and move to the top. Follow how the reports are related through the three levels of responsibility. All variances may be subdivided for further analysis, either in these reports or in supporting schedules.

EXHIBIT 22-1   *O'Toole Restaurant Corporation Simplified Partial Organization Chart*

EXHIBIT 22-2 *Responsibility Accounting at Various Levels*

O'Toole Restaurant Corporation
Responsibility Accounting at Various Levels
(in thousands of dollars)

Northern California District Manager
Monthly Responsibility Report

Operating income of branches and district manager office expense:	Budget		Actual		Variance Favorable (Unfavorable)	
	This Month	Year to Date	This Month	Year to Date	This Month	Year to Date
District manager office expense..	$ (150)	$ (600)	$ (158)	$ (620)	$(8)	$ (20)
San Francisco branch	→ 465	1,730	460	1,780	(5)	50
San Jose branch	500	1,800	519	1,890	19	90
Oakland branch.................	310	1,220	341	1,330	31	110
Others	600	2,560	647	2,690	47	130
Operating income	$1,725	$6,710	$1,809	$7,070	$84	$360

San Francisco Branch Manager
Monthly Responsibility Report

Operating income of stores and branch manager office expense:	Budget		Actual		Variance Favorable (Unfavorable)	
	This Month	Year to Date	This Month	Year to Date	This Month	Year to Date
Branch manager office expense ..	$ (20)	$ (306)	$ (25)	$ (302)	$ (5)	$ 4
Geary Store	48	148	47	143	(1)	(5)
Beale Store	→ 54	228	61	244	7	16
Wharf Store	38	160	42	170	4	10
Others	345	1,500	335	1,525	(10)	25
Operating income	$465	$1,730	$460	$1,780	$ (5)	$50

Beale Store Manager
Monthly Responsibility Report

Revenue and expense:	Budget		Actual		Variance Favorable (Unfavorable)	
	This Month	Year to Date	This Month	Year to Date	This Month	Year to Date
Revenue	$170	$690	$178	$702	$ 8	$12
Food expense..................	50	198	45	184	5	14
Paper	15	62	18	64	(3)	(2)
Wages	24	98	28	103	(4)	(5)
Repairs	5	19	4	20	1	(1)
General	12	45	12	47	—	(2)
Depreciation...................	10	40	10	40	—	—
Total expenses	116	462	117	458	(1)	4
Operating income	$ 54	$228	$ 61	$244	$ 7	$16

Trace the $54,000 operating income from the Beale Store manager report to the San Francisco branch manager report. The branch manager report summarizes the final results of the stores under his supervision. In addition, charges incurred by the branch manager office are included in this report.

Trace the $465,000 total from the San Francisco branch manager report to the northern California district manager report. The report of the district manager includes data for her own district office plus a summary of the entire district's operating income performance.

Performance Report Format

OBJECTIVE 2

Prepare a performance report for management by exception

Exhibit 22-2 stresses variances. This focus is a highlight of **management by exception,** a management policy in which executive attention is directed to the important deviations from budgeted amounts. For example, the San Francisco branch's operating income lagged behind the other branches during the current month and for the year to date. The district manager would concentrate her efforts on improving the San Francisco branch. Managers do not waste time investigating smoothly running operations.

The format for reporting operations used in Exhibit 22-2 may be expanded to highlight variances. The expanded performance report for the Beale Store manager follows.

	Budget		Actual Results		Variance: Favorable (Unfavorable)		Variance: Percent of Budgeted Amount	
	This Month	Year to Date	This Month	Year to Date	This Month	Year to Date	This Month	Year to Date
Revenues	$170	$690	$178	$702	$8	$12	4.7%	1.7%

The complete performance report would likely include line-by-line presentations of other data. For example, a report for a restaurant will show the number of customers served and the average selling price per customer. In the hotel industry, managers report the percentage of rooms occupied and the average daily rental rate per room as performance measures.

No single format appeals to all users. Some managers prefer the greater detail shown in the eight-column format, but others prefer less detail. The choice is a matter of personal preference.

Design of a Responsibility Accounting System

A responsibility accounting system can be combined with whatever type of accounting system the company uses, such as a standard cost system, which highlights variances. Recall that process costing works well for goods that are mass-produced as identical units—such as gallons of milk and rolls of paper towels. The key to an effective accounting system is gathering and communicating information to assist the business in achieving its goals. Two factors are important: manager control over operations, and manager access to information.

Consider a furniture manufacturer that uses a standard cost system to measure an efficiency (usage) variance and a price variance for the cost of lumber. The production supervisor is responsible for the quantity of lumber used to manufacture chairs. Good work in the factory wastes little lumber and holds costs down. Careless work wastes lumber and increases production cost. The supervisor must control operations. The efficiency (usage) variance is watched by the supervisor, often by personal observation.

Responsibility for the price variance is assigned to the purchasing manager who buys the lumber. The price of lumber may differ from standard cost because of droughts, crop disease, and forest fires, which are beyond the purchasing manager's control. Nevertheless, the price variance is the responsibility of the purchasing manager because he or she has access to more price information than anyone else in the business. *The reporting responsibility of any manager is to explain the outcome of an action regardless of personal influence over the outcome.* The managers of the energy services divisions in the opening vignette had to explain their business's losses even though prices in the industry were beyond their control.

Responsibility accounting, budgets, standards, and variances are aids to management. They help top managers to delegate decision making to lower levels by assigning responsibility for action and establishing a way to evaluate performance. Such a system frees top managers to work on broad issues affecting the whole organization.

Responsibility accounting systems can also be misused as a way of finding fault and placing blame. The question should not be, Who should be blamed for an unfavorable variance? The question should be, Which individual is in the best position to explain why a specific variance occurred?

Departmental Accounting

Departments are the most widely encountered responsibility centers. Many businesses distinguish between operating, or production, departments and service, or support, departments. The main function of an **operating department** is to add value to products or services sold to customers. In a manufacturing company, each operating department may produce a different product. Alternatively, each department may be responsible for a different stage of production of the same product. Examples are the shaping and finishing departments of a swim mask manufacturer. In a retail company, operating departments typically sell related product lines; examples are the housewares and appliance departments of a department store and the hardware and software departments of a computer store.

The primary function of a **service department** is to provide services to other departments, both operating departments and other service departments. Examples include the production scheduling and central power departments of a manufacturing plant and the purchasing, payroll, and personnel departments of both manufacturers and retailers. Mutual services provided among service departments are called **reciprocal services.** Reciprocal services present special accounting problems, which we discuss in the next section of this chapter.

In departmental accounting systems, both direct and indirect costs are traced to departments. **Direct costs** are costs that are conveniently identified with and traceable to a particular department. Depreciation of a machine used in one department, the department head's salary, the wages of sales clerks, and special advertising of, for instance, a shoe department of a department store are examples of direct costs. **Indirect costs** cannot be traced to a single department only. Examples are building rent and the cost of a general advertising campaign that promotes an entire store. The costs of service departments are indirect costs of the departments they serve.

Allocation of Service Department Costs

Labor costs and various other costs are accumulated for each service department. These costs then are allocated (assigned) to the departments served, for two reasons. First, according to many senior managers, operating department managers should be held accountable for all costs, direct and indirect, that support the activities under their supervision. In theory, operating managers have more incentive to help control support costs when they are assigned a portion of those costs. Second, in manufacturing companies, service department costs are incurred for the purpose of producing products. Thus, these costs should be considered factory overhead costs and applied to products produced. How is this accomplished? Service department costs first are allocated to the production departments that benefit from their services. Then the allocated costs are (1) added to other overhead costs assigned to the production departments and (2) applied to products through departmental factory overhead rates. Our focus here is the first step—allocation of service department costs to production departments.

To allocate a service department's cost, accountants must choose an **allocation base,** which is a logical common denominator for assigning a cost to two or more departments of a business. Exhibit 22-3 offers examples of allocation bases commonly used for selected costs and expenses. The ideal guide for choosing an allocation base is a cause-and-effect relationship. That is, What are the cost drivers, the factors that cause costs? As Exhibit 22-3 implies, generally the more square feet of space, the higher the cost of a janitorial service department. That relationship is relatively easy to understand. Conversely, consider the cost of a general advertising campaign for a department store. The total cost might be allocated to individual departments in relation to budgeted or actual sales, but a cause-and-effect relationship would be much more difficult, if not impossible, to establish.

Let us stress this point: No one "right" allocation base exists for every cost. Managers use their experience and judgment in choosing these bases. Affected managers should participate in the choice of allocation bases, which enhances confidence in the reasonableness of resulting allocations.

We now demonstrate two methods of allocating the costs of service departments to production departments: the direct method and the step-down method. A third method, the reciprocal method, is covered in many cost and advanced managerial accounting texts. These three methods differ only in the way they treat reciprocal services.

Consider TechArt, Inc., which designs, assembles, and installs state-of-the-art integrated electronics systems for both the commercial and residential markets. TechArt has two factory service departments and two production departments in its highly automated manufacturing plant:

Factory Service Departments	**Production Departments**
Engineering & Maintenance	Commercial Systems
Information Systems	Residential Systems

Direct costs of departments are accumulated for planning and control purposes. Then, in order to fully cost installed electronics systems, TechArt

EXHIBIT 22-3 *Bases for Allocating Costs to Departments*

Cost or Expense	Base for Allocating Cost to Departments
Direct material	Separately traced
Merchandise	Separately traced
Packaging materials	Separately traced if feasible
Direct labor	Separately traced
Other labor	Time spent in each department
Supervision	Time spent, or number of employees, in each department
Equipment depreciation and rentals	Separately traced, hours used by each department
Building depreciation, property taxes, and rentals	Square feet of space. Sometimes heavier allocations are made to departments that experience higher customer traffic
Heat, light, and air conditioning	Square feet or cubic feet of space
Janitorial services	Square feet of space
Advertising	Separately traced if possible. Otherwise, in proportion to newspaper space or radio or TV time in advertisement, or in proportion to budgeted sales or actual sales
Payroll Department	Number of employees in each department
Personnel Department	Number of employees in each department
Purchasing Department	Number of orders or dollar amounts of purchases in each department

accountants allocate the costs of the two service departments to the two production departments. Data for our example are shown in Exhibit 22-4.

Exhibit 22-4 shows that $400,000 of direct cost is budgeted for Engineering & Maintenance and $100,000 of direct cost is budgeted for Information Systems. Thus, TechArt has $500,000 of service department costs that must be allocated

EXHIBIT 22-4 *Data for Service Department Cost Allocation at TechArt, Inc.*

	Factory Service Departments		Production Departments		
	Engineering & Maintenance	Information Systems	Commercial Systems	Residential Systems	Total
Direct Department Costs	$400,000	$100,000	$300,000	$250,000	$1,050,000
Services Provided:					
By Engineering & Maintenance					
Budgeted labor hours	—	600	3,000	2,400	6,000
Proportion	—	1/10	5/10	4/10	10/10
By Information Systems					
Budgeted computer hours	600	—	525	375	1,500
Proportion	40/100	—	35/100	25/100	100/100

to the two production departments. TechArt accountants expect Engineering & Maintenance employees will work 6,000 hours: 600 ($\frac{1}{10}$ of the total) for Information Systems, 3,000 for Commercial Systems, and 2,400 for Residential Systems. The accountants anticipate that Information Systems employees will devote 600 computer hours to Engineering & Maintenance, 525 to Commercial Systems, and 375 to Residential Systems.

Direct Method

The **direct method** of service department cost allocation ignores all services provided by one service department to another. It allocates each service department's total cost directly to production departments in proportion to services rendered to them. Exhibit 22-5 illustrates this method, using the data of Exhibit 22-4. Notice that the direct method ignores not only the 600 labor hours of budgeted service provided by Engineering & Maintenance (EM) to Information Systems (IS) but also the 600 hours of computer time budgeted by IS for EM. For each service department, the base number of hours used to compute allocation percentages is the total number budgeted for Commercial Systems and Residential Systems only. That number is 5,400 (3,000 + 2,400) for EM and 900 (525 + 375) for IS.

Step-Down Method

The **step-down method** *partially* recognizes services provided by service departments to other service departments. That is, this method recognizes some, but not all, reciprocal services. With the step-down method, the order of allocation affects the amounts allocated to production departments. For TechArt, the $500,000 ($400,000 + $100,000) of total service department cost is assigned differently to the Commercial and Residential Systems departments if the allocation procedure begins with EM than if it begins with IS.

EXHIBIT 22-5 *Direct Method of Cost Allocation at TechArt, Inc.*

	Factory Service Departments		Production Departments		
	Engineering & Maintenance	Information Systems	Commercial Systems	Residential Systems	Total
Direct Department Costs	$400,000	$100,000	$300,000	$250,000	$1,050,000
Allocation of Engineering & Maintenance: ($\frac{5}{9}$, $\frac{4}{9}$)*	(400,000)		222,222	177,778	
	$ 0				
Allocation of Information Systems: ($\frac{7}{12}$, $\frac{5}{12}$)†		(100,000)	58,333	41,667	
		$ 0			
Total budgeted factory overhead of production departments			$580,555	$469,445	$1,050,000

*Base is (3,000 + 2,400), or 5,400 hours; 3,000/5,400 = $\frac{5}{9}$; 2,400/5,400 = $\frac{4}{9}$
†Base is (525 + 375), or 900 hours; 525/900 = $\frac{7}{12}$; 375/900 = $\frac{5}{12}$

Which department's cost should be allocated first? A popular step-down sequence is to begin with the department that renders the highest dollar amount of services to other service departments and proceed in order to the department that renders the lowest amount. In the case of TechArt, both EM and IS provide $40,000 of services to the other department (EM to IS, $400,000 × 1/10; IS to EM, $100,000 × 4/10). In Exhibit 22-6, EM is allocated first.

Notice that EM's cost is allocated to all departments served by EM, including IS. The allocation proportions are those given in Exhibit 22-4. On the other hand, the total IS cost of $140,000 (the original $100,000 plus the $40,000 allocated from EM) is allocated to Commercial Systems and Residential Systems only. The proportions for IS are the same as those used with the direct method (Exhibit 22-5). Under the step-down method, once a service department's cost has been allocated, no other service department's cost is allocated back to it.

Which method is better? In general, the step-down, because it recognizes the most significant support provided by service departments to other service departments. However, the direct method is simpler. When the two methods produce similar results, many companies use the direct method because it is easier for managers to understand.

Illustration of Departmental Reporting

What information do senior managers need to evaluate past operations and plan for the future? Consider a familiar illustration—the department store. Top managers of a department store want more information than the net income of the store as a whole. At a minimum, they want to know each department's gross margin (sales minus cost of goods sold). In addition, they usually want to know each department's operating income. With these data, managers can identify their most profitable and least profitable departments. This information aids decisions such as whether to expand some departments and phase out others.

EXHIBIT 22-6 *Step-Down Method of Cost Allocation at TechArt, Inc.*

| | Factory Service Departments | | Production Departments | | |
	Engineering & Maintenance	Information Systems	Commercial Systems	Residential Systems	Total
Direct Department Costs	$400,000	$100,000	$300,000	$250,000	$1,050,000
Allocation of Engineering & Maintenance: (1/10, 5/10, 4/10)*	(400,000) $ 0	40,000	200,000	160,000	
Allocation of Information Systems: ($7/12$, $5/12$)†		(140,000) $ 0	81,667	58,333	
Total budgeted factory overhead of production departments			$581,667	$468,333	$1,050,000

*Base is (600 + 3,000 + 2,400), or 6,000 hours; 600/6,000 = 1/10; 3,000/6,000 = 5/10; 2,400/6,000 = 4/10.
†Base is (525 + 375), or 900 hours; 525/900 = $7/12$; 375/900 = $5/12$.

Departmental gross margins are relatively easy to measure because sales and cost of goods sold records are kept by department. Departmental operating income (gross margin minus operating expenses) is not as easy to measure. Why? Primarily because of indirect expenses.

Exhibit 22-7 shows a simplified departmental income statement of a Computer Unlimited store. Supporting details can be shown in various ways. Our discussion focuses on the allocation of selected operating expenses to the store's two departments.

Salaries and wages. These costs, which include each department manager's salary, are direct departmental costs.

Depreciation—equipment. This expense is also direct departmental expense, related to the equipment used only by each specific department.

Supplies. If each department may request supplies as needed, supplies are a direct cost. However, suppose the personnel from both departments help themselves to a companywide pool of supplies without recording usage. In this case, the company must establish a base for allocating supplies expense to the individual departments. The company may use percentage of sales, illustrated as follows for total supplies expense of $200:

Department	Sales	Percent of Total Sales	Allocation of Supplies Expense of $200
Hardware....	$ 7,000	70%	.70 × $200 = $140
Software.....	3,000	30%	.30 × 200 = 60
Total	$10,000	100%	1.00 × $200 = $200

Advertising. Consider a $960 computer store ad that takes up 24 square inches in the Sunday newspaper. Fifteen square inches advertise hardware,

EXHIBIT 22-7 Departmental Income Statement

Computer Unlimited Store
Departmental Income Statement
For the Year Ended December 31, 19X1
(in thousands)

	Total	Department Hardware	Department Software
Net sales..................................	$10,000	$7,000	$3,000
Cost of goods sold	5,500	4,000	1,500
Gross margin...........................	4,500	3,000	1,500
Operating expenses:			
Salaries and wages...................	1,100	660	440
Depreciation—equipment	100	80	20
Supplies	200	140	60
Advertising	1,000	400	600
Rent................................	600	480	120
Heat, light, air conditioning	60	40	20
Purchasing department................	300	230	70
General administration department	200	160	40
Total operating expenses	3,560	2,190	1,370
Operating income......................	$ 940	$ 810	$ 130

and 5 square inches promote software. The remaining 4 square inches carry information about the company as a whole (its address, hours, and so forth). How does the business allocate the overall cost of advertising to the two departments?

Suppose each square inch of advertising costs $40. Then the $960 total cost (24 inches × $40 = $960) may be allocated in two steps, as the accompanying table shows.

Department	Step 1: 20 Inches of Direct Advertising	Step 2: 4 Inches of General Advertising	Steps 1 + 2: 24 Inches of Total Advertising
Hardware	15 × $40 = $600 (75%)	75% × $160 = $120	$720
Software	5 × 40 = 200 (25%)	25% × 160 = 40	240
	$800 (100%)	$160	$960

Step 1 computes each department's direct cost, $600 and $200, respectively. Hardware's percentage of total direct cost is $600/$800, or 75 percent; Software's percentage is $200/$800, or 25 percent. Step 2 uses these percentages to allocate the $160 of general advertising costs ($960 − $800 = $160) to Hardware and Software.

If the computer store had three departments, we would simply total the individual departments' direct expense and use each department's percentage of that total to allocate the general advertising expense. We may allocate other general expenses—for example, salaries, wages, and depreciation—among departments in this way.

Rent.   Rent may be allocated on the basis of square footage, as follows:

Rent for entire store	$600,000
Total square feet	25,000
Rent per square foot ($600,000/25,000)	$24

Suppose that the company considers each square foot of space in the store equally valuable and that the Hardware and Software Departments occupy 20,000 square feet and 5,000 square feet, respectively. The allocation of rent is

Hardware Department:	20,000 square feet × $24 per square foot =	$480,000
Software Department:	5,000 square feet × $24 per square foot =	120,000
Total rent expense	....	$600,000

However, space in certain parts of the store may have different values because of varying potential to generate sales. For example, the space near the entrance may be the most valuable space in the store. The rear of the store may be the least valuable. Managers use judgment, often combined with outside consultants, to arrive at an appropriate allocation of rent. One approach is to weight the square footage. Suppose again that the Hardware and Software Departments occupy 20,000 and 5,000 square feet, respectively, and that Hardware's space is twice as valuable as Software's. In this case, rent of $600,000 is allocated to the two departments as follows:

Department	Space Occupied	Space Weighted By Value	Proportion of Weighted Space	Allocation of Rent of $600,000
Hardware ...	20,000	20,000 × 2 = 40,000	8/9	8/9 × $600,000 = $533,333
Software.....	5,000	5,000 × 1 = 5,000	1/9	1/9 × 600,000 = 66,667
Total	25,000	45,000	9/9	9/9 × $600,000 = $600,000

Heat, Light, Air Conditioning. The most common allocation base is square feet of space occupied. Cubic feet is used if ceiling height varies in different parts of the building.

Purchasing Department. Some of these expenses can be charged directly to specific departments. Any remaining expense is usually allocated in proportion to the dollar amount of purchases made on behalf of each department. Note that this assumes that the total cost of goods purchased is the cost driver. In some cases, the number of orders or the number of units purchased may be better measures of how departments used Purchasing Department resources.

General Administrative Expenses. This category includes depreciation on office furniture and equipment, office utilities, salaries of management and the office staff, and other expenses related to the organization as a whole. Some of these expenses may be charged directly. Others, such as payroll and personnel costs, may be allocated by the number of employees in various departments. The remainder is often allocated in proportion to departmental sales because this allocation base is convenient and no better base is apparent or feasible.

Managers may want expense allocations refined beyond those in Exhibit 22-7. For example, they may desire a statement with the following format to emphasize the difference between direct departmental expense and indirect expense:

Net sales	$XXX
Cost of goods sold	XXX
Gross margin	XXX
Direct departmental expense	**XXX**
Margin before indirect expenses	XXX
Indirect expenses	**XXX**
Operating income	$XXX

The margin before indirect expenses may provide information for deciding whether to expand or cut back a department's operations. Accounting systems can be designed to fulfill these wishes.

Summary Problem for Your Review

Review the data for the allocation of TechArt, Inc.'s, service department costs, Exhibit 22-4. Also review Exhibit 22-6, which shows the step-down allocation of costs when the Engineering & Maintenance Department is allocated first, then the Information Systems Department.

Required

1. Repeat the step-down allocation of TechArt's service department costs, using the alternative sequence of Information Systems first, then Engineering & Maintenance.
2. If this period's results are typical for TechArt, would you expect the company to use the direct or the step-down method? Why?

Requirement 1

	Factory Service Departments		Production Departments		
	Information Systems	Engineering & Maintenance	Commercial Systems	Residential Systems	Total
Direct Department Costs	$100,000	$400,000	$300,000	$250,000	$1,050,000
Allocation of Information Systems: $(^{40}/_{100},\ ^{35}/_{100},\ ^{25}/_{100})^*$	(100,000) $ \underline{\$\qquad 0}$	40,000	35,000	25,000	
Allocation of Engineering & Maintenance: $(^5/_9,\ ^4/_9)^\dagger$		(440,000) $\underline{\$\qquad 0}$	244,444	195,556	$\underline{\qquad\qquad}$
Total budgeted factory overhead of production departments			$\underline{\underline{\$579,444}}$	$\underline{\underline{\$470,556}}$	$\underline{\underline{\$1,050,000}}$

*Base is (600 + 525 + 375), or 1,500 hours; $^{600}/_{1,500} = {}^{40}/_{100}$; $^{525}/_{1,500} = {}^{35}/_{100}$; $^{375}/_{1,500} = {}^{25}/_{100}$.

$\dagger$Base is (3,000 + 2,400), or 5,400 hours; $^{3,000}/_{5,400} = {}^5/_9$; $^{2,400}/_{5,400} = {}^4/_9$.

Requirement 2

If this period's results are typical for TechArt, the company probably would use the direct method. Using this method, the allocations to Commercial and Residential Systems are $580,555 and $469,445, respectively. (See Exhibit 22-5, p. 1024.) As shown in Exhibit 22-6, page 1025, and Requirement 1 above, the allocations using either sequence of the step-down method are very close to the direct method allocations. Because the direct method is simpler and easier for managers to understand, it would probably be used.

Branch Accounting

Many companies establish branch offices or branch factories. Top managers may wish to take advantage of particular benefits that a certain geographical area offers. Materials and labor may be cheaper at a location removed from the home office. Or the company may want to open a new sales market.

Branches are responsibility centers—often cost centers if the branch is devoted to manufacturing or warehousing with no sales responsibility. A branch manager has responsibility for certain aspects of a branch's operations. In turn, he must report the branch's performance to his superior.

Who has the accounting responsibilities in a company that runs branch operations? The home office generally keeps most of the accounting records. The branch maintains only those records needed to manage its own operations. **Branch accounting** is a system for separating the accounts of a branch from those of the home office. The purpose is to establish accountability over the resources entrusted to the branch.

Consider a manufacturer that keeps cost records for direct materials, work in process inventory, and factory overhead at its branch factory. Receivables, finished goods inventory, plant assets, payables, depreciation, and other areas are accounted for in the corporate (home) office. This split of accounting between central headquarters and its branch means dividing the records between the two locations. With such a division, procedures are needed to ensure that all transactions are accounted for. Generally, two reciprocal accounts are used, one in the home office and one in the branch. **Reciprocal accounts** are two or more accounts that have exactly the same offsetting balances and are used to control a general ledger that is kept in two or more locations.

Branch Ledger and Journal

A **branch ledger** is that part of a general ledger kept by the branch, separate from the home-office ledger. The branch ledger contains only those accounts needed to manage its operations plus a special account used to handle its accountability to the home office. If the branch is a manufacturing plant, its ledger is often called a **factory ledger.** Each branch has its own branch or factory ledger.

The **home-office ledger** is that part of a general ledger kept by the home office, separate from the branch ledger. The home-office ledger is identical to the general ledger studied throughout this course except that it includes a special account for the branch and excludes the accounts kept by the branch. The home office and the branch also maintain separate journals for recording transactions.

Suppose Appliance Company of America is headquartered in Chicago but has its manufacturing plant in Indianapolis. The home office makes all purchases and sales, handles cash payments and cash receipts, and incurs all company liabilities. A separate factory ledger is maintained in Indianapolis for managing the branch plant.

When the factory completes the manufacture of inventory, it transfers the finished goods to warehouses, which are managed directly by the home office. Upon transfer of merchandise to the warehouses, the home office debits inventory and credits the factory account for shipments at cost.

The general ledger accounts of the company follow, showing the link between the reciprocal accounts.

Home-Office Accounts	**Branch-Factory Accounts**
Cash	Direct materials inventory
Accounts receivable	Work in process inventory
Finished goods inventory	Factory overhead
Plant and equipment	→ Home-office ledger control
Accumulated depreciation	
Branch-factory ledger control ←	
Accounts payable	
Wages payable	
Common stock	
Retained earnings	
Sales revenue	
Cost of goods sold	
Selling expenses	
Administrative expenses	

The home office's **branch-factory ledger control** account can be viewed as an *investment in,* or a *receivable from,* the branch. Similarly, the branch's **home-**

office ledger control account represents an *owner equity of,* or a *payable to,* the home office.

Illustrative Transactions and Related Journal Entries

Entries for the following transactions illustrate accounting for branch operations:

1. Direct materials purchased on credit $230,000
2. Direct materials used in production 150,000
3. Factory payroll accrued 200,000
4. Miscellaneous factory overhead cost incurred
   (credit Accounts Payable, $150,000; and
   Accumulated Depreciation, $18,000)...................... 168,000
5. Factory overhead applied 165,000
6. Cost of goods shipped to warehouse 425,000
7. Cost of goods sold 400,000
8. Sales (on credit) 600,000
9. Cash collected on account.............................. 440,000

Journal Entries. Illustrative journal entries and postings to the reciprocal accounts are given in Exhibit 22-8 (in thousands of dollars). The entries that would be made in a regular, unified journal are given first in the exhibit. Relating each pair of home office/branch entries to the corresponding unified entry will help you see how branch accounting works. Keep in mind that the focus is on the home office and branch entries. The regular, unified entries are presented solely to aid your understanding. Let's consider the first transaction and related entry—the credit purchase of direct materials by the home office for the branch factory (amounts in thousands of dollars).

OBJECTIVE 5

Account for branch operations

Home-Office Journal		Branch-Factory Journal	
Branch-Factory Ledger Control.... 230		Direct Materials Inventory 230	
Accounts Payable	230	Home-Office Ledger Control .	230
Home-office purchase of direct materials.		Home-office purchase of direct materials.	

The home office is responsible for paying the bill and so records the liability. The branch factory is responsible for using the direct materials and therefore records the inventory. Because accountability is split between the two locations, reciprocal accounts are used to ensure that each transaction is fully accounted for. The home-office debit to the branch account counterbalances the branch's credit to the home-office account. We can regard the $230,000 debit in the first home-office entry as the home office's investment in, or receivable from, the factory. The branch's credit to the home-office account in the branch's entry shows the branch's obligation to the home office for the purchased materials.

Entries 2 and 5 are confined strictly to the branch-factory ledger because these transactions affect factory costs with no home-office involvement. Entries 3, 4, and 6 affect both home office and branch. Entries 7, 8, and 9 are recorded solely by the home office because the branch has no responsibility for sales, cost of sales, or collections of receivables.

Entry 6 deserves special comment. Factory shipments of finished goods transfer inventory from the factory to the warehouses, which are under direct home-office management. Such shipments reduce the home-office investment in the factory because the home office receives inventory. Likewise, the branch decreases the owner equity of the home office by transferring inventory to the warehouses.

Reciprocal Balances. Exhibit 22-8 shows that the reciprocal accounts have identical, offsetting balances. Any difference between the balances signals the accountant to explain the imbalance. A common cause of imbalances is faulty communication. For example, a shipment of finished goods to the warehouse may be in transit at the balance sheet date. The home office may be unaware of the transaction until the goods arrive. At the same time, the factory may have already recorded the shipment. Progress in data processing via computers has reduced problems of this nature.

Accounting for a Sales Branch

Home-office and branch entries depend on the authority given to the branch. In the example shown in Exhibit 22-8, the home office pays branch bills, makes all sales, and collects all cash. Many companies use sales branches to enter new markets. For instance, IBM has sales offices throughout the United States. Sales branches may make sales, collect cash, and make some of their own cash disbursements. Often the home office keeps control of the revenue and expense accounts. Assume an IBM sales branch completed the following transactions:

a. Branch sold merchandise and received cash of $3,000.
b. Branch transferred $3,000 cash to home office.
c. Home office paid commission of $1,100 to salesperson who made the sale in *a*.
d. Branch paid water bill, $90.
e. Branch recorded depreciation on office equipment, $300.

These transactions would be recorded by the home office and branch as follows:

	Home-Office Journal			Branch Journal		
a.	Branch Ledger Control........	3,000		Cash	3,000	
	Sales Revenue		3,000	Home-Office Ledger Control..............		3,000
b.	Cash	3,000		Home-Office Ledger Control ..	3,000	
	Branch Ledger Control ...		3,000	Cash		3,000
c.	Sales Commission Expense....	1,100		None		
	Cash		1,100			
d.	Utility Expense..............	90		Home-Office Ledger Control ..	90	
	Branch Ledger Control ...		90	Cash		90
e.	Depreciation Expense.........	300		Home-Office Ledger Control ..	300	
	Branch Ledger Control ...		300	Accumulated Depreciation- Office Furniture		300

EXHIBIT 22-8 Sample Journal Entries for Branch Accounting (in thousands of dollars)

Transaction	Entries That Would Be Made in a Regular, Unified Journal		Home-Office Journal		Branch-Factory Journal	

1. Direct materials purchases	Direct Materials Inventory
	  Accounts Payable
		230
		230
			Branch-Factory Ledger Control
			  Accounts Payable
				230
				230
					Direct Materials Inventory
					  Home-Office Ledger Control
						230
						230

2. Direct materials uses	Work in Process Inventory
	  Direct Materials Inventory
		150
		150
			None		Work in Process Inventory
					  Direct Materials Inventory
						150
						150

3. Factory payroll	Factory Wages
	  Wages Payable
		200
		200
			Branch-Factory Ledger Control
			  Wages Payable
				200
				200
					Factory Wages
					  Home-Office Ledger Control
						200
						200

4. Miscellaneous overhead	Factory Overhead
	  Accounts Payable
	  Accumulated Depreciation
		168
		150
		18
			Branch-Factory Ledger Control
			  Accounts Payable
			  Accumulated Depreciation
				168
				150
				18
					Factory Overhead
					  Home-Office Ledger Control
						168
						168

5. Overhead application	Work in Process Inventory
	  Factory Overhead
		165
		165
			None		Work in Process Inventory
					  Factory Overhead
						165
						165

6. Shipments to warehouse	Finished Goods Inventory
	  Work in Process Inventory
		425
		425
			Finished Goods Inventory
			  Branch-Factory Ledger Control
				425
				425
					Home-Office Ledger Control
					  Work in Process Inventory
						425
						425

7. Cost of goods sold	Cost of Goods Sold
	  Finished Goods Inventory
		400
		400
			Cost of Goods Sold
			  Finished Goods Inventory
				400
				400
					None	

8. Sales	Accounts Receivable
	  Sales Revenue
		600
		600
			Accounts Receivable
			  Sales Revenue
				600
				600
					None	

9. Collections on account	Cash
	  Accounts Receivable
		440
		440
			Cash
			  Accounts Receivable
				440
				440
					None	

Postings:

Branch-Factory Ledger Control

(1)	230	(6)	425
(3)	200		
(4)	168		
Bal.	173		

Home-Office Ledger Control

(6)	425	(1)	230
		(3)	200
		(4)	168
		Bal.	173

After posting these entries, Branch Ledger Control's credit balance should equal the debit balance of Home-Office Ledger Control.

Computers, Responsibility Accounting, and Remote Processing

Recall Exhibit 22-2, Responsibility Accounting at Various Levels. This report gives managers information on the success of operations at different levels of the business. How might this report be prepared? Each O'Toole restaurant logs its revenues and expenses into its computer and transmits the information to central computer processing.

With complete information from each restaurant, the computer system can sort—that is, arrange in a useful grouping—the revenue and expense information. For example, district managers may want to know which restaurants are way off budget and need attention. The computer program can sort the information by size of budget variance—with additional breakdowns by restaurant, city, district, or region. A system for numbering accounts makes this sorting possible. All restaurant-level accounts have a certain number designation, all city-level accounts have another number designation, and so on. A computerized system like this is called a *database management system*. Managers and accountants can pull up whatever information they need for a particular decision. Ready access to the data enables managers to act on current information.

Consider responsibility accounting for O'Toole Restaurant Corporation. The company's system can provide the information for allocating indirect expenses to individual restaurants. Suppose corporate headquarters purchases much of the food centrally. The O'Toole accountant needs a base for allocating receiving-department costs to the various restaurants. The computer can sort receiving reports by restaurant. The more frequently a restaurant requests food from central headquarters, the higher is that restaurant's share of receiving-department cost. Periodic review of this information reveals any change in use patterns. Accountants can change the allocation base as needed to keep the cost allocation current. Restaurant managers can be evaluated fairly for the expenses under their supervision. The result is likely to be well-motivated managers.

Summary Problem for Your Review

A general ledger may be divided between home office and branch in any manner whatsoever. Reconsider Exhibit 22-8. Suppose the branch factory, instead of the home office, keeps its plant and equipment accounts and the related depreciation records. The plant and equipment accounts would appear in the ledger of the factory but not the home office. Among the nine transactions in our example, what journal entry or entries would be changed? Prepare the changed entry or entries.

Entry 4 would be changed. Accumulated depreciation would appear in the branch-factory ledger but not in the home-office ledger. Moreover, the amounts recorded in the reciprocal accounts would be $150,000 instead of $168,000, as follows (amounts in thousands of dollars):

Home-Office Ledger			Branch-Factory Ledger		
4. Branch-Factory Ledger Control .	150		Factory Overhead	168	
Accounts Payable		150	Accumulated Depreciation		18
			Home-Office Ledger		
			Control		150

Summary

Responsibility accounting is a system for evaluating the progress of managers based on activities under their supervision. This system is especially important in organizations with scattered operations. Most companies are organized into *responsibility centers* to establish accountability. There are different types of responsibility centers: *cost center*, *profit center*, and *investment center*. The most critical factor in designing a responsibility accounting system is gathering and communicating information to help the business achieve its goals.

Performance reports show deviations from budgeted amounts. By focusing on important variances, managers can direct their attention to operations needing improvement and avoid wasting time investigating successful operations. This practice is called *management by exception*.

Departments are the most widely encountered responsibility centers. Gross margin and operating income are important measures of their performance. *Direct costs* are conveniently identified with and traceable to the department. *Indirect costs* are all those costs other than direct costs. Direct costs are easy to allocate to departments because of their natural link to a particular department. Indirect costs are allocated based on some logical relationship between the cost and departments.

Service departments provide services to other departments. Their costs are indirect costs of the departments they serve. *Operating departments* add value to products or services sold to customers. Service department costs are allocated to production departments by the direct method, which ignores reciprocal services, or the step-down method, which recognizes the most significant reciprocal services.

Branch accounting is a system for separating branch accounts from home-office accounts. Its key feature is a set of *reciprocal accounts*. The home office has a *Branch Ledger Control* account for its investment in, or receivable from, the branch. The branch ledger has only those accounts needed to manage its own operations. Its special account, *Home-Office Ledger Control*, represents home-office equity in the branch, or the branch payable to the home office. The debit balance in the Branch Ledger Control account should equal the credit balance in Home-Office Ledger Control.

Self-Study Questions

Test your understanding of the chapter by marking the best answer for each of the following questions:

1. Responsibility accounting is (p. 1017)
   a. An alternative to a standard cost system
   b. A system for assigning responsibility to managers and evaluating their progress
   c. A particular type of home-office/branch accounting system
   d. Designed without consideration of the business's organization structure

2. Which of the following departments is most likely to be a cost center? (p. 1017)
   a. Personnel Department
   b. Housewares Department of a K Mart store
   c. Sales office
   d. Manufacturing plant

3. Budgeted cost of goods sold was $30,000, and actual cost is $33,000. The variance is (p. 1020)
   a. 110 percent favorable
   b. 110 percent unfavorable
   c. 10 percent favorable
   d. 10 percent unfavorable

4. The key to the design of an effective responsibility accounting system is (p. 1020)
   a. Ability of the system to place blame when results are unfavorable
   b. Manager control over all aspects of the business in the department
   c. Gathering and communicating information to achieve the business's goals
   d. Use of a standard cost system

5. One of the more difficult accounting tasks in departmental accounting is (p. 1021)
   a. Measuring departmental gross margin
   b. Allocating direct costs to departments
   c. Allocating indirect costs to departments
   d. Assigning responsibility to department managers

6. Which of the following costs is the most difficult to allocate to departments? (p. 1021)
   a. Direct materials
   b. Janitorial services
   c. Merchandise purchases
   d. Direct labor

7. The most logical basis for allocating building depreciation to departments is (p. 1023)
   a. Square feet of space
   b. Number of employees
   c. Hours used
   d. Building depreciation can be separately traced to each department

8. Which control device is a particular feature of branch accounting? (p. 1030)
   a. Responsibility assignment
   b. Reciprocal accounts
   c. Departmental accounting
   d. Cost allocation

9. Which of these accounts would be the most likely to appear in a branch-factory ledger? (p. 1031)
   a. Accounts Receivable
   b. Branch-Factory Ledger Control
   c. Common Stock
   d. Home-Office Ledger Control

10. A sales branch manages its own operations except for collections on account and cash payments for major expenses such as inventory purchases and salaries, which the home office pays. Which entry would the branch make to record its salary expense? (p. 1032)
    a. Salary Expense.................................. XXX
           Cash XXX
    b. Home-Office Ledger Control XXX
           Cash XXX

c. Salary Expense................................ XXX

       Branch Ledger Control.................... XXX

d. None of the above. The entry would appear on the home-office books only.

Answers to the Self-Study Questions follow the Accounting Vocabulary.

Accounting Vocabulary

Allocation base. Logical common denominator for assigning a given cost to two or more departments of a business *(p. 1022)*.

Branch accounting. System for separating the accounts of a branch of a business from the accounts of the home office *(p. 1029)*.

Branch-factory ledger control. Account in the home office ledger that represents the home office investment in, or receivable from, a branch of the business *(p. 1030)*.

Branch ledger. The part of a general ledger kept by a branch of the business, separate from the home office ledger *(p. 1030)*.

Direct costs. Costs that are conveniently identified with and traceable to a particular department *(p. 1021)*.

Direct method. Method of service department cost allocation that ignores all services provided by one service department to another *(p. 1024)*.

Factory ledger. A branch ledger for a manufacturing plant *(p. 1030)*.

Home-office ledger. The part of a general ledger kept by the home office, separate from the branch ledger *(p. 1030)*.

Home-office ledger control. Account in the branch ledger that represents an owner equity of, or branch payable to, the home office *(p. 1030)*.

Indirect costs. Costs that are not traceable to a single department of a business; a cost other than a direct cost. Often indirect costs arise from activities that serve more than one department simultaneously *(p. 1022)*.

Management by exception. Management strategy by which executive attention is directed to the important deviations from budgeted amounts *(p. 1020)*.

Operating department. Department whose main function is to add value to products or services sold to customers *(p. 1021)*.

Reciprocal accounts. Two or more accounts that have the same offsetting balances and are used to control a general ledger that is kept in two or more locations *(p. 1030)*.

Reciprocal services. Mutual services provided among service departments *(p. 1021)*.

Responsibility accounting. System for classifying financial data by defined areas in an organization in order to evaluate the performance of managers for activities under their supervision *(p. 1017)*.

Responsibility center. Any subunit of an organization needing control, the basic unit in a responsibility accounting system. The three common types of responsibility centers are the cost center, the profit center, and the investment center *(p. 1017)*.

Service department. Department whose primary function is to provide services to other departments, both operating departments and other service departments *(p. 1021)*.

Step-down method. Method of service department cost allocation that recognizes some, but not all, reciprocal services *(p. 1024)*.

ASSIGNMENT MATERIAL _____

Questions

1. Briefly describe responsibility accounting, giving examples of how managers use it in operating a business.
2. Which manager will control expenses better: Grant, whose performance is measured by his departmental sales, or Bruns, whose performance is gauged by her departmental income? Give your reason.
3. Identify three types of responsibility centers, giving examples of each and stating the information they report.
4. A company owns 50 Burger King restaurants in Houston, Dallas, and El Paso, Texas. In each city a local manager oversees operations. Starting at the individual store level, describe a likely flow of information based on responsibility accounting. What information would be reported?
5. What are the goals of management by exception?
6. What is the key to effective design of a responsibility accounting system?
7. What main question is a responsibility accounting system designed to answer? How can a responsibility accounting system be abused?
8. Distinguish between direct expenses and indirect expenses, giving examples of each type.
9. Identify a reasonable allocation base for the following indirect expenses: heating expense, depreciation of equipment used to manufacture products for three separate departments, and advertising expense.
10. Which of the following are likely to be direct expenses? Which are likely to be indirect expenses?
    a. Manufacturing labor
    b. Supervisor labor
    c. Advertising of a specific toy
    d. Cost of goods sold
    e. Depreciation of home-office building
    f. Janitorial services for a manufacturing plant
    g. Expenses of personnel department
    h. Advertising of a storewide sale by a department store
11. Supplies are not charged to departments as used. Instead, supplies expense is allocated at the end of each period based on the period's sales. If a firm used supplies costing $900 and had sales of $5,000, $12,000, and $8,000 in departments X, Y, and Z, respectively, how much supplies expense would be charged to each department?
12. How might rent be allocated in a department store with three floors, one of which is on ground level and opens onto a busy street?
13. Describe a plan for allocating the various components of general administrative expenses.
14. A company has three service departments—A, B, and C—and two production departments—X and Y. Its accountants use the step-down method of service department cost allocation, allocating the departments in

alphabetical order. To which departments are A's costs allocated? B's costs? C's costs?

15. How does branch accounting differ from departmental accounting?

16. What are the special features of a branch accounting system?

17. How does the general ledger of a company with a branch accounting system differ from an ordinary general ledger?

18. What special account does a branch ledger contain? What special account does a home-office ledger contain? Indicate which account normally has a debit balance and which normally has a credit balance.

19. Consider the Branch-Factory Ledger Control account and the Home-Office Ledger Control account. Which account is more like an investment or receivable? Which is more like an owner equity account or payable? Which account is in the ledger of the home office? Which is in the branch ledger?

20. Briefly describe a branch accounting system for a company with two manufacturing plants in distant locations. Identify the special account on the books of the home office and the special account on the books of the branches.

21. A company manufactures its products at three plants. Which of the following transactions is likely to be recorded by the home office only, by the branch only, or by both the home office and the branch?

    a. Use of materials in production
    b. Sale of merchandise
    c. Payment of manufacturing payroll
    d. Purchase of direct materials
    e. Incurrence of overhead cost
    f. Collection of accounts receivable
    g. Shipment of finished goods to home-office warehouse

Exercises

Exercise 22-1 *Identifying different types of responsibility centers* **(L.O. 1)**

Identify each responsibility center as either a cost center, a profit center, or an investment center.

a. A branch manager's performance is judged by the ratio of the branch's net income to the home office's cost of the branch.

b. Accountants compile the cost of surgical supplies for evaluating the purchasing department of a hospital.

c. The hospital pediatrics unit reports both revenues and expenses.

d. The legal department of an insurance company prepares its budget and subsequent performance report based on its expected expenses for the year.

e. A charter airline records revenues and expenses for each airplane for each month. The airplane's performance report shows its ratio of operating income to average book value.

f. The manager of an Exxon service station is evaluated based on the station's revenues and expenses.

Exercise 22-2 *Using responsibility accounting to report on profit centers at three levels* **(L.O. 2)**

Siegfried Newspapers of North Carolina has city managers for its Asheville, Greensboro, and Elizabeth City operations. These managers report to a state manager, who reports to the manager of Southeast operations in Atlanta. The Southeast manager has received the following data for June of the current year:

| | Southeast | | |
| | North Carolina | | |
	Asheville	Greensboro and Elizabeth City	Southeast Totals excluding North Carolina
Revenues, budget	$310,000	$1,800,000	$10,300,000
Expenses, budget	220,000	1,100,000	6,300,000
Revenues, actual	340,000	1,900,000	9,900,000
Expenses, actual	210,000	1,200,000	6,200,000

Required

Arrange the above data in a performance report similar to Exhibit 22-2. Show June results, in thousands of dollars, for Asheville, the state of North Carolina, and the Southeast.

Exercise 22-3 *Preparing a four-column performance report* **(L.O. 2)**

Using the data of Exercise 22-2, prepare a performance report for June in the format illustrated on page 1020. Show June results, in thousands of dollars, for Asheville, the state of North Carolina, and the Southeast. In each case, format your answer in four columns:

Budget	Actual	Variance Favorable (Unfavorable)	Variance: Percent of Budget

Exercise 22-4 *Allocating costs to departments* **(L.O. 3)**

The cost records of West Virginia Foundry, Inc., include the following selected indirect cost data for January of the current year:

Other labor	$14,000
Equipment depreciation	6,000
Building depreciation	3,600
Utilities	2,700
Selling expenses	24,000

Data for cost allocations:

	Department		
	A	B	C
Sales	$60,000	$50,000	$90,000
Other labor—hours	400	500	100
Machine hours	300	450	150
Building—square feet	9,000	3,000	1,500
Selling expense—allocate to departments in proportion to sales			

Required

Show the allocation of these expenses to departments A, B, and C for January.

Exercise 22-5 *Computing departmental rent expense* **(L.O. 3)**

Many department stores grant concessions to other companies to operate the store's shoe departments. Caprice Shoe Company markets its shoes this way. Caprice sells ladies' shoes in a space occupying 500 square feet near the front door of a Sax Third Avenue store. This location is three times as valuable as the average space in the store. Caprice's shoes for men occupy 200 square feet in a back corner of the ground floor, a space with average rental value. Children's shoes occupy 150 square feet on the third floor, which is only 30 percent as valuable as the average space in the store. The entire store has 50,000 square feet, and monthly rent is $300,000.

Required

Compute Caprice's monthly rent expense.

Exercise 22-6 *Preparing a departmental income statement* **(L.O. 3, 4)**

Migdal & Grant, Inc., has two departments, electronics and industrial. The company's income statement for 19X7 appears as follows:

Net sales	$310,000
Cost of goods sold	116,000
Gross margin	194,000
Operating expenses:	
Salaries	70,000
Depreciation	15,000
Advertising	6,000
Other	10,000
Total operating expenses	101,000
Operating income	$ 93,000

Cost of goods sold is distributed $42,000 for electronics and $74,000 for industrial products. Salaries are allocated to departments based on sales: electronics, $124,000; industrial, $186,000. Two-thirds of advertising is spent on electronics. Depreciation is allocated based on square footage: electronics has 28,000 square feet; industrial has 42,000 square feet. Other expenses are allocated based on number of employees, with an equal number working in each department.

Required

Prepare a departmental income statement showing revenues, expenses, and operating income for the company's two departments.

Exercise 22-7 *Recording home-office and branch manufacturing transactions* **(L.O. 4)**

Big Foot Lumber Company manages operations from its home office in Portland. Company sawmills, located in the state of Oregon, are organized as branches. Big Foot uses a branch accounting system. The home office makes all purchases and sales, handles cash payments and cash receipts, and incurs all company liabilities. When a sawmill completes a custom job, it transfers the inventory to central warehouses, which the home office controls. On August 1 Big Foot's investment in the sawmill was $75,000. During August of the current year, the company completed the following transactions:

a. Direct materials purchased on account, $830.
b. Direct materials used in production, $1,090.
c. Sawmill payroll paid, $3,100.
d. Sawmill overhead applied, $4,600.
e. Goods shipped to central warehouse, $7,100.
f. Sales on account, $8,200.
g. Collections on account, $4,690.

Required

Journalize these transactions for the home office and the branch. Post to the reciprocal accounts and show that their balances at August 31 offset each other.

Exercise 22-8   *Recording home-office and branch sales-office transactions* (L.O. 4)

Technology Transfer, Inc., has branch sales offices throughout the Great Lakes states. The company uses a branch accounting system. The branches purchase and sell goods, pay bills, collect cash from customers, and incur selling expenses. The home office, in Cleveland, obtains outside financing as needed and advances cash to, and receives cash from, the branches. During a recent month, the company completed the following transactions:

a. Home office borrowed $7,000 from a bank, signing a note.
b. Home office advanced $2,250 to the Michigan branch.
c. Michigan branch purchased merchandise on account, $2,210 (debit Purchases).
d. Michigan branch paid selling expense, $60.
e. Michigan branch sold goods on account, $2,110.
f. Home office recorded depreciation of $1,040 on home-office building.
g. Michigan branch collected cash from customer, $930.
h. Michigan branch transferred $1,000 cash to home office.

Required

Journalize these transactions for the home office and the Michigan branch. Post to the reciprocal accounts and show that their balances offset each other.

Problems

(Group A)

Problem 22-1A   *Identifying different types of responsibility centers* (L.O. 1)

Identify by letter each of the following as being most likely a cost center, a profit center, or an investment center:

a. Surgery unit of a privately owned hospital
b. Personnel department of Goodyear Tire and Rubber Company
c. Accounts payable section of an accounting department
d. Proposed new office of a real estate firm
e. Branch warehouse of a carpet manufacturer
f. Disneyland
g. Assembly-line supervisory employees
h. Service department of a stereo shop
i. Men's clothing in a department store
j. American subsidiary of a Japanese company
k. Music director of a church or synagogue
l. Catering operation of an established restaurant
m. Executive director of a United Way agency
n. Different product lines of a gift shop
o. The Empire State Building in New York City
p. Work crews of a painting contractor
q. Investments department of a bank
r. Accounting department of a company
s. Eastern district of a salesperson's territory
t. Typesetting department of a printing company

Problem 22-2A *Preparing a profit-center performance report* **(L.O. 2)**

Haltom Oil Company is organized with store managers reporting to a state-wide manager, who in turn reports to the vice-president of marketing. The income statements of the Birmingham store, all stores in Alabama (including the Birmingham store), and the company as a whole (including Alabama stores) are summarized as follows for 19X6:

	Birmingham	Alabama	Companywide
Revenue and expenses:			
Sales..............................	$141,800	$1,647,000	$3,888,000
Expenses:			
State manager/vice-president's office	—	59,000	116,000
Cost of goods sold	53,000	671,900	1,507,000
Salary expense.....................	38,100	415,500	1,119,000
Depreciation.......................	7,200	91,000	435,000
Utilities	3,800	46,200	260,000
Rent	2,400	34,700	178,000
Supplies	1,100	15,600	86,000
Total expenses.....................	105,600	1,333,900	3,701,000
Operating income..................	$ 36,200	$ 313,100	$ 187,000

Budgeted amounts for 19X6 are as follows:

	Birmingham	Alabama	Companywide
Revenue and expenses:			
Sales..............................	$151,300	$1,769,700	$4,400,000
Expenses:			
State manager/vice-president's office	—	65,600	118,000
Cost of goods sold	61,500	763,400	1,672,000
Salary expense................	38,800	442,000	1,095,000
Depreciation...................	7,200	87,800	449,000
Utilities	4,700	54,400	271,000
Rent	2,800	32,300	174,000
Supplies	900	16,100	93,000
Total expenses................	115,900	1,461,600	3,872,000
Operating income..............	$ 35,400	$ 308,100	$ 528,000

Required

1. Prepare a report for 19X6 that shows the performance of the Birmingham store, all the stores in Alabama, and the company as a whole. Follow the format of Exhibit 22-2.
2. Identify the responsibility centers whose operating income exceeds budget and those whose operating income falls short of budget.

Problem 22-3A *Preparing a profit-center performance report* **(L.O. 2)**

The Home Front is organized along product lines, with product managers reporting to department managers, who in turn report to the company vice-president. The vice-president, who has received the following data for August of the current year, needs a performance report to highlight the operating income of bedspreads, the bedding department, and the company in total:

	Company Totals		
	Bedding Department		
	Bedspreads	**Linens**	**Other Departments**
Revenues, actual.....	$3,700	$1,500	$6,500
Expenses, actual	2,100	800	3,100
Revenues, budget....	3,300	1,400	7,100
Expenses, budget	1,600	700	3,600

Required

1. Prepare a performance report for August in a format similar to that on page 1020. Show August operating income for bedspreads, the bedding department, and the company as a whole.
2. Which responsibility centers exceeded budget? Which performed below budget?

Problem 22-4A *Computing and allocating occupancy cost to a department* **(L.O. 3)**

Dillard's occupies a six-story building (including the basement) in downtown Montclair. Assume occupancy cost for a recent month included the following:

Depreciation—building	$ 93,200
Rent—store fixtures	24,700
Utilities	21,300
Janitorial services	16,600
Total	$155,800

Each floor of the building has 8,000 square feet, except for the second floor, which has 6,000 square feet. The company accountant computed the occupancy cost per square foot by dividing the total cost of $155,800 by 46,000 square feet. She charges occupancy to all company departments based on this $3.39 cost per square foot.

The manager of the Budget Buyer Department, located in the basement, objected. He cited a space-usage study conducted for the company by a real estate firm. It estimated that space in the basement is one-fourth as valuable as street level space, one-half as valuable as space on the second floor, and equal in value to the other floors.

Required

1. Based on the space-usage study, compute the occupancy cost of a square foot of space on each of Dillard's floors. Round decimals to three places, and round the cost per square foot to the nearest cent.
2. The Budget Buyer Department occupies 5,500 square feet of the basement. How much occupancy cost should be charged to this department each month?

Problem 22-5A *Allocate service department costs to producing departments* **(L.O. 3)**

The Shaker Heights Valve Company manufactures industrial valve systems in the Cleveland, Ohio, area. The company has two service departments, Power and General Factory Administration (GFA), and two production departments, Machining and Assembly. The following data are budgeted for the month of August, 19X4:

	Service Department		Production Department		
	Power	**GFA**	**Machining**	**Assembly**	**Total**
Direct department cost	$10,000	$40,000	$60,000	$50,000	$160,000
Services provided:					
By Power—kilowatt hours	—	120	600	480	1,200
Proportion		1/10	5/10	4/10	
By GFA—labor hours	50	—	450	500	1,000
Proportion	1/20		9/20	10/20	

Shaker Heights accountants want to know the full cost of manufactured valve systems, including the support cost incurred by Power and GFA. Also, the company's top management holds the two production department heads responsible for the service department costs incurred to support their departments. For these reasons, the costs of Power and GFA must be allocated to Machining and Assembly.

Required

1. Allocate the service departments' costs to production departments using the direct method. Compute the total budgeted cost of both the Machining Department and the Assembly Department.

2. Repeat Requirement 1, using the step-down method. Allocate GFA first, then Power.

Problem 22-6A *Preparing a departmental income statement* (L.O. 3, 4)

Aladdin Travel is organized into a custom department and a group discount department. At August 31, the end of Aladdin's fiscal year, the bookkeeper prepared the following trial balance, which includes the effects of year-end adjusting entries:

Cash	$ 1,300	
Receivables	24,600	
Supplies	3,800	
Prepaid expenses	1,700	
Building	70,500	
Accumulated depreciation—building		$ 20,900
Office furniture	38,100	
Accumulated depreciation—office furniture		7,300
Other assets	3,100	
Accounts payable		11,400
Accrued liabilities		6,900
Unearned service revenue		5,800
Long-term note payable		22,000
Owner equity		19,200
Custom travel service revenue		77,700
Group discount travel service revenue		107,300
Salary expense—travel agents	34,600	
Commission expense—travel agents	26,000	
Salary expense—office manager	25,000	
Salary expense—bookkeeper	16,800	
Lease expense—computer equipment	15,000	
Supplies expense	6,300	
Depreciation expense—office furniture	2,500	
Property tax expense	2,200	
Depreciation expense—building	2,100	
Interest expense	2,000	
Insurance expense	1,700	
Advertising expense	1,200	
	$278,500	$278,500

In January, Aladdin hired a group travel specialist at an annual salary of $25,000. Remaining agent salaries of $9,600 go to part-time agents that handle custom travel plans. The office manager spends 60 percent of her time on group discount plans and 40 percent on custom travel planning. The bookkeeper spends approximately two-thirds of his time on accounting for custom travel planning operations and the remainder on group discount plans. Aladdin leases a computer that it uses 80 percent of the time for custom travel planning and 20 percent of the time for group discount packages. Insurance expense is evenly divided between the two departments. Interest expense relates to the note payable, which the company signed to purchase the building. The company allocates all other expenses based on relative service revenue.

Required

1. Prepare a departmental income statement through operating income.
2. Which department is more profitable? Was the decision to hire the group specialist wise? Give your reason.

Problem 22-7A *Preparing a budgeted departmental income statement* **(L.O. 3, 4)**

Plemmon's is a suburban hardware store with two departments. The most recent annual report to management follows.

	Plemmon's Departmental Income Statement For the Year Ended January 31, 19X2		
	Total	Dept. A	Dept. B
Sales revenue	$400,000	$300,000	$100,000
Expenses:			
Cost of goods sold	160,000	120,000	40,000
Sales salaries	41,000	28,000	13,000
Salary—store manager	35,000	17,500	17,500
Rent expense—building	16,000	8,000	8,000
Advertising	5,000	3,500	1,500
Property tax	3,000	1,500	1,500
Insurance	2,400	1,200	1,200
Depreciation—store fixtures	1,200	600	600
Supplies	1,000	500	500
Interest	800	400	400
Uncollectible accounts	600	300	300
Total expenses	266,000	181,500	84,500
Operating income	$134,000	$118,500	$ 15,500

The company is considering opening a third department early in fiscal 19X3. To plan for the coming year, the store owner seeks your help in preparing a budgeted income statement. Your conversation with the owner reveals the following:

1. Management expects annual sales of the new department to be $80,000, with a gross profit percentage equal to that of the two existing departments.
2. Addition of a third department will also draw customers into Department A and should increase Department A sales by 25 percent. Sales of Department B are expected to increase by only 10 percent.
3. A salesperson can be hired for the new department at an annual salary of $16,000. Other salaries will increase by 5 percent.
4. Thus far, the company accountant has allocated all expenses except cost of goods sold, sales salaries, and advertising equally to Departments A and B. The store owner decides that the equal allocation of indirect expenses to departments is inappropriate.

5. The store manager expects to spend equal amounts of time in the three departments during the coming year.

6. Department A is nearest the door and occupies 2,000 square feet of the most valuable space in the store. Department B also occupies 2,000 square feet, but its space is only half as valuable as that of Department A. The new department will take up 1,000 square feet with the same value per square foot as Department A. Total rent expense under the long-term lease will be unchanged in 19X3.

7. Advertising expense will increase by 10 percent for the two existing departments. The company will commit $2,000 to advertising Department C merchandise.

8. Depreciation of new store fixtures for Department C will be $900. Other depreciation amounts will be unchanged.

9. Interest expense needed to finance Department C will be $1,000. The remaining 19X3 interest of $500 applies equally to the other two departments.

10. All other expenses will increase by 8 percent and should be allocated to departments based on relative sales, except property tax, which is allocated on the same basis used for rent. Round percentages to three decimal places.

Required

1. Prepare a budgeted departmental income statement in multiple-step format for fiscal year 19X3 based on the preceding projections.

2. Based on your budget, would you recommend that Plemmon's add the new department? State your reasons.

Problem 22-8A *Recording home-office and branch transactions* *(L.O. 5)*

Landmark Realty has branch offices throughout the Kansas City area and uses a branch accounting system for control purposes. The home office has a separate Branch Ledger Control account for each branch, and the branches maintain branch ledgers. Branch ledgers contain only asset, liability, and Home-Office Ledger Control accounts.

The home office advances cash to the branches. Branch managers have authority to purchase supplies and office furniture and equipment. They also pay utility and other branch-office expenses. However, only the home office records branch expenses. The branches collect commissions earned from their real estate sales and immediately transfer the cash to the home office. Only the home office records commissions revenue. The home office then pays half the commission directly to the agent who made the sale. During a recent month the following transactions occurred at the Independence Branch of Landmark Realty:

a. Home office advanced $6,900 to branch.
b. Branch sold a house, earning a commission and receiving cash of $4,000.
c. Branch transferred $4,000 to home office.
d. Home office paid commission to agent making sale in *b*, $2,000.
e. Branch paid office cleaning expense, $220.
f. Branch purchased office furniture on account, $1,400.
g. Branch paid cash for office supplies, $160.
h. Branch paid account payable, $700.
i. Branch transferred $2,300 cash to home office.
j. Branch recorded depreciation on office equipment, $380.

Required

1. Record these transactions in the home-office journal and in the branch journal.
2. Post the transactions to the reciprocal accounts. Show the balances of the reciprocal accounts after posting.

(Group B)

Problem 22-1B *Identifying different types of responsibility centers* **(L.O. 1)**

Identify by letter each of the following as most likely being a cost center, a profit center, or an investment center:

a. Quality-control department of a manufacturing company
b. Top management of a company
c. Southwest region of Pizza Inns, Inc.
d. Editorial department of *The Wall Street Journal*
e. A small clothing boutique
f. Payroll department of a university
g. Different product lines of a furniture manufacturer
h. Job superintendents of a home builder
i. A real estate firm
j. Fast-food restaurants under the supervision of a regional manager
k. European subsidiary of an American company
l. Children's nursery in a church or synagogue
m. Lighting department in a Sears store
n. Personnel department of Coca-Cola, Inc.
o. Service department of an established automobile dealership
p. Proposed new office of a CPA firm
q. Branch offices of a bank
r. Police department of a city
s. Delta Air Lines, Inc.
t. Consumer Complaint Division of Procter & Gamble Co.

Problem 22-2B *Preparing a profit-center performance report* **(L.O. 2)**

Eye Pro, Inc., is a chain of optical shops that dispense eyeglasses. Each store has a manager who answers to a city manager, who in turn reports to a state-wide manager. The income statements of Store No. 24, all stores in the Los Angeles area (including Store No. 24), and all stores in the state of California (including all Los Angeles stores) are summarized as follows for April:

	Store No. 24	Los Angeles	State of California
Revenue and expenses:			
Sales	$42,900	$486,000	$3,264,500
Expenses:			
City/state manager office	—	16,000	41,000
Cost of goods sold	14,000	171,300	1,256,800
Salary expense	5,300	37,500	409,700
Depreciation	3,000	26,100	334,000
Utilities	2,700	19,300	245,600
Rent	1,900	16,400	186,000
Supplies	700	5,500	60,700
Total expenses	27,600	292,100	2,533,800
Operating income	$15,300	$193,900	$ 730,700

Budgeted amounts for April are as follows:

	Store No. 24	Los Angeles	State of California
Revenue and expenses:			
Sales	$42,000	$468,000	$3,143,000
Expenses:			
City/state manager office ...	—	15,000	43,000
Cost of goods sold.........	14,200	172,800	1,209,000
Salary expense	5,600	37,900	412,000
Depreciation	3,500	25,400	320,000
Utilities..................	2,100	17,000	240,000
Rent	1,600	15,700	181,000
Supplies	800	5,900	60,000
Total expenses	27,800	289,700	2,465,000
Operating income	$14,200	$178,300	$ 678,000

Required

1. Prepare a report for April that shows the performance of Store No. 24, all the stores in the Los Angeles area, and all the stores in the state of California. Follow the format of Exhibit 22-2.
2. Identify the responsibility centers whose operating income exceeds budget and those whose operating income falls short of budget.

Problem 22-3B *Preparing a profit-center performance report* **(L.O. 2)**

Chi Alpha Corporation is organized along product lines, with product managers reporting to division managers, who in turn report to the company vice-president. The vice-president, who has received the following data for November of the current year, needs a performance report to highlight the operating income of audio products, the audio-video division, and the company in total:

	Company Totals			
	Audio-Video Division			
	Audio Products	Video Products	Other Divisions	
Revenues, actual	$212,000	$867,000	$788,000	
Expenses, actual	138,000	516,000	374,000	
Revenues, budget ...	218,000	907,000	760,000	
Expenses, budget ...	147,000	505,000	368,000	

Required

1. Prepare a performance report for November in a format similar to that on page 1020. Show November operating income in thousands of dollars for audio products, the audio-video division, and the company as a whole.
2. Which responsibility centers exceeded budget? Which performed below budget?

Problem 22-4B *Computing and allocating occupancy cost to a department* **(L.O. 3)**

Cokesbury Book Store occupies three floors in a building in downtown Columbus. Occupancy cost for a recent quarter included the following items and amounts:

Rent	$41,000
Utilities	9,300
Janitorial services	8,200
Depreciation—building fixtures	3,500
Total	$62,000

Cokesbury occupies 5,000 square feet on the street level, 3,000 square feet on the second floor, and 4,000 square feet of the basement. The company accountant computed the occupancy cost per square foot by dividing the total cost of $62,000 by 12,000 square feet. He charges occupancy to all company departments based on this $5.17 cost per square foot.

The manager of the children's books department, located in the basement, objected. She cited an engineering study conducted for the company by a real estate firm. It estimated that space in the basement is one-half as valuable as second-floor space and one-fourth as valuable as space on the street level.

Required

1. Based on the engineering study, compute the occupancy cost of a square foot of space on each of Cokesbury's three floors. Round decimals to three places, and round the cost per square foot to the nearest cent.
2. The children's book department occupies 2,200 square feet of the basement. How much occupancy cost should be charged to this department each quarter?

Problem 22-5B   *Allocate service department costs to operating departments*   (L.O. 3)

Parkland Memorial Hospital has two service departments and two operating departments. The following data are budgeted for the upcoming fiscal year:

	Service Department		Operating Department		
	General Administration	Maintenance	Regular Admissions	Emergency Room	Total
Direct department cost	$400,000	$60,000	$600,000	$250,000	$1,310,000
Services Provided:					
By General Administration— labor hours	—	400	28,000	11,600	40,000
By Maintenance— square feet	7,500	—	37,500	5,000	50,000

Parkland Memorial has a responsibility accounting system in which the managers of the operating departments are held accountable for both direct department costs and the costs of services provided by the hospital's two supporting service departments. Peter Schoenfeld, the accountant who designed the system, gathered input from affected managers concerning the appropriate allocation bases for assigning the service departments' costs to Regular Admissions and the Emergency Room. The consensus bases were labor hours for General Administration and square feet of floor space for Maintenance.

Parkland Memorial's managers decided to use the step-down method of service department cost allocation. They further decided to allocate first the service department that renders the highest dollar amount of services to the other service department.

Required

1. What sequence of allocation should Parkland Memorial follow—General Administration first, then Maintenance, or Maintenance first, then General Administration? Why?

2. Using the sequence you selected in Requirement 1, allocate the service departments' costs to Regular Admissions and the Emergency Room. Compute the total budgeted cost of each operating department.

Problem 22-6B *Preparing a departmental income statement* **(L.O. 3, 4)**

InstilPrinter is organized into a printing department and a copy department. At May 31, the end of InstilPrinter's fiscal year, the bookkeeper prepared the following trial balance, which includes the effects of year-end adjusting entries:

Cash	$ 2,400	
Receivables	3,600	
Supplies	25,400	
Prepaid expenses	1,100	
Land	25,900	
Building	41,200	
Accumulated depreciation—building		$ 16,200
Printing equipment	33,700	
Accumulated depreciation—printing equipment		9,600
Other assets	4,700	
Accounts payable		3,200
Accrued liabilities		1,600
Unearned printing revenue		2,200
Long-term note payable		15,000
Owner equity		61,400
Printing revenue		67,100
Copy revenue		54,900
Salary expense—machine operators	23,600	
Salary expense—store manager	22,900	
Salary expense—bookkeeper	18,300	
Lease expense—copy equipment	12,000	
Supplies expense	9,000	
Property tax expense	2,300	
Insurance expense	1,600	
Depreciation expense—building	1,400	
Depreciation expense—printing equipment	1,400	
Interest expense	400	
Uncollectible account expense	300	
	$231,200	$231,200

InstiPrinter owns its printing equipment and leases a copier from Xerox. Established printing customers do business with the company on a credit basis, but copy services are performed for cash only. Insurance expense is evenly divided between departments. The bookkeeper spends approximately two-thirds of his time on accounts receivable and other printing department matters and the remainder on general accounting. Interest expense relates to the note payable, which the company signed to purchase the printing equipment. The store manager spends 60 percent of her time on printing and 40 percent on copy services. The company allocates all other expenses based on service revenue.

Required

1. Prepare a departmental income statement through operating income.
2. Which department has the higher operating income? What factor contributes most to the profitability difference between departments?

Problem 22-7B *Preparing a budgeted departmental income statement* **(L.O. 3, 4)**

Kellner's is a neighborhood clothing store with two departments. The most recent annual report to management appears below.

Kellner's is considering opening a children's department early in fiscal 19X8. To plan for the coming year, the store owner seeks your help in preparing a budgeted income statement. Your conversation with the owner reveals the following:

1. Management expects annual sales of the new department to be $65,000, with a gross profit percentage equal to that of the two existing departments.

Kellner's
Departmental Income Statement
For the Year Ended January 31, 19X7

	Total	Men's	Women's
Sales revenue	$317,700	$141,800	$175,900
Expenses:			
Cost of goods sold	152,500	68,050	84,450
Sales salaries	44,300	20,800	23,500
Salary—store manager	32,900	16,450	16,450
Rent expense—building	14,000	7,000	7,000
Advertising	8,000	2,400	5,600
Property tax	2,000	1,000	1,000
Insurance	1,800	900	900
Depreciation—store fixtures	1,700	850	850
Supplies	1,000	500	500
Interest	600	300	300
Uncollectible accounts	300	150	150
Total expenses	259,100	118,400	140,700
Operating income	$ 58,600	$ 23,400	$ 35,200

2. Addition of a children's department will draw more women than men into the store and should increase sales of women's wear by 20 percent. Sales of men's wear are expected to increase by only 5 percent.

3. A salesperson can be hired for the children's department at an annual salary of $14,000. Other salaries will increase by 6 percent.

4. Thus far, Kellner's accountant has allocated all expenses except cost of goods sold, sales salaries, and advertising equally to the men's and women's departments. The store owner decides that the equal allocation of indirect expenses to the two departments is inappropriate.

5. The store manager expects to spend equal amounts of time in the three departments during the coming year.

6. The women's department is nearest the door and occupies 3,000 square feet of the most valuable space in the store. Men's wear also occupies 3,000 square feet, but its space is only two-thirds as valuable as that of women's wear. The new children's department will take up 1,000 square feet with the same value per square foot as the women's department. Total rent expense under the long-term lease will be unchanged in 19X8.

7. Advertising expense will increase by 10 percent for the two existing departments. The company will commit $2,000 to advertising the children's department.

8. Depreciation of new store fixtures for the children's department will be $900. Other depreciation amounts will be unchanged.
9. Interest expense needed to finance the children's department will be $1,000. The remaining 19X8 interest of $600 belongs equally to the other two departments.
10. All other expenses will increase by 10 percent and should be allocated to departments based on relative sales, except property tax, which is allocated on the same basis used for rent. Round percentages to three decimal places.

Required

1. Prepare a budgeted departmental income statement in multiple-step format for fiscal year 19X8 based on the preceding projections.
2. Based on your budget, would you recommend that Kellner's open the new department? State your reasons.

Problem 22-8B *Recording home-office and branch transactions* (*L.O. 5*)

Guadalupe Realty has branch offices throughout the El Paso area and uses a branch accounting system for control purposes. The home office has a separate Branch Ledger Control account for each branch, and the branches maintain branch ledgers. Branch ledgers contain asset, liability, and Home-Office Ledger Control accounts.

The home office advances cash to the branches. Branch managers have the authority to purchase supplies and office furniture and equipment. They also pay utility and other branch-office expenses. However, only the home office records branch expenses. The branches collect commissions earned from their real estate sales and immediately transfer the cash to the home office. Only the home office records commissions revenue. The home office then pays a commission directly to the agent who made the sale. During a recent month the following transactions occurred at the Rojo Mesa Branch of Guadalupe Realty:

a. Home office advanced $5,000 to branch.
b. Branch purchased office supplies on account, $400.
c. Branch paid cash for a file cabinet, $700.
d. Branch paid account payable, $600.
e. Branch sold a house, earning a commission and receiving cash of $4,700.
f. Branch transferred $4,700 to home office.
g. Home office paid commission to agent making sale in *e*, $3,100.
h. Branch transferred $1,000 cash to home office.
i. Branch paid electricity expense, $300.
j. Branch recorded depreciation on office equipment, $600.

Required

1. Record these transactions in the home-office journal and in the branch journal.
2. Post the transactions to the reciprocal accounts. Show the balances of the reciprocal accounts after posting.

Extending Your Knowledge

Decision Problems

1. Evaluating Cost Allocation and Departmental Performance (L.O. 2, 3, 4)

Stuarts is a jewelry store located on the main floor of a four-star hotel on the Loop in Chicago. It opened in January of the current year. The store has two entrances, one off the lobby and the other off the street. Stuarts is one of many exclusive stores on the street. There are display windows beside both entrances.

Stuarts places particular departments close to each entrance. Customers entering the store from the street will see the watch department first. Entering from the lobby brings the customer into the diamond department. The watch and diamond departments occupy equal space in the store, and both have the same number of staff behind the counter. The silver and costume jewelry departments occupy relatively little space in the store compared to diamonds and watches.

It is now December, and the Stuarts, Inc., accountant has prepared a departmental statement for presentation to George Stuart, the president.

Required

Evaluate the presentation of the statement. If necessary, redraft the statement. Clearly state any assumptions you make. Analyze the profitability of Stuarts' departments.

Stuarts, Inc.
Departmental Income Statement
For the Year Ended December 31, 19X7
('000)

	Diamonds	Watches	Other
Sales revenue	$1,050	$675	$180
Costs:			
Cost of goods sold	450	337	110
Sales commissions	105	54	4
Salary—manager	22	22	22
Rent expense	72	46	12
Advertising	70	0	0
Insurance	10	6	3
Depreciation—fixtures	8	8	8
Office expenses	12	12	12
Income before interest and taxes	$ 301	$190	$ 9

2. Using Departmental Operating Income to Decide on an Advertising Campaign (L.O. 3, 4)

The accountant of Onondaga Nissan-Toyota has produced the following annual summary of revenue and expense information for management:

	Nissans	Toyotas
Units sold	200	80
Average selling price per unit	$15,000	$22,000
Average cost per unit	12,200	17,300
Average direct expense per unit	1,900	2,320
Average variable indirect expense per unit	500	1,200

Jeff Onondaga, owner of the business, is considering an advertising campaign to increase sales and operating income. He estimates that additional advertising cost of $25,000 will increase sales by 30 automobiles each year. However, because Onondaga is the only Nissan-Toyota dealer in the area, any increase in Nissan sales is likely to decrease sales of Toyotas by an equal number. Likewise, an increase in Toyota sales of 30 automobiles is likely to cause an equal decrease in Nissan sales. Onondaga's fixed expenses, other than the $25,000 of advertising, will be unaffected by this decision.

Required

Prepare an analysis to show whether Onondaga should advertise Nissans or Toyotas, or not undertake the advertising campaign at all. Base your decision on operating income (ignoring fixed expenses other than the $25,000 advertising) under three alternatives: (1) no new advertising, (2) advertise Nissans, and (3) advertise Toyotas.

Ethical Issue

Bertha Bumiller manages the hosiery department of McRae's Department Store in the Metro Mall of Jackson, Mississippi. Bertha buys merchandise, hires sales clerks, arranges displays, and takes the inventory. Her annual bonus depends on departmental income before income tax. The Bumiller family is planning a Christmas vacation to the Virgin Islands and is counting on Bertha's bonus. Sales for 1993 have been sluggish, so Bertha slightly overstates ending inventory.

Required

1. Specify the effect of the inventory overstatement on cost of goods sold, gross margin, income before income tax, and Bertha's bonus.
2. Is overstating ending inventory unethical? Who is helped and who is harmed by Bertha's action?

Chapter 23

Strategy, Cost Management, and Continuous Improvement

Activity-based costing (ABC) is a new accounting method that has executives at both large and small companies singing its praises. Accountants use ABC systems to determine the cost of products by accumulating the costs of all activities necessary to produce and support them. They use the systems to estimate the cost of production processes by adding up the costs of all activities performed in them. The resulting costs generally are regarded as more accurate than costs generated by traditional accounting systems.

Engineers use ABC data to assess alternative product designs. Managers use the data to evaluate different factory layouts, reduce waste in manufacturing, and improve product and service quality.

According to Chrysler president Robert Lutz, his company "is dynamiting the old financial system" and replacing it with ABC. This major decision was influenced by the company's recent experience with a very minor part, the harnesses that yoke together wires under the dashboards of minivans. Each group involved in the decision (for example, product designers and assembly personnel) recommended a different number of distinct harnesses, ranging from one to nine. When Chrysler examined the cost of each activity affected by the decision, everyone involved became convinced that the optimal number was two.

Source: Adapted from Terence P. Paré, "A New Tool For Managing Costs," *Fortune*, June 14, 1993, pp. 124-129.

In today's international marketplace, companies prosper by implementing strategies that lead to a sustainable competitive advantage. A **strategy** is a set of business goals and the tactics to achieve them. Successful implementation of strategies means gathering, organizing, and using resources effectively and efficiently so that goals are attained.

A growing number of companies worldwide, including Chrysler, Boeing, and Caterpillar Tractor, are using a new management process known as **activity-based management (ABM)**. ABM focuses on the management of activities as the way to improve value delivered to customers. Providing that value generates profits. ABM fosters a culture of excellence, which is achieved by:

- Managing those activities that advance the organization's strategy
- Eliminating (or minimizing) activities that do not add value to customers
- Synchronizing activities within business processes
- Promoting continuous improvement of activity cost, time, and quality

The key to successful business management is intelligent decision making. A successful management accounting system provides decision support, that is, tools and information that lead to wise decisions and consequent actions. As the Chrysler vignette illustrates, activity-based management draws on activity-based costing as its major source of information. This chapter begins with activity-based costing and then discusses several other approaches to improving the "critical success factors" of cost, time, and quality.

Activity-Based Costing

Earlier chapters have focused on product costing for *inventory valuation*. To maximize long-term profitability, systems also should serve the planning and control purpose. Many managers plan and control manufacturing, marketing, and other business functions by personal observation and with budget and cost systems. In many companies, these functions are divided into departments.

This section describes an emerging new approach to measuring the costs of various cost objects. A cost object can be anything for which it is worthwhile to compile costs, such as an activity (spray painting), a department (finishing), or a product (a table). **Activity-based costing (ABC)**, also called *activity-based accounting*, is a system that focuses on *activities* as the fundamental cost objects and uses the costs of those activities as building blocks for compiling the costs of products and other cost objects. ABC is generic. It can be used in conjunction with either a job order or a process costing system and by both manufacturing companies and service firms.

If dividing companywide functions into departments helps managers, wouldn't dividing departments into activities further sharpen managers' focus? Exhibit 23-1, Panel A, shows the different functions in a furniture manufacturer's value chain. Panel B divides the manufacturing function into departments, and Panel C lists common activities in a Finishing Department. Note that costs are accumulated for each activity separately. The activity costs then are applied to tables and other products as the products move through production. For example, if a table's finishing calls for polishing, the cost of that activity—polishing—is added to the table. If the table is a less-expensive model, the company may not polish it. In this case, the table bears no polishing cost. Inspecting cost and packaging cost likewise are added to the cost of the table as appropriate. *The product cost of a dining table is "built up" from the cost of the specific activities undertaken to manufacture it.*

Exhibit 23-1 shows how cost objects become ever-more-finely granulated from a particular business function, such as manufacturing, to departments, including painting and finishing, to activities, such as polishing and inspecting. But how do the refinements of ABC translate into better decisions?

EXHIBIT 23-1   *Overview of Business Functions, Departments, and Activities*

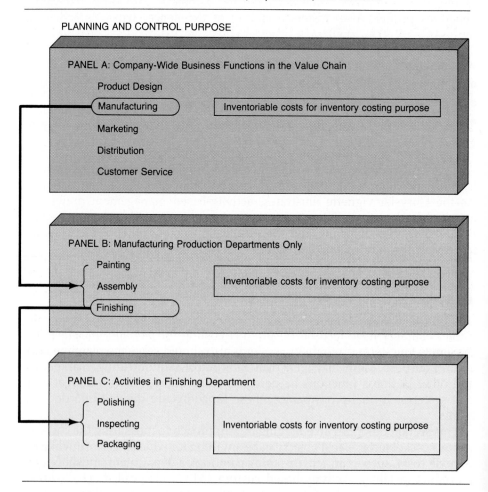

Demand for Activity-Based Costing

Managers often are frustrated by a time-honored cost accounting practice—the allocation of all overhead costs to products on the basis of a single application base, direct labor. There are two problems with this practice. First, in many manufacturing settings, especially those that are highly automated, overhead cost incurrence is not related to direct labor hours or cost. Recall that a *cost driver* is any factor whose change causes a change in a related total cost. Using a cost application base that is not the driver of the cost in question results in inaccurate product costs. Second, no *single* factor drives all indirect manufacturing costs, much less all costs in the value chain. ABC focuses the attention of managers and accountants on the specific activities performed to manufacture and support individual products. A key feature of ABC is allocation of activity costs on the basis of multiple cost drivers. Each driver is selected for its relationship to the activity. The more precise relationships identified by ABC yield more accurate product costs than traditional systems that use a single allocation base for conversion costs. Better cost figures help managers make wiser decisions.

Another reason managers demand ABC information is that activities cut across departmental lines. For example, inspection may take place in a painting department, an assembly department, and a finishing department. Only if detailed records are kept by activities can the total company cost of inspection (or any other activity) be compiled and used by managers. Focusing on cost by department or product instead of by activity can obscure activity costs.

More than ever, managers focus attention on activities. Fundamentally, people manage activities, not products. If activities are managed well, costs will be lower than otherwise, and products will be more competitive.

Developments in information technology make activity-based costing feasible. Optical scanning, bar coding, and robotics have reduced the cost of processing the information demanded by ABC. Before these techniques became available, it was convenient to use direct labor hours or direct labor dollars as the sole basis for allocating overhead cost. Now it is relatively inexpensive to obtain more-precise cost allocations with multiple cost drivers.

Product Costing in an Activity-Based System

Product cost build-up in an ABC system follows the pattern of other cost systems, with one exception. Conversion costs are applied to products on the basis of various manufacturing activities rather than a single measure, such as direct labor hours in traditional systems. Suppose Des Moines, Inc., uses ABC, and the direct material of its wrought-iron lawn chairs costs $4 per unit. Each chair includes eight parts and requires 15 minutes of machine time. Shown below are Des Moines' conversion costs, organized by manufacturing activities, and the associated cost drivers and unit application rates for a batch of 1,000 chairs. Note the procession of analysis:

1. Identify activities.
2. Identify the cost of the activity.
3. Identify the primary cost driver as the application base for each activity.

Manufacturing Activity	Cost of Activity	Cost Driver Chosen as Application Base		Conversion Cost per Unit of Application Base
1. Materials handling	$ 800 ÷	Number of parts (8,000)	=	$ .10
2. Machining	5,000 ÷	Machine hours (250)	=	20.00
3. Assembling	4,800 ÷	Number of parts (8,000)	=	.60
4. Inspecting	1,400 ÷	Number of finished units (1,000)	=	1.40

Each chair's manufacturing cost is $16.00, computed as follows:

Direct materials.	$4.00
Conversion costs:	
Materials handling (8 parts × $.10)	.80
Machining (1/4 machine hour × $20.00).	5.00
Assembling (8 parts × $.60)	4.80
Inspecting (1 finished unit × $1.40)	1.40
Total manufacturing cost per unit	$16.00

The detailed breakdown of conversion costs by activity pinpoints opportunities for cost control. For example, machining costs of $5 per unit may be too high. Managers could take action to bring machining cost down. In a traditional costing system this information may not be available, and cost may escalate without managers' attention.

Managers are also concerned about *full product cost*, which includes the costs of upstream activities and downstream activities in the value chain. Recall that upstream activities precede manufacturing and downstream activities follow. Des Moines' full product cost per chair is $26.60, computed as follows:

Upstream activities:	
Product design (assumed)	$1.40
Total manufacturing cost per unit (as before)	16.00
Downstream activities:	
Marketing, distribution, and customer service (assumed) . . .	9.20
Full product cost per unit	$26.60

Internal decisions, such as product mix and product pricing, will focus on the components of full product cost. However, the external financial statements will report chairs at $16 each because that is their manufacturing (inventoriable) cost. The costs of upstream and downstream activities are expensed as incurred.

Activity-Based Costing and Management Decisions

A major feature of activity-based costing is the use of several cost application bases instead of just one. The following illustration is exaggerated to emphasize the effect of multiple bases on product costs.

Quality Instrument Company manufactures two products, space missile instruments (20 per month) and testing instruments (400 per month). The company has had the same cost accounting system since its founding in 1971. A single plantwide rate based on machine hours of running time has been used for applying all conversion costs to production. Direct materials cost and machine hours are the same for the two products, so their total manufacturing costs are equal. In the following tabulation of total cost per unit, focus on conversion cost:

	Conversion Costs per Unit			Direct Materials	
Product	Machine Hours per Unit	Application Rate per Machine Hour	Total Cost	Cost per Unit	Total Manufacturing Cost per Unit
Space missile instrument...........	5 ×	$120	= $600	$200	$800
Testing instrument	5 ×	120	= 600	200	800

In recent years the cost of each machine setup has soared to $42,000 as precision requirements have tightened. The use of a single cost application rate that is based on machine hours of running time ignores the role of setup cost. To better gauge the cost of each product, management decides to use two bases, machine setups and machine running time, for applying conversion costs to products. Each product requires one machine setup. When machine setup cost is subtracted from total manufacturing cost, the application rate for machine running time decreases to $80 per hour from the previous level of $120. The ABC computations of product cost differ significantly from the earlier figures:

	Conversion Costs						Direct Materials	
		Running of Machines						
Product	Machine Setups	Units	Hours	Rate	Total Cost	Per Unit	Cost per Unit	Total Manufacturing Cost per Unit
Space missile instrument.........	$42,000 +	(20 ×	5	× $80) =	$ 50,000	$2,500*	$200	$2,700
Testing instrument ...	42,000 +	(400 ×	5	× 80) =	202,000	505†	200	705

*$50,000/20 units = $2,500
†$202,000/400 units = $505

Compare the total manufacturing cost per unit under the two methods of allocating conversion costs:

	Total Manufacturing Cost per Unit	
Product	Using Plantwide Rate	Using ABC Rates
Space missile instrument	$800	$2,700
Testing instrument	800	705

OBJECTIVE 2

Use activity-based costs to make management decisions

Activity-based costing is likely to give managers better information for decision making. ABC identifies the various activities and cost drivers that cause costs and uses those relationships to apply costs more precisely. For example, use of a single cost application base ignores the high cost of machine setups. Manufacture of each group of instruments requires one setup costing $42,000, but that information is ignored in the traditional approach. Consequently, the same amount of conversion cost ($600) is allocated to each space missile instrument and each testing instrument. The accounting records indicate that each product's manufacturing cost is $800. A product-pricing decision based on these cost figures can be disastrous. Suppose the marketing department prices each space missile instrument and each testing instrument at $1,500. Managers believe each sale will yield a $700 profit ($1,500 − $800). However, the company will lose $1,200 ($2,700 − $1,500) on the sale of each space missile instrument.

The ABC amounts lead to an entirely different conclusion. Each space missile instrument is allocated $2,500 of conversion costs, and the accounting records indicate that total cost is $2,700. Company managers who know this cost are more likely to price the product appropriately.

Another decision is whether Quality Instrument Company should make these products or buy them from an outside supplier. Suppose an outside company offers to supply each product for $1,000. Using a single cost application base, Quality managers would reject the offer. They would think they could make each instrument for $800. Using ABC, they would accept the outside offer for space missile instruments. The purchase price of $1,000 is much lower than Quality's manufacturing cost of $2,700.

Each of the above decisions may be influenced by other factors. For example, managers should consider the contribution to profits that could be earned if the outside supplier's offer is accepted and freed-up machine time is used to produce a third product. Nevertheless, properly functioning ABC systems provide more accurate figures than systems that use a single cost application base.

A word of caution is in order here. ABC is not easy. Describing the concept is deceptively simple: Activities consume resources and products consume activities. However, implementing an ABC system is not simple, especially in complex organizations with many activities and multiple cost drivers. The business press has reported several failures. One problem is that some managers regard ABC as a "quick fix" for declining profitability or productivity. But ABC is not a stand-alone technique that assures success in the marketplace. Instead it is one of several activity-based *management* initiatives used by companies that seek world-class status. Others include just-in-time (JIT) production systems, product-life-cycle budgeting, target costing, and total quality management (TQM). The remainder of this chapter addresses these topics.

Summary Problem for Your Review

Indianapolis Auto Parts (IAP), a manufacturing company, uses activity-based costing. Chrysler has asked for a bid on 50,000 built-in baby seats that will be installed as an optional item on some Chrysler vans. IAP's costing system has the following features:

Activity	Cost Driver Chosen as Application Base	Conversion Cost per Unit of Application Base
1. Purchasing	Number of purchase orders	$60.00
2. Assembling	Number of parts	.50
3. Packaging	Number of finished units	.90

Each seat has eight parts; total direct materials cost per seat is $5. A total of 200 purchase orders will be necessary if Chrysler accepts IAP's bid.

Required

1. Compute the total cost that IAP will incur to purchase the needed parts and then assemble and package 50,000 baby seats. Also compute the average cost per unit.
2. Assume that for bidding purposes, IAP adds a 30% markup to total cost. What price will the company bid for the Chrysler order?
3. Suppose that instead of an ABC system, IAP has a traditional product costing system that applies all conversion costs to products at the plant-wide rate of $3.20 per direct labor hour. The baby-seat order will require 100,000 direct labor hours. What price will IAP bid on the basis of this system's total cost?

SOLUTION TO REVIEW PROBLEM

1. Direct materials, 50,000 × $5.00 .... $ 250,000
   Conversion costs of activities:
       Purchasing, 200 × $60.00 12,000
       Assembling, 50,000 × 8 × $.50 200,000
       Packaging, 50,000 × $.90...................... 45,000
   Total cost .... $ 507,000
   Divide by number of units .... ÷50,000
   Average cost per unit .... $ 10.14
2. $507,000 × 130% = $659,100
3. Direct materials, 50,000 × $5.00......................... $250,000
   Conversion costs, 100,000 × $3.20 320,000
       Total cost $570,000
   $570,000 × 130% = $741,000

Just-in-Time Production Systems

Traditional Manufacturing Environment

Traditional manufacturing systems often produce enormous waste, in terms of both time and money. Recently, attention has focused on two areas where this waste is especially apparent: (1) inventories and (2) manufacturing processes.

Inventories. Business managers long have favored keeping large stocks of raw materials, work in process, and finished goods inventories. Why? First, to protect against poor quality. Poor quality in raw materials and parts purchased from suppliers means that companies must purchase more materials than are strictly needed for production. Machine breakdowns and poor-quality production *within* departments mean that buffer stocks must be kept *between* departments so that downstream operations can keep busy when upstream problems occur. Consider the sequence of operations shown in Exhibit 23-2 for the production of drill bits. Work in process stocks between the thread grinding and smoothing operations allow smoothing work to continue if thread-grinding machines break down.

A second reason for large inventories is long setup times on production equipment. Some managers view setup times of several hours to several days, and correspondingly high setup costs, as acceptable. They make products in large batch sizes to spread the setup time and cost over many units, thereby minimizing per-unit amounts. A third reason for stocking large inventories is uncertainty, in both deliveries from suppliers and demand from customers. Large stocks of raw materials and parts protect against delays in deliveries; large stocks of finished goods protect against missed sales if customer demand is higher than expected.

Why are large inventory stocks a problem? First, inventories tie up cash. Companies either pay interest expense or forego interest revenue on that cash. Second, inventories hide problems. Quality problems, production bottlenecks, obsolescence, and supplier unreliability often are hidden in inventories. If the drill bit manufacturer improperly grinds threads on a batch of 1,000 bits and the problem is not discovered by the smoothing-machine operator until a week later, the company will have to devote considerable resources to reworking the defective bits. Alternatively, the bits may have to be discarded.

Manufacturing processes. Traditionally, machines have been grouped according to function. Rough-shaping machines might be located in one area of a plant, thread-grinding machines in another area (perhaps hundreds of feet away), and smoothing machines in yet another area. In many cases, raw materials and parts travel several *miles* back and forth through a factory before they are completed as finished goods, perhaps detouring to storage areas along the way. This excessive movement not only wastes time but also increases the chance that an order will be misplaced or damaged. Misplaced orders lead to delayed shipments, and delayed shipments anger customers.

Traditional manufacturing processes are called "push" systems. One goal of their managers is to keep every machine as busy as possible in order to maximize output per hour, a common performance measure. The thread-grinding machine center in Exhibit 23-2 pushes threaded bits to the smoothing machine center whether or not the smoothing machines are ready for them. Too often, the bits are pushed forward whether or not they meet quality standards. The felt need to keep busy regardless of downstream demand for a machine center's output is another reason for high work in process inventory levels.

Production specialists refer to the time between receipt of purchased materials and completion of finished products as **throughput time**. Throughput time may be represented by the following equation:

EXHIBIT 23-2 *Sequence of Operations for Drill Bit Production*

$$\text{Throughput time} = \text{Processing time} + \text{Waiting time} + \text{Moving time} +$$
$$\text{Inspection time} + \text{Reworking time}$$

Processing time often is called "value-added" time. Processing activity adds value to the products a company provides to its customers. The remainder of throughput time is "non-value-added," or simply "waste," time. It represents **non-value-added activities** that do not increase customer value or satisfy a company need. In many manufacturing systems, processing time accounts for less than 10% of throughput time. The remainder is waste.

Characteristics of Just-in-Time Systems

Just-in-time (JIT) production systems are designed to eliminate waste. Indeed, many people regard JIT as a *general philosophy of waste elimination* instead of a particular type of manufacturing system. The production systems of companies that apply the JIT philosophy have several common characteristics.

OBJECTIVE 3

Compare the major features of a just-in-time (JIT) production system and a traditional system

1. *Arrangement of production activities.* JIT processes arrange machines according to the sequence of operations, not by function. In our drill bit example, a production line might manufacture a specific type of drill bit. In that line, a rough-shaping machine located near the cutting operation might be followed by a thread-grinding machine, which in turn might be followed by a smoothing machine. These machines, which perform various functions, would be arranged differently from the clusters of a traditional factory layout. In some JIT cases, machines performing sequential steps are physically joined. The goal is continual production without interruption. Arranging machines in this sequential manner results in great reductions in time and distance traveled, in some reported cases several *miles*.

2. *Setup times.* JIT companies work continually to reduce setup times on machines that are used to make more than one product. Through a combination of employee training, preparation, and technology, the companies have achieved impressive results. Some companies (such as Toyota) have reported reductions in setup times from several hours to a few minutes; others, from minutes to seconds. Lower changeover times—one machine setup to another—give companies greater flexibility in scheduling production to meet customer requirements. The results are increased customer satisfaction and increased profits.

3. *Production scheduling.* JIT businesses schedule production in small batches "just in time" to satisfy needs. Manufacturing usually is activated by receipt of a customer order. The final operation in the production sequence (smoothing, in our drill bit example) "pulls" parts from the preceding operation (thread grinding). That is, the smoothing-machine operator signals the grinding-machine operator to supply the number of threaded bits required to satisfy the order. The grinding-machine operator pulls shaped parts from rough shaping, and so on. This "demand-pull" system extends back not just to the first production operation but also to suppliers of materials. Suppliers are expected to make frequent deliveries of small quantities of defect-free materials just in time to be placed into production. Ideally, this arrangement results in greater coordination of efforts throughout the value chain. Otherwise, it merely shifts inventory carrying costs from purchasers to suppliers.

    Purchasing and producing only what is needed to meet downstream demand results in great reductions in inventory quantities (and dollars tied up in inventory). As inventory quantities decrease, problems hidden by inventory are exposed. Also, floor space devoted to inventories is freed up for more productive use.

Several companies that implemented JIT practices reported finding a "factory within a factory"—enough newly available space to double production capacity. This additional space has allowed some companies to postpone either expensive plant expansions or the purchase of entirely new plants.

The small batch sizes of JIT production, coupled with sequentially arranged operations in close proximity, produce yet another benefit. Production problems are detected quickly and can be corrected before causing a large number of defective units. Early detection saves rework and scrap costs.

4. *Employee roles.* Production employees in JIT systems are trained to do more than operate a single machine. They also are trained to conduct routine maintenance, to perform setups, and to operate other machines. Cross-training increases flexibility and decreases costs.

Our discussion has highlighted how application of the JIT philosophy leads to better quality, less inventory, lower costs, fewer non-value-added activities, and shorter throughput times. The next section demonstrates how JIT leads to simplified cost accounting.

Backflush Costing

Backflush costing is a standard costing system that starts with output completed and works backward to apply manufacturing costs to units sold and to inventories. Backflush costing arose during the 1980s when JIT production systems gained popularity, but the method can be used with any production system. Users of backflush costing typically have the following characteristics:

1. Standard costs for each product
2. Either low inventories or constant inventory levels of direct materials and work in process

Backflush costing differs from the more common standard costing system described in Chapter 21. The latter is a sequential tracking system—it traces costs in each step of the production process, from direct materials to work in process and on through to finished goods and cost of goods sold. The simpler backflush method does not track direct materials requisitions or labor records to individual processes or products. It is less time-consuming and less costly to use than sequential tracking.

Illustration of Backflush Costing

The following illustration shows that backflush systems do not use a separate Work in Process account. Consider the Mintel Company, which makes microdevices (integrated circuits) used in computers. Mintel purchases silicon wafers and converts them into a variety of microdevices. The company uses only two inventory accounts:

- Raw and in Process (RIP), which is a combination of direct materials and work in process
- Finished Goods, which is the usual finished goods account

Mintel has only one type of direct manufacturing product cost: silicon wafers, which are labeled "raw." All other manufacturing costs, including labor and various gases and chemicals, are indirect costs of conversion. No cost, whether direct or indirect, is separately tracked to microdevices in process.

The Mintel backflush system has two **trigger points**, which prompt entries in the accounting records. The trigger points are (1) the purchase of direct materials and (2) the transfer of completed units to finished goods.

Mintel Company has a JIT production system with minimal inventories of $100,000 of raw and in process and $900,000 of finished goods at July 31. In August, the company's accountants take the following steps:

1. Record direct materials purchases of $3,020,000:

   (a) RIP Inventory.......................... 3,020,000
           Accounts Payable   3,020,000
   (Note that the inventory is carried at standard cost. Variances are discussed in a later section of this chapter.)

OBJECTIVE 4

Record manufacturing costs for a backflush costing system

2. Record the actual conversion costs incurred:

   (b) Conversion Costs 18,540,000
           Various Accounts   18,540,000
       (such as payables and accumulated depreciation)

3. Compute the number of finished units manufactured during August. Mintel produced 3,000,000 microdevices.

4. Calculate the standard cost per finished unit. The company develops standard conversion costs for each individual operation or step in the production process. Standard costs are "built up" for each device, depending on the operations that work on it. Assume that August production was limited to one type of device. Its standard cost is $7 ($1 direct materials + $6 conversion cost).

5. Record the standard cost of finished goods completed during the month; 3,000,000 units × $7 per unit = $21,000,000:

   (c) Finished Goods 21,000,000
           RIP Inventory   3,000,000
           Conversion Costs   18,000,000

   This is the second trigger point and the essence of backflushing. The costs were not tracked sequentially, following the product as it moved through the various manufacturing operations. Instead, completion of the units triggered the accounting system to go back and pull costs from RIP inventory.

6. Record costs of goods sold in the usual manner. Assume that 2,930,000 units were sold: 2,930,000 units × $7 per unit = $20,510,000:

   (d) Cost of Goods Sold 20,510,000
           Finished Goods   20,510,000

The August ending inventory balances are:

RIP inventory .... $ 120,000
Finished goods 1,390,000
Total inventories............................. $1,510,000

Other Trigger Points

Exhibit 23-3 shows Mintel Company's backflushing accounts. Using no work in process account eliminates detail. Physical units in process may be tracked, but costs are not assigned to units in the accounting records via materials requisitions or time records. Instead, costs are identified with physical products only at the second trigger point, when goods are fully completed.

Our illustrated two-trigger-point system that uses completion of goods as the second trigger point is the most popular version of backflushing. However, other trigger points may be used. For example, Toyota's cost accounting system for its Kentucky plant uses the sale of units, not their completion, as the second trigger point.

The simplest version of backflush costing has only one trigger point, the completion of output. This version's accounting records do not record the purchase of direct materials. It is appropriate for manufacturing systems that have almost no direct materials inventories and minimal work in process inventories.

Variances in Backflush Costing Systems

All standard costing systems share the same fundamental approach to accounting for variances. (Chapter 21 explains the basic techniques.) In our Mintel Company illustration, assume that the direct materials purchased had an unfavorable price variance of $125,000. Entry (a) would change as follows:

```
(a)  RIP Inventory ...........................   3,020,000
         Direct Materials Price Variance ..............     125,000
             Accounts Payable ....................                   3,145,000
```

Direct materials efficiency variances are measured in total by working backward from the output units completed. Completed output is the key to determining what should remain in RIP inventory (beginning inventory plus purchases less standard materials used for completed units) and comparing it with what does remain. Suppose that such a comparison for Mintel reveals an unfavorable efficiency variance of $9,000. The entry is:

```
(e)  Direct Materials Efficiency Variance.................   9,000
             RIP Inventory ...............................               9,000
```

EXHIBIT 23-3 *The Mintel Company*
Major Backflushing Accounts

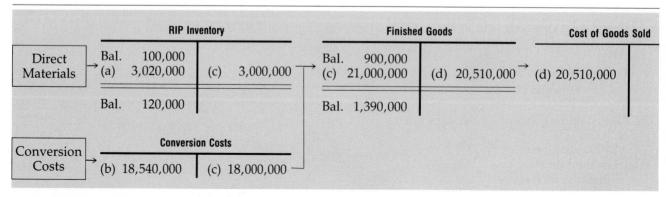

An unfavorable efficiency variance in backflush costing means that more direct materials were used for units *completed* during the month than the standard amount allowed. Entry (e) pulls the cost of that additional, over-standard material out of RIP inventory.

Conversion costs may be overapplied or underapplied in any month. Mintel's conversion costs are underapplied by $540,000 ($18,540,000 incurred − $18,000,000 applied to production) in August. Companies vary in writing off underapplied amounts monthly, quarterly, or yearly. Assume that Mintel favors a monthly write-off. The August entry is:

(f) Cost of Goods Sold 540,000
        Conversion Costs 540,000

If the company used the yearly write-off alternative, debits and credits would accumulate throughout the year in the Conversion Costs account. An entry like the one shown above would be made at the end of the year.

Companies that use backflush costing typically have low inventories. Proration of variances between inventories and cost of goods sold usually is unnecessary. As shown above, variances are written off directly to Cost of Goods Sold.

Summary Problem for Your Review

The Flores Company manufactures telephones. Flores uses a backflush costing system with two trigger points: (1) when direct materials are purchased and (2) when completed telephones are transferred to finished goods inventory. The standard unit cost of a particular model is $37: $24 direct materials and $13 conversion costs. The standard amount paid for direct materials during June was $2,540,000. Actual conversion costs incurred totaled $1,295,000.

Flores completed 102,000 units of the model in June. The company sold 98,000.

Required

1. Prepare June journal entries for the transactions described.
2. Assume that the actual cost of direct materials purchased in June was $2,480,000. Record the purchase under this assumption.
3. Make the entry to close the underapplied or overapplied conversion costs to Cost of Goods Sold.

SOLUTION TO REVIEW PROBLEM

1. (a) RIP Inventory 2,540,000
        Accounts Payable 2,540,000
  (b) Conversion Costs 1,295,000
        Various Accounts 1,295,000
  (c) Finished Goods 3,774,000
        RIP Inventory 2,448,000
        Conversion Costs 1,326,000
  (d) Cost of Goods Sold 3,626,000
        Finished Goods 3,626,000

2. (a) RIP Inventory		2,540,000	
Direct Materials Price Variance			60,000
Accounts Payable			2,480,000
3. (e) Conversion Costs		31,000	
Cost of Goods Sold			31,000

Continuous Improvement and Product-Life-Cycle Costs

To remain competitive, businesses must continuously improve their processes and products. Many companies seek continuous improvement through cost management. The idea is for employees throughout the company's value chain to strive steadily for cost reductions while maintaining high levels of quality, speed, and customer satisfaction.

In the past, many managers sought to determine the "optimal" level of quality. These individuals paid for quality improvements up to the point where the costs began to exceed the apparent benefits. But in today's competitive environment customers demand ever-higher levels of quality. And managers fear that if they don't provide it, their competitors will. They are willing to incur additional costs for quality improvements in order to reduce rework, scrap, and warranty costs and decrease lost sales to dissatisfied customers.

This section of the chapter relates continuous improvement to the planning and control of new products. The next section ties continuous improvement to the management of quality. We focus initially on the Japanese automobile industry, because Toyota and other companies in the industry pioneered the use of continuous improvement techniques. Different companies in the industry use these techniques in different ways; we discuss a general approach that includes proven methods.

Life-Cycle Budgeting

In Japan, a proposal for developing a new automobile model usually is made by a product line's chief engineer. The initial focus is on the marketplace. What product, with what features, will have wide appeal to potential customers? At what sales price? And how many automobiles will customers demand at that price?

As an illustration, suppose that a product-planning committee of a Japanese company predicts that a total of 400,000 units of a new luxury automobile model can be sold to retail dealers for an average price of $36,000. Its product life cycle is predicted to be eight years: three years in product development and five years in the marketplace. A **product life cycle** is the time from original research and development to the end of a product's sales and customer servicing. Some products in high technology have life cycles of less than one year. Other products, such as automobiles and refrigerators, have much longer life cycles.

After the sales price and production volume have been predicted, a planning committee composed of representatives of the five business function areas (design, engineering, manufacturing, marketing, and accounting) calculates desired profit and allowable cost for the model's life cycle. Desired profit often is a set percentage of target sales. Allowable cost is the cost that will allow, or result in, the desired profit. This cost includes all costs in the value chain, but we concentrate on the manufacturing function here. Thus our measure of profit is manufacturing contribution—life-cycle sales less manufacturing costs directly traceable to the product.

The allowable average manufacturing cost over the product's life cycle may be computed as follows:

Life-cycle average sales price	$36,000
Desired life-cycle manufacturing contribution (45%)	16,200
Allowable life-cycle average manufacturing cost	$19,800

The next step in the development process is preparation of the initial **life-cycle budget**. This budget compiles predicted life-cycle revenues and costs of the automobile model using current technology and methods, before any cost-reduction efforts. The budget for our proposed model is given in Exhibit 23-4.

OBJECTIVE 5

Prepare a life-cycle budget for a product

The budget begins with sales minus the most prominent category of manufacturing cost, direct materials and parts. This category often is about 70% of the total manufacturing cost of a Japanese automobile. The Japanese industry depends heavily on its suppliers and works closely with them from early stages of design through the entire product life cycle.

The life-cycle budget shows the costs of all activities in the value chain that can be directly linked to the product. For example, depreciation on new production equipment (such as molds for the model's parts) is included. The budget excludes any allocations of indirect costs. Depreciation on existing equipment is excluded because it will be the same regardless of whether the new product is added. Thus, all costs in the budget are incremental. They will be incurred if the product is accepted, but not otherwise.

EXHIBIT 23-4   Initial Life-Cycle Budget
Proposed Automobile Model
Predicted Sales Volume, 400,000 units

Sales @ $36,000		$14,400,000,000	(100%)
Direct materials and purchased parts @ $15,000		6,000,000,000	
Material contribution margin		8,400,000,000	
Other costs direct to product:			
Variable conversion costs @ $2,425:			
Indirect materials @ $400	$ 160,000,000		
Direct labor @ $1,500	600,000,000		
Indirect labor @ $300	120,000,000		
Utilities @ $200	80,000,000		
Other @ $25	10,000,000	970,000,000	
Variable conversion cost contribution margin		7,430,000,000	
Fixed conversion costs:			
Indirect labor	$ 200,000,000		
Depreciation on equipment	1,270,000,000		
Maintenance	200,000,000	1,670,000,000	
Product manufacturing contribution		5,760,000,000	(40%)
Other fixed costs:			
Design and engineering	$760,000,000		
Marketing	900,000,000		
Customer Service	450,000,000		
Other	50,000,000	2,160,000,000	
Life-cycle operating contribution		$3,600,000,000	(25%)

After preparing the initial life-cycle budget, the planning committee managers decide whether the project is worth pursuing further. The budgeted average manufacturing cost is $21,600 [($6,000,000,000 + $970,000,000 + $1,670,000,000) ÷ 400,000]. Because of fixed costs, this unit amount is sensitive to variations in sales volume. At the predicted volume of 400,000 units, the average cost is $1,800 ($21,600 − $19,800) more than the allowable cost. Nonetheless, top management might approve the model. Why? Because cost-reduction efforts throughout the value chain, especially in the design stage, might bring the budgeted cost down to the allowable amount.

Target Costing

OBJECTIVE 6

Relate target costing and kaizen costing to continuous improvement

To achieve allowable product costs, Japanese auto manufacturers attempt to reduce costs gradually through continuous improvement in manufacturing, marketing, and customer-service activities. However, they usually focus their cost-reduction efforts on the design stage. They have found that reductions built into the auto's design are both considerably larger and more quickly realized than reductions from later efforts. **Target costing** is a cost management technique that helps managers set goals for cost reductions through product design.

Suppose that members of the product-planning committee believe that gradual continuous improvement after production begins will trim $100 from the life-cycle average cost of each car. The target unit manufacturing cost therefore is $19,900 ($19,800 allowable average cost + $100). Designers, engineers, and management accountants work together to develop a model whose average manufacturing cost *at the beginning of production* does not exceed the target cost of $19,900.

In the target-costing process, the planning team budgets a currently attainable cost for each element of the proposed car. Many of these elements will be similar, if not identical, to elements in existing cars. Exhibit 23-5 shows the general approach. Then, cost planners use their experience and company precedents to establish cost-reduction goals for the design divisions in charge of the elements. At that point, value engineering begins.

Value-engineering (VE) refers to design activities aimed at achieving cost targets while designing high-quality, high-performance products that satisfy the customer. Engineers dissect the company's processes and individual activ-

EXHIBIT 23-5 *Approach to Budgeting Manufacturing Costs*

	Product Elements					
Cost	Engine	Body	Drive Train	Electronics	Interior	Other
Direct materials						
Purchased parts						
Indirect materials						
Direct labor						
Other						
Total						

ities, rethinking their whys and hows. After close study, engineers may redesign a painting method or the shape of a part. They may specify new materials or different tolerances or substitute parts that are common to several product lines for parts designed for one product only. For example, *The Wall Street Journal* reported the following comment by an engineer whose design team was instructed to cut the number of unique fasteners used in Nissan vehicles by 50%: "If we use fewer different screws, plant workers can save time changing the heads on their power tools," he explains, drilling an imaginary bolt with his index finger. "We can save 50 seconds per car. And one second equals one yen."

Through VE, design teams reduce the budgeted costs of elements to their target costs. Target costing proceeds as follows (numbers assumed):

Product Element	Budgeted Cost	Value Engineering Cost Reduction	Target Cost
Engine	$3,000	$300	$2,700
Body	6,000	500	5,500
Drive train	2,000	150	1,850
.	.	.	.
.	.	.	.
.	.	.	.
Unit cost	$21,600	$1,700	$19,900

Management accountants play important roles in the value-engineering process. First, accountants help engineers identify those expensive activities where costs can be reduced the most. Second, they help to determine the cost effects of design modifications, which pinpoint when target costs have been reached. In the opening vignette, accountants used activity-based cost data to help Chrysler managers determine the optimal number of wiring harnesses for a new minivan.

Kaizen Costing

The Japanese word for continuous improvement is *kaizen*. Japanese managers describe the relentless pursuit of cost reduction in the manufacturing stage as **kaizen costing**. In manufacturing, continuous improvement means achieving planned reductions in cost drivers such as setup times, waiting times, number of parts, and number of suppliers. Ideally, kaizen costing helps companies to continuously lower the standard costs of their products from their first months of production to the final months of their life cycles. As in target costing, accountants help not only to identify cost drivers but also to measure the financial effects of improvements.

The contributions of target costing and kaizen costing to achieving the allowable life-cycle manufacturing cost of our example automobile model can be illustrated as follows:

	Life-cycle sales price		$36,000
	Desired life-cycle manufacturing contribution		16,200
Product Development and Design	Original budgeted cost	$21,600	
	Value-engineering cost reduction	1,700	
	Target cost	$19,900	
Manufacturing	Continuous improvement Kaizen costing	100	
	Allowable life-cycle cost		$19,800

Life-cycle budgeting, target costing, and kaizen costing are proven techniques for continuous improvement. Companies that combine these cost management tools with JIT production systems can become remarkably efficient. Note especially that target costing requires teamwork among the various functions of the business. Design engineers often lack hands-on production experience. They must work with manufacturing personnel and accountants so that product lines are carefully planned for low-cost manufacturing.

Continuous Improvement and the Management of Quality

The quality of goods and services is a major feature of global competition. Businesses that deliver the best quality in otherwise comparable products gain market share. Throughout the 1980s, Japanese automobile companies' share of the worldwide market soared, principally because of higher-quality products. Indeed, the nature of competition in many industries has been altered because of Japanese leadership in continuous improvement techniques.

Various definitions of quality exist. We define **quality** as the conformance of the attributes of a product or service with a specific set of standards. For example, Holiday Inns has standards for its hotel rooms regarding towels, soap, cleanliness, mattress firmness, light bulbs, television sets, and smoke alarms. The chain even has a standard for how long a customer should have to wait to be registered.

Total Quality Management

Total quality management (TQM) is a formal effort to improve quality throughout an organization's value chain. The focus of TQM extends horizontally across all business functions, from research and development through customer service. Accountants can help operating managers understand how decisions made in product design affect quality (and costs) in manufacturing or distribution. The quality focus also is vertical. Each business function examines its own activities and attempts to improve them.

A hallmark of TQM is its emphasis on educating, training, and cross-training employees in order to increase and broaden their skills and their ability to innovate. Motorola's purchasing department provides an example. The department's managers wanted to reduce the time taken to process a requisition. Before starting the project, the team took a two-day company course called

High Commitment, High Performance Team Training. Course topics included how to set priorities and how to disagree with others without insulting them.

The purchasing department initiative was judged the best of almost 4,000 entries in Motorola's 1992 quality competition. The team reduced the steps in handling a requisition from 17 to 6. Average processing time was slashed from 30 hours to 3. Now the department can process 45% more requisitions with no additional employees.

Types of Quality Costs

Business analysts have identified four types of quality-related costs:

OBJECTIVE 7

Contrast the four types of quality costs

1. **Prevention costs** are incurred to avoid poor-quality goods or services in the first place. For example, accounting firms invest heavily in training personnel to use appropriate auditing and consulting procedures. Better-trained accountants are more likely to follow company policies and make fewer errors.

2. **Appraisal costs** are incurred in detecting poor-quality goods or services. For example, Intel, a manufacturer of integrated circuits, uses several procedures to test its products. One procedure, called *burn-in*, heats the product in an oven to a temperature exceeding 2,000 degrees Centigrade. A circuit that fails the burn-in test has an unacceptably high likelihood of failing when being used by a customer.

3. **Internal failure costs** are incurred when poor-quality goods or services are detected before delivery to customers. An example is an auto-repair-shop mechanic reworking a faulty installation of a brake job after inspection by a supervisor. It is better to detect the problem in-house than to have the customer detect it.

4. **External failure costs** are incurred when poor-quality goods or services are detected after delivery to customers. The auto repair example applies here, except that the flawed brakes are discovered by the customer. External failures can devastate a company's reputation. To cite one example, Ford Motor Company has worked hard in recent years to overcome an earlier reputation for poor quality.

Exhibit 23-6 shows additional examples of the four types of quality costs. Many managers emphasize that investments in the front end of the value chain generate savings in the back end. They want their companies to *design and build* quality into the product or service rather than having to *inspect and repair* it later. Carefully designed products and processes and high levels of employee training reduce the costs of inspections, rework, and warranty claims. The theme of total quality management is to see the big picture of how subpar work in one business function can hurt the whole organization.

Nonfinancial Performance Measures

Review the four types of quality costs in Exhibit 23-6. Many of those costs are difficult to measure. Cost accounting classifications often cannot identify individual components. For example, design engineering, a prevention cost, may have to be divided among quality, product development, process development, and other activities. This allocation is necessarily subjective. It is especially difficult to measure the costs of external failures. Many managers believe that these quality costs dwarf the other three types. The most prominent exter-

EXHIBIT 23-6 *Examples of Costs of Quality*

Prevention Costs	Appraisal Costs
Training of company personnel and supplier personnel	Inspection costs of incoming materials
Improved materials	Costs of overseeing suppliers
Preventive maintenance	Inspection at various stages of production
Design engineering	Inspection of final products or services
Improved equipment and processes	

Internal Failure Costs	External Failure Costs
Yield loss caused by quality-related downtime	Lost profits from lost customers
Rework	Warranty costs
Scrap	Field service costs
Rejected product units	Sales returns and allowances due to quality problems
Disposal of rejected units	Product liability claims

nal failure cost—profits lost because an unhappy customer never comes back—is not recorded in the accounts at all.

TQM programs do not necessarily compile the costs of quality. Instead, they emphasize nonfinancial measures that are useful for day-to-day control purposes. Examples include number of customer complaints, percentage of defective units, and first-time inspection pass rates. Companies use benchmarking to evaluate their performance on these dimensions. **Benchmarking** is the comparison of current performance with some standard. The standard often is the best practice by an outside organization.

Exhibit 23-7 lists examples of nonfinancial measures of quality used by the Cummins Engine Company, a manufacturer of diesel engines and trucks. The company's emphasis on continuous improvement of nonfinancial quality measures exemplifies how businesses are broadening the scope of performance measurement. Many companies no longer are concentrating solely on profitability measures such as operating income or return on investment. Companies are linking managers' compensation to performance on nonfinancial measures of quality, innovation, speed to market, and customer satisfaction. Nonetheless, the ultimate test is long-term profitability.

More and more managers believe that nonfinancial measures are the keys to profitability. They base a strategy for gaining competitive advantage on links such as the following:

EXHIBIT 23-7 *Examples of Nonfinancial Measures of Quality Cummins Engine Company*

Percent of engines passing test first time
Incoming supplier quality—percent of suppliers having acceptance rate of 98% or better
Average machine downtime of bottleneck machines
Number of unplanned machine breakdowns
Number of product failures in the field
Percent of engines delivered on time
Average supplier delivery in percent of parts on time
Training hours as percent of total hours worked

Nonfinancial Performance Measures	Financial Performance Measures

Quality ⎤
⎟
Innovation ⎬ → Customer satisfaction → Long-run profitability → Long-run shareholder value
⎟
Speed ⎦

In short, continuous improvement of critical nonfinancial performance measures is essential for long-run success.

Summary Problem for Your Review

The Ishikawa Motorcycle Company is considering a new product line with a budgeted average sales price of $8,000. The desired life-cycle manufacturing contribution is $3,000 per motorcycle.

Required

1. Compute the allowable manufacturing cost per unit.
2. The kaizen cost reduction for the product line's life cycle is expected to be $250 per motorcycle. The value-engineering cost reduction goal has been set at $900 per unit. Compute the target cost and the budgeted unit manufacturing cost in the initial life-cycle budget.
3. Some of Ishikawa Company's accounts are:
   a. Product callback repairs
   b. Training of supplier personnel
   c. Inspection costs of incoming materials
   d. Scrap

   Identify each cost as belonging to one of the following categories of quality costs: prevention, appraisal, internal failure, or external failure.

SOLUTION TO REVIEW PROBLEM

1. Allowable cost is $8,000 − $3,000 = $5,000.
2. Target cost is $5,000 + $250 = $5,250. Initial budgeted cost is $5,250 + $900 = $6,150.
3. a. External failure
   b. Prevention
   c. Appraisal
   d. Internal failure

Summary

Activity-based costing (ABC) is a system that focuses on activities as the fundamental cost objects. It uses the costs of those activities as building blocks for compiling the costs of products and other cost objects. Activity-based costing is general in that it can be used in either a job order costing system or a process costing system and by either a manufacturing company or a service firm.

Just-in-time (JIT) production systems are designed to eliminate waste. They are characterized by sequentially arranged production activities, low setup times, demand-pull production scheduling, minimal inventories, and highly trained and committed employees. JIT systems rely on dependable suppliers to deliver materials just as they are needed for production. Goods often are sold before they are produced.

Backflush costing is a standard costing system that begins with output completed and works backward to apply manufacturing costs to units sold and to inventories. The more-common standard costing system is a sequential tracking system that moves forward, step by step, from direct materials inventory through cost of goods sold.

To be competitive, companies are focusing increasingly on continuous improvement. *Life-cycle budgeting* compiles predicted revenues and costs of a product line for its entire life. *Target costing* is a cost management technique that helps managers set goals for cost reductions through product design. *Value engineering* refers to design activities aimed at reducing the cost of a product without reducing its ability to satisfy the customer via high quality and high performance. *Kaizen costing* is an explicit plan for cost reduction at the manufacturing stage. Life-cycle budgeting, target costing, and kaizen costing are examples of continuous improvement in action.

Quality is the conformance of the attributes of a product or service with a specific set of standards. *Total quality management* (TQM) is a formal effort to improve quality throughout an organization's value chain. Four types of quality costs are *prevention, appraisal, internal failure,* and *external failure.*

Nonfinancial measures are widely used to measure performance in quality management. *Benchmarking* compares current performance with some standard, which is often the best practice of a leading outsider.

Self-Study Questions

1. Activity-based product costs are likely to be more accurate than product costs computed with *(p. 1059)*
    a. A job order costing system
    b. A process costing system
    c. A plantwide rate
    d. Kaizen costing

2. Activity-based costing is part of an overall process known as *(p. 1062)*
    a. Activity-based management
    b. Total quality management
    c. Just-in-time manufacturing
    d. Backflush costing

3. Investments in activity-based costing systems are justified only if they lead to *(p. 1062)*
    a. More-accurate product costs
    b. More-accurate inventory values
    c. Better cost-driver analysis
    d. Better management decisions

4. Which of the following does not represent non-value-added activities? *(p. 1065)*
    a. Wait time
    b. Processing time
    c. Moving time
    d. Inspection time

5. Just-in-time (JIT) production systems are characterized by *(p. 1065-66)*
    a. Long setup times
    b. Small batch sizes
    c. Machines arranged by function
    d. Employee departments that specialize in machine setups

6. In backflush costing systems, trigger points are points in operations that prompt (p. 1067)
   a. Entries in the internal accounting system
   b. Collections of receivables
   c. Issuances of purchase requisitions
   d. Additions to cost of goods sold

7. Backflush costing is noteworthy because it eliminates the use of the following separate account (p. 1068)
   a. Work in process
   b. Accounts receivable
   c. Finished goods
   d. Cost of goods sold

8. Value engineering is used to reduce costs from (p. 1073)
   a. Life-cycle sales price to allowable cost
   b. Initial budgeted cost to target cost
   c. Target cost to allowable cost
   d. Initial budgeted cost to allowable cost

9. Kaizen costing is a (p. 1073)
   a. Type of standard costing system
   b. Tool for compiling costs over a product's entire life cycle
   c. Tool that assists the product design state
   d. Tool that assists the manufacturing stage

10. Which of the following is an example of an internal failure cost? (p. 1076)
    a. Inspection of services
    b. Product liability claims
    c. Rework
    d. Design engineering

Answers to the Self-Study Questions follow the Accounting Vocabulary.

Accounting Vocabulary

Activity-based costing (ABC). A system that focuses on activities as the fundamental cost objects and uses the costs of those activities as building blocks for compiling the costs of products and other cost objects (p. 1057).

Activity-based management (ABM). A management process that focuses on the management of activities as the way to improve value received by customers (p. 1057).

Appraisal costs. Costs incurred in detecting poor-quality goods or services (p. 1075).

Backflush costing. A standard costing system that starts with output completed and works backward to apply manufacturing costs to units sold and to inventories (p. 1066).

Benchmarking. Comparison of current performance with some standard. The standard often is the best practice by an outside organization (p. 1076).

External failure costs. Costs incurred when poor-quality goods or services are detected after delivery to customers (p. 1075).

Internal failure costs. Costs incurred when poor-quality goods or services are detected before delivery to customers (p. 1075).

Just-in-time (JIT) production systems. Production systems designed to eliminate waste by such means as sequentially arranged production activities, low setup times, demand-pull production scheduling, and a high level of employee training and commitment (p. 1065).

Kaizen costing. The relentless pursuit of cost reduction in the manufacturing stage of a product's life cycle, achieved by planned reductions in cost drivers (p. 1073).

Life-cycle budget. A budget that compiles predicted revenues and costs of a product over its entire life cycle (p. 1071).

Non-value-added activities. Activities that do not increase customer value or satisfy a company need (p. 1065).

Prevention costs. Costs incurred to avoid poor-quality goods or services (p. 1075).

Product life cycle. The time from original research and development to the end of a product's sales and customer servicing *(p. 1070).*

Quality. The conformance of the attributes of a product or service with a specific set of standards *(p. 1074).*

Strategy. A set of business goals and the tactics to achieve them *(p. 1057).*

Target costing. A cost management technique that helps managers set goals for cost reductions through product design *(p. 1072).*

Throughput time. The time between receipt of purchased materials and completion of finished products *(p. 1064).*

Total quality management (TQM). A formal effort to improve quality throughout an organization's value chain *(p. 1074).*

Trigger points. Points in operations that prompt entries in the accounting records *(p. 1067).*

Value engineering. Design activities aimed at achieving cost targets while designing high-quality, high-performance products that satisfy the customer *(p. 1072).*

Answers to Self-Study Questions

1. c   3. d   5. b   7. a   9. d
2. a   4. b   6. a   8. b   10. c

ASSIGNMENT MATERIAL

Questions

1. "Activity-based costing systems provide more-accurate information than traditional systems that use one overhead cost driver. Every company should adopt ABC." Do you agree? Why or why not?

2. In what way do activity-based costing systems emphasize nonfinancial performance measures more than traditional product costing systems?

3. "Activity-based costing systems promote coordination and communication across the various functions within a company." Do you agree? Explain.

4. "For costing-system alternatives, accountants have activity-based costing, job order costing, and process costing." True or false? Explain.

5. Give three examples of technology that have made the gathering of activity-based accounting information less expensive.

6. Contrast the traditional and just-in-time (JIT) approaches to managing machinery setups.

7. Describe "demand-pull" production scheduling.

8. Companies that implement JIT production systems usually reduce the number of suppliers they use. Give two benefits of doing so.

9. The backflush costing account labeled "raw and in process" represents two accounts in a sequential tracking system. What are they?

10. How do management accountants using a backflush costing system compute the amount of a direct materials efficiency variance?

11. "Prevention costs are the most important quality costs." Explain.

12. Why is target costing somewhat more important than kaizen costing for achieving allowable life cycle manufacturing cost?

13. A new car's target cost is $15,000 per unit. Kaizen costing is expected to reduce its life-cycle average cost by $500. The car's life-cycle average sales

price is budgeted at $43,500. If management expects the model to exactly achieve its allowable average cost, what is the desired life-cycle manufacturing contribution percentage (manufacturing contribution ÷ sales price)?

14. "Data from an activity-based accounting system help managers evaluate prevention costs in a total quality management program." Explain.

15. "Financial performance measures are used almost exclusively to evaluate quality management efforts." Do you agree? Why or why not?

Exercises

Exercise 23-1   *Product costing in an activity-based costing system*   **(L.O. 1)**

Amarillo Motor Company uses activity-based costing (ABC) to account for its manufacturing process. Company managers have identified four manufacturing activities: materials handling, machine setup, insertion of parts, and finishing. The budgeted conversion costs for 19X5 and their cost drivers are as follows:

Manufacturing Activity	Total Budgeted Cost	Cost Driver Chosen as Application Base
Materials handling	$24,000	Number of parts
Machine setup	2,400	Number of setups
Insertion of parts	60,000	Number of parts
Finishing	9,000	Finishing direct labor hours
	$95,400	

Amarillo Motor expects to produce 2,000 electric motors during the year. The motors are expected to use 120,000 parts, require 6 setups, and consume 500 hours of finishing time.

Required

1. Compute the four application rates for activity costs.
2. Compute the average manufacturing cost of each motor (excluding direct materials).

Exercise 23-2   *Product costing in activity-based and traditional systems*   **(L.O. 1)**

Panhandle Electric Motor Co. (PEMCO) has an activity-based costing (ABC) system very similar to that of its chief rival, Amarillo Motor Company (Exercise 23-1). PEMCO's system has the same four activity categories and the same activity cost drivers. For 19X6, PEMCO's budgeted ABC application rates are:

Manufacturing Activity	Cost Driver Chosen as Application Base	Cost per Unit of Application Base
Materials handling	Number of parts	$ .25
Machine setup	Number of setups	300.00
Insertion of parts	Number of parts	.75
Finishing	Finishing direct labor hours	20.00

PEMCO produces two electric motor models: standard and deluxe. Budgeted data for 19X6 are as follows:

	Standard	Deluxe
Parts per unit	50.0	70.0
Setups per 1,000 units	3.0	3.0
Finishing direct labor hours per unit	0.1	0.5
Total direct labor hours per unit	2.0	4.0

The company's managers expect to produce 1,000 units of each model during the year.

Required

1. Compute the total budgeted conversion cost for 19X6.
2. Compute the unit conversion cost of each model.
3. Assume that PEMCO budgets conversion costs in the amount computed in Requirement 1. Also assume that PEMCO does not use an ABC system, but applies total conversion cost to products using a plantwide rate based on total direct labor hours. Compute the plantwide rate and use it to determine the conversion cost per motor for each model.

Exercise 23-3 *Activity-based costing and management decisions* *(L.O. 2)*

Refer to Exercise 23-2. For 19X7, PEMCO's managers have decided to use the same conversion costs per motor that they computed in 19X6. In addition to the unit conversion costs, the following data are budgeted for the company's standard and deluxe models for 19X7:

	Standard	Deluxe
Sales price	$110.00	$155.00
Direct materials	15.00	25.00

Suppose that because of limited machine-hour capacity, PEMCO can produce either 2,000 standard motors or 2,000 deluxe motors.

Required

1. If the company's managers rely on the ABC unit cost data computed in Exercise 23-2, which model will they decide to manufacture? (Assume that all nonmanufacturing costs are the same for both models.)
2. If the managers rely on the plantwide-rate cost data, which model will they produce?
3. Which course of action will yield more income for PEMCO?

Exercise 23-4 *Recording manufacturing costs for a backflush costing system* *(L.O. 4)*

Advanced MicroManufacturing (AMM) produces electronic components. AMM uses a backflush costing system with two trigger points: the purchase of direct materials and the transfer of completed units to finished goods. One of the company's products has a standard direct materials cost of $4 per unit and a standard conversion cost of $20 per unit.

During 19X3, AMM produced 500,000 units of the component and sold 480,000. It purchased direct materials having a standard cost of $2,100,000, and incurred actual conversion costs totaling $9,950,000.

Required

1. Prepare summary journal entries for 19X3.
2. Assume that AMM's January 1, 19X3, balance of the raw and in process (RIP) inventory account was $80,000. What is the December 31, 19X3, balance?
3. Is conversion cost overapplied or underapplied for the year? By how much?

Exercise 23-5 *Recording variances in a backflush costing system* **(L.O. 4)**

Ramius Engineering produces sonar components that are used on nuclear submarines. The company uses a backflush costing system with trigger points at direct materials purchase and completion of goods. In 19X4, Ramius Engineering purchased direct materials having a standard cost of $8,000,000.

Required

1. Record the journal entries that correspond to the following variances:
   a. Favorable direct materials price variance of $100,000.
   b. Unfavorable direct materials price variance of $50,000.
   c. Favorable direct materials efficiency variance of $70,000.
   d. Unfavorable direct materials efficiency variance of $40,000.
2. Conversion cost is underapplied by $60,000 in 19X4. Record the entry to close the Conversion Cost account to Cost of Goods Sold.

Exercise 23-6 *Preparing a life-cycle budget* **(L.O. 5)**

Robotic Solutions (RS) produces robots for computer-controlled manufacturing systems. Sue Patrick, the engineering vice-president, is developing a proposal for a new line of robots with an expected life cycle of five years. The sales staff predicts that a total of 10,000 robots can be sold at an average sales price of $15,000. Patrick believes that with today's technology and methods, RS could manufacture the robots for the following direct product-line costs:

Fixed conversion costs	$34,000,000
Direct materials/unit	4,500
Variable conversion costs/unit	1,400

Required

1. Prepare an initial life-cycle budget through the product-line manufacturing contribution.
2. At the predicted volume level of 10,000 robots, what is the original budgeted cost per unit?
3. What percent of sales revenue is the initial product-line manufacturing contribution?

Exercise 23-7 *Using target costing and kaizen costing to achieve cost reductions* **(L.O. 6)**

Refer to Exercise 23-6. The sales staff of Robotic Solutions (RS) is less sure of their original sales volume prediction than they would like to be. They would not be surprised if life-cycle sales volume is as low as 8,000 units or as high as 12,000. Vice-president Sue Patrick is uneasy about the degree of uncertainty that exists.

The top management of RS has set as a goal for each product line a life-cycle manufacturing contribution of 44% of sales revenue. Patrick expects kaizen costing efforts to reduce the life-cycle average manufacturing cost of the robots by $100.

Required

1. Compute the allowable life-cycle average manufacturing cost of the product line.
2. Compute the target cost of the product line.
3. Determine the value engineering cost reduction per robot that is required to achieve the target cost if the life-cycle sales volume is (a) 10,000 units, (b) 8,000 units, (c) 12,000 units.

Exercise 23-8 *Types of quality costs* (L.O. 7)

Household Engineering (HE) makes electronic components for microwave ovens. Fred Rogers, the HE president, recently instructed financial vice-president Ken Madden to develop a total quality control (TQC) program. "If we don't at least match the quality improvements our competitors are making," he told Madden, "we'll soon be out of business."

Madden began his task by listing various "costs of quality" that Household Engineering incurs. The first five items that came to mind were:

a. Costs of inspecting components in one of HE's production processes
b. Labor costs of product design engineers who work to design components that will withstand electrical overloads
c. Costs of reworking defective components after discovery by company inspectors
d. Costs of electronic components returned by customers
e. Travel costs incurred by HE customer representatives in traveling to customer sites to inspect defective products

Required

Classify each of the five items as a prevention cost, an appraisal cost, an internal failure cost, or an external failure cost.

Problems   *(Group A)*

Problem 23-1A *Product costing in an activity-based system* (L.O. 1)

A Texas Instruments factory assembles and tests printed circuit (PC) boards. Using assumed numbers, consider the following data regarding PC Board XR1, which is used in various computers:

Direct materials	$65.00
Conversion costs applied..................................	?
Total manufacturing product cost	?

The activities consumed in building the PC boards follow:

Manufacturing Activity	Cost Driver Conversion Costs Applied for Each Activity	
1. Start station	Number of raw PC boards	1 × $.90 = $ .90
2. Dip insertion	Number of dip insertions	20 × .25 = ?
3. Manual insertion	Number of manual insertions	12 × ? = 7.20
4. Wave solder	Number of boards soldered	1 × 3.50 = 3.50
5. Backload	Number of backload insertions	? × .70 = 4.90
6. Test	Standard time each board is in test activity	.25 × 80.00 = ?
7. Defect analysis	Standard time for defect analysis and repair	.16 × ? = 8.00
Total		$?

Required

1. Fill in the blanks in both the opening schedule and the list of activities.
2. How is direct labor identified with products under this product costing system?
3. Why might managers favor this activity-based accounting system instead of the older system, which applied conversion costs based on direct labor?

Problem 23-2A *Product costing in an activity-based system* **(L.O. 1)**

Blume Furniture Company manufactures rocking chairs in its two plants in West Virginia. The company uses activity-based costing, and its activities and related data follow:

Manufacturing Activity	Budgeted Conversion Costs for 19X8	Cost Driver Chosen as Application Base	Conversion Cost per Unit of Application Base
Materials handling	$ 200,000	Number of parts	$ 0.25
Cutting	880,000	Number of parts	1.10
Assembling	3,000,000	Direct labor hours	15.00
Painting	70,000	Number of painted units	2.00

Two styles of chairs were produced in March, the standard chair and an unpainted chair, which had fewer parts and required no painting. Their quantities, direct materials costs, and other data follow:

Product	Units Produced	Direct Materials Costs	Number of Parts	Assembling Direct Labor Hours
Standard chair	5,000	$90,000	100,000	7,500
Unpainted chair	1,000	15,000	15,000	1,200

Required

1. Compute the total manufacturing costs and unit costs of the standard chairs and the unpainted chairs.
2. Suppose upstream activities, such as product design, were analyzed and applied to the standard chairs at $3 each and the unpainted chairs at $2 each. Moreover, similar analyses were conducted of downstream activities, such as distribution, marketing, and customer service. The downstream costs applied were $21 per standard chair and $16 per unpainted chair. Compute the full product cost per unit.
3. Which costs are used for reporting in the external financial statements? Which costs are used for management decision making? Explain the difference.

Problem 23-3A *Recording manufacturing costs for a JIT backflush costing system* **(L.O. 3, 4)**

Hi-Tek Products (HTP) produces mobile beepers. The company has a JIT production system and uses backflush costing. Its backflush system has two trigger points that prompt entries in its accounting records:

- Purchase of raw materials and parts
- Completion of beepers

HTP has two inventory accounts, raw and in process (RIP) and finished goods. On August 1, 19X3, the account balances were:

- RIP inventory $1,000
- Finished goods 2,500

HTP's standard cost per beeper is: direct materials, $30, and conversion costs, $20. The following data pertain to August manufacturing and sales activity:

Raw materials and components purchased	$301,000
Conversion costs incurred	202,000
Number of units completed	10,000
Number of units sold	9,900

Required

1. What are the major features of a just-in-time (JIT) production system?
2. Prepare summary journal entries for August. Assume that there are no direct materials variances and that underapplied or overapplied conversion costs are closed to cost of goods sold at the end of the year.
3. Now assume that the standard cost of the raw materials and components purchased in August is $300,700. The actual cost remains $301,000. HTP accountants have computed the following variances: direct materials price variance, $300 unfavorable; direct materials efficiency variance, $700 unfavorable. Make the journal entries to record these variances.
4. Refer to Requirement 3. What is the August 31, 19X3 balance of RIP inventory?

Problem 23-4A *Recording backflush costs, second trigger point in sale* (L.O. 4)

Refer to Problem 23-3A. Hi-Tek Products (HTP) has a two-trigger-point backflush costing system, but now assume that the second trigger point is the sale, not the completion, of mobile beepers. The company has only one inventory account, labeled simply "Inventory." Only direct materials costs are assigned to the inventory account; the account balance is the sum of the costs of materials in the storeroom (if any), in process, and in finished units that have not been sold.

Conversion costs are not inventoried. They are applied, at standard, to units sold. Continue to assume that overapplied or underapplied conversion costs are closed to cost of goods sold at the end of the year.

Required

1. Prepare summary journal entries that correspond to the entries you prepared in Problem 23-3A, Requirement 2.
2. Why might a company use the point of sale as the second trigger point instead of the point of completion?

Problem 23-5A *Life-cycle budgeting, target costing, and kaizen costing* (L.O. 5, 6)

The Computron Company makes personal computers that it sells through catalogs. Shown below is the *final* life-cycle budget for a new product line. The budget takes into account both expected value-engineering cost reductions and expected kaizen cost reductions from the company's new total quality management (TQM) initiative.

Final Life-Cycle Budget
Proposed Computer Product Line

Sales	$250,000,000
Direct materials.......................................	67,500,000
Materials contribution margin........................	182,500,000
Variable conversion costs............................	22,500,000
Variable conversion cost contribution margin	160,000,000
Fixed conversion costs	60,000,000
Product-line manufacturing contribution	$100,000,000

This budget allows the new product line to exactly achieve management's desired life-cycle manufacturing contribution.

Required

1. Assume that the final life-cycle budget is based on an expected life-cycle sales volume of 100,000 units. Compute the life-cycle average sales price. Then compute the allowable life-cycle average manufacturing cost.
2. Repeat Requirement 1 for a sales volume of 200,000 units.
3. Again assume that the budget is based on 100,000 units. Suppose that Computron's managers expect kaizen costing efforts to reduce variable conversion costs by $50 per unit and fixed conversion costs by a total of $10,000,000 over the computer line's life cycle. Calculate the target cost.
4. If Computron's engineers predict a value engineering cost reduction of $250 per unit, what is the original budgeted cost per computer?

Problem 23-6A *Analyzing costs of quality* (L.O. 7)

Blade Close, Inc. (BCI) is using a costs-of-quality approach to evaluate design engineering efforts for a new electric shaver. BCI's senior managers expect the now-concluding engineering work to yield sizable savings in the costs of appraisal, internal failure, and external failure activities. The predicted reductions in activities over the two-year life cycle of the shaver are shown below. Also shown are the estimated unit activity costs.

Activity	Predicted Reduction in Activity Units	Unit Activity Cost
Inspection of incoming materials	300	$20
Inspection of work in process	200	25
Number of defective units discovered in-house	5,000	15
Number of defective units discovered by customers	800	30
Lost unit sales to dissatisfied customers	200	45

Required

1. Calculate the predicted quality-cost savings from the design engineering work.
2. Assume that BCI spent $40,000 on design engineering for the new shaver. What is the net benefit of this "preventive" quality activity?
3. What major difficulty would BCI managers have in implementing this costs-of-quality approach? What alternative approach to quality improvement could they use?

Problem 23-1B *Product costing in an activity-based system* **(L.O. 1)**

A National Semiconductor factory assembles and tests printed circuit (PC) boards. Using assumed numbers, consider the following data regarding PC Board J47, which is used in various computers:

Direct materials	$71.00
Conversion costs applied................................	?
Total manufacturing product cost	$?

The activities consumed in building the PC boards follow:

Manufacturing Activity	Cost Driver	Conversion Costs Applied for Each Activity
1. Start station	No. of raw PC boards	1 × $1.30 = $1.30
2. Dip insertion	No. of dip insertions	? × .60 = 6.00
3. Manual insertion	No. of manual insertions	11 × .80 = ?
4. Wave solder	No. of boards soldered	1 × 1.50 = 1.50
5. Backload	No. of backload insertions	6 × ? = 4.20
6. Test	Standard time each board is in test activity	.20 × 90.00 = ?
7. Defect analysis	Standard time for defect analysis and repair	.10 × 1.3? = 7.00
Total		$?

Required

1. Fill in the blanks in both the opening schedule and the list of activities.
2. How is direct labor identified with products under this product costing system?
3. Why might managers favor this activity-based accounting system instead of the older system, which applied conversion costs based on direct labor?

Problem 23-2B *Product costing in an activity-based system* **(L.O. 1)**

Janelli, Inc., manufactures chairs and uses an activity-based costing system. Janelli's activity areas and related data follow:

Manufacturing Activity Area	Budgeted Conversion Costs for 19X0	Cost Driver Used as Application Base	Conversion Cost per Unit of Application Base
Materials handling	$ 100,000	Number of parts	$ 0.10
Cutting	1,000,000	Number of parts	1.30
Assembly	3,000,000	Direct labor hours	18.00
Finishing	60,000	Number of finished units	3.00

Two styles of chairs were produced in March, the standard chair and an unfinished chair, which had fewer parts and required no finishing. The quantities, direct material costs, and other data follow:

	Units Produced	Direct Material Costs	Number of Parts	Assembling Direct Labor Hours
Standard chair	2,000	$24,000	30,000	3,000
Unfinished chair	3,000	27,000	36,000	2,800

Required

1. Compute the total manufacturing costs and unit costs of the standard chairs and the unfinished chairs.
2. Suppose upstream activities, such as product design, were analyzed and applied to the standard chairs at $4 each and the unfinished chairs at $3 each. Moreover, similar analyses were conducted of downstream activities, such as distribution, marketing, and customer service. The downstream costs applied were $18 per standard chair and $15 per unfinished chair. Compute the full product cost per unit.
3. Which costs are used for reporting in the external financial statements? Which costs are used for management decision making? Explain the difference.

Problem 23-3B *Recording manufacturing costs for a JIT backflush costing system* **(L.O. 3, 4)**

Nickoh Time Manufacturers (NTM) produces precision hydraulic system components. The company uses backflush costing for its just-in-time (JIT) production system. Its backflush system has two trigger points that prompt entries in its accounting records:

- Purchase of direct materials
- Completion of hydraulic system components

NTM has two inventory accounts, raw and in process (RIP) and finished goods. On December 1, 19X3, the account balances were:

- RIP inventory $3,000
- Finished goods   5,000

The standard cost of a component is $40: $15 direct materials plus $25 conversion costs. Data for December's activity follow:

Direct materials purchased	$227,000
Conversion costs incurred	373,000
Number of components completed	15,000
Number of components sold	14,800

Required

1. What are the major features of a just-in time (JIT) production system?
2. Prepare summary journal entries for December. Assume that there are no direct materials variances. Also assume that underapplied or overapplied conversion costs are closed to cost of goods sold monthly.
3. Now assume that the standard cost of direct materials purchased in December is $228,000. The actual cost remains $227,000. NTM accountants have computed the following variances: direct materials price variance, $1,000 favorable; direct materials efficiency variance, $800 favorable. Make the journal entries to record these variances.
4. Refer to Requirement 3. What is the December 31, 19X3, balance of RIP inventory?

Problem 23-4B *Recording backflush costs, second trigger point is sale* **(L.O. 4)**

Refer to Problem 23-3B. Nickoh Time Manufacturers (NTM) has a two-trigger-point backflush costing system, but now assume that the second trigger point is the sale, not the completion, of hydraulic system components. The company has only one inventory account, labeled simply "Inventory." Only direct materials costs are assigned to the inventory account; the account balance is the sum of the costs of materials in the storeroom (if any), in process, and in finished units that have not been sold.

Conversion costs are not inventoried. They are applied, at standard, to units sold. Continue to assume that the conversion costs account is closed to cost of goods sold monthly.

Required

1. Prepare summary journal entries that correspond to the entries you prepared in Problem 23-3B, Requirement 2.
2. Why might a company use the point of sale as the second trigger point instead of the point of completion?

Problem 23-5B *Life-cycle budgeting, target costing, and kaizen costing* **(L.O. 5, 6)**

Southwestern Telecom produces telephones. Shown below is the *final* life-cycle budget for a new product line. The budget takes into account both expected value-engineering cost reductions and expected kaizen cost reductions from the company's new total quality management (TQM) initiative.

Final Life-cycle Budget
Proposed Telephone Product Line

Sales	$95,000,000
Direct materials	26,000,000
Materials contribution margin	69,000,000
Variable conversion costs	10,000,000
Variable conversion cost contribution margin	59,000,000
Fixed conversion costs	14,000,000
Product-line manufacturing contribution	$45,000,000

This budget allows the new product line to exactly achieve management's desired life-cycle manufacturing contribution.

Required

1. Assume that the final life-cycle budget is based on an expected life-cycle sales volume of 1,000,000 telephones. Compute the life-cycle average sales price. Then compute the allowable life-cycle average manufacturing cost.
2. Repeat Requirement 1 for a sales volume of 2,000,000 telephones.
3. Again assume the budget is based on 1,000,000 units. Suppose that Southwestern Telecom's managers expect kaizen costing efforts to reduce variable conversion costs by $4 per unit and fixed conversion costs by a total of $2,000,000 over the product line's life cycle. Calculate the target cost.
4. If Southwestern Telecom's engineers predict a value-engineering cost reduction of $14 per unit, what is the original budgeted cost per telephone?

Problem 23-6B *Analyzing costs of quality* **(L.O. 7)**

Popular Electronics, Inc. (PEI) is using a costs-of-quality approach to evaluate design engineering efforts for a new laser disc player. PEI's senior managers expect the now-concluding engineering work to yield sizable savings in the costs of appraisal, internal failure, and external failure activities. The predicted reductions in activities over the two-year life cycle of the player are shown below. Also shown are the estimated unit activity costs.

Activity	Predicted Reduction in Activity Units	Unit Activity Cost
Inspection of incoming materials	500	$ 40
Inspection of work in process	300	20
Number of defective units discovered in-house	2,000	45
Number of defective units discovered by customers	500	70
Lost unit sales to dissatisfied customers	150	100

Required

1. Calculate the predicted quality-cost savings from the design engineering work.
2. Suppose PEI spent $175,000 on design engineering for the new laser disc player. What is the net benefit of this "preventive" quality activity?
3. What major difficulty would PEI managers have in implementing this costs-of-quality approach? What alternative approach to quality improvement could they use?

Extending Your Knowledge

Decision Problems

1. Costing Jobs with a Plantwide Overhead Rate and Then with Activity-Based Costing Rates and Making a Decision That Is Based on the Resulting Product Costs. (L.O. 2)
National Electronics Systems (NES) is a government contractor that specializes in electronics systems for military applications. The company's current job order cost accounting system has two direct cost categories, direct materials and direct labor. Indirect manufacturing cost (overhead) is applied to jobs at the single rate of $23 per direct labor hour.

An NES task force headed by the senior management accountant recently designed an activity-based costing system with five activities. Pertinent data follow:

Activity	Cost Driver Used as Application Base	Cost per Unit of Application Base
Materials handling	Number of parts	$ .50
Machine setup	Number of setups	500.00
Machining	Machining hours	22.00
Assembling	Assembling direct labor hours	18.00
Shipping	Number of shipments	1,200.00

All data necessary for both budgeting and job costing with this ABC system are collected automatically.

National Electronics Systems has been awarded two new government contracts, which will be produced as Job A and Job B. Budget data relating to the contracts are shown below.

	Job A	Job B
Direct materials cost	$30,000	$210,000
Direct labor cost	12,000	160,000
Number of parts	2,000	15,000
Number of setups	4	6
Number of machining hours	700	3,000
Assembling direct labor hours	200	1,500
Number of shipments	1	1
Total direct labor hours	600	8,000
Number of output units	100	1,000

Required

1. Compute the unit manufacturing cost of each job using the current product costing system (with two direct cost categories and a single overhead application rate).

2. Suppose that NES adopts the ABC system for product costing. Compute the unit manufacturing cost of each job with this system, which has the same two direct cost categories as the current system but five activity-based application rates instead of a single plantwide rate.

3. Which costing system more accurately assigns to jobs the costs of the resources consumed to produce them? Explain.

4. A dependable company has offered to produce both jobs for NES for $600 per output unit. NES may subcontract (buy from the outside company) either Job A only, Job B only, or both jobs. Which course of action will NES managers take if they base their decision on (a) current system costs (b) ABC system costs? Which course of action will maximize the company's income? Explain.

2. *Using Life-Cycle Budgeting and Target Costing to Make a Production Decision. (L.O. 6)*

Suppose a U.S. automobile company is using life cycle budgeting and target costing in the development stage of a new luxury car. The predicted average selling price of the car is $33,333. The company's senior managers desire a life-cycle manufacturing contribution of 40% of sales revenue. Company engineers predict that kaizen costing efforts will reduce the average cost of cars over the manufacturing life cycle by $200.

The original budgeted cost of the automobile is $23,100. Should company managers decide to proceed with production if the value-engineering cost reduction is (a) $1,000 (b) $3,000? Explain.

Ethical Issue

Stanislav Precision Engineering manufactures complex metal products used in consumer goods. The company is under extreme pressure to reduce costs. Stanislav's managers have decided to implement a just-in-time production system in an effort to relentlessly pursue and eliminate waste. Company accountants have decided to design a new activity-based costing system to help identify and reduce non-value-added activities. They are seeking the help of all operating personnel to identify and classify activities.

The problem? Stanislav's employees do not want to cooperate with the accounting staff. Many believe that the ABC program is just one more way to cut jobs. Specifically, they are afraid that "non-value-added activities" will be linked to "non-value-added employees," who then will be fired.

Required

Is it ethical to ask employees to participate in a management initiative that may eliminate some employees' jobs? Why or why not?

Chapter 24

Special Business Decisions and Pricing

The Super Bowl is one of America's premier sporting events. It is also one of its most expensive advertising opportunities. To offset the projected $40 million cost of producing and broadcasting Super Bowl XXVII, NBC priced each of its 30-second commercial spots for the game at $850,000.

The 56 commercials that were run during Dallas's 52–17 victory over Buffalo yielded $45.9 million in revenue. But after advertising agency commissions and production costs were subtracted, NBC netted only $39 million—$1 million short of breaking even.

Did NBC lose money on the game? No. The network relied on the $6–$10 million in advertising revenues from pre- and postgame shows, plus revenues generated by its locally owned stations, to make a nice profit.

How did NBC decide to price each 30-second Super Bowl commercial at $850,000? How did NBC decide to allocate $40 million of its NFL contract fee to the Super Bowl? Questions like these require the best of management skills. This chapter shows how to use accounting data to make special decisions, that is, decisions that are not routine in running the business. It also explores the role of costs in making decisions about pricing.

Relevant Information for Decision Making

OBJECTIVE 1

Identify the relevant information for a special business decision

The main financial goals in business are to earn a profit and to have a strong financial position. Decisions center on how to achieve these goals. Decision making includes choosing among several courses of action, which means managers must make comparisons. The process has two steps: (1) identifying the information useful for making the decision and (2) analyzing the information to compare alternatives.

Relevant information is the expected future data that differ between the alternative courses of action. Which alternative will increase sales more? Which alternative will decrease expenses more? By studying expected future amounts resulting from alternative actions, managers can decide which action will help a business reach its goals.

Not all data influence a manager. Irrelevant data will not change a decision. For example, in some short-term situations the cost of fixed overhead will not change regardless of the action the manager takes. The manager, then, need not consider fixed overhead in making the decision. Determining which information is relevant—which data make a difference—is as important a skill as being able to analyze the information.

Let's consider an illustration of decision analysis using relevant information. Suppose Pendleton Woolen Mills is deciding whether to use pure wool or a wool-polyester blend in the manufacture of a line of sweaters. Pendleton predicts the costs shown at the top of page 1095.

Assume that cost is the chief consideration in this decision. The cost of direct materials is relevant because this cost differs between alternatives (the wool costs more than the wool blend). The labor cost is irrelevant because there is no difference in its cost whichever material is used.

We can compute the $4 cost difference between alternatives either from the cost of direct materials only or from total cost. It is helpful to know that there is

	Wool	Wool Blend	Cost Difference
Expected manufacturing cost per sweater:			
Direct materials	$10	$6	$4
Direct labor	2	2	0
Total cost of direct materials and direct labor	$12	$8	$4

a $4 total cost difference between the two alternatives. But it is more helpful for managers to know that the $4 cost difference results from the materials, not from labor. Failure to identify the reason for the difference may lead managers to make an unwise decision.

Let us emphasize this important point about special decision analysis: Relevant information is *expected future data that differ between alternative courses of action*. Managers should base their decisions on the expected future data rather than on historical data.

Historical data are usually supplied by the accounting system and are often useful guides to predictions. Bear in mind, however, that historical data by themselves are irrelevant. They are useful only to the extent that managers use them to help predict future data.

This approach to making decisions is called the *relevant information* approach. This approach applies to a wide variety of decisions, regardless of the specific characteristics of the particular situation. We turn now to a number of special decisions.

OBJECTIVE 2
Make nine types of special business decisions

Special Sales Order

Torino Corporation, a manufacturer of automobile parts, ordinarily sells oil filters for $3.20 each. A mail-order company has offered Torino $35,000 for 20,000 oil filters. That works out to a special sale price of $1.75 per oil filter ($35,000/20,000 = $1.75). This sale will not affect regular business in any way, it will not change fixed costs, it will not require any additional variable selling and administrative expense, it will put idle manufacturing capacity to use, and it will violate no antitrust laws regarding pricing. Torino's total manufacturing cost of an oil filter is $2.00. Should Torino accept the special order and make the sale at $1.75? At first glance, the answer appears to be no, because each oil filter costs $2.00. But more thought must go into making this decision.

To set the stage for the analysis, let's examine Torino's income statement. Exhibit 24-1 presents the income statement in two different formats. The income statement on the left is the standard format presented to stockholders, creditors, and other parties outside the company. It is based on absorption costing. It is called a *functional* income statement because it categorizes expenses by manufacturing, selling, and administrative functions.

The contribution margin format on the right is based on variable costing. It categorizes expenses primarily as variable and fixed. The contribution margin format is more useful for special decision analysis because it highlights how costs and income are affected by decisions. Recall that the contribution margin is revenue minus *all* variable expenses.

In this illustration, assume that Torino made and sold 250,000 oil filters before considering the special order. Under the functional costing approach,

EXHIBIT 24-1   *Functional Format and Contribution Margin Format for the Income Statement*

Torino Corporation
Income Statement
For the Year Ended December 31, 19X2

Functional Format		Contribution Margin Format		
Sales	$800,000	Sales		$800,000
Less manufacturing		Less variable expenses:		
cost of goods sold	500,000	Manufacturing.............	$300,000	
Gross margin	300,000	Selling and		
Less selling and administrative		administrative	75,000	375,000
expenses	200,000	Contribution margin		425,000
		Less fixed expenses:		
		Manufacturing.............	200,000	
		Selling and		
		administrative	125,000	325,000
Operating income............	$100,000	Operating income............		$100,000

the manufacturing cost per unit is $2.00 ($500,000/250,000 = $2.00). But the contribution margin approach shows that the variable manufacturing cost per unit is $1.20 ($300,000/250,000 = $1.20). We now answer the key question facing Torino: What difference would the special sale make to the company's operating income?

Correct Analysis: Contribution Margin Approach

The correct analysis concentrates on the *differences* in revenues, expenses, and operating income, as Exhibit 24-2 shows.

This special sale is expected to increase revenues by $35,000. The only cost affected by the sale is variable manufacturing expense, which is expected to increase by $24,000. Torino management predicts that the special sales order will increase operating income by $11,000. Fixed expenses do not enter the analysis because they do not change. Variable selling and administrative expenses are unchanged because Torino has to make no special effort to get the sale. To make the decision, Torino should compare the special sale price with the total variable expenses of producing and selling the goods. As long as the increase in revenues exceeds the increase in variable expenses, there is a contribution to fixed expenses and profits.

EXHIBIT 24-2   *Quick Summary of Special Sales Order Analysis*

Expected increase in revenues—sale of 20,000 oil filters × $1.75 each.	$35,000
Expected increase in expenses—variable manufacturing costs 20,000 oil filters × $1.20 each.............................	24,000
Expected increase in operating income	$11,000

Exhibit 24-3 gives Torino's income statements both without the special sales order (column 1) and with it (column 2). It shows operating income under both courses of action. Column 3 of Exhibit 24-3 repeats the quick summary by showing the differences caused by the special sales order. The quick summary presents the result of accepting the special sales order, an $11,000 increase in operating income.

You have just seen two correct ways of deciding whether to accept or reject the special sales order at a price less than total cost per unit: (1) a quick summary of differences (Exhibit 24-2) and (2) total revenues, expenses, and operating income under both courses of action (Exhibit 24-3). Whether to use a quick summary or a total analysis depends on the question you are addressing. The summary answers this question: What will be the *difference* in revenues, expenses, and operating income if the business accepts the special order? The total analysis shows the summary of differences and answers an additional question: What will total revenues, expenses, and operating income be under the alternative courses of action? Whether to accept or reject the special sales order can be decided from either analysis.

Incorrect Analysis: Ignoring the Nature of Fixed Costs

Let's look at an incorrect analysis of the Torino special sales order situation. The functional approach, shown on the left-hand side of Exhibit 24-1, leads to an incorrect measure of the change in expenses resulting from the sale.

> **OBJECTIVE 3**
> Explain the difference between correct analysis and incorrect analysis of a particular business decision

EXHIBIT 24-3 Total Special Order Analysis—Income Statements Without and With the Special Order

	Torino Corporation Income Statement For the Year Ended December 31, 19X2			
	(1) Without Special Order, 250,000 Units	(2) With Special Order, 270,000 Units	(3) Special-Order Difference, 20,000 Units Total	Per Unit
Sales	$800,000	$835,000	$35,000	$1.75
Variable expenses:				
Manufacturing	$300,000	$324,000	$24,000	$1.20
Selling and administrative	75,000	75,000	—	—
Total variable expenses	375,000	399,000	24,000	1.20
Contribution margin	425,000	436,000	11,000	.55
Fixed expenses:				
Manufacturing	200,000	200,000	—	—
Selling and administrative	125,000	125,000	—	—
Total fixed expenses	325,000	325,000	—	—
Operating income	$100,000	$111,000	$11,000	$ .55

Total manufacturing costs	$ 500,000
Units produced	÷ 250,000
Total cost per unit ($500,000/250,000)	$2.00
Expected increase in revenues—	
sale of 20,000 oil filters × $1.75 each	$ 35,000
Expected increase in expenses—*total* manufacturing costs—	
20,000 oil filters × $2.00 each	40,000
Expected decrease in operating income	$ (5,000)

A manager who follows this approach reasons that it costs $2 to make an oil filter. In this view, it is unprofitable to sell the product for less than $2. *The flaw in this analysis arises from treating a fixed cost as though it changes in total like a variable cost.* To manufacture one additional oil filter would increase Torino's expenses by the variable manufacturing cost of $1.20. Fixed expenses are irrelevant to the decision analysis because Torino will incur the fixed expenses whether or not the company accepts the special sales order. The addition of 20,000 oil filters will *not* add to *total* fixed expenses. As volume changes, manufacturing costs will increase at the rate of $1.20 per unit, not $2.00 per unit. In this analysis, the variable expenses are relevant, and the fixed expenses are irrelevant.

Short Run versus Long Run: Other Factors to Consider

The special sales order analysis focused on short-run factors—the expected effect on operating income. We must also consider long-run factors. What will be the impact on customers? Will acceptance of the order at $1.75 per unit hurt Torino's ability to make sales at the standard price of $3.20? Will regular customers find out about the special price and balk at paying the regular price? (Pricing is discussed in greater detail later in this chapter.) How will competitors react? Will they view this sale as the start of a price war?

Accepting the order yields an $11,000 advantage in operating income. Will potential disadvantages offset this $11,000? The sales manager may think so and reject the order. In turning away the business, the manager is saying that the company is better off passing up $11,000 now to protect its long-run market position. Rejecting the special sales order is like making an $11,000 "investment" in the company's long-run future.

Deletion of Products, Departments, or Territories— Fixed Costs Unchanged

To analyze whether a company should drop a product line, a department, or a territory, let's use the Torino Corporation data. Assume that Torino is already operating at the 270,000-unit level, as shown in column 2 of Exhibit 24-3. Suppose Torino is considering dropping the air cleaner product line, which makes up $35,000 (20,000 units) of the company's sales. A manager is given an income statement divided by product line as follows:

	Total	Product Line	
		Oil Filters	Air Cleaners
Units	270,000	250,000	20,000
Sales	$835,000	$800,000	$ 35,000
Variable expenses	399,000	375,000	24,000
Contribution margin	436,000	425,000	11,000
Fixed expenses:			
Manufacturing	200,000	185,185*	14,815*
Selling and administration	125,000	115,741†	9,259†
Total fixed expenses	325,000	300,926*	24,074
Operating income (loss)	$111,000	$124,074	$(13,074)

*$200,000/270,000 units = $.74074 per unit; 250,000 units × $.74074 = $185,185; 20,000 units × $.74074 = $14,815

†$125,000/270,000 units = $.46296 per unit; 250,000 units × $.46296 = $115,741; 20,000 units × $.46296 = $9,259

In determining cost per unit, Torino, like many companies, allocates fixed expenses to units in proportion to the number of units sold. For example, the data show that Torino sold 270,000 units of its products altogether. Total fixed manufacturing expenses of $200,000 divided by 270,000 units equals fixed manufacturing cost of $.74074 per unit. Applying this unit cost to the 250,000 units of the oil filter product line allocates fixed manufacturing cost of $185,185 to this product. The same procedure allocates fixed manufacturing cost of $14,815 to air cleaners. Fixed selling and administrative expenses are allocated in the same manner. Using this allocation method we see that air cleaners have an operating loss of $13,074. Should the air cleaner product line be dropped?

This illustration is basically the same example we studied for the special sales order. The relevant items are the changes in revenues and expenses. But now we are considering a decrease in volume instead of an increase. The difference between the change in revenues and the change in expenses is the change in operating income, as shown in Exhibit 24-4. Again, only the variable expenses are relevant to the decision. In the short run, dropping air cleaners would decrease operating income by $11,000. This analysis suggests that Torino should *not* drop air cleaners.

The decision of whether to delete a product is based on the same analysis used for the special sales order. The only difference is that deleting products leads to decreases in revenues and expenses, whereas accepting a special sales order leads to increased revenues and expenses. Decisions in both cases are based on the expected change in operating income.

EXHIBIT 24-4   *Deletion of a Product—Fixed Costs Unchanged*

Expected decrease in revenues:	
Deletion of sales of air cleaners—20,000 units × $1.75 each	$35,000
Expected decrease in expenses:	
Deletion of variable manufacturing expenses—	
20,000 units × $1.20 each	24,000
Expected decrease in operating income	$11,000

Deletion of Products, Departments, or Territories— Fixed Costs Changed

In our two examples total fixed expenses did not change. But do not jump to the conclusion that fixed costs are always irrelevant. The following example illustrates the role of fixed costs in special decision analysis.

Suppose Torino Corporation employs an engineer to improve the efficiency of the air cleaner product line. This employee is paid a fixed fee of $12,000, which can be avoided if the company phases out air cleaners. The question facing management is whether to drop air cleaners. To make this decision, Torino managers analyze all costs—fixed and variable—affected by the decision. Exhibit 24-5 shows the analysis.

The analysis suggests that operating income will increase by $1,000 if Torino drops air cleaners. In this situation, fixed expenses are relevant, and so the change in the fixed cost must enter the analysis. Special decisions should consider all costs that management expects to be affected by the situation. Managers must ask, What costs—fixed *and* variable—will change?

Which Product to Emphasize

Companies must decide which products to emphasize and which to deemphasize. This decision has a profound impact on profits. If salespersons push a product with a low profit margin, the company's operating income may decrease even though they succeed in selling the product. How should a manager decide which product to emphasize? Decisions like this are important because of limited sales staff, store display space, and advertising budgets.

Assume that a clothing manufacturer has two products, shirts and slacks. The following data are relevant:

	Product	
	Shirts	**Slacks**
Per unit:		
Selling price	$15	$20
Variable expenses	6	16
Contribution margin	$ 9	$ 4
Contribution margin ratio:		
Shirts—$9/$15	60%	
Slacks—$4/$20		20%

EXHIBIT 24-5 *Deletion of a Product—Fixed Costs Changed*

Expected decrease in revenues:		
Deletion of sales of air cleaners		$35,000
Expected decrease in expenses:		
Variable manufacturing expenses	$24,000	
Fixed expenses—engineer fee	12,000	
Expected decrease in total expenses		36,000
Expected increase in operating income		$ 1,000

EXHIBIT 24-6 *Which Product to Emphasize*

	Product	
	Shirts	**Slacks**
(1) Units that can be produced each hour	1	3
(2) Contribution margin per unit	×$9	×$4
(3) Contribution margin per hour (1) × (2)	$9	$12
Capacity—Number of hours	×20,000	×20,000
Total contribution margin for capacity	$180,000	$240,000

The data suggest that shirts are more profitable than slacks. But an important piece of information has been withheld—the time it takes to manufacture each product. This factor is called the *constraint,* or the *limiting factor.*

The **limiting factor,** or **constraint,** is the item that restricts production or sales of a product. In some companies, the constraint is production capacity. The factory or the labor force may be unable to produce more than a specified number of units. This constraint—the limit to how much the labor force can produce—may be stated in terms of labor hours, machine hours, materials, or square feet of shelf space. (For example, storage may be limited to 50,000 square feet of space in a warehouse.) These factors vary from company to company, depending on each company's line of business. Other companies are constrained by sales. Competition may be stiff, and the business may be able to sell only so many units. In other companies, the constraint is time, as we see in the following example: Suppose the company can produce three pairs of slacks *or* one shirt per hour. This company has 20,000 hours of capacity. Which product should the company emphasize?

The way to maximize profits for a given capacity is to obtain the highest possible contribution margin per unit of the limiting factor—in our example, direct labor hours. The analysis includes two steps. First, determine the contribution margin per unit of the limiting factor. Second, multiply this unit contribution margin by the company's capacity, stated in the number of units of the limiting factor.

Exhibit 24-6 shows how to decide which product to emphasize when there is a limiting factor. Slacks should be emphasized because they contribute more profit per hour. When the limiting factor is a part of the analysis, clearly the business should push slacks.

Make or Buy

Manufactured goods often include specialized parts. Overhead garage doors, for example, are activated by electronic controls. A garage door manufacturer may face this question: Should we manufacture the control device ourselves or buy it from an outsider? A furniture company may ask: Should we stain, lacquer, and finish the furniture we manufacture, or should we hire an outsider for the finish work? Assuming that quality is unaffected, at the heart of the make-or-buy decision is *how best to use available facilities.*

Let's see how to answer the make-or-buy question. Torino Corporation's production process uses Part No. 4, which has the following manufacturing costs for 250,000 parts:

	Total Costs (250,000 Units)
Part No. 4 costs:	
Direct materials..	$ 40,000
Direct labor	20,000
Variable overhead...	15,000
Fixed overhead	50,000
Total manufacturing cost	$125,000
Cost per unit of Part No. 4 ($125,000/250,000)...........	$.50

Another manufacturer offers to sell Torino the same part for $.37 a unit. Should Torino make Part No. 4 or buy it from the outside supplier? Torino's $.50 unit cost of manufacturing the part is $.13 higher than the $.37 cost of buying it outside. At first glance, it appears that Torino should purchase Part No. 4 from the outsider. But the correct answer to a make-or-buy question is rarely as clear as this comparison suggests. The key to making the correct decision lies in analyzing the difference in expected future costs between the alternatives. Which costs will differ depending on whether Torino makes or buys Part No. 4?

Assume that by purchasing the part from an outsider, Torino can avoid all variable manufacturing costs and reduce the fixed overhead cost by $10,000. (Fixed overhead will decrease to $40,000.) Exhibit 24-7 shows the difference in cost between the make and buy alternatives.

It would be cheaper to make the part than to buy it outside. Fixed overhead represents a significant amount of cost even in the buy alternative. The total cost savings for 250,000 units of Part No. 4 is $7,500, which is $.03 per unit.

This example shows that *fixed costs are relevant to a special decision if fixed costs differ between the alternatives*. In this instance, fixed costs differ by $10,000. In these situations, this $10,000 amount is often called *avoidable* fixed overhead.

Best Use of Facilities

The cost data in the make-or-buy decision indicate that making the part is the right decision. As we mentioned in that discussion, the focus is on making the best use of available facilities over a particular planning horizon. This decision is illustrated further with a make-or-buy decision that includes three alternative courses of action.

Assume that buying from an outside supplier releases factory facilities that can be used to manufacture another product. Suppose the expected annual profit contribution of this other product is $18,000. The three alternatives become (1) make, (2) buy and leave facilities idle, or (3) buy and use facilities to manufacture another product. The alternative with the lowest *net* cost indicates the best use of facilities. The comparison of *net* cost under the three alternatives is given in Exhibit 24-8.

This analysis of *net* cost indicates that buying the parts outside and using the vacated facilities to manufacture another product is the best choice. If the facilities remain idle, the company will forgo the opportunity to earn $18,000.

Special decisions often include nonquantitative factors. For example, Torino managers may believe they can better control the quality of Part No. 4 by

EXHIBIT 24-7 *Make or Buy*

	Make Part	Buy Part	Cost to Make minus Cost to Buy
Part No. 4 costs:			
Direct material	$ 40,000	$ —	$ 40,000
Direct labor	20,000	—	20,000
Variable overhead	15,000	—	15,000
Fixed overhead	50,000	40,000	10,000
Purchase price from outsider (250,000 × $.37) .	—	92,500	(92,500)
Total cost of Part No. 4	$125,000	$132,500	$ (7,500)
Cost per unit—250,000 units .	$.50	$.53	$(.03)

manufacturing it themselves. Or they may fear that an outside supplier cannot deliver sufficient quantities of the part on time. These factors argue for Torino's making the part itself. However, Torino may not have the employees or the factory facilities to manufacture Part No. 4. Its manufacture may require rare materials that Torino cannot obtain economically, so Torino may decide to buy from the outside supplier. Managers consider nonquantitative factors as well as cost differences in making decisions.

Sell As-Is or Process Further

Inventories become obsolete. Should the company incur the additional manufacturing cost to rework the inventory, or should the company try to sell the inventory as-is? Some companies hold inventory that is only partially finished. These businesses face the decision of whether to finish the inventory or sell it as-is. Of course the finished inventory will bring a higher sale price, but management must consider the additional costs of completing the inventory. Whether the inventory is obsolete or incomplete, managers must decide if further work on it makes financial sense. For this decision, managers must know which costs to analyze. Historical costs are irrelevant to the "sell-or-process-further" decision.

EXHIBIT 24-8 *Best Use of Facilities*

	Make	Buy and Leave Facilities Idle	Buy and Use Facilities for Other Product
Expected cost of obtaining 250,000 units of Part No. 4 (amounts from Exhibit 24-7)	$125,000	$132,500	$132,500
Expected profit contribution from the other product	—	—	(18,000)
Expected *net* cost of obtaining 250,000 units of Part No. 4	$125,000	$132,500	$114,500

EXHIBIT 24-9 *Sell As-Is or Process Further*

	(1) Process Inventory Further	(2) Scrap Inventory (Sell As-Is)	Difference (1)-(2)
Expected revenue	$64,000	$17,000	$47,000
Expected costs	40,000	—	40,000
Expected net revenue	$24,000	$17,000	$ 7,000

Suppose a company has 1,000 obsolete computer parts that are carried in inventory at a manufacturing cost of $200,000. The alternatives facing the company are (1) process the inventory further at a cost of $40,000 with the expectation of selling it for $64,000, or (2) scrap the inventory for $17,000. Which alternative should the company select? The inventory's $200,000 historical cost is irrelevant to the decision. Such a cost is called a sunk cost. A **sunk cost** is an actual outlay that has been incurred in the past and is present under all alternatives. It is irrelevant because it makes no difference to a current decision.

Exhibit 24-9 shows how to make the decision of whether to sell an asset in its present condition or to process it further. On the basis of expected revenues and costs, processing the inventory further appears to be the best alternative. The historical cost—the sunk cost—of the obsolete inventory makes no difference to the decision of whether to scrap the inventory or to rework it for sale at a higher price.

Replacement of Equipment

Another business decision that requires managers to distinguish between relevant and sunk costs is whether to replace plant equipment. Many owners of equipment hold it too long because they want it to be "fully depreciated," or they want their money to be "recovered," before disposal. The point here is important but widely misunderstood: The book value of old equipment is irrelevant. Money invested in the past is down the drain. Book value is a past cost that is common to all decision alternatives; it is not an expected future cost that will differ among alternatives.

The following illustration shows why book value is irrelevant. The manager of a bowling alley is deciding whether to replace some pin-setting equipment with new, more efficient, equipment:

	Old Pin-Setting Equipment	Potential Replacement Equipment
Annual cash operating costs*	$15,000	$ 7,000
Original cost	$35,000	$22,000
Accumulated depreciation	20,000	—
Book value	15,000	—
Current age in years	4	0
Useful life remaining in years	3	3
Current disposal value in cash	3,000	—
Future disposal value in cash (in 3 years)	0	0

*Maintenance, power, repairs, parts, lubricants.

EXHIBIT 24-10 *Cost Comparison: Replacement Decision Relevant Items for Three Years*

	Keep	Replace	Difference
Cash operating costs: $15,000 × 3 for old equipment and $7,000 × 3 for new equipment	$45,000	$21,000	$24,000
Disposal value of old equipment	—	−3,000	3,000
New equipment, acquisition cost	—	22,000	−22,000
Total relevant costs	$45,000	$40,000	$ 5,000

Exhibit 24-10 presents the relevant information for this decision. The advantage of replacement is $5,000 for the three years taken together. The time horizon is not confined to the next year only. Instead, the manager considers the full three-year life of the new equipment. In this way, he or she takes an appropriate long-run view. Exhibit 24-10 focuses solely on the relevant items, those that are expected to differ between the alternatives:

Expected future cash operating costs of the equipment
Disposal value of old equipment
Acquisition cost of new equipment

The following items are *irrelevant* in replacement decisions:

The book value of old equipment. This is irrelevant because it is a past (historical) cost that is common to all decision alternatives.

The gain or loss on disposal, which is the difference between book value and disposal value. Note that while the book value is irrelevant, the disposal value typically is relevant. The difference, that is, the gain or loss on disposal, combines the two, which confuses the issue. It is better to consider each item independently.

Exhibit 24-11 further illustrates the irrelevance of book value. The exhibit includes both relevant and irrelevant items to reinforce the point that irrelevant items, properly analyzed, do not make a difference in the decision.

EXHIBIT 24-11 *Cost Comparison: Replacement Decision Relevant and Irrelevant Items for Three Years*

	Keep	Replace	Difference
Cash operating costs, $15,000 × 3 and $7,000 × 3	$45,000	$21,000	$24,000
Book value of old equipment:			
Periodic write-off as depreciation	15,000[†]		
or			—
Lump-sum write-off		15,000*	
Disposal value	—	−3,000*	3,000
Acquisition cost of new equipment	—	22,000	−22,000
Total costs	$60,000	$55,000	$ 5,000

*The replacement year's income statement would condense these two items into one as "loss on disposal" of $15,000 − $3,000 = $12,000.

[†]Assuming straight-line depreciation, the income statement would show depreciation of $15,000 ÷ 3 = $5,000 in each of three years.

To underscore the important concepts of relevance and irrelevance, we deliberately postpone the roles of income taxes and interest until the next chapter. As is explained on page 1152, book value is irrelevant even if income taxes are considered. The relevant item is the *tax* cash flow, not the book value. Book value is essential information for predicting future tax cash flows, but by itself, book value is irrelevant.

Joint Products

Characteristics of Joint Products

A manufacturing process that produces more than one product simultaneously is called a joint process. **Joint products** are goods that are specifically identified as individual products only after a juncture in the production process called the **split-off point.** To be called a joint product, an item must have a sales value that is significant in relation to other items produced. For example, refining crude oil produces gasoline and natural gas as joint products. Exhibit 24-12 diagrams this joint process.

OBJECTIVE 4

Allocate joint processing costs to joint products

Many industries have manufacturing processes that create joint products. Soap making, for example, produces lanolin and other oils for cosmetics, in addition to soap. Refining copper also produces ammonia, which has many uses.

How do we assign costs to individual products that are manufactured by a joint process? After the split-off point, costs are easily assigned. For example, after gasoline and natural gas are separated in the refining process, further costs can be separately identified with the two products. But what costs incurred *before* split-off are assigned to the individual joint products? For example, how should we allocate the cost of exploring and drilling for oil to final products (gasoline and natural gas)? These *joint processing costs* may be allocated using the *relative sales value* method, which most accountants consider to be the best of several available methods.

Assume that the joint cost of processing 65,000 gallons of gasoline and liquid natural gas is $72,000. Exhibit 24-13 shows how to allocate this joint cost to the two products.

The relative sales value of each joint product is computed by dividing its individual sales value by the total sales value. In the exhibit, the gasoline sales value makes up two-thirds of the total and liquid natural gas makes up one-third. Multiplying joint cost of $72,000 by these fractions gives the two products' individual costs of $48,000 and $24,000. Any cost of processing gasoline after split-off is added to $48,000 to determine the total cost of the gasoline. The cost of liquid natural gas is computed similarly.

EXHIBIT 24-12   *Joint Products*

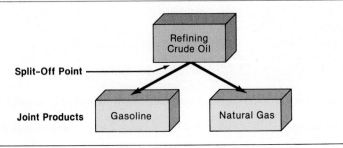

EXHIBIT 24-13 *Allocation of Joint Cost to Joint Products*

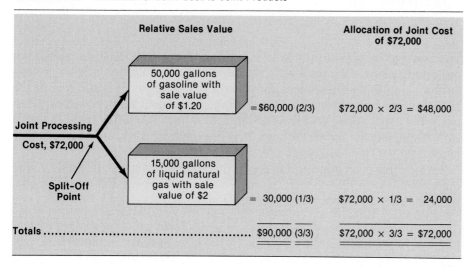

Sell at Split-off or Process Further

Should a joint product be sold at split-off, or should it be processed further? Managers need to understand which costs are relevant. For example, let us determine whether a special additive should be added to the gasoline to make it a premium product. The additional costs of materials and other resources in the subsequent process would be $.11 per gallon, resulting in a total cost of $5,500 for 50,000 gallons. However, the net sales price would increase to $1.40 per gallon, for a total of $70,000. There would be no difference in the liquid natural gas because it will be sold at the split-off point.

Joint processing costs are not relevant to the decision to sell at split-off or process further. Why? Because they do not differ between alternatives. In contrast, separable costs are relevant. **Separable costs** are those costs that occur after the split-off point that can be exclusively identified with an individual product. The correct analysis focuses on the separable costs and revenues after split-off, as Exhibit 24-14 shows.

Because this is a business decision that specifies two alternative courses of action, the concept of opportunity cost applies.

EXHIBIT 24-14 *Separable Costs and Revenues after Split-off*

	Sell at Split-Off	Process Further
Expected revenue from selling 50,000 gallons of regular gasoline at $1.20 per gallon	$60,000	
Separable costs of $.11 per gallon required to convert 50,000 gallons of regular gasoline into premium gasoline		($5,500)
Expected revenue from selling 50,000 gallons of premium gasoline at $1.40 per gallon		70,000
Total	60,000	64,500
Difference in net revenue		$ 4,500

Opportunity Cost

OBJECTIVE 5

Use opportunity cost in decision making

The concept of opportunity cost is often relevant to special decisions. An **opportunity cost** is the maximum available profit contribution forgone (rejected) by using limited resources for a particular purpose. It is the cost of the forsaken next-best alternative. This definition indicates that opportunity cost is not the usual outlay cost recorded in accounting. An **outlay cost** requires a cash disbursement sooner or later. It is the typical cost recorded by accountants.

An example of an opportunity cost is the salary forgone by an engineer who quits his job with IBM to start his own business. Suppose this engineer analyzes the two job opportunities as follows:

	Open an Independent Business	Remain an IBM Employee
Expected salary income from IBM ..		$60,000
Expected revenue	$200,000	
Expected total expenses............	120,000	
Expected net income	$ 80,000	$60,000

The opportunity cost of staying with IBM is the forgone $80,000 of net income that the independent business is expected to earn. The opportunity cost of starting a new business is the $60,000 salary that could be received from IBM for the next year.

The concept of opportunity cost applies to all business decisions that specify alternative courses of action. For example, in Exhibit 24-3, page 1097, the opportunity cost of rejecting the special sales order is $11,000 of operating income. In Exhibit 24-6, page 1102, the opportunity cost of manufacturing shirts is the $240,000 of contribution margin that could be earned on slacks. The opportunity cost of manufacturing slacks is the $180,000 contribution margin available on shirts. In Exhibit 24-9, page 1104, the opportunity cost of scrapping the inventory in its present condition is the $24,000 that can be earned by processing the inventory further. The opportunity cost of processing the inventory further is $17,000, which can be received immediately by selling the inventory as-is.

Summary Problems for Your Review

Problem 1

Ariz, Inc., has two products, a standard model and a deluxe model, with the following per-unit data:

	Standard	Deluxe
Selling price	$20	$30
Variable expenses	16	21

The company has 15,000 hours of capacity available. Seven units of the standard model can be produced in an hour, compared with three units of the deluxe model per hour. Which product should the company emphasize?

Problem 2

Suppose Zenith Corporation has the following manufacturing costs for 20,000 of its television cabinets:

Direct materials	$ 20,000
Direct labor	80,000
Variable overhead............................	40,000
Fixed overhead	80,000
Total manufacturing cost	$220,000
Cost per cabinet ($220,000/20,000)	$11

Another manufacturer has offered to sell Zenith similar cabinets for $10, a total purchase cost of $200,000. By purchasing the cabinets outside, Zenith can save $50,000 of fixed overhead cost. The released facilities can be devoted to the manufacture of other products that will contribute $60,000 to profits. Identify and analyze the alternatives. What is Zenith's best decision?

SOLUTIONS TO REVIEW PROBLEMS

Problem 1

Decision: The company should emphasize the standard product because its contribution margin at capacity is greater by $15,000:

		Product	
		Standard	Deluxe
(1)	Units per hour that can be produced	7	3
(2)	Contribution margin per unit	× $4*	× $9*
(3)	Contribution margin per hour (1) × (2)	$28	$27
	Capacity—Number of hours	×15,000	×15,000
	Total contribution margin for capacity	$420,000	$405,000

*Contribution margins: Standard: $20 − $16 = $4; Deluxe: $30 − $21 = $9.

Problem 2

| | Alternatives | | |
| | | Buy and Leave Facilities Idle | Buy and Use Facilities for Other Products |
	Make		
Cabinets for televisions:			
Direct materials	$ 20,000	—	
Direct labor	80,000	—	
Variable overhead	40,000	—	
Fixed overhead	80,000	$ 30,000	$ 30,000
Purchase price from outsider (20,000 × $10)	—	200,000	200,000
Total cost of obtaining cabinets	220,000	230,000	230,000
Profit contribution from other products............................			(60,000)
Net cost of obtaining 20,000 cabinets	$220,000	$230,000	$170,000

Decision: Zenith should buy the television cabinets from an outside supplier and use the released facilities to manufacture other products.

Costs and Pricing Decisions

Setting the selling prices of a company's products is an important decision facing management. In addition to market conditions, both customers and competitors influence this decision. Management also needs to know the relationships of costs to prices. For example, earlier in this chapter we described how to analyze costs in relation to pricing a special sales order. Other examples of decisions regarding costs and prices include:

Competitive bidding
Cost plus a "fair" profit, which is used in defense contracting
Deciding which products to emphasize
Pricing new products

OBJECTIVE 6
Identify three factors that influence pricing decisions

In the remainder of this chapter, we discuss several influences on pricing, focusing on costs. We show how desired selling prices may be set by marking up various unit costs. We then present arguments for both contribution and full-cost approaches to pricing. The chapter concludes with a brief discussion of antitrust laws.

Influence of Customers on Pricing

Three major factors that affect pricing decisions are customers, competitors, and costs. Customer satisfaction is a major theme of many businesses. To be satisfied, customers must approve of the price and the quality of a product, as well as the service they receive. Otherwise, customers will go elsewhere, or perhaps make the product themselves. For instance, Apple Computer can either manufacture particular computer components or purchase them from outside suppliers. If the price of purchasing a component is too high, Apple might redesign the component or change the construction material in order to make it profitably.

Target costing, which is described in Chapter 23, page 1072, illustrates the prominent role of customers in setting prices. Recall that target costing begins with research by the marketing department regarding how much customers will be willing to pay for a product having a particular set of features. For example, when Toyota Motor Corporation prices a new model, its sales division begins with the price of the existing model on which the new model is based. To that price, managers add the amount they believe customers will pay for new functions, such as four-wheel steering or better engine performance.

Influence of Competitors on Pricing

Competitors typically react to the price changes of their rivals. Consequently, pricing decisions may be influenced by predictions of how competitors will respond. For example, Compaq might cut prices for its personal computers if it expects price cuts from its rivals. Compaq's justification for this price cut may be its prediction that the increase in overall demand for its personal computers will offset the reduction in its unit profit margins.

Companies sometimes are reluctant to reduce prices because the resulting price wars could harm the profitability of the entire industry. Profitability is harmed when overall industry demand is not significantly increased by price cuts. The key factors are changes in market share and in overall demand for the industry's products. Thus, we may hear the president of a large airline complaining about a small airline's price-cutting moves. The president's complaint is that the small airline will not gain market share because the large airline will match the lower prices. Furthermore, the entire airline industry may suffer lower profits because overall demand will not rise significantly.

Global competition has forced companies to consider how their pricing decisions will affect rivals from beyond their country's borders. The amount of worldwide idle manufacturing capacity may affect predictions of how competitors will react to changes in prices.

Predictions of competitors' reactions also are affected by knowledge about rivals' technology, operating policies and procedures, and costs. Hence, many companies systematically gather as much information as practicable about competitors.

Influence of Costs on Pricing

Do costs influence prices? The answer depends on the industry involved. Costs do not influence prices in industries where the market price is regarded as a given, such as agricultural commodities and metals. For example, a copper-mining company faces prices set by fluctuating demands and supplies of copper. The company's profitability depends on how it manages its costs and volume. Cost data do not help the company's executives set prices, but they do help them control operations.

Costs do influence prices most directly in defense and other industries where "fair" prices are set on the basis of cost reimbursement plus some negotiated amount that provides a profit. In a sense, the cost accounting system becomes a substitute for markets in determining mutually agreeable prices. The resulting "cost-plus" contracts usually specify how costs should be measured and which costs are allowable. For example, some travel costs (such as rentals of luxury automobiles) may be prohibited. Cost-reimbursement contracts usually require laborious, detailed cost accounting procedures.

Costs *may* influence prices in situations where managers claim that they set prices by cost-plus pricing. For example, executives in the computer components industry describe the procedure as calculating an average unit cost and then adding a markup that will produce a desired return on investment. But there is leeway here in the size of the "markup" or "plus" that determines the actual price. Market conditions are strong factors in setting the final prices.

A general answer to whether costs influence prices is that the market, not costs, sets prices. Managers test the pricing waters. The maximum price they should set for a product is the one that does not cause their customers to leave them.

Pricing decisions are affected by particular decision situations and time horizons. The minimum acceptable price of a special order, for example, should be equal to the costs that will be avoided if the order is rejected. That usually is all variable costs of manufacturing and selling plus any one-time lump-sum costs related to the order. An example of the latter is a machinery changeover cost. For long-run decisions, the price should exceed all costs, including fixed costs of running the business, that can be related to the products or services in question. Exhibit 24-15 uses assumed numbers to show how costs may be computed for an electric razor.

In the long run, managers want prices that exceed the full total cost per unit. In the short run, they might settle for less. For example, managers might set a price slightly in excess of total variable cost per unit to gain entry to a new market. The special sales order decision at the beginning of this chapter illustrated that pricing strategy.

In Exhibit 24-15, the **total variable cost** per unit of $18 is computed in the first column. This is the additional cost incurred when one unit of product is manufactured, sold, distributed, and serviced. The **full absorption cost** of $19 is computed in the second column. This is the average manufacturing cost per

EXHIBIT 24-15   *Various Unit Costs for a Product: Electric Razor*

	Cost per Unit of Product		
	Total Variable Cost	Full Absorption Cost	Full Total Cost
Variable manufacturing cost (direct materials, direct labor, variable overhead)	$14	$14	$14
Variable nonmanufacturing cost*	4		4
Total variable cost	$18		
Fixed manufacturing cost		5†	5
Full absorption cost		$19‡	
Fixed nonmanufacturing cost*			9§
Full total cost			$32

*Nonmanufacturing costs might be shown in more detail. They consist of all business functions other than manufacturing. Examples are product design, marketing, distribution, and customer service.

†$10,000,000/2,000,000 units = $5

§This amount must be used for inventory valuation by U.S. companies in reports to shareholders.

‡$18,000,000/2,000,000 units = $9

unit at a production volume of 2,000,000 units. The **full total cost** (often called **fully allocated cost**) of $32 per unit, computed in the third column, is the average unit cost to design, manufacture, market, distribute, and service the product, again at a 2,000,000-unit volume. You will find each of these terms, and others, used in practice.

Desired Prices and Marketing Formulas

Companies have many ways of setting desired prices. Influential factors include anticipated sales volume and desired levels of operating income and return on investment. Suppose a company budgets sales of an electric razor, one of its many products. The budgeted sales would be computed by multiplying a desired price by expected sales volume. The desired sales price might be set by marking up any one of several costs from Exhibit 24-15, depending on the policies of the company. The chosen cost plus the chosen markup would equal the desired price.

OBJECTIVE 7

Use four cost-based formulas to achieve a desired sales price

Exhibit 24-16 displays various costs and markup percentages that will lead to the same desired selling price. The exhibit illustrates four frequently used formulas for calculating the markup:

a. Percentage of variable manufacturing cost
b. Percentage of total variable cost
c. Percentage of full total cost
d. Percentage of full absorption cost

Exhibit 24-16 shows a 133-1/3% markup on total variable cost, a 31-1/4% markup on full total cost, and a 121% markup on full absorption cost. Assume that for a budgeted volume of 2,000,000 razors the desired unit selling price is $42. No matter which markup formula is used, the same $42 selling price, and the same total sales revenue and operating income will result.

EXHIBIT 24-16   *Calculations for Markup Percentages*

		Alternative Markup Percentages to Achieve Desired Selling Price
Desired selling price	$42	
Variable costs:		
(a) Manufacturing	$14	$\dfrac{(\$42 - \$14)}{\$14} = 200\%$
Nonmanufacturing	4	
(b) Total variable cost	$18 $18	$\dfrac{(\$42 - \$18)}{\$18} = 133\tfrac{1}{3}\%$
Fixed costs:		
Manufacturing	$ 5	
Nonmanufacturing	9	
Total fixed cost	$14	
(c) Full total cost	$32	$\dfrac{(\$42 - \$32)}{\$32} = 31\tfrac{1}{4}\%$
Desired operating income	$10	

(d) Another popular formula is based on full absorption cost, the sum of variable and fixed manufacturing costs: $\dfrac{[\$42 - (\$14 + \$5)]}{(\$14 + \$5)} = \dfrac{\$23}{\$19} = 121\%$

Suppose the manager of the electric razor company prices razors by marking up the product 200% above variable manufacturing cost. Exhibit 24-16 illustrates computation of the 200% markup. Exhibit 24-17 gives the product pricing formula. The manager would add the variable manufacturing cost ($14) to the 200% markup ($28 = 2.00 × $14) to determine the razor's selling price of $42.

Variable-Cost versus Full-Cost Approaches

Exhibits 24-16 and 24-17 demonstrate that managers may use either variable-cost approaches—exhibit items (a) and (b)—or full-cost approaches—items (c) and (d)—to develop markup formulas for pricing. When used carefully, variable-cost approaches have a key advantage over full-cost approaches. Variable-cost methods routinely distinguish between variable and fixed costs. As illustrated earlier in this chapter, such distinctions are especially helpful to guide special business decisions. For example, analyzing variable and fixed costs separately helped Torino Corporation evaluate a special sales order for oil filters at a price ($1.75) substantially below its regular market price ($3.20, p. 1097).

Full-cost approaches do not *routinely* separate variable and fixed costs. Instead, firms that use these methods often must conduct expensive special studies in order to calibrate the relevant costs of particular courses of action. However, managers more widely favor full-cost approaches to pricing. The most frequently encountered argument for these approaches is that all costs (the full total cost of $32 in our razor example) must be recouped in the long run. Many managers reject variable-cost approaches because they are concerned that marketing personnel will regard variable costs as the only costs that prices must "cover." The result will be unjustifiable price cutting.

Adherents of variable-cost methods believe that any problems associated with them are due to their faulty use, not to any inherent weaknesses. These individuals state that variable-cost approaches are neutral. The approaches do not say "Go forth and slash prices."

In addition to concerns about long-run cost recoupment and unwise price cutting, the following arguments support full-cost approaches:

1. Managers are uncertain about which business costs really are affected by individual products and individual customer orders. They may think that measures of both a product's variable costs and its fixed costs are inaccurate. Consequently, managers prefer to reduce risks by using a full-cost measure. They often feel safer if they believe that the marked-up amount tends to overstate relevant costs rather than understate those costs.

2. Full-cost pricing is regarded as more defensible for justifying prices to customers and antitrust investigators.

EXHIBIT 24-17 *Formulas for Setting Desired Selling Price of $42*

Percentage of	Formula
(a) Variable manufacturing cost	$14 + (2.00 × $14) = $42
(b) Total variable cost	$18 + (1.333 × $18) = $42
(c) Full total cost	$32 + (.3125 × $32) = $42
(d) Full absorption cost	$19 + (1.21 × $19) = $42

3. Full-cost pricing may lead to better approximations of the potential prices of competitors, especially if they have similar efficiency and capacity.

Among companies that use full-cost approaches, absorption-cost methods are more often used than full-total-cost methods. Accounting systems have tracked manufacturing costs to individual products for years, but nonmanufacturing costs are not so widely traced to products. Therefore, most pricing formulas use absorption cost rather than full cost as the base for computing pricing formulas. Nevertheless, more and more companies are attempting to trace all costs in the value chain to products so that pricing and product mix decisions can be improved.

Antitrust Laws

The United States and other countries have antitrust laws that affect pricing decisions. In general, predatory pricing is banned. **Predatory pricing** is a scheme to temporarily reduce prices in order to eliminate competition and thereby restrict supply, so that prices then may be raised above their original levels. Prices are legal if they are set both to meet competition and without predatory intent.

U.S. court decisions have usually maintained that pricing below average variable cost may be predatory. Note that *average variable cost* includes all variable costs, not just variable manufacturing costs.

Discriminatory pricing is charging different prices to different customers for identical services or products. Pricing is not discriminatory if costs or other features are different in relation to different customers, services, or products.

Managers can defend against antitrust laws by keeping detailed records of all costs. Such records should be designed to capture the additional costs of various activities or features that justify differing prices. For example, a company may charge a higher price to customers in remote locations because of higher distribution costs. Our discussion here has assumed that pricing alternatives abide by antitrust and fair-trade laws.

Summary Problem for Your Review

Consider the following cost data for a company that manufactures and sells cellular telephones:

Total budgeted units of production	100,000
Total fixed nonmanufacturing cost	$5,000,000
Total fixed manufacturing cost	3,000,000
Unit variable nonmanufacturing cost	40
Unit variable manufacturing cost	90

Required

1. Compute the following unit costs: Total variable cost, full absorption cost, and full total cost.

2. Compute the markup percentage for each of the three unit costs in Requirement 1 (that will yield a desired selling price of $390).
3. Use the percentages you computed in Requirement 2 to compute the $390 selling price by marking up (a) total variable cost and (b) full absorption cost.

SOLUTION TO REVIEW PROBLEM

Requirement 1
Unit costs for cellular telephones

	Cost per Unit of Product		
	Total Variable Cost	**Full Absorption Cost**	**Full Total Cost**
Variable manufacturing cost	$90	$90	$90
Variable nonmanufacturing cost	40		40
Total variable cost	$130		
Fixed manufacturing cost		30	30
Full absorption cost		$120	
Fixed nonmanufacturing cost			50
Full total cost			$210

Requirement 2

Cost	Markup Percentage to Achieve Desired Selling Price of $390
Total variable = $130	($390 − $130) ÷ $130 = 200%
Full absorption = $120	($390 − $120) ÷ $120 = 225%
Full total = $210	($390 − $210) ÷ $210 = 85.7%

Requirement 3
(a) Total variable cost: $130 + (2.00 × $130) = $130 + $260 = $390
(b) Full absorption cost: $120 + (2.25 × $120) = $120 + $270 = $390

Summary

Special business decisions are those that are not routine in running the business. They have both short-run and long-run consequences. These decisions include whether to accept or reject a special sales order; whether to delete a product, department, or territory; which product to emphasize; whether to make or buy a part; how to make the best use of facilities; whether to sell inventory as-is or process it further; whether to replace current equipment; and whether to sell a joint product at split-off or process it further. In each decision, management usually selects the alternative course of action that will produce the largest income from operations.

In making special decisions, managers focus on relevant information, that is, expected future data that differ between alternative courses of action. Often, historical data are irrelevant, except for helping to develop predictions of future data for the decision analysis. Managers also consider nonquantitative factors, such as long-run effects on customers and competitors.

Opportunity cost is another factor in special decisions. Opportunity cost is the maximum available profit contribution forgone by using limited resources for a particular purpose. It differs from the usual outlay cost recorded by accountants.

A contribution margin income statement, which shows variable expenses and fixed expenses, is helpful in decision analysis. Variable expenses often are relevant in decisions because alternative courses of action frequently result in different volumes of activity. Fixed expenses are less-often relevant. Failure to account for fixed expenses correctly is a common mistake. When fixed expenses do not differ between alternatives, they should not enter the analysis. But when they do differ, decision makers must consider their effect.

Prices are affected by customers, competitors, and costs. Various measures of variable and full cost may be marked up to set desired sales prices. Both variable-cost and full-cost approaches are used in practice.

Self-Study Questions

Test your understanding of the chapter by marking the best answer for each of the following questions.

1. Relevant information for decision analysis *(p. 1094)*
   a. Remains constant regardless of the alternative courses of action
   b. Is used in some but not all business decisions
   c. Varies with the alternative courses of action
   d. Excludes direct materials and direct labor because they are fixed
2. Assume that fixed costs remain unchanged. To decide whether to make a sale at a special price, compare *(p. 1096)*
   a. Expected change in gross margin (sales minus cost of goods sold) with the sale
   b. Expected change in revenue with expected change in fixed expenses
   c. Expected change in revenue with expected change in selling expenses
   d. Expected change in revenue with expected change in variable expenses
3. To decide whether to delete a product, a manager should *(pp. 1099–1100)*
   a. Consider all costs that change
   b. Consider only variable costs
   c. Consider all costs that remain unchanged
   d. Consider only fixed costs
4. Pontchartrain's $.47 cost per unit (incurred in manufacturing its inventory) includes fixed cost of $.19. Another company offers to sell the product to Pontchartrain for $.35 per unit. The make-or-buy decision hinges on the comparison between Pontchartrain's $.47 manufacturing cost and the total cost if the products are purchased from the other company. That total cost is *(p. 1103)*
   a. $.28
   b. $.35
   c. $.53
   d. $.66

5. Sunk costs are *(p. 1104)*
   a. Relevant to most business decisions
   b. The cost of the next-best alternative
   c. Equal to the residual value of a plant asset
   d. Irrelevant to most business decisions
6. The joint cost of manufacturing cardboard and linerboard is $160,000. Cardboard can be sold for $240,000 and linerboard for $80,000. The individual costs of the products are *(p. 1107)*
   a. $240,000 and $80,000
   b. $160,000 and $80,000
   c. $120,000 and $40,000
   d. Cannot be determined from the given information
7. Which of the following is irrelevant in deciding whether to replace equipment? *(p. 1104)*
   a. Cost of the new equipment
   b. Book value of the old equipment
   c. Expected future cash operating costs
   d. Disposal value of old equipment
8. Which of the following is the cost term that describes how U.S. companies must value inventories for reporting to shareholders? *(p. 1112)*
   a. Full total cost
   b. Total variable cost
   c. Full absorption cost
   d. Contribution cost
9. Which of the following is *not* an argument that favors the variable-cost approach to pricing? *(p. 1113)*
   a. Shows variable and fixed costs separately
   b. Markup formulas can be easily developed
   c. Quantifies potential short-run effects of cutting prices on orders
   d. Shows how unit fixed costs change with volume
10. U.S. court decisions have usually maintained that pricing may be predatory if it is below *(p. 1114)*
    a. Average variable cost
    b. Average absorption cost
    c. Average full cost
    d. None of the above

Answer to the Self-Study Questions follow the Accounting Vocabulary.

Accounting Vocabulary

Constraint. *See* limiting factor.

Discriminatory pricing. Charging different prices to different customers for identical services or products *(p. 1115).*

Full absorption cost. The sum of variable and fixed manufacturing costs *(p. 1112).*

Full total cost. The total of all manufacturing and nonmanufacturing costs. This is also called **fully allocated cost** *(p. 1113).*

Joint products. Goods that are specifically identified as individual products only after a juncture in the production process, which is called the split-off point *(p. 1106).*

Limiting factor. The item that restricts production or sales of a product *(p. 1101).*

Opportunity cost. The maximum available profit contribution forgone (rejected) by using limited resources for a particular purpose *(p. 1108).*

Outlay cost. A cost that requires a cash disbursement sooner or later *(p. 1108).*

Predatory pricing. A scheme to temporarily reduce prices in order to eliminate competition and thereby restrict supply, so that prices then may be raised above their original levels *(p. 1115).*

Relevant information. Expected future data that differ between the alternative courses of action in a decision *(p. 1094).*

Separable costs. Costs beyond the split-off point that can be exclusively identified with individual products *(p. 1107).*

Split-off point. The juncture in the production process where goods become specifically identified as individual products *(p. 1106).*

Sunk cost. An actual outlay that has been incurred in the past and is present under all alternatives in a decision *(p. 1104).*

Total variable cost. The additional cost incurred when one unit of product is manufactured, sold, distributed, and serviced *(p. 1112).*

Answers to Self-Study Questions

1. c
2. d
3. a
4. c Fixed cost ($.19) + Cost of outside units ($.35) = $.54
5. d
6. c Cardboard: [$240,000/($240,000 + $80,000)] × $160,000 = $120,000
   Linerboard: [$80,000/($240,000 + $80,000)] × $160,000 = $40,000
7. b
8. c
9. d
10. a

ASSIGNMENT MATERIAL _____

Questions

1. How do special decisions differ from ordinary day-to-day business decisions? Give examples.
2. Briefly describe how relevant information is used in making special decisions.
3. Discuss the roles of expected future data and historical data in special decision analysis. On which set of data are special decisions based?
4. Identify two income statement formats. Which is more useful for deciding whether to accept a special sales order? Why?
5. Identify two income amounts on which special decisions are based.
6. What is "special" about a special sales order? How does a manager make a special sales order decision?
7. Identify two long-run factors to be considered in making a special sales order decision.
8. What is the similarity between a special sales order decision and a decision to delete a product? What is the difference?
9. Which type of cost is more likely to change in a special decision situation, a fixed cost or a variable cost? Can both costs change?
10. Outline how to decide which product to emphasize when there is a limiting factor. Give four examples of limiting factors.
11. Which is relevant to special decision analysis, an asset's sunk cost or its residual value? Give your reason, including an explanation of each.
12. What is opportunity cost? How does it differ from an ordinary accounting cost?

13. Give an example of a decision that would be based on opportunity cost. Discuss the role of opportunity cost in making this decision.

14. What is the role of joint costs in deciding whether to sell a joint product at the split-off point or process it further?

15. What is discriminatory pricing? How can managers defend against charges of discriminatory pricing?

16. Name three major factors that affect pricing decisions.

17. Identify four unit costs that may be marked up to produce a desired sales price. How is each cost computed?

18. Of the variable-cost or the full-cost approach, which is better for quantifying the short-run impact on operating income of accepting a special order? Why?

19. Why do managers often feel safer using a full-cost approach to pricing?

Exercises

Exercise 24-1   *Accept or reject a special sales order?   (L.O. 1, 2)*

Top-Flite Marketing approaches McDade Manufacturing Company with a special offer. Top-Flite wishes to purchase 100,000 monogrammed golf balls for a special promotional campaign. Top-Flite offers $.38 per ball—a total of $38,000. McDade's total manufacturing cost per ball is $.40, broken down as follows:

Variable costs:	
Direct material	$.06
Direct labor	.03
Variable overhead	.11
Total variable cost	.20
Fixed overhead cost........	.20
Total cost	$.40

Required

Prepare a quick summary to help determine whether McDade should accept the special sales order. Assume that McDade has excess capacity.

Exercise 24-2   *Retain or drop a product line (fixed costs unchanged)?   (L.O. 1, 2, 3)*

Top managers of Merchants & Planters Supply Co. are alarmed that operating income is so low. They are considering dropping the building materials product line. Company accountants have prepared the following analysis to help make this decision:

	Total	Hardware	Building Materials
Sales.....................	$460,000	$290,000	$170,000
Variable expenses	240,000	140,000	100,000
Contribution margin	220,000	150,000	70,000
Fixed expenses:			
Manufacturing....................	120,000	70,000	50,000
Selling and administrative	90,000	55,000	35,000
Total fixed expenses..............	210,000	125,000	85,000
Operating income (loss)	$ 10,000	$ 25,000	$(15,000)

Fixed costs will not change if the company stops selling building materials.

Required

Prepare a quick summary to show whether Merchants & Planters should drop the building materials product line. Explain the error of concluding that dropping building materials will add $15,000 to operating income.

Exercise 24-3 *Retain or drop a product line (fixed costs change)?* **(L.O. 1, 2)**

Refer to the data of Exercise 24-2. Assume that Merchants & Planters can avoid $35,000 of fixed expenses by dropping the building materials product line. Prepare a quick summary to show whether Merchants & Planters should stop selling building materials.

Exercise 24-4 *Which product to emphasize?* **(L.O. 1, 2)**

Impala Fashions sells both designer and moderately priced women's wear. Profits have fluctuated recently, and top management is deciding which product line to emphasize. Accountants provide the following relevant data:

	Designer	Moderately Priced
Per item:		
Average sale price	$100	$60
Average variable expenses	35	18
Average contribution margin	$ 65	$42
Average contribution margin ratio	65%	70%

The store, in Tulsa, Oklahoma, has 8,000 square feet of floor space. If moderately priced goods are emphasized, 300 items can be displayed in the store. Only 200 designer items could be displayed for sale.

Required

Prepare an analysis to show which product to emphasize.

Exercise 24-5 *Make or buy?* **(L.O. 1, 2, 3)**

The production process of Danon Company uses an electronic control that has the following manufacturing cost per unit:

Direct materials	$2.45
Direct labor	.55
Variable overhead	.62
Fixed overhead	2.04
Total manufacturing cost per unit	$5.66

Another company has offered to sell Danon the electronic control for $4 per unit. If Danon buys the controls from the outside supplier, the manufacturing facilities that will be idle cannot be used for any other purpose in the business. Should Danon make or buy the electronic controls? Show how you made this decision. Explain the difference between correct analysis and incorrect analysis of this decision.

Exercise 24-6 *Best use of facilities?* **(L.O. 1, 2)**

Refer to Exercise 24-5. Assume that Danon needs 100,000 of the electronic controls. By purchasing them from the outside supplier, Danon could use its idle facilities to manufacture another product that can be sold for a $42,000 profit. Identify the *net* costs that Danon may incur to acquire 100,000 electronic controls under three alternative plans. Which alternative makes the best use of Danon's facilities? Support your answer with analysis.

Exercise 24-7   *Scrap inventory or process further?*   **(L.O. 1, 2, 5)**

Garcia Milling has damaged some custom cabinets, which cost the company $8,000 to manufacture. Luis Garcia, the owner, is considering two options for disposing of this inventory. One plan is to sell the cabinets as damaged inventory for $1,400. The alternative is to spend an additional $600 to repair the damage and expect to sell the cabinets for $2,200. How should Garcia dispose of this inventory? Support your decision with an analysis that shows expected net revenue under each alternative. Identify the opportunity cost of each alternative.

Exercise 24-8   *Equipment replacement*   **(L.O. 1, 2)**

Hudson's Catalog Sales is thinking of buying, at a cost of $220,000, some new packaging equipment with expected cash operating costs of $5 per order packed. The new equipment's useful life is predicted to be four years, with a disposal value in four years of $10,000. The current packaging equipment it would replace was purchased two years ago for $150,000. It has four years remaining useful life and a predicted disposal value at that time of zero. The current equipment has cash operating costs of $7 per order; it can be sold now for $30,000.

Required

Hudson's president expects to pack 25,000 orders per year over the next four years. Compute relevant costs of the two alternative courses of action to determine whether the company should replace the current packaging equipment.

Exercise 24-9   *Determining the cost of joint products and byproducts*   **(L.O. 4)**

Catawba Paper Corporation manufactures cardboard and linerboard by a joint process that costs $300,000 on average each month. Cardboard sells for $32 per ton and linerboard for $12 per ton. Each month the manufacturing process generates 5,000 tons of cardboard and 20,000 tons of linerboard. Use the relative sales value method to determine the cost of each ton of the two products.

Exercise 24-10   *Computing unit costs*   **(L.O. 7)**

McCloud Office Products has variable manufacturing cost of $10 per pen and variable nonmanufacturing cost of $2 per pen. For 19X6, its fixed manufacturing cost totaled $3,000,000; its fixed selling and administrative cost was $2,900,000. For the 19X6 volume of 500,000 pens, compute (a) total variable cost per unit, (b) full absorption cost per unit, and (c) full total cost per unit.

Exercise 24-11   *Developing markup formulas*   **(L.O. 7)**

Refer to Exercise 24-10.   Angus Gunn, the marketing vice-president of McCloud, wants to develop markup formulas that yield a target selling price of $30 per pen. Determine three markup percentages (one for each of the three unit costs computed above) that will give the $30 price. How else might the target price be computed?

Problems   *(Group A)*

Problem 24-1A   *Accept or reject a special sales order?*   **(L.O. 1, 2)**

Casavas Toy Corporation manufactures toys in Torreón, Mexico. Casavas's contribution margin income statement for the most recent month contains the following:

Sales—units		630,000
Sales		$ 63,000
Variable expenses:		
Manufacturing	$ 12,600	
Selling and administrative	14,900	
Total variable expenses		27,500
Contribution margin		35,500
Fixed expenses:		
Manufacturing	17,400	
Selling and administrative	11,300	
Total fixed expenses		28,700
Income from operations		$ 6,800

Pan American Promotions, Inc., wishes to buy 120,000 toys from Casavas. Acceptance of the offer will not increase selling and administrative expenses. Cavasas's fixed plant has unused capacity to manufacture the additional toys. Pan American has offered $.07 per toy, which is considerably below the normal sales price of $.10.

Required

1. Prepare a quick summary to help determine whether Casavas should accept this special sales order.
2. Prepare a total analysis to show Casavas's operating income with and without the special sales order.
3. Identify long-run factors that Casavas should consider in deciding whether to accept the special sales order.

Problem 24-2A *Retain or drop a product line?* (L.O. 1, 2, 3)

Members of the board of directors of Alarm Systems, Inc., have received the following income statement for the year just ended:

	Total	Industrial Products	Household Products
Sales	$866,000	$445,000	$421,000
Cost of goods sold:			
Variable	$119,000	$ 64,000	$ 55,000
Fixed	327,000	241,000	86,000
Total cost of goods sold	446,000	305,000	141,000
Gross margin	420,000	140,000	280,000
Selling and administrative expenses:			
Variable	178,000	86,000	92,000
Fixed	89,000	58,000	31,000
Total selling and administrative expenses	267,000	144,000	123,000
Operating income (loss)	$153,000	$ (4,000)	$157,000

Members of the board are shocked that the industrial products division is losing money. They commission a study to determine whether the company should delete the industrial products line. Company accountants estimate that dropping industrial products will decrease the fixed cost of goods sold by $65,000 and decrease fixed selling and administrative costs by $19,000.

Required

1. Prepare a quick summary to show whether Alarm Systems should drop the industrial products line.
2. Prepare a total analysis to show Alarm Systems' operating income with and without industrial products. Prepare the income statement in contribution-margin format.
3. Explain the difference between correct analysis and incorrect analysis of the decision whether to drop the industrial products line.

Problem 24-3A *Which product to emphasize?* (L.O. 1, 2)

Suntex Corp., located in Youngstown, Ohio, produces two lines of household appliances: deluxe and standard models. The owners are expanding the plant, and they are deciding which product line to emphasize. To make this decision, they assemble the following data, which suggest that the deluxe product line is more profitable:

	Deluxe	Standard
Per unit:		
Sale price	$40	$30
Variable expenses	12	10
Contribution margin	$28	$20
Contribution margin ratio . . .	70%	66⅔%

After the plant expansion, the factory will have production capacity of 1,200 machine hours per month. By devoting the machine hours to deluxe appliances, the plant can manufacture 20 units of merchandise each hour. If standard appliances are emphasized, they can produce 30 units per hour.

Required

1. Identify the limiting factor for Suntex Corp.
2. Prepare an analysis to show which product to emphasize.

Problem 24-4A *Make or buy/best use of facilities?* (L.O. 1, 2)

Glastron Company manufactures ski boats. Currently the company makes the seat covers. The cost of producing 1,000 seat covers each year is

Direct materials	$1,100
Direct labor	1,100
Variable overhead	760
Fixed overhead	2,210
Total manufacturing cost per 1000 units	$5,170

Xavier Corporation will sell the seat covers for $3 each. Glastron would pay $.14 per unit to transport the seat covers to its manufacturing plant and add its own Glastron label at a cost of $.05 per seat cover.

Required

1. Glastron accountants estimate that purchasing the seat covers from Xavier will enable the company to avoid $700 of fixed overhead. Prepare an analysis to show whether Glastron should make or buy the seat covers.
2. Assume that the Glastron factory space freed up by the company's purchasing the seat covers from Xavier can be used to manufacture another product that can be sold for a $1,610 profit. Fixed costs will not change. Prepare an analysis to show which alternative makes the best use of Glastron's factory space: (a) make, (b) buy and leave facilities idle, or (c) buy and make another product.

Problem 24-5A *Sell or process further?* **(L.O. 1, 2, 5)**

Propylene Corporation's manufacture of chemicals produces a wide variety of products. Assume that Propylene has spent $290,000 to refine 84,000 gallons of acetone, which can be sold for $3.32 a gallon. Alternatively, Propylene can process the acetone further and produce 77,000 gallons of lacquer thinner that can be sold for $4.80 a gallon. The additional processing will cost $.89 a gallon. To sell the lacquer thinner, Propylene must pay a transportation charge of $.23 a gallon and administrative expenses of $.16 a gallon.

Required

1. Identify the sunk cost in this situation. Is the sunk cost relevant to Propylene's decision?
2. Prepare an analysis to indicate whether Propylene should sell the acetone or process it into lacquer thinner. Show the expected net revenue difference between the two alternatives.
3. Identify the opportunity cost of each alternative. State how managers use the notion of opportunity cost in making their decision.

Problem 24-6A *Equipment replacement decision* **(L.O. 1, 2)**

Consider the following data regarding Providence Hospital's photocopying requirements:

	Old Equipment	Proposed Replacement Equipment
Original cost	$25,000	$9,000
Useful life in years	5	2
Current age in years	3	0
Useful life remaining in years	2	2
Accumulated depreciation	$15,000	—
Book value	10,000	—
Current disposal value in cash	2,000	—
Future disposal value in cash (in 2 years)	0	0
Annual cash operating costs (power, maintenance, supplies)	13,000	7,500

Roberta Sullivan, the hospital administrator, is evaluating replacement of the old equipment. Because of rapid changes in technology, she expects the replacement equipment to have only a two-year useful life.

Required

1. Prepare a cost comparison that includes both relevant and irrelevant items for the next two years.
2. Repeat Requirement 1, but compare relevant items only.
3. What course of action should the hospital administrator take?

Problem 24-7A *Joint cost allocation; sell at split-off or process further?* **(L.O. 1, 2, 4)**

A BP America refinery produces two products, S and M, in a joint process. Both products are sold to manufacturers as fertilizer ingredients.

Product S sells at the split-off point for $.50 per gallon; Product M, for $.60 per gallon. Data for April, 19X3, are:

Joint processing cost	$2,800,000
Gallons produced and sold:	
S	8,000,000
M	5,000,000

Suppose that in April the 5,000,000 gallons of M could have been processed further into 5,000,000 gallons of Super M at an additional cost of $500,000. The Super M could have been sold for $.76 per gallon.

Required

1. Allocate the joint processing cost to Product S and Product M using the relative sales value method.
2. Should Product M have been processed further into Super M? What is the role of the allocated joint cost (Requirement 1) in the decision to sell at split-off or further process?

Problem 24-8A *Computing unit costs and pricing formulas* **(L.O. 7)**

For 19X5, Ben Franklin Company budgeted the sale of 10,000 surge protectors.

The following data are from its budgeted income statement:

Target sales	$600,000
Variable costs:	
Manufacturing	300,000
Nonmanufacturing	60,000
Total variable costs	360,000
Fixed costs:	
Manufacturing	100,000
Nonmanufacturing	40,000
Total fixed costs	140,000
Total cost	500,000
Operating income	$100,000

Required

1. Compute both (a) the target unit selling price and (b) the unit cost for each cost category above.
2. Compute markup formulas that could be used to obtain the target selling price as a percentage of (a) variable manufacturing cost, (b) total variable cost, (c) full absorption cost, and (d) full total cost.
3. The volume for 19X6 is expected to be 12,000 surge protectors. The unit selling price and unit variable costs are expected to be the same as in 19X5. The total fixed cost in each category (manufacturing and nonmanufacturing) is predicted to remain the same. What will be the 19X6 markup percentage on variable manufacturing cost? On full absorption cost? Comment on the results.

(Group B)

Problem 24-1B *Accept or reject a special sales order?* **(L.O. 1, 2)**

Goodfellow Rubber Company's contribution margin income statement for the most recent month reports the following:

Sales—units	38,000
Sales	$95,000
Variable expenses:	
Manufacturing	$19,000
Selling and administrative	27,000
Total variable expenses	46,000
Contribution margin	49,000
Fixed expenses:	
Manufacturing	29,000
Selling and administrative	8,000
Total fixed expenses	37,000
Income from operations	$12,000

American Marketing Associates wishes to buy 5,000 industrial belts from Goodfellow. Acceptance of the offer will not increase selling and administrative expenses. Goodfellow's fixed plant has unused capacity to manufacture the additional belts. American has offered $1.60 per belt, which is considerably below the normal sale price of $2.50.

Required

1. Prepare a quick summary to help determine whether Goodfellow should accept this special sales order.
2. Prepare a total analysis to show Goodfellow's operating income with and without the special sales order.
3. Identify long-run factors that Goodfellow should consider in deciding whether to accept the special sales order.

Problem 24-2B   *Retain or drop a product line?   (L.O. 1, 2, 3)*

The income statement of Vito's Pasta Company highlights the losses of the ravioli division:

	Total	All Other Products	Ravioli
Sales	$920,000	$630,000	$290,000
Cost of goods sold:			
Variable	$170,000	$100,000	$ 70,000
Fixed	140,000	90,000	50,000
Total cost of goods sold	310,000	190,000	120,000
Gross margin	610,000	440,000	170,000
Selling and administrative expenses:			
Variable	410,000	270,000	140,000
Fixed	150,000	80,000	70,000
Total selling and administrative expenses	560,000	350,000	210,000
Operating income (loss)	$ 50,000	$ 90,000	$(40,000)

Luigi Vito, owner of the company, is considering deleting the ravioli product line. Accountants for the company estimate that dropping ravioli will decrease fixed cost of goods sold by $30,000 and decrease fixed selling and administrative expenses by $20,000.

Required

1. Prepare a quick summary to show whether Vito's should drop the ravioli product line.
2. Prepare a total analysis to show Vito's operating income with and without the ravioli division. Prepare the income statement in contribution margin format.
3. Explain the difference between correct analysis and incorrect analysis of the decision whether to drop the ravioli product line.

Problem 24-3B   *Which product to emphasize?   (L.O. 1, 2)*

Copeland Appliances is located in Cody, Wyoming. The business specializes in washers/dryers and televisions. Jim and Mary Sue Copeland, the owners, are expanding the store, and they are deciding which product line to emphasize. To make this decision, they assemble the following data, which suggest that televisions, with the higher contribution margin ratio, are more profitable:

	Washers/Dryers	Televisions
Per unit:		
Sale Price	$450	$320
Variable expenses.	235	136
Contribution margin	$215	$184
Contribution margin ratio	47.8%	57.5%

After the renovation, the store will have 6,400 square feet of floor space. By devoting the new floor space to washers/dryers, the Copelands can display 35 units of merchandise in the store. If televisions are emphasized, they can display only 32 units.

Required

1. Identify the limiting factor for Copeland Appliances.
2. Prepare an analysis to show which product to emphasize. Round contribution margin per square foot to five decimal places.

Problem 24-4B   *Make or buy/best use of facilities?*   *(L.O. 1, 2)*

Recreation Corp. of America manufactures snowmobiles. Currently the company makes the seats. The cost of producing 2,000 seats each year is

Direct material	$ 3,900
Direct labor	2,800
Variable overhead.	1,040
Fixed overhead	5,110
Total manufacturing costs	$12,850

Toledo, Inc., will sell the seats for $5 each. Recreation would pay $.22 per unit to transport the seats to its manufacturing plant and add its own Recreation insignia at a cost of $.06 per unit.

Required

1. Recreation accountants estimate that purchasing the seats from Toledo will enable the company to avoid $1,800 of fixed overhead. Prepare an analysis to show whether Recreation should make or buy the seats.
2. Assume that the Recreation factory space freed up by the company's purchasing the seats from Toledo can be used to manufacture another product that can be sold for a $3,700 profit. Fixed costs will not change. Prepare an analysis to show which alternative makes the best use of Recreation's factory space: (a) make, (b) buy and leave facilities idle, or (c) buy and make another product.

Problem 24-5B   *Sell or process further?*   *(L.O. 1, 2, 5)*

The refining of crude oil by Phillips Petroleum Company produces a variety of petroleum products. Assume that Phillips has spent $300,000 to refine 60,000 gallons of petroleum distillate. Suppose Phillips can sell the distillate for $5.75 a gallon. Alternatively, Phillips can process the distillate further and produce cleaner for tape heads in cassette decks. The additional processing will cost another $1.33 a gallon. The tape-head cleaner can be sold for $7.50 a gallon. To make this sale, Phillips must pay a sales commission of $.10 a gallon and a transportation charge of $.15 a gallon.

Required

1. Identify the sunk cost in this situation. Is the sunk cost relevant to Phillip's decision?

2. Prepare an analysis to indicate whether Phillips should sell the distillate or process it into tape-head cleaner for cassette decks. Show the expected net revenue difference between the two alternatives.

3. Identify the opportunity cost of each option. State how to use opportunity cost to make this decision.

Problem 24-6B   *Machine replacement decision   (L.O. 1, 2, 3)*

Earl Martin of Grace Street Metal Works is considering purchasing a new $135,000 machine that is expected to have a three-year life and a terminal value of zero. It can produce 40,000 units of an aftermarket engine part per year at a variable cost of $7 per unit. If purchased, the new machine will replace old equipment with a variable cost of $8.50 and book value of $60,000. The old machine is being depreciated on a straight-line basis at $20,000 per year. Because it is highly specialized, both its current and expected future disposal values are zero.

The sales representative for the new machine prepared the following comparison:

	New Machine	Old Machine
Units	40,000	40,000
Variable cost	$280,000	$340,000
Depreciation	45,000	20,000
Total cost	$325,000	$360,000
Unit cost	$8.125	$9.00

According to the representative, "The new machine is obviously worth purchasing. You will save $.875 on every unit you produce."

Required

1. Do you agree with the sales representative's analysis? If not, how would you change it?

2. The predicted demand for the engine part is 20,000 per year for the next three years. Prepare an analysis of the total and unit costs for each machine.

3. At what annual volume would the relevant costs of the old and new machines be equal?

Problem 24-7B   *Joint cost allocation; sell at split-off or process further?*
   (L.O. 1, 2, 4)

McLennan County Dairy purchases raw milk from area farmers and processes it up to the point where it becomes two products, cream and liquid skim. Cream may be sold at split-off for $6 per gallon and liquid skim may be sold for $3 per gallon. During August, 19X4, the dairy's accountant recorded the following amounts:

Joint processing cost	$20,000
Gallons produced:	
Cream	2,000
Liquid skim	6,000

Both cream and liquid skim may be further processed past split-off: cream into butter cream and liquid skim into condensed milk. One gallon of cream, combined with other ingredients, yields one gallon of butter cream. McLennan County Dairy's cost of processing 2,000 gallons of cream into 2,000 gallons of butter cream is $3,100. Butter cream sells for $7.50 per gallon.

All of the August production of cream and liquid skim was sold at split-off.

Required

1. Allocate the joint processing cost to the gallons of cream and liquid skim produced in August. Use the relative sales value method.
2. Why did the dairy's managers decide not to process cream into butter cream? Be specific.

Problem 24-8B *Computing pricing formulas* **(L.O. 7)**

Michaels Corporation, a building contractor, constructs as many as 15 houses simultaneously. The company's accounting manager, Lauren Gray, has budgeted costs for 19X6 as follows:

Direct materials......................	$1,500,000
Direct labor	750,000
Job construction overhead:	
Variable............................	450,000
Fixed	300,000
Total construction cost	$3,000,000
Selling and administrative costs	750,000
Total cost	$3,750,000

The selling and administrative costs include $150,000 of variable costs, such as sales commissions and bonuses, that vary with sales volume. Gray has set a target operating income of $750,000 for the year.

Required

Compute markup formulas that could be used to set the target selling prices of homes as a percentage of

1. Variable construction cost
2. Total variable cost and selling and administrative costs
3. Full absorption cost of construction
4. Full total cost

Extending Your Knowledge

Decision Problem

Using Relevant Cost Analysis to Make Business Decisions (L.O. 1)

Sam Webb is a second-year business student at the University of Cincinnati. He will graduate in two years with an accounting major and a marketing minor. It is now April, and Sam is trying to decide where to work this summer. He has two choices: work full-time for a bottling plant, or work part-time in the accounting department of a meat-packing plant.

    If Sam works part-time, he can take two courses toward his degree for no extra tuition. This option will reduce his workload next year. It might also allow him to work part-time during the regular term in the bottling plant. In addition, the experience gained this summer will qualify Sam for a full-time position with the meat-packing company next summer.

    The meat-packing company and the university are close enough to Sam's home that he could ride his bike. However, if he works at the bottling plant he must drive. Sam's car is a 1975 Dodge Swinger that he bought two years ago for $2,000; he is not sure how much longer the car will run.

Sam is able to work 12 weeks during the summer. This year the bottling plant is paying $300 per week; average annual increases have been 6%. At the meat-packing plant, Sam could work 20 hours per week at $6.90 per hour. Sam thinks he could work at the bottling plant again next summer. In a full-time position at the meat-packing company, he would earn $500 per week next summer.

Required

Advise Sam on the better course of action. Identify opportunity costs and sunk costs in the decision. Also identify any assumptions that you make.

Ethical Issue

Missoula Construction Company, a corporation, builds highways for the state of Montana. Geoff Duggins, the company president, needs a new earth-moving vehicle and is evaluating three alternatives. Vehicles 1 and 2 cost the same amount, but the variable operating cost of vehicle 1 is expected to be $3,000 per year less than the variable cost of vehicle 2. Vehicle 3 is a new experimental machine that costs $5,000 more than the other two pieces of equipment. Because it has just recently been developed, its variable operating costs are difficult to predict. Company accountants expect the variable cost to be approximately the same as that of vehicle 1, but they tell Duggins that the cost may range from $4,000 per year less than the variable cost of vehicle 1 to $4,000 per year more.

A close friend of Duggins owns the company marketing the new experimental machine. Duggins wants him to get the business.

Required

1. Which vehicle should Duggins purchase? Why?
2. What is your opinion of Duggins's ethics if he buys vehicle 3? Who is helped and who is harmed by this action? Would your answer change if Missoula Construction Company were a proprietorship instead of a corporation?

Appendix

Absorption and Variable Costing

Chapters 17 and 24 briefly compare the two alternative approaches to income measurement. These approaches are the conventional, or functional, approach, which is based on absorption costing, and the contribution approach, which is based on variable costing. Recall that with absorption costing, fixed manufacturing cost (fixed overhead) is applied to products produced through the budgeted factory overhead rate (Chapter 19). That is, fixed overhead is "absorbed" into product cost and expensed as part of cost of goods sold. On the other hand, fixed manufacturing cost is not applied to products but instead is expensed as a lump-sum period cost under variable costing. Only variable manufacturing costs—direct materials, direct labor, and variable overhead—are assigned to products.

In both Exhibit 17-4, p. 813, and Exhibit 24-1, p. 1096, operating income is the same on both absorption (functional) and variable (contribution) costing income statements. This is not always the case; we implicitly assumed in both examples that the number of units of output produced was equal to the number of units sold. Actually, manufacturing companies sometimes produce more units than they sell during a year (or other period) and sometimes sell more than they produce. This appendix presents comparative income statements for both these circumstances.

Our examples are based on the Torino Corporation production and cost data used for Exhibit 24-1. *The only change is the assumed sales volume.* For convenience, the data are repeated in Exhibit 24A-1.

Under absorption costing, the fixed overhead portion of the budgeted factory overhead rate is $.80 ($200,000 ÷ 250,000 oil filter units). The manufacturing cost per unit, and therefore unit cost of goods sold, is $2.00 ($1.20 variable and $.80 fixed). The unit gross margin is $1.20 ($3.20 − $2.00). Under variable costing, the unit contribution margin is $1.70 [$3.20 − ($1.20 + $.30)].

We now demonstrate how differences between production and sales volume result in differences between absorption costing and variable costing operating income.

Operating Income When Units Produced Exceed Units Sold

Exhibit 24-A2 presents absorption costing and variable costing income statements for an assumed sales volume of 240,000 units. Absorption income is $8,000 ($91,000 − $83,000) greater than variable income. Why? The difference is due solely to the amount of fixed overhead cost expensed. Under absorption costing, the year's fixed overhead cost of $200,000 is applied to the 250,000 oil filters produced, at the rate of $.80 per unit. Of that amount, $192,000 (240,000 × $.80) is expensed as part of manufacturing cost of goods sold. The remaining $8,000 [(250,000 − 240,000) × $.80] is held back in Finished Goods Inventory,

Oil filters produced....................................	250,000
Unit sales price	$3.20
Unit variable manufacturing cost	$1.20
Unit variable selling and administrative cost	$.30
Total fixed manufacturing cost...........................	$200,000
Total fixed selling and administrative cost	$125,000

assigned to the 10,000 filters produced but not sold. That cost will be expensed in 19X3, when the 10,000 filters are sold.

On the variable costing statement, the entire $200,000 of fixed overhead cost is expensed as a lump-sum. The $8,000 ($192,000 − $200,000) difference in fixed overhead expensed accounts for the $8,000 difference in incomes.

Operating Income When Units Sold Exceed Units Produced

Exhibit 24-A3 presents income statements for a 19X3 sales volume of 260,000 oil filters. All other data are assumed to be the same as for 19X2, including the budgeted and actual production volume of 250,000 units.

For 19X3, variable costing income is $8,000 greater than absorption income. The difference again is due entirely to the fixed overhead cost expensed. With absorption costing, the $200,000 of 19X3 fixed overhead cost is assigned to the

EXHIBIT 24A-2   Functional Format and Contribution Margin Format Income Statements.
Units Produced = 250,000; Units Sold = 240,000

Torino Corporation
Income Statement
For the Year Ended December 31, 19X2

Absorption Costing Functional Format		Variable Costing Contribution Margin Format		
Sales $768,000		Sales		$768,000
Less manufacturing cost of		Less variable expenses:		
goods sold 480,000		Manufacturing	$288,000	
Gross margin 288,000		Selling and administrative..	72,000	360,000
Less selling and administrative		Contribution margin		408,000
expenses 197,000		Less fixed expenses:		
		Manufacturing	200,000	
		Selling and administrative..	125,000	325,000
Operating income .... $ 91,000		Operating income		$ 83,000

Torino Corporation Income Statement For the Year Ended December 31, 19X3				
Absorption Costing Functional Format		**Variable Costing Contribution Margin Format**		
Sales	$832,000	Sales		$832,000
Less manufacturing cost of		Less variable expenses:		
goods sold	520,000	Manufacturing	$312,000	
Gross margin	312,000	Selling and administrative..	78,000	390,000
Less selling and administrative		Contribution margin.........		442,000
expenses	203,000	Less fixed expenses:		
		Manufacturing	200,000	
		Selling and administrative..	125,000	325,000
Operating income	$109,000	Operating income		$117,000

250,000 units produced that year, just as in 19X2. All these units are sold in 19X3; thus, all $200,000 is expensed as part of the year's cost of goods sold. However, this is not *all* the fixed manufacturing cost expensed in 19X3. The 10,000 units produced but not sold in 19X2 also are sold in 19X3, and the $8,000 of fixed cost assigned to them also is expensed. The total fixed overhead portion of 19X3 cost of goods sold therefore is $208,000 [(250,000 + 10,000) × $.80] under absorption costing. By contrast, only the actual cost of $200,000 is expensed on the variable costing statement. As before, the difference in fixed overhead expensed ($208,000 − $200,000 = $8,000) accounts for the difference in incomes.

Summary of Income Effects

The preceding examples illustrate the differences in operating income reported under absorption and variable costing systems. The effects of differences between production and sales volumes may be summarized as follows:

Circumstance	*Effect*
Units produced equal units sold	Absorption costing income equals variable costing income
Units produced exceed units sold	Absorption costing income exceeds variable costing income
Units sold exceed units produced	Variable costing income exceeds absorption costing income

Bear in mind that individual-year differences are likely to be small for companies that seek to minimize inventories and produce only to satisfy actual customer demand. Also, year-to-year differences cancel out each other, as production volume exceeds sales volume in some years and sales volume exceeds production volume in others. Total operating income over the life of a company (assuming that all output produced is eventually sold) is the same for either approach.

Appendix Review Problem

Refer to Exhibit 24A-1. Assume that Torino Corporation's unit variable costs and total fixed costs are the same as those in the exhibit. Also assume that the budgeted sales volume for 19X4 is only 200,000 oil filters and that 200,000 are both produced and sold.

Required

1. Under absorption costing, what is the fixed overhead portion of the budgeted factory overhead rate for 19X4? What is the manufacturing cost of goods sold per unit?
2. What is the unit contribution margin for 19X4?
3. Prepare functional format and contribution margin format income statements for 19X4.

SOLUTION TO REVIEW PROBLEM

1. $200,000 ÷ 200,000 oil filter units = $1.00 per unit, the fixed overhead portion of the budgeted factory rate. The manufacturing cost of goods sold per unit is $2.20 ($1.20 variable and $1.00 fixed).
2. The unit contribution margin remains $1.70 [$3.20 − ($1.20 + $.30)]. It is not affected by production or sales volume.

3.

Torino Corporation
Income Statement
For the Year Ended December 31, 19X4

Sales	$640,000	Sales		$640,000
Less manufacturing		Less variable expenses:		
cost of goods sold	440,000	Manufacturing	$240,000	
Gross margin	200,000	Selling and administrative	60,000	300,000
Less selling and administrative		Contribution margin		340,000
expenses	185,000	Less fixed expenses:		
		Manufacturing	200,000	
		Selling and administrative	125,000	325,000
Operating income	$ 15,000	Operating income		$ 15,000

Chapter 25

Capital Budgeting

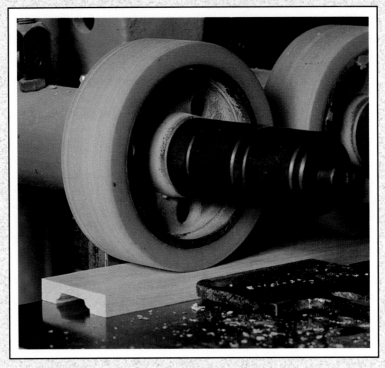

Grant Gummelt, manager of the engineering department of Bangor Desk Company, closed his office door and strode over to the coffee machine. He had only 24 hours to decide whether to recommend the purchase of a new sanding machine.

The sanding machine, designed to replace four-year-old general-purpose equipment, could be purchased for $600,000, delivered and installed. The older general-purpose equipment could be sold to a nearby company.

Bangor executives, Gummelt realized, demanded capital expenditures of this great an amount to generate at least a 15 percent return on a discounted basis. He believed that now would be a good time to buy the machine. The industry to which Bangor sold its products was booming. Also, the prices of sanding machines had dropped recently. It was likely that they would go up again within the next year. What should Gummelt recommend? Keep the old machine or purchase the new?

Popular Capital-Budgeting Models

A factory building may be used for 50 years. Equipment for successful products such as Ivory soap and Coca-Cola may be used for decades. The term *capital asset* refers to an asset that is used over a long period of time. Plant assets such as land, buildings, machinery, equipment, and furniture and fixtures are capital assets. The decisions for the purchase of such long-term assets often require long-range planning and large risks. Many uncertain factors—such as consumer preferences, manufacturing costs, and government legislation—enter into the decisions on the purchase of capital assets. Successful organizations quantify as many of these factors as they can before making long-range decisions. Grant Gummelt in the chapter-opening vignette is in the pressured position of having to make a long-range decision in a short period of time. The method, or technique, he will use for evaluating and choosing among alternative courses of action is called a **decision model.**

Capital budgeting is a formal means of analyzing long-range investment decisions. Examples include plant locations, equipment purchases, additions of product lines, and territorial expansions. The diagram below shows where capital budgeting fits into the process of purchasing and using long-term assets.

In this chapter, we discuss four popular capital-budgeting decision models (methods of making choices): payback, accounting rate of return, net present value, and internal rate of return. In large measure, the models use *net cash inflow from operations*. Generally accepted accounting principles are based on the accrual accounting model, but capital budgeting focuses on cash. The desirability of a capital asset depends on its ability to generate cash inflows that exceed required cash outflows over its useful life.

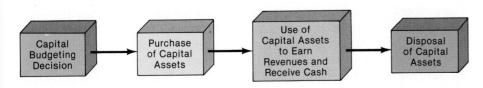

EXHIBIT 25-1 *Payback—Equal Annual Net Cash Inflows*

$$\text{Payback period (P)} = \frac{\text{Amount invested (I)}}{\text{Expected annual net cash inflow from operations (O)}}$$

$$P = \frac{I}{O}$$

$$= \frac{\$24,000}{\$6,000} = 4 \text{ years}$$

Payback—Equal Annual Cash Flows

Payback is the length of time it will take to recover, in net cash inflow from operations, the dollars of a capital outlay. Suppose a business pays $24,000 for an assembling machine with an estimated useful life of six years and zero estimated residual value. Managers expect use of the machine to generate net cash inflow from operations of $6,000 annually. This increase in cash could result from an increase in revenues, a decrease in expenses, or a combination of the two.

Payback is expressed as a period of time, as shown in Exhibit 25-1. The payback model measures how swiftly investment dollars may be recovered. The shorter the payback period, the more attractive the asset.

A major criticism of the payback model is that it does *not* consider or measure profitability. Consequently, the payback technique can lead to an unwise decision. Suppose an alternative to the $24,000 machine is a comparable machine that also costs $24,000 but which will save $8,000 annually during its three-year life. The two machines' payback periods are computed as follows:

OBJECTIVE 1

Use four capital-budgeting models to make investment decisions

$$\text{Payback period for Machine 1} = \frac{\$24,000}{\$6,000} = 4 \text{ years}$$

$$\text{Payback period for Machine 2} = \frac{\$24,000}{\$8,000} = 3 \text{ years}$$

The payback criterion favors the second machine because it recovers the asset cost more quickly. But consider useful lives. Suppose the second machine's useful life is the same as its payback period—three years. Its use will merely cover cost and provide no profits. Machine 1, on the other hand, will be more profitable. It will generate net cash inflows for six years—two years beyond its payback period—which will give the company additional net cash inflow of $12,000 ($6,000 × 2 years).

Payback—Unequal Annual Cash Flows

The payback equation can be used only when net cash inflows are the same each period. When periodic cash flows are unequal, the payback computation has a cumulative form. Each year's net cash inflows are accumulated until the amount invested is recovered. Suppose Machine 1 in our example will produce annual net cash inflows of $10,000 in the first year, $8,000 in Year 2, and $5,000 in Years 3 through 6. Exhibit 25-2 shows the payback computation when annual cash flows are unequal.

Years 1, 2, and 3 together bring in $23,000. Recovery of the amount invested ($24,000) occurs during Year 4. We can compute that payback (P) occurs in 3.2 years:

$$P = 3 \text{ years} + \left(\frac{\begin{array}{c}\$1{,}000 \text{ needed to complete recovery} \\ \text{in Year 4}\end{array}}{\begin{array}{c}\$5{,}000 \text{ net cash inflow during the} \\ \text{year when recovery is completed}\end{array}} \times 1 \text{ year} \right) =$$

$$= 3 \text{ years} + \qquad\qquad .2 \text{ year} \qquad\qquad = 3.2 \text{ years}$$

How does a manager use the payback model in capital budgeting? Managers often compare the payback period with the asset's useful life. The asset's payback period must be shorter than its useful life. Let's take an extreme example. If a machine has a payback period of five years and a useful life of three years, the company will never earn a profit from using the asset. How much shorter than the useful life the payback period must be is a matter of personal preference. When the business is deciding between two or more assets, the asset with the shortest payback period is the most profitable—if all other factors are the same.

The payback method highlights cash flows, an important factor in business decisions. Moreover, payback is easily understood. Advocates view it as a way to eliminate proposals that are unusually risky (for projects with lengthy payback periods). A major weakness of payback is that it ignores profitability.

Accounting Rate of Return

A primary goal of business is to earn profits. One measure of profitability is the **accounting rate of return** on investment. The rate of return is computed by dividing income by the amount of the investment made to earn the income:

$$\text{Rate of return} = \frac{\text{Income}}{\text{Investment}}$$

In capital budgeting, the income amount is income from operations (operating income) that results from use of the asset. Operating income on an asset can be computed as net cash inflow minus depreciation on the asset. Accounting rate of return is computed in Exhibit 25-3 for the machine in the payback illustration. Recall that the machine costs $24,000 and has a useful life of six years with no estimated residual value. Annual straight-line depreciation is,

EXHIBIT 25-2   Payback—Unequal Annual Net Cash Inflows

Year	Amount Invested	Net Cash Inflow	
		Each Year	Accumulated
0	$24,000	—	—
1	—	$10,000	$10,000
2	—	8,000	18,000
3	—	5,000	23,000
3.2	—	1,000	24,000

therefore, $4,000 ($24,000/6 years). Use of the machine is expected to generate annual net cash inflows of $6,000.

Accounting rate of return is an *average*. It measures the average rate of return from using the asset over its entire life. The computation is average annual operating income divided by the average amount invested in the asset. If annual operating income varies by year (as in the preceding payback illustration), compute the average annual operating income over the asset's life and use this amount (as O) to compute the accounting return. Also, the book value of the asset decreases as it is used and depreciated. Thus the company's investment in the asset declines. Average investment in the asset is computed as the average of its cost and estimated residual value.

When the asset's residual value is not zero, the average amount invested will *not* be half the asset's cost. For example, assume the asset's residual value is $3,000. Annual depreciation is $3,500 [($24,000 − $3,000)/6]. The accounting rate of return computation becomes

$$R = \frac{\$6,000 - \$3,500}{(\$24,000 + \$3,000)/2} = \frac{\$2,500}{\$13,500} = .185 = 18.5\%$$

Suppose a company is purchasing a machine. The company can use the accounting rate of return to make the capital-budgeting decision. Suppose the machine under consideration is the one in Exhibit 25-3, with an accounting rate of return of 16.7 percent. Many companies demand a minimum rate of return on their investment projects. They invest only in assets with accounting rates of return equal to or greater than the minimum rate. Assume that the company's minimum rate is 20 percent. Would managers approve an investment in the illustrated machine, which is expected to generate an average return of 16.7 percent? No, because the asset's average annual return is less than the company's minimum rate.

Rates of return can be computed on a before-tax or after-tax basis. For simplicity, we ignore income taxes until later in this chapter.

Discounted Cash Flow Models

Although the accounting rate of return model measures profitability, it has a major weakness. It does not recognize the time value of money. It fails to

EXHIBIT 25-3 *Accounting Rate of Return*

$$\text{Accounting rate of return (R)} = \frac{\text{Average annual operating income from investment*}}{\text{Average amount invested}} = \frac{\text{Average annual net cash inflow from operations (O)} - \text{Annual depreciation (D)}}{[\text{Amount invested (I)} + \text{Residual value (RV)}]/2}$$

$$R = \frac{O - D}{(I + RV)/2}$$

$$= \frac{\$6,000 - \$4,000}{(\$24,000 + \$0)/2} = \frac{\$2,000}{\$12,000} = .167 = 16.7\%$$

*Operating income can also be computed as revenues minus expenses consider the timing of the cash outlay to purchase the asset and the timing of the annual net cash inflows. Discounted cash flow models are popular because they overcome this weakness. In the chapter-opening vignette, top management of Bangor Desk Company requires at least "a 15 percent return on a discounted basis." The reference to a "discounted basis" means that this company uses discounted cash flow models for capital budgeting.

Discounted cash flow models are conceptually superior to payback models and accounting rate of return models. They are used by over 85 percent of the large industrial firms in the United States. There are two main variations of discounted cash flow models: (1) net present value (NPV) and (2) internal rate of return (IRR). Both variations are based on the concept of compound interest.

Choosing the Minimum Desired Rate of Return

The **minimum desired rate of return** (*hurdle rate, cutoff rate, required rate, discount rate, cost of capital*) is the rate that can be earned by the best alternative use of investment capital. Selecting the rate is a complex problem that is discussed fully in finance texts. The rate of return differs by types of investments, depending on the risk (the degree of variability in likely outcomes). For example, petroleum companies use higher minimum rates for exploration projects than for refining operations.

Capital-budgeting decision models focus on *investing* decisions, not *financing* decisions. The models avoid a piecemeal approach; that is, the hurdle rate for a specific project is unaffected by whether the project is financed by all debt, all ownership capital, or some of both. The piecemeal approach would lead to the acceptance of any project as long as its expected rate of return on invested capital exceeds the interest rate on any cash borrowed to finance the project. Therefore, a project would be accepted if its expected rate of return is 11 percent and the borrowing rate is 10 percent. The flaw here is that a series of such decisions will produce enormous debt that will cause the borrowing rate to soar or will prohibit any additional borrowing. During a subsequent year, inability to borrow might prevent the company from accepting a project with a substantially higher expected rate of return.

Net Present Value

Appendix A, "Time Value of Money," discusses the concept of present value. The present value of $1 to be received in the future is less than $1 today. The logic is this: to receive $1 a year from now, we would pay less than $1 today. Why? Because if we pay $1 or more now to receive $1 a year later, we earn no income. Instead, we could deposit our $1 in a bank to earn interest of, say, $.08 during the year and have $1.08 a year later. We would rather have $1.08 than $1.00. The fact that we can earn income by investing money for a period of time is called the **time value of money**.

The present-value concept can be applied to the acquisition of capital assets. A company purchases an asset in order to earn revenues and receive cash. The excess of cash revenue received over the cash paid for costs associated with an investment is called the investment's net cash inflow. Ordinarily net cash inflow is stated in an annual amount. The advantage of analyzing net cash inflows instead of analyzing accounting income is that the focus is on the premier asset, cash.

The timing of the net cash inflows from operations is important because of the time value of money. Consider two $10,000 investments. Both investments promise future cash receipts of $11,000. Investment 1 will bring in cash of $5,500 at the end of each of two years. Investment 2 will return the full $11,000 at the end of the second year. Which investment is better? Investment 1, because it brings cash home sooner, and so the cash can be invested for a longer period of time.

The **net present value (NPV)** model is a discounted cash flow approach to capital budgeting. It computes the expected net monetary gain or loss from a project by discounting all expected future cash inflows and outflows to the present time, using a minimum desired rate of return. A zero or positive NPV indicates that the investment should be accepted. A negative net present value indicates that the investment should be rejected. If this model is used to compare several assets, the asset with the highest net present value is the best.

Assume that the business is considering the manufacture of two products, tape decks and VCRs. Each would require different specialized equipment costing the same amount, $1 million, and having zero residual value. Each piece of equipment is expected to have a five-year life. The two products have different patterns of expected net cash inflows:

	Annual Net Cash Inflows	
Year	Tape Decks	VCRs
1	$ 305,450	$ 500,000
2	305,450	350,000
3	305,450	300,000
4	305,450	250,000
5	305,450	40,000
Total	$1,527,250	$1,440,000

Total net cash inflows are greater if the company invests in the manufacture of tape decks. However, these net cash inflows will occur in the future. In the net-present-value model, we base the capital-budgeting decision on present value, not future values. In present-value language, we say that we *discount* these future cash flows to present value. Discounted cash flow is a representation of cash inflows and outflows at a common time so that they can be compared (added, subtracted, and so on) for decision making.

The manufacture and sale of tape decks is expected to generate $305,450 of net cash inflow each year—a total of $1,527,250. A stream of equal periodic amounts is called an **annuity**. The present value of an annuity is computed by multiplying the periodic amount ($305,450 annually, in this case) by the present value of an annuity of $1 from Table 25-2, page 1146. Let's assume that the minimum desired rate of return is 14 percent. The table indicates that the present value of an annuity of $1 for five periods discounted at 14 percent is 3.433. Exhibit 25-4 shows the computation of the present value of the net cash inflows from investing in the tape-deck project—$1,048,610.

The annual net cash inflows from investing in the manufacture of VCRs are unequal—$500,000 in Year 1, $350,000 in Year 2, and so on. Because these amounts vary by year, the present value of each annual amount is computed separately. For example:

Year	Find the Present Value Factor From Table 25-1 page 1145 14% Column		Net Cash Inflow		Present Value of Net Cash Inflows
1	.877	×	$500,000	=	$438,500
2	.769	×	350,000	=	269,150

Exhibit 25-4 includes these present-value computations.

The exhibit indicates that the VCR project has a net present value of $78,910, compared with $48,610 for the tape-deck project. The analysis favors VCRs because an investment in that project will earn the company's hurdle rate of 14 percent plus an additional $78,910. This expected excess is greater than the net present value of the tape-deck project, which also meets the hurdle rate of 14 percent but returns only an additional $48,610.

This example illustrates an important point about net-present-value analysis. The tape-deck project promises the greater total amount of net cash inflows, but the timing of the VCR cash flows—loaded near the beginning of the project—causes the VCR project to have a higher net present value. The VCR project is more attractive because of the time value of money. Its nearer dollars are worth more now than the more-distant dollars of the tape-deck project.

Another important point about net-present-value analysis is this: Either project, considered alone, is acceptable because its net present value is at least zero. Thus, both projects earn at least the minimum desired rate of return of 14 percent.

Net Present Value of a Project with Residual Value

When the asset to be acquired is expected to have a residual value at the end of its useful life, that amount also should be considered in the NPV analysis. It must be discounted to its present value and added to the present value of the annual net cash inflows to determine the total present value of the project. The residual value is discounted as a single amount—not an annuity—because it

EXHIBIT 25-4 Net Present Value

	Present Value at 14%		Net Cash Inflow		Present Value of Net Cash Inflows
Tape-Deck Project:					
Present value of equal annual net cash inflows for 5 years	3.433*	×	$305,450 per year	=	$ 1,048,610
Investment					(1,000,000)
Net present value of the tape deck project					$ 48,610
VCR Project:					
Present value of net cash inflow by year: **Year**					
1	.877†	×	$500,000	=	$ 438,500
2	.769	×	350,000	=	269,150
3	.675	×	300,000	=	202,500
4	.592	×	250,000	=	148,000
5	.519	×	40,000	=	20,760
Total present value of net cash inflows					1,078,910
Investment					(1,000,000)
Net present value of the VCR project					$ 78,910

*Present value of annuity of $1 for 5 years at 14%, Table 25-2, page 1146.
†Present value of $1 for 1 year, 2 years, 3 years, and so on, at 14%, Table 25-1, page 1145.

will be received only at the end of the asset's useful life (that is, when the asset is sold).

Suppose the equipment to manufacture tape decks (in Exhibit 25-4) is expected to be worth $100,000 at the end of its five-year life. To determine the tape-deck project's NPV, we discount $100,000 for five years at 14 percent—using Table 25-1 on page 1145—and add its present value ($51,900), as shown in Exhibit 25-5.

Compare the tape-deck project's NPVs in Exhibits 25-4 and 25-5. The residual amount raises the project's NPV to $100,510, which is higher than the VCR project's NPV. If the VCR equipment is expected to have zero disposal value, then the tape-deck project is more attractive. This illustrates the difference that residual value can make to a business decision. Although the amount may often be insignificant, it can change an investment decision.

There is a slightly different way to use present-value analysis for making capital-budgeting decisions. Suppose the company starts the decision process by determining the present values of the expected future net cash inflows from the two projects—$1,048,610 for tape decks and $1,078,910 for VCRs. Managers may ask, What is the most we can invest in the tape-deck project and still earn our minimum desired rate of return of 14 percent? With zero residual values, the answer is $1,048,610. Similarly, the maximum acceptable investment for VCRs is $1,078,910. Negotiations with the seller of the tape-deck manufacturing equipment may drive the required investment down to only $850,000. This would increase the tape-deck project's attractiveness, especially if the cost of the VCR manufacturing equipment remains $1,000,000. In any event, managers would not want to pay more than $1,048,610 for the tape-deck equipment or more than $1,078,910 for the VCR equipment. At prices above these present-value amounts, the company would not be able to earn 14 percent on its investment.

Internal Rate of Return

Another discounted cash flow model for capital budgeting is the *internal rate of return (IRR)* model. The **internal rate of return—the IRR**—of an investment project is the rate of return that makes the net present value of the project equal to zero. As the name implies, a project's IRR is the rate of return that a company can expect to earn by investing in the project. The higher the IRR, the more desirable the project; the lower the IRR, the less desirable.

Exhibit 25-6 shows why 16 percent is the IRR of our tape-deck project. The 16 percent rate produces a net present value of zero. There are three steps:

EXHIBIT 25-5 *Net Present Value of a Project with Residual Value*

Tape-Deck Project	Present Value at 14%	Net Cash Inflow	Present Value of Net Cash Inflows
Present value of equal annual net cash inflows for 5 years (from Exhibit 25-4)	3.433	× $305,450 per year =	$ 1,048,610
Present value of residual value	.519*	× $100,000 =	51,900
Present value of the project's net cash inflows			1,100,510
Investment			(1,000,000)
Net present value of tape-deck project			$ 100,510

*Present value of $1 for 5 years at 14%, Table 25-1, pg. 1145.

TABLE 25-1 *Present Value of $1*

					Present Value of $1				
Periods	6%	7%	8%	10%	12%	14%	16%	18%	20%
1	0.943	0.935	0.926	0.909	0.893	0.877	0.862	0.847	0.833
2	0.890	0.873	0.857	0.826	0.797	0.769	0.743	0.718	0.694
3	0.840	0.816	0.794	0.751	0.712	0.675	0.641	0.609	0.579
4	0.792	0.763	0.735	0.683	0.636	0.592	0.552	0.516	0.482
5	0.747	0.713	0.681	0.621	0.567	0.519	0.476	0.437	0.402
6	0.705	0.666	0.630	0.564	0.507	0.456	0.410	0.370	0.335
7	0.665	0.623	0.583	0.513	0.452	0.400	0.354	0.314	0.279
8	0.627	0.582	0.540	0.467	0.404	0.351	0.305	0.266	0.233
9	0.592	0.544	0.500	0.424	0.361	0.308	0.263	0.225	0.194
10	0.558	0.508	0.463	0.386	0.322	0.270	0.227	0.191	0.162
11	0.527	0.475	0.429	0.350	0.287	0.237	0.195	0.162	0.135
12	0.497	0.444	0.397	0.319	0.257	0.208	0.168	0.137	0.112
13	0.469	0.415	0.368	0.290	0.229	0.182	0.145	0.116	0.093
14	0.442	0.388	0.340	0.263	0.205	0.160	0.125	0.099	0.078
15	0.417	0.362	0.315	0.239	0.183	0.140	0.108	0.084	0.065
16	0.394	0.339	0.292	0.218	0.163	0.123	0.093	0.071	0.054
17	0.371	0.317	0.270	0.198	0.146	0.108	0.080	0.060	0.045
18	0.350	0.296	0.250	0.180	0.130	0.095	0.069	0.051	0.038
19	0.331	0.277	0.232	0.164	0.116	0.083	0.060	0.043	0.031
20	0.312	0.258	0.215	0.149	0.104	0.073	0.051	0.037	0.026

Appendix B provides a fuller table for the present value of $1.

1. Identify the expected net cash inflows ($305,450 for five years) exactly as in calculating the net present value in Exhibit 25-4.
2. Find the interest rate that equates the present value of the cash inflows to the present value of the cash outflows. If one outflow is followed by a series of equal inflows, use the following equation to solve for the value of the present-value (PV) factor:

Investment = Expected annual net cash inflow × Annuity PV factor
$1,000,000 = $305,450 × PV factor

$$PV\ factor = \frac{\$1,000,000}{\$305,450} = 3.274$$

EXHIBIT 25-6 *Internal Rate of Return, Tape-Deck Project*

	Present Value at 16%		Net Cash Inflow		Present Value of Net Cash Inflows
Present value of equal annual net cash inflows for 5 years ...	3.274	×	$305,450	=	$ 1,000,000*
Investment					(1,000,000)
Net present value of the tape deck project					$ 0 †

* Slight rounding error.
† The zero difference proves that the rate of return is 16%.

TABLE 25-2 *Present Value of Annuity of $1*

Periods	6%	7%	8%	10%	12%	14%	16%	18%	20%
1	0.943	0.935	0.926	0.909	0.893	0.877	0.862	0.847	0.833
2	1.833	1.808	1.783	1.736	1.690	1.647	1.605	1.566	1.528
3	2.673	2.624	2.577	2.487	2.402	2.322	2.246	2.174	2.106
4	3.465	3.387	3.312	3.170	3.037	2.914	2.798	2.690	2.589
5	4.212	4.100	3.993	3.791	3.605	3.433	3.274	3.127	2.991
6	4.917	4.767	4.623	4.355	4.111	3.889	3.685	3.498	3.326
7	5.582	5.389	5.206	4.868	4.564	4.288	4.039	3.812	3.605
8	6.210	5.971	5.747	5.335	4.968	4.639	4.344	4.078	3.837
9	6.802	6.515	6.247	5.759	5.328	4.946	4.607	4.303	4.031
10	7.360	7.024	6.710	6.145	5.650	5.216	4.833	4.494	4.192
11	7.887	7.499	7.139	6.495	5.938	5.453	5.029	4.656	4.327
12	8.384	7.943	7.536	6.814	6.194	5.660	5.197	4.793	4.439
13	8.853	8.358	7.904	7.103	6.424	5.842	5.342	4.910	4.533
14	9.295	8.745	8.244	7.367	6.628	6.002	5.468	5.008	4.611
15	9.712	9.108	8.559	7.606	6.811	6.142	5.575	5.092	4.675
16	10.106	9.447	8.851	7.824	6.974	6.265	5.669	5.162	4.730
17	10.477	9.763	9.122	8.022	7.120	6.373	5.749	5.222	4.775
18	10.828	10.059	9.372	8.201	7.250	6.467	5.818	5.273	4.812
19	11.158	10.336	9.604	8.365	7.366	6.550	5.877	5.316	4.844
20	11.470	10.594	9.818	8.514	7.469	6.623	5.929	5.353	4.870

Appendix B provides a fuller table for the present value of an annuity of $1.

Scan the row in Table 25-2 that represents the relevant life of the project, the 5-period row in our example. Choose the column with the number closest to the annuity PV factor that was calculated. The 3.274 annuity factor is in the 16 percent column. Therefore, the IRR of the tape-deck project is 16 percent.

3. Compare the IRR with the minimum desired rate of return. If the IRR is equal to or greater than the minimum desired rate, the project should be accepted. Otherwise, it should be rejected.

If tape decks are the only investment under consideration, managers will invest in the project because its 16 percent IRR exceeds the 14 percent hurdle rate.

Varying Cash Flows and Internal Rate

In the situation of Exhibit 25-4, the VCR project has a higher net present value than the tape-deck project. The VCR investment also has a higher IRR. Many calculators can compute the VCR project's IRR. However, in hand calculations, trial-and-error methods are necessary to compute the rate. Why? Because cash inflows are not equal every year.

In our example, note that the internal rate of the tape-deck project is 16 percent. Hence, because the net present value of the VCR project is higher than that of the tape-deck project, its internal rate also is higher. Use Table 25-1 (p. 1145) and try an 18 percent rate. First, focus on the 18 percent trial that follows:

		Trial at 18%		Trial at 20%	
Year	Cash Inflows	Present-Value Factor	Total Present Value	Present-Value Factor	Total Present Value
1	$500,000	.847	$ 423,500	.833	$416,500
2	350,000	.718	251,300	.694	242,900
3	300,000	.609	182,700	.579	173,700
4	250,000	.516	129,000	.482	120,500
5	40,000	.437	17,480	.402	16,080
			$1,003,980		$969,680

Because $1,003,980 is higher than the $1,000,000 investment, the true internal rate is slightly higher than 18 percent.

Capital-budgeting models deal with uncertain predictions. For that reason many managers would say that the 18 percent computation is sufficiently accurate for decision-making purposes. If a manager wants a more precise calculation, he or she can try 20 percent (or 19 percent, if such a table is available). The 20 percent total present value of $969,680 is below the required investment of $1,000,000. The IRR therefore is between 18 percent and 20 percent.

Comparison of the Capital-Budgeting Models

How do the net-present-value approach and the IRR approach compare? The net-present-value method indicates the amount of the excess (or deficiency) of a project's present value of net cash inflows over (or under) its required investment—for a specified rate of return. Net present value, though, does not show the project's unique rate of return. The IRR shows the project's rate but fails to indicate the dollar difference between the project's present value of future cash flows and its required investment. In most cases the two methods lead to the same investment decision.

The discounted cash flow models are better than the payback or accounting-rate-of-return models because they are based on cash flows and because they consider both profitability and the time value of money. The time value of money enters the analysis through the discounting of future dollars to present value. Profitability is also built into the discounted cash flow models. Managers specify the earnings rate that they demand of investment projects. Use of this minimum earnings rate—10 percent, 15 percent, or whatever—as the discount rate for the computations produces the maximum price for the

OBJECTIVE 2

Compare and contrast popular capital-budgeting models

EXHIBIT 25-7   Capital-Budgeting Decision Models

Model	Strengths	Weaknesses
Payback	Easy to understand Based on cash flows Highlights risks	Ignores profitability and the time value of money
Accounting rate of return	Based on profitability	Ignores the time value of money
Discounted cash flow models: Net present value Internal rate of return	Based on cash flows, profitability, and the time value of money	None of the above

project. At this price, the project is expected to earn the specified rate of return.

Exhibit 25-7 summarizes the strengths and weaknesses of the payback, accounting rate of return, and discounted cash flow models. In practice, managers often use more than one model simultaneously to gain different perspectives on risks and returns.

Lease or Buy

The capital budgeting decisions considered thus far have centered on which investment project to acquire. The first decision is whether to acquire a particular asset. After that decision is made, managers must decide how to finance the acquisition. There are several possibilities. The business may be able to purchase the asset with internally generated cash or with cash obtained by borrowing. In many cases managers can acquire the use of assets through leasing—that is, renting on a long-term basis.

A recent survey of 600 companies indicated that only 70 companies did not acquire the use of some of their assets through leasing. Why is leasing so popular? One factor is rapid change in technology. Rather than buy a computer and risk getting stuck with a machine made obsolete by new developments, a company may prefer to lease one. Then if IBM, Apple, or Compaq develops a new generation of computer, the company can let its lease expire and switch to a new, more powerful machine. For similar reasons, airline companies lease some of their aircraft.

A professional sports team may lease its arena or its stadium from the city. It is easier to move a sports franchise to another city if the team does not own the stadium. Consider, too, tax advantages. In 1990, the city of Arlington, Texas, where the Texas Rangers play baseball, voted to build a new stadium. The city owns the stadium, so no property taxes are levied on the structure. Thus, by leasing the stadium from the city, Ranger management can save money by avoiding property tax.

The role of leasing should be kept in perspective. There are two steps: (1) deciding whether or not to acquire an asset, which is an investment decision using a discounted-cash-flow model, and (2) deciding whether to finance the acquisition by borrowing or leasing. The second step is *not* an investment decision. It is a financing decision that is covered in textbooks on finance.

Summary Problem for Your Review

The data for a machine follow:

Acquisition cost of machine	$48,000
Estimated residual value	6,000
Estimated annual net cash inflow	13,000
Estimated useful life	5 years
Minimum annual rate of return required . .	16%

Required

1. Compute the payback period.
2. Compute the accounting rate of return.
3. Compute the net present value (NPV).
4. Indicate whether each decision model leads to purchase or rejection of this investment. Would you decide to buy the machine? Give your reason.

SOLUTION TO SUMMARY PROBLEM

Requirement 1

$$P = \frac{I}{O} = \frac{\$48,000}{\$13,000} = 3.7 \text{ years}$$

Requirement 2

$$R = \frac{O - D}{(I + RV)/2} = \frac{\$13,000 - \$8,400^*}{(\$48,000 + \$6,000)/2} = \frac{\$4,600}{\$54,000/2}$$

$$= \frac{\$4,600}{\$27,000} = .170 = 17\%$$

$$^*D = \frac{\$48,000 - \$6,000}{5 \text{ years}} = \$8,400$$

Requirement 3

Present value of equal annual net cash inflows ($13,000 × 3.274†)	$ 42,562
Present value of residual value ($6,000 × .476‡)	2,856
Present value of the machine	45,418
Investment	(48,000)
Net present value	$ (2,582)

†Present value of annuity of $1 for 5 years at 16%, Table 25-2, page 1146.
‡Present value of $1 for 5 years at 16%, Table 25-1, page 1145.

Requirement 4

Payback: Purchase machine because payback period (3.7 years) is less than useful life (5 years).

Accounting rate of return: Purchase machine because return on machine of 17 percent exceeds minimum desired rate of 16 percent.

Net present value: Reject machine because it has negative net present value.

Decision: Reject machine because of negative net present value. The net-present-value model considers cash flows, profitability, and the time value of money. Each of the other models ignores at least one of these factors.

Income Taxes and Capital Budgeting

General Features and Assumptions

Income taxes are cash disbursements that frequently have a significant impact on the amount and timing of cash flows. Managers tend to follow the "least, latest" rule regarding income tax outflows. That is, they seek to obtain the maximum deductions from revenues as soon as possible so that not only the least amount of taxes is paid but also taxes are paid as late as legally allowed.

Income tax laws are prominent parts of the fiscal policies of nearly all states and countries. There is an old saying that the only certainties in life are death and taxes. But there is another certainty: Tax rules and rates change almost yearly. Depending on economic conditions, jurisdictions often change rates or offer special incentives to encourage or discourage capital investments. We will describe and illustrate some general concepts that hold regardless of specific income tax laws. Knowledge of these concepts will enable you to understand and quickly apply any particular rates or other special income tax provisions. The following assumptions pertain to our examples:

Corporate entities, not partnerships or proprietorships, are our focus. They can obtain immediate benefits from any deductions. For example, any losses from the sale of an asset may be offset against gains elsewhere on the corporate tax return.

The applicable combined federal and state corporate income tax rate is 40 percent.

There are no lags in cash flows. That is, pretax cash flows and their related tax effects occur simultaneously. Suppose pretax cash operating savings in 19X5 are $50,000. The related tax effect is .40 × $50,000, a $20,000 cash outflow in 19X5.

Tax Savings from Depreciation

Depreciation often is a prominent deduction in income tax computations. It can affect capital budgeting decisions. Consider the following illustration. The president of Chan Co., a food manufacturer, is considering the acquisition of some special materials-handling equipment. The cost is $625,000, the useful life is three years, and the expected terminal disposal value is $25,000. Because of production cost savings, annual pretax cash inflows from operations would increase by $301,900. The income tax rate is 40 percent, and the minimum desired after-tax rate of return is 14 percent.

To see how depreciation affects cash flows, distinguish between the cash effects of operations excluding depreciation and the cash effects of the depreciation deduction:

Cash effects of operations:
Pretax cash savings from operations.....................	$301,900
Income taxes at 40% on resulting increased income.......	120,760
After-tax effect on cash each year for 3 years............	$181,140

Cash effects of depreciation deduction:
Straight-line depreciation, ($625,000 − $25,000) ÷ 3 = $200,000
Income tax savings at 40% each year, .40 × $200,000	$80,000

By itself, depreciation is a noncash item. However, the depreciation deduction reduces the annual cash outflow for income taxes by $80,000. The yearly after-tax cash flow of the investment is $261,140, not the $181,140 that it would be without the depreciation effect.

Disposal of Capital Assets

The sale, or disposal, of a capital asset produces a gain (loss) if the sales price of the asset is greater than (less than) the book value of the asset at the time of sale. Like depreciation, gains and losses themselves are noncash items that affect income tax cash flows. Gains increase both taxable income and income taxes in the year of sale; losses reduce both amounts.

In the Chan Co. example, the book value at time of sale equals the sales price. Thus, there is no gain or loss, and the cash flow from disposal is equal to the sales price:

Sales price	$25,000	$25,000
Book value	25,000	
Net gain (or loss)	$ 0	
Income tax at 40%		0
After-tax effect on cash		$25,000

On the other hand, if the sales price is $30,000 instead of the $25,000 predicted at the time of purchase, a gain will be recorded, and the after-tax cash flow will be different:

Sales price	$30,000	$30,000
Book value	25,000	
Net gain	$ 5,000	
Income tax at 40%		2,000
After-tax effect on cash		$28,000

Exhibit 25-8 shows how income taxes, depreciation, and disposal affect the discounted cash flow analysis of the Chan Co.'s special-equipment proposal. The net present value is negative. Therefore, the analysis does not favor the investment.

OBJECTIVE 3
Demonstrate how income taxes affect the cash flows of investments

EXHIBIT 25-8 *Present Value Analysis with Income Tax Effects*

	Annual Cash Flow	Present Value Factor at 14%	Present Value of Net Cash Inflows
Cash effects of operations			
$301,900 − .40 ($301,900)	$181,140	2.322*	$420,607
Cash effects of depreciation deduction, savings of income taxes, .40 ×			
$200,000	80,000	2.322*	185,760
Cash effects of disposal	25,000†	.675‡	16,875
Total after-tax effect on cash flows			$623,242
Investment			(625,000)
Net present value			$ (1,758)

*From Table 25-2
†For year 3 only
‡From Table 25-1

Roles of Depreciation and Book Values

Depreciation and book values are widely misinterpreted. Consider the following equipment-replacement example. A construction business has some computer equipment with a book value of $50,000, a remaining life of four years, an expected terminal value of zero, and a current disposal value of $10,000. Assume that the firm has been taking straight-line depreciation for tax purposes of $12,500 yearly. The business is considering replacement.

Exhibit 25-9 focuses on how these factors should be analyzed as a part of the overall replacement decision. Concentrate on the boxes in the exhibit before looking at the numbers. Note the steps:

1. Search and gather *information*, including data from historical experience with the equipment, data concerning potential new equipment, and income tax effects.
2. Formulate *predictions* based on the information in step 1.
3. Use the predicted cash flows as inputs to the *decision model*, whether the model is a discounted cash flow model or another decision model.

After pondering these three steps, examine how our data are analyzed. Note that the book value and the yearly depreciation on the old equipment are historical data that, by themselves, have no effect on cash. However, they do affect predictions of income tax cash flows. These predictions are the inputs to the decision model.

The following points summarize the concepts of the preceding chapter and this one regarding book values and depreciation:

1. *Initial investment.* As Chapter 24 explained (p. 1105), the past investment outlay for old equipment and its current book value are irrelevant by themselves. However, the amount invested in new equipment is relevant; it is an expected future cost that will be avoided if replacement is rejected.

EXHIBIT 25-9   *Overview of Depreciation and Book Value*

	Keep		**Replace**		
Information	Depreciation	$12,500	Book value	$50,000	$10,000
	Predicted tax	×.40	Sales price	10,000	
	savings		Net loss	$40,000	16,000
Historical costs Other information			Predicted tax	×.40	
			savings		
Predictions	Yearly after-tax effect on cash	$5,000	Total one-time after-tax effect on cash	$26,000	
Decision Model	Inputs to decision model	$5,000 each year for 4 years	$26,000 at time of sale		

2. *Avoid double-counting.* In discounted cash flow analysis, the original lump-sum investment is a cash outlay, but its yearly depreciation is not. Deducting depreciation from operating cash flows would be a form of counting the lump-sum twice.

3. *Impact on income tax cash flows.* Book values and past depreciation are irrelevant to all capital-budgeting decision models. As Exhibit 25-9 shows, the relevant items are the predicted income tax cash effects that are inputs to the decision model.

Accelerated Depreciation and MACRS

Depending on the types of depreciable assets purchased, income tax laws often permit businesses to use accelerated depreciation instead of straight-line depreciation. Accelerated depreciation is any pattern of depreciation that writes off depreciable assets more quickly than does the straight-line method. Moreover, businesses sometimes may ignore residual values and use shorter life spans than the expected useful lives of the assets.

Suppose Chan Co. takes advantage of a special U.S. tax depreciation method, the **Modified Accelerated Cost Recovery System (MACRS),** regarding its proposed investment. Estimates of future disposal prices are ignored. MACRS specifies a table of allowable lives (called the recovery period) and a pattern of allowable depreciation that is geared to the recovery period. Double-declining balance depreciation applies to assets having recovery periods of ten years or less.

Knowledge of the MACRS allowable lives and allowable depreciation patterns for specific assets is not nearly as important as the general idea: to permit faster and earlier depreciation deductions than would be obtained using the straight-line method. Suppose that instead of straight-line depreciation, the government permitted accelerated depreciation on the Chan asset as follows:

OBJECTIVE 5

Show how accelerated depreciation and investment tax credits increase the net present values of investments

Year	Depreciation Deduction	Cash Savings at 40% Tax Rate	Present Value Factor at 14%*	Present Value of Net Cash Inflows
1	$300,000	$120,000	.877	$105,240
2	200,000	80,000	.769	61,520
3	100,000	40,000	.675	27,000
Net present value				$193,760

*From Table 25-1

Note how accelerated depreciation encourages investment. It improves the net present value in the Chan case:

Income tax effect of accelerated depreciation, from above ... $193,760
Income tax effect of straight-line depreciation, from
  Exhibit 25-8 185,760
Increase in net present value $8,000

By itself, using accelerated depreciation would change the overall net present value in Exhibit 25-8 from the existing negative $1,758 to a positive $8,000 − $1,758 = $6,242. The analysis now favors investment.

Investment Tax Credit

Governments periodically attempt to spur business investments by allowing investment tax credits. An **investment tax credit** is a direct reduction of income taxes in conjunction with the acquisition of a depreciable asset. This credit is not a *deduction* like depreciation. Instead it is a lump-sum *reduction* of the income tax cash outflow in the same period as the investment outlay.

In our Chan illustration, suppose that the $625,000 investment qualified for a 10% investment tax credit, or .10 × $625,000 = $62,500:

Reduction in income tax cash outflows at time of purchase	$62,500
Net present value in basic analysis from Exhibit 25-8	(1,758)
New net present value	$60,742

This positive effect of the investment tax credit demonstrates why such credits encourage investments throughout the economy.

Investments in Current Assets

OBJECTIVE 6

Identify the special features of investments in current assets and high technology

Most capital-budgeting literature and illustrations focus on investments in machinery and equipment. However, almost all investments require outlays for current assets. Typical examples are investments in such working capital items as cash, receivables, and inventories. These investments are analyzed in the same manner as investments in plant and equipment.

In discounted cash flow models, all initial investments are regarded as cash outflows at the beginning of projects' lives. At the end of their lives, investments in property, plant, and equipment often are only partially recovered as disposal values. Indeed, some investments, such as mining, may result in environmental obligations that require additional cleanup outlays upon disposal.

By contrast, investments in working capital items usually require initial outlays, sometimes require more outlays at intermittent subsequent times, and are fully recovered during the investment's final year. For example, suppose inventories are necessary to sustain sales over the ten-year life of a product. Money is tied up constantly in the acquisition and storing of inventories, even if they are being steadily sold and replaced.

The following computations, based on assumed numbers, demonstrate the discounted cash flow effects of investments in current assets:

	Cash Flows	Present Value Factor at 12%*	Present Value
Original investment	$(400,000)	1.000	$(400,000)
Additional investment at end of year 6	(200,000)	.507	(101,400)
Recovery of investment	600,000	.322	193,200
Net present value effect			$(308,200)

*Assumed 12% rate, factors from Table 25-1

This analysis shows that a $400,000 initial investment and a $200,000 additional investment at the end of year 6 have a net investment cost of $308,200 in today's dollars—if the investments are fully recouped at the end of year 10.

Effects of High Technology

Many industries face rapidly changing competitive conditions that are caused by technological advances such as new microtechnology, automation, and robotics. Such advances often require enormous investments. For example, a new microchip factory costs over $500 million to build and make operational.

Capital-budgeting approaches to investments in high technology are basically no different than approaches to other investments. However, they are more complicated because of numerous factors that affect predictions. Examples are effects on factory support costs, software costs, employee training costs, cycle time, scrap rates, manufacturing flexibility, product quality, and customer satisfaction.

Investments in technology often entail comparisons of existing equipment and processes (the status quo) with expensive replacement equipment and processes (the alternative). At first glance, predictions of future cash flows may show that a proposed investment has a negative present value. However, a common error in these analyses is too much optimism concerning sticking with the status quo. The cash inflows currently being experienced with the status quo may decline rapidly if a company fails to match or exceed competitors' investments in new technology.

Sensitivity Analysis and Capital Budgeting

In this and Chapter 24, we work with expected values (single dollar amounts) of operating cash flows, useful lives, and disposal values. In this way, we emphasize various important points. In actual decision situations, these predictions are subject to differing degrees of risk or uncertainty.

Managers are painfully aware of risk. They cope in assorted ways. A favorite tack is to prepare pessimistic, optimistic, and most-likely predictions. Then the managers can see an array of possible outcomes that may influence their ultimate decisions.

Sensitivity analysis is the most widely used tool for analyzing risk. **Sensitivity analysis** is a "what-if" technique that asks how a result will change if an original predicted amount is not achieved or if an underlying assumption changes. In capital budgeting, sensitivity analysis answers a question such as, How will the net present value change if my predictions of useful life or cash flows are inaccurate?

Let us apply sensitivity analysis to the Chan illustration. Suppose management wants to know the effect of changing the predicted terminal disposal value to $40,000 instead of $25,000. (To focus on this change, we assume no change in depreciation deductions.) The analysis changes as follows:

After-tax impact of disposal on cash:

Sales price	$40,000	$40,000
Book value	25,000	
Net gain	$15,000	
Income tax at 40%		6,000
After-tax impact on cash		$34,000
Present value, using Table 25-1, .675 × $34,000....		22,950
Present value in basic analysis from Exhibit 25-8...		16,875
Increase in present value		6,075
Net present value in basic analysis from Exhibit 25-8		(1,758)
New net present value		$ 4,317

The increase in disposal value improves the net present value of the equipment. The analysis now favors investment. Note that various estimates regarding the value upon disposal could change the net present value in various ways. If the disposal value is lower than the basic prediction of $25,000, the net present value will be lowered.

Computers in Capital-Budgeting Analysis

Computers are ideally suited for decision analysis. They can compute the outcomes of alternative courses of action quickly and without computational error. Consider the net-present-value analysis of three possible investments. Suppose the assets under consideration promise irregular net cash inflows for 20 years. The 60 (3 × 20) present-value computations would be time consuming and present a great possibility for error. However, a computer can be programmed to handle these multiple computations. The manager can then use the program over and over. He or she can alter the annual cash flows, the earnings (discount) rate, or the timing of the cash flows. The manager simply enters the data, and the entire sensitivity analysis is performed in seconds.

The computer can greatly assist management in making capital-budgeting decisions. Suppose a large manufacturer of lawn-maintenance equipment, such as Toro, is considering opening a new production facility to meet increasing demands for its lawn mowers. Where will the new facility be? Company management has examined 25 possible sites and narrowed the choice to five. And which of six alternative factory designs that management is considering is best? Analyzing the data with a spreadsheet allows the computer to quickly run through all the calculations to reach the optimal combination of site and design based on net present value and internal rate of return.

Summary Problem for Your Review

The chief financial officer of Holtz Company, a large fast-food restaurant chain, is trying to decide whether to buy some new cooking equipment that will improve quality and shorten cooking times. The cost is $1,050,000, and the terminal disposal value after three years of useful life is expected to be $150,000.

Annual pretax cash operating savings are expected to be $500,000. The income tax rate is 40 percent, and the minimum desired after-tax rate of return is 12 percent.

Assume that tax laws permit accelerated depreciation for a "capital recovery" period of three years that ignores terminal disposal values. The amounts applicable are $525,000 in year 1, $350,000 in year 2, and $175,000 in year 3.

Required

1. Compute the net present value of the investment.
2. Suppose that the tax authorities permit only straight-line depreciation and that the terminal disposal value of $150,000 must be considered when computing depreciation. By how much will the net present value in Requirement 1 change? Will the decision change?
3. Assume straight-line depreciation and that a terminal disposal value of $150,000 must be considered when computing depreciation for tax purposes. However, assume that for planning purposes the terminal disposal value is actually expected to be only $5,000. By how much would the net present value in Requirement 1 change? Would the decision change?

SOLUTION TO SUMMARY PROBLEM

Requirement 1

		Cash Flow	Present Value Factor at 12%	Present Value of Net Cash Inflows
Cash effects of operations:				
Pretax cash savings from operations		$500,000		
Income taxes at 40% on resulting increased income		200,000		
After-tax effect on cash each year for 3 years		$300,000	2.402*	720,600
Cash effects of depreciation deduction:				
Year	Depreciation Deduction			
1	$525,000 × 40%	210,000	.893†	187,530
2	350,000 × 40%	140,000	.797†	115,580
3	175,000 × 40%	70,000	.712†	49,840
Cash effects of disposal value:				
Sales price	$150,000 $150,000			
Book value	0			
Net gain (or loss)	$150,000			
Income tax @ 40%	60,000			
After-tax impact on cash		90,000	.712†	64,080
Total after-tax effect on cash flows				$1,137,630
Investment				(1,050,000)
Net present value				$ 87,630

*From Table 25-2
†From Table 25-1

Requirement 2

Depreciation effects on present value:
Present value of depreciation deduction in Requirement 1:
$187,530 + $115,580 + $49,840 .... $352,950
Straight-line depreciation, $1,050,000 − $150,000 = $900,000
$900,000 ÷ 3 years = $300,000 yearly
Income tax savings at 40% each year,
.40 × $300,000 = $120,000
Present value of $120,000 each year is:
2.402 factor from Table 25-2 × $120,000 288,240
Decrease in net present value .... $ 64,710
Disposal value effects on present value:
Present value of disposal value in Requirement 1 .... $64,080
New cash effects of disposal value:

Sales price	$150,000	$150,000
Book value	150,000	
Net gain (or loss)	0	
Income tax @ 40%		0
After-tax impact on cash		$150,000

Present value of $150,000 to be received
at end of Year 3,
$150,000 × .712 106,800
Increase in net present value $42,720
Total decrease in net present value of Requirement 1,
$64,710 − $42,720 .... $21,990

Note that the assumptions of Requirements 1 and 2 changed concerning disposal values as well as depreciation methods. In this example, the $21,990 change in net present value would not be large enough to offset the positive net present value of $87,630 in Requirement 1.

Requirement 3

Depreciation effects, same as in Requirement 2,
decrease in net present value $64,710
Disposal value effects on present value:
Present value of disposal value in Requirement 1 .... $64,080
New cash effects of disposal value:

Sales price	$ 5,000	$ 5,000
Book value	150,000	
Net gain (or loss)	$(145,000)	
Income tax savings @ 40% ...		58,000
After-tax impact on cash		$63,000

Present value of $63,000 to be received
at end of Year 3, $63,000 × .712 44,856
Decrease in net present value $19,224
Total decrease in net present value $83,934

The $83,934 decrease in net present value is almost large enough to offset the $87,630 in Requirement 1. Nevertheless, the equipment remains attractive even if straight-line depreciation and a large taxable loss upon terminal disposal are assumed.

Summary

Capital budgeting helps managers make long-range decisions. *Payback, accounting rate of return*, and *discounted cash flow* are three basic models for making capital-budgeting decisions. Payback is the simplest. Discounted cash flow is the best of these because it is based on cash flows and also considers profitability and the time value of money. Two widely used variations are *net present value* and *internal rate of return*. Companies may use more than one method in practice.

The *minimum desired rate of return*, or hurdle rate, is the rate that can be earned by the best alternative use of investment capital. The minimum rate varies within a business, depending on risk. The higher the risk, the higher the desired rate.

Income taxes can significantly affect capital-budgeting decisions. When investments are being made in depreciable assets, insights can be obtained from dividing the analysis into three major parts: (1) after-tax operating cash flows, (2) impact of depreciation on tax cash flows, and (3) after-tax proceeds from asset disposals.

Depreciation and book values, by themselves, are irrelevant in capital-budgeting models. However, they help in predicting income tax cash flows.

Accelerated depreciation and investment tax credits make investments in depreciable assets more attractive by boosting their net present values and internal rates of return.

Investments in such working capital items as cash, receivables, and inventories are analyzed essentially in the same way as investments in depreciable assets. However, the former's disposal values are usually much higher, often 100 percent of their original investment amounts.

Managers analyzing investments in high technology should not overlook the likely drops in operating cash flows that will result if they fail to replace present equipment and processes with state-of-the-art alternatives.

Sensitivity analysis is widely used in analyzing capital-budgeting options. It helps managers answer the question, How will our basic answer be affected if we change our assumptions or predictions? Computers are ideally suited for sensitivity analysis because they can quickly compute net present values and internal rates of return under a variety of assumptions and with numerous alternative predictions.

Self-Study Questions

Test your understanding of the chapter by marking the best answer for each of the following questions.

1. Capital budgeting is a (an) (*p. 1137*)
   a. Depreciation method
   b. Short-run decision
   c. Alternative to the payback method
   d. Way to make long-range investment decisions
2. A machine costs $45,000. It is expected to earn operating income of $6,000 and to generate $7,500 net cash inflow annually. Expected residual value is $0 at the end of 30 years. What is the asset's payback period? (*p. 1138*)
   a. 5 years   c. 7½ years
   b. 6 years   d. 9 years
3. The accounting rate of return of the machine in the preceding question is (*p. 1140*)
   a. 15 percent   c. 26.7 percent
   b. 24 percent   d. 37.5 percent
4. The time value of money is an important part of (*p. 1147*)

a. Payback analysis
c. Net-present-value analysis
b. Accounting rate of return analysis
d. All capital-budgeting methods

5. Payback analysis and net-present-value analysis indicate that a particular investment should be rejected, but the accounting rate of return is favorable. What is the wisest investment decision? Give your reason. (*p. 1147*)
   a. Reject because of net-present-value analysis
   b. Reject because of payback analysis
   c. Accept because of favorable accounting rate of return
   d. Cannot decide because of differences among the methods' results

6. The hurdle rate is usually the (*p. 1141*)
   a. Interest rate paid on financing of a specific project
   b. Rate that can be earned by the best alternative use of investment capital
   c. Interest rate paid on long-term debt
   d. Rate earned by the best existing investments of the business

7. Depreciation expense (*p. 1150–51*)
   a. Increases operating cash flows
   b. Increases terminal disposal values
   c. Reduces income tax cash outflows
   d. Reduces net present values

8. The following is *not* an example of sensitivity analysis in a discounted cash flow analysis (*p. 1155*)
   a. Computation of "best guess" of net present value
   b. Computation of net present value using a new income tax rate
   c. Assuming a change from straight-line to accelerated depreciation
   d. Assuming a change from accelerated depreciation to straight-line

9. As compared with straight-line depreciation, the use of accelerated depreciation for tax purposes (*p. 1153*)
   a. Decreases net present value
   b. Is prohibited by generally accepted accounting principles
   c. Causes more taxes to be paid sooner
   d. Increases net present value

10. Investment tax credits (*p. 1154*)
    a. Increase net present value
    b. Decrease operating cash flows
    c. Are special income tax deductions
    d. Decrease net present value

Answers to the Self-Study Questions follow the Accounting Vocabulary.

Accounting Vocabulary

Accounting rate of return. The average annual income from operations minus the average amount invested to earn the income. The higher the accounting rate of return, the better the investment (*p. 1139*).

Annuity. A stream of equal periodic amounts (*p. 1142*).

Capital budgeting. Formal means of making long-range decisions for investments such as plant locations, equipment purchases, additions of

product lines, and territorial expansions (*p. 1137*).

Decision model. A method or technique for evaluating and choosing among alternative courses of action (*p. 1137*).

Internal rate of return (IRR). The rate of return that makes the net present value of a project equal to zero (*p. 1144*).

Investment tax credit. A direct reduction of income taxes in conjunction with the acquisition of a depreciable asset. *(p. 1154)*

Minimum desired rate of return *(hurdle rate, cutoff rate, required rate, discount rate, cost of capital).* The rate that can be earned by the best alternative use of investment capital. *(p. 1141)*

Modified Accelerated Cost Recovery System (MACRS). A special U.S. tax depreciation method that specifies a table of allowable lives and a pattern of allowable depreciation that is geared to the recovery period. *(p. 1153)*

Net present value (NPV). A discounted cash flow approach to capital budgeting. It computes the expected net monetary gain or loss from a project by discounting all expected cash flows to the present value, using a minimum desired rate of return. A zero or positive net present value indicates that the investment should be accepted. A negative net present value indicates that the investment should be rejected *(p. 1142)*.

Payback. The length of time it will take to recover, in net cash inflow from operations, the dollars of a capital outlay. The shorter the payback period, the better the investment, and vice versa *(p. 1138)*.

Sensitivity analysis. A "what-if" technique that asks how a result will change if an original predicted amount is not achieved or if an underlying assumption changes. *(p. 1155)*

Time value of money. The fact that one can earn income by investing money for a period of time *(p. 1141)*.

Answers to Self-Study Questions

1. d
2. b $45,000/$7,500 = 6$ years
3. c $\dfrac{\$6,000}{(\$45,000 + \$0)/2} = \dfrac{\$6,000}{\$22,500} = 26.67\%$
4. c
5. a
6. b
7. c
8. a
9. d
10. a

ASSIGNMENT MATERIAL _____

Questions

1. What are decision models? Why are they helpful in capital budgeting?
2. What is capital budgeting? Are capital-budgeting decisions made before or after long-term assets are purchased?
3. Name three capital-budgeting decision models. State the strengths and the weaknesses of each model. Which model is best? Why?
4. Name the capital-budgeting model that fits each description: (a) based on operating income only; (b) based on cash flows without regard for their timing or for profitability; (c) based on the time value of money.
5. How is payback period computed? How does the estimated useful life of a capital asset affect the payback computation?
6. Your company is considering purchasing a manufacturing plant with an expected useful life of 15 years. What is the maximum acceptable payback period on this plant? Justify your answer.

7. How can managers use accounting rate of return in capital-budgeting decisions?

8. How can accounting rate of return be computed when the annual amounts of operating income are expected to vary each period?

9. State why a positive net present value indicates an attractive investment project and a negative net present value indicates an unattractive project.

10. A project's net present value may be either (1) positive, (2) zero, or (3) negative. In each case, what is the relationship between the project's internal rate of return and the company's minimum desired rate of return?

11. Which capital-budgeting strategy is best? (1) Pick out the best model and use it exclusively. (2) Use all three models. Support your answer.

12. Give two reasons a company might lease a capital asset instead of buying it.

13. What is the role of depreciation expense in the computation of net present value?

14. A machine with a book value of $30,000 is sold for $20,000. The applicable tax rate is 40%. What is the after-tax cash flow from the sale?

15. "The benefit of MACRS and other accelerated depreciation methods is that they increase the total tax savings from depreciation over the asset's life." True or false? Explain.

16. Why is a $50,000 investment tax credit, or other tax *reduction*, better than a $50,000 depreciation expense, or other tax *deduction?*

17. How do investments in current assets differ from investments in capital assets?

18. "The cash inflows currently being experienced with the status quo may decline rapidly if a company fails to match or exceed competitors' investments in new technology." Explain.

19. Identify three inputs (predictions) to discounted-cash-flow capital budgeting models that managers subject to sensitivity analysis. What is the key question that sensitivity analysis helps managers answer?

20. A company is investing in a 20-year project. The managers, who use the net-present-value model for capital-budgeting decisions, expect the net cash inflow amounts to vary considerably each year. How can a computer help the managers decide the amount to invest in this project?

Exercises

Exercise 25-1 *Payback analysis of an investment—equal cash flows* **(L.O. 1)**

Gloff & Sons is considering acquiring a manufacturing plant. The purchase price is $700,000. The owners believe the plant will generate net cash inflows of $95,000 annually. It will have to be replaced in five years. Use the payback model to determine whether Gloff & Sons should purchase this plant.

Exercise 25-2 *Payback analysis of an investment—unequal cash flows* **(L.O. 1)**

Seco Manufacturing is adding a new product line that will require an investment of $750,000. Managers estimate that this investment will generate net cash inflows of $110,000 the first year, $180,000 the second year, and $200,000 each year thereafter. What is the payback period for this investment? Compute a fraction of a year if necessary.

Exercise 25-3 *Accounting rate of return analysis of investments* **(L.O. 1)**

Braddock Textiles is shopping for new equipment. Managers are considering two investments. Equipment manufactured by Ling, Inc., costs $220,000 and will last for five years, with no residual value. The Ling equipment should generate annual operating income of $24,000. Equipment manufactured by Johnson Controls is priced at $310,000 and will remain useful for six years. It promises annual operating income of $32,000, and its expected residual value is $30,000.

Required

Which equipment offers the higher accounting rate of return? What is the opportunity cost of purchasing the Ling equipment? How would managers use the notion of opportunity cost in making their decision?

Exercise 25-4 *Net-present-value analysis of investments* **(L.O. 1)**

Use the net-present-value model to determine whether Tropical Products should invest in the following projects:

Project A costs $550,000 and offers 10 annual net cash inflows of $89,500. Tropical demands an annual return of 12 percent on investments of this nature. *Project B* costs $330,000 and offers 7 annual net cash inflows of $81,700. Tropical requires an annual return of 14 percent on projects like B.

What is the maximum acceptable price to pay for each project?

Exercise 25-5 *Internal rate of return analysis of investments* **(L.O. 1, 2)**

Refer to the data of Exercise 25-4. Compute the internal rate of return of each project, and use this information to identify the better investment.

Exercise 25-6 *Internal rate of return analysis of investments* **(L.O. 1)**

The management of Governers Tap, Inc. is evaluating a new metal-working machine. The machine costs $171,650 and has an expected life of five years, with no residual value. It will generate savings of $50,000 annually in after-tax net cash outflows. Compute the internal rate of return of the machine. Should management buy it if the company's hurdle rate (cost of capital) is 14 percent? 12 percent? 16 percent?

Exercise 25-7 *Net present value analysis of investments. Comparison with internal rate of return* **(L.O. 1, 2)**

Refer to the data of Exercise 25-6. Compute the net present value of the machine if Governers Tap's hurdle rate (cost of capital) is (1) 14 percent, (2) 12 percent, and (3) 16 percent. In each case, should management purchase the machine? Compare your answers with your answers in Exercise 25-6.

Exercise 25-8 *Effect of accelerated depreciation on net present value* **(L.O. 3, 4, 5)**

The managers of Texas Beef Products are considering a new food-handling machine that will cost $100,000 and will have zero disposal value at the end of its five-year life. It may be depreciated either (1) over five years, using the straight-line method, or (2) over three years, using the MACRS percentages of 67 percent, 20 percent, and 13 percent in the first, second, and third years, respectively. The company's cost of capital is 12 percent, and the applicable tax rate is 40 percent.

Required

How much higher is the net present value of the machine if the company uses accelerated depreciation instead of straight-line depreciation?

Exercise 25-9 *After-tax effect of disposal* **(L.O. 3, 4)**

The Waco Force semi-pro soccer team is considering the purchase of a new team bus. If the new bus is purchased, the old bus will be sold for $8,000. What is the after-tax effect on cash from the sale if the current book value of the bus is (1) $15,000? (2) $8,000? (3) $5,000? The team's tax rate is 40 percent.

Exercise 25-10 *Investments in current assets* **(L.O. 3, 6)**

Dillards Department Stores is evaluating the addition of a new line of designer women's accessories. If the line is added, the chain will invest $100,000 in inventory and accounts receivable. Dillards expects to carry the line for two years, after which the full investment in current assets will be recovered.

Required

The company's cost of capital is 10 percent, and its tax rate is 40 percent. What is the total net-present-value effect of the proposed investment in inventory and receivables?

Exercise 25-11 *Sensitivity analysis in capital-budgeting decisions* **(L.O. 1, 3, 7)**

Refer to the Chan Co. data in Exhibit 25-8. Suppose Ms. Chan, the company president, believes that the special materials-handling equipment may provide more than the originally predicted savings of $301,900 in pretax cash inflows from operations. She wants to know the net present value (NPV) of the investment based on predicted pretax savings of $320,000 annually. What is the new NPV? If Ms. Chan believes the savings will be between $301,900 and $320,000, with each amount in that range equally likely, what would you advise her to do?

Problems   *(Group A)*

Problem 25-1A *Capital-budgeting decision using four models* **(L.O. 1, 2)**

Robert Manning, president of the Birmingham Product Design Group, is considering an investment in computer-aided design equipment. The equipment costs $80,000, has a five-year useful life, and has no terminal disposal value. Manning predicts the machine will generate $26,750 annually in net after-tax cash inflows.

The company's minimum desired rate of return for design equipment is 14 percent. Manning requires that all design equipment have a predicted payback period of four years or less.

Required

1. Compute the payback period, accounting rate of return, net present value, and internal rate of return on this investment.
2. On the basis of the computations in Requirement 1, should Birmingham Product Design Group buy the equipment? Why or why not?

Problem 25-2A *Capital-budgeting decision—unequal cash flows* **(L.O. 1, 2, 3, 4)**

Parnelli's Auto Parts is considering a new special-purpose shaping machine for manufacturing brake-system components. The machine is expected to have a three-year life, with no residual value. Company president Joe Parnelli predicts the machine will generate pretax cash flows of $60,000 the first year, $50,000 the second year, and $40,000 the third year. If the machine is purchased, its $120,000 purchase price will be depreciated on a straight-line basis.

The company's tax rate is 40 percent; its minimum desired rate of return is 14 percent.

Required

1. Using the format of Exhibit 25-8, compute the present value of (1) the cash effects of operations and (2) the cash effects of depreciation.
2. Compute the payback period and the accounting rate of return on the investment.
3. What is the net present value of the shaping machine investment? Should Parnelli invest in the machine?
4. What should Parnelli consider to improve the net present value?

Problem 25-3A *Effect of accelerated depreciation and investment tax credit*
(L.O. 1, 3, 4, 5)

Refer to the data of Problem 25-2A. Company president Joe Parnelli has discovered that the special-purpose shaping machine qualifies for an MACRS three-year recovery period, with accelerated depreciation deductions of $80,000 the first year, $26,667 the second year, and $13,333 the third year. The machine also qualifies for a 10 percent investment tax credit, which takes effect at the date of purchase.

Required

1. What is the net present value of the machine investment? Should Parnelli buy the machine?
2. What is the effect of using accelerated depreciation instead of straight-line depreciation on (1) the total depreciation expense over the life of an asset, (2) the total tax savings from depreciation over the asset's life, and (3) the present value of tax savings from depreciation over the asset's life?
3. What is the effect of using accelerated depreciation instead of the straight-line method on the asset's payback period? On its accounting rate of return?

Problem 25-4A *Capital budgeting—different assumptions about depreciation*
(L.O. 1, 3, 4, 5)

As an accountant for Ontime Distributors, which operates a distribution network for medical supplies, you have been asked to compute the net present value of a proposal for automated materials-handling equipment for the company's main warehouse. The before-tax cash operating savings from the automation are predicted to be $700,000 per year. The equipment costs $2,000,000 and is expected to have a disposal value of $200,000 at the end of its four-year life.

Suppose that the government allows the asset's cost (as opposed to cost less disposal value) to be depreciated over three years at the following rates: 66 percent the first year, 22 percent the second year, and 12 percent the third year. Also suppose the applicable tax rate is 40 percent and the cost of capital is 12 percent.

Required

1. Compute the net present value of the automated materials-handling equipment. Do you recommend that the company make the investment?
2. Your supervisor is curious about the effect of depreciating cost only instead of cost less predicted disposal value. Prepare an analysis that shows the total effect on the proposal's net present value of depreciating cost less disposal value.

Problem 25-5A *Capital-budgeting decision with investment in inventory*
(L.O. 1, 3, 4, 6)

Westex, Inc., purchases used oilfield equipment and "rehabilitates" it for resale. A major problem in this process is the welding activity. Many welders have had industrial accidents. The management of Westex is considering an investment in robots, which would be used for the most dangerous welding assignments. The robots cost $3,000,000. They would reduce labor costs, worker insurance costs, and materials costs by $1,600,000 per year, but would require an increase in cash operating costs of $500,000 per year. Thus, the net before-tax cash operating savings from the robots would be $1,100,000 per year. Because of increased efficiency, the amount invested in inventory of welding supplies could be reduced immediately by $25,000. In addition, senior managers believe the robots would reduce the number of industrial accidents involving welders by approximately 80 percent.

The robots Westex is considering have a useful life of four years, with no disposal value. The company would use straight-line depreciation for the $3,000,000 cost. Its tax rate is 40 percent, and its minimum desired rate of return for this type of investment is 16 percent.

Required

1. How do investments in current assets, such as inventory, differ from investments in capital assets, such as robots?
2. What is the net present value of the investment in robots? Should Westex buy them?
3. How should the human safety factor affect the investment decision?

Problem 25-6A *Sensitivity analysis in capital budgeting* *(L.O. 1, 3, 4, 5, 6, 7)*

Refer to the data of Problem 25-5A. Uncertainty exists about several of the predictions in Westex, Inc.'s investment decision. Company controller Tommie Clack is concerned, because she considers the several alternative predictions to be equally as likely as the initial amounts.

Required

Compute the present value of net cash inflows for each item below. Then compute both the change from the initial present value and the new net present value of the investment. Consider each item separately.

1. Before-tax cash operating savings of $1,200,000 per year instead of $1,100,000.
2. MACRS depreciation over three years instead of straight-line depreciation. The deductions are $2,000,000 the first year, $700,000 the second year, and $300,000 the third year.
3. Disposal value of $100,000 instead of zero. (Disposal value not considered for depreciation purposes.)
4. Useful life of three years instead of four years.

(Group B)

Problem 25-1B *Capital-budgeting decision using four models* *(L.O. 1, 2)*

Irving Wiltse, president of Wiltse's Fine Foods, is considering an investment in automated packaging equipment. The equipment costs $138,000, has a six-year useful life, and has no terminal disposal value. Wiltse predicts the machine will generate $30,000 annually in net after-tax cash inflows.

The company's cost of capital is 10 percent. Wiltse requires that all investments have an expected payback period of four years or less.

Required

1. Compute the payback period, accounting rate of return, net present value, and internal rate of return on the packaging equipment investment.
2. On the basis of the computations in Requirement 1, should Wiltse's Fine Foods buy the equipment? Why or why not?

Problem 25-2B   *Capital-budgeting decision—unequal cash flows*   **(L.O. 1, 2, 3, 4)**

Stan's Custom Metal Works is considering a new special-purpose metal-cutting machine. The machine is expected to have a three-year life, with no residual value. Company president Stan Bates predicts the machine will generate pretax cash flows of $50,000 in its first year in operation, $40,000 the second year, and $25,000 the third year. If the machine is purchased, its $60,000 purchase price will be depreciated on a straight-line basis. The company's tax rate is 30 percent. Its hurdle rate is 12 percent.

Required

1. Using the format of Exhibit 25-8, compute the present value of (1) the cash effects of operations and (2) the cash effects of depreciation.
2. Compute the payback period and the accounting rate of return on the investment.
3. What is the machine's net present value (NPV)? Should Stan Bates buy the machine?
4. How could the NPV of the machine be increased?

Problem 25-3B   *Effect of accelerated depreciation and investment tax credit*
(L.O. 1, 3, 4, 5)

Refer to the data of Problem 25-2B. Stan Bates has discovered that the special-purpose metal-cutting machine qualifies for an MACRS three-year recovery period, with accelerated depreciation deductions of $40,000 the first year, $13,333 the second year, and $6,667 the third year. The machine also qualifies for a 6 percent investment tax credit, which takes effect on the date of purchase.

Required

1. What is the net present value of the machine investment? Should Bates buy the machine?
2. What is the effect of using accelerated depreciation instead of the straight-line method on (1) the total depreciation expense over the life of an asset, (2) the total tax savings from depreciation over the asset's life, and (3) the present value of tax savings from depreciation over the asset's life?
3. What is the effect of using accelerated depreciation instead of the straight-line method on the asset's payback period? On its accounting rate of return?

Problem 25-4B   *Capital budgeting—different assumptions about depreciation*
(L.O. 1, 3, 4, 5)

As an accountant for County Hospital, you have been asked to compute the net present value of a proposal for state-of-the-art diagnostic equipment for the hospital's laboratory. The before-tax operating cash flows from the equipment are predicted to be $200,000 per year. The equipment costs $600,000 and is expected to have a disposal value of $60,000 at the end of its four-year life.

Suppose that the equipment's cost (as opposed to cost less disposal value) may be depreciated over three years at the following rates: 60 percent the first year, 25 percent the second year, and 15 percent the third year. The tax rate is 30 percent, and the hospital's cost of capital is 10 percent.

Required

1. Compute the net present value of the diagnostic equipment. Do you recommend that the hospital purchase it?
2. Your supervisor is curious about the effect of depreciating cost only instead of cost less predicted disposal value. Prepare an analysis that shows the total effect on the proposal's net present value of depreciating cost less disposal value.

Problem 25-5B *Capital-budgeting decision with investment in current assets (L.O. 1, 2, 3, 4, 6)*

Jennifer Sullivan is the manager of Smith's Department Store. She is considering whether to renovate some space in order to increase sales volume. New display fixtures and equipment costing $90,000 will be needed. They are expected to be useful for three years, with no terminal disposal value. The renovation is expected to generate pretax cash operating inflows of $50,000 per year.

In addition to fixtures and equipment, the project will require an initial investment of $40,000 in merchandise inventory and accounts receivable. This investment must be maintained continuously. At the end of the three-year period, the inventory and receivables can be liquidated for their full carrying value.

Smith's hurdle rate for space renovations is 14 percent. The applicable income tax rate is 40 percent.

Required

1. Compute both the net present value and the accounting rate of return on the proposed renovation. Assume straight-line depreciation of the investment in display fixtures and equipment.
2. As store manager, which capital-budgeting model would you prefer for the purpose of making this decision?

Problem 25-6B *Sensitivity analysis in capital budgeting (L.O. 1, 3, 4, 5, 6, 7)*

Refer to the data of Problem 25-5B. Uncertainty exists about several of the predictions and methods in Jennifer Sullivan's investment decision. She is concerned, because she considers the alternative predictions to be equally as likely as the initial amounts.

Required

Compute the present value of net cash inflows for each item below. Then compute the change from the initial present value—that is, the effect on the project's net present value of assuming the alternative prediction or method instead of the initial prediction or method. Consider each item separately.

1. Pretax cash operating inflows of $60,000 per year instead of $50,000.
2. MACRS depreciation deductions of $60,000 the first year, $20,000 the second year, and $10,000 the third year instead of straight-line depreciation.

3. Disposal value of $5,000 instead of zero. (Disposal value not considered for depreciation purposes.)
4. Useful life of four years instead of three years.

Extending Your Knowledge

Decision Problem

Evaluating a New Machine   (L.O. 1,3,4)

Texas Instruments (TI) is considering a new computer-controlled etching machine for etching trenches in the surfaces of silicon wafers. The company processes these wafers into semiconductor chips. The etching machine costs $800,000, and an additional $300,000 would be required for installation. The installation cost would be capitalized, making $1,100,000 the investment amount subject to straight-line depreciation.

The expected useful life of the new machine is five years. TI managers believe use of the machine would save $370,000 per year in materials and conversion costs. This savings would be reduced by $40,000 per year in additional maintenance costs.

The new etching machine would replace an existing machine that was purchased five years ago for $500,000. That machine has five years of useful life remaining. Its annual depreciation deduction is $50,000.

Disposal values of the two machines are:

	Old Machine	New Machine
Now	$60,000	—
In 5 years	0	$100,000

The predicted disposal value of the new machine would be deducted from its $1,100,000 cost for the purpose of computing the asset's depreciation deduction.

TI's tax rate is 40 percent. Its minimum desired rate of return on assets of this type is 14 percent.

Required

1. Is the $500,000 cost of the old machine relevant in deciding whether to keep the old machine for five more years or sell it now and replace it with the new machine? Why or why not?
2. What is the difference between the annual depreciation deduction of the new machine and the annual depreciation deduction of the old machine? Why is this difference relevant for the capital-budgeting decision?
3. What is the net present value of the new machine? On the basis of the quantifiable data given, should TI buy it?
4. Suppose that TI managers have identified several intangible benefits associated with the new etching machine. These include greater flexibility, improved quality, and shorter manufacturing throughput time. What dollar amount per year would the managers have to assign to these intangible benefits to make the new machine an acceptable investment?

Robert Morrison is the chief financial officer (CFO) of Standard and Smith, a diversified company with a broad range of products in the food service and household products industries. Morrison recently convinced Standard and Smith's top management to sell the company's old mainframe computer and replace it with a system of minicomputers and microcomputers located at the company's twenty plants and offices.

The CFO and his task force asked two vendors to propose systems that meet Standard and Smith's operating needs. The first vendor's proposal would require a $1,000,000 up-front investment for hardware, software, and training. Its relevant net cash inflows are predicted to be $400,000 per year for the four-year decision period. The second vendor's proposal would require a $2,000,000 initial outlay. Its relevant annual net cash inflows are $750,000. Both systems would have no residual value at the end of four years.

Standard and Smith uses the net-present-value model to evaluate investment proposals. The company's minimum desired rate of return on investments of this nature is 16 percent. However, the specific dollars used to finance the computer system investment will be borrowed at 14 percent interest. Morrison would like to accept the proposal of the second vendor, a company owned by a close friend of his.

Required

1. Compute the net present value of the two computer system proposals. Which proposal should the company accept?
2. Compute the net present value of each proposal using 14 percent as the discount rate. Is this rate acceptable in this case? Would it be unethical for Morrison to make his selection on the basis of the 14 percent computations?

Chapter 26

Decentralization: Transfer Pricing and Performance Measurement

"If we didn't fix things, we'd be in the same shape as IBM is today," asserts David Packard of computer giant Hewlett-Packard (HP). When the value of HP's stock began to decline in 1990, Packard and fellow founder William Hewlett came out of retirement to identify the problems and stop the slide. They discovered that Hewlett-Packard had become too centralized and bureaucratic to be either innovative or effective in bringing new products to market.

To foster innovation and initiative, Packard and Hewlett focused on *decentralizing* the company. From HP's beginning, they had provided each division its own engineering, marketing, manufacturing, and personnel staffs. They also had split apart any segment that amassed more than 1,500 workers. Before the company's drift toward centralization, one of its independent business units had captured the laser printer market for personal computers, which it continues to dominate today.

The result of Hewlett-Packard's decentralization effort is quite telling. The revitalized company recently replaced the Digital Equipment Corporation (DEC) as number two in computer workstations, and it led competitors in bringing to market its "personal digital assistant." Also, HP's stock currently is trading at considerably more than that of either IBM or DEC.

Source: Adapted from Julie Pitta, "It Had to Be Done and We Did It," *Forbes*, April 26, 1993, pp. 148–152.

Who in Hewlett-Packard Co. (HP) should have the authority to launch a new line of laser printers? In some companies, a decision of this importance could be made only by executives at the highest corporate level. At Hewlett-Packard, a division manager could have this authority. What price should the Delco Division of General Motors (GM) charge the Cadillac Division for a compact disc (CD) player? What is the process involved in making such a decision? How should Monsanto's management evaluate the performance of its Nutrasweet Company—on the basis of net income, return on investment, or some other performance measure? Senior managers often ask such questions. The answers depend on how the corporation expects its operating managers to function.

A **management control system** is a set of rules and techniques that aid and coordinate decision making within an organization. All organizations have a management control system; some are more elaborate than others. The best management control system is the one that best motivates managers to achieve top management's goals. But it is not easy to determine the benefits and costs of alternative ways of making decisions. Senior managers study the central issues and select the plan they believe will produce the greatest net benefits.

Like Hewlett-Packard, many companies are highly decentralized. Their executives have delegated much authority to lower-level managers. In this chapter we discuss the benefits and costs of decentralization. We also cover two issues that create special problems for managers of decentralized companies: transfer pricing and performance measurement.

Decentralization

Decentralization is the freedom to make decisions. *It is a matter of degree.* Maximum decentralization means maximum freedom for responsibility-center managers at the lowest levels of a company. Recall from Chapter 22 that a *responsibility center* is a part, segment, or subunit of an organization whose managers are accountable for specified activities. A responsibility center can be an entire company (Nutrasweet) owned by a corporation (Monsanto) or a small group—for example, a two-person legal services department.

Maximum centralization means maximum constraints on lower-level managers. In general, the greater the degree of centralization, the greater the number of management layers and people (or committees) that have to approve any proposed action. One sign of Hewlett-Packard's troublesome move toward centralization was that 38 committees had to approve a division's new networking product. The company's management control system sapped any division manager's initiative.

Benefits and Costs of Decentralization

Decentralizing decision making within organizations can result in the following benefits:

Better decisions. The managers of operating units are often closer to customers than upper-level managers and therefore have better information about market demand. They are more likely to make wise decisions regarding customers and suppliers than managers who are farther removed from local conditions. An actual example makes this point. In 1987, a company-level committee at Hewlett-Packard designed a computer workstation that was both more expensive and slower than its primary competitor. The committee was more concerned with the workstation's effect on the sales of other HP products than with providing maximum value to the customer. The product failed. If lower-level managers had been more involved in the workstation's design, the outcome might have been different. This episode helped convince HP to reorganize.

Faster decisions. A company that empowers lower-level managers to make decisions quickly has an advantage over competitors that require decisions to be approved by layer after layer of management. At one time, HP managers had to submit price-change requests for their personal computers (PCs) to the designated committees 45 days in advance. By contrast, other PC manufacturers were able to reduce their prices in a week. Which approach do you think results in more sales?

Greater creativity and motivation. Managers are motivated by the ability to use their initiative. They are more likely to stay on the cutting edge of market opportunity when they believe they will reap rewards from their efforts. The Dial Corporation decentralized its management information system (MIS) by putting hardware, software, and MIS staff personnel under the direct control of business unit managers. Those managers now feel like they own their MIS system, and they are motivated to search for creative ways to use it. This attitude enables the managers to compete more effectively.

Increased development and learning. Managers learn to make decisions through experience. People learn from their failures as well as their successes. Diffusing decision making throughout a company creates a broad pool of managerial talent available for upper-level positions. Consider a recent counter-example. After incurring unprecedented losses, IBM went outside the corporation to find a chief executive. The company's centralized management structure had not developed its own leader.

The costs of decentralization include the following:

Suboptimal decisions. **Suboptimal, or dysfunctional, decisions** are those whose costs *to the organization as a whole* outweigh the benefits. Managers in a decentralized setting make decisions that are in the best interests of their own responsibility centers. Thus, they may make decisions that are not in the best interests of the entire company. This situation occurs when goal congruence is lacking. **Goal congruence** is harmony between the goals of the manager for the subunit and the goals of top management for the overall organization. Harmony between goals is evidenced by decisions. If the manager of GM's Pontiac Division makes a decision that results in an increase in Pontiac's income but a decrease in the income of GM, that decision is suboptimal. Goal congruence is lacking.

Duplication of activities. Decentralized subunits tend to duplicate some activities. This result often occurs with staff functions such as accounting, personnel, and legal services. Centralization can decrease these fixed costs.

High costs of information. Decentralized decision making increases the demand for information, and generating information costs money. An example is the cost of negotiating prices for goods and services transferred between subunits. In a centralized organization, top management sets the price and avoids the cost of the negotiation process.

Top management compares the benefits and costs of decentralization on a function-by-function (product design, manufacturing, and marketing) basis if not on a decision-by-decision basis. This cost-benefit analysis usually leads to some decentralized decisions and some centralized decisions. For example, within the manufacturing function, the decision to build a new plant may be made at a very high level in the organization, but the day-to-day production decisions may be made by lower-level managers.

Decentralization is most successful when the subunits of a company are relatively independent. When two or more subunits purchase materials from the same suppliers, it may be cheaper to centralize the purchasing function. When two or more subunits sell to the same customers, it may cost less to centralize the marketing function. The cost savings may outweigh any benefits lost because of the higher degree of centralization.

Responsibility Centers and Decentralization

As discussed in Chapter 22, there are three types of responsibility centers:

Cost center: The manager is accountable for costs only

Profit center: The manager is accountable for costs and revenues

Investment center: The manager is accountable for costs, revenues, and investments

Organizations with profit centers and investment centers may appear to be more highly decentralized than companies with cost centers. However, this is not always the case. In one company, investment-center managers may be tightly constrained in their decision-making authority. They may require headquarters' approval for all but minor capital outlays and may have to seek corporate-level input on routine matters. In another company, cost-center managers may have great leeway in purchasing materials and deciding how to use resources in production.

Consider a manufacturing plant whose manager has no say in decisions about marketing its products. Even in such a case, top management may designate the plant as a profit center because of the anticipated effect on the manager's behavior. As a cost-center manager, he or she would focus on achieving budgeted costs. But with a profit-center focus, the manager also must be concerned about quality and timeliness—in short, about all the factors that affect customer satisfaction. A manager who is responsible for revenues and costs will be even more concerned with preventing defects in order to reduce the downstream costs of warranty claims and lost sales. Thus, top managers work hard to predict the behavioral effects of their management control system.

At the start of this chapter we discussed the Delco division of GM selling CD players to the Cadillac division of GM. Now, let us suppose that GM allows Delco to sell CD players to customers other than GM divisions and also allows Cadillac to buy CD players from other external sources. What should the divisions do in order to maximize GM's operating income? What will their managers decide to do in this decentralized setting? The answers depend on an important part of the corporation's management control system—the transfer price of CD players.

Transfer Pricing

Nature of Transfer Pricing

A **transfer price** is the price one subunit of an organization charges for a product or service supplied to another subunit of the same organization. Usually, accountants use the term *cost allocation* for transfers between cost centers and *transfer pricing* for transfers between profit or investment centers. A transfer price is revenue to the transferring (selling) subunit and cost to the receiving (buying) subunit. Thus, the transferring division favors a high transfer price and the receiving division favors a low transfer price, as is true in any other buy-sell transaction. The difference with transfer pricing is that both the seller and the buyer are part of the same company. Top management wants to maximize total company profit but at the same time wants to give division managers enough freedom to gain the benefits of decentralization.

Transfer pricing most often is associated with the transfer of intermediate products or finished goods. **Intermediate products** are products transferred from one subunit of a company to another subunit for further processing. Let us consider the Alabama Board and Box Company (ABBCo), which is illustrated in Exhibit 26-1. ABBCo has two product lines, corrugated linerboard, or cardboard, and boxes. The Linerboard Division makes linerboard in square

EXHIBIT 26-1 *Alabama Board and Box Company Profit Centers*

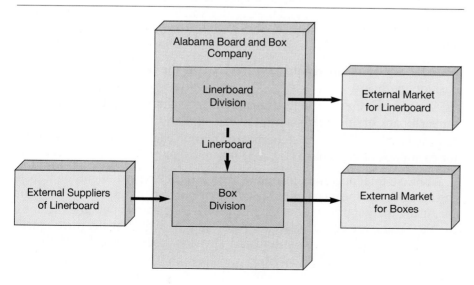

sheets. It can sell packs of 100 sheets to outside customers or transfer them to the Box Division. The Box Division prints, cuts, and shapes linerboard into boxes, which also are sold in packs of 100. The Box Division may buy from the Linerboard Division or from outside suppliers. Alabama Board and Box is highly decentralized. The division managers have the authority to decide whether to buy or sell internally or externally.

What will the divisions do? If the transfer price is higher than the external market price of linerboard, the Box Division will buy from external suppliers in order to maximize the division's income. In that case, the Linerboard Division will sell to external customers. If the external market price of linerboard is higher than the transfer price, the Box Division will buy from the Linerboard Division. Ideally, the transfer price should motivate each division manager to do what is best for ABBCo as a whole. That is, the method used to set the transfer price should lead to decisions that maximize ABBCo's operating income.

We will discuss two general types of transfer prices. The first is based on market prices. These may be either publicly available prices of similar products or services or prices charged by subunits to outside customers. For example, if the Linerboard Division of ABBCo charges outsiders $42 per pack for linerboard, it also may charge the Box Division $42 per pack.

The second type of transfer price is based on costs. Examples of cost bases for transfer prices include variable manufacturing cost, full absorption cost, and full total cost across the entire value chain. For example, a company may use as a general guideline that transfer prices should be 120% of the full total cost of the selling division. The 20% above full total cost provides income to the selling division, which gives that division the incentive to produce and sell the intermediate product.

The Nature of Transfer Pricing: An Illustration

Let us now consider how the choice of transfer pricing method affects the operating incomes of individual subunits. Exhibit 26-2 gives the variable cost per pack, the fixed cost per pack, the full total cost per pack, and the market sales price for Alabama Board and Box Company's two divisions. The number of packs produced is the sole driver of variable costs in each division. Unit fixed costs are based on the budgeted annual volume of linerboard and boxes.

Suppose that 100,000 packs of linerboard are transferred to the Box Division, processed into boxes, and then sold. Exhibit 26-3 presents division operating incomes that result from applying three transfer-pricing methods to the ABBCo data, as follows:

Market Price: The Linerboard Division charges the Box Division $42 for each pack of linerboard

125% of Variable Cost: The Linerboard Division charges the Box Division $25 for each pack of linerboard (1.25 × $20)

120% of Full Total Cost: The Linerboard Division charges the Box Division $36 for each pack of linerboard (1.2 × $30)

OBJECTIVE 2

Calculate the income of a company's divisions using different transfer prices

ABBCo's total operating income will be $600,000 regardless of the transfer price. However, the incomes of the two divisions vary dramatically. For example, using market pricing, the Linerboard Division earns operating income of $1,200,000 and the Box Division loses $600,000. With the transfer price equal to 125% of variable cost, the Linerboard Division loses $500,000 and the Box Division earns $1,100,000.

EXHIBIT 26-2 *Alabama Board and Box Company: Data for Illustration*

Per Pack	Linerboard Division	Box Division
Variable cost	$20	$16
Fixed cost	10	2
Full total cost	$30	$18
Market sales price	$42	$54

To maximize its profit, the Linerboard Division would set the transfer price at market price. The Box Division would much prefer the 125%-of-variable-cost price. This illustration demonstrates why the choice of method, especially in companies where the receiving division *must* buy from the transferring division, is so important to profit-center managers. The evaluation of their performance by top management hinges on the operating incomes of their divisions.

Different approaches to transfer pricing can have broad implications. In a decentralized company, the choice of transfer-pricing method can affect the total amount of operating income as well as how the income is divided among divisions.

Market-Based Prices

When a competitive market exists for an intermediate product, the market price often will lead to optimal decisions by subunit managers. Suppose the Linerboard Division can sell its entire production to external customers for the market price of $42 per pack. The manager of the Linerboard Division will not sell this product for less than $42 to the Box Division, because to do so would reduce the Linerboard Division's profit. The Box Division manager will refuse to pay a transfer price of more than $42 because he or she can buy linerboard on the open market for that price. Paying more would reduce the Box Divi-

EXHIBIT 26-3 *Alabama Board and Box Company: Division Operating Incomes for Three Transfer-Pricing Methods*

	Market Price	125% of Variable Cost	120% of Full Total Cost
Linerboard Division			
Revenue: $42, $25, $36 × 100,000	$4,200,000	$2,500,000	$3,600,000
Division variable cost: $20 × 100,000 . .	2,000,000	2,000,000	2,000,000
Division fixed cost: $10 × 100,000	1,000,000	1,000,000	1,000,000
Operating income (loss)	$1,200,000	$ (500,000)	$ 600,000
Box Division			
Revenue: $54 × 100,000	$5,400,000	$5,400,000	$5,400,000
Transferred-in cost	4,200,000	2,500,000	3,600,000
Division variable cost: $16 × 100,000 . .	1,600,000	1,600,000	1,600,000
Division fixed cost: $2 × 100,000	200,000	200,000	200,000
Operating income (loss)	$ (600,000)	$1,100,000	$ 0
Total operating income	$ 600,000	$ 600,000	$ 600,000

sion's profit. Thus, one of the profit-center managers will refuse an internal transfer at any price other than $42.

Market price, however, is not the answer to every transfer-pricing question. Sometimes intermediate products are so specialized that no outside market exists for them. Or market prices may be unreliable because of the different requirements of different customers. In these situations, companies frequently use a cost-plus-profit method in order to provide a fair substitute for market prices. Examples of this method are the 125%-of-variable-cost method and the 120%-of-full-cost method we discussed above.

Capacity Issues

OBJECTIVE 3

Determine the effect of idle capacity on transfer decisions

Alabama Board and Box Company's top managers want the two division managers to act in the best interests of the company as a whole. That is, they want the managers to make decisions that maximize ABBCo's income. A transfer price that will produce optimal (profit-maximizing) decisions depends on the answer to a key question: Does the selling division (the Linerboard Division) have idle capacity? **Idle capacity** is production capacity in excess of what is needed to satisfy external customer demand for a division's product. Whether the Linerboard Division is operating at capacity affects its pricing strategy.

Suppose the Linerboard Division has enough capacity to produce 100,000 packs of linerboard, but external customers demand only 90,000 packs. The Linerboard Division can transfer 10,000 packs to the Box Division without losing any external sales. In that case, the Linerboard Division manager may be willing to transfer the 10,000 packs to the Box Division for less than the market price of $42. Why? Because any price above the Linerboard Division's variable cost of $20 will add to the division's income.

Exhibit 26-4 presents data for the linerboard and box products of ABBCo. The exhibit gives the contribution to the operating income *of the company as a whole* when the Linerboard Division sells to outside customers and when the Linerboard Division makes a transfer to the Box Division. Top management of ABBCo can use these data to determine the course of action that maximizes the company's income in different capacity situations.

The variable cost of $20 is the only additional cost needed to produce linerboard for each box. Likewise, the $16 variable cost of the Box Division is the only incremental cost of processing the linerboard into boxes. Therefore, the unit contribution margins are the relevant unit profits for determining the course of action that will maximize profits for the company.

EXHIBIT 26-4 *Alabama Board and Box Company: Product Contribution Margins If Sales Price of Linerboard Is $42 and Box is $54*

Per Pack	Sell Linerboard Outside	Use Linerboard to Make Box
Sales price	$42	$54
Variable costs:		
Linerboard Division...............	20	$20
Box Division	—	16 36
Contribution margin	$22	$18

Per Pack	Company As a Whole		Box Division	
Sales price		$54		$ 54
Variable costs:				
Linerboard Division........................	$20		$42	
Box Division	16	36	16	58
Unit profit		$18		$(4)

Idle Capacity

Suppose the Linerboard Division has enough capacity to produce 10,000 packs of linerboard beyond what external customers demand. ABBCo will be better off if Linerboard produces the packs and transfers them to the Box Division. The total cost *to the company* of producing a pack of boxes is $36 ($20 + $16). The sale of each pack of boxes provides an $18 contribution margin to ABBCo.

Idle capacity motivates the Linerboard Division's manager to find ways to generate income even if it means cutting prices. How much can the Linerboard Division reduce its price? All the way down to its variable cost. With idle capacity, the variable cost of the Linerboard Division is a better guide to this pricing decision than the market price. If the transfer price is set at $20, the Box Division will buy the packs and produce the boxes. Income for the company as a whole will increase by $180,000 [10,000 × ($54 − $36)]. But if the $42 market price is used as the transfer price for the 10,000 packs, the Box Division will refuse to buy them because that division would then be $4 worse off for every box produced, as shown in Exhibit 26-5. In this idle-capacity situation, a market-based transfer price would lead the manager of the Box Division to make a dysfunctional decision.

No Idle Capacity

If the Linerboard Division has no idle capacity, ABBCo will be better off selling all linerboard packs outside for $42. If transfers between divisions take place, the Box Division spends $16 for additional processing but adds only $12 ($54 − $42) to the company's revenue. Every pack transferred would reduce the company's overall income by $4 ($16 additional cost − $12 additional revenue).

Market price is the appropriate transfer price in this situation because the market price motivates the manager of the Box Division to refuse to buy from the Linerboard Division. If the Box Division paid $42 per pack it would lose money, as we have shown. For the same reason, the Box Division will not pay $42 to outside suppliers of linerboard. Unless the Box Division can reduce its own processing cost below $16, it will not produce this box.

The variable-cost pricing method also can lead to dysfunctional results. Suppose the market sales price of a box is $60 rather than $54. Will the Linerboard Division transfer packs of its product to the Box Division for $20? No. With no idle capacity, the Linerboard Division can sell every pack for $42. Its income would decrease by $22 ($42 − $20) for every pack transferred at variable cost. But the Linerboard Division's decision is suboptimal for ABBCo. Exhibit 26-6 shows why the company's top management prefers the transfer.

Per Pack	Sell Linerboard Outside	Use Linerboard to Make Box	
Sales price	$42		$60
Variable costs:			
Linerboard Division...............	20	$20	
Box Division	—	16	36
Contribution margin	$22		$24

Alabama Board and Box earns $2 more income ($24 − $22) for every pack of linerboard processed further and sold as boxes.

These possibilities demonstrate that no single transfer-pricing method always leads subunit managers to act in the best interests of the organization as a whole. In general, when a selling division has idle capacity, a price based on its variable cost is more likely to produce goal-congruent behavior than a market-based price. But when a selling division can sell all its output to external customers, market prices usually serve as better guides. But market prices are absent in many situations, especially those in which the selling division produces a specialty product only for the buying division. In such cases, conflicts between divisions are inevitable.

Conflict Resolution

To see how companies resolve transfer-pricing conflicts, let's look again at the idle-capacity situation. The variable-cost transfer price leads to the optimal decision by the manager of the Box Division. He or she will purchase the 10,000 linerboard packs if they are offered at the Linerboard Division's variable cost of $20. But what incentive does the Linerboard Division have to make the transfer at its variable cost? None. Such a transfer yields no contribution to the Linerboard Division's profit.

In this situation, ABBCo's top management may allow the two division managers to negotiate a transfer price that is mutually agreeable. That price will be somewhere between $20 (the Linerboard Division's variable cost) and $38 (the Box Division's $54 sales price minus its own $16 variable cost). For example, a negotiated price of $29 will give each division a $9 profit per unit:

Per Pack	Linerboard Division	Box Division
Sales Price.....................	$29 →	$54
		→ $29
Variable cost...................	20	16 45
Unit profit.....................	$ 9	$ 9

This negotiated price increases the income of each division. By leading to the transfer, it also maximizes the company's income.

In some cases, executives at the corporate level consider it necessary to intervene. Suppose ABBCo's top management mandates the transfer from the Linerboard Division to the Box Division and prorates between the two divisions the $180,000 income from the sale of boxes. The income might be prorated on the basis of the variable cost incurred in each division:

Variable cost of Linerboard Division $20
Variable cost of Box Division   16
                                                                         $36

The income is prorated as follows:

To Linerboard Division . . . . $^{20}\!/_{36}$ × $180,000 = $100,000
To Box Division . . . . $^{16}\!/_{36}$ × $180,000 = $ 80,000

In this solution to the transfer-pricing problem, top managers have taken back the decision-making power they delegated to division managers. In effect, top management has centralized this specific decision. Many managements are reluctant to interfere in this way. They would rather make sure that both the selling and buying managers have all the facts and then let them negotiate a price. As long as dysfunctional decision making is not widespread or too damaging, managements often are willing to accept occasional loss of profits in order to gain the benefits of decentralization. These benefits frequently generate greater overall profits in the long run.

Multinational Transfer Pricing

Domestic companies often set transfer prices with goal congruence and managerial motivation in mind. Other factors may take precedence in **multinational companies** (MNCs), which have divisions in more than one country. Complications arise because countries differ both in terms of their tax rates and in the extent to which they enforce their tax codes. MNC managements often impose the transfer prices that minimize their worldwide taxes and import duties or tariffs. Also, they tend to prefer paying taxes to the headquarters country instead of to foreign countries where they have subsidiaries. Other considerations in multinational transfer pricing may occur as a result of legal restrictions within a specific country. For example, France may want to protect its domestic aerospace industry and therefore limit the value of certain high-tech goods that the French division of a U.S. company may import. If the company sets the transfer price low, the French division can import a larger *quantity* of items from other divisions.

A country may also restrict the amount of cash that leaves its borders in the form of dividend payments to foreign stockholders. This practice occurs mostly in less-developed countries that need to accumulate hard currencies such as the U.S. dollar, British pound, and German mark. Thus, a British multinational company operating in Peru may set a high transfer price for goods transferred to its Peruvian division. This practice allows the British company to remove the desired amount of cash.

Taxes and Tariffs

Suppose Texas Instruments (TI) makes silicon wafers and transfers them to a TI division in an Asian country that has a low tax rate. There the wafers are processed into semiconductor chips. With a low transfer price, the Asian division's costs will be lower and its income higher. More of TI's total profit will be earned in the Asian country, and the company will pay less total tax. Conversely, if the transfer price is high, the U.S. division will earn more income subject to the higher U.S. rate, and TI will pay more tax.

Income tax effects may be offset by import duties on intracompany transfers. Import duties are based on the prices paid for items. Thus, low transfer prices lead to low tariffs.

Consider International Electronics, Inc., whose Division A in Thailand produces VCR components and transfers them to Division B in the United States for final assembly. Suppose Thailand's income tax rate is 20% and the United States' is 35%. Assume that the United States places a 7% import duty on the price of goods. Suppose that at a market-based transfer price, Division A transfers to Division B components worth $1,000,000 in 19X4. At a lower, cost-based price, the transfer is priced at $800,000. Does the higher or the lower price minimize International Electronics' total tax and tariff payment? Exhibit 26-7 shows the analysis, using assumed figures for Division B's revenue and both divisions' processing costs.

If management sets the higher transfer price, the total payment is $220,000, compared with $236,000 at the lower transfer price. By using the higher price, International Electronics earns more income in Thailand, which has a lower tax rate. Using the higher price saves $30,000 in taxes ($150,000 versus $180,000). This tax savings more than offsets the additional $14,000 in tariff payments ($70,000 instead of $56,000). Overall, the company is $16,000 better off with the higher transfer price.

Multinational companies are not free to manipulate transfer prices at will in order to minimize taxes and tariffs. For companies falling under U.S. jurisdiction, the Internal Revenue Service (IRS) specifies that all transfers should be made at "arm's-length" prices—that is, prices that would be used if the divisions were independent companies. As in purely domestic transactions, companies have considerable leeway in applying this rule to specific situations.

OBJECTIVE 4

Minimize worldwide taxes and tariffs through transfer-pricing strategy

EXHIBIT 26-7   *Taxes and Tariffs under Different Transfer Prices*

Panel A—Higher Transfer Price

	Division A	Division B	Total Tax and Tariff
Revenue	$1,000,000	$1,300,000	
Cost—A Division	600,000	→1,000,000	
B Division		100,000	
Operating Income	$ 400,000	$ 200,000	
Tax, at 20% and 35%	$ 80,000	$ 70,000	$150,000
Tariff, at 7%		70,000	70,000
		$ 140,000	$220,000

Panel B— Lower Transfer Price

	Division A	Division B	Total Tax and Tariff
Revenue	$ 800,000	$1,300,000	
Cost—A Division	600,000	→800,000	
B Division		100,000	
Operating Income	$ 200,000	$ 400,000	
Tax, at 20% and 35%	$ 40,000	$ 140,000	$180,000
Tariff, at 7%		56,000	56,000
		$ 196,000	$236,000

"Transfer pricing: A scheme by which foreign companies evade paying U.S. taxes." What led Sam Donaldson to define transfer pricing in this way on a segment of ABC News' "Primetime Live"? According to a spokesman for the Ways and Means Committee of the U.S. House of Representatives, over 70% of foreign companies with U.S. subsidiaries pay no U.S. taxes, and many of the rest pay very little. How do these companies avoid paying their fair share of taxes?

Consider the situation depicted in Exhibit 26-8. A Japanese electronics company has subsidiaries in Singapore and the United States. Singapore and Japan have a "tax holiday" agreement that allows Japanese companies to pay no tax on sales to Singaporean firms or subsidiaries. A component needed for a laser disc player is produced in Japan at a cost of $90, sold to the Singapore subsidiary for $100, resold as-is to the U.S. subsidiary for $200, and sold as final product for $200. No tax is paid to the U.S. government on a transaction that produced a net profit of $107 ($200 − $90 − $3) for the Japanese company. A U.S.-made player of similar quality and price would net its domestic producer $71.50 at the tax rate of 35%:

Sales price	$200.00
Cost	90.00
Operating income	$110.00
Income tax at 35%	38.50
Net income	$ 71.50

The Japanese company can use this $35.50 ($38.50 − $3) difference in tax to undercut the prices of U.S. competitors. Or it can reinvest the savings in research and become an even stronger competitor in the future.

Is the sale of the component by the Singaporean division to the U.S. division an arm's-length transaction? Certainly not. But Japanese and other foreign companies routinely do business in this way without penalty. How can they? IRS agents cannot travel all over the world demanding to inspect the records of every foreign multinational that does business in the United States.

EXHIBIT 26-8 *Multinational Transfer Pricing Scenario*

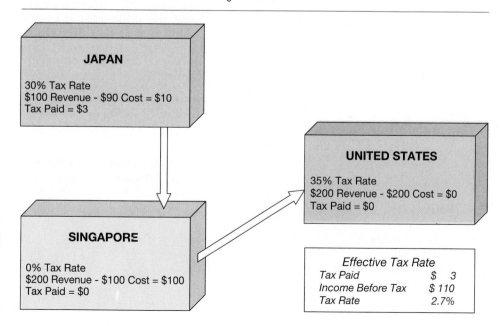

Without agreements between the United States and other nations that go beyond their respective tax laws, this non-level-playing-field situation is likely to continue to plague U.S. firms.

Summary Problems for Your Review

Problem 1

Suppose Seidel Corporation makes color television sets and their principal components, picture tubes. Its two profit centers are the Tube Division and the Set Division. A particular 20-inch picture tube made by the Tube Division can be either sold to external customers for $90 or transferred to the Set Division. The Set Division uses the tube to produce a television that sells for $300. The variable production costs of the two divisions are: Tube Division, $40, and Set Division, $150.

Required

1. Suppose the Tube Division has no idle capacity. From the perspective of Seidel's top managers, should transfers be made? Why or why not?
2. Refer to Requirement 1. If Seidel uses the market price for picture tubes as the transfer price, will that price lead to the optimal decision? Explain.
3. Now suppose that the Tube Division has sufficient idle capacity to produce 1,000 tubes. Will the market transfer price produce the optimal decision in this case?
4. Refer to Requirement 3. If the two division managers are allowed to negotiate a transfer price, in what range will it fall? That is, what is the lowest price the Tube Division will accept and what is the highest price the Set Division will pay? Explain.

Problem 2

Suppose Seidel's Tube Division is located in Japan and its Set Division is in the United States. The applicable income tax rates are Japan, 30%, and the United States, 40%. How much more or less tax will Seidel pay if the transfer price is $90 instead of $70?

SOLUTIONS TO REVIEW PROBLEMS

Problem 1

1.

	Sell Tubes Outside	Use Tubes to Make Sets	
Sales price	$90	$300	
Variable costs:			
Tube Division	40	$ 40	
Set Division	—	150	190
Contribution margin	$50		$110

Transfers should be made. The Set Division adds $210 ($300 − $90) to company revenue for each tube transferred, but adds only $150 to variable cost. Seidel will be $60 better off for each tube transferred.

2. The market price will lead to the optimal decision. Tube will transfer to the Set Division because the Tube Division will receive no more from an external sale. The Set Division will buy from the Tube Division because the Set Division will have to pay the same amount to an external supplier. Divisions typically transfer internally if there is no advantage to external transactions.

3. Yes, the market price will produce the optimal decision in this case. Seidel Corporation will earn a contribution of $110 with the transfer, as shown in the answer to Requirement 1. The Tube Division will sell to the Set Division in order to increase its income by $50 per tube. The Set Division will buy from the Tube Division because the transfer price is no higher than the outside market price. The Set Division's unit contribution margin is $60 regardless of its source of supply:

Sales price		$300
Variable costs:		
For tube	$ 90	
Set Division.	150	240
Contribution margin		$ 60

However, if the Set Division's variable cost were $215 instead of $150, the market price would produce dysfunctional behavior. The company as a whole would be better off by $45 per tube transferred ($300 per set sales price minus $40 per *tube* variable cost and $215 per *set* variable cost). But the Set Division would be $5 per unit worse off with the transfer:

Sales price		$300
Variable costs:		
For tube	$ 90	
Set Division	215	305
Contribution margin		$ (5)

In this case, the Set Division would refuse the transfer.

4. The Tube Division will want more than $40, its variable cost. The Set Division will want to pay less than $150, its sales price minus its variable cost. Thus, the range will be between $40 and $150.

Problem 2

Seidel Corporation pays $2 per unit less by transferring at $90 instead of $70.

Income of Tube Division is $20 higher;	
Tube Division pays 30% of $20 more tax	$(6)
Income of Set Division is $20 lower;	
Set Division pays 40% of $20 less tax	8
Net tax savings per set	$ 2

Performance Measurement

Performance measures are an important part of a management control system. Top management must decide how to measure the performance of responsibility centers—and their managers—at every organizational level. In this section we discuss issues that affect management's choice of measures. We focus on investment centers, which often means the division level and above. For example, Ford Motor Company has two domestic automobile divisions, the Ford Division and the Lincoln-Mercury Division.

Experience shows that people are motivated to perform in a way that leads to rewards. Managers focus their efforts on areas where performance is measured and their efforts affect performance. In designing a performance measurement system, executives seek measures and rewards that promote goal congruence and managerial effort. That is, they seek incentives that motivate responsibility-center managers to work toward top management's goals. Relationships among these variables may be represented this way:

Consider a manufacturing plant manager. Top management may make the plant a cost center and evaluate the plant on the basis of its manufacturing cost. What will the plant manager be motivated to do if his or her reward (bonus) depends on favorable manufacturing efficiency variances? Minimize manufacturing cost, perhaps at the expense of quality. But what if the plant is designated a profit center, and product-line profit is the performance measure and thus the basis for reward? Now the manager has incentives both to help control costs across the entire value chain and to help boost sales. He or she is more likely to cooperate with companywide efforts to increase customer value, and thus long-term profitability.

Nonfinancial and Financial Measures

Management control systems often include nonfinancial measures of performance. Exhibit 26-9 lists examples of nonfinancial measures. Top managers can use these measures to focus the attention of subunit managers on specific factors that enhance profitability. But profitability, a financial measure, is the ultimate test of a business's success. And financial measures are relatively objective—more so, for instance, than customer survey scores. Research shows that the more objective the performance measure, the more effort managers give to the job. For these reasons, companies usually tie rewards to financial results.

Recall that investment-center managers are accountable for costs, revenues, and investments. Many business analysts believe that income, which is revenues minus costs, is inadequate to measure investment-center profitability. Income alone does not indicate the size of the investment required to generate it. For example, two divisions of a company each earn $1,000,000 in income.

EXHIBIT 26-9 *Nonfinancial Performance Measures*

Market share of products	Manufacturing throughput time
Third-party quality ratings of products	Machine setup time
	On-time order delivery rates
Customer survey scores	Number of checks processed per hour
Number of new products introduced	

But one requires an investment of $4,000,000 and the other requires an investment of $8,000,000. In this case the first division is clearly more profitable than the second.

Two performance measures incorporate the amount of invested capital as well as income. They are return on investment (ROI) and residual income.

Return on Investment (ROI)

Return on investment (ROI) is income divided by invested capital, as follows:

$$\text{Return on investment} = \frac{\text{Income}}{\text{Invested capital}}$$

This popular approach to performance measurement enables managers to compare subunit investments with investments elsewhere, both inside and outside the company. For example, General Motors' management might compare the ROI of the Pontiac Division with that of the Buick Division, all other GM divisions combined, or the average for all U.S. auto companies. Also, GM managers might consider abandoning Pontiac, selling its assets, and investing the freed-up capital in the data-processing industry. A useful comparison in that case is Pontiac's ROI versus the ROI of, say, EDS. GM did in fact purchase EDS, Inc., a major computer systems company.

ROI is especially useful for management control when it is divided into its two components, investment turnover and profit margin, as shown below.

$$\text{ROI} = \text{Investment turnover} \times \text{Profit margin}$$

$$\frac{\text{Income}}{\text{Invested capital}} = \frac{\text{Revenue}}{\text{Invested capital}} \times \frac{\text{Income}}{\text{Revenue}}$$

Investment turnover gives the number of revenue dollars that are generated by each dollar of invested capital. The goal is to make each dollar invested generate more sales. The **profit margin** (also called **income-to-sales ratio**) gives the amount of each revenue dollar that goes to income. The goal is to get more income per revenue dollar. The product of these ratios, return on investment, tells the amount of income that each dollar of invested capital generates.

How does a company increase its ROI? By increasing either investment turnover or profit margin without decreasing the other.

One way to increase the turnover of invested capital is to reduce investments in such assets as cash, receivables, and inventories. Historically, managers have recognized the need to increase sales and to control costs. They have paid less attention to managing current assets. Investment turnover highlights the benefits of investing idle cash, managing credit extended to customers, and minimizing inventories. Companies that have implemented just-in-time production systems, as discussed in Chapter 23, have realized dramatic improvements in turnover by reducing both inventories and throughput time.

A company's profit margin may be increased by decreasing costs without a proportional reduction in sales revenue or by increasing sales revenue without a proportional increase in costs. Let us examine Casa del Sabór ("House of Flavor"), the family-style restaurant division of CaliMex, Inc. For 19X4, Casa del Sabór's $4,000,000 investment in restaurants generated the results below:

Sales revenue	$6,250,000
Variable expenses	2,100,000
Fixed expenses	3,150,000
Operating income	$1,000,000

The division's restaurants sold 500,000 meals at an average sales price of $12.50. The average variable cost was $4.20, and the average full total cost was $10.50 [($2,100,000 + $3,150,000)/500,000]. Casa del Sabór's profit margin was 16%. Its ROI was 25%, computed as follows:

$$\textbf{ROI} \quad = \textbf{Investment turnover} \times \textbf{Profit margin}$$

$$\frac{\$1,000,000}{\$4,000,000} = \frac{\$6,250,000}{\$4,000,000} \quad \times \quad \frac{\$1,000,000}{\$6,250,000}$$

$$25\% \quad = \quad 1.5625 \quad \times \quad 16\%$$

Casa del Sabór could increase its profit margin by reducing its variable cost per unit or its total fixed cost. It could increase both its profit margin *and* investment turnover by increasing sales. Suppose the division sold 600,000 meals in 19X5 without changing sales prices, unit variable costs, or fixed costs. The results are:

Sales revenue (600,000 × $12.50)	$7,500,000
Variable expenses (600,000 × $4.20) .	2,520,000
Fixed expenses	3,150,000
Operating income	$1,830,000

$$\textbf{ROI} \quad = \textbf{Investment turnover} \times \textbf{Profit margin}$$

$$\frac{\$1,830,000}{\$4,000,000} = \frac{\$7,500,000}{\$4,000,000} \quad \times \quad \frac{\$1,830,000}{\$7,500,000}$$

$$45.75\% \quad = \quad 1.875 \quad \times \quad 24.4\%$$

Casa del Sabór increased its investment turnover by achieving greater sales volume with no increase in invested capital. The division improved its profit margin by decreasing its fixed cost per sales dollar. In 19X4, this amount was $0.504 ($3,150,000/$6,250,000). In 19X5, it was $0.42 ($3,150,000/$7,500,000). Less fixed cost per sales dollar means more income per sales dollar.

Separating ROI into investment turnover and profit margin makes the measure more useful to managers. If CaliMex's management considers Casa del Sabór's ROI to be too low, the individual components give the group a place to start for planning improvements. For example, suppose the division's turnover is significantly below industry average. Managers may focus their efforts on better asset management. On the other hand, if the profit margin is the problem, they should concentrate on cost control or ways to increase revenue. Segmenting ROI also enhances comparability. Managers may compare both the turnover numbers and the profit margins of divisions instead of their overall profitability only.

Residual Income

Residual income is income minus imputed interest on invested capital.

Residual income = Income − Imputed interest on invested capital

Imputed interest represents the cost of the division's invested capital. It is termed "imputed" because the business did not necessarily borrow the capital and pay cash interest on it. The imputed interest rate is the division's *cost of capital*, which we discussed in Chapter 25. The charge for imputed interest is the minimum income acceptable to management—the income that can be earned by the best alternative use of the capital.

In 19X4, Casa del Sabór earned $1,000,000 of operating income with $4,000,000 of invested capital. Suppose the division's cost of capital was 12%. Its residual income was $520,000, as follows:

Residual income = Income − Imputed interest on invested capital
= $1,000,000 − .12($4,000,000)
= $1,000,000 − $480,000
= $520,000

Casa del Sabór earned $520,000 more income than the $480,000 minimum amount acceptable to CaliMex's top managers.

ROI or Residual Income?

Why do some companies use residual income rather than ROI to measure the performance of investment centers? Because in some circumstances, residual income better promotes goal congruence and managerial effort by motivating managers to maximize an *absolute amount* of income instead of a *percentage rate* of return.

OBJECTIVE 6
Determine how performance measures affect investment decisions

Casa del Sabór's 19X4 ROI was 25% ($1,000,000/$4,000,000). Its cost of capital was 12%. Suppose the division's managers are considering building a restaurant in a new market area. The new restaurant is expected to earn an ROI of 18% per year for its first three years of operation. If corporate headquarters uses ROI to evaluate Casa del Sabór, the division's managers will be reluctant to invest the required capital because acceptance of the project will decrease the division's overall ROI (18% < 25%). But if the subunit's performance is measured by residual income, its managers will build the restaurant. Regardless of Casa del Sabór's base residual income, any project that earns more than the 12% imputed interest rate will increase the amount. All such projects also will improve the profitability of the corporation as a whole.

CaliMex, Inc., has a second division that operates a chain of fast-food restaurants called Burrito Bueno. In 19X4, the Burrito Bueno Division earned $560,000 of operating income. Like the Casa del Sabór Division, Burrito Bueno has $4,000,000 of invested capital and its cost of capital is the companywide rate of 12%. Now suppose CaliMex managers propose a new project that can be undertaken by either Casa del Sabór or Burrito Bueno. The project is expected to earn $180,000 annually on an investment of $1,000,000—an 18% rate of return. From the perspective of CaliMex as a whole, the project should be accepted because its rate of return is greater than the cost of capital. But will either division want to invest in it? Exhibit 26-10 helps answer this question.

We assume that the 19X5 operating results of each division will be unchanged from 19X4 if the division does not accept the new project. The ROIs and residual incomes both without and with the additional investment are shown in Exhibit 26-10.

If the divisions are evaluated on the basis of ROI, Casa del Sabór will reject the project because its ROI will decrease from 25% to 23.6%. Burrito Bueno will accept, because the division can increase its rate of return from 14% to 14.8%. These results illustrate that with ROI, the acceptability of a new project depends on a division's profitability without the project as well as the profitability of the project itself.

What will happen if the divisions' performance is judged by residual income? Now both divisions of the company will invest. The project adds $60,000 to the residual income of either division: $180,000 of additional revenue minus the $120,000 cost of capital. The acceptability of the new project depends on *its* merits only, not on the performance of unrelated investments also.

Despite this key advantage of residual income, most companies prefer ROI, because it is easier for many managers to understand and it is more useful for comparing subunits of different sizes. Consider subunits A and B of a company:

	A	B
Operating income	$ 14,000	$ 140,000
Invested capital	$100,000	$1,000,000
Return on investment	14%	14%
Imputed interest (at 12%)	$ 12,000	$ 120,000
Residual income	$ 2,000	$ 20,000

Both divisions earn $0.14 of operating income for each dollar of capital invested, but Division B has ten times the residual income of Division A. Thus, residual income is said to favor larger divisions.

Regardless of the performance measure used, a comparison of actual results with budgeted results is an attractive way to overcome the measure's weaknesses. In our example, top management may solve their problem by comparing each division's actual residual income to its budgeted residual income instead of the actual amount of the other division.

EXHIBIT 26-10 *Project Evaluation Using ROI and Residual Income*

	Casa del Sabór		Burrito Bueno	
	Without Project	With Project	Without Project	With Project
Operating income (A)	$1,000,000	$1,180,000	$ 560,000	$ 740,000
Invested capital (B)	$4,000,000	$5,000,000	$4,000,000	$5,000,000
Return on investment (A/B)	25%	23.6%	14%	14.8%
Imputed interest (C = 12% × B)	$ 480,000	$ 600,000	$ 480,000	$ 600,000
Residual income (A − C)	$ 520,000	$ 580,000	$ 80,000	$ 140,000

Ideally, the performance of a manager and the performance of the manager's responsibility center should be evaluated separately. Managerial performance and division results certainly are related, but factors beyond the control of managers also affect results. As discussed previously, top managements of multinational companies often dictate international transfer prices to minimize worldwide taxes and tariffs and to avoid restrictions on cash and other international transfers. These transfer prices are revenues of the selling subsidiaries and costs of the buying subsidiaries, but they are not under the control of subsidiary managers. Some accountants believe that central control of multinational operations is so great that subsidiary managers should not be evaluated by the same criteria as domestic investment-center managers even when their segments are evaluated as investment centers.

Different concepts of income. To use either ROI or residual income, businesses must define what they mean by "income." Various definitions are possible. Some firms use operating income and some use net income. Some companies allocate corporate service department costs to manufacturing divisions (see Chapter 22), while others do not.

To measure the performance of division managers separately from that of their divisions, companies may use a contribution approach to income. For instance, the 19X4 income of Casa del Sabór might be computed as in Exhibit 26-11. The idea is to separate *discretionary fixed costs*, which are controlled by the division manager in the short run, from *committed fixed costs*. Committed fixed costs are not under his or her control in the short run, but they *are* directly traceable to the division.

The $2,800,000 contribution controllable by the Casa del Sabór manager can be used as the income measure to evaluate the manager's performance. The $1,000,000 division operating income may be used as the income measure for evaluating *the division* as an investment of CaliMex, Inc.

Different Concepts of Invested Capital. Various alternatives also exist for invested capital. A company might use *total assets assigned to a division* as the investment measure for evaluating the division's performance. *Total assets employed* could be used for the division manager's evaluation. For example, unused land purchased for the division but set aside for future expansion is excluded from total assets employed.

> **OBJECTIVE 7**
> Distinguish between performance of a division and performance of a division manager

EXHIBIT 26-11 *Casa del Sabór Division: Contribution Approach to Income Measurement*

Sales revenue	$6,250,000
Less: Variable expenses	2,100,000
Contribution margin	4,150,000
Less: Fixed expenses controllable by division manager*	1,350,000
Contribution controllable by division manager	2,800,000
Less: Fixed costs controllable by others†	1,800,000
Division operating income	$1,000,000

*Examples are division advertising, restaurant managers' salaries, and training costs. These costs are discretionary.
†Examples are depreciation, property taxes, and insurance. These costs are committed.

Summary Problem for Your Review

In 19X5, the Fountain of Youth Division of DeLeon, Inc., sold 100,000 cases of bottled mineral water for $12 per case. Its variable costs were $4 per case, and its fixed costs totaled $584,000. The division's invested capital balance was $1,000,000. Its cost of capital was 10%.

Required

1. Compute Fountain of Youth's investment turnover, profit margin, and ROI for 19X5.
2. Compute the division's residual income.
3. Fountain of Youth's managers are considering a new line of flavored water. The expected annual ROI of the line is 16%. Will the managers be inclined to add the line if the division is evaluated on the basis of ROI? Of residual income? Explain.
4. DeLeon's management expects the Fountain of Youth Division to improve its ROI for 19X6. Assuming no other changes, calculate the effect on turnover, profit margin, and ROI of each of the following proposals:
   a. An increase in the sales price to $13 per case.
   b. A decrease in invested capital to $900,000.
5. Which proposed action in Requirement 4 is more effective in increasing the division's ROI? Why?

SOLUTION TO REVIEW PROBLEM

Requirement 1 Fountain of Youth's operating income in 19X5 was $216,000:

Sales revenue	$1,200,000
Variable expenses	400,000
Fixed expenses	584,000
Operating income	$ 216,000

$$\text{ROI} = \text{Investment turnover} \times \text{Profit margin}$$

$$\frac{\text{Income}}{\text{Invested capital}} = \frac{\text{Revenue}}{\text{Invested capital}} \times \frac{\text{Income}}{\text{Revenue}}$$

$$\frac{\$216,000}{\$1,000,000} = \frac{\$1,200,000}{\$1,000,000} \times \frac{\$ 216,000}{\$1,200,000}$$

$$21.6\% = 1.2 \times 18\%$$

Requirement 2

$$
\begin{aligned}
\text{Residual income} &= \text{Income} - \text{Imputed interest on invested capital} \\
&= \$216,000 - .10\ (\$1,000,000) \\
&= \$216,000 - \$100,000 \\
&= \$116,000
\end{aligned}
$$

Requirement 3   If Fountain of Youth is evaluated on the basis of ROI, its managers *will not* be inclined to add the new line. Adding a 16% project would decrease the 21.6% ROI the division would achieve without it. The managers *will* be inclined to accept the project if residual income is the performance measure. The flavored-water line will add to the division's current residual income because its 16% return is greater than the division's cost of capital.

Requirement 4

$$\text{ROI} = \text{Investment turnover} \times \text{Profit margin}$$

a. $\dfrac{\$316,000}{\$1,000,000} = \dfrac{\$1,300,000}{\$1,000,000} \times \dfrac{\$316,000}{\$1,300,000}$

$\qquad 31.6\% = \qquad 1.3 \qquad \times \qquad 24.3\%$

b. $\dfrac{\$216,000}{\$900,000} = \dfrac{\$1,200,000}{\$900,000} \times \dfrac{\$216,000}{\$1,200,000}$

$\qquad 24\% = \qquad 1.33 \qquad \times \qquad 18\%$

Requirement 5   The sales price increase is more effective. Increasing revenue while holding other factors constant increases both investment turnover *and* profit margin. Decreasing invested capital increases investment turnover only.

Summary

Many business organizations are highly decentralized. *Decentralization* gives lower-level managers the freedom to make decisions. Decentralization often produces better and faster decision making, greater creativity and motivation, and increased development and learning. However, it can result in *suboptimal decisions,* duplication of activities, and high information costs. The extent of decentralization within a company should not be confused with the type of responsibility center used for management control purposes.

A *management control system* is a set of rules and techniques that aid and coordinate decision making within an organization. The transfer-pricing system is part of the management control system. A *transfer price* is the price one subunit of a company charges for an *intermediate product* or service supplied to another subunit of the same company. In many cases, subunit managers may sell and buy products either internally or externally. Ideally, transfer prices should lead to decisions by subunit managers that are in the best interests of the organization as a whole.

A selling subunit may or may not have *idle capacity*. In general, when a division has more capacity than it needs to satisfy external demand, a transfer price based on the division's variable cost is likely to produce the optimal decision. When the seller has no idle capacity, a market-based price serves as a better guide. In *multinational companies,* top managers often impose transfer prices in order to minimize worldwide taxes and tariffs and to avoid restrictions on cash and other international transfers.

The performance measurement system is another part of the management control system. Top managers seek performance measures and rewards that promote *goal congruence* and managerial effort. The most popular performance measure for investment centers is *return on investment (ROI)*. ROI is income divided by invested capital. ROI also is the product of *investment turnover* and *profit margin*. Companies may increase ROI by increasing revenue, decreasing costs, or decreasing investment while holding the other factors constant.

Another popular measure is *residual income*. Residual income is income minus imputed interest on invested capital. Any project whose rate of return is greater than a subunit's cost of capital increases its residual income.

The best approach to performance evaluation is to compare actual results with budgeted results, whether ROI or residual income is used. Some factors that are beyond a subunit manager's control affect the profitability of the subunit. Thus the performance of the manager and the performance of the subunit should be evaluated separately.

Self-Study Questions

Test your understanding of the chapter by marking the best answer for each of the following questions.

1. Which of the following is not a benefit of decentralization? *(p. 1173)*
   a. Better decision making
   b. Duplication of activities
   c. Faster decision making
   d. Greater creativity and motivation

2. Suboptimal decisions are likely when which of the following is lacking? *(p. 1173)*.
   a. Goal congruence
   b. An external market for an intermediate product
   c. Idle capacity
   d. Residual income

3. If a company uses profit centers in its responsibility accounting system, then it is *(p. 1174)*
   a. Highly centralized
   b. Highly decentralized
   c. Moderately decentralized
   d. Impossible to tell from the information given

4. The variable cost of an intermediate product is $15 per unit. The full total cost at the current volume level is $25. The intermediate market price is $35. If the selling division has idle capacity, which transfer price is likely to produce goal-congruent behavior by the manager of the buying division? *(p. 1179)*
   a. $15   c. $35
   b. $25   d. $10

5. A division of a multinational company is located in a country that has a high income tax rate. The division transfers an intermediate product to a division in a country that has a low income tax rate. Other factors being equal, the company's total tax payment will be minimized if the transfer price is *(p. 1182)*
   a. A high price
   b. A low price
   c. An arm's-length price
   d. A cost-based price

6. The number of revenue dollars that are generated by each dollar of invested capital is called *(p. 1187)*
   a. Return on investment (ROI)
   b. Profit margin
   c. Investment turnover
   d. Residual income

7. Holding other factors constant, decreasing a product's variable cost increases *(p. 1188)*

a. Investment turnover
b. Profit margin
c. Investment turnover and profit margin
d. None of the above

8. Using return on investment (ROI) to measure a division's performance leads to suboptimal decisions when a project's rate of return is *(p. 1189)*
   a. Greater than the division's cost of capital
   b. Less than the division's cost of capital
   c. Greater than the division's ROI without it
   d. Less than the division's ROI without it

9. To evaluate the performance of a division manager, which of the following is the most appropriate measure of income? *(p. 1191)*
   a. The contribution margin of the manager's division
   b. The operating income of the manager's division
   c. The contribution controllable by the manager
   d. The net income of the manager's division

10. An attractive approach to performance evaluation is to compare *(p. 1190)*
    a. Division A's actual results with Division A's budgeted results
    b. Division A's actual results with the actual results of other divisions
    c. Division A's actual results in the current year with Division A's actual results in the preceding year
    d. Division A's actual results with the industry average

Answers to the Self-Study Questions follow the Accounting Vocabulary.

Accounting Vocabulary

Decentralization. The freedom to make decisions *(p. 1172)*.

Goal congruence. Harmony between a subunit manager's goals for the subunit and top management's goals for the overall organization *(p. 1173)*.

Idle capacity. Production capacity in excess of what is needed to satisfy external customer demand for a division's product *(p. 1178)*.

Intermediate product. A product transferred from one subunit of a company to another subunit for further processing *(p. 1175)*.

Investment turnover. The number of revenue dollars that are generated by each dollar of invested capital *(p. 1187)*.

Management control system. A set of rules and techniques that aid and coordinate decision making within an organization *(p. 1172)*.

Multinational company. A company that has divisions in more than one country *(p. 1181)*.

Profit margin (income-to-sales ratio). The amount of each revenue dollar that goes to income *(p. 1187)*.

Residual income. Income minus imputed interest on invested capital *(p. 1189)*.

Return on investment (ROI). Income divided by invested capital *(p. 1187)*.

Suboptimal (dysfunctional) decisions. Decisions whose costs to the organization as a whole outweigh the benefits *(p. 1173)*.

Transfer price. The price one subunit of an organization charges for a product or service supplied to another subunit of the same organization *(p. 1175)*.

Answers to Self-Study Questions

1. b	2. a	3. d	4. a	5. b
6. c	7. b	8. d	9. c	10. a

ASSIGNMENT MATERIAL

Questions

1. Name three benefits and two costs of decentralization.
2. "Companies usually adopt a consistent centralization or decentralization approach to all decisions in all business functions (for example, manufacturing, marketing, and distribution)." Do you agree? Explain.
3. "Profit-center managers are concerned about transfer prices. Cost-center managers are not." Do you agree? Why?
4. What are two general methods for setting transfer prices?
5. Describe a situation in which a "125% of full total cost" transfer-pricing method could lead to a dysfunctional decision.
6. Name two ways firms handle transfer-pricing disputes between subunit managers.
7. "A difference in income tax rates between the jurisdictions of selling and buying divisions is exclusively a *multinational* transfer-pricing issue." Is this statement true? Why or why not?
8. Why is it important for a company's management to carefully select performance measures and rewards for the management control system?
9. Name two nonfinancial performance measures. Tell why a company might use them in its performance measurement system.
10. What are two major strengths of the return on investment (ROI) performance measure?
11. "The residual income measure 'favors' larger divisions." Do you agree? Explain.
12. In measuring the performance of a division manager, what is the importance of the distinction between *discretionary fixed costs* and *committed fixed costs?*

Exercises

Exercise 26-1 *Using different transfer prices to calculate division income* **(L.O. 2)**

Thompson Industries is a decentralized company with an Electric Motor Division and a Ceiling Fan Division. An external market exists for electric motors. At a volume of 8,000 motors and 8,000 fans per year, the following are the unit revenues and costs of the two divisions:

Per Unit	Electric Motor Division	Ceiling Fan Division
Sales price	$40	$200
Variable cost	25	95
Fixed cost	6	35

The variable cost of the Ceiling Fan Division does not include the cost of the electric motor required for each fan.

Required

Compute the operating incomes of the two divisions that result if the Ceiling Fan Division buys 8,000 motors from the Electric Motor Division at each of these transfer prices:

1. a. Intermediate market price of $40
   b. 140% of the Electric Motor Division's variable cost of $25
2. What is the total operating income of Thompson Industries in Requirement 1a? In Requirement 1b?

Exercise 26-2 *Transfer-pricing decision with no idle capacity* (L.O. 3)

Refer to Exercise 26-1. Suppose the Electric Motor Division has no idle capacity. External customers will pay $40 for each of the 8,000 motors the division can produce. The division managers have been delegated full authority to sell and buy internally or externally.

Required

1. From the perspective of Thompson Industries' top management, should the Electric Motor Division transfer 8,000 motors to the Ceiling Fan Division or should the two divisions sell and buy externally? Why?
2. Will a transfer price equal to the intermediate market price lead to goal-congruent decisions by the two managers? Will the 140%-of-variable-cost price? Explain.

Exercise 26-3 *Transfer-pricing decision with idle capacity* (L.O. 3)

Massachusetts Technologies makes calculators and their electronic components. Its two profit centers are the Component Division and the Calculator Division. Calculator components may be either sold to external customers for $11 per assembly or transferred to the Calculator Division. The Calculator Division uses the component assembly to produce a calculator that sells for $32. The variable production costs of the two divisions are: Component, $6, and Calculator, $22.

The Component Division has sufficient idle capacity to produce 10,000 component assemblies.

Required

1. To maximize the income of Massachusetts Technologies, should the 10,000 component assemblies be produced and transferred to the Calculator Division? Why or why not?
2. Will a market-based transfer price for component assemblies lead to the optimal action by the division managers? Explain.
3. What is the highest transfer price acceptable to the manager of the Calculator Division? What is the lowest price acceptable to the manager of the Component Division?

Exercise 26-4 *Transfer-pricing decision with idle capacity* (L.O. 3)

Refer to Exercise 26-3. The Component Division has 10,000 units of idle capacity. Now suppose the variable cost of the Calculator Division is $17 rather than $22. Will a transfer price of $11—the market price of component assemblies— lead the two division managers to act in the best interests of Massachusetts Technologies as a whole? Explain.

Exercise 26-5 *Minimizing taxes and tariffs through transfer pricing* (L.O. 4)

Data for Starnes International Corporation are shown on page 1198. Fill in the blanks to determine whether a higher transfer price or a lower transfer price will minimize worldwide taxes and tariffs on transfers from the company's Taiwan subsidiary to its U.S. division.

	Higher Transfer Price		Lower Transfer Price	
	Taiwan Division	U.S. Division	Taiwan Division	U.S. Division
Revenue	$1,700,000	$2,900,000	?	?
Expenses:				
Taiwan Subsidiary	1,400,000	→ 1,700,000	1,400,000	→ 1,500,000
United States Division	—	1,000,000	—	1,000,000
Operating income	$ 300,000	?	$ 100,000	?
Tax, at 25% and 35%	$ 75,000	?	?	$ 140,000
Tariff, at 7%		$ 119,000		?
Tax and tariff		?		?

Exercise 26-6 *Computing return on investment, investment turnover, and profit margin* (L.O. 5)

Three companies operate in the same industry. Fill in the blanks below and comment on the relative performance of the companies:

	A	B	C
Revenue	$10,000,000	$5,000,000	?
Income	1,000,000	500,000	?
Invested capital.............	4,000,000	?	$10,000,000
Profit margin	?	?	2.5%
Investment turnover	?	?	2
Return on investment (ROI) ..	?	5%	?

Exercise 26-7 *Considering how performance measurement affects an investment decision* (L.O. 6)

Grant Newton is the manager of the Big Sky Division of Backwoods Outfitters, Inc. He has just completed his operating budget for the upcoming fiscal year, 19X5. Newton expects to earn an operating income of $2,000,000 with the division's invested capital of $10,000,000.

Suppose Newton is approached by Backwoods Outfitters managers about adding a new clothing line to his product offerings. The line will require an additional investment of $2,500,000. The headquarters managers believe it will generate operating income of $375,000 in each of the next two years.

Required

1. If Backwoods Outfitters evaluates the Big Sky Division on the basis of ROI, will Newton want to add the clothing line? Why or why not?
2. Suppose the company's top managers evaluate each division by comparing its budgeted ROI with its actual ROI. What action could the managers take to make the clothing line acceptable to Newton?
3. Suppose Big Sky's cost of capital is 12% and the division is evaluated on the basis of residual income. Now will Newton want the project? Explain.

Exercise 26-8 *Distinguishing the performance of manager and division* (L.O. 7)

The 19X4 operating results of Midwest Industries' two divisions are as follows:

	Illinois Division	Indiana Division
Sales revenue	$2,000,000	$2,000,000
Variable expenses	900,000	900,000
Contribution margin	$1,100,000	$1,100,000
Less: Fixed expenses:		
Depreciation, property taxes, and insurance	550,000	400,000
Managerial salaries	200,000*	200,000*
Training costs	80,000	—
Advertising and sales promotion	50,000	50,000
Other discretionary fixed costs	20,000	150,000
Operating income	$ 200,000	$ 300,000

*Includes division manager's salary of $75,000.

The senior executives of Midwest Industries separately evaluate the performance of the division managers and the performance of their divisions. The managers are not held accountable for fixed costs they cannot control in the short run. Because the divisions sell identical products in very similar markets, top managers budget the same rate of return on investment (ROI) for both divisions and also budget the same rate for both division managers.

Midwest Industries had $1,500,000 of capital invested in each division in 19X4. This amount is used as the invested capital base to evaluate both division managers and divisions.

Required

1. According to Midwest Industries' performance evaluation system, which manager performed better in 19X4? Which division was the better economic investment for the company?
2. If the performances of managers and divisions were not evaluated separately, which division manager would be evaluated more favorably? Explain.

Problems   *(Group A)*

Problem 26-1A   *Transfer-pricing decision with no idle capacity* (L.O. 2, 3)

The Mississippi Valley Hardwood Lumber Company is a decentralized company with two divisions, Unfinished Lumber and Finished Lumber. The Unfinished Lumber Division has 1,000,000 board-feet of capacity. Sufficient customer demand exists for the division to sell all its production in the external intermediate market. The Unfinished Lumber Division's fixed cost is $500,000 per year.

The external market sales prices and the variable costs of the two divisions are:

Per Board-Foot	Unfinished Lumber Division	Finished Lumber Division
Market sales price	$3.00	$3.60
Variable cost	1.50	1.00

The variable cost of the Finished Lumber Division does not include the cost of unfinished lumber, its direct material input.

Required

1. To maximize the income of the company as a whole, should the Unfinished Lumber Division transfer unfinished lumber to the Finished Lumber Division or sell all its production in the external intermediate market?
2. Will a transfer price equal to the intermediate market price of $3 per board-foot lead to the action that is best for the company? Why or why not?
3. Suppose Mississippi Valley Hardwood Lumber Company uses a transfer-pricing method of 120% of the full total cost of the transferring division. At the volume level of 1,000,000 board-feet, will this method produce a transfer price that leads to the action you determined in Requirement 1? Explain.

Problem 26-2A   *Transfer-pricing decisions with idle capacity*   *(L.O. 3)*

New Mexico Metal Works is a decentralized company with two profit centers. The Metals Division produces sheet metal that is either sold to outside customers or transferred to the Consumer Products Division. The Consumer Products Division stamps the sheet metal into various forms on a special-order basis. Most of this division's work is done for customers in the automobile industry.

The Metals Division produces an aluminum sheet that it sells to outside customers for $18 per sheet. The division's variable production cost is $12 per sheet. The Metals Division has sufficient idle capacity to produce 80,000 sheets in 19X4.

The Consumer Products Division has recently accepted an order from the Ford Motor Company for 80,000 aluminum bumpers. Each bumper requires one sheet of aluminum. Other data pertaining to the order are:

Sales price per bumper	$30
Variable cost of Consumer Products Division (excluding aluminum sheet)	$ 8

Required

1. From the perspective of New Mexico Metal Works' top management, should the Metals Division produce the 80,000 aluminum sheets needed for the Ford Motor Company order and transfer them to the Consumer Products Division? Or should Consumer Products buy the sheets from external suppliers? Explain.
2. Will a transfer price equal to the market price of $18 lead to the course of action that maximizes the company's operating income? Why or why not?
3. Now suppose the Consumer Products Division's variable cost per bumper is $13 rather than $8. Will the market-price transfer price produce the optimal decision? Will a transfer price equal to the Metals Division's variable cost of $12?
4. Refer to Requirement 3. Suppose the top managers of New Mexico Metal Works intervene and mandate an internal transfer. If the executives prorate the total companywide contribution margin from the bumpers to the two divisions on the basis of their respective variable costs, what amount will be prorated to each division?

Problem 26-3A   *Minimizing worldwide taxes and tariffs through transfer-pricing strategy*   *(L.O. 4)*

Worldwide Gems, Inc., has two profit centers. The Australian Mining Division operates two mines that are rich in raw diamonds. The U.S. Processing Division processes the raw diamonds into industrial diamonds. Two pounds of raw diamonds are required for each pound of industrial diamonds. Industrial diamonds sell for $2,500 per pound.

The senior managers of Worldwide Gems expect to process 2,000 pounds of raw diamonds into 1,000 pounds of industrial diamonds in 19X5. At that volume, the budgeted unit costs of the two divisions are:

Per Pound	Australian Mining	U.S. Processing
Variable cost......................	$100	$300
Fixed cost	200	600

The unit costs of the Australian Mining Division are per pound of raw diamonds mined and shipped to the United States. The unit costs of the U.S. Processing Division are per pound of industrial diamonds produced; the $300 variable cost of the division does not include the cost of raw diamonds.

Suppose the corporate income tax rates of Australia and the United States are 20% and 35%, respectively. Also suppose the United States places a 7% tariff on imported goods.

The managers of Worldwide Gems want to minimize total taxes and tariffs paid to Australia and the United States. They are considering two transfer-pricing methods:

400% of the Australian Mining Division's variable cost
200% of the Australian Mining Division's full total cost

Required

1. Which of the two transfer-pricing methods being considered by Worldwide Gems minimizes the company's taxes and tariffs?
2. How should the top management of Worldwide Gems evaluate the Australian Mining Division manager?

Problem 26-4A *Computing investment turnover, profit margin, and return on investment* **(L.O. 5)**

The 19X3 contribution-margin income statement for Great Plains, Inc., is given below:

	Total	Per Unit
Sales revenue..................................	$2,000,000	$50
Less: Variable expenses.....................	1,200,000	30
Contribution margin	800,000	20
Less: Fixed expenses	640,000	16
Operating income.............................	$ 160,000	$ 4

The company had operating assets of $1,000,000 during the year.

Required

1. Compute the 19X3 investment turnover, profit margin, and ROI for Great Plains, Inc.

For 19X4, Great Plains' top executives are considering several changes to increase the company's ROI. Compute the new investment turnover, profit margin, and ROI if each of the events in Requirements 2 through 5 takes place. Consider each item separately, starting in each case with the 19X3 data.

2. The company saves $20,000 in expenses by redesigning its product to require fewer parts.
3. By implementing a just-in-time (JIT) production system, the company achieves an inventory reduction of $100,000. (The released capital is used to pay off bank loans.)

4. Great Plains raises its sales price to $55. Sales volume in units remains unchanged.

5. The company issues bonds and uses the proceeds to buy new, more-efficient machinery for $250,000. The new machinery reduces production costs by $10,000 per year.

6. Which action in Requirements 2 through 5 is most effective in increasing Great Plains' ROI? Comment on its effectiveness.

Problem 26-5A *Determining the effect of performance measures on investment decisions (L.O. 6)*

Homewood Foods, Inc., has two divisions—the Frozen Food Division and the Canned Food Division. Summary financial data (in thousands) for 19X3 (actual) and 19X4 (budgeted) are:

	Operating Income		Invested Capital	
	19X3	19X4	19X3	19X4
Frozen Food Division	$2,000	$2,050	$10,000	$10,000
Canned Food Division	1,500	1,800	8,500	9,000

Homewood Foods has a bonus plan based on division return on investment (ROI). The top manager of each division receives a large bonus if his or her division reports an increase in ROI from the previous year. If the division's ROI does not increase, no bonus is paid.

As 19X4 begins, each division manager is considering a separate proposal to invest $400,000 in a new food line that is expected to generate annual operating income of $56,000. Homewood Foods' cost of capital is 12% for both divisions.

Required

1. Would you accept the proposed investment project if you were the manager of the Frozen Food Division? Of the Canned Food Division? Explain.

2. Suppose the bonus of each division manager were based on residual income instead of ROI. Would your answer to Requirement 1 change? Why or why not?

3. What is your opinion of a bonus plan that is based on improving last year's performance measure, whether ROI or residual income? How would you change the plan, if at all?

Problem 26-6A *Distinguishing the performance of manager and division (L.O. 7)*

The Consumer Products Division of Glendale Industries earned an operating income of $1,160,000 in 19X3. The division's contribution-approach income statement showed:

Sales revenue	$6,560,000
Variable expenses	3,860,000
Contribution margin	2,700,000
Fixed expenses	1,540,000
Operating income	$1,160,000

The total fixed expense comprised several components:

Depreciation, property taxes, and insurance	$1,000,000
Managerial salaries*	250,000
Employee training	40,000
Advertising and sales promotions......................	100,000
Research and engineering	150,000
	$1,540,000

*Includes division manager's $90,000 salary.

Glendale Industries' top managers separately evaluate the Consumer Products Division and the division's manager, Helen Miller. Miller is not held accountable for fixed costs that she cannot control in the short run. For evaluating both division and manager, headquarters assigned $5,200,000 of invested capital in 19X3.

Required

1. Calculate the total discretionary fixed cost for 19X3.
2. Compute the contribution controllable by Helen Miller.
3. Compute the rate of return on investment (ROI) appropriate for measuring the performance of (a) Helen Miller and (b) the Consumer Products Division.
4. Which rate in Requirement 3 is higher? If Miller's rate is higher, does that mean that her performance will be evaluated more favorably than that of the Consumer Products Division? Explain.

(Group B)

Problem 26-1B   *Transfer-pricing decision with no idle capacity*   *(L.O. 2, 3)*

Montgomery Molded Products, Inc., is a decentralized company with two divisions, Plastic Powder and Molding. The Plastic Powder Division produces powdered plastic that can be either sold to external customers or transferred to the Molding Division. The Molding Division mixes powdered plastic with other ingredients, liquefies it, and injects it into molds to produce various plastic products. One product of the Molding Division is a car-top carrier that requires 1 kilogram of powdered plastic. (The company defines 1 kilogram as a "unit" of powder.) The external market price and the variable cost per unit of powder and per car-top carrier are:

Per Unit	Plastic Powder Division	Molding Division
Market sales price	$20	$90
Variable cost.................................	8	50

The $50 variable cost of the Molding Division does not include the cost of powdered plastic.

The Plastic Powder Division has 200,000 units of production capacity. Sufficient external market demand exists for the division to sell all its production to outside customers.

Required

1. To maximize the income of Montgomery Molded Products as a whole, should the Plastic Powder Division transfer powdered plastic to the Molding Division to make car-top carriers or sell all its production in the external intermediate market?

2. Will a transfer price equal to the intermediate market price of $20 per unit of powder lead to the action that is best for the company? Why or why not?

3. Suppose Montgomery Molded Products uses a transfer-pricing method of 200% of the full total cost of the transferring division. Assume that the full total cost of the Plastic Powder Division is $15 per unit. Will this method produce a transfer price that leads to the action you determined in Requirement 1? Explain.

Problem 26-2B *Transfer-pricing decisions with idle capacity* **(L.O. 3)**

Griggs and Paxton, Inc., is a decentralized company with two profit centers. The Motor Division produces 4-horsepower gasoline motors that are used in lawn mowers and other products. The market price of the motors is $75, and their variable production cost is $50. The Motor Division has sufficient idle capacity to produce 20,000 motors.

The second profit center of Griggs and Paxton is the Mower Division, which produces a line of lawn mowers. The Mower Division has recently received approval from top management to produce a new mulching mower that requires a 4-horsepower motor. Other data pertaining to the mulching mower are:

Sales price	$155
Variable cost of Mower Division (excluding motor)	$ 70

Required

1. From the perspective of Griggs and Paxton's top managers, should the Motor Division produce 20,000 motors and transfer them to the Mower Division, or should the Mower Division buy all the motors it needs from external suppliers? Explain.

2. Will a transfer price equal to the market price of $75 lead to the course of action that maximizes the company's operating income? Why or why not?

3. Now suppose the variable cost of the Mower Division is $81 rather than $70. Will the market-based transfer price produce the optimal decision? Will a transfer price equal to the Motor Division's variable cost of $50?

4. Refer to Requirement 3. Suppose the top managers of Griggs and Paxton intervene and mandate an internal transfer. If the executives prorate the overall companywide contribution margin from the sale of 20,000 mulching mowers to the two divisions on the basis of their respective variable costs, what amount will be prorated to each division?

Problem 26-3B *Minimizing worldwide taxes and tariffs through transfer-pricing strategy* **(L.O. 4)**

Computer Accessories, Inc., is a multinational firm with two profit centers. The South Korean Division produces semiconductor chips and transfers them to the Consumer Products Division in the United States, which uses them to make modems and other computer accessories. Consumer Products expects to produce and sell 50,000 items in 19X4 at an average sales price of $100. At that volume level, the budgeted unit costs of the two divisions are:

Per Unit	South Korean Division	Consumer Products Division
Variable cost	$11	$49
Fixed cost	9	11

The average variable cost of the Consumer Products Division does not include the cost of semiconductor chips.

Suppose the corporate income tax rates of South Korea and the United States are 15% and 35%, respectively. Also suppose the United States places a 10% tariff on imported goods.

The top managers of Computer Accessories want to minimize total taxes and tariffs paid to South Korea and the United States. They are considering two transfer-pricing methods:

200% of the South Korean Division's variable cost
150% of the South Korean Division's full total cost

Required

1. Which of the two transfer-pricing methods being considered by Computer Accessories, Inc., produces the lower total of taxes and tariffs?
2. How should the corporation's top management evaluate the manager of the South Korean Division?

Problem 26-4B *Computing investment turnover, profit margin, and return on investment (L.O. 5)*

The 19X4 contribution margin income statement for the Atlantic Division of European Products, Inc., is given below:

	Total	Per Unit
Sales revenue	$1,500,000	$75
Less: Variable expenses	960,000	48
Contribution margin	540,000	27
Less: Fixed expenses	300,000	15
Operating income	$ 240,000	$12

The company had operating assets of $1,200,000 during the year.

Required

1. Compute the 19X4 investment turnover, profit margin, and return on investment (ROI) for the Atlantic Division.

For 19X5, the Atlantic Division's top managers are considering several changes to increase the division's ROI. Compute the new investment turnover, profit margin, and ROI if each of the events in Requirements 2 through 5 takes place. Consider each item separately, starting in each case with the 19X4 data.

2. The division changes its distribution system and reduces distribution cost by $30,000.
3. The division uses new credit management procedures that reduce the average balance of accounts receivable by $20,000.
4. The Atlantic Division sells 5,000 more items than in 19X4.
5. The division issues bonds and uses the proceeds to buy new, more-efficient packaging equipment for $100,000. The equipment reduces packaging costs by $10,000.
6. Which action in Requirements 2 through 5 is most effective in increasing the ROI of the Atlantic Division? Comment on its effectiveness.

Problem 26-5B *Determining the effect of performance measures on investment decisions (L.O. 6)*

The Green Earth Company has two profit centers, the Fertilizer Division and the Herbicide Division. Summary financial data (in thousands) for 19X4 (actual) and 19X5 (budgeted) are:

	Operating Income		Invested Capital	
	19X4	19X5	19X4	19X5
Fertilizer Division	$1,600	$1,650	$7,000	$7,200
Herbicide Division...............	1,000	950	7,700	7,300

The Green Earth Company has a bonus plan based on division return on investment (ROI). The top manager of each division receives a large bonus if his or her division reports an increase in ROI from the previous year. If the division's ROI does not increase, no bonus is paid.

As 19X5 begins, each manager is considering a separate proposal to invest $500,000 in a new product line that is expected to generate annual operating income of $75,000. Green Earth's cost of capital is 10%.

Required

1. Would you accept the proposed investment project if you were the manager of the Fertilizer Division? Of the Herbicide Division? Explain.
2. Suppose the bonus of each division manager were based on residual income instead of ROI. Would your answer to Requirement 1 change? Why or why not?
3. What is your opinion of a bonus plan that is based on improving last year's performance measure, whether ROI or residual income? How would you change the plan, if at all?

Problem 26-6B   *Distinguishing the performance of manager and division* (L.O. 7)

The Clear Lake Division of Scott Products earned an operating income of $1,710,000 in 19X4. The division's contribution approach income statement showed:

Sales revenue	$9,840,000
Variable expenses..................	5,800,000
Contribution margin	4,040,000
Fixed expenses	2,330,000
Operating income	$1,710,000

The total fixed expense comprised several components:

Depreciation, property taxes, and insurance	$1,450,000
Managerial salaries*	350,000
Management consulting	70,000
Advertising and sales promotions ...	180,000
Research and engineering	280,000
	$2,330,000

*Includes division manager's $100,000 salary.

Scott Products' executives separately evaluate the Clear Lake Division and the division's manager, James O'Hara. O'Hara is not held accountable for fixed costs that he cannot control in the short run. For evaluating both division and division manager, headquarters assigned $9,500,000 of invested capital in 19X4.

Required

1. Calculate the total discretionary fixed cost for 19X4.
2. Compute the contribution controllable by James O'Hara.

3. Compute the rate of return on investment (ROI) appropriate for measuring the performance of (a) James O'Hara and (b) the Clear Lake Division.

4. Which rate in Requirement 3 is higher? If O'Hara's rate is higher, does that mean that his performance will be evaluated more favorably than that of the Clear Lake Division? Explain.

Extending Your Knowledge

Decision Problem

Effect of Performance Measures on an Investment Decision (L.O. 6)

The Venegoni Corporation is a decentralized company that evaluates its two divisions on the basis of return on investment (ROI). The Naples Division of Venegoni makes precision electric motors that are either sold to external customers or transferred to the Florence Division of the company. The Florence Division manufactures and sells a high-quality line of printers, modems, and CD-ROMs.

The Florence Division has recently received an order for 100 units of a combination fax machine/printer. The division has identified an outside supplier from which Florence can buy the 100 motors for $350 each. The Florence Division has asked the Naples Division to price the motors for an internal transfer.

Diana Fiori, the Naples Division manager, expects to achieve an ROI of 20% without the new order from Florence. Her accounting staff predicts that the additional cost to produce each motor will be $200. Fiori has determined that the division will have to invest additional capital of $100,000 to produce the motors. This capital is fully recoverable at the end of the year. Venegoni's companywide cost of capital is 10%; interest is not charged against either division's income in the computation of ROI.

Required

1. From the viewpoint of Venegoni Corporation's top executives, should the Florence Division buy the 100 motors from the outside supplier or should the Naples Division manufacture and transfer them?

2. What transfer price will enable the Naples Division to achieve the same ROI with the new order as without it? Will the Florence Division pay that price?

3. Would Fiori be willing to supply the motors for $350 if the corporation's top executives used residual income to measure each division's performance?

Ethical Issue

Refer to Exhibit 26-8. In the situation depicted there the Japanese multinational corporation has subsidiaries in Singapore and the United States. The Singaporean subsidiary adds no value to the final product sold in the United States, but it "earns" $100 of the total $110 income on each item sold. (In a variant of this situation, the product is shipped directly from Japan to the United States. The Singaporean subsidiary never takes physical custody of the items; it simply "buys" them from the Japanese division and "sells" them to the U.S. division.) The U.S. division adds value to the product by marketing it, delivering it to customers, and servicing it after the sale. Yet the U.S. division pays no income tax. Scenarios such as this are commonplace. But is this practice ethical?

Chapter 27

Using Accounting Information
to Make Business Decisions

E ugene Lerner is a rumpled, pipe-smoking professor of finance at Northwestern University in Evanston, Ill. He lectures in Thailand, quotes Moses, write books on investing, and is "closest to heaven" when he hooks a big fish.

Lerner, 58, also fishes for hot stocks, using some mechanical quantitative rules he and fellow professor William Breen, 49, developed at Northwestern. Both men, still full-time professors, are putting their academic research to work. Their company, Disciplined Investment Advisors Inc. [DIA] of Evanston, manages $462 million for 68 clients.

It took DIA a lot of wading through financial databases to develop its system for buying stocks. But now the . . . partners are sitting pretty. The buy signals are generated on a computer, and little human intervention is called for. . . . The basic rule, elicited from a study of stock price behavior over a 15-year

period, is as simple as looking for earnings gains. DIA buys . . . stocks whose earnings for the past four quarters are above those of the year-earlier period.

Among the other criteria: a [dividend] yield of at least 1 percent, a return on equity between 5 percent and 50 percent, and a price/earnings [P/E] multiple between 2 and 60. Companies with unusually high returns or low P/Es may look like bargains but are excluded as likely freak situations. . . . Companies that meet these criteria are ranked according to the ratio of price to book value, with the cheapest stocks topping the shopping list. The firm also has a simple sell strategy. When per-share earnings in the most recent four quarters drop 5 percent from the year-earlier period, DIA dumps the stock.

Source: Charles Siler, "Strictly by the Numbers," *Forbes*, November 2, 1987, p. 187.

As this vignette illustrates, sophisticated investors such as Disciplined Investment Advisors rely on accounting information to make business decisions. Creditors and individual investors do, too. Should the bank loan officer lend money to the Joneses? Should the investor buy more stock in Xerox or sell those shares presently owned? People need information to make these decisions. The balance sheet, the income statement, and the statement of cash flows provide a large part of the information that is used for making decisions such as these. In Chapters 1 through 15, we have described the process of accounting and the preparation of the financial statements. We have tried to relate each topic to the real world of business by showing the relevance of the accounting data. In this chapter, we discuss in more detail how to use the information that appears in these statements. (Appendix C features the financial statements of The Goodyear Tire & Rubber Company. You may apply the analytical skills you learn in this chapter to those real-world data.)

Financial Statement Analysis

Financial statement analysis focuses on techniques used by analysts external to the organization, although managers use many of the same methods. These analysts rely on publicly available information. A major source of such information is the annual report. In addition to the financial statements (income statement, balance sheet, and statement of cash flows), annual reports usually contain

1. Footnotes to the financial statements
2. A summary of the accounting methods used
3. Management's discussion and analysis of the financial results
4. The auditor's report
5. Comparative financial data for a series of years

Management's discussion and analysis of financial results is especially important. For example, the 1990 annual report of The Boeing Company includes eight pages of top management discussion ranging from company revenues and earnings to the market environment and the company's backlog of unfilled sales orders. Under Market Environment, Boeing managers reveal that in 1990, world airline passenger traffic increased by 7.4 percent. The greatest growth came from routes linked to the Pacific Rim. Management predicted that airline traffic would grow by approximately 5.2 percent annually from 1991 to 2005. The discussion covered bargain air fares, the effects of jet fuel prices on airline profits, and the expectation that one major airline will cease operations. What have these facts and predictions to do with the use of accounting information to make decisions about Boeing? Everything, because they help investors and creditors interpret the financial statements. The balance sheet, income statement, and statement of cash flows are based on historical data. The management discussion offers top management's glimpses into the company's future. Investors and creditors are primarily interested in where the business is headed.

Companies also prepare reports for the Securities and Exchange Commission (SEC). Form 10-K presents financial statement data in a standard format and is generally more comprehensive than the financial statements published in annual reports. Form 10-Q includes quarterly financial statements, so it provides more timely information than the annual reports, although the 10-Q reports are less complete.

Annual reports and SEC reports are issued well after the events being reported have occurred. More timely information is often available from company press releases and articles in the business press. *The Wall Street Journal, Business Week, Forbes, Fortune,* and *Barron's* are among the more popular publications. Moody's Investors Services, Standard & Poor's Industrial Surveys, and other private investment services supply information to their subscribers. Trade creditors rely on published information and reports from credit agencies such as Dun & Bradstreet. The techniques of financial statement analysis presented in this chapter will be important to anyone who wants to gain a thorough understanding of a company's position and prospects.

Objective of Financial Statement Analysis

Investors purchase capital stock expecting to receive dividends and an increase in the value of the stock. Creditors make loans with the expectation of receiving interest and principal. Both groups bear the risk that they will not receive their expected returns. They use financial statement analysis to (1) predict the amount of expected returns and (2) assess the risks associated with those returns.

Because creditors generally expect to receive specific fixed amounts and have the first claim on assets, they are most concerned with assessing short-term liquidity and long-term solvency. **Short-term liquidity** is an organization's ability to meet current payments as they become due. **Long-term solvency** is the ability to generate enough cash to pay long-term debts as they mature.

In contrast, investors are more concerned with profitability, dividends, and future security prices. Why? Because dividend payments depend on profitable operations, and stock price appreciation depends on the market's assessment of the company's prospects. Creditors also assess profitability because profitable operations are the prime source of cash to repay loans.

How can financial statement analysis help creditors and investors? After all, financial statements report on past results and current position, but creditors and investors want to predict future returns and their risks. Financial statement analysis is useful because past performance is often a good indicator of future performance. Current position is the base on which future performance must be built. For example, trends in past sales, operating expenses, and net income may continue. Furthermore, evaluation of management's past performance gives clues to its ability to generate future returns. Finally, the assets a company owns, the liabilities it must pay, and other indicators of current position all affect its future prospects.

We divide the tools and techniques that the business community uses in evaluating financial statement information into three broad categories: horizontal analysis, vertical analysis, and ratio analysis.

Horizontal Analysis

Many business decisions hinge on whether the numbers—in sales, income, expenses, and so on—are increasing or decreasing over time. Has the sales figure risen from last year? From two years ago? By how many dollars? We may find that the net sales figure has risen by $20,000. This may be interesting, but considered alone it is not very useful for decision making. An analysis of the *percentage change* in the net sales figure over time improves our ability to use the dollar amounts. It is more useful to know that sales have increased by 20 percent than to know that the increase in sales is $20,000.

The study of percentage changes in comparative statements is called **horizontal analysis.** Computing a percentage change in comparative statements requires two steps: (1) Compute the dollar amount of the change from the earlier (base) period to the later period, and (2) divide the dollar amount of change by the base period amount. Horizontal analysis is illustrated as follows:

| | | | | Increase (Decrease) | | | |
| | | | | During Year 3 | | During Year 2 | |
	Year 3	Year 2	Year 1	Amount	%	Amount	%
Sales	$120,000	$100,000	$80,000	$20,000	20%	$20,000	25%
Net income	12,000	8,000	10,000	4,000	50%	(2,000)	(20%)

The increase in sales is $20,000 in both year 3 and year 2. However, the percentage increase in sales differs from year to year because of the change in the base amount. To compute the percentage change for year 2, we divide the amount of increase ($20,000) by the base period amount ($80,000), an increase of 25 percent. For year 3 the dollar amount increases again by $20,000. However, the base period amount for figuring this percentage change is $100,000. Dividing $20,000 by $100,000 computes a percentage increase of only 20 percent during year 3. Observe that net income *decreases* by 20 percent during year 2 and increases by 50 percent during year 3.

Detailed horizontal analyses of a comparative income statement and a comparative balance sheet are shown in the two right-hand columns of Exhibits 27-1 and 27-2. McColpin, Inc., is a small retailer of office furniture.

The comparative income statement in Exhibit 27-1 reveals that net sales increased by 6.8 percent during 19X7 and that the cost of goods sold grew by much less. As a result, gross profit rose by 17.3 percent. Note that general expenses actually decreased, and so the company significantly increased income from operations and net income during 19X7. Our analysis shows that 19X7 was a much better year than 19X6. We see that the growth in income resulted more from slowing the increase in expenses than from boosting sales revenue.

No percentage increase is computed for interest revenue because dividing the $4,000 increase by a zero amount would produce a meaningless percentage. Also, we compute no percentage change when a base-year amount is negative. For example, when a company goes from a net loss one year to a profit the next year, we would be dividing a positive number by a negative amount.

(Throughout this chapter, we discuss only some of the elements of the various statements that we present. For example, we mention McColpin's cost of goods sold but not its selling expenses. Understand, however, that the

EXHIBIT 27-1 *Comparative Income Statement—Horizontal Analysis*

McColpin, Inc.
Comparative Income Statement
Years Ended December 31, 19X7 and 19X6

	19X7	19X6	Increase (Decrease) Amount	Increase (Decrease) Percent
Net sales	$858,000	$803,000	$55,000	6.8%
Cost of goods sold	513,000	509,000	4,000	0.8
Gross profit.................	345,000	294,000	51,000	17.3
Operating expenses:				
Selling expenses	126,000	114,000	12,000	10.5
General expenses	118,000	123,000	(5,000)	(4.1)
Total operating expenses ...	244,000	237,000	7,000	3.0
Income from operations......	101,000	57,000	44,000	77.2
Interest revenue.............	4,000	—	4,000	—
Interest expense.............	24,000	14,000	10,000	71.4
Income before income taxes ..	81,000	43,000	38,000	88.4
Income tax expense	33,000	17,000	16,000	94.1
Net income	$ 48,000	$ 26,000	$22,000	84.6

manager of the sales staff—and likely top management also—would examine the selling expenses in conducting a full analysis of the company's operations.)

The comparative balance sheet in Exhibit 27-2 shows that 19X7 was a year of expansion for the company. Property, plant, and equipment increased from $399,000 to $507,000, a growth rate of 27.1 percent. Total assets increased by 22.2 percent. To help finance this expansion, McColpin borrowed heavily, increasing short-term notes payable by 55.6 percent and long-term debt by 46 percent. The increase in assets was also financed in part by profitable operations, as shown by the 26.9 percent increase in retained earnings.

The sharpest percentage increase on the balance sheet is in long-term investments (100 percent). However, the dollar amounts are small compared with the other balance sheet figures. Note this key point of financial analysis: percentage changes must be evaluated in terms of the item's relative importance to the company as a whole. In this instance, the large percentage increase in long-term investments means little because the company holds such a small amount. The 27.1 percent increase in property, plant, and equipment is more important because their cost represents the largest asset and their use is intended to generate profits for years to come.

Trend Percentages

Trend percentages are a form of horizontal analysis. Trends are important indicators of the direction a business is taking. How have sales changed over a five-year period? What trend does gross profit show? These questions can be answered by an analysis of trend percentages over a representative period, such as the most recent five or ten years. To gain a realistic view of the company, it is often necessary to examine more than just a two- or three-year period.

EXHIBIT 27-2 *Comparative Balance Sheet—Horizontal Analysis*

McColpin, Inc.
Comparative Balance Sheet
December 31, 19X7 and 19X6

	19X7	19X6	Increase (Decrease) Amount	Increase (Decrease) Percent
Assets				
Current assets:				
Cash	$ 29,000	$ 32,000	$ (3,000)	(9.4%)
Accounts receivable, net	114,000	85,000	29,000	34.1
Inventories	113,000	111,000	2,000	1.8
Prepaid expenses...........	6,000	8,000	(2,000)	(25.0)
Total current assets.......	262,000	236,000	26,000	11.0
Long-term investments	18,000	9,000	9,000	100.0
Property, plant, and				
equipment, net	507,000	399,000	108,000	27.1
Total assets	$787,000	$644,000	$143,000	22.2
Liabilities				
Current liabilities:				
Notes payable	$ 42,000	$ 27,000	$ 15,000	55.6
Accounts payable	73,000	68,000	5,000	7.4
Accrued liabilities	27,000	31,000	(4,000)	(12.9)
Total current liabilities	142,000	126,000	16,000	12.7
Long-term debt	289,000	198,000	91,000	46.0
Total liabilities	431,000	324,000	107,000	33.0
Stockholders' Equity				
Common stock, no-par	186,000	186,000	—	0.0
Retained earnings	170,000	134,000	36,000	26.9
Total stockholders' equity .	356,000	320,000	36,000	11.3
Total liabilities and				
stockholders' equity	$787,000	$644,000	$143,000	22.2

Trend percentages are computed by selecting a base year, with each amount during that year set equal to 100 percent. The amounts of each following year are expressed as a percent of the base amount. To compute trend percentages, divide each item for years after the base year by the corresponding amount during the base year. Suppose McColpin, Inc., showed sales, cost of goods sold, and gross profit for the past six years as follows:

	(amounts in thousands)					
	19X7	**19X6**	**19X5**	**19X4**	**19X3**	**19X2**
Net sales	$858	$803	$781	$744	$719	$737
Cost of goods sold	513	509	490	464	450	471
Gross profit....................	$345	$294	$291	$280	$269	$266

Assume we want trend percentages for a five-year period starting with 19X3. We use 19X2 as the base year. Trend percentages for net sales are computed by dividing each net sales amount by the 19X2 amount of $737,000. Likewise, dividing each year's cost-of-goods-sold amount by the base-year amount ($471,000) yields the trend percentages for cost of goods sold. Gross-profit trend percentages are computed similarly. The resulting trend percentages follow (19X2, the base year = 100%):

	19X7	19X6	19X5	19X4	19X3	19X2
Net sales.................	116%	109%	106%	101%	98%	100%
Cost of goods sold.........	109	108	104	99	96	100
Gross profit	130	111	109	105	101	100

McColpin's sales and cost of goods sold have trended upward since a downturn in 19X3. Gross profit has increased steadily, with the most dramatic growth coming during 19X7. What signal about the company does this information provide? It suggests that operations are becoming increasingly more successful. A similar analysis can be performed for any related set of items in the financial statements. For example, an increase in inventory and accounts receivable, coupled with a decrease in sales, may reveal difficulty in making sales and collecting receivables.

Vertical Analysis

Horizontal analysis highlights changes in an item over time. However, no single technique provides a complete picture of a business. Another way to analyze a company is called vertical analysis.

Vertical analysis of a financial statement reveals the relationship of each statement item to a specified base, which is the 100 percent figure. For example, when an income statement is subjected to vertical analysis, net sales is usually the base. Suppose under normal conditions a company's gross profit is 50 percent of net sales. A drop in gross profit to 40 percent may cause the company to report a net loss on the income statement. Management, investors, and creditors view a large decline in gross profit with alarm. Exhibit 27-3

EXHIBIT 27-3 *Comparative Income Statement—Vertical Analysis*

OBJECTIVE 2

Perform a vertical analysis of financial statements

McColpin, Inc.
Comparative Income Statement
Years Ended December 31, 19X7 and 19X6

	19X7 Amount	19X7 Percent	19X6 Amount	19X6 Percent
Net sales	$858,000	100.0%	$803,000	100.0%
Cost of goods sold	513,000	59.8	509,000	63.4
Gross profit.................	345,000	40.2	294,000	36.6
Selling expenses...........	126,000	14.7	114,000	14.2
General expenses..........	118,000	13.7	123,000	15.3
Total operating expenses ...	244,000	28.4	237,000	29.5
Income from operations......	101,000	11.8	57,000	7.1
Interest revenue............	4,000	0.4	—	—
Interest expense............	24,000	2.8	14,000	1.8
Income before income tax	81,000	9.4	43,000	5.3
Income tax expense..........	33,000	3.8	17,000	2.1
Net income	$ 48,000	5.6%	$ 26,000	3.2%

shows the vertical analysis of McColpin, Inc.'s income statement as a percentage of net sales. Exhibit 27-4 shows the vertical analysis of the balance sheet amounts as a percentage of total assets.

The 19X7 comparative income statement (Exhibit 27-3) reports that cost of goods sold dropped to 59.8 percent of net sales from 63.4 percent in 19X6. This explains why the gross profit percentage rose in 19X7. The gross profit percentage is one of the most important items of information in financial analysis because it shows the relationship between net sales and cost of goods sold. All other things equal, a company that can steadily increase its gross profit percentage over a long period is more likely to succeed than a business whose gross profit percentage is steadily declining. The net income percentage almost doubled in 19X7, mostly because of the decrease in the cost-of-goods-sold percentage.

Vertical analysis gives a view of the income statement that differs from the view provided by horizontal analysis. Decision makers use these two forms of analysis together. For example, Exhibit 27-1 reports that gross profit increased by 17.3 percent, and net income increased by 84.6 percent from 19X6 to 19X7. Exhibit 27-3 indicates that gross profit grew from 36.6 percent of sales in 19X6 to 40.2 percent of sales in 19X7 and that net income increased from 3.2 percent

EXHIBIT 27-4 *Comparative Balance Sheet—Vertical Analysis*

McColpin, Inc.
Comparative Balance Sheet
December 31, 19X7 and 19X6

	19X7		19X6	
Assets	Amount	Percent	Amount	Percent
Current assets:				
Cash	$ 29,000	3.7%	$ 32,000	5.0%
Accounts receivable, net	114,000	14.5	85,000	13.2
Inventories	113,000	14.3	111,000	17.2
Prepaid expenses	6,000	.8	8,000	1.2
Total current assets	262,000	33.3	236,000	36.6
Long-term investments	18,000	2.3	9,000	1.4
Property, plant, and equipment, net	507,000	64.4	399,000	62.0
Total assets	$787,000	100.0%	$644,000	100.0%
Liabilities				
Current liabilities:				
Notes payable	$ 42,000	5.3%	$ 27,000	4.2%
Accounts payable	73,000	9.3	68,000	10.6
Accrued liabilities	27,000	3.4	31,000	4.8
Total current liabilities	142,000	18.0	126,000	19.6
Long-term debt	289,000	36.7	198,000	30.7
Total liabilities	431,000	54.7	324,000	50.3
Stockholders' Equity				
Common stock, no-par	186,000	23.7	186,000	28.9
Retained earnings	170,000	21.6	134,000	20.8
Total stockholders' equity	356,000	45.3	320,000	49.7
Total liabilities and stockholders' equity	$787,000	100.0%	$644,000	100.0%

of sales to 5.6 percent of sales. Together, vertical analysis and horizontal analysis paint a favorable picture of McColpin's operations

We can apply trend analysis to the balance sheet of McColpin, Inc., as Exhibit 27-4 shows. For example, among the changes that occurred in the one-year period from 19X6 to 19X7, we note that current assets have become a smaller percentage of total assets. A decrease in current assets may make it difficult for the company to pay its bills. However, this does not present a problem for McColpin, Inc., because current liabilities also decreased as a percentage of total assets during 19X7. This kind of comparison is used in vertical analysis.

Common-Size Statements

The percentages in Exhibits 27-3 and 27-4 can be presented as a separate statement that reports only percentages (no dollar amounts). Such a statement, called a **common-size statement,** is a type of vertical analysis. On a common-size income statement, each item is expressed as a percentage of the net sales amount. Net sales is the "common size" to which we relate the statement's other amounts. In the balance sheet, the "common size" is the total on each side of the accounting equation (total assets *or* the sum of total liabilities and stockholders' equity). A common-size statement eases the comparison of different companies because their amounts are stated in percentages.

Common-size statements may identify the need for corrective action. Exhibit 27-5 is the common-size analysis of current assets taken from Exhibit 27-4. Exhibit 27-5 shows cash as a smaller percentage of total assets at December 31, 19X7, than at the previous year end. Accounts receivable, on the other hand, is a larger percentage of total assets. What could cause a decrease in cash and an increase in accounts receivable as percentages of total assets? McColpin may have been lax in collecting accounts receivable, which may explain a cash shortage and reveal that the company needs to pursue collection more vigorously. Or the company may have sold to less-creditworthy customers. In any event, the company should monitor its cash position and collection of accounts receivable to avoid a cash shortage. Common-size statements provide information useful for this purpose.

EXHIBIT 27-5 *Common-Size Analysis of Current Assets*

McColpin, Inc. Common-Size Analysis of Current Assets December 31, 19X7 and 19X6		
	Percent of Total Assets	
	19X7	**19X6**
Current assets:		
Cash	3.7%	5.0%
Accounts receivable, net........	14.5	13.2
Inventories....................	14.3	17.2
Prepaid expenses	.8	1.2
Total current assets	33.3%	36.6%

Industry Comparisons

We study the records of a company in order to understand past results and predict future performance. Still, the knowledge that we can develop from a single company's records is limited to that one company. We may learn that gross profit has decreased and net income has increased steadily for the last ten years. While this information is helpful, it does not consider how businesses in the same industry have fared over this time. Have other companies in the same line of business increased their sales? Is there an industrywide decline in gross profit? Has cost of goods sold risen steeply for other businesses that sell the same products? Managers, investors, creditors, and other interested parties need to know how one company compares with other companies in the same line of business.

Exhibit 27-6 gives the common-size income statement of McColpin, Inc., compared with the average for the retail furniture industry. This analysis compares McColpin with all other companies in its line of business. The industry averages were adapted from Robert Morris Associates' *Annual Statement Studies*. Analysts specialize in a particular industry and make such comparisons in deciding which companies' stocks to buy or sell. For example, financial-service companies like Merrill Lynch have airline-industry specialists, health-care-industry specialists, and so on. Boards of directors evaluate top managers based on how well the company compares with other companies in the industry. Exhibit 27-6 shows that McColpin compares favorably with competing furniture retailers. Its gross profit percentage is virtually identical to the industry average. The company does a good job of controlling operating expenses, and as a result, its percentage of income from operations and net income percentage are significantly higher than the industry average.

Another use of common-size statements is to aid the comparison of different-sized companies. Suppose you are considering an investment in the stock of an automobile manufacturer, and you are choosing between General Motors (GM) and Chrysler. GM is so much larger than Chrysler that a direct comparison of their financial statements in dollar amounts is not meaningful.

EXHIBIT 27-6 *Common-Size Income Statement Compared with the Industry Average*

McColpin, Inc. Common-Size Income Statement for Comparison with Industry Average Year Ended December 31, 19X7		
	McColpin, Inc.	**Industry Average**
Net sales	100.0%	100.0%
Cost of goods sold	59.8	59.7
Gross profit	40.2	40.3
Operating expenses:		
Selling expenses	14.7	23.6
General expenses	13.7	13.4
Total operating expenses	28.4	37.0
Income from operations	**11.8**	**3.3**
Other revenue (expense)	(2.4)	(0.4)
Income before income tax	9.4	2.9
Income tax expense	3.8	0.9
Net income	**5.6%**	**2.0%**

OBJECTIVE 3

Prepare common-size financial statements

However, you can convert the two companies' income statements to common size and compare the percentages. You may find that one company has a higher percentage of its assets in inventory and the other company has a higher percentage of its liabilities in long-term debt.

The Statement of Cash Flows in Decision Making

The chapter so far has centered on the income statement and balance sheet. We may also perform horizontal and vertical analysis on the statement of cash flows. In the preceding chapter, we discussed how to prepare the statement. To discuss its role in decision making, let's use Exhibit 27-7.

Some analysts use cash flow analysis to identify danger signals about a company's financial situation. For example, the statement in Exhibit 27-7 reveals what may be a weakness in DeMaris Corporation.

First, operations provided a net cash inflow of $52,000, which is much less than the $91,000 generated by the sale of fixed assets. An important question arises: Can the company remain in business by generating the majority of its cash by selling its property, plant, and equipment? No, because these assets will be needed to manufacture the company's products in the future. Note also that borrowing by issuing bonds payable brought in $72,000. No company can long survive living on borrowed funds. DeMaris must eventually pay off the bonds. Indeed, the company paid $170,000 on older debt. Successful companies like Xerox, Coca-Cola, and Procter & Gamble generate the greatest percentage of their cash from operations, not from selling their fixed assets or from borrowing money. These conditions may be only temporary for DeMaris Corporation, but they are worth investigating.

EXHIBIT 27-7   *Statement of Cash Flows*

DeMaris Corporation Statement of Cash Flows For the Current Year		
Operating activities:		
Income from operations		$ 35,000
Add (subtract) noncash items:		
Depreciation	$ 14,000	
Net increase in current assets other than		
cash	(5,000)	
Net increase in current liabilities	8,000	17,000
Net cash inflow from operating activities .		52,000
Investing activities:		
Sale of property, plant, and equipment	$ 91,000	
Net cash inflow from investing activities . .		91,000
Financing activities:		
Issuance of bonds payable	$ 72,000	
Payment of long-term debt	(170,000)	
Purchase of treasury stock	(9,000)	
Payment of dividends	(33,000)	
Net cash outflow from financing activities		(140,000)
Increase in cash		$ 3,000

The most important information that the statement of cash flows provides is a summary of the company's use of cash. How a company spends its cash today determines its sources of cash in the future. The company may wisely use its cash to purchase assets that will generate income in the years ahead. However, if a company invests unwisely, cash will eventually run short. DeMaris's statement of cash flows reveals problems. The exhibit information indicates that DeMaris invested in no fixed assets to replace those that it sold. The company may in fact be going out of business. Also, DeMaris paid dividends of $33,000, an amount that is very close to its net income. Is the company retaining enough cash to finance future operations without excessive borrowing? Analysts seek answers to questions such as this. They analyze the information from the statement of cash flows along with the information from the balance sheet and the income statement to form a well-rounded picture of the business.

Summary Problem for Your Review

Perform a horizontal analysis and a vertical analysis of the comparative income statement of TRE Corporation. State whether 19X3 was a good year or a bad year and give your reasons.

TRE Corporation
Comparative Income Statement
Years Ended December 31, 19X3 and 19X2

	19X3	19X2
Total revenues	$275,000	$225,000
Expenses:		
Cost of products sold	$194,000	$165,000
Engineering, selling, and administrative expenses	54,000	48,000
Interest expense	5,000	5,000
Income tax expense	9,000	3,000
Other expense (income)	1,000	(1,000)
Total expenses	263,000	220,000
Net earnings	$ 12,000	$ 5,000

SOLUTION TO REVIEW PROBLEM

TRE Corporation
Horizontal Analysis of Comparative Income Statement
Years Ended December 31, 19X3 and 19X2

			Increase (Decrease)	
	19X3	19X2	Amount	Percent
Total revenues	$275,000	$225,000	$50,000	22.2%
Expenses:				
Cost of products sold	$194,000	$165,000	$29,000	17.6
Engineering, selling, and administrative expenses	54,000	48,000	6,000	12.5
Interest expense	5,000	5,000	—	—
Income tax expense	9,000	3,000	6,000	200.0
Other expense (income)	1,000	(1,000)	2,000	—
Total expenses	263,000	220,000	43,000	19.5
Net earnings	$ 12,000	$ 5,000	$ 7,000	140.0

TRE Corporation
Vertical Analysis of Comparative Income Statement
Years Ended December 31, 19X3 and 19X2

	19X3		19X2	
	Amount	Percent	Amount	Percent
Total revenue	$275,000	100.0%	$225,000	100.0%
Expenses:				
Cost of products sold	$194,000	70.5	$165,000	73.3
Engineering, selling, and				
administrative expenses	54,000	19.6	48,000	21.3
Interest expense	5,000	1.8	5,000	2.2
Income tax expense	9,000	3.3	3,000	1.4
Other expense (income)	1,000	0.4	(1,000)	(0.4)
Total expenses	263,000	95.6	220,000	97.8
Net earnings	$ 12,000	4.4%	$ 5,000)	2.2%

The horizontal analysis shows that total revenues increased 22.2 percent. This percentage increase was greater than the 19.5 percent increase in total expenses, resulting in a 140 percent increase in net earnings.

The vertical analysis shows decreases in the percentages of net sales consumed by the cost of products sold (from 73.3 percent to 70.5 percent) and the engineering, selling, and administrative expenses (from 21.3 percent to 19.6 percent). These two items are TRE's largest dollar expenses, so their percentage decreases are quite important. The relative reduction in expenses raised 19X3 net earnings to 4.4 percent of sales, compared with 2.2 percent the preceding year. The overall analysis indicates that 19X3 was significantly better than 19X2.

Using Ratios to Make Business Decisions

The preceding analyses were based on each financial statement considered alone. Another set of decision tools develops relationships among items taken from throughout the statements.

Ratios are important tools for financial analysis. A ratio expresses the relationship of one number to another number. For example, if the balance sheet shows current assets of $100,000 and current liabilities of $25,000, the ratio of current assets to current liabilities is $100,000 to $25,000. We simplify this numerical expression to the ratio of 4 to 1, which may also be written 4:1 and $\frac{4}{1}$. Other acceptable ways of expressing this ratio include (1) "current assets are 400 percent of current liabilities" and (2) "the business has four dollars in current assets for every one dollar in current liabilities."

We often reduce the ratio fraction by writing the ratio as one figure over the other, for example, $\frac{4}{1}$, and then dividing the numerator by the denominator. In this way, the ratio $\frac{4}{1}$ may be expressed simply as 4. The 1 that represents the denominator of the fraction is understood, not written. Consider the ratio $175,000:$165,000. After dividing the first figure by the second, we come to

1.06:1, which we state as 1.06. The second part of the ratio, the 1, again is understood. Ratios provide a convenient and useful way of expressing a relationship between numbers. For example, the ratio of current assets to current liabilities gives information about a company's ability to pay its current debts with existing current assets.

A manager, lender, or financial analyst may use any ratio that is relevant to a particular decision. We discuss the more important ratios used in credit and investment analysis and in managing a business. Many companies include these ratios in a special section of their annual financial reports. Investment services—Moody's, Standard & Poor's, Robert Morris Associates, and others—report these ratios for companies and industries. They are widely used in all aspects of business-finance, management, and marketing as well as accounting.

Measuring the Ability to Pay Current Liabilities _____

Working capital is defined as current assets minus current liabilities. Working capital is widely used to measure a business's ability to meet its short-term obligations with its current assets. In general, the larger the working capital, the better able the business is to pay its debts. Recall that capital, or owners' equity, is total assets minus total liabilities. Working capital is like a "current" version of total capital. The working capital amount considered alone does not give a complete picture of the entity's working capital position, however. Consider two companies with equal working capital:

	Company A	Company B
Current assets	$100,000	$200,000
Current liabilities	50,000	150,000
Working capital	$ 50,000	$ 50,000

Both companies have working capital of $50,000, but Company A's working capital is as large as its current liabilities. Company B's working capital, on the other hand, is only one-third as large as its current liabilities. Which business has a better working capital position? Company A, because its working capital is a higher percentage of current assets and current liabilities. To use working capital data in decision making, it is helpful to develop ratios. Two decision tools based on working capital data are the *current ratio* and the *acid-test ratio*.

Current Ratio

The most common ratio using current asset and current liability data is the *current ratio*, which is current assets divided by current liabilities. Recall the makeup of current assets and current liabilities. Inventory is converted to receivables through sales, the receivables are collected in cash, and the cash is used to buy inventory and pay current liabilities. A company's current assets and current liabilities represent the core of its day-to-day operations.

The current ratios of McColpin, Inc. at December 31, 19X7 and 19X6, follow (data from Exhibit 27-2).

OBJECTIVE 5

Compute the standard financial ratios used for decision making

Current Ratio of McColpin, Inc.

Formula	19X7	19X6
$\text{Current ratio} = \dfrac{\text{Current assets}}{\text{Current liabilities}}$	$\dfrac{\$262,000}{\$142,000} = 1.85$	$\dfrac{\$236,000}{\$126,000} = 1.87$

The current ratio decreased slightly during 19X7. The average current ratio for furniture retailers is 1.80. Lenders, stockholders, and managers closely monitor changes in a company's current ratio. In general, a higher current ratio indicates a stronger financial position. A high current ratio suggests that the business has sufficient liquid assets to maintain normal business operations. Compare McColpin's current ratio of 1.85 with the current ratios of some actual companies:

Company	Current Ratio
Chesebrough-Pond's, Inc.	2.50
International Business Machines Corporation (IBM)	1.52
General Mills, Inc.	1.05
The Superior Oil Company	1.46

What is an acceptable current ratio? The answer to this question depends on the nature of the industry. The norm for companies in most industries is between 1.60 and 1.90, as reported by Robert Morris Associates. McColpin's current ratio of 1.85 is within the range of these actual values. In most industries a current ratio of 2.0 is considered good.

Acid-Test Ratio

The **acid-test** (or **quick**) **ratio** tells us whether the entity could pay all its current liabilities if they came due immediately. That is, could the company pass this *acid test*? The company would convert its most liquid assets to cash. To compute the acid-test ratio, we add cash, short-term investments, and net current receivables (accounts and notes receivable, net of allowances) and divide by current liabilities. Inventory and prepaid expenses are the two current assets not included in the acid-test computations. These accounts are omitted because they are the least liquid of the current assets. A business may not be able to convert them to cash immediately to pay current liabilities. The acid-test ratio measures liquidity using a narrower asset base than the current ratio does.

McColpin's acid-test ratios for 19X7 and 19X6 follow (data from Exhibit 27-2).

Acid-Test Ratio of McColpin, Inc.

Formula	19X7	19X6
$\text{Acid-test ratio} = \dfrac{\text{Cash + short-term investments + net current receivables}}{\text{Current liabilities}}$	$\dfrac{\$29,000 + \$0 + \$114,000}{\$142,000} = 1.01$	$\dfrac{\$32,000 + \$0 + \$85,000}{\$126,000} = .93$

The company's acid-test ratio improved considerably during 19X7. Its ratio of 1.01 is near the top quartile for the retail furniture industry and significantly better than the industry average of .50. McColpin's ratio value is within range of those of Chesebrough-Pond's (1.25), General Motors (.91), and IBM (1.07). The norm ranges from .20 for shoe retailers to 1.00 for manufacturers of paperboard containers and certain other equipment, as reported by Robert Morris Associates. An acid-test ratio of .90 to 1.00 is acceptable in most industries.

Measuring the Ability to Sell Inventory and Collect Receivables

The ability to sell inventory and collect receivables is fundamental to business success. Recall the operating cycle of a merchandiser: cash to inventory to receivables and back to cash. This section discusses three ratios that measure the ability to sell inventory and collect receivables.

Inventory Turnover

Companies generally seek to achieve the quickest possible return on their investments. A return on an investment in inventory—usually a substantial amount—is no exception. The faster inventory sells, the sooner the business creates accounts receivable, and the sooner it collects cash.

Inventory turnover is a measure of the number of times a company sells its average level of inventory during a year. A high rate of turnover indicates relative ease in selling inventory, whereas a low turnover indicates difficulty in selling. Generally, companies prefer a high inventory turnover. A value of 6 means that the company's average level of inventory has been sold 6 times during the year. In most cases this is better than a turnover of 3 or 4. However, a high value can mean that the business is not keeping enough inventory on hand, and this can result in lost sales if the company cannot fill a customer's order. Therefore, a business strives for the most profitable rate of inventory turnover, not necessarily the highest.

To compute the inventory turnover ratio we divide cost of goods sold by the average inventory for the period. We use the cost of goods sold—not sales—in the computation because both cost of goods sold and inventory are stated *at cost*. Sales is stated at the sales value of inventory and therefore is not comparable with inventory cost.

McColpin's inventory turnover for 19X7 is

Formula	Inventory Turnover of McColpin, Inc.
$\text{Inventory turnover} = \dfrac{\text{Cost of goods sold}}{\text{Average inventory}}$	$\dfrac{\$513,000}{\$112,000} = 4.58$

Cost of goods sold appears in the income statement (Exhibit 27-1). Average inventory is figured by averaging the beginning inventory ($111,000) and ending inventory ($113,000). (See the balance sheet, Exhibit 27-2.) If inventory levels vary greatly from month to month, compute the average by adding the 12 monthly balances and dividing this sum by 12.

Inventory turnover varies widely with the nature of the business. For example, most manufacturers of farm machinery have an inventory turnover close to 3 times a year. By contrast, companies that remove natural gas from the ground hold their inventory for a very short period of time and have an average turnover of 30. McColpin's turnover of 4.58 times a year is high for its industry, which has an average turnover of 2.70. McColpin's high inventory turnover results from its policy of keeping little inventory on hand. The company takes customer orders and has its suppliers ship directly to customers.

To evaluate fully a company's inventory turnover, compare the ratio over time. A sudden sharp decline or a steady decline over a long period suggests the need for corrective action. Analysts also compare a company's inventory turnover with other companies in the same industry and with the industry average.

Accounts Receivable Turnover

Accounts receivable turnover measures a company's ability to collect cash from credit customers. Generally, the higher the ratio, the more successfully the business collects cash, and the better off its operations are. However, too high a receivable turnover may indicate that credit is too tight, causing the loss of sales to good customers. To compute the accounts receivable turnover we divide net credit sales by average net accounts receivable. The resulting ratio indicates how many times during the year the average level of receivables was turned into cash.

McColpin's accounts receivable turnover ratio for 19X7 is computed as follows. (We assume that all sales were on credit.)

	Formula	Accounts Receivable Turnover of McColpin, Inc.
Accounts receivable turnover $=$	$\dfrac{\text{Net credit sales}}{\text{Average net accounts receivable}}$	$\dfrac{\$858,000}{\$99,500} = 8.62$

The sales figure comes from the income statement (Exhibit 27-1). McColpin makes all sales on credit. If the company makes both cash and credit sales, this ratio is best computed using only net credit sales. Average net accounts receivable is figured using the beginning accounts receivable balance ($85,000) and the ending balance ($114,000). (See the balance sheet, Exhibit 27-2.) If accounts receivable balances exhibit a seasonal pattern, compute the average using the 12 monthly balances.

Receivable turnover ratios vary little from company to company. Most companies' ratios range between 7.0 and 10.0. McColpin's receivable turnover of 8.62 falls within this range.

Days' Sales in Receivables

Businesses must convert accounts receivable to cash. All other things equal, the lower the Accounts Receivable balance, the more successful the business has been in converting receivables into cash, and the better off the business.

The **days'-sales-in-receivables** ratio tells us how many days' sales remain in Accounts Receivable. We express the money amount in terms of an average day's sales. This relation becomes clearer as we compute the ratio, a two-step process. First, divide net sales by 365 days to figure the average sales amount for one day. Second, divide this average day's sales amount into the average net accounts receivable.

The data to compute this ratio for McColpin, Inc., for 19X7 are taken from the income statement and the balance sheet.

Formula	Days' Sales in Accounts Receivable of McColpin, Inc.

Days' Sales in AVERAGE Accounts Receivable:

1. One day's sales $= \dfrac{\text{Net sales}}{\text{365 days}}$ $\qquad \dfrac{\$858,000}{\text{365 days}} = \$2,351$

2. Days' sales in average accounts receivable $= \dfrac{\text{Average net accounts receivable}}{\text{One day's sales}}$ $\qquad \dfrac{\$99,500}{\$2,351} = 42 \text{ days}$

The computation in two steps is designed to increase your understanding of the meaning of the ratio. We may compute days' sales in average receivables in one step: $\$99,500/(\$858,000/365 \text{ days}) = 42$ days.

McColpin's ratio tell us that 42 average days' sales remain in accounts receivable and need to be collected. The company will increase its cash inflow if it can decrease this ratio. To detect any changes over time in McColpin's ability to collect its receivables, let's compute the days'-sales-in-receivables ratio at the beginning and the end of 19X7.

Days' Sales in ENDING 19X6 Accounts Receivable:

$$\text{One day's sales} = \frac{\$803,000}{\text{365 days}} = \$2,200$$

$$\text{Days' sales in ending 19X6 accounts receivable} = \frac{\$85,000}{\$2,200} = 39 \text{ days at beginning of 19X7}$$

Days' Sales in ENDING 19X7 Accounts Receivable:

$$\text{One day's sales} = \frac{\$858,000}{\text{365 days}} = \$2,351$$

$$\text{Days' sales in ending 19X7 accounts receivable} = \frac{\$114,000}{\$2,351} = 48 \text{ days at end of 19X7}$$

This analysis shows a drop in McColpin's collection of receivables; days' sales in accounts receivable has increased from 39 at the beginning of the year to 48 at year end. The credit and collection department should strengthen its collection efforts. Otherwise, the company may experience a cash shortage in 19X8 and beyond.

Measuring the Ability to Pay Long-Term Debt _____

The ratios discussed so far give us insight into current assets and current liabilities. They help us measure a business's ability to sell inventory, to collect receivables, and to pay current liabilities. Most businesses also have long-term debts. Bondholders and banks that loan money on long-term notes payable and bonds payable take special interest in a business's ability to meet long-term obligations. Two key indicators of a business's ability to pay long-term liabilities are the *debt ratio* and the *times-interest-earned ratio*.

Debt Ratio

Suppose you are a loan officer at a bank and you are evaluating loan applications from two companies with equal sales revenue and total assets. Sales and total assets are the two most common measures of firm size. Both companies have asked to borrow $500,000, and each has agreed to repay the loan over a ten-year period. The first customer already owes $600,000 to another bank. The second owes only $250,000. Other things equal, which company is likely to get the loan at the lower interest rate? Why?

Company Two is more likely to get the loan. The bank faces less risk by loaning to Company Two because that company owes less to creditors than Company One owes.

This relationship between total liabilities and total assets—called the *debt ratio*—tells us the proportion of the company's assets that it has financed with debt. If the debt ratio is 1, then debt has been used to finance all the assets. A debt ratio of .50 means that the company has used debt to finance half its assets. The owners of the business have financed the other half. The higher the debt ratio, the higher the strain of paying interest each year and the principal amount at maturity. The lower the ratio, the less the business's future obligations. Creditors view a high debt ratio with caution. If a business seeking financing already has many liabilities, then additional debt payments may be too much for the business to handle. Creditors, to help protect themselves, generally charge higher interest rates on new borrowing to companies with an already high debt ratio.

McColpin's debt ratio at the end of 19X7 and 19X6 follow (data from Exhibit 27-2).

	Debt Ratio of McColpin, Inc.	
Formula	**19X7**	**19X6**
Debt ratio = $\dfrac{\text{Total liabilities}}{\text{Total assets}}$	$\dfrac{\$431,000}{\$787,000} = .55$	$\dfrac{\$324,000}{\$644,000} = .50$

Recall from our vertical and horizontal analyses that McColpin, Inc., expanded operations by financing the purchase of property, plant, and equipment through borrowing, which is common.

Even after the increase in 19X7, McColpin's debt is not very high. Robert Morris Associates reports that the average debt ratio for most companies ranges around .57 to .67, with relatively little variation from company to company. McColpin's .55 debt ratio indicates a fairly low-risk debt position in comparison with the retail furniture industry average of .64.

Times-Interest-Earned Ratio

The debt ratio measures the effect of debt on the company's *financial position* (balance sheet) but says nothing about its ability to pay interest expense. Analysts use a second ratio—the **times-interest-earned ratio**—to relate income to interest expense. To compute this ratio, we divide income from operations by interest expense. This ratio measures the number of times that operating income can *cover* interest expense. For this reason, the ratio is also called the **interest-coverage ratio.** A high ratio indicates ease in paying interest expense; a low value suggests difficulty.

McColpin's times-interest-earned ratios follow (data from Exhibit 27-1).

	Formula	Times-Interest-Earned Ratio of McColpin, Inc.	
		19X7	19X6
Times-interest-earned = ratio	$\dfrac{\text{Income from operations}}{\text{Interest expense}}$	$\dfrac{\$101,000}{\$24,000} = 4.21$	$\dfrac{\$57,000}{\$14,000} = 4.07$

McColpin's interest-coverage ratio increased in 19X7. This is a favorable sign about the company, especially since the company's short-term notes payable and long-term debt rose substantially during the year. (See the horizontal analysis in Exhibit 27-2). McColpin's new plant assets, we conclude, have earned more in operating income than they have cost the business in interest expense. The company's coverage ratio of around 4 is significantly better than the 2.60 average for furniture retailers. The norm for American business, as reported by Robert Morris Associates, falls in the range of 2.0 to 3.0 for most companies.

Based on its debt ratio and times-interest-earned ratio, McColpin appears to have little difficulty paying its liabilities, also called *servicing its debt.*

Measuring Profitability

The fundamental goal of business is to earn a profit. Ratios that measure profitability play a large role in decision making. These ratios are reported in the business press, by investment services, and in the annual financial reports of companies.

Rate of Return on Net Sales

In business, the term *return* is used broadly and loosely as an evaluation of profitability. For example, consider a percentage called the **rate of return on net sales,** or simply **return on sales.** (The word *net* is usually omitted for convenience, even though the net sales figure is used to compute the ratio.) McColpin's rate of return on sales ratios follow:

	Formula	Rate of Return on Sales of McColpin, Inc.	
		19X7	19X6
Rate of return on = sales	$\dfrac{\text{Net income}}{\text{Net sales}}$	$\dfrac{\$48,000}{\$858,000} = .056$	$\dfrac{\$26,000}{\$803,000} = .032$

You will recognize this ratio from the vertical analysis of the income statement in Exhibit 27-3. The increase in McColpin's return on sales is significant and identifies McColpin as a leader in its industry. Companies strive for a high rate of return. The higher the rate of return, the more net sales dollars are providing income to the business and the fewer net sales dollars are absorbed by expenses. The 5.6 percent rate compares favorably with General Motors (5.4 percent) and Kraft [Foods], Inc. (4.7 percent) but is less than IBM (13.6 percent) and Chesebrough-Pond's (7.6 percent). As these rates of return on sales indicate, this ratio varies widely from industry to industry.

One strategy for increasing the rate of return on sales is to develop a product that commands a premium price, such as Sony products, Maytag appliances, and certain brands of clothing. Another strategy is to control costs. If successful, either strategy converts a higher proportion of sales into net income and increases the rate of return on net sales.

A return measure can be computed on any revenue and sales amount. Return on net sales, as we have seen, is net income divided by net sales. Return on total revenues is net income divided by total revenues. A company can compute a return on other specific portions of revenue as its information needs dictate.

Rate of Return on Total Assets

The **rate of return on total assets**, or simply **return on assets**, measures the success a company has in using its assets to earn a profit. Creditors have loaned money to the company, and the interest they receive is the return on their investment. Shareholders have invested in the company's stock, and net income is their return. The sum of interest expense and net income is the return to the two groups that have financed the company's operations, and this amount is the numerator of the return on assets ratio. Average total assets is the denominator. McColpin's return on assets ratio follows.

	Formula	Rate of Return on Total Assets of McColpin, Inc.
		19X7
Rate of return on assets =	$\dfrac{\text{Net income} + \text{interest expense}}{\text{Average total assets}}$	$\dfrac{\$48,000 + \$24,000}{\$715,500} = .101$

Net income and interest expense are taken from the income statement. To compute average total assets, we use beginning and ending total assets from the comparative balance sheet. McColpin's 10.1 percent return on assets is higher than the 4.9 percent average return on assets in the retail furniture industry and compares favorably with Superior Oil (8.0 percent) and General Motors (10.4 percent). General Mills, Inc. (12.4 percent) and IBM (15.0 percent) earn somewhat higher returns.

Rate of Return on Common Stockholders' Equity

A popular measure of profitability is **rate of return on common stockholders' equity.** This ratio shows the relationship between net income and common stockholders' investment in the company. To compute this ratio, we first subtract preferred dividends from net income. This leaves only net income available to the common stockholders, which is needed to compute the ratio. We then divide net income available to common stockholders by the average stockholders' equity during the year. Common stockholders' equity is total stockholders' equity minus preferred equity. McColpin's rate of return on common stockholders' equity follows. (Data from Exhibits 27-1 and 27-2.)

		Rate of Return on Common Stockholders' Equity of McColpin, Inc.
Formula		**19X7**
Rate of return on common stock- = holders' equity	$\dfrac{\text{Net income} - \text{preferred dividends}}{\text{Average common stockholders' equity}}$	$\dfrac{\$48{,}000 - \$0}{\$338{,}000} = .142$

We compute average equity using the beginning and ending balances [($356,000 + $320,000)/2 = $338,000]. Observe that common stockholders' equity includes Retained Earnings and any Paid-in Capital in Excess of Par on Common Stock.

McColpin's 14.2 percent return on common equity compares favorably with returns of companies in most industries, which average around 10 percent. However, some leading companies show higher ratios: IBM (22 percent), Chesebrough-Pond's (20 percent), and General Motors (20 percent).

Observe that return on equity (14.2 percent) is higher than return on assets (10.1 percent). This 4.1 percent difference results from borrowing at one rate, say 8 percent, and investing the funds to earn a higher rate, such as McColpin's 14.2 percent return on stockholders' equity. This practice is called **trading on the equity,** or the use of **leverage.** It is directly related to the debt ratio. The higher the debt ratio, the higher the leverage. Companies that finance operations with debt are said to *lever* their positions. Leverage increases the risk to common stockholders. For McColpin, Inc., and for many other companies leverage increases profitability. That is not always the case, however. Leverage can also have a negative impact on profitability. If revenues drop, debt and interest expense still must be paid. Therefore, leverage is a double-edged sword, increasing profits during good times but compounding losses during bad times.

Earnings per Share of Common Stock

Earnings per share of common stock, or simply **earnings per share (EPS),** is perhaps the most widely quoted of all financial statistics. EPS is the only ratio that must appear on the face of the income statement. EPS is the amount of net income per share of the company's *common* stock. Earnings per share is computed by dividing net income available to common stockholders by the number of common shares outstanding during the year. Preferred dividends are subtracted from net income because the preferred stockholders have a prior claim to their dividends. McColpin has no preferred stock outstanding and so has no preferred dividends. McColpin's EPS for 19X7 and 19X6 follow. (Data are from Exhibits 27-1 and 27-2, and the company had 10,000 shares of common stock outstanding throughout 19X6 and 19X7.)

		Earnings Per Share of McColpin, Inc.	
Formula		**19X7**	**19X6**
Earnings per share of common stock (EPS)	$= \dfrac{\text{Net income} - \text{preferred dividends}}{\text{Number of shares of common stock outstanding}}$	$\dfrac{\$48{,}000 - \$0}{10{,}000} = \$4.80$	$\dfrac{\$26{,}000 - \$0}{10{,}000} = \$2.60$

McColpin's EPS rose from $2.60 to $4.80, an increase of 85 percent. McColpin's stockholders should not expect such a significant boost in EPS every year. However, most companies strive to increase EPS by 10 to 15 percent annually, and the more successful companies do so. However, even the most dramatic upward trends include an occasional bad year.

Analyzing Stock as an Investment

Investors purchase stock to earn a return on their investment. This return consists of two parts: (1) gains (or losses) from selling the stock at a price that is different from the investors' purchase price, and (2) dividends, the periodic distributions to stockholders. The ratios we examine in this section help analysts evaluate stock in terms of market price or dividend payments.

Price/Earnings Ratio

The **price/earnings ratio** is the ratio of the market price of a share of common stock to the company's earnings per share. This ratio, abbreviated P/E, appears in *The Wall Street Journal* stock listings. P/E plays an important part in evaluating decisions to buy, hold, and sell stocks. The higher the P/E ratio, the higher the value the stock market places on a company. Managers are delighted when their companies command a high P/E ratio.

The price/earnings ratios of McColpin, Inc., follow. The market price of its common stock was $50 at the end of 19X7 and $35 at the end of 19X6. These prices can be obtained from a financial publication, a stockbroker, or some other source outside the accounting records.

		Price/Earnings Ratio of McColpin, Inc.	
	Formula	19X7	19X6
Price/ earnings = ratio	$\dfrac{\text{Market price per share of common stock}}{\text{Earnings per share}}$	$\dfrac{\$50.00}{\$4.80} = 10.4$	$\dfrac{\$35.00}{\$2.60} = 13.5$

Given McColpin's 19X7 price/earnings ratio of 10.4, we would say that the company's stock is selling at 10.4 times earnings. The decline from the 19X6 P/E ratio of 13.5 is not a cause for alarm because the numerator—market price of the stock—is not under McColpin's control. The denominator—net income—is more controllable, and it increased during 19X7. Like most other ratios, P/E ratios vary from industry to industry.

Dividend Yield

Dividend yield is the ratio of dividends per share of stock to the stock's market price per share. This ratio measures the percentage of a stock's market value that is returned annually as dividends, an important concern of stockholders. *Preferred* stockholders, who invest primarily to receive dividends, pay special attention to this ratio.

McColpin paid annual cash dividends of $1.20 per share in 19X7 and $1.00 in 19X6 and market prices of the company's common stock were $50 in 19X7 and $35 in 19X6. McColpin's dividend yields follow:

		Dividend Yield on Common Stock of McColpin, Inc.	
Formula		19X7	19X6
Dividend yield on common stock	$= \dfrac{\text{Dividend per share of common stock}}{\text{Market price per share of common stock}}$	$\dfrac{\$1.20}{\$50.00} = .024$	$\dfrac{\$1.00}{\$35.00} = .029$

An investor who buys McColpin common stock for $50 can expect to receive almost 2½ percent of her investment annually in the form of cash dividends. Dividend yields vary widely, from 5 to 8 percent for older established firms (like Procter & Gamble and General Motors) down to the range of 0 to 3 percent for young, growth-oriented companies (like Anacomp, Inc., the world's largest maker of microfiche). McColpin's dividend yield places the company in the second group.

Book Value per Share of Common Stock

Book value per share of common stock is simply common stockholders' equity divided by the number of shares of common stock outstanding. Common shareholders' equity equals total stockholders' equity less preferred equity. McColpin has no preferred stock outstanding. Its book-value-per-share-of-common-stock ratios follow. Recall that 10,000 shares of common stock were outstanding at the ends of years 19X7 and 19X6.

		Book Value per Share of the Common Stock of McColpin, Inc.	
Formula		19X7	19X6
Book value per share of common stock	$= \dfrac{\text{Total stockholders' equity} - \text{preferred equity}}{\text{Number of shares of common stock outstanding}}$	$\dfrac{\$356,000 - \$0}{10,000} = \$35.60$	$\dfrac{\$320,000 - \$0}{10,000} = \$32.00$

The market price of a successful company's stock usually exceeds its book value. Some investors buy a stock when its market value approaches book value. Suppose you decided to buy McColpin stock at the end of 19X6, when its market price of $35 was close to book value of $32. That investment would have proved wise. The stock's price increased to $50 in 19X7. Of course, when you bought the stock in 19X6, there was no guarantee the stock price would increase.

The chapter-opening vignette shows one use of book value per share in investment analysis—ranking stocks based on the ratio of market price to book value. Observe, however, that DIA, like other investment advisers, bases its decisions on complex formulas that use many of the ratios described in this chapter. This leads to the next topic.

The Complexity of Business Decisions _____

OBJECTIVE 6

Use ratios in decision making

Business decisions are made in a world of uncertainty. Legislation, international affairs, competition, scandals, and many other factors can turn profits into losses, and vice versa. To be most useful, ratios should be analyzed over a period of years to take into account a representative group of these factors. Any one year, or even any two years, may not be representative of the company's performance over the long term.

For example, a business's acid-test ratio may show a substantial increase over a ten-year period. However, a two-year period during the early part of that decade might show a slight downturn. An evaluation based on the two-year analysis might lead to an unwise decision. To make the best use of ratios, we must consider them within a broad time frame.

As useful as ratios may be, they do have limitations. We may liken their use in decision making to a physician's use of a thermometer. A reading of 101.6 degrees Fahrenheit indicates that something is wrong with the patient, but the temperature alone does not indicate what the problem is or how to cure it.

In financial analysis, a sudden drop in a company's current ratio signals that *something* is wrong, but this change does not identify the problem or show how to correct it. The business manager must analyze the figures that go into the ratio to determine whether current assets have decreased, current liabilities have increased, or both. If current assets have dropped, is the problem a cash shortage? Are accounts receivable down? Are inventories too low? Only by analyzing the individual items that make up the ratio can the manager determine how to solve the problem. The manager must evaluate data on all ratios in the light of other information about the company and about its particular line of business, such as increased competition or a slowdown in the economy.

Uncertainty clouds business decisions. A decision maker can never be sure how a course of action will turn out. For example, a careful analysis of ratios and other accounting information may suggest to management that the business should invest its excess cash in the stock of a microcomputer company. This industry may hold the prospect for the fastest return on an investment. A competing microcomputer company may introduce a new computer that sweeps the market, leaving the first company's stock worthless and the investing company in financial trouble. Ratio analysis cannot predict the future, but knowledge gained by a study of ratios and related information can help the analyst to make informed decisions.

Efficient Markets, Management Action, and Investor Decisions _____

Much research in accounting and finance has focused on whether the stock markets are "efficient." An **efficient capital market** is one in which market prices fully reflect all information available to the public. Stocks are priced in full recognition of all publicly accessible data.

The efficiency of a market has implications for management action and for investor decisions. It means that managers cannot fool the market with accounting gimmicks. As long as sufficient information is available, the market as a whole can translate accounting data into a "fair" price for the company's stock.

Suppose you are the president of Bedford Corporation. Reported earnings per share are $4 and the stock price $40—a price/earnings ratio of 10. You believe the corporation's stock is underpriced in comparison with other companies in the same industry. To correct this situation you are considering changing your method of depreciation from accelerated to straight-line. The accounting change will increase earnings per share to $5. Will the stock price then rise to $50? Probably not. The company's stock price will probably remain at $40 because the market can understand the accounting change. After all, the company merely changed its method of computing depreciation. There is no effect on the company's cash flows, and its economic position is unchanged.

In an efficient market the search for "underpriced" stock is fruitless unless the investor has relevant private information. Moreover, it is unlawful to invest based on inside information, which is available only to corporate managers. For outside investors in an efficient market, an appropriate investment strategy seeks to manage risk, to diversify, and to minimize transactions costs. The role of financial statement analysis consists mainly of identifying the risks of various stocks in order to manage the risk of the overall investment portfolio.

Computers and Financial Statement Analysis

How much can a computer help in analyzing financial statements for investment purposes? Time yourself as you perform one of the financial ratio problems in this chapter. Multiply your efforts by, say, 100 companies that you are comparing in terms of this ratio. Now consider ranking these 100 companies on the basis of four or five additional ratios.

Professional investment consultants may bring an impressive array of computer hardware and software into their analysis, but even individuals can take advantage of the computer in determining their investments—rather than merely "playing a hunch." Individual investors may arm themselves with a microcomputer, a spreadsheet, a modem (which transports data from a centralized storage area into your computer across the telephone lines), and a subscription to any one of several on-line financial databases. These on-line services offer quarterly financial figures for thousands of public corporations going back as much as ten years.

Assume you wanted to compare companies' recent earnings histories to perform an analysis similar to that of DIA in the opening vignette. You might have the computer compare hundreds of companies on the basis of price-earnings ratio and rates of return on stockholders' equity and total assets. The computer could then give you the names of the 20 (or however many) companies that appear most favorable in terms of these ratios. Alternatively, you could have the computer download financial statement data to your spreadsheet (that is, place the data in the appropriate cells of your spreadsheet) and crunch the numbers yourself.

Accountants use computerized financial analysis a great deal. CPAs focus on the individual client. They want to know how the client is doing compared to the previous year and compared to other firms in the industry. Auditors also want to detect any emerging trends in the company's ratios and compare the results of actual operations with expected results. To do so, an auditor can download monthly financial statistics on a spreadsheet and compute the financial ratios to gain insight into the client's situation.

Summary Problem for Your Review

This problem is based on the following financial data adapted from the financial statements of Pizza Inn, Inc., which operates approximately 1,000 pizza restaurants.

Pizza Inn, Inc.
Balance sheets
19X3 and 19X2

	19X3	19X2
	(Thousands of Dollars)	
Assets		
Current assets:		
Cash.................................	$ 4,123	$ 6,453
Marketable securities (same as short-term investments)........	4,236	—
Receivables, net.......................................	6,331	7,739
Inventories	5,840	4,069
Prepaid expenses and others............................	3,830	2,708
Total current assets	24,360	20,969
Net property, plant, and equipment	35,330	28,821
Net property under capital leases	23,346	20,886
Intangibles and other assets	10,493	11,349
	$93,529	$82,025
Liabilities and Stockholders' Equity		
Current liabilities:		
Notes payable	$ 1,244	$ 785
Current installments of long-term debt and		
capital lease obligations	5,220	6,654
Accounts payable–trade	8,631	8,791
Accrued liabilities	5,822	5,983
Total current liabilities	20,917	22,213
Long-term debt, less current installments...................	22,195	15,549
Capital lease obligations, less current portion	24,296	22,350
Deferred income and deferred income taxes	2,211	1,522
Total common stockholders' equity		
(shares outstanding 3,017,381 at year end 19X3 and		
2,729,274 at year end 19X2)	23,910	20,391
	$93,529	$82,025

Pizza Inn, Inc.
Statements of Earnings
Years 19X3 and 19X2

	19X3	19X2
	(Thousands of Dollars)	
Total revenue	$148,889	$140,539
Costs and expenses:		
Cost of products sold.................................	$114,335	$111,188
Selling, administrative, and general expenses................	23,475	20,816
	137,810	132,004
Earnings from operations	11,079	8,535
Interest expense.....................................	5,771	5,902
Earnings before income taxes...........................	5,308	2,633
Income taxes.......................................	1,713	932
Net earnings.......................................	$ 3,595	$ 1,701

Required

Compute the following ratios for Pizza Inn for 19X3:

a. Current ratio
b. Acid-test ratio
c. Inventory turnover
d. Days' sales (total revenue) in average receivables
e. Debt ratio
f. Times-interest-earned ratio
g. Rate of return on sales (total revenue)

h. Rate of return on total assets
i. Rate of return on common stockholders' equity
j. Price/earnings ratio, assuming the market price of common stock is $15.50 and earnings per share is $1.16.
k. Book value per share of common stock

SOLUTION TO REVIEW PROBLEM

a. $\text{Current Ratio} = \dfrac{\text{Current Assets}}{\text{Current Liabilities}} = \dfrac{\$24,360}{\$20,917} = 1.16$

b. $\text{Acid-Test Ratio} = \dfrac{\text{Cash} + \text{Short-Term Investments} + \text{Net Current Receivables}}{\text{Current Liabilities}} = \dfrac{\$4,123 + \$4,236 + \$6,331}{\$20,917} = .70$

c. $\text{Inventory Turnover} = \dfrac{\text{Cost of Goods sold}}{\text{Average Inventory}} = \dfrac{\$114,335}{(\$5,840 + \$4,069)/2} = 23.08$

d. Days' Sales (Total Revenue) in Average Receivables:

1. $\text{One day's sales} = \dfrac{\text{Net Sales}}{365 \text{ Days}} = \dfrac{\$148,889}{365} = \$407.92$

2. $\text{Days' sales in average accounts receivable} = \dfrac{\text{Average Accounts Receivable}}{\text{One Day's Sales}} = \dfrac{(\$6,331 + \$7,739)/2}{\$407.92} = 17 \text{ days}$

e. $\text{Debt Ratio} = \dfrac{\text{Total Liabilities}}{\text{Total Assets}} = \dfrac{\$20,917 + \$22,195 + \$24,296 + \$2,211}{\$93,529} = .74$

f. $\text{Times-Interest-Earned Ratio} = \dfrac{\text{Income from Operations}}{\text{Interest Expense}} = \dfrac{\$11,079}{\$5,771} = 1.92$

g. $\text{Rate of Return on Sales (Total Revenue)} = \dfrac{\text{Net Income}}{\text{Total Revenue}} = \dfrac{\$3,595}{\$148,889} = .024$

h. $\text{Rate of Return on Total Assets} = \dfrac{\text{Net income} + \text{Interest Expense}}{\text{Average Total Assets}} = \dfrac{\$3,595 + \$5,771}{(\$93,529 + \$82,025)/2} = .107$

i. $\text{Rate of Return on Common Stockholders' Equity} = \dfrac{\text{Net Income} - \text{Preferred Dividends}}{\text{Average Common Stockholders' Equity}} = \dfrac{\$3,595 - \$0}{(\$23,910 + \$20,391)/2} = .162$

$$\text{j.} \quad \frac{\text{Price/}}{\text{Earnings}} = \frac{\text{Market Price per Share of Common Stock}}{\text{Earnings per Share}} = \frac{\$15.50^*}{\$1.16^*} = 13.4$$

$$\text{k.} \quad \frac{\text{Book Value}}{\text{per Share of}} = \frac{\text{Total Stockholders' Equity} - \text{Preferred Equity}}{\text{Number of Shares of Common Stock Outstanding}} = \frac{\$23,910,000^* - \$0^*}{3,017,381^*} = \$7.92$$

*All dollar amounts are expressed in thousands except those denoted by *.

Summary

Accounting provides information for decision making. Banks loan money, investors buy stocks, and managers run businesses based on the analysis of accounting information.

Horizontal analysis shows the dollar amount and the percentage change in each financial statement item from one period to the next. *Vertical analysis* shows the relationship of each item in a financial statement to its total: total assets on the balance sheet and net sales on the income statement.

Common-size statements—a form of vertical analysis—show the component percentages of the items in a statement. Investment advisory services report common-size statements for various industries, and analysts use them to compare a company with its competitors and with the industry averages.

The *statement of cash flows* shows the net cash inflow or outflow caused by a company's operating, investing, and financing activities. By analyzing the inflows and outflows of cash listed on this statement, an analyst can see where a business's cash comes from and how it is being spent.

Ratios play an important part in business decision making because they show relationships between financial statement items. Analysis of ratios over a period of time is an important way to track a company's progress. The accompanying list presents the ratios discussed in this chapter:

Ratio	Computation	Information Provided
Measuring the ability to pay current liabilities:		
1. Current ratio	$\dfrac{\text{Current assets}}{\text{Current liabilities}}$	Measures ability to pay current liabilities from current assets.
2. Acid-test (quick) ratio	$\dfrac{\text{Cash} + \text{short-term investments} + \text{net current receivables}}{\text{Current liabilities}}$	Shows ability to pay current liabilities from the most liquid assets
Measuring the ability to sell inventory and collect receivables:		
3. Inventory turnover	$\dfrac{\text{Cost of goods sold}}{\text{Average inventory}}$	Indicates saleability of inventory.
4. Accounts receivable turnover	$\dfrac{\text{Net credit sales}}{\text{Average net accounts receivable}}$	Measures collectibility of receivables.
5. Days' sales in receivables	$\dfrac{\text{Average net accounts receivable}}{\text{One day's sales}}$	Shows how many days it takes to collect average receivables.

Ratio	Computation	Information Provided

Measuring the ability to pay long-term debts:

6. Debt ratio

$$\frac{\text{Total liabilities}}{\text{Total assets}}$$

Indicates percentage of assets financed through borrowing.

7. Times-interest-earned ratio

$$\frac{\text{Income from operations}}{\text{Interest expense}}$$

Measures coverage of interest expense by operating income.

Measuring profitability:

8. Rate of return on net sales

$$\frac{\text{Net income}}{\text{Net sales}}$$

Shows the percentage of each sales dollar earned as net income.

9. Rate of return on total assets

$$\frac{\text{Net income} + \text{interest expense}}{\text{Average total assets}}$$

Gauges how profitably assets are used.

10. Rate of return on common stock-holders' equity

$$\frac{\text{Net income} - \text{preferred dividends}}{\text{Average common stockholders' equity}}$$

Gauges how profitably the assets financed by the common stockholders are used.

11. Earnings per share of common stock

$$\frac{\text{Net income} - \text{preferred dividends}}{\text{Number of shares of common stock outstanding}}$$

Gives the amount of earnings per one share of common stock.

Analyzing stock as an investment:

12. Price/earnings ratio

$$\frac{\text{Market price per share of common stock}}{\text{Earnings per share}}$$

Indicates the market price of one dollar of earnings.

13. Dividend yield

$$\frac{\text{Dividend per share of common stock}}{\text{Market price per share of common stock}}$$

Shows the proportion of the market price of each share of stock returned as dividends to stockholders each period.

14. Book value per share of common stock

$$\frac{\text{Total stockholders' equity} - \text{preferred equity}}{\text{Number of shares of common stock outstanding}}$$

Indicates the recorded accounting value of each share of common stock outstanding

Self-Study Questions

Test your understanding of the chapter by marking the best answer for each of the following questions.

1. Net income was $240,000 in 19X4, $210,000 in 19X5, and $252,000 in 19X6. The change from 19X5 to 19X6 is a (an) *(p. 1213)*
   a. Increase of 5 percent
   b. Increase of 20 percent
   c. Decrease of 10 percent
   d. Decrease of 12.5 percent
2. Vertical analysis of a financial statement shows *(p. 1216)*
   a. Trend percentages
   b. The percentage change in an item from period to period
   c. The relationship of an item to its total on the statement
   d. Net income expressed as a percentage of stockholders' equity
3. Common-size statements are useful for comparing *(p. 1218)*
   a. Changes in the makeup of assets from period to period
   b. Different companies

c. A company with its industry

d. All of the above

4. The statement of cash flows is used for decision making by *(pp. 1220, 1221)*

   a. Reporting where cash came from and how it was spent

   b. Indicating how net income was earned

   c. Giving the ratio relationships between selected items

   d. Showing a horizontal analysis of cash flows

5. Cash is $10,000, net accounts receivable amount to $22,000, inventory is $55,000, prepaid expenses total $3,000, and current liabilities are $40,000. What is the acid-test ratio? *(p. 1224)*

   a. .25   c. 2.18

   b. .80   d. 2.25

6. Inventory turnover is computed by dividing *(p. 1224)*

   a. Sales revenue by average inventory

   b. Cost of goods sold by average inventory

   c. Credit sales by average inventory

   d. Average inventory by cost of goods sold

7. Capp Corporation is experiencing a severe cash shortage due to inability to collect accounts receivable. The decision tool most likely to help identify the appropriate corrective action is the *(p. 1226)*

   a. Acid-test ratio   c. Times-interest-earned ratio

   b. Inventory turnover   d. Days' sales in receivables

8. Analysis of the Mendoza Company financial statements over five years reveals that sales are growing steadily, the debt ratio is higher than the industry average and is increasing, interest coverage is decreasing, return on total assets is declining, and earnings per share of common stock is decreasing. Considered together, these ratios suggest that *(pp. 1228, 1229, 1230, 1231)*

   a. Mendoza should pursue collections of receivables more vigorously

   b. Competition is taking sales away from Mendoza

   c. Mendoza is in a declining industry

   d. The company's debt burden is hurting profitability

9. Which of the following is most likely to be true? *(p. 1231)*

   a. Return on common equity exceeds return on total assets.

   b. Return on total assets exceeds return on common equity.

   c. Return on total assets equals return on common equity.

   d. None of the above.

10. How are financial ratios used in decision making? *(p. 1234)*

    a. They remove the uncertainty of the business environment.

    b. They give clear signals about the appropriate action to take.

    c. They can help identify the reasons for success and failure in business, but decision making requires information beyond the ratios.

    d. They aren't useful because decision making is too complex.

Answers to the Self-Study Questions follow the Accounting Vocabulary.

Accounting Vocabulary

Accounts receivable turnover. Ratio of net credit sales to average net accounts receivable. Measures ability to collect cash from credit customers *(p. 1226)*.

Common-size statements. A financial statement that reports only percentages (no dollar amounts); a type of vertical analysis *(p. 1224)*.

Dividend yield. Ratio of dividends per share of stock to the stock's market price per share *(p. 1232)*.

Efficient capital market. A capital market in which market prices fully reflect all information available to the public *(p. 1234)*.

Horizontal analysis. Study of percentage changes in comparative financial statements (p. 1213).

Interest-coverage ratio. Another name for the Times-interest-earned ratio (p. 1229).

Leverage. Earning more income on borrowed money than the related interest expense, which increases the earnings for the owners of the business. Also called Trading on the equity. (p. 1231).

Long-term solvency. Ability to generate enough cash to pay long-term debts as they mature (p. 1212).

Price/earnings ratio. Ratio of the market price of a share of common stock to the company's earnings per share (p. 1232).

Rate of return on net sales. Ratio of net income to net sales. A measure of profitability. Also called Return on sales (p. 1229).

Return on sales. Another name for Rate of return on net sales (p. 1229).

Short-term liquidity. Ability to meet current payments as they come due (p. 1212).

Times-interest-earned ratio. Ratio of income from operations to interest expense. Measures the number of times that operating income can cover interest expense. Also called the Interest-coverage ratio (p. 1228).

Vertical analysis. Analysis of a financial statement that reveals the relationship of each statement item to the total, which is the 100 percent figure (p. 1216).

Working capital. Current assets minus current liabilities; measures a business's ability to meet its short-term obligations with its current assets (p. 1223).

Answers to Self-Study Questions

1. b $252,000 − $210,000 = $42,000; $42,000/$210,000 = .20
2. c
3. d
4. a
5. b ($10,000 + $22,000)/$40,000 = .80
6. b
7. d
8. d
9. a
10. c

ASSIGNMENT MATERIAL _____

Questions

1. Identify two groups of users of accounting information and the decisions they base on accounting data.
2. What are three analytical tools that are based on accounting information?
3. Briefly describe horizontal analysis. How do decision makers use this tool of analysis?
4. What is vertical analysis, and what is its purpose?
5. What use is made of common-size statements?
6. State how an investor might analyze the statement of cash flows. How might the investor analyze investing activities data?
7. Why are ratios an important tool of financial analysis? Give an example.

8. Identify two ratios used to measure a company's ability to pay current liabilities. Show how they are computed.

9. Why is the acid-test ratio called by this name?

10. What does the inventory-turnover ratio measure?

11. Suppose the days'-sales-in-receivables ratio of Gomez, Inc., increased from 36 at January 1 to 43 at December 31. Is this a good sign or a bad sign about the company? What would Gomez management do in response to this change?

12. Company A's debt ratio has increased from .50 to .70. Identify a decision maker to whom this increase is important, and state how the increase affects this party's decisions about the company.

13. Which ratio measures the *effect of debt* on (a) financial position (the balance sheet) and (b) the company's ability to pay interest expense (the income statement)?

14. Company A is a chain of grocery stores, and Company B is a computer manufacturer. Which company is likely to have the higher (a) current ratio, (b) inventory turnover, and (c) rate of return on sales? Give your reasons.

15. Identify four ratios used to measure a company's profitability. Show how to compute these ratios and state what information each ratio provides.

16. The price/earnings ratio of General Motors was 6, and the price/earnings ratio of American Express was 45. Which company did the stock market favor? Explain.

17. McDonald's Corporation, the hamburger company, paid cash dividends of $.78⅔ (78 and ⅔ cents) per share when the market price of the company's stock was $58. What was the dividend yield on McDonald's stock. What does dividend yield measure?

18. Hold all other factors constant and indicate whether each of the following situations generally signals good or bad news about a company:

a. Increase in current ratio
b. Decrease in inventory turnover
c. Increase in debt ratio
d. Decrease in interest-coverage ratio

e. Increase in return on sales
f. Decrease in earnings per share
g. Increase in price/earnings ratio
h. Increase in book value per share

19. Explain how an investor might use book value per share of stock in making an investment decision.

20. Describe how decision makers use ratio data. What are the limitations of ratios?

Exercises

Exercise 27-1 *Computing year-to-year changes in working capital* **(L.O. 1)**

What was the amount of change, and the percentage change, in Lux Corporation's working capital during 19X4 and 19X5? Is this trend favorable or unfavorable?

	Year 5	Year 4	Year 3
Total current assets	$312,000	$260,000	$280,000
Total current liabilities	150,000	117,000	140,000

Exercise 27-2 *Horizontal analysis of an income statement* **(L.O. 1)**

Prepare a horizontal analysis of the following comparative income statement of Milltown Incorporated. Round percentage changes to the nearest one-tenth percent (three decimal places):

Milltown Incorporated
Comparative Income Statement
Years Ended December 31, 19X9 and 19X8

	19X9	19X8
Total revenue	$440,000	$373,000
Expenses:		
Cost of goods sold	$202,000	$188,000
Selling and general expenses	118,000	93,000
Interest expense	7,000	4,000
Income tax expense	42,000	37,000
Total expenses	369,000	322,000
Net income	$ 71,000	$ 51,000

Why did net income increase by a higher percentage than total revenues increased during 19X9?

Exercise 27-3   *Computing trend percentages*   *(L.O. 1)*

Compute trend percentages for net sales and net income for the following five-year period, using year 1 as the base year:

	Year 5	Year 4	Year 3	Year 2	Year 1
		(amounts in thousands)			
Net sales	$1,510	$1,287	$1,106	$1,009	$1,043
Net income	127	114	93	71	85

Which grew more during the period, net sales or net income?

Exercise 27-4   *Vertical analysis of a balance sheet*   *(L.O. 2)*

Overseas Shipping, Inc., has requested that you perform a vertical analysis of its balance sheet to determine the component percentages of its assets, liabilities, and stockholders' equity.

Overseas Shipping, Inc.
Balance Sheet
December 31, 19X3

Assets

Total current assets	$ 62,000
Long-term investments	35,000
Property, plant, and equipment, net	227,000
Total assets	$324,000

Liabilities

Total current liabilities	$ 38,000
Long-term debt	118,000
Total liabilities	156,000

Stockholders' Equity

Total stockholders' equity	168,000
Total liabilities and stockholders' equity	$324,000

Exercise 27-5 *Preparing a common-size income statement* (L.O. 3)

Prepare a comparative common-size income statement for Milltown Incorporated, using the 19X9 and 19X8 data of Exercise 27-2 and rounding percentages to one-tenth percent (three decimal places).

Exercise 27-6 *Analyzing the statement of cash flows* (L.O. 4)

Identify any weaknesses revealed by the statement of cash flows of Perini Investment Consultants.

Perini Investment Consultants
Statement of Cash Flows
For the Current Year

Operating activities:		
Income from operations......................		$12,000
Add (subtract) noncash items:		
Depreciation	$ 23,000	
Net increase in current assets other than cash..	(15,000)	
Net increase in current liabilities exclusive of		
short-term debt	11,000	19,000
Net cash inflow from operating activities		31,000
Investing activities:		
Sale of property, plant, and equipment..........		81,000
Financing activities:		
Issuance of bonds payable	$114,000	
Payment of short-term debt	(101,000)	
Payment of long-term debt....................	(79,000)	
Payment of dividends	(12,000)	
Net cash outflow from financing activities		(78,000)
Increase in cash		$ 34,000

Exercise 27-7 *Computing five ratios* (L.O. 5)

The financial statements of Union Electric Corp. include the following items:

	Current Year	Preceding Year
Balance sheet:		
Cash	$ 17,000	$ 22,000
Short-term investments	21,000	26,000
Net receivables	64,000	73,000
Inventory	87,000	71,000
Prepaid expenses	6,000	8,000
Total current assets	195,000	200,000
Total current liabilities	121,000	91,000
Income statement:		
Net credit sales..............	$444,000	
Cost of goods sold...........	237,000	

Required

Compute the following ratios for the current year: (a) current ratio, (b) acid-test ratio, (c) inventory turnover, (d) accounts receivable turnover, and (e) days' sales in average receivables.

Exercise 27-8 Analyzing the ability to pay current liabilities (L.O. 5,6)

Premark Associates has requested that you determine whether the company's ability to pay its current liabilities and long-term debts has improved or deteriorated during 19X5. To answer this question, compute the following ratios for 19X5 and 19X4: (a) current ratio, (b) acid-test ratio, (c) debt ratio, and (d) times-interest-earned ratio. Summarize the results of your analysis.

	19X5	19X4
Cash	$ 31,000	$ 37,000
Short-term investments	28,000	—
Net receivables	102,000	116,000
Inventory	226,000	263,000
Prepaid expenses	11,000	9,000
Total assets	553,000	519,000
Total current liabilities	205,000	241,000
Total liabilities	261,000	273,000
Income from operations	165,000	158,000
Interest expense	26,000	31,000

Exercise 27-9 Analyzing profitability (L.O. 5,6)

Compute four ratios that measure ability to earn profits for Lerner Carbide, Inc., whose comparative income statement appears below. Additional data follow:

Lerner Carbide, Inc.
Comparative Income Statement
Years Ended December 31, 19X1 and 19X0

	19X1	19X0
Net sales	$174,000	$158,000
Cost of goods sold	93,000	86,000
Gross profit	81,000	72,000
Selling and general expenses	48,000	41,000
Income from operations	33,000	31,000
Interest expense	9,000	10,000
Income before income tax	24,000	21,000
Income tax expense	6,000	8,000
Net income	$ 18,000	$ 13,000

Additional data:

	19X1	19X0
1. Average total assets	$204,000	$191,000
2. Average common stockholders' equity	$ 96,000	$ 89,000
3. Preferred dividends	$ 3,000	$ 3,000
4. Shares of common stock outstanding	18,000	18,000

Did the company's operating performance improve or deteriorate during 19X1?

Exercise 27-10 Evaluating a stock as an investment (L.O. 5,6)

Evaluate the common stock of Fieldcrest Mills, Inc., as an investment. Specifically, use the three stock ratios to determine whether the stock has increased or decreased in attractiveness during the past year.

	Current Year	Preceding Year
Net income..	$ 58,000	$ 55,000
Dividends (half on preferred stock)................	28,000	28,000
Common stockholders' equity at year end (100,000 shares)................................	530,000	500,000
Preferred stockholders' equity at year end..........	200,000	200,000
Market price per share of common stock at year end .	$7.25	$5.75

Problems (Group A)

Problem 27-1A *Trend percentages, return on sales, and comparison with the industry (L.O. 1,5,6)*

Net sales, net income, and total assets for Evergreen Fragrances for a six-year period follow.

	19X6	19X5	19X4	19X3	19X2	19X1
	(amounts in thousands)					
Net sales	$327	$303	$266	$271	$245	$241
Net income	23	21	12	17	14	13
Total assets	286	244	209	197	181	166

Required

1. Compute trend percentages for 19X2 through 19X6, using 19X1 as the base year.
2. Compute the rate of return on net sales for 19X2 through 19X6, rounding to three decimal places. In this industry, rates above 5 percent are considered good, and rates above 7 percent are viewed as outstanding.
3. How does Evergreen's return on net sales compare with the industry?

Problem 27-2A *Common-size statements, analysis of profitability, and comparison with the industry (L.O. 2,3,5,6)*

Top managers of Golden Key Company have asked your help in comparing the company's profit performance and financial position with the average for the department-store industry. The accountant has given you the company's income statement and balance sheet and also the following actual data for the department-store industry.

Golden Key Company
Income Statement
Compared with Industry Average
Year Ended December 31, 19X3

	Golden Key	Industry Average
Net sales	$957,000	100.0%
Cost of goods sold	653,000	65.9
Gross profit	304,000	34.1
Operating expenses	287,000	31.1
Operating income	17,000	3.0
Other expenses	2,000	.4
Net income	$ 15,000	2.6%

Golden Key Company
Balance Sheet
Compared with Industry Average
December 31, 19X3

	Golden Key	Industry Average
Current assets	$448,000	74.4%
Fixed assets, net	127,000	20.0
Intangible assets, net	42,000	.6
Other assets	13,000	5.0
Total	$630,000	100.0%
Current liabilities	$246,000	35.6
Long-term liabilities	124,000	19.0
Stockholders' equity	260,000	45.4
Total	$630,000	100.0%

Required

1. Prepare a two-column common-size income statement and a two-column common-size balance sheet for Golden Key. The first column of each statement should present Golden Key's common-size statement, and the second column should show the industry averages.

2. For the profitability analysis, compare Golden Key's (a) ratio of gross profit to net sales, (b) ratio of operating income (loss) to net sales, and (c) ratio of net income (loss) to net sales. Compare these figures with the industry averages. Is Golden Key's profit performance better or worse than average for the industry?

3. For the analysis of financial position, compare Golden Key's (a) ratio of current assets to total assets and (b) ratio of stockholders' equity to total assets. Compare these ratios with the industry averages. Is Golden Key's financial position better or worse than the average for the industry?

Problem 27-3A   *Using the statement of cash flows for decision making*   (L.O. 4)

You are evaluating two companies as possible investments. The two companies, similar in size, are in the commuter airline business. They fly passengers from Denver and Omaha to smaller cities in their area. Assume that all other available information has been analyzed and that the decision on which company's stock to purchase depends on the information given in their statements of cash flows. The statements of cash flows of the two companies, Coreland Airways, Inc., and Rocky Mountain Express are given on the following page.

Required

Discuss the relative strengths and weaknesses of Coreland and Rocky Mountain. Conclude your discussion by recommending one of the company's stocks as an investment.

Problem 27-4A   *Effects of business transactions on selected ratios*   (L.O. 5,6)

Financial statement data of Navasota Building Supply include the following:

Cash	$ 47,000
Short-term investments	21,000
Accounts receivable, net...................	102,000
Inventories................................	274,000
Prepaid expenses	15,000
Total assets	933,000
Short-term notes payable	72,000
Accounts payable..........................	96,000
Accrued liabilities.......................	50,000
Long-term notes payable	146,000
Other long-term liabilities	78,000
Net income	119,000
Number of common shares outstanding	32,000

Required

1. Compute Navasota's current ratio, debt ratio, and earnings per share.
2. Compute each of the three ratios after evaluating the effect of each transaction that follows. Consider each transaction *separately*.
   a. Borrowed $56,000 on a long-term note payable.
   b. Sold short-term investments for $34,000 (cost, $46,000); assume no tax effect of the loss.
   c. Issued 14,000 shares of common stock, receiving cash of $168,000.
   d. Received cash on account, $6,000.

Problem 27-3A (continued)

Coreland Airways, Inc.
Statements of Cash Flows
For the Years Ended November 30, 19X9 and 19X8

	19X9		19X8	
Operating activities:				
Income (loss) from operations		$ (67,000)		$ 154,000
Add (subtract) noncash items:				
Total		84,000		(23,000)
Net cash inflow from operating activities		17,000		131,000
Investing activities:				
Purchase of property, plant, and equipment	$(120,000)		$ (91,000)	
Sale of property, plant, and equipment	118,000		39,000	
Sale of long-term investments	52,000		4,000	
Net cash inflow (outflow) from investing activities		50,000		(48,000)
Financing activities:				
Issuance of short-term notes payable	$ 122,000		$ 143,000	
Payment of short-term notes payable	(179,000)		(134,000)	
Payment of cash dividends	(45,000)		(64,000)	
Net cash outflow from financing activities		(102,000)		(55,000)
Increase (decrease) in cash		$ (35,000)		$ 28,000
Cash summary from balance sheet:				
Cash balance at beginning of year		$ 131,000		$ 103,000
Increase (decrease) in cash during the year		(35,000)		28,000
Cash balance at end of year		$ 96,000		$ 131,000

Rocky Mountain Express
Statements of Cash Flows
For the Years Ended November 30, 19X9 and 19X8

	19X9		19X8	
Operating activities:				
Income from operations		$ 184,000		$ 131,000
Add (subtract) noncash items:				
Total		64,000		62,000
Net cash inflow from operating activities		248,000		193,000
Investing activities:				
Purchase of property, plant, and equipment	$(303,000)		$(453,000)	
Sale of property, plant, and equipment	46,000		39,000	
Sale of long-term investments	—		33,000	
Net cash outflow from investing activities		(257,000)		(381,000)
Financing activities:				
Issuance of long-term notes payable	$ 131,000		$ 83,000	
Issuance of short-term notes payable	43,000		35,000	
Payment of short-term notes payable	(66,000)		(18,000)	
Net cash inflow from financing activities		108,000		100,000
Increase (decrease) in cash		$ 99,000		$ (88,000)
Cash summary from balance sheet:				
Cash balance at beginning of year		$ 116,000		$ 204,000
Increase (decrease) in cash during the year		99,000		(88,000)
Cash balance at end of year		$ 215,000		$ 116,000

e. Paid short-term notes payable, $51,000.

f. Purchased merchandise of $48,000 on account, debiting Inventory.

g. Paid off long-term liabilities, $78,000.

h. Declared, but did not pay, a $31,000 cash dividend on the common stock.

Use the following format for your answer:

Requirement 1.		Current Ratio	Debt Ratio	Earnings Per Share
Requirement 2.	Transaction (letter)	Current Ratio	Debt Ratio	Earnings Per Share

Problem 27-5A *Using ratios to evaluate a stock investment* **(L.O. 5,6)**

Comparative financial statement data of Ameron, Inc., are as follows:

Ameron, Inc.
Comparative Income Statement
Years Ended December 31, 19X4 and 19X3

	19X4	19X3
Net sales	$667,000	$599,000
Cost of goods 'sold.............	378,000	283,000
Gross profit..................	289,000	316,000
Operating expenses............	129,000	147,000
Income from operations........	160,000	169,000
Interest expense	47,000	41,000
Income before income tax	113,000	128,000
Income tax expense............	44,000	53,000
Net income	$ 69,000	$ 75,000

Ameron, Inc.
Comparative Balance Sheet
December 31, 19X4 and 19X3
(selected 19X2 amounts given for computation of ratios)

	19X4	19X3	19X2
Current assets:			
Cash	$ 37,000	$ 40,000	
Current receivables, net	188,000	151,000	$138,000
Inventories........................	372,000	286,000	184,000
Prepaid expenses	5,000	20,000	
Total current assets	602,000	497,000	
Property, plant, and equipment, net......	287,000	276,000	
Total assets	$889,000	$773,000	707,000
Total current liabilities	$286,000	$267,000	
Long-term liabilities....................	245,000	235,000	
Total liabilities........................	531,000	502,000	
Preferred stockholders' equity, 4%,			
$20 par	50,000	50,000	
Common stockholders' equity, no-par	308,000	221,000	148,000
Total liabilities and stockholders' equity...	$889,000	$773,000	

Other information:

a. Market price of Ameron common stock: $30.75 at December 31, 19X4, and $40.25 at December 31, 19X3.

b. Common shares outstanding: 20,000 during 19X4 and 19,000 during 19X3.

c. All sales on credit.

Required

1. Compute the following ratios for 19X4 and 19X3:
   a. Current ratio
   b. Inventory turnover
   c. Accounts receivable turnover
   d. Times-interest-earned ratio
   e. Return on assets
   f. Return on common stockholders' equity
   g. Earnings per share of common stock
   h. Price/earnings ratio
   i. Book value per share of common stock

2. Decide (a) whether Ameron's financial position improved or deteriorated during 19X4 and (b) whether the investment attractiveness of its common stock appears to have increased or decreased.

Problem 27-6A *Using ratios to decide between two stock investments* **(L.O. 5,6)**

Assume you are purchasing stock in a company in the hospital supply industry. Suppose you have narrowed the choice to HealthCorp and Providence, Inc., and have assembled the following data:

Selected income statement data for current year:

	HealthCorp	Providence, Inc.
Net sales (all on credit)	$603,000	$519,000
Cost of goods sold	454,000	387,000
Income from operations	93,000	72,000
Interest expense	—	8,000
Net income	56,000	38,000

Selected balance sheet and market price data at end of current year:

	HealthCorp	Providence, Inc.
Current assets:		
Cash	$ 25,000	$ 39,000
Short-term investments	6,000	13,000
Current receivables, net	189,000	164,000
Inventories	211,000	183,000
Prepaid expenses	19,000	15,000
Total current assets	450,000	414,000
Total assets	974,000	938,000
Total current liabilities	366,000	338,000
Total liabilities	667,000	691,000
Preferred stock, 4%, $100 par		25,000
Common stock, $1 par (150,000 shares)	150,000	
$5 par (20,000 shares)		100,000
Total stockholders' equity	307,000	247,000
Market price per share of common stock	$8	$47.50

Selected balance sheet data at beginning of current year:

	HealthCorp	Providence, Inc.
Current receivables, net	$142,000	$193,000
Inventories	209,000	197,000
Total assets	842,000	909,000
Preferred stock, 4%, $100 par		25,000
Common stock, $1 par (150,000 shares)	150,000	
$5 par (20,000 shares)		100,000
Total stockholders' equity	263,000	215,000

Your investment strategy is to purchase the stocks of companies that have low price/earnings ratios but appear to be in good shape financially. Assume you have analyzed all other factors, and your decision depends on the results of the ratio analysis to be performed.

Required

Compute the following ratios for both companies for the current year and decide which company's stock better fits your investment strategy.

1. Current ratio
2. Acid-test ratio
3. Inventory turnover
4. Days' sales in average receivables
5. Debt ratio
6. Times-interest-earned ratio
7. Return on net sales
8. Return on total assets
9. Return on common stock-holders' equity
10. Earnings per share of common stock
11. Book value per share of common stock
12. Price/earnings ratio

(Group B)

Problem 27-1B *Trend percentages, return on common equity, and comparison with the industry (L.O. 1,5,6)*

Net sales, net income, and common stockholders' equity for ConEd Corporation for a six-year period follow.

	19X9	19X8	19X7	19X6	19X5	19X4
			(amounts in thousands)			
Net sales	$781	$714	$621	$532	$642	$634
Net income	51	45	42	38	41	40
Ending common stockholders' equity	386	354	330	296	272	252

Required

1. Compute trend percentages for 19X5 through 19X9, using 19X4 as the base year.
2. Compute the rate of return on average common stockholders' equity for 19X5 through 19X9, rounding to three decimal places. In this industry, rates of 13 percent are average, rates above 16 percent are considered good, and rates above 20 percent are viewed as outstanding.
3. How does ConEd's return on common stockholders' equity compare with the industry?

Problem 27-2B *Common-size statements, analysis of profitability, and comparison with the industry (L.O. 2,3,5,6)*

Mears Illuminating has asked your help in comparing the company's profit performance and financial position with the average for the sporting goods retail industry. The proprietor has given you the company's income statement and balance sheet and also the industry average data for retailers of sporting goods.

Mears Illuminating Income Statement Compared with Industry Average Year Ended December 31, 19X6		
	Mears	Industry Average
Net sales...............	$781,000	100.0%
Cost of goods sold........	497,000	65.8
Gross profit	284,000	34.2
Operating expenses.......	243,000	29.7
Operating income.........	41,000	4.5
Other expenses...........	5,000	.4
Net income	$ 36,000	4.1%

Mears Illuminating Balance Sheet Compared with Industry Average December 31, 19X6		
	Mears	Industry Average
Current assets	$350,000	70.9%
Fixed assets, net	74,000	23.6
Intangible assets, net......	4,000	.8
Other assets..............	22,000	4.7
Total	$450,000	100.0%
Current liabilities	$230,000	48.1%
Long-term liabilities	62,000	16.6
Stockholders' equity	158,000	35.3
Total	$450,000	100.0%

Required

1. Prepare a two-column common-size income statement and a two-column common-size balance sheet for Mears. The first column of each statement should present Mears's common-size statement, and the second column should show the industry averages.

2. For the profitability analysis, compare Mears's (a) ratio of gross profit to net sales, (b) ratio of operating income to net sales, and (c) ratio of net income to net sales. Compare these figures with the industry averages. Is Mears's profit performance better or worse than the industry average?

3. For the analysis of financial position, compute Mears's (a) ratio of current assets to total assets and (b) ratio of stockholders' equity to total assets. Compare these ratios with the industry averages. Is Mears's financial position better or worse than the industry averages?

Problem 27-3B *Using the statement of cash flows for decision making (L.O. 4)*

You have been asked to evaluate two companies as possible investments. The two companies, similar in size, buy computers, airplanes, and other high-cost assets to lease to other businesses. Assume that all other available information has been analyzed, and the decision on which company's stock to purchase depends on the information given in their statements of cash flows. The statements appear on the next page.

Required

Discuss the relative strengths and weaknesses of each company. Conclude your discussion by recommending one company's stock as an investment.

Problem 27-3B (continued)

Southern Leasing Corporation
Statements of Cash Flows
For the Years Ended September 30, 19X5 and 19X4

	19X5	19X4
Operating activities:		
Income from operations	$ 79,000	$ 71,000
Add (subtract) noncash items:		
Total	19,000	—
Net cash inflow from operating activities	98,000	71,000
Investing activities:		
Purchase of property, plant, and equipment	$(121,000)	$(91,000)
Sale of long-term investments	13,000	18,000
Net cash outflow from investing activities	(108,000)	(73,000)
Financing activities:		
Issuance of long-term notes payable	$ 46,000	$ 43,000
Payment of short-term notes payable	(15,000)	(40,000)
Payment of cash dividends	(12,000)	(9,000)
Net cash inflow (outflow) from financing activities	19,000	(6,000)
Increase (decrease) in cash	$ 9,000	$ (8,000)
Cash summary from balance sheet:		
Cash balance at beginning of year	$ 72,000	$ 80,000
Increase (decrease) in cash during the year	9,000	(8,000)
Cash balance at end of year	$ 81,000	$ 72,000

Leasehold Assets, Inc.
Statements of Cash Flows
For the Years Ended September 30, 19X5 and 19X4

	19X5	19X4
Operating activities:		
Income from operations	$ 37,000	$ 74,000
Add (subtract) noncash items:		
Total	14,000	(4,000)
Net cash inflow from operating activities	51,000	70,000
Investing activities:		
Purchase of property, plant, and equipment	$ (13,000)	$ (3,000)
Sale of property, plant, and equipment	86,000	79,000
Sale of long-term investments	13,000	—
Net cash inflow from investing activities	86,000	76,000
Financing activities:		
Issuance of short-term notes payable	$ 73,000	$ 19,000
Issuance of long-term notes payable	31,000	42,000
Payment of short-term notes payable	(181,000)	(148,000)
Payment of long-term notes payable	(55,000)	(32,000)
Net cash outflow from financing activities	(132,000)	(119,000)
Increase in cash	$ 5,000	$ 27,000
Cash summary from balance sheet:		
Cash balance at beginning of year	$ 31,000	$ 4,000
Increase in cash during the year	5,000	27,000
Cash balance at end of year	$ 36,000	$ 31,000

Problem 27-4B *Effects of business transactions on selected ratios* **(L.O. 5,6)**

Financial statement data of Ashkenazy, Inc., include the following items.

Cash	$ 22,000
Short-term investments	19,000
Accounts receivable, net	83,000
Inventories	141,000
Prepaid expenses.........................	8,000
Total assets	657,000
Short-term notes payable	49,000
Accounts payable	103,000
Accrued liabilities	38,000
Long-term notes payable..................	160,000
Other long-term liabilities	31,000
Net income	71,000
Number of common shares outstanding	40,000

Required

1. Compute Ashkenazy's current ratio, debt ratio, and earnings per share.
2. Compute each of the three ratios after evaluating the effect of each transaction that follows. Consider each transaction *separately*.
   a. Issued 5,000 shares of common stock, receiving cash of $120,000.
   b. Received cash on account, $19,000.
   c. Paid short-term notes payable, $32,000.
   d. Purchased merchandise of $26,000 on account, debiting Inventory.
   e. Paid off long-term liabilities, $31,000.
   f. Declared, but did not pay, a $22,000 cash dividend on common stock.
   g. Borrowed $85,000 on a long-term note payable.
   h. Sold short-term investments for $18,000 (cost, $11,000); assume no income tax on the gain.

Use the following format for your answer:

Requirement 1.		Current Ratio	Debt Ratio	Earnings per Share

Requirement 2.	Transaction (letter)	Current Ratio	Debt Ratio	Earnings per Share

Problem 27-5B *Using ratios to evaluate a stock investment* **(L.O. 5,6)**

Comparative financial statement data of Cambridge Development Corp. appear below.

Required

1. Compute the following ratios for 19X7 and 19X6:
   a. Current ratio
   b. Inventory turnover
   c. Accounts receivable turnover
   d. Times-interest-earned ratio
   e. Return on assets
   f. Return on common stockholders' equity
   g. Earnings per share of common stock
   h. Price/earnings ratio
   i. Book value per share of common stock

2. Decide (a) whether Cambridge's financial position improved or deteriorated during 19X7 and (b) whether the investment attractiveness of its common stock appears to have increased or decreased.

Cambridge Development Corp.
Comparative Income Statement
Years Ended December 31, 19X7 and 19X6

	19X7	19X6
Net sales	$462,000	$427,000
Cost of goods sold	229,000	218,000
Gross profit	233,000	209,000
Operating expenses	136,000	134,000
Income from operations	97,000	75,000
Interest expense	21,000	12,000
Income before income tax	76,000	63,000
Income tax expense	30,000	27,000
Net income	$ 46,000	$ 36,000

Cambridge Development Corp.
Comparative Balance Sheet
December 31, 19X7 and 19X6
(selected 19X5 amounts given for computation of ratios)

	19X7	19X6	19X5
Current assets:			
Cash	$ 91,000	$ 97,000	
Current receivables, net	107,000	116,000	$103,000
Inventories	182,000	162,000	207,000
Prepaid expenses	16,000	7,000	
Total current assets	396,000	382,000	
Property, plant, and equipment, net	189,000	178,000	
Total assets	$585,000	$560,000	598,000
Total current liabilities	$206,000	$223,000	
Long-term liabilities	119,000	117,000	
Total liabilities	325,000	340,000	
Preferred stockholders' equity, 6%, $100 par	100,000	100,000	
Common stockholders' equity, no-par	160,000	120,000	90,000
Total liabilities and stockholders' equity	$585,000	$560,000	

Other information:

a. Market price of Cambridge common stock: $39 at December 31, 19X7, and $32.50 at December 31, 19X6.

b. Common shares outstanding: 10,000 during 19X7 and 9,000 during 19X6.

c. All sales on credit.

Problem 27-6B *Using ratios to decide between two stock investments* (L.O. 5,6)

Assume you are purchasing an investment and have decided to invest in a company in the air-conditioning and heating business. Suppose you have narrowed the choice to Odegaard Corp. and Advantage, Inc. You have assembled the following selected data:

Selected income statement data for current year:

	Odegaard Corp.	Advantage, Inc.
Net sales (all on credit)	$371,000	$497,000
Cost of goods sold	209,000	258,000
Income from operations	79,000	138,000
Interest expense	—	19,000
Net income	48,000	72,000

Selected balance sheet and market price data at end of current year:

	Odegaard Corp.	Advantage, Inc.
Current assets:		
Cash	$ 22,000	$ 19,000
Short-term investments	20,000	18,000
Current receivables, net	42,000	46,000
Inventories	87,000	100,000
Prepaid expenses	2,000	3,000
Total current assets	173,000	186,000
Total assets	265,000	328,000
Total current liabilities	108,000	98,000
Total liabilities	108,000	131,000
Preferred stock: 5%, $100 par		20,000
Common stock, $1 par (10,000 shares)	10,000	
$2.50 par (5,000 shares)		12,500
Total stockholders' equity	157,000	197,000
Market price per share of common stock	$51	$118

Selected balance sheet data at beginning of current year:

	Odegaard Corp.	Advantage, Inc.
Current receivables, net	$ 40,000	$ 48,000
Inventories	93,000	88,000
Total assets	259,000	270,000
Preferred stockholders' equity 5%, $100 par	—	20,000
Common stock, $1 par (10,000 shares)	10,000	
$2.50 par (5,000 shares)		12,500
Total stockholders' equity	118,000	126,000

Your investment strategy is to purchase the stocks of companies that have low price/earnings ratios but appear to be in good shape financially. Assume you have analyzed all other factors, and your decision depends on the results of the ratio analysis to be performed.

Required

Compute the following ratios for both companies for the current year and decide which company's stock better fits your investment strategy.

1. Current ratio
2. Acid-test ratio
3. Inventory turnover
4. Days' sales in average receivables
5. Debt ratio
6. Times-interest-earned ratio
7. Return on net sales
8. Return on total assets
9. Return on common stockholders' equity
10. Earnings per share of common stock
11. Book value per share of common stock
12. Price/earnings ratio

Extending Your Knowledge

Decision Problems

1. Identifying Action to Cut Losses and Establish Profitability (L.O. 2,5,6)

Suppose you manage Early Bird, Inc., a sporting goods and bicycle shop, which lost money during the past year. Before you can set the business on a successful course, you must first analyze the company and industry data for the current year in an effort to learn what is wrong. The data appear below and on page 1258.

Early Bird Balance Sheet Data	Early Bird	Industry Average
Cash and short-term investments	2.1%	6.8%
Trade receivables, net	16.1	11.0
Inventory	64.2	60.5
Prepaid expenses	1.0	0.0
Total current assets	83.4	78.3
Fixed assets, net	12.6	15.2
Other assets	4.0	6.5
Total assets	100.0%	100.0%
Notes payable, short-term, 12%	18.1%	14.0%
Accounts payable	20.1	25.1
Accrued liabilities	7.8	7.9
Total current liabilities	46.0	47.0
Long-term debt, 11%	19.7	16.4
Total liabilities	65.7	63.4
Common stockholders' equity	34.3	36.6
Total liabilities and stockholders' equity	100.0%	100.0%

Early Bird Income Statement Data

	Early Bird	Industry Average
Net sales	100.0%	100.0%
Cost of sales	(69.7)	(64.8)
Gross profit	30.3	35.2)
Operating expense	(35.6)	(32.3)
Operating income (loss)	(5.3)	2.9
Interest expense	(6.8)	(1.3)
Other revenue	1.1	.3
Income (loss) before income tax	(11.0)	1.9
Income tax (expense) saving	4.4	(.8)
Net income (loss)	(6.6)%	1.1%

Required

Based on your analysis of these figures, suggest four courses of action Early Bird should take to reduce its losses and establish profitable operations. Give your reasons for each suggestion.

2. *Understanding the Components of Accounting Ratios*   (L.O. 5,6)

a. Harvey Drago is the controller of Hunan Industries, Inc., whose year end is December 31. He prepares checks for suppliers in December and posts them to the appropriate accounts in that month. However, he holds on to the checks and actually mails them to the suppliers in January. What financial ratio(s) are most affected by the action? What is Drago's purpose in undertaking this activity?

b. Janet Wong has asked you about the stock of a particular company. She finds it attractive because it has a high dividend yield relative to another stock she is also considering. Explain to her the meaning of the ratio and the danger of making a decision based on it alone.

c. Limeridge Ltd.'s owners are concerned because the number of days' sales in receivables has increased over the previous two years. Explain why the ratio might have increased.

Ethical Issue

Krisler Corporation's long-term debt agreements make certain demands on the business. Krisler may not purchase treasury stock in excess of the balance of Retained Earnings. Also, Long-term Debt may not exceed Stockholders' Equity, and the current ratio may not fall below 1.50. If Krisler fails to meet these requirements, the company's lenders have the authority to take over management of the corporation.

Changes in consumer demand have made it hard for Krisler to sell its products. Current liabilities have mounted faster than current assets, causing the current ratio to fall to 1.47. Prior to releasing financial statements, Krisler management is scrambling to improve the current ratio. The controller points out that an investment can be classified as either long-term or short-term, depending on management's intention. By deciding to convert an investment to cash within one year, Krisler can classify the investment as short-term—a current asset. On the controller's recommendation, Krisler's board of directors votes to reclassify long-term investments as short-term.

Required

1. What effect will reclassifying the investment have on the current ratio? Is Krisler Corporation's financial position stronger as a result of reclassifying the investment?

2. Shortly after releasing the financial statements, sales improve and so, then, does the current ratio. As a result, Krisler management decides not to sell the investments it had reclassified as short-term. Accordingly, the company reclassifies the investments as long-term. Has management behaved unethically? Give your reason.

Appendix A

Time Value of Money: Future Value and Present Value

LEARNING OBJECTIVES

After studying this appendix, you should be able to

1 Compute the future value of an investment made in a single amount

2 Compute the future value of an annuity-type investment

3 Compute the present value of a single future amount

4 Compute the present value of an annuity

5 Determine the cost of an asset acquired through a capital lease

Interest is the cost of using money. To borrowers, interest is the expense of renting money. To lenders, interest is the revenue earned from lending. When funds are used for a period of time, we must recognize the interest. Otherwise we overlook an important part of the transaction. Consider an example. Suppose you invest $4,545 in corporate bonds that pay 10 percent interest each year. After one year, the value of your investment has grown to $5,000. The difference between your original investment ($4,545) and the future value of the investment ($5,000) is the amount of interest revenue you will earn during the year ($455). To ignore the interest would be incorrect because you would fail to account for the interest revenue you have earned. Interest becomes more important as the time period lengthens because the amount of interest depends on the span of time the money is invested.

The term *time value of money* refers to the fact that money earns interest over time. Because of the time value of money, you would prefer to have $1 (or any amount) now versus having to wait to receive it later. Why? Because by receiving the cash now, you can invest it to earn some interest revenue. If you must wait to receive the cash later, you forego the interest revenue in the meantime.

Let's consider a second example, this time from the side of the borrower. Suppose you purchase a machine for your business. The cash price of the machine is $8,000, but you cannot afford to pay cash now. To finance the purchase you sign an $8,000 note payable. The note requires you to pay the $8,000 plus 10 percent interest one year from the date of purchase. What is your cost of the machine? Is it $8,000, or is it $8,800 [$8,000 plus interest of $800 ($8,000 × .10)]? The cost of the machine is $8,000. The additional $800 you pay is interest expense and not part of the cost of the machine. To ignore the interest would be incorrect because you would overstate the cost of the machine and understate the amount of interest expense.

This appendix first considers future value and then present value.

Future Value

The main application of future value is the accumulated balance of an investment at a future date. In our first example above, the investment earned 10 percent per year. After one year $4,545 grew to $5,000, diagrammed and computed as follows:

$$\text{Present value} \times (1 + \text{Interest rate}) = \text{Future value}$$
$$\$4,545 \quad \times \quad 1.10 \quad = \quad \$5,000$$

Now consider the computational difficulty of determining the accumulated balance of this investment if the money were invested for five years. Following the approach just illustrated, you must perform five such calculations. You must also take into account the compound interest that your investment is earning. Compound interest is not only the interest you earn on your principal amount, but also the interest you receive on the interest you have already earned. Most business applications include compound interest. The following table shows the interest revenue earned each year at 10 percent. The far right column shows the future value of a $4,545 investment at the end of each year for five years.

End of Year	Interest	Future Value
0		$4,545
1	$4,545 × .10 = $455	5,000
2	5,000 × .10 = 500	5,500
3	5,500 × .10 = 550	6,050
4	6,050 × .10 = 605	6,655
5	6,655 × .10 = 666	7,321

Earning 10 percent, a $4,545 investment grows to $5,000 at the end of one year, to $5,500 at the end of two years, and so on. Throughout this discussion we round off to the nearest dollar.

Future Value Tables

The process of computing a future value is called *accumulating* because the future value is *more* than the present value. Mathematical tables ease the computational burden. Table A-1, Future Value of $1, gives the future value for a single sum (a present value) invested to earn a particular interest rate for a specific number of periods. Future value depends on three factors: (1) the amount of the investment, (2) the length of time between investment and future accumulation, and (3) the interest rate.

Refer to Table A-1. Note that the heading states $1. Future value tables and present value tables are based on $1 because unity is so easy to work with. Observe the Period column and the interest rate columns 4% through 16%. In

TABLE A-1 Future Value of $1

Period	4%	5%	6%	7%	8%	9%	10%	12%	14%	16%
1	1.040	1.050	1.060	1.070	1.080	1.090	1.100	1.120	1.140	1.160
2	1.082	1.103	1.124	1.145	1.166	1.188	1.210	1.254	1.300	1.346
3	1.125	1.158	1.191	1.225	1.260	1.295	1.331	1.405	1.482	1.561
4	1.170	1.216	1.262	1.311	1.360	1.412	1.464	1.574	1.689	1.811
5	1.217	1.276	1.338	1.403	1.469	1.539	1.611	1.762	1.925	2.100
6	1.265	1.340	1.419	1.501	1.587	1.677	1.772	1.974	2.195	2.436
7	1.316	1.407	1.504	1.606	1.714	1.828	1.949	2.211	2.502	2.826
8	1.369	1.477	1.594	1.718	1.851	1.993	2.144	2.476	2.853	3.278
9	1.423	1.551	1.689	1.838	1.999	2.172	2.358	2.773	3.252	3.803
10	1.480	1.629	1.791	1.967	2.159	2.367	2.594	3.106	3.707	4.411
11	1.539	1.710	1.898	2.105	2.332	2.580	2.853	3.479	4.226	5.117
12	1.601	1.796	2.012	2.252	2.518	2.813	3.138	3.896	4.818	5.936
13	1.665	1.886	2.133	2.410	2.720	3.066	3.452	4.363	5.492	6.886
14	1.732	1.980	2.261	2.579	2.937	3.342	3.797	4.887	6.261	7.988
15	1.801	2.079	2.397	2.759	3.172	3.642	4.177	5.474	7.138	9.266
16	1.873	2.183	2.540	2.952	3.426	3.970	4.595	6.130	8.137	10.748
17	1.948	2.292	2.693	3.159	3.700	4.328	5.054	6.866	9.276	12.468
18	2.026	2.407	2.854	3.380	3.996	4.717	5.560	7.690	10.575	14.463
19	2.107	2.527	3.026	3.617	4.316	5.142	6.116	8.613	12.056	16.777
20	2.191	2.653	3.207	3.870	4.661	5.604	6.727	9.646	13.743	19.461

business applications interest rates are always stated for the annual period of one year unless the transaction specifies an interest rate for a different period. In fact, an interest rate can be stated for any period, such as 3 percent per quarter or 5 percent for a six-month period. Thus the length of the period is arbitrary. For example, an investment may promise a return (income) of 3 percent per quarter for six months (two quarters). In that case you would be working with 3 percent interest for two periods. It would be incorrect to use 6 percent for one period because the interest is 3 percent compounded quarterly, and that amount differs slightly from 6 percent compounded semiannually. Take care in studying future value and present value problems to align the interest rate with the appropriate number of periods.

Let's use Table A-1. What is the future value of $1.00 invested at 8 percent for one year? $1.08 ($1.00 × 1.080, which appears at the junction under the 8% column and across from 1 in the Period column). The table figure of 1.080 includes both the principal (1.000) and the compound interest for one period (.080).

OBJECTIVE 1
Compute the future value of an investment made in a single amount

Suppose you deposit $5,000 in a savings account that pays annual interest of 8 percent. What will be the account balance at the end of one year? $5,400. To compute the future value of $5,000 at 8 percent for one year, multiply $5,000 by 1.080 = $5,400. Now suppose you invest in a 10-year, 8 percent certificate of deposit (CD). What will be the future value of the CD at maturity? To compute the future value of $5,000 at 8 percent for 10 periods, multiply $5,000 by 2.159 (Table B-1: 8% for 10 periods) = $10,795. This future value of $10,795 indicates that $5,000 earning 8 percent interest compounded annually grows to $10,795 at the end of 10 years. In this way you can find any present amount's future value at a particular future date. This is especially helpful for computing the amount of cash you will have on hand for some purpose in the future—to take a vacation, purchase an automobile, or for a business to acquire land or a building.

Future Value of an Annuity

In the preceding example, we made an investment in a single amount. Other investments, called annuities, include multiple investments of an equal periodic amount at fixed intervals over the duration of the investment.

Consider a family investing for the education of a child. Suppose the Dietrichs can invest $4,000 annually to accumulate a college fund for 15-year-old daughter Helen. The investment can earn 7 percent annually until Helen turns 18—a three-year investment. How much will be available for Helen on the date of the last investment? The following diagram shows the accumulation—a total future value of $12,860.

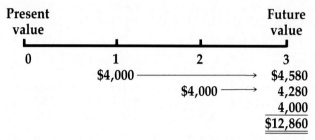

The first $4,000 invested by the Dietrichs grows to $4,580 over the investment period. The second amount grows to $4,280, and the third amount stays at $4,000 because it has no time to earn interest. The sum of the three future values ($4,580 + $4,280 + $4,000) is the future value of the annuity ($12,860), which can be computed as follows:

End of Year	Annual Investment +	Interest	Increase = for the Year	Future Value of Annuity
0				0
1	$4,000		$4,000	$4,000
2	4,000	+ ($4,000 × .07 = $280) =	4,280	8,280
3	4,000	+ ($8,280 × .07 = 580) =	4,580	12,860

These computations are laborious. As they do for the Future Value of $1 (a lump sum), mathematical tables ease the strain for annuities. Table A-2, Future Value of Annuity of $1 gives the future value of a series of investments, each of equal amount, at regular intervals.

What is the future value of an annuity of three investments of $1 each that earn 7 percent? 3.215, which can be found at the junction under the 7% column and across from 3 in the Period column. This table amount can be used to compute the future value of the investment for Helen's education, as follows:

Amount of each periodic × Future value of annuity of = Future value of
investment $1 (Table A-2)   investment

$4,000   ×   3.215   = $12,860

This one-step calculation is much easier than computing the future value of each annual investment and then summing the individual future values. In this way you can compute the future value of any investment consisting of equal periodic amounts at regular intervals. Businesses make periodic investments to accumulate funds for equipment replacement and other uses—an application of the future value of an annuity.

OBJECTIVE 2

Compute the future value of an annuity-type investment

TABLE A-2 *Future Value of Annuity of $1*

Period	4%	5%	6%	7%	8%	9%	10%	12%	14%	16%
1	1.000	1.000	1.000	1.000	1.000	1.000	1.000	1.000	1.000	1.000
2	2.040	2.050	2.060	2.070	2.080	2.090	2.100	2.120	2.140	2.160
3	3.122	3.153	3.184	3.215	3.246	3.278	3.310	3.374	3.440	3.506
4	4.246	4.310	4.375	4.440	4.506	4.573	4.641	4.779	4.921	5.066
5	5.416	5.526	5.637	5.751	5.867	5.985	6.105	6.353	6.610	6.877
6	6.633	6.802	6.975	7.153	7.336	7.523	7.716	8.115	8.536	8.977
7	7.898	8.142	8.394	8.654	8.923	9.200	9.487	10.089	10.730	11.414
8	9.214	9.549	9.897	10.260	10.637	11.028	11.436	12.300	13.233	14.240
9	10.583	11.027	11.491	11.978	12.488	13.021	13.579	14.776	16.085	17.519
10	12.006	12.578	13.181	13.816	14.487	15.193	15.937	17.549	19.337	21.321
11	13.486	14.207	14.972	15.784	16.645	17.560	18.531	20.665	23.045	25.733
12	15.026	15.917	16.870	17.888	18.977	20.141	21.384	24.133	27.271	30.850
13	16.627	17.713	18.882	20.141	21.495	22.953	24.523	28.029	32.089	36.786
14	18.292	19.599	21.015	22.550	24.215	26.019	27.975	32.393	37.581	43.672
15	20.024	21.579	23.276	25.129	27.152	29.361	31.772	37.280	43.842	51.660
16	21.825	23.657	25.673	27.888	30.324	33.003	35.950	42.753	50.980	60.925
17	23.698	25.840	28.213	30.840	33.750	36.974	40.545	48.884	59.118	71.673
18	25.645	28.132	30.906	33.999	37.450	41.301	45.599	55.750	68.394	84.141
19	27.671	30.539	33.760	37.379	41.446	46.018	51.159	63.440	78.969	98.603
20	29.778	33.066	36.786	40.995	45.762	51.160	57.275	72.052	91.025	115.380

Present Value

Often a person knows a future amount and needs to know the related present value. Recall the diagram:

Present value		Future value	
0	1	2	3

Present value and future value are on opposite ends of the same time line. Suppose an investment promises to pay you $5,000 at the *end* of one year. How much would you pay *now* to acquire this investment? You would be willing to pay the present value of the $5,000 future amount.

Present value also depends on three factors: (1) the amount of payment (or receipt), (2) the length of time between investment and future receipt (or payment), and (3) the interest rate. The process of computing a present value is called *discounting* because the present value is *less* than the future value.

In our investment example, the future receipt is $5,000. The investment period is one year. Assume that you demand an annual interest rate of 10 percent on your investment. With all three factors specified, you can compute the present value of $5,000 at 10 percent for one year. The computation is

$$\frac{\text{Future value}}{(1 + \text{Interest rate})} = \frac{\$5,000}{1.10} = \$4,545$$

By turning the data around into a future-value problem, we verify the present-value computation:

Amount invested (present value)	$4,545
Expected earnings ($4,545 × .10)	455
Amount to be received one year from now (future value)	$5,000

This example illustrates that present value and future value are based on the same equation:

$$\text{Present value} \times (1 + \text{Interest rate}) = \text{Future value}$$

$$\frac{\text{Future value}}{(1 + \text{Interest rate})} = \text{Present value}$$

If the $5,000 were to be received two years from now, you would pay only $4,132 for the investment, diagrammed and computed as follows:

By turning the data around, we verify that $4,132 accumulates to $5,000 at 10 percent for two years.

Amount invested (present value)	$4,132
Expected earnings for first year ($4,132 × .10)	413
Value of investment after one year	4,545
Expected earnings for second year ($4,545 × .10)	455
Amount to be received two years from now (future value)	$5,000

You would pay $4,132—the present value of $5,000—to receive the $5,000 future amount at the end of two years at 10 percent per year. The $868 difference between the amount invested ($4,132) and the amount to be received ($5,000) is the return on the investment, the sum of the two interest receipts: $413 + $455 = $868.

Present-Value Tables

We can compute present value by using the formula

$$\text{Present value} = \frac{\text{Future value}}{(1 + \text{Interest rate})}$$

as we have shown. However, figuring present value "by hand" for investments spanning many years becomes drawn out. The "number crunching" presents too many opportunities for arithmetical errors. Present-value tables ease our work. Let's reexamine our examples of present value by using Table A-3 Present Value of $1.

For the 10 percent investment for one year, we find the junction under the 10% column and across from 1 in the Period column. The table figure of 0.909 is computed as follows: $1/1.10 = .909$. This work has been done for us, and only

TABLE A-3 *Present Value of $1*

Period	4%	5%	6%	7%	8%	10%	12%	14%	16%
1	0.962	0.952	0.943	0.935	0.926	0.909	0.893	0.877	0.862
2	0.925	0.907	0.890	0.873	0.857	0.826	0.797	0.769	0.743
3	0.889	0.864	0.840	0.816	0.794	0.751	0.712	0.675	0.641
4	0.855	0.823	0.792	0.763	0.735	0.683	0.636	0.592	0.552
5	0.822	0.784	0.747	0.713	0.681	0.621	0.567	0.519	0.476
6	0.790	0.746	0.705	0.666	0.630	0.564	0.507	0.456	0.410
7	0.760	0.711	0.665	0.623	0.583	0.513	0.452	0.400	0.354
8	0.731	0.677	0.627	0.582	0.540	0.467	0.404	0.351	0.305
9	0.703	0.645	0.592	0.544	0.500	0.424	0.361	0.308	0.263
10	0.676	0.614	0.558	0.508	0.463	0.386	0.322	0.270	0.227
11	0.650	0.585	0.527	0.475	0.429	0.350	0.287	0.237	0.195
12	0.625	0.557	0.497	0.444	0.397	0.319	0.257	0.208	0.168
13	0.601	0.530	0.469	0.415	0.368	0.290	0.229	0.182	0.145
14	0.577	0.505	0.442	0.388	0.340	0.263	0.205	0.160	0.125
15	0.555	0.481	0.417	0.362	0.315	0.239	0.183	0.140	0.108
16	0.534	0.458	0.394	0.339	0.292	0.218	0.163	0.123	0.093
17	0.513	0.436	0.371	0.317	0.270	0.198	0.146	0.108	0.080
18	0.494	0.416	0.350	0.296	0.250	0.180	0.130	0.095	0.069
19	0.475	0.396	0.331	0.277	0.232	0.164	0.116	0.083	0.060
20	0.456	0.377	0.312	0.258	0.215	0.149	0.104	0.073	0.051

the present values are given in the table. Note that the table heading states $1. To figure present value for $5,000, we multiply 0.909 by $5,000. The result is $4,545, which matches the result we obtained by hand.

For the two-year investment, we read down from the 10% column and across from the Period 2 row. We multiply 0.826 (which is computed as follows: .909/1.10 = .826) by $5,000 and get $4,130, which confirms our earlier computation of $4,132 (the difference is due to rounding in the present-value table). We can compute the present value of any single future amount using the table.

Cost of an Asset Purchased by Signing a Note Payable in a Single Amount

Consider another application of the present value of $1. Mid-South Utilities purchases equipment on short-term notes payable. A particular acquisition requires Mid-South to pay $30,000 three years after purchase but specifies no interest rate. Mid-South could borrow at 12 percent interest to purchase this equipment, so 12 percent is the appropriate interest rate.

Mid-South accountants must record the purchase of the equipment now, but what is its cost? The agreement specifies the future amount to be paid ($30,000), but the cost of the equipment today is a present value, not a future amount. The cost of the equipment is the present value of the $30,000, at 12 percent for three years. The computation is:

	Cost (Present value)		Future amount		Present value of $1 at 12% for 3 years (Table A-3)
	$21,360	=	$30,000	×	.712

OBJECTIVE 3

Compute the present value of a single future amount

Mid-South would record the equipment purchase as follows:

19X1
Jan. 2 Equipment 21,360
              Note Payable   21,360

At each year-end Mid-South would accrue interest expense with these entries:

	End of Year		
	1	**2**	**3**
Dec. 31 Interest Expense	2,563	2,871	3,206
Note Payable..........	2,563	2,871	3,206

($21,360 × .12 = $2,563)   ($21,360 + $2,563) × .12 = $2,871
($21,360 + $2,563 + $2,871) × .12 = $3,206*

*Rounded to bring Note Payable balance to $30,000.

For years 2 and 3, adding the preceding year's interest amounts ($2,653 and $2,871) is an example of compound interest. Over the three-year period, the Note Payable account builds to its maturity (future) value of $30,000, as follows:

Note Payable

Beginning balance	21,360
Interest for Year 1	2,563
Interest for Year 2	2,871
Interest for Year 3	3,206
Maturity value	30,000

Mid-South records its payment of the note as follows:

19X4
Jan. 2 Note Payable.............................. 30,000
              Cash   30,000

Present Value of an Annuity

Return to the investment example beginning on page A-6. That investment provided the investor with only a single future receipt ($5,000 at the end of two years). Annuity investments provide multiple receipts of an equal amount at fixed intervals over the investment's duration.

Consider an investment that promises *annual* cash receipts of $10,000 to be received at the end of each of three years. Assume that you demand a 12 percent return on your investment. What is the investment's present value? What would you pay today to acquire the investment? The investment spans three periods, and you would pay the sum of three present values. The computation is

Year	Annual Cash Receipt	Present Value of $1 at 12% (Table A-3)	Present Value of Annual Cash Receipt
1	$10,000	.893	$ 8,930
2	10,000	.797	7,970
3	10,000	.712	7,120
Total present value of investment			$24,020

The present value of this annuity is $24,020. By paying this amount today, you would receive $10,000 at the end of each of three years while earning 12 percent on your investment.

The example illustrates repetitive computations of the three future amounts, a time-consuming process. One way to ease the computational burden is to add the three present values of $1 (.893 + .797 + .712) and multiply their sum (2.402) by the annual cash receipt ($10,000) to obtain the present value of the annuity ($10,000 × 2.402 = $24,020).

An easier approach is to use a present value of an annuity table. Table A-4 shows the present value of $1 to be received periodically for a given number of periods. The present value of a three-period annuity at 12 percent is 2.402. Thus $10,000 received annually at the end of each of three years, discounted at 12 percent, is $24,020 ($10,000 × 2.402), which is the present value.

Present Value of Bonds Payable

The present value of a bond—its market price—is the present value of the future principal amount at maturity plus the present value of the future contract interest payments. The principal is a single amount to be paid at maturity. The interest is an annuity because it occurs periodically.

TABLE A-4 *Present Value of Annuity of $1*

Period	4%	5%	6%	7%	8%	10%	12%	14%	16%
1	0.962	0.952	0.943	0.935	0.926	0.909	0.893	0.877	0.862
2	1.886	1.859	1.833	1.808	1.783	1.736	1.690	1.647	1.605
3	2.775	2.723	2.673	2.624	2.577	2.487	2.402	2.322	2.246
4	3.630	3.546	3.465	3.387	3.312	3.170	3.037	2.914	2.798
5	4.452	4.329	4.212	4.100	3.993	3.791	3.605	3.433	3.274
6	5.242	5.076	4.917	4.767	4.623	4.355	4.111	3.889	3.685
7	6.002	5.786	5.582	5.389	5.206	4.868	4.564	4.288	4.039
8	6.733	6.463	6.210	5.971	5.747	5.335	4.968	4.639	4.344
9	7.435	7.108	6.802	6.515	6.247	5.759	5.328	4.946	4.607
10	8.111	7.722	7.360	7.024	6.710	6.145	5.650	5.216	4.833
11	8.760	8.306	7.887	7.499	7.139	6.495	5.938	5.453	5.029
12	9.385	8.863	8.384	7.943	7.536	6.814	6.194	5.660	5.197
13	9.986	9.394	8.853	8.358	7.904	7.103	6.424	5.842	5.342
14	10.563	9.899	9.295	8.745	8.244	7.367	6.628	6.002	5.468
15	11.118	10.380	9.712	9.108	8.559	7.606	6.811	6.142	5.575
16	11.652	10.838	10.106	9.447	8.851	7.824	6.974	6.265	5.669
17	12.166	11.274	10.477	9.763	9.122	8.022	7.120	6.373	5.749
18	12.659	11.690	10.828	10.059	9.372	8.201	7.250	6.467	5.818
19	13.134	12.085	11.158	10.336	9.604	8.365	7.366	6.550	5.877
20	13.590	12.462	11.470	10.594	9.818	8.514	7.469	6.623	5.929

Let's compute the present value of the 9 percent, five-year bonds of Bethlehem Steel. The face value of the bonds is $100,000, and they pay 4½ percent contract (cash) interest semiannually. At issuance the market interest rate is expressed as 10 percent, but it is computed at 5 percent semiannually. Therefore, the effective interest rate for each of the 10 semiannual periods is 5 percent. We use 5 percent in computing the present value of the maturity and of the interest. The market price of these bonds is $96,149, as follows:

OBJECTIVE 4

Compute the present value of an annuity

	Effective annual interest rate ÷ 2	Number of semiannual interest payments	
PV of principal:			
$100,000 × PV of single amount at 5%	for	10 periods	
($100,000 × .614—Table B-3			$61,400
PV of interest:			
($100,000 × .045) × PV of annuity at 5%	for	10 periods	
($4,500 × 7.722—Table B-4			34,749
PV (market price) of bonds			$96,149

The market price of the Bethlehem Steel bonds shows a discount because the contract interest rate on the bonds (9 percent) is less than the market interest rate (10 percent).

Let's consider a premium price for the Bethlehem Steel bonds. Assume that the market interest rate is 8 percent at issuance. The effective interest rate is 4 percent for each of the 10 semiannual periods.

	Effective annual interest rate ÷ 2	Number of semiannual interest payments	
PV of principal:			
$100,000 × PV of single amount at 4%	for	10 periods	
($100,000 × .676—Table B-3			$ 67,600
PV of interest:			
($100,000 × .045) × PV of annuity at 4%	for	10 periods	
($4,500 × 8.111—Table B-4			36,500
PV (market price) of bonds			$104,100

Capital Leases

OBJECTIVE 5

Determine the cost of an asset acquired through a capital lease

How does a lessee compute the cost of an asset acquired through a capital lease? Consider that the lessee gets the use of the asset but does *not* pay for the leased asset in full at the beginning of the lease. A capital lease is therefore similar to an installment purchase of the leased asset. The lessee must record the leased asset at the present value of the lease liability. The time value of money must be weighed.

The cost of the asset to the lessee is the sum of any payment made at the beginning of the lease period plus the present value of the future lease payments. The lease payments are equal amounts occurring at regular intervals— that is, they are annuity payments.

Consider the 20-year building lease of the Southland Corporation, which owns 7-Eleven stores. The lease requires 20 annual payments of $10,000 each, with the first payment due immediately. The interest rate in the lease is 10 percent, and the present value of the 19 future payments is $83,650 ($10,000 × PV of annuity at 10 percent for 19 periods, or 8.365 from Table A-4). Southland's cost of the building is $93,650 (the sum of the initial payment, $10,000, plus the present value of the future payments, $83,650).

APPENDIX ASSIGNMENT MATERIAL

Problem A-1 *Computing future values* **(L.O. 1, 2)**

For each situation compute the required amount.

1. Langefeld Enterprises is budgeting for the acquisition of land over the next several years. Langefeld can invest $300,000 at 9 percent. How much cash will Langefeld have for land acquisitions at the end of five years? At the end of six years?
2. Mercer Associates is planning to invest $10,000 each year for five years. The company's investment advisor believes Mercer can earn 6 percent interest without taking on too much risk. What will be the value of Mercer's investment on the date of the last deposit if Mercer can earn 6 percent? If Mercer can earn 8 percent?

Problem A-2 *Computing future values* **(L.O. 1, 2)**

Olivia Degas has just received $5,000 from an insurance settlement. A single parent, she seizes this opportunity to establish a fund for the education of her son Hector. Ms. Degas's banker offers an FDIC-insured certificate of deposit (CD). Under this arrangement, Ms. Degas would invest the entire $5,000 for a four-year period and earn 6 percent interest.

After computing the future value of the bank CD, she hopes for a higher rate of return on the investment. A broker at Merrill Lynch suggests that Ms. Degas invest $1,000 at the end of each year for five years. The broker assures Ms. Degas that this investment may earn as much as 16 percent, but it is quite risky.

Required

Write a brief memo to advise Ms. Degas on which investment is better for her purpose. Base your answer on future value and risk, and give your reason.

Problem A-3 *Computing the annual investment for the future value of an annuity*
(L.O. 2)

Fellowship Bible Church of Tallahassee, Florida, needs a new building but refuses to go into debt. An architect has prepared plans for a multipurpose facility (sanctuary, recreation, and classrooms) that will cost $400,000 in five years. To accumulate this fund, the finance committee recommends that the church start setting aside cash from the weekly offerings. These funds can be invested to earn 7 percent per year. How much must the church invest each year to build up to $400,000 on the date of the final deposit? To address this question, set up the computation for the future value of an annuity.

Problem A-4 *Relating future values and present values* **(L.O. 1, 3)**

1. Eastman Kodak's operations are generating excess cash flows that can be used for future projects. During 19X2, Kodak invests $564,400 for a campaign to advertise a new product that will be available six years later, in 19X8. If Kodak's investments can earn 10 percent each year, how much cash will the company have for the advertising campaign in 19X8? Round to the nearest $1,000.
2. Eastman Kodak Company will need $1 million to advertise a new type of photo film in 19X8. How much must Kodak invest in 19X2 to have the cash available for the advertising campaign? Kodak's investments can earn 10 percent annually.
3. Explain the relationship between your answers to *a* and *b*.

Problem A-5 *Recording an asset acquisition by signing a note payable* **(L.O. 3)**

The Red Cross chapter in Cupertino, California, purchased equipment by signing a $7,000 note payable. Because the Red Cross organization does charity work, the seller of the equipment allows Red Cross to pay in a single amount at the end of 10 years. The note payable specifies no interest rate, but Red Cross could borrow the funds at an interest rate of 5 percent.

Required

1. Compute Red Cross's cost of the equipment.
2. Journalize Red Cross's purchase of the equipment on January 2, 19X4, and the entry at December 31, 19X4 to accrue interest expense.
3. How much will Red Cross pay on the maturity date of the note payable?

Problem A-6 *Evaluating customer payment plans* **(L.O. 3, 4)**

Mainline Manufacturing Company is negotiating the sale of a large shipment of office furniture. The customer, a French company, will pay Mainline in French francs. Mainline is considering two proposals from the French concern:

Proposal A—Mainline will receive 2,500,000 francs at the end of two years.
Proposal B—Mainline will receive 1,400,000 francs at the end of one year and another 1,400,000 francs at the end of year 2.

Which proposal should Mainline accept? Base your answer on present value. Considering the fluctuation in the value of the franc and Mainline's other investment opportunities, an appropriate interest rate for this transaction is 12 percent.

Problem A-7 *Computing the present values of notes and bonds* **(L.O. 3, 4)**

Determine the present value of the following notes and bonds:

1. $40,000, five-year note payable with contract interest rate of 11 percent, paid annually. The market interest rate at issuance is 12 percent.
2. Ten-year bonds payable with maturity value of $100,000 and contract interest rate of 12 percent, paid semiannually. The market rate of interest is 10 percent at issuance.
3. Same bonds payable as in 2, but the market interest rate is 8 percent.
4. Same bonds payable as in 2, but the market interest rate is 12 percent.

Problem A-8   *Computing a bond's present value; recording its issuance at a discount and interest payments*   **(L.O. 3, 4)**

On December 31, 19X1, when the market interest rate is 8 percent, Interstate Express Co. issues $300,000 of 10-year, 7.25 percent bonds payable. The bonds pay interest semiannually.

Required

1. Determine the present value of the bonds at issuance.
2. Assume that the bonds are issued at the price computed in 1. Prepare an effective-interest method amortization table for the first two semiannual interest periods.
3. Using the amortization table prepared in 2, journalize issuance of the bonds and the first two interest payments.

Problem A-9   *Computing a bond's present value; recording its issuance at a premium and interest payments*   **(L.O. 3, 4)**

On December 31, 19X1, when the market interest rate is 10 percent, JAX Gold Corporation issues $2,000,000 of 10-year, 12.5 percent bonds payable. The bonds pay interest semiannually.

Required

1. Determine the present value of the bonds at issuance.
2. Assuming the bonds were issued at the price computed in 1, prepare an effective-interest method amortization table for the first two semiannual interest periods.
3. Using the amortization table in 2, journalize issuance of the bonds on December 31, 19X1, and the first two interest payments on June 30 and December 31, 19X2.

Problem A-10   *Deciding between two payment plans*   **(L.O. 3, 4)**

Yokohama Children's Home needs a fleet of vans to transport the children to singing engagements throughout Japan. Nissan offers the vehicles for a single payment of 6,300,000 yen (¥) due at the end of four years. Toyota prices a similar fleet of vans for four annual payments of 1,700,000 yen each. The children's home could borrow the funds at 6 percent, so this is the appropriate interest rate. Which company should get the business, Nissan or Toyota? Base your decision on present value, and give your reason.

Problem A-11   *Computing the cost of equipment acquired under a capital lease and recording the lease transactions*   **(L.O. 5)**

Goldblatt Institute acquired equipment under a capital lease that requires six annual lease payments of $10,000. The first payment is due when the lease begins, on January 1, 19X6. Future payments are due on January 1 of each year of the lease term. The interest rate in the lease is 16 percent.

Required

1. Compute Goldblatt's cost of the equipment.
2. Journalize the (a) acquisition of the equipment, (b) depreciation for 19X6, (c) accrued interest at December 31, 19X6, and (d) second lease payment on January 1, 19X7.

Appendix B

The Foundation for Generally Accepted Accounting Principles

Every technical area seems to have professional associations and regulatory bodies that govern the practice of the profession. Accounting is no exception. During the 1970s and 1980s generally accepted accounting principles in the United States have been influenced most by the Financial Accounting Standards Board (FASB) and its predecessor, the Accounting Principles Board (APB). The FASB consists of seven full-time members. A large staff and an annual budget of $14 million support the FASB. Its financial support comes from various professional associations, such as the American Institute of Certified Public Accountants.

From 1962 to 1973 the APB issued accounting pronouncements called *Opinions,* many of which are still part of generally accepted accounting principles (GAAP). In 1973 the FASB was established to replace the APB. The FASB is an independent organization with no government or professional affiliation. The FASB's pronouncements, called *Statements of Financial Accounting Standards,* currently specify how to account for certain business transactions. Each new *Standard* becomes part of GAAP, the "accounting law of the land." In the same way that our laws draw authority from their acceptance by the people, GAAP depends upon the general acceptance by the business community. Throughout this book, we refer to GAAP as the proper way to do financial accounting.

The United States Congress has given the Securities and Exchange Commission (SEC) ultimate responsibility for establishing accounting rules for companies that are owned by the general investing public. However, the SEC has delegated much of its rule-making power to the FASB. Exhibit B-1 outlines the flow of authority for developing GAAP.

Setting accounting standards is a complex process involving the FASB, the SEC, and occasionally Congress. Also, individuals and companies often exert pressure on all three bodies in their efforts to shape accounting decisions to their advantage. Accountants also try to influence accounting decisions. Although any overruling is rare, the SEC has the authority to override an FASB decision, and Congress itself can override an SEC or an FASB decision, as the authority structure in Exhibit B-1 shows. In most cases, however, the FASB plays the key role.

We have seen that GAAP guides companies in their financial statement preparation. Independent auditing firms of certified public accountants (CPAs) hold the responsibility for making sure companies do indeed follow GAAP.

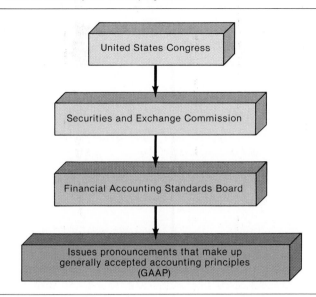

The Conceptual Framework

Throughout the first 14 chapters, we have introduced key concepts and principles as they have applied to the topics under discussion. Now that you have an overview of the accounting process, we consider the full range of accounting concepts and principles. Collectively, they form the foundation for accounting practice—GAAP.

Shortly after its formation in 1973, the Financial Accounting Standards Board (FASB) began the Conceptual Framework Project. The FASB's goal is to develop a constitution that will define the nature and function of financial accounting. As we have studied, accounting is based on historical amounts. From time to time the SEC and the FASB show interest in basing accounting on *current* value amounts. For example, in 1992 the chairman of the SEC proposed current-value accounting in a series of speeches.

Accounting principles differ from natural laws like the law of gravity. Accounting principles draw their authority from their acceptance in the business community rather than from their ability to explain physical phenomena. Thus they really are *generally accepted* by those people and organizations who need guidelines in accounting for their financial undertakings. Exhibit B-2 diagrams how we move from the conceptual framework to the financial statements.

We now look at the objective of financial reporting. This objective tells what financial accounting is intended to accomplish. Thus it provides the goal for accounting information. Next, we examine particular accounting concepts and principles used to implement the objective. What is the difference between a concept and a principle? The concepts are broader in their application, and the principles are more specific. Last, we discuss the financial statements—the end product of financial accounting—and their elements—assets, liabilities, owner's equity, revenues, expenses, and so on.

Objective of Financial Reporting

The basic *objective of financial reporting* is to provide information that is useful in making investment and lending decisions. To be useful in decision making, the FASB believes accounting information should be *relevant*, *reliable*, and *comparable*.

Relevant information is useful for making predictions and for evaluating past performance—that is, the information has feedback value. To be relevant, information must be timely. *Reliable* information is free from significant error—that is, it has validity. Also, it is free from the bias of a particular viewpoint—that is, it is verifiable and neutral. *Comparable* information can be compared from period to period to help investors and creditors track the entity's progress through time. These characteristics combine to shape the concepts and principles that make up GAAP. Exhibit B-3 summarizes the qualities that increase the value of accounting information.

Underlying Concepts

Entity Concept

The **entity concept** is the most basic concept in accounting because it draws a boundary around the organization being accounted for. That is, the transactions of each entity are accounted for separately from transactions of all other organizations and persons, including the owners of the entity. This separation allows us to measure the performance and the financial position of each entity independent of all other entities.

A business entity may be a sole proprietorship (owned and operated by a single individual), a partnership of two or more persons, or a large corporation like Exxon. The entity concept applies with equal force to all types and sizes of organizations. The proprietor of a travel agency, for example, accounts for her personal transactions separately from those of her business. This division

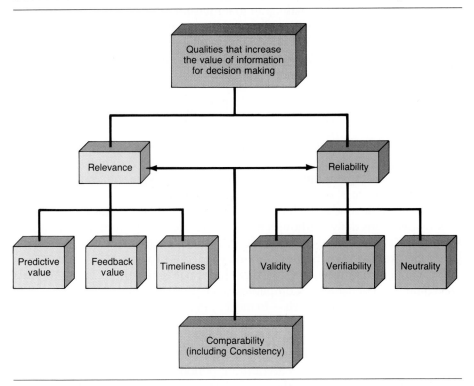

allows her to evaluate the success or failure of the travel agency. If she were to mix her personal and business accounting records, she would lose sight of the information needed to evaluate the business alone.

At the other end of the spectrum, Exxon is a giant company with oil-refining, retail gasoline sales, and chemical operations. Exxon accounts for each of these divisions separately in order to know which part of the business is earning a profit, which needs to borrow money, and so on. The entity concept also provides the basis for consolidating subentities into a single set of financial statements. Exxon reports a single set of consolidated financial statements to the public.

Going-Concern Concept

Under the **going-concern** (or **continuity**) **concept,** accountants assume the business will continue operating for the foreseeable future. The logic behind the going-concern concept is best illustrated by considering the alternative assumption: going out of business.

When a business stops, it sells its assets, converting them to cash. This process is called liquidation. With the cash, the business pays off its liabilities, and the owners keep any remaining cash. In liquidation, the amount of cash for which the assets are sold measures their current value. Likewise, the liabilities are paid off at their current value. However, if the business does not halt operations—if it remains a going concern—how are its assets and liabilities reported on the balance sheet?

For a going concern, the balance sheet reports assets and liabilities based on historical cost. To consider what the asset may be worth on the current market requires making an estimate. This may or may not be objective. Under the going-concern concept, it is assumed that the entity will continue long enough to recover the cost of its assets.

The going-concern concept allows for the reporting of assets and liabilities as current or long-term, a distinction that investors and creditors find useful in evaluating a company. For example, a creditor wants to know the portion of a company's liabilities that are scheduled to come due within the next year and the portion payable beyond the year. The assumption is that the entity will continue in business and honor its commitments.

Time-Period Concept

The **time-period concept** ensures that accounting information is reported at regular intervals. This timely presentation of accounting data aids the comparison of business operations over time; from year to year, quarter to quarter, and so on. Managers, owners, lenders, and other people and businesses need regular reports to assess the business's success—or failure. These persons are making decisions daily. Although the ultimate success of a company cannot be known for sure until the business liquidates, decision makers cannot wait until liquidation to learn whether operations yielded a profit.

Nearly all companies use the year as their basic time period. *Annual* reports are common in business. Companies also prepare quarterly and monthly reports—called interim reports—to meet managers', investors', and creditors' need for timely information.

The time-period concept underlies the use of accruals. Suppose the business's accounting year ends at December 31 and the business has accrued—but will not pay until the next accounting period—$900 in salary expense. To tie this expense to the appropriate period, the accountant enters this adjusting entry, as we have seen:

| Dec. 31 | Salary Expense | 900 | |
| | Salary Payable | | 900 |

Accrual entries assign revenue and expense amounts to the correct accounting period and thus help produce meaningful financial statements.

Stable-Monetary-Unit Concept

Accounting information is expressed primarily in monetary terms. The monetary unit is the prime means of measuring assets. This measure is not surprising given that money is the common denominator in business transactions. In the United States, the monetary unit is the dollar; in Great Britain, the pound sterling; in Japan, the yen. The stable-monetary-unit concept provides an orderly basis for handling account balances to produce the financial statements.

Unlike a liter, a foot, and many other measurements, the value of the monetary unit may change over time. Most of us are familiar with inflation. Groceries that cost $50 three years ago may cost $60 today. The value of the dollar changes. In view of the fact that the dollar does not maintain a constant value, how does a business measure the worth of assets and liabilities acquired over a long span of time? The business records all assets and liabilities at cost. Each asset and each liability on the balance sheet is the sum of all the individual dollar amounts added over time. For example, if a company bought 100 acres of land in 1975 for $60,000 and another 100 acres of land in 1992 for $300,000, the asset Land on the balance sheet carries a $360,000 balance, and the change in the purchasing power of the dollar is ignored. The **stable-monetary-unit concept** is the accountant's basis for ignoring the effect of inflation and making no restatements for the changing value of the dollar. Let's look at the short-comings of this concept.

Suppose another company paid $600,000 for the same 200 acres of land in 1992. Its land would be the same as the preceding company's land, but its balance sheet would show a much higher amount for the land. How do we compare the two companies' balance sheets? The comparison based on the stable-monetary-unit concept may not be valid because mixing dollar values at different times is like mixing apples and oranges.

Many businesspeople believe that accounting information must be restated for changes in the dollar's purchasing power. The FASB encourages large companies to present supplementary inflation-adjusted information in their financial reports. Generally, however, accounting is based on historical costs.

Accounting Principles

Reliability (Objectivity) Principle

The **reliability principle** requires that accounting information be dependable—free from significant error and bias. Users of accounting information rely on its truthfulness. To be reliable, information must be verifiable by people outside the business. Financial statement users may consider information reliable if independent experts would agree that the information is based on objective and honest measurement.

Consider the error in a company's failure to accrue interest revenue at the end of an accounting period. This error results in understated interest revenue and understated net income. Clearly, this company's accounting information is unreliable.

Biased information—data prepared from a particular viewpoint and not based on objective facts—is also unreliable. Suppose a company purchased inventory for $25,000. At the end of the accounting period, the inventory has declined in value and can be replaced for $20,000. Under the lower-of-cost-or-market rule, the company must record a $5,000 loss for the decrease in the inventory's value. Company management may believe that the appropriate value for the inventory is $22,000, but that amount is only an opinion. If management reports the $22,000 figure, total assets and owner's equity will be overstated on the balance sheet. Income will be overstated on the income statement.

To establish a *reliable* figure for the inventory's value, management could get a current price list from the inventory supplier or call in an outside professional appraiser to revalue the inventory. Evidence obtained from outside the company leads to reliable, verifiable information. The reliability principle applies to all financial accounting information—from assets to owner's equity on the balance sheet and from revenue to net income on the income statement.

Comparability Principle

The **comparability principle** has two requirements. First, accounting information must be comparable from business to business. Second, a single business's financial statements must be comparable from one period to the next. The FASB encourages comparability in order to make possible useful analysis from business to business, from period to period.

Standard formats for financial statements promote comparability among different companies. Using the same terms to describe the statement elements—assets, liabilities, revenues, and so on—aids the comparison process.

Even among companies that adhere to standard formats and standard terms, comparability may be less than perfect. Comparisons of companies that use different inventory methods—LIFO and FIFO, for example—are difficult. When GAAP allows a choice among acceptable accounting methods—in inventory, depreciation, and other areas—comparability may be hard to achieve.

Recall that the comparability principle directs each individual company to produce accounting information that is comparable over time. To achieve this quality—which accountants call *consistency*—companies must follow the same accounting practices from period to period. The business that uses FIFO for inventory and straight-line for depreciation in one period ought to use those same methods in the next period. Otherwise, a financial statement user could not tell whether changes in income and asset values result from operations or from the way the business accounts for operations.

Companies may change accounting methods in response to a change in business operations. A company may add a new product line that calls for a different inventory method. GAAP allows the company to make a change in accounting method, but the business must disclose the change, the reason for making the change, and the effect of the change on net income. This disclosure is made in a note to the financial statements.

Cost Principle

The **cost principle** states that assets and services are recorded at their purchase cost and that the accounting record of the asset continues to be based on cost rather than current market value. By specifying that assets be recorded at cost, this principle also governs the recording of liabilities and owner's equity. Suppose a land developer purchased 20 acres of land for $50,000. Additional costs included fees paid to the county ($1,500), removal of an unwanted building ($10,000), and landscaping ($20,000), a total cost of $81,500. The Land account carries this balance because it is the cost of bringing the land to its intended use. Assume that the developer holds the land for one year, then offers it for sale at a price of $200,000. The cost principle requires the accounting value of the land to remain at $81,500.

The developer may wish to lure buyers by showing them a balance sheet that reports the land at $200,000. However, this would be inappropriate under GAAP because $200,000 is merely the developer's opinion of what the land is worth.

The underlying basis for the cost principle is the reliability principle. Cost is a reliable value for assets and services because cost is supported by completed transactions between parties with opposing interests. Buyers try to pay the lowest price possible, and sellers try to sell for the highest price. The actual cost of an asset or service is objective evidence of its value.

Revenue Principle

The **revenue principle** provides guidance on the *timing* of the recording of revenue and the *amount* of revenue to record. The general rule is that revenue should be recorded when it is earned and not before.

Some revenues, such as interest and rent, accrue with the passage of time. Their timing and amount are easy to figure. The accountant records the amount of revenue earned over each period of time.

Other revenues are earned by selling goods or rendering services. Identifying *when* these revenues are earned depends on more factors than the passage of time. Under the revenue principle, three conditions must be met before revenue is recorded: (1) the seller has done everything necessary to expect to collect from the buyer; (2) the amount of revenue can be objectively measured; and (3) collectibility is reasonably assured. In most cases, these conditions are met at the point of sale or when services are performed.

The *amount* of revenue to record is the value of the assets received—usually cash or a receivable. However, situations may arise in which the amount of revenue or the timing of earning the revenue is not easily determined. We turn now to four methods that guide the accountant in applying the revenue principle in different circumstances.

OBJECTIVE 4
Allocate revenue to the appropriate period by four methods

Sales Method.   Under the **sales method,** revenue is recorded at the point of sale. Consider a retail sale in a hardware store. When a sale occurs, the customer pays the store and takes the merchandise. The store records the sale by debiting Cash and crediting Sales Revenue. In other situations, the point of sale occurs when the seller ships the goods to the buyer. Suppose a mining company sells iron ore to Bethlehem Steel Corporation. By shipping the ore to Bethlehem Steel, the mining company has completed its duty and may expect to collect cash for the revenue earned. If the amount of revenue can be objectively measured and collection is reasonably certain, the mining company can then record revenue. The sale entry is a debit to Accounts Receivable and a credit to Sales Revenue. The sales method is used for most sales of goods and services.

Collection Method.   The **collection method** is used only if the receipt of cash is uncertain. Under this method, the seller waits until cash is received to record the sale. Professionals such as physicians and attorneys use the collection method because they often find it difficult to collect their receivables. They may not reasonably assume that they can collect the revenue, so they wait until actual receipt of the cash before recording it. The collection method is conservative in that revenue is not recorded in advance of its receipt.

Installment Method.   The **installment method** is a type of collection method that is used for installment sales. In a typical installment sale, the buyer makes a down payment when the contract is signed and pays the remainder in installments. Real estate companies sell on the installment plan. Under the installment method, gross profit (sales revenue minus cost of goods sold) is recorded as cash is collected.

Suppose a real estate developer sells land for a down payment of $80,000 plus three annual installments of $120,000, $140,000, and $160,000 (a total of $500,000). The developer's cost of the land is $300,000, so the gross profit is $200,000, computed as follows:

Installment sale	$500,000
Cost of the land sold	300,000
Gross profit	$200,000

To determine the gross profit associated with each collection under the installment method, we must compute the gross profit percentage, as follows:

$$\text{Gross profit percentage} = \frac{\text{Gross profit}}{\text{Installment sale}} = \frac{\$200,000}{\$500,000} = 40\%$$

We next apply the gross profit percentage to each collection. The result is the amount of gross profit recorded as revenue at the time of cash receipt.

Year	Collections	×	Gross Profit Percentage	=	Gross Profit
1	$ 80,000	×	40%	=	$ 32,000
2	120,000	×	40%	=	48,000
3	140,000	×	40%	=	56,000
4	160,000	×	40%	=	64,000
Total	$500,000	×	40%	=	$200,000

Accountants would record gross profit of $32,000 in year 1, $48,000 in year 2, and so on. The total gross profit ($200,000) is the same as under the sales method. However, under the sales method, the full $200,000 of gross profit would be recorded at the beginning of the contract.

Of course, companies make installment sales year after year. Each year's sales may have a different gross profit percentage. In the preceding example, year 1 installment sales earned gross profit of 40 percent. Suppose year 2 sales earn gross profit of 45 percent, year 3 sales earn 42 percent, and year 4 sales earn 35 percent. The total gross profit for a year is the sum of all the gross profit amounts recorded on cash collections made that year.

Using assumed cash receipts on installment sales made in years 2, 3, and 4, the gross profit computations for years 1 through 4 follow. All year 1 amounts are taken from our computations above.

	Year 1 Sales	Year 2 Sales	Year 3 Sales	Year 4 Sales
Gross profit percentage	40%	45%	42%	35%

Gross profit by year

	Year 1	Year 2	Year 3	Year 4
Year 1 sales:	$80,000 × .40 = $32,000	$120,000 × .40 = $48,000	$140,000 × .40 = $56,000	$160,000 × .40 = $64,000
Year 2 sales:		90,000 × .45 = 40,500	100,000 × .45 = 45,000	20,000 × .45 = 9,000
Year 3 sales:			75,000 × .42 = 31,500	65,000 × .42 = 27,300
Year 4 sales:				30,000 × .35 = 10,500
Total gross profit	$32,000	$88,500	$132,500	$110,800

The installment method is attractive for income tax purposes because it postpones the recording of revenue and thus the payment of taxes. However, it can be used under limited circumstances—for example, the sale of real estate. Under generally accepted accounting principles, this method is permissible only when no reasonable basis exists for estimating collections.

Percentage-of-Completion Method.   Construction of office buildings, bridges, dams, and other large assets often extends over several years. The accounting issue for the construction company is *when* to record the revenue. The most conservative approach is to record all the revenue earned on the project in the period when the project is completed. This procedure, called the **completed-contract method,** is acceptable under limited circumstances.

Under the preferred method, called the **percentage-of-completion method,** the construction company recognizes revenue as work is performed. Each year the company estimates the percentage of project completion as construction progresses. One way to make this estimate is to compare the cost incurred for the year with the total estimated project cost. This percentage is then multiplied by the total project revenue to compute the construction revenue for the year. Construction income for the year is revenue minus cost.

Assume Combustion Engineering Company receives a contract to build a power plant for a price of $42 million. Combustion estimates total costs of $36 million over the three-year construction period: $6 million in year 1, $18 million in year 2, and $12 million in year 3. Construction revenue and income during the three years are as follows (amounts in millions):

Year	Cost for Year	Total Project Cost	Percentage of Project Completion for Year	Total Project Revenue	Construction Revenue for Year	Construction Income for year
1	$ 6	$36	$ 6/$36 = $\frac{1}{6}$	$42	$42 \times \frac{1}{6}$ = $ 7	$ 7 − $ 6 = $1
2	18	36	18/ 36 = $\frac{1}{2}$	42	42 $\times$ $\frac{1}{2}$ = 21	21 − 18 = 3
3	12	36	12/ 36 = $\frac{1}{3}$	42	42 $\times$ $\frac{1}{3}$ = 14	14 − 12 = 2
	$36				$42	$42 $36 $6

The percentage-of-completion method is appropriate when the company can estimate the degree of completion during the construction period, which most construction companies can do. When estimates are not possible, the completed-contract method is required. If Combustion Engineering had used the completed-contract method, its income statement for year 3 would report total project revenue of $42 million, total project expenses of $36 million, and income of $6 million. The income statements of years 1 and 2 would report nothing concerning this project. Most accountants believe the results under the percentage-of-completion method are more realistic.

Matching Principle

The **matching principle** governs the recording and reporting of expenses. This principle goes hand in hand with the revenue principle to govern income recognition in accounting. Recall that income is revenue minus expense. During any period, the company first measures its revenues by the revenue principle. The company then identifies and measures all the expenses it incurred during the period to earn the revenues. To *match* the expenses against the revenues means to subtract the expenses from the revenues. The result is the income for the period.

Some expenses are easy to match against particular revenues. For example, cost of goods sold relates directly to sales revenue, because without the sales, there would be no cost of goods sold. Commissions and fees paid for selling the goods, delivery expense, and sales supplies expense relate to sales revenue for the same reason.

Other expenses are not so easily linked to particular sales because they occur whether or not any revenues arise. Depreciation, salaries, and all types of home-office expense are in this category. Accountants usually match these expenses against revenue on a time basis. For example, the company's home-office building may be used for general management, manufacturing, and marketing. Straight-line depreciation of a 40-year building assigns one-fortieth of the building's cost to expense each year, whatever the level of revenue. The annual salary expense for an employee is the person's total salary for the year, regardless of revenue.

Losses, like expenses, are matched against revenue on a time basis. For example, if an asset like inventory loses value, the loss is recorded when it occurs, without regard for the revenues earned during the period.

Disclosure Principle

The **disclosure principle** holds that a company's financial statements should report enough information for outsiders to make knowledgeable decisions about the company. In short, the company should report *relevant, reliable,* and *comparable* information about its economic affairs. This section of the chapter discusses and illustrates different types of disclosures.

OBJECTIVE 5
Report information that satisfies the disclosure principle

Summary of Significant Accounting Policies. To evaluate a company, investors and creditors need to know how its financial statements were prepared. This consideration is especially important when the company can choose from several acceptable methods. Companies summarize their accounting policies in the first note to their financial statements. The note may include both monetary amounts and written descriptions. Companies commonly disclose revenue-recognition method, inventory method, and depreciation method.

Dresser Industries, Inc., a manufacturer of oilfield and other industrial equipment, reported the following:

NOTE A—SUMMARY OF SIGNIFICANT ACCOUNTING POLICIES [IN PART]

Long-Term Contracts

Revenues and earnings related to products requiring long-term construction periods, principally draglines and electrostatic precipitators, are recognized for financial reporting purposes on the percentage of completion basis.

Inventories

Substantially all the U.S. inventories of the Company are recorded on a last-in, first-out (LIFO) cost basis. Inventories not on LIFO cost valuation, principally foreign inventories, are recorded at the "lower of cost (principally average cost) or market."

Fixed Assets

Fixed assets are depreciated over the estimated service life. Accelerated depreciation methods are used for financial statement purposes, except for U.S. fixed assets with a service life of 10 years or less which are depreciated on a straight-line basis. Accelerated depreciation methods are also used for tax purposes wherever permitted.

Probable Losses. The disclosure principle directs a business to record and report a probable loss *before* it occurs if the loss is likely and its amount can be estimated. Bethlehem Steel Corporation reported such a loss in its 1990 financial statements. Observe that the restructuring has not occurred yet, but the company does *expect* the transaction to result in a loss.

NOTE C. ESTIMATED RESTRUCTURING LOSSES

On January 24, 1991, we signed a letter of intent with British Steel plc [Inc.] to complete a feasibility study to form an equally owned joint venture in the United States to produce and market structural and rail products. The proposed venture would restructure and combine into a single entity most of the assets of our existing structural and rail business units located in Bethlehem and Steelton, Pennsylvania and make a significant capital investment. In 1990, we recorded a $550 million restructuring charge principally in connection with this proposed modernization, restructuring and venture.

The $550 million loss appeared on Bethlehem's income statement as follows (in millions):

	1990
Net Sales	$4,899.2
Costs and Expenses:	
Cost of sales	4,327.2
Depreciation	305.7
Selling, administrative and general expense	159.6
Estimated restructuring losses—net (Note C)	550.0
Total Costs and Expenses	5,342.5
Income (Loss) From Operations	(443.3)

Accounting Changes. Consistent use of accounting methods and procedures is important, as we saw in discussing comparability. When a company does change from one accounting method or procedure to another, it must disclose the change, the reason for making the change, and the effect of the change on net income. Two common accounting changes are *changes in accounting principles* and *changes in accounting estimates*.

A **change in accounting principle** is a change in accounting method. A switch from the LIFO method to the FIFO method for inventories and a switch from the double-declining-balance depreciation method to the straight-line method are examples of accounting changes. Special rules that apply to changes in accounting principles are discussed in later accounting courses. Whatever the change in principle, the notes to the financial statements must inform the reader of the change and its effect on income.

A **change in accounting estimate** occurs in the normal course of business as the company alters earlier expectations. A company may record uncollectible account expense based on the estimate that bad debts will equal 2 percent of sales. If actual collections exceed this estimate, the company may lower its estimated expense to 1½ percent of sales in the future.

An airline company such as American or Delta may originally estimate that a new Boeing 767 airplane will provide fifteen years' service. After ten years of using the plane, the company sees that the plane's full useful life will stretch to eighteen years. The company must recompute depreciation based on this new information at the start of the plane's eleventh year of service. Assume that this plane cost $30 million, has an estimated residual value of $6 million, and is depreciated by the straight-line method.

Annual depreciation for each of the first ten years of the asset's life is $1.6 million, computed as follows:

$$\text{Depreciation per year} = \frac{\$30 \text{ million} - \$6 \text{ million}}{15 \text{ years}} = \$1.6 \text{ million}$$

Changes in estimate are accounted for by spreading the asset's remaining depreciable book value over its remaining life. Annual depreciation after the accounting change is $1 million, computed in the following manner:

$$\text{Depreciation per year} = \frac{\text{Remaining depreciable book value}}{\text{Remaining life}} = \frac{\$30 \text{ million} - \$6 \text{ million} - (\$1.6 \text{ million} \times 10)}{18 \text{ total years} - 10 \text{ years used}}$$

$$= \frac{\$8 \text{ million}}{8 \text{ years}} = \$1 \text{ million}$$

Subsequent Events. A company usually takes several weeks after the end of the year to close its books and to publish its financial statements. Occasionally, events occur during this period that affect the interpretation of the information in those financial statements. Such an occurrence is called a **subsequent event** and should be disclosed in the prior period's statements. The most common examples of subsequent events are borrowing money, paying debts, making investments, selling assets, and becoming a defendant in a lawsuit.

The Clorox Company, maker of bleach and other household products, reported the following subsequent event in its financial statements for the year ended June 30, 19X6:

NOTE 2. SUBSEQUENT EVENT—ACQUISITION

On August 1, 19X6, the Company completed its purchase of American Cyanamid Company's household products brands for $465,000,000. With this acquisition [. . .], the Company acquired the *Pine-Sol* cleaner and *Combat* insecticide brands, including a primary manufacturing facility and a small amount of working capital. An amount in excess of $400,000,000 of the purchase price will be allocated to trademarks, goodwill, and other intangibles to be amortized over the estimated useful lives which are yet to be determined.

Business Segments. Most large companies operate in more than one product line or industry. Each area is called a *business segment.* Sears, Roebuck, and Company, best known for its retail stores, also has real estate, investment banking, and other financial service operations. Union Pacific Corporation, the railroad company, is also active in the oil and gas business. Diversification like this is not limited to large international companies. A realtor may also own a restaurant. A farmer may sell farm implements. An automobile dealer may also own a furniture store.

Suppose you are considering investing in a company that is active in the steel industry but also owns a meat packer and several leisure resorts. Assume the American steel industry is in retreat because of intense foreign competition. With income and asset data broken down by business segments, you can determine how much of the company's assets are committed to each segment and which lines of business are most (and least) profitable. Companies disclose segment data in notes to their financial statements.

The Scott Paper Company data in the accompanying table meet the GAAP requirement for adequate disclosure of business segments.

Year 19X6	(Millions)	Sales	Income before Taxes	Identifiable Assets	Capital Expenditures	Depreciation and Cost of Timber Harvested
Business Segment	Personal Care and Cleaning	$2,349.5	$252.7	$2,105.4	$220.0	$124.1
	Printing and Publishing Papers	921.2	149.2	1,217.4	178.3	62.4
	Pulp, Forest Products and Minerals	166.3	17.6	188.4	16.7	11.6
	Total business segments	$3,437.0	$419.5	$3,511.2	$415.0	$198.1

Disclosure Techniques. Companies use a variety of disclosure techniques in the financial statements. An example is the allowance for uncollectibles, reported as follows by Tandem Computers Incorporated (in millions):

| | December 31, | |
	19X7	19X6
Accounts receivable, net of allowances of $13.4 in 19X7 and $11.6 in 19X6	$462.3	$399.3

Other companies, including CPC International Inc., list the allowance on a separate line of the balance sheet, as follows (in millions):

| | December 31, | |
	19X7	19X6
Notes and accounts receivable [summarized]	$855.8	$684.3
Allowances for doubtful accounts	(16.8)	(12.8)

Both disclosure techniques provide adequate information on the total amount receivable and the net amount expected to be collected.

Constraints on Accounting

Do financial statements report every detail, no matter how small, to meet the need for relevant, reliable, and comparable information? The result would be an avalanche of data. To address this problem, accountants use the *materiality concept*. Also, a company's top managers are responsible for its financial statements. To add balance to managers' optimism—which could bias the statements and present too favorable a picture of company operations—accountants follow the *conservatism concept*. This section discusses these constraints on accounting information.

Materiality Concept

The **materiality concept** states that a company must perform strictly proper accounting only for items and transactions that are significant to the business's financial statements. Information is significant—accountants call it *material*—when its inclusion and correct presentation in the financial statement would cause a statement user to change a decision because of that information. Immaterial—insignificant—items justify less than perfect accounting. The inclusion and proper presentation of *immaterial* items would not affect a statement user's decision. The materiality concept frees accountants from having to compute and report every last item in strict accordance with GAAP. Thus the materiality concept reduces the cost of accounting.

OBJECTIVE 6
Apply two constraints to accounting

How does a business decide where to draw the line between what is material and what is immaterial? This decision rests to a great degree on how large the business is. The Coca-Cola Company, for example, has over $4 billion in assets. Management would likely treat as immaterial a $100 purchase of wastebaskets. These wastebaskets may well remain useful for ten years, and strictly speaking, Coca-Cola should capitalize their cost and depreciate the wastebaskets. However, this treatment is not practical. The accounting costs of computing, recording, and properly reporting this asset outweighs the benefits of any information provided. No statement user—a potential investor or lender, for example—would change a decision based on so insignificant (immaterial) an amount. The cost of accounting in this case outweighs the benefit of the resulting information.

Large companies may draw the materiality line at as high a figure as $10,000 and expense any smaller amount. Smaller firms may choose to expense only those items less than $50. Materiality varies from company to company. An amount that is material to the local service station may not be material to General Motors.

The materiality concept does not free a business from having to account for every item. Coca-Cola, for example, must still account for the wastebaskets. Coca-Cola would credit Cash (or Accounts Payable) to record their purchase, of course, but what account would the company debit? Because the amount is immaterial, management may decide to debit Supplies Expense. No matter what account receives the debit, no statement user's decision would be changed by the information.

Conservatism Concept

Business managers are often optimists. Asked how well the company is doing, its president will likely answer, "Great, we're having our best year ever." Without constraints this optimism could find its way into the company's reported assets and profits. Managers may try to present too favorable a view of the company. For example, they may pressure accountants to capitalize costs associated with fixed assets that should be expensed. This would result in less immediate expense and higher current income on the income statement. The balance sheet would report unduly high fixed asset values and owner's equity. The overall result would be that the managers' performance would appear to be better than it actually was. Traditionally, accountants have been conservative, to counter management's optimism.

Conservatism has been interpreted as "Anticipate no profits, but anticipate all losses." A clear-cut example is the lower-of-cost-or-market (LCM) method for inventories. Under LCM, inventory is reported at the *lower* of its cost or market value, which results in higher cost of goods sold and lower net income. Thus profits and assets are reported at their lowest reasonable amount. Other conservative accounting practices include the LIFO method for inventories when inventory costs are increasing, accelerated depreciation, and the completed-contract method for construction revenues. These methods result in earlier recording of expenses or later recording of revenues. Both effects postpone the reporting of net income and therefore are conservative.

In recent years, conservatism's effect on accounting has decreased. The FASB has stated that conservatism should not mean deliberate understatement of assets, profits, and owner's equity. However, if two different values can be used for an asset or a liability, the concept suggests using the less optimistic value. Conservatism is a secondary consideration in accounting. Relevant, reliable, and comparable information is the goal, and conservatism is a factor only after these primary goals are met.

Financial Statements and Their Elements

We have examined the concepts and principles that shape accounting practice. The FASB aims for financial statements that best meet user needs for business information.

This accounting information appears in four statements: the balance sheet, the income statement, the statement of owner's equity, and the statement of cash flows (which we cover in Chapter 15). The FASB provides definitions for the elements that make up these statements. Financial information presentation, to be most useful to the greatest number of statements users, must be presented in a standard format with well-defined terms, as we learned in our discussion of the comparability concept.

FASB Concepts Statement No. 3 provides authoritative definitions of the elements of financial statements.[1]

Balance Sheet Elements

Assets are future economic benefits obtained or controlled by a particular entity as a result of past transactions.

Liabilities are the obligations of an entity to transfer assets or provide services to other entities as a result of past transactions.

Equity (Owner's Equity) is the interest in the assets of an entity that remains after subtracting its liabilities. It is the ownership interest in the entity.

Income Statement Elements

Revenues are inflows of assets that arise from delivering or producing goods, rendering services, or performing other activities that constitute the entity's ongoing central operations.

Expenses are outflows of assets or the incurrences of liabilities that arise from delivering or producing goods, rendering services, or carrying out activities that constitute the entity's ongoing central operations.

Gains are increases in owner's equity that do not result from revenues or investments by owners.

Losses are decreases in owner's equity that do not result from expenses or distributions to owners.

Note that *revenues* and *expenses* arise from the business's ongoing central operations, but *gains* and *losses* do not. Sales and interest earned are revenues because most companies make sales and earn interest as part of their central operations. Selling cars and trucks lies at the heart of an automobile dealership. To this business, a gain on the sale of a truck is revenue, and a loss on the sale is expense. However, a gain on the sale of a truck is not revenue for a trucking company because that entity buys trucks for use rather than for sale. Selling a truck is not a part of central operations. Exhibit B-4 shows how to report revenues, expenses, gains, and losses on a multiple-step and a single-step income statement.

---

[1]The definitions here are paraphrased from *FASB Concepts Statement No. 3*, "Elements of Financial Statements of Business Enterprises" (Stamford, CT: December 1980), Highlights.

EXHIBIT B-4   *Reporting Revenues, Expenses, Gains, and Losses*

Multiple-Step Income Statement		Single-Step Income Statement		
Sales revenue	$XXX	Revenues and gains:		
Cost of goods sold............	XXX	Sales revenue		$XXX
Gross profit................	XXX	Gain on sale of land		XXX
Operating expenses...........	XXX	Total revenues and gains...		XXX
Income from operations	XXX	Expenses and losses:		
Other items:		Cost of goods sold..........	$XXX	
Gain on sale of land .... $XXX		Operating expenses..........	XXX	
Loss due to fire XXX	XXX	Loss due to fire	XXX	
		Total expenses and losses ..		XXX
Net income	$XXX	Net income		$XXX

Statement of Owner's Equity Elements

Investments by owners are increases in owner's equity that result from the owner's transferring to the entity something of value. The most common investment is cash, but owners sometimes invest land, buildings, legal services, or other assets. In some cases, an owner's investment in the business may consist of paying off its liabilities. **Distributions to owners** are decreases in owner's equity that result from the owner's transferring assets or services from the business to himself or herself, or from the business taking on the owner's liabilities. When the business is a corporation, owner withdrawals are called dividends. The most commonly distributed asset is cash, but businesses sometimes distribute other assets, such as stock investments they hold in other companies, to their owners.

Accounting Standards Throughout the World

We have focused on the principles of accounting that are generally accepted in the United States. Most of the methods of accounting are consistent throughout the world. Double-entry bookkeeping, the accrual accounting system, and the basic financial statements are used worldwide. Differences, however, do exist among countries.

In discussing depreciation—Chapter 8—we emphasized that in the United States the methods used for reporting to tax authorities differ from the methods used for reporting to shareholders. In contrast, tax reporting and shareholder reporting are identical in many countries. For example, France has a "Plan Compatible" that specifies a National Uniform Chart of Accounts used for both tax returns and reporting to shareholders. German financial reporting is also determined primarily by tax laws. If accounting records are not kept according to strict tax laws, the tax authorities can reject the records as a basis for taxation.

In some countries, tax laws have a major influence on shareholder reporting even if tax and shareholder reports are not required to be identical. In Japan, for example, certain principles are allowed for tax purposes only if they are also used for shareholder reporting.

A significant difference among countries is the extent to which financial statements account for inflation. In the 1980s, the FASB experimented with requiring supplementary disclosure of inflation-adjusted numbers, but there is no requirement for such supplementary disclosure in the United States. In contrast, some countries have full or partial adjustments for inflation as part of their reporting to both investors and tax authorities. For example, Argentina and Brazil, which have experienced very high inflation rates, require all statements to be adjusted for changes in the general price level.

The globalization of business enterprises and capital markets is creating much interest in establishing common, worldwide accounting standards. There are probably too many cultural, social, and political differences to expect complete worldwide standardization of financial reporting in the near future. However, the number of differences is decreasing. Cooperation among accountants has been fostered by the International Federation of Accountants (IFAC), an organization of accountancy bodies from more than seventy-five countries. International standards are being formulated and published by the International Accounting Standards Committee (IASC).

Summary Problem for Your Review

This appendix has discussed the following principles and concepts:

Entity concept
Going-concern concept
Time-period concept
Reliability principle
Comparability principle

Cost principle
Revenue principle
Matching principle
Disclosure principle
Materiality concept

Indicate which of these concepts is being violated in each of the following situations:

1. A construction company signs a two-year contract to build a bridge for the state of Montana. The president of the company immediately records the full contract price as revenue.

2. Competition has taken away much of the business of a small airline. The airline is unwilling to report its plans to sell half its fleet of planes.

3. After starting the business in February 19X2, a coal-mining company keeps no accounting records for 19X2, 19X3, and 19X4. The owner is waiting until the mine is exhausted to determine the success or failure of the business.

4. Assets recorded at cost by a drug store chain are written up to their fair market value at the end of each year.

5. The accountant for a manufacturing company keeps detailed depreciation records on every asset no matter how small its value.

6. A physician mixes her personal accounting records with those of the medical practice.

7. Expenses are reported whenever the bookkeeper records them rather than when related revenues are earned.

8. The damaged inventory of a discount store is being written down. The store manager bases the write-down entry on his own subjective opinion in order to minimize income taxes.

9. A quick-copy center changes accounting methods every year in order to report the maximum amount of net income possible under generally accepted accounting principles.

10. The owners of a private hospital base its accounting records on the assumption that the hospital might have to close at any time. The hospital has a long record of service to the community.

SOLUTION TO REVIEW PROBLEM

1. Revenue principle
2. Disclosure principle
3. Time-period concept
4. Cost principle
5. Materiality concept
6. Entity concept
7. Matching principle
8. Reliability principle
9. Comparability principle
10. Going-concern concept

Summary

The Financial Accounting Standards Board (FASB) formulates generally accepted accounting principles (GAAP) to provide relevant, reliable, and comparable accounting information. *Relevant* information allows users to make business predictions and to evaluate past decisions. *Reliable* data are free from material error and bias. Accounting information is also intended to be *comparable* from company to company and from period to period.

Four concepts underlie accounting. The most basic, the *entity concept,* draws clear boundaries around the accounting entity. The entity, based on the *going-concern concept,* is assumed to remain in business for the foreseeable future. The *time-period concept* is the basis for reporting accounting information for particular time periods such as months, quarters, and years. Under the *stable-monetary-unit concept,* no adjustment is made for the changing value of the dollar.

Accounting principles provide detailed guidelines for recording transactions and preparing the financial statements. The *reliability* and *comparability principles* require that accounting information be based on objective data and be useful for comparing companies across different time periods. The *cost principle* governs accounting for assets and liabilities, and the *revenue principle* governs accounting for revenues. *Matching* is the basis for recording expenses. The *disclosure* principle requires companies to report their accounting policies, probable future losses, accounting changes, subsequent events, and business-segment data. They use different disclosure techniques.

Two constraints on accounting are materiality and conservatism. The *materiality concept* allows companies to avoid excessive cost in accounting for immaterial items. *Conservatism* constrains the optimism of managers by anticipating no profits, but anticipating all losses.

Financial statements and their elements include:
Balance sheet: assets, liabilities, and *equity (owner's equity)*
Income statement: revenues, expenses, gains, and *losses*
Statement of owner's equity: investments by owners and *distributions to owners.*

Accounting Vocabulary

Change in accounting estimate. A change that occurs in the normal course of business as a company alters earlier expectations *(p. B-13).*

Change in accounting principle. A change in accounting method, such as from the LIFO method to the FIFO method for inventories and a switch from an accelerated depreciation method to the straight-line method *(p. B-13).*

Collection method. Method of applying the revenue principle by which the seller waits until cash is received to record the sale. This method is used only if the receipt of cash is uncertain *(p. B-9).*

Comparability principle. Specifies that accounting information must be comparable from business to business and that a single business's financial statements must be comparable from one period to the next *(p. B-7).*

Completed-contract method. Method of applying the revenue principle by a construction company by which all revenue earned on the project is recorded in the period when the project is completed *(p. B-11).*

Cost principle. States that assets and services are recorded at their purchase cost and that the accounting record of the asset continues to be based on cost rather than current market value *(p. B-8).*

Disclosure principle. Holds that a company's financial statements should report enough information for outsiders to make knowledgeable decisions about the company *(p. B-12).*

Gain. An increase in owner equity that does not result from a revenue or an investment by an owner in the business (p. B-17).

Going-concern concept. Accountants' assumption that the business will continue operating in the foreseeable future (p. B-5).

Installment method. Method of applying the revenue principle in which gross profit (sales revenue minus cost of goods sold) is recorded as cash is collected (p. B-9).

Loss. A decrease in owner equity that does not result from an expense or a distribution to an owner of the business (p. B-17).

Materiality concept. States that a company must perform strictly proper accounting only for items and transactions that are significant to the business's financial statements (p. B-15).

Percentage-of-completion method. Method of applying the revenue principle by a construction company, by which revenue is recorded as the work is performed (p. B-11).

Reliability principle. Requires that accounting information be dependable (free from error and bias). Also called the Objectivity principle (p. B-7).

Sales method. Method of applying the revenue principle in which revenue is recorded at the point of sale. This method is used for most sales of goods and services (p. B-9).

Stable-monetary-unit concept. Accountants' basis for ignoring the effect of inflation and making no adjustments for the changing value of the dollar (p. B-6).

Subsequent event. An event that occurs after the end of a company's accounting period but before publication of its financial statements and which may affect the interpretation of the information in those statements (p. B-14).

Time-period concept. Ensures that accounting information is reported at regular intervals (p. B-6).

ASSIGNMENT MATERIAL

Exercises

Exercise B-1 *Identifying the objective of financial reporting* **(L.O. 1)**

As a financial analyst with Merrill Lynch, your job is to follow the aerospace industry. Specifically, you compare companies in this industry to recommend to Merrill Lynch clients which companies to invest in. What is the basic objective of financial reporting? Briefly discuss some of the predictions and related evaluations of past performance that an investment analyst would make. Also state why the analyst feels more comfortable using information that has been audited by an independent CPA.

Exercise B-2 *Applying accounting concepts* **(L.O. 2)**

The Merrimac Insider is a magazine devoted to cultural affairs in the Tidewater region of Virginia, North Carolina, and South Carolina. Its owner, Marla Griffis, is better attuned to cultural affairs than to the business aspects of running a magazine. Readership is at an all-time high, but the financial position of the business has suffered. For each of the following items indicate the accounting action needed at December 31, the end of the accounting year. Also identify the underlying accounting concept most directly applicable to your answer.

a. On March 31, *The Merrimac Insider* had to borrow $200,000 to pay bills. The interest rate of this one-year loan is 11 percent, payable March 31.

b. Ms. Griffis intermingles her personal assets with those of the business. In applying for the $200,000 loan, she wanted to include on the company books her Lincoln automobile, which was worth $24,000. Her reasoning was that the business is a proprietorship and that her personal assets are available to the magazine if needed.

c. Its financial position is so dismal that *The Merrimac Insider* is in danger of failure. Assets measured at historical cost total $1.3 million, but their current market value is only $900,000, which barely exceeds liabilities of $850,000. For now it appears that the magazine will remain in business.

Exercise B-3 *Reporting assets as a going concern and as a liquidating entity (L.O. 2, 3)*

Ferris-Browning Company has the following assets:

Cash, $9,000

Accounts receivable, $25,600; allowance for uncollectible accounts, $4,300

Office supplies, cost $280; scrap value $70

Office machinery, cost $72,000; accumulated depreciation, $14,000; current sales value, $47,400

Land, cost $85,000; current sales value, $135,000

Required

1. Assume Ferris-Browning continues as a going concern. Compute the amount of its assets for reporting on the balance sheet.
2. Assume Ferris-Browning is going out of business by liquidating its assets. Compute the amount of its assets at liquidation value.

Exercise B-4 *Reporting assets under GAAP (L.O. 3)*

Identify the amount at which each of the following assets should be reported in the financial statements of Charter Corporation. Cite the concept, principle, or constraint that is most applicable to each answer.

a. Charter purchased a machine for $25,000 less a $1,300 cash discount. To ship the machine to the office, Charter paid transportation charges of $500 and insurance of $200 while in transit. After using the machine for one month, Charter purchases lubricating oil costing $150 for use in operating the machine.
b. Inventory has a cost of $72,000, but its current market value is $69,400.
c. Charter purchased land for $175,000 and paid $2,500 to have the land surveyed, $15,400 to have old buildings removed, and $40,300 for grading land. Charter is offering the land for sale at $225,000 and has received a $200,000 offer.

Exercise B-5 *Reporting income under GAAP (L.O. 3)*

Mayfair Building Materials Company failed to record the following items at December 31, 19X4, the end of its fiscal year:

Accrued salary expense, $1,300

Prepaid insurance, $700

Accrued interest expense, $600

Depreciation expense, $500

Instead of recording the accrued expenses at December 31, 19X4, Mayfair recorded the expenses when it paid them in 19X5. The company recorded the insurance as expense when it was prepaid for one year, late in 19X4. Depreciation expense for 19X5 was correctly recorded.

Mayfair incorrectly reported net income of $10,000 in 19X4 and $7,400 in 19X5 because of the above errors.

Required

Compute Mayfair's correct net income for 19X4 and 19X5. Compare the trend in net income, as corrected, with the reported trend.

Exercise B-6 *Reporting revenues under GAAP* **(L.O. 4)**

For each of the following situations, indicate the amount of revenue to report for the current year ended December 31 and for the following year:

a. Sold merchandise for $4,400, receiving a down payment of $1,100 and the customer's receivable for the balance. The company accounts for these sales by the sales method.

b. On April 1 loaned $35,000 at 12 percent on a three-year note.

c. Performed $900 of services for a high-risk customer on August 18, accounting for the revenue by the collection method. At December 31 the company had received $200 of the total; $550 was received the following year.

d. On September 1 collected one year's rent of $12,000 in advance on a building leased to another company.

e. Sold gift certificates, collecting $4,000 in advance. At December 31, $2,200 of the gifts have been claimed. The remainder were claimed during the next year.

Exercise B-7 *Computing gross profit under the sales method and the installment method* **(L.O. 4)**

Hometown Pawn Shop sells on the installment plan. The store's installment sales figures for 19X7 follow.

Sales	$390,000
Down payments received on the sales	80,000
Collections on installments	170,000
Inventory at beginning of 19X7.......	60,000
Inventory at end of 19X7	42,000
Purchases	216,000

Required

Compute the store's gross profit if it uses (a) the sales method of revenue recognition and (b) the installment method.

Exercise B-8 *Computing construction revenue under the completed-contract method and the percentage-of-completion method* **(L.O. 4)**

Ecclesia Construction Company builds bridges for the state of Florida. The construction period typically extends for several years. During 19X5 Ecclesia completed a small bridge with a contract price of $500,000. Ecclesia's $320,000 cost of the bridge was incurred as follows: $20,000 in 19X3, $180,000 in 19X4, and $120,000 in 19X5. Compute Ecclesia's revenue for each year 19X3 through 19X5 if the company uses (a) the completed-contract method and (b) the percentage-of-completion method. Which method better matches expense with revenue?

Exercise B-9   *Changing the useful life of a depreciable asset*   *(L.O. 5)*

Ecclesia Construction Company uses a crane on its construction projects. The company purchased the crane early in January 19X3 for $400,000. For 19X3 and 19X4 depreciation was taken by the straight-line method based on an eight-year life and an estimated residual value of $80,000. In early 19X5 it became evident that the crane would be useful beyond the original life of eight years. Therefore, beginning in 19X5, Ecclesia changed the depreciable life of the crane to a total life of ten years. The company retained the straight-line method and did not alter the residual value.

Required

Prepare Ecclesia's depreciation entries for 19X4 and 19X5. Identify the accounting principles most important in this situation.

Exercise B-10   *Identifying subsequent events for the financial statements*   *(L.O. 5)*

Bavarian Merchants experienced the following events after May 31, 19X8, the end of the company's fiscal year, but before publication of its financial statements on July 12:

a. Increased demand for Bavarian products suggests that the next fiscal year will be the best in the company's history.
b. On July 6 Bavarian is sued for $3 million. Loss of the lawsuit could lead to Bavarian's bankruptcy.
c. Bavarian collected $126,000 of the $480,000 accounts receivable reported on the May 31 balance sheet. Bavarian expects to collect the remainder in the course of business during the next fiscal year.
d. A major customer, who owed Bavarian $220,000 at May 31, declared bankruptcy on June 21.
e. Bavarian sales personnel received a contract to supply Bronson Company with laser equipment.

Required

Identify the subsequent events that Bavarian should disclose in its May 31, 19X8, financial statements.

Exercise B-11   *Using accounting concepts and principles*   *(L.O. 2, 6)*

Identify the accounting concept or principle, if any, that is violated in each of the following situations. You may choose among *disclosure, conservatism, cost, entity,* and *matching.*

a. The inventory of a clothing store has a current market value of $62,000. The store reports the inventory at its cost of $106,000.
b. The owner of a court reporting service used the business bank account to pay her family's household expenses, making no note that the expenses were personal.
c. A manufacturing company changed from the FIFO inventory method to the LIFO method and failed to report the accounting change in the financial statements.
d. A paper company that purchased 1,000 acres of timberland at $300 per acre in 1973 reports the land at its current market value of $3,000 per acre.
e. A railroad records depreciation during years when net income is high but fails to record depreciation when net income is low. Revenues are relatively constant.

Exercise B-12 *Using accounting concepts and principles* **(L.O. 2, 6)**

Indicate the accounting concept or principle that applies to the following situations. Choose among *comparability, materiality, reliability, revenue,* and *time period*.

a. Bert's Barbecue was recently sued for $200,000, but the plaintiff has indicated a willingness to settle for less than that amount. Bert's hopes to settle for $50,000, but its attorneys believe the settlement will be between $90,000 and $100,000. Bert's auditor reports the settlement as a real liability on the balance sheet. The only remaining issue is whether to report the liability at $50,000 or at $95,000.

b. Southern Kraft Company is considering publishing quarterly financial statements to provide more current information about its affairs.

c. POA, Inc., is negotiating the sale of $500,000 of inventory. POA has been in financial difficulty and desperately needs to report this sale on its income statement of the current year. At December 31, the end of the company's accounting year, the sale has not been closed.

d. New Wave Distributors expenses the cost of plant assets that cost less than $300.

e. Although Bracken Company could increase its reported income by changing depreciation methods, Bracken management has decided not to make the change.

Problems

Problem B-1 *Disclosing a change in accounting method* **(L.O. 1, 5)**

Your company's board of directors is debating a change from the FIFO inventory method to the LIFO method. The main points of contention are the effects of the accounting change on net income and cash flow. Two members of the board favor keeping the FIFO method because of its effect on net income during periods of rising prices. Recently, however, prices have risen so fast that other members of the board think the company is wasting money by paying too high taxes. These board members are willing to have the company report lower income in order to save precious cash. All members of the board agree that if the company changes inventory methods, it would be best *not* to disclose the change in the annual report.

Required

Assume the board of directors has decided to change accounting methods. Draft a memorandum to convince the board members of the need to disclose the relevant aspects of the accounting change. Explain to the board in your memorandum the basic objective of financial reporting. Also draft the disclosure note to report the accounting change in the financial statements, using your own made-up figures to disclose relevant information about the change. Discuss how the information in your proposed disclosure note meets the objective of financial reporting. Refer to two accounting principles directly applicable to this situation.

Problem B-2 *Identifying the basis for good accounting practices* **(L.O. 2, 3, 6)**

The following accounting practices are in accord with generally accepted accounting principles. Identify all the accounting concepts and principles that form the basis for each accounting practice. More than one concept or principle may apply.

a. A theater company accrues employee salaries at year end even though the salaries will be paid during the first few days of the new year.

b. Assets are reported at liquidation value on the financial statements of a company that is going out of business.

c. The cost of machinery is being depreciated over a 5-year life because independent engineers believe the machinery will become obsolete after that time. (The company had hoped to depreciate the machinery over 10 years to report lower depreciation and higher net income in the early years of the asset's life.)

d. A manufacturing firm built some specialized equipment for its own use. The equipment would have cost $110,000 if purchased from an outside company, but the cost of constructing the equipment was only $89,000. The firm recorded the equipment at cost of $89,000.

e. Depreciation of the home-office building is difficult to relate to particular sales. Therefore, the company records depreciation expense on a time basis.

f. A company wishes to change its method of accounting for revenue. However, the company does not switch because it wants to use the same accounting method that other companies in the industry use.

g. Because it is often difficult to collect installment receivables, a realtor uses the installment method of revenue recognition rather than the sales method.

h. The cost of office equipment such as staplers and wastebaskets is not capitalized and depreciated because of their relative insignificance.

i. A fire destroyed the company garage after December 31, 19X7, and before the financial statements were published in early February 19X8. Although the fire loss is insured, reconstruction of the garage will disrupt the company's operations. This subsequent event will be reported in the 19X7 financial statements.

j. A paint company accounts for its operations by dividing the business into four separate units. This division enables the company to evaluate each unit apart from the others.

Problem B-3   *Identifying the concepts and principles violated by bad accounting practices*   (L.O. 2, 3, 6)

The following accounting practices are *not* in accord with generally accepted accounting principles. A few of the practices violate more than one concept or principle. Identify all the accounting concepts and principles not followed in each situation.

a. All amounts on the balance sheet and income statement of Cleveland Consulting Company have been adjusted for changes in the value of the dollar during the period.

b. Waterloo Wheat Processor records one-half of the depreciation of its grain silos when it purchases them and the other half over their estimated useful lives.

c. Linda's Threads sells high-fashion clothing to customers on credit. Thus far, collection losses on receivables have been very small. Nevertheless, Linda Vela, the owner, uses the collection method to recognize revenue. The entity's revenue is understated because credit sales are not accounted for properly.

d. Canton Importers changed from the FIFO method to the LIFO method for inventory but did not report the accounting change in the financial statements.

e. Quebec Fisheries, Inc., applied the lower-of-cost-or-market method to account for its inventory. Quebec used an estimate of the inventory value developed by its management. This estimate differed widely from estimates supplied by two independent appraisers. The estimates of the two appraisers were close together.

f. Butler Manufacturing does not report a lawsuit in which it is the defendant. Alvin Butler, the president, argues that the outcome of the case is uncertain and that to report the lawsuit would introduce subjective data into the financial statements.

g. Todd Department Store records cost of goods sold in a predetermined amount each month regardless of the level of sales.

h. Tim Ihnacek is having difficulty evaluating the success of his advertising firm because he fails to separate business assets from personal assets.

i. Tapes Unlimited is continuing in business, but its owner accounts for assets as though the store were liquidating.

j. Major Construction Company recognizes all revenue on long-term construction projects at the start of construction.

Problem B-4 Using the installment-revenue method (L.O. 4)

Indianapolis Realty Company makes all sales on the installment basis but uses the sales method to record revenue. The company's income statements for the most recent three years are as follows:

	Year 1	Year 2	Year 3
Sales	$380,000	$404,000	$370,000
Cost of goods sold	190,000	181,800	199,800
Gross profit	190,000	222,200	170,200
Operating expenses	110,600	130,700	125,100
Net income (net loss)	$ 79,400	$ 91,500	$ 45,100
Collections from sales of year 1	$140,000	$151,000	$ 72,000
Collections from sales of year 2		143,000	209,000
Collections from sales of year 3			163,000

Required

Compute the amount of net income Indianapolis would have reported if the company had used the installment method for revenue. Ignore the effect of uncollectible accounts and present your answer in the following format:

Installment-method net income:	Year 1	Year 2	Year 3
Gross profit	$	$	$
Operating expenses	110,600	130,700	125,100
Net income	$	$	$

Problem B-5 Using the installment-revenue method (L.O. 4)

Harbor Springs Land Company sells land on the installment plan. Collections of installment receivables have deteriorated. The company's accountants are considering the different methods of recording revenues. Revenue, expense, and collection data for the current year are as follows:

	19X3
Installment sales	$2,400,000
Cost of land sold	1,320,000
Collections of installment receivables from sales of 19X2	760,000
19X3	520,000

The gross profit percentage on 19X2 installment sales was 46 percent.

Required

1. Which method should be used to account for revenues if collections are extremely doubtful? If collections are reasonably assured? Which method is more advantageous for income tax purposes? Why?

2. Compute gross profit for 19X3 under the sales method, the collection method, and the installment method.

Problem B-6 *Accounting for construction income (L.O. 4)*

Brooklyn Bridge Company constructs bridges under long-term contracts. During 19X5, Brooklyn began three projects that progressed according to the following schedule during 19X5, 19X6, and 19X7:

| | | | 19X5 | | 19X6 | | 19X7 | |
| | | Total | | | | | | |
Project	Contract Price	Project Cost	Cost for Year	% Completed During Year	Cost for Year	% Completed During Year	Cost for Year	% Completed During Year
1	$2,400,000	$1,800,000	$1,800,000	100%	—	—	—	—
2	3,100,000	2,200,000	484,000	22	$1,716,000	78%	—	—
3	1,900,000	1,400,000	280,000	20	840,000	60	$280,000	20%

Required

1. Assume Brooklyn uses the completed-contract method for construction revenue. Compute the company's construction revenue and income to be reported in 19X5, 19X6, and 19X7.
2. Compute Brooklyn's construction revenue and income to be reported in the three years if the company uses the percentage-of-completion method.

Problem B-7 *Accounting for revenues and expenses according to GAAP*
(L.O. 2, 3, 4)

Kate Krupp established Krupp Home Furnishings in January 19X7. During 19X7, 19X8, and most of 19X9 Krupp kept the company's books and prepared its financial statements, although she had no training or experience in accounting. As a result, the accounts and statements contain numerous errors. For example, Krupp recorded only cash receipts from customers as revenue. The sales method is appropriate for the business. She recorded inventory purchases as the cost of goods sold. When the current market value of her company's equipment increased by $6,200 in 19X7 and by $1,700 in 19X9, Krupp debited the Equipment account and credited Revenue. She recorded no depreciation during 19X7, 19X8, and 19X9.

Late in 19X9 Krupp employed an accountant, who determined that depreciable assets of the firm cost $150,000 on June 30, 19X7, had an expected residual value of $10,000, and a total useful life of eight years. The accountant believes the straight-line depreciation method is appropriate for Krupp's plant assets. The company's fiscal year ends December 31. At the end of 19X9 the company's records reveal the amounts in the accompanying table.

Required

Apply the concepts and principles of GAAP to compute the correct net income of Krupp Home Furnishings for 19X7, 19X8, and 19X9.

	19X7	19X8	19X9
Reported net income (net loss)	$ 24,300	$ (6,200)	$ 62,900
Sales	131,800	164,700	226,100
Cash collections from customers	106,500	151,300	239,600
Purchases of inventory	100,600	136,000	191,700
Ending inventory	20,800	47,400	83,700
Accrued expenses not recorded at year end; these expenses were recorded during the next year, when paid	3,800	2,700	6,800
Depreciation expense recorded	-0-	-0-	-0-
Revenue recorded for increase in the value of equipment	6,200		1,700

Appendix C

Published Financial Statements

Appendix C

Published Financial Statements

Results of Operations

Consolidated

Sales for 1991 were $10.9 billion, which represents a 3.2 percent decline from 1990 but exceeds 1989 levels. During 1991, the Company's traditional markets were impacted by the worldwide weakness in the automotive sector and this, coupled with competitive pricing in certain tire markets, was the main cause of the decline in net sales versus 1990. Results in 1990 were favorably impacted by the currency translation of non-U.S. sales.

Net income in 1991 of $96.6 million, or $1.61 per share, reflects a significant turnaround when compared to the net loss of $38.3 million, or $.66 per share, for 1990. Net income in 1989 was $206.8 million, or $3.58 per share.

Cost of goods sold for 1991 of $8.4 billion decreased 4.5 percent from 1990 but increased 2.1 percent from 1989. Raw material prices in 1991 were the main positive impact compared to 1990 and 1989 cost of sales, but the impact was lessened somewhat by the continued inflation in compensation and benefit costs. Research and development expenditures in cost of sales were $330.0 million, $331.3 million and $303.3 million in 1991, 1990 and 1989, respectively, while expenditures for 1992 are expected to decrease from 1991's level. Charges for environmental cleanup projects totaled $31.5 million in 1991, substantially all of which were included in cost of sales. This compared to charges for environmental cleanup projects of $16 million in 1990 and $7 million in 1989. At December 31, 1991, the Company had reserved $62.2 million ($38.1 million at December 31, 1990) for environmental cleanup costs.

Selling, administrative and general expense for 1991 of $1.9 billion decreased 4.4 percent from 1990 but increased 2.6 percent from 1989. The decrease in 1991 was mainly due to ongoing cost containment measures.

The Company has a goal of reducing overall costs by $350 million over the next three years.

Interest expense for 1991 of $317.8 million decreased 3.1 percent from 1990 but increased 24.5 percent from 1989. Interest expense is expected to decrease again in 1992 due to anticipated lower debt levels. The increase from 1989 was due primarily to the recognition of interest associated with the All American Pipeline System, which had been capitalized until October 1, 1989. Recognition of such interest during all of 1989 would have increased 1989 interest expense by $100.1 million.

Restructuring charges of $17.6 million, $81.4 million, and $109.7 million were incurred in 1991, 1990 and 1989, respectively, and resulted from cost containment programs, realignments of operations, plant closures and sales of facilities. For further discussion, refer to the note to the financial statements No. 2, Restructuring.

Other income and expense primarily included interest income on deposits and miscellaneous expenses. Interest income on deposits (primarily in Latin America) has declined since 1989 due to lower investment levels and lower interest rates on deposits, although related foreign currency exchange expenses also decreased. The major miscellaneous expenses are fees associated with the Company's accounts receivable continuous sale program. In 1990, other income and expense also included a charge of $22.2 million for environmental cleanup costs associated with operations discontinued in 1986. For further discussion, refer to the notes to the financial statements No. 3, Other (Income) and Expense and No. 5, Accounts and Notes Receivable.

The Company's 1991 effective tax rate, while lower than 1990, remained higher than 1989 due to an inefficient mix of foreign taxes and U.S. taxes on foreign earnings. Further improvement is expected in 1992. The tax benefit of foreign loss carryovers, recorded as an extraordinary item, increased earnings by $22.1 million or $.37 per share in 1991 and $17.4 million or $.30 per share in 1989. For further discussion, refer to the note to the financial statements No. 15, Income Taxes.

The Company expects Statement of Financial Accounting Standards No. 96, "Accounting for Income Taxes", to be superseded by a new Statement in 1992. While not in its final form, the Company does not expect the new Statement to have a material impact on future financial statements.

Statement of Financial Accounting Standards No. 106, "Employers' Accounting for Postretirement Benefits Other Than Pensions," (SFAS No. 106) is effective for fiscal years beginning after December 15, 1992. SFAS No. 106 will require accrual of postretirement benefits during the years an associate provides services. The Company intends to take a one-time charge for the transition obligation when it adopts the standard in 1993 or earlier. Preliminary estimates of the amount of transition obligation range from as much as $1.8 billion to as low as $1.5 billion ($1.2 billion and $1.0 billion after tax, respectively). The annual charge to income will not materially differ after SFAS No. 106 has been adopted and the one-time charge recorded by the Company, and no material cash impact is anticipated.

Industry Segments

Operating income was $783.3 million, $604.6 million and $926.3 million in 1991, 1990 and 1989, respectively, and was reduced by restructuring charges of $8.1 million, $81.4 million and $109.7 million in those same years. For further discussion, refer to the notes to the financial statements No. 2, Restructuring and No. 16, Business Segments.

Tires and Related

Sales for 1991 of $9.0 billion decreased 2.8 percent from 1990 but rose 1.2 percent from 1989. Continued weakness in the worldwide automotive sector resulted in slightly lower unit sales (see table right). Competitive pricing in certain markets and adverse economic conditions in Brazil also impacted sales in 1991.

Tires and Related Sales
(Dollars in Billions)

$9.0 $9.3 $8.9
91   90   89

Tires and Related Operating Income
(Dollars in Millions)

$621 $723
      $463
91   90   89

Increase (Decrease) in Tire Unit Sales for the Year

	1991 vs 1990	1991 vs 1989
U.S.	(2.4)%	(.7)%
Foreign	1.5 %	3.9 %
Worldwide	(.5)%	1.4 %

In spite of slow growth in U.S. and European automobile production, continued over-capacity in the tire industry and a soft replacement market, sales are expected to improve in 1992 on the basis of recent price increases and new product introductions.

Operating income for 1991 of $620.8 million increased 34.0 percent from $463.4 million in 1990 but decreased 14.1 percent from $722.6 million in 1989. Operating income increased in 1991 on lower raw material costs and lower selling, administrative and general expenses due mainly to ongoing cost containment measures. Operating income was also favorably affected by the resumption of normal operations in Turkey after a prolonged strike at the Company's tire plants there in 1990. Competitive pricing in the North American and European tire markets, which continued from 1990, partially offset these improvements.

The Goodyear Tire & Rubber Company and Subsidiaries

(Dollars in millions, except per share) Year Ended December 31,	1991	1990	1989
Net Sales	$10,906.8	$11,272.5	$10,869.3
Cost of Goods Sold	8,405.3	8,805.1	8,234.7
Selling, Administrative and General Expense	1,911.7	1,999.6	1,863.7
Interest Expense (Note 14)	317.8	328.2	255.3
Restructuring (Note 2)	17.6	81.4	109.7
Other (Income) and Expense (Note 3)	(83.2)	(83.9)	(171.5)
Foreign Currency Exchange	47.4	72.1	87.9
Minority Interest in Net Income of Subsidiaries	19.5	14.1	18.6
Income before Income Taxes and Extraordinary Item	270.7	55.9	470.9
United States and Foreign Taxes on Income (Note 15)	196.2	94.2	281.5
Income (loss) before Extraordinary Item	74.5	(38.3)	189.4
Extraordinary Item—Tax Benefit of Loss Carryovers	22.1	—	17.4
Net Income (loss)	$ 96.6	$ (38.3)	$ 206.8
Per Share of Common Stock:			
Income (loss) before extraordinary item	$ 1.24	$ (.66)	$ 3.28
Extraordinary item—tax benefit of loss carryovers	.37	—	.30
Net Income (loss)	$ 1.61	$ (.66)	$ 3.58
Average Shares Outstanding	59,875,990	58,215,897	57,727,577

The accompanying notes are an integral part of this financial statement.

(Dollars in millions)
December 31,

	1991	1990
Assets		
Current Assets:		
Cash and cash equivalents	**$ 163.4**	$ 220.3
Short term securities	**71.7**	56.4
Accounts and notes receivable (Note 5)	**1,315.0**	1,495.2
Inventories (Note 6)	**1,312.7**	1,346.0
Prepaid expenses	**255.9**	206.3
Total Current Assets	**3,118.7**	3,324.2
Other Assets:		
Investments in affiliates, at equity	**123.1**	127.6
Long term accounts and notes receivable	**234.0**	292.5
Deferred charges and other miscellaneous assets	**397.8**	410.9
	754.9	831.0
Properties and Plants (Note 7)	**4,636.9**	4,808.4
	$8,510.5	$8,963.6
Liabilities and Shareholders' Equity		
Current Liabilities:		
Accounts payable—trade	**$ 839.5**	$ 986.8
Accrued payrolls and other compensation	**352.8**	442.7
Other current liabilities	**352.2**	282.5
United States and foreign taxes	**245.0**	248.6
Notes payable to banks and overdrafts	**511.6**	247.6
Long term debt due within one year	**91.5**	85.4
Total Current Liabilities	**2,392.6**	2,293.6
Long Term Debt and Capital Leases (Note 8B)	**2,038.1**	3,286.4
Other Long Term Liabilities	**629.9**	550.0
Deferred Income Taxes	**599.1**	622.9
Minority Equity in Subsidiaries	**119.7**	112.8
Shareholders' Equity:		
Preferred stock, no par value:		
Authorized, 50,000,000 shares, unissued	**—**	—
Common stock, no par value:		
Authorized, 150,000,000 shares		
Outstanding shares, 70,663,515 (58,477,890 in 1990)	**70.7**	58.5
Capital surplus	**639.1**	65.1
Retained earnings	**2,208.5**	2,135.4
	2,918.3	2,259.0
Foreign currency translation adjustment	**(187.2)**	(161.1)
Total Shareholders' Equity	**2,731.1**	2,097.9
	$8,510.5	$8,963.6

The accompanying notes are an integral part of this financial statement.

(Dollars in millions, except per share)	Common Stock Shares	Amount	Capital Surplus	Retained Earnings	Foreign Currency Translation Adjustment	Total Shareholders' Equity
Balance at December 31, 1988						
after deducting 53,561,863 treasury shares	57,430,526	$57.4	$ 29.3	$2,175.4	$(235.0)	$2,027.1
Net income for 1989				206.8		206.8
Cash dividends 1989—$1.80 per share				(103.8)		(103.8)
Common stock issued (including 376,369 treasury shares):						
Dividend reinvestment and stock purchase plan	293,823	.3	14.9			15.2
Stock option plans	51,198	.1	1.7			1.8
Key Personnel Incentive Profit Sharing Plan	31,322	—	.6			.6
Foreign currency translation adjustment					(65.7)	(65.7)
Divestiture of South African subsidiary					61.8	61.8
Balance at December 31, 1989						
after deducting 53,185,494 treasury shares	57,806,869	57.8	46.5	2,278.4	(238.9)	2,143.8
Net loss for 1990				(38.3)		(38.3)
Cash dividends 1990—$1.80 per share				(104.7)		(104.7)
Common stock issued (including 671,138 treasury shares):						
Dividend reinvestment and stock purchase plan	588,223	.6	17.2			17.8
Key Personnel Incentive Profit Sharing Plan	82,798	.1	1.4			1.5
Foreign currency translation adjustment					77.8	77.8
Balance at December 31, 1990						
after deducting 52,514,356 treasury shares	58,477,890	58.5	65.1	2,135.4	(161.1)	2,097.9
Net income for 1991				**96.6**		**96.6**
Cash dividends 1991—$.40 per share				**(23.5)**		**(23.5)**
Common stock issued	**12,000,000**	**12.0**	**569.7**			**581.7**
Common stock issued (including 185,988 treasury shares):						
Dividend reinvestment and stock purchase plan	**71,818**	**.1**	**2.0**			**2.1**
Stock option plans	**113,807**	**.1**	**2.3**			**2.4**
Foreign currency translation adjustment					**(26.1)**	**(26.1)**
Balance at December 31, 1991						
after deducting 52,328,368 treasury shares	**70,663,515**	**$70.7**	**$639.1**	**$2,208.5**	**$(187.2)**	**$2,731.1**

The accompanying notes are an integral part of this financial statement.

(22)

(Dollars in millions)

Year Ended December 31,	1991	1990	1989
Cash Flows from Operating Activities:			
Net Income (loss)	**$ 96.6**	$ (38.3)	$ 206.8
Adjustments to reconcile net income to net cash:			
Depreciation	**441.5**	415.0	383.5
Restructuring	**(13.9)**	51.7	109.7
Deferred income tax (Note 15)	**(38.5)**	(56.6)	38.2
Accounts and notes receivable	**169.4**	(196.8)	259.0
Inventories	**5.9**	340.8	(120.1)
Prepaid expenses	**(53.7)**	(32.3)	(74.1)
Other assets	**44.4**	(151.7)	27.4
Accounts payable—trade	**(136.2)**	27.2	169.5
Other liabilities	**56.9**	215.3	(182.1)
Total adjustments	**475.8**	612.6	611.0
Net cash provided by operating activities	**572.4**	574.3	817.8
Cash Flows from Investing Activities:			
Capital expenditures	**(345.1)**	(574.5)	(775.7)
Asset dispositions	**117.6**	18.4	164.2
Short term securities acquired	**(118.2)**	(75.4)	(126.3)
Short term securities redeemed	**101.5**	110.3	44.3
Other transactions	**(4.8)**	(3.9)	(9.1)
Net cash used in investing activities	**(249.0)**	(525.1)	(702.6)
Cash Flows from Financing Activities:			
Proceeds from sale of foreign currency exchange agreements	**51.7**	—	75.4
Short term debt incurred	**1,069.3**	1,519.9	2,359.8
Short term debt paid	**(1,911.3)**	(1,707.4)	(2,083.5)
Long term debt incurred	**4.7**	485.2	237.9
Long term debt and capital leases paid	**(149.6)**	(160.4)	(708.1)
Common stock issued	**586.2**	19.3	17.6
Dividends paid	**(23.5)**	(104.7)	(103.8)
Net cash provided by (used in) financing activities	**(372.5)**	51.9	(204.7)
Effect of Exchange Rate Changes on Cash and Cash Equivalents	**(7.8)**	(3.3)	(22.1)
Net Increase (Decrease) in Cash and Cash Equivalents	**(56.9)**	97.8	(111.6)
Cash and Cash Equivalents at Beginning of the Period	**220.3**	122.5	234.1
Cash and Cash Equivalents at End of the Period	**$ 163.4**	$ 220.3	$ 122.5

The accompanying notes are an integral part of this financial statement.

(23)

NOTE ① Accounting Policies

A summary of the significant accounting policies used in the preparation of the accompanying financial statements follows:

Principles of Consolidation

The consolidated financial statements include the accounts of all majority-owned subsidiaries. All significant intercompany transactions have been eliminated.

The Company's investments in 20% to 50% owned companies in which it has the ability to exercise significant influence over operating and financial policies are accounted for on the equity method. Accordingly, the Company's share of the earnings of these companies is included in consolidated net income. Investments in other companies are carried at cost.

Consolidated Statement of Cash Flows

Cash and cash equivalents include cash on hand and in the bank as well as all short term securities held for the primary purpose of general liquidity. Such securities normally mature within three months from the date of acquisition. Cash flows associated with items intended as hedges of identifiable transactions or events are classified in the same category as the cash flows from the items being hedged.

Inventory Pricing

Inventories are stated at the lower of cost or market. Cost is determined using the last-in, first-out (LIFO) method for a significant portion of domestic inventories and the first-in, first-out (FIFO) method or average cost method for other inventories.

Properties and Plants

Properties and plants are stated at cost. Depreciation is computed on the straight line method. Accelerated depreciation is used for income tax purposes, where permitted.

Income Taxes

Income taxes are recognized during the year in which transactions enter into the determination of financial statement income with deferred taxes being provided for timing differences.

Per Share of Common Stock

Per share amounts have been computed based on the average number of common shares outstanding, and for 1990 and 1989 also included those treasury shares allocated for distribution under the incentive profit sharing plan.

Reclassification

Certain items previously reported in specific financial statement captions have been reclassified to conform with the 1991 presentation.

NOTE ② Restructuring

(In millions)	1991	1990	1989
Cost containment expenses	**$65.1**	$66.4	$ 18.4
Asset sales—(gain) loss:			
Scottsboro plant	**(47.5)**	—	—
South African subsidiary	—	—	43.0
Unused pipe	—	—	48.3
Plant closure expense	—	15.0	—
	$17.6	$81.4	$109.7

1991   The Company incurred charges during the first quarter of $65.1 million ($59.7 million after tax or $1.02 per share) related primarily to costs associated with workforce reductions worldwide and the decision to discontinue efforts to establish a tire factory in South Korea.

The Company implemented a new cost containment program which includes, among other things, the reduction of the salaried workforce of the Company and its subsidiaries by 1,100 persons by the end of 1992 and realignment of certain operations in Argentina and Europe. Charges associated with this program were $50.4 million. The Company incurred charges of $9.5 million which represented its share of personnel reduction costs at its South Pacific Tyre joint venture. Also during the first quarter, the Company incurred a charge of $5.2 million related to the previously mentioned South Korean project.

The Company sold the assets of its Scottsboro, Alabama tire cord textile plant in the fourth quarter to Akzo N.V. for $95.0 million. The Scottsboro plant produces a polyester reinforcing material for tires. A gain of $47.5 million ($43.2 million after tax or $.68 per share) was recorded.

24

Restructuring *(continued)*

1990 The restructuring of United States tire operations during the second quarter resulted in a charge of $20.0 million ($12.2 million after tax or $.21 per share) from the reduction of personnel in various sales, distribution and other operations and other associated costs.

The Company incurred restructuring charges of $46.4 million ($38.2 million after tax or $.66 per share) during the third quarter. The costs resulted from: a realignment of European tire marketing, distribution and production operations, which will eliminate approximately 1,180 jobs by mid-1992; the phaseout of medium and heavy truck tire production at the Valleyfield, Quebec, Canada plant; and the rationalization of certain tire and related production operations in Canada and Argentina.

The decision to close the New Bedford roofing systems plant resulted in a charge of $15.0 million ($9.2 million after tax or $.16 per share) for personnel reduction and other plant closure costs during the second quarter.

1989 The Company accrued expenses of $18.4 million ($10.9 million after tax or $.19 per share) for the reduction of bias-ply truck tire capacity at the Gadsden, Alabama plant and from the realignment of the Canadian operations.

The Company sold its South African tire and general products manufacturing subsidiary for $41.0 million. A loss of $43.0 million ($52.0 million after tax or $.90 per share) was recorded in the second quarter, the majority of which was due to the recognition of the decreased value of the Company's assets in South Africa arising from the devaluation of the South African Rand during the past several years.

The Company's oil transportation subsidiary, All American Pipeline Company, sold about 435 miles of unused 30-inch pipe for $70.0 million in the second quarter. A loss of $48.3 million ($43.0 million after tax or $.75 per share) was recorded on the sale.

NOTE ③ Other (Income) and Expense

(In millions)	1991	1990	1989
Other income	**$(139.3)**	$(180.6)	$(216.1)
Other expenses	**56.1**	96.7	44.6
	$ (83.2)	$ (83.9)	$(171.5)

Other income consists primarily of interest income on deposits. The primary source of interest income was from funds invested in time deposits in Latin America, pending remittance or reinvestment in the region. Interest income of $79.0 million, $86.8 million and $132.4 million was recorded in 1991, 1990 and 1989, respectively. At December 31, 1991, approximately $114.9 million or 48.9% ($128.4 million or 46.4% at December 31, 1990) of the Company's cash, cash equivalents and short term securities were concentrated in Latin America, primarily Brazil. Other income also includes interest on installment sales, technical assistance fees, equity in net income or losses of affiliated companies and other miscellaneous items.

Other expenses consist primarily of fees associated with the Company's accounts receivable continuous sale programs, which are based upon volume and market interest rates, and commitment fees on unused lines of credit. For 1990, other expenses also included $22.2 million ($13.5 million after tax or $.23 per share) for environmental cleanup costs associated with operations discontinued in 1986.

NOTE ④ Research and Development

Research and development cost included in cost of goods sold for 1991, 1990 and 1989 was $330.0 million, $331.3 million and $303.3 million, respectively.

NOTE ⑤ Accounts and Notes Receivable

(In millions)	1991	1990
Accounts and notes receivable	**$1,366.5**	$1,534.1
Allowance for doubtful accounts	**(51.5)**	(38.9)
	$1,315.0	$1,495.2

Throughout the year, the Company sold certain domestic accounts receivable under continuous sale programs. The Company decreased the level of net proceeds from sales under these programs to $580.0 million in December, 1991, from $600.0 million. Under these agreements, undivided interests in designated receivable pools are sold to purchasers with recourse limited to the receivables purchased. Fees paid by the Company under these agreements are based on certain variable market rate indices and are recorded as other expenses.

The Company sold accounts and notes receivable under these and other agreements, the net proceeds of which totaled $4.0 billion, $3.9 billion and $3.1 billion during 1991, 1990 and 1989, respectively. At December 31, 1991 and 1990, the balance of the uncollected portion of these receivables was $663.3 million and $674.8 million, respectively.

The Company ceased operations of Goodyear Financial Corporation (GFC) in 1991. GFC, a wholly-owned subsidiary, purchased certain receivables from Goodyear and domestic subsidiaries. The financial position and results of operations of GFC were not significant with respect to the Company's consolidated results.

NOTE ⑥ Inventories

(In millions)	1991	1990
Raw materials and supplies	**$ 232.0**	$ 234.5
Work in process	**58.1**	67.5
Finished product	**1,022.6**	1,044.0
	$1,312.7	$1,346.0

The cost of inventories using the last-in, first-out (LIFO) method (approximately 35.0% of consolidated inventories in 1991 and 38.4% in 1990) was less than the approximate current cost of inventories by $301.9 million at December 31, 1991 and $335.4 million at December 31, 1990.

NOTE ⑦ Properties and Plants

	1991			1990		
(In millions)	Owned	Capital Leases	Total	Owned	Capital Leases	Total
Properties and plants, at cost:						
Land and improvements	**$ 300.6**	**$ 8.0**	**$ 308.6**	$ 297.2	$ 8.1	$ 305.3
Buildings	**1,194.1**	**68.7**	**1,262.8**	1,137.6	71.5	1,209.1
Machinery and equipment	**5,253.3**	**125.7**	**5,379.0**	5,049.5	125.4	5,174.9
Pipeline	**1,411.4**	**—**	**1,411.4**	1,393.3	—	1,393.3
Construction in progress	**317.4**	**—**	**317.4**	535.4	—	535.4
	8,476.8	**202.4**	**8,679.2**	8,413.0	205.0	8,618.0
Accumulated depreciation	**(3,898.5)**	**(143.8)**	**(4,042.3)**	(3,669.9)	(139.7)	(3,809.6)
	$ 4,578.3	**$ 58.6**	**$ 4,636.9**	$ 4,743.1	$ 65.3	$ 4,808.4

The amortization for capital leases included in the depreciation provision for 1991, 1990 and 1989 was $8.4 million, $11.1 million and $10.1 million, respectively.

㉖

NOTE (8) Credit Arrangements

A. Short Term Debt and Credit Lines

At December 31, 1991, the Company had short term credit lines and overdraft arrangements totaling $888.1 million, of which $391.7 million were unused. Included in Notes payable to banks and overdrafts were loans under revolving credit agreements totaling $114.5 million at December 31, 1991. None of the amounts outstanding under revolving credit agreements at December 31, 1990 were classified as short term.

B. Long Term Debt and Capital Leases

(In millions)	1991	1990
Sinking fund debentures:		
8.60% due 1992–1994	$ 19.0	$ 20.3
7.35% due 1993–1997	30.7	37.2
Promissory notes:		
12.15% due 1992–2000	45.0	50.0
10.26% due 1999	118.4	118.4
Swiss franc bonds:		
5.375% due 2000	175.9	185.5
5.375% due 2006	146.6	155.9
Yen bonds:		
6.875% due 1994	89.1	82.9
7.125% due 1995	194.4	180.8
6.625% due 1996	77.7	72.3
6.30% Yen bank term loan due 1994	39.8	37.0
6.875% Convertible Debentures due 2003	150.0	150.0
Bank term loans due 1992–2000	468.5	544.6
Revolving credit agreements	140.5	160.0
Euro-commercial paper	—	16.0
Other domestic debt	15.5	958.8
Foreign subsidiary debt	333.7	507.3
Capital lease obligations:		
Industrial revenue bonds	62.7	69.2
Other	22.1	25.6
	2,129.6	3,371.8
Less portion due within one year	91.5	85.4
	$2,038.1	$3,286.4

Substantially all of the Company's long term debt is unsubordinated.

At December 31, 1991, the Company had available long term credit sources totaling $4,491.8 million, of which $2,347.0 million were unused.

At December 31, 1991 (December 31, 1990), the Swiss franc bonds totaling $322.5 million ($341.4 million) and $117.5 million ($201.8 million) of Yen bonds and bank term loan were completely hedged by foreign currency exchange agreements with four (five) domestic and international financial institutions whereunder the Company is entitled to purchase 438 million Swiss francs and 15 billion Yen (27.5 billion Yen) for $286.0 million ($330.4 million). At December 31, 1991, $161.1 million ($212.8 million) associated with these agreements was recorded in long term accounts and notes receivable on the Consolidated Balance Sheet. These agreements are subject to changes in market value which offset fluctuations in the dollar amount of the related debt. In addition, various forward contracts and a call option entitling the Company to purchase 36.9 billion Yen (25.3 billion Yen) for $282.8 million ($168.2 million) were in effect at each year end. These arrangements are intended to limit exposure to fluctuations in the currency exchange rate affecting $283.5 million ($171.2 million) of the Yen bonds. At each year end, $10.7 million ($18.5 million) associated with these contracts was recorded in certain receivable accounts on the Consolidated Balance Sheet.

In December 1991, a foreign currency exchange agreement, covering 12.5 billion Yen in place to hedge an equivalent portion of the outstanding Yen bonds due 1995, was sold generating cash proceeds of $51.7 million. The resulting 12.5 billion Yen exposure was rehedged.

The Convertible Debentures due 2003 are convertible into common shares of the Company at $80.25 per share.

The bank term loans due 1992 through 2000 consist of various agreements which provide for interest at either fixed rates ranging between 8 percent and 9.89 percent or floating rates based upon LIBOR plus a fixed spread.

During 1991, the Company renegotiated its bank revolving credit agreements, which were originally established in 1989, for the primary purpose of extending the duration and increasing the amounts of the commitments under such agreements. Non-cancelable commitments totaling $2,320.0 million with 44 domestic and international banks, including 3 new banks, were extended for a term which now expires June 30, 1994 and, thereafter, are automatically renewed for successive one year terms unless a notice of termination is given at least 13 months prior to the end of the current term or annual renewal period. Under each agreement the Company may borrow, for periods of up to at least one year, at any time during the commitment period. Each revolving credit agreement provides that the Company may obtain loans bearing interest at LIBOR or a

Long Term Debt and Capital Leases *(continued)*

defined Certificate of Deposit rate plus spreads ranging from
³/₄ percent to one percent depending upon the amount of the
bank's commitment and extent of utilization by the Company,
or at quoted rates, and requires a commitment fee on the
unused portion ranging from 35 to 50 basis points depending
upon commitment level. Each agreement contains certain
covenants which, among other things, require the Company to
maintain at the end of each calendar quarter a defined interest
coverage and current ratio, a consolidated net worth minimum
and a limitation on consolidated debt. In addition, commitments totaling $255.0 million under the 1989 revolving credit
agreements with six other banks remain available for drawings
through the fourth quarter of 1992. Amounts outstanding
under the Company's Euro-commercial paper program and
other short term facilities are supported by these revolving
credit agreements.

 Certain domestic and foreign subsidiary debt obligations
amounting to $140.5 million and $126.9 million, respectively,
at December 31, 1991 ($1,116.0 million and $256.6 million
at December 31, 1990), which by their terms are due within
one year, are classified as long term. Amounts reclassified at
December 31, 1991 are significantly lower versus year end
1990 due to the reduction in consolidated debt during 1991
and further debt reductions anticipated in the future. Such obligations are incurred under or supported by the revolving credit
agreements, and it is the Company's intent to maintain them as
long term. Short term obligations reclassified to long term at
December 31, 1991 consist primarily of loans under revolving
credit agreements and short term bank borrowings.

 Refer to note No. 9, Leased Assets for additional information on capital lease obligations.

 The Company enters into various interest rate contracts
in managing the cost of its floating rate debt. These contracts
limit the effect of market fluctuations on the interest cost of
floating rate debt. A summary of contracts in place domesti-
cally at December 31 follows:

(Dollars in millions)	1991	1990
Notional principal amount:		
Pay fixed rate; receive variable LIBOR	**$1,373.8**	$1,433.7
Pay variable LIBOR; receive fixed rate	**480.0**	—
Average life to maturity (years)	**3.4**	3.2
Weighted average interest rate	**8.08%**	8.80%

In addition, interest rate contracts with notional principal
amounts totaling $77.7 million were in place at December 31,
1991 ($103.4 million at December 31, 1990) to hedge foreign
subsidiary floating rate debt denominated in Canadian dollars,
whereunder the Company pays a fixed amount and receives a
variable amount equivalent to LIBOR. The average life to
maturity and the weighted average interest rate for these contracts was 1.7 years and 12.12% at December 31, 1991 and
2.2 years and 12.39% at December 31, 1990.

 The annual aggregate maturities of long term debt and
capital leases for the five years subsequent to 1991 are presented below. Maturities of debt incurred under or supported
by revolving credit agreements have been reported on the basis
that the commitments to lend under these agreements will be
terminated effective at the end of their current terms.

(In millions)	1992	1993	1994	1995	1996
Debt incurred under or supported by revolving credit agreements	$ —	$ —	$ —	$239.8	$ —
Other	91.5	121.9	190.1	504.0	150.4
	$91.5	$121.9	$190.1	$743.8	$150.4

C. Foreign Currency Forward Contracts

The Company enters into forward exchange contracts as
hedges relating primarily to identifiable currency positions.
At December 31, 1991, contracts were in place to purchase
$4.4 million ($81.6 million at December 31, 1990) in various
foreign currencies and to sell $34.6 million ($40.8 million at
December 31, 1990) in U.S. and other currencies. The future
value of these contracts and the hedged positions are subject
to offsetting market risk due to foreign currency exchange
rate volatility.

28

NOTE (9) **Leased Assets**

Certain manufacturing, retail store, transportation, data processing and other facilities and equipment are held under leases which generally expire within ten years but may be renewed by the Company. Many of the leases provide that the Company will pay taxes assessed against leased property and the cost of insurance and maintenance.

Minimum lease commitments follow:

(In millions)	Capital Leases	Operating Leases
1992	$ 18.8	$234.5
1993	11.5	192.0
1994	11.3	133.5
1995	11.0	88.5
1996	11.4	60.8
1997 and thereafter	73.7	188.8
Total minimum lease payments	137.7	$898.1
Less estimated executory costs	.6	
Net minimum lease payments	137.1	
Less amounts estimated to represent interest	52.3	
Present value of net minimum lease obligations	84.8	
Less portion due within one year	11.6	
	$ 73.2	

Total rental expense charged to income and contingent rentals included therein follow:

(In millions)	1991	1990	1989
Minimum rentals	$310.8	$337.3	$306.2
Contingent rentals	1.2	1.5	1.2
Less sublease rentals	51.1	51.6	49.5
	$260.9	$287.2	$257.9

NOTE (10) **Stock Compensation Plans**

The Company's 1972, 1982 and 1987 Employees' Stock Option Plans and the 1989 Goodyear Performance and Equity Incentive Plan provide for the granting of stock options and stock appreciation rights (SARs). For options previously granted with SARs, the exercise of an SAR cancels the stock option; conversely, the exercise of the stock option cancels the SAR.

The 1972, 1982 and 1987 Plans expired on December 31, 1981 and 1986 and April 10, 1989, respectively, except for options and SARs then outstanding. The 1989 Plan was adopted at the April, 1989 shareholders' meeting. The 1989 Plan empowers the Company to award or grant, from time to time until December 31, 1998, when the 1989 Plan expires except with respect to Awards then outstanding, to officers and other key managerial, administrative and professional associates of the Company and its subsidiaries Incentive, Non-Qualified and Deferred Compensation Stock Options, Stock Appreciation Rights, Restricted Stock and Restricted Unit Grants, Performance Equity and Performance Unit Grants, other Stock-Based Awards authorized by a committee of the Board of Directors which administers the 1989 Plan, and any combination of any or all of such Awards, whether in tandem with each other or otherwise. The Company issued Performance Equity Grants in 1989 up to a maximum of 83,820 shares of common stock (including possible dividend equivalents payable in stock) of which 3,873 shares were canceled in 1990 under the terms of the Plan. The 1989 Performance Equity Grants were in effect for a 3 year period which expired December 31, 1991. Assuming that there will be full utilization of the shares of Common Stock available for Awards during the term of the 1989 Plan, and that no other increases or decreases in the number of shares of Common Stock outstanding would occur during the term of the 1989 Plan, approximately 10,400,000 shares of the Common Stock would be available for the grant of Awards through December 31, 1998.

Stock Compensation Plans *(continued)*

	1991		1990	
	Shares	*SARs*	*Shares*	*SARs*
Outstanding at January 1	**2,980,527**	**592,005**	1,984,538	339,205
Options granted	**1,921,028**	**—**	971,500	199,500
Freestanding SARs granted	**196,200**	**196,200**	94,000	94,000
Restricted stock granted	**50,125**			
Options without SARs exercised	**(70,605)**	**—**	—	—
Options with SARs exercised	**(213)**	**(213)**	—	—
SARs exercised	**(18,377)**	**(18,377)**	(200)	(200)
Restricted stock issued	**(50,125)**	**—**	—	—
Options without SARs expired	**(176,675)**	**—**	(54,811)	—
Options with SARs expired	**(8,100)**	**(8,100)**	(14,300)	(14,300)
SARs expired	**(1,600)**	**(130,450)**	(200)	(26,200)
Outstanding at December 31	**4,822,185**	**631,065**	2,980,527	592,005
Exercisable at December 31	**2,184,767**	**312,575**	1,765,452	271,705
Available for grant at December 31	**1,965,087**		3,427,552	

All options were granted at an option price of not less than the fair market value of the Company's common stock at the date of grant.

At December 31, 1991, options were exercisable at prices ranging from $22.50 to $67.50 ($18.25 to $67.50 at December 31, 1990). During 1991, options were exercised at prices ranging from $18.25 to $35.50 ($12.00 during 1990).

NOTE (11) Pensions

The Company and its subsidiaries provide substantially all associates with pension benefits.

The principal domestic hourly plan provides benefits based on length of service. The principal domestic plans covering salaried associates provide benefits based on career average earnings formulas. Associates making voluntary contributions to these plans receive higher benefits. Other plans provide benefits similar to the principal domestic plans as well as termination indemnity plans at certain foreign subsidiaries.

The Company's domestic funding policy complies with the requirements of Federal laws and regulations. Plan assets are invested primarily in common stocks, fixed income securities and real estate.

Net periodic pension cost follows:

(In millions)	1991	1990	1989
Service cost-benefits earned during the period	**$ 58.3**	$ 53.3	$ 49.2
Interest cost on projected benefit obligation	**158.3**	139.2	129.7
Actual return on assets	**(208.8)**	49.7	(194.8)
Net amortization and deferrals	**120.5**	(150.3)	113.3
Net periodic pension cost	**$128.3**	$ 91.9	$ 97.4

30

Pensions *(continued)*

The following table sets forth the funded status and amounts recognized in the Company's Consolidated Balance Sheet at December 31, 1991 and 1990. At the end of 1991 and 1990, assets exceeded accumulated benefits in certain plans and accumulated benefits exceeded assets in others.

(In millions)	1991 Assets Exceed Accumulated Benefits	1991 Accumulated Benefits Exceed Assets	1990 Assets Exceed Accumulated Benefits	1990 Accumulated Benefits Exceed Assets
Actuarial present value of benefit obligations:				
Vested benefit obligation	$(136.6)	$(1,430.3)	$(110.3)	$(1,284.1)
Accumulated benefit obligation	$(151.6)	$(1,583.8)	$(120.3)	$(1,404.2)
Projected benefit obligation	$(198.6)	$(1,696.8)	$(158.4)	$(1,512.1)
Plan assets	214.1	1,282.7	153.7	1,054.0
Plan assets in excess of (or less than) projected benefit obligation	15.5	(414.1)	(4.7)	(458.1)
Unrecognized net loss	7.6	1.8	23.3	93.0
Prior service cost not yet recognized in net periodic pension cost	11.9	277.2	9.2	188.7
Unrecognized net (asset) obligation at transition	(6.4)	20.7	(6.6)	21.2
Adjustment required to recognize minimum liability	—	(205.9)	—	(215.3)
Prepaid (accrued) and deferred pension cost recognized in the Consolidated Balance Sheet	$ 28.6	$ (320.3)	$ 21.2	$ (370.5)

Assumptions:	U.S.	Foreign	U.S.	Foreign
Discount rate	9.0%	0%–24.0%	9.0%	0%–22.0%
Rate of increase in compensation levels	5.5%	0%–22.0%	5.5%	0%–20.0%
Expected long term rate of return on assets	9.0%	5.0%–10.5%	9.0%	5.0%–11.0%

During 1991, the Company incurred curtailments and/or settlements in the termination indemnity and pension plans in Canada, Greece, Peru and Turkey. The result was an aggregate loss of $5.0 million.

During 1990, the Company incurred curtailments in the principal domestic hourly and salary plans as a result of the New Bedford closure. The result was an aggregate loss of $3.2 million. These items were recorded as part of restructuring.

(31)

NOTE ⑫ Associates' Savings Plans

Substantially all domestic associates are eligible to participate in savings plans. Under these plans associates elect to contribute a percentage of their pay. In 1991, most plans provided for the Company's matching of these contributions (up to a maximum of 6 percent of the associate's annual pay or, if less, $8,475) at the rate of 50 percent. Company contributions were $25.9 million, $25.4 million and $25.5 million for 1991, 1990 and 1989, respectively.

NOTE ⑬ Postretirement Health Care and Life Insurance Benefits

The Company and its subsidiaries provide substantially all domestic associates and associates at certain foreign subsidiaries with health care and life insurance benefits upon retirement. Substantial portions of health care benefits for domestic retirees are not insured and are paid by the Company. The life insurance benefits and certain health care benefits are provided by insurance companies through premiums based on expected benefits to be paid during the year. The Company recognized the cost of these benefits by expensing the annual insurance premium and the amount of health care costs incurred by retirees during the year. The cost of providing these benefits for retirees for 1991, 1990 and 1989 was $119.9 million, $103.0 million and $93.9 million, respectively.

Statement of Financial Accounting Standards No. 106, "Employers' Accounting for Postretirement Benefits Other Than Pensions," (SFAS No. 106) is effective for fiscal years beginning after December 15, 1992. SFAS No. 106 will require accrual of postretirement benefits other than pensions during the years an associate provides services. The Company intends to take a one-time charge for the transition obligation when it adopts the standard in 1993 or earlier. Preliminary estimates of the amount of the transition obligation upon adoption of the new standard range from as much as $1.8 billion to as low as $1.5 billion ($1.2 billion and $1.0 billion after tax, respectively). The annual charge to income will not materially differ after SFAS No. 106 has been adopted and the one-time charge recorded by the Company. No material cash impact is anticipated.

NOTE ⑭ Interest Expense

Interest expense includes interest and amortization of debt discount and expense less amounts capitalized as follows:

(In millions)	1991	1990	1989
Interest expense before capitalization	$326.1	$362.9	$374.2
Less capitalized interest	8.3	34.7	118.9
	$317.8	$328.2	$255.3

The Company made cash payments for interest in 1991, 1990 and 1989 of $349.1 million, $347.9 million and $367.5 million, respectively.

NOTE ⑮ Income Taxes

The components of income before income taxes and extraordinary item follow:

(In millions)	1991	1990	1989
Domestic Operations	$119.0	$(15.5)	$204.9
Foreign Operations	151.7	71.4	266.0
	$270.7	$ 55.9	$470.9

A reconciliation of Federal income taxes at the U.S. statutory rate to income taxes provided follows:

(In millions)	1991	1990	1989
U.S. Federal income tax at the statutory rate (34%)	$ 98.7	$23.8	$166.4
Differences applicable to foreign operations:			
Additional tax on foreign source income	73.6	31.8	47.0
Losses with no tax benefit and loss carryovers	11.0	35.0	10.0
Tax rate differences and other variations	6.0	13.2	28.9
Sale of South African subsidiary	—	—	23.6
Total Foreign	90.6	80.0	109.5
Rate benefit on U.S. loss carryback	—	(9.0)	—
Other items	6.9	(.6)	5.6
United States and foreign taxes on income before extraordinary item	196.2	94.2	281.5
Extraordinary item—tax benefit of loss carryovers	(22.1)	—	(17.4)
United States and foreign taxes on income after extraordinary item	$174.1	$94.2	$264.1

Income Taxes *(continued)*

The components of the provision for income taxes by taxing jurisdiction follow:

(In millions)	1991	1990	1989
Current:			
Federal	$ 71.2	$ 12.0	$ 26.2
Foreign income and withholding taxes	134.2	136.4	190.9
State	7.2	2.4	8.8
	212.6	150.8	225.9
Deferred:			
Federal	(65.7)	(59.4)	23.7
Foreign	27.6	6.8	16.7
State	(.4)	(4.0)	(2.2)
	(38.5)	(56.6)	38.2
Charge equivalent to the effects of foreign operating loss carryovers utilized	22.1	—	17.4
United States and foreign taxes on income	$196.2	$ 94.2	$281.5

Prepaid and deferred taxes relating to timing differences of revenues and expenses for tax and financial reporting purposes follow:

(In millions)	1991	1990	1989
Depreciation	$ 32.8	$ 35.9	$59.4
Plant closures	(.8)	.3	14.2
Capitalized interest	(2.6)	(20.1)	18.9
Restructuring costs	(2.5)	(6.1)	(2.9)
Pensions	2.9	4.8	(24.2)
Alternative minimum tax	(33.3)	(55.5)	—
Sale of foreign currency contracts	(19.2)	7.4	(30.8)
Environmental costs	(7.1)	(13.0)	—
Other items	(8.7)	(10.3)	3.6
	$(38.5)	$(56.6)	$38.2

At December 31, 1991, the Company had approximately $200.0 million of foreign operating loss carryovers, some of which expire at various times from 1992, and some of which never expire. At December 31, 1991, the Company also had incurred alternative minimum tax of $88.8 million which will be used to offset future regular tax liability.

The Company made net cash payments for income taxes in 1991, 1990 and 1989 of $213.9 million, $118.7 million and $333.6 million, respectively.

No provision for Federal income tax or foreign withholding tax on retained earnings of foreign subsidiaries of $1,252.9 million is required because this amount has been reinvested in properties and plants and working capital.

The Company expects that Statement of Financial Accounting Standards No. 96, "Accounting for Income Taxes" will be superseded by a new Statement in 1992. While not in its final form, the Company does not expect the new Statement to have a material impact on future financial statements.

(33)

NOTE ⑯ **Business Segments**

Tires and related is the principal industry segment, which involves the development, manufacture, distribution and sale of tires and related products. These products include tires, tubes, retreads, automotive repair services and merchandise purchased for resale.

The General products segment involves the manufacture and sale of various kinds of belts, hose, molded products, foam cushioning accessories, tank tracks, organic chemicals used in rubber and plastic processing, synthetic rubber and rubber latices, polyester resins, films, vinyl products and other activities.

The Oil transportation segment consists primarily of the All American Pipeline System, a common carrier crude oil pipeline extending from California to Texas. This segment, which also includes a crude oil gathering pipeline in California, crude oil storage facilities, linefill and related assets, also engages in various crude oil gathering, purchasing and selling activities. Segment sales consist of tariffs charged by the All American Pipeline System and revenues, net of acquisition costs, resulting from various crude oil gathering, purchasing and selling activities. Acquisition costs associated with the gathering, purchasing and selling activities amounted to $1.1 billion, $1.3 billion and $705.2 million for 1991, 1990 and 1989, respectively. On October 1, 1989, the Company began recognizing depreciation and other net operating expenses of the All American Pipeline System. These charges, as well as interest associated with the System, had previously been capitalized.

Operating income for each industry segment consists of total revenues less applicable costs and expenses. Transfers between industry segments were insignificant.

Operating income for each geographic segment consists of total revenues less applicable costs and expenses. Intergeographic sales were at cost plus a negotiated mark up.

Dividends received by the Company and domestic subsidiaries from its foreign operations for 1991, 1990 and 1989 were $118.0 million, $62.1 million and $195.5 million, respectively.

Portions of certain items described in note No. 2, Restructuring were (credited) or charged to the operating income of both the industry and geographic segments as follows:

Industry Segments

(In millions)	Tires and related	General products	Oil transportation	Total
1991				
Gain on sale of Scottsboro assets	$(20.9)	$(26.6)	$ —	$(47.5)
Cost containment expenses	46.9	8.7	—	55.6
	$ 26.0	$(17.9)	$ —	$ 8.1
1990				
Plant closure expense—New Bedford	$ —	$ 15.0	$ —	$ 15.0
Cost containment expenses	66.4	—	—	66.4
	$ 66.4	$ 15.0	$ —	$ 81.4
1989				
Loss on sale of South African subsidiary	$ 33.4	$ 9.6	$ —	$ 43.0
Loss on sale of unused pipe	—	—	48.3	48.3
Cost containment expenses	18.4	—	—	18.4
	$ 51.8	$ 9.6	$ 48.3	$109.7

Geographic Segments

(In millions)	United States	Canada	Europe	Latin America	Asia	Total
1991						
Gain on sale of Scottsboro assets	$(47.5)	$ —	$ —	$ —	$ —	$(47.5)
Cost containment expenses	34.0	.4	5.8	9.9	5.5	55.6
	$(13.5)	$ .4	$ 5.8	$9.9	$ 5.5	$ 8.1
1990						
Plant closure expense—New Bedford	$ 15.0	$ —	$ —	$ —	$ —	$ 15.0
Cost containment expenses	20.0	10.4	31.0	5.0	—	66.4
	$ 35.0	$ 10.4	$ 31.0	$ 5.0	$ —	$ 81.4
1989						
Loss on sale of South African subsidiary	$ —	$ —	$ —	$ —	$43.0	$ 43.0
Loss on sale of unused pipe	48.3	—	—	—	—	48.3
Cost containment expenses	10.5	7.9	—	—	—	18.4
	$ 58.8	$ 7.9	$ —	$ —	$43.0	$109.7

The following items have been excluded from the determination of operating income: interest expense, foreign currency exchange, equity in net income of affiliated companies, minority interest in net income of subsidiaries, corporate revenues and expenses and income taxes.

Corporate revenues and expenses were those items not identifiable with the operations of a segment. Corporate revenues were primarily from certain technical agreements and royalties. Corporate expenses were primarily central administrative expenses.

Assets of industry and geographic segments represent those assets that were identified with the operations of each segment. Corporate assets consist of cash and cash equivalents, short term securities, prepaid expenses, deferred charges and other miscellaneous assets.

Industry Segments

(In millions)	1991	1990	1989
Sales to Unaffiliated Customers			
Tires	**$ 7,848.6**	$ 8,180.1	$ 7,880.7
Related products and services	**1,109.9**	1,035.3	968.3
Tires and related	**8,958.5**	9,215.4	8,849.0
General products	**1,917.4**	2,027.3	2,008.5
Oil transportation	**30.9**	29.8	11.8
Net sales	**$10,906.8**	$11,272.5	$10,869.3
Income (loss)			
Tires and related	**$ 620.8**	$ 463.4	$ 722.6
General products	**214.6**	194.1	260.5
Oil transportation	**(52.1)**	(52.9)	(56.8)
Total operating income	**783.3**	604.6	926.3
Interest expense	**(317.8)**	(328.2)	(255.3)
Foreign currency exchange	**(47.4)**	(72.1)	(87.9)
Equity in net income of affiliated companies	**(4.9)**	3.2	10.9
Minority interest in net income of subsidiaries	**(19.5)**	(14.1)	(18.6)
Corporate revenues and expenses	**(123.0)**	(137.5)	(104.5)
Income before income taxes and extraordinary item	**$ 270.7**	$ 55.9	$ 470.9
Assets			
Tires and related	**$ 5,126.1**	$ 5,156.4	$ 5,206.7
General products	**735.6**	860.8	857.5
Oil transportation	**1,530.1**	1,746.6	1,556.0
Total identifiable assets	**7,391.8**	7,763.8	7,620.2
Corporate assets	**996.6**	1,072.2	714.2
Investments in affiliated companies, at equity	**123.1**	127.6	125.9
Assets at December 31	**$ 8,510.5**	$ 8,963.6	$ 8,460.3
Capital Expenditures			
Tires and related	**$ 244.9**	$ 479.7	$ 576.2
General products	**82.0**	68.1	68.3
Oil transportation	**18.2**	26.7	131.2
For the year	**$ 345.1**	$ 574.5	$ 775.7
Depreciation			
Tires and related	**$ 348.1**	$ 336.5	$ 331.8
General products	**58.3**	46.4	41.1
Oil transportation	**35.1**	32.1	10.6
For the year	**$ 441.5**	$ 415.0	$ 383.5

Geographic Segments

(In millions)	1991	1990	1989
Sales to Unaffiliated Customers			
United States	$ 6,230.8	$ 6,459.6	$ 6,421.3
Canada	554.6	567.3	601.8
Europe	2,281.9	2,301.2	2,039.0
Latin America	1,248.9	1,351.6	1,180.6
Asia	590.6	592.8	626.6
Net sales	$10,906.8	$11,272.5	$10,869.3
Inter-Geographic Sales			
United States	$ 290.5	$ 270.8	$ 268.8
Canada	156.5	151.8	145.1
Europe	60.5	78.8	89.3
Latin America	46.1	52.7	69.3
Asia	37.1	37.7	52.7
Total	$ 590.7	$ 591.8	$ 625.2
Revenue			
United States	$ 6,521.3	$ 6,730.4	$ 6,690.1
Canada	711.1	719.1	746.9
Europe	2,342.4	2,380.0	2,128.3
Latin America	1,295.0	1,404.3	1,249.9
Asia	627.7	630.5	679.3
Adjustments and eliminations	(590.7)	(591.8)	(625.2)
Total	$10,906.8	$11,272.5	$10,869.3
Operating Income			
United States	$ 422.7	$ 326.9	$ 490.7
Canada	(5.9)	(20.7)	9.8
Europe	123.9	36.3	131.7
Latin America	156.4	195.1	244.8
Asia	86.3	74.5	48.6
Adjustments and eliminations	(.1)	(7.5)	.7
Total	$ 783.3	$ 604.6	$ 926.3
Assets			
United States	$ 4,971.3	$ 5,406.5	$ 5,187.1
Canada	592.6	596.2	527.6
Europe	1,597.4	1,535.4	1,452.8
Latin America	820.5	881.8	815.5
Asia	409.9	422.9	365.8
Adjustments and eliminations	(4.3)	(6.8)	(14.4)
Total identifiable assets	8,387.4	8,836.0	8,334.4
Investments in affiliated			
companies, at equity	123.1	127.6	125.9
Assets at December 31	$ 8,510.5	$ 8,963.6	$ 8,460.3

NOTE (17) Commitments and Contingent Liabilities

At December 31, 1991, the Company had binding commitments for investments in land, buildings and equipment of approximately $75.7 million.

Various legal actions, claims and governmental investigations and proceedings covering a wide range of matters are pending against the Company and its subsidiaries. In the opinion of management, after reviewing such matters and consulting with the Company's General Counsel, any liability which may ultimately be incurred would not materially affect the consolidated financial position of the Company, although an adverse final determination in certain instances could materially affect the Company's consolidated net income for the period in which such determination occurs.

NOTE (18) Preferred Stock Purchase Rights Plan

In 1986, the Company authorized 3,000,000 shares of Series A $10.00 Preferred Stock ("Series A Preferred") issuable only upon the exercise of rights ("Rights") issued under the Preferred Stock Purchase Rights Plan adopted in July 1986. Each share of Series A Preferred issued would be non-redeemable, non-voting and entitled to cumulative quarterly dividends equal to the greater of $10.00 or, subject to adjustment, 100 times the per share amount of dividends declared on Goodyear common stock during the preceding quarter, and would also be entitled to a liquidation preference.

Under the Rights Plan, each shareholder of record on July 28, 1986 received a dividend of one Right per share of Goodyear common stock. When exercisable, each Right entitles the holder to buy one one-hundredth of a share of Series A Preferred at an exercise price of $100. The Rights will be exercisable only after 10 days following the earlier of a public announcement that a person or group has acquired 20 percent or more of Goodyear common stock or the commencement of a tender offer for 20 percent or more of Goodyear common stock by a person or group. The Rights are non-voting and may be redeemed by the Company at $.05 per Right under certain circumstances. If not redeemed or exercised, the Rights will expire on July 28, 1996. If a person or group accumulates 35 percent or more of Goodyear common stock, or a merger takes place with an acquiring person or group and the Company is the surviving corporation, or an acquiring person or group engages in certain self-dealing transactions, each Right (except those held by such acquiring person or group) will entitle the holder to purchase Goodyear common stock having a market value then equal to two times the exercise price. If the Company is acquired or a sale or transfer of 50 percent or more of the Company's assets or earning power is made, each Right (except those held by the acquiring person or group) will entitle the holder to purchase common stock of the acquiring entity having a market value then equal to two times the exercise price.

Quarterly Data and Market Price Information

(In millions, except per share)

1991		Quarter			Year
	First	Second	Third	Fourth	
Net Sales	$2,497.0	$2,791.3	$2,838.3	$2,780.2	$10,906.8
Gross Profit	534.4	632.2	687.1	647.8	2,501.5
Income (loss) before Extraordinary Item	(93.4)	16.3	52.3	99.3	74.5
Extraordinary Item	3.3	6.2	6.8	5.8	22.1
Net Income (loss)	$ (90.1)	$ 22.5	$ 59.1	$ 105.1	$ 96.6
Average Shares Outstanding	58.5	58.5	58.6	63.9	59.9
Per Share of Common Stock:					
Income (loss) before extraordinary item	$ (1.60)	$ .28	$ .90	$ 1.55	$ 1.24
Extraordinary item	.06	.10	.11	.10	.37
Net Income (loss)	$ (1.54)	$ .38	$ 1.01	$ 1.65	$ 1.61
Price Range*					
High	$ 24³/₄	$ 35¹/₄	$ 44¹/₄	$ 54¹/₄	$ 54¹/₄
Low	16³/₄	21	31³/₄	41³/₄	16³/₄
Dividends Paid	.10	.10	.10	.10	.40

The Company incurred charges during the first quarter of $65.1 million ($59.7 million after tax or $1.02 per share) related primarily to costs associated with workforce reductions worldwide and the decision to discontinue efforts to establish a tire factory in South Korea.

The Company sold the assets of a tire cord textile plant to Akzo N.V. for $95.0 million in the fourth quarter. A gain of $47.5 million ($43.2 million after tax or $.68 per share) was recorded.

Quarterly per share amounts do not add to the year 1991 per share amount due to issuance of 12 million shares of common stock in the fourth quarter.

1990		Quarter			Year
	First	Second	Third	Fourth	
Net Sales	$2,691.7	$2,870.8	$2,899.7	$2,810.3	$11,272.5
Gross Profit	613.5	637.8	609.4	606.7	2,467.4
Income (loss) before Extraordinary Item	16.5	(10.0)	(56.4)	11.6	(38.3)
Extraordinary Item	4.4	.6	(5.0)	—	—
Net Income (loss)	$ 20.9	$ (9.4)	$ (61.4)	$ 11.6	$ (38.3)
Average Shares Outstanding	58.0	58.1	58.3	58.4	58.2
Per Share of Common Stock:					
Income (loss) before extraordinary item	$ .29	$ (.18)	$ (.97)	$ .20	$ (.66)
Extraordinary item	.07	.02	(.09)	—	—
Net Income (loss)	$ .36	$ (.16)	$ (1.06)	$ .20	$ (.66)
Price Range*					
High	$ 46³/₈	$ 37¹/₄	$ 30³/₈	$ 19¹/₄	$ 46³/₈
Low	32⁷/₈	30	16	12⁷/₈	12⁷/₈
Dividends Paid	.45	.45	.45	.45	1.80

The Company incurred charges during the second quarter of $35.0 million ($21.4 million after tax or $.37 per share) from restructuring of North American tire operations and costs associated with the decision to close the New Bedford, Massachusetts, roofing systems plant.

The Company incurred charges during the third quarter of $46.4 million ($38.2 million after tax or $.66 per share) from the restructuring of certain tire and related production operations worldwide. Also during the third quarter the Company incurred charges of $22.2 million ($13.5 million after tax or $.23 per share) for environmental cleanup costs associated with a business segment discontinued in 1986.

The fourth quarter included favorable adjustments totaling $40.4 million ($11.3 million after tax or $.19 per share) consisting of $12.0 million of LIFO inventory adjustments and $28.4 million of various other expense items that, by their nature, were estimated during the year. The majority of the adjustments affected Gross Profit.

*New York Stock Exchange—Composite Transactions

(Dollars in millions, except per share)	1991	1990	1989	1988	1987
Financial Results					
Net Sales	$10,906.8	$11,272.5	$10,869.3	$10,810.4	$9,905.2
Income (loss) from Continuing Operations					
before Extraordinary Item	74.5	(38.3)	189.4	350.1	513.9
Discontinued Operations	—	—	—	—	257.0
Income (loss) before Extraordinary Item	74.5	(38.3)	189.4	350.1	770.9
Extraordinary Item—Tax Benefit of Loss					
Carryovers	22.1	—	17.4	—	—
Net Income (loss)	96.6	(38.3)	206.8	350.1	770.9
Net Income (loss) per Dollar of Sales	.9¢	(.3)¢	1.9¢	3.2¢	7.8¢
Per Share of Common Stock					
Income (loss) from Continuing Operations					
before Extraordinary Item	$ 1.24	$ (.66)	$ 3.28	$ 6.11	$ 8.49
Discontinued Operations	—	—	—	—	4.24
Income (loss) before Extraordinary Item	1.24	(.66)	3.28	6.11	12.73
Extraordinary Item—Tax Benefit of Loss					
Carryovers	.37	—	.30	—	—
Net Income (loss)	1.61	(.66)	3.58	6.11	12.73
Dividends	.40	1.80	1.80	1.70	1.60
Book Value at December 31	38.65	35.88	37.08	35.30	32.19
Financial Position					
Total Assets	$ 8,510.5	$ 8,963.6	$ 8,460.3	$ 8,618.3	$8,395.9
Properties and Plants—Net	4,636.9	4,808.4	4,615.3	4,427.4	4,128.3
Depreciation from Continuing Operations	441.5	415.0	383.5	357.1	349.9
Capital Expenditures for Continuing Operations	345.1	574.5	775.7	743.7	665.6
Long Term Debt and Capital Leases	2,038.1	3,286.4	2,963.4	3,044.8	3,282.4
Shareholders' Equity	2,731.1	2,097.9	2,143.8	2,027.1	1,834.4
Other Information					
Shareholders of Record	41,706	45,244	43,277	46,435	45,878
Common Shares:					
Outstanding at December 31	70,663,515	58,477,890	57,806,869	57,430,526	56,986,579
Average outstanding during the year	59,875,990	58,215,897	57,727,577	57,322,165	60,564,981
Price Range:					
High	$ 54¹/₄	$ 46³/₈	$ 59³/₄	$ 67⁷/₈	$ 76¹/₂
Low	16³/₄	12⁷/₈	42¹/₈	47	35
Associates:					
Average during the year	99,952	107,671	111,469	114,161	114,658
Total compensation for the year	$ 2,854.1	$ 2,881.4	$ 2,775.0	$ 2,790.7	$2,592.8

The method of consolidating financial statements was changed in 1987. Financial information has been restated where necessary to reflect discontinued operations and the method of consolidating financial statements.

Goodyear Responsibility for Financial Statements

The financial statements of The Goodyear Tire & Rubber Company and Subsidiaries were prepared in conformity with generally accepted accounting principles. The Company is responsible for selection of appropriate accounting principles and the objectivity and integrity of the data, estimates and judgments which are the basis for the financial statements.

Goodyear has established and maintains a system of internal controls designed to provide reasonable assurance that the books and records reflect the transactions of the Company and that its established policies and procedures are carefully followed. This system is based upon written procedures, policies and guidelines, organizational structures that provide an appropriate division of responsibility, a program of internal audit and the careful selection and training of qualified personnel.

Price Waterhouse, independent accountants, examined the financial statements and their report is presented on the following page. Their opinion is based on an examination which provides an independent, objective review of the way Goodyear fulfills its responsibility to publish statements which present fairly the financial position and operating results. They obtain and maintain an understanding of the Company's accounting and reporting controls, test transactions and perform related auditing procedures as they consider necessary to arrive at an opinion on the fairness of the financial statements. While the auditors make extensive reviews of procedures, it is neither practicable nor necessary for them to test a large portion of the daily transactions.

The Board of Directors pursues its oversight responsibility for the financial statements through its Audit Committee, composed of Directors who are not employees of the Company. The Committee meets periodically with the independent accountants, representatives of management and internal auditors to assure that all are carrying out their responsibilities. To assure independence, Price Waterhouse and the internal auditors have full and free access to the Audit Committee, without Company representatives present, to discuss the results of their examinations and their opinions on the adequacy of internal controls and the quality of financial reporting.

Stanley C. Gault
Chairman of the Board
and Chief Executive Officer

Oren G. Shaffer
Executive Vice President
and Chief Financial Officer

BP America Building
200 Public Square
27th Floor
Cleveland, Ohio 44114-2301

Price Waterhouse

February 10, 1992

To the Board of Directors and Shareholders
of The Goodyear Tire & Rubber Company

In our opinion, the accompanying consolidated balance sheet and the related consolidated
statements of income, shareholders' equity and cash flows present fairly, in all material
respects, the financial position of The Goodyear Tire & Rubber Company and Subsidiaries
at December 31, 1991 and 1990, and the results of their operations and their cash flows for
each of the three years in the period ended December 31, 1991, in conformity with generally accepted accounting principles. These financial statements are the responsibility of the
Company's management; our responsibility is to express an opinion on these financial statements based on our audits. We conducted our audits of these statements in accordance with
generally accepted auditing standards which require that we plan and perform the audit to
obtain reasonable assurance about whether the financial statements are free of material mis-
statement. An audit includes examining, on a test basis, evidence supporting the amounts
and disclosures in the financial statements, assessing the accounting principles used and
significant estimates made by management, and evaluating the overall financial statement
presentation. We believe that our audits provide a reasonable basis for the opinion
expressed above.

42

Appendix **D**

Accounting for Partnerships

Forming a partnership is easy. It requires no permission from government authorities and involves no legal procedures. When two persons decide to go into business together, a partnership is automatically formed.

A **partnership** is an association of two or more persons or other entities who co-own a business for profit. This definition stems from the Uniform Partnership Act, which nearly every state has adopted to regulate partnership practice.

A partnership brings together the capital, talents, and experience of the partners. Business opportunities closed to an individual may open up to a partnership. Suppose neither Pedigo nor Lee has enough capital individually to buy a $300,000 parcel of land. They may be able to afford it together in a partnership. Or VanAllen, a tax accountant, and Kahn, an investment counselor, may pool their efforts. Their partnership may offer a fuller range of services than either person could offer alone.

Partnerships come in all sizes. Many partnerships have fewer than 10 partners. Some medical and law firms may have 20 or more partners. The largest CPA firms have almost 2,000 partners and businesses such as Wal-Mart pool their resources with other businesses to form partnerships.

Characteristics of a Partnership

Starting a partnership is voluntary. A person cannot be forced to join a partnership, and partners cannot be forced to accept another person as a partner. Although the partnership agreement may be oral, a written agreement between the partners reduces the chance of a misunderstanding. The following characteristics distinguish partnerships from sole proprietorships and corporations, which we examine in later chapters.

The Written Partnership Agreement

A business partnership is like a marriage. To be successful, the partners must cooperate. However, business partners do not vow to remain together for life. Business partnerships come and go. To make certain that each partner fully understands how a particular partnership operates, and to lower the chances that any partner might misunderstand how the business is run, partners may draw up a **partnership agreement,** also called the **articles of partnership.** This agreement is a contract between the partners, so transactions involving the agreement are governed by contract law. The articles of partnership should make the following points clear:

1. Name, location, and nature of the business
2. Name, capital investment, and duties of each partner
3. Method of sharing profits and losses by the partners
4. Withdrawals of assets allowed to the partners
5. Procedures for settling disputes between the partners
6. Procedures for admitting new partners
7. Procedures for settling up with a partner who withdraws from the business
8. Procedures for liquidating the partnership—selling the assets, paying the liabilities, and disbursing any remaining cash to the partners

As partners enter and leave the business, the old partnership is dissolved and a new partnership is formed. Preparing a separate agreement for each new partnership may be expensive and time consuming.

Limited Life

A partnership has a life limited by the length of time that all partners continue to own the business. When a partner withdraws from the business, that partnership ceases to exist. A new partnership may emerge to continue the same business, but the old partnership has been *dissolved.* **Dissolution** is the ending of a partnership. Likewise, the addition of a new partner dissolves the old partnership and creates a new partnership. Partnerships are sometimes formed for a particular business venture, like a mining operation or a real estate investment. When the mine is depleted or the real estate is sold, the partnership may be dissolved.

Mutual Agency

Mutual agency in a partnership means that every partner can bind the business to a contract within the scope of the partnership's regular business operations. If an individual partner in a CPA firm enters into a contract with a person or another business to provide accounting service, then the firm—not the individual who signs the contract—is bound to provide that service. However, if that same CPA signs a contract to purchase home lawn services for the summer months, the partnership would not be bound to pay. Contracting for personal lawn services does not fall within the partnership's regular business operations.

Unlimited Liability

Each partner has an **unlimited personal liability** for the debts of the partnership. When a partnership cannot pay its debts with business assets, the partners must use their personal assets to meet the debt.

Avilla and Davis are the two partners in AD Company. The business has had an unsuccessful year, and the partnership's liabilities exceed its assets by $120,000. Davis and Avilla must pay this amount with their personal assets.

Recall that each partner has *unlimited* liability. If a partner is unable to pay his or her part of the debt, the other partner (or partners) must make payment. If Davis can pay only $50,000 of the liability, Avilla must pay $70,000.

Unlimited liability and mutual agency are closely related. A dishonest partner or a partner with poor judgment may commit the partnership to a contract under which the business loses money. In turn, creditors may force *all* the partners to pay the debt from their personal assets. Hence, a business partner should be chosen with great care.

Partners can avoid unlimited personal liability for partnership obligations by forming a limited partnership. In this form of business organization, one or more general partners assume the unlimited liability for business debts. In addition there is another class of owners—limited partners. The limited partners can lose only as much as their investment in the business. In this sense limited partners have limited liability that is similar to the limited liability that stockholders of a corporation have.

Co-Ownership of Property

Any asset—cash, inventory, machinery, and so on—that a partner invests in the partnership becomes the joint property of all the partners. Also, each partner has a claim to the business's profits.

No Partnership Income Taxes

A partnership pays no income tax on its business income. Instead, the net income of the partnership is divided and becomes the taxable income of the partners. Suppose AD Company earned net income of $80,000, shared equally by partners Avilla and Davis. AD Company would pay no income tax *as a business entity*. However, Avilla and Davis would pay income tax as individuals on their $40,000 shares of partnership income.

Accounting for a partnership is much like accounting for a proprietorship. We record buying and selling, collecting and paying in a partnership just as we do for a business with only one owner. However, because a partnership has more than one owner, the partnership must have more than one owner's equity account. Every partner in the business—whether the firm has two or two thousand partners—has an individual owner's equity account. Often these accounts carry the name of the particular partner and the word *capital*. For example, the owner's equity account for Larry Insdorf would read "Insdorf, Capital." Similarly, each partner has a withdrawal account. If the number of partners is large, the general ledger may contain the single account Partners' Capital, or Owners' Equity. A subsidiary ledger can be used for individual partner accounts.

Let's see how to account for the multiple owner's equity accounts—and learn how they appear on the balance sheet—by looking at how to account for starting up a partnership.

Initial Investments by Partners _____

Partners in a new partnership may invest assets and liabilities in the business. These contributions are entered in the books in the same way that a proprietor's assets and liabilities are recorded. Subtracting each person's liabilities from his or her assets yields the amount to be credited to the capital account for that person. Often the partners hire an independent firm to appraise their assets and liabilities at current market value at the time a partnership is formed. This outside evaluation assures an objective accounting for what each partner brings into the business.

Assume Benz and Hanna form a partnership to manufacture and sell computer software. Benz brings to the partnership cash of $10,000, accounts receivable of $30,000, inventory of $70,000, computer equipment with a cost of $600,000 and accumulated depreciation of $120,000, and accounts payable of $85,000. Hanna contributes cash of $5,000 and a software program. The development of this program cost Hanna $18,000, but its current market value is much greater. Suppose the partners agree on the following values based on an independent appraisal:

OBJECTIVE 2

Account for partners' initial investments in a partnership

Benz's contributions:

Cash, $10,000; inventory, $70,000; and accounts payable, $85,000 (the appraiser believes the current market values for these items equal Benz's values)

Accounts receivable, $30,000, less allowance for doubtful accounts of $5,000

Computer equipment, $450,000

Hanna's contributions:

Cash, $5,000

Computer software, $100,000

Note that current market value differs only slightly from book value for Benz's computer equipment. However, the appraiser valued Hanna's $18,000 computer software at the much higher $100,000 figure. The partners record their initial investments at the current market values. The title of each owner's equity account includes the owner's name and *Capital*—exactly as for a proprietorship.

Benz's investment:

June 1	Cash	10,000	
	Accounts Receivable	30,000	
	Inventory	70,000	
	Computer Equipment	450,000	
	Allowance for Doubtful Accounts		5,000
	Accounts Payable		85,000
	Benz, Capital		470,000
	To record Benz's investment in the partnership.		

Hanna's investment:

June 1	Cash	5,000	
	Computer Software	100,000	
	Hanna, Capital		105,000
	To record Hanna's investment in the partnership.		

The initial partnership balance sheet reports these amounts as follows:

			Benz and Hanna		

Benz and Hanna
Balance Sheet
June 1, 19X5

Assets			Liabilities	
Cash		$ 15,000	Accounts payable....	$ 85,000
Accounts receivable..	$30,000			
Less Allowance for			**Capital**	
doubtful accounts .	5,000	25,000		
Inventory		70,000	Benz, capital	470,000
Computer equipment		450,000	Hanna, capital	105,000
Computer software ..		100,000	Total liabilities	
Total assets		$660,000	and capital	$660,000

Each owner's capital account appears under the heading Capital. Having more than one capital account distinguishes a partnership balance sheet from a proprietorship balance sheet.

Sharing Partnership Profits and Losses

How to allocate profits and losses among partners is one of the most challenging aspects of managing a partnership. If the partners have not drawn up an agreement, or if the agreement does not state how the partners will divide profits and losses, then, according to law, the partners must share profits and losses equally. If the agreement specifies a method for sharing profits but not losses, then losses are shared in the same proportion as profits. For example, a partner allocated 75 percent of the profits would likewise absorb 75 percent of any losses.

In some cases, an equal division is not fair. One partner may perform more work for the business than the other partner, or one partner may make a larger capital contribution. In the preceding example, Hanna might agree to work longer hours for the partnership than Benz in order to earn a greater share of profits. Benz could argue that he should share in more of the profits because he contributed more net assets ($470,000) than Hanna did ($105,000). Hanna might contend that her computer software program is the partnership's most important asset and that her share of the profits should be greater than Benz's share. Agreeing on a fair sharing of profits and losses in a partnership may be difficult. We now discuss options available in determining partners' shares.

Sharing Based on a Stated Fraction

OBJECTIVE 3

Use different methods to allocate profits and losses to the partners

Partners may agree to any profit-and-loss-sharing method they desire. Suppose the partnership agreement of Cagle and Dean allocates two-thirds of the business profits and losses to Cagle and one-third to Dean. If net income for the year is $90,000 and all revenue and expense accounts have been closed, the Income Summary account has a credit balance of $90,000, as follows:

Income Summary	
	Bal. 90,000

The entry to close this account and allocate the profit to the partners' capital accounts is

Dec. 31   Income Summary   90,000
         Cagle, Capital ($90,000 × ⅔)   60,000
         Dean, Capital ($90,000 × ⅓)..........   30,000
      To allocate net income to partners.

Consider the effect of this entry. Does Cagle get cash of $60,000 and Dean cash of $30,000? No. The increase in the capital accounts of the partners cannot be linked to any particular asset, including cash. Instead, the entry indicates that Cagle's ownership in *all* the assets of the business increased by $60,000 and Dean's by $30,000.

If the year's operations resulted in a net loss of $66,000, the Income Summary account would have a debit balance of $66,000. In that case, the closing entry to allocate the loss to the partners' capital accounts would be

Dec. 31   Cagle, Capital ($66,000 × ⅔)   44,000
          Dean, Capital ($66,000 × ⅓)   22,000
             Income Summary....................   66,000
      To allocate net loss to partners.

Sharing Based on Partners' Capital Contributions

Profits and losses are often allocated in proportion to the partners' capital contributions in the business. Suppose Antoine, Barber, and Cabañas are partners in ABC Company. Their capital accounts have the following balances at the end of the year, before the closing entries:

       Antoine, Capital .... $ 40,000
       Barber, Capital   60,000
       Cabañas, Capital...................   50,000
       Total capital balances.............. $150,000

Assume that the partnership earned a profit of $120,000 for the year. To allocate this amount based on capital contributions, compute each partner's percentage share of the partnership's total capital balance. Simply divide each partner's contribution by the total capital amount. These figures, multiplied by the $120,000 profit amount, yield each partner's share of the year's profits:

       Antoine: $40,000/$150,000 × $120,000   = $ 32,000
       Barber: $60,000/$150,000 × $120,000   =   48,000
       Cabañas: $50,000/$150,000 × $120,000   =   40,000
             Net income allocated to partners   = $120,000

The closing entry to allocate the profit to the partners' capital accounts is

Dec. 31   Income Summary   120,000
          Antoine, Capital....................   32,000
          Barber, Capital   48,000
          Cabañas, Capital   40,000
      To allocate net income to partners.

After this closing entry, the partners' capital balances are

Antoine, Capital ($40,000 + $32,000)	$ 72,000
Barber, Capital ($60,000 + $48,000)	108,000
Cabañas, Capital ($50,000 + $40,000)	90,000
Total capital balances after allocation of net income .	$270,000

Sharing Based on Capital Contributions and Service to the Partnership

One partner, regardless of his or her capital contribution, may put more work into the business than the other partners. Even among partners who log equal service time, one person's superior experience and knowledge may command a greater share of income. To reward the harder-working or more valuable person, the profit-and-loss-sharing method may be based on a combination of contributed capital *and* service to the business.

Assume Randolph and Scott formed a partnership in which Randolph invested $60,000 and Scott invested $40,000, a total of $100,000. Scott devotes more time to the partnership and earns the larger salary. Accordingly, the two partners have agreed to share profits as follows:

1. The first $50,000 of partnership profits is to be allocated based on partners' capital contributions to the business.
2. The next $60,000 of profits is to be allocated based on service, with Randolph receiving $24,000 and Scott receiving $36,000.
3. Any remaining amount is allocated equally.

If net income for the first year is $125,000, the partners' shares of this profit are computed as follows:

	Randolph	Scott	Total
Total net income.........................			$125,000
Sharing of first $50,000 of net income, based on capital contributions:			
Randolph ($60,000/$100,000 × $50,000) ..	$30,000		
Scott ($40,000/$100,000 × $50,000)		$20,000	
Total			50,000
Net income remaining for allocation			75,000
Sharing of next $60,000, based on service:			
Randolph	24,000		
Scott		36,000	
Total			60,000
Net income remaining for allocation			15,000
Remainder shared equally:			
Randolph ($15,000 × ½)...............	7,500		
Scott ($15,000 × ½)		7,500	
Total			15,000
Net income remaining for allocation			$ -0-
Net income allocated to the partners	$61,500	$63,500	$125,000

Based on this allocation, the closing entry is

Dec. 31	Income Summary	125,000	
	Randolph, Capital		61,500
	Scott, Capital		63,500
	To allocate net income to partners.		

Partners may be rewarded for their service and their capital contributions to the business in other ways. In one sharing plan, the partners are allocated salaries plus interest on their capital balances. Assume Lewis and Clark form an oil-exploration partnership. At the beginning of the year, their capital balances are $80,000 and $100,000, respectively. The partnership agreement allocates annual salary of $43,000 to Lewis and $35,000 to Clark. After salaries are allocated, each partner earns 8 percent interest on his beginning capital balance. Any remaining net income is divided equally. Partnership profit of $96,000 would be allocated as follows:

	Lewis	Clark	Total
Total net income..........................			$96,000
First, salaries:			
Lewis.................................	$43,000		
Clark		$35,000	
Total			78,000
Net income remaining for allocation			18,000
Second, interest on beginning capital balances:			
Lewis ($80,000 × .08)	6,400		
Clark ($100,000 × .08)..................		8,000	
Total			14,400
Net income remaining for allocation			3,600
Third, remainder shared equally:			
Lewis ($3,600 × ½)	1,800		
Clark ($3,600 × ½)		1,800	
Total			3,600
Net income remaining for allocation			$ -0-
Net income allocated to the partners	$51,200	$44,800	$96,000

Based on this allocation, the closing entry is

Dec. 31	Income Summary	96,000	
	Lewis, Capital........................		51,200
	Clark, Capital		44,800
	To allocate net income to partners.		

These salaries and interest amounts are *not* business expenses in the usual sense. Partners do not work for their own business to earn a salary, as an employee does. They do not loan money to their own business to earn interest. Their goal is for the partnership to earn a profit. Therefore, salaries and interest in partnership agreements are simply ways of expressing the allocation of profits and losses to the partners. For example, the salary component of partner income rewards service to the partnership. The interest component rewards a partner's investment of cash or other assets in the business.

In the preceding illustration, net income exceeded the sum of salary and interest. If the partnership profit is less than the allocated sum of salary and interest, a negative remainder will occur at some stage in the allocation process. Even so, the partners use the same method for allocation purposes. For example, assume that Lewis and Clark Partnership earned only $82,000.

	Lewis	Clark	Total
Total net income			$ 82,000
First, salaries:			
Lewis	$43,000		
Clark		$35,000	
Total			78,000
Net income remaining for allocation			4,000
Second, interest on beginning capital balances:			
Lewis ($80,000 × .08)	6,400		
Clark ($100,000 × .08)		8,000	
Total			14,400
Net income remaining for allocation			(10,400)
Third, remainder shared equally:			
Lewis ($10,400 × ½)	(5,200)		
Clark ($10,400 × ½)		(5,200)	
Total			(10,400)
Net income remaining for allocation			$ -0-
Net income allocated to the partners	$44,200	$37,800	$ 82,000

A net loss would be allocated to Lewis and Clark in the same manner outlined for net income. The sharing procedure would begin with the net loss and then allocate salary, interest, and any other specified amounts to the partners.

We see that partners may allocate profits and losses based on a stated fraction, contributed capital, service, interest on capital, or any combination of these factors. Each partnership shapes its profit-and-loss-sharing ratio to fit its own needs.

Partner Drawings

Partners, like anyone else, need cash for personal living expenses. Partnership agreements usually allow partners to withdraw cash or other assets from the business. Drawings from a partnership are recorded exactly as illustrated in previous chapters for drawings from a proprietorship. Assume Lewis and Clark are each allowed a monthly withdrawal of $3,500. The partnership records the March withdrawal with this entry:

Mar. 31	Lewis, Drawing	3,500	
	Clark, Drawing	3,500	
	Cash		7,000
	Monthly partner withdrawals.		

During the year, each partner drawing account accumulates 12 such amounts, a total of $42,000 ($3,500 × 12). At the end of the period, the general ledger shows the following account balances immediately after net income has been closed to the partners' capital accounts. Assume these beginning balances for Lewis and Clark at the start of the year and that $82,000 of profit has been allocated based on the preceding illustration.

Lewis, Capital	
	Jan. 1 Bal. 80,000
	Dec. 31 Net inc. 44,200

Clark, Capital	
	Jan. 1 Bal. 100,000
	Dec. 31 Net inc. 37,800

Lewis, Drawing		Clark, Drawing	
Dec. 31 Bal.	42,000	Dec. 31 Bal.	42,000

The withdrawal accounts must be closed at the end of the period. The final closing entries transfer their balances to the partner's capital account as follows:

Dec. 31	Lewis, Capital............................	42,000	
	Lewis, Drawing		42,000
	Clark, Capital	42,000	
	Clark, Drawing		42,000
	To close partner drawing accounts.		

After closing, the accounts appear as follows:

Lewis, Capital			
Dec. 31 Clo.	42,000	Jan. 1 Bal.	80,000
		Dec. 31 Net inc.	44,200
		Dec. 31 Bal.	82,200

Clark, Capital			
Dec. 31 Clo.	42,000	Jan. 1 Bal.	100,000
		Dec. 31 Net inc.	37,800
		Dec. 31 Bal.	95,800

Lewis, Drawing			
Dec. 31 Bal.	42,000	Dec. 31 Clo.	42,000

Clark, Drawing			
Dec. 31 Bal.	42,000	Dec. 31 Clo.	42,000

In this case, Lewis withdrew less than his share of the partnership net income. Consequently, his capital account grew during the period. Clark, however, withdrew more than his share of net income. His capital account decreased.

Partnerships, as we have mentioned, do not last forever. We turn now to a discussion of how partnerships dissolve—and how new partnerships arise.

Dissolution of a Partnership

A partnership lasts only as long as its partners remain in the business. The addition of a new member or the withdrawal of an existing member dissolves the partnership.

Often a new partnership is formed to carry on the former partnership's business. In fact, the new partnership may choose to retain the dissolved partnership's name. Price Waterhouse & Company, for example, is an accounting firm that retires and hires partners during the year. Thus the former partnership dissolves and a new partnership begins many times. The business, however, retains the name and continues operations. Other partnerships may dissolve and then reform under a new name. Let's look now at the ways that a new member may gain admission into an existing partnership.

Admission by Purchasing a Partner's Interest

A person may become a member of a partnership by gaining the approval of the other partner (or partners) for entrance into the firm *and* by purchasing a present partner's interest in the business. Let's assume that Fisher and Garcia have a partnership that carries these figures:

Cash	$ 40,000	Total liabilities	$120,000
Other assets	360,000	Fisher, capital	110,000
		Garcia, capital	170,000
		Total liabilities and	
Total assets	$400,000	capital	$400,000

Business is going so well that Fisher receives an offer from Dynak, an outside party, to buy her $110,000 interest in the business for $150,000. Fisher agrees to sell out to Dynak, and Garcia approves Dynak as a new partner. The firm records the transfer of capital interest in the business with this entry:

OBJECTIVE 4

Account for the admission of a new partner to the business

Apr. 16	Fisher, Capital	110,000	
	Dynak, Capital		110,000
	To transfer Fisher's equity in the business to Dynak.		

The debit side of the entry closes Fisher's capital account because she is no longer a partner in the firm. The credit side opens Dynak's capital account because Fisher's equity has been transferred to Dynak. Notice that the entry amount is Fisher's capital balance ($110,000) and not the $150,000 price that Dynak paid Fisher to buy into the business. The full $150,000 goes to Fisher, including the $40,000 difference between her capital balance and the price received from Dynak. In this example, the partnership receives no cash because the transaction was between Dynak and Fisher, not between Dynak and the partnership. Suppose Dynak pays Fisher less than Fisher's capital balance. That does not affect the entry on the partnership books. Fisher's equity is transferred to Dynak at book value ($110,000).

The old partnership has dissolved. Garcia and Dynak draw up a new partnership agreement, with a new profit-and-loss-sharing ratio, and continue business operations. If Garcia does not accept Dynak as a partner, Dynak gets no voice in management of the firm. However, under the Uniform Partnership Act, the purchaser shares in the profits and losses of the firm and in its assets at liquidation.

Admission by Investing in the Partnership

A person may also be admitted as a partner by investing directly in the partnership rather than by purchasing an existing partner's interest. The new partner contributes assets—for example, cash, inventory, or equipment—to the business. Assume that the partnership of Ingel and Jay has the following assets, liabilities, and capital:

Cash	$ 20,000	Total liabilities	$100,000
Other assets	240,000	Ingel, capital	70,000
		Jay, capital	90,000
		Total liabilities and	
Total assets	$260,000	capital	$260,000

Kahn offers to invest equipment and land (Other assets) with a market value of $80,000 to persuade the existing partners to take her into the business. Ingel and Jay agree to dissolve the existing partnership and to start up a new business, giving Kahn one-third interest in exchange for the contributed assets. The entry to record Kahn's investment is

July 18	Other Assets...............................	80,000	
	Kahn, Capital		80,000
	To admit L. Kahn as a partner with a one-third interest in the business.		

After this entry, the partnership books show:

Cash	$ 20,000	Total liabilities	$100,000
Other assets ($240,000 +		Ingel, capital	70,000
$80,000)	320,000	Jay, capital	90,000
		Kahn, capital	80,000
		Total liabilities and	
Total assets	$340,000	capital	$340,000

Kahn's one-third interest in the partnership [$80,000/($70,000 + $90,000 + $80,000) = ⅓] does not necessarily entitle her to one-third of the profits. The sharing of profits and losses is a separate element in the partnership agreement.

In the previous example, Dynak paid an individual member (Fisher), not the partnership. Note that Kahn's payment (the other assets) goes into the partnership.

Admission by Investing in the Partnership—Bonus to the Old Partners.
The more successful a partnership, the higher the payment the partners may demand from a person entering the business. Partners in a business that is doing quite well might require an incoming person to pay them a bonus. The bonus increases the current partners' capital accounts.

Suppose that Nagasawa and Osburn's partnership has earned above-average profits for 10 years. The two partners share profits and losses equally. The balance sheet carries these figures:

Cash	$ 40,000	Total liabilities	$100,000
Other assets	210,000	Nagasawa, capital	70,000
		Osburn, capital	80,000
		Total liabilities and	
Total assets	$250,000	capital	$250,000

The partners agree to admit Parker to a one-fourth interest with his cash investment of $90,000. Parker's capital balance on the partnership books is $60,000, computed as follows:

Partnership capital before Parker is admitted ($70,000 + $80,000)	$150,000
Parker's investment in the partnership	90,000
Partnership capital after Parker is admitted	$240,000
Parker's capital in the partnership ($240,000 × ¼)	$ 60,000

The entry on the partnership books to record Parker's investment is

Mar. 1	Cash	90,000	
	Parker, Capital		60,000
	Nagasawa, Capital ($30,000 × ½)		15,000
	Osburn, Capital ($30,000 × ½)		15,000
	To admit G. Parker as a partner with a one-fourth interest in the business.		

Parker's capital account is credited for his one-fourth interest in the partnership. The other partners share the $30,000 difference between Parker's investment ($90,000) and his equity in the business ($60,000). This difference is called a bonus and is accounted for as income to the old partners and is, therefore, allocated to them based on their profit-and-loss ratio.

The new partnership's balance sheet reports these amounts:

Cash ($40,000 + $90,000)	$130,000	Total liabilities	$100,000
Other assets	210,000	Nagasawa, capital ($70,000 + $15,000)	85,000
		Osburn, capital ($80,000 + $15,000)	95,000
		Parker, capital	60,000
		Total liabilities and	
Total assets	$340,000	capital	$340,000

Admission by Investing in the Partnership—Bonus to the New Partner. A potential new partner may be so important that the existing partners offer him or her a partnership share that includes a bonus. A law firm may strongly desire a former governor or other official as a partner because of the person's reputation. A restaurant owner may want to go into partnership with a famous sports personality like Jack Nicklaus or Dr. J. (Julius Irving).

Suppose Page and Osuka is a law partnership. The firm's balance sheet appears as follows:

Cash	$140,000	Total liabilities	$120,000
Other assets	360,000	Page, capital	230,000
		Osuka, capital	150,000
		Total liabilities and	
Total assets	$500,000	capital	$500,000

The partners admit Schiller, a former attorney general, as a partner with a one-third interest in exchange for his cash investment of $100,000. At the time of Schiller's admission, the firm's capital is $380,000—Page, $230,000, and Osuka, $150,000. Page and Osuka share profits and losses in the ratio of two-thirds to Page and one-third to Osuka. The computation of Schiller's equity in the partnership is

Partnership capital before Schiller is admitted ($230,000 + $150,000)	$380,000
Schiller's investment in the partnership	100,000
Partnership capital after Schiller is admitted	$480,000
Schiller's capital in the partnership ($480,000 × ⅓)	$160,000

The capital accounts of Page and Osuka are debited for the $60,000 difference between the new partner's equity ($160,000) and his investment ($100,000). The existing partners share this decrease in capital, which is accounted for as though it were a loss, based on their profit-and-loss ratio.

The entry to record Schiller's investment is

Aug. 24	Cash	100,000	
	Page, Capital ($60,000 × ⅔)	40,000	
	Osuka, Capital ($60,000 × ⅓)	20,000	
	Schiller, Capital		160,000
	To admit M. Schiller as a partner with a one-third interest in the business.		

The new partnership's balance sheet reports these amounts:

Cash			Total liabilities	$120,000
($140,000 + $100,000) .	$240,000		Page, capital	
Other assets	360,000		($230,000 − $40,000) ..	190,000
			Osuka, capital	
			($150,000 − $20,000) ..	130,000
			Schiller, capital	160,000
			Total liabilities and	
Total assets.............	$600,000		capital	$600,000

Withdrawal of a Partner

A partner may withdraw from the business for many reasons, including retirement or a dispute with the other partners. The withdrawal of a partner dissolves the old partnership. The partnership agreement should contain a provision to govern how to settle with a withdrawing partner. In the simplest case, as illustrated on page D-12, a partner may withdraw and sell his or her interest to another partner in a personal transaction. The only entry needed to record this transfer of equity debits the withdrawing partner's capital account and credits the purchaser's capital account. The dollar amount of the entry is the capital balance of the withdrawing partner, regardless of the price paid by the purchaser. The accounting when one current partner buys a second partner's interest is the same as when an outside party buys a current partner's interest.

OBJECTIVE 5
Account for the withdrawal of a partner from the business

If the partner withdraws in the middle of the accounting period, the partnership books should be updated to determine the withdrawing partner's capital balance. The business must measure net income or net loss for the fraction of the year up to the withdrawal date and allocate profit or loss according to the existing ratio. After closing the books, the business then accounts for the change in partnership capital.

The withdrawing partner may receive his or her share of the business in partnership assets other than cash. The question arises as to what value to assign the partnership assets: book value or current market value. The settlement procedure may specify an independent appraisal of assets to determine their current market value. If market values have changed, the appraisal will result in revaluing the partnership assets. Thus the partners share in any market value changes that their efforts caused.

Suppose Isaac is retiring in midyear from the partnership of Green, Henry, and Isaac. After the books have been adjusted for partial-period income but before the asset appraisal, revaluation, and closing entries, the balance sheet reports:

Cash...................	$ 39,000		Total liabilities	$ 80,000
Inventory	44,000		Green, capital	54,000
Land	55,000		Henry, capital	43,000
Building $95,000			Issac, capital............	21,000
Less accum.				
depr...... 35,000	60,000		Total liabilities and	
Total assets............	$198,000		capital	$198,000

Assume an independent appraiser revalues the inventory at $38,000 (down from $44,000) and the land at $101,000 (up from $55,000). The partners share the differences between these assets' market values and their prior book values based on their profit-and-loss ratio. The partnership agreement has allocated one-fourth of the profits to Green, one-half to Henry, and one-fourth to Isaac. (This ratio may be written 1 : 2 : 1 for one part to Green, two parts to Henry, and one part to Isaac.) For each share that Green or Isaac has, Henry has two. The entries to record the revaluation of the inventory and land are

July 31	Green, Capital ($6,000 × ¼)	1,500	
	Henry, Capital ($6,000 × ½)	3,000	
	Isaac, Capital ($6,000 × ¼)	1,500	
	Inventory ($44,000 − $38,000)		6,000
	To revalue the inventory and allocate the loss in value to the partners.		
31	Land ($101,000 − $55,000)	46,000	
	Green, Capital ($46,000 × ¼)		11,500
	Henry, Capital ($46,000 × ½)		23,000
	Isaac, Capital ($46,000 × ¼).		11,500
	To revalue the land and allocate the gain in value to the partners.		

After the revaluations, the partnership balance sheet reports:

Cash.	$ 39,000	Total liabilities	$ 80,000
Inventory	38,000	Green, capital	
Land	101,000	($54,000 − $1,500 +	
Building $95,000		$11,500)	64,000
Less accum.		Henry, capital	
depr 35,000	60,000	($43,000 − $3,000 +	
		$23,000)	63,000
		Isaac, capital ($21,000 −	
		$1,500 + $11,500)	31,000
		Total liabilities and	
Total assets.	$238,000	capital	$238,000

The books now carry the assets at current market value, which becomes the new book value, and the capital accounts have been adjusted accordingly. Isaac has a claim to $31,000 in partnership assets. How is his withdrawal from the business accounted for?

Withdrawal at Book Value

If Isaac withdraws by receiving cash equal to the book value of his owner's equity, the entry would be

July 31	Isaac, Capital	31,000	
	Cash		31,000
	To record withdrawal of K. Isaac from the partnership.		

This entry records the payment of partnership cash to Isaac and the closing of his capital account upon withdrawal from the business.

Withdrawal at Less Than Book Value

The withdrawing partner may be so eager to leave the business that he is willing to take less than his equity. This situation has occurred in real estate and oil-drilling partnerships. Assume Isaac withdraws from the business and agrees to receive partnership cash of $10,000 and the new partnership's note for $15,000. This $25,000 settlement is $6,000 less than Isaac's $31,000 equity in the business. The remaining partners share this $6,000 difference—which is a gain to them—according to their profit-and-loss ratio. However, since Isaac has withdrawn from the partnership, a new agreement—and a new profit-and-loss ratio—must be drawn up. Henry and Green, in forming a new partnership, may decide on any ratio that they see fit. Let's assume they agree that Henry will earn two-thirds of partnership profits and losses and Green one-third. The entry to record Isaac's withdrawal at less than book value is

July 31	Isaac, Capital	31,000	
	Cash		10,000
	Note Payable to K. Isaac		15,000
	Green, Capital ($6,000 × ⅓)		2,000
	Henry, Capital ($6,000 × ⅔)		4,000
	To record withdrawal of K. Isaac from the partnership.		

Isaac's account is closed, and Henry and Green may or may not continue the business.

Withdrawal at More Than Book Value

The settlement with a withdrawing partner may allow him to take assets of greater value than the book value of his capital. Also, the remaining partners may be so eager for the withdrawing partner to leave the firm that they pay him a bonus to withdraw from the business. In either case, the partner's withdrawal causes a decrease in the book equity of the remaining partners. This decrease is allocated to the partners based on their profit-and-loss ratio.

Assume Chang, Daley, and Evans share profits in a ratio of 3:2:1. Their partnership accounts include the following balances:

Cash	$ 50,000	Total liabilities	$110,000
Other assets	220,000	Chang, capital	80,000
		Daley, capital	50,000
		Evans, capital	30,000
		Total liabilities and	
Total assets	$270,000	capital	$270,000

Assume Evans withdraws, accepting cash of $15,000 and the new partnership's note for $25,000. This $40,000 settlement exceeds Evans's capital balance by $10,000. Chang and Daley share this loss in equity based on their profit-and-loss ratio (3:2). The withdrawal entry is

Nov. 30	Evans, Capital	30,000	
	Chang, Capital ($10,000 × ⅗)	6,000	
	Daley, Capital ($10,000 × ⅖)	4,000	
	Cash		15,000
	Note Payable to R. Evans		25,000
	To record withdrawal of R. Evans from the partnership.		

The withdrawal entry closes Evans's capital account and updates those of Chang and Daley.

Death of a Partner

Death of a partner, like any other form of partnership withdrawal, dissolves a partnership. The partnership accounts are adjusted to measure net income or loss for the fraction of the year up to the date of death, then closed to determine the partners' capital balances on that date. Settlement with the deceased partner's estate is based on the partnership agreement. The estate commonly receives partnership assets equal to the partner's capital balance. The partnership closes the deceased partner's capital account with a debit. This entry credits a payable to the estate.

Alternatively, a remaining partner may purchase the deceased partner's equity. The deceased partner's equity is debited and the purchaser's equity is credited. The amount of this entry is the ending credit balance in the deceased partner's capital account.

Liquidation of a Partnership

OBJECTIVE 6

Account for the liquidation of a partnership

Admission of a new partner or withdrawal or death of an existing partner dissolves the partnership. However, the business may continue operating with no apparent change to outsiders such as customers and creditors.

Business **liquidation**, however, is the process of going out of business by selling the entity's assets and paying its liabilities. The final step in liquidation of a business is the *distribution of the remaining cash to the owners*. Before liquidating the business, the books should be adjusted and closed. After closing, only asset, liability, and partners' capital accounts remain open.

Liquidation of a partnership includes three basic steps:

1. Sell the assets. Allocate the gain or loss to the partners' capital accounts based on the profit-and-loss ratio.
2. Pay the partnership liabilities.
3. Disburse the remaining cash to the partners based on their capital balances.

In actual practice, the liquidation of a business can stretch over weeks or months. Selling every asset and paying every liability of the entity takes time. To avoid excessive detail in our illustrations, we include only two asset categories—Cash and Noncash Assets—and a single liability category—Liabilities. Our examples also assume that the business sells the noncash assets in a single transaction and pays the liabilities in a single transaction.

Assume that Aviron, Bloch, and Crane have shared profits and losses in the ratio of 3:1:1. (This ratio is equal to ⅗, ⅕, ⅕, or a 60-percent, 20-percent, 20-percent sharing ratio.) They decide to liquidate their partnership. After the books are adjusted and closed, the general ledger contains the following balances:

Cash.................	$ 10,000	Liabilities	$ 30,000
Noncash assets	90,000	Aviron, capital..........	40,000
		Bloch, capital	20,000
		Crane, capital	10,000
		Total liabilities and	
Total assets............	$100,000	capital	$100,000

We will use the Aviron, Bloch, and Crane partnership data to illustrate accounting for liquidation in three different situations.

Sale of Noncash Assets at a Gain

Assume the partnership sells its noncash assets (shown on the balance sheet at $90,000) for cash of $150,000. The partnership realizes a gain of $60,000, which is allocated to the partners based on their profit-and-loss-sharing ratio. The entry to record this sale and allocation of the gain is

Oct. 31	Cash	150,000	
	Noncash Assets		90,000
	Aviron, Capital ($60,000 × .60)		36,000
	Bloch, Capital ($60,000 × .20)		12,000
	Crane, Capital ($60,000 × .20)		12,000
	To sell noncash assets in liquidation and allocate gain to partners.		

The partnership must next pay off its liabilities:

Oct. 31	Liabilities	30,000	
	Cash		30,000
	To pay liabilities in liquidation.		

In the final liquidation transaction, the remaining cash is disbursed to the partners. *The partners share in the cash according to their capital balances.* (By contrast, *gains and losses* on the sale of assets are shared by the partners based on their profit-and-loss-sharing ratio.) The amount of cash left in the partnership is $130,000—the $10,000 beginning balance plus the $150,000 cash sale of assets minus the $30,000 cash payment of liabilities. The partners divide the remaining cash according to their capital balances:

Oct. 31	Aviron, Capital ($40,000 + $36,000)	76,000	
	Bloch, Capital ($20,000 + $12,000)........	32,000	
	Crane, Capital ($10,000 + $12,000)	22,000	
	Cash		130,000
	To disburse cash to partners in liquidation.		

A convenient way to summarize the transactions in a partnership liquidation is given in Exhibit D-1.

EXHIBIT D-1   *Partnership Liquidation—Sale of Assets at a Gain*

				Capital		
	Cash	+ Noncash Assets =	Liabilities +	Aviron (60%) +	Bloch (20%) +	Crane (20%)
Balances before sale of assets	$ 10,000	$ 90,000	$ 30,000	$ 40,000	$ 20,000	$ 10,000
Sale of assets and sharing of gain	150,000	(90,000)		36,000	12,000	12,000
Balances	160,000	-0-	30,000	76,000	32,000	22,000
Payment of liabilities .	(30,000)		(30,000)			
Balances	130,000	-0-	-0-	76,000	32,000	22,000
Disbursement of cash to partners	(130,000)			(76,000)	(32,000)	(22,000)
Balances	$ -0-	$ -0-	$ -0-	$ -0-	$ -0-	$ -0-

After the disbursement of cash to the partners, the business has no assets, liabilities, or owners' equity. The balances are all zero. At all times, partnership assets must equal partnership liabilities plus partnership capital, by the accounting equation.

Sale of Noncash Assets at a Loss

Assume that Aviron, Bloch, and Crane sell the noncash assets for $75,000, realizing a loss of $15,000. The summary of transactions appears in Exhibit D-2. The journal entries to record the liquidation transactions are

Oct. 31	Cash	75,000	
	Aviron, Capital ($15,000 × .60)	9,000	
	Bloch, Capital ($15,000 × .20)	3,000	
	Crane, Capital ($15,000 × .20)	3,000	
	Noncash Assets		90,000
	To sell noncash assets in liquidation and allocate loss to partners.		
Oct. 31	Liabilities	30,000	
	Cash		30,000
	To pay liabilities in liquidation.		
31	Aviron, Capital ($40,000 − $9,000)	31,000	
	Bloch, Capital ($20,000 − $3,000)	17,000	
	Crane, Capital ($10,000 − $3,000)	7,000	
	Cash		55,000
	To disburse cash to partners in liquidation.		

Sale of Noncash Assets at a Loss—Deficiency in a Partner's Capital Account. The sale of noncash assets at a loss may result in a debit balance in a partner's capital account. This situation is called a **capital deficiency** because the partner's capital balance is insufficient to cover his share of the partnership's loss. The unlimited liability of partners forces the other partners to absorb this defi-

EXHIBIT D-2 *Partnership Liquidation—Sale of Assets at a Loss*

				Capital		
				Aviron (60%)	Bloch (20%)	Crane (20%)
	Cash	+ Noncash Assets	= Liabilities +	+	+	
Balance before sale of assets .	$ 10,000	$ 90,000	$ 30,000	$ 40,000	$ 20,000	$ 10,000
Sale of assets and sharing of loss	75,000	(90,000)		(9,000)	(3,000)	(3,000)
Balances	85,000	-0-	30,000	31,000	17,000	7,000
Payment of liabilities	(30,000)		(30,000)			
Balances	55,000	-0-	-0-	31,000	17,000	7,000
Disbursement of cash to partners	(55,000)			(31,000)	(17,000)	(7,000)
Balances	$ -0-	$ -0-	$ -0-	$ -0-	$ -0-	$ -0-

ciency through debits to their own capital accounts if the deficient partner does not erase his deficiency. The deficiency is a loss to the other partners, and they share it based on their profit-and-loss ratio.

DEFICIENT PARTNER UNABLE TO ERASE DEFICIENCY.   Assume that Aviron, Bloch, and Crane's partnership has had losses for several years. The market value of the noncash assets of the business is far less than book value ($90,000). In liquidation, the partnership sells these assets for $30,000, realizing a loss of $60,000. Crane's 20 percent share of this loss is $12,000. Because the loss exceeds his $10,000 capital balance, Crane's account has a $2,000 deficit. Crane is obligated to contribute personal funds to the business in order to meet this debt. Assume that Crane cannot erase the deficiency by contributing personal assets. Because of mutual agency, the other partners must absorb the deficiency before the final distribution of cash.

Because Aviron and Bloch share losses in the ratio of 3:1, Aviron absorbs three-fourths of the deficiency [3/(3 + 1) = ¾] and Bloch absorbs one-fourth [1/(3 + 1) = ¼]. Aviron's share of Crane's $2,000 deficiency is $1,500 ($2,000 × ¾), and Bloch's share is $500 ($2,000 × ¼).

The journal entries to record the foregoing liquidation transactions are

Oct. 31	Cash	30,000	
	Aviron, Capital ($60,000 × .60)	36,000	
	Bloch, Capital ($60,000 × .20)	12,000	
	Crane, Capital ($60,000 × .20)	12,000	
	Noncash Assets		90,000
	To sell noncash assets in liquidation and allocate loss to partners.		
31	Liabilities	30,000	
	Cash		30,000
	To pay liabilities in liquidation.		
31	Aviron, Capital ($2,000 × ¾)	1,500	
	Bloch, Capital ($2,000 × ¼)	500	
	Crane, Capital......................		2,000
	To allocate Crane's capital deficiency to the other partners.		
31	Aviron, Capital ($40,000 − $36,000 − $1,500)	2,500	
	Bloch, Capital ($20,000 − $12,000 − $500) ...	7,500	
	Cash		10,000
	To disburse cash to partners in liquidation.		

The summary of transactions in Exhibit D-3 includes a separate transaction (highlighted) to allocate Crane's deficiency to Aviron and Bloch.

DEFICIENT PARTNER ERASES DEFICIENCY.   A partner may erase his or her deficiency by contributing cash or other assets to the partnership. Such contributions are credited to the deficient partner's account and then distributed to the other partners. Suppose Crane erases his deficiency by investing $2,000 cash in the partnership.

The journal entries to record Crane's contribution and the disbursement of cash to the partners are on the following page.

EXHIBIT D-3 *Partnership Liquidation—Deficient Partner Unable to Erase a Capital Deficiency*

	Cash	+ Noncash Assets	= Liabilities +	Capital Aviron (60%) +	Bloch (20%) +	Crane (20%)
Balance before sale of assets .	$ 10,000	$ 90,000	$ 30,000	$ 40,000	$ 20,000	$ 10,000
Sale of assets and sharing of loss	30,000	(90,000)		(36,000)	(12,000)	(12,000)
Balances	40,000	-0-	30,000	4,000	8,000	(2,000)
Payment of liabilities	(30,000)		(30,000)			
Balances	10,000	-0-	-0-	4,000	8,000	(2,000)
Sharing of Crane's deficiency by Aviron and Bloch				**(1,500)**	**(500)**	**2,000**
Balances	10,000	-0-	-0-	2,500	7,500	-0-
Disbursement of cash to partners	(10,000)			(2,500)	(7,500)	
Balances	$ -0-	$ -0-	$ -0-	$ -0-	$ -0-	$ -0-

Oct. 31	Cash	2,000	
	Crane, Capital.		2,000
	Crane's contribution to erase his capital deficiency in liquidation.		
31	Aviron, Capital.	4,000	
	Bloch, Capital	8,000	
	Cash		12,000
	To disburse cash to partners in liquidation.		

In this case, the summary of transactions, beginning with the balances after payment of the liabilities, appears in Exhibit D-4.

EXHIBIT D-4 *Partnership Liquidation—Partner Erases Capital Deficiency*

	Cash	+ Noncash Assets	= Liabilities +	Capital Aviron (60%) +	Bloch (20%) +	Crane (20%)
Balances after payment of liabilities	$ 10,000	$ -0-	$ -0-	$ 4,000	$ 8,000	$(2,000)
Crane's contribution to erase his deficiency	2,000	-0-	-0-			2,000
Balances	12,000	-0-	-0-	4,000	8,000	-0-
Disbursement of cash to partners	(12,000)			(4,000)	(8,000)	
Balances	$ -0-	$ -0-	$ -0-	$ -0-	$ -0-	$ -0-

Partnership Financial Statements

OBJECTIVE 7
Prepare partnership financial statements

Partnership financial statements are much like those of a proprietorship. However, a partnership income statement includes a section showing the division of net income to the partners. For example, the partnership of Gray and Hayward might report its income statement for the year ended June 30, 19X6, as follows:

Gray and Hayward Income Statement For the Year Ended June 30, 19X6	
Sales revenue	$381,000
Net income	$ 79,000
Allocation of net income:	
M. Gray	$ 36,600
L. Hayward	42,400
Total	$ 79,000

Large partnerships may not find it feasible to report the net income of every partner. Instead, the firm may report the allocation of net income to active and retired partners and average earnings per partner. For example, the CPA firm of Main Price & Anders reported the following:

Main Price & Anders Combined Statement of Earnings For the Year Ended August 31, 19X0	
Dollar amounts in thousands	
Fees for Professional Services	$914,492
Earnings for the year	$297,880
Allocation of earnings:	
To partners active during the year—	
Resigned, retired, and deceased partners	$ 19,901
Partners active at year end	253,270
To retired and deceased partners—retirement and death benefits	8,310
Not allocated to partners—retained for specific partnership purposes	16,399
	$297,880
Average earnings per partner active at year end (1,336 partners)	$223

Exhibit D-5 summarizes the financial statements of a proprietorship and a partnership.

EXHIBIT D-5 *Financial Statements of a Proprietorship and a Partnership*

Income Statements
For the Year Ended December 31, 19X1

Proprietorship		Partnership		
Revenues	$460	Revenues		$460
Expenses	(270)	Expenses		(270)
Net income	$190	Net income		$190
		Allocation of net income:		
		To Smith	$114	
		To Jones	76	$190

Statements of Owner Equity
For the Year Ended December 31, 19X1

Proprietorship		Partnership	Smith	Jones
Capital, December 31, 19X0	$ 90	Capital, December 31, 19X0	$ 50	$ 40
Additional investments	10	Additional investments	10	—
Net income	190	Net income	114	76
Subtotal	290	Subtotal	174	116
Drawings	(120)	Drawings	(72)	(48)
Capital, December 31, 19X1	$170	Capital, December 31, 19X1	$102	$ 68

Balance Sheets
December 31, 19X1

Proprietorship		Partnership	
Assets		**Assets**	
Cash and other assets	$170	Cash and other assets	$170
Owners' Equity		**Owners' Equity**	
		Smith, capital	$102
		Jones, capital	68
Smith, capital	$170	Total capital	$170

Summary Problem for Your Review

The partnership of Taylor and Uvalde is considering admitting Vaughn as a partner on January 1, 19X8. The partnership general ledger includes the following balances on that date:

Cash	$ 9,000	Total liabilities	$ 50,000
Other assets	110,000	Taylor, capital	45,000
		Uvalde, capital	24,000
Total assets	$119,000	Total liabilities and capital	$119,000

Taylor's share of profits and losses is 60 percent, and Uvalde's share is 40 percent.

Required (Items 1 and 2 are independent)

1. Suppose Vaughn pays Uvalde $31,000 to acquire Uvalde's interest in the business. Taylor approves Vaughn as a partner.
   a. Record the transfer of owner's equity on the partnership books.
   b. Prepare the partnership balance sheet immediately after Vaughn is admitted as a partner.
2. Suppose Vaughn becomes a partner by investing $31,000 cash to acquire a one-fourth interest in the business.
   a. Compute Vaughn's capital balance, and record Vaughn's investment in the business.
   b. Prepare the partnership balance sheet immediately after Vaughn is admitted as a partner. Include the heading.
3. Which way of admitting Vaughn to the partnership increases its total assets? Give your reason.

SOLUTION TO REVIEW PROBLEM

Requirement 1

a. Jan. 1 Uvalde, Capital 24,000

                 Vaughn, Capital   24,000

                 To transfer Uvalde's equity in the partnership to Vaughn.

b. The balance sheet for the partnership of Taylor and Vaughn is identical to the balance sheet given for Taylor and Uvalde in the problem, except that Vaughn's name replaces Uvalde's name in the title and in the listing of capital accounts.

Requirement 2

a. Computation of Vaughn's capital balance:

Partnership capital before Vaughn is admitted
($45,000 + $24,000) .... $ 69,000

Vaughn's investment in the partnership   31,000

Partnership capital after Vaughn is admitted $100,000

Vaughn's capital in the partnership ($100,000 × ¼) .... $ 25,000

Jan. 1 Cash 31,000

                Vaughn, Capital   25,000

                Taylor, Capital

                  [($31,000 − $25,000) × .60]   3,600

                Uvalde, Capital

                  [($31,000 − $25,000) × .40]   2,400

              To admit Vaughn as a partner with a one-fourth interest in the business.

b.

Taylor, Uvalde, and Vaughn
Balance Sheet
January 1, 19X8

Cash		Total liabilities	$ 50,000
($9,000 + $31,000)......	$ 40,000	Taylor, capital	
Other assets	110,000	($45,000 + $3,600)......	48,600
		Uvalde, capital	
		($24,000 + $2,400)......	26,400
		Vaughn, capital	25,000
Total assets	$150,000	Total liabilities and capital.	$150,000

Requirement 3

Vaughn's investment in the partnership increases its total assets by the amount of his contribution. Total assets of the business are $150,000 after his investment, compared to $119,000 before. By contrast, Vaughn's purchase of Uvalde's interest in the business is a personal transaction between the two individuals. It does not affect the assets of the partnership regardless of the amount Vaughn pays Uvalde.

Summary

A *partnership* is a business co-owned by two or more persons for profit. The characteristics of this form of business organization are its *ease of formation, limited life, mutual agency, unlimited liability,* and *no partnership income taxes.*

A written *partnership agreement,* or *articles of partnership,* establishes procedures for admission of a new partner, withdrawals of a partner, and the sharing of profits and losses among the partners.

When a new partner is admitted to the firm or an existing partner withdraws, the old partnership is *dissolved,* or ceases to exist. A new partnership may or may not emerge to continue the business.

Accounting for a partnership is similar to accounting for a proprietorship. However, a partnership has more than one owner. Each partner has an individual capital account and a withdrawal account.

Partners share net income or loss in any manner they choose. Common sharing agreements base the *profit-and-loss ratio* on a stated fraction, partners' capital contributions, and/or their service to the partnership. Some partnerships call the cash drawings of partners *salaries* and *interest,* but these amounts are not expenses of the business. Instead, they are merely ways of allocating partnership net income to the partners.

An outside person may become a partner by purchasing a current partner's interest or by investing in the partnership. In some cases the new partner must pay the current partners a bonus to join. In other situations the new partner may receive a bonus to join.

When a partner withdraws, partnership assets may be reappraised. Partners share any gain or loss on the asset revaluation based on their profit-and-loss ratio. The withdrawing partner may receive payment equal to, greater than, or less than, his or her capital book value, depending on the agreement with the other partners.

In *liquidation,* a partnership goes out of business by selling the assets, paying the liabilities, and disbursing any remaining cash to the partners. Any partner's capital deficiency, which may result from sale of assets at a loss, must be absorbed before remaining cash is distributed.

Partnership *financial statements* are similar to those of a proprietorship. However, the partnership income statement commonly reports the allocation of net income to the partners.

Accounting Vocabulary

Articles of partnership. Agreement that is the contract between partners specifying such items as the name, location, and nature of the business; the name, capital investment, and duties of each partner; and the method of sharing profits and losses by the partners. Also called the partnership agreement *(p. D-3)*.

Capital deficiency. Debit balance in a partner's capital account *(p. D-20)*.

Dissolution. Ending of a partnership *(p. D-3)*.

Liquidation. The process of going out of business by selling the entity's assets and paying its liabilities. The

final step in liquidation of a business is the distribution of any remaining cash to the owners *(p. D-18)*.

Mutual agency. Every partner can bind the business to a contract within the scope of the partnership's regular business operations *(p. D-3)*.

Partnership agreement. Another name for the articles of partnership *(p. D-3)*.

Unlimited personal liability. When a partnership (or a proprietorship) cannot pay its debts with business assets, the partners (or the proprietor) must use personal assets to meet the debt *(p. D-3)*.

ASSIGNMENT MATERIAL

Exercises

Exercise D-1   *Organizing a business as a partnership*   (L.O. 1)

Alan Bowden, a friend from college, approaches you about forming a partnership to export software. Since graduation, Alan has worked for the Export-Import Bank, developing important contacts among government officials and business leaders in Czechoslovakia and Hungary. Eager to upgrade their data-processing capabilities, Eastern Europeans are looking for ways to obtain American computers. Alan believes he is in a unique position to capitalize on this opportunity. With expertise in finance, you would have responsibility for accounting and finance in the partnership.

Required

Discuss the advantages and disadvantages of organizing the export business as a partnership rather than a proprietorship. Comment on how partnership income is taxed.

Exercise D-2   *Recording a partner's investment*   (L.O. 2)

Celeste Caballero has operated an apartment-locater service as a proprietorship. She and Julia Wiethorn have decided to reorganize the business as a partnership. Celeste's investment in the partnership consists of cash, $3,700; accounts receivable, $10,600 less allowance for uncollectibles, $800; office furniture, $2,700 less accumulated depreciation, $1,100; a small building, $55,000 less accumulated depreciation, $27,500; accounts payable, $3,300; and a note payable to the bank, $10,000.

To determine Celeste's equity in the partnership, she and Julia hire an independent appraiser. This outside party provides the following market values of the assets and liabilities that Celeste is contributing to the business: cash, accounts receivable, office furniture, accounts payable, and note payable—the same as Celeste's book value; allowance for uncollectible accounts, $2,900; building, $35,000; and accrued expenses payable (including interest on the note payable), $1,200.

Required

Make the entry on the partnership books to record Celeste's investment.

Exercise D-3 *Computing partners' shares of net income and net loss* **(L.O. 3)**

Alice Mitten and Martha Gibney form a partnership, investing $30,000 and $60,000, respectively. Determine their shares of net income or net loss for each of the following situations:

a. Net loss is $31,000, and the partners have no written partnership agreement.
b. Net income is $102,000, and the partnership agreement states that the partners share profits and losses based on their capital contributions.
c. Net loss is $78,000, and the partnership agreement states that the partners share profits based on their capital contributions.
d. Net income is $125,000. The first $60,000 is shared based on the partner capital contributions. The next $45,000 is based on partner service, with Mitten receiving 30 percent and Gibney receiving 70 percent. The remainder is shared equally.

Exercise D-4 *Computing partners' capital balances* **(L.O. 3)**

Alice Mitten withdrew cash of $62,000 for personal use, and Martha Gibney withdrew cash of $50,000 during the year. Using the data from situation d in Exercise E-3, journalize the entries to close the (a) income summary account and (b) the partners' drawing accounts. Explanations are not required.

Indicate the amount of increase or decrease in each partner's capital balance. What was the overall effect on partnership capital?

Exercise D-5 *Admitting a new partner* **(L.O. 4)**

Bob Lemley is admitted to a partnership. Prior to the admission of Lemley, the partnership books show Richard Battistoni's capital balance at $100,000 and Carol Terry's capital balance at $50,000. Compute the amount of each partner's equity on the books of the new partnership under each of the following plans:

a. Lemley pays $50,000 for Terry's equity. Lemley's payment is not an investment in the partnership but instead goes directly to Terry.
b. Lemley invests $50,000 to acquire a one-fourth interest in the partnership.
c. Lemley invests $70,000 to acquire a one-fourth interest in the partnership.

Exercise D-6 *Recording the admission of a new partner* **(L.O. 4)**

Make the partnership journal entry to record the admission of Lemley under plans a, b, and c in Exercise E-5. Explanations are not required.

Exercise D-7 *Withdrawal of a partner* **(L.O. 5)**

After closing the books, Brooks & Linam's partnership balance sheet reports capital of $50,000 for Brooks and $70,000 for Linam. Brooks is withdrawing from the firm. The partners agree to write down partnership assets by $40,000. They have shared profits and losses in the ratio of one third to Brooks and two thirds to Linam. If the partnership agreement states that a withdrawing partner will receive assets equal to the book value of his owner's equity, how much will Brooks receive?

Linam will continue to operate the business as a proprietorship. What is Linam's beginning capital on the proprietorship books?

Exercise D-8   *Withdrawal of a partner*   *(L.O. 5)*

Derek Backus is retiring from the partnership of Backus, Cantu, and Gill on May 31. After the books are closed on that date, the partner capital balances are Backus, $36,000; Cantu, $51,000; and Gill, $22,000. The partners agree to have the partnership assets revalued to current market values. The independent appraiser reports that the book value of the inventory should be decreased by $3,000, and the book value of the building should be increased by $35,000. The partners agree to these revaluations. The profit-and-loss ratio has been 5:3:2 for Backus, Cantu, and Gill, respectively. In retiring from the firm, Backus receives $30,000 cash and a $25,000 note from the partnership. Journalize (a) the asset revaluations and (b) Backus's withdrawal from the firm.

Exercise D-9   *Liquidation of a partnership*   *(L.O. 6)*

Dooney, Casini, and Oleg are liquidating their partnership. Before selling the noncash assets and paying the liabilities, the capital balances are Dooney, $23,000; Casini, $14,000; and Oleg, $11,000. The partnership agreement divides profits and losses equally.

a.   After selling the noncash assets and paying the liabilities, the partnership has cash of $48,000. How much cash will each partner receive in final liquidation?

b.   After selling the noncash assets and paying the liabilities, the partnership has cash of $39,000. How much cash will each partner receive in final liquidation?

Exercise D-10   *Liquidation of a partnership*   *(L.O. 6)*

Prior to liquidation, the accounting records of Sims, Trent, and Udall included the following balances and profit-and-loss-sharing percentages:

		Noncash			Capital		
					Sims	Trent	Udall
	Cash	+ Assets	= Liabilities +		(40%)	(30%)	(30%)
Balances before sale of assets	$8,000	$57,000	$19,000		$20,000	$15,000	$11,000

The partnership sold the noncash assets for $63,000, paid the liabilities, and disbursed the remaining cash to the partners. Complete the summary of transactions in the liquidation of the partnership. Use the format illustrated in the chapter.

Exercise D-11   *Preparing a partnership balance sheet*   *(L.O. 7)*

On October 31, 19X9, Black and White agree to combine their proprietorships as a partnership. Their balance sheets on October 31 are as follows:

Assets	Black's Business		White's Business	
	Book Value	Current Market Value	Book Value	Current Market Value
Cash	$ 8,000	$ 8,000	$ 3,700	$ 3,700
Accounts receivable (net) .	8,000	6,300	22,000	20,200
Inventory	34,000	35,100	51,000	46,000
Plant assets (net)	53,500	57,400	121,800	123,500
Total assets	$103,500	$106,800	$198,500	$193,400

Liabilities and Capital

	Book Value	Current Market Value	Book Value	Current Market Value
Accounts payable	$ 9,100	$ 9,100	$ 23,600	$ 23,600
Accrued expenses payable	1,400	1,400	2,200	2,200
Notes payable	—	—	75,000	75,000
Black, capital	93,000	96,300		
White, capital			97,700	92,600
Total liabilities and capital	$103,500	$106,800	$198,500	$193,400

Required

Prepare the partnership balance sheet at October 31, 19X9.

Problems

Problem 1D   *Writing a partnership agreement*   **(L.O. 1)**

John Haggai and Jody Magliolo are discussing the formation of a partnership to manufacture trapper-keeper ring binders used by schoolchildren. John is especially artistic, and he is convinced that his designs will draw large sales volumes. Jody is a super salesperson and has already lined up several large stores to sell the merchandise.

Required

Write a partnership agreement to cover all elements essential for the business to operate smoothly. Make up names, amounts, profit-and-loss sharing percentages, and so on as needed.

Problem 2D   *Investments by partners*   **(L.O. 2, 7)**

On June 30 Dukakis and Pilot formed a partnership. The partners agreed to invest equal amounts of capital. Dukakis invested his proprietorship's assets and liabilities (credit balances in parentheses).

On June 30 Pilot invested cash in an amount equal to the current market value of Dukakis's partnership capital. The partners decided that Dukakis would earn two thirds of partnership profits because he would manage the business. Pilot agreed to accept one third of the profits. During the remainder of the year, the partnership earned $60,000. Dukakis's drawings were $35,200, and Pilot's drawings were $23,000.

	Dukakis's Book Value	Current Market Value
Accounts receivable	$ 16,300	$ 16,300
Allowance for doubtful accounts	(-0-)	(1,050)
Inventory	22,340	24,100
Prepaid expenses	1,700	1,700
Office equipment	45,900	27,600
Accumulated depreciation	(15,300)	-0-
Accounts payable	(19,100)	(19,100)

Required

1. Journalize the partners' initial investments.
2. Prepare the partnership balance sheet immediately after its formation on June 30.
3. Journalize the December 31 entries to close the Income Summary account and the partner drawing accounts.

Problem 3D *Computing partners' shares of net income and net loss* (L.O. 3, 7)

L. Conway, S. Stroube, and E. Henke have formed a partnership. Conway invested $15,000, Stroube $18,000, and Henke $27,000. Conway will manage the store, Stroube will work in the store half time, and Henke will not work in the business.

Required

1. Compute the partners' shares of profits and losses under each of the following plans.

   a. Net loss is $63,900, and the articles of partnership do not specify how profits and losses are shared.
   b. Net loss is $70,000, and the partnership agreement allocates 40 percent of profits to Conway, 25 percent to Stroube, and 35 percent to Henke. The agreement does not discuss the sharing of losses.
   c. Net income is $92,000. The first $40,000 is allocated based on salaries, with Conway receiving $28,000 and Stroube receiving $12,000. The remainder is allocated based on partner capital contributions.
   d. Net income for the year ended January 31, 19X8, is $162,000. The first $75,000 is allocated based on partner capital contributions, and the next $36,000 is based on service, with Conway receiving $28,000 and Stroube receiving $8,000. Any remainder is shared equally.
2. Revenues for the year ended January 31, 19X8, were $872,000, and expenses were $710,000. Under plan d, prepare the partnership income statement for the year.

Problem 4D *Recording changes in partnership capital* (L.O. 4, 5)

Leading Edge Optics is a partnership, and its owners are considering admitting Curt Benson as a new partner. On March 31 of the current year the capital accounts of the three existing partners and their shares of profits and losses are as follows:

	Capital	Profit-and-Loss Percent
Lee Gingiss	$ 50,000	15%
Diedre Hauk	125,000	30
Paul Kaiser	200,000	55

Required

Journalize the admission of Benson as a partner on March 31 for each of the following independent situations:

1. Hauk gives her partnership share to C. Benson, who is her son.
2. Benson pays Kaiser $145,000 cash to purchase half of Kaiser's interest in the partnership.
3. Benson invests $75,000 in the partnership, acquiring a one-sixth interest in the business.

4. Benson invests $75,000 in the partnership, acquiring a one-fifth interest in the business.
5. Benson invests $50,000 in the partnership, acquiring a 10 percent interest in the business.

Problem 5D   Recording changes in partnership capital   (L.O. 4, 5)

Advantage Investors is a partnership owned by three individuals. The partners share profits and losses in the ratio of 31 percent to Speed, 38 percent to Uzzel, and 31 percent to Ross. At December 31, 19X7, the firm has the following balance sheet.

Cash		$ 31,000	Total liabilities	$ 94,000
Accounts receivable .	$ 22,000			
Less Allowance for uncollectibles	4,000	18,000	Speed, capital	84,000
Building	$310,000		Uzzel, capital.....	49,000
Less Accumulated depreciation	70,000	240,000	Ross, capital...... Total liabilities and	62,000
Total assets		$289,000	capital	$289,000

Uzzel withdraws from the partnership on December 31, 19X7, to establish his own consulting practice.

Required

Record Uzzel's withdrawal from the partnership under the following plans:

1. Uzzel gives his interest in the business to Zagat, his niece.
2. In personal transactions, Uzzel sells his equity in the partnership to Grimes and Hirsh, who each pay Uzzel $50,000 for one-half of his interest. Speed and Ross agree to accept Grimes and Hirsh as partners.
3. The partnership pays Uzzel cash of $15,000 and gives him a note payable for the remainder of his book equity in settlement of his partnership interest.
4. Uzzel receives cash of $10,000 and a note for $70,000 from the partnership.
5. The partners agree that the building is worth only $280,000 and that its accumulated depreciation should remain at $70,000. After the revaluation, the partnership settles with Uzzel by giving him cash of $10,600 and a note payable for the remainder of his book equity.

Problem 6D   Liquidation of a partnership   (L.O. 6)

The partnership of Renoir, Dixon, and Palma has experienced operating losses for three consecutive years. The partners, who have shared profits and losses in the ratio of Renoir 10 percent, Dixon 30 percent, and Palma 60 percent, are considering the liquidation of the business. They ask you to analyze the effects of liquidation under various possibilities about the sale of the noncash assets. They present the following condensed partnership balance sheet at December 31, end of the current year:

Cash.................	$ 27,000	Liabilities	$131,000
Noncash assets	202,000	Renoir, capital	13,000
		Dixon, capital	39,000
		Palma, capital	46,000
Total assets............	$229,000	Total liabilities and capital	$229,000

Required

1. Prepare a summary of liquidation transactions (as illustrated in the chapter) for each of the following situations:
   a. The noncash assets are sold for $212,000.
   b. The noncash assets are sold for $182,000.
   c. The noncash assets are sold for $122,000, and the partner with a capital deficiency pays cash to the partnership to erase the deficiency.
   d. The noncash assets are sold for $112,000, and the partner with a capital deficiency is personally bankrupt.
2. Make the journal entries to record the liquidation transactions in Requirement *ld*.

Problem 7D   Liquidation of a partnership   (L.O. 6)

Clover Associates is a partnership owned by Sen, Sundem, and Dopuch, who share profits and losses in the ratio of 5:3:2. The adjusted trial balance of the partnership (in condensed form) at September 30, end of the current fiscal year, follows.

Clover Associates
Adjusted Trial Balance
September 30, 19XX

Cash	$ 15,000	
Noncash assets	177,000	
Liabilities		$138,000
Sen, capital		57,000
Sundem, capital		53,000
Dopuch, capital		14,000
Sen, drawing	45,000	
Sundem, drawing	37,000	
Dopuch, drawing	18,000	
Revenues		211,000
Expenses	181,000	
Totals	$473,000	$473,000

Required

1. Prepare the September 30 entries to close the revenue, expense, income summary, and drawing accounts.
2. Insert the opening capital balances in the partner capital accounts, post the closing entries to the capital accounts, and determine each partner's ending capital balance.
3. The partnership liquidates on September 30 by selling the noncash assets for $142,000. Using the ending balances of the partner capital accounts, prepare a summary of liquidation transactions (as illustrated in the chapter). Any partner with a capital deficiency is unable to contribute assets to erase the deficiency.

Company Index

Subject Index

Check Figures for Problems

(continued from front cover)

17-4A 2. B/E = 30 cruises; 4. Income = $270,200

17-5A 3. Income, $60,000; 4. B/E = $2,150,400

17-6A 4. New B/E sales, $56,000

17-7A 2. Target sales, $12,375; 4. B/E = 13 units

17-1B No check figure

17-2B 3. B/E sales = $315,429; 5. Income = $16,800

17-3B A. Unit contrib. margin, $5; B. Contrib. margin ratio, .586

17-4B 2. B/E = 51 cruises; 4. Income = $29,000

17-5B 3. Loss, $19,500; 4. B/E = $1,041,463

17-6B 4. New B/E sales, $41,600

17-7B 2. Target sales, $11,306; 4. B/E = 15 units

DP 1 B/E. = $89,143

DP 2 3. CM: Newborn, $225,366; Toddler, $66,025; Preschooler, $142,614

18-1A 1. 1-store income, $43,750; 2-store income, $35,000

18-2A 3. 200 cars sold per salesperson

18-3A 2. $177.6 million

18-4A 4. Total operating cost = $16,250 + $7.50/track mile

18-5A 1. Variable costs = 80%; fixed costs = 20% 3. $7,200 for 75,000 square feet

18-6A 1. $4,302 for 6,000 hours; $5,382 for 4,000 hours

18-1B 1. 1-store income, $66,000; 2-store income, $54,000

18-2B 3. 20 boats sold per salesperson

18-3B 2. $11.8 million

18-4B 4. Total production costs = $35,350 + $75/coat

18-5B 1. Variable costs = 55.6%; fixed costs = 44.4% 3. $4,000 for 40,000 tools

18-6B 1. $2,000 for 200 products; $1,000 for 250 products

DP 2. 400 boats

19-1A Direct mat. used, $78,000; Net inc. $30,800

19-2A April work in process inven., $1,800; April cost of goods sold, $5,400

19-3A 1. Cost of goods manuf., $159.8 mil; 2. Cost of goods sold, $157.6 mil.

19-4A Fin. goods inven. bal., $41,180

19-5A Total job cost, $1,334

19-6A Income from oper., $45,515

19-7A Cost of goods sold, $229,600

19-1B Direct labor, $72,000; Net inc., $54,000

19-2B July work in process inven., $3,200; July cost of goods sold, $3,800

19-3B 1. Cost of goods manuf., $21,200,000; 3. Materials purchased, $3,100,000

19-4B Fin. goods inven. bal., $133,880

19-5B Total job cost, $2,179

19-6B Income from oper., $42,020

19-7B Cost of goods sold, $187,900

DP 1 No check figure

DP 2 New sale price per unit, $10.18

20-1A Cost per unit $1.30; Work in Process bal. $693

20-2A Cost per unit $4.60; Work in Process bal. $3,480

20-3A Cost per equiv. unit: Trans. in $10; Materials $11; Conv. costs $19

20-4A Total cost accounted for $136,380

20-5A Cost per equiv. unit: Transf. in $0.12; Conv. costs $0.07. Cost per screwdriver $0.32

20-6A Cost per equiv. unit: Transf. in $0.115; Conv. costs $0.089. Cost per screwdriver $0.318

20-1B Cost per unit $4.30; Work in Process bal. $17,360

20-2B Cost per unit $24; Work in Process bal. $2,400

20-3B Cost per equiv. unit: Transf. in $38; Materials $21; Conv. costs $89

20-4B Total cost accounted for $94,677

20-5B Cost per equiv. unit: Transf. in $37; Conv. costs $8. Cost per mower $50.82

20-6B Cost per equiv. unit: Transf. in $36.75; Conv. costs $9.174. Cost per mower $50.34

DP 1 Total cost accounted for $208,520

DP 2 Jan. costs per equiv. unit: Materials $1.50; Conv. costs $1.00, Feb. costs per equiv. unit: Materials $1.60; Conv. costs $1.00.

21-1A Net inc. at 100,000 units, $37,730

21-2A Net inc.: Flex. budget var., $3,150F; Sales vol. var., $15,960F

21-3A Gross profit, $370,570; Price var.: Materials, $1,246U; Labor, $1,385F; Efficiency var.: Materials, $15,050F; Labor, $6,820U; Overhead var.: Flex budget, $16,034U; Prod. vol., $10,140F

21-4A Price var., $747U; Efficiency var., $67F

21-5A Price var.: Materials, $1,787.52U; Labor, $678F; Efficiency var.: Materials, $1,436.40F; Labor $1,850F; Overhead var.: Flex. budget, $13,278F; Prod. vol., $10,712U

21-6A Price var.: Materials, $2,688F; Labor, $220F; Efficiency var.: Materials, $5,124U; Labor, $700U; Overhead var.: Flex. budget, $2,140U; Prod. vol., $1,600F; Gross profit, $75,084

21-1B Net inc. at 30,000 units, $77,625

21-2B Net income: Flex. budget var., $7,650U; Sales vol. var., $22,800F

21-3B Gross profit, $336,400; Price var.: Materials, $3,280F; Labor, $579U; Efficiency var.: Materials $9,600U; Labor, $1,800U; Overhead var.: Flex. budget, $11,966U; Prod. vol., $5,600U

21-4B Price var., $660U; Efficiency var., $1,560F

21-5B Price var.: Materials, $624.25F; Labor, $692U; Efficiency var.: Materials, $851.25F; Labor, $220U; Overhead var.: Flex. budget, $983U; Prod. vol., $864F

21-6B Price var.: Materials, $749U; Labor, $80U; Efficiency var.: Materials, $465F; Labor, $200U; Overhead var.: Flex. budget,

$80U; Prod. vol. $300U; Gross profit, $55,996

DP 1 Net inc.: Flex. budget var., $139,854F; Sales vol. var., $166,454U

DP 2 Total receipts: Flex. budget var., $1,034U; Volume var., $2,300U

22-1A No check figure

22-2A Oper. income var: Birmingham, $800; Alabama, $5,000; Companywide, ($341,000)

22-3A Oper. income var., % of budget: Bedspreads, (5.9%); Bedding, (4.2%); Company, (3.4%)

22-4A Cost per square foot: Basement, $2.04; Street level, $8.20; Second floor, $4.10; Floors 3-5, $2.05

22-5A Direct Method, total budgeted cost: Machining, $84,503; Assembly, $75,497, Step-down Method: Machinery, $84,667; Assembly, $75,333

22-6A Oper. income: Custom, $16,284; Group, $33,316

22-7A Oper. income: Dept. A, $166,162; Dept. B, $31,984; Dept. C, $10,430

22-8A Branch Ledger Control, $4,000

22-1B No check figure

22-2B Oper. income var.: Store No. 24, $1,100; Los Angeles, $15,600; California, $52,700

22-3B Oper. income var., % of budget: Audio, 4.2%; Audio-Video (10.1%); Company, (3.0%)

22-4B Cost per square foot; Basement, $2.06; Street level, $8.27; Second floor, $4.13

22-5B 1. Maintenance first
2. Total budgeted cost: Regular admissions, $934,192; Emergency Room, $375,808

22-6B Oper. income: Printing, $14,940; Copy, $13,860

22-7B Oper. income: Men's, $33,366; Women's, $56,122; Children's, $1,055

22-8B Branch Ledger Control, $3,100

DP 1 Income before interest & taxes: Diamonds, $321,000; Watches, $145,000; Other, $34,000

DP 2 Oper. income: No new advertising, $174,400; Advertise Nissans, $126,000; Advertise Toyota, $172,800

23-1A Total manf. cost, $114.50

23-2A Full product cost per unit: Standard chair, $93.50; Unpainted chair, $71.25

23-3A August 31 RIP bal., $1,000

23-4A No check figure

23-5A 1. Allowable life-cycle cost, $1,500. 3. Target cost, $1,650

23-6A 1. Total savings, $119,000. 2. Net benefit, $79,000

23-1B Total manufacturing cost, $117.80

23-2B Full product cost per unit: Standard chair, $85.00; Unfinished chair, $60.60

23-3B December 31 RIP bal. $6,800

23-4B No check figure

23-5B 1. Allowable life-cycle cost, $50 3. Target cost, $56